Contemporary Sport Management

THIRD EDITION

Janet B. Parks, DA
Bowling Green State University, Ohio

Jerome Quarterman, PhD
Florida State University at Tallahassee

Lucie Thibault, PhD
Brock University, St. Catharines, Ontario

Editors

Human Kinetics

Library of Congress Cataloging-in-Publication Data

Contemporary sport management / Janet B. Parks, Jerome Quarterman, Lucie Thibault, editors. – 3rd ed.
p. cm.
Includes bibliographical references and index.
ISBN-13: 978-0-7360-6365-4
ISBN-10: 0-7360-6365-X
1. Sports administration. 2. Physical education and training–Administration. I. Parks, Janet B., 1942- II. Quarterman, Jerome, 1944- III. Thibault, Lucie, 1962-
GV713.C66 2006
796.06'9–dc22

2006022693

ISBN-10: 0-7360-6365-X
ISBN-13: 978-0-7360-6365-4

The Web addresses cited in this text were current as of August 9, 2006, unless otherwise noted.

Acquisitions Editor: Myles Schrag
Developmental Editor: Elaine Mustain
Assistant Editors: Lee Alexander and Melissa McCasky
Copyeditor: Bob Replinger
Proofreader: Joanna Hatzopoulos Portman
Indexer: Susan Danzi Hernandez
Permission Manager: Dalene Reeder
Graphic Designer: Fred Starbird
Graphic Artist: Angela K. Snyder
Photo Managers: Nancy Rasmus and Laura Fitch
Cover Designer: Keith Blomberg
Photographer (cover): Paul Ellis/AFP/Getty images
Photographer (interior): Human Kinetics, unless otherwise noted
Art Manager: Kelly Hendren
Illustrators: Mic Greenberg and Kelly Hendren
Printer: Edwards Brothers

Printed in the United States of America

10 9 8 7 6 5 4 3 2 1

Human Kinetics
Web site: www.HumanKinetics.com

United States: Human Kinetics
P.O. Box 5076
Champaign, IL 61825-5076
800-747-4457
e-mail: humank@hkusa.com

Canada: Human Kinetics
475 Devonshire Road Unit 100
Windsor, ON N8Y 2L5
800-465-7301 (in Canada only)
e-mail: orders@hkcanada.com

Europe: Human Kinetics
107 Bradford Road
Stanningley
Leeds LS28 6AT, United Kingdom
+44 (0) 113 255 5665
e-mail: hk@hkeurope.com

Australia: Human Kinetics
57A Price Avenue
Lower Mitcham, South Australia 5062
08 8372 0999
e-mail: liaw@hkaustralia.com

New Zealand: Human Kinetics
Division of Sports Distributors NZ Ltd.
P.O. Box 300 226 Albany
North Shore City
Auckland
0064 9 448 1207
e-mail: info@humankinetics.co.nz

With sincere appreciation for their unique contributions, we enthusiastically dedicate the third edition of *Contemporary Sport Management* to the authors of the international sidebars that appear throughout the book. We are very grateful to you for providing a stimulating new dimension for our readers! So we say . . .

to Marijke Taks (Belgium),
"Dankjewel!"

to Jun Oga (Japan),
"Taihen arigatou!"

to Allan Edwards, Dwight Zakus, James Paterson,
Sheranne Fairley, and Lisa Kihl (Australia),
"Good on ya!"

to Karen Danylchuk, Joanne MacLean, and Hilary Findlay (Canada),
"Thank you very much!"

to Giorgio Gandolfi (Italy),
"Grazie mille!"

to Hareesh Viriyala (India),
"Dhanyavaadamu!"

to Kamini Sharma (United Kingdom),
"Thank you very much!"

to Abel Correia (Portugal),
"Muito obrigada!"

to James Mandigo, Andy Anderson, and John Corlett (Canada),
"Thank you very much!"

to Makoto Nakazawa (Japan),
"Domo arigatou!"

to Babs Surujlal (South Africa),
"Thank you very much!"

to Rosa Lopez de'Amico (Venezuela),
"Muchas gracias!"

to Win Koo (Korea),
"Gam-sa-ham-ni-da!"

to Todd Beane (Spain),
"Muchas gracias!"

to Bill Gerrard (United Kingdom),
"Thank you very much!"

Contents

A Letter to Students

The goal of *Contemporary Sport Management* is to introduce students to sport management, both as an academic major and as a professional endeavor. Toward that end, the book provides a broad overview of sport management rather than detailed instructions about how to manage sport enterprises. This distinction is important because the book must meet the needs of two types of students: those who have already decided to major in sport management and those who are still thinking about their choice of a major. If you are currently majoring in sport management, you probably anticipate learning more about the field, particularly about the variety of professional opportunities that await you. Those of you who are currently considering a major in sport management probably want to gain general knowledge about the field before making a final decision. After studying the information in this book, some of you will be even more intrigued with the idea of seeking a career in sport management, and you will pursue the remainder of your curriculum with enhanced understanding, insight, and maturity of purpose. On the other hand, others of you will discover that sport management isn't really your cup of tea, and you will choose a different major. In either case, the book will have served a valuable purpose.

Contemporary Sport Management contains 20 chapters written by we three editors in concert with 32 other authors. We invited the 32 contributing authors to participate in this project not only because they are experts in their fields but also because they are committed to sharing their knowledge with the next generation of sport managers. We believe that you will find these authors exceptionally credible and that you will enjoy learning from them. Their photographs and brief biographies are included at the back of the book. We are hopeful that seeing their faces and reading about their accomplishments will personalize the material in the chapters and make the book more meaningful for you. We know you will be impressed with the authors' experience and depth of knowledge.

SCOPE AND ORGANIZATION OF THE BOOK

This edition of *Contemporary Sport Management* addresses each of the content areas that the Sport Management Program Review Council of the National Association for Sport and Physical Education–North American Society for Sport Management (NASPE–NASSM) considers essential to the professional preparation of sport managers. These content areas include sociocultural dimensions in sport (e.g., gender, race, and disability; aggression, violence, and deviance in sport), management and leadership in sport, ethics in sport management, marketing in sport, communication in sport, budget and finance in sport, legal aspects of sport, economics in sport, governance in sport, and field experience in sport management. The book provides basic information in all these content areas. As you progress through the professional preparation curriculum at your college or university, you will study each of them in much greater depth.

The 20 chapters of the book are organized within the following separate parts: "Introduction to Sport Management," "Selected Sport Management Sites," "Selected Sport Management Functions," "Organizational and Managerial Foundations of Sport Management," "Current Challenges in Sport Management," and "The Future of Sport Management." Each of these parts begins with a brief description of its purpose, an explanation of the types of information that you will find in the chapters in that part, and a section titled "For More Information" that identifies additional resources related to the chapter topics. After studying all the chapters, completing selected learning activities within the chapters, and taking advantage of the "For More Information" sections, you should be able to (1) define sport management; (2) discuss the significance of sport as an international social institution; (3) exhibit desirable professional skills and attitudes; (4) describe the nature and scope of professional opportunities in the sport industry; (5) explain a variety of functions that sport managers typically perform; (6) demonstrate an understanding of theories associated with management, leadership, and organizational behavior and how these theories are applied in sport enterprises; (7) critically evaluate major challenges confronting various segments of the industry; (8) explain the relevance of ethical, legal, historical, sociological, and psychological concepts to the management of sport; (9) demonstrate an appreciation of diversity through the use of unbiased language and an inclusive approach to human relations; (10) identify research questions in sport management and demonstrate the ability to analyze and interpret published research; and (11) become a member of the profession who will have a positive influence on the way that sport is managed in the future.

FEATURES OF THE BOOK

This is the third edition of *Contemporary Sport Management*. We are gratified that so many students, faculty, and sport practitioners found the second edition useful, and we hope that the new, improved version will serve your needs even better. In response to suggestions made by students, colleagues, and anonymous reviewers, we have made several changes for this edition.

The most significant new feature of this edition is the increased attention paid to sport as an international pursuit. All chapters now include examples from around the world, and most of them contain international sidebars. Each of these sidebars is written by someone from a country other than the United States and addresses the chapter topic from an international perspective. Examples of sidebar topics are professional basketball in Italy, the organization of sport in Venezuela, and intercollegiate athletics in Canada. Because we respect the linguistic customs of all countries, we have retained the voices of the sidebar authors. Consequently, some of them contain words, expressions, and spellings that might be new to you. We encourage you to take advantage of the opportunities that these new vocabularies provide for you to learn more about cultures outside the United States. We are hopeful that you will find these essays informative and that they will whet your appetite to learn more about sport and its management in other countries.

A second important change is the addition of historical moments that are presented in most chapters. These historical moments are important because sport managers who know and appreciate events of the past are more likely to understand the present and more qualified to plan for the future. We hope these historical moments will capture your attention as they visually communicate historical developments and connections among key events over time. Instructors can incorporate the historical information and the attendant learning activities into their lectures, assignments, and tests.

Third, all chapters have been revised and updated. Moreover, rather than combining ethical and legal aspects of sport management in a single chapter as we did in the second edition, we dedicated a separate chapter to each. This reorganization permitted the authors of these two chapters to provide additional information that is essential to an understanding of the respective topics.

Other key features of *Contemporary Sport Management* include the following:

- Each chapter reflects the inclusion of diverse populations, that is, people of different ages, genders, abilities, social classes, sexual orientations, races, ethnicities, and cultures. No separate chapter is dedicated to a topic such as "opportunities for women," or "sport for the disabled," or "the Black athlete." We believe that the inclusive nature of the text fosters a better understanding and appreciation of the variety of consumers that exist in the sport industry.
- The language used in the book is called gender inclusive language. For example, athletics teams are referred to specifically as either men's teams or women's teams, a practice that acknowledges the existence of teams for both genders. The terms *fair play* and *sporting behavior* are used in place of *sportsmanship* because the inclusive terms avoid the subtle suggestion that sport is reserved for males. This use of unbiased language is a conscious attempt to reflect and embrace the diversity that is celebrated in many other ways throughout the book.
- Although each chapter of the book addresses a particular aspect of sport management, many of the chapters have important similarities. For example, most of the chapters about careers in sport management include lists of publications, governing bodies, and professional associations. Several chapters address ethical, legal, economic, and communication concerns. By including these topics in several chapters, we hope to reinforce important concepts that you will find useful as you progress in your professional preparation program.
- Each of the chapters begins with learning objectives. These objectives serve as an outline for reading and studying the chapter.

• Each chapter contains several learning activities that provide opportunities to practice with the material presented in the text. We included a wide variety of exercises throughout the book to accommodate different learning styles and preferences.

• The review questions at the end of each chapter are linked to the objectives at the beginning of the chapter. These questions reinforce the key points of the chapter.

• Each chapter contains a reference list. Moreover, as previously noted, you will find a "For More Information" section at the beginning of each of the six parts of the book. We hope that you will use the information in these sections for further reading and exploration.

• Some chapters contain real-life scenarios, case studies, profiles of sport managers, or news stories that illustrate a point. We believe these features contribute to the user-friendliness of the book.

• Many chapters include examples of fabricated, but realistic, position announcements related to employment opportunities within particular sport settings. These position announcements will help you understand the skills that prospective employers are seeking and how they communicate the requirements for specific jobs.

• As you would expect in a modern textbook, *Contemporary Sport Management* provides a multitude of Web site addresses. These URLs will enable you to capitalize on the vast amount of information available online. They also enable you to pursue your interests at times and locations convenient for you.

Janet B. Parks, Bowling Green State University
Jerome Quarterman, Florida State University
Lucie Thibault, Brock University

Acknowledgments

Janet Parks and Jerome Quarterman express deep gratitude to Lucie Thibault for joining us as an editor of this edition of *Contemporary Sport Management*. Dr. Thibault teaches sport management at Brock University in St. Catharines, Ontario, Canada. She is an outstanding scholar who brought a keen intellect to bear in the development of the book. She is acutely aware of international developments in sport management and freely shared her knowledge and expertise. Many of the improvements in this edition are attributable to Dr. Thibault's valuable contributions. Welcome!

Anyone who has attempted a project such as this knows that it could not have been done without the assistance of many people. We are, therefore, eager to acknowledge the individuals and groups whose collective contributions made this book a reality.

First, we express our sincere gratitude to the 32 contributing authors who wrote most of the chapters in the book. We are certain that the quality of the book results from the willingness of all of you to share your energy and expertise, and we genuinely appreciate your generosity. We extend a *special* "thank-you" to Dr. Corinne Daprano, University of Dayton, and Dr. Paul Pedersen, Indiana University. Dr. Daprano provided over 400 historical moments and several learning activities associated with them, and Dr. Pedersen contributed photographs that illuminate many of the concepts presented throughout the book.

We owe much of the success of this project to the remarkable talent and efforts of the Human Kinetics team of editors. Myles Schrag, our acquisitions editor, provided valuable advice and assistance as we conceptualized this edition. The quality of the final product is due, in large measure, to Myles' expertise, imagination, energy, and enthusiasm. We were delighted that once again Elaine Mustain served as our capable and committed developmental editor. Elaine, along with Lee Alexander and Melissa McCasky, our assistant editors, actually put the book together while Dalene Reeder helped us through the challenging process of obtaining permissions to reprint or adapt material from published sources. These individuals made our jobs much easier by always being there with valuable information, assistance, and advice. To Myles, Elaine, Lee, Dalene, and all the other personnel at Human Kinetics who were associated with this project—thank you for a great collaborative effort!

We are grateful to Bowling Green State University, Florida State University, and Brock University for providing the resources that facilitated the completion of this book. We are privileged to be university professors and fortunate to work in environments that support our efforts.

Students have made major contributions to this edition. We gratefully acknowledge Omari Aldridge, who was an undergraduate student at Bowling Green State University when he suggested that the third edition should incorporate a wider international perspective. This advice dramatically changed the nature of the book, and we know that it will make the introductory course much more meaningful for students. Bless up, Omari! We also appreciate the contribution of Beth Klocke Fox, a Bowling Green graduate student, for providing the arguments from the concerned parents in chapter 16. In addition, we join the authors of chapter 11 in extending gratitude to Sarah Ratzlaff, a graduate student in sport administration at Wichita State University, for her contributions to that chapter. We sincerely appreciate the suggestions of undergraduate students in the Introduction to Sport Management course at Bowling Green State University who provided us with thoughtful critiques of the second edition. We took their comments seriously and believe that their ideas contributed to major improvements in this edition.

We are indebted to the anonymous reviewers of the 2003 edition for providing many valuable ideas for improving this edition. The results of your efforts appear throughout the book.

We are sincerely grateful to Eric Forsyth of Bemidji State University for creating the ancillary materials that accompany the book. Dr. Forsyth has revised and enhanced the Instructors Guide, adding features such as PowerPoint® slides and numerous test questions. We know that faculty will find his manual to be of high quality and extremely useful.

As always, we extend sincere gratitude to the thousands of students whom we have had the privilege of teaching across the years. You have always been the raison d'être for *Contemporary Sport Management*. We thank you for enriching our lives!

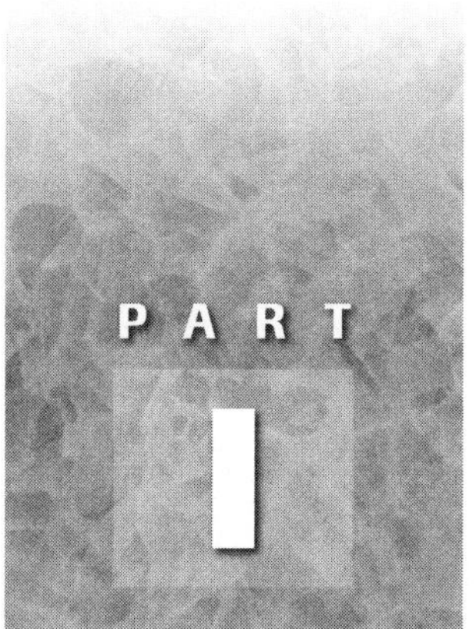

Introduction to Sport Management

The three chapters in this section present basic information and key concepts that form the foundation of professional preparation for all careers in sport management. These chapters take you through an overview of the field in general, an examination of professional considerations vital to success in the sport industry, and an exploration of critical thinking skills and applications. The knowledge that you gain from these chapters will be useful as you study the remaining chapters in the book.

In chapter 1, Janet Parks, Jerome Quarterman, and Lucie Thibault introduce sport management as an academic major and a career field. After defining sport and sport management, the authors delineate settings in which sport occurs, provide examples of traditional and nontraditional sports, and explain different ways of segmenting the sport industry. Parks, Quarterman, and Thibault then discuss several characteristics of sport-related enterprises that distinguish them from other business pursuits, examine two models of organizational design, and describe competencies that will be essential for success in sport management. The chapter concludes with a discussion of personal and professional qualities expected of sport managers as well as opportunities and challenges that will face sport managers of the future. In the international sidebar, Marijke Taks, a native of Belgium who teaches sport management at the University of Windsor in Canada, explains the European Sport for All model of sport.

Chapter 2 contains information that will help you develop a professional perspective on your studies and your career. First, Kathryn Hoff, JoAnn Kroll, and Carol Fletcher provide a preview of the courses and experiences that you can expect in the professional preparation program at your college or university. Next, they discuss four essential elements of a positive professional perspective—attitude, image, work transition and adjustment, and business etiquette. The final component of professional perspective is professional development, a process that begins during your college years and continues throughout your career. The authors close the chapter with special attention to career planning and management and offer sound advice related to finding a career that is compatible with your values, interests, and skills. The international sidebar contains an essay by Jun Oga, a professor of sport management at the University of Electro-Communications in Tokyo, Japan. He discusses several controversies that exist in Japanese professional baseball.

The purpose of chapter 3 is to provide strategies whereby you can develop an appreciation of critical thinking and learn to apply critical thinking skills to issues in sport management. Stuart Keeley, Janet Parks, and Lucie Thibault present examples of contemporary issues in sport and explain why sport managers need to make decisions about these issues based on principles rather than expediency. The authors then discuss the differences between learning *what* to think and learning *how* to think, describe the dispositions of critical thinkers, and incorporate the importance of values and perspective in determining personal beliefs about concerns related to sport. Keeley, Parks, and Thibault present eight critical thinking questions and show how you can use them to resolve a specific issue in sport. The message of this chapter is that sport managers who possess the dispositions of critical thinkers and can think critically about sport-related issues will be competent, reflective professionals with the potential to become influential agents of change. The international sidebar, contributed by Dwight Zakus and Allan Edwards of Griffith University in Queensland, Australia, explains how the process of critical reflection was used to address racial vilification in Australian rules football.

For More Information

Professional and Scholarly Associations

Asian Association for Sport Management

European Association of Sport Management

International Sport Management Alliance

Japanese Society of Management for Physical Education and Sports

Korean Society for Sport Management

North American Society for Sport History

North American Society for Sport Management

Sport Management Association of Australia and New Zealand

Sport Management Council of the National Association for Sport and Physical Education

Professional and Scholarly Publications

Canadian Journal of Sport History

Journal of Sport & Social Issues

Journal of Sport History

Journal of Sport Management

Sociology of Sport Journal

Sport History Review

Women in Sport and Physical Activity Journal

Sport Management Information

Global Sport Management News: http://raider.muc.edu/pe/global.html

North American Society for Sport Management: www.NASSM.com

Sport Business Education: www.sben.org

Sport Management Academic Programs: www.aahperd.org/NASPE/template.cfm?template=programs-smprc.html

Sport Management Related Information: www.unb.ca/SportManagement/links.htm

Sporting Goods Manufacturers Association International: www.sgma.com/index.html

Critical Thinking Resources

Chaffee, J. (1998). *The thinker's way: 8 steps to a richer life.* Boston: Little, Brown.

Critical Thinking on the Web: www.austhink.org/critical

Damer, T.E. (2005). *Attacking faulty reasoning: A practical guide to fallacy-free arguments* (5th edition). Belmont, CA: Thomson/Wadsworth Learning.

Facione, P. (2006). *Critical thinking: What it is and why it counts.* www.insightassessment.com/pdf_files/what&why2006.pdf

Foundation for Critical Thinking: www.criticalthinking.org

Henderson, J.R. (2002). *ICYouSee: T is for thinking: A guide to critical thinking about what you see on the Web.* www.ithaca.edu/library/training/think.html

The Reason Group. (2001-4). *Reasonable: Enabling better reasoning.* www.goreason.com

Sport Management Book Club Selections

Cohen, G.L. (Ed.). (2001). *Women in sport: Issues and controversies* (2nd ed.). Oxon Hill, MD: NASPE.

Eitzen, D.S. (2003). *Fair and foul: Beyond the myths and paradoxes of sport.* New York: Rowman and Littlefield.

Hoberman, J.M., & Møller, V. (Eds.). (2004). *Doping and public policy.* Portland, OR: University Press of Southern Denmark.

King, C.R., & Springwood, C.F. (Eds.). (2001). *Team spirits: The Native American mascots controversy.* Lincoln: University of Nebraska Press.

Maguire, J.A. (2002). *Power and global sport: Zones of prestige, emulation and resistance.* London: Routledge.

Miah, A. (2005). *Genetically modified athletes: Biomedical ethics, gene doping and sport.* New York: Routledge.

Miracle, A.W., Jr., & Reese, R. (1994). *Lessons of the locker room: The myth of school sports.* New York: Prometheus Books.

Putnam, D. (1999). *Controversies of the sports world.* Westport, CT: Greenwood Press.

Sack, A.L., & Staurowsky, E.J. (1998). *College athletes for hire: The evolution and legacy of the NCAA's amateur myth.* Westport, CT: Praeger.

Slack, T. (Ed.). (2004). *The commercialisation of sport*. New York: Routledge.

Sperber, M. (2000). *Beer and circus: How big-time college sports is crippling undergraduate education*. New York: Holt.

Yiannakis, A., & Melnick, M. (2001). *Contemporary issues in sociology of sport*. Champaign, IL: Human Kinetics.

Sport Management Job Market

www.adventuresports.com

www.athleticbusiness.com

www.canada.com/topics/sports/index.html

www.jobsinsports.com

www.nassm.com

www.onlinesports.com/pages/CareerCenter.html

www.onlinesports.com/pages/Jobs.html

www.quintcareers.com/sports_jobs.html

www.teamjobs.com

www.teamworkonline.com

www.ucalgary.ca/library/ssportsite

www.womensportsjobs.com

www.womenssportsfoundation.org/cgi-bin/iowa/index.html

Managing Sport in the 21st Century

Janet B. Parks—Bowling Green State University ▪ **Jerome Quarterman**—Florida State University
Lucie Thibault—Brock University

Learning Objectives

After studying this chapter, you will be able to do the following:

1. Compare and contrast different definitions of sport and identify a variety of activities that fall within these definitions.
2. Differentiate between *sport* and *sports*.
3. Identify several different settings in which sporting activities occur.
4. Discuss examples of traditional and nontraditional sporting activities.
5. Explain three different ways of organizing (segmenting) the sport industry.
6. Identify and explain four unique aspects of sport management.
7. Contrast the bureaucratized and competency-based models of organizational design.
8. Discuss sport management as a career field and as an academic major and identify a variety of positions available in sport management.
9. Identify and explain competencies required for success in a variety of sport management jobs.
10. Identify and discuss personal and professional qualities shared by outstanding sport management students and professionals.
11. Identify and discuss opportunities and challenges facing sport managers of the future, including some of the questions that sport managers will be required to answer and decision-making strategies that they can use.
12. Discuss the International Year of Sport and Physical Education.

In 1957 Walter O'Malley, president and chief stockholder of the Brooklyn (now Los Angeles) Dodgers Baseball Club, anticipated the future growth of organized sport and predicted the need for professionally prepared sport administrators. O'Malley wrote a letter to Dr. James Mason, a faculty member at Ohio University, stating the following:

> I ask the question, where would one go to find a person who by virtue of education had been trained to administer a marina, race track, ski resort, auditorium, stadium, theater, convention or exhibition hall, a public camp complex, or a person to fill an executive position at a team or league level in junior athletics such as Little League baseball, football, scouting, CYO [Catholic Youth Organization], and youth activities, etc. . . . A course that would enable a graduate to read architectural and engineering plans; or having to do with specifications and contract letting, the functions of a purchasing agent in plant operations. There would be the problems of ticket selling and accounting, concessions, sale of advertising in programs, and publications, outdoor and indoor displays and related items . . . (Mason, Higgins, & Wilkinson, 1981, p. 44)

James G. Mason is widely recognized as the founder of academic sport management programs. Since 1966, when Dr. Mason and his colleagues established a master's degree in sport management at Ohio University, hundreds of universities around the world have instituted similar programs, and thousands of students have enjoyed opportunities to pursue this exciting and challenging career field.

Photo courtesy of Ohio University

As a result of that inquiry, Mason and several of his colleagues created a master's-level sport administration program at Ohio University (OU). Inaugurated in 1966, the OU program was the first recorded, university-sponsored attempt to provide a graduate-level curriculum specifically designed to prepare students for jobs in a variety of sport-related industries. The idea caught on, and at last count, there were 158 undergraduate sport management programs and 103 graduate programs in Australia, Canada, Great Britain, New Zealand, and the United States (Comfort, 2005a, 2005b). In addition, hundreds of college students in other countries, such as Switzerland, Spain, Ireland, Netherlands, Italy, Belgium, and Austria, are also studying sport management.

This chapter represents the first step on your journey toward becoming a sport manager. We hope that it will provide you with valuable information, setting the stage for you to study subsequent chapters with greater insight. We have included definitions of basic terms, a discussion of the nature and scope of the sport industry, and explanations of unique aspects of sport management enterprises and careers. You will also learn about desirable sport management competencies, personal and professional characteristics of successful sport managers, and some of the challenges and opportunities that await you as you prepare to take your place among the next generation of sport managers.

DEFINING SPORT AND SPORT MANAGEMENT

At the outset, it might seem unnecessary to define *sport* because you probably already know through experience and intuition what the word means. For most of us, sport implies having fun, but it can also be work (for a professional athlete), a means of employment (for a sport tourism director), or a business (for a sport marketing agency). Sport takes many forms. It might include many participants, as in team sports such as soccer and volleyball; two participants, as in dual sports such as tennis and badminton; or one person, as in individual sports such as golf and surfing. Sport includes a combination of these configurations when it involves team competitions, tournaments, or matches in dual sports (wrestling) or individual sports (in-line skating). What criteria qualify games or activities to be classified as sport? Is horse racing a sport? What about cycling, water skiing, pocket billiards, or Texas Hold 'Em poker and other table games? We know that football, basketball, ice and field hockey, tennis, golf, baseball, and softball are sports. Are they different from sailing, dog racing, marathoning, video gaming, and scuba diving? If so, how are they different? If not, how are they similar?

The Council of Europe (2001) defines sport as "all forms of physical activity which, through casual (informal) or organised participation, aim at expressing or improving physical fitness and mental well-being, forming social relationships or obtaining results in competition at all levels" (p. 1). Similarly, Pitts, Fielding, and Miller (1994) state that sport is "any activity, experience, or business enterprise for which the primary focus is fitness, recreation, athletics, and leisure related" (p. 18). According to these definitions, sport does not have to be competitive, nor does it always require specialized equipment or rules; in fact, sport includes activities such as working out, swimming, running, boating, and dancing. In this book, therefore, the term *sport* will encompass an expansive variety of physical activities and associated businesses.

Many people who are employed in business endeavors associated with sport are engaged in a career field known as sport management. According to Pitts and Stotlar (2002), the term *sport management* refers to "all people, activities, businesses, and organizations involved in producing, facilitating, promoting, or organizing any product that is sport, fitness, and recreation related" (p. 4). This broad definition includes an incredibly wide variety of sport-related careers. One

1950s | 1960s | 1970s

1957 Walter O'Malley letter to Dr. Mason at Ohio Univ.

1966 Ohio Univ. sport administration program established

1970s SMARTS—Sport Management Arts and Science Society, conceived by Univ. of Massachusetts faculty and forerunner of NASSM

NOTHING NEW UNDER THE SUN

Lest we be deluded by the notion that contemporary sport management is markedly different from the ancient art of staging athletic spectacles, let us consider for a moment the following description of the games sponsored in 11 BC by Herod the Great, king of Judea and honorary president of the Olympics:

"The games began with a magnificent dedication ceremony. Then there were athletic and musical competitions, in which large prizes were given not only to the winners but also—an unusual feature—to those who took second and third place. Bloody spectacles were also presented, with gladiators and wild beasts fighting in various combinations, and there were also horse races. Large prizes attracted contenders from all areas and this in turn drew great numbers of spectators. Cities favored by Herod sent delegations, and these he entertained and lodged at his own expense. What comes through most clearly . . . is that gigantic sums of money were spent." (Frank, 1984, p. 158)

The success of such an extravaganza relied in all likelihood on the organizational skills of the individuals charged with planning and executing the games. Certainly there was today's equivalent of a general manager, or CEO, to whom all other personnel were responsible. Additionally, assistants who were knowledgeable in economics, accounting, and finance were indispensable if the event was to become profitable. The "business managers" were responsible for obtaining financial support, purchasing equipment (and perhaps even the requisite beasts), furnishing entertainment and lodging for the VIPs, and generally being accountable for the large sums of money that were spent. Once the financial dimension was secured, there was the challenge of attracting sufficient numbers of contestants and spectators to the games. Enter Herod's "marketing director," armed with unique and unprecedented gimmicks to assure a full complement of participants as well as a full house of onlookers. A new prize structure was devised and, in awarding prizes to musicians as well as athletes, the seeds were sown for the modern spectacle known, among other titles, as the Battle of the Bands.

The marketing director must have enlisted the aid of assistants who were responsible for extending invitations, publicizing the games, and keeping records of the day's activities. In the years prior to the printing press, much less the electronic media, informing the public was no small task—to say nothing of offering enticements sufficient to persuade them to journey for days and endure what must have been extremely undesirable traveling conditions. The marketing and promotions people certainly had their hands full!

The parallel[s] could continue—there was a need for crowd control, rules decisions, award ceremonies, and so forth. After all, certain tasks must be performed regardless of the venue in which the event occurs. Now, 2000 years later, we are reminded once again of Solomon's wisdom in proclaiming in Ecclesiastes 1:9 that "there is no new thing under the sun."

Reprinted, by permission, from J.B. Parks and G.A. Olafson, 1987, "Sport management and a new journal," *Journal of Sport Management, 1*(1), 1-2.

purpose of this book is to provide you with a greater understanding of the vast array of career opportunities that await you as a sport manager.

Sport management is also the name given to many university-level academic programs designed to prepare students to assume positions in the sport industry. These programs provide two additional sources of confusion regarding vocabulary. First, you might have noticed that many professional preparation programs are titled *sport* management, whereas others are called *sports* management. In our view, people prefer one or the other based on the connotations that the words *sports* and *sport* have for them. To many academics, ourselves included, *sports* implies a collection of separate activities such as golf, soccer, hockey, volleyball, softball, and gymnastics—items in a series that we can count. On the other hand, *sport* is an all-encompassing concept. It is a collective noun that includes all sporting activities, not just those that we can place on a list. We have found that students in our classes relate well to the parallel with the different connotations of the words *religions* and *religion*. The word *religions* typically connotes several specific faiths or belief systems—different denominations or sects that we can quantify. *Religion*, on the other hand, is a broad term that we can interpret as a general reverence or faith held by any number of people.

A second source of confusion is the fact that many professional preparation programs are titled sport (or sports) *management*, and others are called sport (or sports) *administration*. In the past, the distinction between administration and management seemed clear; administrators worked primarily in the public sector and managers worked in the private sector. Recently, however, the line

1980 1990 2000

1985 NASSM established

1987—*Journal of Sport Management* (*JSM*) launched

1992 NASSM Code of Ethics adopted

2005 International Year of Sport and Physical Education—United Nations between administration and management has become blurred, making it counterproductive to debate which term is more appropriate. You will find excellent academic programs by either name (Comfort, 2005a, 2005b). Remember that the quality of the curriculum is more important than the title of the program.

NATURE AND SCOPE OF THE SPORT INDUSTRY

Just as there are several definitions of sport, there are many ways to conceptualize the nature and scope of the sport industry. In the following paragraphs, we will elaborate on three concepts that, in different ways, provide overviews of sport: (1) settings in which sports are found, (2) different types of sports, and (3) models of sport industry segments.

Settings for Sporting Activities

One approach involves examining the many different settings in which sporting activities occur. This approach provides ideas about where to look for sites in which sport managers might be needed. VanderZwaag (1998, pp. 4-6) identified 16 settings within the sport industry:

- School and college sports programs
- Professional sport
- Amateur sport organizations (e.g., US Olympic Committee, US Ski and Snowboard Association, USA Swimming)
- Private club sport
- Other commercialized sport establishments (e.g., bowling alleys, ski resorts, public golf courses)
- Arenas, coliseums, civic centers, and stadia
- Community recreation sport programs
- Industrial sport programs
- Sport programs in social agencies (Young Women's Christian Association, Young Men's Christian Association, Jewish Community Center)
- Military sport programs
- Sport marketing and consulting firms
- Developmental programs for sport (e.g., Women's Sport Foundation, National Golf Foundation, Special Olympics)
- Corporate sponsors (e.g., LPGA Jamie Farr Owens Corning Classic, Pilot Pen Tennis Family Classic)
- The sporting goods industry
- The sport news media (e.g., print and broadcast)
- Academic programs in sport management

Learning Activity

The Sports Market Place Directory (2005) lists over 13,000 sports organizations, teams, corporate sponsors, sports agents, marketing and event management agencies, and media companies around the world. Your library might have a copy of the directory or it might subscribe to www.sportsmarketplace.com. Using either source, make a list of 10 sport settings in which you think you might like to pursue a career. Look up examples of each of those settings on the Internet and summarize the information you find there.

If your university subscribes to the Sports Business Research Network (www.sbrnet.com), a market research and publications database, you can also visit that site to investigate hundreds of sport-related organizations.

Types of Sports

Another way to consider the sport industry is to examine the many types of sports that exist. An awareness of the wide diversity of sporting opportunities available to consumers is essential for anyone who anticipates becoming a decision maker in the world of sport. Sport marketers, in particular, must have a good understanding of both traditional and new sports so they can develop effective promotional strategies.

You are already familiar with traditional sports such as basketball, tennis, golf, American football, swimming, and soccer. You might also know that in recent years, numerous new sports and physical activities have emerged. Pitts and Stotlar (2002) identified the following activities and sports that have appeared on the scene lately: several varieties of aerobics, in-line skating (Rollerblading), boogie boarding, snow kayaking, parasailing, ice surfing, beach volleyball, skydive dancing, ice climbing, X Games, and indoor soccer.

Several of these new sports are known as **extreme (action) sports**, and they are becoming more popular. For example, Mawson (2002) reported that people born between 1961 and 1981 demonstrated heightened interest and engagement with action sports such as slam ball, street luge, motocross biking, bungee jumping, and snow bicycling. She further noted that broadcast media had

THE PROSPEROUS '90s!

In 1990 sport was a $63.1 billion USD-a-year business, ranking 22nd among more than 400 industries in the United States (Comte & Stogel, 1990). This figure was predicted to increase to $121 billion USD a year by 2000 (Rosner, 1989), but its growth exceeded this expectation. Meek (1997) estimated the size of the 1995 sport industry as $152 billion USD, while generating an additional $259 billion USD in **associated economic activity**. In 1999 Broughton, Lee, and Nethery estimated the **gross national sport product** (GNSP) to be $213 billion USD. Regardless of the measurements used, one fact is clear: Sport was a booming business in the 1990s!

But will the boom continue?

Mahony and Howard (2001) predicted that the sport boom of the 1990s would not continue. According to these analysts, successful sport managers of the future will need a higher level of sophistication than currently exists as they adopt Internet marketing and other technologies, focus on big competitions and stars, invent new markets, improve efforts to reach target markets, reestablish relationships with traditional consumers, employ creative financing, cut budgets, and promote efficiency.

gross national sport product (GNSP)—The total economic output of the sport industry in the United States.

associated economic activity—Money spent by sport participants, spectators, and sponsors.

embraced extreme sports, as evidenced by the airing of the X Games (ESPN), the Gravity Games (NBC), and the Gorge Games (NBC). Younger people are also learning to enjoy extreme sports. In fact, when Bennett, Henson, and Zhang (2003) asked 367 middle school and high school students about their televised sport viewing preferences, more students preferred watching the X Games than the World Series and the soccer World Cup. More students also preferred watching action sports to watching baseball, basketball, ice hockey, and auto racing. Both Mawson (2002) and Bennett et al. (2003) predicted that the popularity of action sports would continue to rise. Sport managers of the future, therefore, should be familiar with these sports and be prepared to make them accessible to consumers, both as participatory activities and through the media.

The emergence of snowboarding as one of many new activities that have developed in the past few decades exemplifies the constantly changing, challenging, and exciting nature of the sport business.
Eyewire/Photodisc/Getty Images

extreme sports (also known as action sports)—A general term for a collection of newer sports involving adrenaline-inducing action. They often feature a combination of speed, height, danger, and spectacular stunts (http://en.wikipedia.org/wiki/Extreme_Sports).

Sport Industry Segments

A third approach to defining the nature and scope of the sport industry is to create industry models that show the interrelationships among various segments of the sport industries. We will present three of these models, each of which represents a different approach to conceptualizing the sport industry. All three models are useful in showing you interesting and different ways to consider the world of sport.

Product Type Model

Pitts et al. (1994) developed a segmentation model of the sport industry based on the types of products sold or promoted by the businesses or organizations within them. The industry segmentation approach is especially useful to sport marketers, who are typically responsible for formulating competitive strategies. Sport marketers can use their understanding of the sport product segments as they make decisions such as choosing the segments in which they wish to position their products, selecting the types of marketing strategies to use, and determining whether to create new industry segments.

Pitts et al. (1994) proposed three product segments of the sport industry: (1) sport performance, (2) sport production, and (3) sport promotion. As shown in figure 1.1, the sport performance segment includes such varied products as school-sponsored athletics, fitness clubs, sport camps, professional sport, and municipal parks sport programs. Examples of products in the sport production segment are basketballs, fencing foils, jogging shoes, sports medicine clinics, swimming pools, and college athletics conferences. The sport promotion segment includes products such as T-shirts, giveaways, print and broadcast media, and celebrity endorsements. Sport marketers can use this product type model to plan marketing strategies, something you will learn more about in chapter 9.

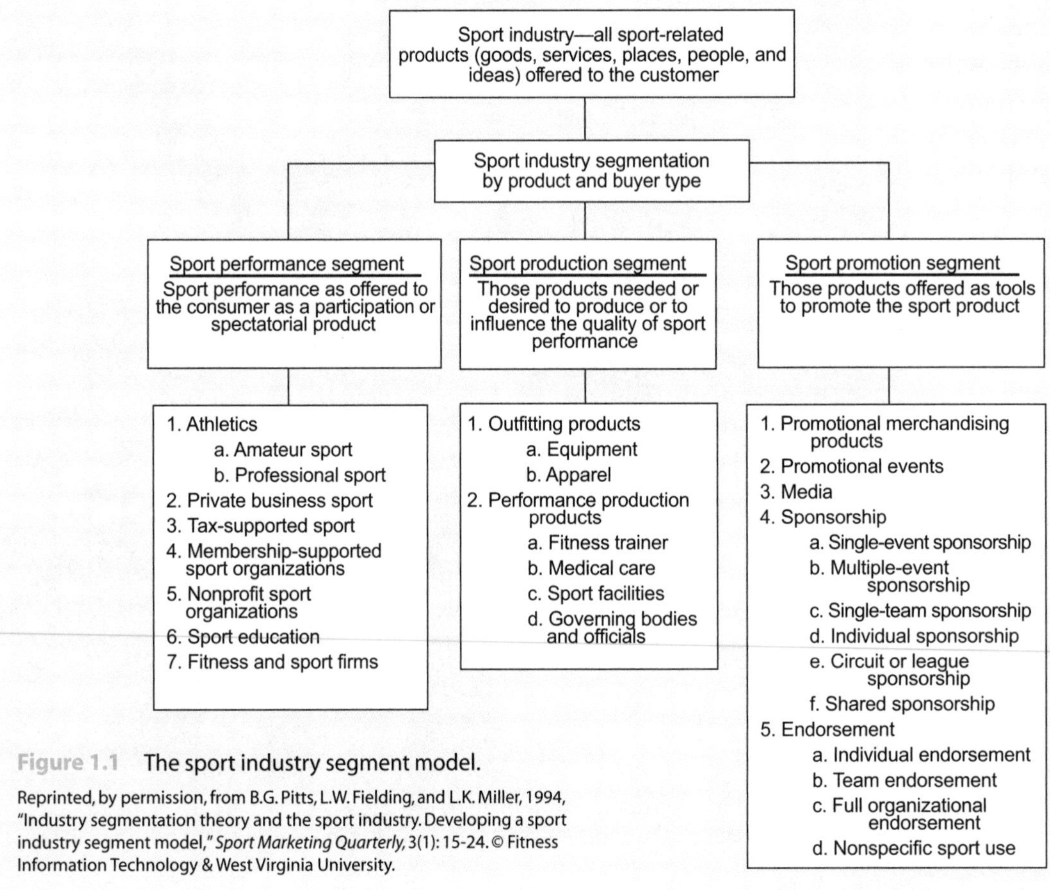

Figure 1.1 The sport industry segment model.

Reprinted, by permission, from B.G. Pitts, L.W. Fielding, and L.K. Miller, 1994, "Industry segmentation theory and the sport industry. Developing a sport industry segment model," *Sport Marketing Quarterly*, 3(1): 15-24. © Fitness Information Technology & West Virginia University.

Economic Impact Model

Meek (1997) took another approach to describing the sport industry. First, he proposed that the industry can be defined by describing three primary sectors:

1. Sport entertainment and recreation such as events, teams, and individual participants; sports and related recreational activities; and [associated] spending
2. Sport products and services such as design, testing, manufacturing, and distribution of equipment, clothing, and instruments
3. Sport support organizations such as leagues, law firms, and marketing organizations (p. 16)

The three sectors of Meek's 1997 model are presented in figure 1.2. Meek proposed that his broad definition of sport enabled an analysis of the economic activity of the teams and businesses within each sector and the economic activity associated with sport. Based on this model, Meek estimated the size of the 1995 US sport industry at $152 billion USD, with an additional $259 billion USD in economic activity generated by sport. You will learn more about what these figures mean in terms of sport economics in chapter 12.

Sport Activity Model

Li, Hofacre, and Mahony (2001) proposed a model of the sport industry based on the single characteristic that differentiates sport industries from all other industries: sport activities (i.e., games and events). These authors defined the sport industry as

1. the firms and organizations that produce sport activities,
2. the firms and organizations that provide products and services to support the production of sport activities, and
3. the firms and organizations that sell and trade products related to sport activities (p. 6).

As shown in figure 1.3, the sport-producing sector is the core of the industry. Six supporting subsectors surround, and overlap with, the activity-producing core. Organizations in these subsectors either (1) provide products and services to the core

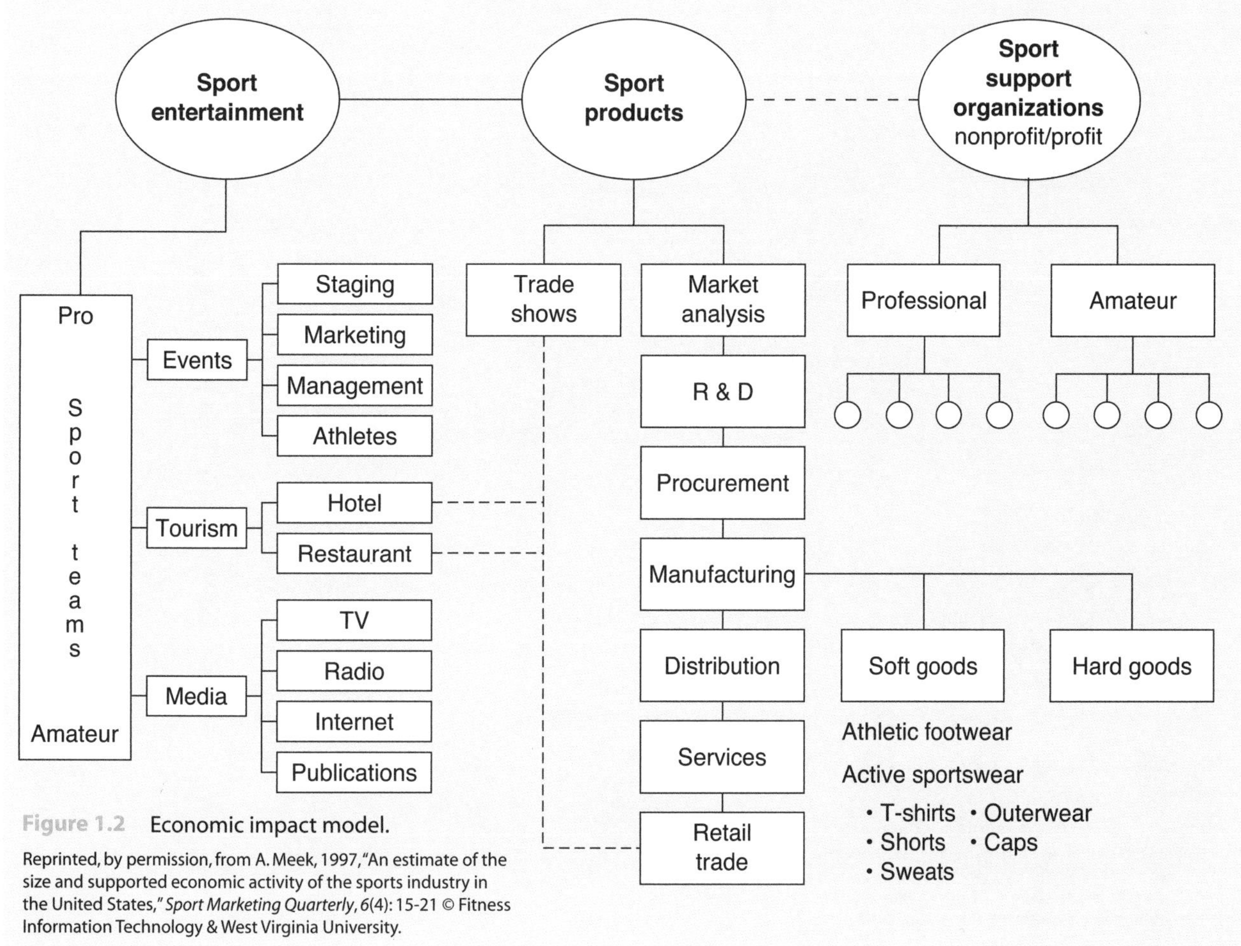

Figure 1.2 Economic impact model.

Reprinted, by permission, from A. Meek, 1997, "An estimate of the size and supported economic activity of the sports industry in the United States," *Sport Marketing Quarterly*, 6(4): 15-21 © Fitness Information Technology & West Virginia University.

organizations or (2) sell or trade products related to sport. This model differs conceptually from the other two models in that it places sport at the center and illustrates the dependence of the subsectors on the production of sporting activities.

Learning Activity

Go to one or more of the Web sites listed in "For More Information" on pages 2 and 3. Make a list of 10 jobs that you find at that site and classify them within the three models of sport industry segmentation. Which jobs are most appealing to you? Why are particular jobs more appealing than others?

UNIQUE ASPECTS OF SPORT MANAGEMENT

Mullin (1980) provided insight into three unique aspects of sport management: sport marketing, sport enterprise financial structures, and sport industry career paths. These three aspects of the sport business make it different from other business enterprises and justify sport management as a distinct area of professional preparation. We would add a fourth unique aspect of sport to Mullin's list: the enormous power and influence of sport as a social institution.

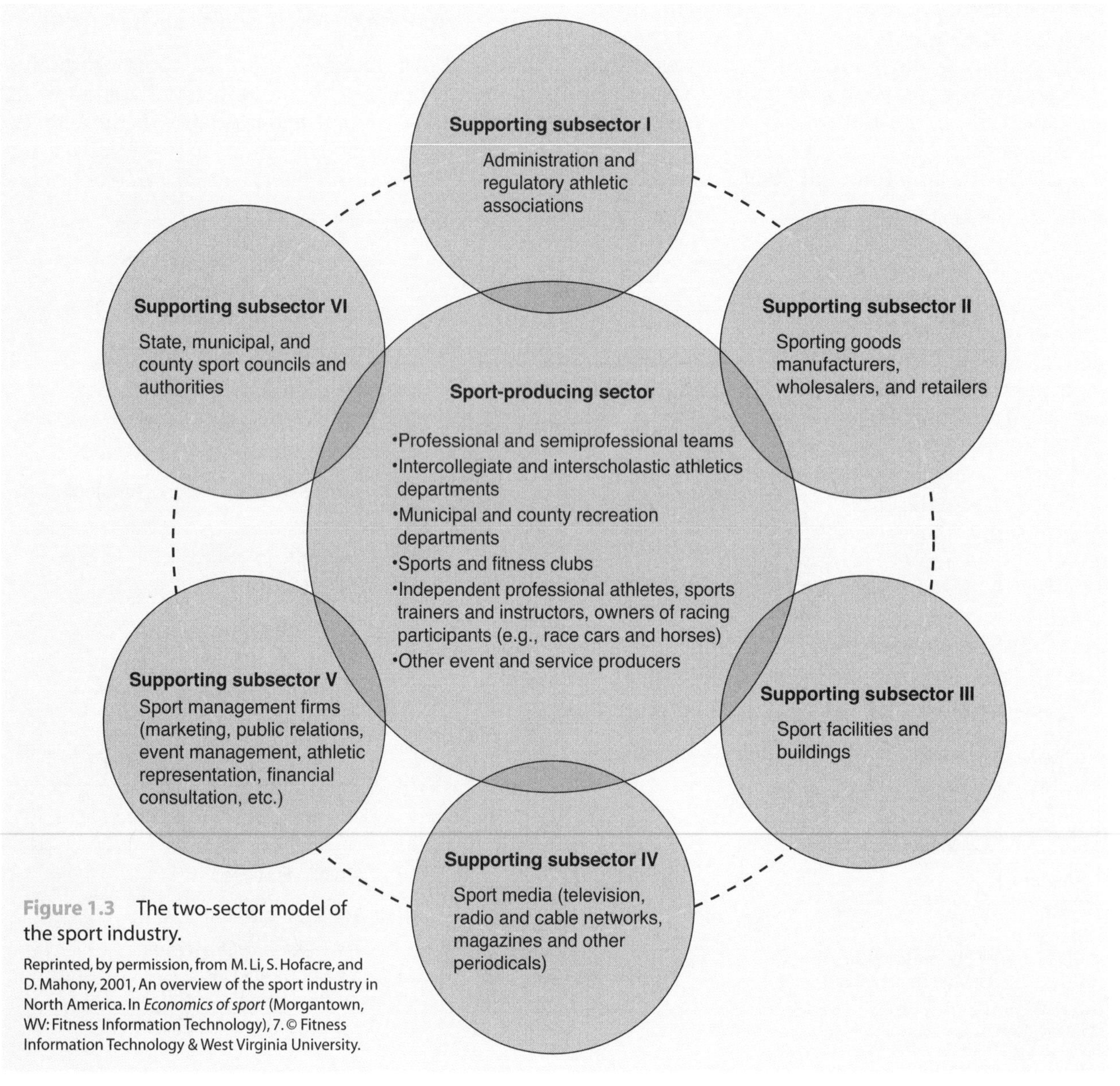

Figure 1.3 The two-sector model of the sport industry.

Reprinted, by permission, from M. Li, S. Hofacre, and D. Mahony, 2001, An overview of the sport industry in North America. In *Economics of sport* (Morgantown, WV: Fitness Information Technology), 7. © Fitness Information Technology & West Virginia University.

Sport Marketing

Sport marketing is unique because the sport product is unlike other products that consumers buy. For example, sport is consumed as quickly as it is produced. It is a perishable product that is not accompanied by any guarantees of customer satisfaction. People who provide the sport experience cannot predict the outcome because of the spontaneous nature of the activity, the inconsistency of events, and the uncertainty surrounding the results. Sport marketers, therefore, face unique challenges. You will learn much more about sport marketing in chapter 9.

Sport Enterprise Financial Structures

Most sport businesses are financed differently from other businesses. Typically, the sale of a product or service such as clothing, food, automobiles, or home cleaning finances the business. But with the exception of sporting goods stores, sport enterprises earn a significant portion of revenue not from the sale of a service such as a game, workout, or 10K run, but from extraneous sources such as television rights, concessions, road game guarantees, parking, and merchandise. Intercollegiate athletics and municipal recreation sport programs might generate revenue from student or user fees, private donations, taxes, rentals, or licensing fees. Sport managers continually compete for the **discretionary funds** of consumers through the sale of items that might or might not be related to the apparent primary focus of the enterprise. One unique aspect of sport is that it invariably attracts consumers who spend more money outside the sporting arena than they spend on the sport itself (e.g., travel, entertainment, souvenirs, and equipment). This unique financial base requires different practices within the sport setting. Sport finance is discussed in more depth in chapter 12.

discretionary funds—Money left over after necessary expenditures (e.g., rent, food, car payment, insurance) have been made.

Sport Industry Career Paths

Career paths in sport management are not as well defined as those in other vocational areas. Traditionally, many sport management practitioners have been hired from visible groups, such as intercollegiate athletics or professional sport. An example of this phenomenon is the basketball star who becomes a basketball coach and eventually an athletics director. We can find similar career advancement patterns within municipal recreation programs, sport clubs, and professional sport teams. In some situations, sport is still a closed society in which obtaining employment might depend less on what the applicant knows than on whom the applicant knows (Clay, 1995). Additionally, the attitude that members of **underrepresented groups** do not have the requisite skills for sport management positions still exists in some organizations, and this attitude creates an obstacle for aspiring sport managers. Arthur Triche, public relations director for the Atlanta Hawks and the first African American public relations director in the NBA, credits volunteering and making contacts in the sport industry as important steps that he took toward overcoming this obstacle (Clay, 1995). Most experts, both academicians and practicing sport managers, agree with Triche that volunteering and **networking** are critical to success in the sport industry. A cautionary note about networking is in order: Mere acquaintance with influential people in the world of sport is not sufficient. Unless those acquaintances have a positive impression of your competence and work ethic, you cannot expect them to assist you in your career.

underrepresented groups—People who traditionally have not been hired in sport management positions (e.g., women, people of color, people with disabilities).

networking—The building up or maintaining of informal relationships, especially with people who could bring advantages such as job or business opportunities (MSWord® online dictionary).

Learning Activity

The book, *Profiles of Sport Industry Professionals* (Robinson, Hums, Crow, & Phillips, 2001), contains the stories of people who work in various facets of the sport industry. Read the stories of people in careers that appeal to you. Write a paper on the steps that they took in their career paths and how they developed the competencies that helped them succeed. What advice do they offer to aspiring sport management professionals?

Growing evidence suggests that success in today's sport enterprise depends on a good understanding of business principles such as finance, marketing, sales, sponsorship, and management. As a result, contemporary sport organizations are abandoning traditional employment practices and attitudes, such as hiring only people with experience as athletes or with specific enthusiasm for sport. The current level of economic competition within sport enterprises mandates that employers recognize and appreciate sound business expertise and that their hiring practices reflect these values. As Jesse Krebs, president and CEO of the Wrestling Mall states on Monster.com (Krumrie, 2006), "Just because you have an interest in sports doesn't necessarily mean you will succeed in sports-industry management." At the same site, Matt Krumrie, a journalist who has been reporting on the employment industry since 1998, states, "The business of sports management is not about wins and losses, stats and glamour. It's about business—that's the bottom line."

In spite of some advances resulting from efforts to diversify the sport management workforce, we have a long way to go before we can claim that sport is truly an equal opportunity environment (Acosta & Carpenter, 2006; Lapchick, 2004-2006; Parks & Roberton, 2002; Schoenfeld, 1999). Opportunities for people of color and women continue to lag behind opportunities for white males, both in the core sport industry (e.g., professional sport senior executives, athletics directors, general managers) and in the support industries (e.g., broadcast media, sport agents, concessions). Someday soon, many of you who are currently preparing for careers as sport managers will be in positions of authority in which you can effect change in the organizational culture of the sport industry. If you pay careful attention to the value of workforce diversity, the world of sport and society at large will benefit from your efforts.

organizational culture—Workplace values, norms, and behaviors that produce patterns of behavior unique to an organization.

workforce diversity—People of different ages, genders, religions, physical abilities, social classes, sexual orientations, races, ethnicities, and cultures working together in an organization.

Sport As a Social Institution

Sport is a distinctive social activity that is frequently the basis of a person's social identity (Coakley, 2004). As such, it is a social institution of almost unbelievable magnitude and influence. What other social pursuit is allotted several pages in the daily newspaper, has its own slot on every television and radio news program, has its own cable channels, and creates what appears to be an international withdrawal crisis when members of its workforce go on strike? The sheer power of sport mandates that people who wish to manage it acquire a sound understanding of its historical, psychological, sociological, cultural, and philosophical dimensions. Understanding sport marketing and management is essential for prospective managers; equally important is understanding and appreciating the social and cultural implications of sporting activities. Parks and Roberton (2000) described the social power of sport:

> The pervasive influence of sport on the values and attitudes of the general population demonstrates its power in American society. One example of this power is the adulation accorded many athletes, both amateur and professional, and the concomitant expectation that athletes should serve as positive role models for youth. The influence of athletes is also reflected in the sizable royalties paid for their endorsements of a multitude of products, ranging from long-distance telephone services to beer to sports bras. An additional example of the influence of sport is the amount of attention devoted to athletic contests and the sport industry by both print and broadcast media. (p. 422)

The General Assembly of the United Nations publicly recognized the power of sport "to promote education, health, development and peace," when it declared 2005 the International Year of Sport and Physical Education (United Nations, 2000-2005, p. 1). Further noting the major role that sport can play in promoting the UN goals of peace, dignity, and prosperity, the executive director of the United Nations Environment Programme (UNEP) stated, "The way sports events are run, the way sporting goods companies do business, and the way sports stars conduct themselves on and off the field can have profound effects far beyond the financial bottom line" (Toepfer, 2003, p. 2). Clearly, the immense power of sport mandates that sport managers understand the social implications of their actions. Contemporary sport enterprises need well-prepared managers who can make sound management decisions in the context of sport as an exceptionally influential social institution. Many chapters of this book elaborate on the social significance of sport.

Learning Activity

On pages 2 and 3 you will find a list of books that address sport as a social and cultural phenomenon. Read one or more of those books, either individually or as a group project. Keep a journal of your impressions of each chapter. Particularly note instances in which you changed your viewpoint on a particular issue or problem and instances in which your viewpoint was affirmed. Explain why you did or did not change your mind.

SPORT MANAGEMENT COMPETENCIES

Bureaucratic processes and emphasis on job specialization characterize contemporary sport organizations. In these organizations, job descriptions define the requirements of various positions, and the organizations hire people to perform the jobs as described. Some scholars have predicted, however, that the organization of the future might focus more on **competencies** of individual employees as well as the ability of those employees to learn new competencies as marketplace demands and organizational cultures change (Lawler & Ledford, 1997). With this approach, people would be hired "for organizational membership, not to fill a job" (p. 240), and the reward system within the organization would be based on how well employees demonstrated the required competencies. The competency approach to hiring and managing an organization will require you, as a prospective employee, to consciously develop the knowledge and skills that are valued by the organizations in your chosen field. Although the transition from the **bureaucratic model** to the competency-based model is not complete, you would be wise to consider the competencies valued by contemporary sport organizations.

competencies—Skills and knowledge necessary for successful performance in the job.

bureaucratic model—An organizational design that stresses specialization, division of labor, hierarchy, formal rules, and standard operating procedures (Lawler & Ledford, 1997).

Research suggests that sport management competencies are universal and have remained relatively stable over time (Cuskelly & Auld, 1991; Danylchuk & Boucher, 2003; Horch & Schütte, 2003; Lambrecht, 1991; Quain & Parks, 1986). In addition to emphasizing competencies required to perform traditional tasks such as personnel management and planning, today's business world places increased importance on communication skills, communication technology, and the ability to interact in a global and multicultural society (Ammon, 2000; Danylchuk & Boucher, 2003; DeSensi, 1994; Li, Kanters, & Ammon, 2002; Masteralexis & McDonald, 1997). In fact, with respect to competencies expected of sport managers, Horch and Schütte noted, "Interpersonal communication, information tasks and external representation as well as social tasks are central components of their activity. This is why they should be given equal consideration in basic and advanced training frameworks" (p. 73).

Although competencies required for specific settings depend on the assigned tasks and the type and size of particular organizations (Horch & Schütte, 2003), the sport management tasks presented in figure 1.4 provide an overview of industry expectations. Most of the competencies required for these tasks are transferable, which means that you should be able to use them in a variety of vocational settings that include, but are not limited to, sport organizations.

COMMUNICATION IS THE KEY

"If I went back to college again, I'd concentrate on two areas: learning to write and to speak before an audience. Nothing in life is more important than the ability to communicate effectively" (Gerald R. Ford, 38th President of the United States, 1979, p. 50).

The tasks in the core of figure 1.4 are general sport management responsibilities, those in which all sport managers must be proficient and, to varying degrees, be able to perform on the job. For example, regardless of whether you work in a sport club, the front office of a professional sport team, a sport governance association, or an intercollegiate athletics department, you need to demonstrate competence in writing, speaking, and public relations as well as in the other tasks presented in the core.

The tasks listed in the clusters branching out from the core reflect distinctions between two types of responsibilities. Leadership and management skills are necessary for performing tasks in the organization management cluster. Sport managers need good organizational skills to direct and supervise subordinates in settings such as sport clubs, municipal recreation programs, or sport associations for

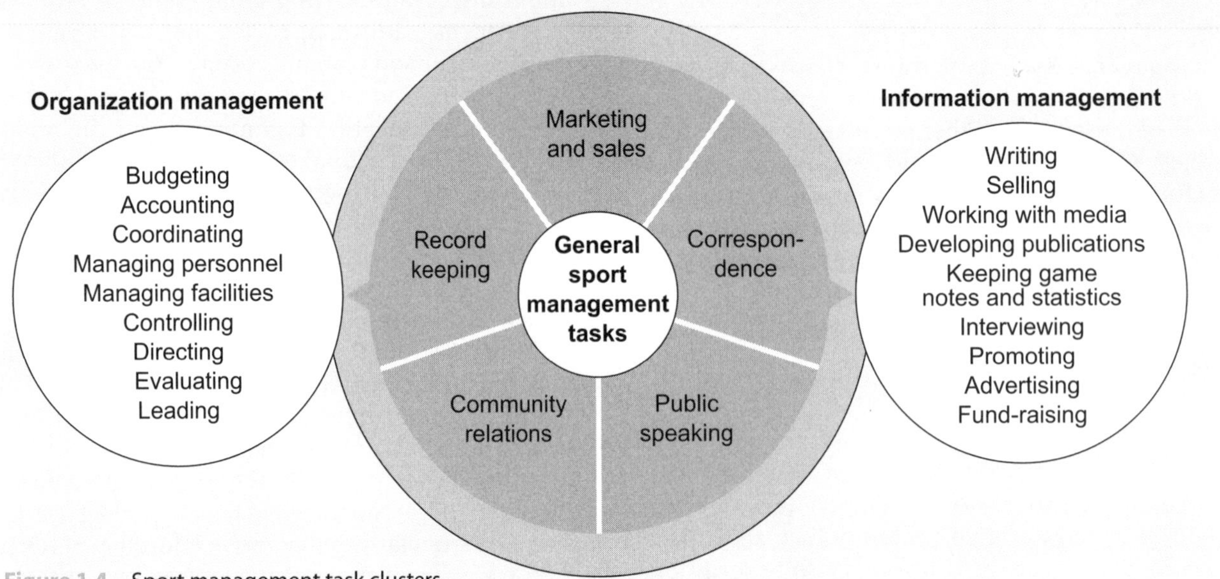

Figure 1.4 Sport management task clusters.

Source: Parks, J.B., Chopra, P.S., Quain, R.J., and I.E. Alguindigue, 1988, "ExSport I: An expert system for sport management career counseling." *Journal of Research on Computing in Education*, 21(2), 196-209.

specific populations, such as seniors or people with differing abilities; in intercollegiate athletics and professional sport; and in the business aspect of any sport-related enterprise.

In the information management cluster, written and oral communication skills are of paramount importance. Information management tasks include identifying information needs, acquiring information, categorizing and storing information, packaging and formatting information, developing information products and services, disseminating information, and analyzing and using information (McGee & Prusak, 1993). Contemporary sport communication practitioners also must be highly skilled in computer technology related to data storage and retrieval as well as Web-based technology. Sophisticated information management competencies are critical in areas such as sport marketing, media relations, and sport writing.

Note that although tasks requiring similar competencies appear within one cluster or the other, the clusters are not mutually exclusive. For example, people employed in media relations (information management cluster) also need to be able to manage and lead personnel (organization management cluster). Conversely, employees in organization management positions need strong communication skills to be successful. In chapters 14 and 15, you will learn more about the types of organizations that exist in the sport industry and the skills and abilities that managers should possess.

Learning Activity

Table 1.1 presents examples of a variety of sport industry positions categorized within the segments of the Pitts et al. (1994) model. Identify the competencies that you believe are required to be successful in the positions that are of interest to you.

Some of you might be planning to obtain professional positions in one of the numerous health-related industries. Some people preparing for careers in these settings focus solely on acquiring the fundamental scientific understanding for such positions and are unaware of the need to develop proficiency in tasks associated with organization and information management. Our experience is that health care professionals soon learn that management skills are required. For example, a contemporary trend is for athletic trainers to work in commercial enterprises such as sport medicine clinics, hospitals, professional sport teams, and industrial fitness programs. In recognition of this trend, students who seek certification by the National Athletic Trainers' Association (NATA) must demonstrate competence in health care management (Board of Certification, 2004; Moss & Parks, 1991). Moreover, after you have been an athletic trainer or other health care professional for a while, you might receive an opportunity to become the director of your clinic or club. If so, competence

Table 1.1

Examples of Job Titles in Three Product Type Segments of the Sport Industry

Sport performance segment	Sport production segment	Sport promotion segment
Collegiate sports information director; assistant director	Sales representative–sporting goods manufacturer	Sport marketing coordinator–rental car agency
Collegiate facility manager; ticket sales manager	Sales representative–sports equipment company	Writer or producer–Internet sport broadcast
Collegiate promotion or marketing director	Manager–sporting goods and apparel retail store	Financial analyst–sport sponsorship management company
Sport tourism company travel manager	Account executive–sporting goods retailer or wholesaler	Sport journalist–print
Marketing director–racetrack	Sales representative–sport surfacing manufacturer or supplier	Sales representative–sports TV channel
Campus recreation director	Assistant media director–collegiate athletics conference	Account executive–sport marketing or management agency
Media director–motor speedway	Events coordinator–professional sport facility	Legal consultant–sport business licensing company
Municipal recreation–assistant athletics supervisor; special events	Executive director–regional sports commission	Sport journalist–broadcast director; assistant general manager
Marketing director–International Special Olympics	Facilities design consultant–sport facility architectural company	Vice president–sport licensing company
Marketing manager–professional golf tournament	Legislative services assistant–governing body	Vice president, sport sponsorship and events–credit card company

in both organization management and information management functions will be prerequisite to your success. So, although none of the chapters in this book will provide you with information regarding the scientific fundamentals of health-related careers, you will benefit from the knowledge that is presented.

Learning Activity

Go to www.career.fsu.edu/ccis/guides/infoint.html for suggestions about how to conduct informational interviews. Then conduct an informational interview with someone who has worked in either a sport or a commercial health-related setting for five years or longer. Ask your interviewee about the use of management skills in the position and how she or he acquired those skills. Write a paper about this person's position and skills. Focus particularly on her or his experiences in managerial situations, both as a manager and as a lower-level employee. What elements of this person's experience can help you become a better employee and a better manager?

The model in figure 1.4 includes only the technical responsibilities involved in managing sport. Employers are also looking for specific personal and professional qualities in graduates of sport management programs. In addressing the characteristics shared by outstanding sport management students and professionals, Cuneen and Sidwell (1998) noted that, in general, such students

> (a) possess a good work ethic, (b) are flexible in both their personal and professional schedules, (c) are people-oriented, (d) are able to perform in committee-type work or other group projects, (e) are goal-oriented self-starters who have the ability to close-out tasks absent of supervision, (f) are creative, and (g) are intellectually curious. (p. 12)

You will learn more about the importance of these characteristics in chapter 2.

Assume that you possess the qualities and characteristics delineated by Cuneen and Sidwell (1998), that you achieve the required level of education, and that you obtain that coveted job in sport. The question then arises, Will your job bring you satisfaction? Data collected from sport managers in both the United States and Europe suggest that you can expect to be satisfied with most facets of your job (Madella, 2003; Parks & Parra, 1994; Parks, Russell, Wood, Roberton, & Shewokis, 1995; Robinson, Peterson, Tedrick, & Carpenter, 2003; Smucker & Kent, 2004). These studies have also shown, however, that you might be somewhat less satisfied with your pay and your opportunities for promotion. Of course, all jobs are different, and you might find a job that brings you immense satisfaction in all aspects, including pay and advancement. In some cases, however, the fulfillment that sport managers find in their jobs comes from their passion for sport, the camaraderie they enjoy with their coworkers, or their love of the duties the jobs entail, with salary and promotion being of lower priority.

Learning Activity

Read an article about job satisfaction of sport managers. List the facets with which the participants in the study tended to be satisfied. List the facets with which they were less satisfied. Based on what you know about sport management jobs, why do you think that the participants answered as they did? What insights does this study provide you with respect to your future career in sport management?

FUTURE CHALLENGES AND OPPORTUNITIES FOR SPORT MANAGERS

The future will present sport managers with many challenges and opportunities, some of which have already begun to emerge and others that we can only imagine. In the remaining chapters, you will learn about a variety of challenges facing specific segments of the sport industry. For this chapter, we have chosen to address four of the opportunities and challenges that sport managers in all segments of the industry will face—challenges associated with technology, ethics, globalization, and social responsibility.

Technology

The technology explosion of the past several decades has been mind boggling, and this is only the beginning! As Danylchuk and Boucher (2003) noted, ". . . the sport industry is already information driven. This will continue to increase and the demand for technically competent employees will continue to accelerate" (p. 293). In the epilogue to their book *Sport Business in the Global Marketplace* (2003), Hans Westerbeek and Aaron Smith provided a hypothetical glimpse into the future with their prediction of a sport scenario in the year 2038. (See "Brilliant Orange Finally Go All the Way!" on p. 19.)

Regardless of whether the future will be exactly as Westerbeek and Smith (2003) predict, their scenario does provide food for thought. One notion to consider, however, is that technology is not an end unto itself; it is a means to an end—an innovation that facilitates progress and helps us realize other accomplishments. In the future, scientific advances in computers and communication technology will play an increasingly significant role in our society and in sport management. This progress will likely be accompanied by acknowledgment of the human need for "high-touch" activities, many of which the sport experience can provide. The challenge, therefore, is to become proficient in using technology while remaining aware of the need for human interaction in people's lives and understanding how sport can facilitate such interaction.

Learning Activity

Robin Gunston (2005) identified five key drivers of change in contemporary sport: the lack of a clear difference between work and leisure, the need for instant entertainment, the increasing control of commercial enterprises over sport, the politicization of sport governing bodies, and the decline of core social values. He predicted that the influence of these drivers could result in the development of four possible types of sport: religiosport, machosport, technosport, and valuesport. Read Gunston's article and write a paper in which you (1) explain each of the drivers of change, (2) describe each of the possible outcomes, and (3) discuss which outcomes you believe are most probable, giving reasons for your choices.

Ethics

Sport managers must deal with a multitude of questions that require an understanding of ethical principles and moral psychology. Consider the following:

- How can we best achieve gender, race, and class equity in sport?

BRILLIANT ORANGE FINALLY GO ALL THE WAY!

Amsterdam, 10 July 2038. Celebrations are under way in Amsterdam where a whole nation indulges in the "Orange Eleven's" victory in the World Cup final against Cameroon. In a capacity filled Manage-to-Manage Dome, 100,000 on-site spectators and 6 billion people worldwide celebrated a three-hour entertainment extravaganza culminating in a World Cup final that will be remembered for its brilliant soccer and mind-boggling drama.

First Time Ever Sell-Out of Virtual Stadium

Pre-match entertainment started off in spectacular fashion with hologrammatic appearances by Elvis Presley, Marilyn Monroe and Frank Sinatra, complemented by a live appearance of the Rolling Clones. Presley and Monroe performed the World Cup hymn, Sinatra treated the crowd to some classics from the last century and the Clones performed three songs from their first album, before they took the honours of kicking off the World Cup final.

The Dutch turned around what proved to be a high-scoring and equal contest throughout the four quarters of the match during extended play, when the score was still level at 4-4. Twenty minutes into extra time, after both teams were forced to take six players off the pitch (one player every three minutes) and goals were increased in height by 20 centimetres, cloned veteran striker Hans Westerbeek scored the golden goal. Westerbeek II was the first person in the world to be genetically modified with the help of "top striker" DNA. Former Dutch great Marco van Basten donated his superior genetic material through FIFA's soccer development foundation, for a modest fee of course.

Nationality gene chip measurements indicate that 88.02 per cent of all Dutch in the world witnessed this moment live, 3.02 per cent on free to air television in the continent of Africa, 1.90 per cent on pay television, 23.12 per cent on the mobile Internet, 0.1 per cent on-site (predominantly backpackers who were willing to cope with the inconvenience of actually attending the event live at no cost) and a staggering 59.52 per cent virtually live, having bought tickets in the virtual Manage-to-Manage Dome. The Quantum Entanglement technology that was trialled first at the 2006 Commonwealth Games in Melbourne, Australia, has become so popular that the virtual Manage-to-Manage Dome was sold out for the first time in the history of digital virtual stadia. The technology has become so sophisticated that it only takes a contact lens-based microchip, with a wireless link to a MoGMeD (Mobile Global Media Device) to be transported to the stadium and interact with those who also subscribed to the match. So many people (3.2 billion worldwide) wanted to log on to the server powered through the international Duff beer space station that memory capacity to interact as a live spectator in the Dome ran out. The newly introduced violence protection chip was reported to work very well, with only minor clashes reported among non-football interested cyberspace fringes. Given the effectiveness of the violence protection chip, denying access to the stadium by any spectator who is genetically predisposed to cyber violence, the virtual police had little trouble containing the culprits. (Westerbeek & Smith, 2003, pp. 229-230)

H. Westerbeek and A. Smith, Sport business in the global marketplace, 2003, Palgrave Macmillan. Reproduced with permission of Palgrave Macmillan.

- Do professional team owners owe primary allegiance to themselves or to the communities that support the team?
- Should sport teams appropriate the sacred rituals and symbols of American Indians?
- How can we balance academic integrity with the demands of intercollegiate competition?
- Should gymnasts and wrestlers sacrifice their youth and health for victory?
- Is winning really the bottom line of sport?
- Is intercollegiate sport an entertainment business for public consumption or an extracurricular opportunity for student development, or both, or something else?
- Should sport programs for men be negatively affected in the name of providing equal opportunity for women?

The list is endless, and no doubt you could add your concerns to it. Malloy and Zakus (1995) suggested that sport management students should understand the need to "challenge the assumptions, both overt and covert, of sport and society to enable themselves to make ethically sound decisions" (p. 54). Malloy and Zakus further noted that helping students develop the knowledge and skill necessary to challenge traditional assumptions and to make ethically defensible decisions requires the integration of instruction and practice into the professional preparation program. Toward that end,

SPORT CLUBS AND THE "SPORT FOR ALL" MOVEMENT IN WESTERN EUROPE

Marijke Taks, Belgium

Participant sport is delivered differently in Western Europe than it is in North America. In North America, the educational system delivers most participant sport. In Europe, however, community-based sport clubs play a dominant role in the sport delivery system. Although a school sport system outside regular physical education classes does exist in Belgium and in most Western European countries, it does not receive much attention or exposure, and people are hardly aware of its existence. Most participant sport takes place in sport clubs.

Sport clubs, which are an integral part of European communities, have a long history and strong tradition in European society. Sport clubs are voluntary organizations led by a board of directors, who are often a group of friends. The directors make the decisions and run the club. Besides the participants, the clubs have coaches, trainers and technical staff, administrative volunteers, parents, facility operators, cafeteria owners, and so forth. Through cooperation among all stakeholders, clubs create social networks outside the work or school environment. Much socializing occurs during after-sport hours in bars, pubs, or cafeterias—the so-called 19th holes or fifth quarters. This camaraderie is an integral part of the sport experience and often takes up more time than the sport participation itself!

In 1966 Sport for All was adopted as the major long-term objective for the sports program of the Council of Europe. The Sport for All philosophy includes the right to participate in sport, human development, cooperation between public authorities and voluntary organizations, safeguarding sport from exploitation, accessibility of facilities and nature for the purpose of recreation, and the need for qualified personnel at all levels. The Sport for All movement reflected the strong social values of the 1960s—democratization, participation, inclusion, and pluralism. The movement strengthened the position of the sports clubs because as the Sport for All movement grew, so did the involvement of the state. National, regional, and local governmental agencies started to provide direct and indirect support to voluntary sport clubs, and they still do so. For example, a strong partnership between local sport authorities (e.g., municipal departments of sport and recreation) and the sport clubs has always been in place. The local sport authorities mainly provide the facilities, whereas the sport clubs offer the sport programs. Nowadays, a third partner, the school, is being targeted for providing additional facilities during after-school hours.

Sport clubs in Europe offer a wide variety of sport programs and provide opportunities to children, adolescents, and adults to become involved in sport at all levels. Involvement can be as a recreational participant or interclub competitor; as a coach, administrator, or member of the board of directors; as a facility provider; or even as a bartender. Each of these actors has a role to play in the sport delivery system of Europe as it strives to offer "sport for all."

---

you will find information about ethical crises facing sport in many chapters of this book. Now is the time to begin reflecting on these concerns because you surely will face them in the years to come.

The following ethical maxims represent simple and quick considerations that a sport manager can use when making decisions (Laczniak, 1983, p. 7; 1985, p. 10). We have added specific examples of each maxim to help you understand how a sport manager might put them into action.

- ***The golden rule***: Act in the way you would expect others to act toward you (e.g., providing superior customer service to the fans attending a sporting event staged by your organization).
- ***The utilitarian principle***: Act in a way that results in the greatest good for the greatest number of people (e.g., increasing resources as necessary and appropriate to pay for enhanced security at an athletic competition between two teams that are staunch rivals).
- ***Kant's categorical imperative***: Act in such a way that the action taken under the circumstances could be a universal law or rule of behavior (e.g., enabling a person to cancel a contract within three days of signing).
- ***The professional ethic***: Take only actions that a disinterested (objective) panel of professional colleagues would view as proper (e.g., requiring athletic trainers in your organization to be accredited by the National Athletic Trainers' Association).
- ***The television test***: Always ask, "Would I feel comfortable explaining to a national television audience why I took this action?" (e.g., commenting on a recent allegation that a colleague had been arrested on criminal drug violations).

Jelske Snoeck and Elie Balligand during the 2006 Belgian national badminton championships mixed doubles final. Because badminton is less visible than soccer or tennis, the clubs had to stage this tournament without government assistance. It appears, then, that the concentration of public resources on a few popular sports is a public health issue on both sides of the Atlantic in terms of encouraging widespread participation in sport.

Photo courtesy of Sport for All.

As noted by Laczniak, these maxims are oversimplifications of complex, multifaceted ethical frameworks. They can serve well, however, as a basic introduction to the place of ethics in a sport manager's decision-making process.

principled decision making—Basing decisions on the "Six Pillars of Character"—trustworthiness, respect, responsibility, fairness, caring, and good citizenship (responsible participation in society) (Josephson Institute of Ethics, 2002).

Learning Activity

Excerpts from the code of ethics established by the North American Society for Sport Management are presented on p. 24. This code is designed to serve as a guide to **principled decision making**. Choose five of these principles and explain how each could influence a specific decision in one, or more, of the sport management positions listed in table 1.1.

Globalization of Sport

The need to understand and appreciate other countries and cultures cannot be overstated. In recognition of this fact, most chapters of this book contain information on the sport industry in other nations. Because the need for students to learn about other cultures is so urgent, several sport management scholars have suggested that the curriculum should provide students with a global view of sport and the sport industry (Ammon, 2000; Danylchuk & Boucher, 2003; Li, Kanters, & Ammon, 2002; Masteralexis & McDonald, 1997). Regardless of the requirements of your curriculum, you can take several actions to prepare yourself to interact effectively in the global community. For example, although students in many countries consider mastery of the English language a basic skill, most students in the United States do not master languages of other countries. Consequently, US students can distinguish themselves from their peers by learning a language other than their native tongue. Studying in another country for an extended period and completing courses that focus on other cultures are additional steps that you can take to broaden your horizons and enhance the quality of your life as you increase your value in the marketplace.

Learning Activity

Investigate sport management jobs in countries other than your own. Information in chapters 7 and 8 will be helpful to you. You can also visit some of the numerous Web sites identified throughout the book. Make a list of at least 10 jobs that appeal to you. What qualifications are required for those jobs? How would you go about acquiring each of those qualifications?

Social Responsibility

In the future, enlightened sport managers will be more aware of their social responsibilities and will deliver their services in ways that reflect this understanding. For example, sport managers worldwide will be conscious of environmental concerns and will incorporate this understanding into their business practices. Environmental concerns that are important to sport managers include air and water quality, land and water use, waste management, energy management, transportation design and services, accommodation design and services, and facilities construction. Indeed, the United Nations Environment Programme (UNEP) has the following objectives for its Sport and Environment Strategy (Toepfer, 2003, p. 1):

1. To promote the integration of environmental considerations in sports
2. To use the popularity of sports to promote environmental awareness
3. To promote the development of environmentally friendly sports facilities and the manufacture of environmentally friendly sports goods

Additional evidence of sport managers' sense of social responsibility will include the routine provision of professional childcare services in sport facilities and the targeting of previously untapped and undertapped target markets, such as women and people of differing ages, abilities, and sexual orientations. Sport managers of the future will also recognize the importance of keeping the sport experience accessible to all socioeconomic groups. Several chapters of this book address socially responsible sport management.

Learning Activity

Visit the Vermont Frost Heaves of the American Basketball Association at www.vermontfrostheaves.com/about. Make a list of the ways in which this club demonstrates social responsibility.

FUTURE OF THE SPORT INDUSTRY

Pitts and Stotlar (2002) observed that the world of sport is growing rapidly. This growth is reflected not only in the introduction of many new sports but also in the increasing number of opportunities to participate in sports and activities, an upsurge in the number and variety of sport-related magazines and sport-related sites on the Internet, enhanced mass media exposure of sporting activities, growth in the number and types of sport facilities and events, increased interest in sport tourism and adventure travel, and the provision of sport-related goods and services for a greater variety of market segments. Moreover, new professional sports have emerged, sport opportunities are being offered to a more diverse population, endorsements and sponsorships are on the rise, sport industry education is becoming more prevalent and sophisticated, marketing and promotion orientation is growing in the sport industry, sport managers are becoming more competent, and the globalization of the sport industry is progressing rapidly (Pitts & Stotlar). Undoubtedly, these advances will create numerous job opportunities for aspiring sport managers. Madella (2003), however, cautions that the quality of these jobs should be carefully monitored.

In 1989 an entire issue of a now-defunct sport magazine titled *Sports inc*, was devoted to predictions about the nature and scope of sport in the 1990s ("What Will Happen to Sports in the '90s," 1989). Over a decade later, in a special issue of the *Journal of Sport Management*, several authors reflected on those 1989 predictions and provided new predictions for the ensuing millennium (Cuneen & Schneider, 2001a). As shown in table 1.2, these authors' predictions encompassed sport economics, professional sport, women's sport, sport gambling, and Canadian intercollegiate sport. The information in table 1.2 raises several questions that you, as a future sport manager, will need to address. These questions include whether sport will continue to grow; how North American social,

Table 1.2

Summary of *Journal of Sport Management* Reflections on 1990s Sport and Forecasts for 2000-Era Sport

Topic	General points
Sport business in a new decade (Mahony & Howard)	• 1990s sport industry climbed to a new high • Abundant new venues led to greater disparity among teams • Increased need for financing affected professional sport economics • Attendance declined at most major league venues • Future economic stability depends on creativity and technology • Big events, rivalries, and marquee players will have to be exploited in order to maintain profit and interest
Managing professional teams (Gladden, Irwin, & Sutton)	• Taxpayers rejected many facility proposals • Increased ticket prices reflected financial necessity rather than supply and demand • Fan loyalty decreased due to many factors, including player mobility • Future management will focus on strategies associated with long-term franchise stability rather than short-term profit associated with winning • Relationship-building efforts will increase in an attempt to keep/build fan bases • Strategic alliances, mergers, and regional sport networks will continue to form • Consumer interaction and customer management will be paramount
Reflections on women's sport (Spencer & McClung)	• Tennis experienced a crisis in title sponsorship • Individual tennis and golf stars earned millions in product/company endorsements • Sex appeal remains a prime consideration in endorsement and marketing strategy • Summer and Winter Olympic sport stars and events grew at rapid-fire pace • Women's professional and amateur team sports such as basketball and ice hockey grew steadily • Great gender disparity remains in coaching ranks
Sport gambling (Claussen & Miller)	• Expansion of opportunities reflected expansion of public interest in gambling • "Governmental endorsement" in the form of lotteries helped to triple gambling-related games • Improved TV access generated public interest • Internet gambling is growing and prompting legal responses • Sport administrators will need to protect the integrity of sport contests
Canadian intercollegiate sport (Danylchuk & MacLean)	• Canadian Interuniversity Athletic Union implemented changes in decision making, communication, programmatic orientation, and delivery • Gender and sport equity drive many sport and financial decisions • Athletic awards (first party scholarships) spur debates among coaches and administration • Funding crises will prompt more emphasis on marketing • Technology will change sport delivery and environments on Canadian campuses

Reprinted, by permission, from J. Cuneen and R. Schneider, 2001b, "Sport in the third millennium: A retrospective and perspective on 1990 and 2000-era sport," Journal of Sport Management, 15(4): 270-271.

political, cultural, and economic trends will affect sport; how global developments will affect sport; and whether the global influence of North American sport will continue unabated (Cuneen & Schneider, 2001b). Of course, a major question for you is how the answers to these questions will affect your future as a sport manager.

Learning Activity

Select five of the positions presented in table 1.1. Make a list of at least one specific action that sport managers in each of those positions can take to address each of the environmental concerns listed at www.greengold.on.ca/index.html (Chernushenko, 2001).

CODE OF ETHICS, NORTH AMERICAN SOCIETY FOR SPORT MANAGEMENT

The following canons or principles, arranged according to category or dimension, shall be considered by the sport manager in the performance of professional duties:

- The sport manager should hold paramount the safety, health, and welfare of the individual in the performance of professional duties.
- The sport manager should act in accordance with the highest standards of professional integrity.
- The sport manager's primary responsibility is to students/clients.
- When setting fees for service in private or commercial settings, the sport manager should ensure that they are fair, reasonable, considerate, and commensurate with the service performed and with due respect to the students'/clients' ability to pay.
- The sport manager should adhere to any and all commitments made to the employing organization. The relationship should be characterized by fairness, non-malfeasance, and truthfulness.
- The sport manager should treat colleagues with respect, courtesy, fairness, and good faith.
- The sport manager should uphold and advance the values and ethical standards, the knowledge, and the mission of the profession.
- The sport manager should promote the general welfare of society.

North American Society for Sport Management, 1992.

YOU CAN MAKE A DIFFERENCE!

The future will most assuredly bring change, something that can be frightening and is frequently resisted. Progressive sport managers who can anticipate and embrace change will have opportunities to be agents of change who will transform the way that sport is managed. We hope that you will be one of those managers!

Learning Activity

Read one of the articles published in the special issue of the *Journal of Sport Management* (Cuneen & Schneider, 2001b). Write a synopsis of the reflections and predictions it contains. How will each of these predictions affect the sport job market? Describe your role in the sport environment of the future as described in the article. How will you cope with the predicted challenges and opportunities?

Join the sport management student organization at your university. Run for an office or volunteer to work on a project. The experience that you gain through these sorts of activities will be valuable when you take a position in the sport industry.

SUMMARY

In this chapter, sport is broadly defined as (1) "all forms of physical activity which, through casual (informal) or organised participation, aim at expressing or improving physical fitness and mental well-being, forming social relationships or obtaining results in competition at all levels" (Council of Europe, 2001) and (2) "any activity, experience, or business enterprise focused on fitness, recreation, athletics, or leisure" (Pitts et al., 1994). The sport industry can be conceptualized based on (1) the settings in which it occurs, (2) the many types of sporting activities that exist, and (3) the industry segments into which different sport businesses and organizations can be categorized. Three models of segmentation describe the sport industry: the product type model, the economic impact model, and the sport activity model. Four unique aspects of sport management are sport marketing, the sport enterprise financial structure, career paths, and the power of sport as a social institution. Sport managers should possess general, transferable competencies as well as competencies specific to organization management responsibilities and information management responsibilities. People who work in the health care industry should also possess these competencies. The next generation of sport managers will face challenges associated with technology, ethics, globalization, and social responsibility. Enlightened sport managers of the future will be competent in the technical aspects of their jobs and will be agents of change, both in the management of sport and in the larger society.

Review Questions

1. Using the definitions of sport presented in this chapter, make a list of 10 activities that qualify as sports and explain why they qualify as sports.
2. What is the difference between *sport* and *sports*?
3. List and discuss five sport business settings that might represent job opportunities for sport managers.
4. Name five new sports that have emerged in the last few years. How has their emergence affected career opportunities in sport management?
5. Describe the three models of segmentation that have been applied to the sport industry and provide examples of sport organizations in each segment of each model.
6. Identify four unique aspects of sport management and explain how each aspect acts to make the sport business different from other businesses.
7. Contrast the bureaucratic and the competency-based models of organizational design and explain the implications of each for aspiring sport managers.
8. Explain the task clusters into which sport managers' responsibilities can be classified. Explain how the competencies required for those tasks overlap those of different professional positions.
9. Describe personal and professional characteristics of successful sport management students and professionals and explain how you might acquire and develop those competencies.
10. Describe what forecasters predict for the future of the sport industry with respect to sport economics, professional sport, women's sport, sport gambling, and Canadian intercollegiate sport.
11. Describe opportunities and challenges in technology, ethics, globalization, and social responsibility that all sport managers will face in the future.
12. Define principled decision making and give examples of when and how sport managers need to make principled decisions.
13. Explain why the United Nations proclaimed 2005 as the International Year of Sport and Physical Education.

Developing a Professional Perspective

Kathryn S. Hoff—Bowling Green State University ■ **JoAnn Kroll**—Bowling Green State University
Carol Fletcher—St. John's University

Learning Objectives

After studying this chapter, you will be able to do the following:

1. Discuss your perspective on professional preparation, professional attitude, and career planning and management as three important elements for success in sport industries.
2. Explain the three components of an undergraduate sport management curriculum.
3. Describe the content areas required by the National Association for Sport and Physical Education (NASPE) and the North American Society for Sport Management (NASSM) for undergraduate sport management programs.
4. Discuss field experiences in sport management, including information about how to obtain them, what steps you can take during them, and what to do following them.
5. Identify differences between master's and doctoral sport management programs.
6. Discuss ways in which your personal appearance, work transition and adjustment, and business etiquette can enhance your employability and advancement.
7. Describe the four stages involved in career planning.
8. Identify several resources that are useful in planning a career in sport management.

Achieving success in most business settings requires specific knowledge, skills, values, and understanding that students are expected to begin to acquire as undergraduates. The first step toward acquiring these requisites to success involves adopting the perspective that you are now more than simply a student. You are a professional. You cannot wait until four years from now to begin to accept the responsibilities of being a professional. Your professors will expect you to conduct yourself with professionalism, and you will gain more from your degree program if you consider yourself a professional rather than just a student. Your perspective of yourself and sport management as an academic pursuit will influence how you approach your course work, your extracurricular activities, and your relationships with your fellow students and instructors. Now is the time to begin to develop a professional perspective.

This chapter addresses three components of a professional perspective:

- **Professional preparation**—the courses and experiences that you can expect in your undergraduate curriculum and beyond
- **Professional attitude**—how to present a professional image, suggestions for entering the world of work and being comfortable and productive there, and the fundamentals of business etiquette
- **Career planning and management**—purposeful steps that you can take and helpful resources available to you as you contemplate entering the world of work

PROFESSIONAL PREPARATION

Sport management preparation programs exist at the baccalaureate (undergraduate), master's, and doctoral levels. Baccalaureate programs prepare students for entry-level positions in the sport industry. Master's-level education prepares students for more advanced, specialized responsibilities. The doctorate usually emphasizes research. Students who seek the doctorate typically wish to become professors or work in some other capacity in a college or university setting.

Currently, you might be enrolled in an undergraduate program. Or you might be a high school student or a university student in another major field who wants to learn more about opportunities in sport management. In any case, you will benefit from an explanation of what to expect in a sport management curriculum at the undergraduate level. Most undergraduate sport management professional preparation programs include three components: general education courses, major courses, and field experiences.

General Education

The general education component of the undergraduate curriculum is vital because university graduates should demonstrate understanding and capabilities beyond those acquired in their major courses. As a university graduate, you will be expected to express yourself well, both in writing and in speaking. You should understand and be able to discuss—at least on a topical level—areas such as art, music, literature, drama, history, political science, dance, psychology, sociology, anthropology, physical sciences, and human movement. With a firm foundation provided by general education courses, you should be able to deal with a changing society that reflects the cultural diversity of our world. Indeed, awareness of other cultures, as well as an understanding and appreciation of them, is essential in addressing the sport management needs of the global community (Chelladurai, 2005).

Learning Activity

Identify a classmate, teacher, friend, or other person who is demographically different from you, that is, a person of a different gender, race, ethnicity, or sexual orientation. Interview that person, asking questions about his or her experiences in school, work, sport, recreation, and society in general. Make a list of how these experiences differ from yours. What differences might these experiences make in the workplace? As a manager, how could you use these differences to create a better workplace?

As a sport manager, you will also be expected to use critical thinking skills, which you can acquire and develop in general education courses. These skills will be useful in generating original ideas and creative solutions to a broad spectrum of societal and global concerns. The knowledge that you acquire in your general education courses will also be helpful as you seek to advance in your career. For example, as an entry-level group sales representative for a professional baseball team, you could use your knowledge of sport marketing and enterprise to develop a promotional plan. As you advance to the position of general manager, the analytical, critical thinking, and leadership skills that you developed in your general education courses will become even more important.

> Given the characteristics of the emerging technologies that are increasingly critical to international competition, basic academic skills—literacy, numeracy, communications—are perhaps the ultimate employability skills. . . . Without basic academic skills, it is difficult to comprehend how individuals can possess personal flexibility and teach-ability or be capable of engaging in lifelong learning, a condition that increasingly will be required to maintain personal flexibility. (Herr, Cramer, & Niles, 2004, p. 131)

1980s

- **1986** First NASSM conference held at Kent State Univ.
- **1987**—Sport and Recreation Law Association (SRLA) established
- **1987**—NASPE publishes curricular guidelines

1990s

- **1993**—NASPE-NASSM curricular standards published
- **1994**—Sport Management Program Review Council (SMPRC) created

Major Courses in Sport Management

Standards for sport management academic programs have been developed through a joint effort of the National Association for Sport and Physical Education (NASPE) and the North American Society for Sport Management (NASSM). The NASPE–NASSM (2000) program approval standards require undergraduate programs to offer course content in

- sociocultural dimensions in sport,
- management and leadership in sport,
- ethics in sport management,
- marketing in sport,
- communication in sport,
- budget and finance in sport,
- legal aspects of sport,
- economics in sport,
- governance in sport, and
- field experience in sport management.

NASPE–NASSM approved sport management programs are not required to dedicate a separate course to each of these content areas, but they must cover the subject matter somewhere within the curriculum. As of June 2006, 40 undergraduate, 28 master's, and 5 doctoral programs had received NASPE–NASSM approval (NASPE, 2006).

The course work designated by NASPE–NASSM focuses on preparing you for a career in one of the many sport industries. Remember, however, that as a university student, you are not being trained for a career in sport management; you are being educated for a life in which you hope to enjoy one or more positions in sport management. Your goal of entering the sport management field might not materialize. Moreover, even if you do begin your career in sport management, you might decide later to pursue some other line of work. In either case, the course content prescribed by NASPE–NASSM is sufficiently broad that you should be prepared to assume positions in a variety of other vocational fields such as advertising and promotions, sales, and communications.

Keeping up with current events in your field is essential to your academic preparation. Numerous newspapers, magazines, and journals are available to you. One way to know which ones are most relevant to your career goals is to pay attention to the publications that your instructors use for assignments. When you do the assignments, take a few minutes to look through the publications. If you do this regularly, you will begin to identify the periodicals that you should be reading.

Several chapters of this book include lists of relevant associations and publications specific to various careers in the sport management field. Membership in one or more of these associations will offer you opportunities to read publications, attend conferences, and perhaps present papers. Some organizations have student sections, providing you with opportunities to gain experience in governance. NASSM, for example, is composed of scholars and leaders in the field who are receptive to student involvement. Sharing ideas and networking with professionals of all ages will be enjoyable and helpful in your career development. Your instructors will be able to give you advice about which groups would be most helpful to you, both now and in the future.

Learning Activity

Go to www.nassm.org and click on "students". Make a list of the ways in which NASSM is useful to sport management students.

Other ways to learn more about your field and gain relevant work experience include on-campus employment, community service, and student activities. Student affiliate chapters of professional organizations, often found on campuses that have sport management programs, are an excellent way to become involved in career-related community service activities, networking with professionals in your field, and visiting appropriate sport facilities within your geographic area. Examples of community service activities include volunteering with the Special Olympics or recreational programs within your community. Participation in student organizations also provides opportunities to assume leadership roles and gain experiences to add to your portfolio. Numerous sport- and recreation-related jobs are available on most college campuses in settings such as the student recreation center, the intramural sport office, and athletics department offices.

Extracurricular activities are an important part of professional preparation. In an employer survey conducted at Florida State University, 180 employers rated the importance of student participation in non-classroom-based activities. Paid, job-related

2000s

▶**2002**
Sport Marketing Association (SMA) established

▶**2003**
First SMA conference held in November

COMPETENCIES REQUIRED IN JAPANESE PROFESSIONAL BASEBALL

Jun Oga, Japan

In 2004-2005 several incidents occurred in Japanese baseball that called attention to the need for managers and owners to possess specific professional competencies.

First, the Kintetsu Corporation, owner of the Kintetsu Buffalos, withdrew from the baseball business and disbanded the team. In response, the players and many Buffalos fans protested the corporation's decision. In an effort to stop the action, the Japanese Baseball Players Union struck for the first time in Japanese baseball history. The Kintetsu Corporation gave two main reasons for disbanding the team: First, the Buffalos could not draw enough spectators to the stadium to be profitable and second, its media value was not necessary for the corporation.

With the disappearance of the Buffalos, the Osaka City Dome, where the team played its home games, went bankrupt and requested an application of the corporate revival law. One of the reasons for bankruptcy was that the Dome relied largely on income from the Buffalos' home games.

Second, with the collapse of the Japanese bubble economy, the Daiei Corporation, which managed the biggest supermarket business in Japan, went bankrupt. The corporation, which also owned the Daiei Hawks, sold the team to the SoftBank Corporation. The corporation stated that it sold the team because it could not make a profit and was in debt. On the other hand, SoftBank believes that by changing the team management, it can turn the deficit into a profit.

Third, Rakuten Inc., an Internet-related corporation, has recently shown interest in the baseball business. After the Buffalos disbanded, Rakuten created a new professional baseball team that joined the Pacific League. Rakuten believed that professional baseball games would become important content for its Internet business. In addition, Rakuten bought a majority stock interest in TBS (Tokyo Broadcasting System), the corporate owner of the Yokohama Bay Stars. The aims of Rakuten are to combine TV and the Internet and distribute sport content through the media.

Fourth, the investment fund corporation M & A Consulting Inc. became a primary stockholder in the Hanshin Electric Railway Corporation, owner of the Hanshin Tigers, the 2005 Central League champion. One of the reasons given for embarking on the business was that the Tigers had approximately 130,000 fan club members and had drawn 3.13 million spectators in 2005. M & A Consulting requested that the Hanshin Corporation offer stocks of the Tigers to the public. M & A Consulting estimates that the pubic offering of stocks can significantly raise the asset value of the Tigers.

Fifth, the Chiba Lotte Marines, a team led by Bobby Valentine, a former manager of the New York Mets, became champion of the Pacific League and won the 2005 Japanese championship after an interval of 31 years. The team had stayed in second place for many years. The owner, Lotte Corporation, had wanted to sell the team. Over a two-year period, the team tried to change the managerial system and developed many ideas and plans for attracting more fans and raising profits. One idea was to create a uniform with the number 26 on the back. In Japanese professional baseball, 25 players can be on the bench. The uniform with the number 26, which is always hung on the wall behind the Lotte bench, shows that the 26th player is the fans. Lotte fans in the stadium also put on replica uniforms with the number 26 and cheer the team. These changes in the system have decreased the deficit of the team from $34 million USD to an estimated $19 million USD.

work was rated important or above average in importance by 88% of respondents. Leadership in student organizations was the second most valued activity, with 86% of the employers rating it important or above average in importance. Membership in preprofessional organizations was rated important or above average in importance by 73% of employers, and participation in volunteer community service experiences received a rating of important or above average in importance by 58% of employers (Reardon, Lenz, & Folsom, 1998).

Field Experiences

A field experience is typically called either a practicum or an internship, both of which are supervised, practical experiences. These experiences are opportunities to learn about managerial responsibilities and the scope of the sport business while working in a sport setting. Field experiences also present opportunities for students to apply what they have learned in the classroom to a real-life situation, thus connecting theory with

Courtesy of Koyo Fukasawa.

Japanese Hanshin Tigers fans release balloons at the beginning of a lucky seventh inning instead of singing "Take Me Out to the Ball Game." The Tigers, drawing more than 3 million spectators, have the best draw among the 12 professional Japanese baseball teams.

International Learning Activity

Match the competencies required for each of the organizations described in the essay on page 30 with the course content required by the National Association for Sport and Physical Education–North American Society for Sport Management (NASPE–NASSM) curriculum standards. Then explain how the managers and owners of baseball teams in Japan can use these competencies to improve the status of the teams. What information does this exercise reveal about the NASPE–NASSM curriculum standards relative to your sport management education?

practice (Cuneen & Sidwell, 1994; Sutton, 1989). Moreover, as Williams (2003) noted, most sport organizations do not recruit on college campuses or advertise their openings. Consequently, professional opportunities in the sport industry are "part of the 'hidden' job market" (p. 28). Given this reality, practical experience in the professional setting is a vital first step into an environment where you might be seeking employment after graduation.

According to Casella and Brougham (1995), "work experience gained while still in college is an important factor in career success, particularly in the first year after graduation" (p. 55). They further note that students benefit from work experiences before graduation by building networks, improving self-organization, establishing a greater sense of responsibility, expanding work skills, learning more about personal strengths and values, and gaining self-confidence. Students can also use these experiences to strengthen their oral and written communication skills, learn daily business functions, and find out what it's like to work full time every day in a business environment (Gordon, 2002).

Courtesy of Paul M. Pedersen

One wide-open area for internships is sport communication, including both on-air and off-air positions in electronic journalism and media. Student internships are invaluable preparation for positions such as that of TV sports reporter Doris Burke, shown here interviewing J.J. Redick.

After meeting the selection criteria of your university, you can obtain a field experience at one of a variety of organizations and agencies. You might even have the opportunity to engage in a practicum or internship in a foreign country, either through your sport management program or through the international studies program on your campus. The following suggestions will help you find a field experience interesting and useful:

- Start your search for an internship at least six months in advance to give you sufficient time to write a resume, prepare cover letters, and acquire and practice your interviewing skills. Your career center is a valuable source of assistance.
- Identify your specific areas of interests and make a list of companies and organizations that interest you. The *Sports Internship Book 2005* (2004) is an excellent directory that profiles organizations providing good-quality learning and work experiences for students in sport management. Your internship coordinator might maintain a database of available positions or a list of employers who have provided internships in the past.
- After you have identified an opening, conduct research on the organization to learn about its products, services, and key customers and markets. Read the internship description carefully to determine the primary duties and requirements of the position and personality traits and attitudes sought. Tailor your resume and cover letter to highlight your qualifications for the position, including relevant academic background, work experience, skills, personal qualities, and professional interests (see figure 2.1). After sending your resume and cover letter, be sure to follow up by telephone or e-mail to confirm receipt of your application and your interest in the position. This would be a good time to request an interview.

JUAN C. RIVERA

jcrivera@stateunet.edu

Campus Address: 2000 Main Street, University, OH 43403 • (419) 555-2112
Permanent Address: 1553 Huron Road, Somewherein, NJ 55221 • (908) 555-4489
Title: Director of Community Relations, Kansas City Royals

QUALIFICATIONS SUMMARY:

- Organized and energetic team player with background in technology, marketing, and sport management.
- Strong leadership and communication skills with a proven ability to analyze and solve problems.
- Creative, innovative thinker who enjoys learning new concepts.
- Willing to travel extensively and relocate.

EDUCATION:

Bachelor of Science in Sport Management, December 2006
The State University, University, OH

- Overall GPA: 3.1; Major GPA: 3.5
- Courses in Sport and Event Promotion, Sport and Society, Sport Facility Management, Sport Marketing, Financial Management, and Sport Law

RELEVANT EXPERIENCE:

Intern, Dallas Sports Association • May 2006–August 2006

- Created a business plan to produce and market a sports directory for the city of Dallas.
- Conducted market research to identify past and potential customers.
- Determined ways to manage an existing database of sport-related organizations and to customize it to user requests.
- Identified ways to generate revenue for the association.
- Updated the association's outdated Web site and recommended changes to improve usability.

Intern Assistant to the Director, University Athletics • January 2005–May 2005

- Completed rotational assignments in various areas of college sport management, including facilities operations, purchasing, inventory management, and concessions.
- Revised the Athletics Department Policy and Procedures Manual, a fifty-page document.
- Assisted with game operations of baseball, basketball, and ice hockey games.

Student Assistant, University Athletics • May 2004–December 2004

- Updated the Athletics Department's Web site and composed biographies of student-athletes.
- Used the Internet during home football games to assist media outlets with their broadcasts.

COMPUTER SKILLS:

- Working knowledge of Dream Weaver and other web design software, MS Office, and Adobe applications.
- Familiar with C++, Visual Basic. Extensive use of Windows and Mac OS.

ACTIVITIES:

- **Sport Management Alliance** (2004–2006), vice president of New Member Recruitment and Treasurer
- **Wood County Special Olympics** (2003–2005), volunteer
- **University Activities Organization** (2002–2003), member of the Sport and Promotions Committees

REFERENCES:

Available upon request

Figure 2.1 Resume of a sport management graduate.

• Before the interview, develop in-depth examples from your experience that demonstrate your knowledge, skills, and past accomplishments. The interviewer might ask you to tell her or him about yourself and will probably ask questions such as these: What motivates you? How have you changed since starting college? What work experiences have been most valuable to you and why? Of the sport management courses that you have completed, which have you enjoyed the most? How have your educational and work experiences prepared you for this internship? Why are you interested in our organization? What goals do you want to achieve in this internship?

The interviewer may ask you to give specific examples of your past performance on the job or in school. For instance, he or she may say, "Give me an example of your role on a successful team project. Tell me about a time at work where you did more than was required. Describe the steps that you took to resolve a complex problem." A useful exercise is to write out your answers to these questions and practice your responses by participating in a **mock interview**.

> **mock interview**—A practice interview in which you can rehearse your responses to questions that interviewers are likely to ask you.

• During the interview, focus on the organization's needs rather than your own. Talk about your desire to help the organization achieve its goals. Your goal is to be remembered as the candidate who was the most enthusiastic about the internship and the most prepared for the interview. Emphasize your strengths by giving detailed examples of your accomplishments. Incorporate information that you learned in researching the organization into your responses. Focus the questions that you ask the employer on the key responsibilities of the job. Be prepared to summarize your interest in and qualifications for the internship.

• Attempt to arrange your field experience with an agency at which you would like to work after graduation. If you present yourself well and do high-quality work, the agency might consider you for full-time employment. But you should not have your heart set on being hired by your field experience agency. Among other reasons, the agency may not have any positions available for which you would be qualified.

Before beginning a practicum or internship experience, identify learning goals with your faculty advisor and field supervisor. For example, you may be asked to complete a specific project, such as developing a marketing plan, writing a manual, or coordinating an event. Be ready to meet the challenge of the level of responsibility that you are given. Research has shown that the best field experiences in sport management are those that require interns to expand their knowledge and learn new skills (Dixon, Cunningham, Sagas, Turner, & Kent, 2005).

Besides meeting the academic requirements for your internship, you should keep a journal of your experiences and reflect on your new knowledge, professional skills, attitudes, values, and ways of thinking and behaving. Develop a new set of learning goals and an action plan to achieve them. Throughout the process, maintain open communication with your on-site supervisor and faculty supervisor.

During your internship, try to identify a professional mentor. A mentor in your workplace can provide career-related support (e.g., coaching and counseling) as well as psychosocial support (e.g., role modeling, friendship, and confirmation). Your mentor can help you clarify job responsibilities, appropriate behavior in the particular organizational culture, and the reality of your expectations of the field experience. Many students find that their enthusiasm for the field and motivation to excel academically increase because of their internship experience. After completing your internship, remember to send a thank-you letter to your internship supervisor. You also might want to ask your supervisor for a letter of recommendation to use in your search for a postgraduation job.

Learning Activity

According to the National Commission for Cooperative Education (NCCE, 2005), field experiences (i.e., co-op experiences) provide benefits to students, employers, colleges and universities, and society. Go to the NCCE Web site (www.co-op.edu/aboutcoop.htm) and, following the links that you find there, identify ways in which a field experience in sport management can result in the benefits described. Discuss your findings in class.

Advanced Education

As you look toward career advancement and additional responsibilities, you may choose, or be asked by your employer, to pursue a graduate degree. Even now, early in your academic career, you may want to begin thinking about an advanced degree. The first graduate degree after the baccalaureate is the master's. Programs that culminate in master's degrees typically require one or two years of additional study. Special features associated with sport management curricula and programs are the location of the program within the university, the industry focus of the program, and the experience and research interests of the faculty.

Some sport management programs are located in departments of physical education or sport management, whereas others are housed within schools of business administration, departments of sport administration, or a variety of other units. The location of the program is of particular concern for advanced-degree students because its location "unquestionably influences its orientation" (Parkhouse, 1987, p. 109). For example, students interested in the study of sport (e.g., sociology of sport, psychology of sport, or cultural anthropology) as well as the study of sport business will probably find relevant course work in units housed in departments of physical education or sport management and administration rather than in schools of business.

Another concern is the industry focus of the graduate program. Some programs are geared toward preparing students for positions in athletics administration within the educational structure (e.g., intercollegiate or high school athletics). Other programs focus on sport management in the private sector (e.g., professional sport), and some programs encompass both sectors. As you investigate graduate programs, you will notice that the content and requirements of each program reflect the competencies, skills, and experiences valued by the sector that serves as that unit's focus. You will also notice that graduate programs expect candidates to have high grades, involvement in extracurricular activities, experience in the sport industry, and a good work ethic. Moreover, most graduate schools require high scores on entrance exams such as the Graduate Records Exam (GRE) or Graduate Management Admission Test (GMAT).

Examining the experience and research interests of the faculty is a critical step in selecting a graduate program. Many faculty are actively involved in some type of scholarship. If you consciously choose a major professor (advisor) whose research and scholarly interests are compatible with yours and who has a record of scholarly productivity, you will increase the probability of gaining valuable research experience at the master's level. This advice is especially important for students who plan to enroll in doctoral studies after earning the master's degree.

During the past several years, because of proliferating sport management curricula in colleges and universities, many sport management professorial positions have become available. Doctoral-level education, which builds on the background gained at the undergraduate and master's levels and is much more specialized in its focus, is essential for anyone who aspires to be a college professor. Currently, gender and racial diversity is absent among sport management professors, with the vast majority being white, able-bodied males (Moore & Parkhouse, 1996; Parks & Bartley, 1996). Many faculty and administrators are committed to expanding diversity in the professoriate and would be receptive to applications from qualified doctoral candidates who could contribute to that objective.

In many institutions, sport management professors are expected to conduct and publish research in an effort to build the body of knowledge. Consequently, if you aspire to the professoriate, you should acquire the research skills needed to perform this aspect of your responsibilities. As you plan your doctoral studies, you will want to find a major professor who is an established researcher in your area of interest, has experience helping students learn to conduct and publish research, and is interested in helping prospective professors learn the **pragmatics** of university life.

> **pragmatics**—Relating to matters of fact or practical affairs often to the exclusion of intellectual or artistic matters; practical as opposed to idealistic (Merriam-Webster online dictionary).

PROFESSIONAL ATTITUDE

Planning your future in sport management includes paying attention to one of the most important elements of your portfolio—your professional attitude. "Cultivating a positive, assertive outlook on life is the most crucial factor in the difference between those people who have a successful, satisfying life/career and those who don't" (Sukiennik, Bendat, & Raufman, 1995, p. 21). A professional attitude will enhance your opportunities for employment and advancement and will make you a more pleasant person for others to be around. That alone is a worthy goal.

Attitudes are demonstrated by behaviors. As noted in chapter 1, the professional codes of many organizations frequently articulate acceptable behaviors. Professionals in these organizations are expected to adhere to these codes, and those in sport management are no exception. For example, a quick search of the Internet using the keywords "sport code of ethics" will yield more than 29,000 hits. The Institute of Sport Management sponsors one of those Web sites (www.ismhome.com/). This company, located in New South Wales, Australia, is committed to the development of the profession of sport management. The code of ethics of the Institute of Sport Management (2005) Web site states the following:

> The Institute of Sport Management's Code of Ethics & Professional Conduct recognizes that the objectives of the Sport Management profession are to work to the highest standards of professionalism, to attain the highest levels of performance and generally to meet the public interest requirement. These objectives require four basic needs to be met: (a) Credibility, (b) Professionalism, (c) Quality of Services, and (d) Confidence. Users of the services of professional Sport Managers should be able to feel confident that there exists a framework of professional ethics that governs the provision of those services.

Learning Activity

What are the implications of the Code of Ethics and Professional Conduct of the Institute of Sport Management for the attitudes of sport managers?

Employees display their professional attitude in the image they project, in the ways in which they approach work transition and adjustment, and in their business etiquette. Recruiters usually evaluate these attributes during interviews.

Professional Image

When first meeting you, other people rely on your physical appearance to make judgments about you. "Studies on the overall impression that people make in the first few minutes . . . show that 7 percent of that impression is based on what a person says, 38 percent on how he or she says it, and 55 percent on what the other person *sees*" (Mitchell, 1998, p. 10). Although this way of judging you might seem unfair, and although initial impressions can change after someone gets to know you, you can make a first impression only once—so why not make it a good one?

The impression that you make through your physical presentation during interviews and on the job is related less to physical attractiveness than to other factors, all of which are within your control. The following items are among the many aspects of a professional image.

- ***Grooming***—Of the 254 employers responding to the *Job Outlook 2005* survey (National Association of Colleges and Employers [NACE], 2005), 70% indicated that grooming had a strong influence on their opinion of a candidate's suitability for employment. Paying attention to your grooming, therefore, could pay off. Aspects of grooming to consider include care of hair, nails, and teeth, as well as neatness and cleanliness.
- ***Attire and accessories***—While in college, you have wide discretion in your choice of clothing and accessories, but as you move into the workplace, you will be expected to conform to the norms of your employer. You might want to avoid political or religious insignia in the form of ties, pins, or rings. Clothing with logos, slogans, or phrases may be inappropriate in some settings. Although baseball caps are a staple of college students' wardrobes, caps are inappropriate in certain situations (e.g., the classroom, meetings, mealtime, conferences with faculty or administrators, class presentations, and employment interviews) (see figure 2.2). With regard to personal taste, however, only you can decide whether conforming to the norms of a particular workplace will compromise your values so much that you should look for a job elsewhere.
- ***Posture***—Your sitting, standing, and walking posture (body language) conveys an impression of your attitude. People will draw different conclusions about the attitude of a person who is slouching as opposed to one who is sitting erect, with feet firmly planted on the floor, or leaning slightly forward to indicate good listening skills, interest, and enthusiasm.

Work Transition and Adjustment

Are you ready to face the challenges that will present themselves in the workplace? Are you confident in your abilities and competent in your specific job skills? Are you knowledgeable about the social, political, legislative, technological, and economic trends that have influenced your field? Now is the time to begin practicing for life in the work environment.

How you enter a new organization, approach the challenges of your new position, learn the organi-

Peanuts

Figure 2.2 Hats off!

Learning Activity

You are the manager of a sport-related business. On a quarterly basis, you conduct evaluations of your employees. This quarter, you will evaluate a member of your class. Select a person in your sport management class to be your employee. Do not reveal the person's identity. In your hypothetical role as that person's supervisor, describe the person's attitude with respect to the following areas:

- Attitude toward himself or herself
- Attitude toward her or his role as a student (job)
- Attitude toward the importance of etiquette

Now answer the following questions:

- What cues did you use to make your judgments?
- If this person were your employee, how would you deal with her or his attitudes? This question applies regardless of whether you have judged the attitude as good or bad.
- If someone in the room chose you as his or her employee, what do you think the person would say about your attitude toward yourself, your attitude toward your role as a student, and your etiquette? On what cues might the person have made these judgments?
- What did you learn from this exercise?

zational culture, develop positive working relationships with bosses and colleagues, participate in departmental and team meetings, communicate your ideas to others, and establish your reputation as a bright, capable, and valuable employee will have a major influence on your success within that organization. "Successful employees recognize that the workplace is really a mini-society that sends out a constant stream of information about what is expected of its members and what the rules and limits are" (Carney & Wells, 1995, p. 178). The following sections offer tips on learning your job, understanding the organizational culture, demonstrating your work ethic, developing written communication skills, using electronic communication, writing thank-you notes, refining teamwork skills, managing conflict, embracing diversity, being evaluated, and continuing your professional development.

Learn Your Job

When you start a new job, make sure that you understand the duties listed in your job description, what you are expected to do, and how to proceed. Listen carefully to directions and ask for clarification of any instructions that you do not comprehend fully before beginning an assignment. Taking notes as you receive oral instructions is perfectly appropriate, to assure understanding and thorough recall of expectations. Set up periodic meetings with your supervisor to confirm and clarify your progress on assignments to ensure that your work is accurate, thorough, and of high quality.

Understand Organizational Culture

As you will learn in chapter 14, each organization has a unique culture; therefore, new employees must learn what behaviors are expected in the workplace. These expectations are sometimes stated in the organization's policy manual, but more often informal structures and unwritten ways of getting things done have evolved over time. New employees learn these unofficial procedures by observing the behaviors of others and by listening to stories told about the organization at informal gatherings, during lunch conversations, and at celebrations.

Some of the key factors to pay particular attention to as a new employee are "the mission of the organization, guiding philosophies, basic values and norms, behavioral expectations, work ethic, what gets rewarded, social norms, management philosophies, ethical standards, sacred beliefs and events, general atmosphere, attitude of employees, communication norms, work norms, and office climate" (Nardo, 1999, p. 54). Many organizations offer formal or informal mentoring programs to assist new professionals in learning about and adapting to the culture of the organization. Developing a mentoring relationship with a seasoned professional whom you trust and admire is an excellent idea.

Demonstrate Your Work Ethic

Demonstrate your commitment to the organization, supervisors, and colleagues by enthusiastically completing all job assignments within the agreed-upon deadlines, keeping your word, offering assistance, and supporting others in achieving the organization's goals. Your attitude toward work is referred to as your work ethic. "Your work ethic is a set of values you work and live by. The strength of your work ethic is based on the solidarity of your values" (Curtis & Associates, 1999, p. 2). Thinking about people whom you admire and the qualities and characteristics that you admire in them may help you determine your work values. Strive to become known as a person who prepares before meetings, contributes ideas, listens to others, supports colleagues, is team oriented, and follows through on work commitments.

Develop Your Written Communication Skills

The ability to express thoughts and ideas in writing is one of the most important competencies of a good sport manager. Among the many types of writing that you will have to produce are business correspondence (e.g., memos, e-mail messages, and responses to complaints), reports, and technical manuals. Learn to organize your thoughts logically and use grammar and punctuation correctly. Investing time and energy in learning to write well will pay huge dividends when you enter the professional world. See figure 2.3 for a humorous illustration of the role that punctuation plays in communicating with others.

Use Electronic Communication Appropriately

Although e-mail is an informal mode of communication, adherence to the conventions of good business writing is expected in business-related e-mail messages. Good judgment regarding the content of e-mail messages is essential. Avoid using off-color humor, slang, and profanity. A number of excellent Web sites address the appropriate uses of e-mail and provide tips for composing business correspondence (use the keywords *netiquette* or *e-mail etiquette*). Observe established protocols for various electronic mailing lists and other communications on e-mail. For example, although you might enjoy exchanging jokes of questionable taste on humor electronic mailing lists or with your friends, the same jokes would be inappropriate on electronic mailing lists established for professional or scholarly discussions.

Dear Jack,
I want a man who knows what love is all about. You are generous, kind, thoughtful. People who are not like you admit to being useless and inferior. You have ruined me for other men. I yearn for you. I have no feelings whatsoever when we're apart. I can be forever happy—will you let me be yours?
Jill

Dear Jack,
I want a man who knows what love is. All about you are generous, kind, thoughtful people, who are not like you. Admit to being useless and inferior. You have ruined me. For other men I yearn! For you I have no feelings whatsoever. When we're apart, I can be forever happy. Will you let me be?
Yours,
Jill

Figure 2.3 An example of the importance of punctuation.

From *Eats, Shoots and Leaves* by Lynne Truss, copyright © 2004 by Lynne Truss. Used by permission of Gotham Book, an imprint of Penguin Group (USA) Inc.

Thank Others

Through thank-you letters, you can express gratitude to someone who provided you with information or with his or her time. A good practice to follow is to send a thank-you letter within 24 hours of a social or business contact or event. You may send thank-you letters within an organization as well as to outsiders. Making a habit of thanking people who help you will go a long way toward establishing your reputation as a true professional.

Refine Your Teamwork Skills

Throughout the course of your career you will be a member of many work teams (e.g., problem-solving teams, special project teams, or cross-functional teams). A work team is a group of people who work in relationship with one another to accomplish a task or solve a problem. Team members identify themselves as part of the team, are interdependent, use one another as resources to accomplish their tasks, support one another, and see team success as personal success. To be an effective team member, you need to develop skills along several dimensions including commitment to the task, communication, collaboration, confrontation, consensus building, and caring for and demonstrating respect for other team members.

Learn to Manage Conflict

Conflict is energy among groups of people or individuals; it is not about winning or losing. Conflict is an opportunity to acknowledge and appreciate our differences. Carney and Wells (1995) note that workplace differences or conflicts are most likely to occur "when workers are under pressure, when their responsibilities are not clear, or when their personal expectations or needs are violated. . . . Conflict situations offer ideal opportunities for clarifying personal differences and for team building" (p. 179). If you disagree with a colleague, supervisor, or customer, try to do so without being disagreeable. You can take several steps to resolve minor workplace conflicts:

- Stating specific needs, concerns, and fears
- Citing examples of behaviors (do not attack the individual personally)
- Expressing your feelings
- Inviting the other person to respond
- Repeating what you heard to check for understanding (active listening)
- Eliminating the words *yes, but* from your vocabulary
- Looking for the common ground in each of your needs
- Determining next steps

When handled in this way, conflict can be healthy. Imagine that your team is brainstorming possible solutions to a marketing problem. You express your ideas, listen to the ideas of your colleague, and then look for elements of each of your ideas that could be merged to result in a solution to your problem. The idea here is to look for the best of all possible solutions, rather than shoot down the ideas of others.

Embrace Diversity

Appreciate and celebrate diversity of gender, race, religion, sexual orientation, ability, age, and so on. Do not engage in racist, ageist, or sexist behaviors, and let others know, tactfully, that you do not appreciate such behaviors in others. Laws protect people

WORKFORCE DIVERSITY

Workforce diversity will bring with it questions about how business people should conduct themselves. Letitia Baldrige (1993) captured the essence of the new demands created by the changing workplace:

"There is a new informality at work in how we meet and greet, entertain, dress, and socialize with one another, and yet a new formality as we deal with a diversity of people from and in other countries, where we increasingly do business.

"The needs of families, of women and men who are parents as well as respected workers, are increasingly sensitive issues in the workplace. The relations of men and women working together not only as equals, but also as new configurations of peer and superior in terms of gender and age, changes a lot of preconceived behavior codes. Also transforming life at work are the new concerns for the rights of the disabled, for more attention to ethnic equality, diversity and pluralism." (p. xxix-xxx)

From "Why We Need a New Book on Business Manners." Reprinted with permission of Rawson Associates/Scribner, an imprint of Simon & Schuster Adult Publishing Group, from *Letitia Baldrige's New Complete Guide to Executive Manners* by Letitia Baldrige. Copyright 1985, 1993 by Letitia Baldrige.

from racial and sexual harassment and discrimination, but the sensitive person does not need laws to enforce kindness and inclusiveness.

Performance Appraisals

Organizations typically incorporate goal setting and identification of professional development needs into the performance appraisal process. As a novice professional, you should welcome the evaluation process, recognizing that the aim of constructive criticism is to improve your performance. Expect to be involved in setting goals that will challenge your learning process but not be unreachable. Be prepared to discuss your specific needs for development and strategies to improve your job performance. Setting goals and measuring the attainment of those goals on a recurring basis will help you and your supervisor identify appropriate professional development activities so that your performance appraisals will reflect the best performance that you are capable of delivering. The most important question to ask your supervisor is "What should I be doing to improve my job performance?"

Continue Your Professional Development

As the concept of a successful career continually changes in our global marketplace, personal flexibility and the ability to adapt to change become even more important (Herr, Cramer, & Niles, 2004). Underlying the assumption that professionals can be flexible and can adapt to change is the concept of lifelong learning. Your professional education is just beginning, and it will continue throughout your life.

You should make an early commitment to lifelong learning, both formal and informal, so that you can continue to grow professionally and personally. Participation in business and professional associations increases your knowledge and expands your network of associates throughout your career. A well-developed career network is vital to your professional advancement. Your network members can provide information, guidance, support, honest feedback, and access to career opportunities. Interaction with colleagues is stimulating and allows you to grow professionally and contribute to your field.

Business Etiquette

The importance of correct business etiquette cannot be overstated.

> Manners are the very keystone of good human relationships. They govern how people treat each other, whether in the coalmines or in a mahogany-paneled boardroom. When people who work together in either place adhere to the rules of social behavior, their workplace becomes efficient. There is an absence of confusion and wasted time. When people treat each other with consideration, they do not run into each other; there is a minimum of stumbling about feeling awkward, groping for words, or wondering what to do next. (Baldrige, 1985, pp. 5-6)

Although a discussion of manners might seem out of place in the classroom, research has revealed that quite the opposite is the case. Lilienthal (2004) interviewed 15 managers from five sport organizations in the Bay Area of Northern California to identify the professional behavior that they expected of their new or young employees. She found that almost all these managers had recurring issues with employees' unprofessional behavior with regard to dress code and courtesy. These managers believed that classroom and workplace training in professional etiquette would be helpful. Based on the managers' suggestions, Lilienthal recommended the following strategies for teachers and managers to increase students' professionalism in the sport industry.

- Teach about the critical importance of frontline personnel and the influence that they have on customer care and customer satisfaction.
- Teach students about customer expectations and the service quality gap.
- Ensure that teachers and managers display the level of professionalism expected from subordinates.
- Practice setting, communicating, and reinforcing customer-oriented employee professionalism standards.
- Teach students about measuring employee performance and the importance of rewarding good service.
- Develop scenarios in which employees can practice responding to customers in difficult situations, so that when the situation arises, they have a prepared response and the self-confidence to respond appropriately.
- Use the classroom for scenario development and practice sessions to increase student professionalism under a range of situations.

As you prepare for a career in sport management, we encourage you to consider the following reminders of good manners:

• ***Telephone***. Answering the telephone in a professional manner includes clearly identifying yourself and your organization or department; giving each caller your full attention; restating important information to check for understanding and accuracy; projecting a tone that is cheerful, natural, and attentive; ending the conversation with agreement on what is to happen next; and following up appropriately. When leaving your phone number on someone's voice mail system, speak distinctly and at a reasonable speed. Remember to leave your name, phone number, and a brief message so that the caller will be prepared when she or he returns your call.

• ***Voice mail and answering machine messages***. Refrain from leaving cute or suggestive greetings on your voice mail system, especially when you are searching for an internship or professional employment. Busy callers do not appreciate long messages, cleverness, or loud music in the background.

• ***Language***. Practice using inclusive language rather than gender-biased or racially biased language. In the workplace of the 21st century, employees will interact with managers, clients, and customers who are women, people of color, or from other cultures. Mastery of inclusive language is a good way to demonstrate your sensitivity to such concerns and to create a more pleasant workplace (Parks, Harper, & Lopez, 1994).

• ***Meeting participation***. You will find that certain behaviors are expected in business meetings. Behavior may vary by organizational culture, but general conventions include being prepared, arriving at least 10 minutes early, turning cell phones to the vibrate option or off, staying on task, participating openly, giving your full attention through active listening, and encouraging others to participate and offer their ideas.

• ***Dining etiquette***. Many business meetings include a meal, and prospective employers, customers, and other business associates will judge your table manners. You will be more comfortable when you know what to expect. First, be prepared to engage in light conversation. Appropriate topics include current events, sports, and the arts. On the other hand, politics, religion, and sex are taboo topics. Although alcohol is never appropriate at a business lunch in the United States, know your organization's policy on alcohol at business functions or follow your host's lead. A glass of sparkling water with a twist of lime is always a safe choice. Order foods that are easy to manage with a knife and fork. Place your napkin in your lap immediately upon being seated. After your napkin is on your lap, if you leave the table for any reason, place the napkin on the back or arm of the chair, never on the table. The order of silverware use is from farthest from your plate to closest. A spoon or fork placed at the top of your plate is for dessert. After you use a utensil, place it on a bread plate or other piece of tableware. Many career services offices now offer dining etiquette workshops. You might benefit from taking advantage of these opportunities.

• ***Travel***. If you use laptop computers, cellular phones, or personal digital assistants on public transportation, be considerate of the people who are sharing the limited space with you. Do not appropriate the middle seat and tray for your papers and be sure to mute the sound function. Ask your seatmates if they mind your typing or talking, and obey the captain when she or he directs you to put away your electronic devices.

• ***International experiences***. From an international perspective, good manners can be defined in different ways. Advice posted on the main page of the Web's Leading Resource for International Business Etiquette and Manners (www.cyborlink.com/) states, "As international business, multinational business, transnational business, multi domestic business, and global business continues to expand and bring people closer, the most important element of successful business outcomes may be the appreciation and respect for regional, country, and cultural differences—known as cultural diversity."

Communicating with and relating to people from other cultures requires that you learn the protocols, courtesies, customs, and behaviors of those from other countries. To avoid embarrassment, investigate the customs prevalent in foreign countries before traveling there and before entertaining international visitors. For example, in Russia you will receive gifts and will be expected to give gifts. In Japan you present your business card with both hands, making sure that the type is facing the recipient and is right side up; when receiving a business card, read and digest the information printed on the card—it is considered rude to just pocket it. Never give a Hindu anything made of cowhide or an Indian Muslim anything made of pigskin. Such gifts are insulting to their religious beliefs. Excellent resources are available through your local or campus library, as well as on the Internet (e.g., www.cyborlink.com/).

- ***Introductions and greetings***. The host is responsible for introducing those who are meeting for the first time. When making an introduction, use the name of the most senior person first and introduce everyone else to him or her. As a general rule of respect, do not use a person's first name until invited to do so. Regardless of your gender, stand when being introduced to others (e.g., supervisors, customers, guests), especially if they are older than you are or outrank you. When you shake hands, use a firm grip but do not crush the other person's hand. Grasp his or her entire hand, not just the fingers, and adjust your grip to the state of health and physical strength of the person whom you are greeting.
- ***Office etiquette***. Refrain from chewing gum and using toothpicks, tobacco, and cigarettes at work, during an interview, or while others are eating. Many organizations today use dividers rather than walls, so you may find yourself working in a small space with a number of coworkers. Be conscious of their need for privacy and a quiet workplace. Be cautious in your use of radios, speakerphones, and other devices that can be distracting in a small work space.
- ***Romantic relationships***. The office is not an appropriate place to engage in flirting or in more overt forms of affectionate behavior. Charges of sexual harassment are serious and can have a profoundly negative effect on your career. Moreover, people involved in these relationships often are hurt and bewildered when they end.

In summary, a positive, professional attitude—as reflected in your professional image, work habits and behavior, and business etiquette—is essential to your future success. Look on the positive side of every situation. Optimistic people view problems as opportunities to exercise creativity, resolve difficult situations, and make things happen. The ability to stay calm and composed in stressful situations is a sign of professional maturity. Enthusiasm and a positive self-image are important parts of a professional attitude.

CAREER PLANNING AND MANAGEMENT

To thrive in the 21st century, employees will need to assume responsibility for their own career planning and management. Gone are the days when a college graduate could expect to find a job after graduation and spend his or her entire career working for one organization. You will make multiple career and job choices throughout your lifespan. Estimates are that US workers will change career fields 3 to 5 times and switch jobs as many as 10 times during their working lives. Although frequent job changes will become the norm, you can achieve employment security by continuing to develop new skills through lifelong learning and by assuming personal responsibility for managing your career.

The complex process of making career decisions involves four stages: self-awareness and exploration, occupational exploration, decision making, and career implementation (Hoff, 2000). Career planning can be fascinating because you will gain new insights about yourself as well as knowledge about the variety of career options available to you. The following steps will help you in your career planning. You do not have to complete them in the order presented, and you may need to repeat a step or two as you gain new information about yourself and your career options or encounter obstacles or barriers.

- ***Self-awareness and exploration*** entails identifying and understanding your personal and work values, interests, abilities, aptitudes, personality traits, and desired future lifestyle.
- ***Occupational awareness and exploration*** entails taking a broad look at career fields and researching specific occupations, work environments, and employers that may be a match with your unique career profile as identified through your self-assessment.
- ***Career decision making*** is the process of consciously analyzing and weighing all information that you have gathered about yourself, various occupations, and career paths. At this stage you will make a tentative career decision, formulate educational and vocational goals, and develop plans to achieve them. The more you learn about yourself and the world of sport management, the better and more realistic your educational and career choices will be.
- ***Career implementation*** involves sharpening your job search skills. You will learn to prepare an effective resume and cover letter, identify sources of job leads, present yourself professionally in interviews, evaluate and accept a job offer, and adjust to a new position.

Career planning is not a single, once-in-a-lifetime event. You are continually developing new interests, knowledge, and skills through your course work, leisure activities, volunteer experiences, summer and part-time jobs, and internships. Throughout your career you may be motivated to reevaluate your options when changes in duties or work conditions of a job cause you to become less satisfied with it. Each time you face a career or job change, you will go through the career planning stages.

Your college career center offers services and programs to help you develop career goals, find the right academic and experiential programs to achieve those goals, and gain employment upon graduation. Career counselors can be extremely helpful in providing guidance and direction in assessing your vocational interests, identifying skills, writing resumes and cover letters, preparing for interviews, developing a professional portfolio, and conducting the job search. As Williams (2003) noted, positions in the sport industry are frequently in the "hidden" job market, so you should take advantage of the expert assistance available at your career center.

A relatively new tool for job seekers is the electronic portfolio. An electronic portfolio, which you record on a CD-ROM or DVD, contains items that you have chosen to show prospective employers. These portfolios use "sounds, text, video/audio testimonies, voice-over explanations, and scanned images" as evidence of what you have done and, by implication, what you will be able to do as a professional (Fletcher, Kelley, & Ridinger, 2005). Kadlecek and Thoma (1999) suggest that the essential items in the portfolio of a sport management student are a sport marketing plan, a budget project, a sponsorship proposal, an ad media campaign, and a ticket sales campaign. Although time consuming to develop, electronic portfolios are valuable to students in providing examples of skills, and in the process of creating them, students will have an opportunity to reflect on their competencies and proficiencies. More information on electronic portfolios is available at http://electronicportfolios.com/portfolios.html.

Values

Your values are fundamental to career planning and indicate what you consider most important in your life. "Values are the qualities, attitudes, beliefs, traits, and concepts that have special significance or meaning for a person" (DiMarco, 1997, p. 23). Raths, Harmin, and Simon (1978) developed seven criteria that will help you determine your values. Your actions and decisions truly reflect your values when they are (1) prized and cherished, (2) publicly affirmed, (3) chosen freely, (4) chosen from alternatives, (5) chosen after consideration of consequences, (6) acted on, and (7) acted on repeatedly and consistently to form a definite pattern.

The choices that you make about your occupational life need to be in harmony with your basic values and belief systems; otherwise you will not find personal satisfaction in your job. Ultimately you should seek an occupation and job that will enhance, strengthen, and support the values that you consider important. For example, a high school coach may possess values different from those of a sport entrepreneur. While the high school coach is demonstrating his or her value of assisting with the physical, mental, and moral development of young people, the sport entrepreneur may be demonstrating his or her value of providing a high level of financial security for family members. More information about the relationship between your values and your career awaits you in chapter 17.

Learning Activity

Congratulations! You have just won $25 million in the lottery. You will never again have to worry about money. All of life's options are available to you. You have many choices to make about your future—where to live, how to spend your days, who will share your life, how to spend and invest your money, and so on. Write a few paragraphs outlining your new life decisions now that your financial future is secure. What would you like to accomplish in your life, both personally and professionally? What does success really mean to you? How are the choices that you make a reflection of what you value in life?

Interests

Interests are activities in which you enthusiastically engage and find enjoyable, and subjects that arouse your curiosity or hold your attention. Interests are an integral part of your personality and are related to your values. Throughout your life, your personal experiences shape your interests. These interests often lead to competencies in the same areas. When your occupation matches your interests, you experience greater job satisfaction. If you have difficulty identifying or articulating your interests, you might want to seek the assistance of a career counselor at your university career center. Using interest inventories, career counselors can help you assess your measured interests and match those interests with appropriate occupations.

Skills

A skill is the developed aptitude, ability, or personal quality needed to perform a task competently. The three basic types of skills are job content skills, functional skills, and adaptive skills. Job content skills are the specialized knowledge or abilities needed to fulfill a specific job responsibility. Knowing the rules of basketball is an example of a job content skill for a basketball referee. Functional skills are general abilities that transfer to many jobs or situations. For example, a basketball referee uses functional skills to make quick, accurate decisions and to resolve player conflicts that occur on the court. Adaptive skills are personal attributes or personality traits. In our example, a basketball referee must remain calm and poised under stressful conditions.

Patterson and Allen (1996) identified the following skills necessary for success in careers of the 21st century:

> (a) Computer literacy in all types of technology; (b) flexibility and adaptability to handle ever-changing roles and management styles; (c) diversity in ability to function and work with people from a broad range of ages, cultures, and learning styles; (d) language skills—especially knowledge of multiple languages for the global marketplace; (e) team players—networking and negotiating skills a must; (f) learning skills and continuous reeducation; (g) personal career planning skills (self-assessment, inner worth, current skills); (h) global awareness/orientation—knowledge of a country and region as well as the culture of the people there; (i) oral and written communications skills—become even more valuable as corporations flatten; (j) people must be self-starters; (k) self-comfort—the company no longer defines the worker; (l) strong ethical framework; (m) environmental scanning skills—knowing where your company is going, where the opportunities will be, see which direction to flex forward. (p. 61).

A survey of 254 employers revealed the top 20 skills and qualities sought in new college hires (NACE, 2005), listed here in order of importance:

> Communication skills, honesty/integrity, interpersonal skills (relates well to others), strong work ethic, teamwork skills (works well with others), analytical skills, motivation/initiative, flexibility/adaptability, computer skills, detail-oriented, leadership skills, organizational skills, self-confidence, friendly/outgoing personality, tactfulness, well-mannered/polite, GPA (3.0 or better), creativity, entrepreneurial skills/risk-taker, and sense of humor. (p. 15)

As career success is being redefined throughout the world and our global economy becomes more competitive, "workers must be able to function with quality and efficiency at the levels of creativity, invention, and innovation as well as at the implementation and application levels, in customer service, in quality control, in goods production, and in services delivery" (Herr, Cramer, & Niles, 2004, p. 6). Knowing which skills are required to be successful in today's workplace is a good starting point for assessing your level of skill attainment. After you have identified the skills that you possess and to what degree, you can develop a plan for enhancing your level of those most pertinent to your career goals.

Occupational Information

Many positions are available in existing sport management settings. You could also create your own opportunities by becoming an **entrepreneur**.

> **entrepreneur**—One who organizes, manages, and assumes the risks of a business or enterprise (Merriam-Webster online dictionary).

Making solid career decisions requires you to gather extensive information about the occupations that you wish to consider. By using a systematic approach, you will be able to compare occupations and make decisions that are compatible with your values, interests, skills, personality, and desired future lifestyle. For each occupation that you are considering, gather the following information: the nature of the work, work setting and conditions, educational and personal qualifications required, earnings, employment outlook and competition, methods of entering the occupation, opportunities for advancement, opportunities for exploring the occupation, related occupations, and sources of additional information. See "Sport Management Career Resources" on page 45 for sources that will be useful in your research.

Another way of collecting data is through a computerized career information system. Most career centers provide an interactive, Web-based career guidance and education planning system, such as

SPORT MANAGEMENT CAREER RESOURCES

Books

- Fischer, D. (1997). *The 50 coolest jobs in sports: What they are, who's got them, how you can get one too!* New York: Macmillan.
- Field, S. (2004). *Career opportunities in the sports industry* (3rd ed.). New York: Ferguson.
- Heitzmann, W. R. (2003). *Opportunities in sports and fitness careers.* Boston: McGraw-Hill.
- *Sports Market Place Directory.* (2004). Millertown, NY: Grey House Publishing.

Online Resources

- Nike, Inc. Web site (www.nike.com/nikebiz)
- National Basketball Association (www.nba.com/help/jobs.html)
- America's Career InfoNet (www.acinet.org/acinet)
- America's Job Bank (www.ajb.org)
- Canada's Sport Information Resource Centre (www.canadiansport.com/)
- Career Voyages (www.careervoyages.gov)
- CareerBuilder.com (http://careerbuilder.com)
- CareerOneStop (www.careeronestop.org)
- Jobs in Sports (www.jobsinsports.com)
- Monster.com (http://monster.com)
- *Occupational Outlook Handbook* (www.bls.gov/oco/home.htm)
- Ontario Sport Alliance (www.sportalliance.com/new/home.html)
- Sport Careers (www.sportscareers.com/jobs/jobs.htm)
- SportsInternshipJobs.com (www.sportsinternjobs.com/)
- The Official Sports Industry Job Board (www.sports-jobboard.com)

Additional Web sites are listed on pages 2 and 3.

FOCUS (Career Dimension Inc., 2004), designed to help students with important career planning tasks, including (1) understanding their interests, work values, personality, skills, and educational preferences; (2) identifying and discovering how their personal qualities relate to occupations; and (3) narrowing down their options by interactively exploring and analyzing occupations.

Interviewing employees on site is an excellent way to gain additional information about jobs and work environments. Most sport managers are willing to help eager college students learn about the field. Through informational interviews you can gain an insider's view on a sport management job, obtain referrals to other professionals, and create a network of contacts. Good preparation and practice are the keys to effective informational interviewing.

Learning Activity

To find out more about sport management positions that are compatible with your interests, go to http://personal.bgsu.edu/~jparks/ExSport/ and run *ExSport II* (Parks & Sun, 2001). This expert (artificial intelligence) computer program simulates the career counseling process by asking questions about your career interests and providing you with information about sport-related careers associated with those interests.

To learn more about informational interviewing, read the article "Information Interviewing: Get the Inside Scoop on Careers" posted at www.bls.gov/opub/ooq/2002/summer/art03.htm. Practice asking questions and having a conversation with a friend before you meet with the professional. Next, identify a sport manager to interview and call to arrange an appointment. Ask a variety of questions about how you can prepare to enter the occupation. Remember to take notes. After the interview, send a thank-you letter within 24 hours.

SUMMARY

Three elements necessary for success in sport management are (1) professional preparation, (2)

Learning Activity

Access Women Sports Jobs at www.womensportscareers.com/default.htm. Go to the "Career in Sports—Resources" page and read about various career paths in sport management, job descriptions, qualifications, experience and educational requirements, and salaries. Write a paper answering the following questions: Which positions do you find most interesting? Why do these jobs appeal to you? What knowledge and experiences would you need to succeed in these positions?

professional attitude, and (3) career planning and management. You can find sport management professional preparation programs at the bachelor's, master's, and doctoral levels. The typical undergraduate curriculum consists of general education courses, major courses, and field experiences. Field experiences give you opportunities to apply what you learn in the classroom in sport settings. Master's and doctoral programs will be more specific to your career goals.

Professional attitude is reflected in your personal appearance (e.g., hygiene, posture, self-confidence), your adjustment to the workplace (e.g., academic preparation, writing skills, dependability, ethics, work habits), and your business etiquette (e.g., telephone, e-mail, thank-you letters). Recruiters evaluate professional attitudes during interviews, and employers evaluate them in performance appraisals.

Career planning and management consists of self-awareness and exploration (e.g., values, interests, skills), occupational awareness and exploration (gathering information from a variety of sources), career decision-making, and career implementation. College career centers can provide valuable guidance and direction, including directing you to a multitude of resources and helping you create an electronic portfolio.

Review Questions

1. How can professional preparation, a professional attitude, and career planning and management contribute to your success in sport management?
2. List the three components of your undergraduate sport management curriculum and explain which elements within each of them fulfill the content requirements of the NASPE–NASSM program approval standards.
3. Define field experiences and explain how they benefit students, employers, colleges and universities, and society.
4. Outline a plan for finding a field experience in sport management.
5. According to *Job Outlook 2005* (NACE, 2005), what skills and competencies will you need for a successful career in sport management? Explain how you plan to acquire these skills and competencies while in college.
6. List important elements of personal appearance, work transition and adjustment, and business etiquette and explain what your conduct might reveal regarding your personal perspective on each.
7. Describe and explain the four stages involved in career planning.
8. Identify print and electronic resources that you could use in seeking employment in sport management.

Thinking Critically About Sport Management

Stuart M. Keeley—Bowling Green State University ▪ **Janet B. Parks**—Bowling Green State University
Lucie Thibault—Brock University

Learning Objectives

After studying this chapter, you will be able to do the following:

1. Recognize the benefits of applying critical thinking skills to issues in sport management.
2. Distinguish between learning *what* to think and learning *how* to think.
3. Appreciate the implication of the fact that experts disagree on many issues.
4. Define critical thinking.
5. Describe the dispositions of critical thinkers.
6. Identify and understand the meaning of core critical thinking questions.
7. Recognize the importance of values and perspectives in determining personal beliefs about sport management.
8. Apply core critical thinking questions to controversial topics in sport management.
9. Use your critical thinking skills in the process of personal decision making.

In a thought-provoking address to the members of the North American Society for Sport Management (NASSM), Bob Boucher (1998) explained that "a true measure of whether [sport management] graduates are truly prepared is *not* the courses listed on their transcripts but whether they have been educated to *think* intelligently and *make decisions* about issues they will face in the dynamic world of managing a sport enterprise" (p. 81). Similarly, Janet Harris (1993) urged sport management educators to give greater emphasis to students' development of critical and reflective competencies. She surmised that such an emphasis would prepare professionals who would be able to "free themselves from traditional ways of identifying and solving problems, [and] to look at problems from new perspectives" (p. 322). In the same vein, Allan Edwards (1999) suggested that **critical reflection** should receive more attention than it currently receives in sport management so that we can find "new, less oppressive, and more just ways of creating and managing sport" (p. 79). Wendy Frisby (2005) proposed that sport management educators become "versed in critical social science theories" so that they can help students become "strong critical thinkers who will make positive contributions to society" (p. 5). The clear implication of all these suggestions is that, as the managers of the future, you will need exceptional thinking skills to make the decisions necessary to deal effectively and responsibly with the myriad challenges that you will encounter.

critical reflection—Making judgments about whether professional activity is equitable, just, and respectful of persons (Edwards, 1999, p. 69).

Sport managers of the 21st century will have to solve problems that we cannot even conceptualize today. To develop the ability to make good decisions—decisions that are consistent with values and perspectives on which you have seriously reflected—you first need the ability to integrate critical thinking skills with the legal and ethical principles that you will learn in chapters 16 and 17. Such a need becomes obvious when you consider the types of issues that future sport managers will face. Following are a few examples of contemporary issues:

- Should intercollegiate athletes receive salaries?
- Should professional athletes undergo testing for drugs?
- Should the Confederate flag be flown at athletic contests in the United States?
- Should male and female coaches receive equal salaries if they coach the same sport?
- Should athletes participating at the Olympic Games receive a share of the revenues of the International Olympic Committee?
- Should child athletes be subjected to an intense high-performance training regimen?
- Should boys' and men's sport programs be adversely affected so that athletics programs can comply with Title IX?

You can probably think of many more such questions. How do you make good decisions about these and other issues? Good decisions are not based on expediency, the easy way out, or what will cause the least turmoil or make the most money. As noted in chapter 1, you are most likely to make good decisions if you make it a point to work toward a principled justification for your beliefs. Becoming a critical thinker is an important step toward providing such a justification.

The aim of this chapter is to provide you with helpful tools for thinking critically about issues relevant to sport management so that you can develop confidence in your ability to make decisions concerning such issues. First, we will help you discriminate between critical thinking and other forms of thinking and become aware of the essential components of critical thinking. In doing so, we will stress critical thinking dispositions and questions. We will define a set of critical thinking questions and then apply them to an essay concerning a controversial topic so that you can see critical thinking in action. Our hope is that when you have completed the chapter, you will be better prepared to solve problems and make decisions in sport management.

BECOMING A CRITICAL THINKER

As a professional, you will often find yourself in situations that require you to make decisions that affect a large number of people. Many times, you will have to make these decisions quickly. In all likelihood, you will base your decision on your personal values while also considering the values of others. Two important components of critical thinking, therefore, are conscious reflection on personal values and recognition of conflicting values. The scenario below clearly demonstrates the role of values in decision making—and the importance of knowing your values before the occurrence of a crisis that requires you to make an important decision.

WHEN TRAGEDY STRIKES

A high school basketball player collapsed during a tournament game. Rescue personnel administered mouth-to-mouth resuscitation and closed-chest heart massage for 90 minutes, but to no avail. The young man was taken from the game on a gurney and subsequently was pronounced dead. The decision makers had two choices—to continue the game or postpone the game.

If the decision had been your responsibility, what would you have done? If you had been the coach of the injured player's team, what would you have recommended? What would you have thought if you had been the player's parent, a parent of a player on the opposing team, a student, or anyone else associated with the event?

On what values would you have based your recommendation or decision? What additional information do you need to answer the question? What value conflicts are you experiencing as you reflect on the decision that you would make?

Recognizing value conflicts and making judgments about your preferred values are just two of the important ingredients for becoming a successful critical thinker. For example, in the basketball scenario, the values of competition, the integrity of the game, and convenience are in conflict with the values of compassion and respect for the individual. Considering your own preference with regard to this value conflict helps you make a more reflective decision on the issue. What is the best way to become a better decision maker? An essential step is to develop critical thinking skills.

What Is Critical Thinking?

You probably have encountered the term *critical thinking* many times in your daily life and in the classroom. You may also have noticed that when the term is used, its meaning is often unclear. One reason for the confusion is that the term *critical thinking* means different things to different people. Thus, you must understand the meaning of critical thinking as we are using it in this chapter. Our definition is an adaptation of definitions that are widely used among scholars who systematically study critical thinking, and it should be helpful to you in distinguishing between critical thinking and other kinds of thinking.

First, to better understand what we do mean by critical thinking, you need to understand what we do not mean. For example, critical thinking is not any of the following:

- Simply thinking—Critical thinking is "thinking," but it is a special form of thinking. For example, developing a good understanding of something is an important dimension of (just) thinking, but it is quite distinct from critical thinking.
- Negative thinking—To many people, critical thinking does not sound agreeable. It sounds negative. But critical thinkers are not naysayers! Critical thinkers are seeking something positive—as solid a basis for their beliefs as they can find in a world full of uncertainty. Criticisms are simply part of their search for better arguments. In this respect, critical thinking, if practiced appropriately, is positive, caring, and productive.
- Creative thinking—Certain aspects of critical thinking do require our best creative efforts. That is one of its appealing components. But critical thinking stresses making evaluative judgments rather than the imaginative leaps associated with brainstorming or generating novel ideas or strategies.

We have provided examples of what we do *not* mean, so what *do* we mean by critical thinking? A common feature of all critical thinking activity is systematic evaluation of arguments (reasons and their companion conclusions) according to explicit standards of rationality—careful thinking that helps us move forward in a continual, ongoing search to improve our opinions, decisions, or judgments. Critical thinking, as we use the term, refers to the following:

- The awareness of a set of interrelated critical questions
- The ability to ask and answer critical questions at appropriate times
- The desire to use those questions and accept their results as a guide to behavior

Thus, the following equation captures the essence of critical thinking:

Critical thinking = Questioning skills + Desire to question and to accept the results of the questioning

People can practice critical thinking in a number of ways, some of which are much more desirable than others. For example, individuals might apply critical thinking with selfish motives, using their skills to support their own selfish interests. These people are not seeking solutions; rather, they are seeking to destroy the arguments of those who disagree with them. Such motivation interferes with the pursuit of furthering our understanding of an issue.

On the other hand, ideal critical thinkers possess a particular set of dispositions, or tendencies. Although many dispositions facilitate the critical thinking process (see, for example, Facione, Facione, & Sanchez, 1995), we believe that the set of three dispositions summarized by Ennis (2000) is especially useful for the critical thinker to pursue. According to Ennis, ideal critical thinkers

- care that their beliefs are true and that their decisions are justified; that is, they care to get it right to the extent that it is possible;
- care to present a position honestly and clearly, theirs as well as others'; and
- care about the dignity and worth of every person.

CRITICAL THINKING

Dealing With Racial Vilification in Australian Rules Football

Dwight Zakus and Allan Edwards, Australia

The sport of Australian rules football is governed by the clubs that make up the league. A professional management team known as the Australian Football League (AFL) manages it. Since the early 1990s the AFL has expanded and relocated clubs to make the league a truly national competition. Throughout its history, the sport has attracted Aboriginal youth to its playing ranks, and these athletes comprise some of the most talented players ever in the AFL.

Traditionally, Australian rules football condoned racial vilification. Verbal attacks based on Aboriginal or other ethnic origins were routinely employed to gain an advantage by distracting a player from the flow of play or by causing a physical altercation. This practice was seen as a form of gamesmanship and was not deemed a major issue.

Initially the league condoned this behaviour by not addressing it. Following a 1995 incident between a star Aboriginal player and an opposing White player, however, the league had to act upon this gamesmanship. Although racial slurs and taunts were not new, this behaviour went against the leagues' mission statement and its inherent values of equality and fairness. The league ultimately instituted a policy and attendant procedures to deal with racial (and religious) vilification.

Through his public actions, the Aboriginal player had forced the AFL to do something about racism at last. Although the exact decision-making processes are not known, AFL management clearly went through a critically reflective process to deal with the issue. Critical reflection in this case refers to thinking about how the broader social, cultural, and value frameworks impinge on the structure and flow of Australian rules football. No longer could the AFL condone behaviours that were contrary to those in the wider Australian society. So, first it was an issue of values.

Second, racial vilification became a management issue within the game. Historically, the assumption was that AFL players should be able to challenge opponents verbally and mentally to gain a tactical advantage. Because this jousting was regarded as just part of the game, it really didn't matter what players said to one another. Although racial vilification was not new, public response to the 1995 incident demanded a change in the way the game was played.

The league's reaction was to institute a policy to deal with racial vilification. The AFL chose to use player education programs and mediation between players as a first response, as well as the imposition of fines and suspensions. The vilification policy was written into the league's statutes, and the issue of appropriate player behaviour became sanctioned in the laws of the game.

The establishment of this policy and its procedures were reactive, and the AFL recognised that the policy alone would not resolve the underlying problem of racism. Therefore, the league set up other programs to deal with racism at the development level of the game. Community awareness programs, indigenous participation programs, and AFL player visits to indigenous communities were developed and funded to address racism at all levels of the sport. These programs demonstrate that the league management critically reflected on the issue and thought of ways to deal with the issue beyond standard, normative reactionary approaches (e.g., punishments, fines). In this way, critically reflective thinking led to more proactive, holistic ways of managing racial vilification in the AFL.

Note that caring is a central aspect of the critical thinking process. The ideal critical thinker cares enough about what others have to say to make an active attempt to discover and listen to others' reasons and to be sensitive to others' feelings and levels of understanding. An important component of this caring is being truly and seriously open to points of view different from one's own, recognizing that one's own beliefs may not be sufficiently justified. Clearly, achieving this openness is more easily said than done. For a more complete list of dispositions, see Ennis (1995).

Moving From the Sponge Approach to the Panning-for-Gold Approach

One approach to thinking about issues related to sport management is to think in a way similar to how a sponge reacts to water—by absorption. The problem with the sponge approach is that it is passive; it fails to provide you with a method for actively choosing which information and opinions to believe and which to reject, or which values to incorporate as your personal values. If you were to rely solely on the

Recently retired Aboriginal AFL player Darryl White, in a trademark move, soars to secure the football. Murry Bird, former AFL operations manager, describes White as "a proud man who stands up for his people," who has been an inspiration in the fight against racism in Australian rules football.
© Just Photography

International Learning Activity

Analyze the Australian Rules Football issue in terms of the eight critical thinking questions presented in this chapter.

sponge approach, you would be dependent on the last expert whom you encountered, the last argument that you read, or the person who spoke the loudest. The sponge approach is also ineffective because experts often disagree for many reasons (e.g., differing values, training, and cultural backgrounds).

We think that you would prefer a model of learning different from the sponge approach because you would rather choose for yourself what to believe and what to reject. To make your own choices, you should read and listen with a special attitude—a questioning attitude, assisted by a strong sense of curiosity. Such an attitude requires you to interact with information and arguments. We call this interactive style the panning-for-gold approach. Such an approach assumes that by actively sifting through all the information that bombards you, you can choose what to believe with a sense of self-confidence; you can provide good justification for your beliefs. Such beliefs are the gold nuggets that you are seeking.

To distinguish the gold from the gravel as you sift through information, you must ask frequent questions and reflect on the answers—the essence of critical thinking. Using critical thinking as the method for panning for gold is a challenging task, but the reward is great. If you incorporate the interactive critical thinking process that we are emphasizing in this chapter, you can feel the same sense of pride in your reading and listening that you normally get from successful participation in physical activities. You will no longer have to depend on experts. In fact, you will be able to challenge the opinions of experts, including your instructors, by asking critical questions about those opinions. You will, therefore, be able to construct your own knowledge and make your own decisions. You will have the satisfaction of knowing why you should either ignore or accept a particular bit of advice. As you learn to evaluate information and opinions systematically, you will become an active member of the growing field of sport management and not just a passive observer.

UNDERSTANDING AND ASKING CRITICAL THINKING QUESTIONS

Central to your success as a panning-for-gold thinker is having a good understanding of a set of questions that you need to ask to evaluate someone's reasoning. To help you achieve such an understanding, we first briefly describe a set of core questions that you should find helpful as you critically evaluate the reasoning of others. Next, to help clarify these questions, we then apply each of them to a reasoning example related to a contemporary sport management issue.

What Are the Critical Thinking Questions?

There is no single correct set of critical thinking questions. We will present eight selected critical thinking questions with a brief description of their meanings and suggestions for how to put them into practice. If you nurture the habit of asking these questions, you will be successful in your panning-for-gold quest, and you will be better equipped to come up with your own questions as situations demand. Thus you will be in an excellent position to decide what to accept and what to reject. (Our discussion of each question is necessarily somewhat brief. For an in-depth discussion of the eight questions, see Browne & Keeley, 2007.)

The first set of questions will help you determine the reasoning of the argument. Some aspects of the reasoning will be stated (explicit), and some will be hidden (implicit). Before you can critically evaluate reasoning, you need to have as clear a picture of the reasoning as possible. Some communicators make their reasoning clear; others present it in a confusing manner.

Critical Thinking Question 1: What Are the Issues and the Conclusion?

Usually, writers and speakers are reacting to some issue, and they are trying to persuade you to accept their point of view on it. You start the critical thinking process by identifying the issue and the conclusion. Issues and conclusions will be either descriptive or prescriptive. Value preferences will have much greater influence over prescriptive conclusions than they will over descriptive conclusions. For example, values will heavily influence the claim that there should be more African American athletics directors (prescriptive). Conversely, the claim that in 2003-2004 only 5% of all NCAA Division I athletics directors were people of color (descriptive) will depend largely on empirical evidence, such as surveys of university athletics departments (Lapchick, 2004-2006). Look for the issue and conclusion at the beginnings and endings of essays, articles, or chapter sections. Titles and headings (especially in newspapers and magazines) are also excellent clues. Also, to help locate the conclusion, look for words that signal its presence, such as the following: *thus*, *therefore*, *consequently*, *hence*, and *but*.

> **descriptive**—Concerns about the way the world is, was, or will be.
>
> **prescriptive**—Concerns about the way the world should or ought to be.

Critical Thinking Question 2: What Are the Reasons?

Reasons are ideas that writers and speakers use to justify their conclusions. Reasons answer the *why* question: Why do you believe what you believe? Most reasoning is in the form "*This* (conclusion) because of *that* (reasons)." To discover reasons, you need to ask this: If the writers were sitting across from me, what reasons would they give to support their conclusion? When you have the combination of a reason or a set of reasons and a conclusion, then you have an argument. Thus,

Reasons + Conclusion = Argument

You should decide the merits of the conclusion based on the quality of the reasons. Conclusions not supported by reasons are mere opinions, and thus you should usually ignore them—especially if they are controversial. Anyone who is trying to persuade you should have to answer the question, What are your reasons?

Critical Thinking Question 3: What Words or Phrases Are Ambiguous?

We cannot determine whether we agree or disagree with someone's reasoning if key terms in the reasoning could have more than one meaning and those different meanings would influence how we would react. Such terms or phrases are importantly ambiguous. Critical thinkers attempt to clarify the meaning of key terms and phrases (those that are in the reasoning structure) that are ambiguous before they make judgments about the quality of the reasoning. When faced with reasoning that is importantly ambiguous, ask for clarification if it is possible to do so. If you cannot ask, then you will want to make a conscious effort to recognize how the changes in meaning will influence your reaction to the reasoning. For example, in evaluating a coach's success, if you define success solely as winning percentage, you may reach a different conclusion than if you define success as motivating athletes to achieve their full potential.

Critical Thinking Question 4: What Are the Value Conflicts and Assumptions?

Assumptions are ideas that people take for granted when they engage in reasoning. Assumptions are usually implicit in the reasoning, rather than explicit, so you have to fill in the blanks. A full reasoning structure, with the blanks filled in, usually looks like the diagram in figure 3.1. Reasons support the conclusion only if the assumptions are reliable.

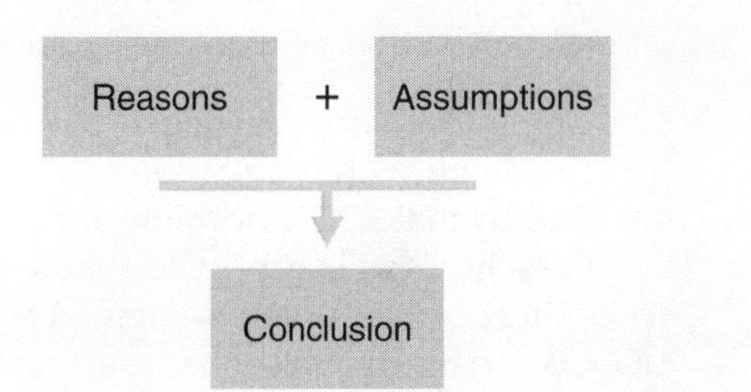

Figure 3.1 A full reasoning structure with the blanks filled in.

Browne, M. Neil; Keeley, Stuart M., *Asking the right questions: A guide to critical thinking,* 7th Edition, © 2004. Reprinted by permission of Pearson Education, Inc., Upper Saddle River, NJ.

There are two kinds of assumptions—value assumptions and descriptive assumptions. As we use the term, values are abstract ideas about what individuals or groups care about. For example, honesty, compassion, competition, and justice are all values for most of us. In many cases, however, such as the basketball game in which the player collapsed, values are in conflict, such that embracing one value means rejecting another. Such conflicts are pervasive in prescriptive issues, and within such issues people assume certain value preferences—they take for granted that some values are more important than others. The following reasoning example illustrates the influence of value conflicts and value assumptions:

> Conclusion: Sport teams should cease using American Indian symbols and traditions, such as Indian ritual dances.
> Reason: These practices are inaccurate, disrespectful, and offensive to American Indians and to others who are sensitive to such stereotyping.

values—The unstated ideas that people see as worthwhile (Browne & Keeley, 2007, p. 57).

This reason might be true, but for it to support the conclusion, a value assumption must be made: The value of *human dignity* is more important than the value of the *right to freedom of expression*; otherwise the writer would be less concerned about disrespect of Indians and more concerned about the rights of teams to promote whatever symbolic image they wished. Thus, within this controversy, the values of human dignity and freedom of expression are in conflict; and the writer has assumed that human dignity is the preferred value. Other writers might place higher value on the right to freedom of expression. When you encounter prescriptive conclusions, remember to search for the underlying value assumptions.

Critical Thinking Question 5: What Are the Descriptive Assumptions?

Descriptive assumptions are beliefs about how the world is, was, or will be, which, much like value assumptions, usually fill the gaps between reasons and conclusions and are usually unstated. We discover these important missing links—the glue that holds the reasoning together—by asking the question, What does the writer have to take for granted in order for the reason to support the conclusion or for us to believe that the reason is accurate? The following scenario illustrates the discovery of a descriptive assumption (Women's Sports Foundation, 2001-2005):

> Conclusion: Female athletes perform at higher levels when coached by men rather than women.
> Reason: Teams with male coaches have won more championships than teams with female coaches because female coaches are not as intense and demanding as male coaches are.

What descriptive beliefs do we need to take for granted to agree with the reasoning? A good way to discover such hidden beliefs is to ask, How could we disagree with the reasoning? In so asking, we discovered several beliefs that were taken for granted:

- Assumption 1: Teams coached by females have had the same recruiting resources as teams coached by males. It is possible, for example, that the schools willing to invest the most in the recruiting process have also tended to be the schools that hire male coaches, and that the discrepancy in expenditure is the cause of the difference in championships won.
- Assumption 2: It is acceptable to attribute standard characteristics to all members of a given group. If we accept that assumption, we also have to accept other stereotypes, such as all football players are stupid, all African Americans have rhythm, and white men can't jump (Women's Sports Foundation, 2001-2005).
- Assumption 3: Intense, demanding coaches are more likely to help women athletes reach their potential. It is more probable that different female athletes respond to different coaching personalities. Diverse coaching methods can determine how much individual athletes flourish, and successful coaching styles vary greatly both between and within genders.

Locating assumptions is well worth the hard thinking effort. Although usually hidden, assumptions are crucial to holding reasoning together. If the assumptions are faulty, as they are in the previous example, then you should reject the reasoning.

Learning Activity

Form a book club among sport management majors and read a book about issues in sport. You will find examples in the section "For More Information" on pages 2 and 3. Additional titles will be available in your library. Keep a journal and discuss your journal entries during club meetings. Encourage club members to use critical thinking skills in the discussions. Pay special attention to finding assumptions.

Critical Thinking Question 6: Does the Reasoning Contain Fallacies?

Fallacies are mistakes in reasoning that usually do not seem to be mistakes. Often, they represent reasoning that requires erroneous or false assumptions. The following brief claim illustrates a fallacy: Either we raise public moneys to finance a sport stadium, or we will have to move the team to another city. This reasoning assumes that only two choices are available. If, for example, it is possible to raise private moneys to build the stadium, then the assumption is false and the reasoning contains a fallacy. We recommend that you familiarize yourself with the several types of fallacies by referring to some of the Web sites and books listed in the section "For More Information" on page 2.

Critical Thinking Question 7: How Good Is the Evidence?

Consider the following claims:

- Relaxation and imagery training enhance gymnastics performance in Olympic athletes.
- The graduation rate of nonathletes is higher than the graduation rate of athletes.
- The mandates of Title IX have forced several colleges to drop some men's sports.
- Participation in sport builds good character.
- If we accommodate athletes who are differently abled, then sports as we know them will be destroyed.

Should we believe these claims? Are they accurate? Are they facts or merely unsupported opinions? To evaluate such claims, we must ask the question, How good is the evidence?

All reasoning includes claims, or assertions, about the way the world is, was, or is going to be; these are descriptive beliefs. As critical thinkers we must decide which claims to believe. Because establishing the absolute truth or falsity of most descriptive beliefs is extremely difficult, we find it most useful to view beliefs along a continuum of dependability. The greater the quality and quantity of evidence supporting a belief, the more we can depend on it and the more we can legitimately call the claim a fact. Thus, for us, facts are beliefs that are supported with abundant evidence. The major difference between claims that are opinions and those that are facts is the present state of the relevant evidence.

Before we can judge the persuasiveness of a communication, we need to know which descriptive claims we can count on. How do we decide? We ask questions such as the following: Where's the evidence? How good is the evidence? What is your proof? How do you know that?

The value of the evidence depends on what kind of evidence it is. Evidence comes in many forms, including the following:

- Intuition
- Appeals to authorities
- Testimonials
- Personal experience
- Case studies and examples
- Scientific research studies
- Analogies

Each kind of evidence can be good evidence—when used appropriately. Learning to evaluate evidence well is a lifelong learning task. The more that you read and study across the various disciplines, the more familiar you will become with which kinds of evidence are most suitable for which kinds of descriptive claims. We can best help you at this point by briefly mentioning the most common kinds of evidence used in the field of sport management and alerting you to the strengths and weaknesses of such evidence. Even if you are not an expert on evidence, you can usefully ask the question, How good is the evidence? Let's examine the various kinds of evidence and some central questions that you can ask about each kind.

Appeals to Authority As Evidence

In today's world, the most common way to support a belief is to appeal to statements of an expert, or of an authority. Purported experts appear everywhere—on TV, in magazines, on the Internet, and in your textbooks. Appeals to the statements of credible authorities are often valuable evidence. Authorities, however, vary in degrees of expertise, and they often disagree. Thus, we need to be highly critical when appealing to authority. Questions that we need to ask when evidence is an appeal to authority include the following:

- How much expertise or training does the authority have on the relevant subject?
- Has the authority been in a position to have especially good access to pertinent information?
- Does the authority provide any specific information or reasons to support the claim?
- Is there good reason to believe that the authority is relatively free of distorting biases or influences?
- Has the authority developed a reputation for making dependable claims?

Personal Testimonials As Evidence

The editors of this book, of course, would be pleased to hear personal testimonials (see figure 3.2) from our readers. But praise from a single reader provides scant evidence for the quality of the book. After all, how typical is the reader? Does she have special expertise in reading such books? Does she have something to gain by her statement? As critical readers, we should be wary of such evidence. Communicators often try to persuade us by quoting particular persons as saying that a given idea or product is good or bad, citing their personal experiences with the product. Such personal testimonials are always highly suspect as evidence because they are highly selective, likely to be biased, and often void of any special expertise on the product or idea.

Case Studies As Evidence

Case studies possess many of the same problems that personal testimonials do. We define a case study as a report of detailed observations of a single individual or event made by another individual. A case study may be formal and systematic, such as the cases completed by Sigmund Freud, or it may be informal. Journalists, for example, often begin persuasive essays with vivid, rather informal descriptions of people to whom they wish to refer. Writers and reporters often present such cases to generate emotional reactions.

Single case studies usually can best be viewed as striking examples, or as possibilities, and not as proof or good evidence. Like personal testimonials, they are highly selective and subject to major biasing influences. Generalizing from them is difficult. Be suspicious of case studies as evidence. Look for further evidence for the claim.

Scientific Studies As Evidence

"Research studies show . . ."
"Investigators have found . . ."
"A new study in the *Journal of Sport Management* has shown . . ."

Dear Publisher:

This book on sport management has changed my life. I now truly understand the opportunities open to me in this field. I strongly recommend this book to anyone who plans a career in sport management.

Jane Feelgood, student

Figure 3.2 Personal testimonial.

One kind of evidence that often carries special weight as support for beliefs or ideas is scientific research, which we define as a systematic collection of observations made by people who have followed some form of scientific methodology. In the field of sport management, such research studies are most likely to rely on surveys, in-depth interviews, or experiments.

Although the scientific method attempts to minimize many of the built-in biases in our observations of the world and in our intuitions, even the best studies have important limitations. Beliefs that appear to be scientific facts one day may turn out to be tomorrow's myths. Like appeals to an authority, such findings are of undetermined value until we ask important critical thinking questions, such as the following:

- How reputable is the source of the report?
- Does the research have any special strengths?
- Have other researchers found the same results? (Do not be overly influenced by a single study. Findings often vary from time to time and from researcher to researcher. In general, we should be most influenced by research findings that have been repeated by many researchers over a period of time.)
- How selective has the writer or speaker been in choosing studies to support a belief? Has she or he omitted relevant studies with contradictory results?
- Would someone have had a reason to distort the research or research interpretations? For example, are certain findings likely to benefit the researcher or the person citing the research?
- How far can we generalize, given the kinds of people or events studied? (Research results can be applied only to people and situations similar to those studied in the research.)
- Did biases or distortions occur in the way that the surveys, questionnaires, ratings, or other measurements were used? Did interviewers ask leading questions? Did research participants know what kinds of answers were expected? Were survey questions ambiguous?

Analogies As Evidence

Our last kind of evidence is quite different from the others. Look closely at the form of the following brief argument, paying special attention to the reason supporting the conclusion.

"It's a mistake to hire a former star as a coach of an NBA basketball team. Look at what has happened the last several times teams hired great players to coach. They knew the game, but they just didn't know how to manage the players."

The evidence presented is a comparison between two things (hiring a star in the past and hiring a star today) to prove something about one of the things (the possible success of hiring a star now). When we compare something with which we are less familiar with something with which we are more familiar to support a conclusion, then we argue from **analogy**.

> **analogy**—A form of logical inference in which we reason that if two things are alike in some ways, they are alike in other ways.

Analogies can stimulate insights, but they can also deceive us. For example, the previous analogy makes us consider potential problems with hiring a star athlete as a coach. But the situation may contain important differences, which we need to consider. Perhaps recent stars are different from former stars in how they have tried to learn coaching methods. If so, this analogy may be faulty.

Because analogical reasoning is so common and has the potential to be both persuasive and faulty, you need to recognize such reasoning and know how to evaluate it systematically. To do so, try to focus on two factors: (1) the number of ways the two elements being compared are similar and different and (2) the relevance of the similarities and the differences. Strong analogies will be ones in which the two elements compared possess relevant similarities and lack relevant differences.

Try to evaluate the following reasoning, in which an analogy provides the evidence:

"This baseball team needs a manager who will use strict discipline. Baseball players are like children in a family. They need a strong parent who will set clear limits. Otherwise, they will keep testing the limits and disrupting the team."

Learning Activity

Using an Internet search engine, locate two essays by credible authorities that provide arguments for different conclusions to an issue in sport or sport management (see issues on p. 48 for examples). Identify differences in value preferences, the selection of reasons, and the selection of evidence.

Critical Thinking Question 8: What Significant Information Is Omitted?

What is *not* said by a writer or speaker is often as important as what *is* said. The information we receive is highly selective and incomplete. Communicators with limited space who are trying to persuade you are likely to select and use information that supports or confirms their view. Thus, you need to ask an important additional question before judging the quality of reasoning: What significant information is omitted or missing?

How do we discover something that is missing? You can ask many different questions to identify relevant omitted information, including many of the critical thinking questions described earlier. The following list, adapted from Browne and Keeley (2007), highlights some important kinds of omitted information:

- Arguments, research studies, examples, testimonials, or analogies that support conclusions that differ from those of the author
- Plausible definitions of key terms that differ from the author's definition
- Other value perspectives from which one might approach this issue
- Origins and details of "facts" and research findings referred to in the reasoning
- Omitted effects, both positive and negative, and both short and long term, of what is advocated and what is opposed, including possible unintended consequences
- Context of quotations and testimonials that would provide a clearer sense of their meaning
- Possible benefits that authors might gain by convincing others of their position

By explicitly looking for missing information, you can decide whether you have enough information to judge the author's reasoning. If the writer has left too much out, which is often the case, you should be cautious about accepting the conclusion. If you wish to make an informed judgment about the reasoning, you will want to seek out more information.

Asking the Core Critical Questions

Let's go through the critical thinking steps with an example of a situation in which a sport manager needs to make a decision. Assume that you recently took a position as the children's soccer league coordinator in your community. The program has a long tradition of offering soccer skill development and competitive opportunities for youth. Recently, however, some parents have challenged the way that the league and the coaches operate. You are not sure what to do. To add to the confusion, you receive a letter from a child's parents who are irate that you are not ensuring that children have equal playing time during the soccer games. What will you decide to do? Will you continue to allow the coaches to decide how much time each child gets to play during games or will you introduce new policies, rules, or strategies to ensure equal playing time? How will you make your decision? Perhaps reading the letter in figure 3.3 and the accompanying discussion will help you decide.

Learning Activity

Go to your library and check out a copy of *Sport in Contemporary Society, an Anthology* (2005), edited by Stanley Eitzen. Find a chapter that covers a topic of interest to you and analyze the issue using the core critical thinking skills described in this chapter. Or check out a copy of *Controversies of the Sports World* (1999) by Douglas T. Putnam. Find a chapter that covers a topic of interest to you and, using core critical thinking questions, answer one of the issue-related questions at the end of the chapter.

What Are the Issues and Conclusion? (Question 1)

The letter in figure 3.3 asks the question, Should community youth sport emphasize equal participation and skill development rather than winning? This is a prescriptive issue because it asks what *should* be done rather than what *is*, *was*, or *will be* the state of the world. The major clue to the issue is the conclusion, which is stated in the last sentence: "Shouldn't the emphasis for youth sport be on participation and fun rather than on performance, competition, and winning?"

What Are the Reasons? (Question 2)

Your willingness to accept someone's conclusion should depend on the quality of the reasons. Just how well do the reasons support the conclusion? Writers often fail to make their reasons clear to the reader, in which case you will need to work hard to construct the reasons from the argument. You may need to reread the essay several times and write notes in the margins. Keep asking yourself how the author would answer the question, Why do you believe your conclusion? An idea is not a

Dear league organizers,

We are deeply concerned about the state of youth sport in our community. Our eight-year-old daughter wanted to play soccer in a summer league. We were very happy with her decision because she has never been extensively involved in sport or physical activity. We thought this was the beginning of something great for our daughter—a more active and healthy lifestyle. We were able to find a team in your league, and the beginning of the season was great. Our daughter was initiated to the sport easily with regular weekly practice and game days. The coach (the parent of a boy on the team) made sure all children were actively involved in all aspects of the practice. There were enough parents willing to help and enough soccer balls so that everyone could be involved in the drills and exercises. Our daughter's skills were improving and more importantly, she was making friends and having fun.

Unfortunately, when it came to the games, our daughter did not get to play extensively. Our daughter is by no means a soccer star—she is a beginner. And because it appears that the coach wants the team to do well on the field, he is overly concerned with winning. As a result of the emphasis on winning, only the highly skilled 'athletes' on the team get the maximum playing time during games. The coach's focus on winning is not necessarily shared by all the children on the team or for that matter by many parents on the sidelines. Several parents have the same concerns that we have about their children's time on the field during games. Our daughter is one of only a few children who do not get to play much during games. She is now completely turned off the sport, and she no longer wants to go to the practices or to the games. In fact, immediately following the team's last game, she spent hours crying, and she remained upset for several days following the game. She doesn't understand why, as a member of the team, the coach doesn't want her to play.

In an attempt to help our daughter, we did some reading on the topic of youth participation in sport and realized that our daughter's issue with organized sport is not unique. We read a chapter in a book where a sociologist named Jay Coakley discussed how sport could be valuable for children's psychological, social, and physical development. The chapter also addressed the value of sport in building character as well as instilling self-esteem and self-confidence. This Coakley fellow also discussed a number of problems that can be associated with organized youth sport. One of the problems is an overemphasis on performance and winning, which leads to having only the highly skilled children play during games. In fact, he said that playing time was related to a child's reputation among peers and that not getting enough playing time was the most likely cause of a player's disappointment and often resulted in loss of interest. Coakley suggested several strategies a coach could use to make sure all the kids got to play a reasonable amount of time, but our daughter's coach isn't using any of them.

We believe we must protect our child from over-eager coaches, an over-emphasis on performance, and an obsession with winning. We are bombarded by news stories and research reports about the negative impact of inactivity among Americans. The Centers for Disease Control and Prevention (CDC) and the National Center for Health Statistics (NCHS) report alarming statistics with respect to the prevalence of childhood obesity (NCHS, 2004, October 6). In light of our country's obesity epidemic among children and the increasing popularity of sedentary activities among our youth (watching television, playing video games, listening to music), it seems ironic that we are not doing more to encourage our children to be and stay more physically active. We must find a way to keep children motivated to practice sports without turning them off.

Your organization took in a motivated young girl; and with the actions of your leaders, you have discouraged her and other marginally skilled players from ever wanting to play organized sports again. We paid the same registration fee that all other parents paid for their children to be involved in this team, which helped pay for the costs of the fields, the equipment, and other things. Why can't our daughter play as much as the other kids during games? Shouldn't all children have access to equal playing time during practice sessions and games? Shouldn't the emphasis for youth sport be on participation and fun rather than on performance, competition, and winning?

Sincerely,

LaTasha's parents

Figure 3.3 Letter describing a prescriptive issue.

reason unless it answers this why question. Trying to state reasons in your own words helps you check your understanding of them. As you study the essay, try to list each reason and supporting reason; then check how adequately you have grasped the reasons by determining whether you believe that the author wanted to use these ideas to support the conclusion.

The writers of this letter present several reasons and have supported them with other reasons.

- ***Reason 1.*** Active participation in sports has many potential benefits for youth.
  - Research shows that participating in sports has psychological, social, and physical benefits.
  - Sport participation builds character, contributes to self-esteem and self-confidence, and helps participants establish social connections and interactions with peers.
- ***Reason 2.*** An overemphasis on winning turns less skilled youth off to sports.
  - Jay Coakley states that the overemphasis on performance and winning is a common problem.
  - Letter writers' daughter initially enjoyed her soccer involvement, but then she didn't play much in games and is now turned off to the sport.
- ***Reason 3:*** Inactivity of Americans is causing health problems; the increase in obesity and the popularity of sedentary activities suggest that we need a way to keep children motivated to participate in sports.
  - The CDC and the NCHS report an alarming presence of childhood obesity.
- ***Reason 4:*** Parents each pay the same registration fee, which contributes to the cost of things like fields and equipment. Having equal access to game experience is the same right as having equal access to the equipment needed to practice and play.
- ***Reason 5:*** Many parents and children share the concern about an overemphasis on winning.

These parents have presented many reasons to support their conclusion. We now need to evaluate this reasoning by asking further critical thinking questions.

Which Words or Phrases Are Ambiguous? (Question 3)

The place to look for important ambiguity is in the reasoning structure, which we have just completed; thus, our focus is on the reasons and the conclusion. Do you need more information about the meanings of certain terms or phrases before you decide whether to agree with the beliefs that the parents state in the reasoning structure?

A potential important ambiguity is "lack of playing time," a phrase used in support for the second reason. An emphasis on winning can lead to many different levels of playing time for the less skilled players. Some coaches who emphasize winning may play the less skilled players for one-fourth of the game, whereas other coaches may play them only for a token minute or two. The negative effect on participants is likely to be much greater in the latter instance. Coaches may be able to emphasize winning while still providing significant playing time for all players.

Another potentially misleading ambiguity occurs in the fifth reason, the phrase "many parents and children share the concern." First, the phrase fails to make clear just how much parental dissatisfaction exists in terms of numbers and intensity of the concern. If "many" refers to the majority of parents of potential youth participants, regardless of the talent of their own children, then the reason provides better support to the conclusion than if "many" refers to a minority of parents or just those parents whose children are receiving limited time.

What Are the Value Conflicts and Assumptions? (Question 4)

A central value assumption for these parents is that the goals of participation and equal opportunity, in the sense that all players have the same chance to take part actively and improve their skills, are more important than the goals of competition and individual excellence. The parents' letter emphasizes the physical and psychological benefits that *all* children will gain by staying active in sport and deemphasizes the potential benefits of a highly competitive atmosphere in which *some* children will have more opportunity to excel than others, and in which there are winners and losers.

What Are the Descriptive Assumptions? (Question 5)

To get a more complete picture of the parents' reasoning, we need to know more than their value preferences. We also need to know what beliefs about the state of the world they take for granted. In order for the second reason to support the conclusion, one must assume that reactions to actual game experiences are more important for participants than the more holistic experience of involvement in a sport,

Sheila Johnson speaks at a press conference in 2005 in Washington, DC, where she was named president of WNBA team the Washington Mystics. Critical thinking has been crucial to Ms. Johnson's success.
© Getty Images

such as practicing together, making friends, becoming sport educated, and preparing for a competitive world. Even if the less skilled players become bored in games, they may still find the experience of being members of a team more beneficial to them in the long run than activities that they might have pursued had they not been members of the team. In addition, one must assume that this child's experience is typical of the experience of less skilled children. Perhaps most children are less dissatisfied with limited playing time than she is and appreciate the opportunity just to be part of a team.

Another questionable assumption must be true in order for the fourth reason to be acceptable: Children who are turned off to a single sport because of lack of playing time are unlikely to participate in other sports or find other activity outlets. A related assumption is that the primary determinant of a child's activity level is the degree of success in a given sport. If other factors shape children's disposition to be active, then the third reason is unlikely to be true. A further assumption is that most children will react to "failure" experiences by quitting sport, or by ceasing to make efforts to improve, rather than by working harder to become more competitive.

Does the Reasoning Contain Fallacies? (Question 6)

Reasoning fallacies in this essay include several fallacies of irrelevance, including an appeal to common opinion, using the wrong reasons, an appeal to questionable authority, and an emotional appeal. Using the reason, for example, that a number of parents feel the same way (i.e., that they are concerned about their children's playing time during games and that they feel that too much emphasis is placed on performance and winning) urges us to accept a position simply on the grounds that a large number of people accept it. Broad acceptance does not make a claim worthy of our acceptance. In addition, the claim that other parents have similar concerns regarding their children's lack of playing time during games is unsubstantiated; we don't know whether the information is accurate, and we don't know how many (if any) parents feel the same way. In addition, the first reason is irrelevant; it focuses on some of the positive elements of sports, not on the central issues of unequal playing time during games and overemphasis on performance and winning. Reason 3 commits the fallacy of using the wrong reason; the issue is not about childhood obesity or inactivity among youth per se but about community youth sport. The parents also use emotional appeals by claiming that their daughter "spent hours crying and remained upset for several days following the game." The use of emotional appeals distracts the readers from evidence that is more relevant.

How Good Is the Evidence? (Question 7)

First, we need to ask the question, What kinds of evidence did the parents use? They used appeals to authority (e.g., Centers for Disease Control and Prevention and the National Center for Health Statistics), several research studies (see reasons 2 and 3), an analogy (see reason 4), and a personal experience (see support for the second reason). The credibility of these authorities for making these particular judgments is questionable. For example, the relevance of the research is questionable because the writers provide no information about sample size, breadth, and randomness; or about the purpose of the research; or about the wording and context of the research questions. Thus, we cannot judge the generalizability or transferability of the results to large populations of Americans or whether the questions were validly measuring the concepts to which they are referring. For example, the research (Coakley, 2004) alluded to in the letter does not provide specific details about age of research participants, skill levels, sports, and so on. The research from the CDC and the NCHS lacks context. Also, the claim that other parents feel the same way is insufficiently supported. Systematic research would be needed to determine the degree of parental dissatisfaction, as well as the basis for whatever discontent exists.

Furthermore, the analogy provides weak support for the notion that each child participant should have equal playing time in games. For example, there are important differences between having the right to the same equipment, fields, and coach and having the right to play the same amount of time. To participate on a team sport at all, one needs equipment, field access, and a coach. Equal playing time, however, is not something that a player must have to participate actively in a team sport.

In summary, the parents' letter provides weak evidence.

What Significant Information Is Omitted? (Question 8)

Much information that could help us judge the persuasiveness of the parents' reasoning is missing. We would like to see the following information:

- What are possible downsides to deemphasizing winning? Might players put forth less effort? Would coaches focus less on the learning of strategies? Would parent spectators lose interest and leave?
- If competition were deemphasized, would children be less prepared for the competitive world outside the school environment? What benefits might children gain by having to work through disappointments in their lives?
- What has other research shown about the short-term advantages and disadvantages of emphasizing equal playing time?
- Do most of the most skilled athletes believe that they should get equal playing time even if others do not get to play much?
- How is playing time during games measured or calculated? How much playing time would be enough to keep less skilled players motivated?
- How many players are registered on the team?
- Do parents of other children on the team really feel the same way as the parents who wrote the letter?
- Does the coach really emphasize team performance, competition, and winning during games?
- Did the coach's actions discourage marginally skilled players from ever wanting to play organized sports again?
- How does the coach really decide who plays during the games? Study of this issue is necessary. (Perhaps children really do have equal playing time during games; perhaps some of the children are not comfortable playing in games yet; perhaps a child has missed a number of practices and sending that child into the games unprepared could lead to negative experiences or increase the potential for injuries for that child or other children.)

- What are the particulars about the research used to support the arguments—especially the nature and type of the research, who was involved in the research (i.e., sample), and how the results were interpreted and presented?

Can you think of other relevant information that the writers omitted?

Learning Activity

Go to www.womenssportsfoundation.org and click on Issues and Action. Choose any of the issues listed and read the accompanying articles. Critically analyze the ideas presented in the articles using the critical thinking skills presented in this chapter.

Go to www.idebate.org, click on Debatabase, and search "sport." Choose any of the issues listed and read the accompanying documentation. Critically analyze the ideas presented in the debates using critical thinking skills presented in this chapter. Debatabase is a product of the International Debate Education Association (IDEA).

A sound bite—a simple yes or no—cannot answer the question of whether community youth sport should emphasize performance, competition, and winning or whether it should focus exclusively on skill development and learning how to play the game. Regardless of your personal position on this issue, we hope that the foregoing scenario provided a useful example of how to think about it. You can be certain that issues such as this are in your professional future. If you begin now to reflect on your values and the values of others, develop critical thinking dispositions, and learn to ask and answer critical questions, you will be able to resolve them with greater confidence.

SUMMARY

Several scholars have suggested that sport managers of the future will be better prepared for their careers if they acquire critical thinking skills. Critical thinking is different from simply thinking, negative thinking, or creative thinking. It involves the awareness of a set of interrelated questions, the ability to ask and answer critical questions at appropriate times, and the desire to use those questions and accept their results as a guide to behavior. Acquiring and developing critical thinking skills obliges you to engage in reflection, to demonstrate certain dispositions, and to ask core critical questions. Reflection implies evaluating your values and the values of others. The critical thinking dispositions are caring that you "get it right," caring to present a position honestly and clearly, and caring about the dignity and worth of every person. The core critical questions involve identification of (1) the issues and the conclusion, (2) the reasons or justifications for the conclusions, (3) ambiguities, (4) value conflicts and value assumptions, (5) descriptive assumptions, (6) fallacies in the reasoning, (7) the quality of the evidence, and (8) information that was omitted. Sport managers can use critical thinking skills to solve problems in sport management and make personal decisions.

Review Questions

1. Define critical thinking and explain the benefits of applying critical thinking skills to important issues in sport management.
2. What is the difference between learning *what* to think and learning *how* to think? Give examples of both types of activities as they can be applied to specific issues in sport management.
3. Identify an issue in sport on which experts have different opinions. What are the different opinions? Do you accept one opinion over another? Why or why not?
4. List the dispositions that critical thinkers should possess and indicate whether you possess each of them. Explain your answers.
5. What are the core critical thinking questions, and how would you use them in resolving issues in sport management?
6. Choose one or more of the issues listed on page 148. What questions would you ask in reflecting on these issues?
7. Reflect on the academic major of sport management. Discuss how your values and perspectives determine your personal beliefs about the choice of a major.

Selected Sport Management Sites

The sport industry offers a wide variety of career opportunities to aspiring sport managers. The purpose of the chapters in this section is to introduce you to five sites within the sport industry in which possibilities exist for you. These five sites are representative of settings in which you could find careers in sport, but they do not constitute a complete inventory of sport-related job possibilities. If you take advantage of the additional resources included in the reference lists in each chapter and the section "For More Information" on pages 64-65, you will discover many more opportunities available to you in the world of sport.

Intercollegiate athletics is the topic of chapter 4. First, Ellen Staurowsky and Robertha Abney present an overview of the history of intercollegiate athletics in the United States. Then, the authors describe several governing bodies associated with intercollegiate athletics, discuss problems within intercollegiate athletics, and explain attempts that have been made to reform intercollegiate athletics. Next, Staurowsky and Abney identify administrative positions and related responsibilities within intercollegiate athletics departments and discuss current challenges in college sport. Finally, they present information about several professional associations, organizations, and publications related to intercollegiate athletics. In the international sidebar, Karen Danylchuk, Western Ontario University (London, Ontario, Canada), and Joanne MacLean, Brock University (St. Catharines, Ontario, Canada), describe intercollegiate athletics in Canada.

In chapter 5 Jay Gladden and Bill Sutton define professional sport and discuss its history in the United States. The authors address the unique characteristics of professional sport, such as its governance structure and the relationship between labor and management. The significance of television for pro sport is also presented, as is a discussion of the major revenue sources for professional sport teams. Gladden and Sutton then describe several types of employment opportunities available in pro sport. The international sidebar addresses professional basketball in Italy. Giorgio Gandolfi, editor-in-chief of *FIBA Assist Magazine* and *Giganti del Basket Magazine*, contributed this essay.

In chapter 6 Mark McDonald and Bill Sutton define sport management and marketing agencies and present valuable information about their roles, scope, and influence. The authors then differentiate among four types of agencies—full service, general, specialty, and in-house—and explain the evolution of each. In conclusion, McDonald and Sutton discuss career opportunities associated with sport management and marketing agencies. In the international sidebar, James Paterson, general manager of sponsorship information services at Griffith University, Canberra (Australia), discusses sports sponsorship as it is practiced Down Under.

Chapter 7 addresses one of the newer career opportunities in sport management—sport tourism. Heather Gibson describes tourism and the tourism industry and then explains the intersection of tourism and sport. The author provides a thorough explanation of the different types of sport tourism: active sport tourism (e.g., traveling to participate in physical activities), event sport tourism (e.g., traveling to watch sporting events), and nostalgia sport tourism (e.g., traveling to sport museums or halls of fame). Gibson concludes with a discussion of the sociocultural, economic, and environmental impacts of sport tourism. In the international sidebar, Sheranne Fairley, a native of Australia who teaches sport management at the University of Massachusetts at Amherst, discusses sport volunteer tourism associated with the Sydney and Athens Olympic Games.

In chapter 8 Ted Fay and David Snyder define international sport and provide a snapshot of key historical moments that led to the current balance of power and dominance among international sport teams. Then they discuss current practices related to the recruitment of international athletes and international sport marketing. Fay and Snyder provide a comprehensive discussion of China as the awakening giant of sport in the 21st century and conclude the chapter with a discussion of the knowledge and skills necessary for a successful career in international sport. The importance of cricket in India is the topic of the international sidebar. Hareesh Viriyala, development manager at IMG Academies Bharata (IMGB), in Hyderabad, Andhra Pradesh, India, contributed this essay.

An understanding of the wide variety of opportunities available in the sport industry will enable you to plan your professional life more realistically. Rather than concentrating only on the chapters that address the careers in which you are currently interested, we hope that you will study the material in each of these five chapters and reflect on the possibilities that each site might hold for you. Who knows? As you learn more about the possibilities that exist, you might develop new interests and revise your career goals!

For More Information

Intercollegiate Athletics

The Drake Group: www.thedrakegroup.org

National Christian College Athletic Association: www.thenccaa.org

National Collegiate Athletic Association: www.ncaa.com

National Junior College Athletic Association: www.njcaa.org

Professional Teams

Arena Football League: www.arenafootball.com

American Hockey League: www.theahl.com

East Coast Hockey League: www.echl.com

National Association of Professional Baseball Leagues: www.minorleaguebaseball.com

National Basketball Association: www.nba.com

National Football League: www.nfl.com

National Hockey League: www.nhl.com

Women's National Basketball Association: www.wnba.com

Sport Management and Marketing Agencies

www.business.com/directory/media_and_entertainment/sports/agencies_and_management

Tourism Associations

Audubon International's Cooperative Sanctuary System, Golf Program: www.audubonintl.org/programs/acss/golf.htm

Canadian Tourism Commission: www.canadatourism.com

Golf Environment Europe: www.golfenvironmenteurope.org

Travel Industry Association of America: www.TIA.org

US Olympic Committee: www.usoc.org

World Tourism Organization: www.world-tourism.org

World Travel and Tourism Council: www.wttc.org

Special Issues of Journals on Sport Tourism

Current Issues in Tourism, 2002, vol. 5(1)

Sport in Society, 2005, vol. 8(2)

Journal of Sport Management, 2003, vol. 17(3)

Journal of Vacation Marketing, 1998, vol. 4(1)

Tourism Recreation Research, 1997, vol. 22(1)

European Sport Management Quarterly, 2005, vol. 5(3)

Visions in Leisure and Business, 1999, vol. 18 (Spring)

Sport Tourism Companies or Attractions

National Association of Sports Commissions: www.sportscommissions.org

American Skiing Company: www.peaks.com

Basketball Hall of Fame: www.hoophall.com

Disney's Wide World of Sports: www.dwws.disney.go.com

Intrawest Ski Company: www.intrawest.com

LPGA Hall of Fame: www.worldgolf.com/wglibrary/history/lpgahoff.html

National Baseball Hall of Fame: www.baseballhalloffame.org

Norwegian Cruise Lines: www.ncl.com

Olympic Museum, Geneva, Switzerland: www.olympic.org/uk/passion/museum/index_uk.asp

Pinehurst Resort, North Carolina: www.pinehurst.com

Women's Basketball Hall of Fame: www.wbhof.com/main.html

World Golf Village: www.wgv.com

Professional and Scholarly Publications

Amusement Business

Athletics Administration

Journal of Sport Management

Journal of Sports Tourism

National Aquatics Journal

NCAA News

Sports Illustrated

Sports Market Place

Street & Smith's SportsBusiness Journal

The Chronicle of Higher Education

The Paralympian Online

The Sporting News

The Sports Business Daily

International Sport

Cerebral Palsy International Sports & Recreation Association: www.cpisra.org

General Association of International Sports Federations: www.agfisonline.com

Institute for International Sport: www.internationalsport.com/index.html

International Committee of Sports for the Deaf/Deaflympics: www.deaflympics.com

International Paralympic Committee: www.paralympic.org/release/Main_Sections_Menu/index.html

Maccabiah Games: www.maccabiusa.com

Olympic Games: www.olympic.org/uk/index_uk.asp

Pan-American Games: www.cob.org.br/pan2007/ingles/indexing.asp

Books

Foer, F. (2004). *How soccer explains the world: An unlikely theory of globalization.* New York: Harper Perennial.

Jennings, A. (2001). *The great Olympic swindle: When the world wanted its games back.* New York: Simon & Schuster.

Pound, R.W. (2004). *Inside the Olympics.* Montreal: Wiley.

Smith, A., & Westerbeek, H. (2004). *The sport business future.* London: Palgrave Macmillan.

Whiting, R. (2004). *The Samurai way of baseball: The impact of Ichiro and the new wave from Japan.* New York: Warner Books.

Intercollegiate Athletics

Ellen J. Staurowsky—Ithaca College ■ **Robertha Abney**—Slippery Rock University

Learning Objectives

After studying this chapter, you will be able to do the following:

1. Define intercollegiate athletics.
2. Demonstrate an understanding of the events surrounding the development of intercollegiate athletics.
3. Describe the purposes of organizations that govern intercollegiate athletics.
4. Identify key athletic administrative personnel within intercollegiate athletics departments.
5. Identify the duties of the various administrators who manage intercollegiate athletics departments.
6. Discuss several current challenges within intercollegiate athletics.
7. Identify key associations, organizations, and publications related to intercollegiate athletics.

From the intrigues of the Bowl Championship Series (BCS) to March Madness, US college sport occupies as prominent a place in the sports scene as any professional or Olympic-level sporting enterprise. The fate of favored and favorite teams is the subject of much attention. Internet chat rooms churn out speculation about who will be recruited by whom, what team will come out on top, and which shoe company has reached an agreement with which university for a multiyear, big-money sponsorship deal. Through sport media coverage, which includes television, radio, and print, players and coaches become celebrities, while the games themselves entertain millions of fans around the country.

There is much more to college sport than meets the eye. The financial stakes are high, as evidenced by the 11 year, $6 billion USD agreement that the National Collegiate Athletic Association (NCAA) reached with CBS in spring 2002 for the broadcast rights to the men's Division I basketball tournament and selected other championships. Of equal importance are the reputations of the schools that sponsor these athletics programs. The purpose of this chapter is to provide an overview of contemporary US college athletics in the 21st century and to create a snapshot of what goes on behind the scenes. After reading this chapter, you should have a better understanding of the organizations that govern and regulate college sport, how college athletics programs operate, and the kinds of careers that you might wish to pursue in this segment of the sport industry.

Learning Activity

Visit the NCAA Web site at www1.ncaa.org/finance/pie_charts. Locate the revenues and expenses data for the association. Using the charts provided, track how the revenue from the $521 million USD budget is distributed to the NCAA membership.

GOVERNANCE OF INTERCOLLEGIATE ATHLETICS

Most secondary and postsecondary educational institutions in North America provide varsity athletics programs for their students. In US secondary schools these programs are called interscholastic athletics. Programs offered by four-year colleges, universities, and junior and community colleges are known as intercollegiate athletics. Initially, students controlled intercollegiate athletics. They began with class games that eventually became intercollegiate contests. The contests were so low-key that, when the owner of a railroad proposed the idea of a regatta between the Yale and Harvard boat clubs in 1852, "The crew members thought of it as a 'jolly lark' which provided them with an eight-day, all-expense paid vacation on Lake Winnipesaukee" (Lucas & Smith, 1978, p. 197). This unpretentious event marked the beginning of intercollegiate athletics in the United States.

The nature of intercollegiate athletics quickly changed from being social occasions to becoming highly competitive events. By 1905 football competition had become so intense that some people advocated reform or elimination of the sport. One way of implementing reform was to establish associations to govern intercollegiate athletics.

National Collegiate Athletic Association (NCAA)

Prompted by deaths and charges of brutality in college football, President Theodore Roosevelt hosted two White House conferences on football in 1905. Roosevelt summoned coaches, faculty, and alumni representatives from Harvard, Yale, and Princeton to the conference. The purpose of the conference was to encourage the representatives to carry out both the letter and the spirit of the football rules. Roosevelt's decree led to the formation of the Intercollegiate Athletic Association of the United States (IAAUS), which was officially constituted on March 31, 1906, and became known as the National Collegiate Athletic Association (NCAA) in 1910 (Crowley, 2006).

The NCAA headquarters is located in Indianapolis, Indiana. Many people believe that the NCAA rules college athletics; however, it is a bottom-up organization in which the members rule the NCAA. The members appoint volunteer representatives to serve on committees that introduce and vote on rules called bylaws (NCAA, 2005a). With a membership of more than 1,250 colleges, universities, conferences, and sport organizations dedicated to the sound administration of intercollegiate sport, it is the largest and most influential governing body in the field (NCAA, 2005b).

The NCAA membership was divided into three competitive divisions in 1973 (NCAA, 2005a). Each NCAA member institution is classified as Division I, II, or III (see figure 4.1). Division classification is based on several criteria, among which are the size of the financial base, the number and types of sports offered, the focus of the program, and the existence of athletics grants-in-aid. Examples of Division I, II, and III athletics department organizational charts are shown in figures 4.2, 4.3, and 4.4, respectively.

Athletics programs at Division I schools are major financial enterprises that generate significant revenue. They must offer at least seven sports for men and seven for women (or six for men and eight for women), and they must have at least two team sports for each gender. Division I schools offer full grants-in-aid based on athletic ability, are highly competitive, and consider many athletic contests as entertainment for spectators. Depending on their resources, Division I programs may be financed through student fees, gate receipts, television revenues, **licensing revenues**, and private donations. Division I colleges and universities are further divided into Divisions I-A (117 active members), I-AA (118 active members), and I-AAA (91 active members), each with specific classification criteria (NCAA, 2005b). Refer to the NCAA Web site at www1.ncaa.org/membership/membership_svcs/membership_breakdown.html for a complete list of institutions in NCAA Divisions I, II, and III.

> **licensing revenues**—Royalties paid to athletics departments by second parties in return for the right to produce and sell merchandise bearing a logo or other mark associated with its sports program (Irwin, 2001).

Division II institutions must offer at least four sports for men and four for women and must have two team sports for each gender. The 281 active member institutions in Division II offer grants-in-aid based on athletic ability, but they offer fewer per capita than do Division I schools. Division II institutions finance their athletics programs in the

1850s

- **1852**—First intercollegiate sport competition: Yale-Harvard Regatta

1860s

- **1869**—Rutgers plays Princeton in first intercollegiate football game (the rules were akin to soccer)

1870s

- **1872**—Yale plays Columbia in first intercollegiate football game with admission charge
- **1873**—Intercollegiate Football Conference (IFB) created; established rules for football
- **1876**—Thanksgiving Day football championship games

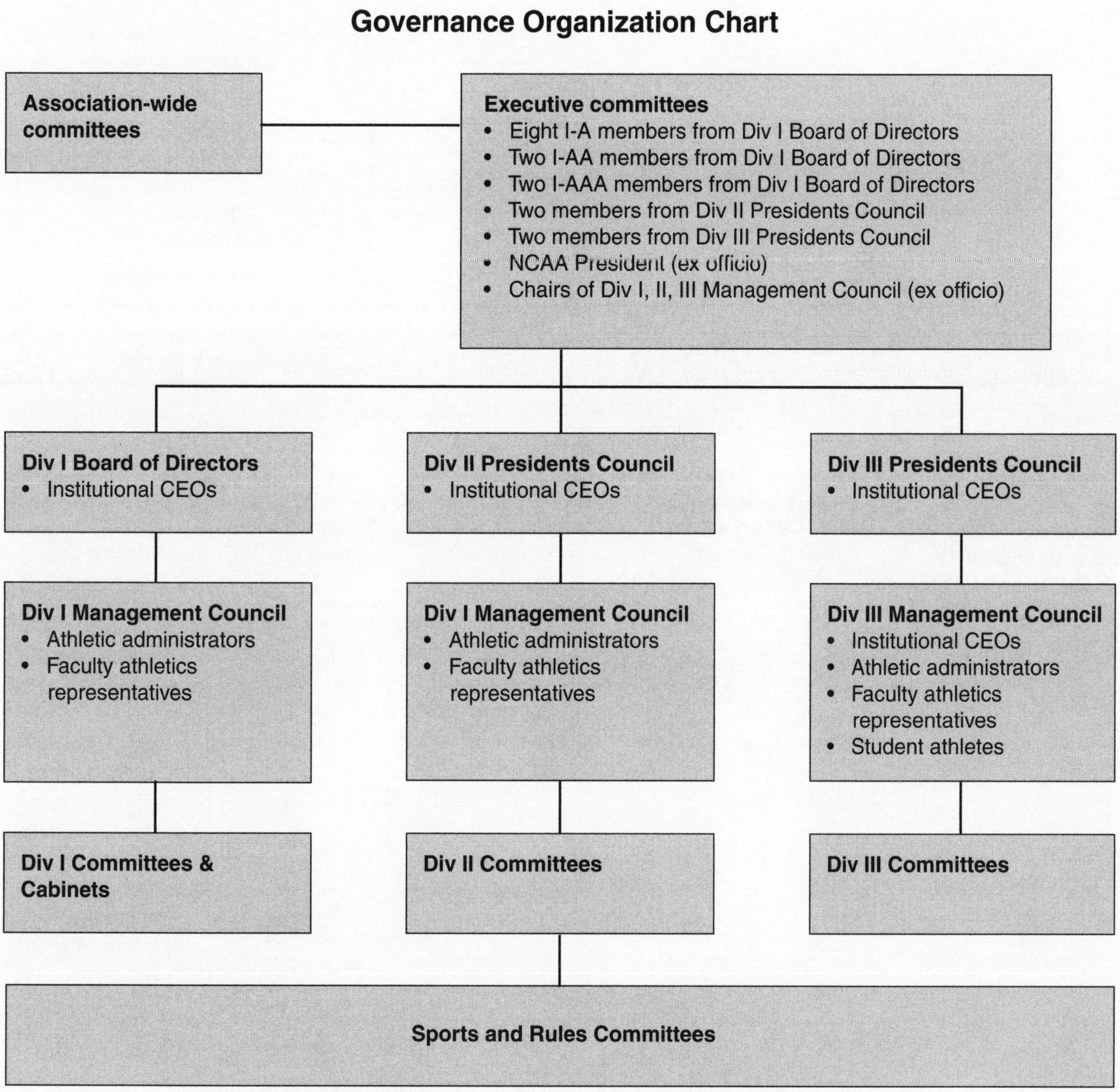

Governance Organization Chart

This chart available on the NCAA Web site at www.ncaa/org on February 5, 2006.

Figure 4.1 NCAA organizational chart and governance structure (2006).

same way that they do their academic programs on campus and focus primarily on regional competition. In Division III, with 421 members, the focus is on participation rather than competition or entertainment. These schools, which must offer at least five sports for women and five sports for men, including two team sports for each gender, do not offer athletics scholarships. Athletes are treated the same as other students with respect to admission policies, academic advisement, and scholarships. Participation opportunities for student–athletes are the primary concern of these programs, and they generally focus on regional and conference competition (NCAA, 2005b).

1880s

▶**1888**—Amateur Athletic Union formed

1890s

▶**1895**—Big 10 founded as Intercollegiate Conference of Faculty Representatives

1900s

▶**1905**—White House Conference on football, encouraged by Theodore Roosevelt

▶**1906**—Intercollegiate Athletic Assoc. of US (IAAUS) formed

▶**1910**—IAAUS name changed to National Collegiate Athletic Assoc. (NCAA)

▶**1912**—Central Intercollegiate Athletics Assoc. founded, oldest Black athletic conference, comprising 12 institutions of higher education

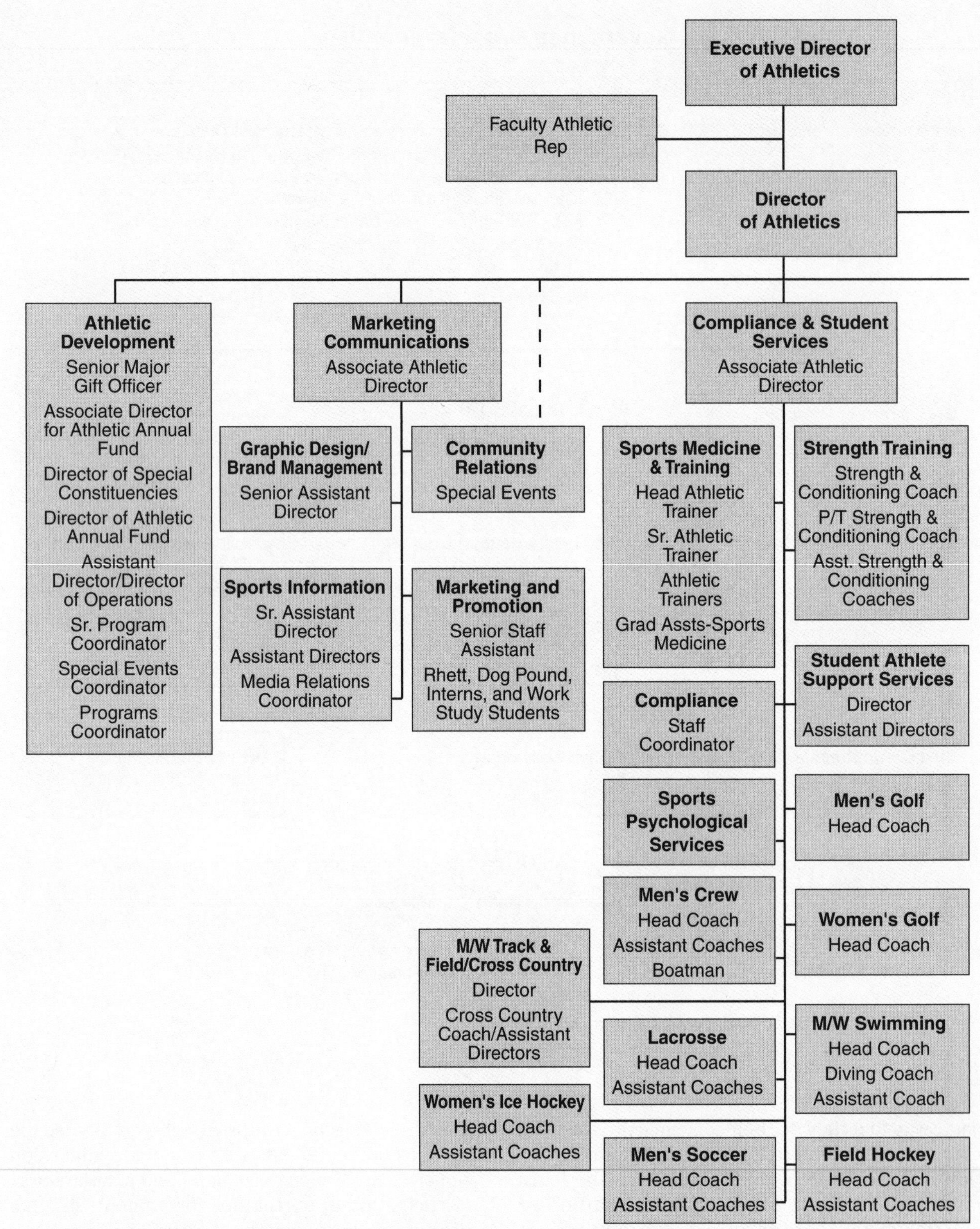

Figure 4.2 Organizational chart for Boston University, an NCAA Division I athletics department (2006).

Reprinted, by permission, from Boston University.

1920s

▷**1920**—Univ. of Texas v. Texas A&M football—first radio broadcast on WTAW AM (Bryan, TX)

▷**1922**—College football national radio broadcast—Univ. of Chicago v. Princeton-WEAF (NY)

1930s

▷**1935**—Heisman Trophy first presented

▷**1938**—National Invitation Tournament (NIT) for men's college basketball, founded

▷**1938**—National Junior College Athletic Assoc. (NJCAA) established, headquartered in Colorado Springs, CO

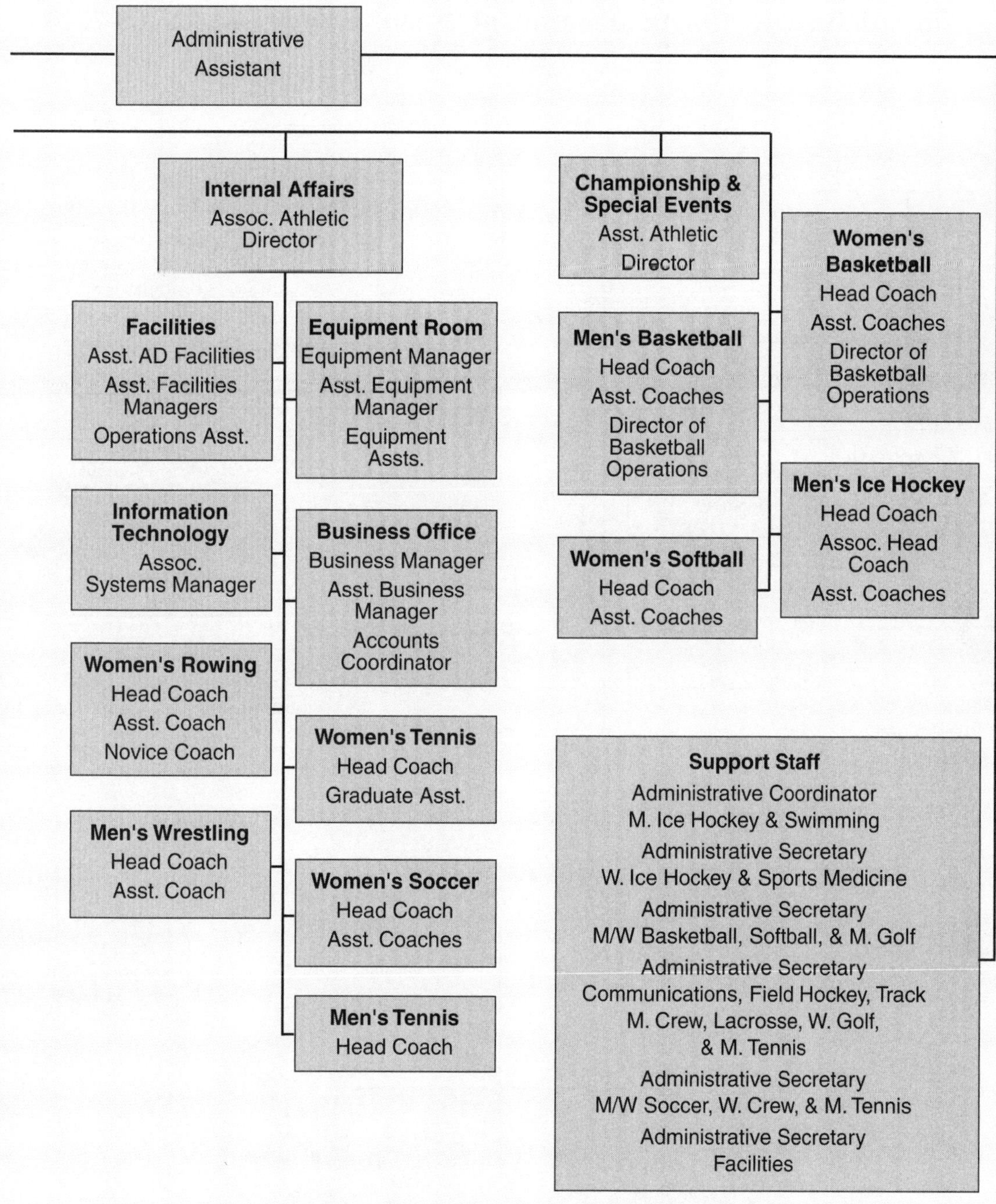

Figure 4.2 *(continued)*

Other National Governing Bodies

Established in 1940, the National Association for Intercollegiate Athletics (NAIA), located in Olathe, Kansas, has more than 360 member institutions (NAIA, 2005a). It is open to four-year and upper-level two-year colleges and universities in the United States and Canada. With an emphasis on academic achievement, the NAIA is also dedicated to respect, integrity, responsibility, servant leadership, and

1930s

▶ **1938**—Eastern College Athletics Conference founded as Central Office for Eastern Intercollegiate Athletics; largest athletics conference in US

▶ **1939**—First NCAA Men's Basketball Championship game: Univ. of Oregon over Ohio State, 46-33

1940s

▶ **1940**—National Assoc. of Intercollegiate Athletics (NAIA) founded as National Assoc. of Intercollegiate Basketball

▶ **1940**—First college basketball doubleheader telecast (NBC)—NYU v. Georgetown and Univ. of Pittsburgh v. Fordham (Feb. 28)

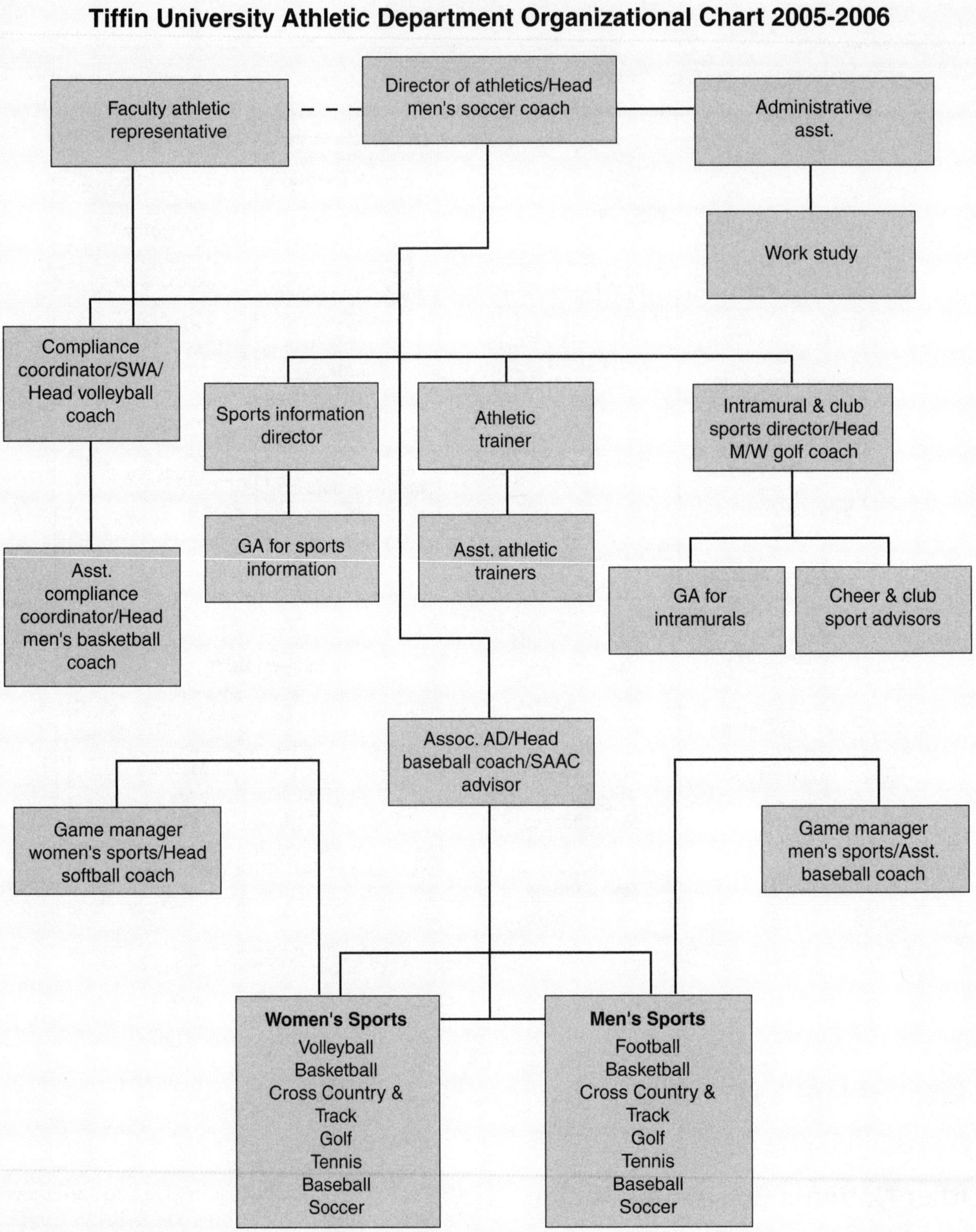

Tiffin University Athletic Department Organizational Chart 2005-2006

Figure 4.3 Organizational chart for Tiffin University, an NCAA Division II athletics department (2006).

Reprinted, by permission, from Tiffin University.

1940s

▶**1942**—Eddie Robinson becomes head coach of Grambling State Univ.; retires, 1997

▶**1948**—NAIA becomes first organization to offer postseason opportunities to Black athletes

1950s

▶**1951**—Walter Byers appointed first executive director of NCAA

▶**1951**—First live, coast-to-coast telecast of a sporting event (NBC)—college football Duke v. Pittsburgh

▶**1951**—City College basketball scandal

▶**1953**—HBCUs voted into NAIA

▶**1954**—NCAA publishes first PR manual for intercollegiate athletics

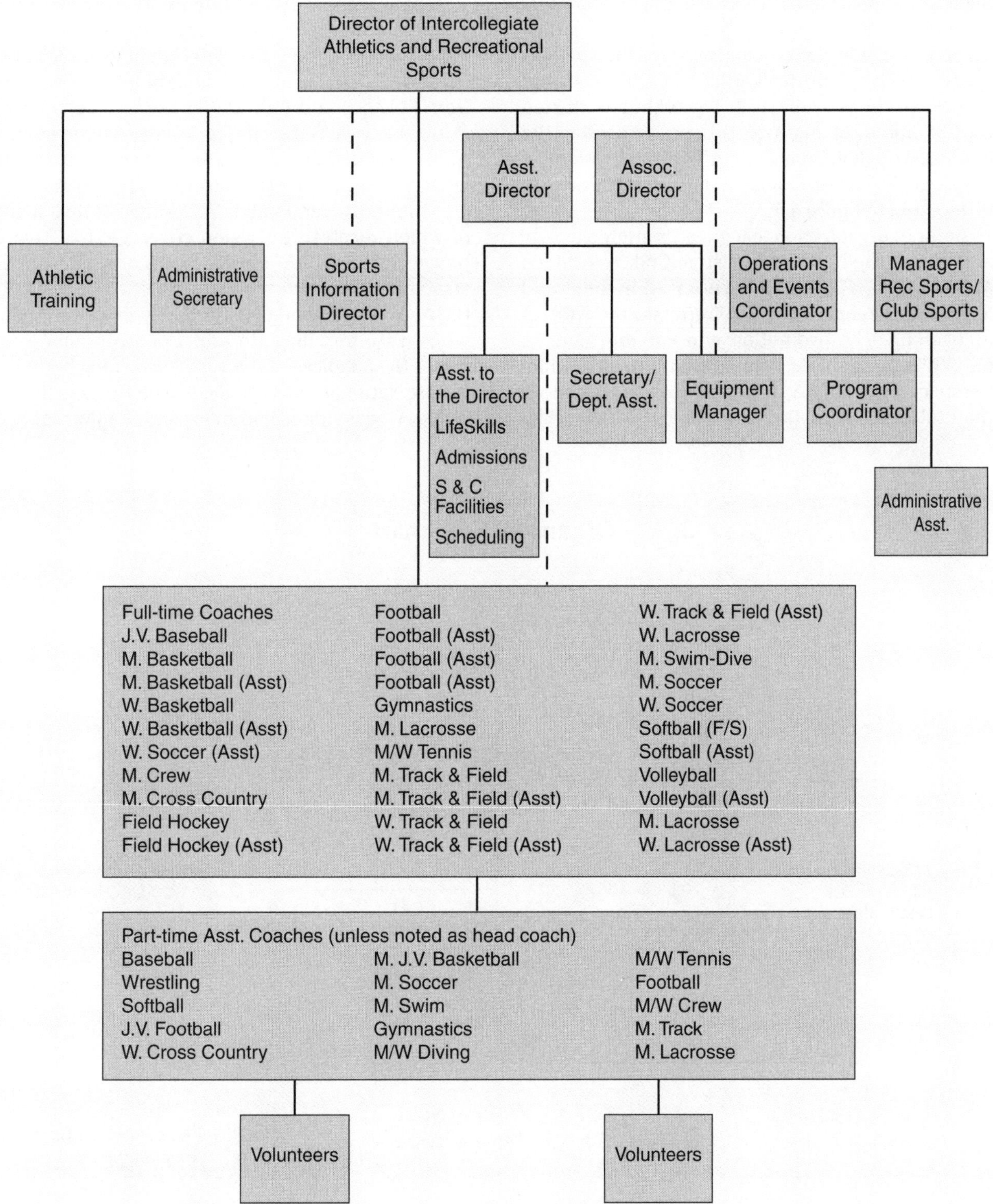

Figure 4.4 Organizational chart for Ithaca College, an NCAA Division III athletics department (2006).
Reprinted, by permission, from Ithaca College

1960s | **1970s** | **1980s**

- **1963**—Instant replay—first used during Army v. Navy football game (Dec. 7)
- **1968**—National Christian Colleges Athletic Assoc. (NCCAA) forms
- **1971**—Association of Intercollegiate Athletics for Women (AIAW) formed; disbands in 1982
- **1972**—Title IX adopted
- **1973**—NCAA splits its membership into Divisions I, II, and III
- **1980**—NAIA offers first national athletics association to offer collegiate athletics to men and women

fair play. In 1948, the NAIA was the first national organization to offer postseason opportunities to Black student–athletes. It was also the first national organization to sponsor men's intercollegiate athletics and to offer athletic championships for women's sports (1980). Historically Black institutions were voted into the NAIA in 1953. The NAIA has started the Champions of Character program to continue its emphasis on developing integrity through athletics (NAIA, 2005b). The organizational chart for the NAIA is depicted in figure 4.5.

Another organization that governs intercollegiate athletics is the National Christian College Athletic Association (NCCAA). Incorporated in 1968 and located in Greenville, South Carolina, the NCCAA focuses on "the promotion and enhancement of intercollegiate athletic competition with a Christian perspective" (NCCAA, 2005). The NCCAA has more than 100 member institutions in two divisions. Division I consists of 47 liberal arts institutions, and Division II consists of 48 Bible colleges.

A national governing body exclusively for women's intercollegiate sport emerged in 1971 when the Association for Intercollegiate Athletics for Women (AIAW) was established by female physical educators from colleges and universities across the country (Morrison, 1993). During its 10-year existence, the AIAW provided many opportunities for female athletes, coaches, and administrators. The organization also offered several national championships, many of which received television coverage. Eventually, however, the NCAA and the NAIA expanded their structures to include women's athletics, and in 1982 the AIAW was dismantled. Currently, both men's and women's intercollegiate athletics programs exist under the auspices of the same governing bodies.

The National Junior College Athletic Association (NJCAA) was conceived in Fresno, California, and

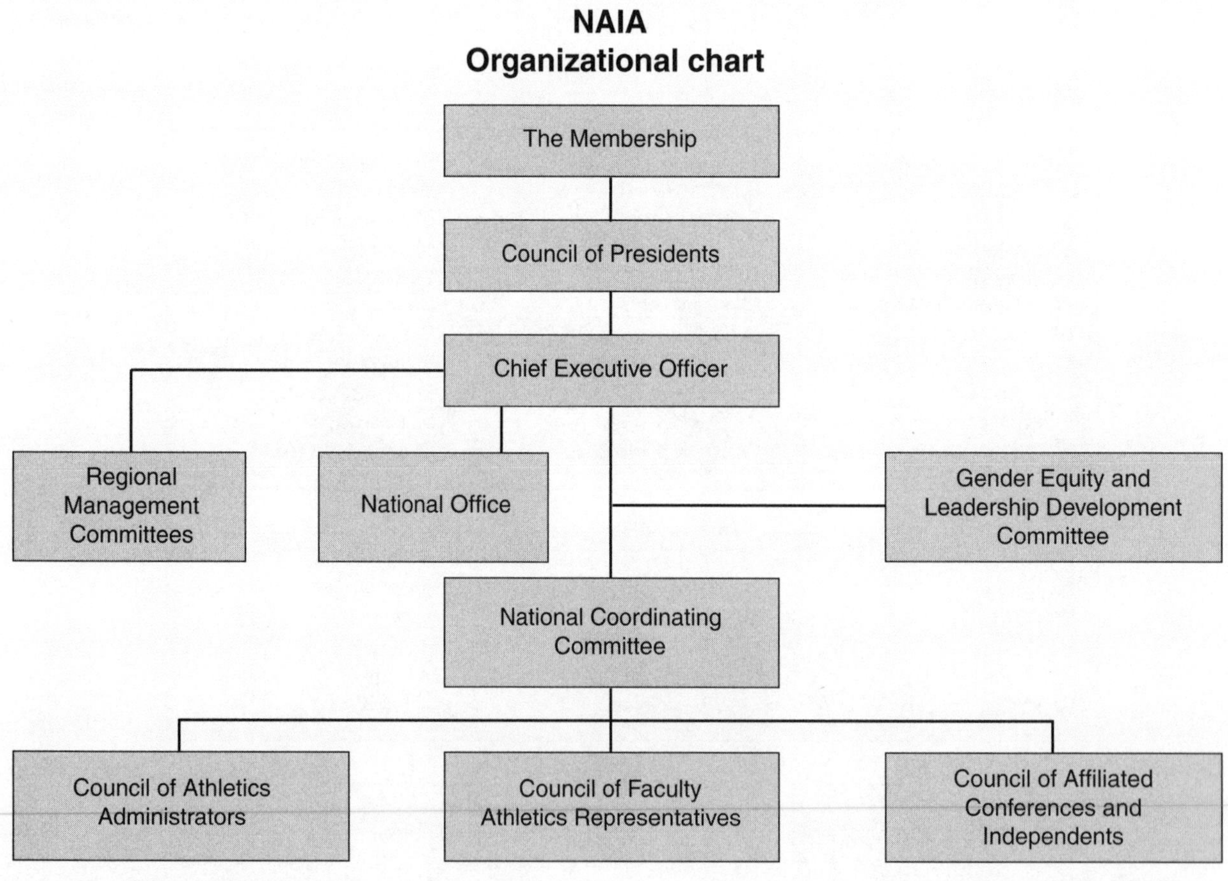

Figure 4.5 NAIA organizational chart (2006).

Reprinted, by permission, from NAIA.

1980s

- **1988**—Civil Rights Restoration Act
- **1989**—Knight Commission formed by the Knight Foundation in response to scandals in college sports

1990s

- **1991**—Judith Sweet becomes first female president of NCAA
- **1994**—Equity in Athletics Disclosure Act
- **1995**—Atlantic Women's Colleges Conference forms comprising eight women's liberal arts colleges
- **1998**—BCS established

became a functioning organization in 1938. The NJCAA seeks to promote and supervise a national program of junior college sports and activities consistent with the educational objectives of junior colleges. Its membership comprises approximately 550 institutions. The NJCAA is organized into 24 geographic regions and is headquartered in Colorado Springs, Colorado (Karlin, 1997; NJCAA, 2006).

Athletics Conferences

A conference is a group of colleges or universities that governs the conduct and organizes the competition among its member institutions' athletics programs. All conferences are responsible to their respective governing bodies (e.g., NCAA, NAIA). The first athletics conference, the Intercollegiate Conference of Faculty Representatives, was established in 1895; later it became known as the Western Conference or the Big Ten Conference. Besides establishing rules of competition and conducting conference championships, conferences have functions related to the following areas:

- Communication within and beyond the membership
- Scheduling
- Officiating
- Crowd control and contest management
- Compliance and enforcement (rules and regulations)
- Eligibility of student–athletes
- Television contracts
- Informational services
- Merchandising (e.g., procuring commercial sponsorship of conference championships)
- Endorsement of an exclusive line of clothing or equipment
- Conducting surveys of its members
- Fostering collegiality among member institutions
- Record keeping (Kinder, 1993)

Examples of conferences are the Central Intercollegiate Athletics Association (CIAA), Mid-America Intercollegiate Athletics Association (MIAA), the Ivy League, the Atlantic Coast Conference (ACC), the Mid-Eastern Athletic Conference (MEAC), the Pennsylvania State Athletic Conference (PSAC), the Mid-American Conference (MAC), the Southeastern Conference (SEC), the Southwestern Athletic Conference (SWAC), the Eastern College Athletic Conference (ECAC), the New York State Women's Collegiate Athletic Association (NYSWCAA), the Atlantic Women's Colleges Conference (AWCC), and the Big Ten Conference. A typical conference organizational chart is presented in figure 4.6.

The ECAC, the nation's largest athletics conference, was founded in 1938 as the Central Office for Eastern Intercollegiate Athletics. In 1983 the Eastern Association of Intercollegiate Athletics for Women (EAIAW) was merged into the ECAC structure. According to an article which appeared in *The Harvard Crimson* in May of 1983, the merger resulted in eight more regional championships than had been provided for previously (Williams, 1983).

Membership within the CIAA, MEAC, and AWCC conferences is unique in comparison with the major conferences. The member institutions within the CIAA and MEAC are exclusively historically Black colleges and universities (HBCUs). See figure 4.7 for the organizational flow chart for Mississippi Valley State University, an HBCU that was founded in 1950. Established in 1912, the CIAA is the nation's oldest Black athletic conference. It consists of 12 historically African American institutions of higher education (CIAA, 2005). The AWCC, formed in 1995, includes only women's colleges. It is committed to promoting the highest level of excellence for women in academics and athletics. Each member institution must be a women's college; an accredited, four-year, liberal arts institution; and an NCAA Division III member. The AWCC comprises eight institutions.

Learning Activity

Eddie Robinson, a retired head coach of Grambling State University, is the African American head football coach with the most football wins.

- What is an HBCU?
- What conference does Grambling belong to?
- How long did Eddie Robinson coach?
- Who was the first African American head coach of a football program in the United States, and when was this coach hired?
- Examine the most recent Race and Gender Report Card: College Sports, posted at www.bus.ucf.edu/sport/cgi-bin/site/sitew.cgi?page=/ides/index.htx. How many African Americans are NCAA head football coaches in Divisions I, II, and III? Which division has the highest percentage of African American head football coaches? What do you think accounts for the differences among the divisions?

1990s

- **1999**—NCAA moves to Indianapolis
- **1999**—The Drake Group holds its first meeting in Des Moines, Iowa
- **1999**—Alfred University hazing study

2000s

- **2001**—*Game of Life* by Shulman & Bowen published
- **2001**—Collegiate Athletics Coalition, Ramogi Huma (former UCLA football player) attempts to start a Division I college players association

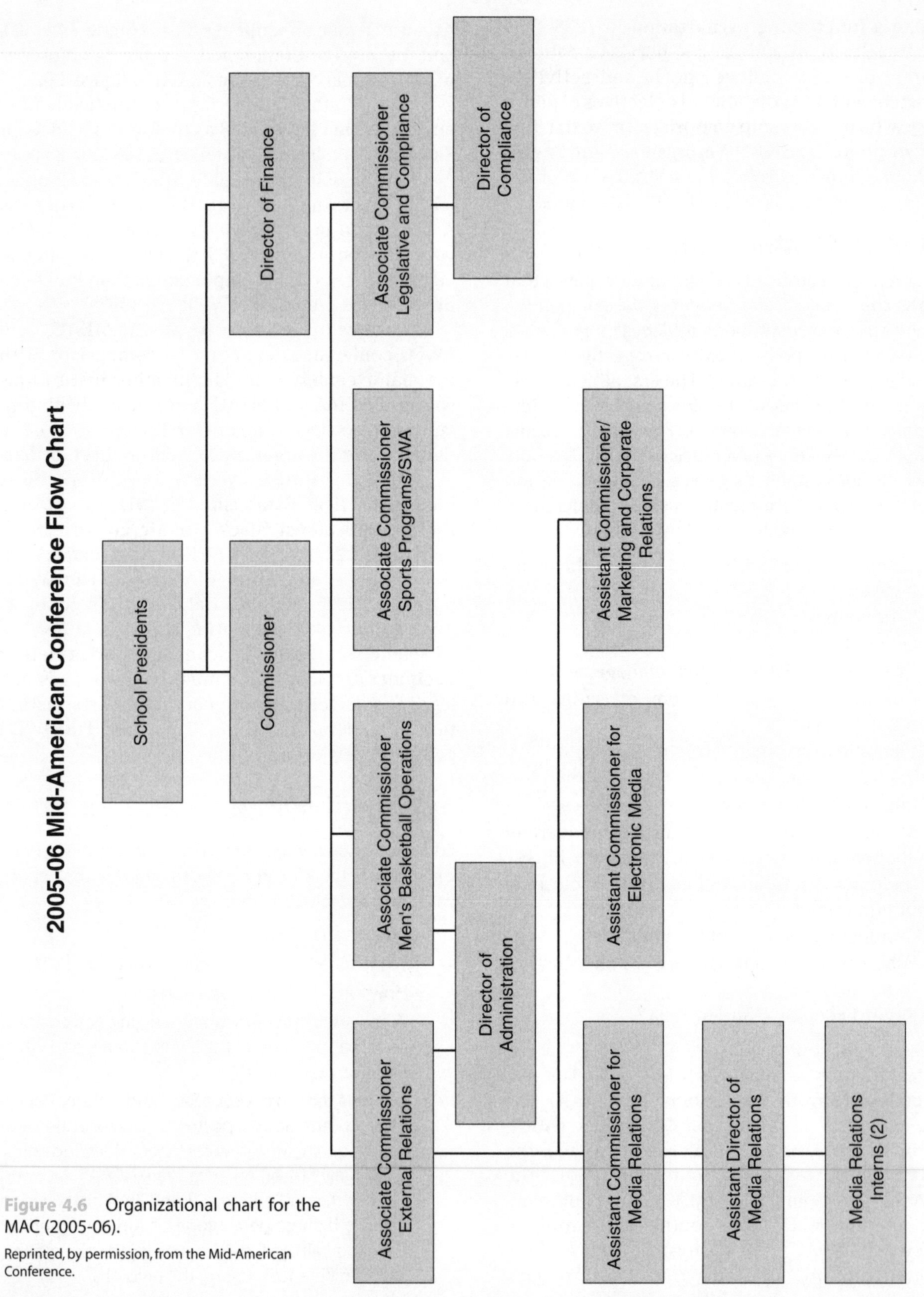

Figure 4.6 Organizational chart for the MAC (2005-06).

Reprinted, by permission, from the Mid-American Conference.

2000s

- **2001**—Billboard ad in Times Square promotes Heisman trophy candidate Joey Harrington of Univ. of Oregon
- **2002**—CBS TV signs 11 year rights deal with NCAA for $6 billion USD
- **2003**—College Sport TV begins programming
- **2005**—ESPNU begins programming
- **2005**—ESPN and Fox college sports begin programming

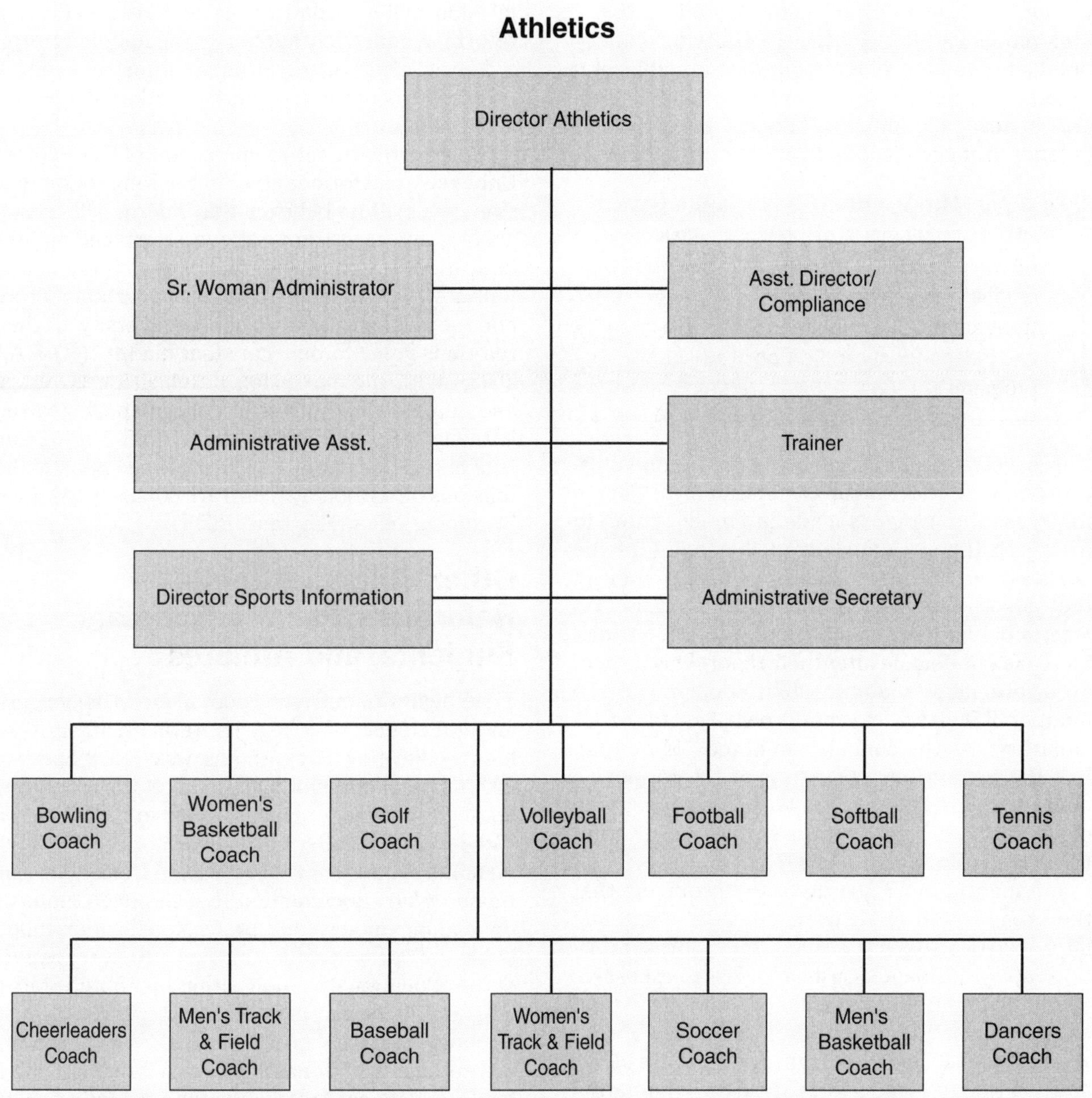

Figure 4.7 Mississippi Valley State University Athletic Department organizational chart (2006).

Reprinted, by permission, from Mississippi Valley State University.

HBCUs—Historically Black colleges and universities.

College Sport Reform

Since the founding of the NCAA, the question of who controls athletics on college campuses has been a point of contention. The history of college sport is replete with stories of repeated academic and financial scandals that have led to college sport being described periodically as out of control and in need of reform. Before 2001 the most significant college athletics reform movement in recent memory was initiated by the Knight Commission on Intercollegiate Athletics in the late 1980s. In response to one of the most scandal-ridden and publicly embarrassing moments in college sport history, a moment in which just over half of the Division I-A programs (57 of 106) had been censured, sanctioned, or put on probation for major violations of NCAA rules, the commission proposed a **one-plus-three model for intercollegiate athletics** (Knight Foundation

Commission on Intercollegiate Athletics, 1991). This model emphasized the necessity for college presidents to control intercollegiate athletics and to direct their attention to three aspects of the programs: academic integrity, financial integrity, and independent certification of athletics programs.

one-plus-three model for intercollegiate athletics—A model of intercollegiate athletics reform proposed by the Knight Commission that emphasized individual presidential control over three areas: academic integrity, financial integrity, and independent certification of athletics programs.

Ten years after the unveiling of the one-plus-three model, the Knight Commission met again to assess the progress made in implementing it. Although they acknowledged that some of the goals set out in the late 1980s had been achieved, they also found that problems in big-time college sport had not diminished and, in fact, had increased. A decade after their report was issued, no appreciable reduction had occurred in the number of Division I-A schools penalized for NCAA violations. As the commission noted, "More than half the institutions competing at the top levels continue to break the rules. Wrongdoing as a way of life seems to represent the status quo" (Knight Foundation Commission, 2001).

Among the most glaring of the problems that the commission cited were repeated academic improprieties (e.g., academic fraud, low graduation rates), a "financial arms race" (e.g., excessive spending and poor financial accountability), and escalating commercialization as evidence of "the widening chasm between higher education's ideals and big-time college sports" (Knight Foundation Commission, 2001). This time around, the commission proposed another one-plus-three model of athletics reform. The centerpiece of this model was no longer individual college presidents but a coalition of presidents who represented the most powerful athletics conferences, which the commission believed had the potential to achieve a reform agenda that addressed academic reform, a de-escalation of the athletics arms race, and a de-emphasis of the commercialization of intercollegiate athletics.

academic fraud—Inappropriate conduct in academic areas such as having tutors write papers for athletes, providing athletes with copies of tests in advance, changing athletes' grades so they can remain eligible, and other practices that violate principles of academic honesty.

Thomas Hearn, retired president of Wake Forest University and former chair of the Knight Commission, has said he believes that reform will remain an ongoing issue for college sport and higher education. Hearn stated, "As long as there is this pull between the entertainment-television culture and the academic culture of the university . . . then reform is going to be a constant matter" ("Q & A," 2005). With the expansion of television coverage and commercial interest in college sport, as seen in the launch of ESPNU in March 2005, joining College Sport Television and Fox College Sports, the tensions described by Hearn are not likely to lessen in coming years (Hiestand, 2005).

Other College Athletics Reformers: Faculty, Scholars, Students, and Athletes

The Knight Commission is not alone in its concern about the effect of college sport on the integrity of higher education (Sack & Staurowsky, 1998; Sperber, 2000). The commission's model of reform is only one among a number to be discussed in recent years. Well-respected college administrators James Shulman and William Bowen (2001), in their book *The Game of Life*, documented that the overemphasis on winning, money, and professionalization found in big-time programs had seeped into every aspect of the educational system within the United States, reaching all the way to the elementary school level. Shulman and Bowen reported that even among institutions traditionally known for maintaining a balance between academics and athletics, such as the Ivy League and private liberal arts colleges, progressively more resources have been allocated to intercollegiate athletics programs over the years to the detriment of the academic experience of students on those campuses. They concluded that presidents, trustees, alumni, faculty, and students should seriously reconsider the role that athletics plays on college campuses and reallocate resources accordingly.

Even before the Knight Commission reconvened in the year 2000, the Drake Group, composed of sport scholars from around the United States, met to develop a reform platform for intercollegiate athletics (Lords, 2000). In response to the reality

Omari Aldridge, an NCAA Division I soccer athlete, successfully balanced the demands of athletics and academics. An excellent student, he was also a first team All Mid-American Conference selection as well as the Most Valuable Player on the 2006 Bowling Green soccer team.
Photography by the Bowling Green State University, Office of Marketing and Communications (Craig Bell and Brad Phalin).

located in athletics departments, and that consideration be given to replacing one-year renewable scholarships that place athletes in dependent relationships with coaches with need-based financial aid.

Other faculty groups that have offered statements regarding athletics reform include the Coalition for Intercollegiate Athletics (COIA) and the American Association of University Professors (AAUP). Athletes have also been involved in reforming intercollegiate athletics. Under the leadership of former UCLA football player Ramogi Huma, the Collegiate Athletes Coalition was formed in January 2001. With both support and money from the United Steelworkers of America, the coalition has targeted full health care coverage, better life insurance plans, reductions in class-disrupting mandatory practices and workouts (including those falsely labeled "voluntary"), increased in-season stipends, and greater flexibility in the restrictions governing employment (Farmer, 2001).

that "college athletics has been transformed into a multi-billion dollar entertainment industry that has compromised the academic mission of the university," members of the Drake Group have strongly advocated for faculty to play a more forceful role in preserving academic integrity and safeguarding against the corrosive effect of big-time college sport on the daily practices of higher education. Among the Drake Group's proposed solutions are a recommendation that public policy makers consider requiring public disclosure of academic information about athletes, that institutions offer academic support and counseling services equally to all students rather than have special services

INTERCOLLEGIATE ATHLETICS ADMINISTRATORS

As a student, you may want to find a definitive answer to the question of what athletics administrators do. To some degree, athletics administrators resemble managers in other business settings and industries. Athletics administrators must be able to execute the fundamental managerial functions of planning, organizing, staffing, directing, coordinating, reporting, and budgeting.

A definitive answer to the question of what athletics administrators do is elusive, however, because of the unique nature of athletics departments and

Learning Activity

What is the Knight Commission on Intercollegiate Athletics?

- What recent reforms have been put into place by the NCAA in response to the reports of the Knight Commission on Intercollegiate Athletics?
- Look at the Knight Commission Foundation's Web site. What reports on intercollegiate athletics has the commission issued and when were they issued? What issues within intercollegiate athletics did these reports respond to?
- Read a review of the *Game of Life* (Shulman & Bowen, 2001). What issues related to intercollegiate athletics does this book discuss?
- Use your library search engine to find other individuals or groups (Drake Group) who have called for reform in intercollegiate athletics.
- In January 2006 the Knight Commission hosted an athlete summit. Find more information about the summit at www.knightcommission.org/index_working.php.

how they are structured within specific colleges and universities. On one hand, the business of college sport is big business. As ESPN.com writer Ivan Maisel (2005) points out, "Athletic departments have eight-figure budgets and bosses who are referred to as CEOs. The title of athletics director is almost quaint, a relic of a time before anyone had heard of a 'corporate partner.'" Indicative of this reality, *Fortune* magazine has referred to the athletics department at the University of Texas as Longhorn Inc. and athletics director DeLoss Dodds as the chief executive officer (CEO) responsible for overseeing a business (Johnson, 1999). During the 2004-2005 academic year, Longhorn Inc. generated revenue just under $90 million USD (as reported in the EADA Report filed with the United States Department of Education, 2005). An athletics director at a Division III institution or junior college, with responsibility for a budget of less than $1 million USD, faces different job demands and responsibilities. In many respects, the difference in these situations resembles the distinction between a major corporation and a locally owned business. Both require managerial skills and experience, but the demands on the leaders of the enterprises vary markedly.

In chapter 15 you will learn about top-level (senior) managers, middle-level (responsible to top-level managers and oversee supervisory and technical personnel) managers, and supervisory-level, or first-line, managers (report to middle-level managers and oversee nonmanagerial employees). As figures 4.2, 4.3, 4.4, and 4.7 show, you can find all three types of managers in most intercollegiate athletics departments. An important point to remember is that many administrators have assistants. Novice athletics administrators often pursue and occupy these assistant positions at the beginnings of their careers.

As a rule, the more prominent the athletics department is, the larger the annual operating budget will be; and the more complex the organizational structure is, the larger the full-time and part-time athletics department staff will be. Thus, administrators working in Division I-A colleges and universities will occupy positions with narrowly defined responsibilities. In contrast, administrators in athletics departments in Division II, Division III, and at the junior and community college levels may be responsible for a wider array of responsibilities. Consequently, people employed in those settings might have to perform duties other than those related to their athletics management role, such as teaching in sport-related areas, coaching, or working in an area related to student life.

The size of the school and the scope of the athletics department are not the only factors that can affect the approach that athletics administrators take to their jobs. Most of what we know about intercollegiate athletics management today pertains to traditionally White institutions. Although management functions overlap significantly in every athletics department, we cannot assume that what we know about intercollegiate athletics management based on that information can be uniformly generalized and applied to HBCUs, such as Tennessee State, Mississippi Valley State, Howard University, South Carolina State, Florida A&M, Tuskegee University, and Grambling State University (Jackson, Lyons, & Gooden, 2001). In fact, historically Black colleges are among the nation's leaders in I-AA football attendance (NCAA, 2005c). For example, *USA Today* sportswriter Bryan Burwell (1993) noted that the Bayou Classic and other HBCU men's football classics offer a "radical cultural departure" from the prevailing image of men's college football. In contrast to most highly publicized men's college football games, audiences for these events are composed primarily of people of color. The events themselves are often staged as cultural festivals with step shows, beauty pageants, and music performances scheduled in conjunction with the games. Ketra Armstrong's (2001, 2002) research on marketing sport to Black consumers reinforces this point.

> **Bayou Classic**—Considered to be the granddaddy of historically Black college football rivalries, this game features Grambling State University versus Southern University. Described as "a three-day celebration of football, black culture, state pride and school loyalty," the Bayou Classic was featured in *Sports Illustrated*'s 50th anniversary celebration as a centerpiece of Louisiana's sporting culture (Bamberger, 2003). Other events between the two schools in track and field and women's basketball are labeled classics as well.

The notion that not all athletics programs fit the dominant model of college sport management is borne out not only by the HBCUs but also by women's college athletics programs. Located in small liberal arts institutions and falling under the rubric of Division III, the women's athletics programs in schools such as Smith, Bryn Mawr, Mt. Holyoke, and Mills College employ management models that are consistent with single-sex women's education institutions.

Because of the variability of the college sport marketplace, no two positions are identical nor are the job titles used to describe them the same. As you explore career opportunities in this sector, therefore, you will discover that although two people in separate institutions may hold the same job title, their jobs may differ considerably. When you begin to search for internships or positions in intercollegiate athletics, study each job description carefully to determine whether the responsibilities of the position match your career interests and your areas of expertise. This investment of time and attention will yield a more satisfying result and will increase the likelihood that you will be successful in your search. The following sections offer overviews of positions in typical athletics departments along with outlines of job responsibilities for each.

Athletics Director (AD)

In a book about strategic planning for college athletics programs (Yow, Migliore, Bowden, Stevens, & Loudon, 2000), ADs were described as "pilots [of a jumbo airliner], responsible for taking off, landing, conferring with the navigator, and communicating with the air traffic controller" (p. 3). The metaphor is an apt one. An AD assumes oversight for the following: budget and finance, facilities, risk management, television contracts, compliance with laws and regulations of national and conference governing bodies, academic progress of college athletes, communication with the media, scheduling, marketing games and other events, corporate sponsorships, ticket sales, community relations, alumni relations, campus relations, fund-raising, and personnel management, including the hiring and termination of coaches (Karlin, 1997). For discussions of the multifaceted nature of the AD position in the context of job satisfaction, see Robinson et al. (2003), and in the context of leadership style and occupational stress, see Ryska (2002).

Although ADs once focused primarily on providing leadership and direction in the creation of playing opportunities for athletes, the ever-increasing demands of revenue generation have reshaped the emphasis that ADs place on certain responsibilities (Copeland & Kirsch, 1995). Notably, the skills sought in ADs are virtually the same as those required of managers in traditional business settings (Huggins, 1996). Several researchers in recent years have documented the growing importance of fund-raising within the overall scheme of what an AD is expected to do (Curtis, 2000; Staurowsky, 1996). Further, the transformation of college sport into a **mass-mediated** spectacle with high visibility has, in turn, transformed the responsibilities of the AD and other administrators within an intercollegiate athletics department (Nichols, Moynahan, Hall, & Taylor, 2001).

> **mass mediated**—Distributed through media such as newspapers, television, radio, and the Internet.

Obviously, the AD cannot perform all these duties. Thus, athletics directors who work in the major conferences (e.g., SEC, ACC, Conference USA, Big East, and Big Ten) identify the ability to delegate responsibility as the key skill needed to run a successful athletic team or organization (Christian, 2000). Most of these ADs also believe that the abilities to influence and motivate individuals are essential leadership skills. These skills are crucial in an organizational structure in which middle-level and first-line administrators in charge of specific areas report to, and are supervised by, an AD. In most Division I and Division II institutions, the AD reports directly to the university president or through a vice president to the president. Division III athletics directors most commonly report to the Office of Student Affairs (Sanders, 2004).

When asked about qualities they find most important when hiring athletics directors, college

IN PROFILE: Gene Smith

Title: Director of Athletics, Ohio State University

Photo courtesy of Arizona State University.

If there is a prototype for the 21st century athletics director, Gene Smith might well be it. Growing up in Cleveland, Ohio, Smith attended Chanel High School, where he distinguished himself in football, basketball, and track while receiving the football team's most valuable player award. Smith went on to pursue a bachelor's degree in business administration at the University of Notre Dame, where he also played defensive end for the Irish, achieving distinction again as a member of the Associated Press 1973 national championship team.

Smith made the successful transition from player to coach at Notre Dame. Notably, during the famed 1976-1977 season when Notre Dame emerged as the undisputed national champions, Smith was on staff as an assistant coach. Following his coaching experience, Smith chose to make a career move, becoming a marketing representative for IBM, a decision that would eventually lead to his being hired as the director of athletics at Eastern Michigan University, Iowa State, and Arizona State University.

In 2005 Smith was appointed the eighth director of athletics at The Ohio State University. In his role as director of athletics at Ohio State, he must demonstrate command of an array of organizational management skills in running a Division I-A athletics department that is a member of the Big Ten Conference. Smith is responsible for providing the vision and direction for one of the most comprehensive and successful university athletics programs in the United States. Overall, Smith oversees an athletics program that sponsors 36 teams, provides for over 900 athletes, has a staff of close to 300 (many of whom are charged to execute marketing, operating, and information management functions), and operates with a $90 million USD budget. Smith took over at a time when Ohio State was nearing the end of a major campaign that had resulted in the renovation of existing facilities and new construction, including renovation of historic Ohio Stadium and completion of the largest arena in the Big Ten, the Jerome Schottenstein Center, a $116 million USD multipurpose facility.

In March 2005 *Black Enterprise* named Smith one of the "50 Most Powerful People in Sports." Recognized as a national leader, Smith currently serves on numerous NCAA committees including the Football Officiating Committee, Committee on Infractions, and the Management Council. Additionally, Smith is a member of the Bowl Championship Series (BCS) Athletic Director's Advisory Committee and the Fiesta Bowl Board.

The authors thank Mark Brand, assistant director of athletics and sports information director at Arizona State University, for information in this profile. Additional information comes from http://ohiostatebuckeyes.collegesports.com/genrel/030505aab.html and http://ohiostatebuckeyes.collegesports.com/genrel/EADA/eada-2000.html.

presidents across all three divisions identified a solid foundation in budget and finance along with skills in management and leadership, marketing, and communication (Schneider & Stier, 2005). A key element of success for ADs who wish to move up the ranks is mastering the art of networking (Whisenant & Pedersen, 2004).

Associate or Assistant Athletics Director

Associate and assistant ADs are clearly middle-level managers. These titles generally represent either the level of administrative responsibility assigned to the person in the role or the level of seniority and experience that the person has. In many respects, the associate or assistant AD supports the AD in achieving the overall mission of the department by working closely with the AD and overseeing specific areas, such as marketing, fund-raising, event management, facilities management, or athletics communications. In large athletics departments, several people will be designated as associate or assistant ADs. Senior associates usually serve as the second in command within an athletics department and assume responsibility for the overall operation of the department in the absence of the AD. As mentioned previously, to determine what people in these positions do, you have to read their job descriptions or speak with them directly.

First-Line Managers

First-line managers are responsible for specific work groups in the athletics department. These managers typically report to an associate or assistant AD. Note

INTERCOLLEGIATE ATHLETICS IN CANADA

Karen Danylchuk and Joanne MacLean, Canada

The original Canadian Interuniversity Athletic Union (CIAU) was founded in 1906, existed until 1955, and was composed of universities from Ontario and Québec. In 1923 the Women's Interuniversity Athletic Union (WIAU) was founded to provide athletics competition for female students in Ontario and Québec. The modern CIAU was reconstituted in 1961 with members from all geographical regions across the country. In 1978 the CIAU absorbed the WIAU. In June 2001 the CIAU membership changed the name and logo of the organization to Canadian Interuniversity Sport (CIS).

The CIS, composed of the majority of Canadian universities (51 of them), now governs university athletics programs in Canada. Each year over 11,000 male and female student–athletes participate in 11 sport disciplines (basketball, cross country, field hockey, football, ice hockey, rugby, soccer, swimming, track and field, volleyball, wrestling) that lead to national championships. A volunteer general assembly, board of directors, and executive committee, with full-time staff housed in the national office in Ottawa, govern the CIS.

The CIS is composed of four regional conferences—Atlantic University Sport (AUS), Québec Student Sport Federation (QSSF), Ontario University Athletics (OUA), and Canada West Universities Athletic Association (CWUAA). Universities within these conferences compete for the opportunity to advance to national championships. A number of conference sports (e.g., figure skating, squash, tennis) do not lead to national championships. Their culminating championships occur at the regional conference level.

Two organizational models for sport exist within Canadian universities. At some institutions, athletics programs are located in an academic unit (e.g., kinesiology, human kinetics), and the athletics personnel (administrators and coaches) might have additional duties such as teaching, research, and service. At other universities, athletics is separate from academic units, and athletics personnel are charged solely with organizing and delivering the intercollegiate sport program.

All Canadian university sport programs employ an athletics director and typically one or more associate athletics directors, commonly titled intercollegiate coordinators. Frequently, although dependent on program size and resources, other positions exist, such as the sport information director, marketing director, facility manager, and ticket manager. The athletics training staff is usually linked to the program as well. There are no compliance officers per se, because the athletics directors are charged with ensuring that all athletes meet the rules and regulations of the CIS. The traditional career path of an athletics director has been from athlete to coach to athletics director. Some universities, however, have placed greater emphasis on marketing and business expertise for recent hires.

A number of issues and challenges face university sport in Canada. One of these issues is institutional diversity in areas such as size and breadth of program, geographical differences, structural placement of athletics within the university, different ways of calculating student–athlete grade point averages, and size of operational budget. Because of this diversity, equity is a constant challenge. The CIS has not moved to a tiered competitive structure that would group institutions based on athletic performance, although this possibility has been discussed. Policies and initiatives within the CIS and regional conferences have been formulated to address the additional challenges of gender and sport equity. Funding is also a challenge. The CIS allows athletics scholarships that pay full tuition for second-, third-, and fourth-year student–athletes. First-year athletes may receive assistance retroactively if they maintain a 65% average. Ontario institutions continue to reject offering assistance to first-year athletes, and they cap the amount for continuing athletes at $3,500 CAD.

Intercollegiate sport in Canada is not big business as it is in the United States. Television revenues are virtually nil, with few university events appearing on television. Canadian university athletics is pure amateur sport, and the emphasis on student first, student–athlete second is legislated, reinforced, and operationalized.

that many of these positions have emerged within the past two decades. These positions include academic coordinator, business and finance manager, compliance officer, development and public relations director, event and facility manager, marketing and promotions director, sports information director, ticket manager, senior woman administrator, head athletic manager, and equipment manager. Brief descriptions of these jobs follow.

Academic Coordinator

According to the National Association of Academic Advisors for Athletes (N4A), fewer than 10 full-time academic advisors for athletes existed in 1975. As of 2005 the N4A had a membership of over 600 (National Association of Academic Advisors for Athletics, 2006). This phenomenal growth has resulted from the passage of NCAA bylaw 16.3.1, which requires all Division I programs to offer

Rugby is one of the newer but more popular sports in Canadian women's intercollegiate athletics. Here players from the University of Western Ontario (dark jerseys) and the University of Waterloo (light jerseys) battle for the ball during an Ontario University Athletics game.
Photo courtesy of The Western Gazette.

International Learning Activity

Identify similarities and differences between the Canadian intercollegiate sport system and the intercollegiate sport system of your country. Note the instances in which you prefer the Canadian system and those in which you prefer your country's system. In each case, give reasons for your preference.

academic support and tutoring services to athletes, and the existence of the Academic Enhancement Fund Program, which allocates $54,000 USD per year to each Division I athletics program in support of these programs. During the academic year 2004-2005, the NCAA distributed $18.24 million USD to Division I institutions through that program (NCAA Membership Report, 2005d).

Athletics academic advisement services are designed to assist athletes in addressing the dual and sometimes conflicting demands of being both a student and an athlete. As with all areas that we have addressed, the structure of these offices and the range of services that they provide can vary from one institution to another. In general, athletics academic offices assist athletes in the broad areas of admission, academic orientation, academic standards, registration, financial aid, housing, and student life. The academic coordinator monitors the academic activities of athletes and maintains records on their academic progress. To do their jobs effectively, academic coordinators work closely with coaches, faculty, the compliance officer, and other administrators.

One of the programs that the athletics academic support office may offer to athletes is the CHAMPS–Life Skills Program (Challenging Athletes' Minds for Personal Success). This program was created through the collaborative efforts of the NCAA Foundation and the Division I-A Athletic Directors' Association. The program is built around five "commitment statements" that address academic excellence, athletic excellence, personal development, career development, and service to the community (www1.ncaa.org/eprise/main/membership/ed_outreach/champs-life_skills/program.html).

People interested in working as athletics academic advisors need to understand the business of college sport and the regulations that affect athletes. They must be equally familiar with the processes of social adaptation and human development, academic performance assessment, and career guidance strategies. In large athletics programs, the athletics academic support services staff might include several academic counselors, mentors, and tutors, some of whom will be undergraduate and graduate students.

Business and Finance Manager

The business and finance manager for an intercollegiate athletics department recommends and implements policies, procedures, and methods of accounting that ensure strict compliance with sound business practices in accordance with the rules and regulations of the institution, the conference, and the national governing body. As the financial officer for the athletics department, the business manager assists the AD in preparing, administering, and monitoring the budget. This job includes determining charges and arrangements associated with the rental of athletics facilities by both internal and external groups. Business managers oversee the processing of all reimbursements and payments while assuming responsibility for the creation, generation, and distribution of monthly financial statements for review by the AD, middle-level managers, coaches, and staff members. Depending on the athletics department, the athletics business and finance office may also be responsible for handling the payment of wages to part-time and student personnel hired to assist with athletics and special events. Further, this office may be charged with the task of arranging housing, hotel, and meal accommodations for teams. Business and finance managers must have a solid background in financial accounting.

Compliance Officer

Compliance with NCAA regulations is not solely the responsibility of the person designated in an athletics department to serve as the compliance officer or coordinator. Compliance is technically a shared responsibility among all parties who come in contact with the athletics program, including the AD, coaches, current athletes, prospective athletes, boosters, and alumni, as well as representatives from various campus offices (e.g., admission, financial aid, residence life, health services). The process of compliance in its contemporary form evolved in the 1990s in conjunction with the development of the NCAA program certification process (Lagesse, 2002).

Broadly stated, the role of compliance coordinators is to develop educational processes that help everyone directly or indirectly involved with the athletics program understand and comply with the rules of the institution, the conference, and the national governing body. The span of responsibilities to which compliance officers may be assigned includes assessment of student initial eligibility, continuing eligibility, and transfer eligibility as well as adherence to regulations that govern athlete recruitment. Because of the complexity of rules, compliance coordinators often have the task of developing and implementing record-keeping methods to demonstrate that compliance in various areas is monitored. Much of this record keeping is done with computer software programs. Compliance officers play a crucial role in the formulation of compliance reports that institutions must submit to the NCAA on a regular basis.

Those interested in working in the compliance area must be detail oriented and have an exhaustive understanding of NCAA and conference rules and regulations along with the management and communication skills necessary to explain rules and regulations effectively. Although a law degree is not a requirement for this type of position, the nature of the job lends itself to someone with this kind of interest and background.

Development and Public Relations Director

Depending on the institution, the process of raising money from friends of an athletics program is called athletics fund-raising, development, or advancement. Athletics fund-raising organizations may be called fan clubs, booster clubs, friends associations, alumni clubs, or athletics foundations. Athletics development officers are responsible for raising funds to support various aspects of the athletics department by identifying and implementing fund-raising projects and cultivating potential and current donors. In athletics fund-raising, several basic principles apply. The fund-raiser wants to encourage people who donate to the program to continue to donate, and ideally to donate more over time, while searching out and contacting new donors to expand the program's financial base. The importance of development efforts to college athletics programs cannot be underestimated. For the fiscal year 2002-2003, 18% of the revenue generated by Division I-A programs came from alumni and booster contributions, which translates to millions of US dollars in support (Fulks, 2005). This type of position requires a combination of marketing, management, and media relations skills.

One extremely important element in this area is vigilance with regard to the donors involved with the program. The potential for rules violations in this area has proven to be high. Donors and friends of athletics programs may offer athletes under-the-table payments, improper gifts, and other benefits that violate NCAA rules. Athletics development officers are required to show the steps that they take to educate friends of the program about rules and regulations that govern athletics programs so as to avoid problems in this area.

Event and Facility Manager

In recent years, a marked expansion of athletics facilities on college campuses has occurred. Because of limitations of space and resources, athletics departments must find ways to use facilities to serve the multiple needs of campus constituencies and generate income through the rental and use of multipurpose facilities for special events, such as concerts. The position description for an event and facility manager reflects this trend. Facility scheduling, maintenance, improvements, and contest management are the major duties assigned to event and facility managers (Ammon, Southall, & Blair, 2004; Solomon, 2001). Because so many people use athletics facilities, and for so many different activities, facility and event managers must be attentive to the reduction of risk and liability while finding ways of being user-friendly through creating as much availability and accessibility as possible. One of the major responsibilities of the event and facility manager is game management for home athletics events. This task entails arranging for appropriate levels of security at games; hiring, training, and supervising ushers; marking and lining fields and courts; making arrangements for ticket sellers and ticket takers; managing the time schedule of the game, including such things as the National Anthem, bands, and halftime shows; and attending to the needs of game officials. A more detailed description of event and facility management is presented in chapter 13.

Marketing and Promotions Director

In summer 2001 the University of Oregon bought a 10-story billboard in New York City's Times Square, on which it displayed a picture of its Heisman Trophy nominee, quarterback Joey Harrington. The cost of that billboard was a tidy $250,000 USD—a quarter of a million dollars! Although the amount of money invested in the Harrington campaign was exceptionally high, the promotion itself was not unusual. Schools routinely invest $15,000 to $20,000 USD to promote their Heisman nominees (Posnanski, 2001). Marketing and promoting the contemporary college athletics program happens at all levels and is motivated by the need to generate interest in the program through enhanced visibility, increased attendance, and expanding revenue streams (see chapter 12).

Marketing and promotions directors may be responsible for promoting ticket sales for individual games, nonrevenue sports, season packages, and championship events along with a complete line of apparel, fan support merchandise, and items for retail sale by direct mail and through the university's bookstore and concessions area. Marketing and promotions directors are also responsible for identifying potential corporate sponsors, developing sponsorship proposals, and ensuring that proposals are implemented according to agreements reached with sponsors (Irwin, Sutton, & McCarthy, 2002). In an age in which product branding, merchandising, and licensing have become such integral parts of the marketing of intercollegiate athletics programs, marketing and promotions directors must have a comprehensive understanding of trademark licensing and be familiar with trademark principles, terms, and definitions used in trademark law (Pitts & Stotlar, 2002). See chapter 9 for more information on sport marketing and promotions.

Sports Information Director

Media have played a significant role in the development and evolution of all forms of sport in the United States, including college sport. The popularity and revenue-generating potential of college football and men's basketball are not, as some seem to believe, accidental or happenstance. Rather, the intensity of the interest and financial investment in those sports is the result of a long-standing relationship between college sport and the media (Oriard, 2001). The emergence of the NCAA and the formalization of college football in 1910 coincided with an era in which newspapers were struggling to gain a foothold in US popular culture. As John Marrs (1998) noted, "Serious-minded newspaper editors of the 1920s found sports too popular to fight and sports coverage claimed 40 percent of all local news space" (p. 5).

The advent of televised sport in the mid-1950s dramatically changed the relationship between college athletics departments and journalists. Before the 1950s, sport publicists sought to gain coverage for their teams in newspapers and on radio. Television introduced the element of revenue-generating potential through access to national audiences and immediate, live game coverage. Emblematic of the changing times, the NCAA published its first public relations manual for intercollegiate athletics in 1954. Reflecting the background and training of the NCAA's first executive director, Walter Byers, who had been a journalist, the association went on to persuade colleges and universities that they needed to have a full-time sport publicist on staff. Simultaneously, the NCAA pursued television contracts to enhance the public profile of college sport (Byers, 1995; Marrs, 1998).

The introduction of 24-hour-a-day, every-day-of-the-week sport coverage, along with the Internet, other emerging technologies, and the increase in women's sport, has substantially affected the way that intercollegiate athletics programs manage and handle communications (Hardin & McClung, 2002; Nichols et al., 2001). Sports information directors, also referred to as athletics communications specialists, sport publicists, and college sport public relations directors, are responsible for both technical and management functions. As a public relations practitioner, a sports information director must be adept at developing an array of publication materials, including media guides, press releases, recruiting brochures, game programs, feature stories, and newsletters, along with the background work (e.g., research, interviews with coaches and players) to support those publications. Besides executing the technical demands of the job, sports information directors are also responsible for managing budgets, organizing events, and supervising personnel (Stoldt, Miller, & Comfort, 2001). Successful sports information directors need to have excellent writing and research skills, firm understanding of mass communication and media technologies, awareness of and ability to appeal to internal and external audiences, and capacity to maintain a calm demeanor while working in high-stress, high-pressure situations. Practicing sports information directors offered this advice for students who want to pursue careers in this field: "Get as much writing experience as possible," "Gain as much experience as possible as an undergraduate," "Be prepared to work long hours," and "Plan on a career with little pay and little appreciation, but also plan on it being a lot of fun" (Hardin & McClung, 2002). For more information about sports information directors, see chapter 11.

Learning Activity

Identify a story about a college athletics program, coach, or athlete from a media source. Based on the information in the story, track the source of the story. Did the story originate with a press release distributed by the sports information office? Was it a feature idea suggested by the sports information director to the writer of the story? Were the statistics in the story drawn from a media guide or game program? Put together a summary of your findings and be prepared to present your findings in class.

Ticket Manager

The primary responsibilities of the ticket manager are coordinating all ticket operations, designing the ticketing plan, and accounting for all money expended and received for tickets. Responsible for a major area of revenue generation and customer service, ticket managers are called on to assist in setting the price of tickets, determining staffing, ensuring that ticket distribution is handled in a secure manner, and understanding state laws that pertain to ticket scalping (Reese, 2003). A major resource for the ticket manager is the International Ticketing Association (INTIX). Members of INTIX include an array of businesses and organizations in sport and entertainment fields around the world (e.g., amphitheaters, ballet and opera companies, festivals, sport teams, state fairs, theaters, and universities). Ticketing software and hardware development workers, ticket agents and printers, and Internet-based ticketing companies also belong to INTIX. INTIX sponsors an annual conference as well as an intensive certification program to help people in the industry stay current on trends and techniques to provide the best service possible to consumers. Additional information can be found at www.intix.org.

ticket operations—Process by which tickets are distributed to customers (season ticket holders and fans) coupled with attention to a high level of customer service (Reese, 2003).

ticket scalping—Selling a ticket for a price in excess of the price printed on the ticket (Reese, 2003).

Senior Woman Administrator (SWA)

When you read biographies of people working in intercollegiate athletics, you may come across the term *senior woman administrator*. The term itself is not a position title per se. In Divisions I and III, it designates "the highest-ranking female administrator involved with the conduct of a member institution's intercollegiate athletics program" (NCAA Member Services Staff, 2004a, p. 22; NCAA Member Services Staff, 2004c, p. 22). At the Division II level it refers to a "member of the institution's senior management team" (NCAA Member Services Staff, 2004b, p. 26). The purpose of the senior woman administrator concept is to ensure that women have a role in the decision-making process in college sport while also ensuring representation of women's interests at the campus, conference, and national levels. Research about senior woman administrators reveals that 79% of Division I SWAs serve in some administrative role within their departments, occupying assistant, associate, or senior associate athletics director positions. In other divisions, fewer senior woman administrators have significant administrative responsibilities (Claussen & Lehr, 2002).

Despite the intention of the SWA designation to integrate women in the decision-making process of athletics departments, a significant number of SWAs have little decision-making power and serve only as figureheads. Research has revealed a disconnect between the perceptions of athletics directors and senior woman administrators regarding the role of SWAs in decision making at the senior management level. Whereas ADs perceived that SWAs were instrumental in advancing the interests of the athletics department, SWAs perceived that they encountered barriers because of the limits placed on their assignments or authority (Claussen & Lehr, 2002; Tiell, n.d., 2004).

The concept of the senior woman administrator can sometimes be confusing. Although some SWAs are assigned sole responsibility for women's athletics programs and teams, the range of responsibilities assigned to SWAs can encompass all that goes on in a coeducational athletics department. According to Jane Meyer, the senior associate director of athletics at the University of Iowa, the scope of responsibilities for SWAs should contribute to decision making in the following areas: business affairs and budget management; Equity in Athletics Disclosure Act (EADA) oversight; personnel decisions; gender equity and Title IX; athlete welfare; promotions, sponsorship, marketing, and development; the legislation process at the NCAA and conference levels; strategic planning; and the formulation of a mission or philosophy for the department. In recent years steps have been taken to designate an SWA within athletics conferences as well.

EADA—Equity in Athletics Disclosure Act, www.ed.gov/finaid/prof/resources/athletics/eada.html.

Learning Activity

In recent years, some have come to question the effectiveness of appointing an SWA, arguing that the title has not encouraged the involvement of women in the decision-making process as intended. If you were considering this issue as a member of the NCAA's Committee on Women's Athletics, would you take the position that the SWA should be eliminated or retained? Present five key points to support your position.

Head Athletics Trainer

According to the National Athletic Trainers' Association (2006), "certified athletic trainers are health care professionals who specialize in preventing, recognizing, managing and rehabilitating injuries that result from physical activity." Most full-time athletic trainers in US colleges and universities are certified by the National Athletic Trainers' Association (NATA), the primary professional organization for athletic trainers.

Most athletics programs have a head athletic trainer and any number of assistant athletic trainers, depending on the size of the institution. The head athletic trainer ensures that personnel are assigned to all home and away events for which an athletic trainer is appropriate and that the necessary staff is provided for all championship events. Typically, the head athletic trainer also oversees decisions regarding injured athletes. Decisions related to practice, competition, treatment, therapy, and rehabilitation are usually coordinated with the full participation of the athletes, the head coach, and the athletic training staff in consultation with a team physician. Increasingly, athletic trainers are members of health care teams that include nutritionists, psychologists, and other appropriate medical personnel.

Equipment Manager

According to the Athletic Equipment Managers Association (AEMA, 2005), equipment managers purchase equipment; fit equipment such as football helmets; check, clean, and inspect uniforms and equipment to reduce wear and risk of injury while preserving the life of the equipment and garments as part of the budget management process; and establish a comprehensive accountability system that includes inventory (pre- and postseason), reconditioning, and storage. As with all other positions mentioned in this chapter, an equipment manager's job includes a significant management component (Olson, 1997). Effective communication with top-level, middle-level, and other first-line administrators is essential. Equipment managers must develop educational programs for the purposes of training professional and student staff (Momentum Media, 1999).

Since 1991 AEMA has promoted a certification program for equipment managers to ensure a high standard of performance and professional preparation. In 2005 there were over 500 certified athletic equipment managers in the United States (AEMA, 2005).

Administrators in Governing Bodies

Administrative positions in conferences and national governing bodies parallel many of those in colleges and universities. The major difference between them is that administrators in conferences and governing bodies must consider the welfare of many institutions and the conference as a whole rather than focus on a single university. As you will learn in chapter 15, conference commissioners in all NCAA divisions perform their duties within three major role classifications: interpersonal, informational, and decisional (Quarterman, 1994). Examples of these functions are shown in table 15.8 in chapter 15. You will notice that these functions are similar to those of an AD, except that an AD is acting on behalf of a university and the commissioner is acting on behalf of member institutions. The organizational charts in figures 4.1, 4.5, and 4.6 contain additional positions in the NCAA, the NAIA, and conference offices, respectively.

CAREERS IN INTERCOLLEGIATE ATHLETICS ADMINISTRATION

For some people, money, praise, prestige, and short workweeks are motivational factors for pursuing a career in intercollegiate athletics. These benefits, however, are unlikely to accompany the vast majority of positions. Intercollegiate athletics administrative positions do not typically pay high salaries, administrators have to contend with Monday morning quarterbacks who are always willing to tell them how they could improve their performance, the hours are long, and the work is challenging. Rewards might occasionally include the excitement of watching their teams in conference, regional, or national championship tournaments. More frequently, however, athletics administrators feel sufficiently rewarded to know that they are doing something they enjoy and, at the same time, touching the lives of young men and women and making a difference.

Career paths in intercollegiate athletics vary widely. No established path will lead the aspiring athletics administrator to his or her goal. The following discussion of career paths of ADs and first-line administrators is designed to provide insight into this competitive career field.

Becoming an Athletics Director

The traditional path to the AD position has been from collegiate athlete to collegiate coach to AD. Currently, however, at least two alternative paths to that destination are available. In some cases, athletics departments are recruiting successful businesspeople to take the helms of their financially challenged departments. In other situations, people who aspire to be ADs are gaining formal education through sport management programs (Berg, 1990).

Although there is no one best path to the AD position, the appropriateness of the athlete-to-coach-to-AD path has been challenged, particularly for NCAA Division I institutions. Reflecting widely held sentiments, Cuneen (1992) stated, "Managerial expertise and business acumen have become such essential characteristics for directors of major collegiate athletics programs that the long-standing career path of player to coach to athletic director is no longer sufficient" (p. 16). She suggested that prospective ADs should pursue a doctoral program to prepare them for job responsibilities such as business management, strategic planning, marketing, facility management, legal aspects of sport, finance, accounting, organizational theory, and personnel management.

Fitzgerald, Sagaria, and Nelson (1994) examined the career patterns of 200 athletics directors in NCAA Division I, II, and III institutions. They found that most respondents had been either college athletes or college coaches. Consistent similarities ended there, however, because career paths differed unpredictably within divisions and between genders. ADs in HBCUs have followed a slightly different path (Quarterman, 1992). Like their counterparts in predominately White institutions, most administrators at HBCUs were intercollegiate players and coaches before they became ADs. The difference is that most of them have teaching experience and are faculty members or coaches while serving as ADs. According to Quarterman, the career experiences of ADs in HBCUs (athlete to coach or instructor to AD) are similar to those of ADs in NAIA and NCAA Division II and III institutions.

First-Line Administrators

First-line administrators, such as marketing directors, academic coordinators, and sports information directors, spend their entire careers within a work unit focused on one aspect of a program. For these administrators, career advancements are typically

IN PROFILE: Judith Sweet

Title: Senior Vice President for Championships and Education Services, National Collegiate Athletic Association (NCAA)

What does it take to become one of the most influential people in college sport? Ms. Judith Sweet's profile offers abundant lessons for anyone wishing to learn the answer to that question.

After graduating with honors from the University of Wisconsin-Madison with a BS in physical education and mathematics, Ms. Sweet taught and coached at Tulane University and the University of Arizona before being appointed as a coach and teacher at the University of California, San Diego (UCSD), where she became involved in athletics administration. In the course of her professional career, she also earned two master's degrees, one in education from the University of Arizona and a second in business administration from National University.

A distinguished leader, Ms. Sweet started her odyssey to the NCAA by serving as director of athletics at UCSD. At the time of her appointment as director in 1975, she was one of the first women in the United States to direct a combined men's and women's athletics program at the university level. Under Ms. Sweet's leadership, UCSD emerged as one of the dominant NCAA Division III athletics programs in the nation, being awarded the NACDA Directors Cup for most successful Division III athletics program in 1998. By the time she left UCSD in 2000 to accept the position of VP for NCAA Championships, Ms. Sweet had left her mark. UCSD teams had won 26 national championships, and the budget and facilities had improved dramatically. The budget increased from less than $100,000 USD at the time of her hire to just short of $1 million USD on her departure, and the UCSD campus was altered forever, with new baseball, softball, tennis, soccer, and aquatics facilities, an all-weather track, and a $34 million USD multipurpose recreation and athletics center all being built during her tenure.

Ms. Sweet has been described as someone with an unparalleled depth of knowledge regarding intercollegiate athletics. She acquired this level of expertise through extensive involvement in NCAA governance, with significant responsibilities on various NCAA committees, including those with budget and financial responsibilities. Ms. Sweet holds the distinction of being the first woman and first director of a Division III program to be elected to a two-year term as membership president of the NCAA, in January 1991 (a position that no longer exists as a result of NCAA restructuring in the mid-1990s). Notably, she chaired the NCAA Budget Committee and also chaired the NCAA Revenue Distribution Committee that was formed after the signing of a $1 billion USD contract with CBS to broadcast men's basketball. In the position of Senior VP for Championships and Education Services, Ms. Sweet had oversight over 84 championships in 24 sports and was the national office senior woman administrator. In the process, she influenced the lives of roughly 360,000 athletes and viewing audiences around the world.

A defining quality of Ms. Sweet's leadership style is her ability to build consensus and help groups with competing interests or viewpoints find common ground. About her strategy for working in the high-stress environment that can sometimes exist around intercollegiate sport, she commented, "It's important to not make assumptions, to get all the facts, listen to people, give everyone an opportunity to have a fair hearing, then to identify what the appropriate decisions and solutions should be" (Becker, 1992).

Ms. Sweet's accomplishments are all the more significant when one considers that at the time she was in college, varsity sports for women were rarely offered. At the University of Wisconsin-Madison in the late 1960s, women played in recreational leagues only. About the significance of her rise through the ranks in intercollegiate athletics for women and minorities, Ms. Sweet observed, "For individuals who may have thoughts of taking leadership responsibility in the organization, but felt there may have been a lot of hurdles in the way, the message should be that with patience and persistence and a willingness to put in the effort, the opportunity will be there" (Weiberg, 1991). Every aspiring sport manager should consider this message.

Ms. Sweet retired from the NCAA in August 2006. Upon her departure, NCAA President Myles Brand stated, "Judy has made a significant difference to intercollegiate athletics in multiple ways . . . Her contributions to the NCAA—both from the campus and on the national office staff—frankly are beyond calculation. College sports is fortunate she chose athletics administration as the place to make her contribution" (NCAA News Online, May 8, 2006).

Photo courtesy of the NCAA brochure *Senior Woman Adminstrator.*

in the form of a vertical move from assistant director of a work unit to director of that unit. Occasionally, first-line administrators relocate to similar positions at other universities (i.e., a horizontal or lateral move) to advance their careers. Other first-line administrators, particularly in NCAA Division I programs, might move into associate or assistant AD positions (Fitzgerald et al., 1994; Quarterman, 1992). As these administrators move vertically, whether to director of a work unit or to associate or assistant AD positions, they will be expected to perform additional managerial and administrative functions.

Academic Preparation for Athletics Administration

The typical AD has at least one degree beyond the baccalaureate. In 1994, 85% of the ADs in NCAA I, II, and III institutions held master's degrees, with 21.5% of them possessing doctorates (Fitzgerald et al., 1994). Quarterman (1992) found that more than 95% of the ADs in HBCUs held master's degrees, and 36% of them had doctorates. An advanced degree was also prevalent among NCAA Division I-A middle-level and first-line administrators. Parks, Russell, Wood, Roberton, and Shewokis (1995) found that more than 60% of these administrators held either master's or doctoral degrees. Clearly, if you want to pursue a career in intercollegiate athletics, a master's degree will probably be necessary.

You can begin your career path in athletics administration by studying sport management at the undergraduate level; engaging in service learning or field experiences in athletics administration; or volunteering or completing an internship with an athletics department or a conference office. Your program should provide you with knowledge about sport in society and the role of athletics in institutions of higher education as well as an understanding of the business and technical aspects of the field. If you aspire to a position in an HBCU, NAIA, NCAA Division II, or NCAA Division III institution, you should also develop a field of academic or coaching expertise because you will probably be a professor or a coach as well as an administrator (Quarterman, 1992).

Field experiences (e.g., practica, internships) and volunteer positions will give you practical experience, one of the most valuable assets that you can acquire. While you are observing, learning, and performing career-related tasks for an athletics department or conference office, you are proving your competencies to professionals who are working in the positions for which you strive. In some cases, an internship serves as a stepping-stone to a job with either the internship organization or another organization. Although you may perform menial tasks at times, the observations that you make and the interaction that you have with professionals in the field can be invaluable for ongoing professional development. Volunteer for as many related events as possible to gain experience that you can place on your resume. Potential employers want to see real accomplishments and practical work experience obtained through field experiences, volunteering, and service learning. An internship is vital to your career development.

Next, you should select a graduate school that will complement the knowledge and experience that you gained at the undergraduate level. If you have no experience in intercollegiate athletics, an important element of the master's degree might be an internship with the university athletics department or conference office. This experience will permit you to learn more about the day-to-day operations of athletics administration. If you perform well, you will also begin to develop a valuable network of professionals who can vouch for your ability when you are looking for a job. If you want to be an AD, particularly at a major institution, you should consider including doctoral studies in your professional preparation plans.

Current Challenges

Numerous challenges await the next generation of intercollegiate athletics administrators. Major concerns include diversity, gender equity, racial equity, homophobia, age, disability, financial stability, ramifications of the socioeconomic status (SES) of student–athletes, program cost containment, corporate sponsorship, institutional control of athletics, academic integrity, and financial compensation for athletes. One of the challenges that athletic administrators face is reconciling the often conflicting and competing demands of the job. These conflicts often affect the level of satisfaction that athletic administrators have about their chosen career path. This section introduces selected issues that athletic administrators face, but space limitations prevent us from presenting any of these in depth. We will limit our discussion to just a few of these issues.

Diversity

Current discussions of affirmative action and equal opportunity might lead a person to believe that gender and racial balance has been achieved in intercollegiate athletics administration, particularly at the middle-level and first-line positions. On the contrary, studies of NCAA member institutions have shown a marked lack of diversity in athletics administrative personnel. For example, 92% of the 200 ADs in Fitzgerald and colleagues' 1994 study were White, and 71.5% of them were men. Parks, Russell, and Wood (1993) found a similar racial and gender imbalance among 402 NCAA Division I-A top-level, middle-level, and first-line administrators; 92% of the respondents were White, and 83% were male. More recent data a decade later show that little has changed. Of the 119 NCAA Division I-A athletics directors who oversee football, 10 (8.4%) are African American men, 3 (2.5%) are Latino men, and 5 (4.2%) are White women. No Asian or Native American men hold these positions, and women of color are not represented at all (University of Central Florida Report, 2004).

Similar patterns have been found in other areas of college sport administration. In athletic training, racial and ethnic minorities from historically underrepresented groups make up less than 10% of NATA membership (Geisler, 2003). The gender and racial imbalance found in these two studies presents a major challenge to the next generation of sport managers, who will be responsible for equalizing opportunities in intercollegiate athletics administration. In the more enlightened age of the 21st century, intercollegiate athletics administration should reflect greater participation not only by women and minorities but also by people with differing abilities, a population that is currently underrepresented in athletics administration (Abney & Richey, 1992). The NCAA annually conducts diversity education workshops for athletics administrators, coaches, faculty, and student–athletes to enhance their understanding and respect for multiculturalism and diversity. Additional NCAA professional development programs that target ethnic minorities are (1) the NCAA Fellows Leadership Development Program, (2) NCAA Leadership Institute for Ethnic Minorities, and (3) Ethnic Minority Enhancement Postgraduate Scholarship for Careers in Athletics.

Gender Equity

Progress has been made toward achieving gender equity in intercollegiate athletics, but much remains to be done. In 2006 women held 35.2% of the administrative positions. Division I included the smallest percentage of programs with a female athletics director (9.3%). Women held the AD position at 17.8% of Division II institutions and 26.6% of Division III schools (Acosta & Carpenter, 2006). Title IX of the Education Amendments Act of 1972 requires athletics administrators to ensure equity in scholarship support, number of female coaches, promotion of women's athletics, salaries, scheduling of women's games, inclusion of female administrators up to the highest levels, and budgets (Tillman, Voltmer, Esslinger, & McCue, 1996). The Equity in Athletics Disclosure Act of 1994, which went into effect in October 1996, requires institutions of higher education to make public all information by gender about participation rates of student–athletes and expenditures associated with coaching salaries, grants-in-aid, recruiting costs, and equipment (US Department of Education, 2002). Although this legislation enhances efforts to enforce the provisions of Title IX, equity in athletics is as much a moral responsibility as it is a legal mandate. The next generation of athletics administrators will be challenged to expand opportunities for women while controlling the costs associated with providing a quality athletics experience (Howard & Crompton, 2004).

Racial Equity

With the increase in participation rates, the implementation of affirmative action policies, the passage of Title IX, and the **Civil Rights Restoration Act** of 1987 (1988), one would expect to see an increase in the opportunities for minorities in coaching and managerial positions in intercollegiate athletics. This has not occurred. African American male and female coaches and administrators have not attained parity and remain underrepresented in college athletics. According to Dr. Richard Lapchick (University of Central Florida, 2006), who conducted a study assessing diversity among campus and conference leaders for Division I-A schools in January 2006, ". . . the most powerful people in college sport are still white. In Division I-A, this includes 94.1 percent of the presidents, 89.1 percent of the athletics directors, 94.1 percent of the faculty athletics reps and 100 percent of the conference commissioners."

> **Civil Rights Restoration Act**—Passed by Congress in 1987, vetoed by President Ronald Reagan, and passed (over his veto) in 1988. For more information, go to www.fhwa.dot.gov/environment/ejustice/facts/restoration_act.htm.

According to information gathered by the NCAA for the 2003-2004 academic year, 8% of all athletics administrators were Black. Members of racial and ethnic minorities were concentrated in positions such as academic advisors (20%), life skills coordinators (19%), and compliance officers (13%) as compared with fund-raising, marketing, and business affairs. As industry insiders point out, administrators who pursue upper-level athletics director jobs need access to positions that allow them to exhibit competencies and skills in fund-raising, negotiation, and administration (Suggs, 2005). As Alan Hughes (2005) of *Black Enterprise* wrote, "Sadly, while African Americans continue to dominate on the field, there remains a gross disparity between blacks and nonblacks when it comes to the decision makers in sport" (p. 88).

Abney and Richey (1991) investigated barriers that Black female administrators face in HBCUs and traditionally White institutions. In both settings, the women reported "inadequate salary," "lack of support groups," and "being a woman" as obstacles to their career development. The women who worked in HBCUs identified the additional barriers of "sexism" and "low expectations by administrators." The women who worked in the White institutions reported that "being Black" was an additional obstacle to their development as was the "lack of cultural and social outlets in the community."

In the 21st century, athletics administrators will be increasingly sensitive to the effects of gender and race on a person's career aspirations. Abney and Richey (1992) summed it up when they stated, "For minority women to enjoy the benefits of Title IX, there must be individuals in positions who are knowledgeable, committed, and sensitive to the differences and the hiring of minority women. Until this occurs, opportunities will remain limited" (p. 58).

Job Satisfaction

Intercollegiate athletics administrators in Divisions I-A and III have reported a high degree of satisfaction with most aspects of their jobs (Parks et al., 1995; Robinson et al., 2003; Robinson, Tedrick, & Carpenter, 2001). Middle-level and first-line administrators, however, tend not to be satisfied with their salaries and their promotion opportunities. Dissatisfaction with salaries is probably a reaction to the lower salaries paid for managerial positions in intercollegiate athletics compared with salaries in other industries. The appeal of sport is so strong, however, that many people are content to work long hours for relatively low pay. Moreover, the benefits that come with university employment (e.g., vacation time, life and health insurance, travel opportunities, access to academic courses, retirement benefits, association with student–athletes) are attractive, frequently offsetting modest salaries.

The dissatisfaction of athletics administrators with opportunities for promotion is probably a reflection of career paths in intercollegiate athletics. In this field, a person typically starts out as an assistant to a first-line administrator (e.g., assistant director of marketing) and eventually works his or her way up to the director's position in the same functional area (e.g., director of marketing). Only in rare instances does this path lead to the top position (i.e., AD). Consequently, first-line administrators might not perceive many opportunities for promotion.

Learning Activity

Richard Lapchick, head of the Center for Diversity and Ethics in Sport at the University of Central Florida, has suggested that the NCAA consider adopting something similar to the NFL's Rooney rule as a way to address diversity issues in hiring. The Rooney rule requires NFL teams to interview members of racial and ethnic minorities when head coaching positions become vacant. The rule further provides that franchises will be fined if they do not interview qualified candidates from racial and ethnic minorities. Write a two-page opinion paper on whether you believe this would be an effective approach to hiring in intercollegiate athletics. Provide reasons for your position.

JOB OPPORTUNITIES

Assistant AD

Assistant athletics director for media relations. Duties include coordinating and supervising media relations for 17 intercollegiate sports including copywriting, designing, and editing media guides and game programs; coordinating interviews and press conferences; writing stories, game notes, and press releases; overseeing all media operations at athletics events; supervising media relations staff; overseeing department's Internet application. Qualifications: bachelor's degree required and five years' experience in collegiate athletics administration.

Associate AD

Associate athletics director for an NCAA Division II program that sponsors cross-country running and skiing, rifle, basketball (men's and women's), and women's volleyball and Division I men's ice hockey. Responsibilities include

(continued)

assisting the athletics director with daily departmental operations; direction of coaching, facility, and sports medicine staff; education and enforcement of NCAA, conference, and university policies and regulations; sports programs and game scheduling; academic advising; liaison to booster clubs and Intercollegiate Athletic Committee; promoting collaboration with community; advisor to student–athlete board. Bachelor's degree in administration or relevant experience required, master's preferred.

Academic Counselor

Academic counselor—Division I athletics: We invite candidates to apply for this full-time, fixed-term 12-month position. The counselor will monitor the academic progress of students on the men's and women's basketball teams, softball team, and baseball team. This responsibility will include supervision of study hall, tutorials, and other academic assistance. The counselor will be responsible for end-of-the-year and term-to-term outcome reports. The counselor will assist in the communication of eligibility issues between the Compliance Office and the students in compliance with university, conference, and the NCAA rules and regulations. The counselor will also assist the NCAA Life Skills staff and the university's Student Affairs staff with the coordination and creation of programming for all students. The position will be responsible for coordinating the Student–Athlete Orientation Program, assisting with orientation classes for student–athletes, monitoring the Learning Zone, and coordinating tutor requests and other academic requests. Master's in education, college personnel, higher education administration, counseling, or other related field required. Two years' experience working with a diverse college population in a counseling or advising capacity required. Applicants with experience working with student–athletes in a major university setting (NCAA Division I) are preferred. Organizational, interpersonal, and communication skills are essential. Some evenings and weekends required.

Sports Information

Twelve-month renewable contract position available at an NCAA Division I-A institution. Responsibilities: design and create media guides, news releases, and other publications for athletics programs; assist in the updating of the Internet Web site; other duties as assigned by the director. Minimum qualifications: bachelor's degree by date of employment; at least two years of work in a sports information, athletics communications, or media relations office; good organizational and management skills; working knowledge of the Internet. Preferred qualifications: bachelor's degree in journalism, telecommunications, or related field; three to five years of experience.

Public Relations

A California university is seeking an assistant director for community and youth programs. Qualifications include strong organizational skills; excellent computer skills (including MS Word®, MS Excel®, MS Access®, MS Publisher®, and Web design); professional and friendly demeanor; strong interpersonal skills; and team orientation. General knowledge of NCAA rules and regulations preferred. The assistant director functions as the division's primary computer support entity, while also serving as a significant resource in the areas of marketing, promotions, and financial affairs. Operating under minimal to general supervision, the person in the position assumes the lead role in all computer-related issues ranging from Web design, to database management, to desktop publishing, while also functioning as a vital liaison in the areas of public relations and community outreach. This 12-month, contract position includes comprehensive health (medical, dental, optical) and retirement benefits.

Athletic Marketing

An NCAA Division I institution has an immediate opening for the position of director of athletic marketing. This is a full-time 12-month position. Responsibilities include but are not limited to developing and implementing comprehensive marketing plans to increase attendance at home events, soliciting and maintaining corporate sponsorships, managing and fulfilling sponsorship agreements, coordinating and managing game-day event operations, developing and designing various athletic publications, creating and organizing advertising, managing community relations program, and serving as a liaison to university student organizations and community groups for the Athletics Department. Qualifications: bachelor's degree required, master's degree preferred; a minimum of three years' experience in NCAA intercollegiate athletics is desired; strong oral and written communication skills; experience with computers with proficiency in desktop publishing preferred (Pagemaker, Illustrator, Photoshop); ability to work a flexible work schedule including some evenings and weekends; ability to organize multiple tasks, meet deadlines, and plan schedules. The successful candidate will be a person of integrity with high ethical standards and will exhibit strict adherence to NCAA, university, and departmental rules and regulations. Salary is commensurate with qualifications and experience.

(continued)

JOB OPPORTUNITIES *(continued)*

Promotions

A Midwestern university is seeking qualified applicants for a director of promotions position. Directs the daily promotional activities for 18 varsity sports with emphasis on football, men's and women's basketball, volleyball, and special events. Responsible for developing promotional plans for all revenue sports; developing effective ticket sales strategies; designing and copying all ticket brochures; disseminating ticket sales and advertising materials throughout the university and community; overseeing the copy, design, production, and placement of all print, television, radio, and billboard ticket advertising; planning and implementing special athletic events; and supervising of staff. A bachelor's degree, preferably in marketing, communications, management, or related field of study, is required. Three years' experience in promotions or event management is required. Athletic promotions experience is preferred. Word processing, desktop publishing, and excellent oral and written communication and editing skills are required. Ability to interact effectively with and serve diverse customers, organize and prioritize multiple tasks to produce high-quality work with attention to detail, meet established deadlines, and take initiative to see projects through to completion is necessary. Interest in and knowledge of sports preferred.

Ticket Office

Athletics ticket manager—Manages operations and supports ticket office personnel, especially supervising all operations of the Paciolan system. Responsibilities include upholding, creating, and implementing policies and procedures that produce optimum customer service and efficient ticket operations; performing and managing financial activities of the office from processing orders to reconciling transactions with university records; overseeing the allocation of seating for all sports in conjunction with customer priority level; coordinating all ticket printing, packaging, and delivery for individual customers and game-day sales. Must have great foresight with planning, financial and auditing knowledge, and excellent communication skills. Requires understanding customer needs; knowledge of ticketing operations and sport management policies and procedures; in-depth understanding of Paciolan system; fluency in Windows® and Microsoft Office®; general understanding of the role of the department within the university. Requires good interpersonal and leadership skills, data entry skills, telephone communication skills, and general understanding of basic accounting procedures. Undergraduate degree or equivalent experience required; master's degree preferred. Five or more years of related experience required.

Compliance

A major college conference invites applications for the position of assistant director of compliance and championships. Responsibilities include administering the NLI, secondary violations, interpretations, rules education, eligibility and squad lists, NCAA legislative issues, administrative management for select conference championships, awards, merchandising, and other duties as assigned. Qualifications: Candidates must have a bachelor's degree; minimum of two years' professional experience in collegiate athletics or related field; excellent interpersonal, writing, and computer skills. Salary commensurate with qualifications.

Development

The booster club of a Florida university is accepting applications for the position of assistant director of development. Bachelor's degree and at least two years of successful development-related experience and knowledge of intercollegiate athletics are required. Excellent leadership, communication, and organizational skills are necessary. Position requires some weekend work, after-hours work, and travel.

Primarily responsible for assisting with the day-to-day operations of the booster club's annual fund, administering major donor recognition and benefits, and coordinating away-game donor travel. Some identification, cultivation, and solicitation of donors is involved. Must work closely with a variety of university and athletics department staff. Must also assist with other duties in the athletics development office as assigned.

These position descriptions were fictionalized from positions found at www.ncaa.org.

SUMMARY

Intercollegiate athletics began in the 1850s as class games and evolved into highly competitive programs. National governing bodies and conferences regulate these programs. The first line of control, however, lies with the institution. The Knight Foundation Commission on Intercollegiate Athletics (1991) issued a report calling for presidential control, academic integrity, financial integrity, and certification. Athletics administrative positions include athletics director, associate and assistant athletics director, academic coordinator, business and finance manager, compliance officer, development and public relations director, event and facility manager, marketing and promotions director, sport information director, and ticket manager. Additional personnel include the equipment manager and the athletic training staff. The SWA (senior woman administrator) is the NCAA designation given to the highest-ranking female athletics administrator.

Career progression in intercollegiate athletics occurs on divergent paths. Most administrators have at least one academic degree beyond the baccalaureate. Those who want to become ADs in major institutions should consider earning a doctorate. Challenges that intercollegiate athletics administrators must deal with include diversity, gender and racial equity, homophobia, age, disability, financial stability, ramifications of differences in socioeconomic status (SES) of student–athletes, cost containment, corporate sponsorship, institutional control, academic integrity, and financial compensation for athletes.

Review Questions

1. How much is the CBS broadcast deal for the NCAA men's Division I basketball tournament and selected other championships worth?
2. When was the NCAA founded?
3. In the 1980s what organization initiated a call for intercollegiate athletics reform?
4. Describe that organization's one-plus-three model for intercollegiate athletics.
5. What did Shulman and Bowen, authors of the book *The Game of Life*, conclude about the effect of big-time college sport programs on education?
6. What is the Drake Group?
7. Are intercollegiate athletics administrators like managers in other business settings? Explain your answer.
8. Identify two factors that can affect how athletics administrators approach their jobs.
9. Identify three key skills that athletics directors who work in major conferences believe are necessary to run a successful program.
10. An academic coordinator may be asked to run something called the CHAMPS–Life Skills Program. What is this program?
11. What does a business and finance manager oversee in an athletics department?
12. What are athletics development officers required to do to demonstrate that they have educated donors about NCAA rules and regulations?
13. What is the Equity in Athletics Disclosure Act of 1994?
14. Discuss several challenges that intercollegiate athletics administrators must face during the 21st century.
15. What is the purpose of the senior woman administrator position?

Professional Sport

James M. Gladden—University of Massachusetts at Amherst ▪
William A. Sutton—University of Central Florida, National Basketball Association

Learning Objectives

After studying this chapter, you will be able to do the following:

1. Define, explain, and discuss the development of professional sport.
2. Describe the unique facets of professional sport, including its governance and the labor–management relationship that professional team sports depend on.
3. Document the significance of the relationship between television and professional sport.
4. Describe the major revenue sources for a professional sport team.
5. Identify the types of employment opportunities available in professional sport.

Professional sport is any sport activity or skill for which the athlete is compensated. Compensation can be in the form of salary, bonuses, reimbursement for expenses, or any other form of direct payment. The activity the athlete performs can be a team sport such as basketball, a dual sport such as tennis, an individual sport such as figure skating or skateboarding, or a sport entertainment performance such as World Wrestling Entertainment (WWE). Although these professional sports usually imply the presence of spectators, an audience is not a criterion by which professional sport is defined. For example, some sport organizations such as the Ladies Professional Golf Association (LPGA) and the Professional Golf Association (PGA) have a classification of membership called the **teaching professional**. Although these professionals might occasionally compete in tournaments for prize money, they typically earn their livings instructing others in the skills and strategies of the game. They may direct their skills to a small group of students or perhaps only one person. Teaching pros also are involved in clinics, lessons, club management, and merchandising ventures, all of which can be lucrative revenue sources. A representative list of professional sports in North America includes the following:

Auto racing	Ice skating
Baseball	Motocross
Basketball	Racquetball
Billiards	Rodeo
Bodybuilding	Skateboarding
Bowling	Skiing
Boxing	Snowboarding
Curling	Soccer
Football	Surfing
Golf	Tennis
Hockey	Triathlon
Horse racing	Volleyball

teaching professional—A professional athlete who focuses primarily on teaching other athletes the intricacies of the sport. Most prevalent in golf, teaching professionals also compete in tournaments but typically do not compete on such high-profile tours as the PGA or LPGA Tours.

Professional sport events such as the Super Bowl, World Series, Masters, Indianapolis 500, Wimbledon, Kentucky Derby, and X Games now occupy the heart of North American sport. Although we have mentioned both team sports and sports featuring the individual, this chapter will concentrate on professional team sports because of their profound economic effect and the number of job opportunities that they provide. Most jobs associated with professional individual sports are found in sport management and marketing agencies (see chapter 6). The purpose of this chapter is to provide information and insight about four primary aspects of North American professional team sport—its historical development, its unique aspects, its revenue sources, and the variety of career opportunities associated with professional sport.

NATURE OF PROFESSIONAL SPORT

David Guterson (1994) described professional sport in this way:

> Like money, it is something we love, a first waking thought and a chronic passion, as well as a vast sector of the economy, a wellspring for myth and totem, and a media phenomenon of the highest order. Our sports can fend off the brute facts of existence, temporarily arrest the sadness of life, briefly shroud the inevitability of death and provide the happy illusion of meaning through long enchanted afternoons. . . . Sport is a language we all speak. Sport is a mirror. Sport is life. Through sport we might know ourselves. (p. 38)

Guterson's description accurately portrays the powerful role that professional sport occupies in the everyday lives of many people. Professional sport exemplifies sport at its highest level of performance, and it generates the majority of coverage devoted to sport through the print and electronic media. As packaged events, professional team sports (e.g., men's and women's football, men's and women's ice hockey, men's soccer, men's baseball, women's softball, and men's and women's basketball) provide considerable entertainment and pleasure for spectators. As such, demands on the three principals that form the professional sport industry—labor, management, and governance—are complex, diverse, and ever changing. **Labor** aggressively continues to protect and procure additional resources for its membership, which is made up of the professional athletes. **Management**, or the owners of professional teams, is trying to win back some leverage and control lost to labor over the past three decades. Finally, **governance**, made up of the professional sport leagues, attempts to regulate, but not completely control, both labor and management.

labor—A term that typically refers to the collective group of athletes in team sports that unionize so that they can bargain collectively with the league owners (management). A union head typically represents labor in negotiations with management.

management—When referring to the collective bargaining process, management refers to the collective group of ownership that is negotiating with the players, or labor. A league commissioner, technically an agent for the owners, typically represents management in negotiations with labor.

governance—In professional team sport, governance is the league structure that oversees both the competitive and the business elements of the sport. The National Football League, Major League Baseball, National Hockey League, and the Women's National Basketball Association are all forms of governance.

HISTORY OF THE MAJOR AMERICAN PROFESSIONAL SPORTS

Professional sport can be traced to ancient Greece where, beginning with the Olympic Games in 776 BCE, a class of professional sportsmen known as

1800s
- **1807**—First Canadian curling club, Montreal Curling Club, founded

1830s
- **1834**—First organized lacrosse game
- **1838**—First baseball game in Canada

1850s
- **1851**—First America's Cup race
- **1858**—National Association of Base Ball Players organizes

1860s
- **1860**—Salaried players begin invading amateur baseball
- **1862**—William E. Commey charges admission to baseball games
- **1863**—Football Association (FA) established

athletai existed. These athletai were well-paid men recruited from mercenary armies and trained exclusively for brutal competition (Freedman, 1987). In exchange for competing and winning, athletai often received remuneration in the form of prizes and money. Although the notion of amateurism might suggest that professional sport did not exist before the late 19th century, an element of professionalism has pervaded sport throughout its development.

Origins of Professional Sport in America

Although baseball is often considered America's national pastime, it was not the first sport that professionals played. Boxers, jockeys, and runners were paid for their prowess during the early and mid-19th century. Baseball, however, was the first team sport to employ professionals. In 1869 the Cincinnati Red Stockings became the first professional baseball team. Their appearance was closely followed in 1871 by the National Association of Professional Base Ball Players, the first professional sport league (Rader, 1983). In 1876 William Hulbert formed the National League, the precursor to Major League Baseball (MLB) as we know it today. Middle-class entrepreneurs owned these early teams. Hoping to see their teams serve as a source of civic pride, individual owners built stadia and arenas in city centers (White, 1996). That approach is in contrast to current circumstances, in which some of the publicly financed stadia and arenas are constructed at least partially under the threat that the owner will relocate the team if a publicly financed stadium or arena is not built.

A recognized professional league in another sport did not form until after the turn of the 20th century. In 1917 the National Hockey League (NHL) emerged after the National Hockey Association of Canada Limited suspended its operations (National Hockey League, 1996). This was closely followed in 1921 with the creation of the National Football League (NFL). The National Basketball League (NBL), founded in 1937, was the first professional basketball league. In 1949 the National Basketball Association (NBA) resulted from a merger between the NBL and the Basketball Association of America (BAA) (Staudohar & Mangan, 1991).

Inclusion (and Exclusion) in Professional Sport

Although professional team sport has been in existence for more than 100 years, only in the past 70 years have professional sport opportunities been available to many minority segments of the American population. Professional sport opportunities were segregated until 1947, when Jackie Robinson broke baseball's color line with the Brooklyn Dodgers. Before 1947 African Americans played in separate, segregated professional leagues. The National Colored Baseball League was founded in 1887 as an outlet for African American baseball players, who were not allowed to play in the all-White major leagues. This league failed quickly because of lack of attendance. But in 1920 the Negro National League was formed. This league and others, such as the Eastern Negro League and Negro American League afforded players such as Satchel Paige, Josh Gibson, and even Jackie Robinson an opportunity to play (*Negro League baseball*, 2005). In addition, most owners, club managers, reporters, and umpires in the Negro leagues were also African American. The demise of the Negro leagues began with the integration of professional baseball in 1947; they ultimately ceased operations in 1960 (*Leagues & Teams*, 2005).

Professional sport outlets for women have arisen only in the past 60 years. In the 1940s the first women's professional league, the All-American Girls Professional Baseball League (AAGPBL), was formed. Created in 1943 in response to decreased player quality in Major League Baseball during World War II and the popularity of women's amateur softball, the AAGPBL played 11 exciting seasons before folding in 1954 because of poor management (Browne, 1992). Since 1954 a number of other women's professional leagues have operated, mainly in the sport of basketball. From 1979 to 1991 there were four attempts to capitalize on the growing participation and interest of women in basketball: the Women's Professional Basketball League (1979-1981), the Women's American Basketball Association (October-December 1984), the National Women's Basketball Association (October 1986-February 1987), and the Liberty Basketball Association (February-March 1991). Each league was unsuccessful because of financial difficulty ("A History," 1996).

In the mid-1960s, women began playing semipro tackle football, and by the 1970s teams were competing in Ohio, New York, Michigan, and Pennsylvania. In 1974 the Women's Professional Football League (WPFL) was established with teams in Dallas, Fort Worth, Columbus, Toledo, Los Angeles, and Detroit. During the ensuing years, a number

1860s

- **1865**—Montreal and McGill Univ. play first rugby game in Canada
- **1868**—Montreal Football club, Canada's first organized football team, forms
- **1869**—Cincinnati Redstockings become first all-professional baseball team

1870s

- **1871**—National Association of Professional Base Ball Players organizes as first professional baseball league
- **1873**—Royal Montreal Golf Club becomes first golf club in North America

LaShawn Foust, running back for the D.C. Divas, eludes the Mass Mutiny defense and heads toward the goal line. Quarterback Allyson "Smooth" Hamlin led the Divas to win the 2006 North Atlantic Division championship, while the Mutiny won the 2006 North East Division title with Allison Cahill in the quarterback slot. The Divas and the Mutiny are members of the National Women's Football Association (NWFA).
Photo courtesy of The National Women's Football Association.

of leagues emerged as women expressed interest and ability in tackle football. Today three professional football leagues for women are active: the Women's Professional Football League (WPFL), the National Women's Football Association (NWFA), and the Independent Women's Football League (IWFL). The NWFA, with 35 teams, is the largest tackle football league for women in the world. As of 2006, more than 80 women's football teams were competing in the United States. Each league has its own Web site where you can go for more information: http://womensprofootball.com/ (the WPFL); http://womensfootballcentral.com (the NWFA); and http://iwflsports.com/ (the IWFL).

The past 10 years has seen a resurgence of interest in women's professional sport. In 1996 two women's professional basketball leagues were formed: the American Basketball League (ABL) and the Women's National Basketball Association (WNBA). The ABL played two and a half seasons before folding halfway into the 1998-99 season because of financial difficulties, which were at least partially due to competition from the NBA-sponsored WNBA (which still exists today). In June 1997 the Women's Professional Fastpitch (WPF) softball league began. Finally, during the summer of 2001 the Women's United Soccer Association (WUSA) began play. Both the WNBA and women's pro softball still exist, but the WUSA ceased operations in 2003 because of financial problems.

Factors Affecting the Growth of Professional Sport

As professional sport progressed throughout the 20th century, its success was largely tied to the media, which both promoted and financed professional sport. As early as the 1920s baseball games were broadcast on the radio. By the mid-1930s radio networks were paying $100,000 USD for the rights to carry the World Series (Rader, 1983). The popularity of professional sport (mainly baseball) on the radio reached its apex in the 1940s and 1950s. During the 1950s televised sporting events became commonplace.

After Congress passed the Sports Broadcasting Act in 1961, the relationship between

Learning Activity

Jackie Robinson broke the color barrier in MLB in 1947 with the Brooklyn Dodgers.

- Who broke the color barrier in the American League later that same year?
- Who were the first African American players to play in the NFL, NBA, and NHL?
- When were these three leagues integrated?
- What opportunities were available for African Americans to play professional baseball before Jackie Robinson's historic debut? Trace the history of the Negro leagues before the 1950s. Searching for stories about Moses "Fleetwood" Walker, Welday Walker, and Bud Fowler will help you get started.

1870s

- **1875**—First running of Kentucky Derby
- **1876**—National League Base Ball, precursor to MLB, forms
- **1876**—Spalding opens Baseball & Sporting Goods Emporium (Chicago)
- **1876**—First soccer game played in Canada (Toronto)
- **1879**—Baseball reserve clause established

1880s

- **1880**—Cincinnati Reds expelled from National League
- **1882**—Canadian Rugby Union forms

Learning Activity

Although much is known and has been written about male professional athletes throughout time, less is known about the history of women in professional sport. Using resources in your library, find a book or article about a professional female athlete who competed before 1970. Write a paper about the highlights and disappointments of her career. How might her career have been different if she were participating today? Why?

the media and professional sports changed dramatically. Until that time, antitrust law had prohibited leagues from negotiating network television contracts on behalf of their members. But the leagues believed they needed to negotiate a collective (on behalf of all league teams) agreement to ensure the financial viability of their member teams. This rationale suggested that the major television networks (ABC, CBS, NBC) would pay significantly larger sums of money to obtain leaguewide rights rather than rights to individual teams. As a result, the NFL successfully led a lobbying effort to create an exemption in antitrust law. The Sports Broadcasting Act of 1961 gave sport leagues an exemption from antitrust law, granting them the right to negotiate fees collectively with the networks. This legislation paved the way for the highly lucrative leaguewide television deals that pervade professional sports today (Gorman & Calhoun, 1994). As you will learn later in this chapter, these broadcasting deals now make up a large portion of the revenues generated by major professional sport teams.

UNIQUE ASPECTS OF PROFESSIONAL SPORT

Four aspects of professional sport distinguish it from other industries: interdependence, structure and governance, labor–management relations, and the role of the electronic media.

Interdependence

The central premise that differentiates professional team sport from any other business organization is the need of the teams to compete and cooperate simultaneously (Mullin, Hardy, & Sutton, 2000). In other words, the teams depend on one another to stage the games that constitute the product. In his classic work on the NFL, *The League*, David Harris (1986) describes this unique situation as **league think**. According to former NFL commissioner Pete Rozelle,

> One of the key things that a sports league needs is unity of purpose. It needs harmony. . . . When you have unity and harmony and can move basically as one, you can have a successful sports league. The objective of "League Think" is to reverse the process by which the weak clubs get weaker and the strong clubs get stronger. Favorable results are a product of the degree to which each league can stabilize itself through its own competitive balance and league wide income potential. (pp. 13-14)

league think—Pioneered and most effectively implemented by the National Football League, league think is the notion that teams must recognize the importance of their competition and share revenues to ensure that their competitors remain strong.

When teams function together collectively, some teams sacrifice the potential for higher revenue in the interest of league stability. For example, the Dallas Cowboys and Oakland Raiders typically sell a disproportionate amount of NFL licensed merchandise. This money, however, is pooled and shared equally among all 32 NFL teams. The presence of the Dallas Cowboys and Oakland Raiders in the collective bargaining agreement increases the revenue generated for all NFL member teams. Because of their location in large television markets, the New York Giants and Chicago Bears function in much the same way during television negotiations. The key is that all members make sacrifices and concessions for the long-term benefit and growth of the league.

Although major professional sport leagues differ in the extent to which they share revenues, each league pools its revenues to some extent. For example, NFL teams all share equally in their national television packages (cable and network), whereas baseball teams share only their national contracts and keep all revenue from their local agreements. These local agreements can vary significantly in the

1880s

▶ **1884**—First baseball postseason championships

▶ **1887**—National Colored Baseball League forms

1890s

▶ **1893**—Stanley Cup awarded

▶ **1894**—USGA forms

▶ **1898**—Golf ball patent

1900s

▶ **1903**—First MLB World Series

▶ **1909**—In first Grey Cup game, Univ. of Toronto defeats Parkdale Canoe Club

Learning Activity

The American Basketball League (ABL) and the Women's United Soccer Association (WUSA) both failed to exist beyond three seasons. The ABL folded in 1998, and the WUSA folded in 2003. Using either library research or research available on the Internet, compare and contrast the reasons these two women's professional sports leagues failed. Based on your research, do you see a way in which one or both of these leagues could have succeeded? If so, how?

amount of revenue produced. Large-market teams (teams located in large cities that can negotiate large local television packages), such as the New York Yankees, have local broadcast packages that are significantly larger than those of small-market teams (teams located in smaller cities), such as the Kansas City Royals. Over the past 10 years the disparity in local media revenues has created significant discrepancies in the amount of money that Major League Baseball (MLB) teams are able to pay their players. Such revenue disparities led Major League Baseball to implement a luxury tax on teams that had the highest payrolls. Teams with disproportionately high payrolls pay a tax to MLB, which is then shared among teams with lower payrolls.

large-market teams—Professional teams located in large markets that offer high potential for lucrative local media contracts.

small-market teams—Professional teams located in midsize or smaller markets (for professional sport) that offer modest potential for local media contracts.

luxury tax—a device used by Major League Baseball and the National Basketball Association to tax the teams that spend the most (or too much as defined by the collective bargaining agreement) on player payroll and share those taxes with teams that do not have high payrolls.

Structure and Governance

Each professional sport has its own structure and system of governance, typically referred to as the league office, which usually involves the following components:

1. League commissioner
2. Board of governors or committee structure composed of the team owners
3. A central administrative unit that negotiates contracts and agreements on behalf of the league and assumes responsibility for scheduling, licensing, and other functions, such as coordinating publicity and advertising on behalf of the teams as a whole

For example, Major League Baseball is composed of 30 teams situated in two leagues (National and American—see table 5.1). Each league consists of three divisions (East, Central, and West). Each league has a president, who reports to a commissioner. The commissioner is responsible for representing the interests of all parties associated with professional baseball. These parties include owners, players, fans, television networks, corporate sponsors, host cities and venues, and the minor leagues. Contrast this organizational structure to mainstream business. For example, no authority governs the actions of candy manufacturers Hershey's and M & M Mars in their attempts to make money.

Baseball is unique in having an extensive minor league system, which provides an elaborate way of preparing players to participate in the major leagues. Each major league team has at least four affiliate teams in the minor leagues. As long as they meet certain standards in terms of the size of their facilities, owners of minor league teams can enter into contractual relationships with major league clubs whereby the minor league team becomes an affiliate of a major league team. The major league team pays the players' salaries, and the minor league affiliate is responsible for all franchise operations (including sales and facility management) and travel expenses for the players (Tannenbaum, 1994). A current trend in minor league baseball is for one corporation to own several minor league baseball teams. For example, Mandalay Baseball Properties, a division of Mandalay Entertainment, owns the Dayton Dragons (single A affiliate of the Cincinnati Reds), the Erie SeaWolves (AA affiliate of the Detroit Tigers), the Frisco Rough Riders (AA affiliate of the Texas Rangers), the Hagerstown Suns (single A affiliate of the San Francisco Giants), and the Las Vegas 51's (AAA affiliate of the Los Angeles Dodgers) (*Mandalay Sports Entertainment Information*, 2005). An organization that owns several minor league teams gains a number of advantages, including the sharing of expertise and the ability to promote its

1910s

- **1911**—First Indy 500 held
- **1912**—First Calgary Stampede
- **1916**—First PGA Championship
- **1917**—NHL established
- **1919**—Farm system created by Branch Rickey of St. Louis Cardinals
- **1919**—Black Sox Scandal

1920s

- **1920**— American Professional Football Association forms—renamed National Football League (NFL) in 1922
- **1920**— Babe Ruth sold to Yankees
- **1920-31**—Negro National League
- **1921**—In first East-West Grey Cup game, Toronto Argonauts defeat Edmonton Eskimos

Table 5.1

Organization of Major League Baseball

National League East	National League Central	National League West	American League East	American League Central	American League West
Atlanta Braves	Chicago Cubs	Arizona Diamondbacks	Baltimore Orioles	Chicago White Sox	Los Angeles Angels of Anaheim
Florida Marlins	Cincinnati Reds	Colorado Rockies	Boston Red Sox	Cleveland Indians	Oakland Athletics
New York Mets	Houston Astros	Los Angeles Dodgers	New York Yankees	Detroit Tigers	Seattle Mariners
Philadelphia Phillies	Milwaukee Brewers	San Diego Padres	Tampa Bay Devil Rays	Kansas City Royals	Texas Rangers
Washington Nationals	Pittsburgh Pirates	San Francisco Giants	Toronto Blue Jays	Minnesota Twins	
	St. Louis Cardinals				

Learning Activity

Using your library resources, find an article that discusses local broadcasting agreements in Major League Baseball. According to the article, which teams make the most money from local broadcasting agreements? Which teams make the least? Do you notice differences in how these teams perform based simply on the amount of revenue that they generate from local television contracts? Explain your observations.

best employees on the business side of the organization across the different teams owned.

The cultivation of minor league systems is increasingly popular among the other major professional sport leagues as the following examples illustrate:

- The American Hockey League (AHL) is the premier development league for the National Hockey League (NHL).
- NFL Europe (formerly known as the World League of American Football) is a summer professional football league in Europe that serves as a training ground for future NFL players.
- Starting with the 2006-2007 season, NBA teams will have player development relationships with teams in the NBA Development League. Players drafted by NBA teams may be placed with NBA Development League teams for the first two years.

During the past decade a variation on the typical league structure and governance has emerged—the **single-entity structure**. In the single-entity structure the league is the de facto owner of all member teams in the league. Introduced by Major League Soccer upon its formation, this structure has also been employed by the now defunct WUSA as well as the WNBA and the NBA Development League (formerly the National Basketball Development League, or NBDL). In its purest form, the single-entity structure has no individual team owners. Rather, individual investors pay for the right to "operate" teams. Along these lines, teams do not hire players; the league does. In theory, this type of ownership allows the league to control labor costs because it is the employer of all the athletes. The legality of single-entity structures has been challenged under antitrust law (*Fraser et al. v. Major League Soccer*, 2000), but thus far the courts have refused to deem the structure to be in violation of antitrust law.

Economically and operationally, the single-entity system has not been successful in professional sports. The WUSA is no longer operating, and the owners of NBA teams now own and operate WNBA teams, with the exception of two franchises—the

1920s

▶**1923**—Ty Cobb breaks Honus Wagner's career hits record

▶**1924**—NHL adds Boston Bruins, first non-Canadian team

▶**1925**—Victoria Cougars win Stanley Cup, last non-NHL team to do so

▶**1927**—First Ryder Cup—US team defeated Great Britain

1930s

▶**1932**—PGA Tour formed

▶**1934**—First Masters Golf tournament

▶**1937**—NBL (National Basketball League), first professional basketball league, forms

Chicago Sky, which is owned by private investors, and the Connecticut Sun, which is owned by the Mohegan Tribal authority. Like the WNBA, the NBA Developmental League is no longer a single-entity structure. The NBA currently owns and operates only two of the seven NBA Developmental League teams that operated in the 2005 season. Both the WNBA and NBA Developmental League have become attractive to investors who want more than just operating rights—they want to have a voice in the governance of not only a team but the league itself. Thus the traditional model of ownership has emerged, and the single-entity structure has been almost totally abandoned. Only Major League Soccer (MLS) remains a single-entity structure.

single-entity structure—A form of league governance in which teams are owned by the league and the players sign contracts with the league.

Labor–Management Relations

Five unique circumstances and conditions are related to the labor–management relationship in North American professional sport: baseball's antitrust exemption, collective bargaining, free agency, salary caps, and player draft. Some aspects are the opposite of common business practices and philosophies. But the participating parties consider such idiosyncrasies essential to preserving the financial stability of the professional sport product. In the following sections we will examine each element and explain its uniqueness and significance to professional sport.

Baseball's Antitrust Exemption

Perhaps the most exceptional condition in professional sport is Major League Baseball's exemption from the rules and regulations of the Sherman Antitrust Act. The Sherman Antitrust Act was created to prohibit companies from dominating their respective markets in interstate commercial activity, thus creating a monopoly in which consumers have only one product choice rather than several. Laws prohibit normal businesses from attempting to eliminate all competitors from the marketplace. For example, the federal government has scrutinized many corporate mergers in the telecommunications and airline industries to determine whether they result in decreased competition.

But as a result of the U.S. Supreme Court's ruling in the *Federal Base Ball Club of Baltimore, Inc. v. National League of Professional Base Ball Clubs* (1922), Major League Baseball was granted an exemption to antitrust law. In its decision, the court deemed that baseball was local in nature, did not involve the production of a tangible good, and thus was not subject to interstate commerce law. In effect, this ruling granted Major League Baseball the right to undertake strategies that would prevent the establishment of competitive leagues. This exemption gives professional baseball team owners significant leverage over the cities in which they operate. In some cases, owners have threatened to leave their host cities if new stadia are not built. Although Major League Baseball's exemption from antitrust regulations has been challenged on several occasions, the courts have not overturned the decision.

Learning Activity

Justice Oliver Wendell Holmes is responsible for the opinion of the court that granted an antitrust exemption to baseball (*Federal Base Ball Club of Baltimore, Inc. v. National League of Professional Base Ball Clubs*, 259 U.S. 200, 1922). Find the case in your local law library or on the Internet through LexisNexis and read the opinion. Write a two-page essay answering the following question: Should MLB continue to receive the antitrust exemption? Why or why not?

Collective Bargaining

Workers involved in interstate commerce, which includes all professional team sports (except Major League Baseball because of its antitrust exemption), are covered by the National Labor Relations Act (NLRA). The NLRA provides three basic rights that are at the center of labor relations policy in the United States: (1) the right to self-organization, to form, join, or assist labor organizations; (2) the right to bargain collectively through agents of one's own choosing; and (3) the right to engage in concerted activities for employees' mutual aid or protection (Staudohar, 1989). In professional team sports, the NLRA provides players the right to join a union, to have a basic player contract (establishing a minimum salary, benefits, and working conditions) negotiated collectively by union representatives, and to strike or conduct other activities that help

1930s

▶**1939**—Baseball Hall of Fame opens

1940s

▶**1941**—Ted Williams compiles .406 batting average

▶**1942**—Negro World Series resumes after 16-year break

▶**1945**—Maurice Richard breaks single-season record for goals, set by Joe Malone with 44 in 1918

▶**1946**—Basketball Assoc. of America (BAA), forerunner of NBA, forms

▶**1947**—Jackie Robinson becomes first African American MLB player

▶**1948**—NBL and BAA merge to form new league named NBA

▶**1947**—NASCAR established

achieve objectives. The term *collective bargaining* is used because all active league players are in the bargaining unit and thus form a collective unit (labor) for negotiating and bargaining with the owners (management). Teams join as a league in bargaining with the players union so that in each league the negotiated contract applies to all teams uniformly.

Greenberg (1993) suggested that common elements of a collective bargaining agreement (the agreed-upon settlement by all parties) might include the following:

- Specification of contract length
- Compensation (minimum salary), which also includes pensions and other fringe benefits
- Rules for use of labor—in professional sports, the number of games played in a week, starting times related to travel, and most important, free agency
- Individual job rights—seniority, time served, and possibly morals clauses related to conduct and drug testing
- Rights of union and management in the bargaining relationship—collecting union dues, providing for union security, and so on
- Methods for enforcing, interpreting, and administering the agreement—grievance procedures, arbitration, no-strike clauses, and so on
- Rules for agent certification
- Option clauses
- Injury protection and safety issues
- Economic benefits such as severance pay, travel expenses, meal allowances, and so on
- Discipline—suspensions, fines, dismissal, and so on

Free Agency

Free agency is the ability of players, after fulfilling an agreed-upon (through a collective bargaining agreement) number of years of service with a team, to sell their services to another team with limited or no compensation to the team losing the players. Thus the terms *free agent* and *free agency* have evolved to signify the relative freedom that all professional team sport players have to move from one team to another.

Professional team sport, however, still imposes significant restrictions on its labor. For example, players do not immediately become free agents. Instead, free agency is a negotiated item in the collective bargaining agreement of all professional team sport leagues. The collective bargaining agreement recognizes the investment that the team has incurred in developing the player, while also recognizing the fair market value of the player in the open market. Thus, the collective bargaining agreement provides free agency after the player has played an agreed-upon (by both labor and management) number of years.

Therefore, rights are granted to the team that initially drafts a player for a specified time. Following that specified period, players are free to seek employment from the highest bidder. Free agents may also be classified according to talent and years of service to a particular team. Based on such classifications, the team that signs a particular player might or might not be required to provide compensation to the team that loses the player. Again, this process differs from mainstream business practice. For example, a brand manager for Procter & Gamble is under no restriction to work for that company for three years before being allowed to take a job with Kraft.

The implementation of free agency in the mid-1970s had a profound effect on the economics of professional sport. After professional athletes gained the freedom to negotiate with the highest bidder, their salaries escalated astronomically. In 1976, when the players first earned the right to become free agents, the average salary in professional baseball was $46,000 USD. In 2005 the average salary in Major League Baseball was $2.63 million USD (Mullen, 2005). Similar salaries exist in the other men's major professional sport leagues (NHL, NFL, NBA). At the time of writing, average salaries for women's professional sport teams were much lower. See figure 5.1 for a graph depicting the salary growth in each of the four major North American professional sport leagues from 1993 to 2005. The heightened power of the players unions and increased salaries of players contributed to an increase in labor stoppages in the professional sport leagues. With player salaries continuing to rise, owners of professional sport teams are facing the challenge of generating sufficient revenue to match those increased costs. Such concerns have led owners to take an increasingly tough stance during collective bargaining negotiations. Because of management–labor salary disputes, work stoppages have become a frequent occurrence.

1950s

- **1950**—LPGA founded
- **1950**—NBA integrated
- **1953**—MLB Players Association forms
- **1954**—Roger Bannister becomes first to run mile under 4 minutes at Iffley Road track in Oxford
- **1955**—Canada's Sports Hall of Fame founded
- **1956**—Don Larsen pitches only no-hitter (and a perfect game) in postseason
- **1956**—NFL Players Union forms
- **1958**—Brooklyn Dodgers move to Los Angeles
- **1959**—American Football League forms, led by Lamar Hunt

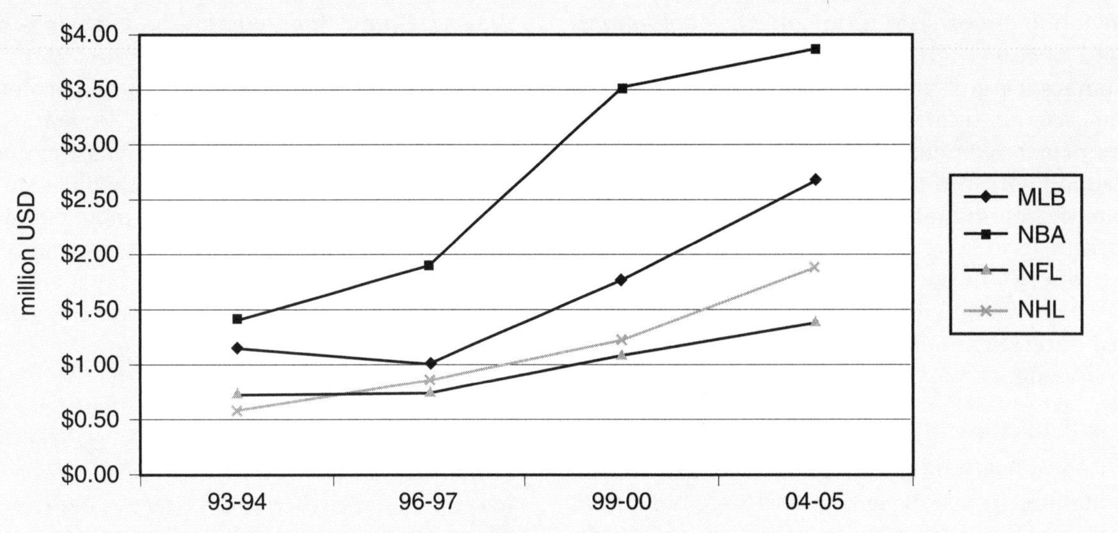

Figure 5.1 Salary growth in MLB, NBA, NFL, and NHL: 1993-2005.

Source: Based on data provided in the following articles: "Salary growth since 1993 in the big four team sports." (2000, January 31). *Street & Smith's SportsBusiness Journal*, p. 29; Mullen, L. (2005, May 30). "NFLPA looks at cutting agent fees." *Street & Smith's SportsBusiness Journal*, p. 4.

Salary Caps

With the onset of free agency in the 1970s, the professional sport industry allowed players to sign with the highest bidder. Consequently, the spending on player salaries increased greatly, particularly among teams with significant financial resources. In response, salary caps that set a ceiling on player payrolls were created to protect owners from one another. According to Gary Roberts, editor of *The Sports Lawyer*, the owners in every sport claim that the inherent need for every team to be successful on the field, coupled with the reality that half the teams will always lose, will inevitably fuel an upward escalation of salaries that will make profits impossible for many league members, especially those in smaller markets (Roberts, 1995). This is exactly what happened in Major League Baseball for a short period. Between 1995 and 1999, teams whose payrolls were in the top 25% of all MLB payrolls won all 158 postseason games (Rofe, 2000a). One way that the leagues, owners, and players have worked together to keep costs down is through the implementation of salary caps.

Salary caps are agreements collectively bargained between labor and management that establish a leaguewide team payroll threshold that cannot be exceeded. The salary cap is typically set using a percentage of league gross revenues as a starting point. Pioneered by the NBA in 1983 and implemented for the 1985-1986 season, the salary cap guaranteed that NBA players would receive 53% of all gross revenues. Since then, the NFL, Major League Soccer (MLS), and the National Hockey League (NHL) have all adopted salary cap structures. These agreements are designed to provide greater parity between teams in large cities (markets), such as the New York Knicks and Los Angeles Lakers, and small-market teams, such as the Portland Trailblazers and Milwaukee Bucks. A salary cap places a limit on the total compensation (salaries and bonuses) that a team can use for player salaries. All teams in the league must comply with the provisions of the salary cap. Salary caps are put into effect through the collective bargaining agreement, which also includes a minimum player salary.

> **parity**—Also known as competitive balance, refers to the notion that every team has a legitimate chance to win the championship based on the resources available.

To illustrate the salary cap and how it works, we will examine the salary cap structure of the NBA. In general terms, the salary cap is calculated, subject to certain adjustments, by multiplying projected basketball-related income (which generally includes all income received by teams as a result of basketball operations—ticket sales, sponsorship,

1950s

▶**1959**—Jacques Plante becomes first goalie to wear a mask regularly

1960s

▶**1960**—Pete Rozelle becomes NFL commissioner

▶**1960**—Gordie Howe becomes leading scorer in NHL history

▶**1960**—Montreal Canadiens defeat Toronto Maple Leafs to win fifth consecutive Stanley Cup

▶**1961**—Sport Broadcasting Act allows leagues to negotiate one television contract for all its teams

▶**1962**—Marvin Miller becomes first executive director of MLBPA

▶**1962**—Rod Laver achieves his first tennis Grand Slam; does the same in 1969 to become only person to do it twice television revenue, and so on) by 51%, subtracting player benefits, and then dividing the result by 30 (the number of teams in the league). The minimum team salary is then calculated by multiplying the salary cap by 75%. Under the NBA collective bargaining agreement established on June 21, 2005, the players were guaranteed to receive no less than 57% of basketball-related income in any given year.

basketball-related income—For the purposes of the NBA collective bargaining agreement, basketball-related income includes:

- Regular season and playoff gate receipts
- Broadcast rights
- Proceeds from exhibition games, team sponsorships and promotions, summer camps, non-NBA basketball tournaments, mascot and dance team appearances, beverage sale rights, and those received by NBA Properties, including international television, sponsorships, revenues from NBA Entertainment, the All-Star Game, the McDonald's Championship, and other NBA special events
- Novelty, program, and concession sales (at the arena and in team-identified stores within a 75-mile [121-kilometer] radius)
- Parking
- Arena club revenues
- 40% of proceeds from arena signage and luxury suites

The most notable exception to the salary cap is the qualifying veteran free agent exception, or as it is most commonly called, the Larry Bird rule. The Bird rule permits a team to re-sign its own free agent for any amount up to the maximum player salary if the player played for the team for some or all of each of the three previous seasons. This rule was implemented to make it more financially attractive for free agents to remain with their current teams, providing a stable team for the hometown fan base. An unintended consequence of the Bird rule was that teams began to exceed the salary cap with more regularity and to a much greater extent. Thus, the NBA created a luxury tax system (implemented in the 2002-03 season) that taxes teams that exceed the cap. The system permits teams to exceed the cap and sign free agents (their own and those of other teams) but places a higher cost on them through the tax. Although Major League Baseball does not currently have a salary cap, it too has a luxury tax for teams that exceed a set salary level. In 2004 teams exceeding payrolls of $120.5 million USD faced the luxury tax penalty (Zimbalist, 2004). Under the NBA–NBA Players Association collective bargaining agreement that runs through the 2010-2011 season, all teams will share in the distribution of luxury tax revenue regardless of whether they paid the tax.

Learning Activity

Disputes between labor and management in professional sport have sometimes resulted in work stoppages, either in the form of a strike (initiated by the players) or a lockout (initiated by the owners). In both cases, the players negotiate for better benefits, including a better pay scale, while the owners claim that they are losing money because the players' salaries are too high. Clearly, the sides must ultimately work together if professional sport is going to succeed. Why, then, have labor and management in nearly all the professional sports had such a long history of problems? Prepare a 10-minute speech highlighting your response. Also, in this speech, identify the argument that you think is right and explain why.

Player Draft

In accordance with the principles of league think, the player draft is designed to be an equitable system for distributing new talent among all league members. The draft provides each professional sport league with a mechanism for the teams with poor records to have an advantage over teams with winning records in acquiring talented new players. Through the draft, teams voluntarily agree to restrict competition for new talent. As a result, the team that drafts a player determines the player's destination and salary. Phenomena such as the player draft do not exist in other areas of the labor market. Imagine a scenario in which top sport management graduates were restricted as to whom they could work for and where they could work by an annual draft held by sport businesses throughout the country!

Collective bargaining agreements in men's basketball and men's football have sought to limit the number of rounds of the draft. This limitation results in fewer players being drafted and more players being free agents to sign with anyone who offers them a contract. The players unions would

1960s

- **1962**—In "Fog Bowl," Grey Cup game between Hamilton and Winnipeg halted because of severe fog; Winnipeg wins 28-27 the next day
- **1964**—CBS buys 80% of Yankees, becoming first media outlet to own pro team
- **1965**—NHL expands by adding new six-team division for 1967-68 season
- **1966**—Bobby Hull becomes first NHL player to score more than 50 goals in a season
- **1967**—American Basketball Assoc. (ABA) forms

prefer this to be the case for all players but recognizes the need for some type of equal and formal player distribution to maintain competitiveness among the members of the league.

A player draft exists in modified form in leagues that have single-entity structures. For example, in Major League Soccer, the league allocates the best players (called marquee players) among the teams as a means of maintaining competitive balance. After the marquee players have been allocated, the teams then draft from the remaining pool of players (*Fraser et al. v. Major League Soccer*, 2000).

Role of the Electronic Media

The electronic media—network television, cable television, radio, and the Internet—play a critical role in driving the popularity of professional sport and generating additional revenue for professional sport teams. Although radio was the first electronic medium to bring professional sport to the masses, television (both network and cable) has had a profound effect on the development of professional team sport over the past 50 years. As we move forward in the 21st century, new media sources such as satellite television and the Internet could be the next important horizons in broadening the reach of professional team sport and the enhancement of league revenue streams.

Importance of Television

No single factor has influenced the popularity of sport, the escalation in player salaries, free agency, and the growth and increase of corporate involvement in professional sport more than television. Television has helped elevate professional sport beyond competition and athleticism into the realm of entertainment.

ABC's *Monday Night Football*, which entered its 36th and final season in 2005 (sister company and cable operator ESPN took over *Monday Night Football* in 2006), was a pioneering effort to package professional sport as entertainment. This prime-time extravaganza sought to reach more than just traditional football fans by adding analysis, commentary, special guests, additional camera angles, video replays, graphics, and highlights to enhance the event and broaden its appeal to women and other nontraditional viewing groups (Roberts & Olson, 1995). Concurrent with the success of *Monday Night Football*, the ultimate television sport spectacle, the Super Bowl, was created. Born from the rivalry and merger of the National Football League and the American Football League, the Super Bowl has become one of the most successful televised events of all time, viewed by millions around the world.

Because of the success in packaging sport for entertainment, **hallmark events** such as the Super Bowl, baseball's World Series, all-star games, and the NBA Finals are now shown during prime time (8 to 11 p.m.). Additionally, these events are telecast in many other countries. The 2005 Super Bowl reached approximately 800 million viewers throughout the world (Zimbalist, 2005). On a somewhat smaller scale, all LPGA tournaments are hallmark events in the cities in which they are held. Tournaments attract not only local, regional, and national followers of the LPGA Tour but also worldwide audiences. For example, the LPGA planned to reach more than 200 million households worldwide with its tournaments in 2004 (Lee, 2004). According to information posted at www.medialifemagazine.com/News2005/jun05/june20/1_mon/news3monday.html, the goal of 200 million households in 2004 was achieved. Such hallmark events also can provide an identity as well as a source of tourism revenue for a city or region. Hallmark events affect the perception of a town or region through media coverage of the event, most notably television coverage. Further, hallmark events contribute economically through expenditures relating to lodging, local transportation, and tourism, such as entertainment and shopping (see chapter 7).

Learning Activity

ABC's *Monday Night Football* debuted in 1970.

- Investigate the NFL TV rights deals. Who negotiates the TV rights deals? How have TV rights affected the NFL?
- What significant legislation has affected the televising of sport events on TV? Why have TV rights played such a significant role in the sport industry?

hallmark events—Highly visible events that are attended by many people, watched by even more on television, and followed on the Internet.

On the other side of the coin, professional sports (and in this case men's football) need television for three reasons. First, as already discussed, the

1960s

- **1967**—North American Soccer league becomes first outdoor pro soccer league in US; folds in 1984
- **1967**—Super Bowl I—AFL v. NFL World Championship Game (Jan. 15)
- **1968**—NFL "Heidi" game—Raiders v. Jets (Nov. 17)
- **1968**—US Open Tennis Tournament
- **1968**—Montreal awarded MLB franchise; plays first home game against St. Louis Cardinals in Jarry Park on April 14, 1969
- **1969**—Grey Cup stolen in Dec. from the Ottawa Rough Riders offices and found in Toronto hotel locker room on Feb. 16, 1970

leagues and member teams receive significant revenue outlays from network and cable television agreements. Second, television enhances the enjoyment associated with watching professional sport events. Third, television helps increase the amount teams and leagues can charge for sponsorships because of the increased exposure that television provides. Consider the following factors in viewing a football game:

- Depending on proximity to the field in a large stadium, the action in a football game can be difficult to follow.
- Only a certain number of fans can attend the game in person.
- Football with its numerous formations and free substitution can be confusing. Television offers commentary and explanation, replays, isolations, and other variations of camera angles, all of which allow the viewer to understand and follow the game more effectively.
- Television provides an expansive (and increasingly international) audience, regardless of the weather.

Emerging Sources of Media Coverage

Imagine that you grew up in Chicago and now live on the East Coast. Because of where you grew up, you are an ardent follower of the Chicago professional sports teams (Bulls, Bears, Cubs, White Sox, Blackhawks, Fire, and Sky). Unless these teams make the playoffs, however, you are rarely able to follow your team through radio or cable television broadcasts. Thousands of North American fans face this dilemma. But solutions are becoming increasingly available to such fans. Most notably, satellite television and the Internet have greatly increased the access of sport fans to a full menu of sport events.

Satellite technology and satellite television providers such as DirecTV have worked with the leagues to create packages whereby the average sport fan can access any game during the season by either paying an up-front fee for season-long access or subscribing (paying a one-time fee) on a game-by-game basis. For example, in 2006, for $280 USD, owners of a satellite television system received NFL Sunday Ticket, which provided them access to all regular season games. Satellite radio providers such as XM and Sirius also allow displaced fans to follow their favorite teams on a regular basis for a monthly fee.

The Internet is affording fans increased access to games of interest. Currently, fans can access radio broadcasts of their favorite games, typically through league-run Web sites. For example, in the scenario described earlier, the Bears fan living on the East Coast could listen to every Bears game by tuning in through NFL.com. The Internet is also increasingly allowing people to watch games online. For example, those with high-speed connections can see almost any MLB game through streamed video. Increasingly, the major professional sport leagues are taking complete control of Internet rights and negotiating collectively on behalf of all member teams. This approach allows the leagues to increase the number of hits on, or visits to, their Web sites during the season. Table 5.2 depicts the average number of unique visitors that MLB, the NBA, the NFL, and the NHL received per month in 2004.

Learning Activity

Using the World Wide Web, locate schedules and determine how you can view or listen to the next game of the following teams:

- Los Angeles Sparks (WNBA)
- Denver Nuggets (NBA)
- Kane County Cougars (Minor League Baseball)
- Houston Texans (NFL)
- Hartford Wolfpack (Minor League Hockey)

REVENUE SOURCES FOR PROFESSIONAL SPORT TEAMS

Revenue sources for sport organizations will be discussed in chapter 12. We will discuss here some unique aspects of revenue generation in professional sport. Professional sport has three primary constituencies: management, labor, and the fans. Each has a unique perspective regarding revenue sources. Management regularly claims that teams are not making money or have a hard time making money because of the exorbitant salaries paid to the players. On the other hand, labor (the players) suggests that, although salaries have increased, teams have remained profitable and franchise values have increased dramatically (Zimbalist, 1992). In addition, players say that owners regularly

1970s

- **1970**—AFL and NFL merge
- **1970**—Monday Night Football launched (1970-2005 on ABC) on Sept. 21 with Browns v. Jets (Cleveland, OH)
- **1970**—Vancouver Canucks join NHL
- **1971**—Ferguson Jenkins wins Cy Young award; becomes first Canadian elected to Baseball Hall of Fame in 1991
- **1972**—Flood v. Kuhn reserve claus ruling
- **1972**—Bobby Orr of the Boston Bruins becomes first defenseman to win scoring title
- **1972**—First World Hockey Association (WHA) season
- **1975**—Baseball's reserve clause struck down; Dave McNally and Andy Messersmith become free agents

Table 5.2

Number of Unique Visitors in an Average Month to MLB, NBA, NFL, and NHL Web Sites

League	Number of visitors
MLB	6,454,000
NBA	4,241,000
NFL	9,438,000
NHL	1,400,000

Source: Based on data presented in Street & Smith's SportsBusiness Journal, *March 7, 2005, p. 23.*

underestimate their profits in the interest of keeping players' salaries low. Claims by the owners that the teams are not profitable and the players' skeptical reaction to such claims have led to collective bargaining disputes and work stoppages in the NBA, NFL, NHL, and MLB.

Fans often see both sides as greedy. They frequently suggest that escalating players' salaries have led owners to increase the price of tickets, concessions, and parking. Further, during work stoppages, fans are likely to become angry with both sides rather than side with one or the other in the dispute. Regardless of the point of view, professional teams are under constant pressure to generate revenue. Beyond what will be discussed in chapter 12, some unique aspects of revenue production exist in the areas of media contracts, gate receipts, licensing and merchandising revenues, and sponsorship.

Media Contracts

The details of the national media contracts for a variety of sport leagues are presented in table 5.3. When looking at this table, please note the increased influence and revenue provided by new technologies such as satellite television and radio. However, we must make two important distinctions with respect to media revenues in professional sport. First, the NBA, NHL, and MLB allow their member teams to negotiate local television contracts. In the case of MLB, this policy leads to great disparities in the incomes of its member teams. The NFL, under the notion of league think, does not allow local television deals, except for preseason games. Finally, the NHL does not distribute national television revenues equally; Canadian teams receive a smaller portion because they lack influence on US television markets.

local television contracts—Agreements made between professional teams and local television stations and regional sport networks. These agreements provide teams with additional media revenue beyond what they receive from the national television contract.

Second, toward the end of the 20th century and the beginning of the 21st century, media revenues began to level off after a period of rapid increase. This slowing of the growth rate occurred at least partially because of the large amount of sport programming now available. Given the growth and capabilities of both cable television and satellite television, the amount of sport programming available to the average viewer has increased dramatically. For example, 21,000 hours of sport programming was available from 13 national networks in 1994. By 2000 more than 87,000 hours of sport programming was available from 20 national networks (Brockinton, 2000). Given the proliferation of choices available to the average sport fan, the number of viewers tuning in to the telecasts of professional sport events has declined, making it more difficult for the leagues to negotiate lucrative television contracts.

Gate Receipts

As late as 1950, gate receipts and concessions accounted for more than 92% of the revenue of a typical professional team (Gorman & Calhoun, 1994). With the increasing importance of media revenues, however, professional teams have become less reliant on gate receipts, although gate receipts remain the major source of revenue for minor league professional sports. In addition, they are the most prevalent source of revenue for newer professional leagues such as MLS and the WNBA (Horovitz, 1996). The home team retains the majority of the gate receipts, but to varying degrees, depending on the league, a portion of the gate receipts are given to the league (to cover league operating expenses), and a portion of the proceeds may be given to the visiting team.

Teams can increase gate receipts by increasing attendance or increasing ticket prices. The ability

1970s

- **1976**—Darryl Sittler of the Toronto Maple Leafs sets single-game scoring record with six goals and four assists
- **1977**—Tomjanovich-Washington fight (Dec. 9)
- **1977**—In their first game, Toronto Blue Jays defeat Chicago White Sox 11-5 in Toronto
- **1978**—Edmonton Eskimos win first of five Grey Cups
- **1978**—Women's Professional Basketball League forms; disbands in 1981
- **1979**—NHL and WHA merge; Quebec, Winnipeg, Edmonton, and Hartford join NHL

Table 5.3

Media Contracts of Various Professional Sport Leagues

League	Network	Amount (USD)	Number of years	Expires
NFL	Fox	$4.3 billion	6	2011
	CBS	$3.7 billion	6	2011
	NBC	$3.6 billion	6	2011
	ESPN	$8.8 billion	8	2013
	DirecTV	$3.5 billion	6	2010
	Sirius Satellite Radio	$220 million	6	2010
MLB	Fox	$2.5 billion	6	2006
	ESPN	$851 million	6	2005
	XM Satellite Radio	$650 million	11	2015
NHL	NBC	Revenue sharing	2	2006
NBA	ABC, ESPN, Time Warner	$4.6 billion	6	2008
	DirecTV	Licensing fee for NBA TV; $5-$7 million annually	6	2008
NASCAR	NBC, Turner	$1.2 billion	6	2006
	Fox	$1.2 billion	6	2006

Adapted from data from J. Rofe, 2000b, "What new sponsorship can we sell?" Street & Smith's SportsBusiness Journal *(April 3): 24; L. Brockinton, 2001, "NBC/TNT adds 6 big Winston Cup race sponsors to NASCAR advertising roster,"* Street & Smith's SportsBusiness Journal *(May 28): 4; A. Bernstein, 2002a, "Increases in NBA's new TV deal tied to new net,"* Street & Smith's SportsBusiness Journal *(January 28): 1; J. Lombardo, 2002, "NBA will try to make switch to cable TV add up,"* Street & Smith's SportsBusiness Journal *(July 29): 19; A. Bernstein, 2002b, "DirecTV paying licensing fee for NBA TV, less upfront for League Pass,"* Street & Smith's SportsBusiness Journal *(November 25): 4; R. Adams, 2005, "Is MLB extending its reach or overreaching?"* Street & Smith's SportsBusiness Journal *(March 28): 21; A. Bernstein, 2005, "NFL restores NBC's clout,"* Street & Smith's SportsBusiness Journal *(April 25): 1.*

to increase attendance varies dramatically by both team and league. For example, during the 2004 season, the WNBA's Connecticut Sun filled 69.1% of their available seats. Meanwhile, the Charlotte Sting filled only 28.8% of their seats, and the Minnesota Lynx filled only 38.7% of their available seats (Callahan, 2005). Clearly, Minnesota and Charlotte had much more potential to increase attendance. Table 5.4 provides a sampling of attendance information from a variety of professional sport leagues. As evidenced by this table, the potential for attendance growth in MLB, MLS, and the WNBA is much greater than it is in the NFL and NBA. In addition, given the rapid escalation of ticket prices since the early 1980s, increasing the price of tickets may not be possible. For the 2004-05 NBA season, the average price of an NBA ticket was $45.28 USD, and the average price of an NFL ticket during the 2004 season was $54.75 USD (*TMR's Fan Cost Index: National Basketball Association: 2004-2005*, 2005; *TMR's Fan Cost Index: National Football League: 2004*, 2005). Considering the other costs associated with attending a professional sport event (parking, concessions, souvenirs, and so on—see chapter 12), a family can attend a major professional sport event only at great expense, further limiting the capacity of major professional sports teams to increase ticket prices.

1980s

- **1980**—Atlanta Flames move to Calgary under new owner Nelson Skalbania
- **1980**—Gretzky scores 164 points, breaking Phil Esposito's single-season record of 152 points
- **1980**—Gordie Howe retires from Hartford Whalers
- **1981**—MLB strike interrupts season; 713 games cancelled
- **1982**—Gilles Villeneuve killed during qualifying race for Belgian Grand Prix

Table 5.4

Attendance Information From Selected Major Professional Sport Leagues for 2004-2005

League	Average attendance	Percent of capacity	Number of teams at 90% of capacity or greater
NFL (2004)	68,428	97.4%	29 out of 32
NBA (2004-2005)	17,319	89.2%	15 out of 30
MLB (2004)	28,034	67.1%	6 out of 30
MLS (2004)	15,559	65.0%	0 out of 10
WNBA (2004)	8,360	48.4%	0 out of 13

Source: Derived from: Street & Smith's SportsBusiness Journal *issues of October 11, 2004 and November 1, 2004; Callahan (2005); and ESPN.com (2005); Rank by Capacity (2005).*

Licensing and Merchandising Revenues

Licensing revenues are generated when leagues and teams grant merchandise and apparel manufacturers the right to use their names and logos. In return for that right, the leagues and teams receive a royalty (i.e., a percentage of the selling price) for each item sold by the manufacturers. These agreements have been an increasingly lucrative source of revenue for professional teams. Licensing programs, administered by the league offices, distribute the revenue equally among the teams. Domestic licensing revenues, however, have begun to plateau as the market for such merchandise has become saturated. For example, from 1995 to 1999, retail sales of NFL licensed merchandise increased only slightly, from $2.8 billion to $3.0 billion USD ("On the Racks," 2000). This modest growth has continued into the 2000s as NFL licensed merchandise sales reached only $3.2 billion USD in 2004 (Sosnowski, 2005). The ability to continue to increase licensing revenues depends partly on the growth and demand for league-licensed video games and the demand for league-licensed products overseas.

Sponsorship

Consider for a moment the magnitude of these sponsorship agreements:

- Title sponsorships and LPGA partnerships can run as high as $3 to $4 million USD per year (Liberman, 2005).
- MLS and adidas agreed on a 10-year, $150-million USD sponsorship (Warfield, 2005).
- The WNBA entered into a three-year sponsorship deal with Proctor & Gamble that includes promotional rights for seven P&G brands—Secret, Head & Shoulders, Herbal Essences, Cascade, Swiffer, Cheer, and Joy (Cassady, 2003).
- MLB has sponsorship agreements with General Motors worth $50 million USD, with Bank of America worth $90 to $100 million USD, and with Taco Bell worth $25 million USD ("How We See It," 2005).

Most leagues and teams have tens if not hundreds of sponsorships in place. Clearly, sponsorship is a significant source of revenue for professional teams and sports leagues. One major benefit of a professional team sponsorship deal is visible corporate signage. The demand for signage locations visible to the television viewer has led sport marketers to seek new and innovative display techniques. Rotating signage (stationary signage around the playing area), LED signage (computer-generated signage typically found on the fascia above the lower bowl and below the upper bowl of an arena), and virtual signage during television broadcasts are devices used to increase revenues. Additionally, teams are helping to fund these facilities by selling naming rights. In exchange for a large sum of money, a team will agree to include the name of a corporation in the name of the facility. For example, the WNBA's Washington Mystics play in the MCI Center. To obtain these naming rights, MCI agreed to pay $44 million USD over 20 years ("Naming Rights Deals," 2001). Table 5.5 presents a sampling of naming rights deals in professional sport.

1980s

- **1984**—NBA salary cap instituted
- **1984**—Women's American Basketball Association, fall league founded by Bill Byrne
- **1985**—Pete Rose breaks Ty Cobb's career hits record
- **1985**—North American Soccer League folds
- **1986**—Nancy Lieberman becomes 1st woman to play in men's pro league, USBL's Springfield Fame
- **1986**—Bill Buckner boots ground ball in 1986 World Series Game 6, Red Sox v. Mets
- **1988**—Wayne Gretzky traded from Edmonton to Los Angeles Kings
- **1989**—Pete Rose banned from baseball

Table 5.5

Sampling of Naming Rights Deals for Professional Sport Arenas

Building	Company	Teams	Amount paid	Years of contract
Reliant Stadium	Reliant Energy	Houston Texans (NFL)	$300 million USD	30
FedEx Field	Federal Express	Washington Redskins (NFL)	$205 million USD	27
Phillips Arena	Phillips Electronics	Atlanta Hawks (NBA), Atlanta Thrashers (NHL)	$185 million USD	20
TD Banknorth Garden	TD Banknorth	Boston Celtics (NBA), Boston Bruins (NHL)	$120 million USD	20
Ameriquest Field	Ameriquest Mortgage	Texas Rangers (MLB)	$75 million USD	30
Comerica Park	Comerica Bank	Detroit Tigers (MLB)	$66 million USD	30
Verizon Wireless Arena	Verizon Wireless Inc.	Manchester (NH) Monarchs of the American Hockey League (AHL)	$11.4 million USD	15
Pizza Hut Park	Pizza Hut	FC Dallas (MLS)	$30 million USD	20
Fifth Third Field	Fifth Third Bank	Dayton Dragons of the Midwest League (A baseball)	$6.5 million USD	20
Louisville Slugger Field	Louisville Slugger	Louisville River Bats of the International League (AAA baseball)	$2 million USD	Indefinite
CanWest Global Park	CanWest Global Comm.	Winnipeg Goldeyes of the Northern League	$1.1 million CAD	25

Source: Data generated from information presented in Street & Smith's SportsBusiness Journal, *August 13, 2001; November 3, 2003; May 17, 2004; March 14, 2005; and June 20, 2005.*

Learning Activity

Start with the naming rights deals noted in table 5.5. Then do some research to identify other naming rights deals. As you look at the naming rights deals presented in table 5.5 and the additional naming rights agreements that you find, what seems to make certain naming rights sponsorships worth more than others? Are there differences between naming rights deals for brand new facilities versus those for existing facilities? Explain your answer.

FUTURE CHALLENGES FACING PROFESSIONAL SPORT

As professional team sports move to the future, they face a variety of challenges, many of which we have already discussed in this chapter. Although the challenges are too many to enumerate in this section, we have isolated four major challenges that professional teams face in the future: maintaining reasonable labor–management relations, developing new revenue streams, managing new technology, and dealing with globalization.

1990s

- **1991**—Liberty Basketball Association, a women's pro basketball league, plays one exhibition game before disbanding
- **1992**—Toronto Blue Jays become first non-US team to win World Series
- **1994**—Salary cap established in NBA and NFL
- **1994**—MLB World Series cancelled because of player strike
- **1994**—New York Rangers win Stanley Cup for first time in 54 years

• ***Maintaining labor–management harmony in the face of rising salaries.*** First, given the history of acrimony between the players and the owners (labor and management), and the history of work stoppages (strikes or lockouts), a continual challenge for professional sport will be ensuring that the games go on. As evidenced by the NHL lockout that cancelled the entire 2004-2005 season, accomplishing this goal is not always easy. Although typically a variety of issues create tension between labor and management, the most visible conflict is associated with the owners' desire to manage costs, mostly tied to player salaries. At the same time, the players are seeking their fair share of the ever-increasing revenues generated by teams and their owners. For this reason, labor disputes are likely to keep occurring.

• ***Developing new revenue streams.*** As shown in figure 5.1, salaries of professional athletes rose significantly between 1993 and 2005. To fund these continued increases, team owners are looking for new revenue streams or ways to enhance existing revenue streams. Technological advances, such as the ability to make advertisements appear as if they are on stadium walls during telecasts (virtual signage) and satellite television and radio, have already provided significant new revenues to leagues and teams. Such quests for revenue enhancement are likely to continue in the future, and technology will probably be involved. Think for a minute about how our world is shrinking because of technology. Professional sport crosses international barriers with increasing regularity. The Manchester United professional football (soccer to North Americans) team is so popular in Asia that they can operate merchandise stores there. The sales of professional sport products globally, whether through broadcasts or apparel, will continue to be a focus for professional sport organizations.

• ***Meeting the challenges created by technology.*** The same technologies that have helped spread the popularity of professional sport and increase revenues have also created the most competitive entertainment and leisure landscape ever. Twenty-five years ago people could access four or five television channels. Today they can access hundreds of channels and choose from a wide variety of entertainment without leaving their homes. Further, think about all the other leisure options that compete with the consumption of sporting events. Video games, movies, numerous outdoor activities, e-mail, instant messaging, and other activities occupy people's time as never before. Couple this with the fact that new sports and sporting genres such as action sports appear to be here to stay, and you can clearly see how professional teams have to compete for consumers' attention and money as never before. This competition is likely to continue in the future. Technology will also present challenges to the traditional business models employed by professional sport. For example, digital video recorders (DVRs) such as TiVo allow people to consume sporting events and shows at their leisure and more quickly because they can skip through commercials. This practice may significantly affect the broadcast advertising models that are currently in place. Similarly, the streaming of video content to handheld devices such as cell phones creates a new way for athletes, teams, and leagues to deliver broadcasts. The challenge is to determine what consumers want and how to provide it. Further, at the league level, the emergence of such new sources of revenue will challenge traditional league revenue-sharing concepts.

• ***Dealing with globalization.*** New technologies are also helping spread professional sport across international boundaries as never before. Thanks to technology, Japanese sport fans can watch Ichiro Suzuki play for MLB's Seattle Mariners and Chinese fans can watch Yao Ming play for the NBA's Houston Rockets. Similarly, new means to facilitate the spread of sport across international boundaries are emerging every day. During the 2005 NFL season, a regular season game was played in Mexico. Similarly, MLB has held season-opening games in other countries. These efforts have been geared toward increasing the global popularity of the sports as a means to generate more revenue. One obvious decision facing the leagues is whether to put a professional team outside North America. This issue raises several challenges, such as how to deal with cultural differences and account for exchange rates. At a league-specific level, NFL Europe, the NFL's development league that plays games in the spring and summer, has never been profitable. Its long-term viability is in question. These issues are just a few of the challenges facing professional sport in the future.

1990s

▶ **1995**—Cal Ripken broke Lou Gehrig's record of playing in 2,130 consecutive games (Sept. 6)

▶ **1995**—Patrick Roy traded from Montreal Canadiens to Colorado Avalanche

▶ **1996**—MLS established

▶ **1996**—American Basketball League (ABL) forms; disbands during 1998-99 season

▶ **1996**—Wayne Gretzky traded from Los Angeles Kings to St. Louis Blues; he then decides to play for New York Rangers, his third team in a year

▶ **1996**—Winnipeg Jets become Phoenix Coyotes

▶ **1997**—Women's Professional Fastpitch (WPF) begins play

sponsorship—"The acquisition of rights to affiliate or directly associate with a product or event for the purpose of deriving benefits related to that affiliation or association" (Mullin, Hardy, & Sutton, 2000, p. 254).

rotating signage—A form of sign placed on scoreboards and adjacent to playing surfaces that can rotate the advertisements shown.

LED (light-emitting diode) signage—Signage located in the arena bowl and primarily found on the fascia below the upper bowl. This signage is computer generated and has the capability to add sound, animation, and other visual effects to present a colorful, eye-catching message. LED signage is usually sold in 30-second increments with a predetermined number of rotations per game. In many arenas this type of signage has replaced traditional rotating signage.

virtual signage—Signage generated by digital technology and placed into a sport event telecast so that the sign appears to be part of the playing surface or adjacent to the playing surface.

naming rights—Rights granted to a corporation to have its name on a professional sport facility in exchange for payment. For example, United Airlines paid for the right to have the stadium where the Chicago Bulls and Blackhawks play called the United Center.

CAREER OPPORTUNITIES IN PROFESSIONAL SPORT

Like any business, a professional sport organization constantly attempts to upgrade its efficiency through its personnel. In searching for new employees, management often looks to sport management and administration programs, to other professional sport organizations, or to people working in the corporate sector who may have skills essential to the sport industry.

The organizational hierarchies of professional sport are far from uniform. Employment opportunities vary greatly in terms of titles and responsibilities not only from sport to sport but also from team to team within the same sport. Additionally, a variety of jobs are available at the league level. One area where many professional sport jobs exist is ticket sales. For an example of what a ticket sales representative for a professional sports franchise does on a day-to-day basis, see "A Day in the Life of Jeff Ianello."

Some professional sport organizations have a single owner (e.g., Bob Johnson owns the NBA's Charlotte Bobcats), and others may have several owners (e.g., John Henry, Larry Lucchino, and Tom Werner lead a group that owns the Boston Red Sox). Additionally, some owners own more than one professional team. For example, it is becoming common for owners of NFL teams to own teams in the Arena Football League. Still other teams may be corporately owned. For example, Comcast owns the Philadelphia Flyers and Philadelphia 76ers.

Particularly with the rise of the WNBA, owners increasingly own multiple teams across different sport leagues. NBA team owners control WNBA teams in the same market. In cases in which one owner or ownership group operates multiple teams, some personnel might fill positions in two or more organizations. That arrangement used to be common with the WNBA, which operates during the summer when NBA arenas are more available. Recently, however, WNBA teams have moved away from sharing staff with their NBA counterparts and have begun creating their own business staffs.

Common Categories of Work Responsibility

The types and existence of positions in professional sport organizations vary from team to team and sport to sport. For example, Major League Baseball teams, because of their extensive minor league systems, employ more people in player personnel than teams in the National Basketball Association or the National Football League do. In addition, minor league organizations (Minor League Baseball, the International Hockey League, and the East Coast Hockey League) typically employ fewer people than major league organizations (NFL, NBA, MLB, NHL) do. This section highlights positions that may be available within any professional sport organization. Major professional sport teams typically have several executives on board:

1990s

- **1997**—WNBA's first season
- **1997**—Dee Kanter and Violet Palmer become first females to officiate an NBA game (Oct. 31)
- **1997**—NHL expands by adding teams in Columbus, Atlanta, Nashville, and St. Paul
- **1997**—Canadian Larry Walker ends season with most home runs (49) and is named MVP; he wins batting title in 1999 with .375 average
- **1997**—Jacques Villeneuve wins Formula One world auto racing title
- **1998**—WPF changes name to Women's Pro Softball League (WPSL)

A DAY IN THE LIFE OF JEFF IANELLO

Toward the end of my senior year of college I had little idea where and how my career was going to begin. I had learned that breaking into the world of sport was going to be difficult, even with a degree from one of the top sport management programs in the country. Also, every job that I was being interviewed for was a sales position. (In retrospect, I realized that companies were seeking help in sales because they always need people who can produce revenue.) Through the interview process with a number of companies, both in and out of the sport world, I realized that to succeed, people must pursue what they are passionate about. For me it was sports. About this same time I was recommended for an entry-level ticket sales program with the NBA's Hornets, who were just moving from Charlotte to New Orleans. The job entailed selling season tickets as well as ticket packages and group sales. If not for the relationships and advice that my professors had given me, I would not have been recommended for the position, nor would I have accepted it.

My first month as an inside sales representative for the New Orleans Hornets was a rollercoaster ride. Sales consultants recommended by the NBA were sent in to train the staff of 10 new hires. Considering that I had minimal sales experience, the consultants' word was gospel to me. Even today, I use on a day-to-day basis all the basic principles that I learned then. After training we were thrust into the fire of making sales calls. We did most of this by phone, attempting to contact decision makers at businesses, with an occasional face-to-face appointment mixed in. Dealing with rejection, both soft and harsh, was new to me. I quickly learned that thick skin is vital to being successful in sales! A hitter in baseball is considered a superstar if he gets a hit 3 or 4 times out of 10 at bats. A salesperson who makes 1 sale out of roughly 100 dials will be that same superstar. I quickly identified two things that could give me a competitive advantage—my call volume (it seemed logical that more opportunities would produce more sales) and my technique (the more I worked at it, the better I would be on every call). These two factors paid off as I rose to the top of my inside sales class. After six months in New Orleans I accepted a job as a season ticket account executive on the senior staff with the Phoenix Suns.

I have been in Phoenix for about two and a half years. The basic principles that I learned in New Orleans and the tutelage that I received from my managers in Phoenix, who are regarded as among the best in the business, have led me to become one of the top producers on a senior level. With my knowledge and productivity, I hope to have the opportunity to manage my own inside sales staff in the near future.

I always feel refreshed when I go to work in the morning because my office is inside a sports arena! My workday begins at 7:30 a.m., because I have found that the best time to get busy work done is before and after hours. I also like to set a good example for our current inside sales staff about the importance of work ethic and time management. Early mornings and late afternoons are usually the best times to contact key decision makers at businesses, so I hit the phones promptly at 8:00. I try to make between 60 and 80 quality phone calls a day. The beauty of what I do is that the quality can always improve as my technique improves, so in this respect my job has no ceiling. Mixed in with these calls are usually a couple of face-to-face appointments in America West Arena. Face-to-face appointments usually lead to a greater conversion rate on sales, as well as a higher dollar amount. Thus, the way I see the sales process is call–appointment–sale. Mixed into my day are calls to current clients. My clients' happiness and overall feeling that I am accessible to them leads to a higher renewal rate as well as referrals. Both are key in an organization's overall sales numbers. During games I am responsible for setting up sales tables strategically around the arena. These tables attract single-game buyers who may be interested in becoming package or season ticket holders. Also, during games I make seat visits to current clients to check on their experience.

Why sales? What about it is so attractive to me that it is hard to imagine myself working in any other field? First, it provides a highly competitive, fast-paced environment in which productivity is rewarded. Literally every phone call or face-to-face appointment provides a unique challenge. Learning to deal with different personalities and becoming more adept at countering a wide variety of objections has helped me grow as a professional. Another benefit is that the harder I work and the better I become at my craft, the greater the financial reward. More specifically, the great thing about ticket sales is that it offers a path for career growth. Those who are successful can pursue opportunities in premium sales (suites leasing), sponsorship, and management.

The old saying goes "It is not what you know, but who you know." I would have to modify that way of thinking. Those with both the passion to succeed and the willingness to gain knowledge from those who are successful in the field will thrive. Find people who are successful in your field and ask questions about how they have succeeded. This knowledge is key in bettering your performance, and superior performance will ultimately lead to opportunities opening up.

1990s

1998—Mark McGwire hits 70 home runs and Sammy Sosa hits 66, both breaking Roger Maris' record of 61, set in 1961

1998—Sportvision debuts its 1st and Ten system, a yellow computer-generated line to aid TV viewers (Sept. 27)

1999—Toronto Maple Leafs play last game at Maple Leaf Gardens

1999—Wayne Gretzky retires after playing in NHL for 21 years

1999—NHL Canadian teams petition federal government for financial aid

2000s

2000—Fraser v. MLS—single-entity league structure challenged

2000—Maurice "Rocket" Richard dies (May 27)

- Chief executive or operating officer (CEO or COO)—Responsible for the day-to-day functioning of the entire organization, both on the field (performance) and off the field (revenue generation)
- Chief financial officer (CFO)—Responsible for the organization's accounting and financial planning
- Chief marketing officer (CMO)—Responsible for coordinating the marketing mix among communications, ticket sales, and corporate sponsorship and partnership sales
- General counsel—Responsible for overseeing all legal matters associated with the team including, but not limited to, player contracts, liability issues, and marketing contracts
- General manager—Typically responsible for acquiring, developing, trading, and releasing talent, as well as creating a development system for young players

Beyond these executive positions, jobs with professional sport teams typically fall into two categories:

1. Player personnel
2. Business

Player Personnel Positions

A variety of jobs focus on player personnel or putting the best possible team on the field or court. Descriptions of these jobs follow. Before you examine the individual jobs on this side of the professional sport organization, recognize the difficulty and competitiveness associated with these positions. Because many of the positions require intricate knowledge of the sport, being a former athlete, or even a former professional athlete, in the particular sport may be a prerequisite for success.

- ***Player personnel.*** This department is involved in identifying, evaluating, and developing potential and current players. In baseball, this department would also be involved in observing players assigned to the minor leagues. Typical jobs in this area include being a scout, in which researching potential draft picks and upcoming opponents are central responsibilities. The pinnacle position within the player personnel side of the organization is typically the general manager position. The general manager is the final decision maker on drafting and trading decisions.

- ***Medical, training, and team support.*** These people assume responsibility for the physical (and sometimes mental) preparation and readiness of the players. Responsibilities include medical care, treatment of injuries, rehabilitation, dental care, nutrition, strength training and conditioning, career counseling, and after-care programs.

- ***Coaching staff.*** This group concentrates on all activities occurring between the lines. In other words, they are primarily concerned with coaching, managing, and training the players on their rosters.

- ***Player education and relations.*** People in these positions are typically responsible for educating players on issues like financial management, substance abuse, nutrition, image management, and additional higher education. Other responsibilities may include working as a liaison between the team and players with respect to player appearances in the community.

- ***Video support staff.*** Responsibilities of the video support staff include producing and editing videos, purchasing and maintaining video hardware and software products, supervising and coordinating satellite feeds, and coordinating all broadcasting that originates at the home facility. The video support staff also is responsible for filming games and maintaining the team's library of game films and player evaluation videos.

- ***Equipment and clubhouse staff.*** These personnel maintain, clean, order, repair, distribute, inventory, ship, and pack all uniforms and equipment. They also negotiate with manufacturers and sales personnel for equipment and uniforms. They are responsible for determining the suitability of the product and making appropriate recommendations regarding purchasing. In addition, these personnel have security responsibility for the locker room both at home and on the road.

- ***Stadium and facility staff.*** This group is responsible for the maintenance, upkeep, and repair of the playing surface. They are also responsible for preparing the team's offices, locker rooms, training facilities, practice facilities, and playing fields. They must be familiar with artificial surfaces as well as natural grass playing surfaces. The stadium and facility staff members ensure that the playing surface is safe, and they work in inclement conditions to make the field playable. In terms of playing surfaces and related areas, these people are the liaisons between the venue management team and the professional franchise.

2000s

- **2000**—Patrick Roy wins 448th career game; owns career wins record
- **2001**—WPSL has season suspended
- **2001**—XFL plays its only season
- **2001**—Sept. 11 terrorist attacks in US
- **2002**—WPSL changes name to National Pro Fastpitch (NPF)
- **2002**—Yao Ming drafted #1 by Houston Rockets
- **2002-3**—NBA luxury tax system implemented
- **2004-5**—Steve Nash becomes first Canadian to win NBA MVP

CASE STUDY

The phone rang in Tonya Mertz's apartment. As a senior in the sport management program at Southeastern University, Tonya was hoping that this would be a return phone call about an internship. It was late April, and Tonya was hoping to start her career by interning with a professional basketball team for the summer.

"Hi, Tonya, this is Kristin Carter of the Raleigh Flyers [in the WNBA]. I'm calling to offer you an internship in our community relations department. As we discussed in the interview, your basic responsibilities will include assisting with our charitable efforts and events in the community. We want the people of the Raleigh–Durham area to know that the Flyers care about the community. Your background working in the community with your team at Southeastern is what convinced us that you were right for this internship. What do you think?"

"Ms. Carter, I am flattered and excited about your offer," said Tonya. "But I would like a little bit of time to think about it. Would it be possible to think about this over the weekend?"

"No problem, Tonya. We would love to have you on our staff this summer. I will look forward to hearing your response on Monday," concluded Carter.

Tonya hung up the phone thinking that the opportunity was interesting and well suited to her skills and experiences. As a four-year starter on the Southeastern basketball team, Tonya's career had just ended. Knowing that she was not quite good enough for the WNBA, Tonya had decided to parlay her passion for basketball into a career in professional basketball. This opportunity with the Flyers could provide the start she was looking for . . . until the phone rang again.

"Hello, Tonya. This is Paul Butterworth of the Topeka Trackers [a new team in the NBA's National Basketball Development League]. I'm calling to offer you an internship position in marketing. As you know, we are a new organization. So, although this is an internship, we are poised to integrate you into the workings of our ticket sales, corporate sales, and promotions efforts. I think you will be hard pressed to find an organization that will give you more responsibility as an intern."

Tonya was stunned, but she collected herself enough to say, "Wow, Mr. Butterworth, that sounds great. I am thrilled by your offer. But would you mind terribly if I took the weekend to think about it?"

"No problem, Tonya. I'll wait for your call on Monday." With that Butterworth hung up.

Tonya did not know what to do. She was stunned. Five minutes ago, she was all but headed for the Raleigh–Durham area. Now another company was offering her an internship. What should she do?

Based on what you learned in this chapter and what you can garner from outside research, consider the following questions:

1. What does Tonya need to consider before making a decision?
2. What are the advantages and disadvantages of each opportunity?
3. What is the potential for growth with each opportunity?

Business Positions

Unlike the player personnel side of the organization, the business side of the organization does not have any control over team performance issues. But people in these positions play an important role in the organization because they are responsible for generating revenue, marketing the product, developing a fan base, and working with the many customers of the organization.

- ***Ticket sales.*** One of two types of sales representatives within the organization, ticket sales people typically focus on selling season tickets, partial season tickets, and group tickets. They target not only individual ticket purchasers but also groups and corporations that can buy either a larger number of tickets or expensive season tickets. Ticket sales is a good first position in professional sport. Many openings are available in this area because teams must sell a large number of tickets to maximize team revenues.
- ***Corporate sales.*** In contrast to those who primarily sell individual tickets, corporate salespeople target corporations exclusively. Corporate salespeople may sell corporate sponsorships, luxury suites, or club seats.
- ***Game experience.*** Responsibilities for these positions focus on enhancing the experience of people who attend games. Specific tasks may include overseeing the music, video boards, and

2000s

- **2003**—Patrick Roy retires
- **2004**—Inaugural season of NPF
- **2005**—NHL cancels season (Feb. 16)
- **2005**—Manchester United bought by American Malcolm Glazer
- **2005**—Club Deportivo Chivas joins MLS
- **2006**—Effa Manley becomes first woman elected to Baseball Hall of Fame

THE ITALIAN BASKETBALL LEAGUE
The Oldest One in Europe
Giorgio Gandolfi, Italy

In Italy, soccer is the national sport and pastime. Basketball is the second most popular sport. This essay focuses on Italian men's professional basketball.

Lega A Organization and Revenues

The Lega (League) A, the First Division, is the oldest professional basketball league in Europe. Founded in 1970 in Milano, the headquarters was later moved to Bologna. The Lega A consists of 18 clubs. Commissioner Enrico Prandi administers the league. The title sponsor of the Lega A is TIM (an Italian cellular phone company), which contributes the equivalent of over $1 million USD. The Lega A also counts on SKY TV, the Murdoch pay-per-view channel that broadcasts three games per week, and other sponsors and technical partners, such as the sport clothing company Champion and the Japanese basketball manufacturer Molten.

Season Format

The Italian Championship is based on 32 regular-season home and away games per team, running from the end of September until the middle of May. The top 8 teams then compete in playoffs. The playoffs consist of best-of-five series, with the finals played in a span of nine days. The last two teams, the 17th and the 18th in the standings at the end of the regular season, go down to Lega Due (League Two), and the top two teams of Lega Due move up the following season to replace them.

Collateral Events

The Lega A organizes three collateral events. In the Supercup, which occurs during the week before the beginning of the season, the winner of the Italian Championship in the previous season plays the winner of the Final Eight (also called the Italian Cup). The All-Star Game, in which a selection of the best foreign players compete against the men's national team, is played in December. The Final Eight, a competition among the top eight teams in the standings at the end of first part of the season, is played at the end of February.

Budgets and Revenues

A team's revenues from the title sponsor, the ancillary sponsors, and the commercial partners cover approximately 60% of the budget. Revenues from ticket sales contribute about 20%. The owner of the team or the other members of the board often cover the rest of the budget.

Most teams have title sponsors, whose contributions vary from $250,000 USD to over $1,000,000 USD. Partners (i.e., minor sponsors) and technical sponsors (i.e., shoe and sport clothing companies) also support part of the budget. The team takes the name of the title sponsor, which also appears on the game jersey, along with the names of the partners and technical sponsors. Examples of title sponsors are Benetton Treviso (the clothing company), Armani Jeans Milano (of the famous fashion guru Giorgio Armani), Montepaschi Siena (the oldest bank in Italy), Lottomatica Rome (the lotto play), and Snaidero Udine (the kitchen manufacturer).

Attendance and Arenas

From the 2003-2004 season to the 2004-2005 season, attendance increased by 17.2%. In 2005 total attendance was over 1 million, with an average of over 3,600 per game. In Bologna, where the two Lega A teams—Fortitudo (2005 Italian Champion) and Virtus—play in two different arenas, all the games were sold out. The season-long sell-outs were attributable in part to the large number of season ticket holders—7,000 for Virtus and 5,000 for Fortitudo.

The largest arena, with 11,200 seats, is the Forumnet in Milano. Second largest is Palalottomatica in Rome (10,100 seats), followed by Bologna (the arena of the Virtus team) and Livorno with 8,000 seats each. The smallest arena is in Teramo, with 3,500 seats.

public address messaging during a game. Opportunities in this area have increased as stadia and arenas have become more sophisticated and as teams have increasingly focused on providing an entertaining experience both on and off the field, court, or ice.

- ***Advertising.*** Responsibilities in advertising include designing and writing advertising copy and identifying, securing, and placing advertisements in a variety of media. The sport organization may handle this responsibility in house or outsource it to an advertising agency that specializes in ad creation and placement.

- ***Promotions.*** Like the game experience area, this area offers increasing opportunity as organizations focus on providing an optimal experience to

Ramunas Siskauskas (left) and Uros Slokar (right), of Benetton, are unable to prevent Stefano Mancinelli, of Fortitudo Bologna, from dunking the ball. Exciting plays like this keep Italian fans coming back for more.
Courtesy of Italian Legabasket.

International Learning Activity

Construct a table in which you compare the Lega A with the NBA and the WNBA relative to organization and revenues, season format, collateral events, budget and revenues, attendance, and arenas.

spectators. Responsibilities in promotions typically include overseeing all promotional activity that occurs on the field of play or in the stands during the game.

- ***Web site management.*** As the importance of the Web site as a marketing communications tool has increased over the past 10 years, a need for people trained in Web site management has arisen. The responsibilities of the Web site manager include uploading and downloading content, working with the league office to ensure conformity to appearance standards, working with corporate sponsors to place advertisements, and creating content that will increase traffic to the site.
- ***Community relations.*** This department may be part of the public relations or marketing department. The community relations staff is responsible for creating and administering grassroots functions, such as clinics and other charitable events that the team sponsors. Staff members are also responsible for implementing leaguewide programs, such as the NBA Reads program.
- ***Media relations.*** This department is involved in assisting and working with the media by providing information necessary for game coverage and publicity. This job includes ensuring that the needs of the media are met at every sporting event. People in media relations positions are also responsible for all publications, such as media guides, yearbooks, and game programs.
- ***Database marketing coordinator.*** People in this area focus on building databases of information about the team's customers so the team can more effectively serve its customers and better meet their needs. This position may also include overseeing the marketing research efforts of the organization.

• ***Hospitality coordinators.*** Hospitality coordinators are responsible for the game-related needs of corporate clients, club seat holders, and luxury box owners. This responsibility would include coordinating the provision of food, beverages, and any other special needs, such as computer and Internet connections, required by corporate clients.

• ***Information technology (IT) staff.*** The computer support staff is responsible for information technology hardware and software used in all operations of the franchise. This department handles purchasing, network maintenance, and report generation.

• ***Ticketing.*** This department may or may not include the ticket sales staff. Ticketing personnel manage the ticket inventory. They are responsible for ticket distribution, printing, accounting, game-day box office sales, complimentary tickets, and the financial settlement for the visiting team.

> outsource—The process of hiring a company to perform an organizational function of the team or league. For example, professional teams often outsource their advertising to advertising agencies because of the expertise these agencies possess.

Securing Employment and Working in Professional Sport

Without question, an internship is essential to securing a position in professional sport. You should begin to construct an informational file on the teams and organizations with whom you would like to intern and gain employment. Increasingly, online sources such as teamworkonline.com, workinsports.com, and even monster.com can be helpful in identifying potential job opportunities in professional sports. Your information file should contain the names, phone numbers, and addresses of department heads within the organization. Supplement the file with information about the business activities of the franchise. Such information might include newspaper and journal articles, sales brochures, advertising examples, promotional schedules, and so on. Recognize that the business area of the team is most likely where you will be working. Accordingly, you should be prepared to make a difference in that aspect of the organization. Although the box score is often interesting, knowing who hit .300 or the name of the leading rusher won't necessarily help you gain employment. Besides knowing the business aspect of sport, you must understand the social role of sport and the place that it occupies as a cultural institution. Only by understanding both the sport business and the influence of sport on culture can you truly comprehend the role and scope of sport.

In addition to developing and maintaining the file, supplement your experience while still in school. Obtaining a worthwhile internship with a solid organization is sometimes as difficult as finding employment. Part-time employment and volunteer experience in sales, game management, or customer service and hospitality are valuable assets on your resume. You can obtain these experiences while still in school or during the summer. Whenever possible, meet and interview people in your chosen field. To interview effectively for internships and permanent positions, you should have a good understanding of the industry, its leaders, and its issues. You can develop this knowledge through studying secondary sources in your file, conducting personal interviews, and attending conferences and other presentations featuring industry leaders. Chapter 2 has some good ideas about informational interviewing.

Internship

Ideally, the internship should be a mutually beneficial relationship between you and the host organization. You should be able to develop a range of employment experience that translates into attractive job skills to a prospective employer. In exchange, the host organization should receive competent and reliable assistance in the performance of assigned tasks. Be aware that many professional sport organizations want interns to remain throughout the entire season, not just for a semester. This arrangement is beneficial for both parties. Organizations benefit because they do not have to recruit and train new people in the middle of the year. You benefit because you are able to be part of the entire cycle of franchise operations. Your goal as an intern should be to make yourself indispensable so that the team feels that they must hire you into a full-time position.

A Word of Advice

Although an internship is critical for employment in professional sport, successful completion of an internship does not guarantee you a job with that franchise. Other factors affect the ability of a professional sport franchise to offer part-time, contractual, or full-time employment to a deserving intern. These factors include employee turnover, the economic climate, organizational goals and objectives, and the hiring philosophy and financial stability of team ownership. Even so, as an intern working in professional sport you should strive to be an integral part of the organization and perform every assigned task to the best of your ability. In addition, you must demonstrate initiative.

Learning Activity

Identify the professional sport franchises, teams, or organizations in your area. Conduct an informational interview with a person who holds a position that interests you. What are the most attractive aspects of this job? What are the least attractive aspects?

JOB OPPORTUNITIES

Promotions Coordinator

The Worcester Warthogs Baseball Club has an entry-level position available in its promotions department. The promotions coordinator will be responsible for the implementation of all in-game promotions that occur at Warthogs' games. Responsibilities will include scheduling promotions, working with sponsors to implement promotions, and implementing the promotions during games. The successful candidate will be a college graduate with some game promotion experience.

Director of Ticket Sales

The Peoria Predators of the Indoor Football League are seeking a person to oversee the sales of individual, group, and luxury suite tickets. This person will also oversee a staff of four other salespeople. The ability to work under pressure and meet sales objectives is necessary. Additionally, the candidate should possess at least three years of ticket sales experience with a professional sport organization.

Media Relations Assistant

An individual with excellent writing skills is sought for a position with the Virginia Robins Basketball Team. This person will be primarily responsible for the media guide and writing press releases. Some coordination with media, particularly during games, will be required as well. Bachelor's degree in journalism or sport management preferred. Some media relations experience is a plus.

Chief Marketing Officer

The Minnesota Lakes of the United Hockey League is seeking a person to coordinate and oversee the entire marketing operations for this highly competitive professional hockey club. Responsibilities include overseeing ticket sales, corporate sales, advertising, promotions, media relations, broadcasting, and community relations. The successful candidate will have at least 10 years of experience with professional sport organizations in various capacities. A proven track record in generating revenue and increasing attendance is also important.

Video Coordinator

The Utah Coyotes Baseball Club seeks a person to coordinate the videotaping of Coyotes games, opponents' games, and the games of potential draftees. The person should be well versed in various digital technology systems. Knowledge of the Pinnacle Systems video system is preferred. One to two years of video experience with another professional team is preferred.

Web Site Manager

The El Paso Eels of the Women's Professional Basketball League is seeking a person to coordinate the design, layout, and content of its Web site. Because we are competing in a new league, this person will be responsible for overhauling the existing Web site and generating new ideas for attracting more visitors to the site. Additionally, the person will be responsible for coordinating the content with all other departments within the organization, including media relations, marketing, and broadcasting. Knowledge of HTML, Java, and additional Internet programming languages is important.

SUMMARY

Professional sport is a large part of the entertainment, social, political, economic, legal, and cultural fabric of North America. The continued growth of the media and related technology, particularly television, ensures that professional sport is prevalent and highly accessible throughout North America, regardless of the demographic characteristics of its audience. Because of this accessibility and prevalence, the importance of the roles that labor, management, and governance play often seem out of balance when compared with their roles in other forms of business. For the most part, reserve clauses, free agency, league think, and antitrust exemptions exist only in the context of professional sport. These concepts are not essential in conducting the traditional activities of mainstream business operations, but they appear to be essential to the survival of the business of professional sport. Further, these concepts will be crucial for new professional sport leagues, such as the WNBA, to understand if they are to be successful. By understanding the unique limitations and opportunities of professional sport as well as the revenue sources and the influence of the media, you will be able to appreciate the career challenges and possibilities in the field.

Review Questions

1. Briefly describe the historical evolution of major professional team sports.
2. Explain how the professional team sport product is different from a mainstream product.
3. What is league think and why is it such an important concept for professional sport leagues?
4. Why have television ratings for professional sport leagues been decreasing lately?
5. What are the five most prevalent revenue sources for a professional sport team?
6. Describe the two areas of opportunities within a professional sport organization.
7. Based on your reading, what areas do you think will offer a growing number of jobs?

CHAPTER 6

Sport Management and Marketing Agencies

Mark A. McDonald— University of Massachusetts at Amherst ▪
William A. Sutton—University of Central Florida, National Basketball Association

Learning Objectives

After studying this chapter, you will be able to do the following:

1. Explain the role, scope, and influence of sport management and marketing agencies as they relate to the business of sport.
2. Differentiate between the types of sport management and marketing agencies to determine which agencies are most appropriate for particular tasks and assignments.
3. Describe the evolution and growth of sport management and marketing agencies.
4. Define the functions performed by sport management and marketing agencies.
5. Appraise career opportunities associated with sport management and marketing agencies.

A sport management and marketing agency is a business that acts on behalf of a sport property. This sport property can be a person, a corporation, an event, a team, a place, or even a concept. The actions undertaken on behalf of the property may include one or more of the following: representation, negotiation, sales, licensing, marketing, or management. Given the scope of potential activities that encompass the arts, festivals, sport events, resorts, and music, a more appropriate term to describe these agencies is *sport and lifestyle management and marketing agencies*.

The first sport management and marketing agencies were formed primarily to represent athletes in contract negotiations and to seek endorsements and other revenue streams for these athletes. Honus Wagner of the Pittsburgh Pirates was the first professional athlete compensated for endorsing a product—Louisville Slugger baseball bats. The International Management Group (IMG), established in 1960 by Mark H. McCormack in Cleveland, Ohio, was the first agency dedicated to representing professional athletes. In their own words, "IMG literally 'invented' sports management and marketing more than three decades ago" (International Management Group, 2000). As time has passed and the marketplace and opportunities have changed, sport marketing agencies have become diverse in their scope and focus. Today, sport marketing agencies are involved not only in contract negotiations but also in numerous other functions.

The purpose of this chapter is to provide an overview of sport management and marketing agencies and to introduce career opportunities within this rapidly growing segment of the sport industry. We will shed light on these unique and multifaceted companies by classifying the many agencies into four categories: full service, general, specialty, and in-house. Examples of each type of agency will help delineate the similarities and differences. Finally, this chapter will give basic information about career opportunities and challenges.

FUNCTIONS OF SPORT MANAGEMENT AND MARKETING AGENCIES

Sport management and marketing agencies perform a vast scope of functions. As you read the following list, you can appreciate the degree of specialization necessary to discharge each duty. Although an agency might perform several or perhaps only one function, some agencies, such as IMG and Octagon, perform all of them.

- Client management and representation
- Client marketing and product endorsement
- Event creation and development
- Event management and marketing
- Property representation and licensing
- Television development and production
- Negotiation of media contracts
- Sponsorship solicitation and consulting
- Hospitality management services
- Grassroots and participatory programs
- Research and evaluation
- Financial planning and management

grassroots programs—Programs targeted to people at the primary level of involvement, usually participants rather than spectators.

• ***Client management and representation.*** Client management and representation involves representing a client in contract negotiations and making marketing decisions to manage the client's income potential and earnings. The contract negotiations could be between player and team, licensee and licensor, or product and endorser. The management function involves the agency in a strategic planning process for its client that may involve any of the following: financial planning, investment and management, marketing, personal appearances, and other forms of revenue production and management. For example, Philadelphia Eagles quarterback Donovan McNabb's agency, Chicago-based CSMG, not only negotiates McNabb's NFL player

SPORT MARKETING AS PART OF A COMMUNICATION STRATEGY

It's a Tuesday morning at First National Bank in River City, USA. At a staff meeting, Ms. Smith, the regional president, states that First National is continuing to lose customers to Second City Federal—a bank that seems to appeal to younger and more upscale clients. Ms. Smith feels that First National's attempts to communicate with its market through traditional outlets such as advertising and direct mail have become too routine, and consequently that customers are not receiving the message. "It is for that reason," says Ms. Smith, "that I have asked Sport Properties Ltd., an international sport marketing agency, to assist us in developing a new communication strategy through sports and special events to help us retain our current customer base and, we hope, attract new customers."

The room begins to buzz with questions: What is a sport marketing agency? What type of sport or special event is best associated with a bank? What services should we promote through the event? What exactly will the agency do?

At the same time, in the regional offices of Sport Properties Ltd., Mr. Brown, regional vice president, is meeting with his staff to discuss their upcoming presentation to First National Bank. "We have an excellent opportunity to use some of our existing properties, such as skiing, kayaking, and in-line skating, to create **grassroots programs** that appeal to younger, more upscale individuals in each of First National Bank's primary markets." At that point, Ms. Perez, senior project director, asks about developing a tie-in with participants from each grassroots venue competing in a championship or finals at the headquarters of First National in River City. "Excellent concept, Ms. Perez!" says Mr. Brown. "Perhaps we should also consider finding other sponsors who might want to become part of this opportunity with First National. Let's begin preparing our agenda."

▷**1921** Sports agents—Christy Walsh ghostwrites columns for Babe Ruth

▷**1960** IMG founded

▷**1994** Big 12 Conference forms

▷**2002** First Battle of Bighorn; Sergio Garcia defeats Tiger Woods contracts but also manages and advises McNabb on financial and marketing opportunities. In 2005, McNabb had endorsement deals with Campbell's Soup, Visa, Lincoln Financial, Pepsi, DirecTV, and Reebok (Mullen, 2005a).

- ***Client marketing and product endorsement.*** Similar to the management function, client marketing involves the agency in the promotion and total marketing of the client. For a professional athlete, this may involve securing endorsement opportunities, product endorsements, personal appearances, book contracts, movie and television roles, interviews and feature stories, video games, and so on. IMG, for example, secures Tiger Woods' endorsements for Nike and Buick.

- ***Event creation and development.*** The growth of sport television in the 1970s, the proliferation of sport networks in the 1990s, and the development of new satellite technology such as DirecTV have led to fiscally rewarding opportunities to create new sports and events (Crespo, 1995). Sports such as Arena Football and Major Indoor Lacrosse, have increased numbers of college football bowl games, and a wider array of collegiate basketball doubleheaders have emerged to capitalize on this opportunity. Some television entities such as ESPN, ESPNU, Fox Regional Sports Networks, and Turner Broadcasting have created events to fill their inventory. For example, ESPN created the Great Outdoor Games and the X Games for this purpose. Other events, such as the Quarterback Challenge, which was developed by former Buffalo Bills quarterback Jim Kelly through his agency Jim Kelly Enterprises, were created as primary revenue sources for their originators ("A New Era," 1995). SFX Sports has either created or partially owns events ranging from the American Celebrity Golf Championship to the Legg Mason Tennis Classic (Mullen, 2005c).

inventory—The assets a sport property has to sell. This term refers not only to quantity but also to characteristics and traits.

Learning Activity

Select a sport event or activity (property). What criteria would you use in selecting an agency to represent that sport property? Construct a marketing inventory of the characteristics of that activity or event that you believe have value and are marketable.

- ***Event management and marketing.*** Given the high cost of personnel (i.e., salaries and benefits), the need for specific expertise, the seasonality of some events, and the geographic scope of the activities, many sport organizations now hire outside agencies to manage and market their events. Event management and marketing agencies are involved in activities such as golf and tennis tournaments, festivals, bowl games, and other sport and lifestyle special events. Event management may involve any of the following areas: tournament operations, hospitality and entertainment, sponsorship and ticket sales, licensing and merchandising, television production, public relations, and promotion. PGI Inc., for example, is responsible for everything from lighting to buses for major sport events for clients such as Major League Baseball, the NFL, the NBA, and the PGA Tour. According to Wendy Nipper, director of marketing with PGI Inc., "As more and more people become involved in the sponsorship side of the sports industry, the leagues increasingly are outsourcing a lot of their event work" (Menninger, 2000). (For more information on outsourcing, see chapter 5.) Hyatt Hotels has a division called Regency Productions, an event management company that specializes in hospitality, event production, and setup (Conklin, 1994). The National Basketball Association contracts Regency Productions for the NBA Jam Session held during the NBA All-Star Weekend.

- ***Property representation and licensing.*** Sport management and marketing agencies often represent sport properties in promotional licensing and sponsor solicitation and procurement. A sport property can be defined as any sport or lifestyle entity that has name or event recognition, desirability, perceived value, and that chooses to offer itself for some type of affiliation. Examples of sport and lifestyle properties include the Rose Bowl, the Rock and Roll Hall of Fame, the San Antonio Spurs, Fenway Park, the Rolling Stones, the US Tennis Open, Ohio State University, NBC's Dew Action Tour, and the Taste of Cincinnati. The property can be a facility, an event, a team, an athletics program, a band or concert tour, and so on. Property representation can result in the sales of rights fees, promotional licensing opportunities, sponsorship sales, signage and advertising agreements, and endorsements.

solicitation—Requesting support or assistance on behalf of a sport property from a potential sponsor.

procurement—Successful solicitation of financial or other resources on behalf of the sport property.

• ***Television development and production***. The growth and proliferation of cable, satellite, and pay-per-view have created many opportunities and outlets for developing and producing programming for television. Host Communications, Creative Sports Marketing, and Raycom are agencies that have been involved in packaging rights fees for college football and basketball and the subsequent sales of these rights to networks such as CBS, NBC, ABC, ESPN, and TBS. The revenue potential of such television programming and the interest of the networks and their sponsors have had an effect on the traditional conference structure in collegiate sport, resulting in the emergence of 12-team conferences such as the Southeastern Conference and the Big 12 Conference (the former Big Eight plus Texas, Texas A&M, Texas Tech, and Baylor), which began play in 1996. For these new conferences, the result has been a lucrative market for a televised conference championship matching the winners of the two 6-team divisions. In 2004 the Big East Conference lost three football powerhouses—Boston College, the University of Miami (FL), and Virginia Tech—but added five schools well known for prowess in men's basketball—Louisville, Cincinnati, DePaul, Marquette, and South Florida. This conference reconfiguration led to an amended broadcasting contract with ESPN (Bernstein, 2005). Traditional sport management and marketing agencies have recognized the opportunities that television presents and have aggressively moved to capitalize on them. IMG has long had its own television production division, Trans World International (TWI), so that it could maximize the revenue derived from the properties

The explosive growth of television and video outlets has resulted in increased opportunities for those interested in working on both sides of the camera in the sport world. Here an NBC TV camera operator and several still photographers record the extreme sport action at Skateboard Vert.

Courtesy of Paul M. Pedersen.

that it represents. Beginning more than 25 years ago with a made-for-TV competition among athletes from various sports, *The Superstars*, IMG continues to add similar events such as the TELUS Skins Game featuring Jack Nicklaus, Vijay Singh, John Daly, and Stephen Ames and played from July 3 through 5, 2005. TWI currently accounts for more than a third of all IMG profits (Bernstein, 2000).

• ***Sponsorship solicitation and consulting.*** The most common functions of sport management and marketing agencies, regardless of the size or scope of the agency, are consulting about solicitation and securing corporate sponsorships. Corporations spent an estimated $7.2 billion USD on US sports in 2003 ("Sports Sponsorship Up," 2004). Although many properties (e.g., teams, sport events, festivals) handle these functions in-house, most seek outside assistance in determining value and identifying and obtaining appropriate sponsors. Similarly, corporations and other potential sponsors often employ a sport management and marketing agency to identify properties that may assist them in achieving their corporate goals and objectives. Atlanta-based Bevilaqua International, a specialist in Olympic sport marketing, describes itself as a marketing consulting firm that specializes in working with corporations and major special events to enhance, protect, and leverage the marketing investment. "We work closely with our clients to develop cost-effective and results-oriented programs directed at corporate objectives such as improving brand sales, elevating awareness and enhancing corporate image" (Bevilaqua International Inc., 1994). Some corporations, such as Gatorade, Coca-Cola, and Anheuser Busch, have in-house sport marketing departments that work directly with properties or through properties' agencies to reach an agreement. Other companies, most notably PepsiCo, use outside sport marketing agencies for representation and to create activation platforms to capitalize on those sponsorship and licensing agreements.

> leverage—To use a licensing agreement to create additional marketing opportunities that may or may not be directly related to the original agreement.

• ***Hospitality management services.*** A frequently overlooked function of a sport and marketing agency is that of creating, arranging, and managing hospitality management services. Hospitality management services include, but are not limited to, transportation and other logistical issues; menu and food service planning and management; corporate sponsor entertainment; special auxiliary event creation and management; housing; and awards, gifts, and recognition programs. As with most events and activities, the type and scope of these services vary greatly according to the event. In the United States, the Super Bowl is one of the most coveted destinations for hospitality packages in all of sport because of geographic location, appeal, and ticket demand. Corporations reward their best sales personnel, thank their highest volume customers, and court new clients through invitations to this megaevent. The Super Bowl offers a prestigious opportunity to achieve these objectives. Agencies such as Party Planners West arrange transportation; accommodations; meals; auxiliary events such as cruises, golf tournaments, and postevent parties; gifts; and spouse programs (Conrad, 1995). Party Planners West produces the NFL Experience, the fan interactive event in association with the Super Bowl that attracts more than 100,000 attendees annually (Menninger, 2000).

• ***Grassroots and participatory programs.*** Grassroots programs are designed to build a following for a product, service, or organization. Although they may not pay immediate benefits, they contribute to long-term growth by creating interest among potential consumers. Most grassroots programs are aimed at children and adolescents who may or may not be consumers of the product, service, or organization in question but who possess the qualities, abilities, and potential to become consumers in the future. Grassroots programs are often designed to involve participants in activities and events that are held at local sites, which could be thousands of miles or kilometers from the headquarters of the sponsoring organization. These local events and activities are often targeted to certain demographic groups and ethnic markets. For example, Major League Baseball's RBI Program targets inner-city youth and the NBA's Basketball Without Borders is a global program that targets youth.

• ***Research and evaluation.*** Evaluation and documentation are critical factors in determining the success of the various types of sport management and marketing programs discussed throughout this chapter. Reengineering, downsizing, value added, and postevent impact analysis are all concepts that stress a high degree of relevance and accountability, for both the sport organization and the agency or program delivering the services. Research, through mail surveys, on-site surveys, personal interviews, pre- and postevent impact analyses, focus groups, and other methods, is essential to assist the decision maker in justifying a program's cost, value, and relevance to the client.

reengineering—Changing an organization's structure or philosophy to capitalize on existing opportunities or changing business environments.

downsizing—Becoming a smaller organization by reducing personnel or departments. This action may result from a change in the organization's mission or direction.

value added—The perception, by the consumer, of added or augmented product or service benefits.

postevent impact analysis—Research conducted (usually by a third party but commissioned by a sponsor or the event itself) after the event ends to determine the effect that the event had on the sponsor's product (image, awareness, or sales) or on the community in general (economic growth through spending associated with the event).

Most corporations involved in sponsorship or licensing activities perform some type of assessment, either through an in-house department or by contracting with an agency that offers research and evaluation services. The research agency selected is typically not involved in the sponsorship and licensing sales process to ensure that it does not have a stake in the findings. Thus, the research agency selected should be a specialist in evaluating sponsorship and licensing programs or perhaps in sport consumer behavior. Joyce Julius and Associates, Performance Research, and Audience Analysts are examples of research or consulting companies that specialize in such services. The type of research most appropriate and the best agency to employ will vary with the scope and magnitude of the event, whether the event is televised, the types of sponsorship and licensing activities taking place at the event, the budget, and the commitment of the organization to undertake a sound research approach (see "*Sponsors Report* and the NTIV Analysis" below).

- ***Financial planning and management.*** This highly specialized service involves accountants, financial planners and advisors, and investment specialists and portfolio managers. Few sport management and marketing agencies specialize in this type of work. IMG offers this service as part of its client management services. Several of IMG's clients have benefited well enough from the investing and planning services that they have started their own companies or have entered limited partnerships with IMG to create new ventures. The success of both Arnold Palmer and Jack Nicklaus in creating their own companies and ventures is testament to the performance of IMG in discharging its fiscal planning duties. But except for IMG and a few others, sport management and marketing agencies usually contract these services out to reputable financial planners and accountants whose primary function is related not to sport but to fiscal management and planning.

TYPES OF SPORT MANAGEMENT AND MARKETING AGENCIES

More than 1,000 agencies identify themselves as sport management and marketing agencies (Lipsey, 2004). This figure does not include city or state sport commissions, corporations such as Anheuser Busch and MasterCard, or divisions of leagues such

SPONSORS REPORT AND THE NTIV ANALYSIS

The services provided by Joyce Julius and Associates are among the most used and reputable in the industry (Cortez, 1992). Through their primary products—*Sponsors Report* and the National Television Impression Value (NTIV) Analysis—Joyce Julius and Associates arguably set an industry standard. *Sponsors Report* is a publication that focuses on the value of the exposure received directly from national television broadcasts. Value is determined by calculating clear, in-focus exposure time during the broadcast. Exposure time is the amount of time given to logos, signage, displays, and audio mentions during the broadcast. Clear, in-focus exposures are the exposures that television viewers can readily see. These exposures are measured and converted to advertising costs per 30 seconds for the actual advertising costs on that specific broadcast. The NTIV Analysis determines the gross impressions from varied exposure sources and assigns a value to those impressions using a single factor that reflects the comparative cost of national television media purchases (Schreiber, 1994).

as NBA Properties, Inc. If these quasi-agencies were included, the figure would exceed 3,500.

These agencies vary in size, budget, type of clientele, and scope of services. Some agencies perform a variety of services for one client, whereas others work for many clients but perform only one function. For example, ARL Properties represents only pilots of the Unlimited Air Racing Series for licensing and merchandising opportunities. Examining the various types of agencies (full service, general, specialty, and in-house) will illustrate the variety and scope of sport and entertainment management and marketing agencies.

Full-Service Agencies

These agencies offer the full range of services, including client management, event creation, television development, sponsorship solicitation, hospitality services, research and evaluation, and financial planning, and they perform the functions in-house. Attorneys, accountants, sales personnel, public relations personnel, creative personnel, and management information services personnel are all contained in-house. Full-service agencies include the International Management Group (IMG), Octagon, and SFX Sports. An examination of IMG provides an excellent overview of a full-service agency.

IMG, the first completely dedicated sport marketing agency, was initially created to represent the interests of golfer Arnold Palmer. As times changed and marketing forces such as television gained greater influence on the sport scene, the roles of sport marketing agencies expanded to include managing not only athletes but other sport properties and events as well. IMG owes much of its early success to being visionary and recognizing the opportunities that the Golden Age of Sport Television (1958-1973) offered.

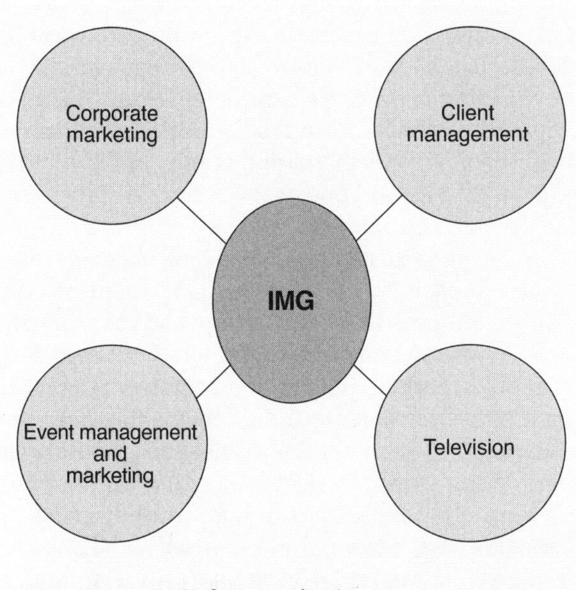

Figure 6.1 IMG's four core businesses.

Data from IMG Corporate Report 2001.

The diversity of IMG's endeavors reflects how successful the company has become. IMG represents athletes, performing artists, writers, fashion models, broadcasters, speakers, world-class events, corporations, resorts, and cultural institutions. IMG has evolved into the largest sport marketing agency in the world, with 70 offices in 30 countries (IMG, 2005). Mark McCormick, founder of IMG, died in 2003. In October 2004, buyout firm Forstmann Little & Co. bought IMG for $750 million (Mullen, 2005d). IMG has four core businesses: client management, event management and marketing, television, and corporate marketing (see figure 6.1). Examining each core business is essential in comprehending the entire scope and magnitude of IMG.

Client Management

IMG's client management activities encompass contract negotiation, personalized strategic planning, endorsement marketing, corporate and resort affiliation, personal appearances, broadcasting, publishing, licensing, and merchandising (IMG, 2000). Because of the size and scope of IMG, as well as the many relationships it has constructed during the past four decades, IMG may enjoy a major advantage over competitors in attracting clients and providing services. Here is a partial listing of IMG clients:

Andre Agassi (Tennis)
Annika Sorenstam (Golf)
Arnold Palmer (Golf)
Bob Costas (Broadcasting)
Brett Hull (Hockey)
Carlos Moya (Tennis)
Chris Webber (Basketball)
Jeff Gordon (Auto racing)
Lindsay Davenport (Tennis)
Itzhak Perlman (Music)
John Madden (Broadcasting)
Kristi Yamaguchi (Figure skating)
Lauren Hutton (Acting)
Pat Conroy (Author)
Julie Foudy (Soccer)
Serena Williams (Tennis)
Peyton Manning (Football)
Tiger Woods (Golf)
Tommy Moe (Skiing)
Tyra Banks (Modeling)
Venus Williams (Tennis)

One key to successful client management is to have satisfied, highly successful, and visible clients involved in a variety of sport and lifestyle activities. The success of the clients ensures successful negotiations and endorsements, and the visibility helps attract new clients, who create a cyclical effect. Given the labor unrest in professional sport in the new millennium, having a client base that ensures income, stability, and diverse sports or activities is extremely valuable.

Event Management and Marketing

IMG is involved in creating, developing, and managing sport and lifestyle activities and events. The company also manages licensing, sponsorship, and broadcast rights for many of the oldest and most distinguished events on the international sport and event calendar. These events include Wimbledon, the America's Cup, the Australian Open, World Championship of Women's Golf, Snowboarding World Championships, and Escape from Alcatraz Triathlon. Given the diverse nature and varying levels and demands of these properties, as well as the combination of rights, duties, and obligations associated with these events, the complexity of the event management and marketing industry becomes clear.

Television

The television appendage of IMG is Trans World International (TWI), the largest independent source

SCENARIO: Interning and Working for IMG

Ann Marie earned a BA degree in economics in 1987. After graduation, she worked for more than two years as a security analyst in New York. She then worked for two years in the product management department of a major commercial bank in the Boston area. After much reflection, she determined that her ultimate goal was to be involved with a sport-related product, so she enrolled in a sport management graduate program.

After completing her course work at the master's level, Ann Marie accepted a yearlong marketing internship with a college in Boston. Although her goal was to obtain a job within the product management department of a sport-oriented company, she viewed this internship as an excellent learning opportunity. In this capacity she was involved in several activities with revenue-producing sports, including corporate sponsorship sales, organization of promotional activities, and collateral production and distribution. Through this internship, she learned that college athletics was not a good fit with her career goals.

Ann Marie's internship coordinator alerted her to another internship possibility with IMG in Boston assisting with two major Boston-area events (a men's professional tennis event and a women's professional golf event). In this capacity, she worked on group ticket sales, print advertising placements, hotel room barters, and gathering ad copy from tournament sponsors. Although not offered full-time employment at the completion of these two tournaments, Ann Marie was given a small stipend to continue with IMG working out of its Chicago office on a women's professional tennis tournament. Fortunately, Ann Marie had sufficient financial resources to allow her to accept the position. Finally, after the initial internship and an extended internship with IMG in Boston and Chicago, the company offered Ann Marie a full-time position in its Boston office.

With IMG, Ann Marie has been involved with professional tennis, golf, and figure skating. Her workday has varied dramatically, depending on whether events are 6 to 12 months or 6 to 12 weeks away. Her largest responsibility involves sponsorship sales. When dealing with companies new to sport sponsorship, she has to educate executives on how sport sponsorship can assist an organization in accomplishing goals such as increased visibility, enhanced corporate image, differentiation of products from competition, and client entertainment. According to Ann Marie, selling takes place 365 days a year, but as an event draws near, other tasks become high priorities. Providing services to event sponsors is obviously a top priority. All sponsor needs must be addressed, and every sponsorship benefit available to the organization must be considered. Tickets, banners, program ads, television and radio spots, logo slicks, on-site promotions, merchandising booths, public address announcements, and on-site parties are all details that must be handled appropriately.

Besides sponsor relations, Ann Marie has many other event responsibilities, including placement of print advertising, group ticket sales, player and sponsor hotel accommodations, and ordering printed materials (e.g., credentials, parking passes, and scorecards). For golf events, she also serves as the tournament coordinator, which involves many responsibilities such as serving as event liaison among the LPGA, tournament volunteers, pro-am participants, and neighborhood residents. Ann Marie says, "Stating that I wear many hats during the weeks before and during an event is an understatement!"

and distributor of sport programs in the world. The main function of TWI is to provide programming to major television networks around the world and to represent the entities owning the rights to those events (Parascenzo, 1993). TWI is able to accomplish this in three ways:

1. By serving as an advisor and consultant to rights holders
2. By negotiating the sale of television rights
3. By creating and producing television series and events for sale or distribution

Overall, TWI packages, produces, and distributes more than 6,000 hours of original programming per year (IMG, 2005).

Corporate Marketing

In much the same way that IMG capitalized on the opportunities afforded by television in the 1960s, it recognized the clutter of television advertising in the 1980s and sought an effective strategy for assisting corporations in communicating to their target markets. IMG decided that the most effective way for corporations to communicate was through sport event and lifestyle marketing.

General Agencies

16W Marketing is a generalist type of agency that uses an integrated approach in the development of client programs. Led by partners Steve Rosner and Frank Vuono, 16W Marketing provides the following business components:

- Athlete, coach, and broadcaster marketing and representation: Full-service representation for all off-field and off-court business and marketing endeavors, including licensing, endorsements, broadcaster contract negotiation, media placement, promotions, speaking engagements, and personal appearances. The company specializes in seeking "ownership" for athletes and celebrities, gaining equity positions with affiliated companies to provide mutual incentives to grow.
- Team and venue services: Helps professional teams, universities, and organizing bodies and sport authorities in franchise acquisition, management, marketing, and integrated sponsorship sales, including venue entitlement, stadium development, merchandising (including e-commerce), concessions, and retail sales.
- Corporate consulting and property marketing: Comprehensive strategic planning and implementation of integrated marketing programs for consumer products or service corporations, online or e-commerce fulfillment companies, manufacturers, retailers, and sport and entertainment management organizations. Services include sponsorship negotiations and evaluation, value-added media packages, licensing, merchandising, and cross-promotional ties.
- Hospitality and event management: Services include turnkey hospitality, event management, promotion coordination, and television packaging for top sport and entertainment events (including the Super Bowl, Masters, US Open, and so on), sponsorship sales, and licensing and merchandising, both on-site and at retail.

venue—A facility or site where a special event or sport activity takes place.

turnkey—A program or product that the vendor executes without further involvement from the client.

Specialty Agencies

A specialty agency specializes in the types of services that it provides or in the scope of its clientele. For example, Velocity Sports & Entertainment, headquartered in Wilton, Connecticut, specializes in sponsorship and event marketing. According to Brian Phillips, vice president of US marketing, "What sets them apart is that they are a marketing agency that happens to specialize in sports and entertainment sponsorship, as opposed to a sports and entertainment agency that dabbles in marketing" (Lefton, 2003).

SportsMark Management Group Ltd. of Larkspur, California, is a specialty agency solely involved in event management and hospitality. SportsMark has entertained 27,000 guests at 50 Olympic hospitality events since the 1992 Winter Games in Albertville, France. Hospitality services include arranging hotel rooms and transportation, obtaining hard-to-get event tickets, and food and beverage services. Using the Olympic Games as a platform, the firm has been able to build strong business relationships with Fortune 500 corporations such as Xerox, Visa, General Motors, and AT&T (Schwartz, 2000).

In-House Agencies—Professional League Departments

In-house agencies are departments of companies (e.g., Anheuser Busch, MasterCard) that perform sport and lifestyle management and marketing

SPORT SPONSORSHIP IN AUSTRALIA

James Paterson, Australia

Whilst Australia and the USA are much the same size in land-mass area, their respective sponsorship marketplaces are vastly different. One of the key reasons for this phenomenon is the dramatic difference in populations. The USA has a population of close to 300 million people. In contrast, Australia's total population is fewer than 20 million people, only 7% of the USA's population. Consequently, professional sports in Australia cannot rely on the enormous revenues that the major US leagues receive from television contracts. For this reason, sponsorship has always been a vital source of revenue for Australian professional sports leagues, explaining why, for instance, sponsor branding appears on all team uniforms and even on the sporting fields themselves.

Because sport is a major part of the Australian way of life, corporations see it as the ideal vehicle to promote their products and services to a passionate fan base. Obviously, sponsorship is expensive, and over the past few years, sponsorship evaluation has become increasingly sophisticated. Corporate sponsors now have to be fully accountable to shareholders and stakeholders for their sponsorship investments, and management must put forward a strong business case for all such major expenditures. Gone are the days when sponsorship deals were done based on a CEO's favourite pastime. Sponsors must be able to access independent, quantifiable information about a given sponsorship.

Sponsorship evaluation is about more than counting how long a logo is on a TV screen and calculating some form of advertising equivalent value. Current evaluation systems being used today focus on measuring the effect of a sponsorship on the specific objectives that a client has for the investment. To capture these vital data from television sporting broadcasts, for example, supremely accurate automated image recognition software, based on the technology used for retina-scanning security systems, is used. The software instantly recognises a corporate logo, records how long that brand was on screen, and notes its size relative to the entire screen. Then, an independent, audited, audience measurement system (e.g., AC Nielsen) analyses the number of people who saw this logo. Subsequently, the effect that the logo would have had upon the average television viewer is examined.

Additional sponsorship evaluation data in which Australian clients are interested include the following:

- Due diligence—whether a sponsorship is worth considering
- Verification of sponsorship media coverage—either domestic or international
- Actual viewing or reading audiences delivered
- Demographic makeup of the audience—age, gender, socioeconomic details
- How one sporting property measures up against other sport sponsorship opportunities
- How best to brand a particular sporting property—from the best signage locations at a sporting venue to how best to maximise brand cut-through from an interview backdrop or sporting uniform
- How much brand exposure a corporate sponsor received and their "share of voice" amongst all other sponsors
- Worth of the brand coverage in dollar terms
- Whether a corporate client received all of its agreed benefits
- How improvements can be made to maximise future sponsorship performance
- Naming rights cut-through and effectiveness broken down by individual journalist or broadcaster
- Effectiveness of a sponsor's public relations and media relations strategies
- Effect of sponsorship on key targeted consumers
- Identification of the most effective source of sponsorship awareness for consumers
- Whether the sponsorship altered consumer loyalties or perceptions about the sponsoring brand
- Whether employees of the corporate sponsor support and understand the sponsorship
- Effectiveness of hospitality programmes and corporate entertaining
- Increased sales of the brand being promoted through the sponsorship.

functions on behalf of the products and divisions of the parent company. In-house agencies have only one client—themselves—and function as gatekeepers in reviewing opportunities presented to them by other entities. Besides performing this gatekeeping function, in-house agencies work with other units of the corporation, such as brand or product managers, advertising departments, public relations departments, and community affairs departments, to create or implement sport

Members of the Australian Wallabies (the Australian national rugby union team) pose on the steps of a Qantas airliner during a 2004 press conference announcing Qantas as the new naming rights sponsor of the team.

International Learning Activity

Compare and contrast sponsorship in the National Basketball League in Australia (NBL) with the NBA and WNBA in the USA. How do the respective leagues and corporate sponsors address concerns such as player drain to other countries, players' conduct on and off the court, and media coverage?

and lifestyle programming useful in achieving corporate objectives.

gatekeepers—Individuals or groups responsible for controlling the flow of proposals or solicitations to the decision maker.

Professional league departments are one example of in-house agencies. Each professional sport league and most sport organizations have departments that focus their marketing and promotional efforts on the entire league or unit. For example, NBA Attractions and Entertainment, an NBA division, markets and promotes the NBA as a holistic product through special events and activities such as NBA Jam Session, the NBA draft, and international tours and activities. NBA Attractions and Entertainment personnel work with the marketing departments of individual teams to promote the growth and development of the league itself. In many cases, these departments, along with their respective corporate partnership divisions, are charged with creating and implementing the activation programs that corporate partners have purchased as part of their sponsorship or licensing agreements. To do so, these personnel must understand the uniqueness and complexities of each team's market and must be prepared to assist teams in maintaining their identity while promoting the image of the whole league.

Learning Activity

Contact a sport management and marketing agency in your area. If there are no sport management and marketing agencies in your area, contact local advertising or public relations firms to determine if they have an appropriate client in the sport and lifestyle marketing area. Arrange an informational interview with someone in the agency who can provide you with an opportunity to learn more about the agency. In conjunction with your faculty advisor, structure a list of questions to ask during your informational interview. If feasible, attend a grassroots program or event managed or marketed by the agency. Observe signage, promotional activities, and agency employees during the activities. Write a critique based on your observations.

SPORT MANAGEMENT AND MARKETING AGENCIES CAREERS AND CHALLENGES

The following section provides an overview of careers in sport management and marketing agencies and some of the challenges currently facing these agencies. Careers in this segment of the sport industry are diverse, requiring a wide range of skills and abilities. Furthermore, mergers and acquisitions and labor unrest in professional sport leagues have created added levels of uncertainty for people working in agencies.

Careers

Careers in sport and lifestyle event management and marketing are challenging and varied. Many sport marketing agencies do not hire entry-level personnel. Instead, they bring in experienced people from other industry segments who have a network in place that they can use to generate new clients. A critical consideration in the hiring process, particularly in smaller agencies, is an assessment of a candidate's ability to get along, communicate, and be productive in a working environment with few staff members who must interact daily. In these smaller agencies, staff members must be compatible because they must act as a team. The ability of a team to work together harmoniously is often called "chemistry."

In terms of educational background, a business degree with a marketing background is preferable. A sport management degree, with several electives in business, is also desirable. An advanced degree in business, law, or sport management is an advantage for the applicant.

Clearly, the sport management and marketing agency segment of the sport economy is diverse and contains both generalists and specialists. Although the personnel in larger sport management and marketing agencies are more likely to function as specialists, those employed in smaller agencies must have a variety of skills and knowledge to perform their duties effectively. Skills essential to working in sport marketing and management agencies can be classified as organizational, technical, and people. Essential skills under each classification are provided in figure 6.2.

Challenges Facing Sport Management and Marketing Agencies

Although the sport management and marketing agency segment of the sport industry is growing in number of firms and job opportunities, agencies still face several difficult challenges in the years ahead. These challenges are similar to those encountered by advertising agencies, public relations firms, and similar enterprises. We can categorize them as follows.

- ***In-house versus outsourcing***. After benefiting from high-level performance by a sport management and marketing agency for several years, a client may believe that he or she knows the functions that the agency performs and decide to dismiss the agency to bring that function in-house. The agency then faces a challenge because it might have to cut personnel and budgets because of losing the account. The agency also may have lost a key staff member to the client, who has hired that person for his or her expertise and familiarity with the organization. This practice is becoming more prevalent in professional sport leagues, such as the NBA and NHL, and in collegiate athletics departments because of the need to maximize revenues. By bringing sponsorship, licensing, and broadcasting in-house instead of outsourcing them to agencies or hiring an outside agency to perform functions on their behalf, organizations feel that they will have more control and generate more income while cutting expenses (agency fees).

- ***Conflicts of interest***. With the growth of full-service agencies, the potential for conflicts of interest has increased. Firms such as IMG represent the interests of leagues, teams, athletes, events, and corporate sponsors. The interests of these parties occasionally come into conflict. For example, an agency may be under contract with

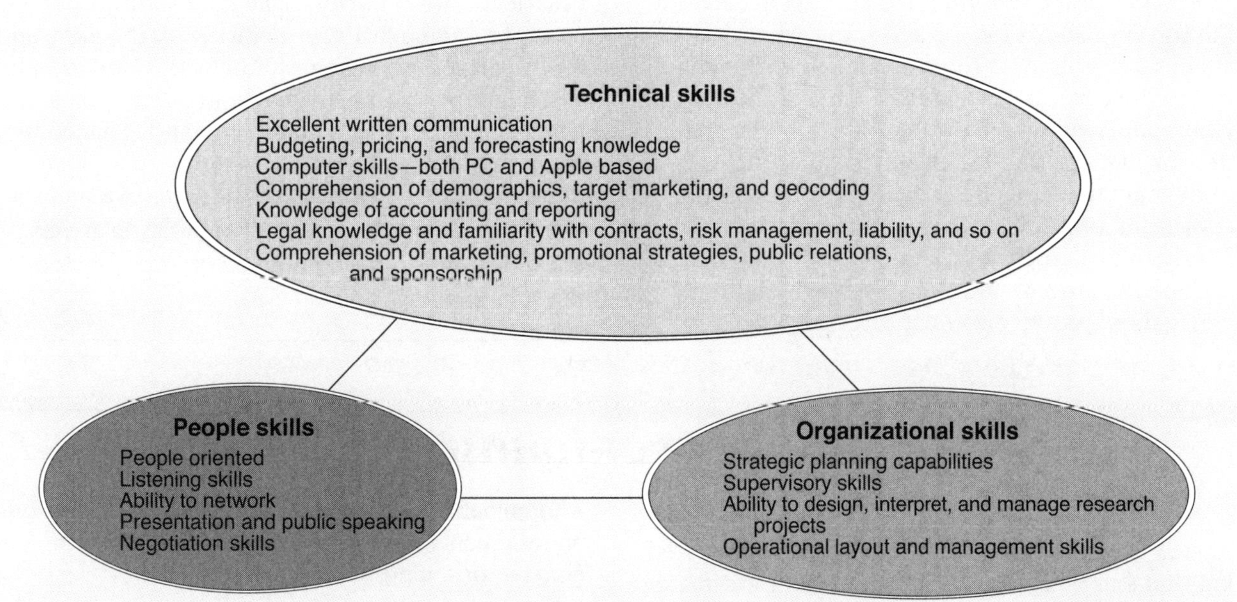

Figure 6.2 Organizational, technical, and people skills essential for sport management and marketing agency personnel.

Learning Activity

Using the scenario outlined in the previous learning activity, interview an employee of a sport management and marketing agency to determine the steps that he or she took in developing a career. What is the person's educational background? Did he or she do an internship? What is the scope of the person's duties on a day-to-day basis? Does the company offer internships or part-time employment? What does the company look for in an entry-level person?

both a free-agent basketball player and several NBA teams, resulting in a potential conflict of interest. Additionally, as noted earlier in this chapter, agencies create and own events in which their athletes participate. Given the charge to maximize profits on agency-owned events, will the agency pay fair market value for the participation of athletes under its representation?

- ***Mergers and acquisitions***. Agencies have traditionally grown organically in size and scope, but the current trend is toward growth through aggressive mergers and acquisitions. Two firms that have used this growth strategy are SFX Sports and Octagon. As a division of advertising conglomerate Interpublic Group, Octagon expanded rapidly in the late 1990s by acquiring firms such as Advantage International; Flammini Group, an Italian motor sports producer; CSI, a large UK-based television rights and production firm; and Koch Tavares, a Brazilian sports agency. In 2005 Octagon acquired IMS Sports, an agency that represents action sports athletes, gaining access to 30 new clients (Mullen, 2005b). The acquisitions strategy allows agencies to reach critical mass quickly and provide a full range of services to clients. A downside of this strategy is the challenge of assimilating new parts into the overall culture of the agency.
- ***Labor unrest***. In 2004-2005, labor strife in the National Hockey League created a situation in which sponsors and product manufacturers, two large revenue sources for agencies, became reluctant to commit advertising dollars and resources to support broadcasts, special events, campaigns, and endorsements to sports and players that could be on strike and thus out of the public's eye and interest. The NHL lockout, for example, resulted in cancellation of the full hockey season, putting strain on all involved stakeholders, including agencies. Some enterprising teams, such as the Florida Panthers, have retained more than 75% of their sponsorship dollars by pulling more events into their arenas. The Panthers have even added new sponsors—Harley Davidson, Norwegian Cruise Lines, and Metro PCS ("Damage Control," 2005). Agencies must be prepared to develop contingency plans and show that these efforts would be effective if implemented. Also, agencies may want to be prepared to help their clients become more diverse in their spending, thus averting dependence on one product or person.

• ***Legislation and judicial review.*** In 1995 the Clinton administration worked with various federal agencies to eliminate tobacco and alcohol signage from sport stadia and arenas. This signage was commonplace in most professional athletics facilities throughout the United States, so agencies had to develop new ways to provide exposure in these sports for their clients. They must also consider alternatives if such restrictions are broadened to include the auto racing industry, in which tobacco and alcohol producers constitute a significant portion (if not the majority) of all sponsorship, entitlement, and signage at the facilities, on the cars, and on the drivers themselves. Might this situation be extended to beach volleyball and other sports that have significant ties with alcohol and tobacco?

entitlement—Associating the name of a sponsor with the name of an event or facility in exchange for cash or other considerations (e.g., the Mobil Cotton Bowl).

JOB OPPORTUNITIES

Event Manager

Agency is looking for a well-qualified and experienced individual to be in charge of operational elements of a major professional golf tournament. Duties include logistics, designing and managing all corporate hospitality venues, planning and scheduling special events for sponsors and guests, scheduling and overseeing preevent activities such as the Longest Drive competition and the Celebrity Pro-Am tournament.

Sponsorship Sales

West Coast agency is looking for experienced sales personnel to become members of a dynamic team-oriented sport marketing company. Client list includes several professional sport franchises, NASCAR, and professional golf. Successful candidates will have previous experience in sponsorship of media sales. Experience with Fortune 500 companies a plus.

Tournament Director

Aggressive East Coast sport marketing company is looking for an enthusiastic, outgoing person with a strong tennis background to manage premier tennis events in Florida, Puerto Rico, and New York. Responsible for securing players, recruiting and training volunteers, scheduling officials, and working with broadcast and cable networks to ensure player availability. Fluency in Spanish, French, or German essential.

Agent

ProPlus, a 10-year-old firm specializing in representing and serving the needs of professional athletes, is searching for two new associates to join our team. Successful candidates will have advanced degrees in law, marketing, finance, or a combination thereof. Duties will include a combination of the following: contract negotiations, endorsements, financial management, appearances, and general consulting.

Product Placement

Large athletic footwear and apparel manufacturing company is seeking an individual to work with its agency of record to secure placement of athletic footwear and apparel products in major motion picture and television programming. Individual should have a background in marketing or communications. Significant travel involved. Individual should have excellent communication skills and familiarity with television and motion picture personalities and product use.

Market Research

Southwest sport marketing agency is looking for a person with a background in marketing research to provide documentation to clients regarding the impact of sport and special events on product preference and use. Candidate should have an advanced degree and training in both qualitative and quantitative research methods.

Sales Agent

NBA team searching for an individual to become part of an in-house agency to generate auxiliary income not directly related to the NBA franchise but using the assets of the franchise. Duties may include developing special events such as camps and clinics and acquiring and marketing minor league franchises. Looking for experienced sales personnel—previous pro sport experience not essential but a plus. Looking for people who can think "outside the box."

SUMMARY

A sport management and marketing agency is a business that acts on behalf of a sport property. Although these agencies initially represented athletes, they have evolved to serve myriad functions, such as representation, negotiation, sales, licensing, marketing, and management. More than 1,000 companies are classified as sport management and marketing agencies. If quasi-agencies such as city and state sport commissions, divisions of leagues, and corporations such as Gatorade are included, the number of marketing and management firms exceeds 3,500. We can classify these agencies into the following four categories:

1. Full-service agencies (e.g., the International Management Group)—Provide a full range of services performed by in-house personnel
2. General agencies (e.g., 16W Marketing)—Provide a variety of services to clients but are not involved in all potential agency functions
3. Specialty agencies (e.g., Bevilaqua International)—Specialize in the type of services that they provide or in the scope of clientele that they serve
4. In-house agencies—Departments of existing companies (e.g., Gatorade, NBA Attractions and Entertainment) that perform many sport marketing functions on behalf of the products or divisions of the parent company

Personnel at larger sport marketing and management agencies tend to function as specialists, whereas those in smaller agencies need to have a greater variety of skills and knowledge. Degrees in business and sport management are preferred, with a background in marketing essential. Careers in sport and lifestyle management and marketing agencies are challenging and varied. Sport management and marketing agencies face several challenges in the coming years—in-house versus outsourcing; labor unrest; conflicts of interest, mergers and acquisitions; and legislative and judicial review.

Review Questions

1. List and briefly describe the functions performed by sport management and marketing agencies.
2. Why is research and evaluation a crucial role performed by agencies?
3. How are specialty agencies different from full-service agencies?
4. What are some of the benefits of bringing functions such as sponsorship in-house instead of outsourcing to agencies?
5. Founded in 1960, IMG benefited from being the first and best known sport management and marketing agency. Which events reviewed in this chapter have affected the competitive situation faced by IMG?

Sport Tourism

Heather Gibson—University of Florida

Learning Objectives

After studying this chapter, you will be able to do the following:

1. Explain tourism and the tourism industry.
2. Describe the intersection between sport and tourism.
3. Distinguish among the three types of sport tourism: active, event, and nostalgia.
4. Discuss the sociocultural, economic, and environmental effects of sport tourism.

Since the mid-1990s, sport-related travel has received more attention as a topic for study from both academics and the sport and tourism industries. The Travel Industry Association of America (TIA), one of the foremost research agencies for tourism in the United States, conducted its first study specifically aimed at sport-related travel in 1999 (Travel Industry Association of America [TIA], 1999). TIA estimated that between 1994 and 1999, 75.3 million US adults traveled to take part in an organized sport event either as spectators or as participants. Moreover, two of the world's most influential agencies for sport and tourism, the International Olympic Committee (IOC) and the United Nations World Tourism Organization (UNWTO, known as the World Tourism Organization, or the WTO, before November 2005) reaffirmed their commitment to sport tourism on World Tourism Day, September 27, 2004. The cooperation between the IOC and the UNWTO began in 1999 and was the impetus for the first world conference on sport and tourism, held in Barcelona, Spain, in 2001. By affirming their cooperation in 2004, they recognized the mutually beneficial relationship that sport and tourism can have as a tool for sustainable economic growth.

Sport-related travel stretches back over the centuries. The Greeks traveled to take part in the ancient Greek Games from as early as 900 BCE, and the Romans regularly staged immensely popular sport competitions that drew large crowds of spectators (Coakley, 2004). In recent years, the term *sport tourism* has become more widely used to describe this type of tourism, and it has gradually become a specialized sector of the sport and tourism industries. Sport tourism as defined today encompasses three main types of travel and sport participation:

- Active sport tourism, a trip in which the tourist takes part in a sport such as golf
- Event sport tourism, a trip in which the tourist watches a sport event such as the Super Bowl
- Nostalgia sport tourism, in which the tourist visits a sport-themed attraction such as the Baseball Hall of Fame in Cooperstown, New York (Gibson, 1998a, 1998b)

The purpose of this chapter is to explore the relationship between sport and tourism, to examine the three types of sport tourism, and to recognize some of the effects of sport tourism such as environmental and sociocultural concerns. The intent is to provide future sport managers with an understanding of the symbiotic relationship between sport and tourism and to present some of the issues related to this growing industry.

TOURISM AND THE TOURISM INDUSTRY

Since 2001 the tourism industry has experienced some rocky times. Economic uncertainty, the terrorist attacks of September 11, 2001, the bombing of a nightclub in Bali (Indonesia), and the SARS outbreak in Asia and Canada all affected the confidence of the traveling public. But during the second half of 2003, the industry experienced its first growth since the record-breaking year 2000, generating $523 billion USD in international tourism receipts compared with $475 billion USD in 2000 (World Tourism Organization [WTO], 2004). Throughout the difficult times, tourism remained the largest industry in the world. In the United States, tourism is either the first, second, or third largest employer in 29 states, employing 7.3 million people in 2004 (TIA, 2005) to take care of the 1.19 billion trips that the TIA predicted tourists would take in the United States in 2005. The TIA also reported that in 2004 the amount of money tourists spent in the United States passed $600 billion USD for the first time, generating $100 billion USD in taxes. Estimates are that without the taxes generated from tourism, each household would pay an additional $806 dollars USD in taxes per year (TIA, 2000).

The enormous size of the tourism industry is partly attributed to the range of services and products associated with it from airlines to rental cars, cruise ships to bus tours, campsites to five-star resorts, and theme parks to national parks. Indeed, Goeldner and Ritchie (2003) proposed that any definition of tourism must include four components:

1. Tourists
2. Businesses providing goods and services for tourists
3. The government in a tourist destination
4. The host community, or the people who live in the tourist destination

The travel and tourism industry also encompasses a wide range of **traveler types**—leisure travelers, business travelers, those visiting friends and relatives, and those traveling for a range of other reasons. In 1991 the WTO held a conference in Ottawa, Canada, to develop a standardized definition of tourism to alleviate some of the inconsistencies that had been occurring around the world in measuring tourism. In 1994 the resulting definition was published: "Tourism comprises the activities of persons traveling to and staying in places outside of their usual environment for not more than one consecutive year for leisure, business and other purposes" (WTO, 1994).

If tourism constitutes the "activities of persons traveling," it would follow that a tourist is the individual who actually does the traveling outside his or her home community. At the simple level this is correct, but the defining characteristic of a tourist is not just the travel component. Attributes also include the reason or the motivation for the trip, the length of the trip, and even the distance traveled. One of the first organizations to define tourists was the United Nations Conference on International Travel and Tourism. In 1963 it defined international tourists as follows:

> Temporary visitors staying at least 24 hours in the country visited and the purpose of whose journey can be classified under one of the following headings:
>
> 1. Leisure (recreation, holiday, health, study, religion, sport)
> 2. Business, family mission, meeting (International Union of Official Travel Organizations [IUTO], 1963)

traveler types—Different types of travelers from leisure tourists to business travelers or people visiting friends and family.

Although the UN's definition of tourism appears to be consistent with the 1991 WTO definition, the two differ in breadth. Both encompass a wide range of travel possibilities, yet the question remains: Are all of them tourism? For many tourism scholars the answer is no. They argue that tourists travel for leisure and that travel for business is a related but separate segment of the travel industry (Cohen, 1974; Smith, 1989; Yiannakis & Gibson, 1992). In the realm of sport tourism it makes sense to adopt the idea that a tourist is a leisure traveler because most sport-related trips constitute our everyday

1970s

- **1975** First General Assembly of World Tourism Organization held in Madrid, Spain
- **1978** First Ironman Triathlon

1980s

- **1987** First National Senior Olympic Games held in St. Louis, MO

1990s

- **1992** National Association of Sports Commissions (NASC) founded
- **1997** Disney's Wide World of Sports opens

understanding of leisure as action that is intrinsically satisfying, noninstrumental in nature, and freely chosen within the constraints of a person's everyday life (Kelly, 1999). Although most leisure scholars currently argue against thinking about leisure as totally separate from work (e.g., see Kelly & Freysinger, 2000), we might want to think of sport tourism in terms of nonwork travel so as to be consistent with the definitions of tourism as leisure travel. Consequently, a sport tourist would be someone who travels to play golf, to watch a favorite team play football, or to visit the Basketball Hall of Fame in Springfield, Massachusetts, during a weekend or while on vacation or school break.

Learning Activity

Access an Internet search engine such as Yahoo or Google, type in the words *sport tourism*, and note how many hits you find. Look at some of the Web sites, especially those linked to the national tourism organizations of various countries. You will find that countries as diverse as Canada and Pakistan have sport tourism initiatives. You will also find that universities around the world offer specialist sport tourism degrees. Write a report comparing the government sport tourism strategies of at least two countries. Your report should contain the following: (1) What type or types of sport tourism are each of the countries trying to attract? (2) How similar or different are the sport tourism strategies that you are analyzing? (3) Do you think that these strategies will be successful? Explain why or why not.

DEFINING SPORT TOURISM

Hinch and Higham (2001) wrote, "Like most social science concepts, there are no universally accepted definitions of sport or tourism. . . . Each concept is rather amorphous and a variety of definitions have been developed to address a broad range of needs" (p. 46). Guided by Loy's (1968) definition of sport and Leiper's (1990) tourism attraction framework, the authors discuss some of the common themes among the existing definitions of sport tourism: time, space, motivation, form of the activity, and behavior.

- ***Time dimension***. Sport tourism includes both the sport excursionist who travels away from home for less than 24 hours (e.g., on a day trip to go skiing) and the sport tourist who is away from home for more than 24 hours (e.g., on a weekend ski trip), with the time away from home still temporary (Nogawa, Yamguchi, & Hagi, 1996).
- ***Spatial dimension***. Travel takes participants outside their home communities, to another town, state, or country (e.g., Gibson, 1998a; Hall, 1992; Hinch & Higham, 2001; Standeven & De Knop, 1999).

sport excursionist—Person who travels for sport and is away from home for less than 24 hours.

sport tourist—Person who travels for sport and is away from home for more than 24 hours. Sport tourists are those whose primary motive for taking a trip is sport, compared with tourism sport, in which sport is a secondary motivation for taking the trip (Gammon & Robinson, 1997).

tourism sport—Trip in which sport is the secondary reason for traveling. Other activities such as visiting friends and family or a trip to the beach are the prime reason for traveling, not sport.

motivation—Reasons or impetus underlying behavior.

- ***Form of the activity***. According to Hinch and Higham (2001), sport tourism is "sport-based travel away from the home environment for a limited time, where sport is characterized by unique rule sets, competition related to physical prowess, and a playful nature" (p. 49). Competition is a motivation that can be placed on a continuum from low to highly competitive. Hinch and Higham suggested that physical prowess is another important characteristic used to define sport. I agree, because one of the major distinctions between sport and other activities is that sport requires physical movement in accordance with prescribed skills associated with a particular sport form. This leads us to a second characteristic of sport, what Loy (1968) called the institutionalized rule set. Although the same sport can be played either in a formal setting with a referee and strict limitations on space and time or in an informal setting where space and time may be freely determined, the rules associated with that sport are consistent.

1990s

- **1998** World Golf Hall of Fame opens in St. Augustine, FL
- **1999** First textbook on sport tourism published
- **1990s** Norwegian Cruise Line introduces Sports Afloat Program

2000s

- **2000** Sydney Olympic Games—The Green Games
- **2001** First World Conference on Sport & Tourism—first such conference, in Barcelona, Spain

institutionalized rule set—The prescribed rules associated with a particular sport (Loy, 1968).

• ***Behavior***. Most existing definitions of sport tourism distinguish between two types of behavior: active, in which a person travels to take part in a sport, or passive, in which the person travels to watch a sport (Hall, 1992; Hinch & Higham, 2001; Standeven & De Knop, 1999). Redmond (1991), in an innovative discussion about sport tourism, recognized the growing popularity of sport-themed destinations such as sport halls of fame, cruises in which tourists have the opportunity to meet their favorite sport personalities, and sport stadia as tourist attractions. Like Redmond, I argue that this type of sport tourism constitutes a third type of behavior—one motivated by nostalgia or a chance to pay homage to a sport personality or stadium associated with a great team or event. I call this third type of behavior **nostalgia sport tourism**.

nostalgia sport tourism—Travel to visit sport halls of fame, sport-themed attractions such as cruises, or sport venues such as the Olympic Stadium in Sydney, Australia.

Thus, the working definition of sport tourism for this chapter will be "leisure-based travel that takes individuals temporarily outside of their home communities to participate in physical activities [active sport tourism], to watch physical activities [event sport tourism], or to venerate attractions associated with physical activities [nostalgia sport tourism]" (Gibson, 1998a, p. 49). Sport in this instance is characterized by differing degrees of competition, is associated with an institutionalized set of rules, and involves physical prowess associated with a specific sport form.

Active Sport Tourism

The first type of sport tourism is travel to take part in sport, or **active sport tourism**. De Knop (1987) suggested that tourism is changing. Tourists now want to be more active while on vacation. Part of this change can be attributed to the increasing sophistication of tourists and the response of the tourism industry in segmenting its product into specialized niche markets, one of which is sport tourism. Elliott-Spivak (1998), in writing about the growth of health spas in the United States, noted the "rapid expansion of health and fitness facilities connected to leisure travel experiences in the USA" (p. 68). In Aburdene and Naisbitt's (1992) book *Megatrends for Women*, Pat Halty, owner of an adventure travel company, said, "Baby boomers don't want to take a cruise and gain five pounds or 'veg out' on a beach. Lots of older people walk every day and like the idea of hiking instead of getting bussed from cathedral to cathedral" (p. 55). Writing in the travel pages of the *Hartford Courant*, Kathy Martin (1995) said, "In these fit times, you don't just stand around admiring exotic destinations; you hike, you float, climb, ski, trek, dive, sail, paddle, dogsled, horseback, mountain bike and sea kayak them" (p. 3).

De Knop (1987) suggested that sport participation on vacation is not a new trend. Taking a lead from his discussion about the growth of active sport tourism, we can identify a number of recent trends that might explain the increased popularity of active sport vacations.

• The range of sports offered to the tourist has increased from the more traditional sports of skiing, golf, and tennis to newer offerings like mountain biking, snowboarding, organized cycling vacations, and learning how to drive a racing car. Even some of the national parks in the United States are using sport vacations to boost the number of visitors during their off-seasons. For example, Yellowstone National Park offers winter sport packages such as the "Experience Yellowstone: Yellowstone on Skis" package, which combines cross-country skiing with talks from naturalists about aspects of the park (Frommer, 2001).

• More people are choosing to take active sport vacations. We need to put this statement in context, however. The 1996 surgeon general's report on physical activity and health (US Department of Health and Human Services, 1996) lamented the lack of physical fitness among the general US population. Indeed, in recent years increased attention has been given to the incidence of obesity and sedentary lifestyles among many people in the Western world (e.g., Blair & Brodney, 1999). Although people who are not regularly physically active at home may take part in sport on vacation (Standeven & De Knop, 1999), those who are active in sport in everyday life are more likely to be active sport tourists (Gibson, 1998b). Standeven and De Knop estimated that sport tourism accounts for between 10 and 20% of the traveling public. Mintel (2000) noted this

2000s

▷2001
Nagano Declaration on Sport, Environment & Sustainable Development

▷2004
World Tourism Day (Sept. 27) reaffirmed by WTO and IOC

pattern in the United Kingdom; 10% of the domestic British special interest vacations taken in 2000 had sport as their primary purpose. Similarly, the Tourism Industry Association of Canada estimates that sport tourism accounts for 4% of the money spent domestically on tourism (Tourism Industry Association of Canada and Canadian Sport Tourism Alliance, 2004).

Active sport tourism is an increasingly popular way to combine physical activity and travel.

- Around the world, awareness of sport vacations has grown. In Europe the term *activity holidays* (Foley & Reid, 1998) has been adopted to describe vacations encompassing activities that Americans would associate with outdoor recreation such as hiking, sailing, and kayaking or resort-based sports such as scuba, tennis, and golf offered by specialist companies such as Mark Warner Holidays and Club Med. In the United States, companies such as Backroads offer biking, walking, and hiking trips (for more information, visit www.backroads.com); ski resorts such as Stratton Mountain, Vermont, offer summer golf schools; and, of course, warm-weather resorts in Arizona, Florida, California, and other states have long offered a range of sports from golf and tennis to various fitness activities. De Knop (1987) suggested that tourists are increasingly choosing particular resorts because of the sports facilities that they offer. Redmond (1991) concurred with this and suggested that comprehensive sports and fitness facilities are becoming almost mandatory for resorts (p. 109).

A review of some of the specific types of active sport tourism will illustrate the growth in opportunities for the active sport tourist. In addition, a look at some of the strategies being used by sectors of the tourism industry supports the idea that sport is increasingly being used to generate tourism.

Cruises

In recent years the cruise industry has begun to emphasize opportunities for both nostalgia sport tourism and active sport tourism through the use of themed cruises. Norwegian Cruise Lines launched its Sports Afloat Program in the late 1990s. Its promotion materials proclaim, "We've got cruises for sports enthusiasts of all kinds: football, hockey, baseball, basketball, and volleyball." Passengers can even take part in an onboard Olympic Games and may have the chance to compete with top athletes (for more information, visit www.ncl.com). Some of the sport-themed cruises offer passengers the chance to take part in clinics, socialize with top athletes, and attend autograph sessions; as such, they fall into the realm of nostalgia sport tourism.

Regular cruises also offer plenty of opportunities to take part in sport. For example, the *SS Norway* has four fitness directors onboard who offer a program of team sports, aerobics, and nutrition classes. According to Cruise2.com, a Web site specializing in cruise travel planning and information, a typical day onboard includes the opportunity to take part in a range of sport- and fitness-related activities including walking a mile (1.6 kilometers) on the Olympic track, aerobics classes, and a table tennis tournament. During ports of call most cruises offer passengers the chance to play golf. Indeed, onboard Royal Caribbean Cruises' ship *Legend of the Seas* is an 18-hole miniature golf course. In 2005 Norwegian Cruise Lines launched its Golf Hawaii Program in which passengers can play a different course each day as *Pride of Aloha* docks at another island.

> **active sport tourism**—Travel to take part in sport, such as a golf vacation.

Amateur Sports

Amateur sport events have grown in recent years. These events are one of those crossover areas encompassing both active tourism and event sport tourism. Amateur sport events at the local, state, national, and even international levels occur throughout the year. Many community organizations host road races that attract not only local residents but also runners from outside the community, both sport excursionists and active sport tourists (Nogawa et al., 1996). Of course, major races such as the New York and Boston Marathons are international events in which professional and amateur runners race side by side. But even lesser known races such as the Manchester Road Race in Connecticut held annually on Thanksgiving morning attract runners not only from local areas but from all over the world, including Europe and Africa.

Amateur sport events are held in a wide range of sports from archery to cycling, soccer to volleyball, swimming to rugby. Some of these events are multisport competitions that are targeted at various population segments. For example, the Junior Olympics holds regional and national events for young athletes, the Special Olympics has events for people with mental retardation, and the Transplant Games are for participants who have undergone transplant surgery. Since 1987 when the first National Senior Games competition was held (www.nsga.com), over 250,000 athletes aged 50 and older have participated at the local, state, and national levels in a wide variety of sports. In a study of Senior Games participants, my colleagues and I (Gibson, Ashton-Shaeffer, Green, & Kensinger, 2002), found that "traveling to the different locations" and "meeting lots of new people" were frequently cited as important reasons for taking part in these events, in addition to the typical motivations of having a chance to compete and participate in the various sports.

Another amateur sport event that draws participants from all over the world is the Gay Games. In an analysis of the lesbian and gay sport tourism industry, Pitts (1999) identified the Gay Games in particular as having "a positive impact on lesbian and gay sports participation travel" (p. 38) in terms of encouraging growth in the number of gay athletes traveling and the profusion of lesbian and gay sport events held each year.

Golf and Skiing

Over the past century two of the most popular forms of active sport tourism have been golf and snow sports, notably alpine, or downhill, skiing. Indeed, a representative for US Airways explained that golf and skiing are the sport tourism foci for the airline. The airline fits its route structure to accommodate golfers and skiers during the appropriate seasons (Zachary, 1997). Interestingly, the growth in popularity of these two sports in the United States paralleled the development of transportation links, notably railroads, and the building of resorts to accommodate rail passengers.

In the 1890s and early 1900s warm-weather winter resorts began to become popular, first in California and then in Florida. Golf, the newly imported game from Scotland, found a home at some of these resorts. Khristine Januzik, of the Tufts Archives at Pinehurst in North Carolina, explained that "nobody put sports with resorts in those days" (cited in Ladd, 1995, p. 8) because the main attractions were the warm weather, eating, drinking, and socializing. But two resort developers with considerable foresight, Henry Flagler and James Tufts Walker, commissioned golf courses for their two new resorts, the Breakers in Florida and Pinehurst in North Carolina, respectively. Although both men faced derision over their decisions to build 18-hole golf courses, just over a century later resort designer John Hill explained that "a resort hotel plus a good golf course adds a great deal of residual value to the property's land value" (Morse & Lanier, 1992, p. 46). Moreover, according to the *North Carolina Travel Guide* (North Carolina Travel and Tourism Division, 1995), the Southern Pines–Pinehurst Area is now called the "golf capital of the world" (p. 105).

With the boom in golf through the late 1980s and 1990s (Aburdene & Naisbitt, 1992), Waters (1989) noted an increasing willingness of golfers to travel long distances to resorts with good golf courses. This readiness extends to international travel; many Japanese golfers come to the United States to play because their own courses are expensive (frequently costing several hundred US dollars for one round) and the number of courses is limited because of lack of space for building new facilities in the country (Pleumarom, 1992). Indeed, as Gee, Makens, and Choy (1989) pointed out, "Travel for golf has spawned a major industry of hotels, resorts and even a golf museum. . . . Pinehurst, North Carolina; Palm Springs, California; and Myrtle Beach, South Carolina owe much of their success as visitor destinations to golf" (p. 372).

These runners in the Senior Olympics in Springfield, Illinois, may be hoping to qualify for the US National Senior Olympics in Florida. Or they may simply be motivated by the desire to meet new people, travel to new places, and engage in physical activity for fun or for health.

Today the United States has 30.3 million golfers (age 12 and over), including 12.8 million avid golfers (who play an average of 37 times per year), and 16,057 golf courses, many of which are located in the southern United States in resort destinations (National Golf Foundation, 2005). The National Golf Foundation estimates that golfers spend $26.1 billion on golf-related travel and favor such destinations as Florida, North and South Carolina, and Arizona. Not surprisingly, as Priestly (1995) pointed out, there is a correlation between the total number of golfers in a country and the number of golf tourists. The more golfers a country has, the more golf tourists it has. Moreover, when golfers live in areas with harsh winter climates or a lack of facilities, they are more likely to travel to pursue their sport, with many harboring a dream to play a round at the ultimate mecca of golf, the Old Course at St. Andrews in Scotland.

The development of downhill skiing in the United States resulted in tourism activities similar to those that occurred with golf. In the 1930s the first cold-weather resorts emerged as the popularity of alpine skiing grew. Sun Valley, Idaho, the first all-inclusive ski resort in the United States, was designed as a way of increasing passenger volume on the new westward expansion of the railroad. Subsequently, ski resorts in Aspen and Vail, Colorado; Park City, Utah; and Lake Tahoe, California, among others, followed. Like the regions of the United States associated with golf, these towns became synonymous with skiing.

Unlike golf, however, which is slated to grow in popularity with the aging population (Aburdene & Naisbitt, 1992), alpine skiing peaked in popularity during the 1970s, leveled off during the 1980s, and began to decline in the 1990s. Waters (1989) attributed the decline partly to the aging population and partly to the popularity of snowboarding among the younger generations. Nonetheless, although participation data from the National Sporting Goods Association shows that 5.9 million Americans skied at least once in 2004, a decline of 12.8% from 2003, and the number of people snowboarding increased by 4.2% to 6.6 million participants (NSGA, 2004), the number of ski resort visits has increased over the past four years (Doyle, 2004). The annual 2003-04 Kottke End of Season Survey showed that during the 2003-04 season, 57.1 million visits were made to US ski areas, which constitutes the third best season in the industry's history (Doyle, 2004).

So how do we explain a decline in skier participation on the one hand and an increase in the frequency of participation on the other? One answer may be the increase in the number of snowboarders. During the 1980s many ski resorts banned snowboarding, but as the number of skiers continued to decline, ski resorts began to court snowboarders by providing terrain parks and specialized lessons. Another explanation may be that the exceptional snowfall experienced by some regions during this time period, coupled with increased snowmaking ability, has encouraged those who enjoy winter sports to participate more often and has extended the season so that there is more opportunity to take part (Mintel, 2004). We do know, however, that the average skier's age is increasing. This is a result of the younger generation of skiers preferring snowboarding over traditional skiing (Doyle, 2004). Thus, faced with uncertainty in participation rates, the ski industry has been engaged in an aggressive marketing campaign, targeting families and foreign skiers over the past 10 years (Rowan & Sandberg, 1990), as well as diversifying its product to entice the nonskier to visit the resorts to enjoy shopping, snowshoeing, spa facilities, and more (Hudson, 2004).

Like those in other segments of the tourism industry, resort managers realized that to maintain profitability they had to combat seasonality. Seasonality refers to the variable pattern of visitation throughout the year at a destination. Most destinations have three seasons, a peak season, a shoulder season (which occurs just before and just after the peak), and an off-season. Ski resorts have a definite season (winter), with fall and spring skiing occurring on either side. With the decline in the number of skiers, operators of ski areas realized at the start of the 1990s that they had to combat the effects of seasonality to remain profitable. Many ski areas added all-weather indoor and outdoor activities and facilities and actively targeted the convention market and nonskiing vacations (US Travel Data Center, 1989). As an article in the Delta Airlines magazine *Sky* proclaimed, "If you only think winter when you think about ski resorts, you're missing out on some serious opportunities for fun." The author goes on to ask and answer several questions: "Which resorts offer the most extreme mountain biking? Where will trophy trout be biting? Where can you ski in a T-shirt?" (Ebisch, 2005, p. 42).

seasonality—The variable patterns of tourist visitation throughout the year at a destination. Most destinations have three seasons: a peak season, a shoulder season (which occurs just before and just after the peak), and an off-season.

Learning Activity

Some of the most famous resorts in North America were developed during the 20th century. As noted, the history of many of these resorts is linked to active sport tourism, notably golf and snow skiing. Trace the history of a famous golf or snow-skiing resort in North America and describe how resorts, the railroads, and the popularity of golf and snow skiing are intricately linked.

For many family-owned resorts, becoming a year-round destination was not enough. Faced with increasing costs because of aging lift equipment, rising liability insurance rates, and the need for snowmaking equipment, many independent resorts merged with or were acquired by one of four corporations—the American Skiing Company, Intrawest, Vail Resorts Inc., and Booth Creek—that emerged as the major players in the North American ski industry (Cohen, 1998). Cohen reported that 8% of the annual skier and snowboarder visits in North America now occur at ski resorts owned by Intrawest. Moreover, in partnering with the French firm Compagnie des Alpes (CDA) in 1998, Intrawest created an intercontinental ski conglomerate and actively targeted British skiers, enticing them to North America. In recent years, aided by a favorable currency exchange rate, North America now attracts 20% of the British ski market (Poon & Adams, 2000) and, as a ski destination, is second only to France among Britons.

Thus, to maintain its profitability in the 21st century in the face of a decline in the absolute number of skiers, the ski industry has actively targeted the destination skier, the active sport tourist who spends more than a day at the resort, buying accommodation, food, and transportation as well as lift tickets. Moreover, golf and skiing continue to forge a closer relationship. Ski resorts use golf to combat seasonality and have begun to diversify their holdings. Intrawest, for example, now owns golf resorts in Florida and Arizona.

Learning Activity

Form a group of three or four students. Your group is on the planning and development committee of a new active sport tourism destination. This destination can be a skiing or golf resort, a small-scale outfitter offering scuba or water-based trips, or any other fictitious active sport tourism company of your choice. Applying your knowledge of sport tourism, address the following issues:

1. Briefly describe your active sport tourism operation. Provide details about geographic location, climate, size, transportation, accommodations, and so on.
2. Who is likely to be your target market? Provide a demographic profile. Also include some information about the kind of participant that your destination or operation is likely to cater to (e.g., hard core; recreational or intermediate, that is, not so committed to the activity; or beginners).
3. What might be some of the potential barriers for tourists considering your destination or operation?
4. How might you encourage a wider participant base for your destination or operation than the profile that you identified in question 2 (e.g., more diverse in race, age, gender, and so on)? This answer might include programming ideas.
5. How might your operation give back to the host community?

After you have finished discussing each of these issues, write a plan of action, making sure that the proposed strategy is consistent with your operation and potential client base. Present your plan of action to the class and be ready to defend and justify any ideas that you have proposed.

Event Sport Tourism

The second type of sport tourism pertains to sport events as tourist attractions and the sport tourists who travel to watch them. To combat seasonality and create or enhance their **destination image**, towns and cities around the United States and the world are increasingly hosting sport events, from **hallmark events**, or **megaevents**, such as the Olympic Games and World Cup Soccer to regional events such as PGA golf tournaments or NCAA-sanctioned college sports to amateur events such as road races and the Senior Games, which draw spectators as well as active sport tourists. The competition among communities to host these events is intense because community leaders focus on the economic impact from event patrons, sponsorship deals, and, for the major events, television rights (Ritchie, 1999). In recent years, as community leaders have recognized the **synergy** between sport and tourism (Standeven, 1998), they are increasingly looking to generate tourism by developing a destination image through hosting sport events. In examining event sport tourism, it is useful to think about two levels: the major events that include hallmark events and the megaevent, that draws international attention, and the **small-scale sport event** (Higham, 1999). We are beginning to realize there is inconsistency in the terms megaevents and hallmark events. Jago and Shaw (1998) do a good job of sorting out these two types of events.

destination image—The impression that people (especially potential tourists) hold of a certain location.

hallmark event—A large-scale event which occurs infrequently (i.e., annually) that is associated with a specific location such as Mardi Gras or the Calgary Stampede. Associated with the culmination of a sporting season such as the Super Bowl or the NCAA Final Four basketball tournament.

megaevent—A one-time international level event of a large scale, such as the Olympic Games or the FIFA World Cup Football (soccer) tournament.

synergy—The interaction between two components, such as tourism and sport.

small-scale sport event—A regular season or a smaller one-off sport event, such as amateur and youth tournaments and college sports.

Hallmark Events

Ritchie (1984) defined hallmark events as

> . . . major one-time or recurring events of limited duration, developed primarily to enhance the awareness, appeal and profitability of a tourism destination in the short and/or long term. Such events rely for their success on uniqueness, status, or timely significance to create interest and attract attention. (p. 2)

Hallmark events include carnivals and festivals such as Mardi Gras in New Orleans, important cultural or religious events such as a British royal wedding, and major sport events such as the Super Bowl or the Calgary Stampede. Ritchie further added the criteria of "relative infrequency," "uniqueness" of the event, "aura of tradition," "excellence" in participants, and international attention (p. 3). Jago and Shaw (1998) suggest that hallmark events are one of two types of major international level events. They suggest that the Olympics and the FIFA World Cup Football tournament constitute megaevents as they are large-scale events that garner international level participation from athletes, spectators, and the world's media.

McFee (1990) observed, "the Olympic Games have become less and less a sporting event and more and more a tourist spectacle" (p. 147). He went on to explain that the idea of the Olympic Games as a tourist attraction is nothing new. Burton Holmes, an American in attendance at the first modern Olympic Games in Athens, Greece, commented, "The chief interest of the Olympic Games of 1896 lay in the splendid setting given them rather than in the Games themselves" (McFee, p. 147). When the United States held the men's FIFA World Cup Soccer Finals in 1994, the expressed intent was to bill them as a tourist event and not just a sport event ("World Cup Soccer," 1993). Likewise, the Australia Tourist Commission actively leveraged the tourism associated with the 2000 Olympic Games in the years following by inviting the international travel media to visit and showcase various aspects of Australia in their travel writing and television coverage. Following the IOC's announcement that London would host the 2012 Olympic Games, VisitBritain, the UK's tourism authority, estimated that over a 7- to 10-year period between 50 and 75% of the economic benefit of hosting the Games would be generated from tourism, a figure predicted to be over 2 billion pounds ($3.5 billion USD) (Travelwirenews.com, 2005).

The concept of destination image drives many communities to invest significant resources in hosting one event. Crompton (1979) developed one of the most widely used definitions. He suggested that destination image is "the sum of beliefs, ideas and impressions that a person has of a destination" (p. 18). The image of a destination is important because it can influence whether tourists choose to visit a particular location (Crompton). If they visit and perceive a discrepancy between the image that they hold and their actual experience (Fakeye & Crompton, 1991), the inconsistency may ultimately affect their feeling of satisfaction with their vacation. Tourist satisfaction is important because dissatisfied tourists may not only decide against future visits to a destination but also influence family and friends against doing so. Word of mouth is an influential factor in vacation decision making because people listen to the opinions of people they know and trust. Dissatisfied tourists can persuade others not to choose a particular destination for a vacation (Goeldner & Ritchie, 2003).

Ritchie and Smith (1991) explained that many event planners assume that the increased awareness of a location following the hosting of an event will lead to increased tourism in the years following the event. The extent to which this occurs is open to debate. Ritchie (1999) suggested that many of the impressions that people hold about a destination are tied to its level of competence in handling a major event and its perceived attractiveness. Transportation efficiency, environmental impacts, ticket distribution, and cost are all associated with this image; the extent to which event organizers can "react with competence and grace" to the unexpected problems is crucial (p. 12). For example, many people still remember the transportation difficulties associated with the 1996 Atlanta Olympic Games, a problem that journalists revisited in the opening days of the 2000 Sydney Olympic Games (NBC, 2000). Moreover, one of the aims of Greece in hosting the Olympic Games in 2004 was to project an image of modernity and efficiency equipped with "a new modern tourist product" accruing from the major infrastructural upgrades in public transportation, sport facilities, and hotels associated with hosting the Games (Coccossis, 2004). Leading up to the Games in 2004, the international media did much to damage this image with its constant coverage of the construction delays associated with the Olympic venues. The Greeks hoped that staging a successful Olympic Games would serve to replace those negative images with more positive ones.

Much of Ritchie's research has been a longitudinal study of the tourism-related impacts of the 1988 Winter Games held in Calgary (e.g., Ritchie, 1999; Ritchie & Aitken, 1984; Ritchie & Lyons, 1990; Ritchie & Smith, 1991). In a study of the image of Canada and its cities and provinces among US and European residents, Ritchie and Smith found that awareness of Calgary increased significantly during the Olympic year and the year following. In comparison, recognition of other Canadian cities such as Edmonton remained relatively stable over the four years of data collection. The authors concluded that hosting the Winter Games certainly raised the profile of Calgary among people around the world. But only a year after the Games, this image was beginning to fade. The authors suggested that tourism officials in a region need to be aware of how image diminishes and take active measures with promotional campaigns.

Unfortunately, as Roche (1994) observed, "Mega-events (large scale leisure and tourism events such as Olympic Games and World Fairs) are short-term events with long-term consequences for cities that stage them" (p. 1). In a broadcast in conjunction with the 2002 Winter Olympic Games in Salt Lake City, ABC provided an update on the Nagano, Japan, site of the 1998 Winter Games (ABC, 2002). The games cost Nagano $10 billion USD, and the city was currently in debt. The facilities cost $12 million USD in operations and maintenance per year, and the revenue generated from renting them out for events had brought in only 10% of these costs. The bullet train built so that Olympic spectators could easily access the Games meant that skiers were now coming to Nagano on day trips and not staying overnight in hotels, which resulted in a loss of revenue for the community. A Nagano resident said, "The Olympics made things great for a while, but it's been downhill since." Another said, "Our advice to Salt Lake is enjoy it while you can."

Stories such as this are more common than not in the aftermath of megaevents. Indeed, the 2004 Athens Olympic Games were budgeted at 4.6 billion euros ($5.52 billion USD) and ended up costing €7.5 billion euros ($9 billion USD), a debt that the Greeks will be paying off for years ("Reality Check," 2004). Although communities continue to vie with one another to host these megaevents, there is a growing realization that hosting smaller scale events might be more beneficial. Indeed, Ritchie (1999) suggested that recurring events such as the Boston Marathon or the Calgary Stampede might be more valuable to a community than one-time events such as the Olympic Games. The long-term effects of hosting megaevents may lie in improved infrastructure and community pride rather than increased tourism.

Small-Scale Event Sport Tourism

Although megaevents such as the Olympic Games are regarded as the pinnacle for a community in terms of hosting a sport event, Higham (1999) suggested that we should pay more attention to what he called small-scale sports events because they may provide communities with more benefits and fewer burdens than the short-lived hallmark events. He defined small-scale sport events as "regular season sporting competitions (ice hockey, basketball, soccer, rugby leagues), international sporting fixtures, domestic competitions, Masters or disabled sports, and the like" (p. 87). He suggested that small-scale sport events usually operate within the existing infrastructure of a community, require minimal investment of public money, are more manageable in terms of crowding and congestion, and may minimize the effects of seasonality for a destination. Indeed, following the failed bid of Dallas–Fort Worth to host the 2012 Olympic Games, Sean Wood (2001) of the *Fort Worth Star-Telegram* suggested that the $8 billion USD generated from hosting amateur sport events each year might be more lucrative than the Olympic Games in the long run.

Many sport events around the United States fit the definition of a small-scale event, from professional and college-level sports to amateur sport events such as the Senior Games and Special Olympics, which represent the crossover between active and event sport tourism discussed earlier. One form of a small-scale sport tourism event with much untapped potential is college sports. In an interview with the owner of a clothing and souvenir shop in Gainesville, Florida, home of the University of Florida Gators, Fisher (2001) found that the shop averaged 1,500 sales on a home football game day compared with 25 sales per day in the off-season. The football game between the University of Texas and the University of Oklahoma in October 2001 was seen as a godsend for the Dallas area tourism industry following September 11, 2001. Dave Whitney, president of the Dallas Convention and Visitors Bureau, said the 100,000 visitors "will spend between $15 million and $17 million" in what "is always a big weekend for us" (Alm, 2001). Other communities around the United States also likely experience similar economic effects from hosting college sport events.

Irwin and Sandler (1998) conducted one of the first academic studies on the tourism-related effects of college sport in the United States. They investigated the travel planning behaviors and expenditures of 1,646 fans attending 10 NCAA championships. As might be expected, fans spent most of their trip expenditures on accommodation and retail shopping. The authors also found that fans who were affiliated with a team participating in the championships (compared with unaffiliated spectators) spent an average of 6% more money per day and tended to stay longer at the destination. Irwin and Sandler recommended that community tourism agencies work closely with universities to market events actively and provide more information about the destination to potential event sport tourists.

One such community tourism agency that should work more closely with universities is the **convention and visitors bureau** (**CVB**) or the chamber of

SPORT VOLUNTEER TOURISM
Travelling to Volunteer at Sporting Events

Sheranne Fairley, Australia

Event organizers are becoming increasingly aware that sporting events might not be financially viable without the substantial economic contribution of volunteer labour. Because many sporting events are not fixed to one particular location, volunteers often must travel some distance to the host venue. Serendipitously, this travel requirement creates a sport tourism opportunity!

Examples of volunteer sport tourists are the members of the Sydney Olympic Volunteer (SOV) Social Club (http://groups.msn.com/SydneyOlympicVolunteers/history.msnw). SOV Club members were among the over 40,000 volunteers at the 2000 Sydney Olympic and Paralympic Games. The stated purpose of the SOV Social Club was to "Keep the [Olympic] Spirit Alive" and to coordinate a concerted effort to volunteer at future Olympic Games and other sporting events. In concert with this purpose, members of the SOV Social Club travelled from Australia to Greece to volunteer at the 2004 Athens Olympic Games.

The SOV Social Club was established as a Web-based community in September 2000, less than a month after the Sydney Games ended. The Web site, designed to foster ongoing dialogue among Sydney Olympic Games volunteers, initially served as the primary communication medium for club members. A discussion section was posted on the Web site to facilitate dialogue among people interested in volunteering at the 2004 Athens Games. The discussion section included information about volunteering in Athens, a link to the official Athens 2004 Web site, and a suggestion that interested people should meet regularly to learn about Greek culture and to organize the trip to Athens collectively.

To prepare for volunteering in Athens, the SOV Club met every three months at a Greek restaurant in Sydney. At these meetings they shared stories about their experiences at the 2000 Games; heard from guest speakers who were key to the Olympic subculture; learned about Greek culture through language, food, and trivia; and exchanged information about logistical issues associated with travel to the Athens Games.

The main reasons that people chose to travel to Athens to volunteer included nostalgia (i.e., wanting to relive the experiences that they had had volunteering at the Sydney Olympic Games), camaraderie, being part of the Olympic subculture, and wanting to use the knowledge and skills that they had acquired while volunteering at the Sydney Olympics. Club members waited patiently to receive their official volunteer assignments in Athens, although many booked their airline tickets and accommodations before receiving an official assignment. Most group members received official notification of their volunteer role less than a month out from the Games.

After arriving in Greece, group members used various means of accommodation, including staying with family or friends, participating in a Greek Homestay program (i.e., living with a local family in Athens), or staying in a community facility that had been converted into a discount accommodation venue for the Games. Although some club members chose to stay only for the duration of the Games, others extended their stay and used the opportunity to explore other parts of Greece and Europe.

On returning to Australia, the club continued to meet every three months. At the first meeting after the 2004 Athens Olympic Games, club members exchanged stories, photos, mementos, and memorabilia from their experiences in Athens. Since then, the club has focused on organizing future volunteer efforts. For example, members have organized volunteer ventures for the 2006 Commonwealth Games in Melbourne, Australia, and for the 2008 Olympic Games in Beijing, China. The meetings have changed to reflect these new opportunities, with the group now meeting at a Chinese restaurant to begin to learn about China and Chinese culture in preparation for the 2008 Games.

commerce. A CVB is a community agency funded by the "bed tax," the local taxes that people pay when they stay in a hotel or other commercial lodging facility. The responsibility of a CVB is to promote tourism in a community and act as a centralized source of information about events, accommodations, and other visitor-related information.

Another local agency responsible for the development of small-scale event sport tourism is a **sports commission**. Some sports commissions are independent, nonprofit organizations; some are divisions of local convention and visitors bureaus; and others are government agencies at the city, county, or state level. In 1992, when the National Association of Sports Commissions (NASC) was established, there were 15 members; just 13 years later there are more than 350 member organizations (see www.sportscommissions.org for more information). This growth reflects the realization among communities of the tourism potential associated with hosting sport events.

Some of the events hosted by the Gainesville Sports Organizing Committee (GSOC) during 2004 illustrate the potential that small-scale event sport tourism has for communities. To put these events in context, the city of Gainesville, Florida, has a population of 117,182 residents (North Central Florida Almanac, 2005) and approximately 4,500 hotel rooms (Alachua County, 2002). The GSOC hosted 21 amateur and youth sports events in 2004. Almost 80,000 people took part in these events, spent $550,000 USD in the community, and yielded 26,279 hotel room nights. The crossover between active sport tourism and event sport tourism is evident in the number of participants and spectators at these events, particularly in youth sports in which parents often accompany the athletes. High school sports, amateur sports, and regional professional events also fall under the umbrella of small-scale event sport tourism.

A core member of the group from Sydney, Australia that has just returned from volunteering at the 2004 Olympics in Athens shares his experience with other members of the Sydney Olympic Volunteer Social Club at a local Greek restaurant.

Photo courtesy of Sheranne Fairley.

convention and visitors bureau (CVB)—A community agency funded by the "bed tax," the local taxes paid for stays in commercial lodging facilities such as hotels. A CVB promotes tourism in a community and acts as a centralized source of information about events, accommodations, and other visitor-related information.

sports commission—Local or state agency responsible for attracting and organizing sport events to help communities capitalize on the potential benefits of sport tourism.

Communities around the United States and the world are recognizing that although hosting the Olympic Games may be out of the question, hosting small-scale sport events is a possibility. Even Walt Disney World in Florida recognized the value of the tourism potential associated with sport tourism by opening Disney's Wide World of Sports in 1997, which caters to both active and event sport tourism (See *Walt Disney World Wide World of Sports* on page 155).

International Learning Activity

Go to www.london2012.com/en and investigate opportunities to volunteer for the 2012 Olympic and Paralympic Games in London. Make a list of what you can do as a volunteer, what sport organizations can do, and what other organizations and companies can do.

For sport to become a successful strategy for tourism development, communities must learn to **leverage** the events. Leveraging entails using strategies to optimize the benefits or outcomes associated with an event. In a study of the Honda Gold Coast Indy race in Australia, an annual event that attracts 250,000 spectators over four days, Chalip and Leyns (2002) found that only 8 of the 22 business owners and managers whom they interviewed actively leveraged the event. The overwhelming attitude was that the "Indy promotes itself" (Chalip & Leyns, 2002). As more communities turn to event sport tourism as an economic and community development strategy, they need to replace the "if we build it, they will come" attitude with increased cooperation between sport and tourism agencies so that they realize all the potential benefits of an event and minimize the negative effects. Certainly, communities are coming to understand the need to leverage the benefits associated with hosting megaevents. For example, a consulting report on the 2010 Winter Olympic Games to be hosted by Vancouver and Whistler, British Columbia, warns that "benefits will not materialize automatically. They must be earned by a focused, adequately funded and skillfully executed marketing campaign. The first step for BC's [British Columbia's] tourism industry is to develop a long-term plan to capitalize on each opportunity to raise awareness" (Tourism Industry Association of Canada and Canadian Sport Tourism Alliance, 2004, p. 4). But as Higham (1999) suggested, for event sport tourism to be successful, "It is important to recognize the need to attract or develop sporting events that complement the scale, infrastructure and resourcing capabilities of the host city" (p. 89). Getz (1997) suggested that perhaps "destinations should also think carefully about developing an appropriate and attractive portfolio of sport events in which the occasional mega-event . . . is balanced by bidding on lesser, occasional events and periodic local or regional-scale events" (p. 62).

leverage—Using strategies to optimize the benefits or outcomes associated with an event.

Nostalgia Sport Tourism

The third type of sport tourism is nostalgia sport tourism. Redmond (1991) identified a type of sport tourism that involves travel to visit sport halls of fame, taking sport-themed vacations on cruise ships or resorts, attending fantasy sport camps, and touring famous sport stadia. In spring and summer 2001, the credit card company MasterCard ran an advertising campaign that showcased the journey of two friends in a Volkswagen bus who visited the 30 major league baseball parks in the United States. This type of trip for a nostalgia sport tourist might be regarded as a dream vacation, a once-in-a-lifetime trip. Other nostalgia sport vacations might be more commonplace and involve such activities as visiting Cooperstown, home of the National Baseball Hall of Fame and Museum (www.baseballhalloffame.org), the LPGA Hall of Fame (www.worldgolf.com/wglibrary/history/lpgahoff.html), or the sport venues for the 2002 Salt Lake Winter Games (which were open to the public for over six years before the Games began).

Most Olympic and major sport stadia provide tours so that visitors can see behind the scenes from the locker rooms to the press boxes and the VIP seating. Somebody who can provide in-depth information about the venue and the history behind it generally guides these tours. On a tour of Stadium Australia, home of the 2000 Summer Games, visitors can even stand on a medal podium and pose for a photograph. In the United Kingdom, soccer fans of a particular team can not only visit the football grounds but also meet the players and relive significant events in the history of the team. Manchester United, perennially a top team in the English Football (soccer) League, pioneered these tours. In the United States, Sports Travel and Tours specializes in baseball tours. Their itineraries usually include four or more major league games with the Northeast itineraries including a side trip to Cooperstown, thereby combining both event and nostalgia sport tourism (www.sportstravelandtours.com).

Another trend over the past 10 years or so has been adult fantasy sport camps. Michael Jordan hosts a basketball fantasy camp in Las Vegas, providing fans a chance to play basketball with him. Golf, baseball, football, and NASCAR all have fantasy sport camps where fans can spend a week or a weekend celebrating the sport of their choice. Walt Disney World in Florida has the Richard Petty Driving Experience, and in the lead-up to the 2002 Winter Games, the Salt Lake Ice Center even hosted a Zamboni driving fantasy camp.

Nostalgia sport tourism is a relatively underdeveloped area of study, yet the growing popularity of this type of tourism suggests that researchers need to pay more attention to it. For example, few scholars have investigated sport tourism associated with sport museums and halls of fame (Adair, 2004; Lewis & Redmond, 1974; Redmond, 1973; Snyder, 1991). Redmond (1973) suggested that the "the ultimate raison d'être for a sports hall of fame, like the ancient Greek statuary, is the glorification of sporting heritage" (p. 42). Gammon (2002) explored the nostalgia sport tourism associated with the sport fantasy camp. He suggested, "Fantasy camps provide both the opportunity to relive the past and the propensity to rewrite it" (Gammon, p. 69). In a study of Australian rules football fans who make an annual pilgrimage by bus to see their team play,

WALT DISNEY WORLD WIDE WORLD OF SPORTS

Walt Disney World Florida: The Ultimate Sport Tourism Destination

Since 1997 Walt Disney World (WDW) in Orlando, Florida, has become an important venue for sport tourism in the state of Florida with the opening of its Disney's Wide World of Sports Complex. Indeed, in June 2005, the Wide World of Sports welcomed its one millionth athlete, a participant in the 32nd Annual AAU Junior National Volleyball National Championships (www.travelwirenews.com). Between 1997 and 2005 the venue has hosted over 1,000 events. The Wide World of Sports Complex contains world-class facilities for hosting a range of sport events from baseball and beach volleyball to basketball and gymnastics. The Milk House, the indoor venue, has over 30,000 square feet (2,800 square meters) of space for competitions and seating for 5,500 spectators. Similarly, the tennis complex has 10 courts and room for 1,000 spectators with the capability of expanding the seating to accommodate 7,500 people when hosting a professional event. The baseball stadium is the spring training venue for the Atlanta Braves and home of the Orlando Rays minor league team. But most of the sport events held at Disney's Wide World of Sport are youth and adult amateur competitions. These include the Pop Warner National Football Championships, high school field hockey championships, NCAA women's basketball, and the Transplant Games. The strategy behind Disney's Wide World of Sports is to use sport to promote its core product, the theme parks. Athletes and spectators are actively encouraged to visit the parks during their stay. In fact, theme park tickets are packaged with tournament fees and on-site hotel accommodation. Just as many communities in the United States have realized that youth and amateur sport events bring both athletes and families to their towns and cities, Disney uses sport tourism as a way to attract more guests to their theme parks.

The Wide World of Sports Complex uses volunteer sports enthusiasts to help run the larger events. On event days, guests can participate in the NFL Experience, a simulated football training camp. Boston's Northeastern University has a branch of its Center for the Study of Sport in Society housed within the complex, thereby providing research resources for use by the center and WDW. Moreover, on the WDW resort properties as a whole, many opportunities are available for guests to take part in sports. They can play a round of golf on one of the five championship courses, play tennis on one of the 12 clay or 8 hard courts, or jet boat across the lagoon in a specially designed two-person water mouse boat. The Richard Petty Driving Experience helps guests realize the dream of being a NASCAR driver. In May each year WDW hosts the Danskin Triathlon for women, which entails swimming across the lagoon, running around the Magic Kingdom, and biking around the backstage area of Epcot. At the former Disney Institute building, the auditorium hosts forums in which fans get a chance to listen to and interact with their favorite athletes. There has even been talk of hosting sport-themed cruises on the Disney Cruise Lines. At the end of the day guests can watch their favorite athletes on the TV screens of ESPN Zone, which is part of the Board Walk shops and restaurants. In its diversity of sport tourism offerings, WDW provides opportunities for active, event, and nostalgia sport tourism in conjunction with visiting the four theme parks.

Fairley (2003) introduced the idea that nostalgia may be associated not only with physical artifacts such as stadia or sports equipment housed in halls of fame but also with the social interactions of the group. She found that the fans reminisced about trips that they had previously taken together and enacted ritual activities as a way of reliving the nostalgia associated with those trips. In another study of nostalgia sport tourists on a tour of Wrigley Field in Chicago, Wilson (2004) found that men and women appear to experience nostalgia in different ways. In general, the male tour participants appeared to express higher levels of nostalgia for the stadium and the Chicago Cubs than did the women, who focused more on the tour as a chance to spend time with their families.

In agreement with these researchers, I hypothesize that this form of tourism appears to be motivated by the need for nostalgia and heritage and may be related to a growing niche in tourism, that of heritage tourism. As Smith (1989) observed, many tourists engage in what she called "the museum and cathedral circuit" touring the "glories of the past." Like sport tourism, heritage tourism emerged through the 1990s as a specialized niche market, with regions of the world such as the United Kingdom specializing in this form of tourism (Watson & Kopachevsky, 1994). The question to be asked by researchers is, Why has nostalgia sport tourism become so popular in recent years? Is it because sport-themed vacations are more prevalent? Or, as a growing body of literature in tourism studies

Michael Clayton of the Tampa Bay Buccaneers signs autographs after morning workouts during training camp at Disney's Wide World of Sports in Lake Buena Vista, Florida.

© Getty Images

postulates (Dann, 1994; Davis, 1979; Fowler, 1992), is it because the need for nostalgia has become more important for people in the late 20th and early 21st centuries? Wilson (1999) observed, "nostalgia oozes out of our popular culture. Even those of us who have not experienced a particular decade (e.g., the fabulous 1950s or the turbulent 1960s) find ourselves looking back to those eras with fondness" (p. 296).

Dann (1994) suggested: "Today a great deal of time and energy is dedicated to looking backwards, toward capturing a past which, in many ways is considered superior to the chaotic present and the dreaded future" (p. 55). This idea raises the question, Why has the past become more highly valued than the future? Urry (1990) spoke of a "postmodern museum culture" (p. 107) in which almost anything can be found in a museum, from a Tupperware exhibit at the Smithsonian in Washington, DC, to Jack Nicklaus' fly-fishing rod at the World Golf Hall of Fame in Florida. Dann postulated that because of the rapid change brought about by technology in the mid- to late 20th century, nostalgia might help people deal with the uncertainty of postmodern life in which many things are unfamiliar. Heritage tourism sites provide us with familiarity and a sense "that we have seen it before" (p. 40).

Similarly, Bale (1988) discussed two concepts that are linked to identity: **place attachment** and **place pride**. In terms of place attachment, he postulated that in Western societies sport might have become a major forum for collective identity, especially because the faster pace of life prevents many people from being active in community life (Schor, 1991). Identifying with a sport team and attending games with thousands of other fans can provide a major source of personal and collective identity. Success in sport generates place pride in a community. Bale discussed the place pride evident in Clemson, South Carolina, home of the Clemson University Tigers. The town is decorated in the university colors, road signs at the entrances to town document sporting successes, and tiger paw prints (the Clemson insignia) are prevalent throughout the community.

THE WORLD GOLF HALL OF FAME
A Case Study in Nostalgia Sport Tourism

The World Golf Hall of Fame, part of the World Golf Village, is located 15 minutes from St. Augustine, Florida. Since it opened in 1998, more than one million visitors have walked through the 18 thematic areas that emulate an 18-hole golf course. Visitors go on a guided or self-guided tour through the history of golf from its beginnings in Scotland to its introduction and development in the United States to the technology now required to broadcast the top tournaments to viewers around the world. Each of the themed areas provides photos and narrative about historical developments in the game of golf. An 1880s-style putting green complete with replica putters of the time allows visitors to try their hand at sinking a shot without the aid of modern high-tech equipment. A video golf swing analysis enables visitors to match their technique to the top player whom they most resemble. Tourists can have their photos taken atop a replica of the Swilkern Bridge on the 18th hole at St. Andrews or feel the pressure of television cameras and a crowd in the viewing gallery as they try to sink the championship putt. Shell Hall contains 109 crystal spheres commemorating the men and women who have been inducted into the hall of fame. Along the opposite wall are computer terminals where visitors can spend hours accessing databases that document the career of each of the 109 inductees. Before leaving, visitors can ascend the 190-foot memorial tower, which offers a panoramic view of the World Golf Village, which includes shops, an IMAX theater, resort hotels, golf courses, and homes for golf enthusiasts. Finally, tourists can try their hand at the 18-hole putting course or the 132-yard Challenge Hole, which offers the opportunity to experience hitting a shot to the Island Green hole number 17 at the famed Tournament Players Club. Although the hall of fame certainly captivates the nostalgia sport tourist, the golf courses and the PGA Tour Golf Academy provide opportunities for active sport tourism, and events such as the Senior Tour's Liberty Mutual Legends of Golf Tournament provide opportunities for event sport tourism. Thus, as a print advertisement for the World Golf Village says, "Built for those of you who think about golf morning, noon and night."

place attachment—The sense of identity that people develop with a location based on a sport team or figure.

place pride—The feelings of pride people have in their community arising from the success of their local sport teams or athletes.

In our Gator football study, many fans referred to Gainesville as the mecca and described their journeys as pilgrimages (Gibson, Willming, & Holdnak, 2002; 2003). Fans, many of whom have come from out of town, can be seen throughout the year walking around the Swamp (Ben Hill Griffin Stadium) on the University of Florida campus. Bale (1988) argued that some sport facilities "can develop, over time, a sufficient mystique to become tourist attractions in their own right" (p. 120). As we noted earlier, tours of famous sport venues have been popular tourist attractions for years. Indeed, Hanis (2000) commented, "With several cities retiring classic stadiums and opening new ones, interest in baseball theme vacations is high" (p. 60). Fodor's, the tour book publisher, has even produced a guidebook on the subject—*Baseball Vacations: Great Family Trips to Minor League and Classic Major League Ballparks Across America*. Perhaps Bales' thoughts about the mystique accompanying these "shrines" might help in our understanding of nostalgia sport tourism.

SOCIOCULTURAL, ECONOMIC, AND ENVIRONMENTAL IMPACTS OF SPORT TOURISM

As sport tourism continues to grow in popularity, we need to be aware of the potential negative effects of this sector of the sport and tourism industries as well as the benefits that we have already discussed. Typically, three types of impacts can be identified, sociocultural, economic, and environmental. We will look at each of these in turn.

Sociocultural Impacts of Sport Tourism

Tourism studies have produced abundant evidence that tourism can have both positive and negative effects on a host community. Some of the positive effects relate to economics; tourism is a major source of income and employment for an area. Tourism may also lead to a renewed sense of pride among community members, whether it is in relation to showcasing their town or city to visitors or the heightened sense of excitement and community identity that frequently accompanies an event, especially if residents take an active role in it through volunteering (Garnham, 1996). This pride in community results in what Burgan and Mules (1992) called the psychic income associated with hosting an event. Tourism has also been shown to open up societies to new ideas and even bring about a liberalization of values in more rigid or closed cultures (Dogan, 1989). Tourism may provide the funding and the impetus to preserve historic buildings, traditional practices (dances, crafts, and so on), and natural settings.

psychic income—The pride that people have in their community, generated by hosting a sport event.

Hosting the America's Cup in 1987 has been credited as being the catalyst for the renovation of the downtown area in Fremantle, Australia (ANZALS, 2001). In a longitudinal study of residents' perceptions of Fremantle toward hosting the America's Cup, Soutar and McCleod (1993) found that before the event residents in general feared the congestion and crowds that the event would bring. These problems never materialized to the extent that residents were anticipating. In fact, with the infrastructural improvements and potential for increased tourism, residents felt that their quality of life would improve in the years to come.

Positive outcomes, however, may not always result from sport events. Indeed, in another study of the 1987 America's Cup, Dovey (1989) found that in Perth (the city adjacent to Fremantle) the event was used as an excuse to manipulate the planning processes for new development, and residents had to live with the negative consequences of those decisions. In a study of the potential costs associated with the 2000 Sydney Olympics, Hall and Hodges (1996) found that a megaevent affected different segments of a host community unequally, with low-income residents suffering the most because they are frequently displaced from their homes by plans to redevelop their neighborhoods with high-priced residences. This displacement of low-income residents has been a common practice in relation to the Olympic Games, as cities hosting the Games face decisions over where to build stadia, athletes' village, and so forth (Olds, 1998; Whitson & Macintosh, 1993).

Event sport tourism is not the only type of tourism to have an effect on a host community. The crowding and congestion experienced by small ski towns or golf resort areas such as Myrtle Beach, South Carolina, also need attention. In most tourism regions, host communities experience a love–hate relationship with tourists. On the one hand residents realize that their economic well-being often depends on tourists, yet the high prices, traffic congestion, and sometimes increased crime that accompany living in a tourist destination may lead to resistance and even hostility among community members (Dogan, 1989). All of these effects need to be carefully thought through in any proposed tourism development. But as Burgan and Mules (1992), among others, argue, emphasis is too frequently placed on the potential economic benefits and the voices of the community are often unheard or ignored.

Economic Impacts of Sport Tourism

As you will read in chapter 12, when community leaders are trying to raise money to build a new stadium, host a professional franchise, or host a sport event, they often point to the projected economic benefits arising out of these projects. But as studies have repeatedly shown over the years, particularly in relation to professional sport, as many as 70% of spectators come from within the metropolitan area (Crompton, 1995; Stevens & Wootton, 1997) and therefore are not event sport tourists according to any definition of a tourist. Thus, although using sport as a tourist attraction is a valuable strategy for economic and community development, we need to be sure when we read studies about the tourism-related impacts accruing from sport events that locals were not included in the people surveyed or the economic estimates generated.

We also need to be clear about how economic impact is measured. As Crompton (1995) explained, at least 11 common mistakes can occur when communities estimate economic impact, including using the wrong multiplier, measuring time switchers and casuals, and including people whose primary motivation was not to attend the event but who happened to be in the vicinity or switched the timing of their visit to coincide with the event. Another phenomenon that appears to be associated with hosting the megaevents is the displacement effect. Some potential visitors avoid a host city and region in the years leading up to, and during, the event discouraged by fear of congestion, construction-related hassles, and terrorism. Mules and Dwyer (2005) suggest that there is no accurate way to estimate how many visitors are displaced. But in conversations with various business owners, I have been told that "regular tourism" disappeared in Victoria, British Columbia, when the city hosted the 1994 Commonwealth Games. Similarly, in the three years preceding the Athens 2004 Games, tourism to Greece declined significantly. Of course, some of that decline was likely related to world events and tourism flows. As we noted earlier, the years 2001 through 2003 were abnormal years for the tourism industry following the various acts of terrorism and the general economic decline that occurred in many parts of the world. Nevertheless, in the media coverage leading up to the 2004 Olympic Games, the threat of terrorism and the construction delays were the major topics of debate.

Certainly, studies associated with the 2002 men's FIFA World Cup (Kim & Chalip, 2004; Toohey, Taylor, & Lee, 2003) have documented perceptions of risk associated with attending an event. As a result, security costs associated with hosting an event have become a major part of an event budget. Likewise, as you will learn in chapter 13, strategies to manage security threats are a major part of contemporary event planning.

Clearly, the lure of the potential economic impacts associated with sport tourism will continue to grow as countries around the world rely more heavily on tourism to boost their gross national product. Members of the Cooperative Research Centre for Sustainable Tourism in Australia suggested from their studies of the 2000 Olympic Games that conducting a cost–benefit analysis may be more appropriate than emphasizing economic impact (Chalip & Green, 2001; Mules & Dwyer, 2005). Indeed, some of the preliminary lessons learned from those Olympics have been to focus not on the effects of an event but to use strategic leveraging to maximize the effects of the event (Chalip, 2001).

time switchers—Visitors who had been planning to visit the destination and then switched their visit to coincide with the event; their spending cannot be attributed to the event.

casuals—People who happened to be visiting the destination and chose to attend the event instead of doing something else. Their attendance at the event is not their prime reason for visiting the destination.

displacement effect—The process whereby potential tourists are discouraged from visiting a destination because of perceptions of such hassles as crowding and construction or fear of terrorism. For example, tourists have already been warned that they may face disappointment if they visit Beijing in the years leading up to the 2008 Olympic Games because many of the famous attractions are undergoing renovations and will not be available for public viewing (Spencer, 2006).

Environmental Effects of Sport Tourism

As the popularity of sport vacations increases, we must consider the effects on the environment. Over the past 10 to 12 years, those in the tourism industry have begun to realize that the environment is the core of the tourism product. Destroy the environment and you destroy the attractiveness of a destination and the reason tourists choose to visit. The growth in ecotourism has been one outcome of this environmental concern. More recently, however, there has been a push toward extending sustainable development practices to all segments of the tourism industry.

sustainable development—The protection of the social and environmental resources of a destination for the long term rather than emphasizing short-term gain (Goeldner & Ritchie, 2003).

Tabata (1992) wrote of the increasing pressure on the environment as the popularity of scuba diving grows. Pollution of the water, littering, anchor damage, trampling, and specimen collecting by divers can destroy the natural resource base. Tensions between environmentalists and the alpine skiing industry have been growing in recent years as well. In Vermont environmentalists have raised an alarm over the amount of water being taken from rivers for snowmaking. In Colorado an activist group called the Ski Area Citizen's Coalition produced a scorecard that ranked resorts on their environmental friendliness so that skiers could choose to ski at mountains employing sustainable practices (Janofsky, 2000). Yellowstone National Park has limited the use of snowmobiles because of the noise and air pollution that they cause and because conflicts have arisen between snowmobilers and cross-country skiers in the western part of the park.

Around the world, ski resort development is causing alarm among environmentalists (Hudson, 1996). As Buckley, Pickering, and Warnken (2000) explained, ski resorts are among the most intensive forms of development in mountain regions, with tree clearing for ski runs and water usage for snowmaking and servicing the resorts. Moreover, a longer season may reduce the economic effects of seasonality, but it leaves little time for grass and plant regeneration and relief from the noise and air pollution caused by the sheer number of people using the mountain roads to access the resorts. Indeed, Bourdeau, Corneloup, and Mao (2004) voice concern over the growing popularity of active sport tourism in the French Alps and suggest a plan of sustainable development to protect the fragile ecosystem. Hudson has suggested that there are ways to implement sustainable practices in mountain resorts, but at present the commitment among resort developers and skiers and the awareness of the need for sustainability are lacking.

Some of the same concerns have been levied at the golf industry (Palmer, 2004; Pleumarom, 1992). Golf courses are land intensive, and the use of chemicals on the greens and the use of water in desert areas have been of particular concern. Some golf courses have adopted strategies to protect the ecological balance of their courses with programs to protect wildlife sponsored by partnerships between the United States Golf Association and the Audubon Society, among others (www.auduboninti.org/programs/acss/golf.htm). More needs to be done in this area, particularly in the lesser developed countries where national governments have identified golf tourism as a source of much needed foreign currency, while ignoring the severe socioeconomic and environmental consequences that golf courses have for their citizens (Palmer, 2004).

In support of the Nagano Declaration on Sport, Environment and Sustainable Development (November 2001), the International Olympic Committee has charged host countries with implementing environmentally friendly practices in relation to the Olympic Games. The 1994 Winter Games in Lillehammer have been labeled the Green Games (Chernushenko, 1996). The Norwegian Parliament mandated Project Environment Friendly Olympics to protect the fragile ecology surrounding the small city of Lillehammer. Chernushenko argued that the 1994 Olympic Games provided a good example of event sport tourism and environmentalism that future events can copy to produce not only a better event but also satisfied tourists and a reputation as a clean and attractive destination.

The organizing committee of the 2000 Sydney Games adopted policies established during the 1992 United Nations Earth Summit in developing their environmental guidelines. Although the Sydney Olympic Games have also been called the Green Games, Sparvero, Trendavilova, and Chalip (2005) contended that Sydney had not kept all its promises, citing the failure to detoxify Homebush Bay, where the main Olympics complex was located. Sparvero et al. questioned the traditional approach of using environmental guidelines mandated by sport governing bodies. They suggested that consensus-building approaches in which the local organizing committees and host communities are integrally involved in establishing environmental policies and practices for their events might be more successful.

Certainly, there is evidence of a growing realization of the need for sustainable development in tourism of all kinds. The question becomes, How do we balance the growing popularity of tourism in general and sport tourism in particular, along with the potential for greater economic profitability, with the need to protect the natural and sociocultural environments? A unified policy between sport and tourism agencies might be one way of balancing sustainability with profitability.

Learning Activity

Prepare a 15- to 20-minute presentation on a sport tourism enterprise, issue, or trend that you have read about in this chapter. Your presentation should make use of visual aids such as PowerPoint®, video, and so on. Engage the class in discussion based on your presentation. Prepare a two-page handout to accompany your presentation. The first page should provide a detailed outline of the major points of your presentation, and the second page should list the major references for your topic. Possible topics include the 2001 Subway World Series (New York Mets vs. New York Yankees), inside Cooperstown, tourism associated with the Field of Dreams, golf tourism in Korea, and sport tourism in Daytona Beach, Florida.

SUMMARY

You should now have a good overview of sport tourism in terms of both academic knowledge and some practices around the world. We started the chapter by analyzing the sport and tourism connection. The focus was on understanding tourism and

JOB OPPORTUNITIES

Sports Commission Associate Director

Individual sought to attract and implement citywide sport events. Duties include assisting in bid documents to compete for events, event management, sponsorship and marketing, coordination with local convention and visitors bureau, supervising event staff and volunteers, and media liaison. Must have public relations skills as well as excellent organizational abilities. Bachelor's degree in tourism or sport management preferred. Experience in event management a plus. Salary commensurate with experience.

Adventure Travel Leader and Coordinator

Adventures Are Yours now accepting applications for travel coordinators and leaders to plan and escort bicycling and hiking trips in the southwestern United States. Trips range from two to four weeks for various age groups. Experience as a trip leader required as well as a strong desire to work with young people. Bachelor's degree required in sport management, recreation, tourism, or related area. Excellent benefits and salary.

Tournament Planner

Sponsoring corporation seeking individual to assist in the planning, development, and execution of international tennis tournament to be hosted in August. Candidate must have tournament planning experience to supervise committees that oversee a variety of events surrounding the four-day tournament. Bachelor's degree in sport management, recreation, leisure, tourism, or related area. Salary commensurate with experience.

Stadium Tour Guide

Energetic and enthusiastic person needed to conduct walking tours of the 2004 Olympic Stadium in Athens. Individual must be bilingual in Greek and one other language. Knowledge of the Olympic Games and the city of Athens required. Interested individual should apply to Hellenic Olympic Stadium Operations. Flexible hours. Excellent salary per hour.

Cruise Line Sports and Fitness Director

Leading cruise line seeks an individual to lead their onboard sports and fitness program. Duties include coordinating the sports and fitness staff, leading sports and fitness classes, planning special events such as the onboard ship Olympics, and generally ensuring that the passengers experience a quality sports and fitness program. Applicants must have at least one year's experience working in the sports and fitness industry. A bachelor's degree in recreation or sport is required. The applicant should also be certified by AFAA, YMCA, or ACSM, or have earned the equivalent certifications from other countries. Salary commensurate with experience.

the tourism industry. Tourism, the world's largest industry, is composed of many segments, including transportation; accommodation; attractions; and the government and nongovernmental agencies responsible for planning, setting policy, and marketing. A tourist is defined in this chapter as a leisure traveler. Sport tourism is defined as travel to participate in sport (active sport tourism), to watch sport (event sport tourism), or to venerate something or somebody associated with a sport (nostalgia sport tourism).

In reviewing the three types of sport tourism, we discussed some possible explanations for the increasing popularity of active sport tourism over the past 15 years or so. Some of this popularity may be related to increased awareness of the benefits of an active lifestyle coupled with increased opportunities to take part in sport on vacation at resorts, on cruises, and at amateur sport events. We took an in-depth look at golf and skiing as the most popular types of active sport tourism. Golf is increasing in popularity as the population ages, while the alpine skiing industry has experienced some difficulties sustaining its market share. All sectors of event sport tourism, on the other hand, are increasing in popularity. Cities around the world compete vigorously to host megaevents such as the Olympic Games and the World Cup Soccer Finals. But communities around the United States are coming to realize that small-scale sport tourism events may be more manageable and beneficial than megaevents. As a result, many communities now have sports commissions whose task is to attract sport events to their towns or cities. Sports commissions coupled with convention and visitors bureaus are helping many towns and cities throughout the United States develop sport tourism. The third type of sport tourism we discussed, nostalgia sport tourism, is the least well developed in terms of research and attention from tourism professionals. Nonetheless, around the United States and the world, sport halls of fame, museums, and sport-themed events are becoming more popular. Even the cruise industry has developed a niche in the nostalgia sport tourism realm by offering cruises with various sport personalities.

We ended the chapter by looking at some of the impacts of the various types of sport tourism, from the effects on host communities, especially of megaevents, to the environmental consequences of those events. Over the last decade most of the Olympic Games' organizing committees have paid particular attention to the environmental effects of their Games, although some critics have suggested that the 2004 Athens Games may have represented a regression in sustainable practices (Grohmann, 2004). The economic impacts of sport always garner much attention. Certainly, many communities have become involved in hosting sports events to boost their local economies. Measuring economic impact, however, may not always be straightforward. Indeed, closer cooperation between sport and tourism agencies at all levels may be one way of reaping both the economic benefits and the social benefits of sport tourism while decreasing the negative impacts. Attaining this goal will become more important because "the economies of cities, regions and even countries around the world are increasingly reliant on the visiting skier and golfer or the traveling football and rugby supporter. In some countries, sport can account for 25% of all tourism receipts" (Sportbusiness.com, 2004).

Review Questions

1. Define the major dimensions of sport tourism and the sport tourism industry.
2. If sport tourism is leisure-based travel, is a professional athlete a sport tourist? Why or why not?
3. Why has golf tourism continued to grow, while winter sport tourism has been uneven in its growth?
4. What strategies might you suggest to your community to leverage the tourism associated with college sports?
5. What are the arguments for and against a city hosting the Olympic Games?
6. Why has nostalgia sport tourism become popular in recent years?
7. How might we alleviate some of the sociocultural and environmental impacts associated with sport tourism?
8. In what ways do you think that sport tourism will grow over the next 10 years?
9. What sorts of career opportunities are available in sport tourism for sport management majors?
10. Do we need to offer a separate degree in sport tourism at the university level? If your answer is yes, explain why a specialist sport tourism degree would be beneficial. If your answer is no, suggest how we might better prepare students for a career in sport tourism from within existing degree programs.

A North American Perspective on International Sport

Ted G. Fay—State University of New York at Cortland
David Snyder—State University of New York at Cortland

Learning Objectives

After studying this chapter, you will be able to do the following:

1. Define international sport.
2. Explain key changes that occurred in international sport between 1972 and 1984.
3. Discuss phenomena that have redefined international sport.
4. With respect to the 2008 Olympic and Paralympic Games, explain (1) the bidding process, (2) Beijing's preparation for the Games, and (3) the potential of the Olympic legacy.
5. Identify future effects of China on international sport.
6. Discuss the issue of relocation of manufacturers of sport-related products to countries that use sweatshop labor.
7. Discuss the impact of corporate sponsorship, drug testing, and the Paralympic Games on international sport governance.
8. Explain how aspiring international sport managers can prepare for the job market.
9. Discuss future trends in international sport.

During the 20th century, a number of events, companies, teams, and personalities transcended the isolation and limitations of regional and national recognition to become international sport brands across a broad cross-section of cultures, religions, and locations around the globe. International events (e.g., the Olympic Games, the Ryder Cup, the FIFA Men's and Women's World Cup, the Tour de France), professional leagues (e.g., the National Basketball Association, the English Premier League in soccer) athletic apparel and shoe companies (e.g., Nike, adidas-Reebok, Puma), and sports teams (e.g., Manchester United and Real Madrid in soccer, New York Yankees in baseball), all share a high degree of global brand recognition. Like pop movie stars and musicians, athletes such as Annika Sorenstam, Michael Jordan, Michael Schumacher, Martina Navratilova, David Beckham, Mia Hamm, and Yao Ming enjoy near cult status (Longman, 2000; Beckham & Watt, 2004; Yao, 2004). Against this contemporary backdrop, this chapter will provide snapshots of individuals, organizations, and historical events that shaped and defined the international sport industry. As you learn about the people, organizations, and events that have been prominent on the international sport scene, we hope that you will gain a better understanding of the ever-changing and expanding dimensions of international sport in the 21st century. This chapter will also emphasize the special skills, experiences, and competencies that will help you, as a new sport management professional, gain access to a career in the management of international sport.

FIFA—Fédération Internationale de Football Association

WHAT IS INTERNATIONAL SPORT?

We will consider two factors in determining whether a sport is international:

1. The degree to which, or the regularity with which, action by an organization, company, event, or individual focuses primarily on international activity
2. The context in which an individual, an organization, or an event operates within the international sport enterprise

For example, are US intercollegiate athletic teams that have one or more foreign players on scholarship or play one or more international teams during their preseason exhibition schedules involved in international sport on a regular basis? In 2005 over 450 foreign male and female athletes received basketball scholarships to play at NCAA Division I colleges and universities in the United States. Besides men's and women's basketball, many top-ranked men's and women's US collegiate ice hockey, ski, track and field, tennis, field hockey, and soccer teams regularly recruit foreign players and play exhibition tours in foreign countries. The number of foreign athletes on all US college sport teams has risen sharply since 1995. A somewhat surprising statistic reveals that in 2005, more Canadian baseball players (648) were on athletic scholarships in the United States than the combined total of male and female Canadian ice hockey players on US collegiate teams (Maich, 2005). Many top-ranked NCAA Division I softball teams tap Australian or Canadian talent, and some field hockey, basketball, swimming, and track and field teams are stocked with European or African athletes.

Frequently, this imported talent makes a big difference in team success. For example, in 1999 the University of Minnesota at Duluth (UMD) hired Shannon Miller, coach of the 1998 Canadian Olympic team that won the silver medal, to help jump-start its new women's ice hockey program. Miller immediately used her international connections to bring in 10 players from six foreign national teams. Subsequently, UMD won three consecutive NCAA Division I Women's Ice Hockey Championships. Miller, a Canadian, has assistant coaches from Finland and Sweden who are responsible for maintaining UMD's European pipeline. As a result, UMD had players or alumnae on seven of the eight women's teams competing in the 2006 Winter Olympic Games in Torino, Italy (Allen, 2006).

The context in which an organization operates within the sport industry is also important in determining whether it can be characterized as being involved in international sport. Clearly, the Olympic and Paralympic Games, world championships in specific sports such as FIFA's Men's and Women's World Cups, and major annual international events such as the Tour de France, the Ryder Cup, and Wimbledon are among the giants of international sport. The same can be said for multinational sport product and service corporations such as Nike, adidas (and its recently acquired Reebok brand), and Puma; sport marketing and representation agencies such as Octagon and International Management Group (IMG); and sport facility design and management firms such as HOK Sport, Ellerbe Becket, AEG, and Global Spectrum (Schoenfeld, 2005; Westerbeek et al., 2005; Mullen, 2006a, 2006b).

Assessing whether an organization is engaged in international sport is more difficult if it oper-

INTERNATIONAL COLLEGIATE SPORT?

In the past, many would have argued that US intercollegiate sport is not a segment of international sport. Although it may still be reasonable to say that members of the National Collegiate Athletic Association (NCAA) do not have international competition as a primary focus, evidence is growing that many universities are intensifying their efforts to recruit foreign athletes. Schools are also looking for ways to expand their name exposure overseas by using merchandising and marketing strategies related to their sport team licensed apparel. Only the naive believe that a sizable number of people in Croatia, Lithuania, Russia, or Australia are aware of top NCAA teams such as Duke, George Mason, North Carolina, or Louisiana State. A number of US schools, however, are attempting to change that situation through promoting their branded apparel in other countries.

1890s

▷**1896**—First Modern Olympic Games held in Athens, Greece

1900s

▷**1900**—Olympic Games in Paris mark first time that women compete

▷**1903**—First Tour de France held

▷**1904**—FIFA established

▷**1904**—St. Louis becomes first US city to host Olympic Games

1910s

▷**1916**—Olympic Games scheduled for Berlin are canceled due to World War I

1920s

▷**1922**—So-called Women's Olympic Games took place in Paris in track and field; led by Alice Millat ates almost exclusively in one nation or is only occasionally involved with international athletes or clients. Examples of these types of organizations, leagues, and events include US-based professional leagues such as the National Basketball Association (NBA), Women's National Basketball (WNBA), Major League Baseball (MLB), National Football League (NFL), National Hockey League (NHL), National Pro Fastpitch Softball (NPF), and Major League Soccer (MLS). These leagues appear to be using strategies to broaden their regional or national bases through marketing, branding, and broadcasting events to an international audience. They are recruiting and marketing international players in hopes of gaining new international fans, starting developmental leagues (e.g., NFL Europe, Australian Baseball League), or allowing their athletes to play for their home countries in the Olympic Games or world championships. The creation of "grand tours" by some of the world's most famous soccer teams (e.g., Manchester United, Chelsea, Real Madrid, Juventus) to play high-profile exhibition matches in the United States and China signals the recognition of the value of creating an international brand (Larmer, 2003; Westerbeek & Smith, 2003; Foer, 2004).

Clearly, then, there are several ways to look at international sport. To avoid confusion, this chapter will address only those organizations, events, and governance structures that are involved internationally on a regular basis or as one of their primary functions.

EXPANSION OF INTERNATIONAL SPORT

During the late 20th century, sport enjoyed unprecedented international growth. This growth can be seen in (1) dramatic changes in the Olympic Games (figure 8.1), (2) the redefinition of international sport involving the advent of corporate sponsorship and a shift in the balance of power, and (3) the expansion of international sport as reflected in the recruitment of international athletes and the extension of worldwide marketing efforts.

Key Historic Changes in International Sport

Before the mid-1980s, the quadrennial Olympic Games and the FIFA World Cup in men's soccer largely defined international sport, with nations and their respective political ideologies clamoring to stake their claims to being the world's best (Maguire, 1999). During this period, the United States was primarily an exporter of sport products and services, while being chauvinist in its view that its men's professional team sports and sport leagues were the world's best, and that their respective championships (i.e., the World Series, Super Bowl, Stanley Cup) were the most important sporting events in the world. With the exception of the former East Bloc countries, led by the former Soviet Union and East Germany, little focus in international sport was placed on women's sports before the 1990s.

chauvinist—Blindly or excessively patriotic.

The Olympics at the Brink

Several events from 1968 to 1984 had lasting effects on international sport governance, sport politics,

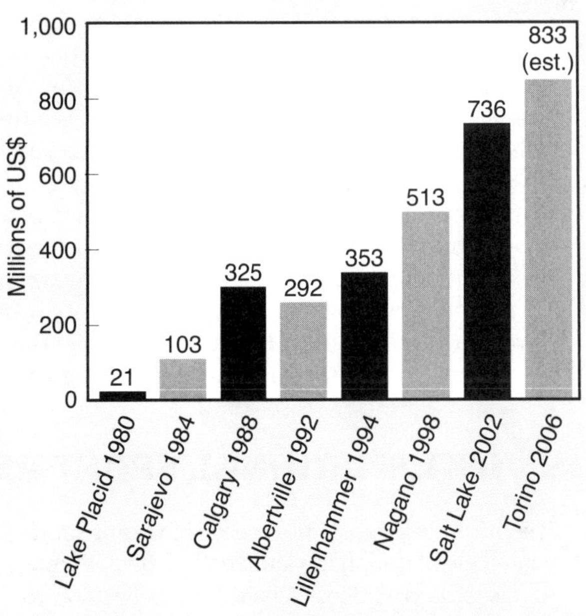

Figure 8.1 The total global broadcast fees paid to the IOC in selected winter Games from 1921 to 2006 illustrates the tremendous growth in IOC revenue from this income source. The IOC has taken advantage of that growth to develop a long-term broadcast rights strategy, enabling future organizing committees and bid cities to plan firm budgets much earlier, ensuring in turn a more stable staging of the Olympics.

Reprinted, by permission, from International Olympic Committee. Available: www.olympic.org.

1920s **1930s**

- **1923**—First World University Games (World Student Games), Paris
- **1923**—First 24 Hours of Le Mans race held
- **1924**—Women formally accepted in Olympic Games
- **1924**—First Winter Olympics held in Chamonix, France
- **1924**—Olympic motto, "Citius, Altius, Fortius," (swifter, higher, stronger) introduced at Paris Games
- **1930**—First British Empire Games (now known as Commonwealth Games) held in Hamilton, Ontario, Canada
- **1930**—First FIFA World Cup held in Uruguay—Uruguay defeats Argentina in final 4-2

and the international sport industry and marketplace. Change began at the 1968 Mexico City Olympic Games with the compelling and symbolic Black Power salute on the medal podium by American sprinters Tommie Smith and John Carlos. Then, in 1976 African nations boycotted the Montreal Games over South Africa's apartheid policies.

The Summer Olympics of 1972, held in Munich, Germany, marked the birth of an international sport revolution. The West German government was eager to demonstrate its rebirth as a peaceful nation free of its dark past associated with the anti-Semitism of Hitler and the Nazis at the 1936 Olympics and the Holocaust of the late 1930s and early 1940s (Reeve, 2000; Wharton, 2002). As the world watched the incredible performances of athletes such as triple gold and silver medalist Olga Korbut of the USSR in women's gymnastics and Jewish American Mark Spitz, with his seven gold medals in men's swimming, the prevailing idealistic sense that the Olympics were above international politics was about to be shattered forever.

The perception that the Olympics were immune to the evils of the world changed dramatically on September 5, 1972, with the tragic murder of 11 Israeli Olympic athletes and coaches and a German police officer by Palestinian terrorists in the Munich Olympic village. This 20-hour saga, watched by a worldwide audience of over 900 million viewers, sent shock waves through the international sports establishment (Reeve, 2000). This horrific catastrophe permanently altered the safety and security procedures required for all subsequent Olympic Games and other major international sporting events (Guttman, 1994; Moore, 1996; Reeve, 2000). The expenditure of vast sums on security and a fortress mentality that included expanded police and military presence became commonplace at subsequent FIFA World Cups and Olympic Games.

The year 1972 also saw the eruption of competing principles of amateurism and professionalism in the Olympics. At both the Winter and Summer Olympic Games, some sporting goods manufacturers (e.g., adidas and Puma) were accused of under-the-table payments to alpine skiers such as Karl Schranz of Austria, track and field athletes such as Michel Jazy of France, and swimmers such as Mark Spitz of the USA (Wharton, 2002). Such payments challenged the concept of amateurism that had been carefully promulgated and fiercely protected by American Avery Brundage, who reigned as International Olympics Committee (IOC) president from 1952 to 1972 (Guttman, 1994; Schenkler, 2000).

The controversy involving individual sport athletes, however, paled in comparison to the debate over inequities in team sports, such as ice hockey and basketball, wherein the USSR was accused of fielding professional teams against the amateurs from Western countries. The fierce debate over the eligibility of professional athletes to participate in the Olympic Games reached a flashpoint in 1972 because of the controversial upset victory by the Soviet Union (51-50) over the favored US team. This game marked the first loss by a US men's basketball team in Olympic history. The game took on epic proportions as a symbol of the ultranationalism and pride associated with international and Olympic sport, intensified because of the cold war being

INTERNATIONAL SPORT AS POLITICAL AND SOCIAL POLICY

The most socially and politically significant sport-related event during the latter half of the 20th century was US president Richard Nixon's decision to use sport as a diplomatic tool by sending a US table tennis team to China in 1972. This historic event, which is often referred to as Ping-Pong diplomacy, marked the beginning of the normalization of diplomatic and economic relations between the United States and China. Between 1976 and 1984, three boycotts of the Summer Olympic Games occurred, thus compromising opportunities for athletes from boycotting nations to fulfill their Olympic dreams after years of training and preparation. The boycotts began with the 1976 Montreal Olympic Games when a group of African nations protested the ongoing apartheid practices of South Africa and Rhodesia by choosing not to participate. In 1980 the United States and some of its Western allies withdrew from the 1980 Moscow Olympic Games in protest over the Soviet invasion of Afghanistan. In 1984 the Soviet bloc skipped the 1984 Olympics in Los Angeles in reprisal for the US-led boycott of 1980. These boycotts caused some within the International Olympic Committee to believe that the Olympic movement was in serious jeopardy and on the brink of dissolving as a viable international sporting event (Simson & Jennings, 1992; Guttman, 1994; Pound, 2004).

1930s

- **1932**—First Maccabiah Games, international Jewish athletic event held in Israel
- **1936**—Berlin Olympic Games

1940s

- **1940**—Olympic Games canceled due to World War II
- **1944**—Olympic Games canceled due to World War II
- **1948**—Olympic Games reinstated with the Winter Games in St. Moritz, Switzerland and the Summer Games in London, England
- **1948**—First televised Olympic Games (in London)

1950s

- **1950**—Inaugural Formula One World Championship held in Great Britain

Learning Activity

Select one international sport league (e.g., the English Premier League, Serie A, or the Bundesliga in soccer; the European Basketball Association; professional baseball leagues in Japan; and so on) or event (Tour de France, America's Cup, Davis Cup, Federation Cup, Ryder Cup, FIFA World Cups, FIS Alpine and Cross Country World Cup series). Trace the history of the league or event and identify specific incidents that have had a significant effect on its development.

waged between the Soviet Union, along with its communist allies, and the US-led Western European alliance of nations. In response to this loss, some within the US National Olympic Committees (NOCs) and Western Europe accused the Soviet players of being quasi-professionals who were paid by their government (Maguire, 1999). Many observers believe that the idea of sending NBA all-stars instead of the best US amateur collegians gained serious momentum as a result of this loss (Smith, 1992).

The professionalism controversy deepened in October 1972, one month after the Summer Olympic Games in Munich, when a team of Canadian NHL all-stars challenged the reigning Olympic and World ice hockey champions ("amateurs") from the Soviet Union for the first time in history. The Canadian professionals barely emerged victorious in what ice hockey historians called the series of the century. That series, which the Canadians won by a single goal after eight games, changed Olympic hockey forever (Terroux & Brodeur, 1972).

New Dawn in Women's Sports

The year 1972 also signaled the passage of US civil rights legislation on gender equity in educational opportunities. Known as Title IX of the Education Amendments Act, this law set off a revolution in women's sports in the United States, and indirectly around the world, because it challenged White, male privilege within the Olympic movement and other international sport federations. As a result, by the 2004 Athens Olympic Games, the level of women's participation in both the Summer and Winter Olympic Games as measured by the number of athletes, number of sports, and number of events had become nearly equal to that of men (King, 2005b).

A critical effect of Title IX has been the slow but steady growth in the number of women who are assuming leadership roles within international sport federations, including increased numbers of women being elected as members of the International Olympic Committee. In 1995 IOC president Juan Antonio Samaranch established a Women and Sport Working Group to advise the IOC Executive Board on new policies regarding women's roles in international sport. This working group, chaired by former US Olympian and IOC vice president Anita DeFrantz, became a full-fledged IOC commission in March 2004.

Redefining International Sport

As social and political forces affected the nature of Olympic Games, the character of international sport itself began to change. These changes appeared in the introduction of corporate sponsorship and the elimination of amateurism, shifting power positions of elite teams, and the emergence of soccer as a worldwide obsession.

The Olympics Go Corporate and Professional

Faced with possible political and financial disaster, the IOC reluctantly altered its rules governing corporate involvement for the 1984 Summer Olympic Games in Los Angeles (Ueberroth, 1985; Pitts & Stotlar, 2002; Payne, 2005). For the first time in Olympic history, the IOC allowed the Los Angeles Olympic Organizing Committee, under the leadership of its entrepreneurial CEO, Peter Ueberroth, to charge significant fees for corporate sponsorship that included the use of the Olympic rings. The financial success of these Games, despite the Soviet-led boycott, touched off a sport marketing and event management revolution (Pound, 2004).

In 1985 the International Olympic Committee completed this sport governance revolution under the leadership of its newly elected president, Juan Antonio Samaranch, when it eliminated all references to the term *amateur* and allowed each international sport federation (IF) to determine its own eligibility rules. This landmark decision opened the door for professional athletes in both individual and team sports to compete in both Summer and Winter Olympic Games and helped level the playing field between the state-supported athletes of the Soviet bloc and their Western counterparts (Wilson, 1994; Pound, 2004).

These changes in IOC eligibility criteria, coupled with the aftershocks of the fall of the Berlin Wall in 1989, had a profound effect on the scope of international sport. The collapse of the Soviet Union and East Germany eliminated some of the most powerful nations in the history of Olympic competition.

1950s

- **1951**—First Pan-American Games, held in Buenos Aires, Argentina
- **1952**—First time cross-country events held for women in Olympic Games in Oslo, Norway
- **1954**—Union of European Football Association (UEFA) founded in Basle, Switzerland
- **1954**—Soviets defeat Canada at World Hockey Championships to win tournament
- **1954**—British Empire Games (now known as Commonwealth Games) in Vancouver, Roger Bannister defeats John Landy in the Race of the Century
- **1954**—Soviets compete for the first time in Olympic Games in Cortina D'Ampezzo

Learning Activity

Write a one-page paper on one of the following aspects of the Olympic Games: women's involvement, professional athletes' participation, commercialism, drug testing, political events, boycotts, environmental impacts, the bidding process, or economic implications.

At the same time, the independence of the former Soviet republics resulted in the addition of a number of new nations to the Olympic family (Powers, 1993; Pound, 2004).

New Kids on the Block: A Shift of Power and Players

Over the past several decades the balance of power in international sport has shifted dramatically with each breakthrough victory by an individual, team, or nation. Beginning with Australia's surprising win in the 1983 America's Cup, to the amazing success of American cyclists in the Tour de France beginning with Greg LeMond in 1986 and including Lance Armstrong's incredible streak of winning seven straight titles (1999-2005), to Chen Liu of China being the first Asian woman to win a World Ladies Figure Skating Championship in 1995, the previously predictable world of international sport has been transformed. The Europeans have taken turns dominating the professional women's and men's tennis tours, while European, African, Asian, and Australian golfers have consistently succeeded on the LPGA and PGA Tours, demonstrating that single nations or regions no longer dominate specific sports.

From Dream Team to Team Nightmare

Perhaps even more dramatic on a team sport level were the difficulties of the Team USA men's basketball team, which was defeated in the 2002 World Championship Games by Team Argentina, which went on to win the 2004 Olympic Gold Medal (Wise, 2005). The overwhelming dominance of the original Dream Team, made up of NBA legends such as Michael Jordan, Magic Johnson, and Larry Bird, is only a distant memory (www.fiba2006.com).

With the appearance of NBA and European league professionals in world championship and Olympic tournaments and the recruitment of foreign players in Division I college basketball, players from Europe, Asia, Africa, and South America became a greater presence in the NBA. Players such as Dikembe Mutumbo (Congo), Tim Duncan (US Virgin Islands), Steve Nash (Canada), Toni Kukoc (Croatia), Yao Ming (China), Manu Ginobili (Argentina), Tony Parker (France), and Dirk Nowitzki (Germany) became stars (Bosman, 2003).

The first foreign-born player selected in the NBA draft was Luc Longley from Australia, by the Chicago Bulls in 1991. By the 2005 season over 80 foreign-born players appeared on NBA rosters, including over 15% of the starters (Larmer, 2005). The increasing prominence of international players in the NBA since 2000 has been astonishing. Pau Gazol of Spain (Memphis Grizzlies) was selected NBA Rookie of the Year in 2001-2002, Yao Ming of China was selected first in the NBA draft by the Houston Rockets in 2002, Steve Nash of Canada (Phoenix Suns) was selected the NBA's Most Valuable Player in 2005 and 2006, and Andrew Bogut of Australia via Croatia was selected first in the draft in 2005 (Pedulla, 2005).

Soccer: The World's Sport Obsession

The period from 1992 through 2002 brought a dramatic shift in both men's and women's soccer. Teams from Africa, Asia, and the United States emerged to challenge the dominance of a few select European and South American teams. In 1994 the United States successfully hosted FIFA's Men's World Cup, played before record crowds of spectators (3.58 million) and television viewers (2.1 billion worldwide). Unfortunately, following the Columbian team's return home after failing to qualify for the second round, the ugly side of international sport appeared. A chilling example of nationalistic soccer fever run amuck was the revenge murder of the Colombian player Andres Escobar. Escobar was a defensive player who had inadvertently scored on his own goal in Columbia's 2-1 loss to the United States (Foer, 2004).

Despite scandals and fan violence, soccer has continued to expand its presence globally. New professional leagues for men have formed in Japan, Korea, and China. An elite professional league in the US was restarted with the Major League Soccer league in 1996, and the 2010 FIFA Men's World Cup was awarded to South Africa. Clearly, FIFA has successfully expanded from its traditional roots in Europe and South America to Asia, North America, and Africa (Foer, 2004).

In 1991 FIFA introduced the first World Cup for women, held in China. The Women's World Cup was held in Sweden in 1995 and in the United States in 1999, where over 90,000 fans watched in the Rose Bowl in Los Angeles as a scoreless tie between China and the United States was settled by a shootout won

1950s

- **1956**—Soviets compete for the first time in Olympic Games in Cortina D'Ampezzo
- **1958**—Munich air disaster—Manchester United players die in plane crash

1960s

- **1960**—Abebe Bikila of Ethiopia becomes the first Black African Olympic champion at the Summer Games in Rome, Italy
- **1960**—First Paralympic Games held in Rome, Italy
- **1960**—United States defeats USSR and Canada for gold medal in Men's ice hockey—1st Miracle on Ice
- **1960**—5BX exercise plan created by RCAF Wing Commander Johnny Tett
- **1962**—Donald Jackson achieves seven perfect scores and lands first triple Lutz in competition at figure-skating competition in Prague

by the United States. This victory gave the US team their second successive World Cup title (Longman, 2000). In the 2003 Women's World Cup, Germany defeated the favored Americans and thus joined the elite group of nations (United States, Norway, and China) that had ruled women's soccer in the 1990s.

The successful US hosting of the Women's World Cup in 1999 and again in 2003 had a tremendous influence on the popularity of the game with girls and women throughout the world (Kaufmann, 2001). Players such as Mia Hamm and Brandi Chastain (US), Su Wen (China), Sasi (Brazil), and Birgit Prinz (Germany) became well known. Endorsements, professional league contracts, and television deals became connected with the women's game for the first time (Longman, 2000). The ascent of the United States as a world power in women's soccer is often attributed to the role that Title IX has played in supporting the development of sport for girls and women at the school, college, and elite club level. Efforts are underway to restart and sustain a US professional women's soccer league based on the initial launch of the Women's United Soccer Association (WUSA) league in 2000 (Kaufmann, 2001).

Assessing the Expanding Market for Sport

A current trend in most professional sport leagues throughout the world is the recruitment and development of top players from nontraditional sources of talent. The NBA is one example, with players from Brazil, Argentina, Canada, Australia, Germany, Croatia, Congo, Nigeria, Senegal, Spain, Turkey, and China. Other examples are the American, Asian, and African players in soccer (premier European leagues); Korean, Japanese, Caribbean, Latin American, Canadian, and Australian players in North American baseball (MLB); European players from Russia, Sweden, Finland, Czech Republic, and Slovakia in North American hockey (NHL); Canadian and Australian players in NCAA softball; and an array of international stars from Europe, Asia, Australia, and South America in women's professional basketball (WNBA) and soccer (WUSA before suspension of the league in 2003) (King, 2005b).

Professional Baseball Expands

The 1990s produced an unexpected star in Hideo Nomo, a pitcher for the Los Angeles Dodgers. Nomo not only became the first Japanese player to play in the major leagues since 1963, when Murakami pitched briefly for the San Francisco Giants, but also was named to the 1995 National League All-Star team and was the National League Rookie of the Year. In 2001 Ichiro Suzuki, another Japanese national, became an overnight phenomenon as the first Japanese position player in Major League Baseball when he won the American League's MVP award, batting title, and Rookie of the Year award in the same season. The success of Nomo and Ichiro set off a groundswell of signings of other Asian players by MLB teams.

position player—Any baseball player other than a pitcher.

The increasing number of international athletes who compete in elite US-, European-, and Asian-based professional sport leagues continues to broaden the definition of what constitutes international sport. The leagues use the influence of these players on fans to market to new audiences at home while expanding their teams' brands through the sale of broadcast rights, team merchandise, and other product extensions overseas. An interesting result of increased access to international stars has been a corresponding drop in fan interest and attendance within regionally focused professional leagues. For example, the rise of Japanese players in Major League Baseball has resulted in a drop in attendance at Japanese professional baseball league games and an increase in interest among Japanese fans in watching Japanese players on television play for MLB teams in the United States (Maguire & Nakayama, 2005).

In light of these developments, major professional leagues in soccer, basketball, baseball, and ice hockey have formed new working agreements. Leagues and franchises have worked to create a climate of cooperation and a more orderly international transfer of players, both of which have been confounded by court rulings in different countries. Beginning in the early 1990s, issues arose over the eligibility of dual nationals to participate in the Olympic ice hockey tournament in which a number of Canadian- and US-based players had migrated to the national teams of their ancestry (Bale & Maguire, 1994). Issues involving transfer fees and freedom of movement of Russian and other European players to the NHL also developed. The case that laid the

1960s

1968—At Olympic Games in Mexico City; Tommie Smith and John Carlos raise black-gloved fists at awards ceremony

1970s

1970—Canada withdraws from world hockey championship to protest rules barring best Canadian players (professionals) from playing

1970—First Arctic Winter Games; Pierre Trudeau opens games in Yellowknife, NWT (March 9)

1972—Series of the Century—Canada beats Soviet Union in ice hockey

1972—First Olympic Winter Games held outside of Europe or United States in Sapporo, Japan

Japan won over Cuba 10-6 in the final game of the inaugural World Baseball Classic (WBC) in March 2006 in San Diego, California. What is the possible impact of the WBC for the game's ability to attract more participants and fans?
© Getty Images

foundation for future decisions occurred in 1995 when Jean-Marc Bosman, a Belgian soccer player, challenged the Belgian Football Association and the European Union of Football Associations over their system that allowed only a certain number of foreign-born players on each professional club. In this case, the European Court of Justice ruled that transfer fees for out-of-contract, foreign-born soccer players who were transferred between clubs from one EU nation to another were illegal and represented a restraint of trade (Maguire, 1999).

Sport Marketing Goes Global

The international expansion of sport has set off a flurry of activity in sport marketing. For example, more than 450 million people worldwide participate in basketball, including over 28 million in the United States alone (www.FIBA.com, 2006). Recognizing the mature market in North America, the NBA launched a global marketing campaign in 1989 to expand the brand awareness of its teams, players, and league-licensed merchandise. This campaign was perfectly positioned to capitalize on the gold medal performance of the 1992 US Olympic men's basketball team (a.k.a. Dream Team I) led by the NBA's best. As much by design as by happenstance, Michael Jordan and Magic Johnson became international sport icons. The NBA is now one of the most recognized sport brands in the world and is poised to consider expansion of team franchises into Europe by 2010 (Lombardo, 2004; Lefton, 2005).

Successful and popular professional sport teams such as the New York Yankees (Major League Baseball) and Manchester United (English Premier League Football) have also experimented with forming unique business partnerships to broaden themselves as worldwide brands, particularly in China. Even the ownership of these teams is undergoing a radical international shift with a change from national to international investment and ownership control. For example, in 2005, an American named Malcolm Glazer, who also owns the Tampa Bay Buccaneers of the National Football League, took over controlling interest of Manchester United (Andrews, 2004; Kaplan, 2005). British soccer fans and sport media were outraged by this

1970s

- **1972**—Ping Pong diplomacy—Nixon sends US table tennis team to China
- **1972**—At Munich Olympics—Israeli athletes taken hostage and killed
- **1972**—Munich Olympics—Mark Spitz wins seven gold medals
- **1972**—Munich Olympics—Soviets upset United States in men's basketball
- **1974**—Cindy Nicholas breaks record for swimming across Lake Ontario
- **1975**—First International Cricket Council (ICC) World Cup, West Indies won by 17 runs over Australia

action, which was seen as anti-British and could be compared to the purchase of the New York Yankees by a Russian business mogul. On the sports apparel side, in 2006 adidas and Reebok, longstanding competitors, merged in a effort to boost their position in the international sport marketplace and to blunt Nike's 21% share of the global sport apparel and shoe markets (Abelson, 2006).

The end of the cold war and the dissolution of the Soviet Union and East Germany in 1989 helped spawn sport market economies in the new nation-states of Central and Eastern Europe in the 1990s. In the first decade of the 21st century, a corresponding rise in sport market economies has occurred in emerging nations in South America and Asia. A vibrant global marketplace based on new sources and pathways in both the production and distribution of goods and services has stimulated a dynamic export–import exchange among many nations and regions of the world. Sport is often seen as a universal product that bridges cultural differences, customs, and belief systems and, thus, is a vital part of the growing international business exchange (Maguire, 1999; Larmer, 2005). The following story of the rise of China as a world force in sport describes the emergence of the ancient Middle Kingdom into the spotlight of the international sport enterprise.

CHINA, AN AWAKENING SPORT SUPERPOWER

During the 20th century, individuals and nations from the developed world (Western Europe, Russia, Japan, and the United States) organized, controlled, and dominated international sport. In the first decade of the 21st century, however, the definition of the international sport industry and its controlling agents will change. The power language of sport business will remain English, but a working grasp of Mandarin and possibly Cantonese will be necessary for multinational sport-related corporations and organizations to be effective in their attempts to be serious players on the world stage (Maguire, 1999).

You might be asking, Why China? The answer: The economy. China is the awakening giant of sport in the 21st century. Both the Olympic Games and World Cup soccer have tied their future growth to the economic reformists within the communist government in Beijing. Although risky, this strategic initiative could yield a tremendous economic windfall to the IOC and FIFA. China, with its population of nearly 1.3 billion people, roughly 20% of the earth's total population, has emerged in the past decade as fertile ground for broad-based sport development.

Sheer population, however, does not necessarily provide the foundation for either sport development or investment. A stable political, financial, and economic infrastructure also must be in place for a real shift of the international sport enterprise to Asia in general, and to China specifically. Corporations must know how to negotiate cautiously and patiently with the power brokers and hierarchies of Chinese business and sport, in which bribery and graft are expected and commonplace. Brand security and intellectual property rights are continually at risk. Relationships with ruling cells, cliques, and power elites must be built carefully and strategically because shifts in power are unpredictable (Chu, 1991; Elashmawi & Harris, 1998).

Over the past decade, China has emerged as the new Olympic power, challenging the traditional powers led by the United States, Russia (formerly the Soviet Union), and other Western countries, such as Germany and Australia. Following the blueprint provided by the former Soviet Union and the former East Germany, China has invested heavily in a government-run and government-sponsored sport model. This model identifies children with talent in specific sports and then trains them intensively in residential training centers for elite and promising athletes.

Similar to its Soviet and East German predecessors, China also has focused on developing women's sports with a specific goal of rapidly boosting its Olympic medal haul in both the Summer and Winter Olympic Games. Although it has not forgotten to support its burgeoning men's program, the Chinese government, beginning in the late 1980s and early 1990s, has sunk significant sums into developing its women's programs in sports such as swimming, track and field, basketball, volleyball, soccer, gymnastics, figure skating, and short-track speed skating. These efforts have produced countless gold, silver, and bronze medals, as evidenced by China's finishing third overall in total medals behind the United States and Russia at both the 2000 and 2004 Olympic Games in Sydney and Athens, respectively (Wallechinsky, 2004). China also dominated the medal count at the 2004 Summer Paralympic Games in Athens, sending shock waves through the traditional Paralympic powers—the United States, Australia, the United Kingdom, and Germany.

1970s

- **1976**—At Montreal Olympics, Nadia Comaneci scores perfect 10 in gymnastics
- **1976**—African nations boycott Montreal Olympics, protesting tour of South Africa by New Zealand rugby team
- **1976**—In first Canada Cup, Canada defeats Czechoslovakia, 5-4
- **1976**—First Paralympic Winter Games held in Örnsköldsvik, Sweden
- **1976**—Women's basketball introduced into Summer Olympic Games in Montreal, Quebec, Canada

This strategy of developing winning international teams in a variety of high-profile sports has created a strong sense of national pride. It has also assisted the government in garnering increased international respect. The convergence of a number of geopolitical and economic forces between 1990 and 2004 propelled China into the elite power circle of international sport (Roberts, 2001a; 2001b). An intentional strategic shift to a more market-based economy over the past 20 years and the emergence of a sizable middle class have aided in creating a new sport culture that is both participant and fan based. Over 100 million Chinese are active in one or more sports, ranging from the traditional sports of table tennis and badminton to sports such as basketball and soccer (Roberts, 2004a, 2004b). In fact, as shown in figure 8.2, soccer is the number one sport in terms of participation, fan, and viewer interest (Ashton, 2001).

The 2008 Olympic and Paralympic Games

The intriguing story of the 2008 Olympics begins with a fascinating series of events associated with Beijing's winning bid. Vast changes made in China in preparation for the Games are noteworthy, as are the effects that the Beijing Games will have on international sport for years afterward.

Olympic Bidding—Chinese Style

In 1993 the Chinese Olympic Committee was expecting a positive vote by the IOC membership on its bid to host the 2000 Summer Olympic Games. It was no secret that China had been a source of sustained support for the favorite initiatives of Juan Antonio Samaranch, the president of the International Olympic Committee (IOC). It was also no secret that Samaranch wished to conclude his nearly 20 years in power by delivering the Games to China. Using the power and purse of the IOC, Samaranch actively courted the Chinese, whom he saw as an emerging Olympic power and a potential political and economic windfall for the IOC as a Summer Olympic host. After five ballots, however, China fell two votes short to Sydney, Australia, in its efforts to become the first country on the Asian mainland (Russia notwithstanding) to host the Olympic Games (Jennings, 2001; Roberts, 2001c).

The Chinese bid was unsuccessful because of a variety of missteps leading up to the vote in 1993. Although official IOC policies prohibit unethical practices such as outright bribery or giving expensive gifts to its voting members as part of the Olympic bidding processes, most bidding cities understood that these common and widely used practices were a necessary part of winning the bid. China's bid committee, however, was less than subtle in its gift of a priceless Ming vase to IOC president Samaranch for the International Olympic Museum. This gift was highly publicized in the US, European, and Australian press as being ill-timed and suspicious at best; thus, it appeared to jeopardize the outcome of the vote for awarding the 2000 Summer Olympic Games (Jennings, 1996, 2001).

In addition, the early 1990s were sensitive geopolitical times with regard to China's hard-line policies on the reannexation of Taiwan, its bloody suppression of the pro-democracy protests in Tiananmen Square, and its inability to stem the proliferation of counterfeiting and trademark abuses. Ironically, while governments argued over China's human rights record and environmental issues, US and European corporations were vying to expand their business ventures in China. Among those who profited were sports apparel and footwear companies (e.g., Nike, Reebok, adidas, Puma, and others), whose relocations of production sites to southeast Asia, including China, were based on the exploitation of workers in sweatshops (Bernstein, Shari, & Malkin, 2000). By 2005 joint ventures and partnerships between Chinese and European- or North America-based multinational corporations were becoming commonplace (Rubinfeld & Hemingway, 2005).

The bid for the 2000 Olympic Games was further compromised by suspicions within various international sport federations and several Western nations regarding the rapid rise of China as a power in the two marquee Olympic sports of track and field and swimming. With the dissolution of East Germany and the Soviet Union that began with the fall of the Berlin Wall in 1989, a number of former East Bloc coaches and exercise scientists disappeared—only to reemerge in China. China's hiring of many former East German coaches and sport scientists in the early 1990s coincided with the discovery of documents in the former East Germany by German police. These documents revealed how the East German sports establishment had systematically cheated for decades by using illegal drugs and **blood doping** techniques to help enhance the speed, strength, and endurance of its Olympic athletes. Many famous East German Olympic coaches and Olympic medal winners, who had been identi-

1970s

▷ **1977**—Cindy Nicholas becomes the first woman to complete a round trip crossing by swim of the English Channel

▷ **1978**—Amateur Sports Act enacted by US Congress creating the US Olympic Committee with oversight over all Olympic sport organizations

▷ **1979**—Trivial Pursuit invented by Chris Haney and Scott Abbott

1980s

▷ **1980**—Miracle on Ice—US Men's hockey team wins gold by upsetting heavily favored Soviet team at winter Olympics (Lake Placid, NY)

▷ **1980**—Speedskater Eric Heiden wins 5 gold medals

▷ **1980**—US, Canada boycott Summer Olympic Games in Moscow

Quick Facts–China

Area: 9,598,032 sq km (3,705,820 sq mi)

Population: 1.31 billion

Capital: Beijing (11,299,000 pop.)

Type of Government: Communist

Famous Leaders: Mao-Zedong, Deng Xiaopeng

Major Cities: Beijing, Guangzhou (Canton), Shanghai, Shenzhen, Macau, Nanjing, Hong Kong, Fuzhan, Wuhan

Tourism: 21 million visitors per year

Religion(s): Daoist, Buddhist, Muslim

Language(s): Mandarian, Cantonese, Shanghaiese, Various Regional Dialects

Literacy: 84.2 % of population

Life Expectancy: 70 years of age

Climate: Northern and western regions have hot, dry summers and cold winters with the coastal areas milder and wetter.

Southern regions have heavy rainfall between May and September.

Currency: Yuan (equivalent to $0.085 USD)

GDP per Capita: $3,460 USD

Economy: Modified market-driven with strong government control. *Industrial*—iron and steel, coal, machine building, armaments, textiles, and apparel. *Agriculture*—rice, wheat, potatoes, sorghum, peanuts, tea, millet, cotton, pork, fish. *Exports*—electrical machinery, clothing, footwear, toys, mineral fuels, leather, and plastics

Source: World Atlas, DK books (2004)

Quick Sport Facts–China

Popular Sports of Interest: Soccer, basketball, table tennis, badminton, swimming, snooker, and tennis

Olympic/International Sports (Winter): Short track speedskating, women's figure skating, women's freestyle skiing

Olympic/International Sports (Summer): Swimming, track & field, table tennis, soccer, badminton, basketball, and volleyball

Major Professional Sport Leagues: Soccer, basketball, volleyball, table tennis and badminton

Famous Athletes: Chen Liu (figure skating), Su Wen (women's soccer), Wang Zhi-Zhi, Yao Ming (basketball), Liu Xiang (Track & Field), Lang Ping (Volleyball)

Leading Sports Manufacturer: Beijing Li Ning Sports Goods Company

Major International Sport Events—Host: 2001 World University Games; 2002 Tennis Masters Cup; 2004 Asian Football Cup (Soccer); 2007 FIFA Women's World Cup (Soccer); 2008 Summer Olympic Games (Beijing); 2008 Summer Paralympic Games (Beijing)

Popular TV/Sports Media: China Central Television (CCTV); ESPN Star TV (cable)

Homes with TV: 310 million

Homes with Cable TV: 125 million

Source: Sport Business International: SBG London (2001)

Figure 8.2 China by the numbers.

fied through evidence, provided so-called doping documents that were presented at trials conducted in Germany and Canada (Ungerleider, 2001). Suspicion followed these coaches and sport scientists to China as the Chinese women had become a world power in swimming and track and field virtually overnight. Several well-publicized drug busts of Chinese swimmers and track athletes confirmed the widely held suspicion that Chinese athletes were not clean (Jennings, 1996; Pound, 2004).

blood doping—The practice of illicitly boosting the number of red blood cells, which transport oxygen, to enhance athletic performance.

So what happened to change things in favor of China's being awarded the 2008 Summer Olympic Games when the IOC gathered in Moscow in July 2001? To begin with, the Chinese had hired Hill and Knowlton, a major US public relations and advertising firm, to manage their image and public relations campaign. The Chinese Olympic Committee and its corresponding national sport federations took a firm stand against some of their own athletes in swimming and track and field in an effort to quell the rumors and suspicions of state-supported drug use. This action took place after the doping scandals of 1998, when Chinese swimmers were caught with vials of human growth hormone (HGH) in their

1980s

- **1980**—Marathon of Hope—Terry Fox halts his marathon in Sept. because cancer reappears in his lungs
- **1981**—Terry Fox dies on June 28, 1981
- **1981**—Soviets defeat Canadian professionals to win second Canada Cup (ice hockey)
- **1982**—Laurie Skreslet becomes first Canadian to reach the summit of Mt. Everest (Oct. 5)
- **1983**—Australia wins America's Cup
- **1983**—Steve Podborski becomes first non-European to win World Cup downhill skiing championship

CRICKET: A National "Religion" in India

Hareesh Viriyala, India

For more than a century, cricket has been played in countries around the world. The International Cricket Council (ICC), the governing body for world cricket, has 10 full-time members—Australia, Bangladesh, England, India, New Zealand, Pakistan, South Africa, Sri Lanka, West Indies, and Zimbabwe—and 88 associate and affiliate member countries. Every four years, the best teams compete in the ICC Cricket World Cup. The international popularity of cricket is growing rapidly, and nowhere is this phenomenon more apparent than in India.

From its humble beginnings as a legacy of British rule, cricket in India has become the epicenter of world cricket. Research estimates that most of the monies in international cricket flow in and out of India. Schedules for One Day Internationals (ODI) are often tailored to meet prime-time viewing in India, and the ICC has recently shifted its headquarters from London to Dubai to move strategically closer to the hub of cricket activity.

Cricket has many factors in its favor in India—high entertainment value, extensive media coverage that elevates cricketers to demigod status, a platform that brings a diverse people together and instills nationalistic feelings, and the thrill of high-voltage drama of sporting encounters. That the sport doesn't require elaborate and expensive equipment—a makeshift wooden bat, ball, and three wooden stumps (or three vertical lines drawn on a wall) are the minimum requirements—has contributed to mass participation. Several pairs of teams and multiple makeshift pitches often occupy the same field. This mass appeal has TV channels, sponsors and advertisers, and bookmakers scampering to grab their share of eyeballs and revenues.

In a country where the culture of active participation in sport is largely absent, cricket has engaged the fancy of the public like no other sport. Cricket terminology and cricket-related similes and metaphors often find their way into conversation. The national cricket team is the de facto national sports team, and the adoration of the sport is such that it is often considered more than religion. Cricket holds the center stage so firmly that India has often had the dubious distinction of being called a one-sport nation. Testimony to this preoccupation with the sport is that cricket holds sway in all sport-related discussions, is covered in nearly 60% of the country's most popular sports weekly magazines, and garners more than 80% of the money spent on sport marketing in India. The popularity and passion of cricket in India is comparable to that of soccer in Brazil, ice hockey in Canada, or American football in the United States.

Cricket in India has also had its lows in the form of match-fixing scandals, strings of poor performances that saw interest levels and TV ratings drop, questionable politics in the Board of Control for Cricket in India (BCCI), legal tangles over TV rights, and a public spat between coach and captain. Despite these events and despite increasing competition from other sports, the Indian public continues to take to the game with unbridled joy and spirit.

No discussion of India's passion for cricket would be complete without a mention of the intensity, fervor, fanaticism, and hype involved in an India–Pakistan cricket tournament or a one-off (one-time) ODI. The long-standing political rivalry between these nations fuels the excitement of encounters between their powerful national cricket teams. Television ratings, media coverage, advertising and sponsorship spending, and wagers skyrocket during such encounters. The immense popularity of these tournaments has served to ease political tensions between the two countries and pave the way toward initiating the peace process over the issue of Kashmir.

Spotlight on India's Favorite Sportsperson

Ever since he began his career in international cricket in 1989 as a 16-year-old batting prodigy, Sachin Tendulkar has been capturing the nation's imagination like no other sportsperson. His popularity and the emotions that he arouses in fans are unparalleled. His iconic status is akin to Wayne Gretzky's in Canada, Michael Jordan's in the United States, or David Beckham's in England. Said to be India's most recognized public figure, he carries the burden of expectations of a billion people every time he steps out to bat.

1980s

- **1984**—1984 Olympic Games in Los Angeles—commercialism and Soviet boycott
- **1984**—Joan Benoit Samuelson wins first Olympic women's marathon
- **1984**—First exhibition events in track and field for wheelchair athletes introduced into Olympic Games
- **1985**—IOC eliminates term *amateur,* opening door to participation by pro athletes
- **1985**—Heysel Stadium disaster—39 soccer fans die—Liverpool v. Juventus
- **1985**—Olympic TOP sponsorship program created

Indian batsman Sachin Tendulkar celebrates after scoring during a cricket match between India and Sri Lanka in New Dehli in December of 2005. Tendulkar is an Indian cricket superstar who is known to hundreds of millions, joining the likes of Gretzky, Jordan, Pele, and Beckham.
© Getty Images

luggage en route to Sydney for the 1998 World Swimming Championships (Ashton, 2001).

Supporters of the IOC decision to award the 2008 Games to China claimed that Beijing had the most compelling bid of all the cities vying for the Games. They further argued that China had addressed the critical political, financial, human rights, environmental, and ethical issues (i.e., drugs) that had been to blame for their near miss in 1993 (Symonds, 2001). Skeptics and cynics who follow the Olympic bidding process, however, have described the vote that gave Beijing the 2008 Games as being a foregone conclusion based on a backroom deal. Many argued that this was essentially a parting gift to Samaranch on his retirement as Olympic chief and that little, if anything, had truly changed in China regarding critical issues before the vote (Jennings, 2001). The realities of the what, who, and why resided somewhere between these conflicting viewpoints.

Before the Games

More than 20 years after the unexpected marketing success of the 1984 Olympic Games in Los Angeles, the IOC has become an international sport marketing juggernaut (figure 8.3). It has been fueled by billions of dollars in television rights fees from NBC and others (Burton, 2000; Payne, 2005) as well as millions from corporations known as the TOP (The Olympic Partner) Program. The TOP Program includes Coca-Cola (with the Olympic Games since 1928), Atos Origin (formerly SchlumbergerSema), Manulife (formerly John Hancock), Kodak (with the Olympic Games since 1896), Lenovo (formerly IBM), McDonald's, Matsushita (Panasonic), Omega, Samsung, Johnson & Johnson, Visa, and General Electric.

Not coincidentally, many of these multinational corporations are already present and doing business in China (Echikson, Webb, & Fonte, 2001). Enormous advertising expenditures are at stake as

International Learning Activity

Write a report on the influence of Martin Bladen Hawke on the world of cricket. Also, write a report on contemporary women's cricket. Include information about the number of women who play organized cricket, what countries have teams, and where women's tournaments are held.

1980s

- **1986**—Greg LeMond from the United States becomes first non-European to win Tour de France
- **1986**—First Goodwill Games
- **1986**—Sharon Wood becomes first American woman to reach summit of Mt. Everest
- **1986**—Canada qualifies for the Men's FIFA World Cup
- **1986**—Gail Greenough becomes first Canadian and first woman to win World Show Jumping championship
- **1987**—First Rugby Union World Cup
- **1988**—Ben Johnson, 100 m winner, disqualified for doping at the Seoul Olympics

RIGHTS AND OPPORTUNITIES FOR TOP COMPANIES

TOP companies receive exclusive marketing rights and opportunities within their designated product category. They may exercise these rights on a worldwide basis, and they may develop marketing programs with the various members of the Olympic Movement—the IOC, the NOCs, and the organizing committees. Besides exclusive worldwide marketing opportunities, partners receive the following benefits:

- Authorization to use all Olympic imagery, as well as appropriate Olympic designations on products
- Hospitality opportunities at the Olympic Games
- Direct advertising and promotional opportunities, including preferential access to Olympic broadcast advertising
- On-site concessions and franchise, and product sale and showcase opportunities
- Protection from ambush marketing (see page 182)
- Acknowledgement of support through a broad Olympic sponsorship recognition program

The strength of the TOP sponsorship program is evident in the fact that the program enjoys one of the highest sponsorship renewal rates of any sport property.

Data from www.olympic.org/uk/organisation/facts/programme/sponsors_uk.asp.

China prepares to host the 2008 Games ("A-B Paces Ad Spending," 2005). Many industry insiders had predicted that awarding the 2008 Games to Beijing would trigger the largest stadium construction program the world has ever witnessed and would create record-setting advertising revenues. China expects to spend $2 to 3 billion USD on new state-of-the art stadia and arenas in preparation for the Olympics and other major international events. American stadium and sport facility design companies such as HOK Sport, Ellerbe Becket, NBBJ Sport & Entertainment, and Sasaki & Associates are all heavily involved in the master planning or building of 18 new stadia and arenas and the renovation of 14 existing arenas in Beijing alone (Cronin, 2001).

The Chinese government expects to spend the equivalent of over $30 billion USD in preparations, including over $12 billion USD on transport infrastructure, $8 to 10 billion USD on cleaning up the environment, $5 billion USD on information technology, and $4 billion USD on improved living conditions (Roberts, 2004b). This total does not include the nearly $3 billion USD expected to be spent in managing and operating the 2008 Olympic and Paralympic Games. For example, the costs associated with the marketing, management, and operation of a series of major international events leading up to the Games will reach several billion US dollars. These events include the 2001 World

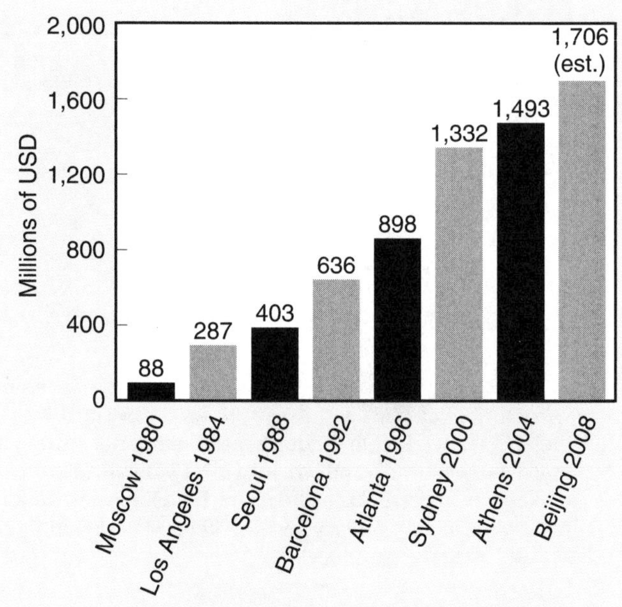

Figure 8.3 The summer Olympic Games have seen massive increases in global broadcast coverage over the past 20 years, despite continuous pressure to alter the principle that all Olympic television agreements be based on free-to-air broadcasting. The IOC has maintained this growth through direct negotiations, without incurring any agency or third-party commissions. From 1984 until 2008, the IOC has concluded broadcast agreements worth more than $10 billion USD.

Reprinted, with permission, from International Olympic Committee. Available: www.olympic.org.

1980s

- **1988**—Canadian Kurt Browning lands first quadruple toe loop in competition
- **1989**—NBA initiates global marketing campaign
- **1989**—Hillsborough Stadium disaster—96 lives claimed during soccer match between Liverpool and Nottingham Forest at the Sheffield stadium in Hillsborough, United Kingdom
- **1989**—Berlin Wall Falls

1990s

- **1991**—First Women's FIFA World Cup held in China
- **1991**—Japanese National Football (soccer) league established in Japan

Learning Activity

Go to www.olympic.org/uk/organisation/facts/programme/sponsors_uk.asp. Using the information posted there, write a report about the rights and opportunities that TOP Partners receive.

University Games, the 2002 Men's Tennis Masters Cup, the 2004 Men's Asian Football Cup (soccer), and the 2007 FIFA Women's World Cup (Roberts, 2004a).

After the Games

Based on past experiences of host cities, all will not be gold for the Chinese as they prepare the infrastructure necessary to host the world's largest sporting event. For example, there are widespread concerns about human rights abuses in China, such as the detention and execution of political dissidents. Global trade and resource production issues associated with sweatshop labor will continue. These issues include the fact that multinational corporations exploit Chinese workers who produce sports apparel and footwear for extremely low wages in oppressive working conditions (Engardio & Belton, 2000). In addition, serious environmental problems could compromise the health of the athletes and spectators. Of particular concern is the air pollution found in Beijing and many of the projected satellite host cities throughout China. The air is expected to be similar to or worse than the air quality in Los Angeles during the 1984 Olympic Games. Responding to the findings of the Kyoto Protocol on Climate Change and the commitment of the IOC to protecting the environment, Beijing has accelerated its environmental planning in preparation for the 2008 Olympic and Paralympic Games (Smith & Westerbeek, 2004).

Other issues concern the lack of a free press and the suspicion that the Chinese government will be unwilling to grant unfettered access to the foreign press. Brand protection and intellectual property rights are serious concerns for many Olympic sponsors, as they weigh the pros and cons of doing business on the mainland. Tension over the status of Taiwan and its inclusion as a separate team recognized by the IOC also poses challenges to diplomacy. The requirement that the host city accommodate the follow-on Paralympic Games initially presented serious challenges for the Chinese because of their historically prejudiced attitude toward people with disabilities and the lack of accessible accommodations throughout the nation, specifically in Beijing. Many in the Paralympic movement were critical of the awarding of the 2008 Summer Paralympic Games to China and did not want the selection of Beijing as the host city to appear as a tacit endorsement of negative attitudes toward athletes with disabilities. Surprisingly, the Chinese have embraced the 2008 Paralympic Games and instituted sweeping reforms related to the rights and access of people with disabilities. They have also launched an aggressive campaign to develop the most dominant Paralympic team in the world.

WHAT DOES IT TAKE TO BROADCAST THE OLYMPIC GAMES?

In 2004 the Athens Olympic Broadcasting Organization carried out the following tasks:

- Televised more than 4,000 hours of live Olympic coverage
- Provided coverage of 300 Olympic events
- Used more than 1,000 cameras and 450 videotape machines
- Employed 3,700 personnel
- Worked with more than 12,000 accredited broadcast personnel

Data from www.olympic.org/uk/organisation/facts/revenue/broadcast_uk.asp.

It remains to be seen what the Olympic Games legacy will be in China. Will China undergo social, political, and economic changes similar to what occurred in South Korea following the 1988 Olympic and Paralympic Games (Pound, 1994)? One could argue that the 1988 Games in Korea created momentum for a shift to a more open South Korean society that was willing to institute changes regarding human rights, the environment, and protectionist trade practices. Although the results will not be evident for some time, preparing to host the Olympics and Paralympics have already had a profound effect on China.

1990s

- **1992**—At Barcelona Olympics, Dream Team debuts, Michael Jordan covers up Reebok label on his warm-ups, Butch Reynolds challenges drug testing.
- **1992**—Court of Arbitration created
- **1992**—International Paralympic Committee (IPC) created
- **1994**—15th FIFA Men's World Cup hosted by US for first time and won by Brazil
- **1994**—Columbian national team soccer player Andres Escobar killed for scoring goal for opposing team in World Cup match against US

Olympic Games legacy—Positive effects of the Olympic Games on the host cities and countries; these effects can be related to architecture, urban planning, economics, sustainable development, ideas and cultural values, and so on.

Learning Activity

Go to the Internet and find a story on the Olympic Games legacy of the 2006 Winter Games in Torino, Italy. Summarize the organizing committee's initiatives, the activities of the Values Committee, and the Charter of Intent.

Effect of China on International Sport

The saga of China's Olympic bid is interesting, but the story does not end with the 2008 Games. For example, China has provided the single largest boom in the growth of fans, viewers, and participants that soccer has ever seen and is now primed to move into the mainstream of soccer (Roberts, 2001a). Building on the international success of its women's national team in FIFA World Cups and Olympic competition and the success of its men's team in qualifying for the 2002 FIFA World Cup held in Japan and Korea, China is on target to define itself as one of the new centers of the world's most popular sport.

China will no doubt continue to influence international sport for quite some time. At this point, it appears that three areas in which China will have its greatest influence are the exportation of athletic talent, the provision of corporate sponsorship opportunities, and the impact of its economy on the world financial system.

Exportation of Talent

China is likely to continue to loosen its control over its prime athletic talent (e.g., athletes and coaches) to make possible the export of this talent to North America and Europe (Kaplan, 2001). At the same time, China will continue growing new generations of elite athletes, sport participants, fans, and viewers at home. The relaxation of rules controlling athletes and coaches is evidenced by two primary examples: Yao Ming, a star with the Houston Rockets of the NBA, and Lang Ping, the head coach of the 2008 US Women's Olympic volleyball team.

Because of Yao Ming's success and the NBA's interest in expanding overseas telecasts of its regular season, all-star, playoff, and championship games, more Chinese viewers (over 30 million) will typically watch the Houston Rockets play on China Central Television (CCTV) by satellite on any given night than the total combined North American audience that would watch the Rockets and every other NBA team (Larmer, 2005). Lang Ping, known as the Iron Hammer when she played for the Chinese national volleyball team, was a member of five winning teams in World Championships, World Cups, and the Olympic Games and is a cultural hero throughout China. According to Al Monaco, USA Volleyball President, "USA Volleyball is sending a loud message—to the world that we are serious about having our women's team be the best, and to the nation that we are committed to the advancement of females at the top levels of coaching" (Embassy of the People's Republic, 2005). Clearly, both of these icons of Chinese sport have had and will continue to have a dramatic effect on international sport.

Sponsorship Opportunities

The professional side of the Chinese sport industry will expand in the first two decades of the 21st century, aided initially by aggressive stadium and arena building as an outgrowth of the 2008 Olympic Games. Professional leagues, such as the China Basketball Association in basketball and the C-League in soccer, will grow. The Chinese Football Association has already garnered additional flexibility from the central government in Beijing, basing its operational strategy (e.g., merchandising, corporate sponsorships) on a Western professional sport model to a greater extent than many experts thought possible.

Whether it is Su-Wen in women's soccer; Yao Ming, Wang Zhi-Zhi, and Bateer Menk in men's basketball (NBA); or Peng Suai and Li Na in women's tennis, China appears poised to evolve from exporting a few emerging sport heroes to developing a critical mass of elite male and female professional players who are able to perform at the highest level in the US- and European-based professional leagues (Kaplan, 2001). These athletes are being represented by American-based sport marketing agencies and already have tie-ins to corporate sponsorship such as adidas, Nike, and other sportswear companies.

Rights to represent elite Chinese players, lucrative exhibition tours and tournaments, and team and league sponsorships are up for grabs among

1990s

- **1994**—Hideo Nomo, of LA Dodgers, becomes first Japanese player in MLB since 1965 when Masanori Murakami pitched for the San Francisco Giants
- **1995**—Chinese Basketball Association (CBA) established
- **1995**—Bosman case changes soccer transfer rules in Europe
- **1996**—Atlanta Centennial Olympic Games
- **1996**—Atlanta Olympics—Donovan Bailey wins 100 m race
- **1996**—Atlanta Olympics—Canada wins 4 × 100 m relay
- **1996**—US defeats Canada at first World Cup of Hockey
- **1998**—NHL players compete in Olympics for first time

firms based in Europe and North America (Larmer, 2005). These firms must carefully build alliances and partnerships within China or risk millions of US dollars in investment as Lucent Technologies did in its attempt to sponsor Chinese professional soccer in the late 1990s. Lucent thought that it could import the Western model of sport advertising and corporate sponsorship as a platform to expand and sell its products to the Chinese market. The company did not understand how to adapt to a more Chinese-centric model of establishing business relationships and networks. Money for billboards and TV advertisements alone were not enough to convince Chinese consumers to buy new products without the reinforcement of word-of-mouth advertising or network marketing coupled with testimonials by Chinese entertainers and sports stars. This dilemma was also repeated in Nike's failure to leverage its contract with Yao Ming (now with adidas) when he entered the NBA to help expand its presence and sales of apparel and sport shoes in the Chinese market (Larmer, 2005).

CAREERS IN INTERNATIONAL SPORT

The international sport industry is complex, and it changes so rapidly that you need an up-to-date road map to keep the facts straight. To work as an international sport manager, you must have a sound understanding of the processes of international business, local and regional culture, and sport, as well as clear recognition of the key stakeholders (e.g., organizations and people). From using sport teams and events to sell tobacco products, alcohol, and automobiles in Europe, to sponsoring Formula One car racing in the United States, to selling tourism associated with an Olympic Games or world championship, there is a direct relationship between sport, leisure, recreation, and *business* in international sport (Warfield, 2005).

What do you need to know as a prospective sport manager to prepare for a journey into international sport? Employees of any company or organization that does business in another country must understand the basics of finance, macroeconomics, manufacturing, distribution of products and services, retailing, and human resource management (Morrison, Conaway, & Douress, 2001; Rubinfeld & Hemingway, 2005). The first step in your journey, therefore, is to develop an understanding of the primary trade treaties and agreements, such as the General Agreement on Tariffs and Trade (GATT), the North American Free Trade Agreement (NAFTA), and the rules and regulations that affect the European Community (EC). This knowledge will provide a rudimentary foundation from which you can research other important trade regulations, currency exchanges, and legal issues concerning brand protection and intellectual property rights. You must also know how free or restricted the movement of goods, services, persons, and capital is from nation to nation. Knowing your rights as a foreigner when doing business in another nation is critical (Morrison et al., 2001). With an in-depth awareness of how well you, your employees, and your investments will be protected by a given legal

AND THE WINNER IS . . . THE SPORT ECONOMY

Despite the protracted international debate over key geopolitical, environmental, and human rights issues prominent in the run-up to China's being voted into the World Trade Organization (WTO) as a full-fledged member in 2001 and Beijing's being awarded the 2008 Olympic and Paralympic Summer Games, the ultimate winner in the emergence of China as a world player is the sport industry itself (Power & Allison, 2000). The potential growth in real gross global sport product (GGSP) for all segments of the international sport industry will come from new sport media and marketing opportunities, the rise of new professional leagues, the exportation of elite athletic talent, the incredible growth of new facilities of all types, and expanded sport manufacturing and product development. These developments will fuel the continued growth of the sport enterprise well into the first two decades of the 21st century (Khermouch, Holmes, & Ihlwan, 2001). With this boom in the establishment of a new sport infrastructure for China, other segments of the sport enterprise, such as finance and licensing, will continue to accelerate. We will also see the creation of joint ventures and alliances between established US and European sport firms and their Chinese partners. A review of the first decade of the 21st century will show that power and profit in international sport will be counted in dollars, euros, and yuan (Cronin, 2001).

1990s

- **1998**—Czech Republic wins gold medal in ice hockey at Nagano
- **1998**—Women's ice hockey introduced and US team upsets Canada for the gold
- **1998**—Athletes with a disability included in Commonwealth Games with full medal status (Manchester, UK)
- **1999**—Lance Armstrong wins first of seven consecutive Tour de France races

2000s

- **2000**—Canadians Daniel Nestor and Sebastien Lareau win men's tennis doubles at Sydney Olympics
- **2002**—Women's World Cup match between US and China draws 90,000 spectators in Rose Bowl; Brandi Chastain rips off jersey after making game-winning penalty shot

system, you will know what recourse you have if problems occur. You also need to be highly attuned to security procedures, including visa requirements and other travel-related regulations.

GATT—An agreement negotiated in 1947 among 23 countries, including the United States, to increase international trade by reducing tariffs and other trade barriers.

NAFTA—A 1994 agreement reached by the United States, Canada, and Mexico that instituted a schedule for the phasing out of tariffs and eliminated a variety of fees and other hindrances to encourage free trade among the three countries.

EC—An organization currently composed of the following Western European nations: Belgium, Germany, France, Italy, Luxembourg, the Netherlands, Denmark, Greece, Ireland, Portugal, Spain, and the United Kingdom. The EC attempts to unify and integrate member countries by establishing common economic policies.

Many professional leagues and teams are concerned about whether trademark and copyright laws of a nation or regional economic group will protect their trademarks. They also need to know whether other countries have laws or regulations that might inhibit the movement of players from one nation to another (e.g., European soccer, Japanese baseball, Chinese basketball), whether they have a system of binding contracts (e.g., the NBA and the NHL with the European leagues and MLB with their Latin American and Japanese counterparts), and in what currency to base the compensation for a given player (e.g., MLB and the NHL with their Canadian-based teams). The following sections will explore two of the most pressing concerns in international sport today: (1) the relocation of sporting goods manufacturing companies and (2) international sport governance issues.

Relocation of Manufacturing Companies

Some sporting goods manufacturing companies have relocated most of their production of footwear and apparel to China, Vietnam, or Indonesia (Katz, 1994). This relocation has created serious financial and ethical questions (Bernstein, et al., 2001). For example, does the availability of a large, cheap labor force outweigh concerns over counterfeiting made possible by weak copyright laws, currency fluctuations and devaluations, and potentially restrictive export and import laws? What are the human rights and ethical considerations when large, multinational corporations such as Nike, adidas, and others profit from the toil of children and women for pennies an hour in sweatshop conditions in Southeast Asian or Central American countries (Jones, 1996; Robson, 2001)? Is it exploitive to move footwear and sport apparel production from one developing nation to another (e.g., from Korea to the Philippines to China and Indonesia) in search of the cheapest labor supply? What responsibility do companies have to the workers and countries that they leave behind?

Ideally, ethical value systems and human rights principles are part of the decision-making process in the relocation of manufacturing centers. Companies must also consider the stability of political regimes and their diplomatic relations with the nations in which the corporate home offices are located. In the aftermath of the September 11 terrorist attacks in New York (2001) and the terrorist bombings in Moscow (2003), Madrid (2004), and London (2005), depending on an uninterrupted supply of cheaply produced goods made in nations where there are large radical, anti-Western movements makes strategic international business planning difficult. Security issues have become paramount in decisions to locate new production facilities.

Learning Activity

Write an op ed (250 to 750 words) about a contemporary issue in international sport. Your topic should cut across sport and the international spectrum (e.g., fair play, international judging, doping and performance enhancing drugs, security, professionalization, commercialization, expansion, governance, ethics). Do not focus on any particular event (such as the Olympic Games); you could, however, include the Olympic Games or some other event or league as a focal point. Use the "Final Word" column in *Street & Smith's SportsBusiness Journal* as an example for this paper.

International Sport Governance

Another key step on your journey into international sport is developing an understanding of compli-

2000s

- **2001**—First NCAA Division I Women's Ice Hockey Championship won by University of Minnesota—Duluth
- **2001**—China voted into World Trade Organization
- **2002**—Japan and Korea co-host 2002 FIFA World Cup
- **2002**—Salt Lake City Olympics: Catriona LeMay Doan wins women's 500 m speedskating gold medal
- **2003**—Canada wins World Hockey Championship
- **2004**—Brian Lara, West Indies, scores a test innings record 400 not out against England

cated international sport governance structures (see figure 8.4). Eligibility for competing in each Olympic-related sport is governed and controlled by an international sport federation (IF) and its related national sport governing federation or body (NSF or NGB). Note that the international sport federations have relationships to the International Olympic Committee (IOC), but they are not formally part of the IOC. These federations, therefore, sometimes differ with the IOC with respect to rules of control, athlete eligibility, and drug-testing procedures and consequences (Hums & MacLean, 2004).

Before 1985 international sport focused on amateur sports that were included in the Olympic Games, Commonwealth Games, or hemispheric games (e.g., Asian, Pan-African, Pan-American Games). As you can see in figure 8.4, over the past 20 years a number of new entities have become involved in international sport governance. These changes reflect the evolution of international sport from a relatively small number of organizations that emphasized amateur sport to a highly complex set of interrelated organizations with billions of US dollars at stake. The principal additions include

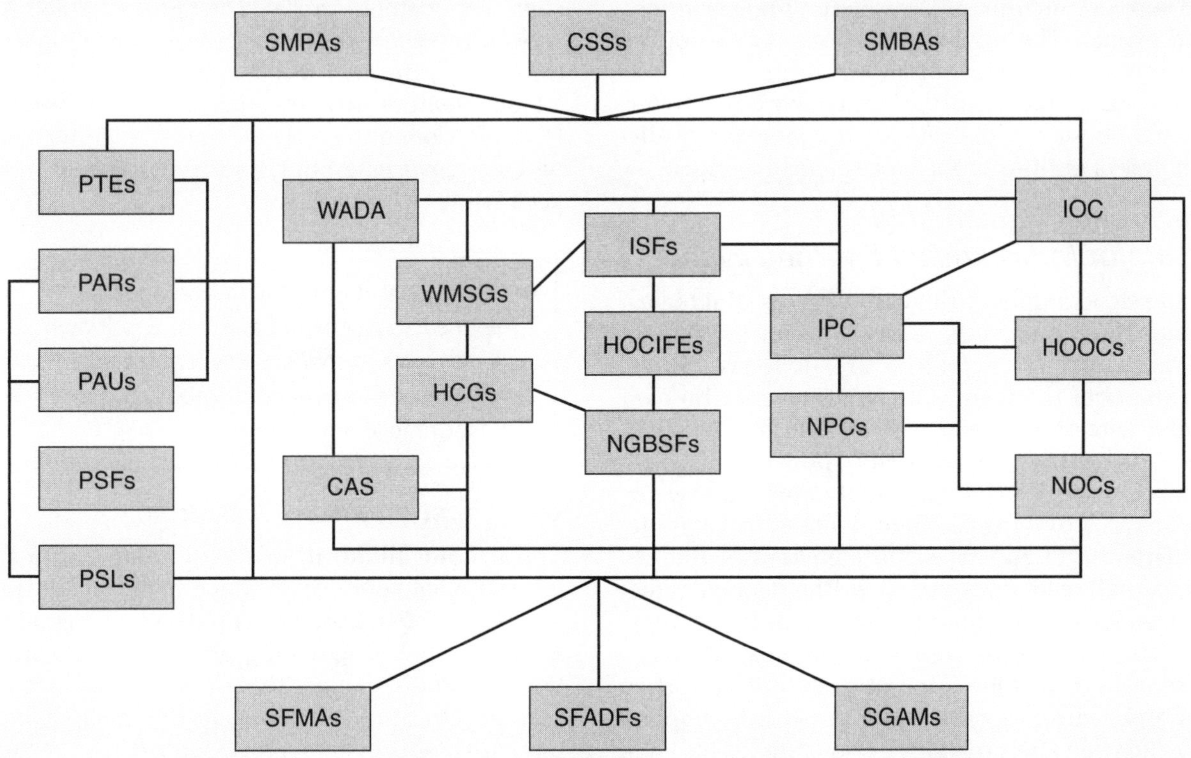

Legend

IOC:	International Olympic Committee	**WADA:**	World Anti-Doping Agency
HOOCs:	Host Olympic Organizing Committees	**CSSs:**	Corporate Sponsors & Suppliers
NOCs:	National Olympic Committees	**HOCIFEs:**	Organizing Committees – IF Events
ISFs:	International Sport Federations	**SMBAs:**	Sport Media & Broadcasting Agencies
NGBSFs:	National Sport Federations	**SMPAs:**	Sport Marketing & Promotional Agencies
IPC:	International Paralympic Committee	**SGAMs:**	Sporting Goods & Apparel Manufacturers
NPCs:	National Paralympic Committees	**SFADFs:**	Sport Facility Architects & Design Firms
CAS:	Court of Arbitration in Sport	**SFMAs:**	Sport Facilities Management Agencies
PTEs:	Professional Sport Tours & Events	**PAUs:**	Professional Athlete Unions
PSLs:	Professional Sport Leagues	**PARs**	Professional Athlete Agents
PSFs	Professional Sport Team Franchises	**HCGs:**	Hemispheric or Continental Games
WMSGs:	World Multi-Sport Games		

Figure 8.4 Universe of key international sport governance and industry interrelationships.

Created by Fay, 2006.

(1) professional sport organizations (PSOs), such as sport franchises, leagues, tours and circuits; (2) professional athlete unions, along with professional athlete representatives (PPUs and PARs); (3) the Court of Arbitration for Sport (CAS), which adjudicates issues such as international athlete eligibility and issues relating to breaches of fair play; (4) the World Anti-Doping Agency (WADA), which acts as an independent testing and research organization designed to eliminate the use of banned performance-enhancing substances and techniques from international sport competition; and (5) sport organization and event sponsors that provide critical support and funding to athletes, organizations, and events. The following sections on corporate sponsorship, drug testing and arbitration, and special concerns regarding the Paralympic Games offer details about the reasons for the increase in the number of entities in the governance structure.

Corporate Sponsorship of Major International Sporting Events

A classic example of the complexities of international sport involved the 1992 US men's Olympic basketball team (a.k.a. the Dream Team). Some members of the team were NBA players who had endorsement contracts with sponsors other than the official US Olympic team sponsors. In 1992 Reebok was the official US Olympic outerwear sponsor, providing warm-up jackets to Olympic athletes in all sports. Some members of the US basketball team chose to cover the Reebok name with American flags as they stood on the victory podium to accept their gold medals. Michael Jordan, a Nike-sponsored athlete, initiated this action because he did not want to be seen implicitly endorsing his company's competitor. This incident thrust the USOC, Nike, Reebok, USA Basketball, the NBA, the NBA Players Association, and Jordan into a high-stakes public relations battle (Katz, 1994). The USOC has since amended its code of conduct to include language that requires all US Olympic athletes to wear the apparel provided by official US Olympic sponsors.

Ambush marketing is another concern related to corporate sponsorship of international events. One way companies engage in ambush marketing in advertising is to link images of sports or athletes to the host city (e.g., "Good luck to our athletes in Torino") while carefully refraining from the use of terms such as *Olympic* or *Olympic Games* in the ad. Even so, consumers psychologically infer a relationship between the product being advertised and the sporting event with which it is being linked.

The IOC and its NOC members have become forceful in limiting and counteracting ambush marketing campaigns by corporations and organizations intent on circumventing the costs of sponsorship. The IOC, NOC, and the local Olympic Organizing Committee (OOC) must be diligent in protecting and supporting their corporate partners who have been granted exclusive advertising rights in exchange for large sums of money in sponsorships ("A-B Paces Ad Spending," 2005). To prevent future conflicts between official Olympic team sponsors and rival companies that have endorsement deals with Team USA's players, the USOC has tightened its contracts and oversight. For example, in 2002 the USOC established a new partnership program called Olympic Properties US (OPUS), through which it sought control over its joint venture partners such as the Salt Lake City Olympic Committee (SLOC) and the winter sport national governing bodies (NGBs) involved in the 2002 Winter Olympic Games (USOC, 2005).

ambush marketing—A tactic whereby a company attempts to undermine the sponsorship activities of a rival, which owns the legal rights to sponsor an event; intended to create the sense that the ambusher is officially associated with the event.

Drug Testing and Arbitration

The second illustration of the complexities of international sport governance involved US track and field athlete Butch Reynolds' challenge of the 1992 Olympic drug-testing procedures. Reynolds failed an out-of-competition drug test and was disqualified from participating in the 1992 Olympic Games. He subsequently filed suit against the International Amateur Athletic Federation (IAAF), claiming that his urine specimens had been tampered with and that the analysis procedures had been flawed. This controversy highlighted new, complex entanglements that involve an athlete's right to sue an international sport federation with respect to the right to compete in the Olympic Games.

The US federal court held for Reynolds and threatened to freeze IAAF sponsorship money from US-based corporations to force the IAAF to fulfill its obligations of a compensatory award (Weiler & Roberts, 2004). The problems caused by this successful legal action prompted several international sport federations to join the IOC in creating the Court of Arbitration for Sport (CAS), which mediates sport-related disputes that cross national boundaries (Thoma & Chalip, 1996).

If this situation had occurred 10 years later, the World Anti-Doping Agency (WADA), headed by ex-IOC vice president Dick Pound, would likely have assumed jurisdiction over the Reynolds case. WADA was established in 2001 because of broad international perception that many world records and gold medal results in the Olympic Games, as well as many world championships in a variety of sports, had been tainted by cheaters who had never been caught (Jennings, 2001). Established as an independent agency, WADA has been willing to challenge sport federations and professional sport leagues by taking on the giants of sport, including star performers such as Lance Armstrong and the International Cycling Union, which takes a more laissez-faire approach to testing. WADA has not been shy about voicing its zero tolerance policies to professional leagues (e.g., Major League Baseball and the National Football League), international and national sport federations, and national sport heroes of host nations (Orkin, 2004; Pound, 2004; McCloskey & Bailes, 2005).

Learning Activity

Search the Internet for stories about Greek track and field stars Katerina Thanou and Kostas Kenteris. Have a class discussion about their withdrawal from the 2004 Athens Olympic Games after they failed to appear for several drug tests before and during the Games. What does the experience of these two athletes reveal about the influence of WADA?

Issues related to the use of drugs, performance-enhancing supplements, steroids, and technologies that aid performance continue to challenge the foundation of international sport (Pound, 2004; King, 2005a). Stemming from the government-sponsored cheating of the East Germans and other countries in the 1970s and 1980s and the free-market approach of companies such as US-based BALCO, the challenges facing sport governing bodies are staggering (McCloskey & Bailes, 2005; Ungerleider, 2001). With billions of US dollars in potential endorsement deals at stake, some athletes are seeking to beat the system. Is the creation of a generation of cyborg athletes who use altered DNA or implants next on the horizon (Smith & Westerbeek, 2004)? Moreover, what are the implications of technology for Paralympic athletes who are currently allowed to use space-age prosthetics? (Joukowsky & Rothstein, 2002; Price, 2005).

BALCO—Bay Area Laboratory Cooperative, whose founder Victor Conte and others have been implicated in providing designer performance-enhancing drugs and steroids to major league baseball players and several Olympic athletes.

Learning Activity

Deliver an oral presentation on a current critical issue or event in international sport. Use a variety of sources that provide information relevant to international sport. At least half the sources should be from periodicals or literature outside your home country. We encourage you to use the Internet and other electronic information sources.

Paralympic Governance Concerns

The Paralympic Games, which involve elite athletes with physical and sensory disabilities, are among the world's largest quadrennial sporting events. Both the Winter and Summer Paralympic Games usually occur two weeks after the Olympic Games and are held at the same location and in the same facilities as the Olympic Games. An Olympic bid awarded to a city, therefore, brings with it an obligation to conduct the Paralympic Games. The host country is expected to modify its infrastructure where necessary to meet the accessibility needs of Paralympians (Hums & MacLean, 2004). Strong historical support for the Paralympic movement and sound planning for the Paralympic Games strengthened both Vancouver's and London's winning bids for the Olympic and Paralympic Games in 2010 and 2012, respectively.

Under the leadership of the International Paralympic Committee (IPC) and its corresponding National Paralympic Committees (NPCs), the Paralympics have emerged as a viable international sport movement (DePauw & Gavron, 2005). As the Paralympic Games have gained prominence, the topic of inclusion of athletes with a disability has arisen. Following the example regarding gender equity in US sport, some people have begun to ask if the national governing bodies of Olympic sports and the US Olympic Committee should be required by law to integrate their structures, teams, management, and governance to include Paralympic athletes (Hums & MacLean, 2004; Fay, Legg, & Wolff, 2005). The US Ski and Snowboard Association (USSA) established precedent in 1986, when it became the first national governing body of

Vietnam's Thi Khoa Nhu powers her way to gold during the women's 400-meter athletics finals at the 2005 ASEAN Paralympics in Manila, Philippines. Nhu clocked 1 minute and 11.83 seconds.

AP Photo/Aaron Favila.

an Olympic sport to integrate Paralympic athletes into its operating structure. When the USSA assimilated the US Disabled Ski Team (USDST), the USDST became, at least in theory, equal to the other US ski teams (i.e., alpine and cross-country teams) of the USSA. This recognition allowed USDST athletes to compete in open USSA sanctioned races, including the US National Championships (Fay, 1989).

In the first decades of the 21st century, sport governing bodies will continue to struggle to find the best path to full and equitable inclusion of athletes with disabilities into international organizations and events (Burton, 2000; Fay, 2001; Grevemberg, Hums, & Wolff, 2001). Not surprisingly, the discussions and debates regarding the integration of athletes with a disability are reminiscent of the dialogue that accompanied a similar movement for equality of treatment for racial minority groups and women.

Essentials for Aspiring International Sport Managers

Important segments of the international sport industry include arenas, stadia, sport products, ticketing, security, fitness centers, rehabilitation and sports medicine centers, accommodations, and travel. These segments are crucial to the conduct of international sport and are the areas in which the most growth will occur in the next decade, thereby providing the most opportunities for entry-level sport managers (Muret, 2005; Woodward & Muret, 2005). To secure work in these venues, sports managers must master a wide knowledge and skill base, discussed in the following section.

International Sport Manager's Skill Set

Computer skills and the ability to use the Internet to conduct research and maintain daily business communications are basic skills for entry-level sport management positions. International sport is a "phone, fax, and e-mail" culture based on strong oral and written communication skills as well as an understanding of electronic etiquette. A sales background or experience as an athlete is not a requirement, but either can be helpful in gaining a job and succeeding in it. International sport managers must be willing and able to travel, necessitating an adequate level of fitness and health. In addition, the position entails long flights, long meetings compressed into tight schedules, and long periods away

Learning Activity

Write a paper about the history of the Paralympic Games. Include facts such as the location of the first Summer and Winter Games, the creator of the forerunner to the Paralympic Games, the athletes for whom the first Games were organized, and the first example of inclusion of athletes with a disability into a national sport federation.

Learning Activity

In small groups, read and discuss one or two of the books listed on page 65.

from home (Rubenfeld & Hemingway, 2005). You need to be patient, able to listen, and respectful of existing hierarchies established by various cultural and religious practices (Morrison et al., 2001).

Being able to communicate in the language of the country where you are working is extremely important. For example, you might be told that your colleagues from other countries understand English better than they do or that you can obtain the services of an interpreter who, as it turns out, cannot or will not convey the nuances of key oral exchanges. Consequently, in international business and sport, even a rudimentary understanding of the language of the country in which you are doing business can gain you an invaluable advantage over the competition (Barnet & Cavanagh, 1994; Morrison et al., 2001).

TOOL KIT FOR INTERNATIONAL SPORT MANAGERS

Essential equipment for a career in international sport includes an up-to-date world atlas, a current passport, appropriate visas, bilingual dictionaries, a pocket guide to currency exchange rates, several credit cards with reasonable credit lines, appropriate transportation tickets, a laptop computer with modem and WiFi capability, a personal digital assistant (PDA), a cellular phone with international calling options, and two bags packed with the items necessary to conduct business. You will be embarking on an adventure that will test your wits with respect to your personal habits, eating preferences, cultural understanding, business etiquette, patience, ability to develop a new network of friendships, and flexibility.

International Sport Manager's Worldview

If you aspire to a career in international sport management, you should consider (1) studying abroad (preferably in country that speaks a language different from yours) for a minimum of one semester while still in school and (2) availing yourself of a wide range of publications, including industry and trade publications, professional journals, newspapers, and magazines to keep you up to date on international political, business, and sport trends. You would be wise to start to assemble a library of books and information that will augment off-the-shelf or library reference material. A daily regimen of reading key periodicals such as the *Wall Street Journal*, *SportBusiness International*, *Street & Smith's SportsBusiness Journal*, *The Economist*, and *USA Today* is vital. This practice will give you knowledge of general business practices in a given culture, keep you current on what is happening in the global economy, and provide up-to-date information about world events. A variety of online services on the Internet offer easy access to key materials and daily periodicals that may not be available in hard copy at a library, bookstore, or newsstand (Brake, Walker, & Walker, 1995).

A basic knowledge of how a sport operates internationally, the specific rules of the game, how the sport is structured, and where the locus of power resides with the sport (politically as well as on the field of play) can enhance your marketability. An understanding of trends in licensing, marketing, promotion, event management, and contracts is also helpful. Familiarity with international geography, such as shifting borders within geopolitical regions, will prevent serious faux pas, such as forgetting that Czechoslovakia is now the separate nations of the Czech Republic and Slovakia; that Burma is now Myanmar; and that Croatia, Slovenia, Bosnia-Herzegovina, Kosovo, and Macedonia are no longer part of Yugoslavia (*The Great World Atlas*, 2004).

Learning Activity

Consult the Web site www.cia.gov/cia/publications/factbook and look up the population, birth rate, death rate, life expectancy at birth, languages, literacy, gross domestic product and gross domestic product per capita, and the population below poverty line for one country of your choice on each continent excluding Antarctica (six countries total). Compare this information with the same data for your country. Identify the sports that are culturally significant to the countries that you have selected.

International Sport Management: "It's Personal!"

Success in the international sport and business sphere is predicated on personal contact and friendship. Attending meetings of national sport federations, professional sport-related associations, and other conferences and symposia helps maintain and expand your network of professional contacts. Time availability, relevance to your professional interests, and financial resources are important factors to consider when choosing the associations or annual conferences and trade shows that you want to attend. Volunteering at a major international sports event, conference, or trade show is an effective way to gain access to the field and demonstrate your capabilities as a potential employee.

No single pathway leads to a career in the expanding and shifting landscape of the international sport marketplace. An informational interview of a professional in the field can be valuable in learning more about the realities of working for sport organizations that do business with other cultures or the challenges of working in a country in which one must speak a different language. One important caveat to remember is that you must experience culture directly to understand it even at a fundamental level; you cannot adequately prepare for a career in international sport management online or from home (Pike & Fay, 1993).

INTERNATIONAL SPORT 2006 THROUGH 2015: FORECASTING THE FUTURE

In the beginning decades of the 21st century, the international sport industry will shift from being a niche in the sport marketplace to constituting the very foundation of the sport enterprise. Based on concepts such as **gross global sport product** (GGSP), both market share and investment in sport products and services are already being measured in terms of worldwide rather than national economic parameters. Although attempts will be made to restrict and protect segments of the industry based on national biases and policies, the decade from 2006 through 2015 will see an almost seamless integration and movement of goods, services, and personnel on a global scale. In the following paragraphs, we will discuss several trends that are destined to affect international sport.

> **gross global sport product**—The total economic output of the sports industry worldwide.

The Shrinking Globe

In the coming years, countries around the world will be drawn closer as national and international sport federations compete more directly with professional leagues and franchises for global market share of trademark licensing and merchandise. All domains of the international sport enterprise, both emerging niche sports and traditional professional sports, will profit from increased advertising revenues made possible through worldwide cable deregulation and integrated technologies that use the Internet and cellular phones to deliver sport content to consumers. Advances in on-demand information technologies will allow the creation of strong fan affiliations and the development of new virtual fans. Cross-marketing and promotional agreements between partners on different continents and in different sports (e.g., Manchester United and the New York Yankees) will change the way in which the sport industry organizes itself. Differences in cultures, national laws, and customs will compound the challenges of these developments ("Who's Wearing?" 2001; Smith & Westerbeek, 2004; Szymanski & Zimbalist, 2005).

Learning Activity

Choose a country and investigate its most popular sport activities, sport facilities, and famous athletes to create a profile for a global sport atlas. Describe the prime sport exports and imports of this country, including the production of goods and services, the existence of prominent sport leagues and events, the development of players and coaches in particular sports, offices of international sport federations (IFs), and so on.

With respect to athletes, international exchanges in a broad cross-section of sports ranging from youth to near elite levels will become commonplace. Such exchanges will continue to include showcase tournaments and camps for the benefit of coaches who use them to recruit athletes from Europe, Australia, and to a lesser extent Africa and South America, who seek prized US athletic scholarships. As the rate of export and import of international talent at all competitive levels escalates, international trade agreements will have a greater effect on the sport industry.

Social Awareness

As noted in chapter 1, the United Nations proclaimed 2005 as the International Year of Sport and Physical Education. In so doing, it drew attention to its focus on a new human rights convention, which included access to sport and leisure activity for all people of the world as a basic human right. This and other trends indicate that the world will soon rediscover the importance and interrelationship of access to play and sport opportunities for all, regardless of socioeconomic status, gender, race, or ethnicity.

The social consciences of elite athletes will become even more pronounced. Already, we see athletes such as Tiger Woods, David Beckham, Julie Foudy, Lance Armstrong, and others give back to society by establishing charities and foundations to support critical causes, from finding a cure for cancer to literacy to HIV and AIDS research. Another example of philanthropy is the generosity of Johan Olav Koss, multiple speedskating gold medalist from Norway at the 1994 Lillehammer Winter Olympic Games. Koss used his accomplishments as an Olympic champion to call attention to a number of human rights needs by creating an organization called Olympic Aid. This organization was originally designed to support the survivors of ethnic cleansing in Bosnia in the 1990s and has since evolved into Right to Play, an international organization focused on bringing sport and physical activity to children in developing countries in Africa, Asia, and South America. American gold medalist speedskater Joey Cheek renewed Koss' pledge and commitment to worldwide human rights needs by donating all $40,000 USD of his 2006 Olympic gold and silver medal earnings from the USOC to Right to Play. Cheek leveraged the publicity surrounding this pledge to challenge more than 10 corporations to match his gift (Weir, 2006).

Within the context of human rights, an expansion and application of the principles of equity will occur throughout all cultures. Such an effort will affect not only who gets to play sports but also who gets to control the sporting enterprise. The growth and expansion of professional team sport leagues for women, particularly in North America, will give rise to expanded marketing and management initiatives (Grundy & Shackelford, 2005; King, 2005b). The Paralympic Games will achieve major-event status through increased television, media, and spectator appeal. These trends will provide expanded job opportunities in the international sport marketplace for women, older people, and people with disabilities. Farsighted, socially responsible, consumer-oriented companies will stand to gain the most from these developments (Fay, Hums, & Wolff, 2000a, 2000b).

A new order of elite decision makers will assume command of a global sport industry based on pragmatic alliances between leagues, international federations, television networks, and corporate sponsors. Corporations will begin to seek brand identification with particular sports, leading to the formation of corporate and national team alliances (Smith & Westerbeek, 2004). Niche and action sports, such as in-line skating, triathlon, snowboarding, and mountain biking, will continue to emerge and grow. Sports such as roller hockey, beach volleyball, and endurance kayaking will redefine themselves and continue to expand. All these sports will flourish because of broad, cross-generational participation and their appeal as televised events.

Environmental Concerns

Expanded leisure time for the elite and the growing middle classes in South America, China, India, Asia, and parts of Africa will continue to fuel worldwide expansion of golf, tennis, and other recreational sports. Extended life expectancy will continue to affect the international sport and leisure travel industry, necessitating significant expansion of facilities. As you learned in chapters 1 and 7, serious concerns about the effect of recreational facilities on the environment will accompany this expansion. For example, conflicts have already emerged regarding the construction of golf courses in sensitive mountain terrain and tropical rain forests. Concerns also exist about building large-scale leisure and sport resorts in the developing world and stadia and arenas in environmentally or economically sensitive areas. These developments have plunged the international sport industry more deeply into debates related to the impact of sport and recreation on the environment (Smith & Westerbeek, 2004). In response, the International Olympic Committee has created a commission and a policy position regarding concerns about the impact of the Olympic Games on local and regional environments (*The Sport and Environment Commission*, 2006).

In the future, more career opportunities will emerge in areas dealing with jurisdiction and dispute resolution related to international athletes' rights, blood doping, drug use and abuse, relocation of franchises from nation to nation, and other policy matters. International and national sport federations, professional leagues, sport marketing agencies, cable and network television and radio, arenas and facilities, fitness clubs, and sport product corporations will begin to give hiring preference to people with backgrounds oriented to the global marketplace.

SUMMARY

International organizations, events, and governance structures are international if they are involved internationally on a regular basis or as one of their primary functions. Beginning in 1972, several events (e.g., the growing commercialization of the Olympics, Nixon's Ping-Pong diplomacy, and the passage of Title IX in the United States) had a profound effect on sport. Subsequently, international sport was redefined by the commercialization of the Olympic and Paralympic Games, a shift from the predictable dominance of specific countries in some sports, recruitment of international athletes, extension of the popularity of soccer around the globe, entry of more Japanese players into MLB, and the growing role of sport in the world economy through successful marketing strategies. In the 21st century, China emerged as a dominant force in international sport. Beijing's successful bid for the 2008 Olympic and Paralympic Games initially created ethical concerns, but massive changes in the country's infrastructure in preparation for the Games and the potential for the Olympics to leave a lasting effect on China allayed many of these concerns. In the future, China will affect sport through an increase in exportation of talent, provision of additional sponsorship opportunities, and contribution to an expanded world economy. Careers in international sport require an understanding of issues such as the relocation of manufacturing operations to countries that use sweatshop labor, governance issues related to corporate sponsorship, drug testing, and the Paralympics. To be successful internationally, aspiring sport managers must have the appropriate tools, skills, worldview, and cultural understanding. The future of international sport will occur in a world that is becoming smaller because of technology, is aware of social concerns that can be addressed through sport, and possesses a heightened commitment to environmental (green) concerns. Career opportunities in international sport will expand for those who are oriented to the global marketplace.

Review Questions

1. Define international sport.
2. Identify three changes that occurred in international sport between 1972 and 1984 and explain their effects.
3. Identify six phenomena that have redefined international sport and explain the particular effects of each.
4. With respect to the 2008 Olympic and Paralympic Games, explain (1) the bidding process, (2) Beijing's preparation for the Games, and (3) the potential of the Olympic legacy.
5. Identify three future effects of China on international sport.
6. Discuss the advantages and disadvantages of relocating the manufacture of sport-related products to countries that use sweatshop labor.
7. Discuss the effects of corporate sponsorship, drug testing, and the Paralympic Games on international sport governance.
8. Explain how aspiring international sport managers can prepare for the job market.
9. Discuss future trends in international sport.

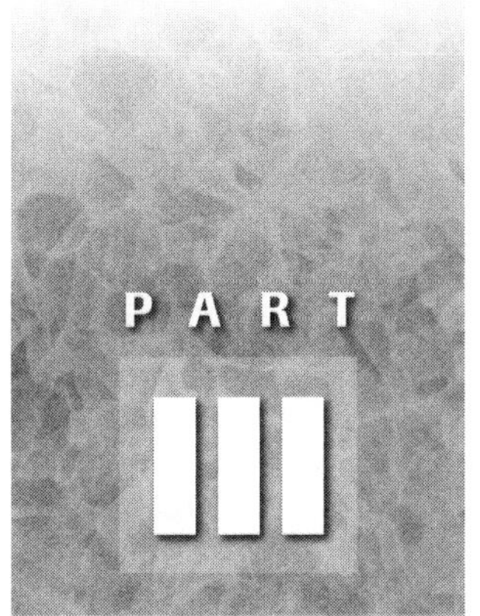

Selected Sport Management Functions

The five chapters in this section present valuable information about sport marketing and promotion; consumer behavior; communication and public relations; finance, economics, and budgeting; and facility and event management. These functions are universal in sport in that they are performed at most sport-related sites, including those discussed in the previous section—intercollegiate athletics, professional sport, sport management and marketing agencies, sport tourism, and international sport.

In chapter 9 Wayne Blann and Ketra Armstrong define marketing and explain the unique aspects of sport marketing. Then they examine the evolution of sport marketing and discuss the importance of the relationship between a sport marketing plan and the organization's mission and core values. Next, the authors present the elements of the marketing mix and show how a marketing plan addresses those elements. They discuss the elements of a SWOT analysis and explain how to use it to assess present and future market climates. Blann and Armstrong then present information on the various dimensions of sport products and events, define product positioning and market niches, and explain the communication of product images. They also cover branding, marketing segmentation, pricing and promotion strategies, distribution channels, and the packaging and selling of sport products. The theme of socially responsible sport marketing runs throughout the chapter. In the international sidebar, Kamini Sharma describes the North American Sports Network (NASN), a TV channel in Europe dedicated to North American sports. Ms. Sharma, who has worked in various roles in the sport industry since 1991, currently lives in London, England, where she is the marketing director for NASN.

Christine Green and Carla Costa address the psyche of the sport consumer in chapter 10. First, they examine people's perceptions and attitudes toward sport and explain the types of factors that motivate individual sport consumers to purchase sport-related products. After discussing the influence of various groups of people on consumers' behaviors, they suggest strategies for building and strengthening relationships with customers. Green and Costa then explain the steps in the decision-making process and suggest ways in which sport marketers can influence those decisions. The underlying theme of this chapter is that understanding how people make decisions about their consumption of the sport product will be valuable to sport managers as they compete with a multitude of other leisure-time diversions for the time and money of consumers. The international sidebar contains an essay on the influence of the 2004 European Soccer Championship on the national identity of Portuguese citizens. Abel Correia, a marketing professor at the Universidade Técnica de Lisboa (Lisbon, Portugal) contributed this essay.

Clay Stoldt, Catherine Pratt, and Steve Dittmore address sport public relations in chapter 11. After presenting basic information about communication in general, they explain several models of public relations practices. Then the authors provide an overview of the development of the relationship between sport and the mass media, including a discussion of the balance of power in the complex relationships among sport, media, and corporations. In the remainder of the chapter, the authors explain careers in media relations and community relations, delineating the responsibilities involved and the skills needed for each. The authors conclude with information on ways in which advances in communication technology have affected the practice of public relations in sport. Attention to ethical practices is included throughout the chapter.

Andy Anderson, from the University of Toronto in Ontario, Canada and John Corlett and James Mandigo, both from Brock University in St. Catharines, Ontario, Canada, contributed the international sidebar for chapter 11. They describe a successful community relations program that provides sport experiences to children in El Salvador.

In chapter 12 Tim DeSchriver and Dan Mahony introduce basic information about finance, economics, and budgeting within the sport industry. After explaining the size and scope of the sport industry in economic terms, they describe the current financial situation of the US professional and intercollegiate sport industries. Then they present basic principles of the macroeconomics of sport, including attention to real gross domestic product, interest rate, and inflation rate. A discussion of microeconomics follows, addressing supply and demand, market structures, and the economic impact of sport. Next, DeSchriver and Mahony further explain the business structure of sport organizations and introduce basic tools of financial management. They conclude the chapter with advice for students who aspire to careers in financial management of sport organizations. The international sidebar contains an essay on the financial aspects of the Japanese Football Association (JFA). Makoto Nakazawa, who teaches sport management at the Institute of Health & Sport Sciences, University of Tsukuba (Tsukuba, Japan), contributed the essay.

Robin Ammon and David Stotlar address sport facility and event management in chapter 13. First, they note the unprecedented boom that has occurred in sport facility construction and the accompanying expansion of employment opportunities. Ammon and Stotlar then differentiate among several types of facilities and explain the current trend toward privatization of facilities. A discussion of ways in which sport managers can minimize risks associated with facilities and events follows. The final sections of the chapter provide in-depth information on facility management personnel and responsibilities as well as examples of event personnel assignments. Real-life scenarios illustrate the importance of proper planning for sporting events. In the international sidebar, Babs Surujlal, who teaches sport management at the University of Technology in Gauteng, South Africa, describes the importance of accurate risk assessment at sporting events in South Africa.

For More Information

Marketing: Professional and Scholarly Associations

Academy of Marketing Sciences

American Marketing Association

American Sports Data, Inc.

Direct Marketing Association

International Sports Marketing Association

Licensing Industry Merchandisers Association (LIMA)

Society of Consumer Affairs Professionals

Sport Consumer Behavior

Research and Markets: www.researchandmarkets.com

Public Relations Professional Organizations

College Sports Information Directors of America (CoSIDA): www.cosida.com

Female Athletic Media Relations Executives (FAME): www.personal.psu.edu/staff/m/j/mjh11/Fame13.html

Football Writers Association of America: www.footballwriters.com

International Association of Business Communicators: www.iabc.com

National Association of Collegiate Directors of Athletics (NACDA): http://nacda.cstv.com

National College Baseball Writers Association: www.sportswriters.net/ncbwa

Public Relations Society of America: www.prsa.org

United States Basketball Writers Association: www.sportswriters.net/usbwa

Sport Finance Books

Fried, G., Shapiro, S., & DeSchriver, T. (2003). *Sport finance*. Champaign, IL: Human Kinetics.

Helyar, J. (1994). *Lords of the realm*. New York: Ballantine Books.

Livingstone, J.L., & Grossman, T. (Eds.). (2002). *The portable MBA in finance and accounting*

(3rd ed.). New York: Wiley.

Noll, R.G., & Zimbalist, A. (Eds). (1997). *Sports, jobs, and taxes: The economic impact of sports teams and stadiums*. Washington, DC: Brookings Institution Press.

Quirk, J., & Fort, R.D. (1997). *Pay dirt: The business of professional team sports*. Princeton, NJ: Princeton University Press.

Quirk, J., & Fort, R.D. (1999). *Hard ball: The abuse of power in pro team sports*. Princeton, NJ: Princeton University Press.

Staudohar, P.D. (1996). *Playing for dollars: Labor relations and the sports business* (3rd ed.). Ithaca, NY: ILR Press.

Facility Management Professional Associations

International Association of Assembly Managers

National Recreation & Park Association

National Swimming Pool Foundation

Stadium Managers Association

US Golf Association

YMCA of the USA

Facility Management Internet Sites

International Association of Assembly Managers: www.iaam.org

International Facility Management Association: www.ifma.org

Job opportunities: www.JobsinSports.com

Rock concerts and crowd safety: www.crowdsafe.com/reports.html

TeamWork Online: www.teamworkonline.com

Stadium and venue news: www.stadianet.com/go.php

Professional and Scholarly Publications

Advertising Age

Amusement Business

Athletic Business

Athletics Administration

CoSIDA Digest

Facility Manager

Journal of Communication Management

Journal of Marketing

Journal of Public Relations Research

Journal of Sport Management

Marketing Communications

National Aquatics Journal

PR Week

Psychology and Marketing

Public Relations Strategist

Special Events Report

Sport Marketing Quarterly

Sports Illustrated

Sports Market Place

Street & Smith's SportsBusiness Journal

Team Marketing Report

Team Marketing Report Newsletter

The Sponsors Report

The Sporting News

The Sports Business Daily

Sport Marketing

F. Wayne Blann—Ithaca College ■ **Ketra L. Armstrong**—California State University at Long Beach

Learning Objectives

After studying this chapter, you will be able to do the following:

1. Recognize how a marketing plan is linked to an organization's mission statement and core values.
2. Assess the present and future market climate for a sport or event by conducting a SWOT (strengths, weaknesses, opportunities, and threats) analysis.
3. Analyze the dimensions of a sport product, such as the game itself or an event.
4. Define product positioning and market niche.
5. Communicate images and messages of a sport product in ethical and socially responsible ways.
6. Define market segmentation and identify viable target audiences.
7. Discuss how sports are distributed to consumers.
8. Define packaging and selling a sport product.
9. Explain what is meant by the "promise" of a marketing plan.
10. Identify two sport marketing needs in the 21st century.

Marketing is a complex function that is extremely important to the overall success of sport organizations. You probably have heard the term *sport marketing* in many contexts, and you might be wondering exactly what it means. That's a good question because sport marketing is composed of several elements, and the term *sport marketing* frequently is used incorrectly. People tend to define marketing in terms of their experiences, instead of recognizing one of the most important roles of marketing—carrying out the mission of an organization.

Some corporate executives might describe sport marketing as selling goods and services to generate a profit. But sport marketing is more than selling. People who work in advertising and public relations might consider sport marketing as obtaining Super Bowl tickets for clients or entertaining a corporate sponsor at the US Open Golf Tournament. But sport marketing is more than advertising and public relations. Those who provide services for professional athletes might view sport marketing as arranging for athletes to attend the grand opening of a shopping mall or arranging to have corporate executives play tennis with Lleyton Hewitt or Lindsay Davenport. But sport marketing is more than community relations.

Pitts and Stotlar (2002) defined sport marketing as "the process of designing and implementing activities for the production, pricing, promotion and distribution of a sport product or sport business product to satisfy the needs or desires of consumers and to achieve the company's objectives" (p. 79). Balancing a company's business objectives with consumer wants and needs is a challenge in any industry, but sport marketing is even more complex because sport has certain characteristics that make it unique. A brief examination of sport's unique combination of characteristics proposed by Mullin, Hardy, and Sutton (2000) will show how sport differs from other products, goods, and services and therefore why the approach to marketing sport is unique.

1. Aspects of sport are intangible. For example, you cannot touch the actual competition that takes place between two football teams. You can, however, touch products associated with the experience such as equipment, the seats in the stadium, hats, T-shirts, videos, and so on. In addition, Brooks (1994) pointed out that sport has an intangible dimension that is internally generated and represented by the emotions and experiences of sport participants and spectators. Examples include the following:

- The emotional high that sport participants experience when running their personal best time
- The thrill that sport spectators experience when watching a spectacular play in sport such as a slam dunk in basketball
- The satisfaction that athletes derive when overcoming challenges posed by competitors or the sport environment
- The agony that sport spectators feel when their favorite team or athlete loses a competition

2. Sport is subjective and heterogeneous because the impressions, experiences, and interpretations about the sport experience may vary from person to person. Two people who attend the same field hockey game might have markedly different experiences. One might view the game as low scoring and unexciting, whereas the other might appreciate the strategy involved in the game and consider it interesting. Because sport marketers cannot easily predict the impressions, experiences, and interpretations that consumers will have about the sport consumption experience, they will find it difficult to ensure that consumers will have satisfying sport experiences.

3. Sports are inconsistent and unpredictable for a variety of reasons. A few of the many factors that influence the sport experience include injuries to players, the emotional state of players, the momentum of teams, and the weather. Sport marketers have little if any control over these factors. On the other hand, although the uncertainty and unpredictability of sport events prevent sport marketers from offering consumers any guarantees, the uncertainty adds an extra appeal and excitement that sport spectators (and sport marketers) enjoy.

4. Sport is perishable because the sport experience is simultaneously produced and consumed. For example, as the athletes are competing (i.e., producing the action and experience), the spectators are watching the competition (i.e., consuming the action and experience). Few people are interested in seeing yesterday's soccer match or field hockey game. Consequently, marketers must focus on generating preevent excitement to promote advance ticket sales. Based on the perishability of sport competitions, sport marketers often offer tangible items (such as T-shirts, souvenirs, and other merchandise) that serve as lasting reminders of the perishable sport experience.

5. As alluded to in the discussion of the intangible aspects of sports, sport involves emotions. Some spectators become emotionally attached to their teams and are referred to as fanatics or fans. Other consumers might buy licensed products with team logos and uniform replicas as a way of identifying with their teams. Consumers do not often display such heightened emotions or psychological attachment to other goods or products, such as vacuum cleaners.

Sport's unique combination of characteristics provides marketers with some interesting challenges and opportunities. Given these characteristics, what factors should we consider in making decisions about packaging, promoting, and delivering sport? Who will be attracted to certain sport events, and how will the packaging, promoting, and delivering of the event influence the consumers' experiences and perceptions? What changes will we need to make in the packaging, promoting, and delivering of sport in the future? This chapter will address these questions. You will learn about the necessity of developing sport marketing plans (strategies and activities) that are responsive to the needs of society; the elements of the marketing mix; how to select consumers for sport; how companies develop socially responsible sport marketing plans; and the integrated process involved in packaging, positioning, promoting, and delivering sport to consumers. In addition, you will learn to appreciate the dilemmas faced by sport managers in implementing sport marketing plans. Finally, we will discuss future challenges and trends in sport marketing.

1870s

1877— Pittsburgh Pirates—team accused of "pirating" Louis Bierbauer from Philadelphia A's and adopted new name

1920s

1928—Coca-Cola begins marketing partnership with Olympic Games

1930s

1934—Lou Gehrig becomes first athlete to appear on Wheaties box

1939—First televised MLB broadcast (NBC)—Cincinnati Reds v. Brooklyn Dodgers (Aug. 26)

1939—First televised NFL game (NBC)—Philadelphia Eagles v. Brooklyn Dodgers (Oct. 22)

1940s

1940—First televised NHL game—NY Rangers v. Montreal

As mentioned at the outset of this chapter, marketing sport is a challenging but exciting undertaking. Nevertheless, the sport industry competes with other industries, such as music and entertainment, for consumers' discretionary time and money. Therefore, sport marketing decisions should be based on sound and rational information. In the United States, the sport industry has been estimated to generate approximately $213 billion USD per year in revenues, making it the sixth largest US industry (Broughton, Lee, & Nethery, 1999). Because of the increased growth and popularity of sport as a business, a number of resources now offer valuable information and insight regarding sport, marketing, and the marketing of sport. See "For More Information" on page 190.

EVOLUTION OF SPORT MARKETING

Fullerton (1988) and Hardy (1990) divide the history of American sport marketing into three periods: (1) the Era of Origins, 1820-1880; (2) the Era of Institutional Development, 1880-1920; and (3) the Era of Refinement and Formulation, 1920-1990.

During the Era of Origins, micromarketing decisions emerged in response to the growth and greater effect of external forces (Pitts & Stotlar, 2002). Pitts and Stotlar describe the tactics of William Fuller, a boxing promoter in South Carolina. In 1824 Fuller enticed paying customers to his "Extravaganza of Fun, Frolic, Fashion, and Flash" through newspaper advertisements and handbills that announced theater plays, boxing, and fireworks. Boxing was thus only one aspect of his complete product. Unlike today's high-powered marketing strategies, Fuller's effort did not include an announcement of the price and the location if the event was hard to reach. Moreover, although the promotions included newspapers and handbills, they still relied heavily on word of mouth among a small sporting fraternity.

During the 1850s and 1860s, Michael Phelan's promotion of billiards and billiard tables marked a significant advance over the earlier boxing promotions. As a means to market billiards and billiard tables, Phelan identified a growing sporting fraternity of White males age 18 to 35 and the proprietors of poolrooms and taverns who catered to this fraternity. Phelan also recognized that the billiard market extended beyond a local market to other cities. By organizing national billiard tournaments, publishing the *Billiard Cue*, and holding a leadership position in the American Billiard Players Association, he was able to achieve brand-name recognition and promote his products as the best billiard events and equipment. As a result, Phelan was able to compete successfully with a growing number of firms, and his control over technological developments in billiard equipment and standardized rules of the game allowed him to influence buyer preferences for different kinds of billiard products. Phelan's marketing tactics were a prelude to more thorough development of micromarketing techniques during the 1865 to 1870 baseball fad, which included charging admission fees for a sport entertainment product; promoting sports rivalries; promoting games, tours, tournaments, all-star games, and championship games through newspapers, weekly journals, and special baseball publications; publishing statistical reviews of games and seasons; and promoting baseball as America's national pastime. Early baseball promoters made decisions about price, promotion, and place based on market size and growth, and they took advantage of the increase in per capita income and discretionary time (Pitts & Stotlar, 2002).

Pitts and Stotlar (2002) note that the micro and macro concepts associated with modern sport marketing evolved during the Era of Institutionalized Development (1880-1920): product planning, product management, distribution, pricing, and promotion. During this period, sport products were branded, trademarked, and packaged to enhance their appeal to consumers. Market analysis to determine customer needs, estimate market potential, and study competition began at the turn of the century. Before 1880 price was a matter of guesswork. After 1880 the pricing decision became an important part of the marketing strategy. Promotional activities expanded in volume and intensity, building on the tactics used by baseball promoters.

Population expansion and concentration were accompanied by a significant increase in discretionary money. Sport benefited from these developments because consumers demanded more sport products and more forms of sport entertainment. Technological changes influenced the distribution and production of sporting goods. The railroad and an overland truck line transport system allowed wide distribution of products to cities, towns, and hamlets. The emergence of the telegraph and telephone provided improved and broadened means of communications that could be used as a business

1940s

▷**1947**—First televised World Series game—New York Yankees v. Brooklyn Dodgers (shown in New York City)

▷**1949**—Babe Didrikson Zaharias lands first major endorsement deal for female athlete

1950s

▷**1951**—Eddie Gaedel, at three feet, seven inches, pinch hits for St. Louis Browns (Aug. 19)

1960s

▷**1960**—CBS pays $50,000 USD for the rights to televise the Olympic Winter Games in Squaw Valley, Calif.

▷**1964**—Blue Ribbon Sports organized; renamed Nike in 1972

DEVELOPING A MARKETING STRATEGY FOR A EUROPEAN-BASED NORTH AMERICAN SPORTS NETWORK

Kamini Sharma, United Kingdom

In most European countries, finding North American-based sports on television, especially live and unedited programming, has been difficult. Traditionally, European channels have shown European-based sports such as football (soccer), rugby, cricket, Formula One racing, and national competitions in sports such as cycling, golf, tennis, and other sports that are viewed much less, if at all, in the United States. When North American sports are shown, they are broadcast late at night or early in the morning, and they have local sport commentators who might not be knowledgeable about the nuances of the sports. A few years ago, these observations led to the conclusion that a market existed for a channel that would broadcast North American sports.

North American Sports Network (NASN) was founded in December 2002 as a premium sports channel based in the United Kingdom and Ireland and airing sports 24 hours a day, 7 days a week, 365 days a year. NASN was formed to fill a perceived gap that existed in the market—the transmission of North American sport content (e.g., MLB, NHL, NBA, NFL, NASCAR, and so on) to a target audience of expatriates—people who were in Europe for a short time, typically working for companies based in North America. The channel would broadcast live games, delayed games, replays, and sport magazine shows to provide as much North American sports coverage as possible. Based on the assumption that most subscribers would be North Americans, a marketing plan was developed to discover where North Americans lived and worked, what publications they read, and where they could be found. A strategy was developed to speak to potential viewers in a North American tone and to develop an identity that was familiar and reminded them of home.

After approximately one year into the development of the channel, it became apparent that although a number of North Americans did watch the channel, the vast majority of viewers (over 80%) were from the UK and Ireland. NASN undertook a market research study using focus groups and surveys to investigate this phenomenon. The research revealed tremendous numbers of potential viewers who could be converted to subscribers if they could be targeted properly.

Management decided that it was time to reassess the channel's marketing strategies. More broad-based print and online advertising was developed. No longer would the channel appeal only to Americans and Canadians. Promotional events such as road shows were developed to highlight the channel experience to malls and local sporting events. More broad-based advertising was developed with the aim of retaining the North American tone while appealing to a larger population and drawing people into a new viewing experience. North American sport catch phrases were introduced, league logos and sports images were included, and the catch phrase "Every Play Every Day" was introduced to create a brand identity that supported the NASN brand position. The identity of the channel was evolving with the change in demographics and the needs of viewers for a product that was different from anything that they had ever seen.

Today, NASN continues to grow. The channel is expanding into additional European territories including Germany, France, Austria, Switzerland, the Netherlands, and many other countries with the goal of becoming a pan-European channel. With this growth come new challenges. NASN must maintain its core identity while appealing to vastly different audiences with significantly different cultures and languages. Eventually, the market will be analyzed again, and a market position will be developed and promoted to highlight the uniqueness of the NASN product—the only TV Channel in Europe dedicated to North American Sports!

and marketing tool. During this era, sporting goods manufacturers and promoters of sports developed and refined micromarketing tactics in response to new and powerful external forces.

During the Era of Refinement and Formulation (1920-1990), sport marketing continued to develop along the lines established during the Era of Institutionalized Development. Pitts and Stotlar (2002) point out that new external forces played an

Learning Activity

An example of an external force that has influenced the development of sport marketing activities is the Title IX federal legislation. Analyze how Title IX has influenced the marketing of high school sports and collegiate sports. Give specific examples of marketing activities that high school and college athletics administrators and coaches are implementing today because of Title IX.

1960s

- **1969**—Internet established

1970s

- **1973**—Battle of the Sexes: Billie Jean King defeats Bobby Riggs in tennis
- **1973**—US Open Tennis Tournament offers equal prize money to men's and women's winners
- **1974**—Ali defeats Foreman in the Rumble in the Jungle
- **1979**—Mike Veeck puts on Disco Demolition Night during Chicago White Sox doubleheader (July 15)

1990s

- **1994**—NHL Diversity Task Force created
- **1995**—Washington Bullets change name to Wizards

NASN news

NEWSLETTER : AUTUMN 2005

LATEST NEWS, SCHEDULES, AUTUMN HIGHLIGHTS AND MUCH MUCH MORE FROM NASN!

FALL INTO ANOTHER PACKED AUTUMN SCHEDULE

Welcome to NASN's Autumn Newsletter

It doesn't seem too long ago that we were eagerly anticipating a new season of baseball and NASCAR, tuning in for the top picks from the NFL Draft and leaping into the NBA Playoffs. And it doesn't seem that long ago that we were reflecting on an NHL season that should have been, but wasn't.

That was Spring. This is Autumn and how things have changed! The NHL is back on the ice and more importantly back on NASN. With a huge sigh of relief, we look at the new season ahead. We couldn't have predicted how close this season's MLB Playoff race would become. As if last year's Playoffs weren't exciting enough, this season we've seen probably one of the tightest ever pennant and wild card races. So, brace yourself for more of the same as we head into this year's Playoffs. With Autumn comes a new addition to our range of NFL programming, NFL Total Access, giving you a unique behind-the-scenes insight into the NFL. The Chase for the Nextel Cup is underway and it's now all about ten drivers, ten races and one winner! We also look ahead to our second season of NBA action and much, much more besides.

AUTUMN/WINTER HIGHLIGHTS

October

• MLB Playoffs • NHL Regular Season • NASCAR Nextel Cup • College Football Regular Season • CFL Regular Season

November

• NBA Regular Season • CFL Playoffs and Grey Cup • NASCAR Nextel Cup • College Football Regular Season • NHL Regular Season • College Basketball Regular Season

December

• College Bowl Season • NBA Regular Season • NHL Regular Season • College Basketball Regular Season

THE NHL IS BACK AND IT'S LIVE ON NASN

Absence makes the heart grow fonder? Or, out of sight out of mind? It certainly wasn't the latter. The teams may not have been playing, but the saga of will they, won't they play held our attention well into last season and until the lock-out was finally announced. Thankfully, that is now well and truly in the past and the NHL is back with a new look, new rules and a new superstar in waiting in the form of Sidney Crosby. Plus, many teams will be welcoming new players into their rosters. The puck dropped on NASN's live coverage back in July when we brought you all the top picks from the NHL Draft. Now the wait is finally over and the much anticipated, eagerly awaited new season is here. So get ready hockey fans, this is what you've been waiting. Follow your favourite team with us all the way to the Stanley Cup Final.

NHL RULES!

The return of the NHL sees the introduction of new rules to make the game faster, offering more scoring chances and fewer stoppages. Some of the more exciting rules include changes to the 'dimensions of the rink' increasing the offensive zone by 4ft, having a shoot-out in the event of a scoreless five minute overtime, reducing the goaltenders equipment by 11 percent and removing the two lined pass by ignoring the centre red line. For more details about the new rules visit www.nasn.com

HOCKEY NIGHT Canada

NASN will be bringing you up to 175 games this season with live double headers each and every Saturday from the Hockey Night in Canada team. We'll also bring you plenty more live and as-live games throughout the week, including live coverage from the Playoffs and as-live coverage of the Stanley Cup Finals. With so much on offer, NASN will once again be your home for ice hockey.

What does the 2005/06 Season have in store for us?

The free agent market was sizzling this past summer with big name players changing colours quicker then you can say 'salary cap'. One of the biggest deals to hit the headlines was the capture of Peter Forsberg by Philadelphia, a player who will surely make the Flyers contenders this year. However, the biggest signing this year came courtesy of a lottery. Pittsburgh were lucky enough to have first pick in the NHL Draft, and jumped at the chance to put Sidney Crosby in a Penguins uniform. It's amazing to think that this guy is only 18 and already he's being touted as the next superstar of the NHL. Whether or not he'll live up to his billing is a tough one to call but what is certain- this guy is special and you can follow 'the Crosby show' right here on NASN.

British Ice Hockey Comes to NASN! (see p3)

MLB SHOWDOWN!

Read on for all this season's baseball action >>>

THE ONLY TV CHANNEL IN THE UK DEDICATED TO NORTH AMERICAN SPORT

NHL NFL NCAA NBA NASCAR

The NASN printed newsletter is an added-value service offering the opportunity to communicate directly with, engage, and inform its subscriber base about the latest news and channel information at key moments in the sporting calendar.

Photo courtesy of NASN.

International Learning Activity

Using the case study on page 196, explain why the positioning and branding of NASN might need to be changed in the future. Describe how you would position and brand NASN for the future.

important role in this development. These forces included increased popularity and diversification of sport interests; developing sport fads that periodically increased market growth rates; government policies (National Industrial Recovery Act, 1933; Title IX, 1972; Consumer Pricing Act, 1975; the Brady Bill 1994); technological advancements (new materials such as plastics, fiberglass, alloys, and so on; computers; and the Internet); and the emergence of specialized sports trade journals, sports radio, and sports television programs. In the 21st century, we can expect that new emerging external forces, especially new technological advancements, will influence sport marketing developments.

MISSION, ETHICS, AND SOCIAL RESPONSIBILITY

Every sport organization exists for a purpose. The organization defines this purpose in its mission statement, which represents the core values of the organization. Sport does not exist in isolation; rather, as illustrated in the previous discussion of the evolution of sport marketing practices, various societal issues and trends affect sport. Therefore, the mission statement of a sport organization must reflect the values and beliefs that are prevalent in the environments in which it operates. If the organization does not have a mission statement, it should create one. Everyone in the organization should be involved in writing the mission statement so that all will be committed to carrying out the mission and acting in accordance with the core values. Covey (1989) said, "An organizational mission statement is important because it creates in people's hearts and minds a frame of reference, a set of criteria or guidelines by which they will govern themselves. . . . They have bought into the changeless core of what the organization is about" (p. 143). A sport marketing plan derived from and consistent with the organization's mission statement and core values is necessary to ensure that the packaging, promotion, and delivery of sport will be conducted in socially responsible ways. The National Basketball Association's (NBA) mission, presented in figure 9.1, provides a good example of a mission statement with core values.

Another good example of a mission is that of the Circle City Classic (CCC), an annual football event hosted in Indianapolis, Indiana featuring

The NBA's mission is to be the most respected and successful sports league organization in the world.

We aim to achieve our mission, and thereby continue to enhance the economic value of our teams, by

working to make basketball the most popular global sport and to maintain the NBA's position as the best in basketball; creating and maximizing business opportunities and relationships arising from basketball; and capitalizing on our key assets and strengths—our people, skills, experience, reputation, and innovative and entrepreneurial spirit—to expand beyond basketball into related activities worldwide.

We have a commitment to excellence

We do every task as well as it can be done, reflecting quality and attention to detail at every stage—from inception, to planning, to execution.

We strive at all times to live by and act in accordance with the following core values:

Innovation We encourage entrepreneurship and innovative thinking. We create opportunities and do not merely react to those that come our way. We aim always to be on the cutting edge and ahead of all competition.

Integrity We conduct ourselves in accordance with the highest standards of honesty, truthfulness, ethics, and fair dealing.

Respect We value our individuality and diversity. We are civil and respectful to each other, to our fans, customers, and business associates. We take pride in our success, but we are not arrogant.

Social responsibility We recognize and embrace our responsibility—as a corporate citizen in the world, in the United States, and in local communities to support causes that help people to achieve an improved quality of life.

Teamwork We work hard together in a true cooperative spirit and without regard for departmental lines or individual goals. Our priority is always to provide the best possible service to all our constituencies.

Workplace environment We believe in equal opportunity, the importance of job satisfaction, and that each employee has an important role in achieving our mission. We empower each employee to make job-related decisions commensurate with the employee's experience and level of responsibility. We promote and reward our employees solely on the basis of merit, and we evaluate not only achievement but also whether the employee's conduct reflects conformity with our mission and values.

Figure 9.1 Mission statement of the National Basketball Association.

Reprinted, by permission, from the National Basketball Association.

two historically Black colleges and universities (HBCUs). The mission of this event is to support educational achievement and promote cultural excellence while showcasing the spirit, energy, and tradition of America's HBCUs. The CCC features HBCU football as the centerpiece for integrating sport, entertainment, business, and education. A substantial percentage of the proceeds of the event are donated to the colleges and universities that participate in the event. The CCC marketing plan, which includes student development initiatives, educational programs, community development, corporate opportunities for Black businesses, and uplifting activities for the Black community, is in direct alignment with its mission statement. To see Web-based outcomes of their marketing plan, view their Web site at www.circlecityclassic.com.

Marketing is critical in encouraging consumers to buy an organization's products or engage in an organization's activities and events. Sport marketers, therefore, should acknowledge societal norms and concerns and should not engage in exploitive or unethical practices (Laczniak, Burton, & Murphy, 1999). An example of failure to meet this expectation was the 2003 NFL Pregame Show held on the National Mall in Washington, DC. This event was staged as a commercial entertainment extravaganza supported by a $10 million USD sponsorship from Pepsi. NFL leaders offered this event, in part, as a marketing tool to reach new target audiences and generate additional revenues for the league. Unfortunately, in staging the event, the NFL violated federal regulations designed to protect the sacred and ceremonial nature of the National Mall, which prohibited commercial activities from being held there. Although the event was undoubtedly aligned with the mission of the NFL regarding marketing and revenue-generating practices, many perceived it to be unethical and socially irresponsible.

The event was presented to show support for the Iraq War effort and military troops. It provided benefits to high-level Pentagon employees and "military brass" and allowed corporations to demonstrate their patriotism through sponsorship. Observers have speculated that high-level government officials must have given the NFL permission to hold this kind of commercial event because officials of the National Park Service, who are responsible for enforcing the regulations that prohibit commercial activity in the National Parks, would not likely have given this authorization. For more information about this event go to *Commercial Alert*, September 2003, www.commercialalert.org/news-archive.php. In this case, NFL leaders may have overreached in their efforts to market an entertainment extravaganza. The event was only indirectly linked to the opening game of the NFL season, and marketing stand-alone entertainment extravaganzas is not consistent with the mission and core values of the NFL, which focus primarily on marketing the game of football.

Sport marketing practices should (1) be consistent with the mission statement and core values of the organization and (2) package, promote, and deliver sport in a socially and ethically responsible manner. Marketing in an honest and ethical manner that creates a distinctive and socially responsible image is the best way to position a sport product or event in the market. Being ethically and socially responsible will also increase the likelihood that the organization will achieve long-term marketing success and customer satisfaction.

DEVELOPING A SPORT MARKETING PLAN

Marketing plans serve as road maps or game plans for an organization's marketing activities. Having a well-developed marketing plan is key to the marketing success of sport organizations. The four primary elements of a marketing plan—product, price, place, and promotion—make up the marketing mix. These elements are well established in the marketing industry and are universally known as the four Ps.

- Product—A tangible good (object), a service, or an intangible quality that satisfies consumers' wants or needs.
- Price—The value of the product and the costs that the consumer must accept to obtain the product. Consumers determine the value of a product by balancing the expected benefits of buying the product against the expected costs of the product. When the benefits derived from a product exceed the costs attached to the product, then consumers believe that the product has value.
- Place—The distribution channels that allow consumers to access or obtain the product.
- Promotion—The integrated communication and public relations activities that communicate, inform, persuade, and motivate consumers to purchase the product.

marketing plans—Comprehensive strategic frameworks for identifying and achieving an organization's marketing goals and objectives.

marketing mix—The elements of product, price, place, and promotion, which sport marketers manipulate (modify, alter, or adjust) to achieve marketing goals and objectives.

To maximize their success, marketers develop strategic plans to manipulate the four Ps in a variety of ways depending on the mission of the organization and the fluctuations of the market (Pitts & Stotlar, 2002). This manipulation is critical to carrying out a marketing plan successfully. But to devise a comprehensive plan for achieving marketing goals and objectives, marketers must consider factors beyond the four Ps. In this chapter we present a 10-step process for developing a sport marketing plan called the 10 Ps—purpose, product, projecting the market, position, players, package, price, promotion, place, and promise. This process, shown in figure 9.2, illustrates that although the four Ps are central to the marketing plan, they must be integrated with other elements to achieve optimal sport marketing success.

Step 1: Identify the Purpose of the Sport Marketing Plan

Step 1 involves clarifying the purpose of the sport marketing plan and linking the plan to the organization's mission and core values. Before packaging, promoting, and delivering can occur, sport marketers must establish a context to provide an orientation and direction for what they are trying to accomplish and how they expect to do so. Establishing a context requires sport marketers to examine the organization's core values as described in its mission statement and propose marketing activities and events with purposes that reinforce and align with the overall mission of the organization.

Besides allowing the mission statement to guide the marketing planning process, marketers must

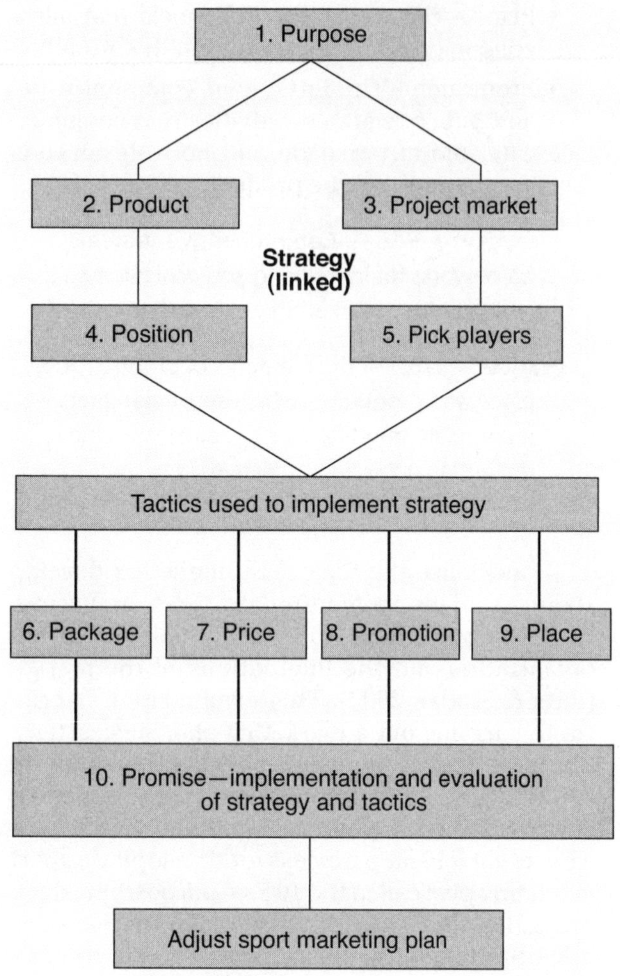

Figure 9.2 Steps in developing a sport marketing plan.

Adapted, by permission, from B.G. Pitts and D.K. Stotlar, 2002, Sport marketing theory. In *Fundamentals of sport marketing*, 2nd ed. (Morgantown, WV: Fitness Information Technology, Inc.), p. 87. © Fitness Information Technology & New West Virginia University.

also have clearly defined and measurable goals and objectives. Goals are general summary statements of expected outcomes. Examples of marketing goals might be to increase attendance by 5% and to increase youth participation in community relations programs by 10%. Objectives are the specific activities that enable the marketer to obtain the expected outcomes. Examples of objectives linked to the earlier mentioned goals might be to increase preseason ticket sales by offering discount prices, adding game promotions giveaway items for youth, and offering youth sports clinics and camps. When the goals and objectives are achieved and are aligned with the organization's mission, the marketing plan is deemed a success.

Step 2: Analyze the Sport Product

In step 2 the marketer analyzes the sport product and determines whether the product is a tangible good, a game or event, or a service. The sport product is three-dimensional (Pitts, Fielding, & Miller, 1994), composed of tangible goods, support services, and the game or event itself (see figure 9.3). Sport goods include tangible items such as clothing (e.g., shoes, aerobic apparel, hats, T-shirts) and equipment (e.g., bats, balls, automobiles and car parts, tack used in horse racing, mountain bikes). Support services include activities or programs ancillary to sport but necessary for its operation (e.g., game officials, athletic trainers, sport psychologists). The game or event itself is composed of two dimensions: the core product and product extensions (Mullin, Hardy, & Sutton, 2000).

The core product of the event is the actual competition (e.g., the players and coaches on the competing teams, the sport activity itself, and the facility in which the competition takes place). Brooks (1994) proposed the following tangible elements in the core sport product:

- Type of sport—football, basketball, gymnastics
- Participants—athletes (beginner, elite, professional), coaches (volunteer, part-time salaried, full-time professionals), and the environment (challenging golf courses, difficult mountains)
- Team—Notre Dame, Michigan, Dallas Cowboys, Chicago Sky

Product extensions are the supplemental ancillary items, such as the mascot, music, halftime entertainment, concessions, bands, cheerleaders, and so on, that are associated with the overall sport experience. Because of the flair and excitement of product extensions that are created around the core product, sport events are often viewed as a form of entertainment (e.g., NBA All-Star Game, Super Bowl, World Series, NCAA Final Four Basketball Championships).

As mentioned in the introduction of this chapter, the unique characteristics of sport as a product as well as the unique emotions experienced by sport consumers make marketing sport a challenging yet exciting endeavor. Marketers must understand and appreciate the elements of the core product of sport as well as the core product extensions before they can develop an appropriate and effective marketing plan.

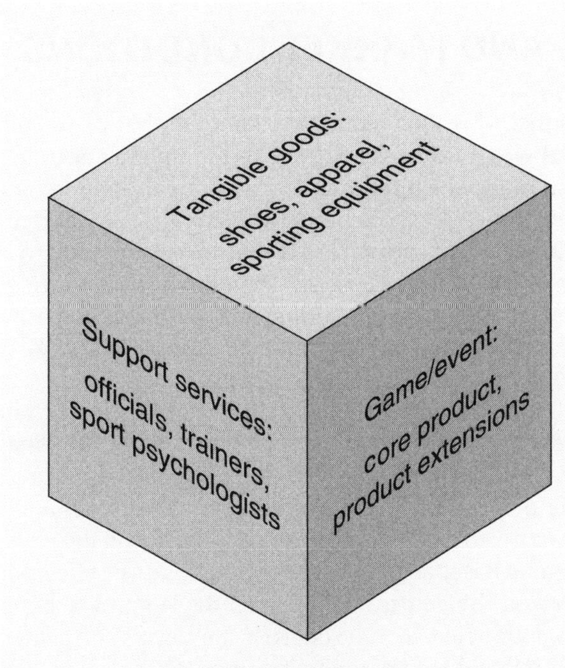

Figure 9.3 Three dimensions of the sport product.

Step 3: Project the Market Climate

As mentioned previously, sport does not exist in isolation; market conditions have a profound influence on it. Therefore, step 3 is an analysis of the past and current market climate in order to project and forecast the future market climate, which will affect marketing practices. Assessing the sport climate requires examination of internal and external factors as they affect marketing efforts. For example, internal factors affecting the climate of Major League Baseball include players, owners, team management, and staff personnel. The media, corporate sponsors, advertisers, spectators, and the federal government represent examples of external factors that affect the climate of Major League Baseball.

internal factors—Factors inside a sport organization that affect the sport marketing climate (i.e., players, owners, team management, and staff personnel).

external factors—Factors outside of a sport organization that affect the sport marketing climate (e.g., media, corporate sponsors, advertisers, spectators, federal regulations, regulations of sport governing bodies).

Learning Activity

Using the NHL or MLB case study, analyze the past market climate of the NHL or MLB to project the future market climate. You might ask these questions: What effect has the media had on hockey or baseball in the past? What effect will the media have on hockey or baseball in the future? What actions has the federal government taken in the past regarding the hockey or baseball industry, and what actions might the federal government take in the future? What kinds of relationships have advertisers and sponsors had with hockey or baseball owners in the past, and what benefits did each party derive? How might the relationships of advertisers and corporate sponsors with hockey or baseball owners change in the future?

Assessing the past market climate enables managers to identify factors associated with successful or failed marketing efforts. On the other hand, forecasting the future market climate requires reexamination of the organization's mission. An assessment of the internal strengths and weaknesses of an organization or event and the external opportunities and threats faced by an organization or event is called a SWOT analysis (Rowe, Mason, & Dickel, 1986). A SWOT analysis usually highlights the manner in which internal and external factors might influence the success of a marketing plan. A SWOT analysis includes four elements: (1) *strengths* are internal factors that are advantageous to the sport organization's ability to achieve its marketing goals and objectives; (2) *weaknesses* are internal factors that are disadvantageous and may prevent an organization from achieving its marketing goals and objectives; (3) *opportunities* are favorable external conditions in the environment that may enhance an organization's ability to achieve its marketing goals and objectives; and (4) *threats* are the unfavorable external conditions in an environment that could interfere with an organization's ability to achieve its marketing goals and objectives. Marketing plans should be designed to maximize the strengths and opportunities and minimize the weaknesses and threats identified in the SWOT analysis. In some instances, the SWOT analysis might reveal a need to revise or develop a new mission statement, which, in turn, will affect the marketing plan.

SWOT analysis—A management technique available to sport marketers to help them assess the strengths and weaknesses of an organization and the opportunities and threats that it faces.

LABOR–MANAGEMENT CONFLICT AND MARKET CONDITIONS

Problems that sport managers confront as a result of player strikes or owner lockouts of players present opportunities for developing and implementing new marketing strategies. The 2003-04 NHL owners lockout case study serves to illustrate this point.

NHL Owners Lockout

During the 2003 and 2004 seasons, National Hockey League (NHL) owners encountered financial difficulties because of rapidly escalating players' salaries. Few teams were able to generate a profit. The owners and league management believed that the league might go bankrupt and go out of business unless they could contain costs. They believed that the only way to achieve "cost certainty" was to persuade the National Hockey League Players Association (NHLPA) to accept a hard cap on players' salaries. The players and the NHLPA believed the players were entitled to receive the higher salaries and argued that the team owners themselves had made the decisions to pay higher salaries to players. The NHLPA was not willing to accept a hard cap on players' salaries.

Given this stalemate, the owners believed they had no option other than to lock out the players and shut down league operations for the 2004 season. In 2005 the NHL and NHLPA signed a new collective bargaining agreement that included a hard cap on players' salaries that provided team owners and league managers with cost certainty so that the league could resume operations for the 2005 season.

Major League Baseball Strike

In 1994 Major League Baseball (MLB) was having one of its best years ever. Several players were striving to break long-standing records, and teams that had not contended for a league championship in many years were leading their leagues in the standings. Newly aligned divisions had created another tier of playoffs and wild-card possibilities. Interest among spectators was high, which resulted in increased attendance and heightened press coverage. The game was reinvigorated and seemed to be making strides to reclaim its place as America's national pastime. Then the dispute between players and owners regarding possible implementation of a salary cap resulted in the longest players' strike in the history of US professional sport.

The strike ended the 1994 season on August 11; there were no league championships and no World Series. The beginning of the 1995 season was delayed because the dispute between players and owners remained unresolved. MLB withdrew its participation in the newly formed Baseball Network and thus limited its television market. The courts finally forced the leagues to begin operations in May 1995 because the players and owners still had not settled their differences. In the fall of 1996 the owners and the players association signed a new collective bargaining agreement. Although the terms of the agreement did not resolve the problems, the agreement did provide stability for the league through the year 2000.

From a marketing perspective, the NHL lockout and the MLB strike were disastrous. The spectators viewed both players and owners as selfish and greedy. Fans believed that the players and owners did not care about them or the game. The situation had serious negative financial consequences for everyone directly or indirectly involved with the industry. Team management and staff personnel; the media; corporate sponsors and advertisers; food, beverage, and lodging businesses; and other support services in the communities all lost in the process. The NHL and MLB needed new marketing strategies to promote and sell themselves.

For example, an assessment of the market climate of MLB between 1990 and 1995 might reveal the following information: escalating player salaries, confrontations between players and owners, federal court actions to settle disputes between players and owners, declining TV viewership, declining ticket sales, and growing public disenchantment with the game. A SWOT analysis of the future market climate of MLB might forecast the following:

- Strengths—History, tradition (America's national pastime), established spectator markets
- Weaknesses—Game too slow and too long, lack of TV viewership, resulting in loss of advertisers and corporate sponsors
- Opportunities—Improve marketing of star players, interleague competition to stimulate team rivalries and spectator interest, new stadia
- Threats—Popularity of other professional sports such as basketball and football; lack of interest in baseball among youth, women, and minority ethnic groups; erosion or loss of antitrust exemption

Given this past, present, and future market analysis, MLB may need to reexamine its mission statement and core values and develop strategic marketing plans in response to favorable and unfavorable internal and external situations and conditions that will influence their marketing success.

Step 4: Position the Sport Product

According to Shank (2005), positioning is establishing a sport entity in the minds of consumers in the target market. The objective of positioning is to differentiate the sport product from competing products by creating a distinctive image of the product. Distinctive images are created in consumers' minds based on (1) the type of consumers who buy the product, (2) the design of the product as well as the benefits offered by the product, (3) the price of the product, and (4) the place where the product is available or where the event occurs (i.e., the arena or facility). Marketers often position products by means of verbal and nonverbal communications to consumers. Sport images can be communicated through logos, symbols, and messages through TV and radio advertisements, public service announcements, jingles, press releases, news articles, and feature articles. For example, in 1995 Reebok developed a new TV advertisement about girls' participation in sport (see *Images that Encourage*). This advertisement communicated a distinctive image to capture the attention of female sport participants, spectators, and volunteers.

IMAGES THAT ENCOURAGE

Video—Scenes from high school, many focusing on girls' sports: team practice, competition, traveling on the bus, hanging out at school, ultimately capturing moments of closeness among the players.

Audio—(girl) If you don't play . . . you can hang out . . . you can watch . . . you can brush your hair a lot . . . but you can never say, "I was a player." And you can never say, "I was on the team." And worst of all, you can never do all this incredible, exciting . . . hilarious stuff . . . with these girls who are like sisters. So all I'm trying to say is . . . my question is . . . wanna play?

Video—Just another chance to play on Planet Reebok.*

Learning Activity

Using the Reebok TV advertisement about girls' participation in sport (in *Images That Encourage*), give specific examples of images that you believe help to differentiate Reebok from its competitors and help to create a distinctive image about Reebok in the minds of girls and women.

A sport product perceived by consumers as being unique is well positioned to compete successfully in selected markets, provided the images are positive. For example, posters and other printed materials used to promote the 1994 Gay Games showed camaraderie and support among the participants, which helped communicate an image of unity. This positioned the 1994 Gay Games for success with consumers in particular markets. The images also conveyed messages that were positive and socially responsible. More recent marketing efforts can be seen on their Web site, www.gaygames.com. Likewise, the Paralympics does an excellent job in communicating positive images of elite athletes who are physically challenged by showing that they can compete in athletic events just like athletes who are not physically challenged. As noted in chapter 4, the New Orleans, Louisiana, Bayou Classic (the largest and most popular Black college sport event in America) has been positioned as a sociocultural and festive entertainment event that contains market features particularly salient to the Black community. Many Black consumers who are not football fans attend the Bayou Classic because of the image they have of the event as one that is exciting and culturally relevant (Armstrong, 1998, 2002). The Bayou Classic Web site, www.statefarmbayouclassic.com/, offers a valuable study in marketing savvy.

As mentioned previously, the type of consumers who are attracted to an event might also contribute to the positioning of the event. For example, ESPN's X Games, OLN's Gravity Games, and so forth are sport events that attract Generation Xers. (Although definitions vary somewhat, persons born between 1964 and 1978 are generally labeled Generation Xers.) Based on the needs and interests of the consumers of these events, the events contain daring and high-energy activities that contribute to their overall image. The effective positioning of sport events contributes enormously to their marketing success.

In their landmark work on public relations theory, Grunig and White (1992) suggested that effective

SWOT ANALYSIS OF WOMEN'S PROFESSIONAL BASKETBALL

A SWOT analysis for two professional women's sport leagues, the Women's National Basketball Association (WNBA) and the now defunct American Basketball League (ABL), provides another illustration of the manner in which internal and external factors can influence marketing success. The major strength of the WNBA was that it was a product of the NBA; a weakness of the ABL was its ownership by a small group of private investors. Consequently, the WNBA had the financial backing (from the NBA) to absorb deficits (a strength), whereas the ABL had a limited budget and did not have the financial resources to absorb the financial losses incurred (a weakness). WNBA teams were located in large cities that were considered major US markets (an opportunity); ABL teams were located primarily in midsize, medium-market cities (a threat). The WNBA games were held in NBA arenas (a strength), whereas the ABL games were held in collegiate and other smaller venues within their respective cities (somewhat of a weakness). Another major strength of the WNBA was its national media distribution (NBC, ESPN, and Lifetime); a major weakness of the ABL was its regional media distribution (regional sports channels, Prime Network, and Black Entertainment Television). The ABL did not allow its players to participate in other basketball leagues (a weakness that limited players' appeal and exposure), whereas the WNBA allowed its players to participate in other professional women's basketball leagues (a strength that maximized the players' appeal and exposure). The WNBA season of competition was held during the summer months and did not compete with other girls' or women's basketball leagues (an opportunity), whereas the ABL season of competition was held during the winter months, competing with girls' high school basketball and women's college basketball games (a threat).

The key to marketing success is for an organization's strengths and opportunities to outweigh its weaknesses and threats. Applying the SWOT analysis to the WNBA and ABL illustrates why the WNBA is still in existence and why the ABL suspended operations midway through its third season. Like the marketers of the WNBA, sportmarketers should examine present market conditions and seek to maximize their products' or events' strengths and opportunities and minimize their weaknesses and threats.

communication practices consisted of several elements:

1. Open and honest communications with the public
2. Images and messages that are socially responsible
3. Cooperation with the public and response to their interests
4. Good faith relationships with the public (see "Renaming the Washington Bullets" on p. 205)

Along the same lines, in order to respect the sacred values and customs of many American Indians, a number of colleges and universities have replaced nicknames of their mascots and eradicated promotional gimmicks that reflected aspects of American Indian traditions and practices. Moreover, as a measure of respect for the many values of its diverse consumers, the NCAA announced that it would not allow universities that contained hostile, abusive, and offensive American Indian mascot nicknames to participate in or host NCAA postseason tournaments. Because of the special circumstances and unique relationships that exist between some American Indian tribes and some NCAA universities, the approval of the use of Native American nicknames and mascots by American Indian tribes will be factored into the NCAA's decision. NCAA President Myles Brand was quoted by the Associated Press (http://msnbc.msn.com, 2006) as saying, "It is vitally important that we maintain a balance between the interest of a particular Native American tribe and the NCAA's responsibility to ensure an atmosphere of respect and sensitivity for all who attend and participate in our championships." Based on the increasing diversity of sport participants and consumers, the best way to position a sport product in the market is to do so by using honest and nonoffensive verbal and nonverbal communication that creates a distinctive and socially responsible image of a sport product.

Positioning the sport product also involves establishing a specific niche for the product in the market. Sport has six distinct markets. Primary markets are composed of (1) participants, (2) spectators, and (3) volunteers; and secondary markets are composed of (4) sponsors, (5) advertisers, and (6) companies that use athletes' endorsement of products and licensed products (Brooks, 1994). Examples of niches in primary markets include the following:

RENAMING THE WASHINGTON BULLETS

A story about the Washington Bullets demonstrates an application of Grunig and White's (1992) four steps. During the 1995-1996 season, Abe Pollin, owner of the Washington Bullets, decided that the team nickname conveyed a negative image because bullets had nothing to do with basketball but everything to do with people being injured or killed by shooting incidents in Washington, DC, and the surrounding communities. Pollin communicated openly and honestly with the public about the need to change the team's nickname (step 1). He involved the public in a promotional contest to determine a new team nickname, one that would convey a positive and socially responsible image of the team (step 2). The contest was an example of how an organization should work cooperatively with the public and respond to the public's interest (step 3). A corporate sponsor contributed prizes for some contestants, thus generating interest and publicity and establishing a good-faith relationship with the public (step 4). Moreover, an antiviolence campaign was launched in conjunction with the team nickname contest. This campaign communicated the message that the Washington Bullets organization was a responsible corporate citizen that wanted to help the community solve an important social problem. The promotional nickname contest resulted in the team being renamed the Washington Wizards.

- Participants—Athletes, coaches, and game officials
- Spectators—Stadium attendees, television viewers, radio listeners, and newspaper or magazine readers
- Volunteers—Social hosts at sports events, statisticians, team managers

Secondary markets function in the following ways:

- Advertisers—Use sports to target and communicate their products to large groups of spectators (e.g., stadium banners and signs, TV and radio advertisements)
- Corporate sponsors—Use sports to target and communicate positive and distinctive images about their products to large groups of spectators (e.g., Cadillac as sponsor of golf tournaments, Volvo as sponsor of tennis tournaments)
- Athletes' endorsement of products and licensed products—Use sports personalities and celebrities or distinctive symbols, logos, or trademarks to create consumer perception of products as popular or prestigious

The process of positioning the product in this way is called branding. **Branding** is the process of using a name, design, symbol, or any combination of them to help differentiate its products from the competition. According to Shank (2005), the purpose of branding a product is to allow an organization to distinguish and differentiate itself from all others in the marketplace. Building the brand will ultimately affect consumer behaviors, such as increasing attendance, merchandising sales, or participation in sports. However, before these behaviors occur, several things must happen in the branding process. The branding process consists of several elements:

- Brand awareness—Making desired consumers recognize and remember the brand name
- Brand image—The consumers' set of beliefs about a brand which, in turn, shape attitudes
- Brand equity—The value that the brand contributes to a product in the marketplace
- Brand loyalty—The consistent purchase or repeat purchase of one brand over all others in a product category

branding—The process of using a name, design, symbol, or any combination of them to help differentiate a product from the competition.

Positioning a product by successfully branding it is the ultimate goal of marketing because consumers subconsciously associate a brand name with a specific product. In sport marketing, brands such as Nike athletic shoes, Louisville Slugger baseball bats, Titleist golf balls, and Penn tennis balls are just a few products that have achieved this status.

Step 5: Pick the Players: Analyze and Target Consumers

In step 5, the marketer analyzes the market and targets particular consumers, a process that we can envision as "picking the players" who will allow the marketing plan to be a success. This approach involves grouping consumers according to common characteristics. As mentioned previously in the discussion of the unique aspects of sport, sport consumers are heterogeneous and have different wants, needs, interests, and behaviors regarding sport. To appeal to the uniqueness of sport consumers, marketers must have information about them. According to Francese (1990), market research is conducted to obtain information about sport consumers in four areas: demographics, psychographics, media preferences, and purchasing behavior (see figure 9.4).

Information collected through market research enables marketers to segment consumers into clusters according to selected characteristics. This process, known as market segmentation, is used to identify target audiences. Demographic segmentation refers to clustering sport consumers based on their age, gender, income, race or ethnicity, education, and place of residence. Psychographic segmentation refers to appealing to consumers' attitudes, interests, and lifestyles (see chapter 10). Market segmentation based on media preference would cluster consumers based on their sport media preferences (such as television, radio, Internet, and magazines or other publications). Purchasing behavior as a means of market segmentation refers to grouping customers according to the frequency of usage behavior, such as how often they attend an event or purchase a product.

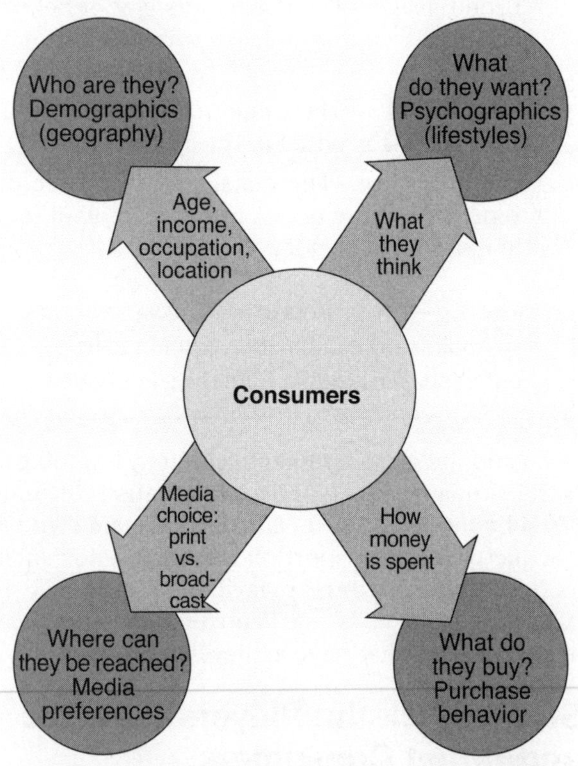

Figure 9.4 Types of information generated by consumers.

Reprinted, by permission, from P. Francese, 1990, How to manage consumer information. In D. Crispell (Ed.), *The insider's guide to demographic know-how* (Ithaca, NY: American Demographics Press), 9-14.

Market segmentation allows the sport marketer to identify smaller clusters of sport consumers who may exhibit similar wants, needs, and interests regarding sport. This process involves target marketing, an approach that zeroes in on specific consumers who are most likely to find the product appealing rather than attempting to sell products to all consumers. Target marketing involves identifying specific consumer groups that will most likely buy the product and therefore help sport organizations meet the goals and objectives of the marketing plan. For example, a sport equipment manufacturer might identify the primary target audience as males 12 to 16 years of age who are interested in in-line skating and who watch MTV.

According to the Selig Center for Economic Growth (2005), a research organization at the University of Georgia, the buying power of US White consumers has been projected to increase modestly (164%) over the 21-year span from 1990 through 2010. During the same time period, substantial increases have been projected for the buying power of ethnic minority consumers; gains of 397% for the Asian consumer market, 413% for Hispanics, 251% for American Indians, and 222% for African Americans. For the period of 2005 to 2010, the Center has projected that Hispanic buying power will increase from $736 billion to $1,087 billion, Asian's buying power will increase from $397 billion to $579 billion, Blacks' buying power will increase from $761 to $1,023 billion, and American Indians' buying power will increase from $51 billion to $69 billion. These trends have made ethnic minority populations economically attractive and potentially profitable consumer segments for sport marketers.

The economic power and sport interests among ethnic minorities represent a huge opportunity (which, as you may remember from "Step 3: Project the Market Climate," refers to favorable conditions in the environment) for sport organizations. A significant increase has occurred in the number of ethnic minority fans, particularly those of Hispanic and Asian descent, of US professional sports such as the NBA, NFL, and Major League Baseball. Consequently, many professional sport leagues and organizations are devising marketing plans that focus on attracting a multicultural base of consumers. For example, the NBA and MLB have many of their games broadcast in languages spoken in Hispanic and Asian cultures. They also have print media in the appropriate languages. The NHL, in partnership with Nike, has devised community relations activities such as street hockey to attract and socialize African American youth from the inner cities to the sport of hockey. A number of professional sport teams are engaging in initiatives to increase the diversity of their corporate and sponsorship partners. For example, the Los Angeles Avengers of the Arena Football League hosted a special event to promote opportunities with local Hispanic businesses, and MLB offered a similar program (seminar) for Native American business owners. MLB also has a Diverse Partners Program in which they use the marketing-related services of minority and women businesses. Many sport marketers also include promotions and special events that celebrate cultural diversity and offer culturally targeted entertainment (music, dance, and so on) in the production of their events to appeal to the interests of a multicultural sport consumer base. As Pons, Larouche, Nyeck, and Perreault (2001) revealed, sport events play a critical role in the culture of most consumers, and many sport events have ethnocultural symbols, rituals, and emblems that may be more salient to some ethnic groups than others. As the consumer base for sport continues to increase in ethnic diversity, so will the need for marketing plans that reflect the multicultural nature of that base.

Besides awakening to ethnic minority markets, sport marketers have also realized the importance of devising marketing strategies to appeal to female consumers. Until recently, women were not considered a viable target market segment for men's sports. But with increased buying of men's sport teams' merchandise by women, women's increased spectatorship of men's sports (such as the NBA, NFL, MLB, and NHL), the growth of women's sports, the financial gains that women have made as consumers, and the general influence that women exert over family purchases and consumption decisions, they have become an important target market for sports (Barbano, 1998; Sutton and Wattlington, 1994). Moreover, the Title IX generation (women and girls born after 1972) is young and relatively affluent, two desirable attributes sought by marketers. NASCAR offers an example of a sport organization that has made concerted efforts to appeal to female consumers. Murphy (2004) reported that 42% of the NASCAR fan base is female. According to Murphy, a Fox Sports spokesman indicated that the fastest growing segment of the television audience for the 2004 Nextel Cup Series, which aired on Fox, was women aged 18 through 34. Women are reportedly attracted to the charismatic NASCAR drivers (many women are also avid viewers of the NASCAR television show *NASCAR Drivers: 360*, which accentuates the human side of the drivers), the family-friendly atmosphere of NASCAR events, and the emotional rush and excitement of the overall race-day experience. NASCAR events feature vendors that provide women with merchandise made specifically for them, such as tank tops, shorts, and T-shirts. The collective marketing efforts of NASCAR appear to be successful in creating a culture that is inviting to segments of female fans.

As mentioned previously, another group of consumers that has attracted the attention of sport marketers are the Generation X consumers (people born between 1964 and 1978). These consumers have exhibited behaviors that differ from other markets and illustrate how demographics (age) and psychographics (attitudes and interests) may interact to influence sport consumer behavior (Turco, 1996). Sport events such as the X Games and the Gravity Games illustrate that Generation Xers are a target market to be reckoned with. In addition, consumer characteristics such as race and ethnicity, age, and gender may be integrated or combined to create specific target markets within the Generation X category.

After identifying target audiences, marketers can develop a strategy to reach them. The strategy involves customizing the elements in the marketing mix to appeal to the wants, needs, and interests of the target markets. A key to success in product positioning (discussed in step 4) is communicating an image for the product that will appeal to the target audience. For example, the 1994 Gay Games and Paralympics advertisements communicated honest and positive images that encouraged participants, spectators, and sponsors from specific target markets to get involved in these events. Regarding Black college sports events such as the Circle City Classic and Bayou Classic previously discussed, advertisements and core product extensions were effective because they were specifically designed to appeal to their target market (i.e., the Black community). The X Games and Gravity Games were also customized to appeal to the target market of Generation Xers.

Picking the players is a critical aspect of the marketing plan. Without consumers, of course, sport organizations would not be successful in reaching their marketing goals and objectives. Therefore, sport marketers must target the right groups of consumers. Criteria for selecting the viable target markets include factors such as the size of the target group, the amount of resources available to the target group, and whether the target group is accessible to the organization. The determination of whether a target market is acceptable varies among sport organizations, based largely on the organization's marketing goals and objectives. For example, a target market of 100 students for a football event that attracts over 100,000 consumers may not be of sufficient size to warrant specific marketing attention. On the other hand, a target market of 100 students for a fitness club with a membership of approximately 200 is an acceptable size and may have a significant effect on the overall marketing success of the fitness club. With the changes that are occurring in demographic representations, psychographic profiles, media preferences, and purchase behaviors of sport consumers, picking the right players is a challenging but necessary undertaking for sport marketers.

After marketers have identified the target consumers for their product, they must engage in a number of strategies that will help draw targeted consumers to the sport organization. Steps 6 through 10 of the 10 Ps process describe strategies that help marketers attract their target audiences.

Step 6: Package the Sport Product

Packaging the sport product includes presenting the product in the best possible manner to encourage selected target audiences to purchase it. Because consumers differ, marketers must present the product in different ways. Packaging tangible or industrial sport products involves explaining the benefits of the products, such as the strength and longevity of metal bats, the comfort and safety of helmets, and the expanded sweet spot of oversize tennis rackets. Packaging the core product of sport (the game or event itself), however, involves communicating the expectations of the product and providing information before the point of purchase. For example, sport marketers might package the game or event as family entertainment and offer family ticket plans. Or marketers might package sport as a good place to make business contacts and offer business ticket plans. A sport organization that wants to be seen as one that cares about the community might offer group discount ticket plans for social service and charitable organizations.

Another aspect of product packaging is the manner in which product extensions (discussed in step 2) are included in the overall sport experience. For instance, music, halftime promotions, and entertainment contribute to the overall packaging of a sport event such as a basketball game. Some consumers may not be specifically attracted to the core product (the basketball game), but they may be attracted to the way in which the core product is packaged (i.e., with music, fun, excitement, and entertainment).

Another aspect of the sport product is the associated licensed merchandise. Many sport teams and events offer goods such as hats, T-shirts, jackets, and other apparel as well as nonapparel items such as watches, novelty items, memorabilia, and decorative items that consumers perceive as extensions and representations of the teams or events. The affinity of sport consumers to teams' licensed products is noteworthy. Based on research by the National Sporting Goods Manufacturers Association, Shank (2005) reported that total retail sales for licensed NFL products had more than doubled in less than 15 years (increasing from $5.35 billion USD in 1990 to $12.1 billion USD in 2003). Therefore, sport marketers should be mindful of the various tangible and intangible extensions of their sport products or events.

Packaging the sport product to secure financial support from corporations is an especially important aspect of the marketing plan called sponsorship. Sponsorship involves an agreement between a sport organization or event and a corporation wherein the corporation pays a fee to the organization or event to acquire the rights to affiliate with it. Sponsorships can help corporations increase sales, change attitudes, heighten awareness, and build and maintain positive relationships with consumers. A sport marketer must conduct research to learn what benefits corporations are seeking through sponsorship. Having this information is necessary before beginning negotiations with corporate sponsors. In negotiations, marketers must be flexible about modifying packages to meet the interests and needs of the corporate sponsor. Being flexible, however, does not mean that the sport product should be misrepresented or that claims of benefits should be exaggerated. To maintain and strengthen a trusting relationship, the exchange between the sport organization and the corporate sponsor must be honest and fair (McCarville & Copeland, 1994).

Crunk and B artist, Ciara, performing in the 2006 Orange Bowl halftime show at Pro Player Stadium in Miami. Including such high-powered performers in pre- and half-time entertainment is one way to pull in significant numbers of fans who might otherwise neither attend the game nor watch it on television.

Courtesy of Paul M. Pedersen.

Sponsorships of women's sport products provide unique opportunities for corporations to communicate to women that they care about women's issues. By sponsoring women's sports, corporations can demonstrate that they are not only promoting their products but also taking a special interest in women and seeking to generate goodwill among women. For instance, State Farm Insurance Company sponsors women's professional skating, tennis, golf, college basketball, and college volleyball with a magazine ad that says, "We will insure that girls will always get to play." This message is most important in women's sponsorship.

The way a product is packaged either directly or indirectly influences or is influenced by every other aspect of the 10 Ps process outlined in this chapter, such as who will be attracted to the product or event, its relevance to the current market climate, what its price should be, how it should be promoted, and how it will be delivered. Therefore, sport marketers must understand how all the elements that contribute to product packaging influence the success of the marketing plan.

Step 7: Price the Sport Product

Step 7 is determining the value of the product by assigning it a price. Price is the most visible and flexible element because of discounts, rebates, and coupons. According to Pitts and Stotlar (2002), marketers should consider four factors when developing a pricing strategy:

1. Consumer—Analyze all aspects of the consumer, including demographics, psychographics, purchasing behaviors, and media preferences.
2. Competitor—Analyze the consumer's perception of the product value compared with all competing products, and analyze the competitors' prices.

3. Company—Analyze the costs involved in producing the product (materials, equipment, salaries, rent) and set a minimum price to cover the costs.
4. Climate—Analyze external factors, such as laws pertaining to pricing, government regulations, the economic situation, and the political situation.

Normally, consumers exchange money for products. In sport marketing, however, trading is a common practice. According to Gray (1996), sport organizations or events frequently trade tickets, stadium signage, and scoreboard advertisement for goods and services. For example, marketers of a tennis tournament might make trades with corporate sponsors, such as tickets for tennis balls, stadium signage for food and beverages for a hospitality tent, and scoreboard advertisement for the use of vehicles to transport players and officials.

Factors other than price help determine the value of a product. Each consumer has attitudes, preferences, beliefs, and a certain amount of expendable money. These factors, along with price, influence how people determine the value of a product. Because the value of a product is unique to each consumer, the pricing strategy must appeal to as many different consumers as possible. For example, sport franchises set different prices for corporate season ticket holders, charitable organizations, group ticket purchasers, miniseason ticket purchasers, family ticket purchasers, and single-ticket purchasers. Prices are generally differentiated based on the consumer's interest, ability, and willingness to commit time and money to participate in the sport experience.

Consumers tend to equate price with value. Therefore, a new sport franchise should price tickets to be comparable with competing products (other sporting events, movies, theater, other entertainment) rather than set a lower price. Consumers might equate a lower price with an inferior product.

Lead time is important to sport pricing. More day-of-the-game or walk-up sales occur at a Major League Baseball game than at an NBA basketball game because many more games and seats are available at lower prices in baseball than in basketball (Mullin, Hardy, & Sutton, 2000).

Sport pricing is complex and critical to the success of the marketing plan. However, price is one aspect of the marketing plan that may be readily changed (i.e., increased or decreased slightly). For example, sport organizations often alter their prices to attract different consumers (e.g., students may pay a different price for event tickets than the general public pays). Sport organizations may also change prices according to the market environment (e.g., lowering prices during a recession or economic downturn) or the team's performance (e.g., increasing prices as a team's performance dramatically improves). In the final analysis, sport marketers must determine how consumers perceive the value of the product compared with all competing products and use that information to set an appropriate price. Additionally, sport marketers should seek to offer consumers a satisfying experience with perceived benefits that surpass the personal and financial costs that consumers incur.

Step 8: Promote the Sport Product

Step 8 involves communicating the image of the product to the selected target audiences. Promoting sport products involves implementing a mix of activities that will best (1) communicate the desired image of the product to the target audiences, (2) educate and inform the target audiences about the product and its benefits, and (3) persuade the target audiences to buy the product.

Promotions, perhaps the most visible aspect of the marketing plan, are related to every aspect of the 10 Ps process. For example, promotions communicate something about the consumers, the product, the packaging and positioning, the price, and the channels in which the product will be distributed. Successful use of the various promotional elements presented in this chapter therefore requires an understanding of the following:

- The factors that influence the thoughts, perceptions, and actions of the target audience
- Clear promotional objectives (regarding sales, promoting awareness, and so on)
- The appropriate promotional mix tool (radio, television, newspapers, and so on) to use given the uniqueness of the sport product or event
- Other aspects of the marketing plan coordinated with the promotional mix elements to create an integrated strategy that will achieve the marketing goals and objectives

Elements that compose a promotion strategy (i.e., the promotional mix) include advertising, publicity, activities and inducements, public relations (including community relations and media relations), personal selling, and sponsorship.

• ***Advertising***. One-way paid messages about the sport product (newspapers, magazines, TV, radio, direct mail, scoreboards, in-arena signage, pocket schedules, game programs, posters, outdoor advertising, the Internet).

• ***Publicity***. Nonpaid communication about a sport product in which the sponsor is usually not identified and the message reaches the public because it is newsworthy (news releases, TV and radio public service announcements).

• ***Activities and inducements***. Promotions to encourage consumers to purchase the sport product (giveaways, coupons, free samples, cash refunds, contests, raffles).

• ***Public relations***. Activities and programs that help the organization develop positive relationships with its target audiences, especially community and media relations activities and programs. For example, through their Be Fit campaign, the WNBA seeks to communicate the importance of being physically active. Moreover, WNBA players, coaches, and administrators are involved in a number of public relations activities that promote awareness of breast cancer and the need for women to take an active role in early detection. Both activities contribute to the WNBA's positioning as a socially responsible sport organization that seeks to address some of the issues that directly or indirectly affect their consumers, both male and female. Public relations also involves assessing the public's opinions and attitudes toward a product. This information provides valuable feedback regarding the ways in which marketing activities and programs are influencing consumers' perceptions of the product and the extent to which the organization is forging positive relationships with its target audiences. With this information, sport marketers can modify promotions activities and programs to ensure that they are communicating positive images and messages about the product and thus fostering positive relationships between the organization and its target audiences.

• ***Community relations***. Activities and programs designed to meet the interests and needs of the public and, by so doing, establish good-faith relationships with the public (youth sport clinics, athlete autograph-signing opportunities, collection of food items at sport arenas to help people in the community). For example, the National Hockey League established the Diversity Task Force in 1994 to introduce economically disadvantaged children of diverse ethnic backgrounds to hockey. The Diversity Task Force implemented several grassroots community relations programs to reach specific target audiences. The Annual Willie O'Ree All-Star Game, named after the first Black player in the NHL, celebrates the successes of the individual inner-city programs, as their top players, ages 10 to 12 years old, compete in an East–West game; the Diversity Task Force Campership program provides economically disadvantaged youth with the opportunity to attend summer hockey camps throughout North America and receive on-ice hockey instruction; and the Coolest Kids Ice Hockey Tournament features boys and girls selected from teams that participated in the summer hockey camps program organized by the Diversity Task Force. With the growing need for sport organizations to be socially responsible, community relations activities that garner favorable relationships with the public are essential for marketing success.

• ***Media relations***. Maintenance of networks and positive relationships with people in the media to obtain positive media exposure for a sport product (informal and formal information sessions with media representatives). Because of the pervasive influence the media has on marketing success, sport marketers must make concerted efforts to create a positive relationship between their sport event and the media. They may accomplish this by providing the media with press releases, having news conferences, having media-day events (in which the media are invited to interact with the players, coaches, and administrators), providing media guides for the respective sport events, and so on. Each of these activities promotes active involvement from the media, which will subsequently contribute to relationship building with the community.

• ***Personal selling***. Direct face-to-face communication with individuals, groups, or organizations to sell tickets, luxury suites or boxes, or sponsorships. Personal selling is one of the most important activities in the promotional mix because it is the revenue-producing element. Sport marketers consider personal selling unique and highly effective because it involves face-to-face interaction with the target audiences rather than mass communication to thousands of consumers. Personal interaction with consumers allows salespeople to adapt messages based on feedback, communicate more information to the target audience, guarantee that the target audience will pay attention to the message being delivered, and develop a long-term relationship with the target audience. Successful salespeople realize they must adapt their sales pitch to the selling situation. For instance, selling women's sports is different from selling men's sports. Research shows that most people who watch women's sports are

Learning Activity

Bill Veeck was considered one of the most innovative owners in MLB history.

- What teams did Veeck own during his tenure with MLB? How did Veeck's marketing and promotions strategy contribute to the success of those teams?
- Bill Veeck's son, Mike Veeck, extended his father's legacy. Mike was responsible for the most infamous promotion in MLB history. What was that promotion and how did it affect Mike Veeck's career?
- Write a paper discussing the contributions that Bill Veeck made to sport marketing and promotions.

either young career professionals with daughters or older, retired people with substantial disposable income. These spectators value the following aspects of sport: quality sport, exemplary graduation rates, high standards of ethical conduct, and articulate young athletes who make contributions to their communities (Lopiano, 2002). In making their sales presentations, salespeople should emphasize these values. For instance, the sales pitch might emphasize hardworking players giving 100% effort, dedicated players who are serious students, talented young athletes who are well spoken, caring athletes who give back to their communities, and an honest sports program. Personal selling complements other promotional activities by educating consumers about what they are experiencing and pointing out the benefits that they are deriving.

- ***Sponsorship***. A form of promotion that involves a partnership between sport organizations or events and corporate entities. Business partnerships are based on exchange theory. Corporations provide money, products, or services to sport organizations or events, and in return sport organizations or events provide rights and benefits of association. If the sponsorship is to be successful, continue, and grow, both parties must perceive the exchange as fair, and the sponsoring corporation must determine that it has achieved an acceptable return on investment (ROI). Sponsorship agreements may include but are not limited to the following rights and benefits: use of the sport organization or event logo, name, or trademark; exclusive association with the event or facility; exclusive association within a product or service category; use of various designations or phrases in connection with the product, event, or facility, such as "official sponsor," "official supplier," "official product," or "presented by"; exclusive use of the product; and authorization to conduct particular promotional activities such as contests, advertising campaigns, or on-site product sales.

return on investment (ROI)—An objective assessment made by managers of a corporation to determine whether the amount of money paid for a sport sponsorship yielded an acceptable amount of earnings.

Sponsorship, then, includes a wide array of activities associated with sport organizations or events that allow corporations to engage in lifestyle marketing to send certain images and messages to target audiences. Sponsorship helps corporations achieve several marketing objectives. It heightens consumers' awareness, builds and maintains (sport lifestyle) relationships with consumers, changes consumer attitudes, and increases sales. It is no wonder that sponsorship is the promotional tool of choice for corporations and continues to grow in importance. Sponsorship has exceeded traditional forms of promotions in the United States and has become quite lucrative. An estimated 69% of the $10.25 billion USD spent on all sponsorships in North America in 2003 was spent on sport events (Shank, 2005).

lifestyle marketing—Form of marketing in which corporations use sponsorships to affiliate with specific sports or sport events as a means of promoting their products to particular groups of consumers (target audiences) who exhibit certain lifestyles (e.g., Generation X, Generation Y, Hip-Hop).

Corporations make significant investments in sport for a number of reasons, such as (1) to establish or improve their image through association with high-visibility events, (2) to promote their products, thereby increasing sales, (3) to display goodwill, and (4) to obtain access and exposure to the events' target markets. For example, sport events such as the Super Bowl, the Olympics, and NCAA football and basketball championships are especially attractive to corporate sponsors. Sport events benefit from the sponsorship arrangement because the corporations often provide the events with products, services, and financial resources. Obtaining sport sponsorships is important for the overall marketing success of sport because sponsorships often provide sport marketers with the resources necessary to package (as discussed in step 6), promote, and deliver their events.

Step 9: Place the Sport Product

Step 9 is analyzing the place of the sport product. **Place** refers to the location of the sport product (stadium, arena), the point of origin for distributing the product (ticket sales at the stadium, sales by a toll-free telephone number), the geographic location of the target markets (global, national, regional, state, communities, cities), and other channels that are important to consider regarding how target audiences may access the product (such as time, day, season, or month in which a product is offered, as well as the media distribution outlets that consumers may use). Factors related to the physical location of the sport can have a favorable or unfavorable effect on the marketing plan. To ensure a favorable effect, the sport facility must be easily accessible (highway systems, parking, walkways, ramps); have an attractive physical appearance (well maintained and painted); have a pleasant, convenient, and functional environment (quick and easy access to concessions, clean restrooms, smoke-free and odor-free environment); and have safe and pleasant surroundings (adequate public safety and security personnel, attractive neighborhood).

place—The comprehensive manner in which sport is distributed to consumers.

Sport is unique in the way it is distributed to consumers. The production and consumption of the product occur simultaneously for spectators attending sport events in stadia or arenas. The sport product is also distributed to consumers, nationally and globally, through the electronic media of television (regular cable and pay-per-view), radio, and Internet broadcasts.

Ticket distribution is another critical aspect of sport distribution. The objective of a ticket distribution system is to make consumer purchases easy, quick, and convenient. Some approaches used by sport organizations include using outside companies such as Ticketmaster; ticket outlets at local banks, shopping malls, and grocery stores; mobile van units that transport ticket personnel and operations to various locations throughout the community; on-site stadium and arena ticket sales with expanded hours of operation; toll-free telephone numbers; and will-call pickup arrangements.

Place is a critical aspect of the marketing plan. Marketers may package a sport product with exciting extensions, communicate effectively to target audiences, and offer the product at a reasonable price, but if consumers cannot access the event (e.g., because of barriers related to time or location), the marketing of the event will not be a success. Therefore, the overall objective of placing, and thus distributing, the sport product is to facilitate consumers' ability to take part in the sport experience, or purchase the sport product, in a timely and convenient manner, thereby promoting marketing success.

Step 10: Promise of the Sport Marketing Plan

Step 10 is evaluating the extent to which the marketing plan met its promise to help achieve the organization's mission. This evaluation requires obtaining feedback about the marketing plan from inside and outside the organization. Some inside sources of feedback are ticket sales; merchandise sales; and customer inquiries, complaints, and suggestions. Some outside sources of feedback include consumers, corporate sponsors, advertisers, and media personnel. The sport marketer must analyze and evaluate the feedback. The evaluation should focus on determining the extent to which the plan helped the organization achieve its mission by acting in accordance with its core values. For example, Reebok might establish a mission "to diversify its products to appeal to girls and women" based on a core value of "establishing positive relationships with all segments of the community." Obtaining feedback from girls and women about the Reebok TV advertisement would be a good way to evaluate this element of the marketing plan. The evaluation might conclude that the TV advertisement achieved the mission and did so in a manner that was consistent with the core values. To evaluate the effectiveness of the marketing plans for some of the Black college sport events that specifically seek to empower the Black community sociologically and economically, marketers may evaluate the number of students who attended the event, examine the financial contributions the event made to the respective HBCU universities, and examine the economic contributions of the event to the local economies.

In some cases, a marketing plan might not have a clear purpose linked with the organization's mission and core values. In these cases, an evaluation of the marketing plan might show that it is not helping the

NIKE SPONSORSHIP OF THE OHIO STATE UNIVERSITY

The essence of sport sponsorship may be illustrated by the sponsorship of the Ohio State University (OSU) by Nike. Because of the popularity of OSU among sport consumers throughout the United States, the high national visibility of OSU athletics, and the tradition of excellence and success experienced by OSU athletes, Nike entered into a sponsorship with OSU valued at $11.4 million USD. Nike contributed $8.4 million USD worth of equipment for OSU's athletic teams and $3 million USD in cash to the OSU account. These product and financial contributions provided significant benefit to OSU's athletic teams and events. Nike received the promotional license or right to have its logo placed on the uniforms of OSU athletic teams and the right to sell Nike products and apparel throughout OSU's campus. Any exposure for OSU athletics also meant exposure for Nike. Thus, the sponsorship between OSU and Nike created a win–win relationship, in which both entities received promotional benefits. Sport marketers seeking sponsorships from corporations must be sure that their sport events will

1. enable the corporation to obtain a competitive advantage and meet their marketing goals and objectives,
2. be a good fit with the image and philosophy of the corporation, and
3. provide a link to the consumers whom the corporation is seeking to attract.

Therefore, sport marketers are usually required to develop sponsorship proposals that outline what the sport event offers to sponsors, what the sport event expects to receive from sponsors, and how the win–win situations will be implemented and evaluated.

organization achieve its mission or, even worse, that it is reflecting poorly on the organization. For example, the Washington Redskins might establish a mission to "be the most respected and successful football team in the NFL" based on a core value of "being civil and respectful to each other, to fans, and business associates." Obtaining feedback from fans, business associates, and others might indicate that the team nickname, Redskins, is offensive to some people, particularly American Indians. An evaluation of the team nickname, as an element of the marketing plan, might conclude that the nickname is not helping the organization achieve its mission and, even worse, is communicating a negative image of the organization. In this case, the management of the franchise might consider selecting a new team nickname that will communicate a positive image and be viewed as socially responsible. The organization should consider its mission and core values in selecting a new team nickname.

As these examples indicate, linking the purpose of the marketing plan to the organization's mission and core values helps ensure that the plan will be socially responsible. Sport marketers who develop marketing plans linked to the organization's mission and core values are being proactive. According to Covey (1989), "Reactive people are driven by feelings, by circumstances, by conditions, and by their environment. Proactive people are driven by values—carefully thought about, selected, and internalized values" (p. 72). Proactive sport marketers will achieve the promise of the marketing plan because their actions will be socially responsible and will help fulfill the mission of the organization.

CHALLENGES AND DIRECTIONS IN SPORT MARKETING

In many segments of the sport industry, sport marketers are pressured to increase their product sales to generate increased revenues for their organizations. This pressure poses a challenge. Because sport marketers are involved in persuading consumers to buy, they run the risk of exaggerating or misrepresenting their products in an effort to sell them. Today, and in the future, sport marketers should recognize this risk and monitor their marketing strategies to ensure that they communicate honest images and messages about their products that are consistent with the core values of their organizations.

Also, even though sport is quite popular, sport marketers must not market sport based on the *Field of Dreams* supposition "If you build it, they will come!" The overall excitement and popularity of sport cannot replace the need for strategic marketing planning. Moreover, as competition (with movies, arts, entertainment, and so on) for consumers increases, and as sport organizations are required to be more profitable, sport marketers will need to increase their understanding of basic marketing principles and apply them to the sport industry.

Technology is a rapidly changing environmental influence, and technological advancements affect the field of sport marketing daily. Sport marketers face the dilemma of how to select technology to stay competitive and remain on the cutting edge without spending money on technology that will quickly become outdated. Whether the new technology is the Internet, satellites, video boards, dynamic in-stadium signage, computers at seats in the stadium, Web hosting, online stores, video sports games, or some other innovation, sport marketers must decide what technology to use to offer a superior sports product and enhance the consumers' experience. A new culture of technology has emerged. In the future, sport marketers will have to decide how to use technology to make the sport product and experience more entertaining for consumers without negatively affecting the nature of sport. Overemphasizing the entertainment aspects that surround sport runs the risk of undermining sport or, worse, transforming sport into what Mark Hall (2002) calls sportainment. According to Hall, sportainment is a marketplace reaction to the consumers' increasing demand for greater human excellence and the desire to feel a sense of escape from ordinary life. Sportainment represents combining sport and entertainment in ways that will fulfill these consumer expectations. Sport marketers will need to guard against the temptation to use technology simply to meet the entertainment expectations of fans without considering its effect on the game or event itself. Failing to do so might jeopardize the integrity of sport and undermine its social value.

Another trend in sport marketing is an infusion of hip-hop nuances into the marketing plan. The term *hip-hop* is grounded in and reflects the burgeoning African American youth-oriented culture that originated in the Bronx, New York, during the 1970s (McLeod, 1999). Hip-hop symbolizes the voice of many urban Black youth and is reflected in the culture of their music, clothes, language, and overall way of life (Dyson, 1996; Midol, 1998). The hip-hop genre has spawned a cultural revolution, and this trend-setting market has exerted a formidable influence on mainstream consumption patterns worldwide. Many companies and industries have made concerted efforts to capitalize on the popularity of hip-hop, and the sport industry is no exception. The overall appeal of the hip-hop culture has not been lost on sport marketers. Hip-hop artists frequently (1) provide the pregame, postgame, and halftime entertainment of sport events, (2) are featured in sport promotions and advertisements, and (3) are often used as sport product endorsers. Reebok has sought to tap into the hip-hop appeal as a measure of reinventing themselves and improving their overall market share position. They have developed advertisements that pair professional athletes with hip-hop recording artists (e.g. Allen Iverson of the NBA and the performer Jadakiss appeared in a Reebok advertisement during NBA All-Star weekend in 2002). Reebok launched the limited edition of sneakers of hip-hop star Jay-Z (whose real name is Shawn Carter) on Easter weekend 2003, and the shoes sold faster than any shoe in Reebok's history (Berfield, Brady, & Lowry, 2003). The gravitation to hip-hop has made a decided difference in the profits of many organizations. The challenge of infusing cultural nuances of hip-hop into marketing practices is to be sensitive to the authenticity and social responsibility needed to reach urban consumers and the markets of consumers that they influence (McLeod, 1999). Sport marketers must obtain and demonstrate a sincere responsiveness and respect for the cultural essence of hip-hop.

Increasing consumer diversity may be the trend that will have the greatest influence on the success of sport marketing plans. As discussed in "Step 5: Pick the Players: Analyze and Target Consumers," sport, like other businesses, operates in a global market and must respond to the rapidly changing racial and ethnic demographics in the societies in which it operates. A person's race or ethnicity generally exerts a profound influence on that person's thoughts, attitudes, and behaviors, including those that pertain to sport consumption. Racial and ethnic influences are often difficult to discern because they may be internal (factors within individuals that may influence sport consumption behaviors) or external (factors prevalent in a sport setting or environment that may influence sport consumption behaviors) (Armstrong, 2001, 2002). Sport consumers' wants and needs may also differ based on a variety of other factors such as gender (e.g., the unique tastes of females compared with males) and age (e.g., the interests of senior consumers compared with Generation Xers).

The changing demographic and psychographic characteristics of sport consumers will increase the overall diversity to which sport marketers must respond as they seek to develop successful marketing plans. The trend toward increased diversity in the national and global market will pose both a special challenge and a unique opportunity for sport managers and marketers of the 21st century (Armstrong, 2001; DeSensi, 1994; Hofacre & Burman, 1992). The

JOB OPPORTUNITIES

Assistant Director, Special Events and Promotions

Responsible for writing press releases, developing mailing lists, making telephone calls, and assisting with the implementation of special events promotions. Candidates must have strong writing, oral, and computer skills and knowledge of the sport industry.

Assistant Sport Marketing Director

Assist ticket coordinator in all aspects of ticket sales and promotions; assist event director with planning and execution of on-site advertising and operations; assist volunteer coordinator in organization and administration of event volunteer workers. Candidates must have communication, organizational, and sales skills.

Assistant Public Relations Director

A professional sport league office is seeking a self-motivated individual with at least three years' experience working in a public relations office with a professional sport team. A bachelor's degree in sport management and communications is required. The candidate must also demonstrate excellent writing and computer skills. Job responsibilities include writing press releases; preparing and distributing daily sport circulation reports; compiling, organizing, and printing statistics for media guide publications for special events such as the All-Star Game Series and League Championship Series; and preparing written materials for press conferences.

Coordinator of New Business Development

A new professional women's ice hockey league is seeking a person with at least five years' management experience with a professional sport team or league office. A bachelor's degree in sport management, management, or marketing is required. Demonstrated skills in strategic management planning, marketing, and community relations are desirable. Job responsibilities include working with the vice president of marketing and special events in developing strategic plans for expanding markets and spectator audiences, strengthening and expanding community grassroots involvement in the sport, and attracting new corporate sponsors.

Tournament Operations Manager

A sport management firm responsible for marketing a professional women's tennis tournament is seeking an individual with one to three years' experience in professional sport tournament operations. A bachelor's degree in sport management is preferred. Job responsibilities include assisting the tournament director with food and beverage operations, managing facilities, and coordinating and servicing on-site booth operations for corporate sponsors. Excellent planning, organizational, interpersonal, and communication skills are required.

Director of Marketing

A major university is seeking an individual with three to five years' experience in marketing or sport marketing. A bachelor's degree in marketing or sport management is preferred. Previous work experience in an NCAA Division I athletics department or with a professional sport team is desirable. Job responsibilities include ticket sales and promotions, promoting individual sport teams, securing corporate sponsorships, selling stadium advertising space and program advertisements, and developing and implementing other marketing and promotions strategies.

Director of Community Relations

A new expansion team in a minor ice hockey league is seeking a creative and highly motivated person to develop and implement a community relations program. A bachelor's degree in sport management is preferred. Job responsibilities include arranging speaking engagements for coaches and players, organizing youth ice hockey clinics, organizing appearances of coaches and players with charitable organizations, and developing other strategies for involving coaches and players in community activities and events. The individual must have excellent planning and organizational skills with the ability to handle details.

Director of Marketing and Promotions

A new professional sports team is looking for an individual to direct marketing and promotions. This position includes raising awareness and interest in a sport never played professionally in this area. Applicants must have at least five years of experience with sport promotion and marketing; preference will be for candidates with previous professional sport promotion and marketing experience. The marketing and promotions director will report directly to the team owner and work closely with the general manager and other team personnel.

increased diversity in the environments in which sport operates will require sport marketers to be equipped with not only the marketing fundamentals but also the skills to adapt them to multicultural sport consumers. Sport marketers will have to develop appropriate and acceptable intercultural communications, packaging features, positioning strategies, and distribution channels to reach culturally diverse consumers in domestic and international environments (Armstrong, 2001; Hofacre & Burman; McCarthy & Stillman, 1998; Pons et al., 2001; Sutton & Wattlington, 1994; Turco, 1996).

SUMMARY

This chapter outlined a 10-step process that you can use to develop a sport marketing plan (see figure 9.1). The core of this process is the marketing mix, traditionally known as the four Ps (product, price, place, and promotion). The process also includes additional factors such as organizational, environmental, and consumer-related considerations (purpose, projecting the market, positioning, picking the players, packaging, and promise). A sport marketing plan will most likely succeed when marketing is viewed as a comprehensive process of packaging, promoting, and delivering sport to consumers in a manner that satisfies consumers' wants and needs and simultaneously meets the sport organization's marketing goals and objectives. Tactical marketing mix strategies (product, price, promotions, place) should therefore communicate a distinct, positive, and honest image of a product and the consumers to whom it is targeted. Such strategies will enable the sport organization to establish a favorable position among its targeted consumers in the market and will subsequently fulfill the promise of socially responsible marketing that is linked to and consistent with the mission and core values of the organization.

Review Questions

1. Explain how a context for a sport organization is established and why establishing a context is important in developing a sport marketing plan. Refer to purpose, mission statement, and core values in the explanation.
2. Explain how a SWOT analysis is used in analyzing a sport organization and its market in an effort to forecast the future market climate.
3. Explain the three dimensions of a sport product and the ways in which a sport product is unique.
4. Explain how positioning a sport product uses other promotion activities to help establish an image of a sport product in the minds of consumers.
5. Explain why a sport product or event should be promoted in ethical and socially responsible ways. Give examples of ethical and socially responsible promotion activities of a selected sport product.
6. Explain methods that are used to segment the market in order to identify viable target audiences for a sport product.
7. Describe strategies that can be used to distribute a sport product to consumers.
8. Explain the role of packaging in selling a sport product to specific target audiences. Give examples of packaging a sport product for a particular target audience.
9. Explain the two sources used to obtain feedback about a sport marketing plan and describe some individuals or groups from each source that can provide information useful to an evaluation of a sport marketing plan.
10. Describe two sport marketing needs in the 21st century.

Sport Consumer Behavior

B. Christine Green—University of Texas at Austin ▪ **Carla A. Costa**—University of Texas at Austin

Learning Objectives

After studying this chapter, you will be able to do the following:

1. Identify key motives for sport participation and spectation, and differentiate between the two.
2. Define consumer perception.
3. Describe the components of consumers' attitudes toward sport.
4. Differentiate between consumer involvement and identification.
5. Analyze the value of consumer loyalty.
6. Explain ways in which groups can influence the consumption behaviors of individuals.
7. Discuss the process of consumer decision making in sport.
8. Identify situational factors that can influence the decision-making process.

Imagine that you have developed a new sport. Who will play your sport? Who might watch it? The success of your new sport depends on your ability to attract customers. You need to know all you can about your customers—what they want, what they need, what they think, what they feel, what they know, and what they value. Most important, you want to know *why* they make the choices that they do. The study of consumer behavior enables you to do just that.

Consumer behavior can be defined as "the processes involved when individuals or groups select, purchase, use, or dispose of products, services, ideas, or experiences to satisfy needs and desires" (Solomon, 2002, p. 5). Consumer behavior helps you understand the personal and group factors that influence consumer decisions and how people make purchase decisions. A good understanding of current and potential consumers enables an organization to develop products and services that meet the needs of customers and to develop marketing strategies that attract and retain customers.

The purpose of this chapter is to provide an overview of consumer behavior in sport. In the first section, you will learn about individual factors influencing sport consumption. This section describes the motives for active (i.e., sport participation) and passive (i.e., sport spectation) sport consumption, and examines consumers' perceptions and attitudes toward sport. Individuals' motives, perceptions, and attitudes influence their involvement with any particular sport and the ways in which they identify with a sport, team, or athlete. The second section examines group influences on the sport consumer. In this section you will examine the influence of culture and ethnicity, reference groups, socialization processes, and sport subcultures on consumer decision making. Ways to build and strengthen relationships between customers and sport organizations are discussed in the third section. The final section introduces you to the decision process itself, and considers ways that sport marketers can influence consumers at each stage of the decision process.

UNDERSTANDING THE INDIVIDUAL AS A SPORT CONSUMER

Think for a minute about buying a gift for two of your close friends. Would you buy each one the same gift? Probably not. How, then, do you decide on the gift best suited to each of your friends? Most likely, you will consider what you know about each friend. What does she like? What might he need? How does she feel about certain types of products? Does he have a favorite brand? The more you know about your friend, the easier it is to choose the perfect gift. The same is true for sport businesses. To sell more tickets, to sell more tennis rackets, or to entice more players and teams to join a league, sport organizations need to know about their customers. The more a sport organization knows about its customers, the better it is able to design products and services to meet the needs of those customers, to design marketing messages that attract new customers and keep existing customers coming back, and to target messages to those most receptive to those messages.

Although no two individuals are the same, people often have some characteristics in common. A standard practice in marketing is to try to group, or segment, people based on common characteristics. In marketing terms, groups that share a number of characteristics are called **market segments**. Marketers then choose to focus their efforts on one or more of the identified market segments. The selected market segments are referred to as **target markets**. Products and services are designed to meet the needs of the target market. For example, many sporting goods manufacturers differentiate male consumers from female consumers. As a result, golf clubs come in men's and women's models. This differentiation makes sense from the standpoint of size and strength. On average, men are taller and stronger than women; women's clubs are shorter and lighter than those designed for men. Thus, women's clubs are designed to meet the physical needs of women golfers. Some golf bags are also designed and marketed as distinctly for men or distinctly for women. On the surface, distinguishing men's bags from women's bags seems unnecessary. Certainly, in this case, no physical need calls for different products. Rather, the distinguishing characteristics of the two models are style and color. The bags are designed to appeal to the different style needs, preferences, perceptions, and attitudes of male and female golfers.

> **market segment**—A portion of the population that is distinctive in terms of its needs, characteristics, or behavior.
>
> **target market**—A market segment or segments identified as the focus of an organization's marketing efforts; a segment chosen to allow an organization to attain its marketing goals most effectively and efficiently.

Gender is just one of a multitude of characteristics that marketers use to define a target market. Age, ethnicity, education, and income levels are demographic characteristics that can also be used to define a particular target market. Although **demographic segmentation** can be useful, it tends to rely on stereotypical images of particular groups. Segmenting based on demographic characteristics alone would be like trying to plan a party for a group of female African American college students whom you've never met. What kind of food would they like? What drinks would you provide? What kind of music would they enjoy? What would they like to do at the party? Because you don't know them, you would have to rely on stereotypes, which are often inaccurate and sometimes offensive. Now consider planning the same party for the same women, only they are your friends and you know them personally. So, besides knowing that they are similar in age and educational background, you also know what they like and don't like. Because you know how your friends think and feel, you know what to give them at your party. When considering demographic segmentation, keep this dynamic in mind.

> **demographic segmentation**—Dividing the market into groups based on demographic variables such as age, sex, family size, income, occupation, education, religion, and ethnicity.

Marketers also seek to understand how customers (and potential customers) think and feel. This information allows them to define their potential market segments more accurately. Grouping people based on their psychological differences is called **psychographic segmentation**. Common psychographic measures include consumer needs and motives, perceptions, learning experiences,

1890s	1900s	1960s	1970s
▷1894 Daily Racing Form debuts	▷1908 Pari-mutuel betting introduced at Kentucky Derby	▷1962 Fantasy football begins among beat writers for the AFL Oakland Raiders	▷1979 Launch of ESPN

attitudes, interests, and opinions. By getting inside the head of the consumer, marketers are better able to meet the needs of their target market. Suppose, for example, that you have been asked to market a summer sport camp to high school girls. What kinds of sports would you offer at the camp? Would you provide elite coaching or recreational instruction? These questions concern the design of your products and services. As a sport marketer, you would want to design your products and services to meet the needs of your chosen target market. A useful approach would be to divide the market of high school girls into smaller, more homogeneous groups based on the girls' motives to participate in sport. So, you might divide this group into three subgroups: (1) athletes who want to enhance their sport skills, (2) players who want to be with their friends or meet new friends, and (3) girls who are trying to lose weight and increase their overall fitness. Notice that these three groups are seeking different benefits from their camp experience.

psychographic segmentation—Dividing a market into different groups based on social class, lifestyle, or personality characteristics.

For the first market segment, you might offer elite coaching in a single sport. You might also provide sessions on strategies and tactics, physical training, and how to get a college scholarship. But if you designed your camp in this manner, do you think that it would be attractive to the other two groups? Probably not. A camp designed for the second group would need to provide plenty of opportunities to socialize. The camp could offer instruction in a number of sports and leave plenty of time for informal activities. Elements of a camp targeting the third group might include a focus on cardiovascular exercise, diet, and nutrition. The key, from a marketing standpoint, is choosing a market segment that fits the products and services that you have to offer or adapting your product to the needs of your target market.

Alternatively, understanding your target market can help you attract customers to an existing product by using messages that appeal to the needs of the target market. Consider again the sport camp for high school girls. It is possible to design a camp (i.e., a product) that could meet the needs of all three groups. Let's say that the camp will offer two sessions of volleyball instruction per day, will include diet and nutrition counseling, and will provide a different social event each evening. Although you now have only one product to sell, you can appeal to each of the three psychographic segments based on their motives for participating in sport. You might emphasize the quality of the coaches in your communications with group 1, the social schedule in advertising targeted at group 2, and the nutrition counseling in a brochure designed to attract girls in group 3. The key aspect of marketing your camp, whether you choose to appeal to one market segment or to all three, is to understand the needs of the customer and to design your products, services, and marketing communications in a way that appeals to the needs of the chosen target market or markets.

Marketers often segment sport consumers based on their motives, perceptions, and attitudes. Consumers build these from experiences, which might depend on their interests and opinions. Sport consumers often are emotionally and psychologically involved with their sports. Many athletes and fans define themselves in terms of their sport identity. The following sections describe consumer needs and motivations, perceptions, attitudes, involvement and identification, and loyalty, and then explore the ways that each can be used to understand the sport consumer.

Consumer Needs and Motivation

The fulfillment of needs is the essence of a marketing orientation (Shank, 2005). Everybody has needs. We are born with innate physiological needs—the need for food, water, air, clothing, and shelter. The fulfillment of these needs is required for life. We also have acquired needs such as the need for esteem, affection, or power. These needs are not necessary for life and tend to vary from culture to culture and from person to person. These needs are better described as wants and desires. Motivation can be defined as "the processes that cause people to behave as they do" (Solomon, 2002, p. 102). The driving force exists in response to an unfulfilled need. The key to the success of a sport organization is to identify and satisfy customers' unfulfilled needs better or faster than the competition does. Consequently, successful marketers define their target markets by the needs that they are trying to satisfy. Although individual needs and motives will vary, researchers have identified some common motives for sport participation.

1980s

1980
Mark Newman starts first Rotisserie Baseball League

1990s

1996
Launch of Speedvision (cable network for motor sport); name changed to Speed Channel in 2001

Participant Motivation

Researchers have identified over 100 motives for participating in sport (Green, 1996). Fortunately, the reasons that people give to explain their participation can be usefully grouped into three key motives: (1) achievement motivation, (2) social motivation, and (3) mastery motivation (Roberts, 1992). The need to compete, to win, and to be the best are examples of achievement motivations. These needs nearly always require an element of social comparison. To attract participants motivated by achievement goals, sport marketers could emphasize the competitive elements of their programs. A competitive league structure and playoff opportunities would be important to players motivated by achievement. These players might also value **extrinsic rewards** such as MVP awards, all-star games, and trophies. Standard programs do a good job of catering to achievement-motivated participants. But many programs stop there, reaching only a narrow market segment—participants with a need for achievement. Sport marketers can attract participants from a much larger pool of potential players by catering to other motivations.

Learning Activity

You have just been hired as the development officer for a regional speedskating organization. Your objective is to increase participation in speedskating. Your organization does not have a large marketing budget, but it does have strong links to US Speedskating, the national governing body for the sport. Because of this relationship, your organization depends on the marketing efforts of US Speedskating. The excerpt from their 2006 Web site shown in figure 10.1 illustrates one of their current marketing campaigns. To leverage the national marketing campaign to recruit new skaters in your region, you have a three-part task:

1. Analyze the benefits of speedskating that the national marketing campaign is using.

To do this, begin by categorizing the reasons listed in the advertisement based on potential motives to participate. The advertisement clearly includes the three main categories of participant motivation. For example, achievement motives are highlighted by items such as "Because you can win an Olympic medal! Because you dream about representing your country in competition! Because you might earn a scholarship for college!" Similarly, social motives appear in the ad. Examples include "Because your friends skate! Because you can meet new friends! Because you like a supportive, social, team environment!" Lastly, the ad includes mastery appeals. Consider the following: "Because you'll learn to skate even faster than you already can! Because you want to be a better in-line skater!"

2. Design one or more speedskating programs and services that meet the needs represented by the motives from task 1.

You could design a single program that tries to deliver all the benefits described. Alternatively, you might design three programs. The first could be highly competitive and emphasize achievement. This program might include opportunities to compete against skaters within and outside the region, and might include a representative team that would compete nationally. A second program could be designed to appeal to social motives. This program would be the most team-oriented and would appeal to all skaters. It could include social (nonskating) events with all program participants. Socially motivated skaters might also enjoy traveling to events in which they could meet new people. Yet another program might focus on providing mastery-oriented benefits. This program could emphasize improvement and might include individualized instruction, support services such as nutrition and weight training instruction, and assistance with goal setting and goal planning.

3. Develop brochures and advertisements that will attract participants to your newly designed programs.

The marketing materials for each program would provide information about the program that would highlight the main benefits of that program. So the achievement program would emphasize the representative and competitive opportunities for skaters. Marketing materials might include images of club skaters receiving medals or an action shot of a skater crossing the finish line first. The social program, on the other hand, would use images of team members enjoying themselves, whereas the brochure for the mastery program might include testimonials from skaters who have made dramatic improvements in their times. In any case, the images and text for the brochures and any supporting advertisements should highlight the particular benefits that potential skaters seek through participation.

Why Should I Try It?

Because you already love to skate! Because it's fun! Because it's fast! Because you are always moving! Because it's like flying without leaving the ground! Because you'll learn to skate even faster than you already can! Because all you have to do is skate! Because your friends skate! Because you can make new friends! Because you can travel, see new places and new people! Because you can win an Olympic medal! Because you need a sport to do in the winter! Because you want to cool off in the summer! Because you want to be a better in-line skater! Because you want an individual sport that you can customize to your needs and goals! Because you want a fast, fun, social recreational activity! Because you want a sport you can do for life! Because you want to beat your Dad or Mom in a race! Because you want a lot of variety and options—short track, long track, pack, time trials, marathon, sprints, indoor, outdoor, intense, recreational, . . . Because you like a supportive, social, team environment! Because it will keep you out of trouble! Because you dream about representing your country in competition! Because you like the speed! Because you like the wind in your face! Because you like to glide fast and far! Because you want a sport that is internationally widespread! Because you want to cross-train for other sports! Because you want to bring the Olympic Spirit to your hometown! Because you want to join the 2006 Winter Olympic Hometeam! Because you want a sport that builds character and self-esteem! Because you want a sport that helps you spend time together as a family! Because you might earn a scholarship for college! Because it will help you get into great shape! Because if you don't, you'll never know if it was your talent, your passion! Because it's fun! Because you already love to skate! Just try it! Won't you join us?

Figure 10.1 Speedskating advertisement.

Reprinted, by permission, from the U.S. Speedskating. Available: www.usspeedskating.org.

extrinsic rewards—Rewards given to a person by someone else.

Marketing efforts directed toward participants seeking social opportunities through their sport participation should highlight social interactions among participants. Advertisers of both sport and nonsport products often use images of athletes enjoying themselves during and after competitions. Many clubs offer coeducational sport in an attempt to provide more extensive social interactions between men and women. Running clubs clearly cater to social motivations. Consider the following excerpt from the Cambridge Running Club Web site (n.d.):

> **Welcome to the Cambridge Running Club.** We are an active, social running club located in Cambridge, Massachusetts (USA). We have runners of all abilities—ranging from the strictly casual to competitive road racers. The club provides professionally coached track workouts on a weekly basis designed to help all of our runners reach their goals. Equally important, we arrange regular social events, including more casual weekend runs, trips to fun races both near and far away, as well as parties and other social gatherings. Almost every workout or run is followed by a meal or drinks. New runners are always welcome to check us out!

Unlike most sports, running does not require participants to train with others, and runners can compete without being a part of a team. But that doesn't mean that people don't run for social reasons or that runners don't value social interactions. The Cambridge Running Club excerpt highlights two important elements of club membership for socially motivated runners: (1) people can run with a group and thus don't have to run alone, and (2) the socializing continues after the run and thus is not limited to the training session itself.

The third key motivational category for participation in sport is mastery motivation. Skill development, learning, and personal challenge appeal to mastery-oriented participants. Programs offering instruction, coaching, or mentoring often appeal to these participants. Like achievement seekers, mastery-motivated participants might seek competition. But for these participants, competition

A SWIM CLUB IN CRISIS

A small suburban swim club was in trouble. Although the club enjoyed moderate success in the local summer swim league, substantial turnover of membership occurred from summer to summer. Each year almost half the families from the previous season did not return. The club conducted a survey at the end of one of its seasons and discovered that families had many different reasons for joining the club. Some wanted their children to win ribbons, medals, and trophies (achievement motivation); some found that the club was a good way to get to know other people in the community (social motivation); and some wanted their children to improve their swimming skills (mastery motivation). The club had always assumed that its primary task was to help children become winning competitive swimmers. The club focused on achievement by helping its swimmers find a specialty event and train to win in that event. All members were required to compete at weekend swimming meets. Although the team had a picnic at the end of the season, the club did little else to foster social interaction among its members.

After the survey, the club changed its policies. Coaches implemented special coaching to help swimmers who wanted to develop swimming skills beyond their primary competitive events (mastery motivation). Members who did not want to compete were not required to enter weekend swimming meets. The club also introduced several social events for members, including pizza parties and midseason picnics (social motivation). Within two years, the club had grown from 62 families to over 300 families, and members typically stayed with the club for several years. By developing its programs to appeal to multiple motivations, the club increased its membership, improved its financial position, and became league champion.

is for **intrinsic rewards** and is less about winning and more about challenging oneself. Training and instruction take place regularly in elite sport settings and in most sport programs designed for children and teens. But what about programs designed for adults? Although instruction is not the only way to appeal to mastery-motivated participants, it is certainly an underused element of adult sport programs. Mastery is intrinsic to timed sports such as swimming and track, and to individually scored sports such as golf and bowling, but it can be built into a wider variety of sport settings through goal setting. Adventure sports such as rock climbing and mountain biking routinely use mastery appeals in their advertising. The advertisement for OuterQuest (n.d.) illustrates the way in which marketers can incorporate mastery appeals into their advertising (see figure 10.2).

> **intrinsic rewards**—Rewards received by a person from the experience itself.

We have identified three fundamental motives for sport participation: achievement, social, and mastery motives. We have also discussed ways in which sport marketers can appeal to each of the three types of motives. Now think of the things that motivate you to participate in your favorite sport. Chances are that more than one thing motivates you. People usually have multiple motives for participating in sport. Rarely do people take up running just to socialize with others. Nor is it likely that a person would join a volleyball team just to best the competition. In marketing your sport to current and potential participants, you would do well to provide elements to appeal to each of the motives and to communicate in ways that highlight benefits appealing to each motivational segment. Consider the example in "A Swim Club in Crisis."

Learning Activity

Collect brochures or advertisements for a variety of sport programs. You might find brochures at fitness centers, campus recreation facilities, sport organizations (such as Ys, Boys & Girls Clubs, Jewish Community Centers), schools, and other sport-related businesses (e.g., REI and other outdoor stores, sporting goods stores). You will find advertisements for sport programs online, in magazines, and in newspapers. What motives do each of the brochures or advertisements cater to? Identify a target market for each program based on the psychographic segmentation variable of motivation. Redesign the brochure or advertisement to heighten the appeal to this target market.

Spectator Motivation

Interestingly, the reasons that people give for watching sport are quite different from their reasons for participating in sport. Like participation motives, spectator motives vary considerably. Eight core

If you are looking for high adventure and great exercise, then you should try mountain biking. Regardless of whether you are completely new to the sport or an experienced biker seeking new skills and terrain, we have a mountain biking course that is perfect for you! Beautiful rolling hills and mountain paths surround the Washington area, and mountain biking is the perfect way to explore and enjoy these natural resources. Use your own bike or borrow one from our quality fleet of front suspension Specialized™ bikes; either way, a great ride and quality instructors await you at OuterQuest.

Figure 10.2 Mastery appeal by OuterQuest.
Reprinted, by permission, from Camp OuterQuest. Available: www.outerquest.com

motives have been found to capture the many reasons given for attending sporting events (Wann, Melnick, Russell, & Pease, 2001):

1. Diversion from everyday life
2. Entertainment value
3. Self-esteem enhancement
4. Eustress
5. Economic gain
6. Aesthetic value
7. Need for affiliation
8. Family ties

The following sections discuss the eight motives.

• ***Diversion***. For many, watching sport is a way to escape from everyday life. It is a **diversion** from the stress or boredom of one's own life. Like other forms of entertainment, such as movies and theater, sport spectating allows people to let their cares slide away as they lose themselves in the drama and spectacle of the contest. To appeal to consumers' desires to escape from everyday life, sport marketers should emphasize what anthropologists call liminality or liminoid space (Turner, 1986). Liminality can be defined as social space outside normal rules that is characterized by a heightened sense of community. In other words, liminoid space is a place where normal rules don't apply, where social boundaries disappear. As social boundaries break down, the sense of connection and bonding with other participants increases. Sport settings often provide liminoid experiences. Where else can people go where it is acceptable (and even encouraged) to scream and yell, to clap and stamp their feet, and to hug complete strangers? Similarly, sport spectators have a ready-made community—other fans of the team. In essence, fans form a community of support for the team and for one another. For fans attracted to sport as an escape from their daily lives, sport marketers can build appeals around images that emphasize the unique behaviors and social relationships found at sporting events. Other entertainment options (e.g., movies and concerts) can provide an escape from everyday life, but few can match the liminality common at most sporting events.

diversion—A distraction from a course or activity.

• ***Entertainment***. Not surprisingly, many fans are motivated to attend a sporting event for its entertainment value. Closely related to the escape motive just discussed, the entertainment motive is driven by a desire for drama and excitement. World Wrestling Entertainment (formerly WWF) is a prime example of sport marketers' ability to create a dramatic context to showcase physical skills that appeals to fans' desire for entertainment. Marketers of more traditional sports can take advantage of the uncertainty built into sport contests to highlight the drama to fans. Further, sport marketers can hype critical player matchups and rivalries to add intensity to the drama. Increasingly, sporting events offer entertainment well beyond the sport contest itself. For example, figure 10.3 lists 30 NFL or NFL-sanctioned events offered at the 2006 Super Bowl (Detroit Super Bowl XL Host Committee, n.d.).

• ***Self-Esteem***. Most of us have felt the glow and satisfaction of a victory by our favorite team. Basking In Reflected Glory (BIRGing), as first labeled by Cialdini and colleagues (1976), is a key driver of

- 2006 Sports Career Expo Series Why Not XL at Your Game Hosted by Robert Porcher
- 4th Annual NFL Alumni Super Bowl Home Tour
- America Online Presents the NFL Experience
- Athletes in Action Super Bowl Breakfast
- Canadian Host Committee Gala
- *Ebony* Magazine Presents . . . The Pathfinders Awards: A Salute to Excellence
- Gridiron Celebrity Hoops VIII
- Nations in Rhythm Detroit
- NFL Alumni Bocce Ball Tournament
- NFL Alumni Player of the Year Awards Gala
- NFL Charities Bowling Tournament Sponsor Party
- NFL Global Junior Championship X
- NFL On Location
- NFL's Black History Month Tribute–Rock My Soul
- One Detroit, One World
- Pepsi Smash Super Bowl Bash Concert
- Player Networking Event
- Players Gala
- PLAYERS INC LIVE!
- Rebuilding Together's Kickoff to Rebuild
- Super Bowl Cheerleading Spirit Clinic
- Super Bowl Diversity Business Forum
- Super Bowl Fitness Challenge
- Super Bowl Football Youth Clinic
- Super Bowl XL Playbook for Small Business
- Taste of the NFL
- The 7th Annual Super Bowl Gospel Celebration
- The Field Generals Reception
- The Field Generals Youth Clinic
- The Touchdown Club

Figure 10.3 Ancillary entertainment at the 2006 Super Bowl.

attendance for fans seeking to enhance their self-esteem by associating themselves with a successful team or player. In effect, the success of the team rubs off onto the fan. Similarly, fans might attempt to maintain their self-esteem by disassociating themselves from a team after a loss or poor performance. This has been described as Cutting Off Reflected Failure, or CORFing (Snyder, Lassegard, & Ford, 1986). Sport marketers can attract new fans who jump on the bandwagon when a team is winning, but marketers must be careful to develop a relationship with these new fans who use the team to enhance their own self-esteem. Remember, marketers have no control over the competitive performance of a team or its athletes, so designing marketing efforts solely on appeals to self-esteem enhancement is dangerous. Marketers might initially appeal to this market segment through opportunities to BIRG and then develop complementary strategies to retain these fans in times when the team is less successful.

• ***Eustress***. Eustress is a form of positive stress or arousal. Fans motivated by **eustress** seek excitement and stimulation. Marketers should appeal to all five senses in efforts to reach fans motivated by eustress. Music, chants, and sound effects can provide auditory stimuli; scoreboards, lighting, movement, and color can provide visual stimuli. Even the smell of hotdogs or automobile exhaust can be stimulating to fans. In many cases, arousal is linked to the suspense associated with prior experience. For example, arousal levels increase when fans are anticipating the first pitch of a baseball game or when the gun goes off at a track meet. As a sport marketer, you can capitalize on existing moments and create new moments of anticipation. For example, clowns often perform before the bull-riding competition in a rodeo. Initially intended to distract the audience, the clown act signals rodeo fans that the bulls are soon to take center stage. As a result, the tension begins to build as the audience's arousal levels increase.

eustress—Positive levels of arousal provided to sport spectators.

• ***Economic gain***. Economic gain is a powerful motive for a small but growing group of people. Although betting on sports is not a new phenomenon, it has become more commonplace since the advent of Internet gambling. Sport gambling has risen alarmingly on college campuses, in part due to the availability of Internet access (Jenkins, 2000). Although ethically you might not want to design your marketing appeals to encourage gambling, it is of interest to explore this motivation. A fan with a bet on a game has a vested financial interest in the outcome. Further, this fan is interested not just in who won but also in the margin of victory. These fans could remain interested and involved in a lopsided game when most fans have long since left for the parking lot. For many sport gamblers, the point spread is what matters. Sport marketers might want to consider ways to encourage this same level of interest in the game without encouraging gambling. **Fantasy** and **rotisserie leagues** are one way to do this. Rotisserie baseball teams draft players from across the league. As a result, these fans

fantasy and rotisserie leagues—Virtual leagues governed by a set of rules by which sport fans can draft players from professional teams onto their own imaginary teams and play weekly games against their friends in a league that rewards the team with the best record. Wins are determined by the aggregate statistics of the individual players on each team. For more information, see www.fftoolbox.com/how_to_play.cfm.

follow players (and teams) throughout the league. The performance of their fantasy teams is based on the performance of players on many major league teams. Thus, these fans have a stake in the outcome of nearly every game played. Scoreboards that provide statistics on other games might be able to keep these fans in the ballpark. Similarly, sport broadcasters might be able to prevent viewers from channel surfing by running other game statistics across the bottom of the screen.

- ***Aesthetic value***. The innate beauty of athletic performance motivates many fans. The aesthetic motive is most clearly associated with sports such as ice dancing and rhythmic gymnastics, but fans of all sports report being fascinated by the aesthetic elements of the sport. Soccer fans, for example, repeatedly mention the pure beauty of well-executed skills. Although it might be less difficult to market stylistic sports by appealing to fans' appreciation for the aesthetics of the sport, marketers can make good use of aesthetic appeals across a variety of sport contexts. Remember, beauty is in the eye of the beholder. Some will see beauty in a linebacker flattening a receiver across the middle, some in the aerial antics of a skateboarder, and still others in the perfect tee shot. To appeal to aesthetic motives, sport marketers should reconsider the elements of skill and beauty in the sport and then highlight those elements using visual imagery, commentary, or music.

- ***Affiliation***. People like to be a part of something, to feel that they belong. Attendance at a sporting event can provide this feeling. Think about attending a WNBA game between the Washington Mystics and the Indiana Fever. You might feel a sense of belonging with several groups. You might feel that you belong to a group of basketball fans or to a group of Mystics fans. These are perhaps the most obvious groups, but there could be others. Many WNBA fans consider attendance as a way of being a part of the women's movement (McDonald, 2000). Others might be motivated to attend because their friends attend; that is, attendance is a way to be part of a social group. As a sport marketer, you can help fans to feel a part of something when they attend your events.

- ***Family Ties***. Similar to those who are motivated by the desire for affiliation, some people attend sporting events to spend time with their families. Sports have the ability to appeal to everyone in the family in some way. Marketers can take advantage of this by appealing to the need for family togetherness. As family schedules become increasingly hectic, sporting events provide a ready source of wholesome, exciting family fun. Minor league baseball and women's basketball have been extremely successful in fulfilling the need for family ties (Rogers, 2000).

Participant and Spectator Markets

Many people believe that the best place to find fans for a sport team is among players of that sport. Although some overlap is present between fans and participants of any particular sport, it varies from sport to sport and is much less common than one might think (Burnett, Menon, & Smart, 1993; Milne, Sutton, & McDonald, 1996). For example, 16.8 million Americans played soccer in 2005 (Soccer Industry Council of America, 2005), yet the Los Angeles Galaxy led all Major League Soccer teams with average attendance of only 24,204 fans per game in 2005 (Major League Soccer, 2005). Given the number of soccer players in the United States, you might expect higher attendance figures for professional soccer matches. Yet if you compare the key motives for participation with those for spectation, it is clear that different needs drive playing sport and watching sport. Consequently, you wouldn't expect active sport consumers (i.e., players) to also be passive consumers of sport (i.e., spectators), nor would you expect spectators to be active participants of the sport.

Consumer Perceptions

As important as they are, needs and motives do not fully explain consumers' sport choices. The degree

Learning Activity

Attend a sporting event. Ask the people seated around you why they chose to attend the event. Make a list of their responses and categorize them within the motives discussed in this chapter. Write two or three paragraphs to describe your results.

UEFA EUROPEAN CHAMPIONSHIP IN PORTUGAL
EURO 2004—Celebration Invaded the Country

Abel Correia, Portugal

Successful management of an international sporting event requires attention to both its tangible and its intangible dimensions. Examples of tangible aspects are technical specifications, rules and regulations specific to the game, and organizational and economic aspects of the event. The symbolic value of the event is usually seen as intangible. To the public, an international sporting event is primarily an opportunity to celebrate with feelings of excitement, euphoria, optimism, and national pride. The unique and ephemeral moments created by and around the sporting event contribute to a country's national identity and to its collective memory.

Specifically, let's focus on the effect of one major sporting event: the UEFA (Union of European Football Association) European Championship (a.k.a. EURO). Portugal hosted EURO 2004. It was the largest sporting event ever organized in Portugal, as measured by the number of spectators, the media involvement, the complexity of the organizational structure, and the expanded national celebration fueled by the successive victories of the Portuguese national team. EURO 2004 was big!

As reported in the official EURO 2004 economic impact study, the total number of spectators was 1,165,192, a number that was substantially higher than the total who attended EURO 2000, hosted by Belgium and Holland. There were 9,870 media accreditation passes issued. Television audiences reached a new high, a 20% increase from EURO 2000. There were 42,270 people involved in security operations, 4,000 volunteers, and 2,500 air flights exclusively associated with EURO 2004. The economic investment amounted to €964.429.397,00, of which 70.6% was allocated to construction and revitalization of stadia, 17.2% to infrastructure, and 12.2% to other investments.

As the organizing committee had hoped, EURO 2004 was deemed a success. It greatly and positively affected the organizational, economic, and social capabilities and perceptions of Portugal, both internally and externally. Specifically, the success of EURO 2004 resulted from the positive and celebratory social environment. The event brought people together. It caught their attention and originated a strong involvement of citizens, media, and public and private entities. EURO 2004 became a common goal, a cause that all Portuguese could work toward. This dynamic was essential during the bidding process and later during the preparation and operational phases of the event. Some say that it was this spirit that gave Portugal the competitive edge over the other hopeful host countries. This same spirit also created the healthy celebratory atmosphere that characterized the country during the event. In addition, this spirit of openness, inclusion, and celebration invited fans visiting from other countries to feel at home and to make the celebrations their own.

Giorgio Marchetti, director of professional football and marketing for UEFA, explained, "The Championship also has a strong symbolic meaning because it is an instrument that strengthens national identity and unites all supporters under the same flag" (www.uefa.com/uefa/Keytopics/kind=4194304/newsId=285889.html). In the case of Portugal, a visible and palpable increase occurred in the collective self-esteem. National identity and pride swelled, as demonstrated by the display of the Portuguese flag and colors on people's homes, cars, and clothing. For the first time the people of Portugal wore green and red, the country colors. This itself was a landmark event! Successfully hosting EURO 2004 created a collective type of trust and confidence capital that will contribute positively to future collective endeavors. EURO 2004 also created an opportunity to shape perceptions of Portugal and its people.

to which a consumer perceives sport as meeting a particular need or motive depends on that person's perceptions and experiences. Consumers must recognize the opportunity to watch or participate in a sport as a means to fulfill a need or motive. That recognition depends on experiences and the ways in which consumers perceive those experiences. This section considers the role of consumer perceptions.

Each of us perceives the world in our own way. Many Americans perceive the sport of curling as an unusual and uninteresting winter sport. The 1.5 million curlers throughout the world would hardly agree with that perception. Similarly, you might consider football an exciting, physically challenging game, whereas your friend thinks of it as brutish and violent. Whose perception is correct? Although perceptions often do not correspond to reality, people tend to act and react based on perceptions rather than objective reality. In fact, marketers spend enormous sums trying to alter people's perceptions of their products and services. So where

The enormous national pride and euphoria generated by Portugal's hosting of EURO 2004 is unmistakable in this sea of Portuguese fans celebrating in the streets of Lisbon.

Photo courtesy of ASF.

do our perceptions come from, and how can sport marketers shape customers' perceptions of their products?

Perception can be defined as a process by which a person selects, organizes, and interprets stimuli to create a meaningful picture of the world. A stimulus can be any input to any of the senses. Stimuli can be physical inputs from the surrounding environment such as sights, sounds, smells, tastes, sensations, or they can be cognitive inputs such as expectations, motives, and learning as a result of experience. Let's examine each of the three facets of perception—selection, organization, and interpretation (Kardes, 2002).

Selection

Consider the following scenario. A group of friends attended a college basketball game. Afterward, they discussed the game at the local pizza shop. Dan, a former high school basketball player, regaled Steve with a play-by-play account of what he called "the most beautiful fast break I've ever seen." No one else in the group even recalled seeing the play under discussion, including Steve. Steve is a high school volleyball coach. He had been impressed with the strategy that the visiting team used. David, a musician with little interest in team sports, talked incessantly about the entertainment at the game—the halftime show, the pep band, the cheerleaders, and the crowd chants. It was almost as if the three friends had attended entirely different events. Each had focused his attention on different elements of the game: Dan on the physical play, Steve on the coaching strategies, and David on the nonsport entertainment. This is an example of selective attention: choosing (often subconsciously) to pay attention to elements that are relevant to one's needs, attitudes, and experiences. In other words, people tend to be aware of stimuli that meet their needs and interests, and they filter out stimuli that are less personally relevant.

Organization

People rarely attend to each stimulus individually. Rather, they group stimuli together and perceive

International Learning Activity

Locate a sports bar or a community center that caters to the international soccer crowd and televises soccer games. Attend a televised game there, during the world championship if possible. Observe the behaviors of the fans around you as well as the behaviors of the spectators on television. Compare them to the behaviors that you would expect from North American football and baseball fans.

them as a unified whole. Sport teams have taken advantage of the grouping effect by associating their teams with particular images. For example, many teams choose their mascots to imply desired characteristics to the team. As a result, American football teams tend to choose mascots such as Bears, Vikings, and Cowboys in the hope that fans will then associate their teams with strength, aggression, and toughness. Similarly, advertisements for a variety of products and services use sport imagery to associate their products with desired characteristics. For example, soft drink ads often show people enjoying a soft drink while watching or playing a sport so that viewers associate the drink with fun, energy, excitement, or camaraderie.

Interpretation

People are selective about the stimuli that they perceive and then organize the stimuli into patterns and groupings. Ultimately, however, perceptions depend on each person's interpretation of the stimuli. The interpretation, and consequently the perception, is uniquely individual. Consider the sport of underwater hockey, a hockey game played on the bottom of a swimming pool by teams whose players wear masks, snorkels, and fins. If you were shown a photograph of people playing underwater hockey and then asked your impression of the sport, your experiences would influence your perception. Your experiences help form particular expectations that might provide alternatives that you would use to interpret the stimuli presented. The broader your experiences, the more interpretations and alternatives you have to draw on. Although you might not have been familiar with underwater hockey, you might draw on your knowledge, experience, and attitudes regarding ice hockey. Someone else might draw on his or her experience with and attitudes toward water sports more generally.

People tend to generalize their experiences and attitudes from one product to another or even from one category to another. When these generalizations are positive, the result is commonly called a halo effect (Mara, 2000). Licensing is a prime example of how sport marketers take advantage of halo effects to sell products. Team logos appear on everything from clothing to golf balls to baby bottles. At least one university offers dog collars, slippers, and sink strainers with their team's logo.

Consumer Attitudes

As the previous section indicates, experiences and existing attitudes greatly influence our perceptions of various sports, teams, athletes, and other sport products and services. Marketing efforts are often directed at shaping people's perceptions of a particular product, service, or brand. Essentially, this marketing tactic attempts to form (in the case of a new product or service) or change (in the case of an existing product or service) customers' attitudes about the product or service. But what exactly is an attitude, and how do we form our attitudes? In its simplest form, an attitude can be an expression of one's inner feelings that reflect whether he or she likes or dislikes something. Attitudes are based on a person's experiences (behavioral component), feelings (affective component), and beliefs (cognitive component) about an object (Shank, 2005). These three components work together to formulate an attitude (see figure 10.4).

Consumer Involvement and Identification

Consumer involvement has been characterized as a combination of one's interest in a sport product (e.g., team, athlete, sport), and the degree to which one considers the product an important part of one's life (Park & Mittal, 1985). Many sport participants become highly involved with their sports. Correspondingly, they think about, talk about, and read about their sports frequently. They tend to feel more deeply about their sports than do less involved participants. Sport marketers value involvement because high levels of involvement

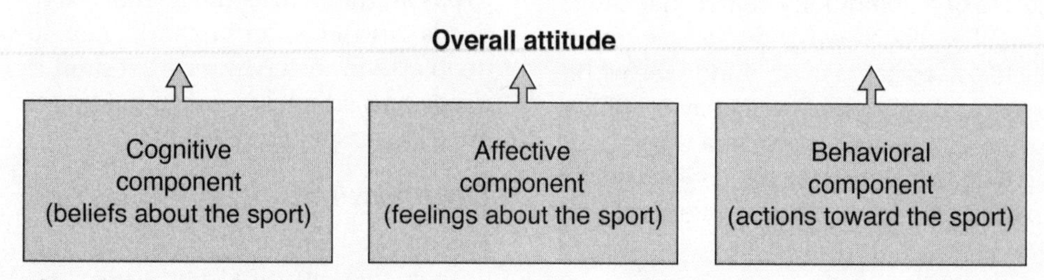

Figure 10.4 Model of attitude formation.

ATTITUDES GET A WORKOUT

Consider the case of Maria. Maria doesn't like health clubs. Let's examine the three components to see how Maria might have formed her attitude toward health clubs.

First, we'll examine the cognitive component of attitude—Maria's knowledge of and beliefs about health clubs. Maria believes that health clubs are expensive. She also believes that health clubs are for fit people. These beliefs might or might not correspond to your beliefs about health clubs and might or might not be true. In fact, much of Maria's knowledge of health clubs comes from two sources: infomercials for home exercise equipment, which highlight the cost savings of home equipment, and magazine ads for a national health club chain that feature ultrafit-looking young professionals working out in a state-of-the-art health club. Now add to those beliefs Maria's feelings about health clubs—the affective component. These feelings are often based on an emotional reaction to one's knowledge, experience, and beliefs. Maria is afraid of health clubs. Her feelings of intimidation stem from her belief that health clubs are only for fit people and from her previous experience with a personal trainer. Her experience is part of the behavioral component and is based on her actions. Last year Maria wanted to get in shape. She contacted a personal trainer whom a friend had recommended. In two months of training, Maria pulled several muscles, sprained an ankle, and felt tired and run down from the flu. Her experience with the personal trainer was not a pleasant one. It is easy to see how that experience, combined with her feelings and beliefs, created a negative attitude toward health clubs.

You might think that it would be nearly impossible to recruit Maria to join a health club. Selling Maria a membership would require a change in Maria's attitude toward health clubs. The three components of attitude offer the sport marketer three points of leverage to change an attitude. Each would require a different approach:

- Maria's belief that health clubs are expensive could be changed through accurate price information, discount promotions, or alternative pricing strategies such as monthly payments rather than annual fees. One might also use testimonials and photos of ordinary-looking, less-than-fit members in brochures and advertisements.
- Emotional appeals emphasizing fun, safety, or comfort might help overcome Maria's fear of health clubs.
- A free trial membership could go a long way toward negating Maria's experience with the personal trainer.

Although these are just a few of the many possible tactics available, each could make a difference. Together, they might work to change Maria's attitude.

Learning Activity

Choose two sports, one that you have a positive attitude toward and one that you have a negative attitude toward. For each sport, develop a list for the components of your attitude, that is, for

- the behavioral component (i.e., your previous experiences of each sport),
- the affective component (i.e., your feelings about each sport), and
- the cognitive component (i.e., your beliefs about each sport).

Compare the lists for the two sports. What did this exercise tell you about the various components of your attitude?

are associated with increased purchasing and consumer loyalty (Kerstetter & Kovich, 1997).

As a marketer, you can facilitate participants' involvement. Imagine for a moment that you are the owner of a local ice rink whose main clientele consists of current and former ice hockey players. How can you deepen their involvement with ice hockey? First, you might want to find ways to stimulate their interest in the sport. Think back to the earlier discussion of participant motivation. You know that your clients might be participating for a variety of reasons. Consequently, they might be interested in different aspects of the sport. Some participants might like the camaraderie of the team atmosphere, some might be interested in skating skills, some might like the strategic elements, and still others might like the physicality of the sport. As a sport marketer, you can build excitement and interest around multiple elements of the sport, thereby broadening participants' interest in the sport as a whole. Further, you could provide products and services such as lessons, magazines, videos, equipment, and other expertise. In this way, you offer your customers materials that engage their thinking about the game and provide fodder for hockey-related conversations.

Finally, you should consider providing space for those conversations to take place. Waiting areas, eating areas, and locker rooms are informal spaces where participants can socialize and share the ice hockey subculture. Involvement does not occur in a vacuum; players learn to value the sport through interactions with others.

The more one becomes involved with a sport, a team, or some other sport product, the more it becomes a part of one's identity. Consequently, involvement and identification are closely related. The process of identification occurs as a person's role (as a participant or as a fan) becomes central to his or her personal sense of self—that is, his or her identity (Shamir, 1992). Hence, the statements "I am a Red Sox fan" and "I am a scuba diver" are expressions of identification with a team and with a sport, respectively. These roles might be part of one's self-identity (the way the person sees himself or herself) or part of one's social identity (the way that others see the person) (Sirgy, 1986). In either case, identification is a form of attachment, and, like any attachment, its object varies.

The most common object of identification is the team, particularly when the team also represents a community. College teams often inspire high levels of identification, particularly among students and graduates. But identification can occur at any level of sport. Entire communities exhibit deep emotional attachment to high school football teams in Texas, Ohio, and other parts of the country. Further, athletes and coaches can also be objects of identification. Advertisers often take advantage of consumers' attachments to individual athletes and coaches by using them in their ads. For example, the "Got Milk?" ad campaign featured pictures of famous athletes sporting milk moustaches. The National Dairy Council believed that consumers would identify with athletes such as Marion Jones, Kristi Yamaguchi, Jeff Gordon, and others (see www.whymilk.com/celebrities/index.htm). The logic goes like this: If they like milk and you identify with them, then you should be drinking milk too.

Highly identified consumers attend more games, are less sensitive to price, and invest more time and effort in being a fan (Sutton, McDonald, Milne, & Cimperman, 1997). They tend to buy and display licensed products. They also tend to be more tolerant of performance slumps and losing seasons. Because performance is beyond the control of sport marketers, the desirability of highly identified fans is obvious. These fans are not fair-weather fans; they are loyal.

Consumer Loyalty

There are few industries other than sport in which customer loyalty carries such a high level of emotional and psychological investment. To get a feel for fan loyalty, you have only to think about the public outrage that occurred in Cleveland when Art Modell moved his NFL franchise from that city to Baltimore. Many people become fans as children and follow a particular team all their lives. This is the essence of brand loyalty—constant preference for one brand over its competitors (Baldinger & Rubinson, 1996). The traditions and rituals of sport and sport teams provide consumers with psychological (and often emotional) hooks to maintain loyalties. For many, team loyalty provides a sense of community and belonging that is difficult to find in modern society (Stone, 1981). For sport marketers, loyalty is a way to shortcut the decision process, to reduce the alternatives available to consumers, and to stimulate continued team-related spending.

Loyalty, involvement, and identification vary considerably from person to person. They are a function of individuals' motives for participating in or watching a sport, their previous experience, and the perceptions and attitudes they form about the sport, sport service, or product. These are largely internal, psychological processes. But sport consumers rarely make decisions or form attitudes or preferences solely based on their own experience. External groups exert tremendous influence on sport consumption decisions, sometimes subtly as in the case of culture and ethnicity, and sometimes blatantly, such as when your friends drag you to a local sporting event. We turn next to an examination of group influences on sport consumption decisions.

GROUP INFLUENCES ON THE SPORT CONSUMER

This section examines external factors that influence sport buying behavior. Each of us is influenced by the people closest to us, by the groups with which we choose to associate, and by the broader society in which we live. Take a moment to think about choosing to play on an intramural team at your university. The types of sports offered are typically those sports valued by your national culture. Consequently, American university students might choose to play basketball, British students might choose to play cricket, and Malaysian students might choose to play badminton. Further, your membership in a group can greatly influence the choice to play or not play intramural sport. Physical education majors would be expected to value sport participation highly, but music majors might not. If you choose to participate, your close friends might then influence your choice of sport.

Clearly, different people will influence each of us, and we will value the opinions of different groups. Thus, each of us has our own reference groups. Reference groups serve as a benchmark for evaluating our participation and purchase decisions. These people and groups influence our values, norms, perceptions, attitudes, and behaviors by providing us with a valued point of comparison. Reference groups can be either direct or indirect. Direct reference groups are groups that require face-to-face interaction; indirect reference groups do not require direct contact. The following sections discuss the two kinds of groups.

Direct Reference Groups

Family and friends exert a great deal of influence on the attitudes, values, and perceptions that we develop. Think about your own sport participation. Who first encouraged you to play sport? Parents or teachers usually introduce children to a sport (Brustad, 1996). Later, peers play a more powerful role in participation choices (Horn & Weiss, 1991). Similarly, you probably shared your first moments as a fan of your favorite team with friends or family members. Furthermore, friends and family usually reinforce your choices. For example, if you are a tennis fan, you might watch the US Open with your family, you might attend a local tournament with friends, or your brother might give you a tennis shirt for your birthday. Each of these actions subtly reinforces your attitudes and behaviors regarding tennis.

Although friends and family can be a powerful influence on one's sport choices and purchases, they are not alone in their influence. Nearly everyone is part of a larger group of some kind. Some of these groups offer formal membership (e.g., sport teams, special interest clubs, service groups), but most do not (e.g., high school sophomores, business majors, residents of a particular neighborhood). The point is that the group shares something and the group's values serve as a point of evaluation for one's own attitudes and behaviors.

Culture is perhaps the largest of the direct reference groups. Each of us is embedded in a national and ethnic culture. You could think of culture as the personality of society. It colors our values, expectations, attitudes, and opinions. It affects our view of the place of sport in society, the sports that we learn to value, and the products and services that we seek. Its effects are subtle, but powerful. Culture profoundly influences our view of what is normal, or at least what is expected. One expects to see American youth shooting baskets at the local park. When a broadcast of a hockey game is scheduled at 8:00 on Saturday night, North Americans expect the game to be ice hockey. In other parts of the world, viewers would expect a field hockey match. If you were in Portugal or Brazil, you would expect to see kids playing soccer in the street or the park. Many people ride bicycles as a means of transportation in Amsterdam, yet most North Americans would wonder what was going on if bicyclists outnumbered motorists on their morning commute.

Culture affects the sports we choose, as well as the way we choose to become involved with sport. Both Japan and North America support professional baseball leagues, but the values inherent in the sport vary by country. In the United States, the purpose of the game is to do your best by contributing to the team in every way you can. In Japan, the purpose of the game is to contribute to the team by not doing certain things (e.g., showing off, being individualistic). This conduct fits the cultural values of Japanese society. Not surprisingly, fan behavior also differs. In Japan, cheering is largely relegated to organized cheering by fans seated behind the outfield, with other fans joining in occasionally. In North America, fans rooting for the home team usually fill the home stadium. In Japan, the fans of the home team always sit on the first-base side of the field, and fans of the visiting team sit on the third-base side. Even when the stadium is not crowded, fans adhere to this tradition (Whiting, 1989).

Social class can sometimes place invisible boundaries on our choices by delineating appropriate and inappropriate behavior. Social class often serves as a referent when choosing to participate (or not participate) in a particular sport (Raudsepp & Viira, 2000). We tend to associate certain sports with participants of a particular social class. Golf, sailing, and polo, for example, are often associated with upper-class participants, whereas bowling and pugilistic sports such as boxing are more likely to appeal to working-class participants.

Social class tends to serve as a global referent; that is, it affects one's choices and behaviors across a variety of settings. But not all reference groups have global influence. Consider the following example. Judy is an executive at XYZ Corporation.

During the week, she interacts with other high-level executives, wears a suit to work, and makes thoughtfully informed decisions about the direction of her company. Her primary reference group is other executives. During work hours, Judy's behavior is constrained by what is seen as appropriate behavior by others like her. But this reference group is not the only influence on Judy's behavior. Judy is also an athlete. On the weekend, she is a football player. Her reference group in this situation is other football players. In her team setting, the unwritten rules of appropriate executive behavior no longer influence her. In fact, Judy the executive would not make a good linebacker. The football subculture might appreciate the thoughtfully informed decisions of an executive but would be far more likely to value big hits, aggression, and trash talk—behaviors that would be entirely inappropriate in Judy's work setting. In this example, Judy physically interacted with others in both the executive subculture and the subculture of women's football. But a subculture does not require direct interaction to serve as a reference group.

Indirect Reference Groups

Indirect reference groups can be highly influential. They might consist of people such as athletes, coaches, actors, or politicians; alternatively they might be groups or subcultures. In either case, the influence of the individual or group is not the result of direct face-to-face contact. Instead, the influence derives from **aspirational reference groups**—groups in which a person is not currently a member but aspires to be one. Accenture's "Go on. Be a Tiger." advertising campaign featuring Tiger Woods is perhaps the most unabashed use of an aspirational reference group to sell a product, but numerous, albeit subtler, examples of advertisements use athletes as aspirational referents.

> **aspirational reference group**—A group to which an individual wishes to belong.

Subcultures operate in much the same way as aspirational reference groups do. Let's assume for the moment that you want to be a surfer. Even before you learn to surf, chances are that you will be influenced by what you know about surfers and the surfing subculture. You might buy *Surfing* magazine, watch surfing events, and talk to people who surf. Your knowledge of the surfing subculture, however superficial, might influence the style and brand of clothing that you choose to wear, the music that you listen to, or even the way that you style your hair. Marketers are more than willing to sell you products that help you to look and feel as though you belong to the group.

As a marketer, you can take advantage of the ability of reference groups to change consumers' perceptions, attitudes, and purchase behaviors. But for the reference group to wield its influence, it must be able to (1) make the person aware of your product, (2) provide a chance for the person to compare himself or herself with the group, (3) influence the person to adopt attitudes and behaviors consistent with the group, and (4) support the person's decision to use the same product or service as the group does (de Mooij, 2004).

Your perceptions and experiences affect your choice of reference groups. Your choice of reference groups can affect your preferences for particular sports and the sport choices that you make. In other words, the reference groups that you choose are based, in part, on what you have learned, and the reference group might affect what you learn subsequently. This process is an effect of consumer socialization.

Consumer Socialization

We have seen that family, friends, teachers, and other reference groups can affect your decisions about participating in sport and about watching sport. Yet the effect of people who are significant in your life reaches even further. Through them you learn not merely *what* you prefer, but also *how* to consume what you prefer. Let's assume that you want to watch a baseball game. You have several choices. You could watch a game played by a local Little League team. You could watch a minor league game. You could watch a major league game. If you choose a major league game, you could attend the game or watch it on television. If you attend the game, you could sit in the bleachers, behind home plate, or behind a dugout. The choices that you make will be influenced, in part, by what you have learned about the ways to watch baseball. If when you were first learning to enjoy watching baseball, your family or friends typically preferred to watch on television, you will be more likely to choose to watch on television. On the other hand, if going to the ball game was something that your family or friends treated as a valuable choice, then you are likely to consider going to the game preferable to watching it on television.

As we grow and mature, we learn how to consume the sport that we prefer. Both direct and indirect reference groups influence the ways in which

Accenture, a company focusing on management consulting, technology services, and outsourcing, appeals to the desire of potential clients to be like high-end sport heroes. Their target audience would not be nearly as responsive had they chosen to highlight a bowling, rather than a golfing, champion. Being able to predict which sport figure or entity will appeal to what audience is crucial to creating effective ads in the aspirational genre.

Photo courtesy of Accenture.

we consume sport. Think of your expectations of appropriate behavior at a baseball game. Your early experiences attending with friends or family might have been the beginning of lifelong rituals. For example, Tom has season tickets to watch the Baltimore Orioles. When he was young, his father took him to watch the Washington Senators. Three things were always part of the baseball experience for Tom. One, he always took his baseball glove to the game; two, his father always bought him peanuts and a hotdog at the ballpark; and three, they always hollered at the umpire. Tom has continued these rituals as an adult. Unintentionally, he has also taught his children that baseball games require one to bring a glove, eat peanuts and hotdogs, and yell at the officials. This is an example of socialization through modeling. Just as Tom did as a child, Tom's children watched their father's behavior at baseball games and began to copy his behavior. Prompting and reinforcement can further assist in the socialization process. For example, Tom might prompt his daughter to bring her glove or ask if she would like some peanuts. Similarly, he might reinforce her jibes at the umpire by laughing or praising her comments.

Socialization is a process that often goes unnoticed. Think of your own sport experiences. How did you develop your fan behaviors? Do you remember someone telling you when to clap, whom you could shout at, or how to show your support for a great play? Chances are that your earlier experiences and reinforcement (or lack of reinforcement) by important reference groups shaped your current behavior. One can perhaps see the effects of socialization best through the absence of expected behaviors. For example, baseball has a long tradition in American culture but is a relatively new sport in Australia. Behaviors that are commonplace at baseball diamonds throughout the United States (e.g., completing a scorecard, yelling at the umpire, singing "Take Me Out to the Ballgame") are missing in Australian baseball. These behaviors are not shown on television broadcasts of major league baseball. Where would Australian fans learn these behaviors? Alternatively, how would you behave at a cricket match or any other sport with which you are unfamiliar? First, you would look to fans around you. Experienced fans model appropriate (or at least valued) behaviors. They might also prompt you to behave in a particular way. For example, music accompanied by the words to a song scrolling across the scoreboard would be an effective prompt to sing. An Australian cricket fan might frown at you for yelling at the cricket linesman, and smile at you for clapping at the end of an over. In this way, appropriate behaviors are positively reinforced and inappropriate behaviors are negatively reinforced.

Each of these processes—modeling, prompting, and reinforcing—also occur through indirect reference groups. Spectators seen on television broadcasts and in movies often influence our attitudes and consumption behaviors. In our current global era, one may not even need to attend live events to be aware of the appropriate behaviors or rituals of specific sports. Media such as pay TV (cable and satellite) and the Internet provide extended and comprehensive broadcasts of global sports and their environments.

Take, for instance, Formula 1 racing. In a 17-race season, just 2 races are held in North America, and only 1 is held in the United States (at the Indianapolis Motor Speedway, the Brickyard). Only these 2 are broadcast on free-to-air TV, and the other 15 are broadcast on pay TV. Most Formula 1 fans have never attended a race. Instead, their fan behavior has been shaped indirectly through reference groups and people such as spectators shown on TV, drivers, commentators, and team owners. Although North American Formula 1 fans have little opportunity to attend a race or meet their favorite drivers, they can access the Internet to build and nurture their fanship. Fans can learn more about the sport, the race series, the teams, and the cars by perusing the official Formula 1 Web site (www.formula1.com). They can obtain more information and interact with other Formula 1 fans through sites such as the official Formula 1 supporters' association site (www.fosagold.org) or subscriber-based sites such as http://f1.racing-live.com/f1. The Internet supports a multitude of potential fan consumption behaviors. Fans can plan a Formula 1 holiday with a travel agency that specializes in package tours to Formula 1 events (i.e., www.formulatours.com), buy merchandise (i.e., www.speedgear.com), and even download a podcast of the latest race (i.e., www.formulapod.com).

Advertisements, broadcasts, Web sites, and other types of indirect reference groups can prompt behaviors or reinforce our perceptions of appropriate ways to enjoy a game or a sport. Over time, we are socialized into a way of consuming sport that is shaped by our reference groups, both direct and indirect. Sport marketers are also interested in ways to socialize customers into particular consumption patterns.

Learning Activity

University athletic events are often filled with rituals known to long-time fans and students. Attend an event at your university. Identify the rituals that are part of the attendance experience. Bring a friend from another school. Sit in the student section. Watch your friend as he or she tries to fit in. How does your friend learn what behaviors are expected? Attend a game at a friend's school. Discuss your experiences with your friend. If possible, invite an international student to join you at both events.

SITUATIONAL INFLUENCES ON THE SPORT CONSUMER

In the previous sections we identified key internal factors and external group influences on sport consumers. In practice, isolating influences of either internal or external forces is difficult. Rarely does a single force influence sport consumption decisions. Rather, one's relationship to a reference group or membership in a particular subculture forms and interprets internal attitudes, perceptions, and experiences. Further, different contexts and situations result in different decisions. Situational influences on the sport consumer are discussed in this section.

A situation is a set of factors outside the individual consumer and removed from the product or advertisement of the product that the consumer is buying. To develop marketing strategies that enhance the purchase of their products, marketers need to know how purchase situations influence consumers. We can identify five categories of **situational influence**:

1. ***Physical surroundings***. The physical surroundings include geographic location, decor, sound, smells, lighting, weather, and crowding. For example, weather would obviously influence the decision to play tennis. Retailing organizations pay particular attention to the physical characteristics of their stores. For example, one Nike Town store has a hardwood basketball court in its basketball shoe section and plays audiotape of the unique sounds of shoes squeaking during a basketball game.

2. ***Social surroundings***. Social surroundings deal primarily with the presence of people who could have an influence on your decision. Whereas reference groups can influence your consumption

decisions even when no one is present at the time of the purchase, social surroundings refer to the effects of the physical presence of others. For example, if you want to go to a movie but the group that you are with prefers to go bowling, you will probably comply with the group and find yourself at the bowling alley.

situational influence—The influence arising from factors that are particular to a specific time and place and are independent of individual customers' characteristics.

3. ***Task requirements***. Task requirements speak to the context of the purchase (that is, the intent or requirement of the purchase). Consider the purchase of a pair of running shoes. If you are buying them for yourself, you might be more concerned with performance functions than with price. But what if you are buying them as a gift? You might be more concerned with price and attractiveness than with performance.

4. ***Temporal perspective***. Time pressures, the time of day, and the season of the year are all examples of potential temporal influences on sport consumption. Most sports are associated with particular times of the year. These associations become entrenched in the minds of consumers. Marketing a sport outside its traditional season can be difficult, as we saw with the failure of the USFL, an alternative professional football league that began league play in spring. Time pressure can affect consumption in a number of ways. Consumers often trade price for convenience. For example, a busy person might pay more to be able to buy tickets online.

5. ***Antecedent states***. Antecedent states encompass momentary moods, such as anxiety, excitement, or even hunger; and momentary conditions, such as cash on hand, fatigue, or illness. If you have ever attended a sporting event and wondered, on your return home, why you bought that gigantic foam finger, you have probably experienced the influence of excitement on the purchase decision process. Let's look more closely at the decision process.

CONSUMER DECISION MAKING IN SPORT

You make hundreds of decisions each day. You decide when to get out of bed in the morning, what to wear, how to comb your hair, and whether to eat breakfast. Your sport-related decisions are equally varied. You decide whether to participate in sport, which sports you will try, whether you will watch sport, which sport you will watch, which team or player you will cheer for, whether you will buy season tickets, and whether you will wear your team jersey. The list of decisions seems endless. You make some easily; others require much thought. In any case, the decision-making process has a common progression. It begins with the recognition of a need or problem that spurs you to gather information about potential solutions. You then evaluate alternatives, with the "best" alternative leading to purchase. The purchase experience is followed by a period of postpurchase evaluation that will influence your future purchase decisions (see figure 10.5). Notice that decision making does not happen in a void. Rather, each of the factors already discussed influences it.

Decision Process

Each of us arrives at a decision in a slightly different way. We begin with motives, perceptions, attitudes, and experiences that are uniquely our own. We are influenced by reference groups and subcultures that are important to us, and we have been socialized in different ways. In fact, we are rarely consistent in the way that we arrive at purchase decisions. We perceive each situation differently. Consumption decisions are not always rational, as can be seen with impulse purchases. As a result, we interpret and react to marketing efforts in varied ways. Despite these differences, the steps in the decision process are remarkably consistent from consumer to consumer.

Need recognition is the first step in the decision process. This stage is likely to occur when you confront a problem or recognize a difference between an actual state and a desired state. This stimulus can be as straightforward as the need to replace a worn-out softball glove or as complex as a desire to be fit. In the first case, the need is obvious: The equipment no longer works, so you must replace it. In the second case, the need is less straightforward. The desired state is to be fit. Currently, however, you have trouble walking up stairs without breathing heavily. What aspects of your lifestyle do you need to change so that you can begin exercising? For example, do you need to wake earlier to make time to exercise? Maybe you need to give up another activity or spend less time at work. In this case, the need emerges from the gap between current fitness level and desired fitness level.

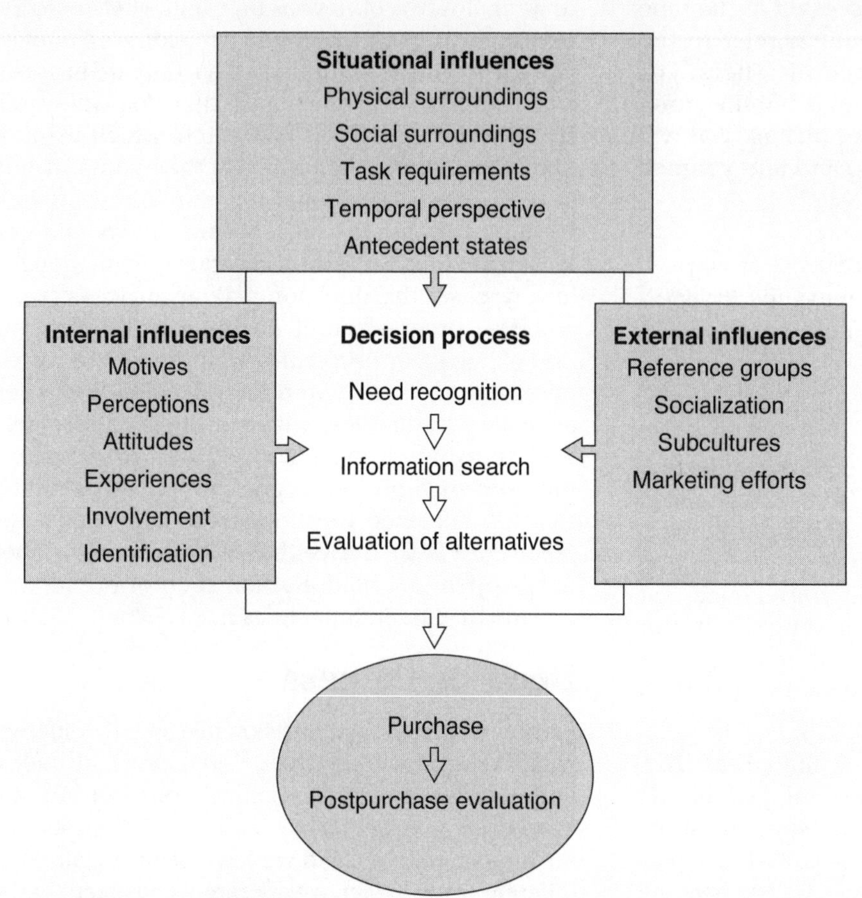

Figure 10.5 Model of the decision process.

need recognition—Perception of a difference between a desired state and the actual situation; the first stage of the decision-making process.

After identifying the need, the consumer seeks information that helps resolve the problem or fulfill the need. Experience or brand loyalty might provide the consumer with enough information to determine alternatives. For example, Carlos' satisfaction with his old glove might be all the information that he needs to decide to buy the latest model of the same glove. If he is loyal to a particular brand, he might limit his search by collecting information only about products produced by that company. He might ask the opinion of respected members of his reference group or be influenced by the acceptability of a brand or style within his softball subculture. He might search out information on the Internet, in magazines, or at the local sport store. In any case, he will collect enough information to determine his purchase options. Potential purchases fall into one of several decision sets. Carlos' list of potential products is called the *awareness set*. This group represents all the alternatives of which Carlos is aware. He will not consider all these products. The group of gloves that he will evaluate in the next step is called the *evoked set*. The gloves that he is not considering, because of an unpleasant experience or negative information, are called the *inept set*. Finally, the *inert set* consists of the products for which Carlos has a neutral evaluation.

When evaluating items in the evoked set, consumers tend to use two types of information: (1) a list of the potential products from the evoked set, and (2) the features and characteristics that they will use to evaluate those products (de Mooij, 2004). Price or convenience might be two features important to Carlos. People will assess features and characteristics differently based on their values, attitudes, motives, and expectations. Notice that one's reference groups also influence the consumer's belief about which features and characteristics are important.

The way in which consumers use information has important implications for sport marketers. First, marketers must ensure that consumers are aware of the product or service. A company might manufacture the best glove on the market, but it will never become part of consumers' evoked sets unless they are aware that it exists. Second, sport marketers need to understand which features are important to their target market. Using the highest quality of leather for softball gloves is useless if consumers evaluate them based on their fit and price.

Consumers make their purchase decision based on an evaluation of products within the evoked set. Note that both internal and external forces influence the evoked set. These forces also influence the relative value attached to product attributes. As you can see, the final purchase decision is based on a personal evaluation of particular products and their attributes.

Postpurchase Evaluation

You might think that the process ends with the purchase, but another step is yet to occur—the postpurchase evaluation (Shank, 2005). As consumers use a product, they evaluate it with respect to their expectations. Let's return to the example of Carlos and the softball glove. Carlos will have developed expectations about the performance of his new glove. He might expect that it will look good, break in easily, and fit his hand well. After using the glove for several practice sessions, he will evaluate its actual performance. If the glove performs as well as or better than expected, Carlos will be satisfied with his purchase. But if the glove does not fit well or is difficult to break in, then he might be dissatisfied with his purchase. From a marketing standpoint, Carlos' satisfaction is important for two reasons. One, his satisfaction will affect his future purchases of the product, and two, it will affect word-of-mouth communication about the product and the brand. He will tell others about his satisfaction or disappointment.

An important part of the postpurchase evaluation is consumers' attempts to reassure themselves that they made the right decision. In other words, they question their own judgment. These feelings of doubt are called **cognitive dissonance**. Consumers attempt to reduce postpurchase cognitive dissonance in several ways. They might rationalize their decision as being a wise choice (e.g., this is definitely the best softball glove because it fits so well). They might search for marketing materials that confirm their decision while avoiding advertisements for competing products. They might try to persuade others to make the same purchase, or they could seek others who are satisfied with their purchase of the same product. Each of these strategies reinforces their satisfaction with the purchase. Consequently, marketers should offer services and information after the sale to reduce consumers' cognitive dissonance. Similarly, selling to existing customers is easier and more cost effective than recruiting new customers. Consequently, reducing consumers' cognitive dissonance in the postpurchase period is a strategy that can increase repeat purchases.

cognitive dissonance—Feelings of anxiety or doubt that can occur after an important decision has been made.

Learning Activity

Consider participating in a new sport. Follow your decision-making process from beginning to end. What information did you collect? From whom? How did you evaluate your alternatives?

CHALLENGES

Analyzing and understanding sport consumer behavior is a complex endeavor. The challenges facing sport marketers are equally complex. Four issues are becoming increasingly important to understanding and marketing to sport consumers:

1. The meaning and emotion of sport consumption
2. The globalization of sport
3. Virtual consumption
4. Compulsive consumption

We know much about the ways that individuals think about sport purchases. Yet consumers consistently report emotional attachments to sport products, teams, events, and other sport services. To understand sport consumers, we need to know how they create these emotional attachments, what influences those attachments, and how the attachments vary as a function of culture or subcultural values. The globalization of sport is creating a related challenge for sport marketers. On one hand, consumers worldwide are being presented with the same sports, broadcasts, products, and advertisements. On the surface, sport is much the same across the globe. On the other hand, we know that culture influences the meaning and value inherent in sport consumption. In this respect, the world is made of a multitude of different consumer groups. We need to understand where similarities and differences exist, and work to tailor our sport products and services for optimal sales.

The other two challenges to understanding and reaching sport consumers are emerging forms of sport consumption—virtual and compulsive. The Internet is a multifunctional space for sport consumption. Participants can purchase hard-to-find equipment; fans can buy tickets and licensed products for teams anywhere in the world. But actual purchases are only the tip of the iceberg. Fans can find a community of other fans online. They can participate in fantasy leagues. Participants can receive or share information about their sport, team, players, and coaches instantly. The list is endless. Wireless technology has made it even easier for fans to stay involved with their teams. Scores and other statistics are routinely delivered to mobile phones. Digital photos and video can be sent by mobile phone. Recently, a college football coach complained that fans were able to see footage of a player getting hurt in practice before he could inform the player's parents. With sport content almost limitless, the challenge is to find ways to use new consumption technologies to reach one's own fans or participants more effectively.

As you can see, sport consumption is not all positive. As sport consumption opportunities become ubiquitous, compulsive consumption is becoming more prevalent. Compulsive consumption refers to the repetitive consumption of sport such that it is addictive. Sports betting is one of the most damaging forms of compulsive sport consumption, but there are others. Fantasy leagues can become a compulsion as well, with participants spending astonishing amounts of time and money managing their teams. Compulsive consumption is not limited to fan behavior. Participants might spend well beyond their means traveling to pursue their sport participation. More likely, participants dedicate outrageous amounts of time to their sports. Compulsive consumption is a delicate issue for sport marketers. After all, effective marketing efforts that take advantage of in-depth knowledge of consumers' psychology, in the case of compulsive consumers, feed their addiction. Yet, most sport consumption is not destructive. The challenge, then, is to use knowledge of consumers to build effective marketing strategies without feeding consumers' addictions.

Today's sport marketers are grappling with these very challenges. Each challenge is representative of the broader society in which sport is embedded. All are interrelated. The emotion elicited by sport might be the high that compulsive consumers seek. Technologies such as the Internet and wireless services provide quick access to sport products and services from all corners of the world, at all times of day and night. Globalization of sport creates content that can be shared, often by technology, with people anywhere in the world. There is much to understand about sport consumers, and many ways to collect information. The challenges identified here also create opportunities for sport marketers to learn more about their consumers.

SUMMARY

The study of consumer behavior in sport helps you understand your customers. A better understanding of your customers can help you develop products and services that meet their needs and design marketing strategies to attract new customers and retain existing customers. This chapter explored the individual, group, and situational factors that influence sport consumption. Individual factors examined were motives, perceptions, attitudes, involvement, and identification. The influence of reference groups, socialization processes, and subcultures were identified as the primary group factors that affect decisions to buy sport products and services.

Rarely, however, does a single force influence sport consumption decisions. Typically, group and individual influences work simultaneously to exert influence over a purchase decision in a given situation. Five situational factors were shown to have an effect on the decision-making process: physical surroundings, social surroundings, task requirements, temporal perspective, and antecedent states. These factors, in combination with the individual and group factors already discussed, exert influence at each stage of the decision process. The recognition of a need or problem is the first step in the process. After identifying a need, the consumer seeks information about potential products and services that can fulfill that need or solve the problem. The consumer then develops a set of possible purchase options and evaluates each before making the purchase.

But the process does not end with the purchase. Customers can evaluate their purchases in two ways. They often evaluate their purchases in reference to prepurchase expectations. If performance meets or exceeds their expectations, then customers are satisfied. Interestingly, customers tend to reassure themselves that they made the right purchase. This action is an attempt to reduce cognitive dissonance. Sport marketers can help customers feel good about their purchase by providing information after the purchase that highlights the benefits and attributes of the product or highlights the use of the product by valued members of customers' reference groups.

As a sport marketer, your job is to entice customers to buy your products, attend your games, compete in your events, and use your services. The consumer decision making process identifies the steps leading to purchase. As a marketer, you can use your knowledge of the situational, group, and individual factors that can influence each step in the decision process to design products, services, and marketing campaigns that meet the needs of your customers.

Review Questions

1. List and explain the key motives for sport participation. Give an example of each.
2. List and explain the key motives for sport spectation. Give an example of each.
3. You and a friend attend a basketball game at your university. Why might you and your friend have different perceptions of the game?
4. List the three components of an attitude.
5. As a sport marketer, how would you try to change a negative attitude toward your product?
6. What is the difference between consumer involvement and fan identification?
7. Why are loyal fans important to a sport organization?
8. Identify potential group influences on a person's decision to attend a sporting event. Give an example of the way that each would influence the decision.
9. Describe the decision process of parents who are choosing a youth sport program for their child.
10. What would you do to reduce postpurchase cognitive dissonance?
11. When was fantasy football introduced? How has it changed fans' television viewing habits?

Public Relations in the Sport Industry

G. Clayton Stoldt—Wichita State University ▪ **Catherine Pratt**—Bowling Green State University
Stephen W. Dittmore—East Stroudsburg University

Learning Objectives

After studying this chapter, you will be able to do the following:

1. Recognize the conceptual knowledge base and skill set necessary to pursue a public relations career in the sport industry.
2. Describe how media relations professionals serve their sport organizations by interacting with members of the sport media.
3. Identify ways in which community relations professionals serve their sport organizations by meeting social needs and connecting with key publics within their localities and surrounding areas.
4. Recognize other types of public relations positions within sport organizations and the functions of people holding those positions.
5. Explain how communication technology affects the practice of sport public relations.
6. Identify ethical issues associated with careers in sport public relations.

Most of us who fantasized about a career in sport eventually realized that professional participation as an athlete was beyond our talents. This reality, however, did not necessarily diminish our interest in and enjoyment of sports, nor does it have to eliminate a career primarily focused on sport. Many of you might find a career in sport **public relations** both enjoyable and rewarding. Organized sport organizations, from small colleges to professional franchises, from YMCAs to the Olympics, need people who can help foster strong relationships between the organization and its most important **publics** (Cutlip, Center, & Broom, 2000; Stoldt, Dittmore, & Branvold, 2006). In some ways public relations can be considered part of the job of every employee, but a substantial number of sport administrators are employed specifically as public relations professionals. Their titles vary, but they usually include words such as *media relations*, *community relations*, *information*, *publicity*, or *communication*.

> **public relations**—An organizational function that fosters the development of positive relationships between the organization and its most important publics.
>
> **publics**—Groups of people who are affected in varied ways by an organization.

In this chapter you will learn about three primary aspects of sport public relations. First, you will learn about communication in general—the basic skills, the general framework, and the application of those concepts to public relations practice. Second, you will learn about the most common sport public relations jobs. These jobs are in media relations, community relations, and several other areas (Jackowski, 2000; Mullin, Hardy, & Sutton, 2000; Stoldt, Dittmore, & Branvold, 2006). The media relations section of the chapter will include a brief overview of the unique relationship between sport and the mass media and highlight some of the most common tactics employed by media relations professionals. The third area discussed in this chapter focuses on community relations in sport, and the fourth section considers other public relations positions in the industry. The fifth section examines the effect of communication technology on sport, specifically the practice of sport public relations. Finally, because understanding and appreciating socially responsible behavior is a bottom-line requirement for a successful career in sport public relations, each of the sections will highlight some relevant ethical issues involved in the practice.

RELEVANT CONCEPTS AND SKILLS

Sport public relations positions include collegiate sports information director, community relations director for a professional sports team, and communication manager for a fitness and recreation provider or sporting goods manufacturer. Regardless of the setting, all the occupational choices in this chapter have a common denominator: They require the ability to communicate effectively. Creating a message that accurately and effectively communicates your ideas to the audience that you want to reach is the foundation for success in sport public relations.

The most basic skills that you need to develop are your writing and speaking abilities. Writing effectively means that you must be able to track down information, organize it, and record it in a way that interests and informs readers. Sentences must be grammatically correct, wording must be succinct, and ideas must flow from one point to another. Speaking effectively also entails organizing information. Strong speakers are able to boil down large amounts of information into key points that they repetitively emphasize, and they are able to build on those points with additional information and humorous or insightful stories (Gregory, 2005). They also connect with their audiences by using appropriate gestures and body language. Because public relations practitioners must routinely reach a variety of audiences, failure to develop effective communication techniques is usually a prelude to unproductive or even counterproductive efforts.

Learning Activity

Who is the best public speaker you have ever heard? Was this person a sport figure? Chances are, the speaker you're thinking of used effective communication techniques. Based on your experience with that speaker, and perhaps others, make a list of the qualities that characterize effective public speakers.

Not all communication is successful communication. Remember the popular game "Gossip," or "Telephone," that involved whispering a sentence to the person in the next seat, who then whispered it to the next person, and so on until everyone playing the game had passed along the message? The outcome was usually a message that differed radically from the original whispered communication. Although this distortion or miscommunication might be amusing in a game, the results are not as funny when we fail to communicate our message in situations in which accurate communication is important.

So how do you become an effective communicator? There's the old joke: How do you get to Carnegie Hall? Practice, practice, practice! When you interview for an entry-level job in the sport public relations field, your prospective employer will expect you to have already developed strong communication skills and gained some related experience. You might get some of this experience through experiential learning activities in your classes, but that kind of practice probably will not be enough to distinguish you competitively. You will likely need to volunteer with a sport organization (e.g., in media relations or community relations) or with a mass media outlet (e.g., a campus newspaper or radio station) to get the repetition necessary to hone your skills adequately. Significant volunteer experience will likely position you to gain a high-quality internship in which you can continue to build the skills necessary for a successful career in the field.

Certainly, experience is a critically important ingredient. But just communicating without understanding the essentials of the process and what has

1830s

▶**1831**—William Trotter Porter starts America's first weekly sport publication, the *Spirit of the Times*

1870s

▶**1870**—Telegraph reports results of baseball, boxing, horse racing, and regattas across the US

1880s

▶**1883**—Joseph Pulitzer establishes first sports department in a daily newspaper in his *New York Herald*

▶**1886**—*Sporting News* established

1890s

▶**1890**—Players League uses media to sway public opinion during battle with National League in professional baseball been learned about effective communication means that you waste a lot of time reinventing the wheel! You can avoid mistakes and eliminate wasted effort if you understand the established principles of effective communication and public relations.

General Communication Models

Communication scholars have suggested that theoretical ideas are easier to understand if they are presented as a diagram or model. Hundreds of communication models, from basic to sophisticated, have been developed to help explain how we communicate, how we ought to communicate, obstacles to communication, and communication effects. The most well-known and useful models share an approach that treats **communication** as a process. Most feature identifiable components arranged to explain the process. The most commonly accepted components are

- the source,
- the message,
- the channel through which the message is delivered, and
- the receiver.

When combined with the concepts of encoding, decoding, feedback, and noise, these components offer a useful description of the communication process with a practical advantage: The better we understand the process, the more likely we are to communicate well.

> **communication**—A process by which senders and receivers share messages of meaning. Communication takes place at multiple levels—interpersonally, in groups, and through the mass media.

The model in figure 11.1 is based on the work of communication scholars such as Harold Lasswell, Wilbur Schramm, Claude Shannon, and Warren Weaver (Severin & Tankard, 1997). In this model, the communication source could be a person addressing the crowd at a community gathering, the person or organization that produces a brochure, the author of a written news release, or the speaker at a news conference. The message in each of these cases is the denotation and connotation of the spoken or written words and pictures that the sender produces. Although we can describe channels literally (e.g., broadcast or cable channels), communication scholars usually use the term to describe the delivery system or the way in which the message gets from the sender to the receiver (e.g., spoken word, gestures, over-the-air broadcast television, film, and so forth). Thus, the channel through which a message is delivered could be face-to-face spoken words (with accompanying voice, expression, and gesture cues) or printed words (with accompanying graphics and layout). The receiver of the communication could be one person or several people who are listening to a speaker, the readers of a magazine, or visitors to a Web site.

The encoding and decoding components of the communication process refer to the inescapable fact that every sender and receiver of communication assigns meaning to the communicated message. This meaning might or might not be readily apparent. Think about the times that you've heard or seen something that didn't communicate the intended message. Key words might not have been familiar, or the speaker's language might have been communicating one message while her facial expressions communicated another. Think, too, about instances in which you thought you knew the meaning of some communication but later discovered that your interpretation was incorrect. (Just think back to a recent test or assignment in which your poor grade was a direct result of not understanding what the instructor expected.)

Noise accounts for elements that interfere with the reception of the message. Noise can be literal; fans yelling at a sporting event might drown out the public address announcer who is relaying an important message. Noise can also be figurative; a poorly printed brochure would certainly hinder communication effectiveness and thus be a form of noise. Another example of figurative noise would be a personal problem that might distract you from focusing on the problem at hand, impairing your ability to speak or write well. The goal in communicating is to minimize controllable noise and cut through uncontrollable noise so that there are as few impediments as possible in the communication process.

Feedback refers to communication that the receiver sends back to the sender through deliberate or inadvertent responses. Feedback helps the communicator understand whether the receiver got the correct message. It provides information for future communication. Phone calls concerning

1890s

▶**1895**—William Randolph Hearst develops first sports section, in the *New York Journal*

1910s

▶**1913**—Western Union grants telegraph rights to MLB

▶**1919**—Notre Dame hires Archie Ward as nation's first full-time sport publicity director

1920s

▶**1920s**—Golden age of sports reporting

▶**1921**—First radio broadcast of World Series—New York Giants beat New York Yankees, 5-3

▶**1921**—First radio sports broadcast of a boxing match—Jack Dempsey (US) defeats Georges Carpentier (France)

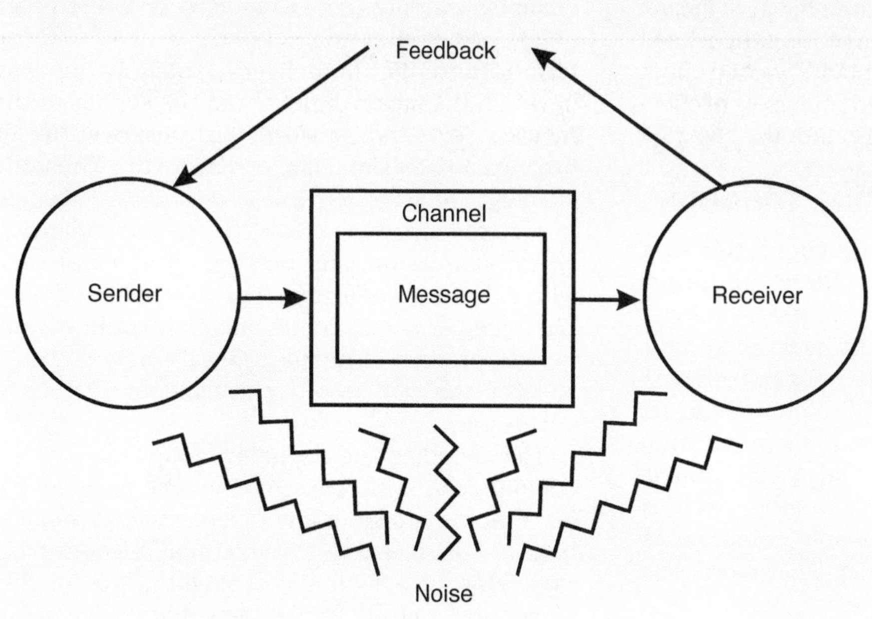

Figure 11.1 The communication process.

a change in the services offered by a recreation facility, fans erupting in cheers at a spirit rally, or the defeat of a municipal ballot initiative to help fund a team's new sports arena are all examples of feedback.

Remember that the receiver may ignore, misinterpret, or forget even the best-intentioned and best-fashioned communication. The terminology for these communication pitfalls is selective attention, selective perception, and selective retention. Selective attention refers to the tendency that we all have to seek communication that relates to topics in which we already have an interest. Selective perception refers to interpreting information in a way that reinforces what we already believe. Selective retention describes our inclination to remember those things that we find comfortable and useful, and forget the things that we dislike or make us uncomfortable. Each concept feeds on the basic human need to avoid conflict or cognitive dissonance—the emotional or intellectual discomfort that we feel when messages conflict with our strongly held beliefs. Effective communication requires an understanding of human nature and of people's need to protect themselves through strategies such as selective attention, perception, and retention.

To simplify our communication model, we can also look to Schramm (1954), who argued that for communication to exist, the sender and the receiver must share something: a common language, vocabulary, or interest in or understanding of the subject being communicated. The more that the sender and receiver share, the easier it is for them to communicate effectively. Schramm's point is a useful one to consider when you communicate. Ask yourself how much you and the receiver of your communication share. If you can increase the level of shared interest, you will increase the likelihood that your communication efforts will be successful.

Models of Public Relations Practice

Although the model in figure 11.1 and Schramm's model present general communication concepts, they also have a direct relationship with many of the key ideas underlying public relations work. For example, some prominent public relations scholars have argued that public relations practitioners work under four basic models of communicating (Grunig & Hunt, 1984): two **one-way models** and two **two-way models**. Table 11.1 summarizes these models. The assumptions made about the communication process and the organization's purpose in communicating usually drive the decision about which model to use.

one-way model of public relations—A communication model focusing exclusively on the flow of information from the sport organization to its publics.

two-way model of public relations—A communication model focusing on communication give-and-take between a sport organization and its key publics.

1920s

- **1923**—Foster Hewitt announces his first hockey game over Toronto Star's radio station (CFCA)
- **1924**—Grantland Rice writes "Outlined against a blue-gray October sky, the Four Horsemen rode again"
- **1924**—The Notre Dame backfield became known as the Four Horsemen

1930s

- **1934**—Ford Motor Company pays $100,000 USD to advertise during the World Series

1940s

- **1946**—In first televised heavyweight championship fight (NBC), Joe Louis beats Billy Conn

1950s

- **1954**—Sports Illustrated launched (Aug. 16)

Table 11.1

Four Models of Public Relations and Communication

Model	Purpose	Nature of communication
Press agentry and publicity	Propaganda	One-way; build media interest
Public information	Dissemination	One-way; truthful disclosure of information
Asymmetrical	Scientific persuasion	Two-way; imbalanced effects
Symmetrical	Mutual understanding	Two-way; negotiated effects

Source: Grunig, J.E., & Hunt, T., 1984, Managing public relations *(New York: Holt, Rinehart and Winston).*

The first model is a one-way publicity and press agentry model. Organizations using this model do not seek input from their key publics, but they are extremely concerned about getting their message out there. Sometimes, to get attention, they are even willing to push the envelope regarding what might be appropriate or ethical. If you've ever watched a news conference promoting an upcoming boxing match turn into a melee, you have seen this model in action at its worst. The boxers, and sometimes the promoters, are willing to risk their credibility, not to mention the well-being of anyone caught in the middle of the fracas, in exchange for the buzz that the prematch fight will generate among the public. This model has many ethical applications as well. Note that Grunig and Hunt (1984) suggest that the entertainment industry commonly employs the limited one-way model (one could argue that sport falls into that category much of the time). In such cases, feedback is limited to responses such as ticket sales.

The second one-way model is the public information model. Organizations that use this model are not as extreme in seeking public attention. Instead, they offer effective service to members of the mass media and the public by providing information in a credible manner. For example, they might assist members of the mass media in setting up interviews, or they might provide a variety of other services to members of the media who are covering a sport event. Many professional organizations and college athletics programs have sports information offices to perform these functions. By offering such services, they hope to receive greater amounts of favorable publicity.

Two-way communication models are based on the assumption that the most effective forms of communication require input from target publics. In other words, communication requires give and take. For example, if the owner of a sport team wants the community to vote in favor of a tax increase to help fund a new stadium, that owner would be smart to gather some information regarding public sentiment toward the team and public projects in general before attempting to craft public relations messages. In such an example, the owner is using the first two-way model, the asymmetrical approach. The goal is to use information about a public in a scientific way to communicate more effectively and induce that public to behave as desired. In the case of our example, the desired outcome would be for the community to vote in favor of the tax increase to fund the new stadium.

The second two-way model is the symmetrical approach. This method also employs planned information-gathering techniques to communicate more effectively, but it recognizes that the outcome of the communication process will likely mean that both the organization and the public will have to change their positions or behavior. In other words, the second model is about negotiating mutually acceptable solutions. In her study of public relations practices in two English cricket clubs, Hopwood (2004) found that one of the clubs made considerable use of two-way symmetrical communication practices whereas the other was less proactive. The more proactive club was at the forefront of public relations practices among the clubs in its league.

MEDIA RELATIONS IN SPORT

The mass media devote considerable attention to sport. Because of that interest, most sport managers find that working with members of the mass media is an important part of their jobs. In many cases, sport organizations hire people specifically

1970s

▶**1974**—Women's Sports Foundation founded

▶**1979**—ESPN debuts

▶**1978**—Female sportswriter gains access to male locker rooms

1980s

▶**1987**—Gayle Sierens provides first female NFL play-by-play coverage

1990s

▶**1992**—Black Women in Sport Foundation established

▶**1994**—Olympic Winter Games' ladies figure-skating becomes the second most-watched TV show ever (~45.7 million US households)

to manage media relations because the work necessary to provide good service to the media requires the complete attention of one or more staff members. Regardless of your level of interest in media relations, you need a good understanding of the relationship between sport and the mass media if you want to be an effective sport manager.

Sport and the Mass Media

The relationship between sport and the mass media has been described as symbiotic (Leonard, 1998), meaning that the two entities are frequently interdependent. Each party uses the other for its own gain.

> mass media—Organizations of professional communicators who deliver messages to large audiences simultaneously or quickly over large geographic areas. The mass media possesses delivery systems capable of transcending the time and space limitations inherent in interpersonal and group communication settings.

The historical timeline featured in this chapter highlights many of the central events relating to sport communication that have occurred over the last 200 years.

Print Media

Newspapers reach a substantial portion of the US population on a daily basis. Readership figures indicate that more than a hundred million adults, or better than 50% of the adult population, read at least a portion of a newspaper each day (Newspaper Association of America, 2004a). Over the span of a typical workweek, 54% of the adult population will read a newspaper, and 63% of all adults read at least a portion of a Sunday newspaper. Sport coverage draws a significant number of those readers, with 60% of newspaper readers reporting that they usually read that section (Newspaper Association of America, 2004b). Sport magazines are also prevalent in the marketplace. These magazines range in scope from general interest periodicals such as *Sports Illustrated* and *The Sporting News* to more specialized publications such as *Golf Digest*.

The print media are also prominent in other nations. On average, 53% of Canadian adults read a newspaper each day, and 79% read at least one issue of a daily newspaper each week (Canadian Newspaper Association, 2006). A recent study conducted in the United Kingdom indicated that citizens spent an average of two hours per week reading newspapers, more time than they spent reading books or magazines or reading on the Internet (BBC, 2002).

Learning Activity

The 1920s are considered the golden age of sports.

- Explain why the 1920s are considered the golden age of sports.
- Who are the important people (Grantland Rice, Knute Rockne, William Hearst, Wrigley family, Gertrude Ederle, and so on) who helped shape the sport industry during this period?
- Select one of these people and discuss his or her contributions to the sport industry.
- What world events happened during the 1920s that affected the sport industry?

Electronic Media

Radio and television stations are ubiquitous in the United States, and a ready audience is willing to listen and watch. Research indicates that 99% of American homes have radios and 98% have television sets (US Census Bureau, 2004). Moreover, 91% have videocassette recorders. Cable television is common as well, with 69% of homes being connected. Serving these households are more than 10,000 commercial radio stations (4,804 commercial AM stations and 6,161 commercial FM stations) and roughly 2,000 noncommercial FM stations. Television stations number 1,714, including 581 commercial VHF stations and 752 commercial UHF stations. There are also 9,339 cable systems operating in the United States. Most offer 60 or more channels. These organizations would not be in business without a large market for programming. The average US household watches 7 hours and 29 minutes of television each day (*Broadcasting and Cable Yearbook*, 2001).

Broadcast media outlets are prevalent throughout much of the world. Table 11.2 displays the number of television and radio stations broadcasting in a number of countries.

Some television and radio stations are noncommercial or educational, but most are commercial. Television stations are either affiliated with a broadcast network (e.g., ABC, CBS, NBC, Fox, CW) or operate as independent stations with limited or

2000s

▷**2003**—NBC pays $1.508 billion USD for the rights to televise the 2006 and 2008 Olympic Games

▷**2005**—Alleged steroid use by Barry Bonds and Jason Giambi no network affiliation. Most major network affiliates have local news and thus sport programming. Many broadcast and television networks have additional sport personnel to cover events on a regular or special basis (e.g., the NFL, Wimbledon). Obviously, ESPN and its sister channels require a large number of sport reporters and anchors to handle their all-sport format. Some programs that air on ESPN, however, are sold to the network as a package complete with announcers and commentators under contract to the company that produces the programs, not the network airing them. Radio stations are less likely to have full-time sport broadcasters on staff, but in large markets, the top stations might have someone who handles sport reporting. Sport talk radio stations tap into a radio network's all-sport programming or have local broadcasters whom they employ on a full- or part-time basis. Sport organizations use the mass media to gain public exposure for their events, facilities, and product offerings. The game preview that you see on the local television news tonight might help sway you to attend that game rather than go to a movie as you had originally planned. The newspaper story about the installation of the latest in exercise equipment at a nearby fitness center might entice you to tour the facility and maybe even buy a membership.

Publicity in the mass media can be an asset or a liability for sport organizations. Positive publicity is the best of all worlds for sport managers. Publicity is less costly than other methods of promotion because the airtime or print space is free. It also tends to be more credible than other methods of promotion because consumers know that the sport organization is not paying for the message. On the other hand, negative publicity is difficult to manage for the same reason. Because sport managers do not control the content of the media's message, they cannot mandate that the media *not* print or broadcast embarrassing stories. Accordingly, many sport organizations have developed crisis communication plans. These plans help sport managers deal with tragic or embarrassing situations such as an accident involving team members or an incident in which a member of a team is arrested.

Crisis communication plans and campaigns designed to generate positive publicity reflect a **proactive** (i.e., defining strategies in advance) rather than a **reactive** (i.e., no planning or scrambling to spin negative situations) approach to media relations.

proactive—Planning that allows individuals or organizations to attain goals and prepare for contingencies that they will likely face in the future. From a public relations perspective, a proactive approach means that the organization develops strategies to maximize positive publicity and to prevent or effectively manage problems that it deems important or likely to occur.

reactive—Using no strategy for attaining individual or organizational goals and dealing with problems only after they have developed. From a public relations perspective, a reactive approach means that the organization simply hopes for positive publicity and fails to anticipate difficult issues that it will likely face.

Just as it is in the sport organization's best interest to cultivate positive coverage in the mass media, it is often in the mass media's best interest to provide considerable sport coverage. Given intense public interest, sport helps sell newspapers and magazines, draw audiences to radio and television newscasts, and generate traffic for Web sites. Therefore, media organizations frequently devote considerable resources to sport journalism.

Table 11.2

Number of Television and Radio Stations

Nation	# of TV stations	# of AM radio stations	# of FM radio stations
Australia	104	262	345
Canada	80	245	582
Japan	211	215	89
Russia	7,306	323	1,500 est.
United Kingdom	228	219	431

Source: Central Intelligence Agency, Field Listing-television broadcast stations: 2006.

PARTNERSHIPS FOR PEACE IN EL SALVADOR

Community Relations from an International Perspective

Andy Anderson, John Corlett, and James Mandigo, Canada

The United Nations (UN) declared 2005 as the International Year of Sport and Physical Education (see www.un.org/sport2005/). Linking to the Millennium Development Goals (www.un.org/millenniumgoals/), the UN challenged the world to consider how sport and physical education could serve as vehicles to address global issues related to violence, inequality, disease, hunger, primary education, environmental sustainability, and global partnerships. The UN embarked on a public relations campaign to encourage key stakeholders who represent government, public and private agencies and organizations, academics, and citizens from around the world to work together through sport and physical education to address the world's most pressing issues.

Inspired by this challenge, the Centre for Healthy Development through Sport and Physical Activity (www.brocku.ca/fahs/research_centres/CHDSPA.php) was formed at Brock University. The centre was designed specifically to work with local, provincial, national, and international partners and act as a catalyst to create, evaluate, and disseminate effective strategies to develop the physical literacy skills necessary to lead healthy, active lives. Based on this vision, the centre's international mandate includes the following:

1. Creating effective ways to make sport and physical activity relevant to as many of the United Nations' Millennium Development Goals (MDGs) as possible
2. Developing effective ways to articulate and achieve the MDGs that can be influenced by sport and physical activity
3. Assisting more groups to share resources devoted to achieving these goals
4. Linking educators in all countries to create genuine global partnerships

Example of an International Community Relations Project

In March 2005 the Ministry of Education in El Salvador launched Plan 2021, a 15-year national public relations plan aimed toward modernizing the country's education system. As part of the plan, sport and physical education in school communities were identified as a pathway for children and youth to develop the competence and confidence associated with peace making. (For an overview of the plan in Spanish, go to www.mined.gob.sv/gestion_mined/Plan_Nacional_2021/principal.asp.)

Programs for peace emphasize participation in a variety of play experiences that enable young people to form identities of courage, compassion, and cooperation. Through play, children and youth can develop images of themselves as strategic thinkers, creative problem solvers, and leaders, which can lead to improvements in self-esteem, self-confidence, decision making, and conflict management. Working constructively and cooperatively with learning partners (parents, teachers, community care providers, peers), they can also experience feelings of affection and affiliation—a deeper sense of belonging, care, and hope. Ultimately, young people build capacity within self and others by expecting more. Through creative challenges, students can expect to have a hand in change, expect their talents to help them learn, expect their working together to build respect and capacity of innovation, and expect their hard work to contribute to the growth of their nation.

Building on the international mandate of the centre, the Partnerships through Peace Project in El Salvador was formed. Together with local partners such as government ministries, current educators, community partners, corporate sponsors, and academics, a coordinated plan to develop instructional programs in school communities was formed. The centre's commitment to the MDGs guides the project. Specifically, the key partners view sport and physical education as important and effective vehicles to address issues of equity and empowerment, affirmation of children's rights, global partnerships for healthy development, and enhancement of primary education. As one of the principals of El Salvador's largest elementary schools commented during a recent visit, "Children do not miss school on days they have physical education."

One of the guiding principles throughout this process is that community relations is about partnership in its truest form. Each member of the partnership must have an equal and shared responsibility. Hence, one of the main tenets of the centre's international work has been to collaborate with partners to craft a version of curriculum and instructional reform that reflects the culture and history of El Salvador. The goal is not to Canadianize the Salvadoran people. Rather, the goal is to help local partners construct curriculum that honours and validates their voice in global discussions about healthy development through physical education, sport, and play.

Canadian delegates from the Partnerships for Peace project observed and participated in PE classes with these El Salvadoran children. They also had the opportunity to discuss with El Salvadoran teachers and administrators the role of physical education in the school. The children are waving Canadian flags as a symbol of the cultural exchange between their two countries.

Photo courtesy of Joanna Sheppard and James Mandigo.

International Learning Activity

Review the United Nations' Millennium Development Goals (www.un.org/millenniumgoals). What role do you see sport playing in helping the United Nations achieve these goals by 2015? Who would be the key partners to help make these goals a reality?

print media—Organizations that mass-produce printed publications for distribution into homes, offices, and businesses. The print media include newspapers of various types (e.g., daily, weekly) and general and specialized magazines.

electronic media—Organizations that transmit radio or television signals through the air or by cable into homes, offices, and businesses. The electronic media include commercial and noncommercial (i.e., public) broadcasting stations and cable networks or stations.

Sport journalists are a diverse lot. Some work as reporters, covering news and writing articles for a newspaper or magazine. These journalists are members of the **print media**. Others work for a radio, television, or cable outlet, covering and packaging reports on sport-related topics. These people help make up the **electronic media**. Increasingly, the work of both print and electronic sport journalists is appearing on the Internet. The World Wide Web is just one aspect of new technologies changing the field of sport journalism and public relations. Although the most prominent area of coverage has traditionally been major professional and top-division collegiate sport, those working for media outlets in sport journalism cover a variety of topics, including nearly every recreational sport activity.

Much of the sport content within the mass media comes in the form of news or feature coverage. The broadcast media also devote significant resources to live coverage of sport events as entertainment programming. These events frequently draw large audiences who possess characteristics that are highly desirable to advertisers (e.g., income, education level). The size of these audiences is commonly measured using ratings and shares. Ratings represent the percentage of the population overall (all households with televisions) that watches a particular program. Shares represent the percentage of the "tuned in" population (all households using television at a given time) that watches a particular program. Super Bowl and Olympics broadcasts account for many of the highest rated television programs ever. Given the ability of sport programming to draw large audiences, many broadcast entities are willing to pay large amounts of money in the form of rights fees to have the exclusive privilege of carrying the events. For example, the National Football League's latest television deals with ESPN, Fox, CBS, NBC and DirecTV will result in more than $3.7 billion USD in annual revenue for the league from 2006 through 2010 (Isidore, 2005).

The primary way that media outlets recoup such investments in sports programming is by securing sponsorships from corporations that seek to market their products and services to audiences of sport fans. The sidebar on page 253 examines relationships among sport organizations, media outlets, and sponsor corporations as they relate to NASCAR.

What Media Relations Specialists Do

Sport **media relations** professionals who work for a team, facility, or organization are responsible for creating, coordinating, and organizing information about that entity and disseminating it to the public indirectly through the mass media or through direct channels (e.g., organizational Web site). Some organizations have staffs large enough to include separate information and promotion functions, but many organizations employ a single person who handles information, promotion, media relations, customer or fan relations, and miscellaneous marketing and other public relations duties. Success as a media relations professional requires a genuine interest in the field, strong interpersonal and written communication skills, and the perseverance to unearth and secure internship and entry-level job opportunities in a highly competitive field.

> **media relations**—An organizational activity resulting in the creation, coordination, and organization of information and the dissemination of it to the public through the mass media.

Those who have studied sport media relations (Helitzer, 2000; Nichols, Moynahan, Hall, & Taylor, 2002; Stoldt, 2000; Stoldt, Dittmore, & Branvold, 2006) indicate that the duties of sports information directors at colleges or universities include the following:

- Writing news releases
- Updating hometown newspapers
- Writing feature stories
- Filing game reports
- Writing, editing, and laying out brochures and media guides
- Preparing game programs
- Overseeing promotional activities
- Compiling records and statistics
- Organizing a photo file system
- Planning and conducting press conferences
- Answering requests from publications and organizations
- Managing a press box staff and managing the press box on game day
- Developing and updating crisis communication plans
- Maintaining the athletics program's Web site
- Any other duties assigned by the athletics director or other supervisor

The following sections offer some elaboration on a few of the more common duties assumed by media relations professionals.

Writing News Releases

The goal of a news release is to release newsworthy information to targeted publics in the most positive light possible. Although sometimes called a press release, *news release* is a more descriptive term for the intent of this media relations tactic. The media usually determine what is and what is not newsworthy. The job of a media relations professional is to get information into the hands of the media and persuade them to use it because it is newsworthy to some segment of the media's audience.

Sports news releases are written about anything relative to the organization. Common types of news releases include straight news, competition previews, competition stories, and hometown releases (Stoldt, Dittmore, & Branvold, 2006). Straight news releases include announcements about personnel, schedules, product launches, event sponsorships, event time changes, and more. Note that not all news releases communicate positive messages. Although distributing a news release that announces the

BALANCE OF POWER

Money has always been a factor in the relationship between sport and the media, and it is becoming increasingly important in the complex relationship among sport, media, and corporations. A 30-second commercial in the 2005 Super Bowl cost advertisers $2.4 million USD. In contrast, the typical prime-time 30-second ad costs only about $400,000 USD. And although it may surprise some people, NASCAR represents another sport property that generates major sums of money for numerous stakeholders.

NASCAR has a fan base of 75 million enthusiasts, and it represents a classic case study of the complex interrelationship between sport, media, and corporate money. In 1979 NASCAR's Daytona 500 was the only Winston Cup Series race on television, although ABC's Wide World of Sports aired NASCAR race highlights. By the late 1990s ESPN, TNN, and TBS aired 28 Winston Cup Series events. By 2003 the entire series was broadcast live. Network television covered 24 of the 36 races (*"The Money in Racing,"* 2003). The increased coverage reflected enthusiastic fan interest. FX's live coverage of NASCAR's 2005 Nextel Cup series (sponsorship shifted from Winston to Nextel in 2004) garnered the highest ratings for the network since it began broadcasting the races in 2001 (Modestino, 2005). Those ratings determine the value of commercials that the networks can sell within broadcasts, and the networks in turn pay NASCAR for the rights to carry the races.

The various racing teams draw major financial support. Primary corporate sponsorship for a NASCAR racing team runs $15 to 20 million USD. Primary sponsors receive prominent logo placement on the cars, and when the cars are shown on the television broadcasts, viewers can easily see the sponsors' brands. In addition, primary sponsors may use the drivers as product endorsers, and the sponsors receive valuable hospitality services from the teams. Secondary sponsorship, which is usually limited to racing car bumper stickers and driver suit patches, can cost a company $500,000 to $1 million USD (Arrington, 2005).

NASCAR itself also sells sponsorships, and the revenue from those deals has tripled to $3.7 billion USD in recent years. Forty-two companies have signed up as official NASCAR sponsors, and other companies back individual drivers or racing teams (Arrington, 2005). Sunoco had been sponsoring NASCAR since the 1980s, and it increased its corporate visibility in 2004 by replacing Union 76 as the official fuel for NASCAR's top three series (Associated Press, 2003).

The loyal NASCAR fan base is attracting some unexpected sponsors as well. In 2004 Kodak highlighted women's health with two pink ribbons framing the theme of Kodak mammography film on the #77 Kodak Racing Dodge driven by Brendan Gaughan (Eastman Kodak Company, 2004). In May 2005 GlaxoSmithKline and Roche took aim at the millions of female NASCAR fans with sponsorship of Joe Gibbs Racing, a high-visibility NASCAR racing team, to promote awareness of a new medicine, Boniva, which treats postmenopausal osteoporosis. GlaxoSmithKline Consumer Healthcare also was the first smoking-cessation sponsor in NASCAR, signing on in 2005 as an associate sponsor with Chip Ganassi's Racing Team. Later in the year the company announced that its Nicorette brand name would replace the Busch name for the March 2006 NASCAR event at the Atlanta Motor Speedway. The Nicorette 300 would be the first NASCAR race sponsored by a product that helps smokers stop using a product whose manufacturers have been long-time NASCAR sponsors (GlaxoSmithKline, 2005).

Not surprisingly, a number of ancillary companies are interested in getting involved in the lucrative sponsorship deals. Verve Sponsorship Group's mission "is to match corporations and their brands with the right race teams to provide a significant ROI for the sponsor" (Verve Sponsorship Group, 2005). Other companies bring together the movers and shakers involved in sport sponsorship for conferences and seminars. In 2003 the Sports Sponsorship Symposium began hosting events for executives representing sport organizations, corporate sponsors, and the media. *Street & Smith's SportsBusiness Journal* calls these "must-attend" events. Among the topics covered have been sports media and technology, intercollegiate athletics, sports facilities and franchises, and sports and social responsibility (Street & Smith's Sports Group, 2005).

Serious scholarship on the issue is also appearing. James Madison University, located in the heart of NASCAR country, has established a Center for Sports Sponsorship, "a nonprofit entity dedicated to sports sponsorship research" (James Madison University, 2004). Its first study, which examined NASCAR sponsorships, found that 36% of 1,000 self-identified NASCAR fans could name, without prompting, the primary sponsors of the top 30 NASCAR drivers. More than half of the people interviewed could identify the sponsors for at least nine drivers. A similar percentage said that they felt as if they were contributing to the sport when they bought the sponsors' products (Arrington, 2005).

hiring of a new women's volleyball coach is appropriate, it is equally appropriate to distribute one that announces the firing of the previous coach.

Competition previews, or game notes, are designed to help media cover an event by providing unique information and trivia that might be incorporated into a reporter's story or broadcast. Hometown releases are common in intercollegiate athletics and national governing bodies and involve spotlighting an athlete to that person's hometown, or high school, community newspaper (Stoldt, Dittmore, & Branvold, 2006).

Planning News Conferences

The goal of a news conference, like a news release, is to disseminate noteworthy information from an organization to its targeted publics. Smith (2002) stated simply, "A news conference is a contrived media happening in which an organizational spokesperson makes a newsworthy statement" (p. 102). After the spokesperson finishes the statement, reporters usually have the opportunity to ask questions.

Key considerations for media relations professionals concerning a news conference include who will speak on behalf of the organization and where the news conference will be held. Nichols, Moynahan, Hall, & Taylor (2002) stated that a senior management person such as the owner, general manager, university athletics director, or university president usually speaks on behalf of the organization at a news conference. But an organization should not automatically assume that senior managers are the best spokespersons. Often they are not. The identity of the best spokesperson can vary for any given subject.

Given that an objective of a news conference might be to generate publicity, an organization should go out of its way to promote attendance at its news conferences by holding them in a location that is convenient for both the media and the organization (Nichols, Moynahan, Hall, & Taylor, 2002). Stoldt, Dittmore, and Branvold (2006) noted that, in most cases, sport organizations should strive to hold news conferences in athletics facilities used by the organization for four reasons: (1) the organization controls the facility, providing a high degree of flexibility in staging the news conference; (2) media personnel who regularly cover the organization should already be familiar with where to go and where to park; (3) senior management who attend the news conference will be less inconvenienced because they will not have to travel to a different location; and (4) the organization is in a position to use atmospherics such as banners and backdrops to help shape the message.

Managing the Press Box

Stoldt et al. (2006) stated that the primary purpose of a press box is to provide accredited, working members of the media with a place to sit and record the actions of the event. The location of this space varies from sport to sport. In baseball, the press box is typically located halfway up the stands behind home plate, whereas in basketball the press box may consist of a row of tables and chairs along the side of the court. Regardless of the location, Stoldt, Dittmore, and Branvold identified some fundamental, and often unstated, rules that govern the workspace.

First, the space is intended to be for the media who are covering the event. Media relations professionals should attempt to remove those who do not meet this criterion. Second, the occupants of the workspace should not cheer. Most members of the media understand the need to remain objective and will adhere to this code. But all people, including organizational employees, must subscribe to this policy.

A third assumed policy of the press box workspace is that some level of hierarchy will be evident through the assignment of seat locations. Separate booths or rooms are generally provided for broadcast media including television, the home organization's radio broadcasters, and the visiting organization's radio team. Within the main press box workspace, media relations professionals should assign space to specific media organizations. No industry-wide formula or protocol governs this process. Helitzer (2000) suggested using a seniority hierarchy for assigning seats. Nichols, Moynahan, Hall, and Taylor (2002) advised providing beat reporters and other regulars the same seat location each week. Public relations professionals may wish to group visiting media together in one section of the workspace.

Sport organizations usually provide results, statistics, and other publicity information to media working in the press box. In addition, some organizations might choose to provide complimentary hospitality, such as beverages and meals, to working media.

Chapter 4 has detailed information on the duties and career paths of collegiate sports information jobs. Media relations specialists in professional sport perform the same functions, although for major league teams, staff responsibilities might be spread among more people. Sports communicators who work with sport recreation facilities also perform some of these functions, but the focus is on the community opportunities available at the facility and the events or activities scheduled.

Learning Activity

You might be surprised to find how much of the information that sport broadcasters share with their audiences comes from materials provided to them by the participating sport organizations. Pick a major professional or college sport event that will soon be televised. Visit the Web site of one of the teams participating in the game. Download the game notes (often available as PDF files). When you later watch the game on television, notice how many of the same facts and figures are shared with the audience!

Careers in Media Relations

North America has thousands of colleges and universities and hundreds of major and minor league professional sports teams, and most North American cities have one or more sport, fitness, health, or recreation facilities. Each enterprise needs to get information to the public, and many of them employ at least one communication specialist to handle the job. You thus have many opportunities for employment as a media relations professional. Remember, however, that the field is so popular and competitive that your career success depends on recognizing and sometimes creating opportunities to get your foot in the door. Prospective employers will be looking for a solid educational preparation that includes strong communication skills. Typical majors are sport management, journalism, public relations, and communications. Beyond your basic education, however, you should capitalize on the opportunity to secure volunteer or internship experiences so that when you graduate you will have more on your resume than just the name of your degree.

A good internship can do more than simply give you experience; it can also give you a network of practitioners to contact for job opportunities, not to mention essentials such as letters of reference. Although some top-level professional teams offer internship opportunities, these internships are hard to come by because of the intense competition to be involved in the "glamorous" world of professional sport. You may find additional opportunities by trying minor league teams or teams in sports other than football, basketball, baseball, and hockey. Don't forget to look for internship opportunities with community recreational facilities such as the YMCA, YWCA, and Jewish Community Centers. Tight budgets and limited staff resources can make these organizations appreciate help from dedicated volunteers and interns.

Your first full-time job will probably be as an assistant sports information director or an assistant promotions director at a college, team, governing body, or facility. You could also start at the director's level with a smaller organization, but you would probably be a one-person staff. If you do your job well and keep your ear tuned for advancement opportunities, you should have the opportunity to advance to a higher-level position or move to a larger organization. The first job you get should provide you with a broad network of contacts who will be valuable as you prepare to move into positions with larger organizations or into a manager or director job. You might also need to evaluate your willingness to relocate. Your pool of opportunities will expand if you are willing to move to organizations in a range of regions.

Competition for jobs in sport media relations is intense. Although the number of available positions has increased as colleges, facilities, and teams have recognized the connection between publicity and profit, the number of people who are competing for those jobs has also increased. Salaries are not always commensurate with similar communication positions in the corporate world because many people seem willing to work in sport almost for free. In addition, sport media relations professionals are frequently called on to work long hours. "First one to arrive, last one to leave" is a common reality in the profession. Work schedules of 60 to even 80 hours a week are not uncommon during a particular season, and for those working at the collegiate level, sport seasons usually run about 10 months.

Ethical Issues in Media Relations

Media relations professionals frequently deal with a variety of ethics-related issues. Perhaps the most sensitive issues center on privacy. Media relations professionals have access to a great deal of information—much of it personal. If you work in the field, you need to be sensitive to this and release only information that will not compromise people's right to privacy. For example, it is unethical (not to mention illegal) for a college media relations professional to publicly release student–athlete grade point averages. An exception might be the authorized release of information about a student–athlete who earns

IN PROFILE: Larry Rankin

Title: Assistant athletic director—media relations, Wichita State University
Education: BS journalism—public relations, Oklahoma State University

Photo courtesy of LWS photography.

Professional Background

- Sports information student assistant, Oklahoma State University (1987-92)
- Assistant sports information director, Wichita State University (1992-94)
- Sports information director, Wichita State University (1994-2000)
- Assistant athletics director—media relations, Wichita State University (2000-present)

Job Responsibilities

- Manage and oversee media relations for Wichita State's 15 Division I sports with specific responsibility for men's basketball, the Internet site goshockers.com, the Pizza Hut Shocker Sports Hall of Fame, and the Pizza Hut Shocker Sports History Museum in Charles Koch Arena
- Oversee an office of two full-time assistants, three graduate assistants, and one student administrative assistant who assist in the media relations office with specific sport responsibility

Career Highlights

- Team media coordinator for the 1989 and 1990 Oklahoma State national championship wrestling teams, the 1991 Sweet 16 Oklahoma State women's basketball team, and the 1996 Wichita State College World Series baseball team
- Event media coordinator for the 1989 NCAA Wrestling Championship in Oklahoma City and the 1995, 1996, 1998, and 1999 NCAA Baseball Regionals in Wichita
- Assistant media coordinator for the 1994 first- and second-round D-I NCAA Basketball Championship in Wichita
- Photo editor and copyeditor for *OSU: History-Making Basketball*, a 250-page book dedicated to the history of Oklahoma State basketball

Advice to Students

Getting involved in athletics as a student, graduate assistant, or volunteer early in your college career will assist you in advancing toward your goals of working in Division I athletics.

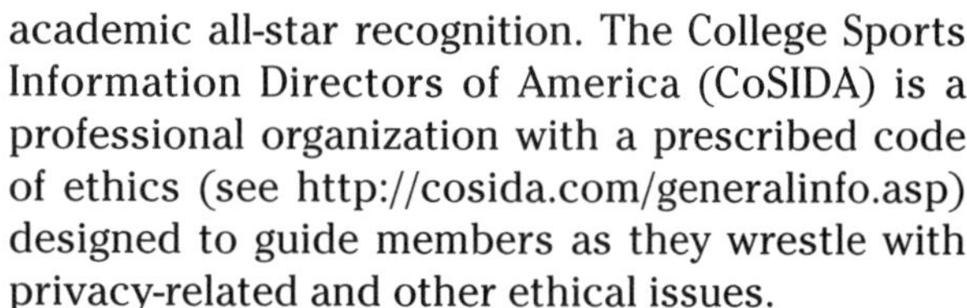

academic all-star recognition. The College Sports Information Directors of America (CoSIDA) is a professional organization with a prescribed code of ethics (see http://cosida.com/generalinfo.asp) designed to guide members as they wrestle with privacy-related and other ethical issues.

Another ethics-related issue relevant to media relations has to do with the one-way and two-way models discussed earlier. Many sport managers think that the job is limited to publicity, to generating coverage of a team or event or practicing damage control when something negative happens or is suspected. But a more complete and sophisticated approach to media relations would classify generating publicity as only one aspect of the work. Sport organizations that rely predominantly on a one-way flow of information might violate the boundaries of ethical relationships with their key constituents. In other words, two parties are unlikely to have a healthy relationship if one does all the talking!

COMMUNITY RELATIONS IN SPORT

Community relations activities tend to center on promoting charitable initiatives and developing opportunities for face-to-face contact with stakeholders, and they often complement media relations work (Lesly, 1998). As stated by one practitioner, media relations publicizes what happens on the field of competition, and community relations promotes what happens off the field (Shani Tate, personal communication, February 13, 2002).

> **community relations**—An organizational activity designed to build relationships with residents and civic-minded organizations in the geographic area in which the sport organization is located.

Sport organizations engage in community relations activities for many reasons. First, community relations has traditionally been viewed as a long-term investment in the image of the sport organization (Mullin, Hardy, & Sutton, 2000). Constituents are likely to have positive perceptions of sport organizations that they see participating in charitable outreach programs and other worthy undertakings. Second, many sport organizations are finding that effectively planned community relations efforts can result in new revenue in the short term. For example, if a player or coach from your organization makes an appearance at an educational assembly for schoolchildren, you can provide the kids with complimentary tickets for an upcoming game. The tickets might stipulate that each child must be accompanied by an adult who purchases his or her own ticket to the game. Finally, community relations is the socially responsible thing for sport organizations to do. Even if your sport organization did not receive long-term image enhancement or short-term revenue gains from your community relations efforts, such activity would be prudent because your organization will benefit from being part of a thriving, vibrant community.

What Community Relations Professionals Do

Sport community relations professionals who work for a team, facility, or organization are responsible for creating, organizing, and executing charitable initiatives and other programs designed to involve the organization in community enhancement. Some organizations have staffs large enough to include community relations specialists who work full time in their assigned areas. Many others employ a single individual or a small staff with other public relations or marketing responsibilities in addition to community relations. Like other sectors of the public relations field, success as a community relations professional requires strong communication and interpersonal skills as well as the determination to seek out opportunities to gain experience and make contacts in the field.

A common form of sport community relations activity is the donation of money to various charities. Some sport organizations, particularly those at the major professional level, execute a variety of fund-raising events throughout the year and then donate the proceeds to charitable organizations.

Community relations in sport runs the gamut from intimate local experiences to international events promoting world peace. Here, FC Barcelona's football (soccer) star, Samuel Eto'o, from Cameroon (center), jokes with Israeli and Palestinian players as they prepare to play a "football for peace" match in Tel Aviv in 2006. Eto'o's participation included initiating the Palestinian–Israeli match and demonstrating football tricks for a group of Palestinian and Israeli children.

© Getty Images

Learning Activity

Visit the Web site of the sport organization of your choice and see whether it contains information on community relations initiatives. Many sport organizations, particularly high-level professional franchises, offer such information online. After reviewing the site, prepare a brief presentation for your class. Questions that you will want to answer during the presentation include the following:

- What community relations activities has the organization implemented?
- Who has been involved in those activities?
- Do the community relations activities listed seem to be a good fit for the sport organization?
- If you were to suggest one other community relations initiative for the organization, what would it be? Why?

For example, the Dallas Stars of the National Hockey League donated more than $300,000 USD to various charities in their metropolitan area in 2000 (Dallas Stars, 2000). The Stars funded those donations through fund-raising events such as a casino night in which donors could join players and coaches for an evening of games, prizes, food, and beverages. Another example is New Balance, a shoe and apparel company that donates to various charities and executes a product donation program for people in need who are located near their main facilities (New Balance, 2001). Sport organizations commonly favor charities that benefit children and young people. Sport organizations may simply contribute autographed merchandise that the charity can then auction off in its own fund-raising activities.

A second form of community relations activities that sport organizations commonly employ involves initiatives to better the community by direct contact. For example, some organizations cultivate youth sport participation by constructing sport venues (e.g., ball fields in the inner city) and sponsoring clinics. Others might engage in partnerships with charitable organizations to advocate important messages (e.g., "stay in school") or generate an important service (e.g., building a home with Habitat for Humanity). These initiatives take place at multiple levels from the professional sport league to the member franchise to the individual player or coach. In addition, some sport organizations are looking to take their community relations efforts to a new level of effectiveness by creating strategic partnerships with corporate sponsors to serve their communities more effectively. The Washington franchise of the National Football League has developed one such "leadership council" in which the team and its corporate partners pool resources to maximize the benefit of their community relations programs for all parties involved (Schoenfeld, 2000).

A third form of common community relations activity does not directly benefit charitable organizations but does enable the sport organization to build relationships with various constituents through direct contact. Many community relations professionals coordinate speaking appearances by other members of their organizations. Still others organize promotional events such as the annual winter caravans that many Major League Baseball teams stage to rally support during the off-season. Some organizations, particularly those at the minor league level, find that the most popular personality at such appearances is the team mascot.

Careers in Community Relations

Community relations activity is common in a wide range of sport organizations from professional entertainment organizations to colleges and universities to for-profit fitness centers to sporting goods manufacturers. The larger the organization and the greater its resources, the more likely it is that organization will have one or more employees assigned specifically to community relations. For example, Major League Baseball's Kansas City Royals has four employees working full-time in community relations. One of their minor league affiliates, the Wichita Wranglers, has no one working full-time in community relations. Those responsibilities fall under the job description of the marketing manager.

On balance, fewer full-time positions are available in community relations than in media relations in sport. One primary reason is that hundreds of colleges and universities hire at least one full-time employee in sports information. Many community relations responsibilities are delegated to the student life skills division of the athletics department. Still, community relations is a viable career option within sport. In fact, some believe that the community relations function will grow considerably in the coming years (Jackowski, 2000). If so, sport organizations will likely be looking to increase the number of community relations specialists whom they employ and increase the resources that they are willing to devote to the function.

Competition is fierce for sport community relations positions, so if you're hoping to work in the

IN PROFILE: Catherine S. Marquette

Title: Community relations director, DC United, Executive director, United for DC

Education: 1997: Double major, economics and communications, with distinction; University of North Carolina at Chapel Hill

Professional Sports Background

- 2002: Community Relations Director, DC United, founder and executive director, United for DC
- 2001: Community and fan relations director, DC United
- 2000: Community and fan relations manager, DC United
- 1999: Customer service and community relations manager, DC United
- 1999: Ticket representative, DC United
- 1997: Intern, Raleigh Icecaps (ECHL)
- 1996: Intern, Raleigh Flyers (USISL)
- 1996: Intern, Long Island Rough Riders (USISL)

Job Responsibilities

- Develop and implement all DC United community-based strategies, programs, and activities
- Manage all DC United player and coach public and community appearances
- Oversee all DC United financial and in-kind donations and contributions
- Serve as chief executive officer of team's not-for-profit organization, United for DC
- Develop and implement all fund-raising strategies and special events
- Direct program development and manage financial grant initiative

Career Highlights

- Major League Soccer Community Relations Executive of the Year (2003)
- Three-time DC United Employee of the Month winner (July 1999, February 2001, July 2004)
- Board Member for DC SCORES, a nonprofit organization that combines soccer and creative writing in an after-school program in over 20 elementary schools in Washington, DC (2002 to present)
- Former president and board member for WISE DC, a nonprofit networking organization for women working in the sports and events industries (2001 to 2005)

Advice to Students

The best advice I can provide anyone interested in working in sport is to gain as much experience as possible. If you are lucky enough to receive an internship, which is the best way to gain experience, you must treat it as one long, intensive job interview. Use this as your opportunity to shine, to stand out, to differentiate yourself from other interns. With the increasing number of colleges and universities that offer sport management degrees at the undergraduate and graduate levels, competition for jobs within sport teams is increasing. Unfortunately, I see many students go after internships and even jobs with the attitude that they are entitled to those jobs and internships because they've earned degrees in sport management. Wrong! Despite the increase in the number of students with sport management degrees, the number of full-time positions within sport teams has not increased. One more piece of advice: Don't lock yourself into one particular area of the industry. You'll be limiting yourself and your own marketability. You must be open to all departments and all functions. Currently, I am the head of all of the team's community outreach and affairs, but my first full-time job was in ticketing. I placed my foot in the door, so to speak, and worked my way up from there. I never viewed myself as too good for ticketing. The most important thing that you can do is earn a full-time job within a team. From there, you prove your worth and write your own ticket.

field you must distinguish yourself competitively by honing your communication skills and by securing significant volunteer and internship experience before applying for an entry-level job. Employers are looking for applicants with proven records of accomplishment in executing community relations initiatives. The good news is that with a little creativity and a good dose of initiative, you can gain this experience while you are still in school. Keep in mind that many sport organizations do not have the resources to hire full-time employees in community relations. Rather than pinning your hopes on a major league organization or industry leader in fitness or equipment, consider volunteering for a local minor league organization, a nonmajor college or university, or a locally owned fitness business. Such organizations would likely welcome your help in carrying out initiatives that they have already planned or in implementing creative ideas that you develop.

Thoroughness is the key. Most community relations efforts are hard work. Your credibility depends on your ability to see the project or projects through to completion. You should also carefully document the results of your efforts. Although many community relations activities are certainly worthy endeavors, key decision makers are more likely to value them (and your efforts) if you can document results such as the attendance at a special event; the amount and type of publicity that the initiative generated; or letters, phone calls, and e-mails of appreciation from the constituents served.

If you are fortunate enough to secure a job in community relations, you will likely start in one of two places. You will be either a public relations and marketing generalist with a smaller organization or a lower-level member of a small community relations staff within a larger organization. As you gain experience, expand your network of contacts, and document your effectiveness in community relations endeavors, you will likely have the chance to advance to higher-level positions or larger organizations. Some people in the field believe that those who want to work with a major professional franchise should start by gaining volunteer, internship, or entry-level experience with a major professional franchise.

Community relations professionals in sport will likely be paid less than their counterparts in other industries. This discrepancy occurs because of the demand for jobs in the field. Another factor may be the perception that community relations in sport is somehow easier than it is in other professions because the mass media have great interest in sport. Although that circumstance may be true at the high-profile professional and college levels, community relations professionals in sport also face some challenges unique to the industry. One is that because of their public visibility, many sport organizations receive far more requests for help from worthy organizations than they can possibly fulfill. Saying "no" to deserving organizations is a difficult but often necessary part of the job. In addition, some community relations professionals find it challenging to match community relations initiatives with the interests of key people within the organization, such as high-profile coaches and athletes. Successful completion of such work, however, produces significant benefits for all parties involved.

Ethical Issues in Community Relations

Community relations professionals frequently confront a couple of ethical issues. One is keeping their priorities straight. Sport organizations are in a unique position to capitalize on the publicity that often accompanies their community service initiatives. For example, visits by sport figures to patients in a children's hospital might make for good press and moving visual images. Publicity for such ventures clearly enhances the reputation of the sport organization within the community. But when publicity rather than service becomes the sole force behind a community relations initiative, an ethical boundary has been crossed. As stated by Peak (1998), "The benefits of a community relations program should be in the program, not the publicity" (p. 130).

A second ethical issue that community relations professionals must deal with is giving credit where credit is due (Peak, 1998). Although sport organizations might want to publicize the good deeds done by their member managers, coaches, and athletes, they should be careful to distinguish individual community relations initiatives from organizational programs. In addition, sport organizations that collaborate with other businesses in the community on charitable initiatives must be careful to share the spotlight. Accomplishing this goal might be difficult because the sport organization is frequently the more prominent player in the mix. Nonetheless, a less self-serving approach to publicity is often best if generating goodwill within the community at large and with corporate partners in particular is the sport organization's priority.

OTHER PUBLIC RELATIONS POSITIONS

Many sport organizations employ public relations professionals in positions that extend beyond media relations or community relations. Job titles and scopes of responsibility vary from one organization to another. Some of the common positions related to public relations are the following:

• ***Corporate communications***: As noted by Deeter (1993), the work of corporate communications frequently intersects with multiple public relations areas. These tasks might include marketing communication such as media placement in support of a promotional effort, employee communications, community relations, investor relations, and customer relations. Corporate communications positions tend to be more common in sport organizations with relatively large public relations staffs.

• ***Creative specialists***: These public relations practitioners possess specialized skills in design, layout, graphic arts, and other technical skills. Within college athletics departments these people frequently work with the sports information office, collaborating with their colleagues to produce media guides, game programs, posters, and other organizational media.

• ***Employee and volunteer relations***: Internal constituents are easily overlooked, but they are critical to the success of the sport organization. Some public relations professionals specialize in employee or volunteer relations. Their jobs are to build strong internal relationships by creating forums for communication and staging special events (e.g., volunteer appreciation day). Volunteer relations positions are more prevalent in settings such as state amateur sport festivals in which a large volunteer workforce is critical to successful execution of the event.

• ***Web site manager***: These sport communicators specialize in managing their organizations' Web sites. They might update online information, respond to inquiries from visitors to the Web site, facilitate discussion forums, and serve as liaisons with other staff members whose functions include Web site interests (e.g., sports information, marketing, ticket sales).

Depending on the setting, other public relations jobs in the industry may also focus on donor relations, government relations, or relations with governing bodies within the industry.

COMMUNICATION TECHNOLOGY AND ITS EFFECT ON SPORT

When the electronic media, particularly television, gained widespread use in the last century, sport changed in a profound way. Instead of having to wait to read about a sport event in the morning newspaper, we could watch it live or catch highlights on cable programs such as ESPN's *SportsCenter*. The influx of television money into professional competitive sports and amateur sport events such as the Olympics has affected everything from salaries to rules. Television was the impetus behind night baseball and obviously plays a central role in making the Super Bowl a super event! Some people believe that our national sport shifted from baseball to football because the pace and segmented action of football made for better television.

Similarly, the new communication technologies emerging today are changing and will continue to change the way in which we relate to sport. Now we don't even have to wait for *SportsCenter* to go on the air to catch up on the day's events. We can simply punch up our favorite sport news Web site on the Internet and obtain updates on games just completed and even those in progress. If we're watching a live broadcast of a game on television, we can expand our game experience by going online for additional coverage where we can track game statistics and respond to various poll questions regarding the contest. And if we are unable to watch a game of interest, we may be able to follow its progress by accessing a game tracker online or through our wireless telephone service or by listening to satellite radio.

Learning Activity

Technological advances in TV viewing have enhanced the experience of sport fans.

- When were the first MLB, NFL, NHL, and NBA games broadcast?
- What technological enhancements have occurred since those first broadcasts? What enhancements have occurred in other sport TV broadcasts to improve the viewer's experience?
- How have these advancements improved the experience for fans?

Emerging Technologies

The technological advances of recent years make this an exciting and challenging time for sport public relations professionals. We now possess the capacity for instantaneous communication and access to a pool, perhaps even an ocean, of information.

Learning Activity

Investigate the computer technologies available at your school, in particular any instructional sessions available free to students through either direct instruction or computer-assisted instruction. Become familiar with some of the basic computer applications that would be valuable to sport public relations professionals and keep track of any innovations that received publicity during this school term. What are the implications of the innovation for sport public relations professionals?

The Internet is a global computer network that offers access to information housed on a multitude of smaller networks linked by a common set of computer protocols, or standards (Holtz, 1999). Even those of us who are not computer gurus frequently rely on the Internet for communication. E-mail allows us to transmit messages to designated individuals over the Internet. Senders and receivers of e-mail must have specific designations or e-mail addresses to direct their communications properly. Gaining such an address is relatively simple and inexpensive (some organizations offer free e-mail service). Many of us who now use e-mail can scarcely remember how we functioned without it.

GROWTH OF THE INTERNET

The growth of the Internet has been the single most important development in sport communications in recent years. As of 2000 more than 300 million people worldwide were using the Internet (World Almanac, 2002). Estimates indicate that 39% of the US population goes online to access sports information ("SportsBusiness Journal/ESPN Sports Poll," 2001). Not surprisingly, sport Web sites such as espn.com, sportsline.com, and nfl.com frequently draw heavy traffic.

Although most people speculate that the Internet will continue to grow through the early years of the 21st century, some believe that the rate of adoption of high-speed technologies will dictate growth (Liberman, 2001). Growth in recent years has been significant, with the percentage of US households with high-speed Internet or broadband access growing from 9% to 20% between 2001 and 2003 (National Telecommunications and Information Administration, 2004). One technology group estimates that 80% of US homes will have broadband Internet access by 2010 ("Communications Today," 2001).

Internet—A global network that provides access to computers around the world with an ever-expanding menu of services. "Surfing the Internet" has entered the jargon of our culture to describe the use of Internet services and capabilities.

e-mail—A form of communication available electronically through the Internet. E-mail allows online computer users to transmit messages to individuals with specific designations (i.e., e-mail addresses).

Another dimension of the Internet is the World Wide Web, a collection of Web sites that we can access through a browser such as Internet Explorer or Safari. Surfing the Web is now a user-friendly experience. All we have to do is point and click. We can access all sorts of information by simply clicking on the appropriate link that appears on our computer screen, thus connecting us to the Web site that we want to visit. The World Wide Web allows us to select content from a vast array of sources (some of them credible and ethical; some of them not). The Web also permits a two-way flow of information. We can send messages by participating in an online discussion, responding to surveys, or sending messages to online content providers by e-mail. Sport-related Web sites such as espn.com (ESPN's Web site) and nfl.com (the National Football League's Web site) frequently provide information and interactive forums (e.g., discussions, online games) and sell products (e.g., tickets, merchandise).

World Wide Web—A collection of Web sites accessible to online computer users through an Internet browser.

If you are interested in pursuing a career in sport public relations, you need to become familiar with this technology. Marshall McLuhan, whose 1966 *Understanding Media: The Extensions of Man* was embraced, ignored, and recently revived by communication scholars and media enthusiasts, said, "The medium is the message." He was right. The technological advancements of recent years have changed our world. Technology isn't an option in sport communication; it is the absolute—or virtual—reality.

Learning Activity

Congratulations! You have just landed your first full-time paid position in sport public relations. Specifically, you have just been named the director of public relations for a minor league professional basketball franchise. You are responsible for coordinating all aspects of the organization's public relations efforts. These include media relations, community relations, and other public relations activities.

One of your first priorities is to upgrade the team's Web site. So far, the Web site has provided only basic information, such as the team's schedule and results. You now have the opportunity to work in conjunction with a technical specialist to expand the site. Your part of the equation is content—what to include and how to organize it. As you consider the possibilities, think about the following questions:

- How could the work that you'll be doing in media relations significantly expand the content that you make available to those who visit your Web site?
- What aspects of your community relations program would you want to highlight on the Web site?
- How could you expand the function of the site to make it a tool for a two-way flow of information?

You are likely to find some great ideas by visiting the Web sites of similar organizations and seeing how they are using those sites as public relations tools.

Challenges Posed by New Technologies

The emergence of these new technologies has already had a major effect on the way that many sport public relations professionals practice their profession, and it seems certain that more changes are on the way. In fact, some communication experts believe the communication technologies that have emerged hold the potential to revolutionize the field.

One advantage that many sport organizations have already realized through the Internet is the ability to disseminate messages to a mass audience quickly and inexpensively without having to go through the mass media. Only a few years ago, sport media relations professionals were completely reliant on the mass media to convey messages that originated with the sport organization through news releases. If the media did not use the releases, the information simply was not available to the public. Now, sport public relations practitioners can post that information on organizational Web sites where interested parties can access it at their convenience. Or they can e-mail the information to a distribution list of interested parties who have previously provided their addresses to the organization. These options offer a level of message control previously unattainable in the field.

Additionally, the Internet provides a forum for a two-way flow of communication with the public. Many sport organizations are only now beginning to take advantage of this opportunity. Some sport managers are doing some simple but innovative things. For example, Mark Cuban, the controversial owner of the NBA's Dallas Mavericks, allows fans to e-mail him directly, and he even takes time to reply! Cuban made his fortune in new technology, and now he is using technology to engage in direct communication with his publics. In fact, the Internet may be one of the most effective tools available to public relations professionals who are trying to manage relationships with multiple constituents (Holtz, 1999).

Of course, new technology frequently has a way of making things more complicated, and sport public relations professionals are finding this to be true. Media relations specialists in particular are dealing with a couple of troublesome issues. First, they are finding that more print journalists are able to post information online about games in progress. This practice has raised concerns among broadcast media outlets that have paid rights fees for what they believed to be the exclusive right to carry live game information. Broadcast partners are calling on sport organizations to deny journalists the right to post play-by-play updates as they happen (Schoenfeld, 1999). Media relations professionals are now developing policies that seek to find a balance between the interests of Web site journalists and broadcast partners. Another issue that they are facing is the growing amount of noncredible information (e.g., false rumors about a sport organization) and unauthorized credible information appearing on the Web. One college football team discovered video of its practices on the Internet the week before a game against a conference rival (Matuszewski, 2000)! These issues, and others, will call on sport public relations professionals to adjust their strategies as new technologies continue to develop.

Given the growing importance of technology as it relates to sport public relations practice, one other concern has begun to receive attention in recent years. Some public relations professionals have become so reliant on technology to communicate

JOB OPPORTUNITIES

Assistant Sports Information Director

Midsize university with Division I athletics program for a wide variety of men's and women's sports is looking for an addition to its sports information staff. The successful candidate will have a bachelor's or master's degree in journalism or a sport-related field with at least two years of sports information experience with a college, facility, or professional sport team. Superior oral and written communication skills are a must! Primary responsibilities include writing and editing press guides and programs. The position requires extensive evening and weekend work. Salary is commensurate with experience.

Promotions Director

Health facility in urban area seeks a self-motivated individual with three to five years of experience working in promotion or public relations with some experience in a sport- or fitness-related field. A bachelor's degree in journalism, communication, or sport management strongly preferred. Strong writing and speaking skills, good organization, and a high level of creativity and flexibility are a must. Job responsibilities include special events planning, media relations, membership promotion, and marketing. The individual will work closely with the facility director and the facility's 20-member community board.

Community Relations Assistant

Major-level professional sport franchise seeks qualified applicant to assist in all aspects of the team's community relations program. These include but are not limited to off-season promotional tours, fan festivals, charitable fund-raisers, special appearances, ticket donations, and research projects as needed. Qualifications include two years of related experience. Excellent communication skills required. Must be proficient in word processing and database management software. Must be a self-starter, well organized, and willing to work flexible hours that frequently include evenings and weekends.

Director of Public Relations

Sport-related entertainment company in major market seeks qualified applicant to generate public exposure that will result in increased revenue. The successful applicant will work to promote ticket sales for more than 25 varied sport events each year. Specific responsibilities include media relations, Web site management, and promotional event planning and execution. The ideal candidate possesses five or more years of experience in sport promotion. Excellent communication, interpersonal, and organizational skills required.

Corporate Communications Assistant

Sporting goods manufacturer seeks team-oriented communicator to assist in various public relations initiatives. Specific responsibilities include producing the employee newsletter, creating other promotional materials, and assisting in the execution of a product donations program. Bachelor's degree in a related field required. Solid oral and written communication skills are a necessity. Must be able to meet deadlines and handle multiple project assignments simultaneously.

Director of Communications

Professional sport league office seeks qualified candidate to manage all aspects of the league's public relations and serve as a resource for member clubs as necessary. Responsibilities include producing league publications (e.g., official league magazine), writing support materials for league video productions, and managing the league's Web site. Must possess strong communication skills and be adept with job-related computer programs. Candidates with diverse public relations experience in minor league sports may be particularly well suited to this position.

that they may underuse the direct communication skills necessary to be effective (Battenfield, 2005). Although the ability to develop message content for online distribution is a powerful tool in the public relations professional's arsenal, informal interactions in the workplace and telephone conversations with members of important publics remain important foundations for effective public relations practice.

SUMMARY

Public relations in sport presents an exciting and viable career option for prospective sport managers. At its best, the public relations function allows sport organizations to build healthy relationships with their key constituents. Jobs in the field include positions in media relations, community relations, and related areas. Regardless of the specific job, however, strong written and oral communication skills are a necessity, as is an understanding of communication concepts relevant to professional practice. Because competition for sport public relations jobs is fierce, you must gain substantial volunteer and internship experience while you are still in college.

Given the unique relationship between the mass media and sport, a large number of media relations positions are available in the field. Sport media relations professionals disseminate information to the public through the mass media or through organizational Web sites. They also manage additional media requests, service the media during games or events, and manage records and statistics.

Sport community relations professionals generate goodwill for their organizations. They coordinate organizational participation in charitable endeavors, fund-raisers that benefit various nonprofits, and public appearances by managers and players. They also coordinate special promotional events. By carefully executing these activities, they enhance their communities and the reputations of their organizations within their communities.

Advancements in technology are changing the way that sport public relations professionals operate. Relatively recent developments such as the Internet afford opportunities to reach constituents directly, instantaneously, and interactively. Web technology is also calling on sport public relations professionals to meet new challenges as the amount of sports information available to consumers expands.

Review Questions

1. How would you define public relations? Why is public relations so important to sport organizations?
2. What skills and experiences are most important to prospective public relations professionals? If you were to begin planning now for a career in sport public relations, what sort of experiences should you seek?
3. Select one of the key historical moments listed in this chapter and conduct a little research about it. What details can you learn about the event? Why was it significant?
4. Describe the work of sport media relations professionals. What sorts of tasks are part of their job descriptions? What are the advantages and disadvantages of their jobs?
5. Describe the work of sport community relations professionals. What sorts of tasks are part of their job descriptions? What are the advantages and disadvantages of their jobs?
6. What are some of the other public relations positions sometimes available in sport organizations?
7. What emerging technologies are affecting sport public relations professionals? What do you see as the greatest opportunities and threats that these technologies bring to the profession?
8. What are some of the common ethical issues facing sport public relations professionals? How can professional codes of ethics help sport public relations practitioners?

Finance, Economics, and Budgeting in the Sport Industry

Timothy D. DeSchriver—University of Delaware ▪ **Daniel F. Mahony**—University of Louisville

Learning Objectives

After studying this chapter, you will be able to do the following:

1. Explain the basic principles of microeconomics and macroeconomics.
2. Relate the theories of economics to the sport industry.
3. Discuss the concept of economic impact analysis and its relationship to sport events and facilities.
4. Describe the business structures of sport organizations.
5. Identify the basic tools of financial management.
6. Recognize the basic elements of financial statements for sport organizations.
7. Identify the various professional and career opportunities in the sport industry that are related to economics and financial management.

Sport is one of the most diverse industries in the business world. It is composed of subindustries such as professional sports, collegiate athletics, facility management, health and fitness, and sporting goods. This diversity increases the difficulty of measuring the overall economic size of the industry. For example, should the sale of backpacking equipment be considered sport spending? Should the money that General Motors spends to be an official Olympic Games sponsor be considered sport spending?

One unfortunate result of the lack of an exact definition of the sport industry is that few attempts have been made to measure the economic size of the industry. Meek (1997) estimated that the cumulative spending on sport-related goods and services in the United States was $152 billion USD in 1995. Based on this estimate, sport was the 11th largest industry in the United States, larger than both the insurance and legal services industries (Meek). *Street & Smith's SportsBusiness Journal* estimated that the size of the sport industry was approximately $212.53 billion USD in 1997, with an annual growth rate of 9.9% (Broughton, Lee, & Nethery, 1999). Although the US Department of Commerce does not estimate the overall size of the sport industry, it does provide some financial information on the size of specific sectors within the sport industry (see table 12.1). For example, in 2002 approximately $1.73 billion USD was spent at skiing facilities such as Vail Mountain in Colorado and Killington Ski Area in Vermont. The skiing industry also employed over 63,000 full-time workers (US Census Bureau, 2005).

Although the actual dollar amount that can be attributed to the sport industry might be debatable, all the estimates make it clear that sport contributes a great deal to the US and global economies. Sport

Table 12.1

Economic Activity of Selected Sport Industry Sectors

Sport industry subsector	2002 sales level (USD)	2001 full-time employees
Skiing facilities	$1.73 billion	63,900
Golf courses and country clubs	$16.74 billion	295,100
Fitness and recreational sport facilities	$15.08 billion	399,400
Professional sport teams and clubs	$12.62 billion	40,100
Racetracks (horse and dog)	$5.53 billion	45,200
Agents and managers for artists, athletes, and public figures	$3.67 billion	16,200

Source: U.S. Census Bureau, Statistical Abstract of the United States: 2004-2005.

and recreation produce enormous sums in sales and employ hundreds of thousands of workers. In addition, the sport industry has experienced significant growth in recent years, which has increased its importance within the US economy (Mahony & Howard, 2001).

Recognition of all this growth and expansion leads us to a discussion of the economic and financial issues related to the sport industry. This chapter will present basic principles of economics and financial management, address their relationship to the sport industry, and discuss career opportunities related to the financial management of the sport industry.

CURRENT FINANCIAL SITUATION OF US PROFESSIONAL SPORT

One segment of the sport industry that has seen tremendous growth over the past decade is professional sport. For example, the National Football League (NFL) in 2004 had operating revenues in excess of $5.3 billion USD, and the league's teams had an overall operating income of about $851 million USD (Ozanian, 2005a). Throughout the last decade, major professional men's sport leagues have seen their revenues increase over 10% annually. Despite this growth in revenue, there are economic problems.

For example, Major League Baseball has seen a widening gap between the high- and low-revenue teams. In 2004 *Forbes Magazine* estimated that the New York Yankees generated over $260 million USD, making them the highest revenue team in MLB. The same year, the Montreal Expos ranked last in revenue with only $80 million USD (Ozanian, 2005b). This imbalance is an economic concern because all teams, regardless of revenue, compete for the same players. The current revenue disparity makes it difficult for teams who have older stadia or are located in small markets, such as the Expos, to acquire the best players and be competitive on the field. The financial problems became so acute for the Expos that the team was relocated to Washington, DC, before the 2005 season. In the long run, this disparity might lead to a decrease in overall fan interest in Major League Baseball, particularly for fans of teams that are consistently poor.

To try to avoid this problem, most professional leagues attempt to equalize the differences in team revenues through revenue sharing. For example, all of the traditional four major men's leagues (National Basketball Association, National Hockey League, Major League Baseball, and National Football League) share revenue from national television rights fees and merchandise sales. Therefore, although a team such as the New York Giants might be more popular than the Cincinnati Bengals, both receive the same amount of money from the NFL's $2.2 billion USD annual television deals, the league's largest single source of revenues. Revenue sharing equalizes team revenues and allows teams in smaller markets (e.g., the Green Bay Packers) to compete financially with the big-market teams. This equalization is important for professional sports leagues. As you learned in chapter 5, professional teams within a single league both compete and cooperate. Although their teams attempt to beat

1960s

▷**1966**—Naming rights—Busch Memorial Stadium, St. Louis

1970s

▷**1971**—NFL New England Patriots Stadium changed to Schaefer Field in $150,000 deal with Schaefer Brewing Company

▷**1973**—Buffalo Bills Stadium changed to Rich Stadium in $1.5 million deal with Rich Foods

1980s

▷**1980s**—Sport licensed products become big sellers

1990s

▷**1990s**—Approximately 170 new pro sport teams and 13 new leagues form during decade of US economic expansion each other on the field, team managers must cooperate to ensure financial success for all. If some teams struggle financially, the entire league could decline.

As you might have already noticed, professional men's sport leagues rely heavily on the media. For example, teams in the NFL generate more money from their national and local media deals than they do from gate receipts. Table 12.2 shows the amount of money that some professional leagues and college events generate from media rights. An interesting facet of these media deals is the financial connection between media companies such as Time Warner, News Corporation, and Chicago's Tribune Corporation and professional sport. For example, the Tribune Corporation owns the Chicago Cubs and WGN, a national cable network. Therefore, when the Cubs negotiate their local television rights deal with WGN, they are signing a contract with a fellow corporate subsidiary. Currently, individuals or corporations involved in the media industry own teams such as the Cubs, Atlanta Braves, and Boston Red Sox. Another trend in major professional men's sport leagues is the development of local sport networks by team owners. For example, the New York Yankees, in conjunction with the New Jersey Nets, started the YES Network in 2002 (*About YES*, 2005). By starting their own network the Yankees no longer generate local rights fees, but they profit from the operation of the television outlet. The YES Network has been lucrative for Yankees owner George Steinbrenner over the last several years.

Despite the fact that most major professional men's sport leagues have seen media and other revenue sources grow substantially over the past

Learning Activity

TV and naming rights are important revenue sources for sport teams and leagues.

- When was the first naming rights deal signed?
- When were the first national TV rights deal signed? What was the dollar amount and length of that contract?
- How has the TV or naming rights industry grown since that first deal (size and scope of deals)?
- Select one of the following organizations (NCAA, NFL, NBA, NHL, MLB) and examine the history of its TV rights deals. Have the value of these TV rights deals continued to escalate? Why do you think that this has occurred?
- Select five of your favorite sport venues and trace the history of the naming rights for that venue (length and dollar amount of contract). Has the value of these naming rights deals continued to increase? In your opinion, will they continue to increase in value?
- Compare the current naming rights deals of these five venues. Why are they so different?

Table 12.2

Sport Television Rights Deals

Property	Network(s)	Annual average (USD)	Length
NFL	CBS, Fox, ABC, ESPN	$2.2 billion	1998-2006
NBA	ABC, ESPN, TNT	$766.7 million	2002-2008
MLB	Fox, ESPN	$558.5 million	2001-2006
NHL*	OLN, NBC	$69 million	2006-2008
NASCAR	NBC, TBS, Fox, FSN	$400 million	2001-2008
NCAA Men's Basketball Tournament	CBS	$545 million	2003-2013
Bowl Championship Series	ABC	$100 million	2002-2006

*The NHL has a three-year, $200 million USD deal with OLN. NBC and the NHL have a revenue-sharing deal in which the NHL and NBC split advertising revenues from the game telecasts, but there are no guaranteed rights fees.

Sources: Street & Smith's SportsBusiness Journal, By the numbers, 2004: The authoritative annual research guide & fact book, vol. 6, number 36; and Bernstein, A. (2005, August 22). NHL rights put OLN in big leagues. Street & Smith's SportsBusiness Journal, page 1.

2000s

- **2001**—Alex Rodriguez signs 10-year, $252 million USD contract with Texas Rangers
- **2002**—YES Network, joint venture between Yankees and Nets, established
- **2003**—East Tennessee State University eliminates football program
- **2003**—CBS signs TV contract for men's NCAA basketball championship for over $500 million USD per year
- **2005**—Montreal Expos relocate to Washington, DC; renamed the Nationals
- **2005**—MLB salary average reaches $2.6 million USD, up from $1.07 million in 1995
- **2005**—Super Bowl ads cost $2.4 million for 30 seconds

decade, this increase has not guaranteed overall profitability. Note that both revenues and costs determine the profits of a business. The following equation can be used to calculate the profit level for a sport organization:

Profit = Total revenues – Total costs

Thus, MLB has seen tremendous growth in revenues over the past decade, but owners still claim to be losing money. They base this claim on cost increases in areas such as team payroll, travel expenses, and coaching and staff salaries. In December 2001 Commissioner Bud Selig released financial information for the league showing that the 30 teams combined lost $232 million USD in the 2001 season (*2001 MLB profits and losses*, 2001). These data are the most current financial information available to the public about the overall finances of MLB. More recently, the owners in the National Hockey League claimed that they lost over $270 million USD during the 2002-2003 season (Bernstein, 2004).

Although many have questioned the accuracy of these numbers, some teams in major professional sport leagues are clearly not profitable because revenue growth has not kept up with the large increases in team operating costs. Specifically, team owners have been unable to control their spending on players. The average player salary in Major League Baseball was over $2.6 million USD for the 2005 season (*2005 Salaries*, 2005). In comparison, the average player salary just 10 years earlier in 1995 was $1.07 million USD (*MLB News*, 2005). The most noteworthy salary is probably that of Alex Rodriguez, the shortstop for the New York Yankees who originally signed his current contract with the Texas Rangers. Texas' owner, Tom Hicks, signed Rodriguez to a 10-year, $252 million USD contract beginning with the 2001 season. At $25 million USD per year, Rodriguez's salary is almost as much as the total payroll of teams such as the Washington Nationals and Kansas City Royals.

As you learned in chapter 5, NHL team owners have also had difficulty controlling player salaries. As stated earlier, this problem has led to substantial losses for teams that have not been able to increase their revenues. The situation in the NHL became a crisis in the fall of 2004. In an attempt to change the economic system in the league, the owners agreed to lock out the players before the start of the 2004-2005 season. The owners and players' union were unable to agree on a new economic system, and an entire season was lost. After more than a year of negotiation, the two groups reached an accord on a new collective bargaining agreement in the summer of 2005 and the players returned to the ice for the 2005-2006 season.

In contrast, the NFL and NBA owners have been able to negotiate agreements with players through the collective bargaining process, thus helping to control salaries. For these leagues, the amount of money that owners spend on players' salaries is based on the level of revenues that they produce. Therefore, player salaries will increase only if teams are generating additional revenue. This arrangement reduces the likelihood that NBA and NFL owners will become as financially stressed as some owners in the NHL and MLB are. Team profitability is also more consistent in the former two leagues. This financial arrangement, however, does not guarantee harmony between the players and owners. Recently, the players unions in both the NFL and NBA have stated that they want a bigger piece of the revenue-sharing pie. If the players and owners in these leagues are unable to agree on how to divide the revenues, work stoppages could occur in those leagues as well.

The four leagues discussed so far have frequently had trouble deciding how to distribute the large amounts of money that they generate, but a number of other leagues are struggling just to survive. During the 1990s, around 170 new professional sport teams and 13 new leagues were created (Mahony & Howard, 2001). Because of the intense competition for sport fans, some of the new leagues have folded and others continue to lose money each year. Although there are certainly some success stories (e.g., the Arena Football League), creating a new sport league is challenging and those involved must be prepared to sustain their investment over the long term. These leagues face challenges from the more established leagues and each other, as well as the large number of popular individual sports (e.g., golf, tennis).

CURRENT FINANCIAL SITUATION IN US COLLEGE ATHLETICS

Rising costs are also an important issue in collegiate athletics. Most collegiate athletics programs, even at the Division I level, do not produce enough revenue to cover their costs. A study of the finances in collegiate athletics for the 2002-2003 academic year found that only 75% of Division I-A athletics departments produced revenues that exceeded costs, and in many cases this profit occurred only because the university provided institutional resources

Micky Arison, owner of the Miami Heat since 1995, at the courtside seat from which he watches all home games. In 2005 Mr. Arison was elected chair of the NBA's board of governors and as such is involved with negotiations for everything from fees for television rights to labor issues and global expansion.

Courtesy of Paul M. Pedersen.

to the athletics department. Only 40% of Division I-A athletics departments reported that their revenues would be greater than their expenses if they didn't receive university support (Fulks, 2005). In addition, the percentage of schools at which costs exceed revenues is greater at the Division I-AA, II, and III levels.

Many athletics departments face a difficult financial future as costs increase in areas such as team travel, equipment, coaches' salaries, and grants-in-aid. Some colleges and universities have also seen their costs increase as they increase opportunities for women. In response to the financial pressure from rising costs in all areas of collegiate athletic spending, some athletics departments have taken measures such as the elimination of sport teams and the reduction of scholarships. For example, in the spring of 2003 East Tennessee State University eliminated their football program, which had been operating at an annual $1.1 million USD loss (*East Tennessee State*, 2003).

Rising costs have also put additional emphasis on the need to increase revenues. Athletics administrators have turned to private donations, corporate sponsorship, television, and merchandising for additional revenue. At the Division I level, athletics administrators have used television rights fees and ticket sales to help their financial situation. Within the past decade schools such as Penn State, Florida State, Virginia, and Texas A&M have expanded their football stadia to increase ticket sales revenue and meet spectator demand. The University of Michigan can generate over $4 million in ticket revenue from one home football game at 110,000-seat Michigan Stadium (Lee, 2001). But not all institutions are able to find additional revenue sources so easily. Many athletics departments are increasingly relying on student fees and other forms of institutional support to avoid large budget deficits. Even Division I-A institutions are applying this remedy, and it becomes increasingly common at lower division levels in the NCAA and at NAIA schools where other revenue sources are more limited.

The largest single source of revenue in collegiate athletics is the annual men's basketball championship. In 2003 CBS began paying the NCAA an average of over $500 million USD per year for the right to televise three weeks of men's basketball in March ("By the Numbers," 2004). The $500 million will be about 90% of the overall revenues generated by the NCAA. Division I universities are quite pleased with this new deal because over 75% of this money is distributed from the NCAA to them. The new contract provided a sizable increase over the more than $100 million USD per year received in the prior contract (NCAA, 2001). This additional revenue has aided big-time college athletics departments as they attempt to pay for their growing expenses, but most programs will likely continue to experience annual deficits.

ECONOMICS OF SPORT

The word *economics* intimidates many people. For some, it brings back memories of studying how intangible items such as widgets and utils are produced and sold. But this example is far from the whole story. Economics is one of the few academic disciplines that can be applied to almost any human action. Within the field of sport management, economics can help us understand issues such as the price paid by consumers for a pair of shorts in a sporting goods store, the escalating salaries of

Major League Baseball players, and the decision made by a high school athlete to forgo college and play professionally.

Definition of Economics

The economics of sport can be defined as the study of how people within the sport industry deal with scarcity. This statement leads to the obvious question, What is scarcity? Scarcity is present in today's world because sufficient resources are not available to meet the wants and needs of society. For example, a health club might want 200 machines available to its members. Unfortunately, because of the scarce amount of resources available to club management, the club might be able to provide only 50 machines. Economics helps determine how the health club management will decide to distribute its scarce resources, not only on machines but also on staff salaries, rent, utilities, and office supplies.

economics of sport—The study of how people within the sport industry deal with scarcity.

scarcity—The basic economic problem facing all societies. A product is considered scarce if people want more of the product than is freely available for consumption.

Scarcity is an important issue in sport management because all managers encounter it. Managers have a maximum quantity of resources available for their use. Even the ultrarich New York Yankees have a limited amount of resources that they are willing to devote to players' salaries. The most successful managers are those who make the best use of these limited resources. Although the fact that the Yankees have the most resources gives them a greater probability of winning the World Series, it does not guarantee a championship. Indeed, the team has not won the World Series since 2000. Their management must make wise decisions about how to allocate these resources most efficiently to be successful.

The limited resources available to managers are used to produce goods and services that are then sold to consumers. Goods and services are exchanged through the economic interaction of individuals and organizations. For example, the purchase of a new tennis racket at a store is an example of economic interaction. One product of value, a tennis racket, is exchanged for another product of value, cash. Note that not all economic interactions involve cash. For example, a business might provide free equipment or services, such as a computer, to an event organizer in exchange for advertising space on the event T-shirt.

goods—Tangible products such as a pair of soccer cleats, a tennis racket, or a mountain bike.

services—Intangible products such as marketing advice, business consulting, and financial planning.

economic interaction—The exchange of one product of value for another product of value.

Transactions such as those just described occur in markets. A market could be an actual physical location such as a sporting goods store or a bicycle shop. It could also be an intangible idea such as a computerized stock exchange or the market for players in the WNBA. For teams such as the Washington Mystics and the Los Angeles Sparks, a market exists in which players are bought and sold, but the market is not an actual physical location. These markets are the core of economic activity. Without markets, the exchange of goods and services could not occur.

markets—Arrangements by which economic exchanges among people or businesses occur.

Economics has been traditionally separated into two areas of study: macroeconomics and microeconomics. The following sections discuss these two areas and relate them to the sport industry.

Macroeconomics and the Sport Industry

Macroeconomics can be thought of as the big picture of economics. Topics such as economic growth and recession, the unemployment rate, and interest rates all come under the study of macroeconomics. An individual sport business might focus on issues such as profits, employee costs, and the price of its product, but it should also be concerned with the macroeconomic environment in which it operates. For example, companies such as Callaway Golf, Rawlings, and New Balance, that produce sport products, might see their labor costs increase when unemployment is low. In another instance, country clubs could experience an increase in membership applications when the economy is strong. Both scenarios show how macroeconomic conditions can affect individual sport organizations.

> **macroeconomics**—The study of the problems and workings of the economy as a whole (Taylor, 2001).

The decade of the 1990s was one of robust macroeconomic growth in the United States. It was the longest economic expansion in US history. As stated earlier, the sport industry was similar to most other industries in that it saw unprecedented financial growth during the decade (Mahony & Howard, 2001). Indeed, many young sport managers had never experienced an economic recession. As the 21st century began, it became obvious that the US economy was entering a downturn. Some sport managers struggled as they faced a difficult business environment. Companies such as Starter, MVPsports.com, and Quokka Sports went out of business in part because of the downturn in the economy.

Real Gross Domestic Product (GDP)

The most important aspect of macroeconomics is the measurement of the value of goods and services produced by a country, as explained by the **real gross domestic product** (**GDP**). For the year 2004 the real GDP of the United States was approximately $10.841 trillion USD (US Bureau of Economic Analysis, 2005). As mentioned earlier, several estimates have been made of the real GDP of the sport and recreation industry. From these studies, let's assume that the real GDP of sport industry is about $250 billion USD. The sport and recreation industry composes approximately 2% of the overall real GDP for the United States. To put this in perspective, $2 out of every $100 of production is spent on sport- and recreation-related goods and services.

> **real gross domestic product (GDP)**—The value of all the goods and services newly produced in a country during some period of time, adjusted for inflation.

Real GDP fluctuates over time. Over the course of several years, these fluctuations are known as **business cycles**. Overall, an economy is usually in a state of either economic **expansion** or economic **recession**. Most economists state that real GDP must decline for at least six months for the economy to be in a state of recession. At some point an economy will switch from expansion to recession. The point at which real GDP hits its highest point before it starts to decline is known as a **peak**. On the other end, the point at which real GDP hits its lowest point and then begins to increase is the **trough**. Figure 12.1 provides a graphic representation of the business cycle.

> **business cycles**—The highs and lows in the level of economic activity over several years.
>
> **expansion**—A period of at least three consecutive quarters in which positive economic growth occurs.
>
> **recession**—A decline in economic activity, or real GDP, that lasts for at least six months.
>
> **peak**—A point at which economic activity reaches a temporary maximum level.
>
> **trough**—A point at which economic activity reaches its lowest level.

Successful sport managers must be able to determine how economic expansions and recessions will affect their individual businesses. Many retail businesses such as sporting goods stores experience declines in sales during periods of recession and vice versa during expansions. Ironically, many economists believe that some sport events experience increased ticket sales during recessions. Sport events, especially minor league sports, are fairly inexpensive. Therefore, during a recession, consumers who have less spending money than usual might attend low-cost sport events such as minor league baseball and hockey games.

Interest Rates

Interest rates are another important aspect of macroeconomics. The **interest rate** is the amount that financial institutions, such as banks, charge when they lend money. The interest rate is presented as a percentage of the amount of money loaned. For example, let's that say a business borrows $1,000 from a bank for a year at an interest rate of 5%. At the end of the year, the business will owe the bank $1,050:

$$\$1{,}000 + (1{,}000 \times .05) = \$1{,}050$$

> **interest rate**—The amount that a financial institution charges when it lends money, stated as a percentage of the amount borrowed.

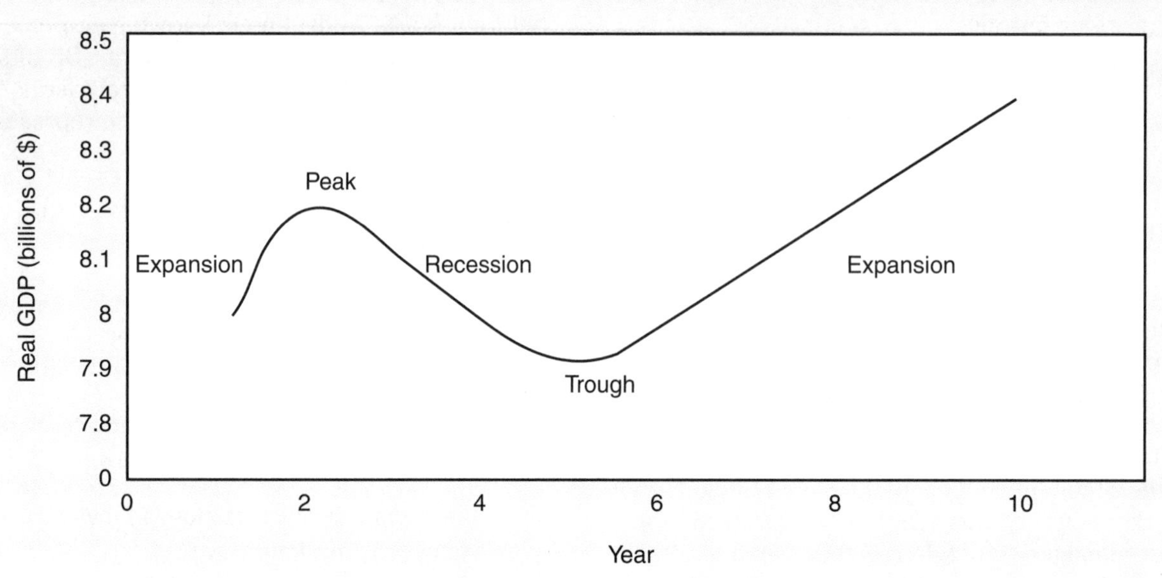

Figure 12.1 Components of the business cycle.

The interest rate is important because many sport organizations must borrow money to operate. For example, two people who want to open a new sport marketing agency might need to borrow money to start their business. They likely do not have enough money to pay for start-up costs on items such as computers, rent, utilities, and office supplies. Therefore, they will borrow money from a financial institution. The owners believe that the agency will generate sufficient revenues to pay for their operating costs as well as the annual payment to the bank for the money that they borrowed plus the interest.

A boom in new construction of sports facilities for professional sports organizations occurred in the early 21st century. Cities such as Philadelphia, Cincinnati, San Diego, Houston, and Seattle have all built new stadia or arenas since 2000. In every case, the team's ownership has borrowed money to pay for their share of the construction expenses. For the New England Patriots' Gillette Stadium, team ownership borrowed $312 million USD to pay for their share of the $350 million USD total construction cost (Kaplan, 2000). When dealing with such large sums of money, a change in the interest rate of only 1% means a difference of millions of dollars. Clearly, when borrowing funds, the general goal of the sport manager should be to obtain the lowest possible interest rate.

Inflation Rate

Another aspect of macroeconomics that sport managers should be concerned with is the inflation rate. The **inflation rate** is the percentage increase in the overall price level of goods and services over a given period, usually one year (Taylor, 2001). For example, if the current inflation rate is 4%, we would expect that a product that costs $100 today will cost approximately $104 in one year. Inflation is closely tied to the real GDP. Historically, we have seen inflation increase just before periods of economic recession and decrease during and after recessions. Because inflation measures the general trend of prices, it has a great effect on sport organizations. A minor league sport team might see its costs for items such as equipment, uniforms, and fuel rise because of inflation. To remain profitable, the franchise could raise ticket prices or attempt to attract new corporate sponsorship money. Both actions would be attempts to increase revenues. If the program does not increase its revenues, it will become less profitable as costs rise or because of inflation.

inflation rate—The percentage increase in the overall price level of goods and services over a given period, usually one year.

As you can see, macroeconomics plays an important role in the field of sport management. The field of macroeconomics is complex, however, and this section has provided only some of the basic concepts. An introductory course in macroeconomics will offer much more information.

Learning Activity

How do you believe that an economic recession would affect the following aspects of the sport industry?

- Corporate sponsorship of sport events
- Luxury sailing vessels
- Minor league professional hockey games

Microeconomics and the Sport Industry

Microeconomics is the study of the behavior of individual businesses and households (Keat & Young, 2003). It uses economic theories to explain specific industries such as sport and recreation, automobile manufacturing, and health care. Microeconomics studies variables such as price, revenues, costs, and profits for individual industries and organizations. For example, microeconomics helps to explain why you might walk into two sporting goods stores and see different prices for the same model of running shoe.

microeconomics—The study of the behavior of individual businesses and households.

Supply–Demand Model

Microeconomists often use models to explain the behavior of producers and consumers. These models are simplified descriptions of how markets operate. A market comprises two fundamental aspects: demand and supply. The supply–demand model is the most widely used and most powerful model in economics. As you will see, an accurate supply–demand model can provide information on the amount of a product or service that consumers are willing to buy at different prices, the amount that suppliers are willing to produce at different prices, and the final price that consumers will pay.

We will begin by discussing demand. Demand is the relationship between the price of a product and the amount of the product that consumers are willing to buy. The amount that consumers are willing to buy at various prices will be referred to as the quantity demanded. In general, consumers will demand less of a product as its price increases, and they will demand more of a product as its price falls. This relationship is known as the law of demand. Demand can be shown through either a table or a graph. Let's use the example of a hypothetical market for mountain bikes. Table 12.3 shows the quantity of mountain bikes demanded by consumers at different price levels. Figure 12.2 illustrates the same relationship graphically. As you can see, the demand curve is downward sloping, as will always be the case because of the law of demand.

demand—The relationship between the price of a product and the amount of the product that consumers are willing to buy.

quantity demanded—The amount of a product that consumers are willing to buy at various price levels.

law of demand—Consumers will demand less of a product as its price increases and more of a product as its price falls.

The other side of the supply–demand model is supply. Supply is the relationship between the price of a product and the amount of the product that suppliers are willing to produce and sell. The amount that suppliers are willing to produce and sell at various prices is known as the quantity supplied. Overall, suppliers will increase production as the price of the product increases and decrease production as the price falls. This relationship is referred to as the law of supply. Like demand, supply can be represented in both tabular and graphic forms. Let's continue with the mountain bike example. Table 12.4 shows the number of mountain bikes supplied by businesses in the market at various prices, and figure 12.3 presents the information in graphic form. Note that the supply curve will generally have this upward-sloping shape. Again, this relationship occurs because suppliers will increase production as the price that they can charge for their product increases.

supply—The relationship between the price of a product and the amount of the product that suppliers are willing to produce and sell.

quantity supplied—The amount that suppliers are willing to produce and sell at various price levels.

law of supply—Suppliers will increase production as the price of the product increases and decrease production as the price falls.

The last phase of the supply–demand model is to determine market equilibrium. By analyzing tables 12.3 and 12.4, you can determine that at a price of

Table 12.3

Demand Schedule for Mountain Bikes

Price	Quantity demanded
$1,400	20
$1,200	40
$1,000	60
$800	80
$600	100
$400	120
$200	140

Table 12.4

Supply Schedule for Mountain Bikes

Price	Quantity supplied
$1,400	140
$1,200	120
$1,000	100
$800	80
$600	60
$400	40
$200	20

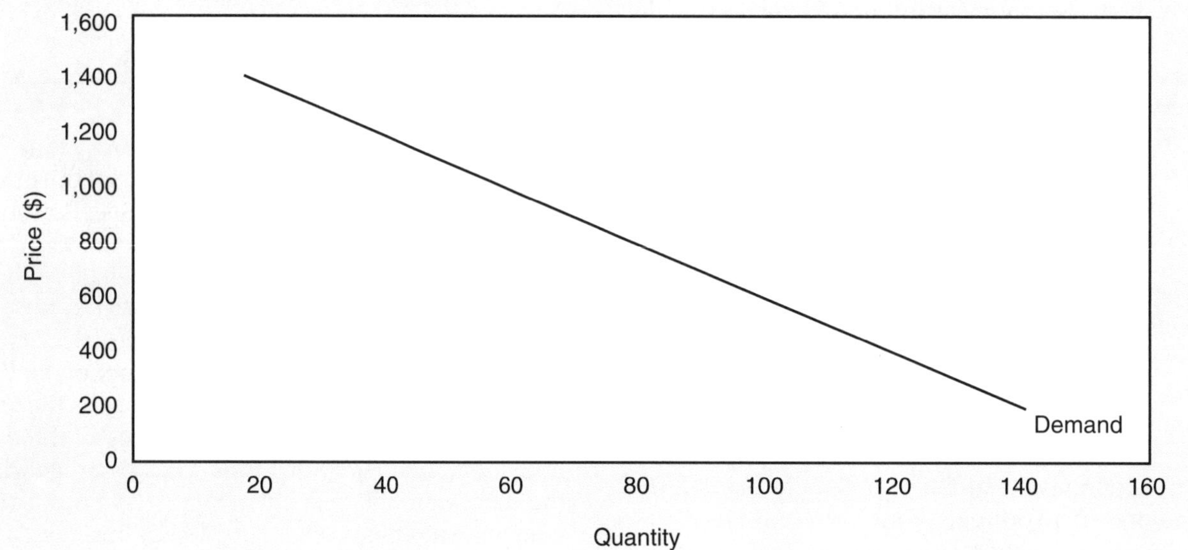

Figure 12.2 Demand for mountain bikes.

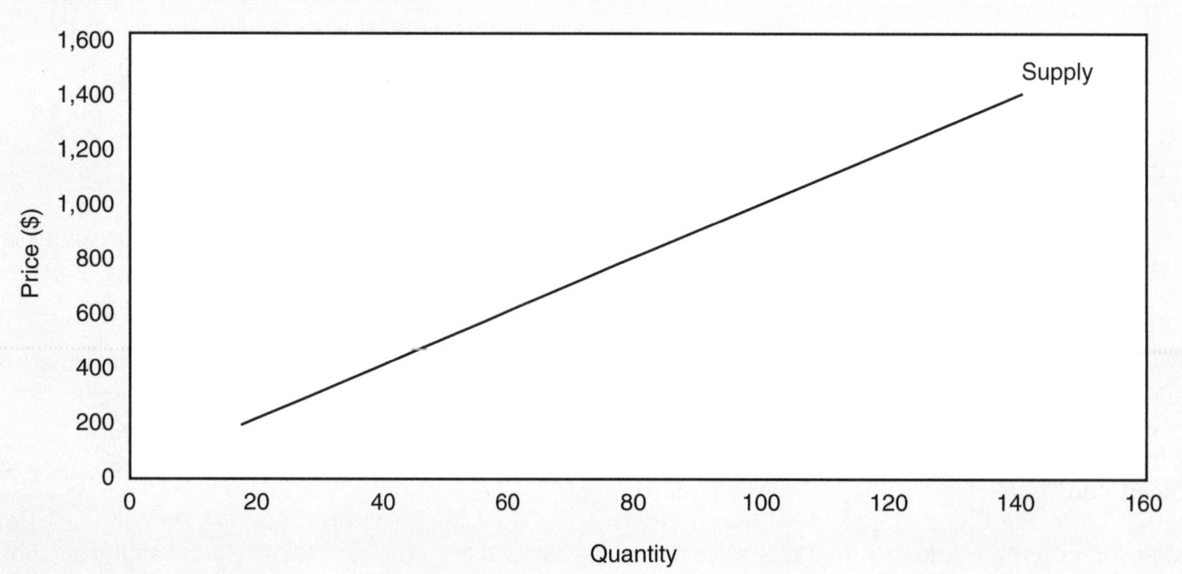

Figure 12.3 Supply of mountain bikes.

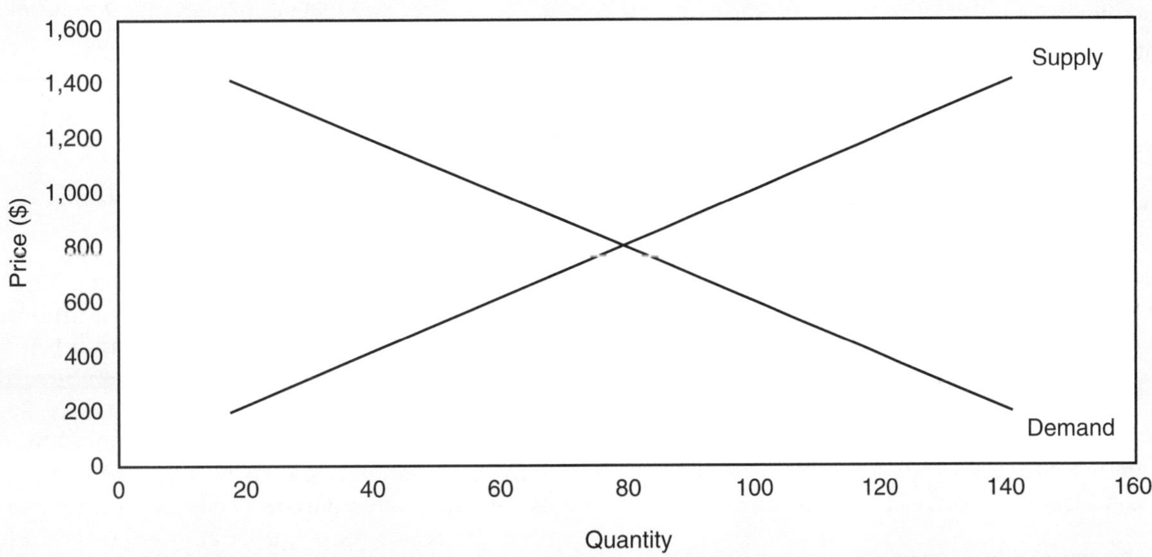

Figure 12.4 Mountain bike market.

$800 consumers are willing to buy 80 mountain bikes and suppliers are willing to produce and sell 80 mountain bikes. Thus, this point would be the market equilibrium. Graphically, the intersection of the supply and demand curves represents market equilibrium. As shown in figure 12.4, when the supply and demand curves intersect, the equilibrium price and quantity are $800 and 80 mountain bikes, respectively.

market equilibrium—The price at which the quantity demanded equals the quantity supplied.

You might wonder what would happen if the price of mountain bikes were $1,000. Notice that at a price of $1,000, consumers are willing to buy 60 mountain bikes and suppliers are willing to sell 100 mountain bikes. Under these circumstances, the market is not in equilibrium. We would refer to this situation as a market surplus because producers are willing to sell more mountain bikes than consumers are willing to buy. Conversely, a market shortage occurs when consumers are willing to buy more mountain bikes than suppliers are willing to produce and sell. This condition would occur if the price were $600.

market surplus—A price at which the quantity supplied of a product is greater than the quantity demanded.

market shortage—A price at which the quantity demanded of a product is greater than the quantity supplied.

As you can see, the supply–demand model is a powerful tool in microeconomics. The model helps us determine the quantity of a product demanded and supplied at various prices and the equilibrium price and quantity. Additionally, it can show whether the market is in a state of surplus or shortage.

Market Structures

The structure of markets is another important aspect of microeconomics. As we said earlier, all products are sold in markets. Many types of markets operate within the sport industry. For example, the market for the purchasing of stadium naming rights is much different from the market for athletic footwear. Economists attempt to group markets based on characteristics such as the number of sellers, the ability of sellers to differentiate their products from those of the competition, and the ability of producers to enter and exit the market. In general, individual markets fall into four categories: perfect competition, monopolistic competition, oligopoly, and monopoly.

Perfectly competitive and monopolistically competitive markets have the greatest number of organizations involved in the market. In addition, companies that produce and sell their product in a perfectly or monopolistically competitive market have little or no control over the price that they can charge. If one producer attempts to sell its product at a price higher than that of its competition, consumers will simply buy from the competition. Therefore, in the long run, companies in highly competitive markets will be unlikely to make large profits. In most major cities the fitness industry is a highly competitive market. Consumers have their choice of dozens of fitness centers. If one center attempts to increase its prices dramatically, consumers will simply shift to the competition.

perfectly competitive market—A market that has a large number of suppliers and consumers; *all suppliers produce an identical product,* all parties have the same information, and suppliers can easily enter and exit the market.

monopolistically competitive market—A market that has a large number of suppliers and consumers; all parties have the same information, suppliers can easily enter and exit the market, and *suppliers can differentiate their products.*

Oligopolistic markets are characterized by a small number of suppliers. A good example of an oligopoly is the sport drink industry, 90% of which is controlled by Gatorade, Powerade, and Allsport (Keat & Young, 2000). Given the low number of producers, these three companies have greater control over the prices that they charge to consumers. Thus, these companies can more easily make a profit than companies that operate in a perfectly competitive market.

oligopolistic market—A market that has a small number of suppliers and a large number of consumers.

The final type of market is a **monopoly**. A monopoly is a market in which only one company sells the product. For example, the NCAA has the market over televising collegiate basketball championships. It is the only organization that sells that product. Therefore, the television networks must compete against each other to purchase this unique product. Because of the popularity of its product, the NCAA Men's Basketball Tournament, and the monopoly power that it has, the NCAA makes over $500 million USD per year from CBS for the exclusive television rights (*CBS Gets Tourney*, 1999).

monopoly—A market that has only one supplier of the product.

Economic Impact of Sport Events and Facilities

With the growth of the sport industry, major sport events seem to take place every week. Although these events bring enjoyment to a community, they can also bring a substantial amount of economic activity. Community leaders believe that events such as the Olympic Games, the Super Bowl, and the NCAA Final Four will stimulate their local economies because of increased spending by out-of-town visitors. This spending will, in turn, increase local tax revenues and produce jobs (Howard & Crompton, 2004). Although major events such as those mentioned might produce a significant amount of money for a local economy, smaller events such as road races, soccer tournaments, and festivals can also increase economic activity.

Sport economic impact studies are estimates of the change in the net economic activity in a community that occurs because of the spending attributed to a specific sport event or facility (Turco & Kelsey, 1992). These studies are helpful in measuring the increase in revenues, tax dollars, and jobs attributable to a sport event or facility. For example, Rishe (2001) estimated that the 2001 NCAA Division I Women's Basketball Final Four had an economic impact of approximately $16 million USD on the St. Louis, Missouri, metropolitan area. In addition, the event generated about $6 million USD in labor income and $1 million USD in tax revenue. As you can see, although it might not attract the level of interest that the Super Bowl attracts, the NCAA Women's Final Four has a significant economic effect on a community. More recently, Arizona State University economists have estimated that the Tostitos Fiesta Bowl in Tempe, Arizona, has an economic impact of $153 million USD annually on the local economy (Kress & Sunnucks, 2003).

sport economic impact studies—Studies of how expenditures on sport teams, events, or facilities economically affect a specific geographic region.

Researchers conduct economic impact studies by collecting information on the spending patterns of visitors to a sport event or facility. A researcher might distribute survey instruments to event spectators to determine how much they spent on things such as hotels, rental cars, food, game tickets, and merchandise. These data are then used to determine the overall new economic activity. Most often, researchers use computer software packages such as RIMS II and IMPLAN to calculate the final economic impact.

Civic leaders often use economic impact analysis when considering the construction of new sport facilities. Most new facilities are funded in part by public money from sources such as taxes and lottery revenues. For example, $169 million USD of public funds were used in Pittsburgh to build PNC Park, the home of the Pittsburgh Pirates. Also, about two-thirds of the $456 million USD bill for the construction of PETCO Park in San Diego came from public funding (Ballparks.com, 2005). Team owners, business community members, and civic leaders defend the use of public funds by stating that the new facilities will generate economic activity, tax revenues, and jobs. Thus, economic impact studies are an invaluable tool in the effort to obtain public funding.

Experts disagree about the potential of sport events and facilities to generate economic activity. A study completed by the Maryland Department of Fiscal Services concluded that M&T Bank Stadium in Baltimore, Maryland, generates only about $33 million USD per year in economic benefits for the state of Maryland. In addition, the stadium produced only 534 additional full-time jobs for the state. In comparison with other projects in the state, the new job creation was quite small. For example, Maryland's Sunny Day Fund for economic development cost taxpayers $32.5 million USD and produced 5,200 full-time jobs (Zimmerman, 1997). Proponents of the public financing of sport facilities argue that the facilities and teams generate intrinsic benefits for a community that cannot be measured in monetary terms. Unlike the Baltimore Ravens, the Sunny Day Fund cannot produce a team that won the Super Bowl, as the Ravens did in 2001.

Because the assessment of economic impact is far from an exact science, the results are always in question. An economic impact analysis can be misrepresented in several ways. As stated earlier, economic impact should include spending only from out-of-town visitors, not the spending of local residents who attend the games. For some events, the inclusion of spending by locals can cause gross overestimation of economic impact. Spending by locals should not be included because if the event did not occur or the facility did not exist, locals would likely spend their money elsewhere in the community, such as at a restaurant or movie theater.

As you can see, economic impact analysis is an important topic in the economics of sport. Economic impact studies have received a significant amount of media attention as civic leaders, and team owners have used them to justify the use of public funding for new sport facilities. An economic impact study is only as good as the methods used to generate its results. Educated readers should always ask two questions when seeing the results of an economic impact study: (1) Who conducted the research? and (2) How was the research conducted? Unfortunately, economic impact studies can be manipulated to generate a variety of results. A proponent of a new facility might greatly overestimate the economic impact, but a critic of the same facility might underestimate the economic impact. For example, the NFL estimated the impact of the 2001 Super Bowl in Tampa to be about $250 million USD, and economist Phillip Porter estimated that the impact was around zero (Porter, 2001). Ironically, the two sides might be using the same statistical information; they are simply analyzing it in very different ways.

Learning Activity

Conduct an Internet search to find the results of at least one economic impact study conducted for a sport event or facility. Who conducted the study? How did they conduct it? What were the conclusions? What alternative conclusions exist?

OVERVIEW OF FINANCIAL MANAGEMENT

Financial management is the "application of skills in the manipulation, use, and control of funds" (Mock, Schultz, Schultz, & Shuckett, 1968). In other words, financial management is how an organization deals with money-related matters. Generally, the functions of financial management fall into two broad areas—determining what to do with current financial resources (i.e., money) and determining how to procure additional financial resources (Mock et al.). For example, in a given year the San Diego Chargers might earn a profit of $20 million USD. The question

CURRENT FINANCIAL SITUATION OF SOCCER IN JAPAN

Makoto Nakazawa, Japan

As shown in table A, the budget for the Japan Football Association (JFA), the national governing body for soccer in Japan, has been growing steadily since 1990. Much of this growth has resulted from the organization's ability to leverage the success of the J. League, the men's professional league that began in 1993, and the 2002 Korea–Japan World Cup. The J. League and the 2002 World Cup have helped raise the profile of the men's national team, which is now a main source of revenue for the JFA. The JFA relies heavily on sponsor revenue, which tends to be highest when the men's team is successful. This situation is unusual in Japan. In other Japanese sport associations, membership fees from individual players are the main source of revenue. Reliance on the success of the men's team has increased the variability of revenue for the organization, and it could face significant losses if the team's popularity declines. In fact, if the national team had not reached the 2006 World Cup in Germany, the JFA would have lost approximately $25 million USD, almost a quarter of the annual budget

In contrast, women's soccer is still considered a minor sport in Japan. This status is clear from tables B and C. Table B shows that the membership of the JFA is overwhelmingly male. In fact, for every woman who belongs, approximately 36 males belong. Table C shows that the percentage of male soccer players who belong to the JFA is more than five times greater than the percentage of female soccer players who belong. Because of the limited revenue generated by women's soccer, the JFA currently supports it with resources generated by men's soccer. People involved with the JFA see this support as an investment in the future. Developing the competitiveness and popularity of women's soccer in Japan is an important strategic priority for the JFA. Although JFA officials are optimistic that the intensive programs being implemented will soon produce results, it still is not certain whether women's soccer will be able to fund itself in the near future.

Table A

Annual Budget of JFA and J. League

	JFA	J. League	Total
1990	13	0	13
1992	20	8	28
1994	56	83	139
1999	61	63	124
2002	83	93	176
2004	110	98	208

*In $1 Million (1USD=120Yen)

Source: Japan Football Association (2005), Japan Professional Soccer League (2004).

Table B

Numbers of Members of JFA (Figures in 10,000s)

	1980	1985	1990	1995	2000	2004
Women	0.2	0.6	1.2	2.3	1.9	2.3
Men	30.7	56.1	64.8	86.1	77.6	83.9
Total	30.9	56.7	66.0	88.4	79.5	86.2

Source: Japan Football Association (2005).

Table C

Population of Soccer Participation and the Rate of Belonging to JFA

	JFA member*	Soccer participant*	Rate of belonging to JFA
Women	2.3	47.0	4.8%
Men	83.9	330.0	25.4%
Total	86.2	377.0	30.2%

*Figures are in 10,000s

Source: Japan Football Association (2005); SSF Sasakawa Sports Foundation (2004).

Since 1993, the Japan Football Association (JFA) has been cultivating female fans as part of their strategy for encouraging women to become soccer players and not just spectators. The JFA is hopeful that young spectators such as these will be the nucleus for a future Japanese professional women's soccer team.

Courtesy of Narihisa Sozu.

International Learning Activity

Find the Web sites for the soccer World Cup tournaments from 2006 to the present. How often has Japan's men's team competed in the tournament? How often has the women's team competed? Compare the success rates of the two teams. How would you assess the programs that the JFA has implemented to improve the competitiveness and popularity of the women's team from 2006 to today?

International Learning Activity

Go to the JFA Web site at www.jfa.or.jp/eng and click on News and Information. Read a current or archived article about the finances of the JFA. Summarize the article and explain its implications for the future of either men's or women's soccer in Japan.

for the financial manager is, What should the Chargers do with that money? The Chargers could use the money to sign a high-priced free agent, renovate their practice facility, or increase the salaries of current employees. They could also invest the money or distribute it among the current owners.

Even after the organization decides how to use the money, the financial manager must choose the method for distributing the money. For example, the Chargers could decide to spend the money on a free agent. But they still must structure the player's contract. The financial manager would try to determine the difference in cost between giving the player a large signing bonus up front and structuring the deal in such a way that the player would not receive most of the contract money until a few years into the future. Choosing what to spend the money on and how to spend it has significant long- and short-term implications for the team. For example, a team that loads much of the contract on to later years might face financial difficulties when they are paying the player more when he might be less valuable in generating fan interest. In addition, they could have more difficulty trading the player because of the large amount of money that they still owe him. When the Texas Rangers decided to trade Alex Rodriguez and his large contract, only a few teams were interested.

Although the example of the Chargers may generate an interesting discussion, few sport organizations have the luxury of deciding how to spend excess money. Because many sport organizations are struggling financially (Howard & Crompton, 2004), two of the key roles of the financial manager in sport are determining how much money the organization will need to meet long-term obligations and how they will procure those funds. Although most involved with sport immediately think of selling tickets or merchandise as ways to increase available funds, a number of other means have potential. For example, good investments can produce significant income for the organization. Also, some sport teams have sold stock in their organizations to raise funds, and many leagues have collected large fees from expansion teams.

Structure of Sport Businesses

To make financial decisions, the organization must understand its structure and current nature. This section will discuss how sport organizations are structured. We will also introduce the basic financial statements that people inside and outside the organization use to determine the current financial strengths and weaknesses of the sport organization.

Profit Versus Nonprofit Organizations

In the United States, one of the key distinguishing characteristics among organizations is whether they are for-profit or nonprofit. A number of examples of each within the sport industry readily come to mind. Profit-oriented organizations include sporting goods companies (e.g., Nike, Wilson, Callaway Golf), professional sport teams (e.g., Los Angeles Dodgers, New York Liberty, Manchester United, Toronto Maple Leafs, Dallas Mavericks), and some sport participation facilities (e.g., miniature golf courses, bowling alleys, health clubs). Traditionally, the primary goal in a for-profit company, as the name would suggest, is to produce a profit. Although the owners might have other purposes (e.g., helping clients improve their health, winning championships), the pursuit of profit is generally the primary goal of the owners, and it is what drives many financial decisions.

In contrast, pursuing profit as the primary goal is in violation of the laws governing nonprofit organizations. Nonprofit entities in sport include most sport teams and organizations below the professional level (e.g., college, high school, youth, USOC, NCAA), some membership clubs (e.g., YMCAs, private golf courses), and municipal sport organizations (e.g., municipal golf courses, community pools). The primary purpose in these organizations is generally to encourage sport participation among those who would not be served adequately by for-profit organizations. For example, a community pool can provide swimming opportunities for children whose families cannot afford to build a pool or buy a membership in a club with a pool. Although these nonprofit organizations cannot pursue profitability as a primary goal, they can be profitable. Nonprofit organizations may end the year with a profit, but laws govern what they can do with it. For example, a nonprofit organization that operates a ski slope cannot give a bonus to the chief executive officer based on profitability, but it can reinvest the money in new ski lifts to serve its nonprofit purpose better.

Sole Proprietorships, Partnerships, and Corporations

Although nonprofit organizations do not have owners, a distinguishing feature among profit-oriented companies is the partnership structure. Among profit-oriented companies in sport, many organizations (e.g., Nike, Churchill Downs, Boston Celtics, Callaway Golf) are corporations. Corporations have multiple owners, who own stock (i.e., an ownership share) in the company. In some cases, the stock is publicly traded, so that anyone can buy an ownership interest in the company. Some corporations, however, have only a limited number of stockholders, and the stock is not publicly available.

The main advantage of the corporate structure is that the owners' liability is limited to the amount that they invested. If you have $1 million USD invested in Nike, you cannot lose more than that amount even if Nike is sued. This advantage might not sound important, but if your net worth as an individual is $100 million USD, the protection provided by limited liability becomes extremely important. Another advantage for publicly traded corporations is that they can easily raise additional revenue by selling more stock. Owners can sell their share of the company easily, and the death of a stockholder does not have any effect on the business, which is not the case with other ownership structures. The corporate structure has disadvantages as well. Incorporating a business is costly, and corporations are essentially double taxed. When a corporation makes a profit, the profits of the business are taxed. Then, when individual owners receive their share of the earnings (through dividends), they pay tax on that amount. In addition, maintaining control of the organization is more difficult because ownership shares can be easily sold. Outside takeovers of corporations occur on occasion, and some are considered hostile takeovers.

One alternative structure is a partnership. Partnerships are organizations in which two or more people provide the resources needed for the organization to operate. Examples of partnerships include many locally owned sporting goods stores, sport agent firms, sport travel companies, and some professional teams. Some people prefer partnerships to corporations because they are less expensive and easier to form, and the owners are taxed only once. Owners in partnerships however, do not have limited liability. For example, if you invest $1 million USD in a partnership and the partnership is sued, your potential liability is not limited to $1 million. In other words, you can lose everything, even if your partner made the mistake that led to the lawsuit. If you are worth $100 million, this risk is obviously significant. Alternative structures (e.g., subchapter S corporations, limited liability partnerships) are designed to avoid the major disadvantages of both partnerships and corporations, but organizations wishing to use these structures must meet specific regulations. A discussion of these regulations is beyond the scope of this chapter.

The final general structure is a sole proprietorship. Examples of sole proprietorships in sport again include many locally owned sporting good stores and sport agent firms. A growing number of small Web-based companies also have only one owner. Sole proprietorships are similar to partnerships with a few differences. First, a sole proprietorship has only one owner instead of multiple owners. Second, the sole proprietorship is even easier to set up than a partnership. Third, although the sole proprietor still has unlimited liability, he or she is no longer liable for the actions of a co-owner. Many people do not have the resources to be a sole proprietor, so this structure is not available to everyone.

Single-Entity Structure

As is discussed throughout this book, the sport industry is unusual or unique in some areas. One example is the use of the single-entity structure in professional sports. Although professional sport teams are all members in a particular league and often share certain revenue sources and expenses, each *team* is generally operated as a separate entity. Some new sport *leagues* (e.g., MLS, WNBA, as noted in chapter 5), however, have gone with a single-entity structure. The advantage of using the single-entity structure is that the members of the fledgling league can work together more efficiently and make decisions that focus more on what is good for the league than what is good for an individual team. In addition, the single-entity structure allows the league to set limits for player salaries in a way that would be illegal if they were not using the single-entity structure. The long-term success of the single-entity structure is still unknown, but it has been increasingly popular with new leagues.

Financial Statements

Although the structure of the business will have some effect on how the business reports financial information, almost all sport organizations develop financial statements for their organizations on a regular basis. The limited scope of this chapter does not permit discussion of every detail included in financial statements and all the ways in which one might examine those statements to understand an organization's current financial situation. We will, however, provide an overview of the major financial statements and the useful information that they provide.

Balance Sheet

In figure 12.5 you will find the balance sheet for Couch Sporting Goods (CSG). In this example, Gary Couch is the sole proprietor of a sporting goods store. The balance sheet reflects the financial condition of the organization on a particular date. Although the balance sheet is generally reported at the end of a given financial period (e.g., the end of the year), a financial manager could generate a balance sheet at any time such information is needed. The balance sheet includes three categories—assets, liabilities, and owner's equity. Assets are the financial resources of the company and include both current assets and long-term assets. Current assets are generally items that are cash or expected to be converted into cash within the next year and will be used to meet current obligations.

Couch Sporting Goods Balance Sheet December 31, 2006	
Assets:	
Current assets:	
Cash	$265,000
Accounts receivable	150,000
Inventory	300,000
Prepaid expenses	50,000
Total current assets	765,000
Long-term assets:	
Land	200,000
Building	70,000
Equipment	75,000
Less: Accumulated depreciation	40,000
Long-term investments	50,000
Total long-term assets	435,000
Total assets	$1,200,000
Liabilities:	
Current liabilities:	
Accounts payable	$250,000
Notes payable	150,000
Accruals payable	100,000
Total current liabilities	500,000
Long-term liabilities:	
Notes payable	200,000
Bonds payable	200,000
Total long-term liabilities	400,000
Total liabilities	900,000
Owner's equity:	
Paid-in capital	200,000
Retained earnings	100,000
Total owner's equity	300,000
Total liabilities and owner's equity	$1,200,000

Figure 12.5 Couch Sporting Goods balance sheet.

Long-term assets are items that are not expected to be turned into cash during the next year. Some examples include CSG's land, building, and equipment. All these items are initially recorded at the price paid for them, and some are reduced as their value declines (i.e., accumulated depreciation). Long-term assets also include CSG's long-term investments, which might include investments such as government bonds that will not be converted to cash for a number of years.

Liabilities are obligations to pay money or provide goods or services to another entity. In other words, liabilities are money, goods, or services owed to others. Current liabilities are those that are due to be paid in the next year (i.e., current obligations), and long-term liabilities are those that are due sometime after the current year. Owner's equity is Gary Couch's share of the resources of the business. It includes both the money that Gary has personally put into the company (i.e., paid-in-capital) and Gary's earnings from the sporting goods store that he decided to leave in the company (i.e., retained earnings). As you can see in figure 12.5, total assets are equal to liabilities plus owner's equity. This relationship is always true. Logically, all the resources (i.e., assets) either belong to the owner (i.e., owner's equity) or are owed to another entity (i.e., liabilities).

Income Statement

In figure 12.6 you will see the income statement for Couch Sporting Goods. The income statement provides the financial results of the organization's operations over a specific period. As with the balance sheet, the income statement is often reported at the end of the year but can be generated at any point and for any period. For many people, the income statement is the most important financial statement because it presents the organization's bottom line (i.e., the net profit or net loss). Developing a complete understanding of the organization's financial situation requires thorough examination of all the financial statements. The bottom line gives the user a quick assessment of the organization and its success in achieving the primary goal of profit-oriented companies—profitability.

The income statement includes two categories—revenues and expenses. Revenue is the inflow of value to the business. Note that revenue is the inflow of value, not the inflow of cash. Therefore, revenue is recorded when the good or service is delivered to a customer, not when the cash is received for that transaction. For example, when the New York Rangers sell a ticket to a December 4 hockey game

Couch Sporting Goods
Income Statement
For the Period Ending December 31, 2006

Net sales	$1,200,000
Cost of sales	600,000
Gross profit	600,000
Operating expenses:	
Salaries	150,000
Rent	10,000
Utilities	5,000
Insurance	50,000
Advertising	10,000
Payroll taxes	20,000
Depreciation	5,000
Total operating expenses	250,000
Net operating income	350,000
Other income (expenses):	
Land sale	50,000
Interest income	2,000
Interest expense	(7,000)
Total other income (expenses)	45,000
Net taxable income	395,000
Income tax expense	100,000
Net income	$295,000

Figure 12.6 Couch Sporting Goods income statement.

in July, the revenue from that sale is not recognized until the game is played on December 4. Likewise, if a customer receives a ticket for the December 4 game with the promise that payment will be made in January, the revenue is recognized on December 4, not when the cash is received in January.

At the top of the income statement for Couch Sporting Goods (CSG) is net sales. This figure represents the amount of merchandise that CSG sold in 2006. You will note that some other revenue items (e.g., land sale, interest income) appear toward the bottom of the income statement. These items are separate from net sales because most financial analysts are more concerned with revenue from the company's main business, which is generally more useful for predicting future revenue. This point will become clearer to you when you take a class in sport finance.

The expenses are generally broken up into four categories—direct expenses (or cost of sales), operating expenses, other expenses, and income tax expense. Again, the income statement is more useful to analysts if the expenses are reported in this way. Direct expenses, or cost of sales, are expenses that can be directly matched to the main sources of revenue. For example, cost of sales for CSG is the total cost to CSG of all the items sold in 2006. Operating expenses are other normal business expenses, such as salaries, rent, and utilities, that cannot be directly matched to specific revenue items. Other expenses are those that occur outside the normal business operations for a given company. Items such as interest expense and unusual losses are often recorded here. For example, if CSG lost $10,000 in a lawsuit, the company would report that loss as an other expense. Finally, income tax expense is the amount the company pays to the Internal Revenue Service (IRS) related to the profits for the year. After subtracting all the expenses from all the revenue, the income statement provides the user with the net income (or loss) at the bottom of the statement; this number is, literally, the bottom line.

Statement of Cash Flow

The final financial statement that we are going to discuss is the statement of cash flow shown in figure 12.7. The purpose of the statement of cash flow is to show the inflow and outflow of cash during a given period. As previously discussed, the income statement does not record revenue and expenses when the cash is received or disbursed. Additionally, the income statement focuses on the items of value that are not cash in nature, such as depreciation. But financial managers must specifically monitor the inflow and outflow of cash. Too much money in cash might mean that the organization should direct more of its money to interest-earning investments or expand business operations. Too little in cash could mean that the company needs to borrow money or limit its expenditures. The statement of cash flow allows financial managers to monitor cash-related activity and make those types of decisions. Figure 12.7 shows that Couch Sporting Goods increased the cash on hand significantly in 2006. Because of the small size of this company, CSG might want to shift some of that cash to long-term investments that would earn more interest for the company or look to expand the business.

SOURCES OF REVENUES AND EXPENSES FOR SPORT ORGANIZATIONS

Organizations in the sport industry have various types of revenues and expenses, depending on the type of organization. In this section we will briefly discuss some of the business types in the sport industry and examine some sources of revenues and expenses in those businesses.

Types of Sport Organizations

As previously discussed, sport organizations can take many forms and have varied goals. Some organizations are geared toward encouraging sport participation. These include youth sport organizations, community recreation programs, and high school sports. Other organizations seek to make a profit by providing participation opportunities not offered, or not offered as well, by nonprofit organizations. These include sport organizations that rent their facilities to participants (e.g., bowling alleys, health clubs), organizations that seek to train people (e.g., personal trainers, others who provide lessons in a particular sport), and organizations that provide the equipment necessary to participate in a certain sport (i.e., sporting goods companies).

Many companies focus more on the sport spectator. These organizations include both professional sports (e.g., WNBA, NASCAR, PGA) and big-time college sports. Although these organizations receive a large portion of the money generated by sport spectators, other entities also benefit from sport spectating, including independent sport facilities that host sporting events, the sport media that bring sport events and information related to sport events to the consumer (e.g., television, radio, magazines,

Couch Sporting Goods
Statement of Cash Flow
For the Period Ending December 31, 2006

		Operating activities
Net income		**$295,000**
Other additions (increases in cash)		
Depreciation	5,000	
Increases in accounts payable	50,000	
Increases in accruals payable	20,000	
Subtractions (decreases in cash)		
Increase in accounts receivable	(25,000)	
Increase in inventory	(75,000)	
Net cash flow from operations		270,000
Long-Term Investing Activities		
Acquisition of fixed assets		(20,000)
Financing activities		
Increase in notes payable	20,000	
Increase in bonds payable	30,000	
Removal of cash by owner	(150,000)	
Net cash flow from financing		(100,000)
Net increase in cash		$150,000
Cash at the beginning of the year		115,000
Cash at the end of the year		$315,000

Figure 12.7 Couch Sporting Goods statement of cash flow.

the Internet), and companies that sell products licensed by these professional and college sport organizations.

The diversity of the sport industry produces a variety of revenue and expense sources. Some are common among these companies. For example, many sport organizations are involved in some way with product sales on the revenue side and salaries, building costs, and supplies on the expense side. The next two sections will focus on types and aspects of revenues and expenses that are unique in the sport industry.

Sources of Revenues

Some of the sources of revenue unique to sport are items related to game attendance (e.g., concessions, personal seat licenses, luxury suite rentals, booster club donations), media rights, sponsorships, and licensed merchandise. Although the ticket price is generally the major source of revenue related to attendance at events outside sport, this is not always true in sport. The total price of attendance is often much greater than the cost of the ticket. Consider the following:

1. Most sport organizations charge fans an additional fee for parking during the event.
2. Fans typically spend money on concessions at the stadium. Purchasing hot dogs, beer, soda, and so on is considered by many fans to be an important part of the game experience. Some sport teams and facilities maintain complete control over the concessions at the stadium, but many prefer to hire a company with expertise in handling concessions. In the latter case, the contract outlines how these organizations will share the profits from concessions.

3. Some professional and college sport teams now charge fans for personal seat licenses, which give them the right to buy a particular seat. For example, a fan may buy a personal seat license for 10 years for $5,000 USD. The fan must then pay for season tickets each year for the next 10 years. If the season ticket price is $500 USD per year, the fan will end up paying $10,000 USD [5,000 + (500 × 10)] over 10 years for the privilege of watching games from that particular seat.
4. A fan who wants a more exclusive setting for watching games might decide to rent a luxury suite. As with the personal seat license, the fan must still buy tickets for the game after paying the cost of renting the luxury suite. The average annual lease price for a luxury suite in major professional team sports ranges from $77,000 USD for an NHL-only arena to $199,000 USD for an NBA–NHL shared arena (Howard & Crompton, 2004).
5. College sport fans often donate money to an athletics department so that they can buy better seats or, in some cases, so that they can buy any seat. For example, a college sport fan might donate $2,000 USD each year for the right to buy two $400 USD season tickets. In this case, the fan is actually paying $2,800 USD (2,000 + 400 + 400) for the season tickets, or $1,400 USD per seat. Overall, donations to college athletics departments have increased from 5% of athletics department revenue to 17% of revenue over last 40 years (Howard & Crompton, 2004). Many athletics departments believe that this area has potential for further increases.

Because of the increasing cost of attending games—Americans spend around $12 billion USD annually for sport tickets (Howard & Crompton, 2004)—many sport spectators watch or listen to most games at home. Because of the large audience for sport beyond those who attend games, many professional sport teams make a large percentage of their revenue from media contracts. For example, the NFL signed six-year contracts with CBS and FOX in 2004 worth $8 billion USD for the television rights (Keating, 2004). In 2005 the NFL negotiated an eight-year contract with ESPN for the Monday night games worth an average of $1.1 billion USD annually and a six-year contract with NBC for Sunday night games worth $650 million USD annually ("NFL on Television," 2006). In addition, big-time college sports receive large amounts of money for their broadcasting rights. The NCAA's contract for the men's basketball tournament is at the top of the list with an 11-year contract that began in 2003 and is worth $6.2 billion USD, a 252% increase from the previous contract (Hiestand, 1999). Because the tournament takes place on only 10 days, the NCAA will receive an average of over $50 million USD per day for the broadcast rights. In many cases television networks make little or no money directly from the broadcast of sporting events. They believe, however, that broadcasting games will be beneficial because they can use the broadcasts to promote other programming and will benefit from a positive association with sport.

Corporations also seek to take advantage of positive associations with sport events, leagues, teams, and players. Spending by corporate sponsors now exceeds $10.5 billion USD in North America and $26 billion USD worldwide, with much of that spent on sport events, leagues, and teams (IEG, 2002). Companies invest heavily in sport sponsorship because they believe that association with these sport organizations will create a more positive image of their company and influence people to buy their product or service. The largest sums of money, such as the $300 million USD paid by Reliant Energy to the Houston Texans, have generally been paid for naming rights of stadia ("Stadiums and Arenas," 2002).

Likewise, corporations pay large amounts of money to athlete endorsers to promote their products and services. For example, Nike became the dominant force in the athletic footwear industry just as the career of their top endorser, Michael Jordan, was taking off. Nike, like other corporations, continues to sign large endorsement deals with athletes, including the 2003 deal with the young NBA star LeBron James. That contract was estimated to be worth over $90 million USD (Rovell, 2003).

Also looking to take advantage of the positive feelings that sport spectators have about teams and players are the sellers of licensed products. Once a rather small industry, sales of sport licensed product became big business during the 1980s (Howard & Crompton, 1995). Although most people immediately think of players' jerseys and team hats, the licensed products industry includes a variety of items, including video games, blankets, framed pictures, and sport equipment. Although most of the money from these sales goes to the producers of these products, sport organizations receive a percentage of the sales revenue.

Sources of Expenses

Two critical sources of expenses for most sport organizations are the cost of sport facilities and the cost of salaries. Sport facilities can be extremely expensive. Most sport organizations try to persuade local communities to pay for stadia, but many are finding that they have to pay at least part of the cost. This arrangement results in long-term debt payments, which can affect the financial stability of the organization for many years. Sport facilities are also costly to maintain, particularly large open-air facilities that might not be used for much of the year but must be maintained year-round. Sport facilities also tend to become obsolete fairly quickly. If an organization has to make debt payments for 30 years, it could end up making payments on a facility that it is no longer using. Some large sport facilities have been torn down before reaching their 30th birthday. Many teams that have built stadia are facing significant issues related to the size of their long-term debt (Mahony & Howard, 2001). All these factors combined mean that any organization that decides to build a new facility must proceed carefully and explore all available options. For example, some sport organizations have been able to offset some of the cost of a new facility by collecting personal seat license and rental fees for luxury suites before the opening of the stadium.

Learning Activity

In 2005 the average MLB salary had increased to $2.6 million USD, highlighted by the $252 million USD contract that Alex Rodriguez signed in 2001.

- What was the average salary for MLB in 1970?
- What significant historical events (players' attempts to change salaries and owners' attempts to control salaries) have occurred in the past 35 years to cause the dramatic change in the MLB salary structure?

Salaries in both professional and college sport have increased dramatically during the last 40 years (Howard & Crompton, 2004). Players' and coaches' salaries often make up more than 50% of the expenses in professional sport, and big-time college coaches are often by far the highest paid employees on campus. The contract that Alex Rodriguez signed with the Texas Rangers in 2001 for $25 million USD per year was still the largest as of mid-2006, but many other contracts are nearly as large. Average salaries in each of the four principal men's team sport leagues exceed $1 million USD per year. Some college coaches are also signing deals worth about $2 million USD per year, and salaries above $1 million USD are not unusual. Although many suggest that the salaries are justified because of the revenue that players and coaches generate for an organization, some have questioned this assumption. Zimbalist (1999) suggested that even the best college coaches are worth less than $200,000 USD extra per year, and it is hard to explain how one player is capable of generating an additional $25 million USD per year. Therefore, although profits are important to these organizations, some of these salaries are not related to the bottom line. Some organizations might pay more than they can afford because the owner or university official cares more about winning than about profits. The strong desire to win has probably led many sport organizations to make unwise financial decisions.

Learning Activity

Pick three sport organizations. Use sources such as Web sites to identify as many sources of expenses and revenues as possible for each. Compare and contrast the revenues and expenses for the three organizations.

CAREERS IN FINANCIAL MANAGEMENT FOR SPORT ORGANIZATIONS

An increasing variety of jobs relate to financial management in sport. In the past, financial management jobs in sport were generally not complicated. Many organizations had business managers who were basically bookkeepers. They recorded receipts and distributions of money and made sure that the organizations' financial records were in order. Although these jobs still exist, many jobs today require far more sophisticated financial management skills. For example, the Cleveland Indians' decision to issue public stock required sophisticated financial skills that the typical bookkeeper would not possess. Likewise, negotiation of a player's contract requires both the team and the player to hire representatives who have a strong understanding of financial management. As the sport industry becomes more sophisticated at all levels, the need for people with sophisticated financial skills will become increasingly important.

A number of jobs are available for people who are interested and have ability in the area of financial management. Some of the jobs that require financial management skills include ticket or box office manager, staff accountant, and athletics business manager. Because sophisticated financial management skills are needed for some activities, many professional teams and other large for-profit sport organizations have people with such skills in positions of assistant general manager or vice president for financial operations. This arrangement is particularly common if the general manager or president does not possess the financial management skills necessary to make complicated financial decisions. To help them in making particularly complicated financial decisions, some sport organizations hire outside consulting firms. A number of companies provide such advice, and some, including many of the major accounting firms, have people who specialize in sport consulting.

As a student of sport management, you must understand that the skills needed for many of these jobs, particularly those that require highly sophisticated financial skills, require the student to take coursework beyond that required for a typical undergraduate degree in sport management. One course in sport finance will not prepare you to handle a public stock offering.

Learning Activity

Interview two people involved with financial management in sport organizations. Determine their educational background, experience, competencies, and current job responsibilities. Write a one-page paper about each, describing their career paths.

JOB OPPORTUNITIES

Associate Director, Athletics and Finance

Bachelor's degree in accounting, business administration, finance, or related field required, with five to eight years of experience in managing a complex accounting operation. Advanced degree preferred. Previous significant experience in budgeting and expense analysis required, as are strong interpersonal, supervisory, written, and oral communication skills, as well as computer skills, including Excel®, database management, and word processing. Certified public accountant highly preferred.

Athletic Ticket Manager

Duties: Administer all aspects of the athletic ticket office; manage and supervise ticket office staff; design ticket applications; coordinate sales and distribution; assign seats; maintain a system of internal controls to ensure that accounting and auditing procedures are followed; maintain computer ticketing system; compile game reports; and maintain cash flow. Qualifications: Experience in ticket office procedures, knowledge of basic accounting principles, demonstrated management skills, and excellent interpersonal skills. Bachelor's degree preferred with experience in a college sport arena. Willingness to work extended days, weekends, and holidays.

Accounting Manager

Local entertainment group seeks an individual who will be responsible for all accounting, budgeting, and reporting for the parent company. The ideal candidate will be a solution-finding, hands-on financial manager with solid accounting, diplomatic, interpersonal, and leadership skills. Past work experience in accounting and financial management of an organization or business is desired. A bachelor's degree in accounting, finance, or business is a minimum requirement.

Accountant

This position is responsible for maintaining some accounting and all accounts receivable requirements for an NBA team. Essential duties and responsibilities include the following: Assist in the preparation of monthly preliminary internal financial records. Assist in the preparation and monthly monitoring of the annual budget, including variance analysis, monthly forecasting for revenue accounts, and some expense accounts. Support accounts payable with coding accruals, journal entries, and assessment of sales and use tax. Prepare game audit reconciliations. Prepare ticket tests for home games. Assist with monitoring cash flow. Assist senior accountant with various ad-hoc projects. Prepare timely invoicing of sponsorship deals, broadcast contracts, executive suite contracts, and other miscellaneous accounts. Record deposits. Make collection calls. Prepare cash reconciliations for ticket system. Prepare monthly ticket accounts receivable report. The successful candidate will have two or more years of accounting and accounts receivable experience, excellent attention to detail and organizational skills, extensive computer knowledge, including Excel®, and ability to work in a high-pressure environment with strict deadlines. We are looking for a team player with a customer service focus.

SUMMARY

This chapter has introduced the basic concepts of economics and finance. Sport economics is the study of how people within the sport industry deal with scarcity. Ideas such as supply, demand, and price equilibrium are important for sport businesses such as professional teams, sporting goods manufacturers, and sport facility operators. Additionally, sport managers must understand the different types of economic markets such as perfect competition, monopolistic competition, oligopoly, and monopoly.

Financial management is the application of skills in the manipulation, use, and control of funds. Students need to have a thorough of understanding of financial information available through financial statements. Balance sheets, income statements, and statements of cash flow contain a plethora of data that are vital to the successful management of a sport organization. Lastly, students must have knowledge of the different types of revenues and costs that are present for sport organizations.

Table 12.5

Supply and Demand for Basketballs

Price	Quantity demanded	Quantity supplied
$50	30	180
$40	60	160
$30	90	140
$20	120	120
$10	150	80
$5	180	20

Review Questions

1. Describe the difference between macroeconomics and microeconomics.
2. What is an interest rate? Why is the interest rate important to owners of a sport organization who are in the process of getting started?
3. What are the four types of market structures? Provide sport examples of each.
4. Explain the meaning of economic impact.
5. Construct supply and demand curves from table 12.5 to show the supply and demand for basketballs.
6. From table 12.5 determine the market equilibrium price and quantity for basketballs. What would happen if the price level were $10?
7. What are the different types of business structures in the sport industry? Give examples of each.
8. What is the main purpose of each of the financial statements?
9. What type of useful information does each financial statement provide?
10. What are the major sources of revenues and expenses in the sport industry? How are they different from or similar to revenues and expenses of nonsport organizations?
11. What types of positions are available in financial management in the sport industry? How are they similar and different?

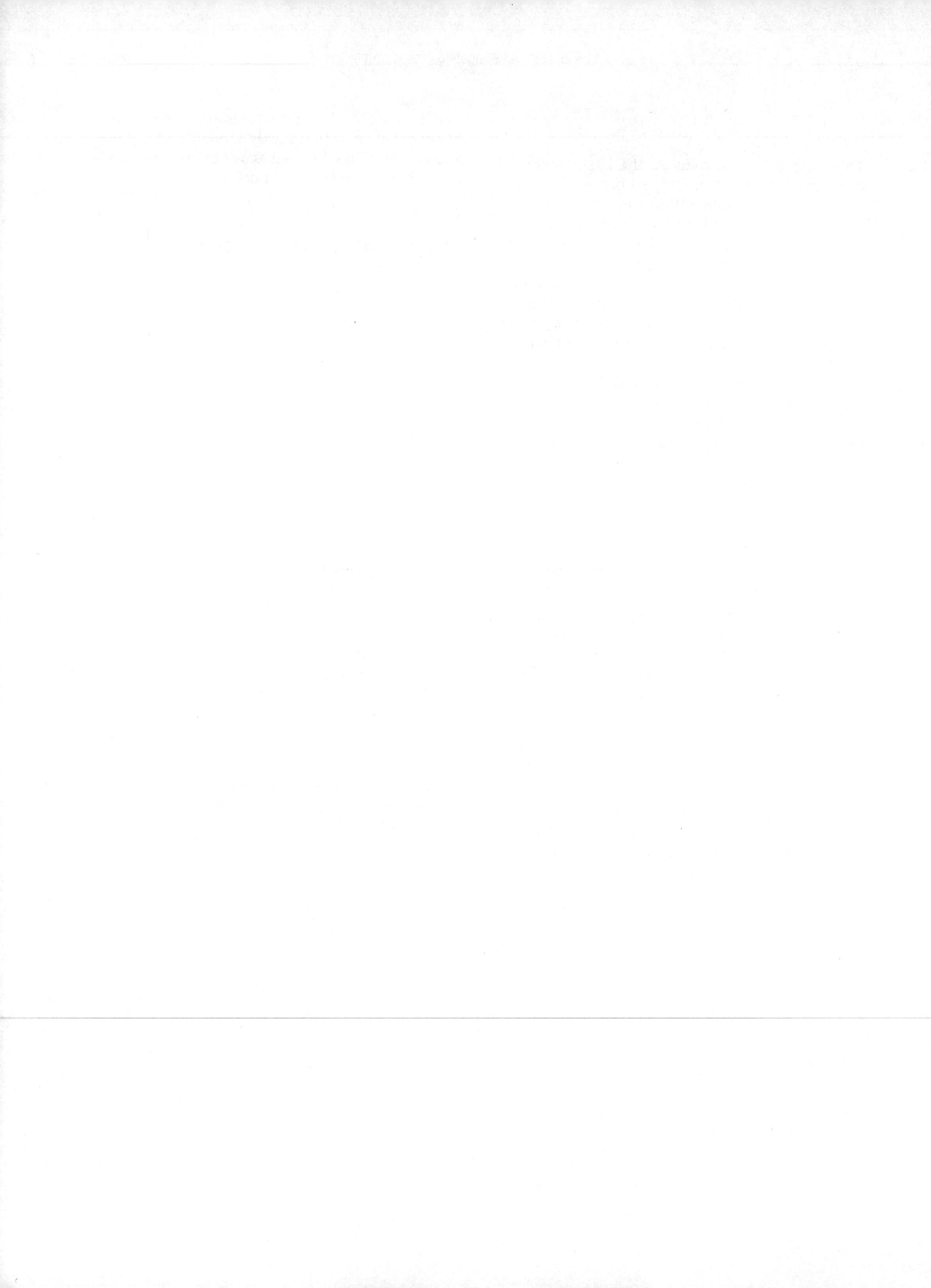

Sport Facility and Event Management

Robin Ammon, Jr.—Slippery Rock University ▪ **David K. Stotlar**—University of Northern Colorado

Learning Objectives

After studying this chapter, you will be able to do the following:

1. Recognize the necessary steps in managing a facility.
2. Identify the differences between public assembly facilities and those managed by private companies.
3. Discuss the similarities and differences between event and facility management.
4. Demonstrate an understanding of the procedures, principles, and current trends in planning and managing an event or facility anywhere in the world.
5. Create an organizational chart with appropriate job descriptions for event staff.
6. Explain the need for effective risk management of facilities and events.

The number of sport and entertainment facilities constructed or renovated in the United States has increased dramatically during the past 10 to 15 years. For example, during 2005 seven new minor league ballparks, four new minor league arenas, six new college baseball stadia, three new college arenas, and four college football renovation projects were completed. Estimates of total cost now approach $1.29 billion USD ("This Year," 2005). This surge in construction is by no means specific to the United States. In Russia eight major facilities are being constructed or renovated. This construction includes a new $200 million USD stadium for the national team. The Chinese have spent an estimated $2 billion (USD) developing 11 new arenas for the 2008 Summer Olympics (Staff, 2005).

Professional positions in these facilities provide students from a variety of majors, including sport management, with opportunities to work with facility operations, schedule events, oversee facility finances, equip facilities with TV and video connections, supervise maintenance and custodial services, conduct facility marketing and promotions, engage in event merchandising, and direct risk management services. The distinction between sport and entertainment has blurred to the point that sport and entertainment events are more similar than they are different. The events are similar, and the skills and competencies required to manage the facilities that host the events are comparable.

TYPES OF FACILITIES

Types of sport and entertainment facilities are as diverse as the events they host (see table 13.1).

Some facilities are designed for only one sport. Coors Field (Colorado Rockies) and Lincoln Financial Field (Philadelphia Eagles) are examples of single-purpose facilities. Golf courses and skate parks are also single-purpose facilities. Swimming pools, bowling alleys, motor sport tracks, and water parks exist for a single purpose. Other facilities are built for specialized events but might not be single-purpose facilities. For example, ice arenas can be used for instructional and recreational skating, figure skating competitions, ice hockey, and curling, but not for rugby matches.

Learning Activity

Search the Internet for the oldest venue in professional sport and the oldest venue in collegiate sport. Compare and contrast the features of these two venues with sport venues of the 21st century.

Other facilities, called multipurpose facilities, host a variety of events, such as concerts, truck pulls, motocross races, home and garden shows, and recreational vehicle shows. In addition, these facilities might be home to intercollegiate and professional sport competitions. Originally, these types of events were held in large outdoor stadia, going as far back as the chariot races in ancient Rome. In recent years, many stadia and large arenas, some of them covered, have been built. You might be familiar with some of these, such as PETCO Park, 2004 (San Diego, CA); Glendale Arena, 2003 (Glendale, AZ); Reliant Stadium, 2002 (Houston, TX); and the AT&T Center, 2002 (San Antonio, TX). You might not be as familiar with venues such as Allianz Arena, in Munich, Germany, which has a translucent shell that will be lit in red, blue, or white lights, depending on whether it is hosting Bayern Munich, TSV 1860 Munich, or German national team games. Croke Park, in Dublin, Ireland, contains more than 80,000 seats and until recently hosted only hurling and Gaelic football. The Daegu Stadium, located in Daegu City, Korea, is a new 70,000-seat stadium. It is the largest stadium in Korea and hosted the 2002 FIFA World Cup. Oita Stadium in Oita, Japan, is another stadium that was used for the 2002 FIFA World Cup. Called Big Eye Stadium, it uses a retractable roof mechanism composed of two Teflon membrane structures that act like giant eyelids as they close the oval opening (Kurokawa, 2001).

Movable stands and convertible floors enable these massive facilities to accommodate a variety of events, from small gatherings to large concerts, ice extravaganzas, conventions, athletic events, and festivals. Covered or not, most of these multipurpose facilities have large video screens and video monitors that provide close-ups, instant replays, and special features to entertain the spectators.

Miscellaneous and Nontraditional Facilities

Not all sport and entertainment facilities are restricted to spaces that are roofed and walled. Golf courses, ski areas, and amusement parks are classified as sport and entertainment facilities. Another mistake would be to think that all facilities contain seating areas for large numbers of spectators. A fitness center might provide activity spaces for gymnastics, a swimming pool, tennis and racquetball courts, jogging trails, a cardiovascular area, fitness machines, and free weights. Finally, in some situations, the mission of a facility is broad and will incorporate many sports or activities. For example, a multipurpose high school gymnasium might be designed for interscholastic sport practices and competition, physical education classes, school plays, and graduation ceremonies.

Table 13.1

Types of Sports Facilities

Type of facility	Example
Single purpose	Softball complex, bowling alley
Single purpose, specialized	Ice arena
Multipurpose	Large stadium (e.g., Chase Field), high school field house
Nontraditional	Skateboard park, convertible indoor–outdoor facility

1860s	1870s	1900s	1910s	
1863—First covered skating rink in Canada opens in Halifax	**1879**—The first Madison Square Garden opens (May 30)	**1906**—Centennial Field, baseball's first ballpark, opens	**1912**—Fenway Park opens **1912**—First electronic timers introduced at 1912 Stockholm Olympic Games	**1914**—Wrigley Field opens

Learning Activity

What significant changes have been made to sport venues over the past century that have affected the management of events in these facilities?

At the same time, the global appeal of high-risk activities has boosted the growth of nontraditional facilities such as indoor climbing walls and in-line skating rinks. Even the once frowned-upon activity of skateboarding now has its own parks replete with half-pipes and various jumps. Snowboarding, once banned at most ski areas, has reached mainstream popularity. Many ski areas now promote special events only for snowboarders. Amusement parks and enormous water sport parks are becoming extremely popular throughout the world. In 2001 the largest-grossing Disney Park was located in Tokyo, Japan. Chelsea FC Stadium in Stamford Bridge (London) includes hotel rooms similar to those contained in the Rodgers Centre in Toronto, Ontario. One team in England's Premier Soccer League, West Ham United, has converted its luxury suites into hotel rooms that can be rented to the public. Some international stadia have become involved in scheduling nontraditional events. The new 60,000-seat indoor stadium near Essen, Germany, has a retractable roof and a sliding field. The field was used when Germany hosted the 2006 Men's Soccer FIFA World Cup. With the field removed, an artificial lake can be set up for indoor windsurfing with the interior blowers creating various wind conditions (Cameron, 2001). Other facilities use renovation to give the illusion that an aging facility is new. For example, in 2005 over $15 million USD was spent on improvements to Turner Field, which was constructed in Atlanta in 1996. These renovations included cosmetic changes to the concession stands, a private restaurant, and one of the largest and tallest high-definition video display in any stadium in the world (Sherborne, 2005).

Mounted police were an important element of risk management at the 2006 Men's Final Four at the RCA Dome in Indianapolis. Since September 11, 2001, few would disagree with NCAA president Myles Brand's comment on security at large venue sport events: "We'd be remiss if we didn't do the very best possible job we could. . . . That is not the place to save money."

Photo courtesy of Paul M. Pedersen.

1920s

- **1923**—Yankee Stadium opens
- **1926**—Maple Leaf Stadium, for minor league baseball, opens on Toronto's Fleet Street

1930s

- **1931**—Maple Leaf Gardens opens in Toronto
- **1935**—Cincinnati Reds play seven games under the lights

1950s

- **1955**—NHL president Clarence Campbell suspends Maurice Richard, causing a riot at the Montréal Forum
- **1959**—First Daytona 500 at Daytona International Speedway

Regardless of the size or type of the facility or the kinds of events that it hosts, one factor remains consistent: To maintain a safe and enjoyable environment, managing the facility and events properly is crucial.

During the past 20 years, many sport and entertainment facilities have turned to private companies to handle their management tasks. Privatization is the term used to describe this move from public to private management. Either private owners or municipalities still own the facilities, but they outsource the management of their facilities to professionals who specialize in facility management (Steinbach, 2004).

> **privatization**—Moving the management of facilities from the public sector to private companies or organizations.
>
> **outsource**—The subcontracting of services to an independent contractor.

The trend toward privatization began with US professional team facilities and spread to intercollegiate facilities, the minor professional leagues, and sport and entertainment facilities in other countries. Some high schools and municipal recreation centers in the United States have also privatized. Often, the owners of private sport and entertainment venues and the managers of public facilities are not prepared to engage in the facility management business. In such cases, poor management can lead to less than optimal operational efficiency, and venue operations become a drain on financial resources. In public facilities, variables such as political red tape and even patronage (hiring people in repayment for political favors) have caused financial difficulties. In most of these cases, gross operating expenses exceed gross revenues, causing the facilities to operate at a deficit. As you can imagine, this situation has led to reductions in services and elimination of events, which in turn has led to privatization (Ammon, Southall, & Blair, 2004).

The future of privatization presents many possibilities, but currently the main reason that a facility would use a private management group is to create new revenue sources. Thus, the priority for a private management company is to make the facility profitable. Because most of these facility management companies operate on a national basis, they can bring negotiating leverage to bear on tenants, promoters, and concessionaires. They are, therefore, able to negotiate lucrative deals based on multiyear contracts that encompass multiple venues. The clout of a national private management firm often leads to more bookings at a lower price than a single facility can achieve. In addition, private management companies usually are able to improve tenant relations by enhancing the physical property and hiring more efficient and accountable employees.

Learning Activity

Among the larger private facility management companies are Spectacor Management Group (SMG), Clear Channel Entertainment, Global Spectrum, and Delaware North. Go to the Web sites of each of these companies and make a list of the services that they provide.

After a municipal facility has decided to use a private management company, the facility manager negotiates the contract, which normally runs from three to five years. The contract usually specifies a base management fee plus incentives. For example, SMG was chosen to manage the Idaho Center, in Nampa, Idaho. This facility contains a 10,000-seat indoor arena, an 11,000-seat outdoor amphitheater, a track and field complex, and a riding center. SMG signed a three-year deal with an annual management fee of $125,000 USD, which will be adjusted upward at an annual rate of 3%. This base fee was to cover site supervision by SMG personnel and any administrative support necessary from the corporate office. Depending on how well SMG manages the facility, the company can earn an additional $125,000 USD in incentives (Deckard, 2005d).

Although private companies currently manage a minority of college and university sport facilities, Steinbach (2004) noted, "If you are looking to test whether this might be a viable alternative, you need to talk to a management company to get a feeling for how much activity it can generate" (p. 28). Anyone considering hiring a private management company would need to be certain that the revenues generated by additional business could offset the management fees.

1960s

- **1962**—Los Angeles Dodger Stadium becomes first municipally financed stadium since Yankee Stadium
- **1965**—Houston Astrodome opens; called eighth wonder of the world
- **1966**—Astroturf developed; first used in Astrodome

1970s

- **1973**—Rehabilitation Act focuses on rights, advocacy, and protections for individuals with disabilities

1980s

- **1983**—BC Place opens in Vancouver
- **1989**—World Series earthquake causes 10-day interruption in play of A's v. Giants Series
- **1989**—Toronto Blue Jays play first game in Skydome, featuring retractable roof stadium, against Milwaukee Brewers (June 5)

Learning Activity

You are the manager of an 18,000-seat municipally owned arena in a midsize city in the central United States. The facility has not shown a profit in the past three years, and you have been asked to make a presentation to the city council describing the advantages and disadvantages of hiring a private company to manage the facility. At this meeting the council expects you to recommend which option they should choose. What will you say?

RISK MANAGEMENT

Terrorist attacks in the United States and elsewhere around the world have dramatically changed the ways in which sport and entertainment facilities are managed. We live in an unstable world, and sport and entertainment events remain inviting targets for potential terrorists. Experts estimate that an attack against the large number of spectators drawn to a major stadium event could result in 10 to 15 times the number of fatalities that the United States suffered in the terrorist attacks of September 11, 2001 (Abernethy, 2004). Thus, regardless of the type of facility involved or whether it is publicly or privately managed, one principle applies in every case: The safety of everyone in the facility is the top priority. Consequently, constructing and implementing an effective risk management plan is the most important duty of facility and event managers.

Risk management is "the control of financial and personal injury loss from sudden, unforeseen, unusual accidents and intentional torts" (see chapter 16) (Ammon et al., 2004). For example, facility managers commonly check the integrity of the air conditioning system and water supply of the venue to detect any unwanted intrusions. A well-trained staff that is knowledgeable about risk management procedures can help a facility or event manager identify other potential risks. Facility managers must be aware of risk locations unique to their facilities and be in constant communication with fans or clients who may witness undiscovered risks that exist in the sport venue.

Frequently, governmental agencies that are involved in protecting citizens from danger assist managers who are developing risk management plans. In the United States, for example, facility managers received assistance from the Department of Homeland Security, which worked closely with the International Association of Assembly Managers (IAAM) to develop a tool to assess the vulnerability of sport and entertainment facilities to terrorist attack. The Vulnerability Self-Assessment Tool (ViSAT) is an online program designed for stadium managers to integrate into their standard operating procedures. ViSAT is modeled after programs successfully used by the Transportation Security Administration to identify vulnerability at airports and other transportation facilities. ViSAT was "adapted to incorporate industry safety and security best practices for critical infrastructure to assist in establishing a security baseline for each facility" ("Launch," 2005, p. 1).

Risk management is an expensive endeavor. For example, estimates are that security costs at the Olympics were $310 million USD at the Salt Lake City Winter Olympics, $1.4 billion USD at the Athens Summer Olympics, and nearly $110 million USD at the Torino Winter Olympics (David, 2006).

Threats of terrorism are not the only problems facing the sport and entertainment industry. Many headlines point out additional concerns for venue and event management: "Man Arrested for Interfering With Monday's Boston Marathon," "Crowd Control Legislation Considered in Ohio," "SEC Fines South Carolina for Fans on Court," and the ubiquitous "Basketball Brawl Prompts NBA Reassessment." Each of these situations represents possible danger, and each reinforces the need for an effective, efficient risk management plan.

Learning Activity

Lawsuits in sport and recreation have increased over the past 10 to 15 years. List three factors that you believe could explain this increase. How could risk management plans control these factors and concomitantly eliminate some of the litigation?

Risk management techniques are continuously changing and improving, and they frequently involve technological advances. One such example is the use of bar codes on tickets. This code allows facility and event personnel to track the sale and use of a ticket. From information embedded in the code, they can determine where the ticket was originally purchased and who purchased it. The bar code also allows the transfer of e-tickets to other fans

2000s

- **2000**—Pacific Bell Park (now AT&T Park), opens: 1st privately funded MLB stadium built since 1962
- **2001**—Game between Cleveland Browns and New Orleans Saints stopped when bottles and other debris thrown on field (Cleveland, OH)
- **2002**—Reliant Stadium and SBC Center (now AT&T Center) constructed
- **2004**—25 sport facilities constructed or renovated, including PETCO Park

STADIUM DISASTERS IN SOUTH AFRICA
A Case Study of Ellis Park

Babs Surujlal, South Africa

Ellis Park Stadium, which accommodates 60,000 spectators, is one of South Africa's showcase stadiums. Part of the Ellis Park Sports Precinct, the stadium is within walking distance of the Johannesburg central business district. Although the stadium is easily accessible by road and rail, it has no formal parking for spectators, except for some areas reserved for VIPs. On event days, the streets surrounding the stadium are congested with parked vehicles.

The stadium is accredited for soccer by the South African Football Association (SAFA) and Fédération Internationale de Football Association (FIFA) and for rugby by South African Rugby Football Union (SARFU) and International Rugby Board (IRB). The stadium has a Sony Jumbotron screen, an advertisement scroll, a medical surgery unit, a media centre, internal and external public address systems, a South African Police Services office, refreshment kiosks, a ticket printing and issuing office, eight change rooms, and standby generators for emergencies. Electronic shutter gates can be controlled jointly and individually, either manually or by an electronic switch. In spite of all these mechanisms, some of the worst stadium disasters in Southern Africa have occurred at Ellis Stadium.

For example, at the 1998 football game between the Kaiser Chiefs and Orlando Pirates, an estimated 90,000 people turned up at the stadium. Spectators jammed the aisles, gangways, and passages, making the management, policing, and evacuation of spectators difficult. When access to the stadium was restricted, spectators broke down the perimeter fence, pelted the police with bottles and stones, and set fires. Police used rubber bullets to quell the disturbance.

Several problems with regard to security were identified: Security personnel had allowed spectators through the gates after corruptly receiving monies from them, keeping legitimate ticket holders from entering the stadium; thousands of unsupervised complimentary tickets had been issued; and untrained security personnel had been more interested in watching the game than in attending to their primary responsibilities.

Three years later, in April 2001, at a football match between the same two teams at the same stadium, 43 fans were crushed to death, 160 were injured, and many more were traumatised. This disaster occurred despite the fact that five security companies had been contracted for the day of the game. A disaster report noted poor forecasting of match attendance, failure to learn from the lessons of the past, overcrowding, inappropriate and inadequate response of security personnel to screams and signals from spectators, use of tear gas or a similar substance, failure to identify and designate areas of responsibility, failure to adhere to FIFA and SAFA guidelines, unacceptable spectator behaviour, corruption and dereliction of duty, inadequate public address system, unsatisfactory attitude of private security companies, poorly managed ticket sales, and failure to use the big screen.

Potential sport managers should realize that cultural differences in spectator behaviours can create risks peculiar to specific countries. In South Africa, for instance, football fans are excessively rowdy, blow trumpets (vuvuselas), and wave banners and flags. On the other hand, in English football, fans' bugles are banned. In India, fireworks are set off during cricket matches. Risk managers must be aware of differences in cultural practices and create plans that adequately address them.

through cell phones or other wireless equipment, and the print-at-home capability of the bar-coded ticket reduces the possibility that customers will present duplicate tickets.

Another example of technological advances in risk management is seen in the effort to reduce the possibility of injuries that result from the tearing down of goal posts. Some universities, such as Southern Methodist University, have invested large sums of money ($90,000 USD or more) to buy collapsible goal posts. These hydraulically lifted goal posts take five to seven seconds to collapse (Deckard, 2005b). If these posts become popular, the risky practice of tearing down goal posts at the end of an exciting football game will become a relic of the past.

FACILITY MANAGEMENT

The number of managers in a given facility, as well as their specific titles and duties, will vary depending on the size and purpose of the facility. Consequently, if you are interested in working in facility management, you will need to read job descriptions carefully to determine the precise duties associated with particular titles. In the sections to follow, we

A number of the 43 fatalities that resulted from the panic in Johannesburg's Ellis Stadium occured here, as several fans were crushed under the weight of the railing that can be seen collapsing in the middle of the photo.
Touchline Photo

International Learning Activity

Using information presented in this chapter, construct a risk management plan for the Ellis Park Stadium.

will describe several management positions and accompanying responsibilities with the caveat that specific situations might differ. In general, however, three positions that exist in most facilities are the facility director, the operations manager, and the event coordinator.

The facility director (also called the facility manager or the chief executive officer) has the overall responsibility for the entire facility. This person is mainly responsible for the creation and proper administration of the facility's standard operating procedures (SOPs). As previously noted, large private management corporations manage many of the large facilities around the world. In such an environment, facility directors are considered experts in the field of facility management and can be thought of as chief executive officers (CEOs).

The operations manager reports directly to the facility director and is responsible for all personnel, procedures, and activities related to the facility. This manager has a variety of duties, such as defining the roles, responsibilities, and authority of facility staff; recruiting personnel to coordinate the various areas of the facility; coordinating personnel, policies and procedures, and activities within the facility; evaluating facility operations; and making recommendations to the facility director.

The ***event coordinator,*** who also reports to the facility director, is responsible for managing individual events held in the facility. These events can vary from concerts to ice shows, to political rallies, to sport events. The event coordinator's responsibilities usually include transporting, assembling, erecting, and storing equipment; establishing a control system for venue and equipment logistics; recruiting, training, and supervising specific personnel, assisting in maintaining venues and equipment during the event; facilitating ticketing and ticket distribution at venue sites; and evaluating venue and equipment operations.

EVENT MANAGEMENT

Every event is a product, an outcome, and an occurrence. An event will occur in a specific year and month, on a specific date, and at a specific place.

Learning Activity

Numerous sport venues are mentioned in this chapter. Go the Web sites of at least five and make a list of the staff positions that you find there. Beside each position, identify the duties of the person in that position. If that information is not on the Web site, use information in this chapter to hazard a guess.

All preparation must be completed before the event begins. The total effort is much like the preparation of an actor who is waiting in the wings for the cue to go on stage. The pressure for perfection in event management is high. Many students in the United States think that obtaining a 90% (A) grade for academic work constitutes excellent performance. But if you are managing an event for 70,000 people and the satisfaction level is 90%, you will have 7,000 dissatisfied patrons.

Events come in many shapes and sizes, from a small corporate 5K run to the New York Marathon, from an 18-hole community golf tournament fundraiser to the Masters, from a Little League Baseball game to the World Series. Event management includes the planning, coordinating, staging, and evaluating of an event. Most events have similar components, regardless of their scope. Successful event management requires attention to each of the following areas:

- Alcohol management and training
- Box office management and ticketing
- Building maintenance
- Contract negotiations with promoters
- Crisis management
- Crowd management
- Customer service
- Evaluating the final result
- Facility rental and venue logistics
- Food service management and catering
- Hospitality and VIP protocol
- Marketing, advertising, and public relations
- Medical emergency and evacuation plans
- Merchandise, concession, and novelty sales
- Parking and traffic control
- Recruitment and training of personnel
- Risk management
- Securing proper permits and licenses
- Specific concerns for people who require assistance (e.g., wheelchair seating)

Whether the event is a small golf tournament or the NFL Super Bowl, the planning of many components is crucial to its success. The components involved depend on the nature of the event, the time, the place, and the clientele. For example, Donna, who is planning the golf tournament in the scenario on page 302, has no need for a box office or ticket management because the event will not have a seated audience. On the other hand, a ticket to an event such as the Super Bowl is a prized possession, so serious attention is paid to ticketing in the NFL. Likewise, think of the preparation of the stadium maintenance crew for an NFL playoff game. Donna doesn't have to attend to maintenance, but she does have to deal with parking logistics for the tournament. Marketing and merchandising are strategic assignments for both Donna and the NFL. Events like NCAA postseason championships present unique challenges because teams do not know where they will play until a few days before the competition.

Good recruitment policies for both volunteer and paid personnel are an important element in event management. The training of event personnel will make or break the success of the production. A good training program will pay for itself many times over by providing quality performance for the event.

Event Personnel Assignments

Establishing an organizational structure for events is one of the first steps in event management (Steadman, Neirotti, & Goldblatt, 2001). Done well, this step prevents confusion regarding tasks and responsibilities for the event (Supovitz, 2005). Because of the varied nature of events, no two events will have identical organizational structures. Many elements, however, are common across the industry of event management. Figure 13.1 shows a typical event management structure for a moderately large (2,000 to 3,000 participants) sporting event. As you study figure 13.1, you will notice that the facility director is at the top of the hierarchy, division managers are in the second tier, and the remainder are primarily coordinators. For the sake of brevity, we will discuss only six of the positions identified in figure 13.1: facility director; administrative division manager; technical services division manager; operations division manager; public relations, marketing, and hospitality division manager; special services division manager.

- The ***facility director*** is responsible for the overall administration of the event. Some of the responsibilities include developing operational and strategic plans, preparing the financial statements and budgets for approval, and anticipating

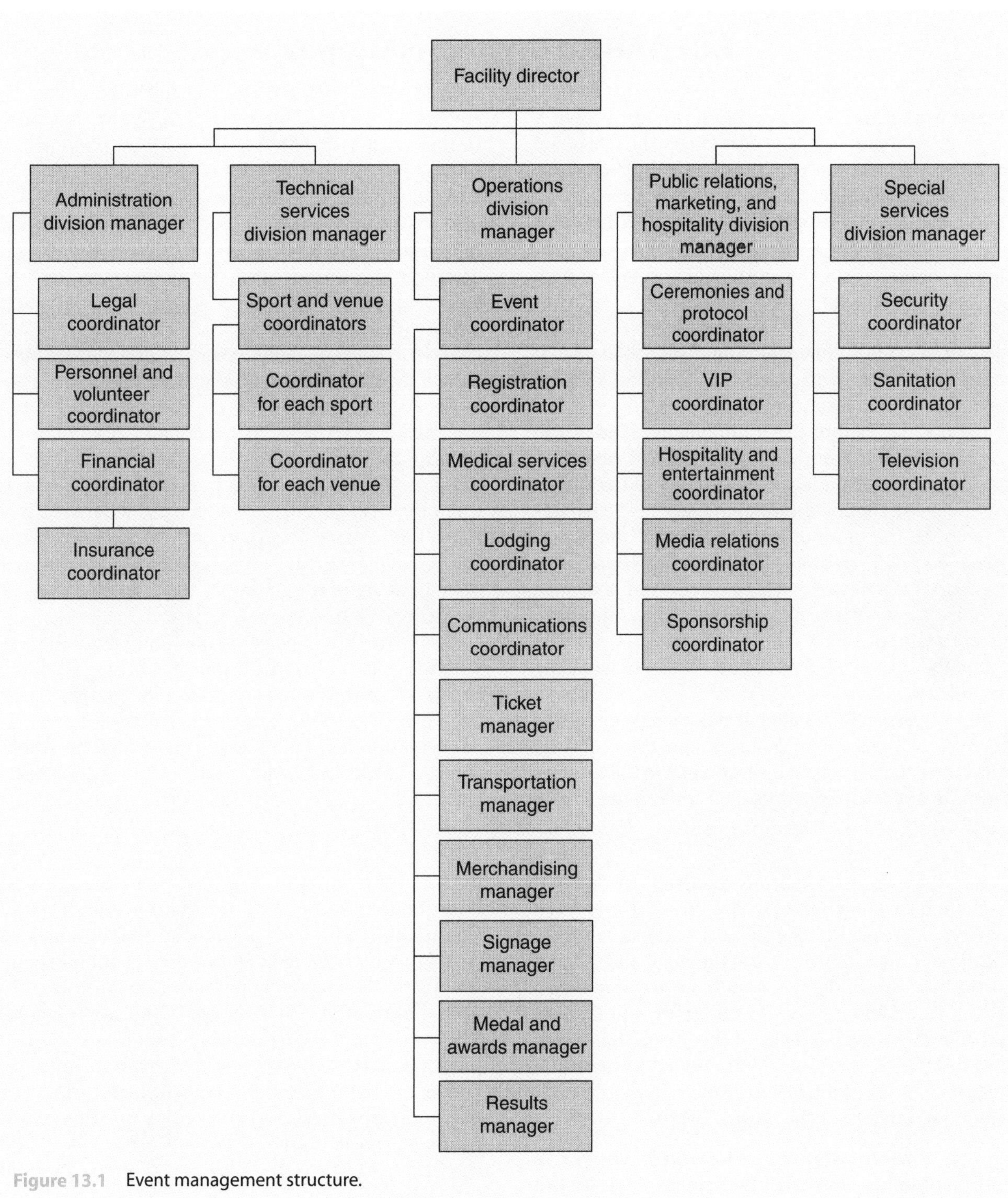

Figure 13.1 Event management structure.

problems and implementing solutions. The director is responsible for hiring and recruiting division managers and coordinators, and defining their roles, responsibilities, and authority. The director also needs to provide administrative support for division managers and coordinators in the overall planning for each area.

The facility director also must prepare an event manual with guiding principles, policies and procedures, roles and responsibilities, and so on. The manual should clearly define the roles, responsibilities, and authority of each division manager and facilitate communication among the divisions. The director assumes responsibility for organiza-

SCENARIO: Depressed Donna

Donna Clark was the activities coordinator for the Department of Parks and Recreation in a midsize town in western Pennsylvania. Following tradition, she scheduled an 18-hole golf tournament called the Spring Swing as a fund-raiser for the Parks and Recreation Department. The tournament was to be held at the local public course in late April. During the two weeks before the tournament, Donna conducted preliminary planning meetings with her staff and local volunteers. She communicated with the golf course administrators to make sure that they remembered the tournament. Donna was confident that most logistics were in place and that the golf tournament fund-raiser would be a success.

On the day before the tournament, a Friday, the groundskeeper responsible for the public course notified Donna that an underground cistern used to irrigate the course had flooded, making the number 10 tee box unplayable. The groundskeeper informed Donna that the situation occurred almost every spring. After several discussions, Donna decided to construct a temporary tee box next to the course parking lot. The head groundskeeper assured Donna that constructing the tee box before the start of the next day's tournament would be no problem.

At 4:00 p.m. on Friday, after the flooding problem had been solved, the only remaining pretournament agenda items were the delivery of the trophies and the catering setup for the tournament lunch. Eighteen teams had prepaid a $200 entry fee, which included a buffet lunch and six categories of trophy awards. Tammy Wannabe, Donna's assistant, convinced her to go home while Tammy awaited the tardy trophies.

Around 7:30 p.m., after a relaxing dinner, Donna received several disturbing phone calls. Tammy called to explain that the trophy manufacturer had production problems and that the plates on the tournament trophies read "Sing Spring" not "Spring Swing." Tammy apologized profusely but said that little could be done at this late date. No sooner had Donna hung up the phone than Mike Munch, the caterer, called. He explained that because the tee box had been moved to the parking lot, there was not enough room to set up the tent for the buffet lunch. Unfortunately, when the company that was contracted to set up the tent discovered that there wasn't enough room, they had gone home. Mike explained that he had called the subcontractors to get them to return to the course, but the company office had closed and would not open until the next morning at 10:00. The tournament was scheduled to begin at 8:00 a.m.

Donna had not anticipated these problems. She was stunned and confused. Besides everything else, the groundskeeper called again and said that the water leak on number 10 was more severe than expected and that the first 210 yards of the 380-yard par 4 was unplayable. Donna was paralyzed with indecision. What should she do?

tional duties not specifically assigned to division managers or coordinators. The director approves all overall plans, strategies, and budgets while at the same time monitoring the financial and human resources (e.g., budget, revenues and expenditures, and staff and volunteers). The director is ultimately accountable for all aspects of the event. In the scenario above, Depressed Donna would assume the responsibilities of the facility director (i.e., the chief executive officer) of the Spring Swing.

- The ***administration division manager*** is responsible for clerical activities associated with the general administration of the event office and other administrative duties as defined by the facility director. This person's responsibilities include maintaining contacts, as directed, with administration division coordinators. Administration division coordinators include legal, financial, insurance, and personnel and volunteer coordinators. This manager coordinates personnel, policies and procedures, and activities within the administration division and provides the necessary support to coordinators and committees within the division. The administration division manager communicates with other division managers while facilitating communication among all administration coordinators and among other division personnel as directed. The person in this position also supervises clerical personnel, evaluates the administration division, and makes recommendations to the facility director, to whom he or she reports directly. In the Depressed Donna scenario above, Tammy Wannabe would be the administration division manager for the golf tournament.

- The ***technical services division manager,*** who reports directly to the facility director, oversees the technical needs of the event, such as parking, lighting, staging, video presentation, sound systems, and HVAC (heating, ventilation, and air conditioning). For all sports, the technical services manager is responsible for operational, logistical, and sanctioning concerns. Operational concerns include all systems, people, and procedures necessary to provide service to customers. Logistical responsibilities include such responsibilities as making sure that the necessary equipment is available, that the court or field markings are accurate, and that the timers' table is set up. Attending to sanctioning concerns involves obtaining official approval from appropriate governing bodies. These tasks are accomplished through the development of a formal, workable structure and planning process that leads to event specifications that clearly illustrate the order of responsibility and authority. A small event such as the Spring Swing would not have a technical services division manager. Another staff member would assume responsibility for those duties.

- The ***operations division manager*** is responsible for all personnel, procedures, and activities contained in the operations division. These items include registration, lodging, medical services, communications, merchandising and concessions, transportation, signage, medals and awards, and results. The operations division manager is also responsible for clearly defining the roles, responsibilities, and authority of each coordinator and manager while recruiting personnel to coordinate each operations area. The person in this position helps coordinators and managers complete their assigned tasks and assists them in the overall planning for each area. He or she coordinates personnel, policies and procedures, and activities within the operations division and facilitates communications among all operations coordinators and managers and among other division personnel, as needed. The operations division manager communicates with other division managers while supervising personnel and approving policies. Finally, he or she evaluates the operations division and makes recommendations to the facility director, to whom he or she reports directly. In the Depressed Donna scenario, Tammy Wannabe would also be classified as the operations division manager for the Spring Swing.
- The ***public relations, marketing, and hospitality division manager*** works at the direction of the facility director in all matters pertaining to public relations, marketing, and hospitality. This person is responsible for personnel, procedures, and activities contained in this division, including, but not limited to, ceremonies and protocol, sponsorship, VIP services, media and public relations, and hospitality entertainment. He or she recruits personnel to coordinate each activity and helps staff complete assigned tasks and responsibilities. While coordinating personnel, policies, procedures, and activities within the division, this manager also assists other divisions with public relations, marketing, and hospitality needs. The public relations, marketing, and hospitality division manager develops, implements, and manages the overall event marketing plan and facilitates communications among personnel in other divisions as needed. He or she reports directly to the facility director. In addition, he or she evaluates the public relations, marketing, and hospitality division and makes recommendations. In a small event such as the Spring Swing, the operations division manager would undertake this duty as well.
- The ***special services division manager*** is responsible for all personnel, procedures, and activities associated with security, sanitation, and television. This manager develops and implements plans for each special services area. He or she recruits personnel to coordinate each special services area while clearly defining the roles, responsibilities, and authority of each coordinator and committee. The special services division manager coordinates personnel, policies and procedures, and activities within the special services division while assisting the coordinators in the overall planning for each area. This manager supports the coordinators and committees within his or her division, while also facilitating communication among special services coordinators and other divisions as needed. He or she supervises personnel, approves policies, evaluates the special services division, and makes recommendations to the facility director, to whom he or she reports directly. The Spring Swing would be a small enough event that a special services division manager would not be necessary. These tasks would become the responsibility of the operations division manager.

An effective organizational structure facilitates effective event planning. All events—from Donna's golf tournament to the Lawn Tennis Championships at Wimbledon—need effective event management plans. A management plan should include seven basic steps: scheduling, negotiating, coordinating, staging, settling with the promoter, cleaning up, and evaluating. The facility director will ultimately be responsible for developing this plan.

SCENARIO: Dynamic Donna

Donna Clark was the activities coordinator for the Department of Parks and Recreation in a midsize town in western Pennsylvania. Following the traditional pattern, she scheduled an 18-hole golf tournament called the Spring Swing as a fund-raiser for the Parks and Recreation Department. The tournament was to be held at the local public course in late April. A year earlier, when the project had been scheduled, Donna began planning the event in detail using a work order that included times, schedules, deadlines, and various committees. She had also held in-depth formal planning meetings with the course groundskeeper, during which they had discussed a variety of "what-if" scenarios and implemented alternative plans. A temporary tee box 170 yards from the green had been constructed two weeks before the tournament, turning the hole into a par 3, in case the annual spring flooding occurred. The trophies were outsourced by contract, with delivery guaranteed two weeks before the tournament. The marketing plan was successfully implemented (see chapter 9), and news releases and interviews were well received by the print and broadcast media (see chapter 11). All project personnel were well prepared and on task. Every committee coordinator performed well. After the golf tournament, Donna's team of volunteers and the course administrators evaluated the event. Donna added all comments, complaints, and suggestions for improvement to her event folder for implementation for the next year. With a great turnout and good weather, the golf tournament was a success. By the way, Donna had been working on more than this one event. The annual Fourth of July 5K road race was coming up, and she was ahead of schedule with her event planning.

Learning Activity

Compare your notes on Depressed Donna with the actions taken by Dynamic Donna. How could you use this comparison to train event management personnel?

Preevent Tasks

The major tasks to be done before the event comprise scheduling the event, negotiating the details with the organization involved, and coordinating how every aspect of the event is to be managed.

Scheduling the Event

Scheduling an event entails a reservation process in which events are planned according to the philosophy of the facility. Because most facilities maintain a profit-oriented philosophy, a facility director will try to schedule the largest possible number of events without overburdening the facility or employees. Securing and contracting one specific event or attraction is known as **booking** an event.

> **scheduling**—A reservation process for a facility's events.
>
> **booking**—Securing and contracting one specific sport or entertainment event.

Scheduling may often involve difficult decisions about what events are acceptable to the owners and management of the facility. For example, a Harley-Davidson motorcycle rally or an Ultimate Fighting competition might be considered too controversial for some constituents, or might be distasteful to owners or managers. But these types of events might produce a large profit margin from increased ticket sales and the accompanying concession and merchandise revenues. The facility builds its reputation on how its directors handle such conflicts.

Thus, the facility director's decision about booking an event becomes a balancing act. Facility directors must ask themselves, Does facility management want or need to book this event? In this context *want* relates to making money, and *need* relates to community satisfaction. In making such decisions, directors must remember that the facility has a reputation in the community; they must not let personal opinion dictate their decision about whether to book a particular event. Obviously, the event travels on to the next tour date, and the director must remain to face any criticism or controversy, which could affect future ticket sales.

Negotiating the Event

After making the decision to schedule the event, the facility director (or their representative) negotiates the terms of the contract with a representative of the event, usually the promoter. Most facilities use a **boilerplate** contract that addresses the specific terms (e.g., cost of facility, division of revenue, and so on) agreed upon by the facility and the promoter. This type of document uses standard language and a fill-in-the-blanks format (similar to most apartment leases) to describe the various clauses in the contract. Normally a prearranged percentage known as a **split** is used to divide revenue from the sale of tickets, merchandise, and sometimes concessions. These financial negotiations are a critical factor in establishing the cost of an event. If the amount is too high, additional negotiations ensue to determine which costs to adjust and which splits to modify.

> boilerplate—Generic document that uses standard language and a fill-in-the-blank format.
>
> split—A prearranged percentage used to divide various sources of revenue between the promoter and the facility.

Coordinating the Event

After completing the preliminary negotiations with the promoter and calculating the cost analysis, the event coordinator sits down and studies all aspects of the event. The event coordinator is responsible for providing specific venue and equipment needs as requested by the promoter or appropriate representatives. An event coordinator will need to transport, assemble, erect, and store equipment while establishing procedures and guidelines for the rental, purchase, storage, and transportation of venue equipment. Securing a warehouse area for equipment storage and distribution as well as establishing a control system for venue and equipment logistics (e.g., inventory management, storage, and transportation of equipment) is crucial. After completing these tasks, the event coordinator works with the facility director to recruit and hire event personnel who will assist in maintaining the venues and equipment during the event. The event coordinator then trains and supervises these personnel.

> cost analysis—An estimation of the revenue and expenses of an event.

The event coordinator designs a plan or work order for all employees to follow. The work order is the game plan for the event. It documents all requirements discussed with the promoter or other company representative. Anything not documented will be the responsibility of the event coordinator. The work order also defines the time required to do each assigned task.

As this plan develops, problems pertaining to the original contract might occur, causing the contract to be revised. The event coordinator will schedule orientation meetings with various staff to address the specific concerns of the work order such as type of seating, search policy, and alcohol policy. Risk management concerns will also need to be discussed. In a research study, 98% of facility managers identified slips and falls as the most common injury, and 95% of the facility managers mentioned that these cases were normally settled out of court (Ammon & Fried, 1998). Such issues need to be discussed beforehand in a proactive manner rather than ignored until after an accident has occurred.

> work order—A document that illustrates all requirements of the event.

One secret to successful planning is accurate plotting of time restrictions for the event. Coordinators should start with the date of the event and calculate the time needed for each step, from last-minute tasks just before the event back to the initial meeting for the event. Additional time for emergencies should be added into the work order schedule. One way to avoid running out of time and to make sure that everything gets done is to plan in reverse. Gannt charts are useful in reverse planning (Ammon et al., 2004, p. 14).

> Gannt charts—Horizontal bar charts used in project planning and management; developed in 1917 by American engineer and sociologist Henry L. Gannt.

Various preliminary planning meetings should take place with all staff members and other people whose cooperation is critical to the success of the event. In Depressed Donna's case, people such as local police and volunteers should have been consulted, informed, and involved at each step along the way. During this process, any necessary permits should be obtained, a factor that Depressed Donna neglected to consider. In addition, organizers must continually anticipate potential problems, thus avoiding surprises such as the ones that Donna faced.

Staging the Event

After much planning and anticipation, the day of the event arrives. During smaller events such as a local golf tournament, the event coordinator makes certain that items such as longest-drive and closest-to-the-pin markers are in place and that each group has received its electric carts or caddies. Finally, refreshments, award tables, and portable toilets should be properly located. For large events such as concerts and ice shows, an entire day is usually allowed for load-in and setup after the trucks carrying the equipment for the event arrive.

The USA Taekwondo Union took an interesting approach in 2005. Citing problems with past event productions, the new management team purchased a semitrailer truck, adorned it with organizational and sponsor logos, packed it with all the equipment needed for its regional qualifiers, and sent the truck on the road. The issue related to accountability. The competition directors, who were employed by the USA Taekwondo Union, now had the responsibility of making sure that all the needed equipment was delivered on time and set up properly.

At the designated hour on the day of the event, the doors or gates are opened, the crowd flows inside, and the event begins. At this point, the event coordinator discovers whether he or she was effective in planning and coordinating the many facets of staging the event, including parking, seating, alcohol policies, and crowd control.

Parking

As with every plan, the various officials involved must be allowed to provide input into the work order. With regard to parking and traffic, campus, city, county, and state law enforcement agencies should have input. The Oklahoma City bombing incident in 1995 demonstrated the need for venue managers to eliminate parking at close proximity to the facility, especially for medium- or large-sized trucks (Abernethy, 2004). Additional parking spaces might be lost because of weather (mud or large puddles of water) or special promotions such as fireworks, and limited access might cause traffic flow problems. Closed circuit television (CCTV) cameras should be located in the parking areas to identify suspicious vehicles as well as protect spectators as they walk to the venue. Providing bus and emergency access lanes will reduce the number of vehicles that can park at the event. Intersections with higher than normal accident rates must be identified, and extra officers should assist out-of-town fans through these problem areas. Posting adequate signs on major thoroughfares to direct arriving spectators also decreases potential problems. Altering the duration of signal lights during ingress and egress can assist vehicular traffic through congested areas. Notifying local residents and businesses of event-day traffic plans helps maintain positive community relations. Finally, establishing emergency routes for police, fire, and medical personnel lessens the likelihood that dangerous situations will occur.

Seating

Many facilities in the United States use reserved seats for events. This policy has not always been in place in sport stadia around the world. Standing-room areas or terraces were permitted in many European stadia until the late 1980s. In April 1989 thousands of football fans flocked to Hillsborough stadium in Sheffield to watch the FA (Football Association) Cup semifinal between Liverpool and Nottingham Forest. Too many fans were allowed into an already full terrace at one end of the stadium. In the resulting crush, 96 people were killed or received serious injuries ("On This Day," n.d.). As a result, a government report (Lord Justice Taylor's report) required reserved seats and phased out the terraces from the Premiership levels of British soccer, although standing room is still allowed in the lower divisions (Warshaw, 2004).

With a reserved ticket, a spectator is assured of a specific seat, in a specific row, in a specific section at the event. With the use of trained ushers and an effective crowd control plan, few problems occur at events with this type of seating. Other types of seating are not as easy to manage. General admission (GA) seating is a first-come, first-served process that sometimes causes fans to line up outside for hours before the facility opens, in the hope of gaining that prestigious front-row seat. Festival seating is a type of GA seating, but it is actually a misnomer because no actual seats exist. Festival seating allows spectators to crowd together standing shoulder to shoulder in open floor space. This type of seating has proved tragic in several instances. In 1991 three teenagers died in Salt Lake City at an AC/DC concert because of a crowd surge. Ironically, legislation that prohibited festival seating in Salt Lake had been passed but was not enforced. During the 2000 Roskilde Festival near Copenhagen, while Pearl Jam was playing, nine concertgoers near the front of the stage were crushed after the crowd surged (Baugus, 2002). Although promoters can sell more tickets for festival seating than by using reserved or general admission seating, it is a potentially deadly arrangement and continues to be a controversial topic in event management.

Customer Service

Tod Leiweke, CEO of the NFL's Seattle Seahawks, emphasizes that for any sport or entertainment event to be a success, facility and event managers must concentrate on three fundamentals: brand, audience, and experience. The brand is the venue (the place). The audience comprises all those people driven by a passion for the product (the event), and the experience is the relationship between the ticket buyer and the event itself (Deckard, 2005a). Customer service, guest relations, and fan services are all terms used to describe the relationship that exists between the event (or facility) management and the people who attend the event. The courtesy and attention provided by the customer service staff as well as their efficiency in finding a solution to patrons' problems reflect on the organization and will affect the success of the event (Nagy, 2001).

The customers, or guests, are the fuel that the sport and entertainment industry relies on. Without patrons there would be neither events nor the facilities to house them. But the guests who attend sport and entertainment events are products of a society that has come to expect immediate results or instant gratification. Everyone knows that most businesses must have repeat customers to be profitable. In the same way, event managers also depend on repeat customers to produce a profit. Thus, to guarantee repeat customers, event and facility managers must listen to their guests and respond effectively to their concerns. These managers must adopt a customer-centered business philosophy, because, as we all know, putting on an event without an audience is difficult (Deckard, 2004). Leiweke believes that the customer is always right. Deckard (2005a) stated, "But more important than serving one person is serving all the people" (p. 2).

Guest relations must begin at the top of the organization (owner) and permeate down through every level all the way to the part-time concessionaires and program hawkers. Each employee working at an event (or facility) must be a proponent of customer service for it to be successful. Although providing superior customer service may sound difficult, it is not impossible. Consider the ABCs of customer servive.

- **A**—the attitude of the staff. Everyone who works with customer services needs to be positive. They need to appear cheerful and helpful to the distraught patron. The staff must also be willing to demonstrate their competence, and competence comes only with training.
- **B**—the importance of being well informed. All pertinent staff must know the locations of restrooms, first-aid stations, and concession stands. The guest relations staff must be knowledgeable about facility policies such as items not allowed into the facility, locations of designated smoking areas, and the camera and refund policy for the event.
- **C**—courtesy. The spectators or fans need to be treated with respect, no matter how trivial their problems may seem. Customer service personnel must be able to recognize patrons' problems and solve them, or find someone who can solve them. The staff must listen to customers' concerns and eliminate the word *no* from their vocabulary.

Unfortunately not every event or facility has the type of customer service that the ticket-buying public seeks. Unknowledgeable and unsympathetic staffers continue to ignore various consumer problems. For example, in 2001 Nagy asked 242 fans and 33 employees of a National Hockey League team in the Midwestern United States to list their pet peeves about customer service. Some of their responses are listed in table 13.2. Perhaps you share some of these concerns and will be particularly mindful of them when you are in a position that requires you to train customer service employees.

Learning Activity

List your top three pet peeves about customer service. As a manager, how would you use your knowledge of these pet peeves in your employee training program?

Alcohol Policies

A potential liability exists if intoxicated patrons create dangerous situations for themselves and others. Some people argue that revenue generated from beer sales is worth the risk, and some facilities would find it difficult to generate a profit without beer sales. Others have determined that the increased revenue produced by selling alcohol does not outweigh the liabilities. For example, up to the end of the 2004 football season, the University of Southern California (USC) was the only Pacific-10 school that allowed the sale of alcohol at its stadium. But the problems caused by the abuse of alcohol during games prompted the university to halt the sale of alcohol at all home Trojans football games, making the alcohol ban unanimous in that league. USC's President Steven Sample stated, "I have received dozens of letters from irate Trojan fans who say they can't and they won't take their families to USC games anymore because drunken fans create a hostile and frightening environment" (Deckard, 2005c, p. 14).

During the 2001 NFL season, games in Cleveland and New Orleans were briefly suspended after fans protested game officials' calls by littering the fields with plastic beer bottles. Miller Brewing Company

Table 13.2

Selected Pet Peeves of Fans at a National Hockey League Game

Category	Sample comments
Attitude	"The employees at the concession counter seem like 'robots.' What happened to service with a smile?"
	"People who think they are too good to help anyone. People who don't smile."
	"Not greeting customer. . . . Seem annoyed that you are asking questions. No 'thank you,' etc."
	"People who say 'I don't know, that's not my job.'"
Being well-informed	"Lack of knowledge of sporting arena."
	"When a customer service employee doesn't know the answer to a question they are supposed to have knowledge of (e.g., where's a seat or a concession stand?)."
	"When purchasing single-game tickets, often the clerk has trouble determining whether a ticket is available in a certain price range."
	"When the team reduced the price of certain areas earlier in the season, the people at the ticket windows knew nothing about it."
	"Blaming the customer when there is a legitimate problem."
	"Apologize but do not ask how they can make it right for you."
	"When they don't know answers but not being willing to try to obtain the answer for you."
Courtesy	"Carrying on side conversations with other employees while assisting customers; making customers wait while employees finish side conversations."
	"No eye contact and smiling. Unfriendly interaction."
	"Impoliteness, no eye contact, not speaking up, showing no concern."
	"Smacking gum when they talk. Profanity. Talking about a person as soon as they turn and leave."
	"Rudeness . . . annoyed (acting as if you are troubling them)."
	"Wait on me when I come up to you. Do not talk to other employees or talk on the phone when I want service!"

Source: T.M. Nagy, 2001, Customer service in professional sport. *Unpublished master's project, Bowling Green State University, Bowling Green, OH.*

had introduced the plastic bottles the year before. The company found that the use of plastic bottles helped reduce spillage from cups, kept the beer from going flat, and obviously increased brand awareness (Hiestand & Woods, 2001).

Some government officials have become concerned enough to legislate dram shop laws. These statutes provide plaintiffs who have been injured by an intoxicated person with a cause of action to sue the defendant and the owners of the bar or restaurant where the defendant became drunk. An example of applying such a law occurred in a 2005 court decision that awarded $105 million USD in favor of a plaintiff who sued the concessionaire Aramark over damages sustained from an incident in 1999. The court found that during a 1999 NFL game at Giants Stadium, Aramark vendors illegally sold beers to a visibly intoxicated spectator. The spectator left the stadium and was involved in a car accident that paralyzed a two-year old girl ("Aramark Hit," 2005). That verdict was overturned by an appellate court in August 2006. The appellate court stated the trial court had allowed the plaintiffs to introduce improper testimony about the "drinking environment" at Giants Stadium. In addition, the appellate judges believed the jury should not have been allowed to compensate the plaintiff for her shortened life expectancy. The New Jersey state appeals panel has ordered a new trial (Court overturns, 2006). No matter the outcome of this case, facility managers have been warned that alcohol serving policies must be implemented and strictly followed.

Foreseeing alcohol risks and instituting measures to protect patrons from those risks is a reasonable way to reduce liability. Several strategies have been successfully employed:

- Employing crowd control techniques to limit the abuse of alcohol at facilities and events
- Erecting signs that inform patrons about a ban on bringing alcohol into the stadium and training crowd management staff at facility entrances to confiscate any alcohol beverages brought into the facility to reduce the likelihood of intoxication among the spectators
- Requiring servers and crowd control staff to be trained in TIPS or TEAM

TIPS (Training for Intervention Procedures by Servers of Alcohol)—Developed by the founding director of the National Institute on Alcoholism and Alcohol Abuse, and TEAM (Techniques for Effective Alcohol Management), a program of the National Highway Transportation Safety Administration, are nationally known alcohol education programs that most U.S. sport and entertainment facility managers use to train their staffs. In Ontario, Canada, the program that parallels TIPS is called SmartServe. "Smart Serve Ontario is a nonprofit organization dedicated to developing and delivering responsible server training to all individuals who serve alcohol beverages or work where alcohol beverages are served in the province of Ontario" (www.smartserve.org/home.asp). A similar program in British Columbia is called Serving It Right (www.servingitright.com).

- Specifying that concessionaires should check IDs thoroughly and place wristbands on those who are of legal age, enforce a two-beer limit on any fan at one time, and reduce the size of servings to 12 ounces (350 milliliters)
- Eliminating beer sales at a specific point during the event and creating a designated driver program for fans who drink too much (Ammon et al., 2004)

The practice of serving alcohol at sporting events is controversial, but Miller and Anheuser-Busch are two of the five largest spending sport advertisers on television. Moreover, drinking beer at sport events has been occurring for over 100 years. It has become a part of the culture of sport spectatorship, and many spectators consider it a right. As Carmen Policy, the president of the Cleveland Browns, stated after the beer-bottle-throwing incident during the 2001 NFL season at Cleveland Browns Stadium, "I think beer is a part of sports, just like it is part of family picnics" (Hiestand & Woods, 2001, p. 3A). Therefore, although the controversy continues, alcohol probably will continue to be a part of many sporting events, and facilities managers must continue to devise tactics to reduce the risks created by alcohol consumption.

Crowd Management

A facility or event manager needs a crowd management plan even when managing an event with a small number of spectators. Whether employed at a small high school basketball game, a local YMCA, or the NCAA Division I Softball Championships, every facility or event manager should have a crowd management plan.

First, facility and event managers must try to provide a safe and enjoyable environment. The crowd control plan must be an integral element of a larger risk management plan. The components of such a plan are staff training, emergency planning, ensuring accessibility for spectators with disabilities, procedures for ejecting disruptive people, an efficient communication system, and effective signage.

- ***Staff training***. Training competent staff to carry out the plan is the first component of an effective crowd control plan. Management at some facilities chooses to use its own staff to conduct crowd control duties. This approach is known as in-house security or crowd control. Management at other facilities contracts out, or outsources, crowd control services to independent contractors.

in-house—Services provided by the facility staff.

- ***Emergency planning***. An emergency plan is the second component of an effective crowd control plan. The intent of an emergency plan is to ensure that minor incidents do not become major incidents and that major incidents do not become fatal. The plan must have an anticipatory and a reactionary component. The anticipatory component pertains to inspections and preventive maintenance, and the reactionary component pertains to the procedures implemented after an emergency occurs. Emergencies take many forms, such as medical problems (life-threatening and minor injuries), severe weather (lightning, tornadoes), natural disasters (earthquakes, floods), fire, bomb threats, power loss, and, in today's society, terrorist activities. Managers must not only design and implement an emergency plan but also practice it, because the courts will ask for documentation about when the plan was practiced. Because of the terrorist threat, managers at several venues use practice sessions to test the ability of their emergency services during a mock attack. In April 2005 the Amsterdam ArenA used 2,000 fire, ambulance, police, and other officials as well as thousands of volunteers to simulate a terrorist attack on a soft target. The drill cost around 1 million euros ($1.2 million USD) to put in place ("Amsterdam ArenA," 2005). On May 7, 2005, the Pittsburgh Pirates conducted a mock terrorist bombing at PNC Park. Over 600 police officers, firefighters, medics, doctors, and ballpark ushers joined almost 5,500 volunteers for the $750,000 USD training exercise. Public officials lauded the drill "as an opportunity to measure how well emergency workers communicate and respond to a mass emergency" (Simonich & Srikameswaran, 2005, p. A1).

• ***Ensuring accessibility for spectators with disabilities***. The third component of an effective crowd control plan should address the procedures necessary to ensure facility accessibility for all citizens. Congress passed the Americans with Disabilities Act (ADA) in 1992. The ADA has had a major effect on sport, entertainment, and arts facility design. Sport and entertainment event managers must be familiar with requirements of the ADA as they pertain to facility features such as signage, restrooms, telephones, parking, and shower stalls. In July 2004 new guidelines were issued by the US Access Board to improve accessibility and compliance with the ADA. The new guidelines ensure that spectators who sit in wheelchairs have the same line of sight afforded to other patrons. Additional guidelines pertaining to ATM technology were provided for people with visual impairment (Yanchulis, 2005). Furthermore, event managers must also develop plans for the evacuation of spectators with disabilities or special needs.

> **Americans with Disabilities Act (ADA)**—Legislation that protects people with disabilities from discrimination. Specific to sport facilities, the law states that managers must provide "reasonable accommodations" for people with disabilities (Ammon et al., 2004, p. 68).

• ***Procedures for ejecting disruptive people***. The fourth component of an effective crowd control plan addresses the procedures necessary to eject disruptive, unruly, or intoxicated patrons. The ejection duties should remain the responsibility of trained crowd control staff and, in some jurisdictions, police officers, sheriff's department personnel, or state troopers. These individuals must understand the concepts of "reasonable prudent person" and "excessive force," and understand that they might be sued for negligence if they eject patrons incorrectly. Ushers should not undertake these duties if they are not trained in proper crowd control procedures. Removing disruptive or intoxicated fans will provide a safer environment for the remaining spectators and help protect the facility or event manager from potential litigation (Ammon & Unruh, 2003).

• ***An efficient communication system***. An efficient communication network is the fifth component of an effective crowd control plan. Communication is critical in providing spectator safety, enjoyment, and security. The use of a centralized area for representatives from each group involved in the management of an event (law enforcement, maintenance, medical, and security) will facilitate communication and improve decision making.

• ***Effective signage***. The creation and use of proper signage is the sixth and final component of crowd control. Informational and directional signs build a support network between fans and facility management staff. Spectators appreciate being treated fairly and if previously informed will normally abide by facility directives pertaining to no-smoking sections, alcohol policies, and prohibited items. Directional signs have several important uses. As spectators approach the facility, road signs can indicate the correct exits and provide relevant parking information. Other signs serve to indicate the correct gate or portal and direct ticket-buying patrons to the box office. Signage will help facility patrons locate concession stands, first-aid rooms, telephones, and restrooms. Informational signs regarding prohibited items assist patrons in making decisions before entry (Ammon & Unruh, 2003).

Settling With the Promoter

While the event is in progress, the promoter and a representative of the facility sit down together for the settlement. This process involves reconciling the revenues versus the expenses and dividing any resulting profit between the promoter and the facility representative according to the split determined during the preliminary negotiation phase (Farmer, Mulrooney, & Ammon, 1996).

settlement—Reconciling the expenses and revenues of an event and dividing the profits according to a contracted arrangement.

Postevent Tasks

After the event has occurred, several additional items need to be completed before the event becomes history and the event coordinator can go home.

- ***Event cleanup***. After the event is over and the crowd has filed out, the equipment used in the event is gathered up and put away or stored in trucks, and the cleanup of the facility commences. Usually another entire day is set aside for the load-out. Interestingly, management of the 1994 US Olympic Festival in St. Louis overlooked this element. Some of the venues were booked only until the day of the last event. This timetable necessitated the frantic dismantling and loading of sport equipment from the venues into trucks because the venues were scheduled for other events on the following day. The trucks were subsequently unloaded and the equipment was inventoried and returned to suppliers and sponsors as needed. Had the managers

JOB OPPORTUNITIES

Food and Beverage Manager

Looking for a general manager to oversee all aspects of our small arena concession business. Major responsibilities include event-day operations, developing and implementing operation and inventory controls, training programs for concessions employees, and special projects. The candidate must have excellent organizational and interpersonal skills.

Event Coordinator

Established Mid-Atlantic municipal arena seeking applications for hands-on event coordinator with additional responsibility of employee training. Include resume and salary history.

Director of Arena Operations

Full-time position available for a director of operations responsible for day-to-day operation of the arena, including ticketing, guest relations, security, and first aid. Duties will also include ensuring guest satisfaction through employee hiring and training, design of safety and risk management programs, and the day-to-day supervision of six managers and staff.

Promotion Manager

Currently seeking an enthusiastic, creative, and results-oriented promotion manager who is eager to promote live sporting events. Will be responsible for researching assigned markets; ticket pricing and sales; setup; media planning, buying, and negotiating; local sponsorship sales; and event publicity planning and coordinating. Candidate must have a degree in marketing or sport management. Travel required.

Operations Manager of Water Park

This position reports to the corporate offices in New Jersey and is responsible for the day-to-day operations of the water park. Primary responsibilities include facility maintenance, aquatics, park services, guest services, and admissions. Secondary responsibilities require supervising group services and marketing.

Sport Facility Manager

Professionally based sport and entertainment group seeking individual to manage its stadium and ancillary facility development process. The ideal candidate should possess experience in facility development and start-up, along with related aspects such as concession negotiations and supervision of facility architectural firms. Facility operations experience a plus.

Branch Manager and Guest Services Managers

Event staffing company is seeking dynamic individuals to fill immediate and future openings in major arenas and stadiums. Proven management skills and hands-on experience in the crowd and facility management industry preferred. Financial management and budgetary planning experience a plus. Communication and leadership skills are necessary to excel in this rewarding environment.

Public Facility Manager

Edwards Amphitheater is seeking a public facility professional to assume the position of facility manager. This position requires supervising marketing and box office personnel, negotiating with outside promoters, and coordinating all self-promoted events. In addition, the facility manager will supervise and oversee all group sales and special events. Individual should possess a background in facility management.

Learning Activity

The Pilot Pen International Tennis Tournament is scheduled for your facility. Prepare an event management plan. Begin by listing all the activities that need to take place before the event. Include such items as reserving the facility, advertising, arranging hotel accommodations, ticket printing and sales, and personnel scheduling. Next, place all the activities in the sequence in which they must occur. Then calculate the time needed to accomplish each task. Finally, place the items on a project calendar that shows each activity in sequence, the time required to complete it, and the overall chain of events.

scheduled time for equipment load-out, they could have avoided this situation.

- ***Evaluating the event***. Immediately after the event, the management team evaluates the process. Documentation of the entire process is critical, not only for protection against subsequent litigation but also for reference in planning future events.

> **documentation**—Completing detailed records that describe the event.

SUMMARY

The FIFA World Cup, the Olympic Games, concerts, and high school track meets have two common denominators: They take place in some type of facility, and they are events. All facilities and events need people to manage them.

The management of many sport and entertainment facilities is being outsourced to several private management companies. These private management companies have been successful in raising the profit margin of many sport and public assembly facilities across the United States.

To ensure a successful event, facility directors must perform several important tasks. They need to know and understand how these tasks relate to the successful completion of every event. Scheduling and booking an event begins the overall process, and a cost analysis is a critical element in this initial operation. After the facility director has decided that the event will be held, the necessary contracts need to be signed, and the event coordinator must create and communicate a work order to the others on the event management team. Items such as seating arrangements, crowd management, alcohol policies, settlement, and event evaluation must be carried out for an event to be successful.

In light of high-profile terrorist activities, risk management has become a tremendously important responsibility for all personnel working with facilities and events. The duty to provide a safe and enjoyable environment creates the need for sport managers who can anticipate potential areas of loss and injury and take action to reduce them. Interested sport management students with knowledge of law and facilities can obtain a position in the facility or event risk management field.

The number of facilities has grown significantly in recent years, and many of these facilities schedule sport and entertainment events with global implications. Worldwide terrorist attacks have changed the facility and event management industry dramatically. In addition, some areas of sport have downsized because of factors such as changes in the economy, corporate mergers, and business failures. Because of these trends, the future of facility and event management is not as clear as once imagined. Slower revenue growth has affected profit margins. The influence that this domino effect has on facility and event management needs to be continually monitored.

Review Questions

1. Name a single-purpose facility. Name a multipurpose facility. List the types of personnel who would be involved in facility management at either type of facility.
2. Currently, several companies privately manage more than 300 facilities nationally and internationally. List these companies. Why would a facility choose to contract with one of these companies?
3. What is a work order similar to? What is the purpose of a work order? Who compiles the work order?
4. Why does the management team need to meet to evaluate the overall production after the event ends? Why should the team complete all the proper documentation at this meeting?
5. Why is employing trained people to reduce facility risks a less expensive alternative than reacting to potential disasters or litigation without such people? How can much of this litigation be avoided?
6. Although sport and entertainment productions continue to be extremely popular and continue to result in extensive media coverage, what are two of the factors that may affect future travel to and spending at these events?

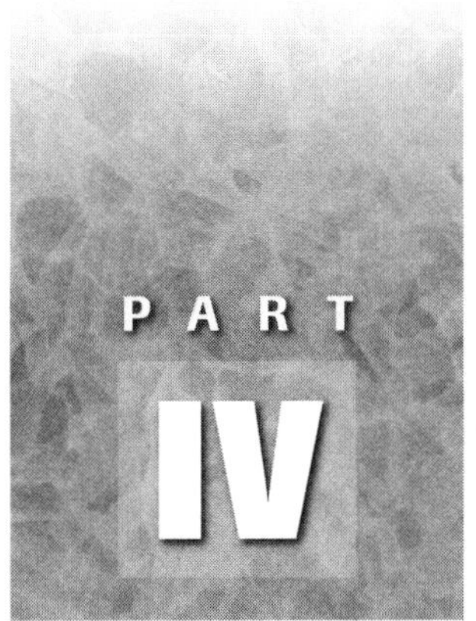

Organizational and Managerial Foundations of Sport Management

Aspiring sport managers should become familiar with theories of organizational behavior, management, and leadership and be able to apply these theories in practical settings. The two chapters in this section address the structure and processes of sport organizations and present desirable attributes of managers and leaders in the sport industry. The underlying theme of this section is that managers have a responsibility to themselves, their employees, and their constituents to appreciate and apply theoretical concepts that will improve the effectiveness and efficiency of the workplace as well as the quality of the sport product or experience.

In chapter 14 Lucie Thibault and Jerome Quarterman define the term *organization* and describe three types of sport organizations—public, nonprofit, and commercial. This discussion is followed by an explanation of organizational effectiveness along with several approaches to evaluating effectiveness and centralization. Then the authors cover organizational structure, focusing on specialization, formalization or standardization, and centralization. In addition, they present various organizational designs, such as entrepreneurial, diversified, innovative, missionary, and political. The remainder of the chapter addresses organizational environment, strategy, culture, change, and diversity. Throughout the chapter, Thibault and Quarterman present completed research on sport organizations and explain how the research findings apply to real-world situations in organizations. In the international sidebar, Rosa López de D'Amico, a professor at the Universidad Pedagógica Experimental Libertador (Maracay, Venezuela), explains how sport is organized in Venezuela.

Chapter 15 examines the concepts of management and leadership in sport organizations. First, Jerome Quarterman, Ming Li, and Janet Parks define management and leadership, pointing out similarities and differences between them. After explaining management as a process, the authors explain theoretical approaches to the study of leadership—trait, behavioral, situational (contingency), transactional, and transformational, ending the discussion with the integrative concept of managerial leadership. Quarterman, Li, and Parks then present three levels of managers, explain managerial skills and roles, and discuss the characteristics of successful leaders. The international sidebar is an essay about prominent Korean sport organizations. Gi-Yong Koo, a native of Korea who teaches sport marketing at the University of Tennessee at Knoxville, contributed the sidebar.

For More Information

Professional and Scholarly Associations

American Alliance for Health, Physical Education, Recreation and Dance (AAHPERD)

North American Society for Sport Management (NASSM)

Sport Management Council of the National Association for Sport and Physical Education (NASPE)

Sport Management Association of Australia and New Zealand (SMAANZ)

European Association for Sport Management (EASM)

International Sport Management Alliance

Asian Association for Sport Management (AASM)

Professional and Scholarly Publications

Athletic Business

European Sport Management Quarterly

International Journal of Sport Management

International Journal of Sport Management and Marketing

International Journal of Sports Marketing and Sponsorship

Journal of Sport Management

Sport Business International

Sport Management Education Journal

Sport Management Review

Sport Marketing Quarterly

Sports Business Daily

Street & Smith's SportsBusiness Journal

CHAPTER 14

Management Theory and Practice in Sport Organizations

Lucie Thibault—Brock University ▪ **Jerome Quarterman**—Florida State University

Learning Objectives

After studying this chapter, you will be able to do the following:

1. Identify principles of management theory and how these principles can help leaders and managers better manage their organizations.
2. Define organizational effectiveness and explain how it is measured in organizations.
3. Discuss the structure and design of organizations.
4. Define organizational environment and describe its influence on organizations.
5. Explain the importance of strategy, culture, and change in organizations.
6. Explain the importance of diversity in organizations.

We are surrounded by organizations. Most of us are born in hospitals, we are educated in schools, we regularly shop for goods and services in stores, and we are protected by organizations (e.g., hospitals, fire services, police services). Even in death, we rely on organizations. Organizations associated with sport also surround us. Most children are introduced to active participation in sport and develop sport skills through the school system. Children often stay involved in sport through physical education courses, intramural activities, and interschool competitions. They may also take advantage of community sports organized by local governments and nonprofit sport clubs. For highly skilled, competitive athletes, opportunities are available in college and university sport programs, amateur sport organizations, and professional sport organizations.

Other types of organizations provide us with opportunities for passive participation in sport. For example, media organizations keep us informed about sport in newspapers and magazines or on radio and television. We might even attend sporting competitions in person at our community facilities, in school facilities, and in professional sport venues. Anyone who consumes sport either actively or passively will be exposed to many different types of organizations.

Learning Activity

Think back over the past year. Identify all the sport organizations that you used as an active or passive participant.

In the first issue of the *Journal of Sport Management*, Earle F. Zeigler (1987) wrote,

> "In North America within the past 100 years, organized physical education and organized athletics, both within education and within various public, private, and commercial

programs of physical activity for people of all ages and abilities, have blossomed into a large and complex enterprise that demands a multitude of good managers" (p. 10).

Slack and Parent (2006) emphasized this point:

> "Throughout many countries, sport is a rapidly growing and increasingly diverse industry. Increased amounts of discretionary income, a heightened awareness of the relationship between an active lifestyle and good health, and a greater number of opportunities to participate in sport have all contributed to this growth" (p. 3).

Street and Smith's SportsBusiness Journal, *Sports Business Daily*, and *Sport Business International* consistently report on the financial and economic state of high-profile sport around the world. Clearly, in most industrialized nations the sport sector plays an important role in the national economy as well as in the country's social and cultural fabric.

Given the importance of the sport sector, sport leaders and managers must understand the structures and processes of organizations so they can adopt and implement the best managerial and organizational practices. In this chapter we will apply organizational theory in the context of sport. We provide illustrations, exercises, and activities to help you understand how sport organizations function. First, we define the term *organization* and describe three different types of sport organizations. Then we address major topics that are central to understanding how organizations are structured and how they operate: organizational effectiveness, structure and design, environment, strategy, culture, change, and diversity. This chapter provides only a basic introduction to management theory and practice applied to sport organizations. As you progress through your professional preparation program, you will have opportunities to learn much more about them.

DEFINING THE TERM *Organization*

Jones (2004) defines an **organization** as "a tool used by people to coordinate their actions to obtain something they desire or value—that is, to achieve their goals" (p. 2). Coordinated actions lead to the creation of social entities (i.e., organizations) in which people work collectively to achieve goals. In essence, people work collectively because achieving goals is often easier when working together rather than working independently. Shown in figure 14.1 is an organizational chart for a fictitious professional baseball club. Here it is conceptualized that a variety of individuals and groups work collectively. One person would almost certainly be unable to perform all the tasks and responsibilities required for the baseball organization to achieve its goals and objectives.

> **organization**—Social entity created to coordinate the efforts of individuals with the intent to achieve goals.

By working in a collective, organizations can achieve economies of scale and economies of scope:

- Jones (2004) explains that **economies of scale** represent savings that originate from the mass production of goods and services. As an organization produces more goods and services, it can realize savings by buying raw material in larger volume and by maximizing the use of specialized labor or machinery in producing, distributing, and selling these products and services. Economies of scale can result in improved efficiencies within an organization. A greater volume of production and distribution, for example, would enhance the skills of employees in carrying out those tasks. For example, if your sport marketing agency occasionally undertakes market research for professional sport franchises, it will realize economies of scale when it starts to undertake additional market research contracts for different sport organizations. The agency will already have developed the survey tools needed for market research. Refining those tools takes less time than developing them from scratch. In addition, as the employees of the agency undertake more market research contracts from various clients, they will become more knowledgeable, competent, and comfortable with conducting market research.

- **Economies of scope** represent savings originating from the maximization of resources used throughout the organization. When an organization is able to use underutilized resources, it will achieve economies of scope. For example, if you have an employee whose main responsibility is to attend to telephone calls and greet visitors to your organization—tasks that likely do not require full-

1900s

▶**1900-1910—** *Classical Management* school of thought emerges

▶**1900-1910—** Max Weber's concept of bureaucracy incorporated into *Classical Management* school

▶**1904—**Max Weber writes on commercial organizations, trade, accumulation of wealth, and capitalism

1910s

▶**1911—**Frederick Taylor's *Principles of Scientific Management* presents productivity improvement strategies

▶**1917—**Henri Fayol's *Administration industrielle et généralé* proposes 14 principles still considered foundational to management theory

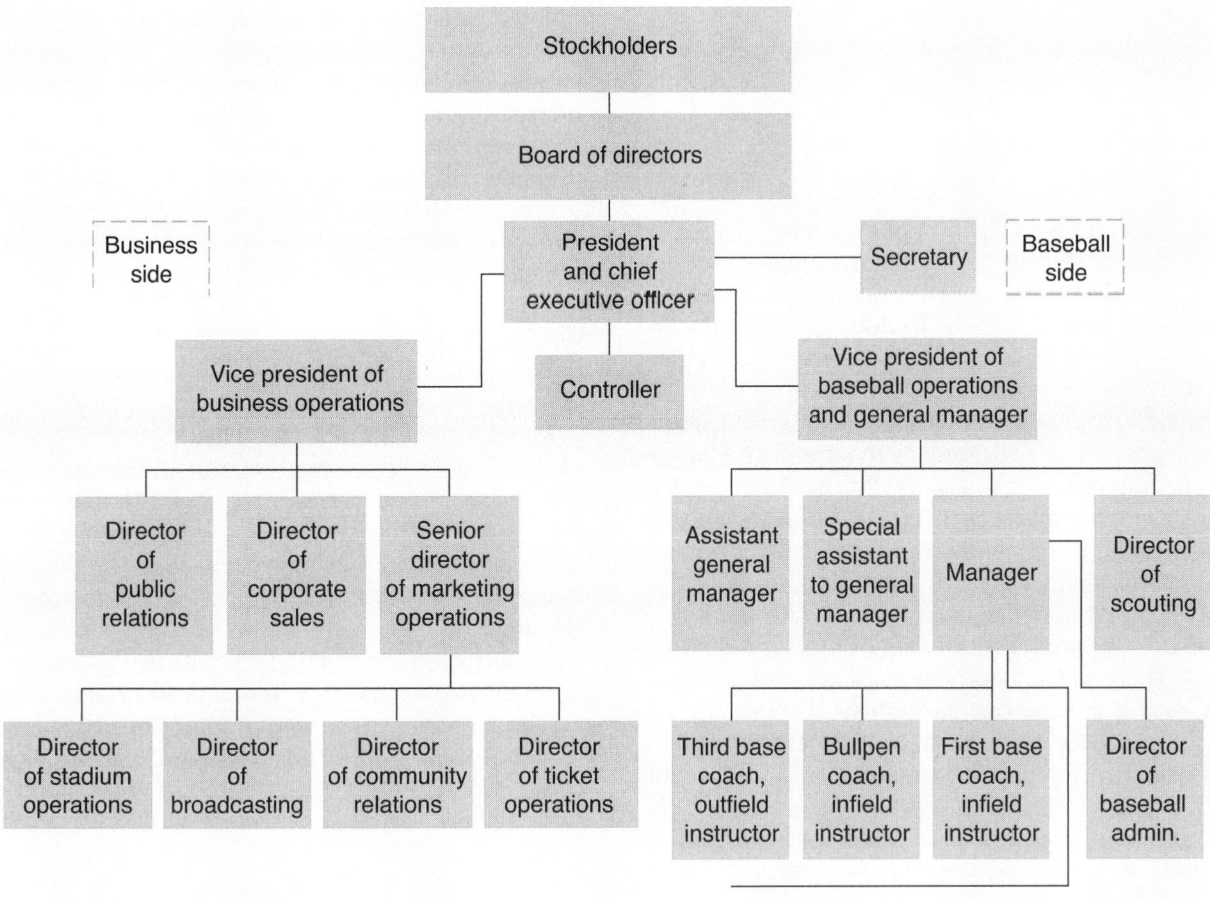

Figure 14.1 Organizational chart of a professional baseball team.

time attention—as the leader of the organization, you may wish to identify other skills this employee has and have him or her capitalize on them between answering telephone calls and greeting visitors. Specifically, if this employee has computer skills, he or she may be able to update your Web site on a regular basis. If the employee has skills with other languages, he or she can translate promotional material for the organization to provide better service for your clients. In this way, the organization is maximizing an underutilized resource.

economies of scale—Savings originating from the mass production of goods and services.

economies of scope—Maximization of resources used throughout an organization.

Organizations are vehicles to achieve goals. In their quest to achieve goals, organizations secure inputs and transform them into outputs. Figure 14.2 outlines these steps.

Organizations fundamentally transform inputs into outputs. They obtain inputs such as financial resources, human resources, raw materials, expertise, and knowledge from the external environment. They then transform those inputs through technology (e.g., through the use of machinery) and through the skills and abilities of the employees to produce outputs, such as goods and services sought by consumers. An organization can also produce other outputs such as dividends for shareholders and salaries for employees (Jones, 2004).

Learning Activity

Select a sport organization and identify what you perceive to be its inputs, its transformation processes, and its outputs.

1920s **1930s** **1940s** **1950s**

1920s—Mary Parker Follett promotes power sharing, employee participation, and negotiations in organizations

1938—Chester Barnard's *Functions of the Executive* focuses on roles of executives in organizations

1940s—*Systems Theory* proposes cross-disciplinary problem solving (e.g., mathematics, statistics, engineering)

1949—Fayol's classic work published in English as *General and Industrial Management*

1950s—Human Resource Management promotes importance of motivation, leadership, and people as assets

Inputs → Transformation → Outputs

Figure 14.2 Organizational systems.

In the quest to achieve goals, organizations must deal with their environments. Environments can be turbulent and uncertain. To address these uncertainties, leaders of organizations devise strategies to divide labor by area of expertise so that the most qualified employees are in appropriate roles. Organizations also use technology to support the ongoing production of goods and services. Additionally, organizations can manage the external environment by exerting power and control over other organizations (Jones, 2004). For example, executives of professional sport organizations may exert some control over local government officials by requesting a share of the revenues from concessions and parking of the city-owned facility.

People play an important role in addressing an organization's environment. People can control organizations, and organizations can control people. More specifically, as people create organizations, they can determine what goals they will seek to achieve, how the organizations will be structured, and the processes that will be used in the organizations' operations. Conversely, through their rules, processes, and structural elements, organizations can control the behavior of employees.

There are three types of sport organizations: public, nonprofit, and commercial.

- ***Public organizations***. Public organizations include federal or state government agencies or units as well as regional and local government departments responsible for the delivery of recreation and sport programs and the maintenance of sport fields, arenas, swimming pools, and parks. The National Park Service (www.nps.gov), the Los Angeles Department of Parks and Recreation (www.laparks.org/info.htm), and the Kansas City Sports Commission and Foundation (www.sportkc.org/about_us/index.htm) are examples of public sport organizations (see www.recreation.gov/).
- ***Nonprofit organizations***. Volunteer executives manage nonprofit organizations. They may hire paid staff to carry out the day-to-day operations of the organization. For example, the US Olympic Committee (www.usoc.org), the International Olympic Committee (www.olympic.org), USA Swimming (www.usaswimming.org), and the US Ski and Snowboard Association (www.ussa.org) are nonprofit organizations. Their volunteer executive members, often referred to as members of the board of directors or executive committee, make policy decisions about the direction of the sport and rely on paid staff to implement and evaluate those policies.

Learning Activity

Go to the US Ski and Snowboard Association Web site (www.ussa.org). Click on About USSA. Review the various elements of the page that describe the organization (i.e., Vision/Mission, USSA Fact Sheet, Management Team, USSA Board of Directors, and Foundation Board of Trustees). Write a one-page paper about the purpose of the organization and how it is structured to achieve this purpose.

Go to the USA Swimming Web site (www.usaswimming.org) and click on Volunteers. Read about the organization's volunteer needs. Click on Governance and read about how USA Swimming operates. Read about the board of directors and the national committees. Write a one-page paper on the governance of USA Swimming.

- ***Commercial organizations***. The main goal of commercial organizations is to make a profit. Professional sports, sport equipment manufacturers and retailers are commercial organizations. Organizations that offer sport or sport-related services, such as private golf clubs, downhill ski and snowboard resorts, fitness clubs, tennis and racket clubs, bowling clubs, and bungee-jumping and wall-climbing facilities, also operate as commercial organizations.

ORGANIZATIONAL EFFECTIVENESS

The effectiveness of an organization is the extent to which it achieves its goals. A related term, efficiency, refers to the achievement of goals using minimum resources. For example, the 2004 Athens Olympic Games were effective because members of the organizing committee achieved their objectives. But did the organizers achieve efficiency? In other words, did they achieve their objectives using the

1950s	1970s	1980s	1990s	
▶**1950s**—*Total Quality Management* movement (Japanese-style focus on quality assurances) emerges	▶**1978**—Concern for performance and excellence prevail in organizational research	▶**1982**—Publication of the ground-breaking book, *In Search of Excellence*, by Peters and Waterman	▶**1990**—Senge's *Learning Organizations* focuses on gaining competitive advantage through training organization members to think critically and creatively	▶**1995-2000s**—With an apparent rise in poor management practices and decision making of executives in organizations, ethics in the workplace is making a comeback

fewest possible resources? Given that members of the organizing committee went down to the wire with the construction of facilities and the training of human resources in advance of the Games, they were not efficient. They achieved their objectives, but they had to invest more resources (i.e., invest more money than budgeted for facility construction) to ensure the completion of the facilities before the Opening Ceremonies.

Efficiency implies the minimal use of resources to produce outputs (ratio of inputs to outputs). As a result, concepts of cost–benefit, return on investment, and budget compared with number of customers served are assessed to evaluate efficiency. As you can see, achieving effectiveness is easier than achieving efficiency. In fact, most managers and leaders of organizations rarely achieve efficiency.

> effectiveness—The extent to which goals are achieved.
>
> efficiency—The extent to which goals are achieved using the fewest possible resources.

Evaluating Organizational Effectiveness

A number of approaches are used to evaluate organizational effectiveness. Traditionally, these include the goal approach, the resource-based approach, and the internal process approach. Contemporary approaches include the stakeholder approach and the competing-values approach (Daft, 2007).

- ***Traditional approaches***. The goal approach focuses on the outputs side of the organization. The organization is considered effective if it achieves its organizational goal (e.g., maximizing profits, winning the game, teaching sport skills to students, healing patients) (Daft, 2007). The resource-based approach focuses on the inputs side of the organization. With this approach, the effectiveness of an organization is assessed by its ability to acquire resources in order to transform them into outputs. The logic behind this approach is that without inputs or the ability to acquire inputs, an organization will be unable to produce outputs (Daft). The internal process approach focuses on the transformation side of the organization—the ability to process the inputs while considering the internal well-being of the organization. Focusing on the transformation of inputs into outputs helps ensure the organization's stability and long-term survival (Daft).

- ***Contemporary approaches***. Although the previous approaches contribute to our understanding of whether an organization is effective, the contemporary approach to organizational effectiveness presents a more integrated perspective (Daft, 2007). Instead of focusing on single parts of the organization, the stakeholder approach and the competing-values approach acknowledges that the assessment or interpretation of organizational effectiveness depends on who you are, what interests you represent, and what values you favor for your organization. With respect to the stakeholder approach, various groups within and outside the organization will assess organizational effectiveness differently. For example, employees in the organizations might not judge effectiveness in the same manner as executives in the organization do or as customers do. More specifically, customers may judge effectiveness by the quality and price of the product they purchased while employees may consider the wages and benefits when they evaluate the effectiveness of their organization (Daft, 1998).

The competing-values approach combines elements of all traditional effectiveness approaches by focusing on the value dimensions of focus and structure. The dimension of focus is represented on a continuum from internal to external while the dimension of structure is represented on a continuum from stability to flexibility. An internal focus means that the organization values the well-being of its employees while an external focus values the well-being of the organization. A stable structure would favor a task-oriented approach while a flexible structure would favor change and innovation in the organization (Daft, 2007). With the competing-values approach, the assessment of your organization's effectiveness will be based on your values with respect to the dimensions of focus and structure.

Those who subscribe to the stakeholder approach and the competing-values approach believe that the organization must consider the values and interest of the various groups, or stakeholders, in the organization and consolidate their interests and views to achieve effectiveness (Daft). As explained by Daft, the stakeholder approach and the competing-values approach address the complexities involved in determining whether an organization is effective.

Learning Activity

Select one sport organization and identify stakeholders, within and outside this organization that have an interest in the activities of the organization. Discuss how these stakeholders may evaluate the effectiveness of the organization. Highlight the differences in these evaluations of effectiveness.

Effectiveness in Sport Organizations

Several sport management researchers have investigated the concept of organizational effectiveness. A number of these studies focused on intercollegiate athletics. For example, Cunningham (2002) examined the multidimensional nature of the effectiveness of NCAA Division I athletics departments. Putler and Wolfe (1999) studied the extent to which individuals' perceptions influenced their assessment of aspects of program performance. In a related study, Wolfe and Putler (2002) investigated the perceptions held by various stakeholders (i.e., faculty members, student–athletes, potential students, university students, members of the athletics department, and alumni) about the priorities of the intercollegiate athletic program. These priorities included win–loss record, graduation rates, violations, attendance, gender equity, number of teams, and finances. In a subsequent study, Wolfe, Hoeber, and Babiak (2002) investigated how perceptions of effectiveness differed according to the values of various intercollegiate athletics stakeholders. Trail and Chelladurai (2000) compared effectiveness in intercollegiate athletics as perceived by faculty members and students. Their results uncovered that students and faculty members were satisfied with their athletic department's emphasis on student-athlete development.

Using a different context, Papadimitriou (2001) evaluated the effectiveness of Greek sport organizations from the athletes' perspectives. Her results showed that athletes perceived their sport organizations' effectiveness to be low because the following factors were poorly addressed: interest in the athletes, long-term planning, caliber of the board, sports science support, and internal and external liaisons. The athletes, as one group of stakeholders of the sport organizations, had different opinions about the sport organizations' levels of effectiveness than did the leaders of those organizations, another group of stakeholders. Papadimitriou concluded that leaders of the organizations should address the concerns of their elite athletes. Given the increasing commitment that athletes make to their sports in training and competition, leaders need to work to improve programs and services to meet the needs of their current athletes as well as their promising athletes.

ORGANIZATIONAL STRUCTURE AND DESIGN

Jones (2004) defined organizational structure as a "formal system of task and authority relationships that control how people coordinate their actions and use of resources to achieve organizational goals" (p. 8). When addressing the topic of organizational structure, we usually refer to formal organizations, or what we typically see when we consult an organizational chart. Figure 14.1 provides an example of a formal organization for a fictitious professional baseball organization. Note, however, that every organization also has an informal dimension. Figure 14.3 depicts informal relationships among members of this baseball organization. The dashed lines illustrate relationships among employees who have lunch together each day and discuss sports and politics. Although the formal elements of an organization are overt, the informal organization is covert. Both formal and informal groups, however, are important to an organization.

Dimensions of Organizational Structure

Organizational theorists generally agree on three dimensions of structure: specialization, formalization or standardization, and centralization. Specialization concerns the division of labor, or the extent to which tasks and duties are divided into separate roles (Daft, 2007). According to Daft, when specialization is high, employees carry out a limited range of tasks and duties, and when specialization is low, individual employees carry out a wide range of tasks.

The dimension of specialization is tied to the concept of complexity. There are three levels of complexity: vertical, horizontal, and spatial.

- Vertical complexity is evidenced by the number of levels that exist between the top executive in the organization (i.e., president, chief executive officer) and the lowest positions and units in the hierarchy (i.e., support positions and departments).

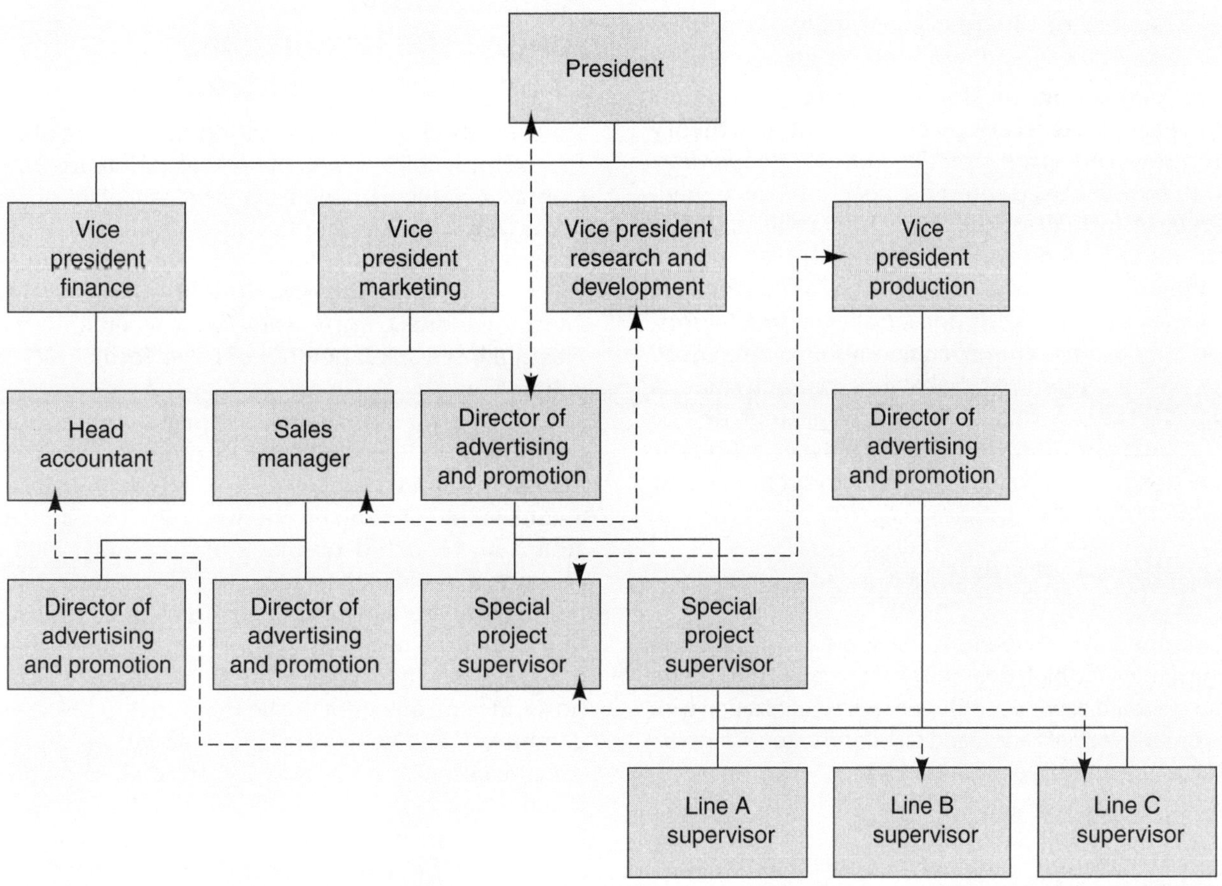

Figure 14.3 Formal and informal groups within a sport organization.

- The more levels there are, the more vertically complex the organization is. For example, compare the different levels of vertical complexity for the organizational structure of positions and departments). The more levels there are, the more vertically complex the organization is. For example, compare the different levels of vertical complexity of the organizational structure of Boston University's athletics department (figure 4.2) with the organizational chart of the athletics department of Ithaca College (figure 4.4). From these two figures, it appears that the Division I Boston University athletics department with four levels (executive director, director, associate or assistant directors, and the various units) is more vertically complex than the Division III Ithaca College athletics department with three levels (the director, associate or assistant directors, sport information director, full-time coaches, and the various sub-units [assistant to the director, equipment manager, part-time coaches]).
- Horizontal complexity is shown in the number of units that exist across the organization. As you can see in figures 4.2 and 4.4, Boston University is also more complex horizontally than Ithaca College because it has more departments (e.g., athletic development, marketing, community relations, and so on) than Ithaca College.
- Spatial complexity refers to the number of geographical locations in which an organiza-

Learning Activity

Go to the Fédération Internationale de Football Association (FIFA) (www.fifa.com/en/organisation/administration/0,1470,2,00.html), go to the International Association of Skateboard Companies (http://skateboardiasc.org/docs/org_chart.pdf), or go to an organization of your choice to examine its organizational chart. Discuss its levels of specialization and complexity. Is the organization complex vertically, horizontally, or spatially? Why or why not?

tion operates. An organization situated in a number of different geographical locations would be considered spatially complex.

Formalization, or standardization, is another dimension of structure. In the organizational theory literature, the terms *formalization* and *standardization* are often used interchangeably because high levels of formalization result in standardization. Formalization refers to "the amount of written documentation in the organization," (Daft, 2007, p. 17) such as job descriptions, policies, procedures, and regulations. This documentation is often used to control employees' behaviors and activities. A high degree of formalization leads to a high degree of standardization because employees who face similar situations will be expected to act in a similar fashion (Daft, 2007).

Learning Activity

Using the Internet, identify one sport organization in which there is a high degree of formalization and, therefore, standardization. Identify one sport organization with no or little formalization and standardization. Compare and contrast the two organizations.

Centralization is the third dimension of organizational structure. It "refers to the hierarchical level that has authority to make a decision" (Daft, 2007, p. 18). When the top of the hierarchy handles decision making, the organization is considered centralized. When decision making is delegated to "lower organizational levels," the organization is decentralized (Daft, p. 18).

Typically, organizations are not completely centralized or decentralized. Some decisions in the organizations may be centralized (e.g., hiring and firing of employees, establishing the strategic direction of the organization), and other decisions may be decentralized (e.g., purchasing of organizational supplies). Several factors affect whether decisions are centralized or decentralized:

- The cost (i.e., organizational resources) of the decision to the organization—the greater the cost, the more centralized the decision will be.
- The timing (how much time does someone have to make the decision?)—the more urgent the decision, the more decentralized it will be.
- The qualifications of employees—the greater the number of expert employees involved throughout the organization, the more decentralized the decision will be.

Relationships Among the Dimensions of Organizational Structure

Specialization and formalization are interrelated. For example, high levels of specialization are typically associated with high levels of formalization. In other words, the greater the number of roles in the organization, the more formalized the organization will be (e.g., more job descriptions, more policies and procedures). In the same way, when an organization has a small number of roles, formalization will be low.

The relationship between formalization and centralization is not as easy to predict. Research in organizational theory has failed to demonstrate a consistent relationship between the two dimensions. As reported by Slack and Parent (2006), research in sport management has not examined the relationship between formalization and centralization. Similarly, research in sport organizations has not analyzed the relationship between specialization and centralization or the relationship between complexity and centralization. In situations where specialization and complexity are high and thus where roles, tasks, and duties within the organization are narrowly defined, one would expect decentralization of decision making. With low levels of specialization and complexity, one would expect centralization within the organization.

Learning Activity

Be prepared to discuss the following questions in class:

- What are advantages and disadvantages of various levels of specialization and complexity?
- What are some advantages and disadvantages of formalization and standardization?
- How might a high level of centralization affect employees?
- With a high level of formalization, should leaders of the organization be concerned about centralization?

Organizational Design

Jones (2004) defined organizational design as the process by which leaders "select and manage aspects of structure and culture" (p. 10) so that the organization can undertake its various activities and achieve its objectives. We will address the concept of organizational culture later in this chapter. For the moment, however, consider organizational design as the structural configurations that leaders use to arrange their organization's activities so that it can reach its goals.

Henry Mintzberg conducted extensive work on organizational design. In a 1979 study he outlined different design configurations for different types of organizations based on the nature of their operations. A sporting goods organization in the business of manufacturing running shoes will be designed differently from a sport marketing agency or an event management business. Mintzberg based his designs on the interplay between five parts of the organization:

- The strategic apex, which represents the leadership within the organization
- The middle line, which represents the managers who are between the leadership of the organization and the employees who are directly involved with the production of goods and services
- The operating core, which represents the group of employees responsible for the production of goods and services
- The support staff, which represents the employees who provide a support function in the organization
- The technostructure, which represents the systems in place to standardize the work processes

Based on the relevance and importance of these five parts of the organization, different designs are proposed. Mintzberg identified several designs, among them the simple structure, the machine bureaucracy, and the professional bureaucracy. Subsequently, new designs were added to reflect emerging realities for organizations. Among these new designs are entrepreneurial, innovative, missionary, and political designs.

The simple structure is typically a suitable design for small organizations that have only two major parts, the strategic apex and the operating core. Simple structures are characterized by low levels of specialization and formalization, and high levels of centralization. A small sport club that operates at the local level might have a simple structure.

Machine bureaucracy is a design appropriate for sporting goods manufacturers that have high levels of specialization, formalization, and centralization. In the machine bureaucracy design, all parts of the organization identified by Mintzberg are important—the strategic apex, middle line, operating core, support staff, and technostructure.

The professional bureaucracy is characterized by an important operating core and support staff along with a limited technostructure, middle line, and strategic apex. This design would be appropriate for national sport organizations (Kikulis, Slack, & Hinings, 1992, 1995) in which professionals (e.g., coaches, sport psychologists, professional administrators) are responsible for the products or services. Decentralization and high levels of specialization and formalization are also characteristics of this design.

Entrepreneurial organizations have a simple design. With a minimal number of staff, the organization has little need for specialization and formalization because the top of the organization coordinates much of the work. As outlined in Sack and Nadim (2002), Starter Corporation, a licensed sports apparel business, was initially structured as an entrepreneurial organization.

Innovative designs allow greater flexibility than the bureaucratic design while providing decentralization not found in entrepreneurial organizations. Organizations featuring an innovative design emphasize a climate of creativity for the experts responsible for developing the product or the service. As a result, the power in the organization resides in the experts, who might be allowed to work in creative teams or on special projects. A marketing agency or ad agency with several accounts could exhibit an innovative design.

A missionary organization will be "dominated by its ideology. Once a new member has been indoctrinated into the organization—that is, once he or she identifies strongly with the common belief—then he or she can be given considerable freedom to make decisions" (Mintzberg & Quinn, 1991, p. 348).

According to Mintzberg and Quinn (1991), organizations with political designs have "no dominant mechanisms of coordination and no stable form of centralization or decentralization" (p. 349). Some organizations are temporarily created using the political design so that they can address challenging transitions. An organization bidding to host a major sport event such as a World Cup or international championship, for example, might be designed as a political organization as it addresses needs to secure resources (e.g., funding, facilities, volunteers) to host the event.

Table 14.1 outlines the structural profiles of all of Mintzberg's organizational designs discussed in this chapter.

Table 14.1

Characteristics of Organizational Designs and Their Structure

Mintzberg's design types	Specialization/ complexity	Formalization/ standardization	Centralization
Simple structure	Low	Low	High
Machine bureaucracy	High	High	High
Professional bureaucracy	High	High	Low
Entrepreneurial	High	Low	High
Innovative	High	Low	Low
Missionary	Low	High	Low
Political	High	Low	Undetermined

Source: Mintzberg 1979; Mintzberg and Quinn 1991; Slack and Parent 2006.

Structure and Design of Sport Organizations

Sport management scholars have investigated the structure and design of various sport organizations. For example, Theodoraki and Henry (1994) examined the designs of British sport organizations following an investigation of their structures, their environments, and other organizational factors such as size and age of the organizations and number of programs they offered. The authors were able to group British organizations into six designs based on a variation of Mintzberg's (1979) configurations. These designs comprised machine bureaucracy, professional bureaucracy, professionalized simple structure, typical simple structure, simple bureaucracy, and specialized simple structure.

In subsequent work, Theodoraki (2001) applied Mintzberg's organizational design theories to Organizing Committees for Olympic Games (OCOGs). She explained how the organizational design of OCOGs changed over time. OCOGs are created seven years before the Olympic Games take place, immediately following the International Olympic Committee's decision about which bid city will host the Games. These organizations have a life span of eight years and are typically dismantled one year after they host the Games. According to Theodoraki, OCOGs initially display a simple structure, Mintzberg's most basic design. She noted that OCOGs eventually display characteristics of the missionary design during the hosting of the Games and in the year following. In other words, as the members and employees of the OCOG becomes indoctrinated and socialized into the organization, they start to work collectively toward the organizational goals without the need for high levels of formalization or centralization.

Learning Activity

Read one of these two articles: Theodoraki and Henry (1994) or Theodoraki (2001). Think of sport organizations in your country that may exhibit similar designs and structures as those discussed in the articles.

ENVIRONMENT

All organizations operate in an environment. As Jones (2004) explained, the environment is a "set of forces surrounding an organization that have the potential to affect the way it operates and its access to resources" (p. 60). The environment can be divided into two categories: general and specific. The general environment includes elements that have the potential to affect all organizations—for example, the economy, technology, politics, social and cultural forces, and demography. The specific environment, or task environment, includes stakeholders external to the organizations. Jones identified stakeholders such as "customers, distributors, unions, competitors, suppliers, and the government" (p. 62) as part of the specific environment of the organization.

First, we will discuss four elements of the general environment: economic conditions, technology, political climate, and social and cultural forces.

- Economic conditions affect the way in which a given organization operates. How does inflation affect the organization? For example, are consumers buying expensive sport equipment when inflation rates are high? How do interest rates affect the organization's ability to acquire the inputs necessary for the fabrication of its products?

- Technology has a powerful effect on most organizations. For example, how do computers, software, and the Internet help the organization reach more consumers, maintain more accurate records of inventory, communicate with suppliers, and monitor purchasing patterns? How does technology help the organization develop better products?
- The political climate is another element of the general environment. As an example, the development of the North American Free Trade Agreement (NAFTA) between the United States, Canada, and Mexico has facilitated trade among the three countries.
- Social and cultural forces as well as **demography** may affect the organization. The age structure of the population, the level of education, and the standard of living are examples of social, cultural, and demographic elements.

demography—Involves the examination of populations, including such elements as size, births, deaths, migration, and aging.

Here are some important questions about elements of the specific environment:

- Who are the consumers? What are their preferences?
- Who are the suppliers? How easy is it for the organization to acquire its resources from suppliers? Does the organization deal with labor organizations or unions for its workforce?
- Who is the competition? Nike, adidas, New Balance, and Asics are competitors of Puma. But does Puma have other competitors? What about nonsport shoe manufacturers? What about clothing manufacturers who also produce leisure wear?
- What role does the government play in the environment? The government might be an element of the specific environment through its imposition of legislation and guidelines for the treatment of employees and consumers. Organizations must also provide details to government agencies for taxation purposes.

Clearly, the environment significantly influences and represents a major source of uncertainty for the organization. As a result, leaders and managers of organizations must understand the environment and carefully monitor its effects on the organization. Figure 14.4 provides a graphic representation of the general and specific environments.

Learning Activity

Select a nonprofit sport organization, a commercial organization, and a public organization and identify the general and specific environments for each.

STRATEGY

The leaders and managers of organizations use strategies, or plans, to cope with the environment. A plan refers to a course of action or a direction in which to move the organization from one point to another (Mintzberg, 1994). According to Jones (2004), the development of a plan involves the following four steps:

1. Identifying the goals, objectives, and mission of the organization. The strategy must be congruent with the goals, objectives, and mission.
2. Determining the strategic objectives. This step involves assessing what the organization wants to achieve with the strategy, and it includes the SWOT analysis. As you learned in chapter 9, a SWOT analysis consists of an assessment of the strengths and weaknesses of the organization and the opportunities and threats emanating from the organization's environment.
3. Identifying the resources required to implement the strategy. Without adequate resources, the organization will find it difficult to implement the strategy.
4. Establishing a timeline for implementing the strategy and identifying milestones to assess whether the organization is on target to achieve its objectives.

Organizations undertake the process of strategy formation to gain a competitive advantage, or edge, over other organizations. They may achieve this advantage by acquiring scarce resources. For sport organizations, scarce resources may be financial resources, sponsorship, media visibility, participants, clients, members and fans, market share,

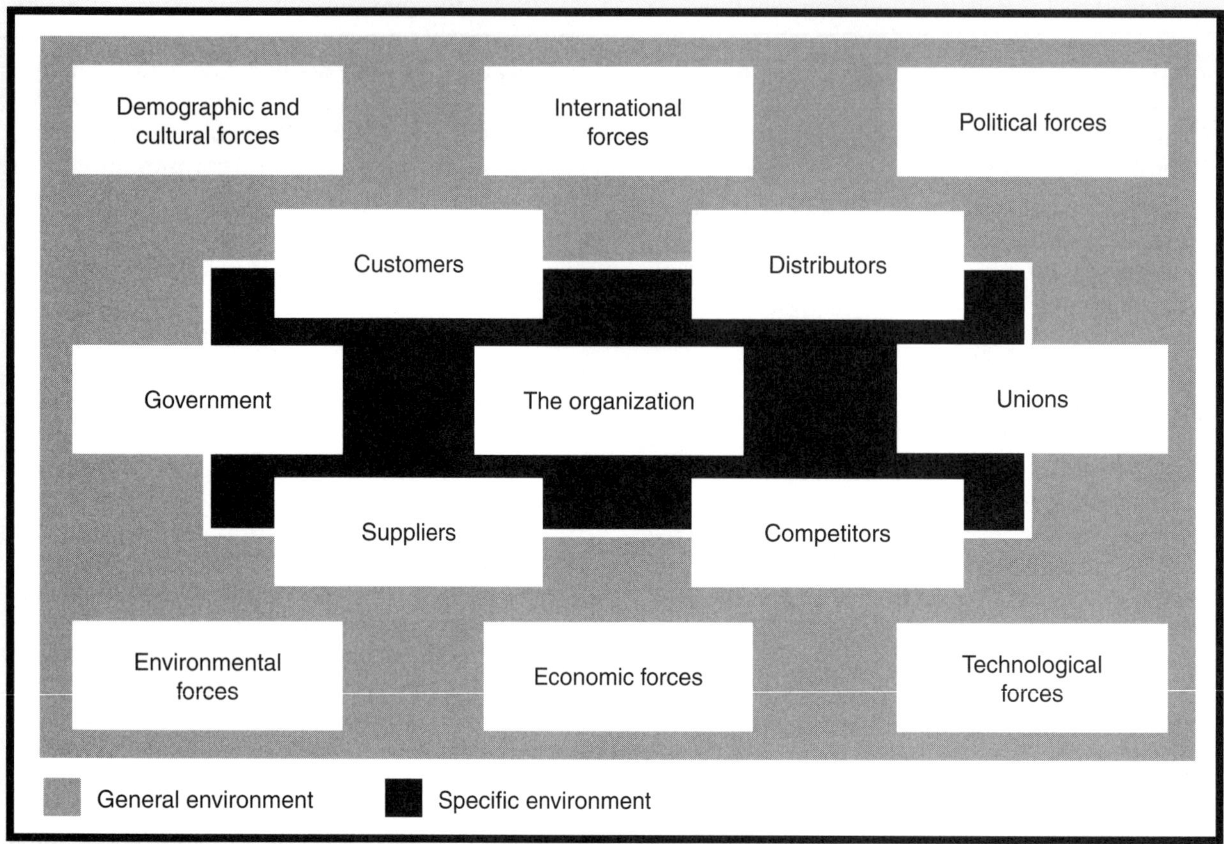

Figure 14.4 Various elements of an organization's environment.

Jones, Gareth R., *Organizational Theory Design & Change: Texts and Cases*, 4th Edition, © 2004. Reprinted by permission of Pearson Education, Inc., Upper Saddle River, NJ.

equipment, or facilities. In turn, access to these resources might lead to success in competition or greater profit because of increased fan attendance at games or increased sales of sporting goods.

Thibault, Slack, and Hinings (1993, 1994) studied the strategies of Canadian nonprofit sport organizations. They divided the organizations' strategies into four types based on the dimensions of program attractiveness (PA) and competitive position (CP). The PA dimension referred to the organization's ability to provide services and programs to its members, and CP referred to the organizations' capacity to attract and retain members, particularly with regard to the costs of joining the sport (i.e., membership and equipment costs). Using the location of the organizations with respect to these two dimensions, Thibault et al. (1994) discussed the types of strategies that these organizations could undertake to increase their PA and CP. The four strategies, outlined in figure 14.5, were called explorer, refiner, innovator, and enhancer.

According to Thibault et al., organizations use the explorer strategy to address low levels of program attractiveness and a weak competitive advantage. Leaders adopt the explorer strategy to increase the number of members by offering new programs and services while seeking ways to reduce the costs of entry into the sport. Explorers may deal with trial and error in their strategic initiatives. The refiner strategy allows organizational leaders to maintain their current level of program attractiveness while entertaining ways to address their competitive advantage. Leaders using the refiner strategies fine-tune their programs and services. Innovator strategies are characterized by a strong competitive advantage but low levels of program attractiveness. Innovators therefore focus on developing new programs and services to increase the number of members and participants in the sport. The potential for successful innovation is promising. The enhancer strategy allows organizational leaders to maintain and enhance their high level of program attractiveness and strong competitive advantage. These organizations are dealing from an advantageous position in their environment, so their strategies focus on maintaining and enhancing this position.

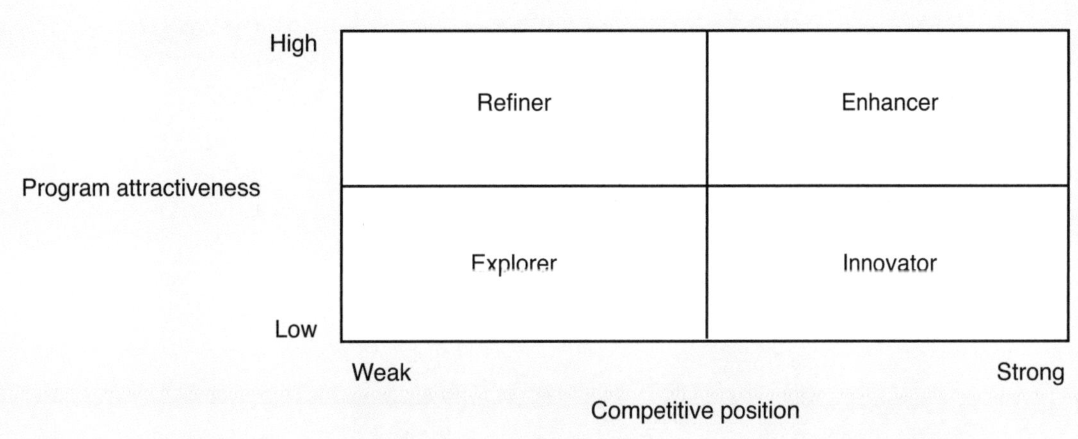

Figure 14.5 Strategic types of national sport organizations.

Building on this research, Olberding (2003) investigated the strategies of 33 Olympic sport organizations in the United States. He examined the following elements: the organization's competitive position relative to other US sport organizations, the domestic sport programs, the level of participation in the sport in the country, the costs involved in taking part in the sport, the level of visibility of the sport, the extent to which the sport was entrenched in the grass roots, the opportunities for competitions in the sport, and the new programs being developed within the organization. Using Thibault et al.'s (1993) framework developed for Canadian sport organizations, Olberding found that US sport organizations used similar strategies (enhancers, refiners, innovators, and explorers).

Legg (2003) examined strategies of the Canadian Wheelchair Sports Association over a 30-year period (i.e., from the creation of the organization in 1967 until 1997). Legg identified three dominant strategies. *Governance strategies* included focus on planning, restructuring, recruitment of volunteers, and communications. *Fund-raising strategies* focused on generating financial resources for the organization's operations, programs, and services. *Inclusion strategies* included communication and negotiation with other sport organizations to include wheelchair sports into the able-bodied system.

Some research on strategy has focused on the development of partnerships (also known as interorganizational relationships) with other organizations as a strategy to retain or gain a competitive advantage. All types of sport organizations (i.e., public, nonprofit, and commercial) are increasingly involved in alliances with other organizations to capitalize on opportunities and access more resources; to increase programs, services, and products offered to members or clients; and to reduce uncertainty. For example, Crompton (1997, 1998a, 1998b); Thibault, Frisby, and Kikulis (1999); Frisby, Thibault, and Kikulis (2004); and Thibault, Kikulis, and Frisby (2004) investigated partnerships in public recreation organizations. All of their findings revealed that in a context of budget shortfalls and cutbacks, local governments in both the United States and Canada developed partnerships with other public organizations, with nonprofit organizations, and with commercial organizations so that they could maintain the levels of programs and services offered to community members.

ORGANIZATIONAL CULTURE

Edgar Schein (1985), one of the pioneers of research into culture in organizations, defined organizational culture as "a pattern of basic assumptions—invented, discovered, or developed by a given group as it learns to cope with its problems of external adaptation and internal integration" (p. 9). Schein explained that organizations consider this set of assumptions valid and as a result promote them to new members as the appropriate and correct way to act in the workplace. Jones (2004) defined organizational culture as "a set of shared values and norms that controls organizational members' interactions with each other and with people outside of the organization" (p. 195).

Slack and Parent (2006) noted that culture is manifested in different ways throughout sport organizations. These manifestations include stories and

Notre Dame's Muffet McGraw embodies Scott's description of successful leadership. McGraw is a collegiate coaching veteran with more than 500 wins and a national championship to her credit. She is on the board of directors of the Women's Basketball Coaches Association (WBCA) and has been honored with awards such as the WBCA National Coach of the Year, Naismith's Women's College Coach of the Year, and the Associated Press Coach of the Year.

Courtesy of Paul M. Pedersen.

myths, symbols, language, ceremonies and rites, physical setting, and symbolic artifacts. Stories and myths are narratives that may be based on truth, fiction, or a combination of both. Symbols consist of events, objects, or acts that convey meanings for the organization. Organizational logos, slogans, and mission statements are symbols. Language refers to the terminology and jargon that organizational members use to communicate with each other. Ceremonies and rites include social events and award and recognition events that leaders organize. These events often reinforce organizational values. Physical setting includes the office space and objects found in the organization. Artifacts are items found in the organization's physical setting. Photographs of past successes or ceremonies, banners, copies of past marketing campaigns, and displays of awards, achievements, and products are examples of artifacts that could be evident in the physical setting. The setting and these artifacts are representative of the organization.

Colyer (2000) investigated organizational culture in nonprofit Australian sport organizations. She drew the cultural profile of three organizations using Quinn and Spreitzer's (1991) competing-values culture instrument. Her findings revealed the existence of "tensions between two of the main groups of people (employees and volunteers) in sport organizations" (p. 338). She explained that if leaders were to draw cultural profiles of their organizations, they would become aware of tensions and could develop strategies to change the culture and thus enhance organizational effectiveness. She also discussed the presence of subcultures—an important element in any examination of an organization's culture.

Scott (1997) discussed the distinction between uncovering the culture (and subcultures) of organizations and the management of these cultures and subcultures in the context of intercollegiate athletics. He examined the relationship between culture and leadership in organizations that seek effectiveness and success. Although his research is not empirical, Scott discussed implications for athletics departments and provided suggestions for athletics administrators and head coaches about how to manage the dominant culture and, specifically for head coaches, their team's culture. The author concluded by stating, "Establishing a distinct vision, collaborating with group members, setting and communicating clear objectives, allowing participation in decision making, providing principled leadership, and establishing a proper and timely reward system are keys to successful culture development" (p. 414).

Other studies have focused on the values held in sport organizations. According to Schein's and Jones' definitions, values are central to an organization's culture. Milton-Smith (2002) discussed the scandals, corruptions, and controversies involving the International Olympic Committee (IOC) in the late 1990s and early 2000s. He discussed how concerns about the Olympic Games mirror concerns about the movement toward globalization. Concerns regarding "winning at any price; commercial exploitation by MNCs [multinational corporations]; corruption; intense national rivalry; [and] the competitive advantage of advanced nations" were identified (Milton-Smith, 2002, p. 132). Milton-Smith discussed the IOC and its scandal in the late 1990s and early 2000s. In analyzing the case of the Sydney 2000 Olympic Games, he drew on the values espoused by the Olympic Movement and demonstrated how members of the IOC and members of the Sydney Organizing Committee for the Olympic Games (SOCOG) violated those values. According to Milton-Smith's analysis, the IOC and SOCOG compromised values such as honesty, transparency, objectivity (i.e., avoiding conflict of interest), fairness, dignity, and loyalty. Although it was not the purpose of his work to discuss the organizational culture of the IOC or the SOCOG per se, Milton-Smith explained that the leadership of the IOC cultivated a culture of excess while overlooking questionable and unethical practices of its members. In other words, the Olympic ideals and the core values of the Olympic Movement were used as marketing tools to showcase the IOC but were never translated into the culture of the organization.

ORGANIZATIONAL CHANGE

Organizational change is defined as "the process by which organizations move from their present state to some desired future state to increase their effectiveness. The goal of planned organizational change is to find new or improved ways of using resources and capabilities" (Jones, 2004, p. 301).

Change in Sport Organizations

To remain competitive, relevant, and viable, organizations constantly undergo change. Several frameworks have been developed to study organizational change. One such model is the contextualist approach developed by Pettigrew (1987, 1990; Pettigrew, Ferlie, & McKee, 1992). The contextualist approach acknowledges that change does not take place in isolation or in a brief period. Understanding change is important but it must be accomplished over a long term by considering three elements: content, context, and process.

To acquire a full understanding of change, one must first examine the content of change, which is best done by answering the question, What changed? The next element of Pettigrew's framework is the context of change. The focus is on answering the question, Why did the change occur? Context includes two sections: the inner context and the outer context. Inner context consists of internal elements at play within organizations, for example, strategy, culture, and the structure of organizations. Outer context refers to general political, economic, and social forces at work within the organizational environment. After content and context of change have been uncovered, the process of change needs to be examined. The process of change is concerned with answering the question, How has change occurred? In uncovering the process of change, leadership is often a key component because change agents often contribute to the adoption of change within the organization. By answering the what, why, and how, leaders are in a better position to understand change in their organizations.

A few studies have applied Pettigrew et al.'s (1992) contextual approach on organizational change to the sport context. Specifically, Cousens, Babiak, and Slack (2001) investigated changes in the National Basketball Association (NBA) over a period of 17 years, focusing on the relationship marketing approach adopted by the league. They discussed the relevance of Pettigrew's approach to

ORGANIZATION OF SPORT IN VENEZUELA

Rosa López de D'Amico, Venezuela

In Venezuela, sport is organized by the Instituto Nacional de Deportes (IND), which is located in the Ministry of Education and Sport and coordinated by the vice minister of sport. The organization of sport is divided into two sectors—official and private. The official sector coordinates, directs, plans, protects, promotes, and supervises sport activities in the country. The private sector is composed of the Venezuelan Olympic Committee, sport federations, sport associations, sport leagues, and clubs.

The 66 registered national sport federations that control the development of sport in Venezuela are financially autonomous. Each federation receives an annual budget from the IND for all activities related to competitive and developmental sport. The government finances most activities, and little marketing or sponsorship takes place.

At the state level—24 states and a capital district—are the sport associations, which receive financial and administrative benefits. The smallest units are the clubs, which do not receive direct financial support from the state, although most of them use state facilities. Each state has a sports foundation sponsored by the state government. The foundations provide financial support for sport development at the state level. Organized activities also take place at the municipal level. The state associations are autonomous administratively and financially and depend largely on volunteers.

Venezuelan sport was highly influenced by Europeans in the 1950s and 1960s. Hence, clubs are the centers of sport activities, but they lack financial independence and rely on parental support. Nowadays, nearly all investment in sport is the responsibility of the national budget prepared by the IND. The federations and associations are not involved in fund-raising, marketing, or sales.

Every two years, different states organize National Games, and new facilities are built accordingly. Individual corporations and government organizations (e.g., police, doctors, and engineers) also hold games. School-level sport is required by law, and government-sponsored National Student Games are held. Nevertheless, students are not incorporated into the federations of organized sports.

Baseball is the national sport of Venezuela, and many organizations work with grassroots development. The second most popular sport is soccer. Professional sport, until recent years, included only baseball and boxing. In the 1990s sports such as tennis, basketball, volleyball, and soccer slowly started to develop at the professional level. Venezuela is now beginning to have better results in the international arena in these sports.

Many people believe that Venezuela has not had better results in the international arena (e.g., Olympic Games) because of the absence of government policies that would enhance participation in sport and make it part of the national culture. Sport management, therefore, needs attention in Venezuela (e.g., Bello 1977, Machado 1990, Agudo 2004). Traditionally, volunteers and supporters have run sport, but common sense and good intentions are clearly insufficient (e.g., Chalip 1995). More managerial competence is required at all levels of organization. In recent years the financial support for sport has been excellent, and important results have occurred in the international arena. The study of sport management, however, has not been considered a necessity because it does not produce immediate results. Nevertheless, decision makers now understand that the only way to obtain better results is with improved management of sport.

better understand the need to foster relationships within and outside the NBA. In another example of Pettigrew's work applied to the context of sport, Caza (2000) examined the adoption of innovative practices in a Canadian provincial sport organization. His investigation looked at the extent to which organizational members were receptive to the implementation of two initiatives. Caza found that Pettigrew's framework was useful in understanding challenges related to the implementation of innovations in the sport sector.

Thibault and Babiak (2005) also used Pettigrew's framework to investigate changes in Canada's sport system. They were specifically interested in examining how and why the Canadian sport system changed to accommodate greater involvement from the athletes. They found that increased representation by athletes on decision-making boards of sport organizations, greater funding of athletes, the creation of national sport training centers, and the creation of a forum for athletes to resolve conflicts between themselves and sport organizations or coaches all contributed to an athlete-centered sport system. Thibault and Babiak were able to understand the nature of the change that had occurred in light of the context in which Canada's sport

The sport complex comprising everything in this image other than the numbered areas was initially built for the National Sport Games held in San Carlos, Cojedes State, Venezuela, in December 2003. The numbered buildings (including residential, dining, and academic facilities) were then added, and in 2006 the entire facility became the Iberian American University of Sports, charged with the mission of transforming society, based on the principles of human dignity and social justice, through sport.

Photo courtesy of Department of Cojoes State Government.

International Learning Activity

In February 2006 Venezuela opened the Iberian American University of Sports in Cojedes State. Find this university on the Internet and examine its academic and extracurricular offerings. List at least five ways in which this new university will contribute to the improvement of sport management in Venezuela.

system operated. They were also able to examine the leadership role assumed by change agents to bring about the adoption of more athlete-centered change in the sport system.

Organizational Diversity

As noted in chapter 1, leaders and managers of organizations are working with an increasingly diverse workforce. Although some may believe that the existence of diversity in the workforce is not important, others understand that a diverse workforce represents an advantage for organizations. A diverse workforce can better respond to consumers' needs and can provide consumers with better goods and services. Diversity can also improve organizational effectiveness by improving managerial decision making. Diversity, therefore, is an important resource for organizations.

Diversity can represent variation in age, gender, race and ethnicity, religion, sexual orientation, socioeconomic status, and ability. Managing diversity in organizations can be challenging, but leaders should not be deterred from ensuring that the workplace is diverse. Although "effectively managing diversity makes good business sense" (Jones, George, Hill, & Langton, 2002, p. 139), diverse employees are often subjected to unfair treatment. Jones et al. identified three factors that may lead managers and employees to treat diverse employees unfairly:

- Biases: systematic tendency to use information about others in ways that result in inaccurate perceptions
- Stereotypes: simplistic and often inaccurate beliefs about the typical characteristics of particular groups of people

- Overt discrimination: knowingly and willingly denying diverse individuals access to opportunities and outcomes in an organization (Jones et al., pp. 140-141)

Dass and Parker (1999) proposed four strategies that leaders use to manage organizational diversity: reactive, defensive, accommodative, and proactive. Leaders usually adopt reactive strategies when they do not value diversity. In some cases, reactive strategies have been used to maintain and protect the status quo. Although reactive strategies are often used to resist diversity in the workplace, a reactive strategy may be appropriate in some cases. For example, the LPGA might consider using a reactive strategy if male athletes wanted to join the organization.

Defensive strategies typically emerge from a discrimination and fairness perspective. In this context, leaders are interested in leveling the playing field for members of diverse groups. Legislation (i.e., affirmative action policies, equal opportunity for employees) may force organizations to adopt this strategy.

With the adoption of accommodative strategies, leaders have embraced the notion that a diverse workforce is beneficial for the organization. Differences are celebrated. This strategy ensures that a diverse workforce results in access to more consumers, often from diverse groups.

The last strategy, proactive, represents a more ingrained perspective about diversity in organizational activities compared with accommodative strategies. Proactive strategies originate from the idea that educating managers and employees of the organization will result in the complete adoption of diversity. In this case, diversity is central to the core operations of the organization. Ideally, all leaders would choose to adopt the proactive strategy.

To protect diverse employees, equal employment opportunity initiatives and affirmative action programs have been developed in the United States. Matton and Hernandez (2004) conducted a study of the success and challenges of diversity and compliance initiatives in 10 organizations. The authors examined training, goal setting and targets for gender and race, equal employment opportunities and affirmative action initiatives, and mentoring and succession planning. Their findings revealed that several factors in the organization favored the success of diversity initiatives:

- Leadership: commitment, passion for diversity, and sustained involvement from the leaders in the organization
- A diversity or compliance professional: creation of a position within the organization and the hiring of a strong individual to implement diversity efforts in the workplace
- Employee involvement: the role of employees in communicating with the leaders and informing, assisting, and recruiting diverse employees
- Ties to performance evaluation and reward system: connection to performance evaluations and rewards to middle managers and diversity officers to encourage them to meet their diversity goals
- Availability and communication of data: information allowing leaders and employees in the organization to monitor patterns, problems, and opportunities for diversity in the organization

Matton and Hernandez (2004) noted that the organizational culture was among the challenges associated with the successful implementation of diversity initiatives. Organizational culture was also tied to the difficulty that some organizations had in generating buy-in from current employees and middle managers. Achieving diversity initiatives is extremely difficult when the culture and the employees are not open to diversity in the organization.

In October 2006 the *Journal of Sport Management* featured a special issue on the topic of diversity in the sport industry. In their introductory article for this special issued, guest editors George Cunningham and Janet Fink (2006) discussed the major diversity issues facing sport organizations. These issues include differences in the quality of the work experience for employees who are judged to be different. Elements of power, inequality, and conflict often ensue in the workplace. Some studies on the work experiences of employees have focused on the effect of diversity on organizational commitment and turnover (Cunningham & Sagas, 2004). Other studies have investigated the issue of diversity from the perspective of consumption patterns (Armstrong, 2002; Armstrong & Stratta, 2004).

These studies and several others clearly suggest that diversity can promote the success of organizations. If an organization does not have strategies in place to embrace a diverse workforce, consumers, members, and clients may choose to buy their products and services from a competing organization that better understands their interests and responds more effectively to their needs. Using a hand analogy, Chelladurai (2005) clearly demonstrated the value of diversity in the workplace—all the fingers of the hand are different, but each plays an important role, particularly in concert, to open a door, to give a handshake, to hold, to throw a ball, and to write a note.

SUMMARY

The organizational theory topics covered in this chapter—structure and effectiveness, design, environment, strategy, culture, change, and diversity—are all important to consider and monitor. Left unchecked, problems in these areas can reduce the effectiveness of an organization and, ultimately, cause its demise. Note that these topics are interrelated. For example, the structure and design of the organization may affect, or be affected by, the culture. Similarly, the ability to develop and implement a strategy or to cope with change may affect, or be affected by, the structure and design of the organization.

These interrelationships take on even more complexity with consideration of the role that people play in the development and management of organizations. The following chapter addresses the topic of individuals and their roles in organizations.

Review Questions

1. What is the difference between effectiveness and efficiency? What is the best approach to the study of organizational effectiveness?
2. Select one sport organization and describe its structure using the three structural dimensions featured in this chapter.
3. What organizational design would be most appropriate for a sporting goods manufacturer? For a sport marketing agency? For an organization bidding for the right to host a major international event?
4. What is the difference between the general environment and the specific environment?
5. Why would organizations choose to develop strategies?
6. Discuss how some organizational cultures can be positive for an organization and how other cultures can be negative for an organization.
7. Describe how you might use Pettigrew's contextual approach to study change in one organization of your choice.
8. Define diversity and identify the advantages of a diverse workplace.

Managerial Leadership in Sport Organizations

Jerome Quarterman—Florida State University ▪ **Ming Li**—Ohio University
Janet B. Parks—Bowling Green State University

Learning Objectives

After studying this chapter, you will be able to do the following:

1. Define management and leadership.
2. Differentiate between the terms *manager* and *leader*.
3. Name and describe the underlying processes of management.
4. Explain the major findings of a study of the management process in sport industry organizations.
5. Compare and contrast the major theories and models of leadership.
6. Explain the major findings of a study of leadership theories and models.
7. Identify three basic roles that managers assume in sport organizations.
8. Explain how to classify managers in sport organizations.
9. Discuss the characteristics of a successful leader.

In this chapter, we introduce two important processes that occur in sport organizations: management and leadership. After defining both management and leadership, we explain how they function as processes in sport organizations. We then differentiate between management and leadership, explore theoretical approaches that have been proposed for the study of leadership, and discuss the integrative concept of managerial leadership. We describe three different levels of management, discuss a variety of management skills, and present characteristics of successful leaders. We end the chapter with a discussion of the various roles that managers play and an example of how the duties of NCAA conference commissioners fit into these roles.

MANAGEMENT AND LEADERSHIP

As noted in several chapters of this book, sport has been estimated to be at least a $213 billion USD industry and to rank sixth among all industries in the United States (Broughton, Lee, & Nethery, 1999). The success of organizations in this large and competitive industry ultimately depends on how effectively managers apply their management and leadership skills. Before discussing effective management and leadership, however, we need to address the following questions: What is **management**? What is **leadership**? How are they similar and how are they different?

The literature offers many definitions of both management and leadership. Hersey, Blanchard, and Johnson (2001) provided one of the most comprehensive definitions of management as "the process of working with and through individuals and groups and other resources (such as equipment, capital, and technology) to accomplish organizational goals" (p. 7). They defined leadership as "the process of influencing the activities of an individual or a group in efforts toward goal achievement in a given situation" (p. 91). The two roles are similar in that they both involve people working with other people. They are different with respect to the ways in which they accomplish the objectives.

management—The process of working with and through individuals and groups to accomplish organizational goals.

leadership—The process of influencing the activities of an individual or group in efforts to achieve a goal in a given situation.

Managers are often leaders, but not all leaders are necessarily managers. The term *leader* is broader than the term *manager* because people need not be in management positions to be leaders. Depending on the situation, all employees of the organization can act as leaders. Any time a person influences the behavior of others, regardless of the reason, that person is demonstrating leadership. For example, a sport management intern might have special skills using the Excel® computer program to draw charts and graphs. When that intern assists the controller or director, she or he is taking the lead during that time. Conversely, when employees in an organization rely on others, those others are acting as leaders, even if they are not in official decision-making positions.

As dynamic and often complex structures, organizations in the sport industry require managers who are skilled in both management and leadership. In the next two sections of this chapter, we discuss the topics of management and leadership as separate entities. We then integrate the two concepts in a discussion of managerial leadership in sport organizations.

MANAGEMENT AS A PROCESS IN SPORT ORGANIZATIONS

Numerous theoretical approaches to management have been used. We classify management theory into three basic types: scientific management, human relations management, and the process approach (also known as administrative management). Thus, before we look at the process approach, we will briefly summarize the other two:

- ***Scientific management approach***. Early theorists believed that the primary responsibility of managers was to increase workers' output. Frederick Taylor (1911) developed this approach, in which the major concern was to scrutinize the performance of individual workers. The key was that workers who produced more than others would receive greater rewards. This approach advocated paying people by the number of units produced or sold rather than by the length of time (e.g., hours) that they worked. In the sport industry, this approach is best illustrated when employees work on a commission basis. For example, a sport promotion employee might earn a commission based on the number of memberships sold for the booster club of an intercollegiate football or basketball program. The sport manager working under such conditions would focus primarily on how effective each individual sport promoter was in selling memberships. The scientific management approach considers pay and working conditions to be the most important factors in increasing a worker's performance.
- ***Human relations management approach***. The human relations approach grew out of studies conducted at Western Electric's Hawthorne, Illinois plant during the late 1920s and early 1930s (Mayo, 1933). Mayo's research on more than 20,000 employees found that when employees felt important, they became more cohesive and productive. His conclusion was that being concerned for the workers would lead to higher rates of job satisfaction, which would result in better performance (Straw, 1986). The human relations approach has been enhanced by modern behavioral scientists such as Abraham Maslow (1954; the hierarchy of needs theory), Frederick Herzberg (1966; the two-factor theory) and Douglas McGregor (1960; theory X and theory Y). Many experts believe that managers who are seeking to maximize organizational productivity should consistently approach nonmanagers in the ways that Mayo, Maslow, Herzberg, and McGregor have documented in the human relations approach.

1920s

▷**1920s**—Hawthorne Effect first observed: productivity improvements occur when workers know they are being observed

1950s

▷**1954**—Maslow's *Hierarchy of Needs* promotes understanding employees' commitment in the workplace

1960s

▷**1960**—McGregor's Theory X and Theory Y change the way employees are perceived in organizations

▷**1964**—Blake and Mouton's *Managerial Grid* describes managerial focus in terms of concern for people and concern for task

Learning Activity

Conduct an online or traditional library search in the *Journal of Sport Management, International Journal of Sport Management*, or *Sport Marketing Quarterly* and locate a study that illustrates the human relations approach. Explain in your own words how the approach of Mayo or one of the more recent behavioral scientists supports the conclusions of the article.

- ***Process approach to management***. The process approach, also known as the administrative approach, has been the chief theoretical approach to the study and practice of management in recent times. Unlike the scientific and human relations management approaches, the process approach focuses on managing the organization as a whole entity. The process approach will guide the remainder of the discussion in this chapter.

The process approach to management uses a set of ongoing, interactive activities, known as the underlying processes of management, to accomplish the goals and objectives of their organizations, departments, or work units. Such processes were first introduced more than six decades ago as POSDCORB (Gulick & Urwick, 1937). POSDCORB is the acronym for Planning, Organizing, Staffing, Directing, Coordinating, Reporting, and Budgeting. The original seven processes have since been reduced to five functions: planning, staffing, organizing, directing, and controlling and evaluating (Hersey, Blanchard, & Johnson, 2001; Koontz, O'Donnell, & Weihrich, 1984). Figure 15.1 illustrates that these underlying processes flow in all directions and that decisions made in each component affect all other components. Ultimately, all the processes revolve around the manager's actions and decisions.

In sport organizations, the process typically starts with planning and ends with controlling and evaluating. Managers might engage in the activities in various sequences, and sometimes they perform several activities simultaneously as they carry out the responsibilities of their jobs. The element that is universal in all of the processes, however and whenever they are performed, is decision making. Table 15.1 provides definitions of each of the underlying processes, as well as examples of how the general manager of a private sport club might practice them.

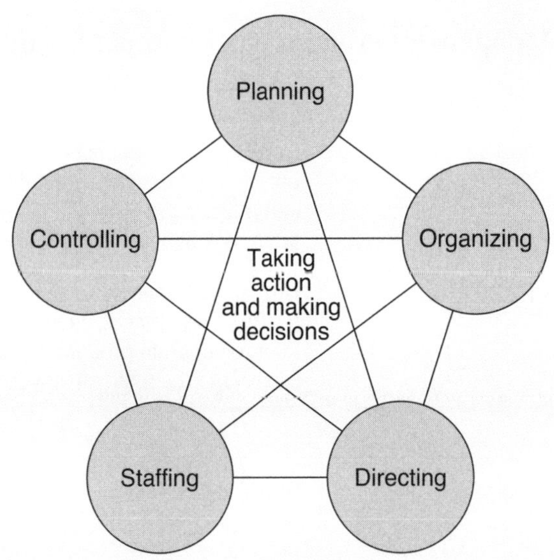

Figure 15.1 The management process approach.

Learning Activity

Using the information in table 15.1 as a guide, construct a similar table for a different organization in the sport industry. It might be interesting for small groups of students to work on this activity because participants will bring different experiences and viewpoints to the decision-making process.

LEADERSHIP AS A PROCESS IN SPORT ORGANIZATIONS

Like management, leadership is also conceptualized as an interactive process. The primary goal of leadership is to exert influence on individual and group behaviors, either toward the leader's goals or toward the organization's goals. Although the terms *manager* and *leader* are sometimes used interchangeably, the two concepts are not the same. When people function as managers, they are primarily focused on efficiency and "doing things right." When people function as leaders, they are concerned with effectiveness and "doing the right things" (Bennis & Nanus, 1985). Differences between management and leadership are further elaborated in table 15.2, which shows that managers cope with complexity in the workplace and that leaders cope with change (Kotter, 1990).

1960s

1960s—Contingency Theory proposes fit between organizational processes and organizational contexts as key

1970s

1973—Mintzberg's *The Nature of Managerial Work* published

1975—Pat Summitt wins first game as head coach of Tennessee Lady Vols

1980s

1984—David Stern named NBA commissioner

1989—Paul Tagliabue named NFL commissioner

1990s

1992—Donna Lopiano becomes executive director of Women's Sport Foundation

Table 15.1

Management Process of a General Manager in a Private Sport Club

Underlying process	Definition	Example
Planning	Developing and implementing goals, objectives, strategies, procedures, policies, and rules to produce goods and services in the most effective and efficient manner.	The general manager of a private sport club predicts the increase in enrollment at the start of the new year and arranges for the facility to be open 18 hours per day instead of 15 hours per day.
Organizing	Arranging resources (e.g., human, financial, equipment, supplies, time, space, informational) to produce goods and services in the most effective and efficient manner.	After conducting an assessment, the general manager establishes a work unit for teaching golf at the club. The general manager appoints a full-time coordinator who will coordinate three teaching pros and a new golf course with an adequate budget.
Staffing	Recruiting, selecting, orienting, training, developing, and replacing employees to produce goods and services in the most effective and efficient manner.	The general manager advertises the positions: three teaching pros, one maintenance person, and one administrative assistant. The general manager then holds interviews, checks references, makes job offers, and selects the staff needed for the golf program.
Directing	Influencing members (subordinates, peers, and supervisors) as individuals and as groups to produce goods and services in the most effective and efficient manner.	The general manager encourages the golf teaching pro to prepare weekend course packages for local executives who have expressed an interest in learning golf skills.
Controlling/evaluating	Evaluating whether the employees are on task and making progress toward achieving the goals and adhering to the guidelines and standards for producing goods and services in the most effective and efficient manner.	After three months the general manager monitors the progress of the new golf program with the coordinator and discusses ways to make the program more attractive to potential new members.

Table 15.2

Comparative Summary of the Management–Leadership Dichotomy

Management (coping with complexity)	Leadership (coping with change)
Planning and budgeting. Setting goals for the future, establishing procedures for achieving the goals, and allocating adequate resources to effectively achieve the goals.	*Setting a direction.* Developing a vision of the future and strategies for producing the changes needed to achieve the vision.
Organizing and staffing. Creating an organizational structure for accomplishing the plan, staffing the organization with qualified workers, delegating responsibility for carrying out the plans, and constructing a system to monitor implementation.	*Aligning people.* Communicating the new direction to those who can create coalitions that understand the vision and are committed to its achievement.
Controlling and problem solving. Monitoring results in some detail, both formally and informally, by means of reports, meetings, and other tools; identifying deviations; and then planning and organizing to solve the problems.	*Motivating and inspiring.* Keeping people moving in the same direction, despite confronting major obstacles, by appealing to basic but often untapped human needs, values, and emotions.

Source: Kotter, J.P. (1990). What leaders really do. Harvard Business Review, *68(3), 103-111.*

1990s

▶ **1996**—Valerie Ackerman becomes president of WNBA; serves until 2005

▶ **1998**—Bud Selig named MLB commissioner

2000s

▶ **2001**—Tyrone Willingham hired as Notre Dame head football coach; fired in 2004

▶ **2003**—Myles Brand becomes NCAA CEO

▶ **2005**—Donna Orender named President of the WNBA

Learning Activity

Read the article "Management Behaviors of an Elite Intercollegiate Baseball Coach" (Bennett & Hardin, 2002). Summarize the purpose of the study, describe the method, and report the results regarding the underlying processes of management. List at least five implications of the findings for managers in a different segment of the sport industry.

Several approaches to the study of leadership have been developed. Among the most common approaches are (1) theories that attempt to explain why some people are good leaders and others are not, and (2) models that represent observed patterns of effective leadership that can be learned. In the following paragraphs, we will present trait theory, behavioral theory, three situational (contingency) leadership models, and the full range of leadership model. The latter model includes transactional, laissez-faire, and transformational leader behaviors. As you progress in your curriculum and study leadership in more depth, you will discover additional leadership theories and models. You will also learn that some leader behaviors overlap categories and defy neat classifications. Nonetheless, brief discussions of several of these approaches will provide you with a basic understanding of current thought regarding leadership in organizations.

Trait Leadership Theory

The earliest attempt to explain the influence of managers was guided by trait theory, which implied that leaders were endowed with particular characteristics that differentiated them from their followers (Wofford, 1982). Underlying the trait approach was the notion that effective leaders could be identified based on physical factors (e.g., age, gender, height, weight, ethnicity), intellectual qualities (e.g., intelligence, speaking ability), or personality attributes (e.g., emotional stability, sensitivity) (Slack & Parent, 2006). Overall, the notion was that people destined to be leaders were born, not made. One problem with this approach was that it grouped all successful leaders together without examining their specific situations. Thus, many scholars disputed the early version of trait theory (Kirkpatrick & Locke 1991; Stogdill, 1974).

Although trait theory fell into disfavor for many years, it appears to be making somewhat of a comeback as reflected in an interest in the characteristics of some visionary and charismatic leaders (Bass & Stogdill, 1990; Northouse, 2004). The current version of trait theory envisions leaders possessing a core of identifiable traits such as drive, the desire to lead, honesty and integrity, self-confidence, cognitive ability, and knowledge of a business (Kirkpatrick & Locke, 1991). Although core traits do not guarantee successful leadership, they are assumed to be good predictors of the potential to lead (Kirkpatrick & Locke). For example, Roger Goodell (NFL), David Stern (NBA), Donna Orender (WNBA), and Bud Selig (MLB) might have some traits in common. Analysis of those commonalities might provide people in professional sport with ideas about whom to hire as commissioners or presidents of professional sport leagues. The five-factor personality approach (McCrae & Costa, 2003) presented in table 15.3 is a widely accepted taxonomy of personality traits.

Behavioral Leadership Theory

Behavioral leadership theory suggests that if key behaviors of effective leaders can be identified, a blueprint for success can be created (Likert, 1961). The behavioral approach grew out of an effort to explain trait theory. Whereas the trait approach focuses on characteristics of leaders, the behavioral approach focuses on what a leader actually does.

The behavioral approach conceptualizes leaders as being either job centered or employee centered (Likert, 1961; Katz & Kahn, 1978; Blake & Mouton, 1985). **Job-centered leaders** are primarily concerned about attaining the goals of an organization. **Employee-centered leaders** are primarily concerned with developing and maintaining good relationships with their peers and followers in the workplace. They care about having mutual trust and respect and being considerate of followers' ideas and feelings.

Several other terms have been used to describe the behaviors of job-centered and employee-centered leaders: initiating structure versus consideration (Katz & Kahn, 1978); task oriented versus relationship oriented (Bass, 1985); and concerned for production versus concerned for people (Blake & Mouton, 1985). Although the terms are different, their meanings are essentially the same.

Learning Activity

You are the director of the sports commission in a major US city. The year after next, the NCAA Women's Final Four will be held in your city. Using the information about management and leadership presented in table 15.2, outline the steps that you would take to prepare for this event. Indicate which steps require management skills and which require leadership skills.

Table 15.3

Five-Factor Model of Personality

Factor	Selected representative traits
Neuroticism	Calm–worrying; self-satisfied–self-pitying; even-tempered–temperamental
Extraversion	Reserved–affectionate; quiet–talkative; passive–active
Openness to experience	Uncreative–creative; conventional–original; uncurious–curious
Agreeableness	Ruthless–soft-hearted; suspicious–trusting; irritable–good-natured
Conscientiousness	Lazy–hard-working; disorganized–well-organized; aimless–ambitious

Source: McCrae, R.R., & Costa, P.T., Jr. (2003). Personality in adulthood: A five-factor theory perspective (2nd ed.), New York: Guilford Press, p. 4.

Learning Activity

Search the Internet for stories about David Stern, Roger Goodell, Donna Orender, and Bud Selig. Make a list of the traits they share. Compare these traits with the ones listed in table 15.3. Make a list of differences among these leaders. What conclusions can you draw regarding the use of the trait approach to hiring CEOs of sport leagues?

Learning Activity

Go to table 15.4 and find the studies conducted by Branch (1990) and Snyder (1990). In your own words, describe the participants, the purpose, and the results of both studies. What are the implications of the findings of these studies for managers of intercollegiate sport organizations?

Another behavioral approach to leadership is the notion that effective managers must use both job-centered and employee-centered behaviors in the workplace. Following this approach, a manager would adapt his or her behaviors to changing situations. Growing out of this idea was the leadership grid (Blake & Mouton, 1985; Blake & McCanse, 1991), which plots a leader's task-versus-people behaviors on four scales: high task–low people, high task–high people, low task–high people, and low task–low people. The underlying concept of the leadership grid is that managers are most effective when they have high concern both for their subordinates and for getting the work done (i.e., high task–high people).

job-centered leaders—Primarily concerned about the technical or formal aspects of jobs and consider followers primarily as the means for accomplishing the organization's goals.

employee-centered leaders—Primarily concerned about interpersonal relations, meeting personal needs of followers, and accommodating personality differences among followers.

In recent years several studies of management have been conducted in sport and recreation organizations. Table 15.4 presents examples of such studies.

Situational (Contingency) Leadership Models

Behavioral leadership theory fell into disfavor when situational leadership theorists began to provide empirical evidence that no single leadership style was best. To the contrary, they found that a variety of styles could be adopted in different situations or that the environment could be altered to meet the needs of the situation. Several models of situational leadership theory have been applied to leadership. Four examples of such models are (1) Fiedler's contingency model, (2) the path–goal model, (3) the Situational Leadership® Model, and (4) the full range of leadership model.

Fiedler's Contingency Model

Fred Fiedler (1967) developed the first situational theory of leadership, which postulates that the effectiveness of a leader depends on (1) the leader's personal style, and (2) the amount of control the leader has over a given situation (Ayman, Chemers, & Fiedler, 1995). According to this model, a person's leadership style is primarily either task oriented (e.g., highly concerned about getting tasks done through his or her followers) or relationship oriented (e.g., highly concerned about developing a good working relationship with followers). Three situational variables determine the degree to which the leader can control a situation: the leader's

Table 15.4

Selected Studies of Management and Leadership in Sport and Recreation Organizations

Researchers	Participants	Purpose	Major findings
Bourner & Weese (1995)	32 executive leaders in the Canadian Hockey League	"To investigate the linkages that exist between executive leadership and organizational effectiveness in the Canadian Hockey League." (p. 88)	"No significant linkage was uncovered between executive leadership and organizational effectiveness." (p. 88)
Branch (1990)	78 ADs and 87 assistant or associate ADs at 105 NCAA Division I-A member institutions	"To examine athletic director and selected assistant[s] perceptions of leader behavior to determine whether their perceptions contributed significantly to the prediction of intercollegiate organizational effectiveness." (p. 161)	The directors who focused on goals and tasks (job centered) were more effective than those who concentrated on relationships (employee centered).
Doherty (1997)	114 Canadian university level coaches	To examine coaches' ratings of the transformational/ transactional leader behavior of 30 interuniversity athletics administrators	" . . . female and younger athletic administrators were found to exhibit transformational leader behavior more often, and transactional leader behavior less often, than their male and older counterparts . . . " (p. 275)
Doherty & Danylchuk (1996)	32 athletic administrators and 114 coaches in Canada	To examine "the leader behavior of inter-university athletic administrators according to Bass' (1985) transformational/ transactional leadership model." (p. 292)	"Leader-centered behavior . . . was used more than subordinate-centered behavior. . . . Coaches' satisfaction . . . was positively and strongly associated with transformational leadership and contingent reward behavior, whereas negative relationships were observed for management-by-exception (passive) and nonleadership behaviors." (p. 292)
Kent & Chelladurai (2001)	108 employees of NCAA Division I-A member institutions	"To test various relationships between perceived leader-member exchange quality, perceived transformational leadership behaviors, organizational commitment, and organizational citizenship behaviors." (p. 135)	"Two of the three dimensions of transformational leadership–charismatic leadership and individualized consideration–were significantly correlated with leader-member exchange." (p. 146)
Kent & Weese (2000)	46 employees of Ontario Provincial Sport Organizations (PSOs), 10 of which had been identified as effective and 10 of which had been identified as ineffective	"To analyze the concepts of organizational effectiveness, executive leadership and organizational culture within the Ontario Sport and Recreation Centre (OSRC)." (p. 4)	"The majority of the Executive Directors studied in both effective and ineffective organizations exhibited transactional leadership styles." (p. 14) Effective organizations rated higher than ineffective organizations on three aspects of culture building: managing change, achieving goals, and customer orientation.

(continued)

Table 15.4

(continued)

Researchers	Participants	Purpose	Major findings
London & Boucher (2000)	129 employees of 41 athletic programs in the Canadian Interuniversity Athletic Union	"To determine whether Canadian university athletic directors' levels of transformational leadership and transactional leadership differed significantly with regard to the organizational effectiveness of their respective athletic programs." (p. 74)	"Significant effects were found for transformational leadership on organizational effectiveness. Conversely, no significant effect resulted from transactional leadership on athletic program organizational effectiveness." (p. v)
Pruijn & Boucher (1995)	Employees of 38 Dutch National Sport Organizations	"To determine the relationship of transactional and transformational leadership to the organizational effectiveness of Dutch National Sport Organizations (DNSO)." (p. 72)	"Medium transformational leaders were more effective than high transformational leaders. The results of this study do not provide general support for Bass' (1991) argument that transformational leadership is universally applicable." (p. 72)
Snyder (1990)	117 intercollegiate coaches in California (36 women, 81 men)	To analyze "the effects of leader behavior and organizational climate on the job satisfaction of intercollegiate coaches." (p. 59)	"The degree of consideration shown by the athletic director had a strong effect on satisfaction with work and supervision. . . . Consideration helped female coaches feel integrated into the department and supported by the administration. Male subjects viewed consideration as important to the development of morale and rapport with colleagues." (p. 59)
Wallace & Weese (1995)	69 CEOs in Canadian YMCAs	"To investigate the links between transformational leadership, organizational culture, and employee job satisfaction . . ." (p. 182)	"Significant differences in organizational culture existed between the YMCA organizations led by high transformational leaders and YMCA organizations led by low transformational leaders." (p. 182)
Weese (1995)	Employees of campus recreation programs in the Big Ten and Mid-American Conferences in the United States	"To investigate the concepts of transformational leadership and organizational culture within the administrative levels of campus recreation programs of Big Ten and Mid-American Conference Universities." (p. 119)	"High transformational leaders direct programs that (a) possess stronger organizational cultures, and (b) carry out culture-building activities . . . to a greater extent than other leaders do." (p. 119)
Weese (1996)	19 directors of campus recreation programs of the Big Ten and Mid-American Conferences in the United States	"To explore the relationships that exist between transformational leadership . . . organizational culture . . . and organizational effectiveness . . .in the campus recreation programs of both the Big Ten and Mid-American conferences." (p. 197)	"Significant differences were uncovered in both conferences for executive transformational leadership and organizational effectiveness. . . . No significant relationship was uncovered between transformational leadership and organizational effectiveness." (p. 197)

personal relations with group members, the power and authority of the leader, and the structure (or lack thereof) of the assigned task. Fiedler proposed that leadership styles are not easily changed but that situational variables can be modified so that "task leaders" and "relationship leaders" are given followers who are compatible with their styles. Fiedler called this approach "organizational engineering" and based it on the assumption that changing the environment is easier than changing a leader's style. Alternatively, rather than altering the situation, leaders who recognize and understand their own styles can seek employment situations that are more compatible with them (Hersey, Blanchard, & Johnson, 2001).

Path–Goal Model

Initiated by Evans (1970) and elaborated by House (1971) and House and Mitchell (1974), the path–goal model of leadership is based on the expectancy theory of motivation. In the context of management, this theory essentially suggests that followers are motivated by two factors: (1) their estimates of the probability that their behaviors will result in specific, desirable outcomes, and (2) the personal satisfactions that they anticipate deriving from their efforts. Evans proposed that a primary function of leaders is to be clear about the behaviors that will lead to reward, a process that he called path clarification. House and Mitchell (1997) clearly and succinctly stated the basic tenets of the path–goal theory:

> The motivational functions of the leader consist of increasing the number and kinds of personal payoffs to subordinates for work-goal attainment and making paths to these payoffs easier to travel by clarifying the paths, reducing road blocks and pitfalls, and increasing the opportunities for personal satisfaction en route. (p. 262)

In this model, two contingency variables affect the relationship between leader behavior and follower satisfaction: personal characteristics of the followers (i.e., the degree of control that they perceive they have over the outcome) and environmental factors (i.e., the task structure, the hierarchy of the organization, and the primary work group). Leaders who are sensitive to these factors can engage in behavior that is either directive, supportive, achievement oriented, or participative, depending on their assessment of which behaviors would be most motivational under the circumstances (House & Mitchell, 1997).

Situational Leadership Model

Initially proposed by Hersey and Blanchard (1969), the third situational approach to leadership emphasizes the leader's behaviors in relation to the followers' readiness to accomplish specific tasks. As shown by the text associated with the "Leader Behaviors" box in figure 15.2, the leader's behavior

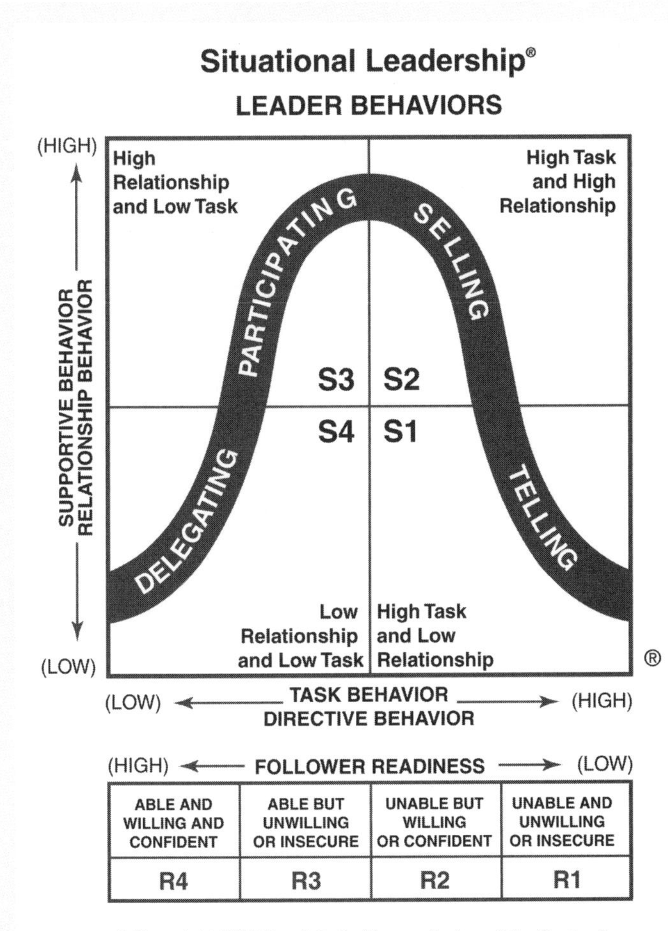

Figure 15.2 The Situational Leadership Model.

Management of Organizational Behavior: Leading Human Resources/Paul Hersey, Kenneth H. Blanchard, Dewey E. Johnson—8th Edition (ISBN 0-13-032518-X)

is composed of two dimensions of style—task behavior (directive) and relationship behavior (supportive). The four styles, which are labeled S1, S2, S3, and S4, reflect leadership behaviors composed of different combinations of task and relationship behavior. When leaders employ Style 1 (high task, low relationship) they closely supervise the follower and use a "telling" mode of communications to provide detailed instructions. In Style 2 (high task, high relationship), leaders use a "selling" mode of communication to explain the task and allow the follower to ask for clarification. Style 3 (high relationship, low task), in which the leader communicates with the follower as a "participant" in the task, emphasizes the sharing of ideas and the facilitation of decision-making. In Style 4 (low relationship, low task), the leader "delegates" the task to the follower, giving the follower responsibility for its completion.

The other component of the leadership situation is the readiness level of the followers. *Readiness* is "the extent to which a follower demonstrates the ability and willingness to accomplish a specific task" (Hersey, Blanchard, & Johnson, 2001, p. 175). Four readiness levels are described at the bottom of the model in figure 15.2—R1, R2, R3, and R4. As shown, followers exhibit various combinations of ability and willingness to perform particular tasks; hence, the leader must interact with each type of follower in different ways. When leaders can identify the readiness level of a given follower for a given task as either R1, R2, R3, and R4, they can use the model in figure 15.2 to choose the most appropriate style and communication pattern for the situation. By drawing a perpendicular line from the readiness level to the curved line that describes the four modes of communication, they will arrive at a description of the leadership style and mode of communication recommended for followers at that readiness level.

Full Range of Leadership Model

Bass and Avolio (1994) developed the full range of leadership model based on research investigations of a variety of leader behaviors. An overview of this model, which includes transactional, laissez-faire, and transformational leader behaviors, is presented in table 15.5.

As shown in table 15.5, the transactional leadership style implies a deal between leaders and followers whereby they agree on the types of performances that will lead to reward or punishment for the followers (Bass, 1985). Transactional leadership includes three types of reinforcement behaviors: contingent reward, active management by exception, and passive management by excep-

Table 15.5

Brief Overview of the Full Range of Leadership

Leadership behaviors	Transactional style
Contingent reward	Gives followers a clear understanding of what is expected of them; arranges rewards for satisfactory performance
Management by exception (active)	Monitors followers' performances and takes corrective action when mistakes are observed
Management by exception (passive)	Waits for mistakes to be made and then corrects them
	Nontransactional style
Laissez-faire	Avoids leadership; is inactive
	Transformational style
Idealized influence	Serves as a good role model; can be trusted to do the right thing
Inspirational motivation	Encourages the optimism and enthusiasm of followers
Intellectual stimulation	Encourages followers to consider new ways of looking at old methods and problems
Individualized consideration	Gives personal attention to followers; listens to them; serves as a coach or mentor

Sources: Bass, B.M. (1985). Leadership and performance beyond expectations. New York: Free Press; Bass, B.M., & Avolio, B.J. (1994). Improving organizational effectiveness through transformational leadership. Thousand Oaks, CA: Sage.

Learning Activity

As the manager of a State Special Olympics Basketball Tournament, you are supervising four employees—one at each of the four levels of readiness described in figure 15.2. You have assigned all four followers the task of recruiting volunteers for the event. Describe the style and mode of communication you would use with each follower in attempting to elicit successful accomplishment of the task. Provide specific examples of your behavior.

tion (Bass). In contingent reward, leaders attempt to be clear about their expectations of followers. When followers' performances are satisfactory, leaders can provide rewards, such as praise or an increase in pay. When followers' performances are unsatisfactory, leaders can respond with notification of the inadequacies and, ideally, with additional clarification. Management by exception (MBE) is a more negative approach. Adherents to this leadership style ascribe to the "If it ain't broken, don't fix it" philosophy (Bass, p. 122). MBE-active leaders keep track of the followers' performances. When followers make mistakes, they take corrective action. MBE-passive leaders do not monitor followers' performances. Rather, they wait passively and make corrections only when mistakes occur.

The second leadership style in table 15.5 is characterized as nontransactional. In reality, it is not a leadership style at all because these types of people are extremely passive. They avoid all forms of leadership. They neither monitor nor correct their followers. Consequently, this style is the least effective.

As shown in table 15.5, the third type of leader behavior is the transformational style (Bass, 1985; Burns, 1978; Yukl, 1989). Transformational leaders practice the "four I's": idealized influence, inspirational motivation, intellectual stimulation, and individualized consideration (Avolio, Waldman, & Yammarino, 1991). They are trustworthy, encouraging, risk taking, and considerate. They raise their followers' consciousness about the importance of outcomes and explain how followers can reach those outcomes by placing organizational interests ahead of self-interests.

Although most leaders engage in the full range of leadership styles, they do so to differing degrees. Many studies in a variety of organizations have suggested that the leaders who were most effective used the transformational style most frequently, the transactional style occasionally, and the nontransactional (laissez-faire) style rarely, if at all (Bass, 1985; Bass & Avolio, 1994).

Learning Activity

In small groups, construct specific scenarios in which each leadership style presented in table 15.5 might be displayed in a sport organization. Share your group's scenarios with the rest of the class. Decide which scenarios most accurately represent each leadership style.

MANAGERIAL LEADERSHIP

Modern management theorists tend to believe that both management and leadership are essential to the efficient and effective functioning of organizations. In concert with this idea, the term *managerial leadership* has emerged to describe the job of the manager–leader. **Managerial leadership** combines the notions of management and leadership into a single construct (see figure 15.3) and expresses the notion that they are two sides of the same coin. As Kotter (1990) observed, good management skills are needed to maintain "a degree of consistency and order," and good leadership skills are needed to "produce movement" in a business (p. 103).

> **managerial leadership**—The combination of management and leadership into a coherent, integrated concept.

Learning Activity

Figure 15.3 presents eight roles of managers and eight roles of leaders. In small groups, make a list of specific scenarios in sport organizations that would call for each of these roles. Describe the actions that you recommend in each of these scenarios.

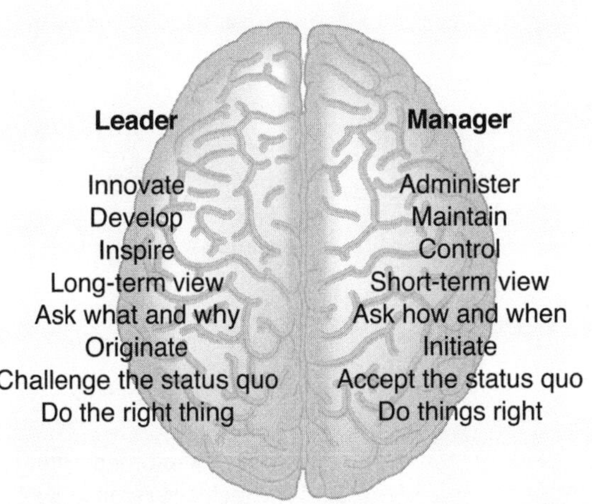

Figure 15.3 The integrative concept of managerial leadership.

Sport management scholars also conceptualize leadership and managerial behaviors as a unified concept. Soucie (1994), for example, suggested that management and leadership are qualitatively different and that each complements the other, resulting in more effective and efficient sport managers. Quarterman (1998) provided further support for this notion when he found that NCAA conference commissioners used both management and leadership skills, depending on the given situation.

Classifications of Managers

Although all managers have formal authority for directing the work activities of others, managers possess different degrees of authority. In the hierarchy of an organization, managers are usually classified as top level, middle level, or supervisory level (Glueck, 1980).

- ***Top-level managers***. The number of managers in this group is small. Also known as executive or senior-level managers, they have the most power and authority. They are usually responsible for the entire organization or a major part of it.
- ***Middle-level managers***. Also known as administrative-level managers, these individuals are usually selected by top-level managers. They are, therefore, accountable to top-level managers and responsible for the employees who are below them in the hierarchy. The managers at the middle level are, in general, responsible for (1) managing a department or unit that performs an organizational function (Petit, 1975) and (2) ensuring that the assigned tasks are done efficiently. To their subordinates, middle-level managers are the source of information and solutions to problems because they know the technical side of the products and services. Middle-level managers are unique because they must be both leaders and followers. They are connected to supervisors and to subordinates, both of whom are also managers.
- ***Supervisory-level managers***. These managers, also known as first-line managers or supervisors, report to middle-level managers and are responsible for the employees who work in their units. The employees for whom these managers are responsible can be classified as operatives or technical specialists. Supervisory managers have the least amount of authority. They are primarily responsible for a single area in a work unit, division, or department, in which they supervise the work of the operatives or technical specialists. Their job is to communicate with, inspire, and influence their subordinates to get the job done in the

Table 15.6

Selected Titles for Managers at Different Levels in Three Typical Sport Organizations

Levels of management	Professional baseball organization	Investor-owned health and fitness club	NCAA Division I-A intercollegiate athletics program
Top-level managers (executive- or senior-level)	President Chief executive officer Vice presidents • Business operations • Baseball operations	Owner(s) General managers Regional directors • Corporate wellness • Health promotion	Board of trustees University president Athletics director (AD)
Middle-level managers (administrative-level)	Director of public relations Director of corporate sales Director of marketing operations Team manager Director of scouting	Site managers • Corporate wellness • Health promotion	Associate ADs • Director of development • Director of business operations • Senior associate AD
	Director of stadium operations Director of broadcasting Director of community relations Director of baseball administration	Coordinators (supervisors) • Aerobics • Fitness • Golf • Pro shop • Weight training	Assistant AD • Sports communication director • Coordinator of athletic training • Marketing director • Academic coordinator

most effective and efficient way. Supervisory managers represent the contact point between the technical specialists (operatives) and middle-level managers.

Examples of titles of managers at these different levels in three types of sport organizations are shown in table 15.6.

Because many current sport management students will assume supervisory positions relatively early in their careers, we give it special attention here. Being a supervisory manager can be challenging, rewarding, and stressful. One of the most challenging areas that you will encounter in your first management position is exercising authority over subordinates, especially your former colleagues. Most often, newly promoted managers must distance themselves from their former colleagues and friends and thus contend with being lonely at the top (well, not really the top, but closer to the top than before being promoted). On the other hand, the promotion brings the rewards of elevated status, higher salary, and additional opportunities to make important contributions to the organization as well as to subordinates. "Tips for New Supervisory Managers" offers several guidelines to help new

Learning Activity

Review an issue of *Athletic Business*, *Fitness Management*, or the *NCAA News*. Find an example of a job announcement for a top-level manager, a middle-level manager, and a supervisory-level manager. Explain your classification rationale—that is, what characteristics of the jobs made you decide that one was top, one was middle, and one was supervisory?

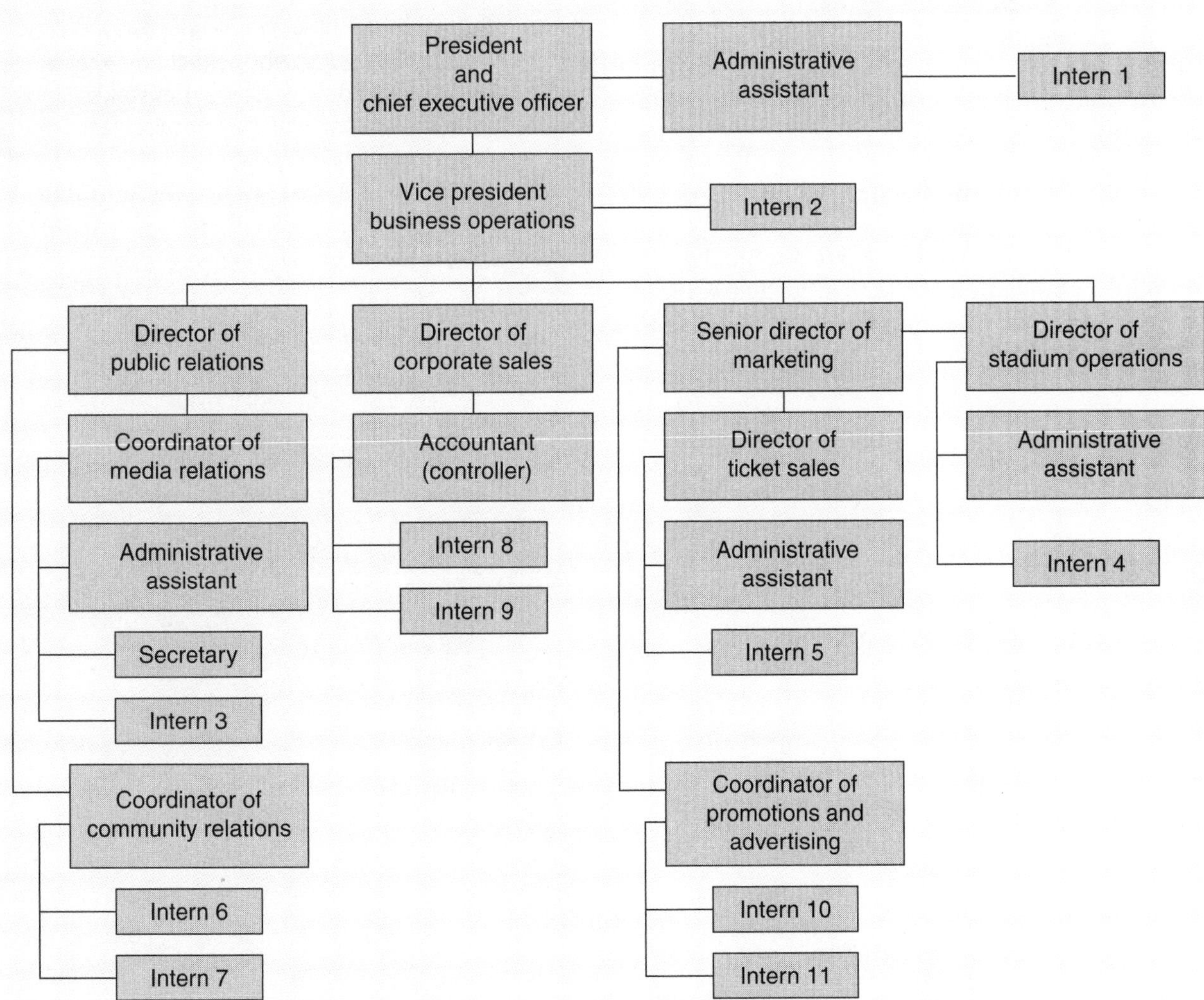

Figure 15.4 Partial organizational flow chart for the business side of a hypothetical professional baseball club.

Learning Activity

A partial organizational flow chart for a hypothetical baseball club is presented in figure 15.4. Identify those managers who are top level, middle level, and supervisory level. Also, identify the operatives (technical specialists). Justify the placement of the positions into the various classifications.

supervisory managers ease into management positions and gain confidence in the new roles.

Managerial Leadership Skills

As noted in chapter 1, competencies are the combination of the skills and knowledge necessary for successful performance. We are not born with skills. We learn and develop them through experience and training. Katz (1974) categorized the skills needed by managers as conceptual skills, interpersonal (human) skills, and technical skills. Managers at all levels use all three of these skills. As shown in figure 15.5, however, managers at the different levels (top, middle, supervisory) use them to differing degrees.

Conceptual skills are required for managers to see the sport organization as a whole and to see the relationships among the parts that make up the entire organization. As shown in figure 15.5, top-level managers often devote a major portion of their time to long-range planning; therefore,

TIPS FOR NEW SUPERVISORY MANAGERS

- Establish a positive relationship with employees—respect your subordinates, ask them for information or advice, and be receptive to their ideas.
- Let go of the old job—train workers to do your old job so that you can concentrate on your supervisory responsibilities.
- Set a good example—be the kind of worker that you expect your subordinates to be.
- Perform the job with your own style—continue to be yourself, even as you improve your strengths and gain new ones.
- Give recognition to employees—remember that sincere praise, attention, and approval for a job well done are powerful motivators.
- Support the employees—accept the mistakes of subordinates and work with them to correct their errors; admit your own mistakes, and defend subordinates if they are falsely accused of making mistakes.
- Be a leader—show that you are motivated to get things done and to involve your subordinates in accomplishing the objectives.

Source: Kumagai, B.T., & Kleiner, B.H. (1995). Managing the transition to supervision. *Work Study, 44*(1), 8-10.

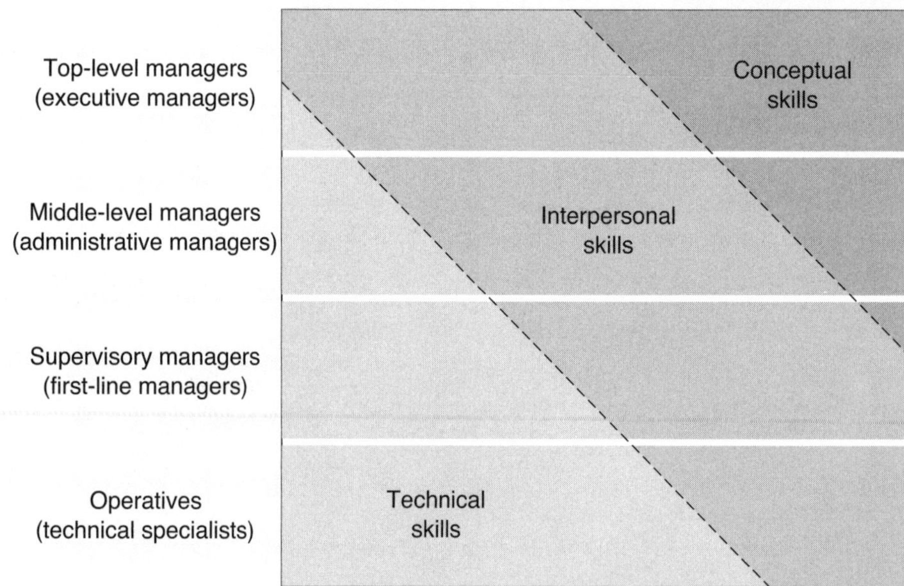

Figure 15.5 Typical distribution of time that managers spend using conceptual, interpersonal, and technical skills.

they typically spend more time using conceptual skills than do middle- and supervisory-level managers. Paul Tagliabue, former commissioner of the NFL, was a top-level sport manager recognized for using conceptual skills. "I don't want to be involved in things that are repetitive and things that are day-to-day," Tagliabue noted. "If it involves a new concept, then I want to know the concept is being implemented the way I conceived it, not the way someone else dreamed of it. I don't want to micromanage" (Weisman, 1993, p. 2C). Middle-level managers use conceptual skills somewhat less than top-level managers do and somewhat more than first-line managers do.

Managers use interpersonal skills to interact with others and to coordinate individual and group efforts in achieving the organization's goal. This responsibility implies that managers must be able to work with both internal and external **constituents**. Interpersonal skills are important to managers at all levels of sport organizations because they are responsible for designing ways for others to do the work. They work with and through others to attain the goals of the organization, so they must be able to communicate effectively. Middle-level managers use interpersonal skills more often than they use technical or conceptual skills (see figure 15.5). For example, if students who are dissatisfied with campus recreation programs and services lodge their complaints with the director of campus recreation, she or he will need interpersonal skills to deal constructively with the situation.

constituents—People who are involved in or served by an organization (Merriam-Webster Online Dictionary).

Technical skills include the specialized knowledge, tools, techniques, and resources necessary for achieving an organization's goals. Managers must master these skills and be able to teach them to their subordinates. A middle-level manager, such as the marketing director for a national athletics footwear firm, would have to be competent in preparing the annual report or annual budget for the marketing division of the firm. He or she must also be able to teach others who work in the division how to prepare such reports. In a sport club, supervisory (first-line) managers use technical skills when they show workers new teaching techniques and how to set up equipment. Because supervisory-level sport managers spend most of their time directing (i.e., motivating, leading, and communicating) subordinates, they use technical skills more often than do top- or middle-level managers. Conversely, top-level managers (i.e., owners, executive directors, or general managers) will use fewer technical skills and will spend far more time using conceptual skills (e.g., developing and implementing long-range goals and monitoring the resources used by the club) and interpersonal skills.

Notice in figure 15.5 that technical specialists must be well trained in both technical and interpersonal skills. This does not mean, however, that technical specialists cannot or should not use conceptual skills; in fact, the best ones do.

Learning Activity

Management consultants, business school professors, and CEOs of America's largest companies identified seven key skills that a person needs to be an effective and efficient leader (Labich, 1988). These skills are presented in table 15.7. For each skill, give one reason that managers who apply it are effective and efficient. Then, for each skill, give one consequence that might occur if managers do not apply it.

Managerial Roles

Besides using a wide range of skills, managers must also assume a variety of roles (Mintzberg, 1973, 1975/1990). Mintzberg defined a role as a set of expected behaviors associated with a managerial position. Based on Mintzberg's theory, the typical manager performs 10 roles, which are classified into three categories: interpersonal, informational, and decisional.

Interpersonal Roles

Mintzberg (1975/1990) identified three specific interpersonal roles: figurehead, leader, and liaison. When managers engage in these roles, they are primarily involved in interpersonal relationships with others. As **figureheads**, managers perform a variety of symbolic and ceremonial duties. Managers are engaged in the figurehead role when they attend a subordinate's wedding, welcome visitors to an organization, represent the organization at a public function, or cut the ribbon for a new facility.

figureheads—Managers acting in symbolic and ceremonial ways.

The leader role relates to managers' relationships with their followers. As leaders, managers recruit, select, train, motivate, evaluate, and direct

KOREAN SPORT ORGANIZATIONS

Gi-Yong (Win) Koo, Korea

Over the past few decades, Korea's sport industry has grown tremendously, particularly in the development of international sport. Specifically, Korea has successfully organized worldwide sporting events such as the 1988 Seoul Olympic Games and the 2002 Korea–Japan FIFA World Cup. These events have drawn attention to three sport organizations that are pioneers in the sport business and academic fields: the Korea Sports Council (KSC), the Seoul Olympic Sports Promotion Foundation (SOSFO), and the Korea Society for Sport Management (KSSM).

The KSC is the largest sport governing organization in the country. Located in Seoul, this organization began functioning in 1920. The core activities of the KSC are facilitating international sports exchanges, disseminating the Olympic Movement in Korea, and promoting sport marketing in Korea. Through its efforts, the Korean sport industry receives remarkable attention from people all over the world. The KSC has jurisdiction over 53 sport member associations, 16 state organizations, and 14 international associate branches.

The KSC has a hierarchical organizational structure; therefore, all work units communicate with their immediately superior work units and with their immediately subordinate work units. Annually, the Korea Institute of Public Administration evaluates the organizational effectiveness of the KSC based on five criteria: fulfillment of long-term goals, completion of annual business plans, appropriateness of goal setting, suitability of the strategic plan for achieving goals, and potential for obtaining funds. These evaluations are designed to keep the organization running efficiently.

Another significant sport organization in Korea is the SOSFO, established as a public foundation in 1989. The major business of the SOSFO is to provide support for the promotion of national sports and research in sports science as well as to create sound direction of youth sport activities. Its mission involves developing "healthy people and a strong country."

The SOSFO has focused on the construction of a healthy society since its successful hosting of the 1988 Seoul Olympic Games, which still receives high marks as one of the best Games in history. Specifically, the SOSFO has performed pivotal roles in expanding the significance of sport and the sport industry to increase the national desire for sport. The SOSFO will continue to support sports facilities and projects related to the development of youth and to promote the sport industry so that the whole nation will be able to enjoy a healthy and pleasant lifestyle. This financial support will pave the way to a society that delivers energy and hope to all people in Korea.

Lastly, the KSSM, which developed the academic field for the Korean sport industry, has established itself as a significant sport organization in Korea. Since its establishment in 1995, the KSSM has played a critical role in lending a scientific hand to the management of sport. The KSSM has focused on the promotion of research and the professional development of sport management. The executive council of the society consists of more than 50 researchers with doctorates in sport management and 20 practitioners from the sport business industry. The KSSM hosts an annual international conference and publishes the *Korean Journal of Sports Management* in both Korean and English. The society has been active in promoting international exchanges. It has played a pivotal role in organizing the Asian Association for Sport Management (ASSM), which includes among its members China, Hong Kong of China, Japan, South Korea, Malaysia, Singapore, Chinese Taipei, and Thailand.

Because the KSC, SOSFO, and KSSM are active and productive, we are confident that the sport industry has a bright future in Korea.

the followers' energies and efforts toward accomplishing the organization's goals. Leaders are also responsible for coordinating the work of followers. Examples of the leader role are conducting a workshop on computer programming for the support staff and rewarding staff for outstanding job performance. The director of ticket sales exhibits the role of leader when providing flexible working hours for the telemarketing staff.

The **liaison** role refers to a manager's ability to develop and cultivate relationships with individuals and groups outside the work unit or organization. For instance, coordinators of concessions usually maintain contact with vendors to determine when special sales will occur on certain supplies. Directors of campus recreation often meet with peer directors to discuss important issues before official voting sessions. These managers are acting in the liaison role.

liaison—Managers in the role of developing and cultivating relationships with individuals and groups outside the work unit or organization.

These Korean teenagers are on teams that are largely supported by private companies. This corporate support is one result of the work of SOSFO and similar government organizations.

Photographed by Seok-Kyun Hong.

International Learning Activity

Compare and contrast similar sport organizations in your country with the KSC, SOSFO, or KSSM.

Informational Roles

When managers exchange and process information, they engage in the informational role. This role includes monitor, disseminator, and spokesperson. As **monitors**, managers scan the environment for information about trends and events that can affect the organization. They collect information from a variety of sources, including subordinates, peers, superiors, contacts, news media, electronic mail, the Internet, gossip, and hearsay. A supervisor who has a coffee-lounge conversation with other supervisors about the organization's plans to downsize the support staff is engaging in the monitor role.

> **monitors**—Managers in the role of scanning the environment for information about trends and events that can affect the organization.

As managers collect information, they become the nerve centers of their work areas. When they transmit the information to others, they are disseminators and spokespersons. As **disseminators**, managers selectively pass on information to others in the organization or work unit. A supervisor who attends an athletic conference meeting and then informs the subordinates of the rules changes that were enacted is engaging in the role of disseminator.

> **disseminators**—Managers in the role of passing information on to others in the organization or work unit.

As **spokespersons**, managers transmit information to persons or groups outside their organizations or work units. For example, when the director of public relations of a professional baseball organization speaks to the local Kiwanis club, she or he might tell the members about the upcoming season and special events. In this situation, the PR director is assuming the role of spokesperson for the baseball organization.

Table 15.7

Characteristics of Successful Leaders

They trust their subordinates.	A good leader will make use of employees' energy and talent. The key to a productive relationship is mutual trust.
They develop a vision.	Employees want to follow a visionary leader. They want to know where they are going and why.
They keep their cool.	Leaders demonstrate their mettle in crisis and under fire. They inspire others to remain calm and act intelligently.
They are experts.	Employees are much more likely to follow a leader who radiates confidence, is intuitive, and continues to master the profession.
They invite dissent.	A leader is willing to accept a variety of opinions and integrate them.
They simplify.	Leaders focus on what is important and reach elegant, simple answers to complex problems by keeping the details to themselves.
They encourage risk.	Leaders encourage employees to take chances, readily accept error, and not fear failure.

Source: Labich, K., 1988, The seven keys to business leadership. Fortune, 118(9), 58-62, 64, 66.

spokespersons—Managers in the role of transmitting information to persons or groups outside the manager's respective organization or work unit.

Decisional Roles

Decisional roles occur in four categories: entrepreneur, disturbance handler, resource allocator, and negotiator. As **entrepreneurs**, managers search for ways to effect change and improve an organization. A manager who provides the latest computer technology for the ticket office is acting in an entrepreneurial role. The director of operations of a professional football team who finds and uses information worldwide is also fulfilling an entrepreneurial role.

entrepreneurs—Managers in the role of searching for ways to effect change and improve an organization.

As **disturbance handlers**, managers respond to unexpected situations that might disrupt the organization's normal operation. Usually, managers must react to such disruptions immediately. For example, if all the support staff of a sport marketing agency become ill with influenza and cannot report to work during the week of a major tennis tournament sponsored by that agency, the normal operation of the tournament will be disrupted. The event manager at the agency would need to hire temporary help and recruit volunteers to handle the disturbance effectively.

disturbance handlers—Managers in the role of responding to unexpected situations that might disrupt the organization's normal operation.

As **resource allocators**, managers determine how best to allocate resources such as people, money, equipment, supplies, time, and information to each employee, group, or work unit, or to the entire organization. For example, the coordinator of marketing and promotions of a state sport festival must provide the support staff and assistants with adequate office supplies to develop literature for informing the public about upcoming events.

resource allocators—Managers in the role of determining how best to allocate resources to each employee, group, or work unit, or to the entire organization.

As **negotiators**, managers confer with people inside or outside the work unit or organization to obtain concessions or to agree on pivotal issues. Bargaining and reaching an agreement with subordinates, a regulatory agency, an interest group, or a vendor are examples of the negotiating role. A purchasing manager for the Women's National Basketball League who negotiates with a vendor for lower prices and faster delivery times on equipment and supplies is performing the negotiator role.

The degree to which managers perform each role described above will vary with managerial level. For example, Pavett and Lau (1983) found that the disseminator, figurehead, negotiator, and spokesperson roles are closely associated with top-level managers. The leadership, resource allocator, and disturbance handler roles are more closely associated with first-line supervisory managers (Kerr, Hill, & Broedling, 1986). Table 15.8 illustrates the role delineation revealed in a study of NCAA conference commissioners (Quarterman, 1994).

negotiators—Managers in the role of conferring with people inside or outside the work unit or organization to obtain concessions or to agree on pivotal issues.

Learning Activity

Working in small groups, select a segment of the sport industry other than athletic conferences. Using table 15.8 as a model, construct a table describing the roles of a manager in the chosen segment. Provide examples of how the manager would fill each of the 10 roles.

Table 15.8

Adaptation of Mintzberg's Managerial Roles for Intercollegiate Athletic Conference Commissioners

Role	Description of role	Examples
Interpersonal		
Figurehead	Performing ceremonial duties on behalf of the conference	Welcoming dignitaries, greeting visitors, participating in groundbreaking ceremonies
Leader	Influencing subordinates to get the work done at the conference office	Conducting performance evaluations, acting as a role model in the workplace, praising an employee for doing a good job
Liaison	Maintaining a network of outside contacts to gather information for the conference	Attending meetings with peers, listening to the grapevine, participating in conference-wide meetings
Informational		
Monitor	Perpetually scanning the environment for information that may prove useful to the conference	Lobbying for information at an NCAA meeting, staying in contact with other commissioners by telephone, reviewing the athletic literature
Disseminator	Transmitting information received by individuals or groups outside the conference	Sending information to the coaches and athletic directors, having a review session on NCAA rules with the athletic directors
Spokesperson	Transmitting information to individuals or groups outside the conference	Speaking at community and professional meetings, briefing the state legislature about athletics
Decisional		
Entrepreneur	Searching for new ideas and implementing changes for the betterment of the conference	Initiating a new marketing concept for increasing revenue, bringing new technology to the conference
Disturbance handler	Making decisions to deal with unexpected changes that may affect the conference	Resolving a conflict among member institutions, dealing with changes in game schedules
Resource allocator	Making decisions concerning resource use—people, time, money, space, or the conference	Making a decision about a tournament site, adding or deleting a sport program
Negotiator	Bargaining with individuals, groups, or organizations on behalf of the conference	Negotiating a television contract, negotiating with vendors

Reprinted, by permission, from J. Quarterman, 1994, "Managerial role profiles of intercollegiate athletic conference commissioners," Journal of Sport Management 8(2): 131-132.

Table 15.9

Selected Studies of Managerial Roles in Intercollegiate Athletics Organizations

Researchers	Participants	Purpose	Major findings
Danylchuk & Chelladurai (1999)	37 Canadian intercollegiate directors	To describe and analyze managerial work in Canadian intercollegiate athletics	Financial management, leadership, policy making, disturbance handling, revenue generation, and athletic affairs were perceived to be the most important activities. Information seeking, maintenance activities, and league responsibilities were rated the least important." (p. 148)
Quarterman (1994)	63 athletic NCAA conference commissioners	"Examined the managerial role profiles of 63 intercollegiate athletic conference commissioners." (p. 129)	The commissioners rated the disseminator role as most important. Remaining roles were rated in the following order: liaison, disturbance handler, monitor, leader, entrepreneur, spokesperson, figurehead, negotiator, and resource allocator.
Quarterman, Allen, & Becker (2005)	151 athletics directors of National Association of Intercollegiate Athletics (NAIA) member institutions	To examine the athletics directors' roles and to investigate relationships between roles and types of institutions (e.g., private and public).	Most ADs ranked the leadership role (interpersonal category) as the most important; more ADs at private institutions ranked the leadership role as the most important; more ADs at public institutions ranked the negotiator role (decisional category) as the most important.

Learning Activity

Three studies of managerial roles in intercollegiate athletics organizations are summarized in table 15.9. Examine those summaries and discuss their implications for the professional preparation of students who aspire to become intercollegiate athletics administrators.

SUMMARY

Management and leadership are two distinct yet complementary functions. Management refers to the process of working with and through individuals and groups to accomplish organizational goals. Leadership is the process of influencing individual and group behavior for some desired result. Contemporary management theorists have cited five underlying processes that guide the concept of management: planning, organizing, directing, staffing, and controlling and evaluating. Two of the most common leadership theories are trait and behavioral. Three situational leadership models are Fiedler's contingency model, the path–goal model, and the Situational Leadership Model. Another model, known as the full range of leadership model includes transactional, laissez-faire, and transformational styles. The latter model includes transactional, laissez-faire, and transformational styles.

Managerial leadership is a concept that integrates management and leadership. Managers "do things right," and leaders "do the right thing." Organizations are more likely to experience success when the administrators serve as both managers and leaders.

Managers in sport organizations are classified as top level, middle level, and supervisory level. The executive or senior-level managers of an organization have the most power and authority. Middle-level managers are selected by and accountable to top-level managers. Middle-level managers, sometimes referred to as administrative-level managers, are responsible for supervisory managers and technical specialists. Supervisory-level managers report to middle-level managers and are responsible for operations or technical specialists.

Conceptual, interpersonal, and technical skills are three types of managerial skills. Conceptual skills are the ability to see the organization as a whole and the relationships among the parts that make up the whole organization. The abilities to interact with others and to coordinate individual and group efforts in achieving an organization's goal are referred to as interpersonal skills. Technical skills are concerned with the specialized knowledge, tools, techniques, and resources used to achieve an organization's goal.

Managers in sport organizations commonly assume three basic roles: interpersonal, informational, and decisional. When managers perform the interpersonal role, they are primarily involved in interpersonal relationships with others. When they exchange and process information, they engage in the informational role. When executing the decisional role, managers search for ways to effect change and improve their organization, respond to unexpected situations that might disrupt their organization's normal operation, or determine how best to allocate resources.

Review Questions

1. Define management and leadership and, using examples from sport organizations, explain the differences between them.
2. Identify the underlying processes of management and give an example of each.
3. Explain one study of management in sport organizations.
4. Explain one study of leadership in sport organizations.
5. Briefly review each of the leadership theories and models.
6. Explain the major classifications of managers.
7. Discuss the managerial skills needed in sport organizations.
8. Discuss the roles that sport managers assume.
9. Explain the managerial skills used at each level of management in a sport organization.

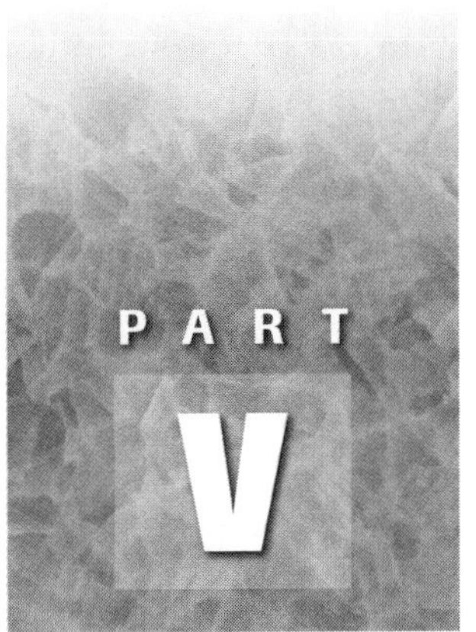

Current Challenges in Sport Management

A critical step in the process of becoming a responsible and effective manager of sport enterprises is recognizing the significance of sport as a major social institution. The three chapters in this section provide the foundation for understanding the challenges presented by legal, ethical, and social aspects of sport. An appreciation of these facets of sport will increase the likelihood that you will make wise managerial decisions within the context of the broad social environment in which sporting activities occur.

In chapter 16 Lori Miller and Anita Moorman introduce basic concepts related to legislation affecting the management of sport in the United States. After presenting a brief introduction to the American legal system, the authors discuss the influence of the federal Constitution on sport management, using as an example the decision on whether prayer should be permitted at public school athletic contests. Next, Miller and Moorman explain the effects of federal legislation, explicitly the Americans with Disabilities Act and Title IX of the Education Amendments Act. Then they discuss state legal systems, including tort law, negligence, intentional torts, and contracts. Miller and Moorman conclude the chapter with a discussion of legal challenges that await prospective sport managers. The topic of the international sidebar is legal considerations in sport management in Canada. Hilary Findlay, who teaches sport law at Brock University (St. Catharines, Ontario, Canada), contributed this essay.

In Chapter 17 Joy DeSensi and David Malloy establish the need for the study of ethics and philosophy in sport management, with particular emphasis on the philosophy of existentialism. After defining ethics, they discuss the influence that values have on the approaches that sport managers take to their responsibilities. Then DeSensi and Malloy define three types of values—immediate, instrumental, and intrinsic—and explain ways in which you can evaluate your values. Then they thoroughly explore the concept of existential leadership, one of several philosophical approaches to leadership available to sport managers, explaining why they believe in the utility of this approach. DeSensi and Malloy conclude the chapter with a discussion of the importance of translating values and beliefs into action. Rather than a sidebar, this chapter contains a collection of quotations from ethicists and philosophers from many countries. These quotations convey the generalizability of ethical concepts and philosophical principles.

Chapter 18 focuses on the role of sport sociology in the management of sporting activities. Mary Jo Kane defines sport sociology, explains the role of theory in understanding sport in the US culture, and discusses the social significance of sport. Kane then examines possible benefits of sport, such as its ability to socialize participants and unify people. Next, she presents several examples of the darker side of sport, including an overemphasis on winning and the encouragement of eating disorders as well as sexism, racism, homophobia and heterosexism, and violence. Kane concludes the chapter with a discussion of how sport can serve as a vehicle for social transformation and how you can apply your knowledge of sport sociology in the management of sport. Throughout the chapter, Kane presents relevant research findings and highlights the role of the media in the perpetuation of the influence of sport on society. The international sidebar is an essay on spectator violence in Australia. Lisa Kihl, a native of Australia who teaches sport management at the University of Minnesota, contributed the essay.

For More Information

Legal Resources

www.findlaw.com

www.washlaw.com

www.law.cornell.edu

www.marquette.edu/law/sports/links.html

www.srlaweb.org

Ethics Resources

www.sportsethicsinstitute.org

Professional and Scholarly Associations

Academy of Legal Studies in Business: www.alsb.org

American Alliance for Health, Physical Education, Recreation and Dance (AAHPERD): www.aahperd.org

American Sociological Association (ASA): www.asanet.org

Australia and New Zealand Sports Law Association: www.anzsla.com.au

Center for the Study of Sport in Society: www.sportinsociety.org

Institute for Diversity and Ethics in Sport: www.bus.ucf.edu/sport/cgi-bin/site/sitew.cgi?page=/ides/index.htx

International Association of Sports Law: http://iasl.org

National Association for Girls and Women in Sport (NAGWS): www.aahperd.org/nagws/template.cfm

North American Society for Sport Management: www. NASSM.org

North American Society for the Sociology of Sport (NASSS): http://playlab.uconn.edu/nasss.html

Sport and Recreation Law Association: http://srlaweb.org

Sports Lawyers Association (SRLA): www.sportslaw.org/

Tucker Center for Research on Girls & Women in Sport: www.tuckercenter.org

Women's Sports Foundation (WSF): www.womenssportsfoundation.org

Scholarly and Legal Journals

Journal of Legal Aspects of Sport

Sport Management Review

Journal of Sport Management

Sport Marketing Quarterly

Marquette Sports Law Review

Seton Hall Journal of Sports and Entertainment Law

American Business Law Journal

International Review for the Sociology of Sport

Journal of Sport & Social Issues

Sociology of Sport Journal

Women in Sport and Physical Activity Journal

CHAPTER 16

Legal Considerations in Sport Management

Lori K. Miller—Wichita State University ▪ **Anita M. Moorman**—University of Louisville

Learning Objectives

After studying this chapter, you will be able to do the following:

1. Identify select legal issues affecting sport management operations.
2. Explain the legal concepts associated with the legal system, tort law, ADA, Title IX legislation, constitutional issues, and contracts.
3. Identify situations in which legal issues may influence decision making.
4. Engage in critical thinking and problem solving regarding how the law can influence sport management decisions.

As you learned in chapter 3, sport managers make numerous decisions each day. These decisions will be of various levels of importance and difficulty. All of them, however, will require the sport manager to engage in a process of decision making. The manager's decisions are likely to affect numerous constituencies, including coworkers, supervisors, the media, spectators, and participants, just to name a few. All these groups are entitled to hold the sport manager accountable for her or his decisions. Chapter 3 also introduced you to the value of critical thinking skills in responding to constituencies who challenge decisions that have been made and who may demand justification for chosen strategies. Now that you have acquired a fundamental understanding of the importance of critical thinking and have learned to ask the core critical questions, you can move on to a deeper understanding of how the law affects both your decision-making process and the results of your decisions.

constituencies—For purposes of this chapter, constituencies are any people influenced by a particular decision.

This chapter will introduce you to situations that require sport managers to examine how legal principles can influence decisions. We will introduce selected legal issues, discuss the situations in which these legal issues arise, and present questions for you to ponder. This chapter focuses on the law and the legal system of the United States, but you should remember that as the sport industry continues to expand into the global marketplace, international law affects many sport organizations. Although we cannot include a complete discussion of international law in this text, we will briefly explore some Canadian legal issues in our international sidebar.

THE BASICS OF LAW

There are varied interpretations and definitions of the law. As defined by Black (1990), the law represents a "body of rules of action or conduct prescribed by controlling authority and having binding legal force" (p. 884). The law is an accumulation of rules and regulations that govern our behavior. Failure to abide by the defined rules of law results in either civil or criminal penalty. In the United States, judges, juries, or congressional representatives do not arbitrarily define the law. Rather, the citizens of the country, in part, define the law. Legislatures (state and federal) enact **statutes**, which create the need for agencies to write or **promulgate** rules and regulations. Then, the courts are required to interpret the statutes or rules and fill in any gaps left by legislatures.

statutes—Laws established by legislatures.

promulgate—To formally proclaim new legislation to the public. This occurs when the law receives final formal approval.

The American judicial system is divided into distinctly separate federal and state systems. The United States Constitution is the supreme law of the land. It governs conduct of the federal and state governments, as well as providing for the fundamental rights of private citizens. Each of the 50 states similarly has a state constitution that governs the conduct of the state government and protects citizens of that state. The United States Congress and 50 state legislatures also enact laws (i.e., statutes) that address issues ranging from enforceability of contracts, to product liability, to the registration of trademarks. Each of the 50 states and the federal government have their own court systems. These court systems, both federal and state, are hierarchical in structure. The highest court is usually a supreme or superior court. An intermediate appellate court is at a middle level, and a district or trial court is at the bottom. Most cases originate at the trial or district court level and work their way up through the court system. It can take years for a case to move through all levels of the court system.

A fundamental premise of the law includes the concepts of **precedent** and ***stare decisis***. A precedent is simply a prior decision that is used to guide and influence subsequent decisions containing similar facts and questions of law (Teply, 1999). The doctrine of *stare decisis* is the legal principle that compels courts to follow a previous decision or precedent when deciding a subsequent case, in the same district or jurisdiction. These two concepts work together to provide predictability and consistency to judicial decisions. This predictability and consistency are important because those bound by the law are then able to make sound decisions and conduct themselves and their affairs in accordance with the law. For example, consider a situation in which a football player injures another player during a game and the injured player threatens to sue the other player. If players had to worry about being sued every time that another player was injured, many sport competitions would probably never occur. The majority rule as established by numerous judicial decisions, however, provides that a player is liable to another player for an injury only if the player causing the injury acted recklessly (i.e., with conscious indifference to an extreme risk). The reckless standard is a much higher standard for determining liability than a traditional negligence standard (i.e., failing to act reasonably). Thus, the concepts of precedent and stare decisis would lead to the conclusion that a player is not liable to another player for accidental or negligent injuries. This precedent helps guide how sport participants conduct themselves and how sport organizations manage sport contests. Players, coaches, and event organizers can predict this judicial outcome because courts will rely on precedents when facing the same or a similar situation.

precedent—A legal case establishing a principle or rule that a court may need to adopt when deciding subsequent cases with similar issues or facts. The term may also refer to the collective body of case law that a court should consider when interpreting the law.

stare decisis—Literally means "to stand by things decided." This principle expresses the notion that prior court decisions must be recognized as precedents, according to case law, and followed accordingly.

But the law is also dynamic because of different fact scenarios, jurisdictional differences, legislative changes to existing laws, creation of new laws, and

1920

▷**1922**
Federal Base Ball Club of Baltimore v. National League of Professional Base Ball Clubs (259 U.S. 200) establishes MLB antitrust exemption

1970

▷**1972**
Flood v. Kuhn—Curt Flood (St. Louis Cardinals) challenges MLB's reserve clause

2000s

▷**2001**
PGA Tour v. Martin—Supreme court rules that Casey Martin can use a golf cart in PGA events

changing societal values (Shapo, Walter, & Fajans, 1999). Legislatures adopt statutes reflecting, in part, the desires of those whom they represent, and many of these laws will affect sport managers or sport organizations either directly or indirectly. For example, many states have adopted the Uniform Athlete Agent Act, which provides protection for student–athletes from unscrupulous sport agents and establishes uniform agent registration and disclosure requirements. Many of the athlete agent statutes have not yet been the subjects of lawsuits; consequently, the courts have not yet interpreted many of the statutes and statutory components. As litigation occurs, courts will decide how the law is to be interpreted, thus setting precedent that will serve as the foundation for later decisions with similar facts. Other societal influences and behaviors have spawned statutes governing ticket scalping, steroid use, gambling, drug testing, and discrimination in athletics. It is the function of the courts to decide disputes to determine whether statutes were properly and legally interpreted and applied (Shapo et al.).

SOURCES OF LAW

- Constitutions: United States Constitution and individual state constitutions
- Statutes: Federal laws enacted by Congress: United States Code (USC); state laws enacted by state legislatures
- Administrative Law: Rules and regulations created by federal agencies: Code of Federal Regulations (CFR); rules and regulations created by state agencies
- Common law: federal and state court decisions

The remainder of this chapter provides a basic overview of US legal principles that affect sport management.

FEDERAL CONSTITUTION

As succinctly stated by Jesse Wilde (2001), the United States Constitution "governs American governments, not Americans" (p. 415). The following sections explore the protective intent of the United States Constitution and several fundamental protections that it affords to citizens of the United States.

Protective Intent of the US Constitution

A fundamental purpose of the Constitution is to protect the people from government's unwarranted intrusion, discrimination, arbitrary and capricious treatment, and infringement of liberty and property rights without **due process**. Sport organizations governed by the Constitution include, for example, athletics programs in public schools, state university athletics departments; federal, state, and municipally owned park and recreation departments; and possibly even a person or organization that leases state-owned property to host a sporting event. The Constitution was not intended to govern the operation of privately owned and operated sport organizations such as retail sporting goods stores, fitness clubs, private golf courses, or professional sport teams.

due process—Law that is administered in the regular course by a court of justice (Black, 1990). But what due process means as it is embodied in the 5th and 14th Amendments to the United States Constitution is that a law shall not be unreasonable, arbitrary, or capricious and that the means selected for enforcing a law shall have a reasonable and substantial relation to the government objective sought.

The passage of the 14th Amendment to the US Constitution in 1868 provided citizens within a given state the same protections against unwarranted actions by state government. The provisions that regulated the acts of the federal government as embodied within the first 10 amendments were passed down to the operations of state governments. Thus, the 10 amendments to the federal Constitution (also known as the Bill of Rights) prohibited state-related, unwarranted behaviors and intrusions on the people.

A Critical Thinking Case Study

An issue that requires sport managers to use critical thinking skills to evaluate a constitutional issue is the question of prayer at public school sporting events (Keeley & Parks, 2003). This controversy, which is particularly prominent in the United States, presents an excellent opportunity for you to practice critically evaluating an issue of great

2000s

2003 Glenbrook North High School (IL) hazing incident

2004 Todd Bertuzzi severely injures opponent Steve Moore during NHL play (March 8)

concern to the public while also learning about how the law, specifically the US Constitution, can be interpreted.

Assume that you were recently named to the position of athletics director at a public high school with a long tradition of offering prayers over the public address system at athletic contests. Recently, however, some students and parents have challenged the prayers, and you aren't sure what to do. To add to the confusion, you receive a letter from a student's parents, who are irate that you are even considering eliminating the prayers (figure 16.1). What will you decide to do? Will you continue the tradition, eliminate it, or alter it? How will you make your decision? Read the letter in figure 16.1 and then consider several critical questions that were presented in chapter 3.

What Are the Issues?

The letter in figure 16.1 asks the question, Should prayer be permitted at public school contests? The major clue to this prescriptive on the issue is found in the first sentence: "Public prayer at public school athletic contests should be permitted." Thus, you, as an administrator, must be able to evaluate what this question requires you to do, if anything. To answer the question, you must understand the reasons behind the request.

What Are the Reasons?

The writers of this letter present several reasons, which are listed here:

- Reason 1: Restriction of personal voices violates the First Amendment, which guarantees freedom of speech and religion, and young people need to have opportunities to proclaim their faith publicly through prayer. The supporting reasons are as follows:

  1. President Clinton has argued that the Constitution doesn't require our schools to be religion-free zones.
  2. Students have the same rights and liberties as all American citizens, and we send them a wrong message when we permit open discussions about sex but not about God.

- Reason 2: Research shows that most Americans believe in God, and most support public prayer. The supporting reasons are as follows:

  1. A 1999 *Newsweek* poll found that 94% of Americans believe in God.
  2. Another poll found that 83% of Americans favored student prayer at graduation ceremonies.
  3. A survey conducted in 2000 showed that 74% of respondents believed that "school prayer teaches children that 'faith in religion and God is important.'"

- Reason 3: Religion is good for our health. The supporting reason is that research by the Centers for Disease Control and Prevention found that regular church attendees lived eight years longer than infrequent attendees did, were less apt to die of coronary disease, and were less apt to commit suicide or die of cirrhosis.
- Reason 4: Prayer at athletic events is a longstanding tradition, and the practice of these traditions should be up to American citizens, not the government.
- Reason 5: Congressional sessions and other public meetings are opened with prayer, so why shouldn't athletic contests open with prayer?
- Reason 6: Even if the government acts against public prayer, some schools will continue to practice it anyway. The supporting reason is that a Texas coach says that his locker-room tradition of prayer will not end.
- Reason 7: President George W. Bush supports voluntary student-led prayer.
- Reason 8: People voluntarily choose to attend athletic contests; if they don't want to hear prayer, let them come late.

As you learned in chapter 3, we need to evaluate the parents' reasoning with more questions.

Which Words or Phrases Are Ambiguous?

In determining relevance, we first want to identify any ambiguous or unclear statements or arguments. For example, in the conclusion, the phrase "public prayer at public school athletic contests" is ambiguous. Although the meaning may seem obvious at first, our reaction to the conclusion and its supporting arguments may reflect the choice of one of the following definitions of public prayer:

1. A school administrator asks those present at the contest to stand and join her in a prayer, which she reads over a microphone.
2. A student representative spontaneously asks those around him to join him in a moment of silent prayer.

Dear Athletics Director:

Public prayer at public school athletic contests should be permitted because the First Amendment gives American citizens the right to freedom of speech and freedom of religion. Any restriction on a citizen's personal view or voice is a violation of these fundamental American rights. This country was founded on the principle of freedom of religion, and the young people of our country need to have opportunities to publicly proclaim their faith through prayer. As President Clinton stated, "I have never believed the Constitution required our schools to be religion-free zones, or that our children must check their faith at the schoolhouse door" ("Public Schools and Religion," 2000). Students have the same rights and liberties as all American citizens. In fact, we are sending students the wrong message when we allow open discussions about sex in our public schools but forbid discussions about God (MacLeod, 2000).

Research has revealed that most Americans believe in God and most support public prayer. For example, a 1999 *Newsweek* poll found that 94% of Americans believe in God while only 4% are atheists (MacLeod, 2000). Another 1999 poll found that 83% of Americans favored allowing students to say prayers at graduation ceremonies (*The Closet Atheist,* n.d.). A survey conducted in 2000 revealed that 74% of the respondents believed that "school prayer teaches children that 'faith in religion and God' is important" (Walsh, 2001).

Religion is also good for our health. Research financed by the Centers for Disease Control and Prevention found that people who attended church frequently had, on average, a life expectancy of eight more years than infrequent attendees (as cited in Myers, 2000). Moreover, religious people are 53% less apt to die of coronary disease, 53% less apt to commit suicide, and 74% less apt to die of cirrhosis (as cited in Myers).

Athletics plays a huge part in the lifestyles of many Americans. With athletics come traditions, which often include prayer. The government does not have the right to forbid its youth from praying, particularly when it is such an integral part of the athletics tradition.

It is the right of American citizens to decide what they want to say when addressing any group publicly. Congressional sessions and other public meetings are opened with prayer, so why shouldn't athletic contests be started with prayer? People who want to pray have the right to believe in and say what they choose, even at public school events. If the government chooses to take any action against public prayer, some schools will continue practicing public prayer at all athletic events anyway. In Abernathy, Texas, the high school's head football coach, Dewayne Sexton, says that their locker-room tradition of prayer will not end: "We enjoy it and feel good about it; that's what we do" (Alford, 2000, p. 19). President George W. Bush agreed as he stated, "I support the constitutionally guaranteed right of all students to express their faith freely and participate in voluntary student-led prayer" (Mauro, 2000, p. 4). The fact is that people attend athletic contests voluntarily; so if they don't want to hear prayer, let them come late.

Angrily,

Chris and Pat Johnson

Figure 16.1 Letter from irate parents to the athletics director.

If the parents are using the first definition, then we may be less willing to agree with them because the first definition seems to create a more coercive environment for those who do not wish to join in. The second example, on the other hand, would seem to represent a private person exercising his or her freedom of religion. Those around him appear to be free not to participate. Notice that the term *public prayer* also is a key term used in reason number 2, and we should be reluctant to agree or disagree with this reason until we have a better sense of just what kind of public prayer most Americans support.

Another importantly ambiguous phrase is *freedom of religion*, which appears in reason 1. Just what does the First Amendment mean by guaranteeing freedom of religion? The extent to which that reason supports the conclusion will depend greatly on how broadly we interpret freedom of religion and how much we actually know about the US Constitution.

What Are the Value Conflicts and Assumptions?

What do these parents care about that leads them to take this position on the issue and to choose the reasons that they use to support their conclusion?

A central value assumption that links reasons 1 and 2, as well as reason 6, to the conclusion is a preference for the value of the right of religious expression over the value of separation of religion and civil or government authority. All these reasons emphasize religious rights and activities while ignoring concern about the rights of students and other spectators to be free from the imposition of religious practices.

A value assumption that links reason 4 to the conclusion is a preference for tradition over government intervention. Also, for the results of public opinion polls in reason 2 to be supportive of the conclusion, we must assume that majority rule is an important value.

What Are the Descriptive Assumptions?

In order for reason 1 to support the conclusion, the parents must assume that schools cannot provide outlets for people to express their religious beliefs and pray while at the same time maintaining a separation of church and state. This assumption is questionable because students can practice religious beliefs in many ways other than at school-sponsored events such as athletic contests.

Also, in order for reason 6 to support the parents' conclusion, the assumption must be made that because some people will ignore government acts, such acts are wrong. For example, people frequently ignore government-regulated speed limits. Does that mean that our government should abolish speed limit laws?

Does the Reasoning Contain Fallacies?

Using a survey that shows that most Americans favor student prayer at graduation ceremonies to support the belief that most Americans support public prayer urges us to accept a position simply because a large number of people accept it. This argument is an example of the fallacy of appealing to common opinion. Popularity of a belief is not good evidence for its truth. In addition, the first and third supporting reasons for reason 2 support irrelevant points. They focus on belief in God and what school prayer teaches, not on legal protection for public prayer, which is the central issue. Also, reason 3 commits the fallacy of using the wrong reason; the issue is not about religion per se but about public prayer at athletic events.

How Good Is the Evidence Supporting the Request?

The parents used appeals to authority (e.g., Presidents Bush and Clinton), several research studies (see reasons 2 and 3), an analogy (see reason 5), and a personal testimonial (see supporting reason for reason 6) as evidence. The credibility of this evidence is questionable. First, we do not know whether Presidents Bush and Clinton have carefully studied the legal arguments on the issue; thus, his public statements of support do not represent specific legal authority that we can rely on. Moreover, it is possible that political considerations may influence any elected official's public statements, so we must be careful to examine the legal authority on which they base their statements. Second, the surveys are of questionable relevance because no information is given about sample size, breadth, and randomness, or about the wording and context of the survey questions. Since we cannot evaluate the survey methodology, we cannot assess the validity of the survey questions or generalize the results to large populations of Americans. Third, a single testimonial such as that from the Texas coach is of limited value because we do not know how representative his view is of other coaches' opinions. It is entirely possible that different coaches will have different attitudes toward public prayer. Finally, the analogy between an opening prayer before Congressional sessions and prayer at a football game is not a particularly strong one. Can you think of important differences between prayer in Congress and prayer at a football game? Why might prayer be all right for Congress but not for a public school sporting event?

Considering this discussion, would you describe the evidence provided in the parents' letter as strong or weak?

What Significant Information Is Omitted?

The parents have left out much information that could help us judge the persuasiveness of their reasoning. Information that we would like to see includes the following:

- A clearer legal definition of public prayer and freedom of religion
- Recognition and rebuttal of common counterarguments, such as the argument that school sponsorship of a religious message sends a message to some that they are outsiders and to others that they are insiders of the community
- President Clinton's actual legal reasons for his claim that the Constitution doesn't require our schools to be religion-free zones
- Further details about the most relevant surveys—especially information about the people surveyed, how the survey was presented to them, and the wording of the survey items

Can you think of other relevant research that the letter writers omitted?

Learning Activity

Read the article "Balancing the First Amendment's Establishment and Free Exercise Clauses: A Rebuttal to Alexander & Alexander" by P. Batista, which appeared in 2002 in the *Journal of Legal Aspects of Sport, 12*(2), 87-116. Identify two examples of religious activities that must be permitted during a public school function such as a football game based on the free exercise clause, and two examples of religious activities that must not be permitted during a public school function based on the establishment clause.

The 1st Amendment to the federal Constitution passed in 1791 provides that "Congress shall make no law respecting an establishment of religion, or prohibiting the free exercise thereof." This portion of the 1st Amendment contains two conflicting and interdependent clauses—the establishment clause and the free exercise clause. These two provisions are often in conflict with each other. The establishment clause prohibits a public school from taking actions that endorse or establish one religion over another. At the same time, that same public school may not take any actions that prohibit the free exercise of individual religious beliefs. Thus, determining what actions satisfy both clauses can be challenging. The 1st Amendment, as applied to state public schools by the 14th Amendment, has been interpreted as requiring a clear demarcation between any religious activity or practice and the public schools. In other words, a religious activity or practice is not to become entangled within an educational institution that receives state moneys or is governed by state employees. The government is not to promote or inhibit any religious practices.

Now, let's look at the issue in the context of the language of the federal Constitution regarding religion. As you read the following section, consider the extent to which your new knowledge of critical thinking might influence how you would react to the letter on prayer at public school sporting events. For example, did the letter fail to address issues that it should have mentioned?

Common law decisions have held that because young students have impressionable minds, what might begin as a tolerance for religious expression can later become coerced indoctrination. Common law is the body of law derived from the judgments and decrees of the courts rather than those laws created by legislatures. Further, in holding against the constitutionality of prayer, courts have considered the nature of events at which prayer is present (e.g., high school football games) (see *Santa Fe Independent School District v. Doe*, 2000). Courts have concluded that attendance at these various events is not totally voluntary because of, for example, peer pressure, music credit given for band participation, and physical education credit given for athletic team participation. In other words, attendance at a high school football game, although not compulsory, is required for some students who want to obtain the overall education experience. Although only a few students may experience a diminished educational experience because of their unwillingness or inability to participate in events at which a prayer occurs, it is indisputable that the role of the courts includes protecting the rights of the minority. Hence, the establishment clause of the First Amendment is violated when what may be viewed as **de minimis** (or minimal) religious activity become entangled with school activity. A moment of silence has become a common alternative to prayer as a means of preserving the convivial attitudes and respectful behaviors of both the audience and the participants (see Thompson & Edmonson, 2002).

common law—The body of law derived from the judgments and decrees of the courts rather than those laws created by legislatures.

de minimis—Literally meaning "about minimal things"; means something that is trivial or seemingly unworthy of the law's attention.

FEDERAL LEGISLATION

The federal Constitution empowers Congress to enact legislation in a variety of subject areas (e.g., copyrights, patents, trade and commerce, taxation, securities regulation). Congressionally enacted legislation reflects societal interests regarding future conduct about a variety of issues including, for example, discrimination and business practices (e.g., ticket scalping). Statutory language may appear general in nature because of its emphasis on governing uncertain future conduct (i.e., situations demanding statutory application that have not yet arisen). In turn, judges, through their written judicial opinions, establish the application and interpretation of a statute having no legislative history. Many federal laws affect sport, some specifically and others only indirectly. For example, the Americans with Disabilities Act and Title IX (discussed later) apply to a broad range of individuals and entities. In other words, when Congress enacted these laws, the elimination of discrimination was a broad and sweeping goal, not just in sport programs but also in employment, education, and public places throughout the United States. The legislation has had, and continues to have, a significant effect on sport managers' decision making. Other federal legislation such as the Ted Stevens Olympic and Amateur Sport Act (2005) and the Sport Agent Responsibility and Trust Act (2005) were enacted specifically to regulate an aspect of the sport industry.

Learning Activity

Look up the Ted Stevens Olympic and Amateur Sport Act, 36 USC § 220501 et. seq. What is a national governing body? A paralympic sports organization? Next, locate the Sports Agent Responsibility and Trust Act, 15 USC § 7801 et seq. (2005). What disclosures and warnings must sport agents give to student–athletes? You can locate these using LexisNexis, the government access Web site at www.gpoaccess.gov/uscode, or the Web site of the Legal Information Institute of Cornell Law School at www.law.cornell.edu/.

Americans With Disabilities Act

The Americans with Disabilities Act (ADA), which was passed in 1990, prohibits discrimination against people with disabilities as well as people who are perceived to have a disability. Under the ADA, a person is defined as having a disability if he or she has (1) a physical or mental impairment that substantially limits one or more major life activities, (2) a record of a disability, or (3) a perception of possessing a disability. Title I of the ADA prohibits discrimination in employment. Employers cannot discriminate against a person with a disability who meets essential job qualifications with or without reasonable accommodation. Title III prohibits discrimination in places of public accommodation. In other words, all people must be provided reasonable accommodations that permit them access to places where the public congregates or participates for purposes of recreation or leisure (e.g., bowling centers, health and fitness centers, skating rinks, sport arenas, and stadia). An accommodation is not required if accommodating the disabled person poses a direct threat to other participants or if a requested accommodation creates an undue hardship by fundamentally changing the nature of the product offering (e.g., aerobic dance class), represents an excessive financial burden, or disrupts the environment itself.

Title IX of the Education Amendments Act

In the United States a law known as Title IX, which was passed in 1972, precludes discrimination based on sex in any education program that receives federal financial assistance. With regard to sport, compliance with Title IX is generally evaluated in three areas. The first area looks at the school's distribution of financial aid among the women's and men's athletic teams. The second area evaluates other benefits, opportunities, and treatments within men's and women's sports programs. Areas evaluated include, but are not limited to, the following:

1. Provision of equipment and supplies
2. Scheduling of games and practice times
3. Travel and per diem allowances
4. Opportunity to receive coaching and academic tutoring
5. Provision of locker-rooms and dining facilities
6. Publicity and recruitment procedures
7. Other support services provided (e.g., clerical or administrative)

The third area examines whether the interests and abilities of the underrepresented group have been accommodated.

The Department of Education has identified a three-prong test for examining the extent to which the interests and abilities of the underrepresented group have been accommodated. The first prong compares the proportionality of the university's male and female students to the proportionality of male and female student–athletes. For example, if the population of the student body at State University is 52% female, the percentage of female

The Americans with Disabilities Act (ADA) has made a tremendous difference in the lives of those with disabling conditions or injuries. Consider what this swimmer might have missed had that legislation not been passed.

student–athletes should also be 52%. Few college athletics programs meet this challenging standard. The second prong allows a school to demonstrate compliance by showing that the school has either a history or a continuing practice of program expansion responsive to the interests and abilities of the underrepresented sex. The third prong allows a school to demonstrate compliance by proving that it is fully and effectively meeting the interests and abilities of its students with its current athletic programs. In other words, this prong conveys that although a disparity may exist between the percentage of males and females within the general student population versus the percentage of males and females among student–athletes, this inequity is due to legitimate, nondiscriminatory factors.

Proving interest levels is not an exact science. The courts have identified several ways to obtain information about athletic participation interest levels: (1) student requests that a sport be added; (2) requests to elevate a club team to varsity status; (3) participation levels in club or intramural sports; (4) interviews with students, newly admitted students, coaches, administrators, or others regarding interest in a particular sport; (5) results of questionnaires of current and newly admitted students; (6) participation levels in interscholastic sports; (7) discussions with amateur athletic associations or community sports leagues; and (8) inclusion of participation and interest questions on university admissions forms (see *Pederson v. Louisiana State University*, 2000).

A controversial clarification letter from the Department of Education in March 2005 stated that a school could demonstrate effective accommodation of current interest and abilities by conducting an online interest survey of its student body. Many critics challenge both the propriety and methodology of these interest surveys, and this topic will likely continue to cause controversy. The majority of Title IX litigation has focused on this three-prong analysis (i.e., proportionality, history or continuing practice, and effectively accommodating current interests).

STATE LEGAL SYSTEMS

As discussed previously, the legislature of each state is responsible for enacting laws to govern its citizens. Each state also has a constitution that sets forth the rights of its citizens and the limitations of the state government. And each state has a court system to interpret and apply the laws of that state. Two areas of law that are based solely on state law are torts and contracts. Thus, although the concepts of prec-

Learning Activity

Assume that you are a senior high school female athlete who aspires to play soccer at a US university 250 miles (400 kilometers) from home. As an all-state varsity soccer player, you have numerous scholarship opportunities in the fall of your senior year. Unfortunately, the university 250 miles down the road does not have a women's soccer program. Your grandfather, father, brother, and sister all attended this university, and you are enthusiastic about following the family tradition and becoming another loyal fan and alumna. In the spring you joyously celebrate the news that your school of choice has added women's soccer as an NCAA varsity sport. Besides announcing the new competitive opportunity for women, the school announces its plans to eliminate the men's varsity wrestling team and the men's swim team. You are perplexed by this situation and wonder whether the school's move to eliminate the men's teams is necessary for compliance with Title IX. What are your thoughts? Is the school's decision to eliminate the men's teams the only option available? What other options might the school explore?

edent and stare decisis apply within the state court systems, a state court is not compelled to follow a precedent from another state. For example, if Florida had already decided a case similar to a case pending in Oklahoma, the Florida decision would be informative or perhaps even persuasive to the Oklahoma court, but the Oklahoma court would not be required to follow the precedent established in Florida.

Tort Law

A tort is a civil wrong or injury for which the law permits a recovery. Typically, a wrong or injury is either a negligent act or an intentional act by one person that causes an injury to another person or his or her property. Tort law focuses on whether a particular person (or persons) failed to perform appropriately based on her or his (or their) relationship with the injured plaintiff. The purpose of tort law is to remedy a wrong. Compensatory or punitive damages (or both) can provide a remedy for the wrong. Compensatory damages can reflect monetary damages for medical bills, lost days of work, payment for hired hands, lost earning potential, and pain and suffering. Punitive damages, in comparison, can impose additional monetary damages on the defendant that serve to punish the defendant for his or her wrongdoing and make an example of the defendant's conduct so that others do not engage in similar acts. Punitive damages often greatly exceed the actual costs of the injury and are generally available only for intentional torts.

tort—A tort is a civil wrong or injury for which the law permits a recovery. Typically, the wrong or injury is either a negligent act or an intentional act by one person that causes an injury to another person or his or her property.

As mentioned earlier, a person may have a cause of action in tort because of the negligent or intentional acts of another. Unintentional torts encompass claims based on negligence. Claims based on defamation, invasion of privacy, assault, and battery represent intentional torts.

Negligence

Negligence represents the failure to act as another reasonably prudent person would have acted in a like or similar circumstance. To prove negligence, a plaintiff must prove the following four elements: duty, breach of duty, proximate cause, and injury. The duty can be based on (1) relationship with the plaintiff (e.g., coach and student–athlete, teacher and student, general manager of a sport team and spectator), (2) voluntary assumption of a duty (e.g., a volunteer coach who agrees to assist a student–athlete with her or his college application materials), or (3) duty imposed by a statute (e.g., a state law that requires lifeguards at all public swimming pools). Breach of duty, the second element, represents an act that was not performed as another reasonable, prudent person would have performed it in the same or similar situation. Typically, liability is eminent when an injury is foreseeable by another reasonable, prudent professional or the defendant's actions reflect a disregard for the relevant professional standards. Proximate cause relates to the linkage between the defendant's failure to adhere to the standard of care (breach of duty) and actual injury suffered (van der Smissen, 2004). For example, although the defendant may be negligent, the injury may have resulted from some other intervening act. Consider the following example: A swimming pool manager has a duty to provide a lifeguard and fails to do so, and a child is injured when a table umbrella falls on top of him. The failure of the pool manager to provide a lifeguard did not cause the injury. And if the umbrella fell because of an unexpected gust of wind, the gust of wind is the cause of the injury. But if the table umbrella fell because of the pool operator's failure to install or inspect the umbrella properly, then the injury would be a result of the operator's breach of duty. Lastly, an injury must actually occur. For example, a swimming pool operator could both fail to inspect the table umbrella and fail to provide a lifeguard, but if no one is injured from these acts, a claim for negligence would also fail. Defenses for negligence can include, but are not limited to, assumption of risk, comparative negligence, failure to meet one of the four elements of negligence, failure to meet procedural guidelines (e.g., statute of limitations), governmental immunity, volunteer immunity statutes, and recreational use immunity statutes.

Intentional Torts

Tort claims may also result from intentional rather than negligent conduct. A number of intentional torts provide a plaintiff with a legitimate cause of action. Intentional torts include invasion of privacy, defamation, assault, and battery. Invasion of privacy and defamation are closely linked.

Invasion of privacy is a tort claim allowing a person to recover for the publication of truthful information and is intended to protect people from unwarranted intrusions into their private lives. Invasion of privacy claims can be based on excessive intrusion into private areas and the unwarranted disclosure of private facts. The fundamental principle underlying invasion of privacy claims is a person's right to be let alone (*Rosenbloom v. Metromedia, Inc.*, 1971). A three-prong test is used to determine invasion of privacy liability based on intrusion or disclosure. The three-prong analysis asks three questions: (1) Did intentional intrusion or disclosure occur regarding private information? (2) Was the intrusion or disclosure something viewed as private to the plaintiff? (3) Would another member of society be reasonably offended? Invasion of privacy claims can also be based on commercial misappropriation that can occur when a person attempts to profit from another's name or likeness. For example, if you printed up hundreds of T-shirts that bore Tiger Woods' image and then sold them, you would be using Woods' image for profit and misappropriating his likeness without his permission.

Defamation claims are intended to protect a person's reputation and allow him or her to recover from the publication of damaging, false information. A plaintiff who alleges defamation must prove four elements to win a defamation claim: (1) a false communication, (2) communication with a reckless disregard for the facts, (3) communication reported to a third party, and (4) communication causing damage to his or her reputation. These elements can be found in the Restatement (Second) of Torts, § 559 (1963). (**Restatements** are secondary legal research sources that seek to restate the legal rules that constitute the common law in a particular area. The American Law Institute [ALI], a prestigious legal organization composed of noted professors, judges, and lawyers, writes the restatements. The ALI has completed restatements in 15 areas of law including torts, contracts, property, conflict of laws, foreign relations law, and products liability). The tort of defamation strives to protect a person's right to her or his reputation, pride, and integrity. For example, a coach who is terminated during on ongoing NCAA recruiting scandal investigation would find it difficult to find other employment if information were published implying that he or she had committed or contributed to the violations. Truth, however, is a defense to a defamation allegation. Thus, if the coach did in fact commit the violations, a defamation claim would be inappropriate. The proof required in defamation claims tends to be subjective. Hence, a successful defamation claim is difficult to prove and can take years to litigate.

TYPES OF INTENTIONAL TORTS

- Invasion of privacy: protects against unwarranted intrusions into private areas and disclosure of private facts
- Defamation: protects against publication of false statements that are harmful to a person's reputation
- Assault: protects against threats that could result in physical harm
- Battery: protects against actual physical harm or offensive touching

restatements—Secondary legal research sources that seek to restate the legal rules that constitute the common law in a particular area such as contracts, torts, property, foreign relations, and product liability.

Sport managers are better able to protect themselves and their employer, while also serving their fans, spectators, consumers, clients, and employees when they understand the distinction between invasion of privacy and defamation, as well as the behaviors that can subject them and the sport entity to liability.

Contracts

The law of contract is also known as the law of private agreements. Contract law enables private

LEGAL CONSIDERATIONS IN CANADIAN SPORT

Hilary Findlay, Canada

In Canada, two main sources of law are common law and statute. The province of Quebec comes from a different legal tradition: that of the civil law. The civil law system is based on a comprehensive civil code, or body of rules, as opposed to the evolution of principles. The common law, as described in this chapter, derives from centuries of judicial decision making. Also known as judge-made law, the common law differs from statutes, which are specific laws passed by legislative bodies. Often statutes simply codify principles of the common law. For example, each province in Canada has a statute on occupiers' liability that codifies the principles of negligence previously discussed. Statutes may also be created to deal with new topic areas or to reflect changing societal values, such as laws dealing with intellectual property, human rights, and privacy.

Canadian law can also be divided into public law and private law. Public laws are those that govern relationships between members of the public and the government. Areas of public law include criminal law and constitutional law. Private law encompasses those laws that govern relationships between private individuals and public and private corporations. Areas of private law include contract law and tort law, of which negligence is a part. Some areas of law can apply to both public and private law. Administrative law is one such example because it deals with fairness in decision making—whether by public bodies or private bodies. Although national and provincial sport organizations might receive large portions of their funding from the Canadian government, they are private organizations. When they make decisions that affect their members, they must do so in a way that respects the principles of fairness that are part of administrative law.

Two distinct jurisdictions in Canada affect what laws (i.e., public laws or private laws) might apply to the various sport interests: those aspects that are within federal jurisdiction and those that are within provincial jurisdiction. The Canadian Constitution sets out the areas of authority for each level of government. So, for example, education (and thus, in general, school sport) is the responsibility of the provinces. Likewise, organizations that do business within a single province would incorporate under the incorporation laws of that province. On the other hand, national sport organizations, which do business among all the provinces, would incorporate under the federal laws of incorporation.

The Constitution of Canada also contains a Charter of Rights and Freedoms (i.e., the Charter). It is through the Charter that basic individual and group rights and freedoms are protected, including, but not limited to, the rights of free speech, religion, mobility, due process, and equality. As with the United States Constitution, the Charter applies only to government action. It is not intended to apply to private organizations, such as national and provincial sport organizations, professional sport teams, and private sport clubs. The Charter does, however, apply to school sport, municipal recreation, and to the various statutes of the provinces and territories. For example, in 1986, 12-year-old Justine Blainey successfully used the equality section of the Charter to strike down a section of the Ontario human rights statute that allowed direct sex-based discrimination in athletic activity. (See *Blainey v. Ontario Hockey Association* (1986), 54 O.R. (2d) 513, 26 D.L.R. (4th) 728; revg. (1985), 52 O.R. (2d) 225, 21 D.L.R. (4th) 599 (H.C.).)

Although the Charter has relatively narrow application to sport, both provincial and federal jurisdictions have passed human rights legislation. Such legislation applies to activities that are available to the public and has been found to apply to universities, national and provincial sport organizations, and local sport leagues. It does not apply to purely private organizations such as private health or golf clubs. Although the language of such legislation differs slightly from jurisdiction to jurisdiction, it generally protects individuals from discrimination in the provision of sporting activities and facilities on the prohibited grounds of sex, disability, religion, national or ethnic origin, and family status, among others.

parties to enter into agreements and enforce those agreements legally. A contract represents an agreement between two or more parties to do, or not to do, a particular act. When a contracting party fails to abide by the terms of the agreement, the nonbreaching party has a legal cause of action. Contract law preserves and encourages the right of parties to make and enter into agreements as long as parties abide by the legal tenants associated with contract law, including, for example, (1) legal subject matter; (2) defined offer, acceptance, and consideration; (3) terms within the realm of acceptable public policy;

Clear the track

Here comes Justine

Justine Blainey, 14, is all smiles yesterday after winning her 2½-year fight for the right to play on a boys' hockey team. The Ontario Human Rights Commission ruled sex discrimination in athletics is unlawful — but boys can't play on girls' teams.

Page 5

Justine Blainey-Broker provided the test case that opened the gates for equal access to sport for girls and women in Canada in the 1980s. Here is a copy of a newspaper clipping on the case from Dr. Blainey-Broker's personal files.

Courtesy of Dr. Justine Blainey-Broker B.SC, D.C.
Article and photo © Sun Media Corp.

International Learning Activity

Look up the story of Justine Blainey. In your own words, write a paper about her experiences in Canadian sport. How do you think the same situation would have been resolved in the legal system of your country?

(4) parties in possession of capacity (i.e., appropriate age and without significant mental disability); (5) no economic duress or exercise of excessive bargaining power; and (6) clear and unequivocal contractual language. An offer, acceptance, and consideration represent the three basic tenents associated with contract law. Consideration refers to the bargained-for exchange (e.g., I'll pay you $75,000 USD in exchange for your employment as the State University associate athletics director for marketing, or I'll pay you $100 USD for your vintage rookie baseball card now worth $1,000 USD). In the latter example, the agreed-upon consideration benefits the buyer of the baseball card much more than it does the party selling the baseball card. Common law and statutes that govern contractual agreements do not require that the agreed-upon consideration be equal (or even fair) to both parties as long as the agreement is made without fraud, duress, or deceit. In other words, one party may clearly benefit by the terms of the contract itself. Recourse for breach of contract actions can include court-imposed injunctions, restoring the parties (or a party) to a contract to their (or his or her) precontract condition, reforming the contract so that it better represents the intention of the parties or fairness, or total abandonment of the contract itself (i.e., rescission).

A variety of sport organizations routinely use exculpatory agreements as part of their daily operations. Waivers and releases both reflect exculpatory agreements, that is, agreements used to excuse an organization for its own acts of negligence. For example, health clubs typically require members to sign a waiver before they use the facility's programs and equipment. The signed waiver excuses an organization (e.g., a health club) from ordinary negligence liability even if an employee of the health

Learning Activity

1. As you eagerly enter an Olympic venue to watch the races that you have long looked forward to seeing, a security officer stops you. The officer searches you and your belongings and takes your fingerprints to run through FBI and police databases that contain information about prior criminal behaviors. Does this intrusion bother you? In a balancing test, what societal benefits are gained and what societal privileges are forsaken? In what ways have individual and societal expectations of privacy changed over the past decade?
2. Assume that you are a university sports information director. Although you like your current job, you have applied for another job at a competing university. Days before your interview, chaos and confusion break out at your current university with rumor of a widespread athletics department scandal involving financial dishonesty, misrepresentation, and fraud. Faculty, student–athletes, boosters, and administrators all are allegedly involved. The local broadcast television station opens the nightly news show with the words, "Your local athletics department is in trouble, and individual integrities are suspect." The next day the local newspaper alleges your involvement in the criminal activity. You worry about how this debacle will influence your current and future employment opportunities. A friend mentions suing for defamation. What are some of the costs and benefits associated with a defamation lawsuit filed against the media that broadcast the university scandal and your alleged involvement?

Learning Activity

1. You have decided to do something about that New Year's resolution to improve your physical and mental condition by joining a local health club. As part of the membership process, the health club asks you to sign a one-year membership agreement for a fixed monthly fee. After 8 months, you are no longer regularly using the health club. Have you breached your contract with the health club if you stop paying your monthly fee before the end of the 12-month period?
2. Now assume that at the end of the year you are no longer regularly using the health club and decide that you don't wish to continue your membership. So you stop visiting the club and stop paying your monthly fee. Now have you breached your contract with the club? Would your answer be different if your contract provided that at the expiration of the first year, your membership would continue on a monthly basis until you notified the club in writing of your desire to terminate your membership? This scenario demonstrates (1) the importance of making sure that all important elements of an agreement are included in the contract and (2) that how the parties terminate or exit a contractual relationship is often as important as how they enter into a relationship. Thus, the parties must exercise care to make sure that the contract clearly spells out the rights of the parties when the contract ends, either according to its terms or in some manner not expected by the parties.

club is responsible for negligence and a resultant injury.

Exculpatory agreements represent a conflict with the purpose of tort law. As mentioned earlier, tort law seeks to allow one injured by another's negligence to recover damages as a matter of public policy; that is, the one causing the injury should be responsible to the injured person. On the other hand, contract law seeks to allow the enforcement of agreements entered into between private parties even though the agreed-upon terms may benefit one party more than another. Waivers jeopardize the legal rights of a few so that society may benefit. In sport and physical activity, the realm of possible injuries is extensive, ranging from mild muscle strains to sprains, heat exhaustion, heat stroke, broken bones, and even death. If people were allowed to sue for the minor injuries inherent in sport and physical activity, the expense associated with owning and managing a sport or recreational organization would be exorbitant and likely prohibitive. Insurance costs, litigation-related fees (e.g., discovery, attorney fees, expert witness testimony), and damaged public relations could result in the cessation of the sport and recreational industry. Judicial and legislative approval of the signed waiver, although it denies recovery to an injured plaintiff, benefits society through the continued solvency and sustained profitability of the sport and recreation industry.

If written correctly, waivers can provide legal protection to a sport entity for acts of ordinary negligence. As mentioned earlier, contract law is based on state common law and statues. Some states permit complete enforcement of waiver agreements; others refuse to enforce waivers at all because they conflict with acceptable public policy. It is always important to review individual state statutes and common law cases regarding the enforceability of exculpatory contracts, as well as state and industry specifications required for a legally enforceable contract.

FUTURE CHALLENGES

The daily decisions of sport managers profoundly influence employee and customer recruitment and retention, as well as organizational solvency. Effective and efficient sport management entities require managers who are cognizant of how their actions influence others. Further, the law (e.g., constitutions, statutes, common law) is a dynamic environment that constantly changes and requires managers to adapt and respond. Failure to comply with the law can bring both individual and organizational liability. Liability risk increases when professionals fail to act as another reasonable professional would act in a like or similar circumstance (i.e., negligence).

Several issues will continue to challenge sport managers. For example, office conduct and related policy issues such as maintenance of personnel files, communications with the media, and inspection of employee e-mail communications can subject an organization to invasion of privacy or defamation litigation. Contract negotiation is becoming a vital skill for sport managers as the sport industry continues to expand. An average NCAA Division I coach's compensation often is in the millions of US dollars and flows from a variety of sources (salary, perks, endorsements, licensing, camps, personal appearances, performance bonuses, and so on), all of which must be provided for in a clear and enforceable contractual agreement. Sport managers today must thoroughly understand contract law. Lastly, advances in technology continue to create legal issues that challenge sport managers. The increasing influence of the Internet in the marketing and promotion of sport has led to a number of new legal challenges such as Internet domain disputes, ambush marketing, and defamatory **blogging**.

> **blogging**—*Blog* is a term derived from *Web log*, which is a kind of hybrid diary–guide for a Web site. The act of posting or publishing personal thoughts and Web links is referred to as blogging. There are as many unique types of blogs as there are people.

SUMMARY

This chapter has discussed how to identify legal issues that affect sport management operations and has introduced many basic legal concepts that affect sport managers. It has also identified and explained a number of ways in which legal issues influence the sport industry and has emphasized how important it is for sport managers to make effective decisions when confronting legal issues. To recognize and respond to legal issues successfully, effective sport managers must engage in critical thinking and prudent problem solving.

Review Questions

1. Why does society need laws that govern behavior?
2. Identify the four elements of negligence that the plaintiff must successfully prove.
3. Elaborate on the concept of invasion of privacy based on intrusion, disclosure, and misappropriation and provide an illustration of why a plaintiff may sue for invasion of privacy.
4. Discuss how the Americans with Disabilities Act and Title IX have influenced the sport industry and discuss the continuing challenges regarding legal enforcement of this legislation.
5. How has the establishment clause (i.e., the separation of church and state) influenced prayer before competitive events or practices? Would a prayer before an annual athletic recognition ceremony during which varsity athletes are recognized and given participation plaques for their season efforts be legally permissible?
6. Identify the benefits of contracts as applied to the following parties: (1) the sport organization, (2) the individual, and (3) society at large.

Chapter 17

Ethical Challenges in Sport Management

Joy T. DeSensi—University of Tennessee at Knoxville ■ **David Cruise Malloy**—University of Regina

Learning Objectives

After studying this chapter, you will be able to do the following:

1. Recognize the need for ethical awareness.
2. Have a basic grasp of the nature of values, the way in which values influence behavior, and the way we can assess values hierarchically.
3. Have a basic appreciation of existentialism as it applies to leadership.
4. Know how to assess your own values and behavior through an existential lens.

In this chapter we establish the need for the study of ethics in sport management. We also present the philosophy of **existentialism** as a useful approach to leadership in sport management. We begin by defining ethics and discussing the concept of **values**, both personal and professional. A major feature of this discussion is the effect that values have on sport managers and how they approach their responsibilities. The process of establishing one's values and a discussion of a hierarchy of values and commitment follows. We then present the notion of existential leadership, which includes existentialist concepts of freedom, responsibility, dread, and **authenticity**. The chapter ends with the important step of translating values and beliefs into action.

existentialism—A philosophy based upon free will and the responsibility for action.

value—Those people, actions, and things that are worthwhile to us.

authenticity—Being true to oneself, being genuine.

"Ethics, if nothing else, is about how people ought to live, about preferred values and behavior" (Kretchmar, 2005, p. 186). The goodness or rightness and the badness or wrongness of our actions is the level at which we experience or understand values. Ethics is **prescriptive** in that it is concerned about how we as human beings *should* treat each other rather than how we *do* treat each other (Morgan, Meier, & Schneider, 2001). For sport managers to assume specific responsibilities ethically, they must have an understanding of their personal and professional values, obligations, and rights. They must also know how their values, obligations, and rights affect themselves and people for whom and to whom they are responsible. Knowledge of the difference between right and wrong from an ethical standpoint should inform sport managers' conduct and decision making and serve as a motivator for action.

prescriptive—Established rules that tell us how to act; founded on long-continued customs or laws.

Sport is a pervasive part of our society. Throughout our lives, we participate in sport in a variety of ways—as athletes, coaches, managers, administrators, or spectators. To be ethical participants at any of these levels, we must know what we value about sport and why we hold those values (DeSensi & Rosenberg; 2003, Lumpkin, Stoll, & Beller, 2003; Malloy, 2003).

The balancing of values and actions is difficult, especially when we confront conflicting messages in sport regarding the concepts of competition versus cooperation, profit maximization versus serving the public interest, fair play versus cheating, and violence in the wake of fair play. Although sport possesses some intrinsically valuable traits, it also has the potential to be a negative force in society. Frequently, a good effect of sport or a bad effect of sport can be traced to the choices that sport managers have made. Clearly, then, sport managers need to be cognizant of the ethical and moral issues inherent in sport. They must also know and understand their own personal and professional values so that they can appropriately address ethical and moral challenges. Because they often face situations in which they must choose the right path, they must have a compass to guide their decision making.

We hear much talk regarding athletic excellence, but little about moral excellence. This is the context of our discussion of ethics, values, and behaviors in sport management.

VALUES DEFINED

From ancient Greece to contemporary culture, philosophers such as Aristotle (384-322 BCE), Immanuel Kant (1724-1804), and Simone de Beauvoir (1908-1986) have discussed ethics as a central concern of their discipline. More recently, several contemporary authors have written applied works on ethics in sport and have offered definitions and types of values for our exploration.

BCE—Before the common era; the equivalent of BC in identifying ancient dates.

Definitions and Types of Values

Among the definitions of the term *values* are "a quality that is important to a person or a society" (Zeigler, 2002, p. 250); "anything we assess to be worthwhile, interesting, excellent, desirable, and important" (DeSensi & Rosenberg, 2003, p. 18); "the foundation of the good life" (Kretchmar, 2005, p. 207); "something that has worth or is worthwhile to you" (Lumpkin, Stoll, & Beller, 2003, p. 7); and "concepts of the desirable with a motivating force" (Hodgkinson, 1983, p. 36). This last definition suggests that our values provide the foundation for our behavior (Malloy, 2003, p. 78). All the foregoing definitions express the importance of the establishment of personal values—the recognition of those people, actions, and things that are worthwhile to us. Note as well the relativistic nature of values, in that each of us has values that, in many cases, are different from someone else's values. The process of discovering and exploring our values is central in creating, as Kretchmar notes, "the good life."

The general concept of values falls into four primary categories: moral values, social values, nonmoral values, and core values. Moral values are those that regulate behavior, accompanied by a sense of "oughtness." They are often universal and focus on the advancement of the human condition. These values can also be accessed through logic. Examples of such values would include honesty, justice, responsibility, and respect. In sport, fair play would fall within the category of a moral value. Social values are based on the cultural context (e.g., American, Canadian, Japanese). For example, individualism is generally highly valued in North American culture, whereas collectivism is valued in Japanese culture. Of course, the intent of these values needs to be taken into consideration. For example, individualism could result in either intolerable selfishness or reasonable self-actualization. From a moral standpoint, social values are important, but they are not as significant as moral values. Nonmoral values are defined as things, events, and places that a person regards as central to his or her life. For example, one may value wealth, pleasure, success, a car, home, friendships, and even sport as being critical for her happiness.

moral values—Values that are often universal and focus on the advancement of the human condition.

social values—Values based on the norms of a particular group (e.g., Americans, Japanese).

self-actualization—An internal, natural drive to become the best that one can possibly be; existentialism assumes that if we self-actualize (through being honest, sincere, and open) we will arrive at moral and ethical behavior naturally.

nonmoral values—Values that concern things, events, and places.

Learning Activity

As you learned in chapter 3, sport managers make better decisions if they consciously reflect on their personal values. Consider the following list of common values. As a sport manager, which five of these values are most important to you? Under what circumstances might you change your list of the five most important values? Explain.

Aggressiveness
Adventure
Ambition
Autonomy
Benevolence
Comfort
Commitment
Competition
Cooperation
Courage
Creativity
Environmental responsibility
Equality of condition
Equality of opportunity
Excellence
Fair play
Faster, higher, stronger
Flexibility
Freedom of speech
Harmony
Healthy lifestyle
Honesty
Intimidation
Honor
Justice
Novelty
Order
Patriotism
Peace
Perseverance
Rationality
Reliability
Selflessness
Security
Social Responsibility
Spontaneity
Teamwork
Tolerance
Tradition
Wealth
Wisdom

Adapted from Browne, M.N., & Keeley, S. 2007. *Asking the right questions: A guide to critical thinking* (8th ed). Upper Saddle River, NJ: Prentice Hall.

Hodgkinson's (1983) definition of values ("concepts of the desirable with a motivating force" [p. 36]) is crucial because it implies that the value leads to action. In this respect, Malloy (2003) noted, "If a value does not cause one to act, then it can be concluded that the value is not valued" (p. 61). For example, if I value fair play, then I must, in fact, play fairly. Such values are considered core values. Malloy described **core values** as ones that are acted upon, no matter the circumstance. These values are different from **intended values** (those that we intend to hold but that are affected by other things or situations), **adopted values** (adopted to conform to society out of pressure), or **weak values** (ones that do not lead to action) (p. 78). For example, a core value is the safety of my children—nothing will compromise this for me; fitness is an intended value, because I usually exercise; however, other demands sometimes supercede my noon hour workout. Weak values do not have such a strong effect on my behavior. For example, I may adopt the value of the ecologist when I am camping with friends and family but quickly revert to my normal polluting ways on my return home, or I may say that poverty in my city is a serious issue to me yet do nothing to alleviate the problem.

core value—Held no matter the circumstance; they translate into action.

intended value—We intend to hold these values but may not act on them because of the situation.

adopted value—Adopted to conform to society out of perceived pressure.

weak values—Espoused but do not lead to action.

Learning Activity

Conduct a value audit on yourself. List 10 values that you hold and then determine which of them are core, intended, adopted, and weak.

Hierarchy of Values

By ranking or categorizing values, one can identify lower and higher values. For example, immediate, instrumental, and intrinsic values can be distinguished from each other. Immediate values are those that directly cause pleasure or satisfaction. **Instrumental values** are those that are worthwhile because they are the means to something intrinsically good. **Intrinsic** or **terminal values** (e.g., Rokeach, 1973) are those that are worthwhile on their own, not merely a means to something. A discussion of two other ways of ranking values follows.

instrumental value—A value that leads to another value.

intrinsic value—Value held for the sake of itself with no other reward expected.

terminal value—A value that does not lead to further values (an ultimate value).

THE IMPORTANCE OF ETHICS IN SPORT MANAGEMENT

Ethical and moral concerns in sport management are increasingly significant because of the complexity and extraordinary rate of expansion of modern sport. For those reasons, there are many competing values within sport. Sport managers must learn to identify and evaluate values related to the bureaucratic and business aspects of sport. They must then seek to evoke positive change so that ethical behavior and practices are championed in sport (DeSensi & Rosenberg, 2003, p. 13).

Baier's Criteria As Presented by Kretchmar

Kretchmar (2005) suggested using Baier's (1958) work as a way of ranking a given set of values. This process includes (1) surveying the facts, and (2) weighing the reasons. Baier noted the importance of evaluating the characteristics and benefits of each value. The initial step, surveying the facts, involves examining the short- and long-term benefits, benefits for ourselves and for others, and benefits as ends in themselves and as means to other ends. The next step, weighing the reasons, involves applying three criteria to determine the hierarchy of the values (cited in Kretchmar, 2005). These criteria include intrinsic value, satisfaction, and coherence.

The criterion of intrinsic value indicates that values that are good in and of themselves are superior to values that lead to good things (e.g., knowledge, happiness). Means values (extrinsic values) are good because they lead to those things that are good in and of themselves. For example, although fitness activities may be good in and of themselves, they may not be comfortable at the time, but they are the means to overall fitness. Thus, achieving overall fitness (the intrinsic value) requires doing the fitness activities.

The second criterion is that of satisfaction. Kretchmar (2005) uses Frankena's (1973) work to explain that "all else being equal, experiences that include satisfaction carry more intrinsic power than those that do not" (p. 89). This concept is further explained as the contentment that we might feel from doing what we want to do even if it is difficult work. If the satisfaction produces little or no harm, it is preferred to that which brings harm. For example, running up the score on a less skillful person or team might bring satisfaction, but it could also bring harm. In addition, satisfaction that is durable or recurs is preferred to any satisfaction that is temporary. In the previous instance, the satisfaction gained from the lopsided victory is not nearly as durable as the satisfaction that comes from having a good reputation. The third criterion is that of coherence, which is based on the writings of MacIntyre (1984), Bellah et al. (1985, 1991), and Singer (1995), as cited in Kretchmar. Kretchmar notes that experiences that contribute to a "coherent and meaningful life take precedence over those that are isolated moments of pleasure" (p. 227) and that they bring more durable satisfaction. Each of these claims is debatable. They do, however, provide a good point from which to begin establishing a hierarchy of values.

Hodgkinson's Value Paradigm

The notion of a hierarchy also can be viewed in terms of the rationale for **valuation**. Hodgkinson's (1996) value paradigm (table 17.1) suggests that a value, any value, can be held from four different perspectives, each one commanding a more complex and convincing philosophical rationale. We will describe each of the four orientations in the hierarchy in ascending order.

valuation—To assess or evaluate.

1. As shown in table 17.1, the lowest grounding for a value is that of preference (type IV). Here a value is valued simply because the person likes it. The value is emotionally based, **subrational**, or precognitive. Little or no thought is at work—the value is simply an inclination. An example of preference is "I value fair play because I like the way it makes me feel."

2. Next is the value based on consensus (type III). A value at this level is held because it is commonly held—a simple democratic orientation. In other words, a person holds a particular value because everyone else seems to hold it (Kohlberg, 1984). Cognition begins to enter the valuation process but only in a limited fashion because the person is simply counting heads. "I value fair play because everyone else does" is an example of a value based on consensus.

3. The level of consequence (type II) fully engages the person's cognitive capacities. A value is valued because of the positive outcome that it produces. The person makes choices using sound logic and scientific methods, and if desirable outcomes result, then the person accepts the value. For

Table 17.1

Value Paradigm Abridged

Value type	Grounds of value	Psychological faculty	Philosophical orientation
I	Principle (transrational)	Conation	Existentialism
II	Consequence (rational)	Cognition	Utilitarianism Pragmatism
III	Consensus (rational)	Cognition	Democratic liberalism
IV	Preference (subrational)	Affect	Behaviorism Positivism Hedonism

Adapted from Hodgkinson, The philosophy of leadership, *1983, Palgrave Macmallan. Adapted with permission of Palgrave Macmillan.*

example, if "I value fair play because I am aware of the empirical evidence that illustrates its positive effect on moral development," I am basing my value on its consequences.

4. Finally, the highest rationale for valuing is the principled level. At this level, values are held based on a leap of faith—regardless of the emotional or intellectual justifications. A principle-based value is an authentic or genuine value, one that defines the essential nature of the person's sense of personhood: "I value fair play because this value is part of who I am—if I didn't play fairly, it just wouldn't be me." This level of authentic valuation leads unfailingly to action and to the realm of existential philosophy.

subrational—Implies activity based on emotion, preference, and instinct rather than calculated reasoning; synonymous with precognitive.

Values and Commitment

A number of social injustices often should be, but just as often are not, directly addressed in sport contexts. Examples include the displays of violence in contact sports and subsequent use by the media to market the events, the win-at-all-costs attitude exemplified by some coaches and teams, accepting bribes to win lucrative sport contracts, enticing college athlete recruits with monetary gains, not being able to distinguish game strategies from cheating, violating Title IX, and not upholding the commitment to education in intercollegiate athletics. These are only a few examples of ethical misconduct in sport. Each example denotes a serious violation of social justice and thus challenges the ethical and moral component of sport.

For this reason, you, as a prospective sport manager, should begin the process of consciously developing a moral sensitivity to issues in sport. Additionally, you would benefit from engaging in a personal introspective audit of your value systems with a view toward developing a commitment to treating people fairly and contributing to the overall betterment of sport. Such a commitment depends on conducting a thorough examination of values and developing a commitment to upholding values that lead to good actions. Commitment is the dedication of the self both intellectually and emotionally to a course of action. In this case, you would be acting on your higher-order values for the betterment of sport. Your commitment then becomes putting your values into action, resulting in social responsibility, reliability, trustworthiness, and integrity, as well as upholding your moral and legal accountability to yourself and others.

EXISTENTIAL LEADERSHIP IN SPORT ORGANIZATIONS

Before we embark on a deeper explanation of existentialism, we should note that a person may adopt many other ethical schools of thought to resolve ethical dilemmas. We focus on existentialism here because we believe that it leads more directly to an awareness of the individual's genuine self than its **deontological** and **teleological** counterparts do. In fact, existentialism is arguably a more radical and demanding approach to ethical conduct than the more traditional perspectives. Further, we contend that virtuous leadership begins with self-awareness of one's values and the extent of one's commitment to them. This is the primary focus of existential philosophy. We also encourage students to explore other viewpoints through other university courses and through their own self-directed study of the fascinating literature of ethics.

deontological—Theories that are rule oriented or principle oriented as opposed to outcome oriented (i.e., teleology). Deontological theories can have divine, social, and intuitive sources. In each case, ethical conduct is characterized by doing one's duty to adhere to these rules. A relevant example is "It's not whether you win or lose but how you play the game" (i.e., by following the preset regulations).

teleological—Theories that focus on the consequence or ends of action or behavior rather than the means or process. Goodness, pleasure, or happiness is the outcome sought by either the individual (i.e., hedonism) or the greatest number (i.e., utilitarianism). For example, consider a teleological quotation from American football coach, Vince Lombardi: "If it doesn't matter who wins or loses, then why do they keep score?" (www.vincelombardi.com/about/quotes/index.htm).

In the previous section the term *authentic* was used to describe values that are central to the very personhood of the individual. These core values define who we are and what we aspire to be. The behavior that is the outcome of these values is not the result of a spontaneous or gut reaction to a stimulus or to the dictates of an authority to whose directions or proclamations you feel compelled to conform. Rather, the behavior that is manifested from these core, or authentic, values is the result of your free will to choose. Furthermore, the responsibility for this behavior falls on no one but you because you have freely chosen it.

Inauthenticity

Although it may be true that each person must accept responsibility for his or her own behavior, do any of us take the time to realize that? Generally, we do not. In fact, in our day-to-day activities, the concerns of the everyday run most of us ragged. One of the world's great existential philosophers, Jean-Paul Sartre (1966), suggested that we are so absorbed in the everyday activities of work, of relationship, of the trivial that we fail to address the dread, anguish, and solitude that is our condition as a consequence of our freedom and responsibility. Heidegger (1962) addresses this sense of "bliss" that is evidenced in our avoidance of seeing ourselves as finite beings-unto-death. In other words, because we prefer not to address the fact that we are finite, we can and do waste time on inauthentic activities (i.e., unfulfilling occupations). Let's put this in the context of a typical sport manager. The following scenario describes an average day in the world of the inauthentic.

> Kay wakes up at 7:30 a.m. She showers, carefully selects a conservative outfit for a day of meetings, eats breakfast, drives to the municipal sport center, stopping to grab a cup of coffee before arriving at the office. Kay spends the next 15 minutes preparing for a 9:30 meeting with staff that lasts until 11:30. She spends the next 30 minutes returning e-mails, voice mails, and prepping for a lunch meeting with the boss, whom Kay desperately wants to please. Noon arrives, the lunch goes well, and Kay is exhausted by stress by the time it's over. After returning to the office, Kay has back-to-back meetings concerning sponsorship for inner-city recreation programming. The final appointment that Kay has is with the mayor's office to begin preparation for an upcoming 10K race through the downtown area. A busy and seemingly successful workday is over, and Kay meets some friends for dinner and a movie. Returning home at midnight, Kay watches TV for 30 minutes and goes to bed. She wakes up at 7:30 a.m., showers, eats breakfast, drives to the municipal sport center, stopping to grab a cup of coffee before arriving at the office . . .

Kay has experienced a typical day in the world of the inauthentic. Her day is not unlike the false world described in the movie *The Matrix* in which anti-human forces have plugged the world's population into a gigantic computer program that distorts their sense of reality. Consider the following comment by the character Cypher as he makes a deal with the villainous agent Smith: "I know this steak doesn't exist. I know that when I put it in my mouth, the Matrix is telling my brain that it is juicy and delicious. After nine years, you know what I realize? Ignorance is bliss" (cited in Korsmeyer, 2002, p. 49).

What does this quotation have to do with the daily existence of Kay, or you, or me? The point is authenticity. To what extent did Kay find meaning in anything that she did during this particular day? To what extent were Kay's actions directly driven by others or indirectly by what Kay perceived to be necessary obligations or norms (e.g., dressing conservatively because of a lunch meeting with the boss)? Is Kay an agent or tool of the organization, or is the organization the means through which she can flourish or self-actualize? These questions relate to existential thinking—a rarity in organizational contexts. We argue, however, that existential thinking is an essential aspect of a person's pursuit of happiness and self-knowledge. In the following section we discuss some of the basic concepts of existential thinking and the applicability of these ideas in the sport management context.

Existential Thinking

As a group of thinkers, existentialists are a rather strange mix of philosophers, writers, and artists. Some perceive themselves to be atheists, whereas others are devoutly spiritual. Most would even deny that they could be classified as part of the same intellectual tradition. Regardless of their disparate nature, however, existentialists share a common perspective on at least four major topics: freedom, responsibility, dread, and authenticity. Each of these concepts—freedom, responsibility, dread, and authenticity—is based in existential ontology.

Freedom

Ontology is the study of essence, and in this case the concern is human essence. Human essence for the existentialist is not **deterministic**. In other words, there is no grand plan based on the will of a higher power or on good or bad karma (as divine determinists would say). Similarly, behavior is not a result of inescapable conditioning that occurred in one's environment or culture (e.g., the behavioral determinists). Rather, one's essence occurs after one exists—it is the result of our self-made decisions. Jean-Paul Sartre (1957) phrased this view as "existence precedes essence" (p. 15). Sartre explained his concept in the following paragraph, published in 1975 with masculine language but meant it to include women as well:

> **ontology**—The study of essence (human).
>
> **deterministic**—Belief that behavior or destiny is controlled by external sources (e.g., God, Fate).

> Man turns up, appears on the scene, and, only afterwards defines himself . . . at first he is nothing. Only afterwards will he be something and he himself will make what he will be. . . . Not only is man what he conceives himself to be, but he is also what he wills himself to be. . . . Man is nothing other than what he makes himself. (p. 350)

The belief that we create ourselves has profound implications for what we choose to value, how we behave toward ourselves, and how we treat people and the world around us.

Behaviorism denies the existence of free will and suggests instead that our actions are a function of the explicit or implicit stimuli in our environment and our response to them. We act in a particular manner because of our having been programmed to seek reward and avoid punishment. A rather successful tutoring service in North America rewards students with tokens when they give correct answers to questions. Students then cash in the tokens for merchandise. The behavioral interpretation (and hope) is that eventually the student will outgrow the desire to accumulate tokens and begin reading because of the now-programmed desire to read. In the business context we reward good work performance with a raise in salary or benefits or a corner office. The bottom-line goal is to hard wire behavior to increase the probability for control and reduce or eliminate the possibility of variance due to unanticipated choices. Existentialists disagree with this approach.

The existential view is that humans have free will (**freedom**) and that any attempt to praise or blame behavior on nature or nurture are indications of failure to take responsibility for action. This approach is a blessing or a curse depending on how one views the human predicament. In the case of Cypher and the *Matrix* cited earlier, "Ignorance is bliss." Cypher knows that the Matrix will control every "experience" that he will have, yet he prefers this state of comfort (physical and mental) to the harsh reality of choice and the physical hardship of living in the "real world" in which he would be responsible for his experiences and actions. Let's put this into a more common context:

> **freedom**—The ability to choose a course of action for oneself.

> Kay adheres to her company's code of conduct so that she can keep her job, because it provides for her current financial needs and retirement. She arrives at 8:00 a.m. and leaves promptly at 5:00 p.m. each day, dreams of the weekend, and pines for

ETHICAL REFLECTIONS FROM AROUND THE WORLD AND ACROSS THE AGES

To see what is right and not to do it is want of courage.

Confucius (551-479 BCE), China

Better to be on a runaway horse than to be a woman who does not reflect.

Theano of Crotona (sixth century BCE), Greece

Every art and every inquiry, and similarly every action and pursuit, is thought to aim at some good; and for this reason the good has rightly been declared to be that at which all things aim. . . . Will not the knowledge of it, then, have great influence on life? Shall we not, like archers who have a mark to aim at, be more likely to hit upon what is right?

Aristotle (384-322 BCE), Greece

You should not be impelled to act for selfish reasons, nor should you be attached to inaction

The Bhagavad Gita 2.47 (third or fourth century BCE [?]), India

On three things the world is sustained: on truth, on judgment, and on peace, as it says in Zechariah 8:16: "Speak the truth to one another, render in your gates judgments that are true and make for peace."

Rabban Shimon ben Gamaliel (second century CE), Galilee

Reserve your right to think, for even to think wrongly is better than not to think at all.

Hypatia of Alexandria (355-415 CE), Egypt

Even as the fingers of the two hands are equal, so are human beings equal to one another. No one has any right, nor any preference to claim over another. You are brothers.

Muhammad (seventh Century CE), Arabian Peninsula

Riches and power are but gifts of blind fate, whereas goodness is the result of one's own merits.

Héloise (c. 1101-1164), France

The real meaning of Shakyamuni Buddha's appearance in this world lay in his behavior as a human being.

Nichiren (13th century CE), Japan

To have courage for whatever comes in life—everything lies in that.

St. Teresa of Avila (1515-1582), Spain

Act in such a way that you treat humanity, whether in your own person or in the person of another, always at the same time as an end and never simply as a means.

Immanuel Kant (1724-1804), Prussia

How very seldom an actual case bears out a principle. . . . In moral cases, a man's behaviour may be quite harmless and even beneficial, when he is behaving like a scoundrel. And he may do great harm when he is morally acting on the highest principles. But that does not affect the fundamental truth of morality.

George Bernard Shaw (1856-1950), Ireland

The first step in the evolution of ethics is a sense of solidarity with other human beings.

Albert Schweitzer (1875-1965), Germany

The person who is cruel dies twice.

Traditional Ethiopian proverb, date unknown

"Ethics as the science of Man," according to Watsuji, enables us to study ethics in the concrete. . . . Unless we deal with it as a problem of the proper relation between man and man, we cannot find a true solution to the problem of what makes our actions good or bad, what is our duty, responsibility, or virtue.

Furukawa Tetsushi (1988) on the ethics of Watsuji Tetsuro (1899-1960), Japan

Every human being, no matter how "ignorant" or submerged in the culture of silence he or she may be, is capable of looking critically at the world in a dialogical encounter with others.

Paulo Friere (1921-1997), Brazil

The moral law commands us to make the highest possible good in a world the final object of all our conduct.

Paul Ricoeur (1913-2005), France

One isn't necessarily born with courage, but one is born with potential. Without courage, we cannot practice any other virtue with consistency. We can't be kind, true, merciful, generous, or honest.

Maya Angelou (1928-), United States

International Learning Activity

In small groups, read through the quotations in the sidebar on page 382. What is the point of the quotations? What theme runs through them? Who are those women and men who made the statements? As a group, choose one of the quotations, explain it to the class, and discuss how it could affect the management of sport.

> early retirement. Kay would much rather have been a coach, but she chose this line of work because of the greater security of the municipal environment. Her parents convinced her that secure employment is the best way of meeting her most important objective—providing for herself and her family. Thus, Kay thinks "This is it . . . but it's not such a bad job after all . . . life could be worse as a coach—this makes my parents proud of me—ignorance is bliss."

The existential reaction: Kay has failed to recognize the capacity to choose and believes that she no longer has freedom to change direction—the course is set—and, to some extent, she has a sense of comfort in this resignation to fate. Malloy, Ross, and Zakus (2003), stated

> Though this theory [existentialism] is highly personal, it is neither about selfishness nor is hedonistic [as Cypher in *The Matrix* is hedonistic]. Rather, existentialism is a philosophy that insists that the individual is self-determined and must constantly battle to overcome the "averaging" effect of modern society. (p. 83)

Responsibility

Existentialists tie the individual's freedom to **responsibility** for all resulting action—almost to the extreme. If I have free will and therefore, if all my behavior is a result of this capacity to choose, then I must bear the responsibility—I am *the* cause of my outcome. If I am unhappy with how my life has turned out thus far, I can look only to myself to blame. Other than the fact that I had no choice to be born and arguably that little culpability can rest on my shoulders for decisions that I made as a child or for how I reacted to events that occurred when I was a child, I am the only architect of my present condition. In other words, I now freely select how I will react to the past and every new event that presents itself in my future. The preceding is the most powerful argument against blaming others for one's own disappointments.

responsibility—The acceptance of praise or blame for all of one's actions.

In general, we are quite proficient at avoiding responsibility and deflecting the cause of our misery to our parents, our teacher, our boss, or our significant others. Consider the following statements and the locus of responsibility: "You have upset me!" as opposed to "I have chosen to be upset with you!" The first person places blame on the other. The second person is equally upset but recognizes that she or he has a choice in reaction, and the choice is to be upset. Sometimes managers have a tendency to use rules and regulations to divert blame and avoid responsibility. The locus of control jumps quickly outside oneself, and the manager becomes nothing more than an agent of the organization without perceiving any individual culpability.

How many human tragedies have been caused by the failure to recognize individual freedom and the belief that there was no choice because "I was just following orders"? Whether it is to live or die or to accept or reject policy—existentialists will always claim that we have a choice.

Dread

If we accept this perspective, the weight of freedom and behavioral outcome becomes a significant burden, called dread. This burden results in one of two outcomes:

- Paralysis for fear of responsibility
- Heightened awareness and commitment to make the best efforts to choose wisely.

Note that the burden of responsibility does not focus only on how decisions influence the individual—the responsibility is for all. Sartre (1957) argues that when one makes a choice, it is for everyone. The awareness of this crushing responsibility for the fate of humanity in every choice is anguish. Freedom of choice is a terrible thing, and thus the individual is "condemned" to be free. Although freedom and responsibility are powerful and can cause anguish, angst, and fear, the acceptance of this personal sovereignty is also profoundly liberating.

dread—The realization of responsibility and finitude of life.

Liberation from dread arrives when we come to terms with existential ontology (existence precedes essence), and when we realize that we are constantly in the state of becoming the person whom we choose to be. Furthermore, Heidegger (1966) argues that because we are finite beings (i.e., beings-unto-death) we had better choose wisely. He suggests that time is a critical and profoundly moral concept because it is irreplaceable and limited. In a lifetime (however brief) a person's efforts to be what others expect rather than to be one's own person is time lost. Hours spent in work or in relationships that are less than genuine are hours that could have been directed to defining and pursuing meaningful living. Meaningful living is synonymous with authentic living, which for existentialists is the ultimate purpose of existence.

becoming—The dynamic state of the existential person who is always in the process of developing his or her essence.

Authenticity (and Intent)

Human beings create structures to better the odds of survival. The strength of our structures and systems is directly related to the degree to which we abide by organizational rules, policies, and principles. Behavior that adheres to these ideas is rewarded in a variety of ways (security, approval, power, and so on). Behavior that is contrary to the organizational mandate is dangerous to the status quo and subject to a wide range of potential reprimands. Consequently, the pressure to conform is significant. Although this conformity results in efficient, effective, and productive societal and organizational behavior, it also leads to the loss of authentic and, therefore, meaningful living. We become agents of the organization.

Nietzsche (1886a/1992), Kierkegaard (1975), and Sartre (1966) wrote at length about the pressure to conform and the resulting herd mentality of the average human. Sartre termed this conformity **bad faith**. Bad faith occurs when the person acts on the will or expectation of another (e.g., parent, boss, spouse, society) as opposed to his or her own will. From our earlier example, Kay chose to be an administrator because of implicit and explicit pressure from family members to seek secure employment rather than pursue the authentic desire to coach.

bad faith—Actions based on the will of others.

In contrast, **good faith** implies that the person makes choices freely, regardless of the pressure to conform. In this case, the decision maker is fully aware of the burden of responsibility that accompanies the authentic choice. In the case of Kay, the decision to choose a career as a sport manager could still be authentic (despite the passion for coaching) if, and only if, Kay realizes that

1. sport management was only one of many options;
2. she had an opportunity to travel a different path;
3. she freely chose this path; and
4. no one is to blame or praise other than herself.

good faith—Actions based on authentic values.

If this had been the case, despite the fact that Kay did not pursue the perceived personal ideal of a career in coaching, the role that she selected would have been existentially sound because of the intent behind her choice. In other words, choosing sport management as a result of conformity is bad faith, but choosing sport management as a result of freedom and responsibility is good faith and, thus, authentic. One must be cautious to avoid the misperception that the existentialist is solitary, selfish, hedonistic, abnormal, sociopathic, or belligerent.

What distinguishes the pure existentialist from the nonexistentialist is the reticence to act only to conform with societal, familial, or organizational expectations. The existentialist acts with the intent to be true to oneself. Interestingly, the decision of the existentialist and the nonexistentialist may be the same—the outward fulfillment of duty might be comparable, but the rationales will differ. You should, however, note that the "pure existentialist" is a theoretical 'beast' and that generally speaking, a person may have stronger or weaker existential leanings (as with any other philosophical perspective). Those who tend to bow to societal pressure to act in a particular manner cannot consider themselves as having existential tendencies; on the other hand, those who are motivated to act based upon their own deep commitment to authenticity, can be considered as having stronger existential orientations.

EXISTENTIALISM AND WORK

We work for most of our lives. Work defines, positively or negatively, how we are perceived as a person. Sartre (1966) argues that it is the "look" of another that objectifies us—what we do is part of our "look." Our work can be a meaningful endeavor or meaningless toil. The former implies that a

Runners Jed Bunyan (R) and Mike Lindemann (L) in their fledgling business in Urbana, Illinois, in 1978. After quitting his accounting job, Jed moved to Urbana to get his MBA. But when he and new running buddies couldn't get local merchants to stock the running shoes they wanted, Jed and Mike set up their own tiny outlet for athletic footwear and found their passion. Jed never did begin his MBA program, and today Body n' Sole Sports has grown to become the premier source for running gear in the area. This is a beautiful example of authenticity in the sport business.

Photo courtesy of Jed Bunyan.

person will flourish or achieve self-actualization as an outcome of his or her labor; the latter implies that work will fail to enhance personal growth and will serve only to allow the individual to survive economically as a tool of the organization (the machine). With this in mind, it is curious why existentialism has not been applied to a greater extent in the realm of work because of its primary concern with the search for authenticity and meaning in all aspects of life—work being a major component of our existence.

Applying Existential Ethics to Sport Management

The existentialist is among you. This person is not the brooding, anxiety-ridden bureaucrat of a Kafka novel (or the movie *Kafka* with Jeremy Irons as the lead actor) or the comically defiant new-age hippie who rages against the machine of corporate America while wearing ripped designer jeans for effect. The existentialist is indeed among you. She is the person who questions the rationale for policies before agreeing to act on them. When others simply nod their heads in blank agreement, the existentialist asks why. He is the one who is committed to the organization because it is a medium through which he finds meaningful work, not because it is the source of his livelihood and retirement security. The existentialist is the one who implements or develops organizational policy on good faith. She takes no rule or principle or value lightly, and carefully assesses each against the background of authenticity. The person who can be genuine when executing policy will follow it as part of personal duty (Agarwal & Malloy, 2000).

In contrast, the person who abides by the rules based on bad faith ("I accept rules because I was told to do so") is not authentically committed to the organization and is subject to the whims of conformity from a variety of sources ("I was told to do X, but now I am told to do Z"). This person is legion in the contemporary organization because we seem to be keen to accept direction from others and often fail to explore or understand our own authentic nature. The "good" child, student, athlete, or worker is an obedient one. The troublemaker, on the other hand, is the one who refuses to conform mindlessly.

Nietzsche (1886b/1992) describes this state of human compliance in his fascinating and provoking work the *Genealogy of Morals*. He argues that

> [W]e no longer have anything left to fear in man; that the maggot "man" is swarming in the foreground; that the "tame man," the hopelessly mediocre and insipid man, has already learned to feel himself as the goal and zenith, as the meaning of history,

> as "higher man". . . . The diminution and levelling of European man constitutes our greatest danger, for the sight of him makes us weary—We see nothing today that wants to grow greater, we suspect that things will continue to go down, down to become thinner, more good-natured, more prudent, more comfortable, more mediocre, more indifferent. . . . There is no doubt that man is getting "better" all the time. (pp. 43-44)

Is existentialism the antithesis of organization? Of team? Of leadership? Of followership? In the next section, we discuss the practical application of existentialism and dispel the fear that it equates to loss of managerial control and leads to organizational anarchy.

Existentialism and Leadership

When existentialists lead, they facilitate independence and personal growth so that they can make themselves redundant. Existential leaders see the organization, whether it is sport or business, or health care or music, as a medium through which individuals can thrive. Although it may be sacrilege to suggest it, in the view of the existentialist the activity, the sport, the job is a means to an end—not an end in itself. The end that is sought is for the individual to flourish.

Although seeking this goal may sound profoundly selfish and appear to be the recipe for egoism, nihilism, chaos, and organizational inefficiency, it could lead to a more ordered, fundamentally happy, and productive environment. Why? Because in such an environment, people find meaning in work or sport as opposed to being involved in useless and meaningless toil (see Morris, 1885 and Rinehart, 1987). Let's look at an example that is not so far fetched:

Pat chose to be involved in sport because of a fundamental belief in its capacity to develop moral character. This was a terminal value that he held at the principled level. Pat went to a university, earned a degree in sport management and coaching, and was thrilled to begin a career as a marketer in a professional sport organization. Years later, Pat has become unhappy and stressed at work. The workload is heavy, although not unrealistically so. But Pat perceives that the primary focus of his job is to provide shareholders of the team with maximum **return on investment** (ROI). In this organization, the bottom line of the financial statement is the sole criterion for all decision making. Recall that Pat entered the world of sport because of the capacity of sport for the moral development of the participants—not to ensure a healthy ROI for the organization.

> **return on investment (ROI)**—The amount of profit or goal attainment received from the resource (e.g., money, time) given.

In this hypothetical case, Pat is working in a field of choice and probably making a reasonable wage. Many people would ask him, What more do you want? Existentially, however, Pat possesses relatively little, because his personal existence is inauthentic. Although he is materially wealthy (i.e., earns a good wage), day-to-day involvement in this organization has become, from Pat's perspective, useless toil controlled by the expectations of others. Work is meaningless for him because it does not cohere with his authentic self—his core or principled values. For Pat, work is a means to an end but not his desired end.

In Pat's situation, the existential leader's initial task would be to discover what values Pat holds at the core, authentic, terminal level or the values that he holds at the principled level. After discovering these values, the leader can use the medium of work (i.e., sport management) as a catalyst to help Pat find meaning in his work. Given what we know about Pat's values, it appears that he needs either to change jobs within the organization or to leave the organization altogether. Alternatively, the leader could make Pat aware of the bigger picture in the overall functioning of the organization.

For argument's sake, let's suppose that the organization is the traditional for-profit model, and as such is ultimately responsible to its shareholders. Let's also suppose that the profits are not directed solely to the pockets of a wealthy few but that a substantial percentage is earmarked for inner-city sport development. In this case, the existential leader would make Pat aware of this other dimension of the organization and its obvious commitment to social responsibility. The leader would also explain that the efficiency, effectiveness, and productivity of the organization has a direct effect on the efficacy of its role in cultivating moral character among the participants in the inner-city programs. With this new knowledge, Pat might be able to rethink the nature of his work and see that, in fact, it does cohere with authentic values and that marketing for the organization can fulfill personal development in good faith. If, on the other hand, the organization is driven only by profit and lacks any concern for sport other than its ability to generate revenue, Pat clearly needs to leave this organization and seek authentic employment elsewhere.

Learning Activity

Value and Authenticity Audit

1. List three to five values that you consider core values (i.e., those that you will not compromise for anything).
2. List three to five values that you consider instrumental to those just listed.
3. List three to five careers that you can envision yourself entering upon graduation.
4. Explain how the values listed in numbers 1 and 2 could match the list in number 3.
   a. Are there discrepancies? How and why are they discrepant?
   b. Are there coherencies? How and why do they cohere?
5. Think of a current or former job. What organizational values does (or did) it espouse?
   a. Do (or did) the values of the organization match your authentic values? Why or why not?
   b. Recall a dilemma or conflict that you faced in your current or former job. What values were involved for you and the organization?
6. Interview a professional in your field.
   a. What are the core values of the organization in which he or she works?
   b. What are the interviewee's core values?
   c. Is there congruence between the interviewee's values and the organization's values? If so, did the interviewee make a conscious choice in job selection or was it a fortunate coincidence?
   d. If the values of the organization are not congruent with the interviewee's values, how does he or she deal with the discrepancy?
   e. Is the interviewee's job fulfilling his or her authentic development? Why or why not?

We argue that in-depth knowledge of your own value system is necessary for you to understand your authentic self and to find a match and meaning in your professional practice. Consider the questions in "Learning Activity: Value and Authenticity Audit" to help you identify your authentic value structure.

Future Implications and Explorations

Existentialism has generally fallen out of favor with most North American organizational theorists and practitioners because of the overwhelming acceptance of behaviorism and an underwhelming knowledge of existential theory and its practical implications.

Existential approaches to leadership are undoubtedly slow to demonstrate results because the interaction between leaders and organizational members is intense and personal, and demands respect and dignity for every individual. An existential organization contains no cogs (i.e., unimportant subordinates). Traditional, behavioral organizations are quick to act and respond because the relationship between the leaders and the led is based on simple market exchanges without depth and without the complications inherent in comprehensive human understanding and interaction (i.e., the whole person as opposed to homo *machanicus*). Currently, however, awareness of the dissatisfaction with unfulfilled or meaningless labor appears to be increasing. Consequently, we are seeing a turn toward existentialism as a philosophical theory that gives voice to our latent disappointment with the hours spent at empty toil. Existentialism also gives voice to our search for meaningfulness, not only in work but in all aspects of life. The potential of an existential revolution in administrative thinking may yet be around the corner—unless the herd prevails. Again, Nietzsche (1886a/1992) describes for us this state of human compliance in "Beyond Good and Evil: Prelude to a Philosophy of the Future."

> High and independent spirituality, the will to stand alone, even a powerful reason are experienced as dangers; everything that elevates an individual above the herd and intimidates the neighbor is henceforth called *evil;* and the fair, modest, submissive, conforming mentality, the *mediocrity* of desires attains moral designations and honors. . . . Any high and hard nobility and self-reliance is almost felt to be an insult and arouses mistrust; the "lamb," even more the "sheep," gains in respect. (p. 304)

SUMMARY

In this chapter we have presented a brief overview of ethics, values, and existentialism. We have discussed the effect that these philosophical ideas could have on the sport manager and have illustrated how existential leadership taps into the primary motivator of professional practice—authenticity.

We argue that an in-depth knowledge of your own value system is necessary for you to understand your authentic self and to find a match and meaning in your professional practice. Consider the questions in "Learning Activity: Value and Authenticity Audit" to help you identify your authentic value structure.

Review Questions

1. In your experiences in work settings thus far, have you felt that you were able to be your true self? What was it about the organization that made you feel that way?
2. Most organizations have as their core values efficiency, effectiveness, and productivity. On what other values should an organization base its behavior?
3. What is ontology? What is existential ontology?
4. Describe the four dominant existential themes. How are they relevant to sport management?
5. Define good and bad faith.
6. Is existential leadership an oxymoron? Why or why not?
7. Nietzsche (1992) stated, "We see nothing today that wants to grow greater, we suspect that things will continue to go down, down to become thinner, more good-natured, more prudent, more comfortable, more mediocre, more indifferent.... There is no doubt that man is getting 'better' all the time" (pp. 480). Could there be some truth to this statement in our modern organizational life? Explain.

Sociological Aspects of Sport

Mary Jo Kane—University of Minnesota

Learning Objectives

After studying this chapter, you will be able to do the following:

1. Define sport and sport sociology.
2. Discuss the social, political, and economic significance of sport in our society.
3. Explain the role of theory in analyzing sport.
4. Identify positive and negative social effects of sport and physical activity.
5. Discuss significant research findings in sport sociology.
6. Explain the importance of sport sociology for sport managers.

An important step in becoming a successful sport manager is gaining an in-depth awareness of sport as a social, political, and economic activity that permeates our society and influences both institutions and individuals in a variety of ways. To understand the complex dynamics of how and why people participate in sport and physical activity, you must have knowledge about both individual behavior (e.g., psychological aspects such as motivation to participate) and the social context in which that behavior occurs. For nearly 40 years, the scientific investigation of the social context of sport has been at the heart of an academic discipline called sport sociology.

The purpose of this chapter is to define sport and sport sociology, delineate the nature and significance of sport in US culture, and outline the role of social theory in understanding key aspects of the sporting enterprise. This chapter will also highlight several domains of scholarly inquiry within sport sociology, paying particular attention to those areas most relevant to sport management as an academic field of study and a professional enterprise. The chapter ends with a discussion regarding the interplay between sport sociology and sport management, and how that interplay can help you address social challenges, especially as those challenges relate to real-world concerns such as violence, racism, and changing gender roles.

DEFINING SPORT

No one would argue that activities such as basketball, football, tennis, and golf are sports. However, scholars have also pointed out that a wide variety of other kinds of physical activities can be considered sport (Coakley, 2004; Snyder, 1990). Such activities may include walking, fishing, and hiking. What is clear from these examples is that there exists a **continuum** of physical activity ranging from informal, playlike activity in a leisure setting, to the highly organized, competitive, and pressure-filled world of professional sports. Figure 18.1 depicts this continuum and includes some of the characteristics typically associated with such activity. Notice that as we move along the continuum, what distinguishes sport from other, more informal kinds of physical activity is the element of competition and the added dimensions of physical prowess and ability.

> **continuum**—Continuous whole or series; an element or thing whose parts cannot be separated or separately discerned.

DEFINING SPORT SOCIOLOGY

Given that sport is such a significant part of many societies of the world, it is not surprising that scholars would be interested in studying its dimensions, scope, and influence. Beginning in the mid-1960s, scholars and educators from academic fields such as psychology, sociology, and kinesiology tried to do more than define sport—they also began to develop a scientific body of knowledge related to the nature and significance of sport. This effort led to the emergence of a new academic discipline called sport sociology. According to Jay Coakley, sport sociology is the "subdiscipline of sociology that studies sports as parts of social and cultural life" (2004, p. 6). Sport sociologists rely on sociological theories and concepts to examine institutions and organizations (the International Olympic Committee), microsystems (women's professional basketball teams), or subcultures (gamblers), and to address such questions as, How do sports influence some of our most cherished values such as loyalty and respect for authority? As part of their analysis, sport sociologists do not typically focus on the behavior of specific individuals, but examine instead the social patterns, structures, and organizations of groups actively engaged in sport and physical activity (Carpenter & Acosta, 2005; Sands, 1999; Theberge, 2000).

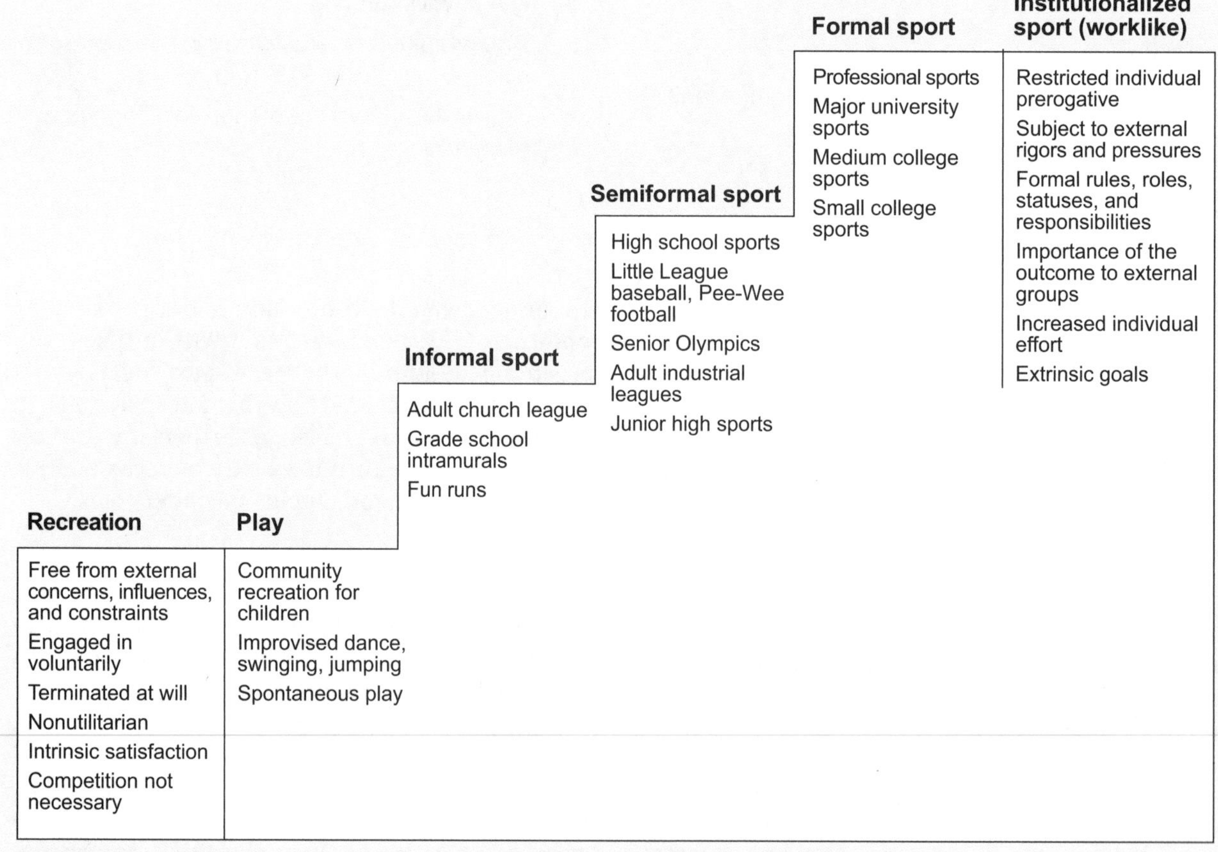

Figure 18.1 A continuum of physical activities ranging from informal play to formal sport.

Reprinted, by permission, from E. Snyder, 1990, *Sport and fitness management,* edited by J.B. Parks and B.R.K. Zanger , p. 215. (Champaign, IL: Human Kinetics).

1920s
- **1926**—Gertrude Ederle becomes first woman to swim the English Channel

1930s
- **1936**—Jesse Owens wins four gold medals in athletics at Olympics

1940s
- **1943**—All-American Girls Professional Baseball League forms; disbands in 1954
- **1948**—Negro National League disbands

1950s
- **1954**—Marilyn Bell becomes first person to swim across Lake Ontario (51 km, or 32 mi)
- **1956**—Althea Gibson wins Wimbledon doubles title with Angela Buxton

An underlying assumption of sport sociology is that sport is an important institution on the same magnitude as the family, the educational system, and our political structure. A fundamental goal of sport sociology is to describe the complex dynamics surrounding patterns of participation (e.g., the number of girls versus boys involved in youth sports) and social concerns (e.g., an overemphasis on winning that may lead to the use of steroids) that make up this all-pervasive institution (Eitzen & Sage, 2003). Keep in mind, however, that sport sociologists do far more than describe sport involvement by, for example, gathering data on how many people participate on an annual basis. They are ultimately concerned with understanding the social context in which this participation occurs, as well as the meaning of sport as an influential social, political, and economic institution.

THE ROLE OF THEORY IN UNDERSTANDING SPORT

When people hear the word *theory*, they often think of something that is boring, abstract, and unrelated to their everyday lives. But if we are to adequately understand the social context in which sport participation occurs, as well as the meaning that underlies that participation, we must use one of the best analytical tools available to social scientists—theory. Theories "provide frameworks for asking . . . questions, interpreting information, and uncovering the deeper meanings and stories associated with sports in particular cultures" (Coakley, 2004, p. 34). In short, theories allow us to make connections among facts and phenomena and organize them into meaningful patterns or explanations that help us make sense of our world.

The principal aim of scientific inquiry is to describe, explain, and predict human behavior. Theory is especially useful for these latter two aims. We could, for example, easily describe the number of professional golfers who are White versus the number who are people of color. But how would we explain, let alone predict, this pattern of participation? By using social theory, we can hypothesize (and empirically test) the notion that such a pattern is a function of race (and racism), as well as social class.

hypothesize—To form a hypothesis, meaning to provide a tentative but logical foundation for further investigation; to assume or suppose.

empirical—Knowledge based on experimental method and observation versus theory or supposition.

Let's take the case of women's sports as a real-world example of how theory can help us not only understand the role and meaning of sport but also create a more balanced and just society. We can readily establish that, historically, women's participation in sport was nowhere near men's participation. This difference was particularly true for certain team-oriented, combat sports such as football and wrestling. One theoretical perspective that allows us to explain such behavior has to do with gender roles. More specifically, the traditional relationship between sport and gender can be summed up in the following theory:

$$\text{Sport} = \text{Male}$$

$$\text{Male} \neq \text{Female}$$

$$\therefore\ \text{Sport} \neq \text{Female}$$

This particular theory allows us to explain why historically, so few women (compared with men) played sports and to predict that when they did participate, especially in sports such as football, they were routinely stigmatized as "not real women". These kinds of theoretical observations led to a classical theory of sport and gender developed in the 1960s by physical educator Eleanor Metheny. She argued that sports were considered sex-"appropriate" or "inappropriate" for females based on the physical and structural requirements of the activity in question. The more the sport allowed a female to conform to traditional expectations of femininity, the more appropriate or acceptable the sport was considered. Sports that required graceful, fluid body movements, along with minimal body contact with one's opponents, would permit appropriate feminine behavior within a sport context (Metheny, 1965). Under this theoretical model, sports such as golf and figure skating would be considered ladylike activities, but sports such as rugby and football would be considered too manly for girls and women.

Although Metheny's theory was useful in explaining the connections between sport and gender for many decades, a great deal has changed since the 1960s. Over the past four decades a revolution

1950s

▶**1957**—Althea Gibson becomes first African-American woman to win Wimbeldon singles title

▶**1957**—Althea Gibson becomes first African American woman to appear on *SI* cover

1960s

▶**1960**—Negro American League folds

▶**1964**—Civil Rights Act becomes law

1970

▶**1972**—Title IX adopted

▶**1977**—Shirley Muldowney wins NHRA Top Fuel Championship

1980s

▶**1985**—Rick Hansen "man in motion" tour raises money for spinal cord research

▶**1987**—Al Campanis makes disparaging remarks toward Blacks on *Nightline*

Learning Activity

1. List at least two other areas within the sport world in which one might apply social theory to explain a particular pattern of athletic participation. Describe in detail (justify) why you picked those two areas.
2. How might you explain, or theorize, why males are much more likely than females to use steroids? Write a two- or three-page report to support your theory and provide four or five references from the Internet (e.g., ESPN.com) to bolster your claim.
3. As part of an in-class discussion, develop a theory to explain why Tiger Woods remains one of the few people of color ever to succeed in men's professional golf.

As you can see from the foregoing examples, the issues and questions—as well as the need for meaningful explanations—are endless. Just remember that as you address such issues, you are often relying on theory to provide those meaningful explanations. Maybe theories aren't boring and irrelevant after all.

has occurred in women's sports, marked by an unprecedented increase in participation rates across a wide variety of sports and physical activities. The beauty of social theory is that, like society, it too is dynamic and ever changing. As a result, rather than categorizing and dividing sport strictly along gender lines, we can now theorize it as a continuum of physical activity ranging from individual, aesthetic sports on one end to power-based team sports on the other. Conceptualizing sport in this fashion can help us explain why high-contact, physically aggressive team sports like soccer and basketball—and sport icons like Mia Hamm and Lisa Leslie—have become socially accepted and widely popular.

THE SOCIAL SIGNIFICANCE OF SPORT

Did you ever wonder why local television newscasts describe their content as "News, Weather, and Sports"? Why not "News, Weather, and Technology"? Why don't they highlight education? Or literature? Perhaps it is because sport influences almost every aspect of our lives. One measure of this influence is the vast amount of resources invested in sport-related activities. Not surprisingly, the sport and fitness industry has an enormous economic impact on US society. With respect to discretionary spending alone, billions of US dollars are spent annually on the sale of licensed sport products such as football jerseys and baseball caps. For example, in 2005 television broadcasting giants CBS, ESPN, and Fox Sports, along with DirecTV, secured the rights to broadcast various NFL events such as Monday Night Football and the Super Bowl for a staggering total of $23.9 billion USD over the next four to seven years (Bernstein, 2005a). At the 2005 Super Bowl in Jacksonville, Florida, advertising rates were astronomical: The average cost of a 30-second ad was $2.4 million USD (Bernstein, 2005b). And at the 2004 Summer Olympics in Australia, advertising revenues alone totaled $1.3 billion USD (Kramer, 2005).

Another way that we can measure the significance of sport is to see how much the on- and off-court behavior of athletes reflects our nation's social ills. Indeed, sport has become so important to our national psyche that sport figures often come to symbolize broader social concerns such as gang and date rape (football players at the University of Colorado), escalating acts of violence and aggression (the "basket-brawl" between the NBA's Indiana Pacers and Detroit Pistons), and drug use and abuse (alleged steroid use among players in Major League Baseball).

These examples clearly indicate that sport holds a prominent place in our society and has both positive and negative consequences. For instance, the positive outcomes of sport are reflected in its role as a unifier of people. Nowhere was this more evident than in the aftermath of the terrorist attacks in New York City on September 11, 2001. All across the United States, in sport stadia big and small, Americans came together and reaffirmed their strength and fortitude as they united as one nation. But sport has its dark side as well. The negative aspects of sport can be seen in—and may even perpetuate—many of the ills that exist in the broader society such as sexism, racism, homophobia, and violence. Keep in mind, however, that in spite of all the negatives, sport has incredible power to serve as a vehicle for social change. As you will see, all these aspects of sport have long been important areas of inquiry for sport sociologists.

Learning Activity

Identify and discuss two recent examples in which sport has served as a catalyst for important social or political change.

1980s

- **1987**—Jackie Joyner-Kersee is 2nd African American female athlete to appear on *SI* cover
- **1989**—First publishing of *Racial & Gender Report Card* by Richard Lapchick and Northeastern University (NU) Center for the Study of Sport in Society

1990s

- **1996**—WNBA launched
- **1998**—US women's ice hockey team defeats Canada 3-1 to win Olympic gold medal at Nagano, Japan
- **1999**—John Rocker makes negative comments about New Yorkers in *SI* interview
- **1999**—US women win the women's World Cup in soccer

THE BENEFITS OF SPORT

Clearly, sport shapes and maintains many social values held in high regard. Such values include hard work and fair play, self-discipline, sacrifice and reliance, and commitment to one's self and others. In short, sport can contribute to the development and stability of both individuals and society as a whole (Coakley, 2004).

Runners at the start of the Twin Cities Twosome, an annual charity race in Champaign-Urbana, Illinois. With its twosomes walking and running subdivisions of youth, parent–child, husband–wife, and combined ages equaling 100+ years, the Twosome offers multiple opportunities for community building and for socializing the younger generation.

Sport as a Socializing Agent

The socialization process refers to the various ways in which a society's dominant values, attitudes, and beliefs are passed down from generation to generation. A major component of the socialization process is **role learning**, whereby young children learn to think and behave in accordance with the various social roles available to them (Greendorfer, 2001). Because many of us are socialized into play, sport, and physical activity at an early age, those pursuits become an incubator for mastering critical social roles such as responsible neighbor, productive student and coworker, loyal friend, and companion. A number of studies have provided empirical evidence that supports the significance of the socialization process in general and role learning in particular. These studies investigated the effects of play, games, and sport and discovered that involvement in such activities enabled children to learn about relationships both inside and outside a sport context (Coakley, 1993; Eitzen & Sage, 2003). Indeed, Coakley (2004) argued that the socialization aspects of sport can be so far reaching that they affect even those who do not actively participate. For example, spectators can learn about the values and attitudes that this country has toward a whole host of issues ranging from respect for authority to teamwork to notions of citizenship. With this in mind, we can readily understand how involvement in sport—whether as participants or as spectators—can influence people to think and behave in ways that enable them to contribute to the larger social agenda.

> **role learning**—A social process by which children learn various roles and the characteristics associated with them such as neighbor, friend, student, sibling, daughter, or son.

Sport as a Unifier

Sport can bring people together by giving them a sense of personal identity, as well as feelings of group membership and social identification (Eitzen, 1999). Sport accomplishes this in a number of ways, from the individual level (an athlete who feels that she is part of something bigger than herself because she's a Minnesota Golden Gopher) to the regional level (the rivalry between—and rabid fan support for—the Pittsburgh Steelers and the Philadelphia Eagles) to the national level (the entire nation rooting

2000s

- **2001**—WUSA forms; disbands in 2003
- **2002**—Esera Tuaolo, former Green Bay Packers and Minnesota Vikings player, publicly announces he is gay
- **2002**—Women's Chinese Basketball Assoc. (WCBA) established
- **2004**—Mean number of women's sport teams per college or university reaches 8.32, up from 2.5 in 1972
- **2005**—T-ball coach encourages player to hit disabled teammate with ball
- **2005**—Dept. of Education issues new Title IX guidelines

for Olympic athletes Brandi Chastain, Michael Phelps, and Jennie Finch). Few, if any, institutions can unite people the way that sport does, largely because the popularity of sport cuts across race, social class, gender, and age barriers.

Because of its enormous visibility and appeal, sport also creates linkages among people that may transcend tension and conflict. In an era of increasing aggression and violence throughout the United States, we must not forget, or fail to employ, sport as a vehicle by which we can bring people together as "team members" of a family, a neighborhood, a city, and a nation. As mentioned earlier, nowhere was the ability of sport to reach across great divides—and unite us in a common bond—more evident than in the aftermath of September 11, 2001. Although some commentators argued that this tragic moment in US history brought into sharp focus what really matters in life, it also showed us that sporting events matter a great deal too. Recall that in October, the World Series rallied the United States and provided a sense of stability and familiarity in the "new normal" way of life after September 11. As **collective ritual**, sport played (and continues to play) an important role, both symbolically and tangibly, in the national process of mourning and healing while reflecting the best of America's values and character.

> **collective ritual**—Groups of people engaging in a set (often traditional) form of rites and practices such as a religious ceremony or athletic event (e.g., the Super Bowl, the Olympics).

THE DARK SIDE OF SPORT

Although sport can produce beneficial outcomes for both individuals and society as a whole, involvement in sport does not bring only good things. As is increasingly and painfully apparent, sport participation can have a darker side. For example, when people are denied the opportunity to experience feelings of competence and self-worth by achieving success in sport, the consequences can be far reaching. The abuses of youth sports programs, in which standards of excellence are often impossible to achieve given the physical, social, and psychological maturation levels of young children, are well documented (Ryan, 2000; Williams, 2001). We also know that the pressure-cooker world of big-time athletics can distort and undermine fundamental values such as honesty and integrity because of its winning-at-all-cost mentality (Murphy, 2005).

Scholars and educators have alerted us to one of the most pressing (and dangerous) issues in all of sport—the prevalence of eating disorders. An alarming number of (mostly female) athletes and their coaches have bought into the dangerous—and potentially fatal—idea that in the world of competitive sport there is no such thing as being too thin (Anderson, 2001). This belief is fostered by the false assumption that reducing body fat and body weight will significantly improve an athlete's performance. How big is the problem, not just for athletes but for the country as a whole? According to the National Association of Anorexia Nervosa and Associated Disorders (2005), seven million women and one million men suffer from anorexia, bulimia, or some other form of eating disorder. Although disordered eating patterns occur among people in all segments of society, some groups are more at risk than others. The risk is especially high for females who are bombarded with unrealistic images and messages from mainstream media that "thin is perfect"; such messages result in far too many young girls struggling with (and dying over) their body image.

We might suppose that participation in sport would make females less vulnerable to unrealistic body images, but in many cases, eating disorders are sport specific. We have all heard horror stories about the pressures that gymnasts feel—and the lengths to which they will go—to be (and stay) petite and dangerously thin. In sports such as basketball and softball, those pressures obviously are not as great. Such variability was behind sport psychologist Mark Andersen's finding that "prevalence rates for eating disorders among athletes are quite variable depending on the sport and who is doing the study" (2001, p. 408). For example, one study indicated that only 8% of elite female athletes could be considered diagnosable with respect to an eating disorder. Another study, however, found that close to 40% of intercollegiate female athletes had a disordered eating pattern (Andersen).

Learning Activity

1. Interview a coach, parent, and teammate who know about a female athlete who may be struggling with an eating disorder. What were the specific signs that led them to believe that the athlete had a problem?
2. If you were a coach or a fellow athlete, how would you deal with the situation? As part of your answer, identify two Internet sites that list resources about eating disorders and female athletes.

Besides the concerns just listed, research findings from sport sociology highlight four areas of sport that reflect and contribute to some of the most troubling aspects of 21st-century America—sexism, racism, homophobia and heterosexism, and violence.

Sexism in Sport

In the wake of the modern feminist movement that began in the early 1970s, a number of women's roles expanded into areas traditionally occupied by men; the world of sport was no exception. As you learned in chapters 4 and 16, Title IX of the Education Amendments Act was passed in the United States in 1972. This landmark federal legislation was designed to prohibit sex discrimination in educational settings (Carpenter & Acosta, 2005; Suggs, 2005). Since its passage and implementation, enormous changes in the world of women's sports have taken place. For example, substantial gains have occurred in the number of sports offered, access to athletic scholarships and facilities, and overall athletic budgets. With respect to sports offered on a nationwide basis, in 2006 the average number of teams (per college or university) that was available for women was 8.45, an all-time high. Compare that with 1972, when the average number was 2.5 sports per school (Acosta & Carpenter, 2006). According to the 2004-2005 report from the National Federation of State High School Associations (2005), almost three million girls are now involved in interscholastic sports nationwide compared with only 298,000 before Title IX. In 2002, 42% of all NCAA participants were women compared with only 15% in the early 1970s (Carpenter & Acosta, 2005, p. 171). And it's not just participation rates that have skyrocketed in the wake of Title IX; the number of fans is exploding as well. Consider women's college basketball, one of the most popular women's sports around. In 2001-02, attendance for this sport surpassed the nine million mark for the first time in history. That season marked the 18th consecutive year for attendance growth for the sport (Campbell, 2004).

Title IX—Federal legislation that amended the 1964 Civil Rights Act: "No person in the United States shall, on the basis of sex, be excluded from participation in, be denied the benefits of, or be subjected to discrimination under any education program or activity receiving Federal financial assistance." To learn the origins and significance of this law, see www.bernicesandler.com/id44.htm.

These statistics make it undeniably clear that because of Title IX, millions of girls and women participate in a variety of sport and physical fitness activities in unprecedented numbers. Change is also reflected in the ever-increasing acceptance of young girls' involvement in sport. According to a national survey sponsored by the Sporting Goods Manufacturers Association (SGMA), girls aged 6 to 17 are very active in organized sports. Noting that approximately 11.5 million girls are members of a team sport, Gregg Hartley, vice president of SGMA, observed, "The flood of girls into team sports is one of the major sports trends [nationwide] in the past decade" (Sporting Goods Manufacturers Association, 2001, paragraph 10). Women are also making great strides at the professional level. In the last few years we have seen the rise of new professional sport leagues such as the Women's National Basketball Association (WNBA) and the Women's United Soccer Association (WUSA). Although the WUSA suspended its operations because of financial difficulties in 2003, a group of former league officers joined with the WUSA Player Association to revive the league (WUSA Player Association, 2004). Another marker of change is the increasing marketability of female athletes in the world of corporate sponsorship. *Sports Illustrated* published its rankings of the highest paid US athletes in 2005. Topping the women's list were Maria Sharapova and Serena Williams, whose annual earnings approached $23 million USD and $22 million USD, respectively. Although women's overall annual earnings paled in comparisons to men's—the number-one ranked male, Tiger Woods, brought in $86 million USD—women were nevertheless a factor in big-time corporate investments.

Although women have made enormous progress in sport, it would be a mistake to assume that they have attained equality. Consider the following examples. In the 2002-03 academic year, three decades after the passage of Title IX, women received 42% of athletic scholarships at the intercollegiate level, even though they represented 54% of all undergraduates nationwide (Carpenter & Acosta, 2005, p. 177). Although 42% is a vast improvement from the pre-Title IX era, Carpenter and Acosta point out that in actual dollar amounts, females received $133 million USD less than their male counterparts. Moreover, athletic budgets, salaries for coaches and athletic administrators, and access to facilities are nowhere near an equitable ratio. At the college level, women in NCAA schools receive about one-third of recruiting and operating budgets. And at the most prestigious level in intercollegiate athletics—Division I—this discrepancy is even more pronounced:

A 2002 statistic from the NCAA reveals that in terms of recruiting budgets, the average amount of money spent per school in men's sports was $1.6 million USD compared with $284,000 USD per school in women's sports (Carpenter & Acosta, 2005, p. 177). This disparity not only puts women's sports at a distinct disadvantage in building a successful program but also sends a powerful message about which sports (and athletes) are considered the real or most important ones. This inequality is particularly troubling given that most Division I sports programs are housed within public institutions.

As these examples clearly indicate, much remains to be done to ensure gender equity in sport. Nevertheless, most observers believe that Title IX has been an overwhelming success. But Title IX also has its critics. Opponents of the law argue that in attempting to comply with Title IX, institutions had to eliminate many men's sports such as gymnastics and wrestling to achieve statistical balance. But the statute does not mandate those decisions; athletics administrators at the local level made those choices. Those administrators are obligated to comply with Title IX, but the statute does not require them to drop a men's sport to do so. Other options are available. For example, athletics directors could pursue cost-cutting strategies such as prohibiting men's football and basketball teams from staying in hotels the night before every home game, a routine practice in big-time sports programs nationwide. The revenue saved from this (and other) unnecessary expenditures could save a men's team from being dropped. Instead, many ADs blame Title IX for their having to eliminate men's sport, thus pitting women's sports against men's, distracting us from taking a closer look at the financial decisions made in men's major sports, and creating unwarranted hostility toward Title IX.

In spite of these realities, critics of Title IX continue to look for ways to challenge the law. An example of this involves compliance guidelines issued by the Department of Education, the federal body responsible for determining whether schools are complying with Title IX. A guideline presented in 2005 allows schools to use e-mail surveys to measure a student's interest and ability in a particular sport. The guidelines, however, offer no guidance about how to write or interpret surveys to determine what level of interest (in terms of either numbers or enthusiasm of respondents) justifies offering new sports. Critics of this approach, then, argue that these surveys are a fundamentally flawed way to assess females' interest in sport and may lower the bar for schools' compliance with Title IX (Brennan, 2005; Sabo & Grant, 2005). For example, many of us receive dozens of e-mails (and their attachments) that we never bother to open, let alone read, fill out, and return. Yet under the new compliance guideline, lack of response to the survey can be interpreted as lack of student interest in a sport.

Males have never been asked to provide evidence of sufficient group support before a sport is offered. Even if the survey approach were valid, what level of interest is needed to trigger the offering of a sport? Would an acceptable level be 40%? Or 60%? Does this procedure seem like a fair way to determine whether to offer opportunities for people to become involved in one of this country's most cherished institutions? Myles Brand, the president of the NCAA, apparently doesn't think so. Asked for his reaction to the e-mail interest survey, he replied: "[This survey] will not provide an adequate indicator of interest among young women . . . nor does it encourage young women to participate—a failure that will likely stymie the growth of women's athletics" (quoted in Samuels, 2005, paragraph 22).

Leadership Roles

Ironically, with respect to leadership positions in women's sports, women have lost far more than they have gained since the passage of Title IX. In terms of national trends, before 1972 over 90% of all head coaches in women's athletics were female; in 2006, that figure was just 42.4% (Acosta & Carpenter, 2006). And although the overall number of head coaching positions in women's sports has increased dramatically since the mid-1980s, males have benefited from this increase far more than their female counterparts. For example, in 2004 there were approximately 8,400 head coaching positions in women's sports, an increase of 631 jobs since 2000. Men, however, filled the majority of these new jobs. During this period, females continued to represent only 2% of the coaches in men's sports (Carpenter & Acosta, 2005, p. 175).

The picture for women in key administrative positions in women's sports is even more disturb-

Learning Activity

Read Donna de Varona's 2006 testimony before the Senate committee on Commerce, Science, and Transportation found at www.womenssportsfoundation.org/cgi-bin/iowa/events/article.html?record=216. Then, construct a table with two columns. In one column, list the positive changes in sport that Title IX made possible. In the other column, list problems that still exist. Identify several actions that could be taken to bring about greater gender equity in sport.

ing. Research indicates that before Title IX, women occupied the vast majority (over 90%) of all athletics director positions throughout women's intercollegiate sports. In 2006, however, they accounted for only 18.6% of those same administrative positions. One particularly shocking finding was that one in seven women's programs had no female *anywhere* in the athletics administrative structure (Acosta & Carpenter, 2006). These facts make it undeniably clear that in terms of employment opportunities, particularly in high-ranking leadership positions, men have fared far better under Title IX than have women. Even more troubling is that in spite of women's increasing experience and expertise, they remain only a token presence as leaders in men's sports and continue to lose ground as leaders in their own domain.

Some have suggested that this employment trend occurred (and persists) because men are better qualified, but empirical evidence does not support this belief. On the contrary, studies have indicated that women are often as qualified, or more qualified, than their male counterparts. In one nationwide study that was undertaken after the occupational trends outlined earlier first became apparent, Acosta and Carpenter (1988) asked those most responsible for recruiting and hiring college head coaches—athletics directors—to list reasons for the dramatic decline in the number of women coaches since the passage of Title IX. Their findings indicated that male ADs perceived the four most important reasons to be (1) lack of qualified female coaches, (2) failure of women to apply for job openings, (3) lack of qualified female administrators, and (4) time constraints because of family obligations. In a follow-up study, researchers empirically tested two such beliefs—that women are less qualified and that women are more restricted than men are because of family obligations (Hasbrook, Hart, Mathes, & True, 1990). These researchers discovered that female coaches were *more* qualified in terms of coaching experience with female teams, professional training, and professional experience. They further discovered that male coaches were *more* restricted because of family responsibilities. These findings suggest that harmful stereotypes can work to the disadvantage of females who want to become coaches because "the beliefs expressed by male athletic directors appear to be based more on a gender-stereotypic bias about female competence than on any objective data" (Stangl & Kane, 1991, p. 49).

Since these early findings, a number of studies have established that such stereotypes are very much alive today and rooted in "assumptions that are frequently made about employment roles and women's and men's perceived abilities to cope within those roles" (Shaw & Hoeber, 2003, p. 348). For example, a long-standing and deep-seated belief about women and their "proper role" in society is that they are (and should be) primarily responsible for child care and other domestic responsibilities. But because there is an equally powerful belief that leadership positions require an extraordinary commitment, a commitment that often intrudes into one's personal life, and that women do not or will not tolerate that intrusion, females start at a distinct disadvantage when trying to secure a top-level leadership position such as head coach or athletics administrator. When you add to the mix that these kinds of management positions require a great deal of travel and night and weekend work, it is no wonder that women, who have to work against gender-role stereotypes and expectations that limit their ability to get hired in the first place, remain significantly underrepresented in leadership positions throughout the sport world. This underrepresentation exists even though research indicates that gender and marital and lifestyle status do not significantly affect a person's organizational commitment (Turner & Chelladurai, 2005).

Why does it matter that fewer and fewer women occupy leadership positions? As anyone involved in sport can easily attest, coaches often serve as important mentors and role models. If young female athletes rarely see women serving in leadership positions, they may think that women do not belong in such roles, and, as a result, may never attempt to enter the coaching profession. Empirical research supports the importance of having women in head coaching positions. In a study examining male and female college athletes, Everhart and Chelladurai (1998) discovered that females who were coached

Learning Activity

1. Conduct a survey of the colleges and universities in your state or region and determine how many women and men occupy head coaching positions in both women's and men's sports.
2. As part of your survey, highlight the results by whether the sport is revenue producing (e.g., basketball) or nonrevenue producing (e.g., track and field). Present the results to your class using bar graphs or pie charts.
3. List three specific strategies that you would use as a sport manager to ensure the hiring of more women as coaches and athletics administrators.

SPECTATOR VIOLENCE IN AUSTRALIAN SPORT

Lisa Kihl, Australia

In 2005 Australian soccer fans engaged in violent clashes at matches in the cities of Sydney, Melbourne, and Perth. For example, as reported online at www.smh.com.au/news/Football/Increased-security-fails-to-prevent-fans-clash/2005/04/30/1114635789393.html# and www.abc.net.au/worldtoday/content/2005/s1358054.htm, approximately 100 fans from the Croatian-backed Sydney United and Serbian-supported Bonnyrigg Eagles clubs fought in the car park of Parramatta Stadium after a New South Wales (NSW) Premier League match. Supporters had brawled the previous time that these two clubs had met. In response, Soccer NSW had moved the game to a neutral site, segregated fans, increased police presence, and stepped up security measures. These actions proved ineffective, however, because security did not allow sufficient time for the Sydney United fans' bus to leave the stadium before Bonnyrigg fans were allowed to depart from the sports ground.

Nonetheless, spectator violence at Australian sporting events is perceived as an uncommon practice and does not reach the levels of hooliganism experienced in Europe or South America (Lynch, 1991). The antisocial behaviors exhibited by fans at Australian sporting events generally occur inside stadia and typically involve only 50 to 100 people. Clashes are often attributed to "ethnic warring," alcohol consumption, antipolice sentiments, working-class culture, and a culture of license in which unruly behavior is almost expected (Lynch; Vamplew, 1994).

Soccer in Australia is mostly identified with ethnic groups, and crowd violence tends to happen when rival ethnic groups are supporting different teams, such as when Croatian-based clubs play Serbian-based clubs or when Greek-based clubs play Macedonia-based clubs (Vamplew, 1994). In rugby league, violent crowd behavior has occurred involving supporters of the Canterbury Bankstown Bulldogs Club, affectionately named the Bulldog Army. The Bulldog Army is a group of youth supporters, predominately of Lebanese and Arabic descent. In an effort to embrace Australian sporting culture, they have adopted the Bulldogs as their team. On several occasions, some members of the Bulldog Army have engaged in antisocial behavior, such as throwing bottles onto the field, damaging seats, fighting opposing fans, and trashing trains. According to journalist Scott Poynting (2005), the ethnic nature of violence at soccer and rugby league games has been labeled by some as un-Australian, and the unruly fans are often not regarded as real fans.

Sport administrators, government officials, and police authorities have collaborated in an attempt to control crowd violence at Australian soccer and rugby league matches. During the 1990s Australian soccer administrators sought to "de-ethnicise" soccer clubs by eliminating the use of ethnic team names (e.g., Melbourne Croatia was renamed Melbourne Knights and Sydney Croatia was renamed Sydney United); however, the Serbian-backed Bonnyrigg White Eagles' home field continued to be named the Serbian Centre Ground (Hughson, 2001). Soccer NSW created a league in which teams represent geographical regions rather than ethnic communities. Soccer administrators employed other social control measures such as seating rival fans at opposite ends of stadiums and banning ethnic flags at matches.

Government- and police-led initiatives have pressured club officials to impose zero tolerance policies for crowd violence and called for clubs to be more responsible for their fans' behaviors. As a result, state soccer officials have imposed strict sanctions (e.g., imposing fines, excluding clubs from competition, barring fans from games) against specific clubs and their fans who engage in violent behavior. The National Rugby League is considering similar types of penalties. Other preventive measures that various Australian sporting venues have implemented include regulation of alcohol consumption, legislation prohibiting offenders from attending or visiting sporting venues, increased security presence, and improved training of security personnel.

by women were more likely to be interested in entering the coaching profession than were females who were coached by men. This finding may be why those who are working to increase the number of females in key leadership positions have pushed for the development and implementation of coaching workshops and clinics for young women (Greenberg, 2005; Women in Higher Education, 2004). A critical part of this approach is to establish formal mentoring relationships between current and aspiring coaches so that "younger women [can] see the embodiment of their visions in such legendary individuals as Pat Summitt and Vivian Stringer" (Kane, 2001, p. 138). In an era when women make significant contributions in the workplace, from science and medicine to the corporate world and everything in between, they must also bring their experience, passion, and commitment to an equally important part of the workplace—the world of sport.

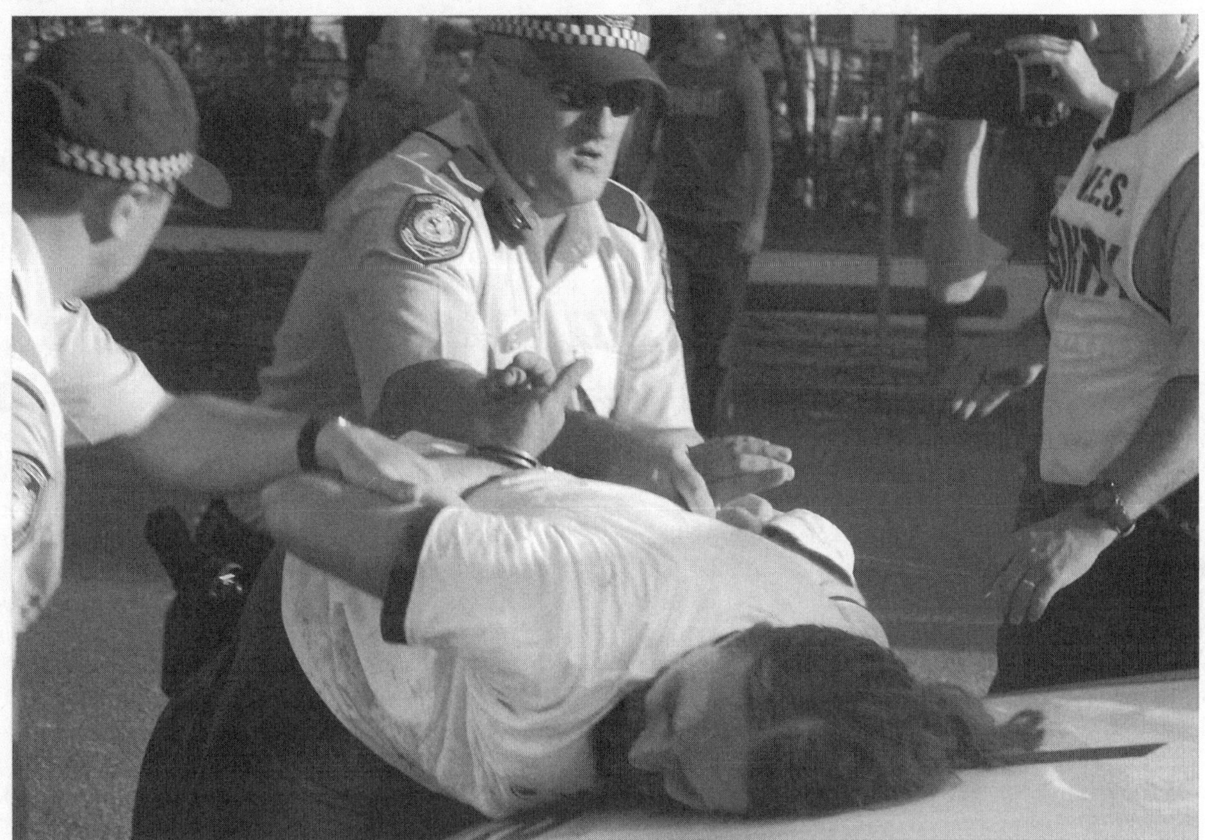

Police officers arrest a Serbian soccer (football) fan after a game between Sydney United and Bonnyrigg at Parramatta Stadium. Fans from the two sides clashed in the parking lot after the game in April 2005.

Fairfax Photos

International Learning Activity

Read Scott Poynting's article "Bulldog Whistling: Criminalization of Young Lebanese Australian Rugby League Fans," which is posted at www.internetjournalofcriminology.com/Poynting%20-%20Bulldogwhistling.pdf. Summarize the article and explain how the collective behavior of some fans resulted in the racial stereotyping and "othering" of those labeled as deviant.

Media Coverage of Women's Sports

A number of female athletes have become household names because of sport media coverage over the last several years. Annika Sorenstam, Michelle Wie, Anna Kournikova, Mia Hamm, Maria Sharapova, Venus Williams, Serena Williams, Justine Henin-Hardenne, Danica Patrick, and Jennie Finch immediately come to mind. In spite of such progress, three decades of sport media scholarship has convincingly demonstrated that the mainstream media treats sportswomen and sportsmen differently in two important ways. First, although females make up approximately 40% of all sport participants, they receive significantly less coverage than do their male counterparts. This finding is true whether we examine periods in relationship to Title IX, the age of the athletes, their race, or the type of sport in which they are involved. A study conducted by Duncan and Messner (2005) not only underscores the lack of coverage given to sportswomen but also indicates that the situation is getting worse. For the third time since 1990, the authors examined TV sports coverage on each of three local network affiliates in Los Angeles (NBC, CBS, and ABC). In the most recent study, they also examined ESPN's *SportsCenter* and Fox's *Southern California Sports Report*. Comparing these results with data from their earlier research, Duncan and Messner found that since 2000, television coverage of women's sports had declined: Sportswomen received only 6.3% of total sports coverage in 2004 compared with 8.7% of total coverage in 1999. An equally unsettling finding was that the percentage of airtime devoted to women's sports in 2004 was as low as it had been 15 years earlier. Women's lack of representation is not confined to network broadcasting; print journalism also underreports women's sport involvement. For example, Eastman and Billings (2000) examined two of the most widely read newspapers in this country—*USA Today* and the *New York Times*. Their findings revealed that although women's participation rates were continuing to skyrocket, men's sports received close to five times as much coverage in *USA Today*. In the *New York Times*, men received a "staggering 10 times as much space as women" (p. 202).

A second way that the mainstream media treats female athletes differently involves type of coverage. Numerous investigations have shown that the media portray males in an array of images and stories that emphasize their athletic strength and mental toughness but present females in narratives that highlight their physical attractiveness and heterosexuality rather than their accomplishments as highly skilled and dedicated athletes (Fink & Kensicki, 2002; Kane & Buysse, 2005). One persistent finding, for example, is that females are significantly more likely than males to be portrayed off the court, out of uniform, and in passive and sexualized poses. Indeed, sexualizing highly skilled sportswomen makes up much of the commentary of male sports reporters. How many times have we heard ESPN's Tony Kornheiser and Michael Wilbon refer to traditionally attractive, well-known female athletes as "hotties"? Consider the case of Anna Kournikova, a professional tennis player who at one point generated the greatest amount of corporate sponsorship ever given to any female athlete even though she had never won a singles tennis championship. Today's latest "hottie" is Danica Patrick, rookie sensation race car driver on the Indy Racing League circuit. Although Patrick has received a good deal of coverage that highlights her skill, poise, and determination, she has also been portrayed in images that bear a striking (alarming?) resemblance to soft pornography.

Although these patterns of representation have remained consistent and unequivocal over the last three decades, scholars remain interested in the gendered aspects of sport media. Not surprisingly, however, the focus of recent research has shifted in that the central issue now under consideration involves change over time. More specifically, sport media studies conducted during the past few years address two central questions: (1) Do gender differences in the amount of coverage remain just as dominant as previous investigations showed them to be? and (2) has a shift occurred in the type of coverage given to sportswomen; that is, does current reporting focus more on women's athleticism than it does on their sex appeal? In terms of current trends related to amount of coverage, Fink and Kensicki (2002) sought to determine "whether there had been any changes in the coverage of women's athletics in *Sports Illustrated*'s historically male-centered magazine" (p. 317). To address this change-over-time perspective, the authors examined photographs and articles from 1997 through 1999. They discovered that athletic females continued to be underrepresented (only 10% of the photographs in their sample featured women's sports), were routinely depicted in narratives that were non-sport related, and engaged in traditionally "feminine" sports.

What about current sports reporting regarding type of coverage? Christopherson, Janning, and McConnell (2002) were interested in the ways in which mainstream media portrayed the 1999 Women's World Cup Soccer Championship. Specifically, they examined newspaper coverage in large metropolitan areas to determine whether a breakthrough moment in women's sports—the 1999 Women's World Cup—would challenge or reaffirm patterns discovered in earlier research. Their findings revealed that although women's participation in, and interest in, soccer was at an all-time high, and although the 1999 Women's World Cup received an unprecedented amount of media coverage, "reporters analyzed the games and the American Women's team through a gendered lens that highlighted and reinforced gender stereotypes about women" (p.183). For example, the authors found that newspaper coverage often contained commentary that focused on aspects of the players' appearance, such as their "smoldering eyes" and "painted toenails."

Like the research by Duncan and Messner (2005) cited earlier, a study by Kane and Buysse (2005) adds additional longitudinal data to contemporary sport media scholarship. This type of research is important for those who wish to investigate questions and issues that require a change-over-time analysis. In short, longitudinal research is a productive methodological technique that enables sport media scholars to make direct, one-to-one comparisons with earlier patterns of coverage. Kane and Buysse were especially interested in intercollegiate athletics given the enormous

Learning Activity

Using an Internet search engine, find photographs of one male and one female athlete from the same sport (e.g., Sam Hornish, Jr. and Danica Patrick from auto racing or Anna Kournikova and Rafael Nada from tennis). Identify differences and similarities in their poses. Which photos highlight athletic prowess, and which ones highlight sexuality? What other characteristics do you see in the photos? What conclusions can you draw from your observations?

explosion in this particular area of women's sports since the enactment of Title IX. They wanted to assess how media guide covers portrayed females and males in the most prestigious athletic conferences in this country—the Atlantic Coast Conference (ACC), the Big East, the Big Ten, the Big 12, the Pacific Athletic Conference (Pac-10), and the Southeastern Conference (SEC). The researchers chose media guide covers because they are consciously constructed products that enable an institution to present its athletics department and sports programs to members of the local and national media, advertisers and corporate sponsors, and alumni, donors, and other campus and community stakeholders (Buysse & Embser-Herbert, 2004). Media guides also serve as important recruiting tools because they are often the first piece of material that a prospective athlete and his or her parents and family members receive.

With this as background, Kane and Buysse (2005) asked two central questions: (1) If images of female and male athletes are examined for the same sports (e.g., basketball, golf, and gymnastics), in the same year, at the same institution, using the same medium, will significant gender differences be apparent? and (2) will significant shifts occur in the patterns of representation over three time periods representing the 1989-90, 1996-97, and 2003-04 athletic seasons? These questions were addressed by measuring "seriousness of presentation," that is, how much do the guides' representations emphasize a sportswoman's athletic competence, strength, and determination? In short, Kane and Buysse measured how frequently females (compared with males) were portrayed on the court, in uniform, and in active, athletic poses.

The study revealed some interesting and unexpected results. The first finding involved images associated with sportswomen during the 2003-04 season. In the most prestigious and influential intercollegiate sport conferences in the nation, females were overwhelmingly portrayed as serious, competent athletes. For example, 97% of the female athletes who appeared on the covers were portrayed in uniform rather than out of uniform, 80% were portrayed on court rather than off court, and 72% were presented in active images rather than passive images. In short, the guides portrayed sportswomen simply and unapologetically as athletes. What was also striking about this finding was how the images surrounding women's sports compared with those for men's sports—there was no significant difference between female and male athletes on all three categories that were measured (i.e., uniform presence, court location, and pose presentation).

The second major finding involved longitudinal comparisons. What was abundantly clear from these change-over-time analyses was that "there were significant shifts in the representations of sportswomen from the early 1990s to 2004, shifts that led to the construction of females as serious, competent athletes . . ." (Kane & Buysse, 2005, p. 231). For example, in the first media guide study (1989-90), only 51% of sportswomen were portrayed on court, but in the 2003-04 season, that figure jumped to 80%. Figure 18.2 highlights these shifts over time and illustrates gender differences as well.

How do we account for these dramatic changes? One explanation involves the role of sport scholars as agents of social change. Over the past three decades scholars and educators have disseminated a vast body of knowledge generated by sport media research. During this same period, there has also been a proliferation of curricula and other educational materials that critique (and criticize) the various ways that mainstream media portray female athletes. This effort has expanded dramatically with the emergence of sport management as an academic discipline. As a result, students majoring in fields of study such as sport psychology, sport sociology, and sport management may well have become the very people who are producing modern-day images of athletic females. Educating future professionals who are aware of research findings that provide empirical evidence of the unfair media treatment given to female athletes, and exposing them to techniques (e.g., marketing strategies) that provide alternative and empowering representations of sportswomen, may be an important legacy of sport scholars.

One final, and pleasantly surprising, result of the media guide study was that representations of intercollegiate female athletes during the 2003-04 season stood in stark contrast to those found in mainstream print and broadcast journalism. For this particular population, why was there such a significant departure from the unrelenting mainstream media images that trivialize and sexualize female athletes? Kane and Buysse (2005) suggest that this finding has to do with the role of media guides in particular and institutions of higher education in general. Media guides are often first-impression statements. They not only provide the facts and statistics of a sports program's on-the-field success but also proclaim the values and attitudes that an institution has toward its athletic teams overall. Those who represent these institutions (e.g., athletics administrators) produce and market media guides to project an appropriate image of women's sports. In the early stages of Title IX, many of those administrators believed that an appropriate

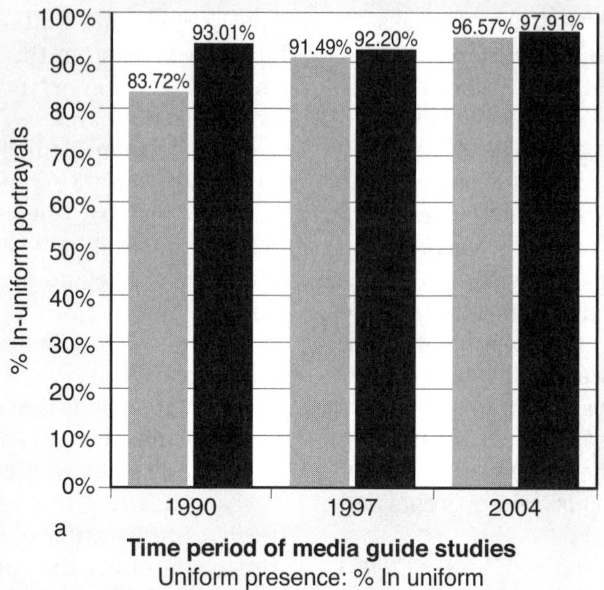

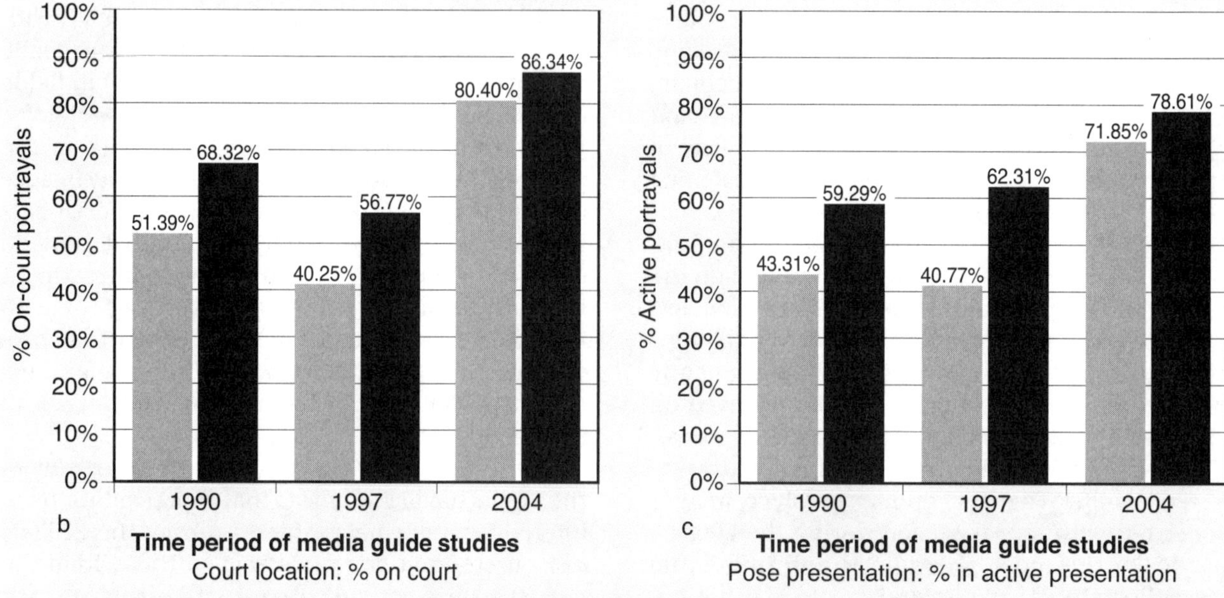

Figure 18.2 Longitudinal comparisons in women's and men's athletics by *(a)* uniform presence (in versus out), *(b)* court location (on versus off), and *(c)* pose presentation (active versus passive). The light bars represent women and the black bars represent men.

From Kane and Bysse, 2005, unpublished.

(not to mention effective) way to market women's college sports was to link female athletes with a traditionally feminine and nonathletic image. Yet Kane and Buysse's findings suggest that today's key decision makers believe that an appropriate, and indeed effective, way to market their teams is to highlight the athletic competence of female athletes. As we move further into the post–Title IX era, the issue of competence becomes an easier sell because sportswomen have much greater access to facilities, better training and coaching, and higher levels of competition. This shift from passive, off-the-court portrayals to images of sportswomen as highly skilled athletes is exemplified on the media guide covers of women's basketball teams at Duke University presented in figure 18.3.

Homophobia and Heterosexism in Sport

Sport scholars are beginning to address one of the most oppressive aspects of sport—homophobia.

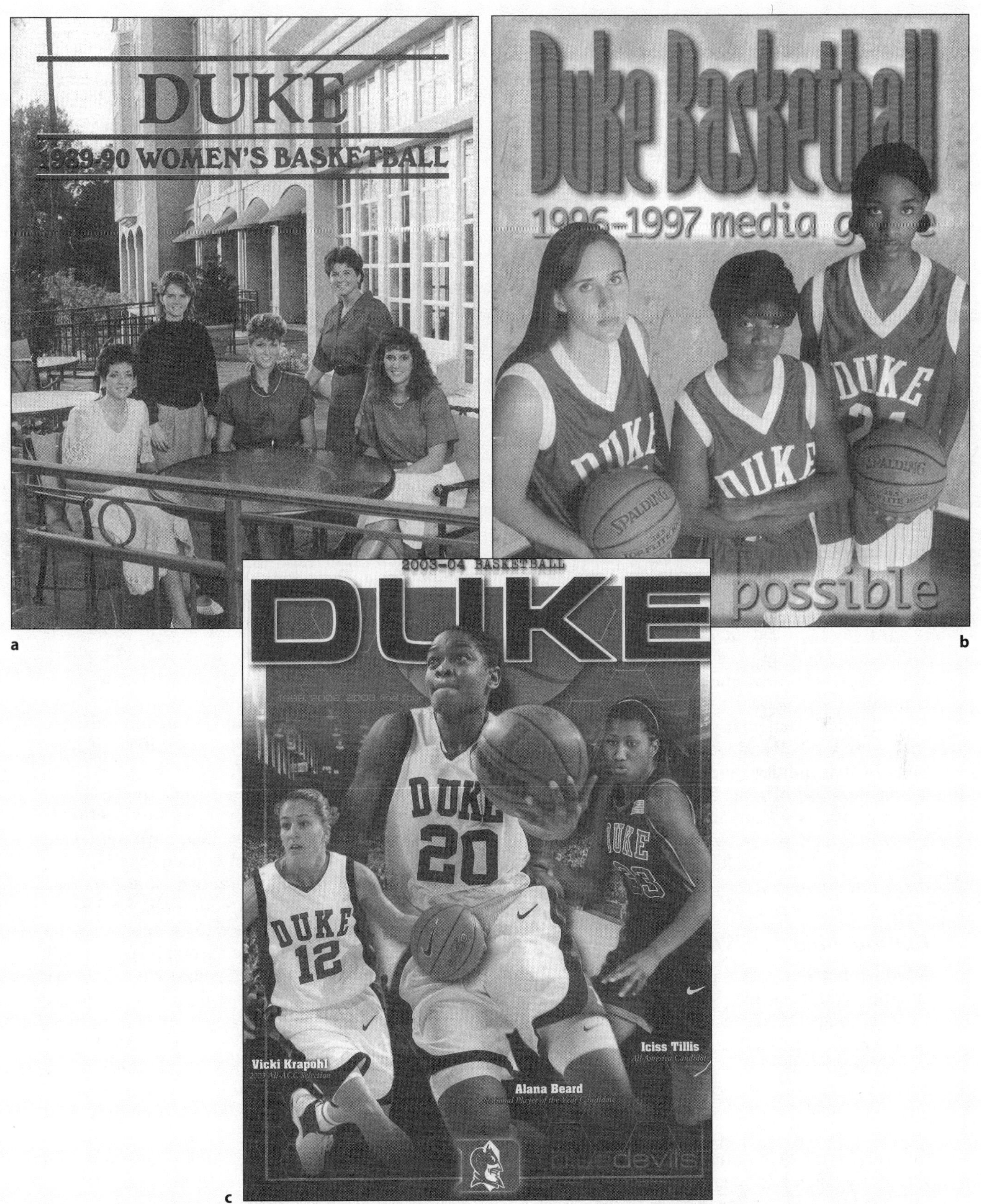

Figure 18.3 Women's basketball at Duke University as an example of change-over-time representations from out-of-uniform, off-court, passive images to live, on-court, athletic images. (*a*) 1989-90 season; (*b*) 1996-97 season; (*c*) 2003-04 season.

Reprinted by permission from the Department of Intercollegiate Athletics, Duke University.

Learning Activity

1. The majority of sport media research focuses on print and broadcast journalism; virtually no research is done on how women's and men's sports are portrayed on the Internet. Visit three major sport sites on the Internet and measure the amount and type of coverage given to both women's and men's sports. Investigate one site at the professional level, another site at the college level, and a third site at the Olympic level.
2. Write a three- to five-page paper on the amount and type of coverage that your local television stations give to female athletes. Does the coverage support or contradict research findings at the national level?
3. Interview the people in your school's athletics department (e.g., sports information director) who are responsible for producing media guides. Ask them how they make their decisions. For example, ask what strategies they use in marketing women's and men's sports.

Pat Griffin, a leading scholar in this area, defines homophobia as a universal fear or intolerance toward gay men, lesbians, and bisexuals (1998). Although significant progress has occurred in this area—especially in women's sports—stereotypes continue to link gender roles with highly competitive athletics, particularly in team contact sports such as basketball and football. Traditional definitions of masculinity (and heterosexuality) were synonymous with "real" athletes. In contrast, traditional notions of femininity—sugar and spice and everything nice—were, by definition, the antithesis of athleticism. As a result, athletes who challenged these stereotypes were often stigmatized as not "real" women or men.

Homophobia and Women's Sports

Although homophobia is present in both women's and men's athletics, fears or concerns about being gay have long been associated with women's sports (Krane & Barber, 2005). Such fears range from historical assertions that women's participation will harm their reproductive capacity (and make them unable to fulfill what are presumed to be appropriate heterosexual roles such as wife and mother) to modern-day claims that athletic involvement will turn women into men (Kane & Lenskyj, 1998). An example of this latter (though false) assertion is the commonly held belief that female athletes, particularly those who engage in more "masculine" sports, are (or will become) lesbians. Alaina Sudeith, a student–athlete at UCLA, experienced firsthand how females engaged in sports such as basketball and softball are automatically assumed to be lesbian. Sudeith, a member of UCLA's water polo team, related her encounter with homophobia: "I've been told from guys on campus that I shouldn't play sports because everybody would think I was a lesbian, and no guys would be interested in me" (quoted in de Jong, 2005, paragraph 7). Her sexual orientation? Straight.

As this example indicates, those associated with women's sports, from athletes to coaches to athletics administrators, have often been stigmatized with the lesbian label. Given this reality, those involved in women's sports feel a great deal of pressure to act or appear to be heterosexual: "The underlying fear is not that a female athlete or coach will appear too plain or out of style; the real fear is that she will look like a dyke or, even worse, is one" (Griffin, 1992, p. 254). To counteract such fears, female athletes have gone to great lengths to assure themselves, their parents and teammates, coaches and corporate sponsors, that sport can (and should be) consistent with traditional notions of femininity and heterosexuality.

Research has demonstrated how homophobic beliefs and practices affect the lives of female athletes on a daily basis. Coaches and athletics administrators often pressure sportswomen to embrace a "feminine image" by dressing in skirts when traveling to out-of-town games and by wearing makeup and jewelry (Krane, 2001; Theberge, 2000). Players suspected of being lesbian may be dismissed from their positions on a team—and lose their scholarships—or could be passed over in the selection of elite teams (Iannotta & Kane, 2002). We should not underestimate the harmful consequences of the homophobic beliefs and practices that surround women's sports. Although conditions for lesbian athletes (and those perceived to be lesbian) are far better than they used to be (Schmid, 2003), it still remains the case that being pejoratively labeled a lesbian is to be stigmatized as abnormal or deviant, and to be threatened with the loss of employment, career, and family (Griffin, 2001; Iannotta & Kane, 2002; Krane & Barber, 2005). Note that this labeling process affects all female athletes, homosexual and heterosexual alike. Just ask Alaina Sudeith.

Homophobia also puts female coaches at risk. Administrators, colleagues, and even their own athletes often monitor coaches' personal lives. For example, when a coaching position opens up, search committee members may place private, discrete phone calls to determine a female applicant's sexual orientation (Griffin, 1998; Wellman & Blinde, 1997). Female coaches are particularly vulnerable to being tagged (or targeted) with the lesbian label because it can affect a critical part of their job—recruiting. A dirty little secret in the world of women's sports involves a specific form of negative recruiting in which a coach suggests to a potential athlete (or her family members) that another coach or team has a lesbian reputation (Galst, 1998; Iannotta & Kane, 2002).

Given such an environment, and the strong (and understandable) desire of many lesbians to keep their private lives private, the subject of homophobia in sport rarely surfaces, at least on any large, public scale. But some controversial (if not well-publicized) incidents brought homosexuality out of the closet. Andrea Zimbardi was the senior captain and record-setting all-star catcher for the women's softball team at the University of Florida. In spite of her on-the-field accomplishments, Zimbardi claimed that once her sexual orientation was known, her coach kicked her off the team and "reneged on an agreement not to retaliate against Zimbardi when she took her concerns to the university's athletic administration" (Buzinski, 2004, paragraph 5). Unfortunately, this type of discrimination is not uncommon for many lesbians involved with sport. Former players of one of the most powerful coaches in women's intercollegiate basketball, Rene Portland at Penn State University, accused her of saying that she would not recruit lesbian athletes. For many years, Portland would not comment on her alleged stance toward lesbians, claiming that, "Team 'training rules' were not public information" (Griffin, 1998, p. 46). In 2005, however, Jennifer Harris, a former Penn State basketball player, filed a discrimination lawsuit against Coach Portland, Tim Curley (Penn State AD), and Penn State University. The outcome of the lawsuit, which is scheduled for May 2007, will be edifying.

The experiences of Andrea Zimbardi and countless others notwithstanding, a number of positive developments have occurred when it comes to lesbians' sport experience. As with society at large, more people (gay and straight) are speaking out against the oppressive, homophobic atmosphere that has been so much a part of women's sports. Grassroots activist groups, institutions of higher education, and even the NCAA have been at the forefront of such efforts. People within these organizations make the case that creating safe and tolerant environments for student–athletes is a matter of student welfare and that student welfare should extend beyond the classrooms to the playing fields (Beck, 2002). Advocacy groups around the country like the National Center for Lesbian Rights and It Takes a Team have held workshops and symposia to educate athletes, coaches, and administrators about policies and practices that would help to create athletic environments that are tolerant of diverse sexual orientations. And in 2002, for the first time in its 95-year history, the NCAA hosted a panel on homophobia in sport at its annual national convention. All of this must be good news to Andrea Zimbardi, currently an SEC honor-roll student in graduate school. In 2004 she agreed to a groundbreaking settlement with the University of Florida. A key part of the settlement is that the university agreed to provide diversity training to all coaches, athletics administrators, and staff members. Zimbardi says that she pushed for diversity training rather than monetary damages "to prevent other athletes from going through this" (Buzinski, 2004, paragraph 7).

Learning Activity

Search the Internet to learn more about the Jennifer Harris lawsuit. Outline the arguments made on both sides of the dispute. As a class, discuss your findings.

Homophobia and Men's Sports

Up to this point we have focused on how homophobia affects women's sports. But as all of us know, men's sports are particularly oppressive and intolerant when it comes to dealing with gay athletes. Scholars have suggested that this is due to the historical role of sport as a training and proving ground for males to establish their masculinity and manhood (Coakley, 2004; Pronger, 1999). Because traditional definitions of masculinity are synonymous with athleticism, it is not surprising that being a male athlete and being gay is seen as a contradiction in terms (Anderson, 2005). Gay male athletes know this formula all too well. Esera Tuaolo, former pro football player with the Green Bay Packers and Minnesota Vikings, is one of the few male athletes ever to "come out." He waited until his career was over to do so, however, because he knew that if his teammates discovered that he was gay, "that would be the end for me. I'd wind up cut or injured. I was sure that if a GM didn't get rid of me for the sake of team chemistry, another player would intentionally hurt me, to keep up the image" (Tuaolo & Cyphers, 2002, paragraph 5).

Although professional female athletes, such as Rosie Jones in golf, Martina Navratilova and Amelie Mauresmo in tennis, and Sheryl Swoopes in basketball, have come out during their playing careers, to date no professional male athlete has ever done so. Given the experience of Esera Tuaolo—who says that he spent hours lying awake, praying for his anxiety attacks and ongoing depression to end—who could blame them? Billy Bean, former professional baseball player and gay man, explained why he too didn't come out until after his career had ended: "A lot of people really, they go to the lowest common denominator and think that just because a person is a homosexual, he is all about sex, and not that he is a human being . . ." (ESPN.com Page 2, 2001, paragraph 68). Another incident that brought to light the stereotypes (and dangers) surrounding gay athletes occurred in 2001 when Brendan Lemon, then editor of *Out Magazine*, told his readers that he had been having a relationship with a major league baseball player. Although his story did not result in a firestorm of slurs and derogatory remarks about gay men, it did generate numerous jokes on television. On a more positive note, the story also started a public—and in many ways sympathetic—discussion about what would happen to a gay athlete if he did come out of the closet, especially if he were still playing.

As this latter example suggests, things are changing, albeit slowly, in men's sports. One indication that a more open and tolerant climate appears to be on the horizon is the advice, in the form of fashion tips, given to the "style-challenged" Boston Red Sox from members of the hit TV series, *Queer Eye for the Straight Guy*. The "Fab Five's" attempt to turn scruffy Red Sox players such as Johnny Damon and Jason Varitek into fashion studs was widely publicized throughout mainstream media and professional (baseball) publications. Far from trying to sensationalize the story (or be repulsed by the very idea), reporters indicated that this was all quite unremarkable. Indeed, many journalists framed the Red Sox players as hopelessly unchic and agreed that they were in desperate need of a "championship makeover" (Donlan, 2005). Although this "encounter" in no way demonstrates that men's sports are ready to accept openly gay players, who would have ever imagined that out-of-the-closet men would be seen as "more acceptable" than male athletes regardless of the circumstances? It is naive to suggest that a safe, tolerant, and open climate will soon be a reality for gay and lesbian athletes. Nevertheless, we as a society should not abandon the principles that embrace social justice in all our institutions, including sport. To achieve that end, we should remember that the "problem" of gays in sport is not the presence of gay and lesbian athletes; it's the presence of homophobia.

Racism in Sport

Since Jackie Robinson broke the color barrier in Major League Baseball in the 1940s, minorities have made important progress in all levels of sport. Despite this, racism remains deeply entrenched throughout the sport world.

Racism and Sport Leadership

One of the most widely studied forms of racial discrimination in sport is a phenomenon called **stacking**, whereby minority groups are steered away from (or into) certain player positions that are more (or less) central to key decision-making and leadership positions on the field (Eitzen & Sage, 2003). For example, in Major League Baseball, Whites have dominated the position of catcher, and African Americans have been overrepresented in the outfield (Woodward, 2004). Another example of stacking is found in the National Football League. Although 68% of all NFL players are African Americans, in 2005 approximately 20% of starting quarterbacks were Black (e.g., Daunte Culpepper, Donovan McNabb, Michael Vick, and Steve McNair). Note, however, that this total is an improvement from historical trends.

> **stacking**—A disproportionate allocation of athletes to central (e.g., quarterback) and noncentral (e.g., offensive tackle) positions as a function of their race or ethnicity.

We should never underestimate the consequences of stacking. If most Black athletes are, for example, steered away from critical decision-making positions such as catcher and quarterback during their playing careers, the practice reinforces the belief that African Americans do not have the leadership skills and judgment necessary to become coaches and managers. Stacking helps explain why, although some progress has occurred, minorities remain underrepresented at all levels of leadership positions. More NFL head coaches are African American than at any time in the league's history, but they still represent only 19% (6 out of 32) of all head coaches. And unlike White head coaches, who are hired repeatedly, few Black coaches are ever hired for the head coaching position a second time. Tony Dungy (Indianapolis Colts) and Dennis Green (Arizona Cardinals) are the only African Americans to have ever coached more than one NFL team.

This pattern of underrepresentation is not confined to the NFL. In 2005, for example, 77% of all Major League Baseball managers were White even though racial minorities (Asians, Blacks, and Latinos) made up 40% of all players (Lapchick, 2006a). African Americans have made the greatest inroads into the coaching profession in the NBA where, in 2005, 37% of head coaches were Black. Although this statistic is noteworthy, keep in mind that in the same year, close to 80% of all players in the NBA were men of color (Lapchick, 2006b). Finally, at the end of the 2003-2004 season, there were 100 teams in the NBA, MLB, NFL, and MLS, combined. Only 10 people of color were general managers (or equivalent) of those teams, and only 3 of the CEOs/presidents were African Americans (Lapchick, 2005a).

According to Lapchick (2005b), minority representation is even lower in intercollegiate athletics. In 2003-2004, only 3.2% of the Division I ADs were African American men. Among head coaching positions in men's football, basketball, and baseball, African Americans occupied just 2.9%, 23%, and .9%, respectively, of these important leadership roles. And although Black men have been hired for prestigious head coaching positions, they remain subject to a "last hired, first fired" occupational employment trend. The hiring and firing of Tyrone Willingham at Notre Dame is the latest (and many consider the most egregious) example of this maxim. Some progress has been noted, however, in that the University of Washington immediately hired Willingham as head coach. But little, if any, progress has occurred when it comes to selecting African American women to occupy leadership positions in intercollegiate sports: In 2003-2004, only 3% of all coaches across Division I were Black women (Lapchick, 2005b). The encouraging news is that all of the men's major professional leagues as well as the NCAA have undertaken diversity initiatives designed to increase the numbers of minorities and women in leadership positions.

Racial Stereotypes in Sport

Stereotypes regarding racial minorities in sport are not confined to beliefs about leadership abilities.

Sport sociologists have identified three areas in which racial myths and prejudices about African Americans in sport abound: assumptions about race and athletic ability, sport media coverage, and the role of sport in racially connected upward mobility.

Race and Athletic Ability

The popularly held belief that Black athletes owe their success to their "natural" abilities suggests that they have some genetic advantage over Whites when it comes to achievement in sport (Buffington, 2005). A parallel belief is that White athletes achieve excellence because of their discipline, intelligence, and hard work. Note, however, that when people of color dominate a particular sport, a strong need develops to explain this dominance, a desire to search for a "black gene." But when Whites dominate sports such as golf and tennis (Tiger Woods and the Williams sisters being notable exceptions), the need to explain patterns of success based on the racial compositions of the players seems to vanish. Jay Coakley makes this point in his discussion of the dominance of Canadians in hockey:

> There have been no claims that White Canadians owe their success in hockey to naturally strong ankle joints, instinctive eye-hand-foot coordination, or an innate tendency not to sweat, so they can retain body heat in cold weather. . . . However, when athletes with black skin excel or fail at a certain sport, regardless of where they come from in the world, many people look for genetic explanations consistent with dominant racial ideology. (Coakley, 2001, p. 249)

Sport Media Coverage

A second area that reflects racial stereotypes can be found in sport media coverage. Sport media scholars Margaret Duncan, Michael Messner, and Cheryl Cookey (2000) found what they called a "hierarchy of naming" pattern whereby those members of a less powerful group (minorities and women) were frequently referred to by their first names only, and those in more powerful groups (White men) were referred to either by their last names or their full names. In 90% of the cases in which male athletes were referred to only by their first names, the athlete in question was a person of color. Some examples from professional sports will illustrate this point. All of us know who Kobe, Magic, KG, and Shaq are, but we do not think of Brett Favre, Larry Bird, and Peyton Manning as Brett, Larry, and Peyton. Although certainly not intentional, this type of coverage can reflect and perpetuate a lack of respect toward minority athletes.

The media's underrepresenting and stereotyping of racial minorities are not confined to male athletes. Although little research has focused on how the mainstream sport media covers Black female athletes, Lumpkin and Williams (1991) discovered that *Sports Illustrated* first placed an African American woman, tennis star Althea Gibson, on its cover in 1957; 30 years passed before a second African American woman appeared there; Jackie Joyner-

and sport are linked together as part of African Americans' biological and cultural destiny, especially in certain sports (Coakley, 2004). In short, the widely held belief is that sport—and in far too many cases only sport—offers a path to upward mobility. Americans believe this largely because Black athletes dominate the most visible and popular sports and because athletes such as Lebron James, Shaquille O'Neal, and Michael Vick earn astronomical salaries and endorsement contracts. In addition, for many years Americans have heard countless rags-to-riches stories about racial minorities making it in professional sports—from Nancy Lopez to Venus and Serena Williams to Lebron James. Probably for that reason, two-thirds of African American adolescent males believe they can have a career in professional sport (Eitzen, 1999). How accurate are those beliefs? How often do African Americans succeed in the big-time world of sport?

Sport sociologists have addressed those questions by pointing out that although African Americans (particularly males) have been enormously successful in the most prominent professional and intercollegiate sports, the likelihood of having a professional sport career is a "dream for all but an infinitesimal number" (Eitzen, p. 136). Consider these statistics: Of all the professional sports available to men, African Americans have found the greatest success in basketball. Yet of the approximately 40,000 Black males who play high school basketball nationwide, only 35 (.09%) will make it to the NBA and only 7 (.02%) will become starters (Eitzen & Sage, 2003).

No one suggests that African Americans (and other racial minorities) should not strive for success in sport, despite the long odds against achieving and maintaining a professional career. But critics point out that achieving upward mobility is easier in other professions, such as medicine, law, educa-

Of these two high school athletes, statistics based on race alone suggest that the African American player is more likely to believe that he has a serious chance of landing a place on an NBA team than does the White player. Ask yourself if this is a healthy situation for American society.

Photo courtesy of Paul M. Pedersen.

Kersee was featured on the cover in 1987. In terms of racial stereotypes, Laurel Davis (1997) examined *Sports Illustrated*'s annual swimsuit issue and discovered that "during the 1980s and early-to-mid 1990s the swimsuit issue featured models with African ancestry, yet these models typically possessed very light-colored skin, and facial features that conform to the Anglo-American beauty ideal" (p. 90).

Sport and Upward Mobility

A third area dominated by racial stereotypes and myths involves the notion that African Americans tion, science, and engineering. Equally important is the fact that people who follow these career paths "have greater *lifetime* earnings than most professional athletes, whose playing careers, on average, last less than five years" (Coakley, 2001, p. 300). The late, great African American Arthur Ashe broke new ground in men's professional tennis. Although he used sport as a way to achieve success, Ashe understood the limitations—and warned against the dangers—of seeing sport as the only, or even the primary, path to social and economic mobility: "We have been on the same roads—sports and entertainment—too long. We need to pull over, fill up at the library and speed away to Congress, and the Supreme Court, the unions, and the business world" (Ashe, 1977, p. 2S). Unfortunately, 30 years after those prescient remarks, the need for African Americans to fill up professions beyond the sport world remains much in play.

Learning Activity

1. While watching televised sports, keep a journal and identify the number of times that announcers refer to athletes of color by their first names only. Compare this coverage with that given to White athletes. Also note the racial backgrounds of sport commentators to see whether an association exists between their racial heritage and the ways in which they refer to Black and White athletes.
2. Conduct a study of your institution's athletics department. Across both women's and men's sports, as well as the athletics administration, determine the occupational employment patterns of coaches and athletics administrators based on race. Break down your findings by specific sports and gender.

Violence in Sport

In the aftermath of the notorious "basketbrawl" between the Detroit Pistons and the Indiana Pacers in 2004—not to mention the role of the fans—NBA commissioner David Stern called the incident repulsive, inexcusable, and unprecedented. Certainly, the episode was repulsive and inexcusable, and the on-court violence may well have been unprecedented for the NBA, but the level of violence was not unprecedented either on or off the court. NFL players, from Rae Carruth to Ray Lewis, have been involved in murder cases. Football players at the Universities of Colorado and Georgia have been accused of gang rape, and in spite of its storied history and clean-cut image, Nebraska's football team has a history of sexual abuse of women (Ray, 1996). Besides accounts of team members engaging in such sordid practices, stories of physical and sexual assault by individual athletes could fill a police blotter on an almost daily basis. In 2005 Kenny Rogers of the Texas Rangers was suspended and fined by Major League Baseball and arrested by local police for assaulting two camera operators. During an NHL game, Todd Bertuzzi of the Vancouver Canucks attacked an opponent, Steve Moore, and left him unconscious and bleeding on the ice. Bertuzzi was fined and suspended by the league and charged with criminal assault and battery. And Kobe Bryant of the Los Angeles Lakers was arrested and brought to trial (though the case was settled before trial) for raping a young woman in Colorado.

This list could include myriad teams, individuals, and sports. More important, the list could also feature one common denominator. The violence that we are talking about is not a generalized, universal practice carried out by all athletes. Violence in sport is really violence in men's sports, particularly team, combat-oriented sports. Indeed, critics suggest that we reap what we sow because physical and sexual violence have become institutionalized in men's athletics (Benedict, 2004; Curry, 1998; Messner & Stevens, 2002). This development may explain why it is virtually impossible to turn on the TV or pick up the newspaper and not learn about the latest assault or even worse. And violence appears to be escalating out of control, both on and off the field.

Why is this happening? One answer lies in what sport has become for men, especially at the elite, financially lucrative echelons of sport. But even if athletes do not reach such lofty heights, an essential part of the sport experience for many men is the glorification of violence—a glorification that encourages them to equate their hyperphysicality with behavior that demeans, intimidates, and sexualizes others (Benedict, 2004; Burstyn, 1999; Kane & Disch, 1993). Not coincidentally, then, men's sports, especially team sports that emphasize physical domination and subjugation of others, have become a place where males learn that their violent behavior is not only acceptable and "normal" but also a source of status and a basis for their (hypermale) identity (Coakley, 2004). Of course, violence in sport is not always rewarded. On the contrary, it is widely, routinely, and publicly condemned. Yet scholars have noted that a powerful mixed message is conveyed, especially in mainstream sport media. For example, NFL broadcasts highlight almost any violent action, with particular attention (tribute?) given to the most spectacular hits in replay after replay. Sportscasters and camera crews are always on the hunt for the most brutal and visually appealing types of contact, often employing slow-motion techniques to hype the late hit, violent collision, or shove in the back (Bryant, Zillmann, & Raney, 1998; Eitzen & Sage, 2003).

Learning Activity

1. Use the Internet to identify three or four current examples from professional sport in which male athletes have been involved in well-publicized incidents of physical and sexual violence. Keep track of which sport (team, individual) and which level of sport (high school, college, pro) were involved.
2. Lead a class discussion in which you, as a future sport manager, would adopt strategies to try to reverse the troubling trend of violence in men's sports. Spell out the advantages and disadvantages of each strategy.
3. Spend a weekend watching men's college and professional sports on TV. List in detail the kinds of images and language that reporters use to glorify violence.

This type of coverage extends beyond football to other professional men's sports, and beyond the games themselves. Messner, Dunbar, and Hunt (2000) examined the dominant themes surrounding televised sport shows and their accompanying commercials. They were most interested in what young boys were seeing and hearing when they watched those programs. The authors found that boys were receiving remarkably consistent messages about masculinity and its relationship to sport and physical violence. In short, they discovered what they called a televised sports manhood formula through which young boys learned, among other things, that boys will be (violent) boys, that sport is war, and that real men are those who show some guts. The result is that aggression and violence are worshiped and glorified in one consistent narrative: "Winners bravely display muscular strength, speed, power, and guts. Bodily harm is (supposedly) intentionally inflicted on opponents. The most ruthlessly aggressive men win, whereas the passive or weaker men lose, often shamefully" (p. 391). Such messages (and practices) combine to create a deadly mix. Male athletes are well aware of the manhood formula that Messner and his colleagues uncovered. They live (and benefit from) it every day. They also know that as "real men" they can engage in an array of criminally violent behavior—from domestic abuse to date rape to assault and battery on strangers—and feel confident that their teams and leagues, not to mention their armies of lawyers and agents, will protect them (Benedict, 2004).

This section of the chapter began with the "basketbrawl" incident. Fittingly, we end with the same incident and a ray of optimism. Although the "basketbrawl" is one of the most embarrassing moments in the history of men's professional sport, it also offers a measure of hope, a possibility that those in charge are finally holding athletes and fans accountable. In the aftermath of this near riot, the NBA handed down lengthy suspensions and hefty fines to players from both teams, most notably Ron Artest of the Indiana Pacers, who was suspended for the remainder of the season and the playoffs, costing him millions of US dollars in salary and endorsements ("Flagrant Fouls," 2004). Besides Artest, five Indiana Pacers were charged with criminal assault. No one is suggesting that these record-setting punishments are a cure-all, but it may be the first step in sending a powerful message that this type of behavior will no longer be tolerated. The NBA also took steps to control fan behavior by banning beer sales after the third quarter and instituting a fan code of conduct. Let's hope that the players, fans, league officials, and owners are listening, because if they're not, we'll continue to live in a society in which the current model of men's sport fosters attitudes and practices of physical and sexual assault that endanger us all (ABC News Internet Ventures, 2006).

SPORT AS A VEHICLE FOR SOCIAL TRANSFORMATION

Although the issues and concerns highlighted through much of this chapter represent some of the most problematic aspects of sport, it is equally true that sport can help us overcome injustice, prejudice, and oppression. Structured and reinforced with appropriate social values, the sport experience can instill people with a deep-seated commitment to make important and long-lasting contributions to society. Although we rarely think of sport in this manner, its enormous popularity, coupled with its ability to reach across social, political, and economic divides, makes sport one of the few institutions that can serve as a catalyst for change. Perhaps the most celebrated example of sport as a vehicle for change occurred in 1947 when Jackie Robinson broke the color barrier in Major League Baseball and paved the way for countless athletes of color to participate across all levels of sport. We can only imagine what sport—and society—would be like were it not for the contributions of Muhammad Ali, Michael Jordan, Magic Johnson, Serena Williams, Venus Williams, and Tiger Woods, to name just a few.

Another area (and era) in which sport confronted society's ills and became a catalyst for significant change involved the turbulent 1960s. That period was marked by social unrest and assassinations of well-known leaders such as John Kennedy, Robert Kennedy, and Martin Luther King, Jr. The decade was also a time of demonstrations in the streets and the killing of students on college campuses over US involvement in Vietnam. Against this backdrop, the 1968 Summer Olympic Games took place in Mexico City. During the Games, two Black athletes, Tommie Smith and John Carlos, who had won the gold and bronze medals in the 200-meter dash, used the awards ceremony to protest racial injustice. During the national anthem, Smith and Carlos lowered their heads and raised their black-gloved, closed fists in a gesture that was widely seen (and criticized) as a Black power salute. Although they were stripped of their medals and vilified back in the United States, their protest brought to light many of the injustices faced by African Americans and (in some quarters) revealed the hypocrisy of America as the "land of the free." As author John Gettings (2002) pointed out, the protest of Smith and Carlos represented not only one of the most memorable moments in Olympic history but also a milestone in the civil rights movement.

In the early 1990s, sport—and a celebrated sports figure—challenged existing stereotypes and again helped to transform society. Near the peak of his career, Magic Johnson stunned not only the NBA but all of America with the revelation of his HIV-positive status. Before his shocking announcement, many Americans were aware that thousands of people had died from AIDS and that millions more were infected with the deadly disease. Although by that time the public knew that celebrities such as Hollywood icon Rock Hudson had died of complications from AIDS, education, treatment, and research about the disease remained almost invisible to the public consciousness. But that all changed with Magic Johnson's announcement. Almost immediately, his medical condition and subsequent retirement from professional basketball became the lead story, not just in the world of sport but throughout society. The event was a dramatic illustration of the power and widespread appeal of sport. It clearly demonstrated how sport, and sport heroes like Magic Johnson, could enable us to see AIDS as an American and world tragedy and allow us to move beyond the stereotypic and inaccurate perception that AIDS was confined to gay men and that contracting AIDS meant a death sentence.

Another example of sport as a vehicle for change is women's increasing and widespread participation in sport and physical activity. Before the early 1970s and the passage of Title IX, many segments of society—including many kinds of sporting activities—were considered off limits to most females. But many women and their male allies began to push for greater opportunities and a more level playing field for any female who wanted to become involved in sport. Such efforts have made an enormous difference in the lives of countless girls and women, their families, and their communities. For the first time in our US history, young girls, like countless young boys before them, grow up with a sense of entitlement to sport. They also experience the benefits of sport, from having a sense of identity, to being a part of something bigger than themselves, to facing (and overcoming) the physical, social, and intellectual challenges found in sport. Because of sport, girls and women feel a sense of pride and accomplishment, learn about their physical limitations and potentials, and create their own destinies, not only in sport but also in every part of the society in which they participate. And because they do, we all benefit.

Finally, and perhaps most amazingly, sport has taken some initial steps in challenging homophobic beliefs and practices. By doing so, this all-powerful institution has created some safe space for gay and lesbian athletes, although it appears limited to individual sports like golf and tennis. Consider the case of professional golfer Rosie Jones. A 20-year veteran of the LPGA tour, Jones decided to come out publicly in 2004. She did so because she had just signed with a new corporate sponsor, Olivia, one of the largest companies in the world that caters to lesbian travelers. Although she had been out to her family and friends for many years, her decision to come out to the world was one that she did not take lightly. Her decision-making process included consulting with family members, friends, other players, business associates, and LPGA staff. In relaying their response, Jones reveals how sport—and courageous athletes—truly make a difference:

> Many of them reminded me that times have changed. I wouldn't have this opportunity as an athlete and our society wouldn't be as liberated as it is if it weren't for all the professional athletes and so many others who have had the courage to come out of the closet. It certainly made my decision easier knowing that others had gone down this road before me. And all of their lives have been enriched as a result. (Jones, 2004, paragraph 11)

IMPLICATIONS FOR SPORT MANAGERS

Sport sociology has a number of implications for sport managers. We have already discussed how individuals face challenges, both on and off the court, and in so doing gain feelings of self-worth and empowerment. We have also examined broader social issues like the various (and harmful) ways in which mainstream media portray female athletes, how racism is perpetuated throughout the sport world, and how homophobic stereotypes put coaches and athletes at great risk personally and professionally. At the same time, however, we have seen how Olympic, professional, and big-time college sports can unify cities and nations, and as a result, challenge and transcend bigotry and oppression. What all these scenarios have in common is people. And knowing about people is critical to one's success as a sport manager. For example, Snyder (1990) pointed out that the management of sport and physical activity ultimately depends on people's desire to become involved, whether as spectators or active participants. A sport manager's ability to get people involved with, and stay committed to, such activity requires a basic understanding of the social context of sport and the meaning attached to that context.

One example that relates to the positive and negative aspects of sport illustrates this point. As we have seen, females' participation in sport and physical activity is a relatively recent phenomenon. As we have also seen, many women who did participate in the pre–Title IX era were often stigmatized as not real women. Yet we all know that people can gain tremendous benefits when they become involved in fitness or competitive sports programs. This is particularly true for females; adherence to sport and exercise can result in significantly lower rates of obesity and heart disease, and can serve as an important counterweight to depression or a negative self-image (Women's Sports Foundation, 2005). Clearly, getting women interested in regular (and serious) physical activity is the right thing to do. But given historical definitions of what it means to be an athlete and a female, many older women may need a more proactive approach by sport mangers to help them get, and stay, involved. Sport managers who understand and respect the concerns of older women can provide creative and sensitive sports programs that reaffirm not only the benefits of participation but also the notion that serious sport involvement can enhance, not undermine, participants' womanhood.

CASE STUDY

The way in which University of Minnesota sport managers used research findings to guide decision making provides a good example of how sport sociology has direct implications for sport management. Anthony Brown is the assistant director of the university's Department of Recreational Sports; his boss, James Turman, is the director. They submitted a long-range proposal for recreational sport facilities to the university planning office. To inform their decisions regarding number of participants, design issues, and other factors related to on-campus sport facilities, they examined longitudinal survey data from the National Sporting Goods Association.

Findings from this survey provide nationwide participation rates related to age, gender, geographic location, and popularity of activity. Brown and Turman concluded that exercise for fitness and physical appearance will remain popular among college students. They also used these research data to conclude that in team sports, interest in basketball will remain strong, soccer will continue to grow, and participation in extreme sports and outdoor pursuits such as snowboarding and skateboarding will increase. Brown and Turman's use of research findings had a direct effect on their facility and program master plan—more soccer fields, facilities for roller hockey and in-line skating, a skateboard park, and inclusion of a climbing wall as well as another basketball gymnasium in the recreation center addition.

SUMMARY

Sport sociology involves the scientific study of the social context of sport. Although sport sociologists study the various ways in which people participate in sport, they are primarily interested in the meaning of sport and its influence on our social, political, and economic institutions. Sport management is directly linked in theory and practice to sport sociology because both areas are influenced by the cultural and societal aspects of sport and physical activity.

Sport has great prominence in society, shaping and perpetuating many important social and cultural values. The social benefits of sport include teaching children positive social roles and unifying diverse groups of people as they cheer for a particular team. Sport can also engender feelings of self-worth and a sense of empowerment. But sport has negative aspects as well—sexism, racism, and violence both in and out of sport settings. Finally, sport may serve as a vehicle for social transformation. Sport figures can enhance awareness of and sensitivity to social problems such as AIDS, racial injustice, and homophobia.

Understanding and appreciating the field of sport sociology will provide an important foundation for understanding the field of sport management. To be effective, sport managers must be aware of the social aspects of sport. Considering that sport managers work with people in social settings, they must understand both the individual and his or her social environment because individuals and their environments are continuously interacting and affecting each other. Sport managers can play an essential role in developing safe, positive, and enriching sport environments. When they do so, people will more fully and effectively participate in all aspects of sport as athletes, fans, clients, or consumers. As we have seen throughout this chapter, sport is a much loved institution. The challenge and the excitement for sport managers is to harness that love in ways that emphasize not only sound management skills but also a sense of social responsibility that enriches us all.

Review Questions

1. What is the definition of sport sociology, and how (and why) is it related to examining the social context of sport?
2. Why are social theories important for understanding the meaning of sport in our daily lives? Give a specific example to support your position.
3. How and why do sports come to symbolize broader social concerns throughout society? List three social causes or concerns in which this has happened.
4. What do we mean when we say that sport is a socializing agent? How does participation in sport allow us to learn important societal roles?
5. Why do eating disorders tend to affect female athletes at significantly greater rates than they do male athletes?
6. What is Title IX, and how has it influenced participation patterns for girls and women on a nationwide basis? Why is Title IX considered a landmark moment in the history of women's sport?
7. What are some of the major criticisms of Title IX? What do the proponents of Title IX say to rebut those criticisms?
8. Why has the number of women in key leadership positions in sport declined dramatically over the past three decades? Identify three specific strategies that you would use as a sport manager to reverse this trend.
9. Identify various ways in which female athletes receive different kinds of media coverage than that received by male athletes. State the reasons that you think account for this difference.
10. List two recent examples of racism in professional sports. Do you think that stereotyping happens more often to African Americans or to Hispanics, or is the stereotyping just of a different type? Explain your answer.
11. Explain how homophobia can negatively affect all women in sport, not just those who are gay.
12. Why are male athletes much more prone to violent behavior on and off the court than are female athletes? How does this tie into societal expectations about maleness and masculinity?
13. Identify the ways in which sport can serve as a catalyst for social change. Give two current examples to support your case.
14. Discuss how and why sport sociology has a number of significant implications for sport managers. How would you use both social theory and research findings from sport sociology to become a more effective sport manager?
15. Identify three of the most significant historical moments highlighted in this chapter. Briefly explain why they are considered significant.

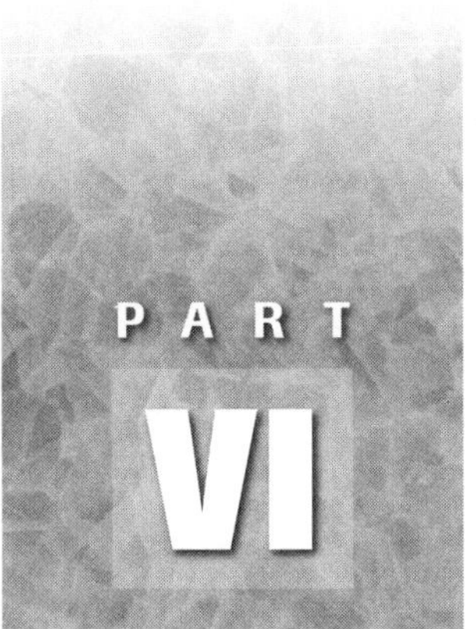

The Future of Sport Management

As you progress through the curriculum at your college or university, some of your instructors will require you to write reports on research articles published in the sport management literature. Instructors assign these reports because they know that when you become a practicing professional, one of your obligations to your employer, to your employees, to the consumers of your products, and to the public will involve being familiar with the research in your field. A problem with these assignments, however, is that students are seldom familiar with why people conduct research, how they conduct it, or how to evaluate the published product. The two chapters in this section will give you a basic understanding of these concepts.

Chapter 19 addresses the important topic of asking questions. First, Bob Boucher and Jess Dixon explain why asking good questions and getting accurate answers are critical to the success of sport management ventures. The authors then explain why sport managers should understand research, why the scientific method is the best route to accurate answers, and why asking the right questions is important. Boucher and Dixon examine questions that researchers have addressed in the sport management literature. The authors then identify additional questions that are awaiting consideration. They explain the role of commercial research companies, demonstrate how statistics can be misinterpreted, and discuss issues and concerns in specific segments of the sport management industry. Numerous examples of sport-related questions and answers are presented throughout the chapter. Todd Beane, Director of Cruyff Academics International (Barcelona, Spain) contributed the international sidebar. The essay describes consequences that can result from failure to ask the right questions and collect purposeful information before taking action.

In chapter 20 Wendy Frisby provides an introduction to sport management research. After explaining why sport managers need to understand research, Frisby defines research and discusses several key research concepts—science and pseudoscience, basic and applied research, quantitative and qualitative data, various research designs, validity and reliability of research instruments. She then identifies and explains the steps in the research process, including attention to factors such as the purpose of the research, the design, the sampling procedure, ethics, data collection and analysis, and communicating the results. The steps in the research process parallel the main sections of most published research articles, and they provide a framework through which you can read and evaluate the articles that your instructors will assign in subsequent courses. Frisby concludes the chapter with examples of research problems that await sport managers of the future, who will need research skills to operate successfully in a knowledge-based economy. The international sidebar examines research topics addressed by European sport management academics. Bill Gerrard, who teaches sport management at Leeds University (Leeds, England), contributed this essay.

We included these two chapters because we know that to perform your sport management job effectively and efficiently, you will need to know how to evaluate research. The better you become at interpreting and evaluating research, the less likely you will be to waste your time and your company's money on unsound suggestions. If you understand research, you will be able to make decisions grounded in the analysis of relevant data rather than depend on hunches or simply perpetuate tradition. The earlier you learn to evaluate research, the more meaningful those research article assignments will be later on. Moreover, as you develop greater skill in evaluating research, you will be more prepared to make the difficult decisions that surely will come your way as a sport manager.

For More Information

Scholarly Publications

Academy of Management Journal

Academy of Management Review

Administrative Science Quarterly

Annals of Tourism Research

European Sport Management Quarterly

Harvard Business Review

Human Relations

International Journal of Sport Finance

International Journal of Sport Management

International Journal of Sport Management and Marketing

International Journal of Sports Marketing and Sponsorship

Journal of Business Research

Journal of Consumer Research

Journal of Marketing

Journal of Marketing Research

Journal of Park and Recreation Administration

Journal of Sport & Social Issues

Journal of Sport Management

Journal of Sports Economics

Sport Management Review

Sport Marketing Quarterly

Strategic Management Journal

Sport Management Research Web Sites

Centre for Leisure Management Research: www.deakin.edu.au/buslaw/bowater/clmr/sport

Institute for Diversity and Ethics in Sport: www.bus.ucf.edu/sport/cgi-bin/site/sitew.cgi?page=/ides/index.htx

International Research Think-Tank: http://playlab.uconn.edu/mylab.html

Michigan Center for Sport Management: www.kines.umich.edu/research/mcsm.html

Research and markets: www.researchandmarkets.com

Sport Business Research Network: www.sbrnet.com/sbr

Sport Industry Research Centre: www.shu.ac.uk/schools/slm/sirc/index.html

Texas A & M Sport Management Research Group: http://smrg.tamu.edu

Tucker Center for Research on Girls and Women in Sport: www.tuckercenter.org

University of Calgary Scholarly Sport Sites: www.ucalgary.ca/lib-old/ssportsite/index.html

Questions, Answers, and Sport Management Research

Robert Boucher—University of Windsor ▪ **Jess C. Dixon**—University of Windsor

Learning Objectives

After studying this chapter, you will be able to do the following:

1. Explain the value of asking questions in sport management.
2. Explain the importance of obtaining accurate answers that are able to stand up to scientific scrutiny.
3. Analyze, interpret, synthesize, and evaluate sport management-related questions that have been asked and answered through academic and professional literature.
4. Identify and explain important current and future questions that relate to specific sport management and commercial sectors.
5. Identify and explain the major issues surrounding the sport management or commercial sector of your choice and construct questions to address those issues or solve the problems associated with those issues.
6. Describe the critical contributions of commercial research firms in answering questions that emerge in sport management sectors.

Scarborough Sports Marketing is a research firm that specializes in measuring the retail shopping patterns, lifestyle characteristics, in-depth consumer demographics, and media habits of American sports fans in more than 75 major US markets (Scarborough Research, 2005). Why are Hollywood movie studios so interested in what Scarborough discovers about Super Bowl spectators? The answer: Super Bowl viewers are avid moviegoers and DVD purchasers. Among Super Bowl XXXVIII viewers, 23% had been to the movies three or more times in the three months leading up to the big game. Furthermore, 31% had purchased a DVD movie in this same three-month period (Mongrain, 2004). Having this information helped justify the decision by six Hollywood studios to pay a combined $16 million USD for television advertising during Super Bowl XXXIX in 2005, outspending both automobile manufacturers and fast-food restaurants in the process (Lefton, 2005a).

Thompson Tregear (2006), an Australian independent consulting company, works one on one addressing the managerial problems of their numerous public- and private-sector sport, recreation, leisure, and tourism clients. Why would companies such as Sydney International Aquatic Centre at Homebush, the Olympic Whitewater Canoe Slalom Complex at Penrith Lakes, and the Arena Sports Complex of Joondalup require Thompson Tregear's help? The answer: Those companies, although able to function steadfastly on a daily basis, have special questions about emerging issues such as strategic facility planning, policy evaluation and development, management restructuring, and a host of other matters that require a unique expertise.

Since 1993 professor Richard Lapchick (2005) has led a team of researchers in preparing the *Racial and Gender Report Card*, which assesses the practices that North American professional and collegiate sport organizations use in hiring women and people of color. Why would a university professor care about the racial and gender composition of these organizations? The answer: This information would be useful to the professor's students as they embark on careers in the sport industry. Each year, the *Report Card* indicates areas where improvement, stagnation, and regression have occurred with respect to the racial and gender composition of players, coaches, and front office or athletics department personnel in such organizations as the National Basketball Association (NBA), National Football League (NFL), Major League Baseball (MLB), National Hockey League (NHL), Major League Soccer (MLS), Women's National Basketball Association (WNBA), and National Collegiate Athletic Association (NCAA). Based on the results presented in this annual *Report Card*, the professor can prepare a series of lesson plans to educate future sport managers about the benefits and challenges of creating and maintaining a diverse workforce, the value of corporate ethics and social responsibility, and the various constitutional issues and civil rights legislation associated with the management of sport personnel. Upon graduating and entering the workforce, sport management students will be in position to put theory into practice (Parks, 1992), by applying this knowledge and shaping a workplace that is more amenable to diversity. Lastly, the information within the *Report Card* can inform sociological, ethical, and legal viewpoints; extend the body of knowledge in sport management; and lead scholars to a better understanding of sport as a social institution. The information is also interesting to the person on the street.

Learning Activity

Did your college or university athletics department make the grade? Using the reference information provided at the end of this chapter, locate and read chapters 1 and 7 of the most recent *Racial and Gender Report Card*. Using the grading keys and weightings provided in chapter 1 of the Report Card and demographic information gleaned from your athletics department's Web site, assess the racial and gender composition of your school's athletics department. Based on the results of your research, report on how your school fares in comparison with the averages reported in chapter 7 of the *Report Card*.

Asking suitable questions and getting accurate answers is critical to every sport management sector in the current information age. Every organization has myriad questions that arise continuously both during and outside working hours. You can answer all your questions by the end of one business day and then come in the next day to a new set of questions that emerged overnight. Questions are important because their answers set the stage for decision, action, profit, satisfaction, and success. If you know how to ask the right questions, can answer questions for your company, or know how to get the answers from available sources or databases, your organization will highly value your contributions. Information of the kind presented in the Q & A elements interspersed throughout this chapter and the kind of information collected by Scarborough, Thompson Tregear, and sport scholars is vital for sport management enterprises in all sectors of the industry.

Wendy Frisby's overview of sport management research in chapter 20 will convince you that the results of the various research processes enable managers to improve their supervisory and decision-making practices in our knowledge-based economy. This chapter relates to Frisby's chapter by addressing the crucial role of questions and answers in the function and conduct of sport management.

exposure—The amount of time, in seconds or minutes, that a company (advertiser) potentially has the viewer's or listener's attention.

Q & A

Do companies benefit from paying athletes to wear their gear and use their equipment?

Answer: CBS TV's final round broadcast of Tiger Woods' playoff victory at the 2005 Masters golf tournament (April 10) was beneficial for his primary endorsement company. Cameras showed logos for Nike, Nike One Ball, and Nike's Tiger Woods Collection for an on-screen total of 30 minutes and 4 seconds. By translating this exposure time into commercial advertising value, Joyce Julius & Associates, Inc. (2005) estimated that Nike received $10,824,000 USD of in-broadcast exposure value. Being associated with Woods appears to be a sound marketing strategy for Nike.

1970s

▶ **1976**—*Arena Review* (now known as *Journal of Sport and Social Issues*) was launched

1980s

▶ **1987**—*Journal of Sport Management* (*JSM*), official journal of NASSM, launched

1990s

▶ **1992**—*Sport Marketing Quarterly* (*SMQ*), SMA-preferred journal, launched

▶ **1994**—*European Journal for Sport Management* (now known as *European Sport Management Quarterly*), published by EASM

▶ **1998**—*Sport Management Review* (*SMR*), published by SMAANZ, launched

Top LPGA money winner with more than $18 million USD in earnings, Annika Sorenstam of Sweden is a walking advertisement for everything from cheese to luxury cars as she plays at the Women's Golf World Cup in South Africa in 2006.

© Getty Images

WHY SPORT MANAGERS NEED TO UNDERSTAND RESEARCH

Research is often unpopular with undergraduate students who aspire to careers in the world of sport and physical activity. Current students, like others who have gone before, appear to gain satisfaction from the practical, hands-on elements of undergraduate preparation and are less enamored with theory and research. In truth, only those who have served in a management position can fully appreciate the role of research in assisting with the managerial role. But there's no time like the present to begin developing an understanding of why research is critical to sport management.

Only Research Can Keep You Current

If your family doctor graduated from a prestigious medical school in 1990, wouldn't you expect him or her to be up-to-date with medical developments in the first decade of the 21st century? Similarly, if the pilot of the 747 that you flew from New York to Paris received a pilot's license 30 years ago, wouldn't you assume that he or she had kept up-to-date with the latest developments in aviation, including safety procedures and technology? The advances that have occurred since our doctors, pilots, and countless other professionals received their initial certifications and credentials have come about largely because of research. Being able to read, understand, and apply scientific findings leads to progress; the world would be a different place without the contributions of millions of scientific studies.

The area of sport management is no different from other professional areas. Through the application of research findings in human resources, leadership, marketing, organizational development, and many other areas, the practicing sport manager has a much better chance of choosing sensible alternatives to everyday managerial problems.

1990s

1999—*International Journal of Sports Marketing and Sponshorship (IJSMS)* launched

2000s

2000—*International Journal of Sport Management (IJSM)* launched; *Journal of Sports Economics (JSE)* launched

Q & A

When is the best time to assess workers' performances in a sport organization?

Answer: The assessment of workers' performances should be an ongoing process, involving a variety of uniform protocols, rather than a finite task with a cut-and-dried timeline (Chelladurai, 2006; MacLean, 2001).

Trial-and-Error Management is Folly

Would any of us drive a car or take a medicine that the appropriate agencies hadn't thoroughly tested? Probably not. In similar fashion, we are well aware of the extensive research conducted on hockey sticks, baseball bats, hardwood floors, running shoes, athletic apparel, and virtually every other piece of equipment related to the world of sport. We consider it progress to conduct experimental studies to improve athletic performance by increments as small as a tenth of a second.

When it comes to the management of sport, however, sometimes the standards are not as exacting. We can easily become enthralled by someone's neat idea or what is being done at another university or in a similar sport in another country. In real terms, trial and error often seems to be the watchword in the everyday management practices of sport. Hundreds of promotions are conducted, marketing plans are formulated, and strategic plans are developed—all without research. Even with a great deal of thought, many of these ventures are doomed to failure. Having sound intuition and a wealth of experience is useful, but trial and error can be expensive. Successful marketing strategies, comprehensive human resources policies, and many other aspects of the sport management domain are based on sound theories derived from research. Admittedly, we are all students of the trial-and-error process in that we make decisions without all possible information or may not have the time or resources to explore all the options. But why do this on purpose? Why not gather information about your question and make your decision based on sound information?

You Need to Know if It Will Play in Peoria

Sport managers face a variety of complicated problems on a daily basis. The general manager of a hypothetical sport organization might handle the following situations in a typical morning at the office: (1) read and approve preliminary budget requests, (2) meet with a small group of disgruntled employees who are not happy with a reorganization of their department, (3) participate in a conference call with league officials to resolve a disciplinary case, (4) chair a marketing committee meeting that finalizes a sponsorship agreement with a blue-chip donor, and (5) view a rehearsal of a halftime show for an upcoming playoff game. In reality no morning could be considered typical in the life of a practicing sport manager.

How the manager reacts to these situations and comes to decisions is the result of many influences. Background, education, values, motives, and numerous other factors blend and provide the impetus for the manager's decisions. Referring to the original list, consider the following questions: (1) What budget items were approved? Why these and not others? (2) How did the manager placate the disgruntled employees? (3) What factors were considered important, and what sanctions were imposed in the discipline case? (4) What approach was taken with the blue-chip donor? (5) How did the manager judge the halftime rehearsal? What do the spectators want, and how does the manager know what they want? Clearly, many alternatives are readily available. As sport managers, we would like to believe that final decisions are based on the best possible information. No one wants sport managers to rely on intuition alone or to fly by the seat of their pants. Notwithstanding the effects of education, background, and the other previously mentioned factors—there must be a better way! Wouldn't it be more efficient to rule out some alternatives to simplify the decision-making process?

When a sport manager learns of a marketing idea that is all the rage of triple A baseball in the southern United States, the manager has to ask, Will it play in Peoria? The point of asking this question is that the astute sport manager must be aware that some geographical, cultural, or economic factor that contributed to the success of the marketing idea in the southern states may not be present in "Peoria," that is, in other parts of North America. From experience we know that the central portion of the United States (represented by Peoria, Illinois) is generally more conservative than other parts of the country. An old adage states that if something works in Peoria, it will probably work anywhere. This idea may be related to the perception that the population of the Midwest is less susceptible to gimmicks, quick fixes, and slick marketing ideas. Or it may just be promoters' perceptions that Midwestern Peoria is a prototype of America, and that if something works there, it will work anywhere.

In any case, deciding whether something will play in Peoria is guesswork. How can we really know whether our scheme will play in Peoria, or in any other part of the world? The answer is research! Carefully conducted research studies can provide important answers to serious questions. As mentioned earlier, trial-and-error approaches can be expensive.

Learning Activity

What is your favorite sport to play in your recreational free time? Using resources available from your library or the World Wide Web (e.g., Sports Business Research Network), research the demographic profile of this sport's participants in your home state or province (e.g., number, age, sex, race, and income levels of participants). Do the same for three other states or provinces. How are the profiles similar or different? If an equipment manufacturer were interested in demonstrating a new product for this sport, which of the geographic regions that you researched would you recommend for doing so? Use the results of your demographic research to support your answer.

TECHNIQUES OF GOOD RESEARCH

Sport managers in the 21st century need to understand the importance of questions, know how and why questions emerge (i.e., know the path of a question), and be able to formulate and pose original and clear-cut questions of their own. Questions are useful to the extent that they are well constructed and able to elicit appropriate and unbiased answers. To be useful in decision making, such questions must precisely address the topics of interest, and the answers must relate explicitly to the needed information.

Addressing Questions and Gathering Information Without Bias

Questions in any industry, but particularly in sport, emerge because of changes in the economy, law, culture, technology, and other sectors that affect sport's operations and bottom lines. Thus, sport companies should not make bottom-line decisions without reliable data. Although many methods exist for obtaining reliable data (see chapter 20), the starting point for any path leading to dependable information is a good question. Questions and their subsequent answers enable sport managers to know their environment, personnel, industry, market, customers, and trends.

According to Peirce's classic theory (cited in Kerlinger & Lee, 2000), there are four ways of knowing (i.e., acquiring knowledge or information or fixing one's beliefs):

1. ***Through tenacity***. One knows that a fact is true because people have always clung to the fact and believe it to be true, even though evidence may exist to the contrary. For example, many people subscribe to the theory that sport participation builds character even though much empirical evidence shows that no relationship whatsoever exists between sport and moral development, good citizenship, and other valued traits (Eitzen, 1999). In fact, some evidence shows that sport might bring out the worst of character traits in athletes. Yet many still hold firmly to the belief that sport builds character because this notion has been firmly ingrained in their consciousness and they believe it to be so in spite of reasonable contradictions.

2. ***Through authority***. One knows that something is right because someone with obvious expertise has said so. For instance, if ABC's Robin Roberts explains that the WNBA plays the game of basketball primarily on a horizontal plane (i.e., back and forth), whereas the NBA plays on a vertical plane (i.e., up and down), and that both styles of play require a unique but equivalent level of proficiency, one accepts her thesis because of her specific talent in sport analysis.

3. ***Through intuition***. One knows that something is true through a sense of reason that is so strong that it might even override experience. Intuitive knowledge is often considered to be common sense or self-evident (Thomas, Nelson, & Silverman, 2005). The case that sport builds character is a good example of intuition (also called the a priori method). Those who have grown up participating in sports may consider the previous statement common sense and would not require factual evidence to substantiate it. Another example might be that Canadians are naturally gifted in the sport of ice hockey. Because this conclusion is self-evident to many around the world, it stands to reason that it must be so—at least according to the method of intuition.

4. ***Through science***. One knows that something is rational because information absent of biases has

been collected, and empirical evidence can support precise conclusions. Nielson Media Research is the sport industry's most widely accepted television ratings firm. The company collects information from approximately 25,000 randomly selected households in 210 US television markets and processes roughly 10 million viewing minutes to produce more than 4,000 gigabytes of research data every day (Nielsen Media Research, 2005). Nielsen reported that game one of the 2004 National League Championship Series between the St. Louis Cardinals and Houston Astros and game two of the American League Championship Series between the New York Yankees and Boston Red Sox combined for a rating of 10.1, corresponding to 15.2 million viewers, on the evening of October 13, 2004. As impressive as these figures may seem, they paled in comparison to the rating produced by the US presidential debate between George W. Bush and John Kerry, which took place on the same October evening. Airing on competing television networks, the debate fetched a combined rating of 32.6 and was viewed by 51.2 million Americans (Puckett, 2004). Most people accept these facts as accurate because they are empirical and the research firm collected these data under controlled conditions with as few outside factors as possible swaying the outcomes.

empirical—Describes data or the results of a study that are verifiable by means of objective observation or experimentation.

rating—The percentage of television households that watched a particular program on a particular date and at a specific time.

In most cases, the scientific method is the most reliable route to information that sport managers can use to answer their questions. The exceptions are those rare occasions when they work in an environment replete with firmly established procedures, when they have impeccable instincts or access to someone else's impeccable instincts, or when they have contacts whose knowledge will not be questioned. In fact, even in the presence of tenacity, authority, and intuition, sport managers must attempt to answer questions without bias. Science, through the data it yields, provides the firmest basis for obtaining answers; it is systematic, controlled, empirical, and self-critical. There can be no better way of arriving at accurate, useful, productive answers.

Q & A

What are the potential attitudinal and behavioral consequences of permitting legalized gambling entities to engage in sport sponsorship activities?

Answer: Because of increased societal and government endorsement of legalized gambling during the 1990s and the concurrent relaxation of many US sport organizations' internal policies, a number of potentially harmful health and socioeconomic risks for sport and its consumers have developed (McKelvey, 2004). Such risks include challenges to the integrity of sport (Farrey, 2003), increases in pathological and problem gambling (especially among adolescents and college-aged students), personal bankruptcies, and crime and corruption (Kindt & Asmar, 2002).

Research Questions and Where They Come From

Questions sometimes emerge merely because of curiosity. The sport management professor described earlier in the chapter was curious about the hiring practices of women and people of color within North American professional and collegiate sports. He set out to answer questions pertaining to these issues and used the results in the classroom to educate future sport managers, shared the findings with the professoriate, and published the results in trade journals so that league executives could benefit from the new knowledge. In sport management practice and in all professional settings, however, questions most often materialize as businesses design or revise strategies.

What if a friend or relative asked you for insight on the feasibility of constructing a new golf course in Myrtle Beach, South Carolina? What questions would you have, and what answers might you need before you could offer sound advice? Would you find it useful to know that the total number of golf rounds played in the United States decreased 4.5% between 2001 and 2003 (World Golf Foundation, 2004)? What questions might you have about this decrease? Would the answers influence what type of golf course you would recommend building? Should the course be accessible to the public or restricted to members only? Should it be a 9-hole executive course, or an 18-hole championship layout? What courses would be the main competitors in the area? You may also want to know that South Carolina has the third highest number of golf courses per capita in the United States ("Market Update," 2005). Given that Myrtle Beach was ranked 9th on *Golf Digest's* list of the 50 greatest golf destinations in the world (Barton, 2000), would it help to know how many golf tourists visited the area in a given season? Thinking more long term, how popular is the sport with kids? According to data collected by the National Golf Foundation (World Golf Foundation, 2004), the total number of junior golfers (aged 5 to 17) increased 37.5% between 2000 and 2003. Perhaps if you were going to recommend building a championship course capable of attracting a PGA or LPGA Tour event, you might even want to know how golf compares with other sports with respect to its popularity as a spectator sport. Between 1996 and 2003, golf experienced a 16.8% increase in fan support, far exceeding the growth in popularity of any other sport during this period (TNS Intersearch, 2004). How many of these new fans are women, and how have the accomplishments of Annika Sorenstam and Michelle Wie helped fuel this growth? As you can see, questions and unbiased answers are vital to the success of sport managers. In other words, you have to know your market. The best way to do that is to ask questions and obtain information through research.

Learning Activity

Using sources that are publicly available on the World Wide Web, determine the feasibility of building a new bowling alley in your hometown. What questions did you have to ask, and subsequently answer, in coming to your conclusion? Compare your findings with a classmate from a different town. What can you conclude about the two markets? Now, combine your efforts in determining the feasibility of opening a new bowling alley in the city closest to your college or university. Discuss your findings with other groups in the class. What is the conclusion of the class?

Planning for Useful Results Through Careful Question Construction

Some of sport's most pressing questions relate to its financial strategies and worth. Recently, concerns about questioning methods have prompted mainstream business to view sport's data-collection processes with skepticism. For example, the use of the **economic impact analysis**, a long-standing tool for assessing the net monetary influence of an event on its community's economy, is being scrutinized in the 21st century for fundamental biases. As you learned in chapter 12, the goal of an economic impact analysis is to determine tangible net income change because of staging an event in a community. But because owners and sponsors have a stake in the event, an economic analysis can produce exaggerated claims about its impact. Crompton (1995) reported that sport facilities, city officials, and other related beneficiaries have sponsored studies with the intent of showing a positive impact. Regrettably, some economic impact studies are neither objective nor impartial and are biased in painting a bright picture for the sponsors of the study. In other words, sport organizations often use economic impact analyses to justify their own positions (Howard & Crompton, 2004). The questions used in these analyses are often designed to influence respondents to answer in certain ways.

economic impact analysis—An analysis used to determine tangible net income change as a result of staging an event in a community.

Take, for instance, the case of the Dallas Cowboys, who in 2004 appealed to residents of Arlington, Texas, to share in the costs of constructing a new stadium to relocate "America's team" from its current home in Irving, Texas. The plan called for Arlington residents to approve an increase in sales, hotel, and rental taxes, as well as new taxes on tickets and parking, to offset the city's share of the $650 million USD construction costs. To educate taxpayers about the costs and benefits of a new NFL stadium in Arlington, as many as four different economic impact analyses were conducted, each offering a different perspective of the same situation. The first study, produced by Economic Research Associates, suggested that the proposed stadium would generate $238 million USD in annual economic impact for the city of Arlington. A second study, prepared by professors Mark Rosentraub and David Swindell on behalf of the Americans for Prosperity Foundation (a taxpayer support group), indicated that the city would lose more than $250 million USD over the 30-year lease with the Cowboys. A third study, presented on behalf of the city of Irving by Turnkey Sports and SportsEconomics, projected that a new stadium in that city would generate $51 million USD in annual economic impact (Muret, 2004). The final study, conducted by economists at the University of North Texas, maintained that the Cowboys and their stadium were worth $346 million USD annually to Dallas County (Fort, 2004).

So who's right and who's wrong? How can such a wide variation occur in the prospective economic benefits that a new NFL venue could bring to the Arlington community? In this particular case, all the estimates are correct! The variation in the results is not due to the disparate interests of the parties represented, but more a reflection of the fact that each study answered different research questions. Whereas the first study reported the total spending that would be diverted from Irving, the second study examined the ongoing dollar subsidy that Arlington taxpayers could expect after luring the Cowboys with a new stadium. The third study looked at the extra spending that would take place in Irving just because the Cowboys are there, and the fourth study assessed the overall worth of the team and stadium to all of Dallas County. The studies did not contradict one another; each generated important yet different information about the issue (Fort, 2004).

Uninformed members of the public and the media attacked the integrity of the analysts and the methods behind these studies because of their inconsistent results. This criticism was unfortunate because it tainted the value that these analyses may have served. Rodney Fort (2004), a leading sport economist, commented that the analysts behind the reports were unfairly branded "as money-grubbing yes-men bent only on twisting data to substantiate the claims of their sugar daddy clients" (p. 26). In the final analysis, improving this sort of process will happen only by addressing more research questions (Fort, 2004).

Learning Activity

Construct at least 20 questions that will address the economic impact of a youth sporting event in your community. Be sure to word the questions properly so that they yield accurate data for the event and its sponsors. Identify any challenges that you might encounter in conducting this research.

Using Statistics Correctly

You don't have to look far to realize that statistical information inundates our daily lives. Television commercials inform us that "Four out of five dentists surveyed recommend Brand X toothpaste." News broadcasts mention that our chances of getting the flu this winter are 1 in 20 without a flu shot and 1 in 100 with the shot. Professional and amateur sport stars break records at what appears to be a record-breaking pace. Goals, home runs, number of coaching victories, and the youngest player to score 10,000 points are all examples of what we count, put in some kind of chronology, and have ready to compare, contrast, or provide information.

North America has clearly demonstrated a preoccupation with sport statistics. Although statistics can be useful, those aspiring to be sport managers should beware of the indiscriminate and in some cases intentional misuse of statistical information. Often, we tend to make decisions based on the stats that have been presented to us. In 1954 Darrell Huff wrote a book entitled *How to Lie With Statistics*. The book was reprinted in 1982 and again in 1993 and has become a best seller in a number of countries. In a lighthearted way, Huff described how the presentation of statistical data can fool us and give us a sense of false confidence because the "numbers back it up." We have adapted two of Huff's examples in the following sections to illustrate how statistics influence sport managers and how they must be careful in using them. Used correctly, statistical information complements the research process. Used improperly, however, statistics can be misleading at best and unethical at worst.

Example 1: The Well-Chosen Average

Since 1988 *USA Today* has conducted an annual survey of MLB player salaries. Results from the 2005 survey indicated that the average opening-day salary increased to $2.64 million USD, up from $2.49 million USD in 2004 and $2.58 million USD in 2003. Of particular interest in 2005 was the amount of money that clubs were spending on pitching. In 2005 the average MLB pitcher was expected to earn $2.3 million USD, up 10% from the previous season, and accounting for a total of $928 million USD in spending by the 30 clubs. The average (arithmetic mean) is a measure of central tendency and certainly provides some information. Yet we must be aware of how this average is used, and what it hides. The $2.3 million USD average fails to inform us that the New York Yankees spent $96.6 million USD on their pitching staff, more than what 26 clubs paid for their entire payroll! Nor does this average indicate that the Tampa Bay Devil Rays had the lowest paid pitching staff, totaling a mere $11.9 million USD, less than what the Yankees paid individually for the rights to Mike Mussina ($19 million USD), Kevin Brown ($15.7 million USD), and Randy Johnson ($14.9 million USD)! Although the same study reported these figures (Bodley, 2005), the $2.3 million USD figure was likely the most quoted and most used in salary negotiation and arbitration cases.

Intuitively, we also would want to question the effect that huge salaries, like those paid to Mussina, Brown, and Johnson, have on this reported average. Given the incredible disparity between the earnings of these pitchers and those making the MLB minimum ($316,000 USD in 2005), the average may not be the best figure for understanding MLB salaries. Of all the measures of central tendency, the arithmetic mean is most affected by extreme measures (either low or high). Perhaps the median (the middle salary) or the mode (the salary most commonly earned) could replace the mean. Some other well-chosen averages to be wary of are (1) the average income of spectators at a professional sport event, (2) the average age of joggers, (3) the average amount spent on sport equipment in a year, and (4) the average length of employment for service employees at a stadium. In short, be careful! These data are useful, but only when combined with other information. As Huff suggested, "An unqualified average is virtually meaningless" (1982, p. 29).

Example 2: Built-In Bias

Huff says, "To be worth much, a report based on sampling must use a representative sample, which is one from which every source of bias has been removed" (1993, p. 18).

Sometimes when we do research, we have a strong desire to get a pleasing answer. Surveys are used to gauge customer satisfaction, fan allegiance, and a host of other factors. Because we can rarely survey the entire population, we draw samples to represent a much larger number of people. If the sample is representative of the larger population, we can draw inferences and be more assured that our conclusions are sound. In some instances, however, the sample is not representative. Analyze the following hypothetical situations to see whether you can spot the problem:

1. Major League Soccer's DC United organization surveys spectators at a game to determine fan allegiance.
2. The city council of Boise, Idaho, hesitates on plans for a multipurpose recreational facility because of an outcry of opposition in the letters to the editor section of the local newspaper.
3. The cost of playing minor lacrosse in a Canadian maritime province was increased to $150 CAD per season based on a survey that determined the average income of the players' parents.
4. A survey of spectators at a local harness racing track revealed that 60% would be receptive to having nutritious offerings replace junk food.

On the surface, each of the scenarios is a legitimate way to use information to improve decision making in sport management. But we must be careful what we ask, whom we ask, how we ask, and most important, what we conclude. Take, for example, the previous hypothetical situations:

1. The information derived from the DC United survey will be biased by the fact that the fan allegiance of spectators would be presumed to be quite high. A comparison between casual fans and regular fans would be more useful, but the best information might come from people who don't attend games at all.
2. People who write letters to the editor are not necessarily representative of the population of a given city. The overwhelming majority may be in favor of a new recreational facility but don't find it necessary to have their thoughts appear in print. Also, a sampling process did not preselect the letter writers—they volunteered to write, and thus they create an imbalance of opinion about which the newspaper readers must be alert.
3. If the average income was self-reported, then the minor lacrosse officials should be careful in using the results because people tend to inflate their earnings when surveyed. And because we already know about the well-chosen average, we know that this income figure may not be representative of the parents of these young players.
4. When surveyed, people almost always support habits and practices that are good for them. The existence of reporting differences between attitudes and actual behavior in survey research is well established (Singleton & Straits, 1999). People may say they would like to see food that is more nutritious at the concession stands, yet junk food will continue to be the biggest seller.

To summarize, we can fairly say that statistics can provide precise information that will assist in making sport management decisions. But we must be extremely careful in drawing conclusions from the numbers alone. They provide only part of the picture!

FROM FOLLY TO FOCUS
Confessions From Cruyff Academics International
Todd Beane, Spain

This chapter rightly claims, "Asking suitable questions and getting accurate answers is critical to every sport management sector of the current information age." I would add that asking suitable questions *to the right people* is critically important. I share this as a lesson learned the hard way.

Cruyff Academics International set out to pioneer a sport management master's program for athletes of Catalonia, the northeast region of Spain. Our mission was to help athletes make the transition from athletic participation into sport management careers. We did so with previous experience in sport management education for athletes in Europe. We did so thinking that we had ample understanding of the needs of these athletes, who typically abandon their education to pursue athletic success.

As we planned the program, we made three assumptions, forgoing any basic research to verify their worth. We assumed that our course should be

1. offered in the evening to be convenient for our student–athletes,
2. hosted at a university campus to promote academic credibility, and
3. marketed through the sport federations (governing bodies) and their leaders.

In line with our assumptions, we set an evening schedule at a credible university, informed the leaders of sport federations, and held a press conference to publicize the program. We followed our marketing and recruitment plan and expected that it would work.

After three months no athletes had enrolled for the course. Failure, which is always a real and present danger in new initiatives, was particularly disturbing because we thought that we had the necessary pieces in place.

This was our folly. The one piece of the plan that was missing was research. As noted in this chapter, questions sometimes emerge because of curiosity, and sometimes they emerge from confusion and desperation. Frustrated but determined, we decided to consult four prominent retired athletes. We engaged an Olympic water polo champion, a professional basketball player, a world-class handball player, and a figure skater, all of whom had trained under the Catalan sport system and were seeking careers in the sport sector. With them, we began a simple participatory action research process (see chapter 20). These athletes graciously served as active contributors to the process. They posed the right questions to the right people, collecting ideas from coaches, players, and sport leaders.

Through this process, we received three recommendations that directly contradicted our previous assumptions. The athletes suggested that the course be

1. offered early in the morning to avoid conflict with athletes' current commitments,
2. hosted at a sport club where athletes would feel comfortable (FC Barcelona), and
3. marketed directly to athletes, bypassing the sport federation leaders entirely.

We had worked through our folly to find a new focus. Once we asked the right questions of the right people, we found the right answers to guide us toward success. After making the appropriate adjustments, we enrolled 25 students within three weeks. The program was launched successfully one month later.

Collecting purposeful information is vital to the success of any initiative. Not all organizations, however, have the financial resources to hire independent research firms. Sport managers often find themselves in organizations with grand goals but modest budgets. This is the reality of our profession. Having said that, what we all can do is follow a process of inquiry, discovery, and communication. That is, we all can develop the skills to ask questions, find answers, and share the results to meet our personal and professional goals.

Problem Solving Through Action Research

Because sport management is an applied field, research questions are less theoretical than those posed in some other fields. Research questions in sport management usually pertain to solving real management problems as opposed to more esoteric concerns that dominate other areas of inquiry. Much like research in engineering and even medicine, research in the sport management field is often judged by its utility. Does it contribute to the building of a stronger bridge? Will it cure an infectious disease? Those sorts of questions are measures of the research in engineering and medicine. Markers in the sport management area are equally

Laura Cierco (center), formerly an elite figure skater, is clearly excited about what she's learning in Cruyff Academic International's Executive MBA program. Had Cruyff Academics not taken the time to understand the unique characteristics of elite Catelonion athletes as a target group, it is unlikely that Laura, now Director of the Cruyff Foundation in Spain, would have had the opportunity to develop her skills in sport management.

Photo courtesy of Cruyff Academics International.

International Learning Activity

Go the Cruyff Academics International Web site at www.cruyffacademics.org. Write a report about this organization. Include information about its purpose, network, programs, foundation, and any other aspects of interest.

Q & A

Do new facilities stimulate competitive success for their tenants?

Answer: In the case of MLB franchises, the construction of a new facility can result in improved competitive quality in the years following the opening of the new venue. But the same does not hold true for franchises in the NFL, NBA, or NHL (Quinn, Bursik, Borick, & Raethz, 2003).

measurable. Solving a labor dispute with umpires, determining the appeal of a new sport in the US Midwest, and improving the profitability of an ailing franchise are problems that are just as meaningful in the world of sport as are structural problems in engineering or medical problems in medicine.

As a consequence of being a practically oriented area of study, the sport management field is an ideal forum for what is commonly known as **action research**. World-renowned sociologist Kurt Lewin (1946) is often given credit for coining the term, which refers to generating knowledge about a social system while at the same time attempting to change it. In sport management circles, this activity would involve solving problems that come directly from the sport enterprise. In short, action research seeks to identify the problem and fix it!

A relatively new area of action research is called **participatory action research** (Argyris & Schon, 1991), in which the subjects of the research become full partners in the process of solving the problem. They provide feedback, help with the research design, and become active contributors to the process. For example, the citizens of a midsize town might participate in a sport and recreation study to determine the facility needs of the town in the next decade. Surveys need to be distributed, interviews must be conducted, and a variety of interest groups must be contacted. Although professional researchers are often hired for such a study, the likelihood of a successful outcome usually rests on the cooperation and candor of civic leaders and townspeople. By going through a systematic process that engages everyone with a stake, participatory action research contributes to solving the problem—in this case, creating a comprehensive facility plan for the town for the next decade.

Critics of action research say that it does not compare favorably with valid scientific experimentation and does not contribute to theory (Tinning, 1992). But given the dynamic nature of the sport management field and the constantly shifting consumer base, action research appears to be a viable option. Action research could address research questions like the following:

1. What crowd control measures would be effective for European soccer games?
2. How can the public sector and private enterprise share in the building and use of major sport venues?
3. How can golf courses be designed to be more accessible to people with disabilities?
4. What new sports should be added to collegiate athletic programs to reflect the changing cultural and ethnic makeup of the student body?

action research—Generating knowledge about a social system while at the same time attempting to change it.

participatory action research—A type of action research in which the subjects of the research are full partners in the process of solving the problem.

COMMERCIAL RESEARCH IN SPORT MANAGEMENT

According to the Council of American Survey Research Organizations (CASRO, 2002), more than 2,000 research companies operate in the United States, each with the mission of answering questions on behalf of other companies. A company might need help in answering questions because in-house personnel lack expertise in newly developing areas or because the company does not wish to hire full-time employees to address questions that need to be answered only periodically. When companies have questions that they are unable to answer themselves, they often hire the services of a research house.

CASRO identified two types of research houses: (1) interviewing companies that specialize in questioning people by either a structured or an open-ended method and (2) full-service companies that act as independent consultants by designing questionnaires, coding participants' responses, analyzing data, and reporting and interpreting results. Headquartered in London, Taylor Nelson Sofres (TNS) is a leading full-service custom research company that provides advice and insight on market segmentation, advertising and communications, new product development and brand performance, and a host of other services to national and multinational organizations. Following their merger with NFO WorldGroup, Inc. in 2003, TNS is now recognized as the world's largest custom research group, with over 14,000 full-time employees who collect, analyze, and interpret information on the wants and needs of consumers in 70 countries (Taylor Nelson Sofres, 2005a). Current TNS clients include a number of sport governing bodies (e.g., UEFA, FIA, World Snooker Association), rights holders (e.g., European Broadcasting Union, Octagon Marketing), sponsors (e.g., Barclays, Budweiser, Fosters, Vodafone), and teams (e.g., Manchester United, Red Bull Racing) (Taylor Nelson Sofres, 2005b).

Several research companies specialize in providing expert research services exclusively to sport organizations. Often, the most pressing questions of teams, manufacturers, and retailers relate to consumers and marketing. Consequently, many commercial companies address marketing and promotional issues on behalf of sport. NASCAR,

Learning Activity

Read an issue of your local daily newspaper. Pay careful attention to articles that report the results of scientific studies. Prepare a one-paragraph summary of three of these articles and explain how the reported findings lead to progress in each respective field. Be sure to include complete and accurate reference information for each article that you choose to summarize.

Nike, and other large and small sport organizations have used the services of commercial research companies in their market and management planning. Table 19.1 lists some of the most visible sport research companies and describes their services.

Q & A

Which North American professional athlete has the greatest fan appeal?

Answer: In two separate studies, one conducted by the ESPN Sports Poll (TNS Intersearch, 2004) and another by Marketing Evaluations, Inc. (Lefton, 2005b), Michael Jordan topped the charts as the respondents' favorite athlete, with Tiger Woods following in second place. Brett Favre and Joe Montana joined Jordan and Woods as the only athletes who appeared in the top 10 of both lists.

ACADEMIC RESEARCH IN SPORT MANAGEMENT

Some authors have noted that sport management has been around since at least 11 BCE when Herod, king of Judea, staged elaborate athletic spectacles (Frank, 1984; see also chapter 1). The study and documentation of research in this area is a much more contemporary occurrence. A number of academic and professional associations formed since the mid-1980s have stimulated research and scholarly activity in sport management. The North American Society for Sport Management (NASSM), the European Association for Sport Management (EASM), the Sport Management Association of Australia and New Zealand (SMAANZ), and the Sport Marketing Association (SMA) are among the notable associations that foster research as part of their mandates. Each association hosts an annual conference during which members and others

Table 19.1

Consultants Specializing in Sport Business Research

Consultant	Specialty
American Sports Data, Inc. Hartsdale, NY www.americansportsdata.com	Specializes in consumer survey research for sport, fitness, and health industries. Provides major research for the Sporting Goods Manufacturers Association and the International Health & Racquet Sportsclub Association. Purveyors of the *Superstudy® of Sports Participation.*
ESPN Chilton (ESPN Sports Poll) White Plains, NY www.sportspoll.com	Analyzes American adults and teens in order to monitor TV viewing, sport and event attendance, and sport industry trends. Their *ESPN-Chilton Sports Poll* is quoted frequently by scholars as well as by various professional literature and the popular press.
Joyce Julius & Associates, Inc. Ann Arbor, MI www.joycejulius.com	Evaluates independent sports and special events programs through their *Sponsors Report* that documents in-broadcast television exposure or their National Television Impression Value (NITV) Analysis that contains full-program sponsorship analysis.
Performance Research Newport, RI Performance Research Europe Ltd. Oxfordshire, UK www.performanceresearch.com	Evaluates sponsorship effectiveness for sports, music, theme parks, arts, and other entertainment industries. Specializes in on-site data collection and research.
Sports Business Research Network Princeton, NJ www.sbrnet.com	Provides continuously updated market research and industry news on sports participation, equipment sales, broadcasting, sponsorships, and marketing.
Turnkey Sports Highland, MD www.turnkeysports.com	Offers highly-specialized market and facility feasibility research services to a variety of private- and public-sector sport clients across North America and worldwide.
Ipsos-Reid Toronto, ON www.ipsos.ca	Part of the Ipsos Group, a global leader in survey-based marketing, advertising, media, customer satisfaction, and public opinion research, Ipsos-Reid is responsible for researching and publishing the *Canadian Sports Monitor*, the most comprehensive study of Canadian sports fans.

IN PROFILE: Daniel Derian

Title: Senior Director of Research, Major League Baseball

Background

In the past decade, many professional sport leagues and franchises have established internal research departments dedicated to collecting, analyzing and explaining research data (Miller, 2003b). Among those participating in this trend is Major League Baseball (MLB), which hired Daniel Derian as its first senior director of research in 2003. Derian joined MLB after spending two years at Blair Television, two years at CBS Network Television, and five years at Universal McCann, the media agency of global ad firm McCann-Erickson.

In a world with a plethora of entertainment options, sport executives are being challenged every day to maintain their current fans and expand to new markets. Although a wealth of information can be derived from subscribing to syndicated sources, the uniqueness of the issues facing today's small- and large-market franchises has driven Derian and his colleagues to pursue customized research undertakings. Accompanying this shift in direction has been a change in the methodologies being used, highlighted by an emphasis on qualitative research, such as focus groups and interviews. These methods complement the more traditional on-site, online, and telephone polls for gaining insight into the demographics, attitudes, and behaviors of baseball consumers.

Derian's research team is responsible for collecting data to answer specific questions, such as the following: What is the profile of MLB's Hispanic fan base? How do National MLB television ratings compare with those of other sports? What effect does interleague play have on attendance and television ratings? How do teens consume MLB in comparison with alternative entertainment options? How can MLB illustrate the value of its fan base to the business of sponsor X? The answers to these and many other questions assist a variety of internal departments that are responsible for managing and marketing the MLB brand at the league level, as well as providing support to all 30 MLB clubs.

By dedicating as much as 25% of its marketing and advertising budget to research (Miller, 2003b), MLB has clearly placed a priority on uncovering new information. "MLB has taken an aggressive approach toward effectively understanding our fans and connecting with them in meaningful ways.... Quality research and information is essential to doing this successfully, and the league has made a commitment to that part of the process" (D. Derian, personal communication, June 28, 2005).

The National Football League and National Basketball Association have also established in-house research departments in recent years. Given the premium that these leagues have placed on information, sales and marketing executives of the future will need to be competent in conducting basic research (Miller, 2003b). Derian suggested, "As decisions within our business are more reliant on measuring the opportunity and the return on investment, research and its associated functions will continue to become more prominent. The acceleration of technology has made the entertainment arena a much more competitive environment, but it has also offered us many more ways to reach out to consumers and to understand what they need and expect from their MLB experience. Because consumers have unprecedented choice and control of their media and entertainment experience, it is essential to be in tune with what is important to them and research is the conduit for that dialogue" (D. Derian, personal communication, June 28, 2005).

Photo courtesy of MLB.

share sport management research in the form of presentations, roundtable discussions, and keynote addresses. In addition, each association publishes a journal to help grow the body of knowledge. The following sections provide an overview of the important issues that contributors have written about in sport management journals over the last several years:

• ***Journal of Sport Management***. The official publication of the North American Society for Sport Management, the *Journal of Sport Management* is the original scholarly journal in the field. Human Kinetics has published the journal since 1987. Following are some research questions posed in this journal:

1. How do athletic administrators distribute resources in intercollegiate athletic departments (Mahony, Hums, & Riemer, 2005)?
2. What are the most important attributes to consider when selecting an endorser for a

women's sporting event (Fink, Cunningham, & Kensicki, 2004)?

3. Which US cities are the most promising candidates for expansion or relocation of NBA franchises (Rascher & Rascher, 2004)?
4. Are there differences in job attitudes between full- and part-time employees in Korean sport organizations (Chang & Chelladurai, 2003)?

• ***Sport Marketing Quarterly.*** Published by Fitness Information Technology Inc. since 1992, this journal now serves as the preferred journal of the Sport Marketing Association. As evidenced by the research questions posed, this journal is designed to service both the academician and the practicing sport marketer:

1. What are the primary motives of people who donate money to college athletic support groups (Gladden, Mahoney, & Apostolopoulou, 2005)?
2. Why do ticket prices differ among teams within the same league (Rishe & Mondello, 2004)?
3. How does race or ethnicity influence sport consumption (Armstrong & Peretto Stratta, 2004)?
4. Do the sponsorship awareness and intent-to-purchase levels of season ticket holders change with repeated exposure to sponsor advertising (Pitts & Slattery, 2004)?

Learning Activity

Conduct an informational interview with a sport practitioner of your choice. During your interview, ask what journals, trade publications, and other sources of information he or she subscribes to or reads in order to stay abreast of current news, trends, and topics within the industry. What kind of information does he or she extract from each of these sources? Summarize the results of your inquiry and briefly comment on the nature of these various information sources (i.e., scientific vs. unscientific, theoretical vs. practical).

• ***European Sport Management Quarterly.*** This journal was first distributed in 1994 as the *European Journal for Sport Management* (1994-2000). It is the official publication of the European Association for Sport Management. Following are some research questions posed in this journal:

1. What factors are considered when participants and parents evaluate the service quality of a children's athletic camp (Costa, Tsitskari, Tzetzis, & Goudas, 2004)?
2. How important are player resources in determining the organizational success of Major League Baseball franchises (Smart & Wolfe, 2003)?
3. Does social integration occur more frequently in voluntary sports clubs than in commercial fitness centers (Ulseth, 2004)?
4. How does the salary cap structure of European football (soccer) differ from those employed by major leagues in the United States (Késenne, 2003)?

• ***Sport Management Review.*** The Sport Management Association of Australia and New Zealand has published this journal since 1998. Distributed as a service to sport industries worldwide, the journal encourages collaboration between scholars and practitioners. Following are some research questions posed in this journal:

1. Do the cultural dimensions of Australian sport organizations differ from those identified in the nonsport sector (Smith & Shilbury, 2004)?
2. What effect do board–executive relationships have on the board performance of voluntary sport organizations (Hoye & Cuskelly, 2003)?
3. How can Australian professional sport organizations stimulate competitive advantage through the Internet and their Web sites (Evans & Smith, 2004)?
4. Do government subsidies increase the technical efficiency of Portuguese sport federations (Barros, 2003)?

• ***International Journal of Sport Management.*** First published in 2000, this journal is geared to sport management and athletic administration professionals at the national and international levels. Following are some research questions posed in this journal:

1. How do auction attributes and seller reputations affect the bidding behaviors and final bid prices for online auctions of sports trading cards (Vizcaino, Mason, & McDaniel, 2005)?
2. What managerial roles are most important for intercollegiate athletic directors in the

National Association of Intercollegiate Athletics (NAIA) (Quarterman, Allen, & Becker, 2005)?

3. To what extent do policies of national sport organizations facilitate the promotion of international relations in the context of Olympic sports (Quick, Taylor, & Gargalianos, 2005)?
4. How engaged are North American professional sport franchises in philanthropic activities (Extejt, 2004)?

• ***Journal of Sport & Social Issues***. Since 1976 this journal has published the ideas and manuscripts of sport scholars who are interested in understanding the relationship between sport and society as a whole. The journal embraces many diverse theoretical and disciplinary perspectives, including those of interest to sport management students. Following are some research questions posed in this journal:

1. How does the use of Native American team names and mascots perpetuate racial hostility and stereotyping in the US public school system (Baca, 2004)?
2. What is it like to be a female college football (soccer) player in the south of England (Harris, 2005)?
3. How have tobacco manufacturers responded to government legislation in marketing their brands to young male consumers through sport publicity and sponsorship (Dewhirst & Sparks, 2003)?
4. Have changing economic forces and league-wide marketing efforts altered the nature of the home-field advantage for North American professional sport franchises (Smith, 2003)?

• ***Journal of Sports Economics***. First appearing in February 2000, this journal appeals to an eclectic audience including people from the fields of business, finance, law, and economics. The journal's editorial board has forged an affiliation with the International Association of Sports Economists. Following are some research questions posed in this journal:

1. Does the old adage "Drive for show and putt for dough" hold true in professional golf (Alexander & Kern, 2005)?
2. What effect do star players have on gate revenues in the NBA (Berri, Schmidt, & Brook, 2004)?
3. How important is competitive balance to maintaining the long-term viability of professional team sport leagues (Sanderson & Siegfried, 2003)?
4. Do the on-field success rates of NFL coaches differ by race (Madden, 2004)?

• ***International Journal of Sports Marketing and Sponsorship***. Catering to sport marketing academics and practitioners across the globe, this journal first appeared in March 1999. Following are some research questions posed in this journal:

1. What is the value of public relations to professional sport organizations (Hopwood, 2005)?
2. Do NASCAR fans exhibit stronger brand loyalty than non-NASCAR fans (Levin, Beasley, & Gamble, 2004)?
3. Has adverse media publicity affected David Beckham's sponsorship potential (Rines, 2004)?
4. Are consumers more likely to buy a product or service from a company that has the naming rights to a NFL stadium (Haan & Shank, 2004)?

Learning Activity

Sport management research is also published in journals from a variety of other academic disciplines including management, marketing, economics, law, sociology, psychology, physical education, recreation and leisure, tourism, and women's studies. Using your library's research databases, locate and read three articles pertaining to the management of sport from three different fields of study. Briefly summarize the research questions and results of each article. Be sure to include complete and accurate reference information for each article that you choose to summarize.

As you can see, much has been accomplished in sport management research in recent decades. In comparison with more established disciplines such as psychology, education, and business, however, the amount of research is limited. Only with systematic and diligent inquiry will the field of sport management progress and flourish. The prospects are excellent, however, because the amount of sound research has increased significantly in the past two decades.

After you have examined some of the recent burning issues in sport management, you may want to read the entire text of these research articles so that you can learn more about the full question-and-answer process. Check the reference listing for the full citation of these articles if you want to find them in your library.

Q & A

Which major North American professional sport provides the most affordable family entertainment?

Answer: Using Team Marketing Report's (2005) exclusive Fan Cost Index (FCI) as the basis for comparison, Minor League Baseball provides the most affordable family entertainment, costing an average of $80.61 to take a family of four out to a game during the 2004 season. Of the other major professional sports tracked by Team Marketing Report, MLB was the second most affordable at an average FCI of $155.71 in 2004, while the NHL ($253.65), NBA ($261.26), and NFL ($301.75) cost considerably more for a family to attend during the 2003-2004 season.

CURRENT CHALLENGES IN SPORT MANAGEMENT RESEARCH

How accessible is sport management research to practitioners? What kinds of events have happened in the world over the last few years that would prompt sport managers to have new questions? What kinds of questions would you have if you were a sport manager dealing with change in your management and leadership? Several major issues will affect sport in the new millennium. The following sections address a few of the most urgent questions.

The Gap Between Research and Practice

In chapter 20 Wendy Frisby will identify several sources of sport management research (e.g., trade journals, the World Wide Web, academic journals, government documents, consulting reports), introduce you to what has been previously researched, and explain how important it is for a discipline to gain acceptance and recognition in society. Research in our field is increasing as the study of sport management spreads to all parts of the globe. Thus, the body of knowledge will continue to grow, providing a solid base for the study and application of sound managerial practices in the sport environment. Although the field is growing and the research is proliferating rapidly, an area of concern has become apparent. Parks (1992) clearly outlined the difficulty when she noted the struggle between those doing the research and those who must apply the knowledge. As stated earlier, the applied nature of sport management makes it doubly important that a strong link exists between what researchers choose to investigate and the needs of those in the field. As Parks communicated it, "Questions still remain how best to translate sport management theory into practice" (p. 221).

fan cost index—Tracks the cost of attendance for a family of four based on the cumulative cost of two adult average-priced tickets, two child average-priced tickets, four small soft drinks, two small beers, four hot dogs, two programs, parking, and two adult-size caps (Team Marketing Report, 2005).

The key word is *translate*, and the meaning of that word leads to an important observation. Over the past decade or even longer, a number of journals have appeared that are dedicated to specific audiences in the larger field of sport management and administration. Some journals cater specifically to the administration of athletic departments or to sport tourism. Others are global in orientation and contain articles of broad generic interest. Put on a continuum with theoretical and practical as polar opposites, the various journals show an interesting and obvious gap (see figure 19.1). No journals translate research findings to the practitioner. Porter and McKibbon (1988) observed that published research is geared toward the academic community and written in such a way that other researchers can understand it but most practitioners cannot. In fact, the readership of the more theoretical journals is almost exclusively made up of professors and graduate students in institutions of higher learning. In contrast, the more practical journals cater to a membership that is involved in the ongoing administration and management of sport venues, athletics departments, marketing firms, health clubs, and professional teams.

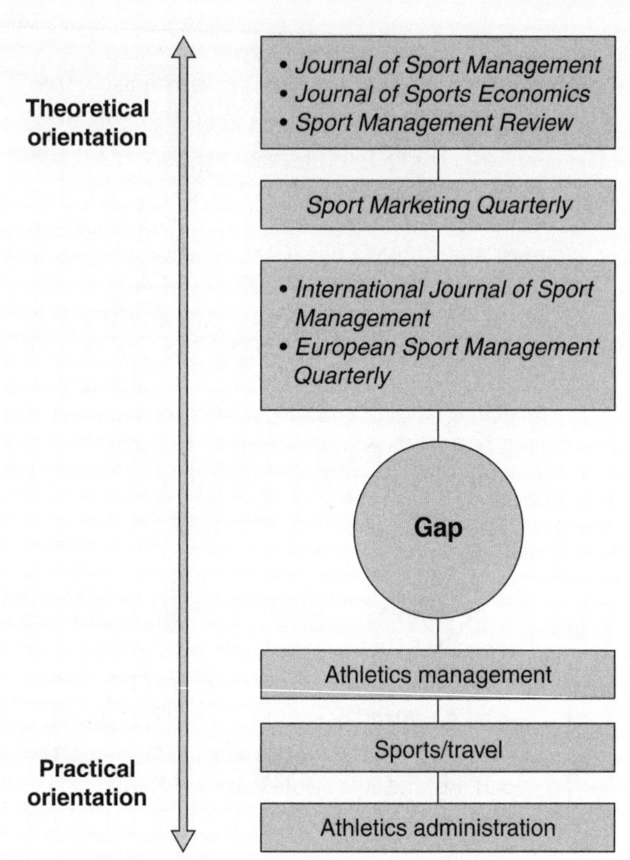

Figure 19.1 A hole in the literature!

Compare the editorial boards of the *Journal of Sport Management* and *SportsTravelMagazine*. A listing of a journal's board members usually appears somewhere inside an issue or on the back cover. What conclusions can you make about the two boards? Notice that the gap between these two groups is magnified by the fact that no journals seem to occupy a common ground, where both researchers and practitioners can contribute. Such a journal might be called *Interface* and would solicit articles with the following characteristics: (1) research explained to the practitioner with emphasis placed on relevance and application, (2) problems that practitioners have faced and how research might help, (3) collaborative efforts between researchers and practitioners who have used research to solve real problems.

The perceived gap between theory and practice in this field may be narrowed by how research findings are reported. Academics cannot assume that the results of their well-conceived and eloquently written studies will reach or have an effect on the field. Similarly, practitioners should not assume that research is too esoteric to be of practical use. Members of both groups must make some effort to answer the questions, What does this really mean? and How can it be of use to me? The establishment of journals and even conferences designed to bridge the gap would contribute to this end. Research questions generated from this kind of collaboration would likely get higher marks for relevance than does most current research.

Q & A

Do the athletic performances of women in international sporting events reflect the labor force participation rates for women in competing countries?

Answer: Yes! Countries whose women performed better in both the 2000 Summer Olympics and the 1999 Women's World Cup tended to be those in which women participated more fully in the labor force. Hence, countries that provide women with greater economic opportunities are those that enable athletically talented women to succeed in both work and play (Klein, 2004).

The Changing Consumer

For decades, North American sport organizations have marketed to the 18- to 34-year-old male. An early-21st-century Sporting Goods Manufacturers Association (SGMA) International (2002) *State of the Industry Report* indicated that 86.2% of all Americans 12 years and older actively follow sports, with 28% of Americans claiming to be avid sports fans. Americans' favorite sports are professional football (NFL), followed by professional baseball (MLB), professional basketball (NBA), and college football (NCAA). When it comes to relieving stress, however, consumers are far more likely to participate in sports or outdoor activities than they are to watch or attend a sporting event (SGMA International, 2002). Knowing this, what questions do you have about the sport consumer of the future? Should sport be promoted thorough the same print and electronic media? What questions come to mind about the future of sport consumption when you consider how the population, and by default sport fans and consumers, may change throughout the 21st century?

First, let's consider the age factor. Although specific date ranges vary from source to source, baby boomers are generally defined as those born in the period from 1946 through 1964. This group has been a much-sought-after market in North America since the 1950s, and will continue to have disposable income and surplus leisure time as they ease into retirement. These aging Americans are well aware of the health benefits that they can gain from regular exercise. During the 1990s the number of people aged 55 and older who worked out twice a week with strength-training equipment rose 345%, whereas the number of those between the ages of 35 and 54 who did so increased by only 133% (SGMA International, 2002). Does that finding motivate you to rethink any promotional strategies to include this affluent group in your marketing plan? More questions may help you decide whether to market exclusively to baby boomers, however. According to SGMA International (2005b), younger Americans participated at least once during 2004 in one or more extreme activities (see table 19.2). Extreme sports have become so popular in recent years that they are attracting more participants than many traditional team sports are (SGMA International, 2005b). Notwithstanding contradictions in date ranges, targeting baby busters (Generation X; born 1965 through 1979), echo boomers (Generation Y; born 1980 though 1995), and millennium busters (born 1996 through 2010) may be a preferred course of action. Mountain Dew has little question about that. In 2004 the soft drink company reportedly committed $3.6 million USD per year for four years to tap this market as title sponsor of the new action sports tour being coproduced by NBC Sports and Clear Channel (Liberman, 2005). The Dew Action Sports Tour, which debuted in 2005, features a series of multiday, multisport events; the largest competitive purse in action sports; and some of the biggest names in skateboarding, BMX, and freestyle motocross (Dew Action Sports Tour, 2006).

Table 19.2

Most Popular Extreme Sports Among Americans Aged 6 and Over

Activity	Number of participants*
1. In-line skating	17,348,000
2. Skateboarding	11,592,000
3. Paintball	9,640,000
4. Artificial wall climbing	7,659,000
5. Snowboarding	7,110,000
6. Trail running	6,486,000
7. Mountain biking	5,334,000
8. Wakeboarding	2,843,000
9. BMX bicycling	2,642,000
10. Mountain/rock climbing	2,161,000
11. Roller hockey	1,788,000
12. Boardsailing/windsurfing	418,000

* Participating at least once in 2004.

Source: SGMA International 2005b.

What about the growing number of young American men who would rather play a sports video game than watch the real thing on television? Between 2000 and 2004, sales of sports video games grew by 34%, to more than $1.2 billion USD (Schiesel, 2005). As the competition for eyeballs intensifies, how will sport managers of the future balance the revenue derived from video game licensing with the revenue from television broadcasting rights? As our society becomes increasingly interactive, consumers will want to play a greater role in the creation of their entertainment experiences, instead of passively watching the entertainment that is being programmed for them. With improved graphics and realism, today's video game systems help to satisfy this need among sports fans (Schiesel). Who else benefits from this increased technology? Brian Billick, head coach of the NFL's Baltimore Ravens, has already acknowledged the potential for incorporating video games and virtual reality technology into his team's training (Schiesel). Similarly, 2004 American League MVP Vladimir Guerrero plays MLB-licensed video games as part of his pregame routine to improve his knowledge of opposing pitchers (Verducci, 2000). Human resource professionals are also finding video games valuable for training and developing employees in the corporate environment (Totty, 2005).

Lastly, what about the trends for women who consume sport? Do you have any ideas on how to reach them? Should advertising to women aged 18 to 34 be different from advertising to men aged 18 to 34? Do women respond to celebrity endorsements by buying the endorsed products? In 1994 Sutton and Watlington found that women were more likely to research a product and make informed purchases than to be motivated by the hero worship associated with endorsements. More than 10 years later, women have far more opportunities to pursue careers as professional athletes, and thus, serve as reputable product endorsers. Given these changes in the sport endorsement marketplace, do Sutton and Watlington's findings still hold true? Not according to Peetz, Parks, and Spencer. In 2004 these authors reported that sport celebrity endorsers have equal influence on the purchase intentions of male and female college students.

How will endorsement trends for athletes and other celebrities change in the next 10 years? How will you advertise to men as well as to the youth sport markets without alienating the increasingly important women's market? Do women respond to cause marketing? As you can see, many issues arise regarding the new sport consumer. Sport marketers will need scientific information based on data to answer their questions and react to consumer needs in a way that builds brand loyalty.

You should have an infinite number of questions about the 21st-century sport consumer. Answers to your questions will become more critical as the century progresses. Appropriate questions and information-based answers will be fundamentally important in solving the emerging problems and vital issues of sport. Questions, answers, and reliable information will be the salvation in the face of dwindling attendance figures and may mean the difference between success and failure for many sport organizations.

Competencies That Sport Managers Will Require in the Next Decade

Chelladurai (2006) identified several key issues associated with sport and recreational management (see table 19.3). As new technologies change the way that we interact with each other and as evolving electronic sources yield updated information almost instantly, we can reasonably presume that sport and leisure managers will need different competencies as we make our way through the new millennium. Many trend analysts see a drastic change in the 21st-century workplace because technology will allow people to complete much of their work from home. Cohen and colleagues (1993) reported that Faith Wohl, human resources director for DuPont, believes that workplaces will be obsolete by the middle part of the 21st century. How will managers' concerns change as a result? Will managers need to be concerned with personalities when the varied personalities within an organization will be working at home instead of interacting on site? How will managers complete job appraisals when they can judge only the final product and not the process itself, which will be hidden at home?

Spectator Services in the 21st Century

Neil Postman of the Department of Culture and Communications at New York University (cited in Cohen et al., 1993) believes that technology will privatize even social activities. In other words, we will all shop, vote, and seek entertainment through our home electronics. Will this extension of the **cocooning** phenomenon described by Popcorn (1992) and Popcorn and Marigold (1998) affect the delivery of sport? How will we use sport as a spectator event? Will we attend sporting events or watch and listen primarily from home? Will stadia and arenas be smaller because of our tendency to stay home? Will stadia and arenas, like the workplace, eventually become obsolete? How will you obtain answers to these questions if your employer asks you to find this information?

cocooning—The tendency of consumers to stay home and order in all forms of entertainment such as movies and videos as well as food and other provisions.

Table 19.3

Chelladurai's Major Sport and Recreation Managerial Issues

Major managerial issue	Associated categorical issues
Managing human resources	Volunteers, professionals, clients
Managing individual differences	Abilities, personality, values, motivation
Human resource practices	Organizational justice, job design, staffing, leadership, performance appraisal, reward systems, internal marketing
Attitudinal outcomes	Job satisfaction, job commitment

For those fans who continue to attend live sporting events, how will the September 11, 2001, terrorist attacks on the World Trade Center and US Pentagon (commonly referred to as 9/11), the outbreak of Severe Acute Respiratory Syndrome (SARS) in Toronto and parts of China, wars in several countries, natural disasters, and other critical events with global ramifications affect their motivations for doing so? What risk management measures must be implemented so that sports fans feel safe at large gatherings? At what point do these risk management strategies detract from the event experience or compromise the reason for attending in the first place? Although attempts at answering some of these questions have already been made (Toohey, Taylor, & Lee, 2003), as technology and globalization continue to transform the sport landscape, many more questions regarding the future of spectator services remain to be asked and subsequently answered.

As you can see, one question brings about several more. Getting precise answers in an efficient manner becomes more imperative as questions multiply.

Dealing With Volunteers

Managing human resources generally entails training, motivating, supervising, and evaluating regular paid employees. How people behave in a sport organization reflects how they view their jobs, their career paths, and other factors related to the exchange of wages for work. In the sport world, many events rely on volunteers to make them successful. From experience we know that virtually all sporting events from the Olympic Games to soap box derbies use unpaid individuals in a variety of capacities.

From a research standpoint, sport managers should know the motivations behind volunteerism, as well as the characteristics of individual volunteers. From limited research to date we know the following about volunteers at sporting events: (1) volunteers are enthusiastic about the event and less enthusiastic about the organization that puts it on (Getz, 1997), (2) recognition is an important element in motivating and retaining volunteers (Wilkinson, 1988), (3) volunteerism increases after retirement (Tedrick, 1990), and (4) volunteers prefer short-term responsibilities (Getz).

Perhaps the most important question to answer through research is, Why do people volunteer? Clearly, people volunteer for personal and specific reasons, but evidence suggests that there is usually something in it for them. Whether for prestige, friendship, self-fulfillment, or altruism, people are "there" because it is better than "not being there." Research leading up to the 1988 Calgary Winter Olympics revealed that personal enrichment and the opportunity to help others were the two most powerful motivations of the almost 1,000 volunteers who were surveyed (Gibbins, 1986). Evidence also suggests that volunteers will become more prominent in sport events of the future. Because people retire at a younger age and because sport organizations are reluctant to hire full-time employees, reliance on the volunteer sector is likely to increase. Many questions need to be answered regarding the management of volunteers, and the following seem to be among them:

1. What are the needs of different sexes, visible minorities, and people with disabilities when they volunteer?
2. What are some effective recruiting strategies?
3. How do you avoid overcommitting volunteers?
4. How can you effectively integrate volunteers with paid employees?
5. How can you overcome boredom related to mundane volunteer tasks?
6. Is your reward system consistent with volunteer needs?
7. How are training requirements different for a volunteer staff?

Q & A

How will the rise in popularity of digital video recorders (DVRs) change sports on television?

Answer: With 3.8 million US households currently owning DVRs, and an estimate that 23.4 million homes will subscribe to the service by 2008, advertisers and television executives are projecting a multibillion US dollar decrease in advertising revenue for sport properties in years to come (King, 2004). James Marsh, senior research analyst at S.G. Cowen & Co., premised that because DVR users can skip through commercial advertisements, those messages reach fewer customers, forcing ad buyers to reduce their spending accordingly. Although many sport properties claim that their products are DVR proof, advertisers will surely need to become more creative and efficient in finding ways to integrate their messages into sport programming, or find alternative means for reaching their consumers (Poole, 2004).

These and other questions must be addressed to ensure that the volunteer workforce is managed as effectively as the paid staff is. Howell (1986) identified the following leading factors related to volunteer frustration:

1. Disagreement about how to reach goals
2. Lack of training
3. Lack of communication
4. Conflict with paid staff
5. The feeling of being useless
6. Lack of influence
7. Too much bureaucracy

Learning Activity

You've now had the chance to read about some of the emerging questions that face sport managers today, but these are merely the tip of the iceberg. What questions remain regarding the future of this industry? Formulate a list of 5 questions that you would like to have answered about the state of the sport industry. Provide reference information for three different sources that you could refer to in finding answers to each of your questions. If sources don't exist or you can't find them, design a study that will elicit the answers that you seek.

WHAT ELSE DO YOU NEED TO ASK?

More sport managerial issues will arise as the field grows and the century progresses. Changing technologies, workforces, spectators, venues, security measures, and a plethora of other factors will influence the sport product and the ways in which it is managed. Sport scholars and practitioners foresee changes in media delivery, the Internet, game management, and fan services to be at the forefront of concern. What issues and problems do you foresee? How will you solve them to the satisfaction of various stakeholders? Do you have the answers? If you do not, then you can find them by designing and asking good questions.

Q & A

Which colleges and universities have the best-selling licensed products?

Answer: According to the SGMA International's (2005a) *Sports Licensing White Paper*, the top-selling institutions, in terms of licensed products, are the University of North Carolina (Tar Heels), University of Michigan (Wolverines), University of Texas (Longhorns), University of Notre Dame (Fighting Irish), and Louisiana State University (Tigers). Sales of collegiate sports licensed products grew by double-digit percentages in the previous three fiscal years, with nearly 40% of sales being attributed to nonapparel products, especially video games.

SUMMARY

Questions and their subsequent answers are critical to sport managers in our information-based economy. Questions emerge continuously in any venture, and well-constructed questions and reliable answers should inform all decisions associated with a venture. The most successful 21st-century sport managers will be those who understand the importance of questions and information in their decision making. Although there are numerous ways of obtaining answers, data-based information provides the most accurate road map for decision making. Questions must be designed to yield unbiased answers, and the resulting information must be used appropriately. Companies that ask good questions and obtain precise answers enhance their planning and improve their profitability. Commercial research firms are often the most suitable sources of questions and answers for sport organizations, regardless of their size and resources. Scholarly, professional, and focus literature also constitute excellent sources of information and often lead readers to ask additional questions of their own. Changing political, economic, and consumer issues that affect the finances, management, and delivery of sport increase the importance of questions, answers, and information as the 21st century progresses.

Review Questions

1. Why will 21st century sport managers need to know how to ask good questions and obtain accurate answers?
2. Explain the importance of scientific data in sport management decision making.
3. Under what circumstances would a commercial research firm be able to make valuable contributions to a sport organization? What might make a commercial firm a better source of questions and answers than the regular employees of a sport organization?
4. What value does a sport organization receive from the answers provided by academic and professional literature?
5. Which area of future concern do you feel is most important for sport managers to address: the gap between research and practice, the changing consumer, managerial competencies, spectator service delivery, volunteer management, or other issues related to sport delivery and fan enjoyment? Why?
6. What other issues do you see affecting the management of sport? How will you identify these major issues? What questions do you have about these issues and their resolution?
7. Which associations have been the most progressive with respect to stimulating academic research and scholarly activity in sport management? For how long have each of these associations been in place? What are the names of the journals affiliated with each association?

CHAPTER 20

Understanding Sport Management Research

Wendy Frisby—University of British Columbia

Learning Objectives

After studying this chapter, you will be able to do the following:

1. Explain what research is and why it is important to sport management students, managers, and researchers.
2. Differentiate between a scientific and a pseudoscientific approach to sport management research.
3. Distinguish between basic and applied sport management research and provide examples of each.
4. Differentiate between quantitative data, qualitative data, and mixed methods approaches.
5. Describe common research designs and data collection methods used to address various research questions or hypotheses in our field.
6. Explain the components of the research process.
7. Know what questions to ask when evaluating the quality of a research article.
8. Provide examples of the growing number of academic journals and other sources that contain relevant sport management research.

Interest in research has paralleled the growth of the sport management industry and sport management educational programs around the world. This interest has occurred because people in business and education understand that research can inform managerial decisions, uncover solutions to managerial problems, improve organizational effectiveness and efficiency, point out inequalities in sport leadership or participation, and help sport management continue to develop a relevant body of knowledge.

Regardless of the area that you are studying, understanding the research process is important for several reasons. For example, if you are embarking on a sport management program at a college or university, you will be required to locate and interpret research from credible sources for various class assignments. You might also have the opportunity to conduct research, either for class projects or during internships. Progressive sport organizations want to find out about the latest trends, evaluate whether their customers are satisfied, update their policies, attract new participants, and stay ahead of their competitors. Increasingly, these sport organizations are looking to sport management graduates for expertise in information searches, feasibility studies, evaluations, and marketing studies, to name a few.

The crucial first step in your education is learning how to conduct Internet and library searches of key sport management journals like the *Journal of Sport Management*, *European Sport Management Quarterly*, *Sport Marketing Quarterly*, *International Journal of Sport Management and Marketing*, *Journal of Sports*

Economics, and *Sport Management Review*. You might also want to seek out additional information in management journals such as *Organization Studies*, the *Harvard Business Review*, and the *Journal of Management*, or in journals in related fields like sport tourism, sport sociology, sport psychology, cultural studies of sport, and recreation management. Other chapters in this book have already introduced you to a variety of government and industry sources that contain relevant sport management research (e.g., Sporting Goods Manufacturing Association, Statistics Canada). Sometimes the answers to questions can be found in these sources, reducing the need to conduct costly and time-consuming research. These sources can also provide valuable information on how to design a study of your own or evaluate research plans proposed by others. If you are planning to pursue a graduate degree or a position in government or industry that requires research skills, you will need a strong foundation in the latest research techniques.

Even if you do not expect research to be a major component of your future career, you will need to be able to understand, evaluate, and use it when problem solving and making professional decisions. But how will you know if the research is credible and reliable? What are the ethical considerations that should be taken into account? Who will benefit from the research? Are there individuals and groups who might not benefit? What are some common mistakes made when conducting research, and what are the implications of depending on erroneous or poorly conceived information? How are advances in technology affecting the way research is conducted? What are the steps in the research process that need to be fully considered before starting a project? Is the project worth doing, that is, will the results be applied in practical situations, or merely sit on a shelf collecting dust?

Although this chapter cannot provide full answers to these questions, it will introduce you to some of the basics of sport management research to get you started. The chapter will introduce key concepts and different types of research conducted in the sport management field. It will present an overview of the research process to provide you with a foundation for becoming both a good producer and a good consumer of research, so that you can become a more informed decision maker. But to develop your skills further, you should seek out the growing list of references and courses in research methods.

WHAT IS SPORT MANAGEMENT RESEARCH?

Sport management research is a systematic way of examining the hunches, assumptions, and questions about a wide range of sport management phenomena. Exercise scientists are interested in questions related to biomechanics, exercise physiology, and motor learning. Sport management researchers are interested in questions related to marketing, finance, human resources, policy, and a number of other topics highlighted in this book. Exercise scientists often conduct research in laboratory settings using experimental designs. Sport management researchers typically use a wide range of research designs in a variety of sport settings to conduct research on people in organizations; their clients, customers, suppliers, sponsors, or partners; the media; and sport products, events, and programs. These findings can inform managerial practice, build knowledge in a subject area, or both.

Sport management research also sometimes considers the broader economic, legal, social, cultural, ecological, technological, and political environment that shapes or is shaped by sport (Slack & Parent, 2006). For example, Thibault, Frisby, and Kikulis (1999) showed how local sport and recreation departments collaborate with other organizations in the public, nonprofit, and commercial sectors to pool resources because of economic, political, and social pressures. These pressures include budget cutbacks, increased calls for accountability by politicians who make decisions about how taxpayer dollars are spent, and increased demand for sport and recreation services by citizens.

Amis and Silk (2005) contend that it is important to consider the historical, social, political, and cultural contexts in which sport management research takes place because these circumstances shape researchers' questions and assumptions, posing implications for how results are interpreted and used. For example, although research might demonstrate the economic benefits of hosting a major event like the Olympic Games, research is also needed to show the negative impacts that could occur, such as harm to the environment or the relocation of poorer citizens to make way for lodging for wealthy tourists (Frisby, 2005).

sport management research—A systematic way of examining the hunches, assumptions, and questions about a wide range of phenomena related to the management of sport.

Sometimes research findings will support our initial hunches and assumptions, while at other times the findings will contradict and challenge them. Such challenges encourage us to consider new and improved ways of managing sport. For example, we might assume that everyone in our community has equal access to the sporting opportunities available, but research might reveal considerable disparities in participation based on income, gender, race and ethnicity, age, sexuality, religion, ability, health status, and other factors. Paying close attention to this evidence will push us to consider new ways of marketing and delivering sport programs so that more people can enjoy the benefits of participation.

Sport managers will sometimes want to conduct research firsthand by evaluating programs, conducting market research to retain or attract customers, comparing financial costs and expenditures over time, or designing feasibility studies before building new sport facilities or starting new sport-related businesses. If sport managers do not know how to design and carry out research properly, they will encounter considerable difficulty and are unlikely to obtain the information required. Inexperienced researchers often underestimate the time, money, and skills required to conduct legitimate research. They might design a survey, send it out, and obtain a reasonable response rate only to discover that they do not know how to enter and analyze the results using a spreadsheet or statistical computer program. As a result, the data obtained from the questionnaire might never be used to inform decisions. Challenges can arise even when sport managers recognize their lack of knowledge in research and hire outside research consultants because they will have to know how to assess the quality of proposals tendered by the consultants who bid on research projects.

Regardless of whether the findings obtained from research confirm or challenge our hunches and assumptions, they will help us make better decisions. Thus, sport managers are increasingly relying on research before investing financial, human, and other types of resources in new or ongoing projects. They want to avoid the costly errors that can occur when decisions are based on false or unfounded assumptions. Successful athletic apparel companies conduct extensive research on their customers and competitors before investing in new products and bringing them to market. A failure to do so could result in major financial losses. Similarly, adults often make decisions about sport for youth, but unless the views of youth are investigated, the decisions made may not be in the youths' best interests. Effective sport managers want assurances that their decisions will help them achieve desired goals based on evidence that has been carefully collected, analyzed, and interpreted.

Learning Activity

Ask one of your sport management professors to describe his or her research interests. How did he or she become interested in sport management research? What challenges did your professor face while conducting research? Ask your professor who benefits most from this type of research. Write a brief report comparing the research interests of your sport management professor with the types of research that you might expect to do when you graduate, given your career goals.

KEY CONCEPTS

Approaches to sport management research vary; the choice of approach will depend on the purpose of the study. Some studies are done to improve the effectiveness and efficiency of operations, whereas others are conducted to solicit the opinions of employees, volunteers, or customers. Other studies are designed to analyze the way that sport organizations are currently managed as a starting point for determining how organizational policies, structures, and practices can be improved or made more inclusive. Familiarity with the following key research concepts will be useful in understanding sport management research: (1) science and pseudoscience, (2) basic and applied research, (3) quantitative and qualitative data, (4) research design, and (5) validity and reliability.

Science and Pseudoscience

When we hear the word **science**, we might associate it with experiments done in high school or with exercise physiology laboratories in which subjects' heart rates are monitored to determine fitness levels. This type of laboratory and experiment-based science is known as natural science, and it has a long historical tradition in physical education and kinesiology programs in colleges and universities. Social science, another type of science, includes areas such as sport sociology, sport psychology, and sport management. In general, a social science approach to sport is concerned with individuals, groups, and organizations as they interact in a complex environment (Slack & Parent, 2006). Chapter 19 provided several examples of the types of research questions of interest to social science researchers in sport management.

Although the natural and social sciences use different research techniques and methods, the goal of both is to collect and analyze data systematically to produce new knowledge that is trustworthy. A systematic approach to research entails the following:

- Clearly stating the purpose of the research
- Developing measures or indicators of key concepts under investigation
- Deciding on the appropriate research methods
- Considering the ethical dimensions involved
- Carefully collecting and analyzing the data
- Drawing on or developing theories to explain the findings
- Making well-founded recommendations

Sport managers who understand the research process are in the best position to judge whether the research has used a systematic approach and thus whether they can base their decisions on the information generated.

science—Information based on systematic research.

A growing body of research, however, appears to have a scientific basis when in fact it does not. Theories promoting the latest managerial or marketing techniques that are not based on systematic research are known as pseudoscience. We can find numerous examples of pseudoscience in popular-press books, in infomercials on television, in newspapers or magazines articles, and on the Internet. "Get rich quick" schemes that provide unsubstantiated evidence to support the claims being made are another example of pseudoscience. Although the latest scheme or trend might be endorsed by a purported expert, explained in technical language, and supported by promises of dramatic outcomes, sport managers must be skeptical of pseudoscience masquerading as science. Although several well-known management gurus have made personal fortunes by speaking about and selling popular how-to books on a variety of management topics, not all their theories and recommendations are supported by the systematic collection, analysis, and interpretation of data. To sort out what types of information are credible and to avoid basing decisions on information that is biased, misleading, or faulty, an understanding of sport management research is essential.

pseudoscience—Information that appears to be based on systematic research when it is not.

One way to determine whether a piece of research qualifies as science or pseudoscience is to analyze it using the 15 questions for judging the quality of research that appear at the end of this chapter. If it is not clear who conducted the research or what their credentials are, if few details are provided about the sample or research methods, and if no mention is made of the validity and reliability of the measures or indicators used, you should be highly suspicious of the claims being made. A systematic approach to research may have been used, but until you can verify that, you should critically question whether the conclusions and recommendations are justified and be hesitant about relying on the information when making decisions.

Learning Activity

Find an example of pseudoscience by locating a popular-press book, magazine, Web site, or a television infomercial that espouses a management theory or trend that does not appear to be backed up by systematic collection and analysis of data. Based on the 15 questions used to judge the quality of research, which appear at the end of the chapter, write a short report on what features of the article appeared to be trustworthy and what features made you skeptical about the claims being made.

Basic and Applied Research

Social science research is of two general types: basic and applied (Neuman, 2003). Although the two types of research can be highly interrelated and may not always be easily distinguishable from one another, understanding some of the differences in their goals and approaches is helpful.

Basic Research

Basic research is usually done in universities or research institutes with the goal of advancing a body of knowledge in a subject area. It focuses on developing or testing theories or explanations for why things operate in certain ways. Direct practical outcomes from basic research are not always immediately apparent, although questions often arise from practical problems and the findings can provide a foundation for developing new managerial systems and approaches.

basic research—Research designed to test or develop theories to add to the body of knowledge.

Simply put, a **theory** provides an explanation for a phenomenon of interest to sport management researchers. Theory is integral to basic research in three main ways: (1) existing managerial theories can be used to explain sport management phenomena, (2) existing managerial theories can be built upon or extended through the study of sport, and (3) alternative theories can be proposed if existing theories do not offer adequate explanations for sport phenomena. Applying, testing, advancing, and developing new theories can further develop the body of knowledge in sport management.

theory—Provides an explanation for a phenomenon of interest to sport management researchers.

Slack and Parent's (2006) book, *Understanding Sport Organizations: The Application of Organizational Theory*, provides an overview of the types of theories that have been or could be used to build the body of knowledge in sport management. In a more specific example, a special issue of the *European Sport Management Quarterly* (*ESMQ*) was devoted to the use of the resource-based view of the firm, a strategic management theory. This theory seeks to explain how companies can gain competitive advantages through the effective use of resources (Gerrard, 2003). In one article in this special issue of *ESMQ*, Mauws, Mason, and Foster (2003) used the resource-based view of the firm to explain why the value of professional sport franchises continue to escalate, despite repeated claims of financial woes by owners. In another article, Smart and Wolfe (2003) were concerned that little research has been done on the contributions of leadership and human resources to the competitive advantages that some firms have over others. In the final article, Amis (2003) demonstrated how the use of sport through direct sponsorship, advertising, and promotions contributed to the intangible resources of enhanced image and reputation for a major transnational firm. Taken together, these three studies not only increased knowledge of how sport organizations operate, but also offered insights into how the study of sport can advance an existing managerial theory.

Sometimes researchers conduct several studies using the same theory to build a body of knowledge in a specific area. Sally Shaw's research program on gender equity in sport provides a good illustration of this approach. Using feminist theory that explains how patterns of gender inequities emerge and are reinforced over time, she and her coauthors provided important analyses about differences in the career experiences of women and men in sport organizations (Shaw & Slack, 2002; Shaw & Hoeber, 2003), the tensions that arise when gender equity policies are implemented (Shaw & Penney, 2003), and the reasons that sponsors invest more in men's sport than they do in women's sport even though women are major consumers of sport products (Shaw & Amis, 2001). Along similar lines, Hums and Mahony and their coauthors have been developing a research program based on the theory of distributive justice in intercollegiate athletics (Hums & Chelladurai, 1994a, 1994b; Mahony & Pastore, 1998; Mahony, Hums, & Riemer, 2002). Distributive justice theory is based on principles of equity, equality, and need. The principle of equity means that those "producing the most, putting forth the most effort, and/or having the most ability receive the larger share of resources" (Mahony et al., 2002, p. 333). In contrast, when the principle of equality is used, all individuals or groups receive the same allocation regardless of contribution, and when the principle of need is used, individuals and groups with the least resources are entitled to receive more. These authors have contributed to theory development by refining definitions of key terms and testing how the theory operates when resources are allocated in intercollegiate athletics.

Applied Research

Most sport managers will be interested in **applied research** because it is designed to help answer practical questions such as how to increase market share and customer satisfaction. Although applied sport management studies often have a narrowly

Learning Activity

Search Slack and Parent's (2006) book or recent issues of leading sport management journals and locate three theories besides the resource-based view of the firm, feminist theory, and distributive justice theory that were briefly described in this chapter. Write a short report that describes the key features of each theory, how the study used the theory, and whether the authors proposed ideas for advancing or building on the theory. In your response, also discuss whether the theories offered practical implications for sport managers.

SPORT MANAGEMENT RESEARCH IN EUROPE

Bill Gerrard, United Kingdom

The defining characteristic of sport management research in Europe is diversity. This diversity is due to the fact that in different European countries, sport management programs developed in different ways, influenced by local institutional structures of government, education, and sport. In the USA sport management roots are in university and college athletics departments. In Europe there was no equivalent common point of origin. College athletics in Europe has never been a commercial enterprise, so there was no internal-led demand for sport management expertise. Consequently, sport management emerged in a variety of university and college departments. In the UK sport management was initially seen as part of leisure and tourism management. But some sport departments, economics departments and business schools, and law schools also have a longstanding involvement in aspects of sport management. A significant number of UK researchers, therefore, have come into sport management from nonsport backgrounds, often from one of the parent business disciplines. Similar heterogeneous growth paths are present in other European countries.

Because of the collectivist political tradition, the sport management research agenda in Europe is more akin to that found in Canada and Australia with an emphasis on the study of government policy toward sport and the behaviour of agencies responsible for delivering sport in both governmental and nongovernmental sectors. As in the USA, Canada, and Australia, considerable research in Europe is conducted on professional team sports and other aspects of the commercial sport business. Unlike sport management research in North America and Australia, European sport management research on the sport business is dominated by a focus on association football (i.e., soccer), reflecting its overwhelming commercial importance in the European marketplace.

The professional body for sport management researchers in Europe is the European Association for Sport Management (EASM). EASM has approximately 500 members drawn from over 30 countries. Unlike its North American counterpart (the North American Society for Sport Management), the membership is not predominantly academic but includes a significant number of practitioners based in national and local government departments and sporting organisations. Apart from providing a facilitating network including a Web site (www.easm.net), EASM has two primary scholarly functions—organising an annual congress and publishing an academic journal. The congress is held in a different venue every September and regularly draws 400 to 500 participants. In recent years it has been held in Spain, Sweden, Finland, Belgium, and England. Reflecting its mixed membership, the congress programme includes both scientific and professional (i.e., practitioner) presentations. A scientific committee selects all presentations, except the invited keynote addresses, based on peer-reviewed abstracts.

EASM publishes an academic journal, *European Sport Management Quarterly (ESMQ)*. *ESMQ* was launched in 2001 (previously EASM published the *European Journal of Sport Management*) and currently publishes approximately 20 peer-reviewed articles annually covering all areas of sport management. Although it is a European-based, English-language journal with a mission to promote academic research in sport management in Europe, *ESMQ* is international in its outlook and open to all scholars in the field, irrespective of geographic location and focus. The journal encourages a diversity of research methods—theoretical and empirical, quantitative and qualitative, statistical sampling and case study. *ESMQ* aims to publish only articles containing research findings that represent a "significant contribution to the field of sport management" defined in the guidelines to authors as "new theoretical developments, methodological innovations and/or new empirical results." *ESMQ* is currently operating with an acceptance rate of around 35%. Submissions are rejected for two principal reasons. First, reviewers may consider the study to have marginal value added, merely replicating previous studies without adding significant innovation in methods or findings. Second, authors may fail to ground their research properly in an appropriate theoretical framework, thus preventing critical interpretation of empirical results.

defined purpose, do not necessarily draw on theories, and aim to produce practical results that are of immediate use, they still must use a systematic approach. That is, researchers must carefully define their research questions, consider how they will measure key concepts, select a sample, collect and analyze the data, and communicate the results. To ensure that the resources and skills required are available, researchers should carefully consider all these steps before starting a study. Some common types of applied research in sport management include marketing research,

In London (May 2006) Union of European Football Associations (UEFA) officials Lennart Johansson (2nd L) and Lars-Christer Olsson (L) and British Sports Minister Richard Caborn (R) exhibit a report compiled by chairman of the Independent Review of European Football Jose Luis Arnaut (2nd R).The report will be used in discussions among the sports ministers of France, Germany, Italy, and Spain, as well as UEFA and FIFA, on governance in European football. It is a high-profile example of the tendency of European sport research to focus on football (soccer).

© Getty Images

International Learning Activity

On EASM's Web site access the list of articles published in *ESMQ* since 2001. Try to classify the articles by subject area. Do you think that *ESMQ* meets its mission statement of offering an international outlook and covering all areas of sport management research? Why or why not?

feasibility studies, economic impact studies, and evaluation research.

> **applied research**—Research designed to answer practical sport management questions.

• ***Marketing research*** covers a broad range of topics, such as testing spectator or client preferences, analyzing the effect of promotional strategies, and determining the effect of competitors' pricing strategies. Geng and Blakemore (2002) conducted an applied marketing study related to China's hosting of the 2008 Olympic Games. They were interested in determining whether there was a gap between sport organizations and commercial corporations in terms of sponsorship strategies. Three types of marketing research were conducted: (1) consulting with sport marketing specialists in the US and China, (2) reviewing historical and current documents about sport marketing and the development of sport in China, and (3) analyzing a questionnaire administered to sport officials in China and business executives connected with China's sport marketing enterprises. The researchers concluded that when Western corporations become involved in sponsoring Chinese athletic events or properties, their capitalistic approach (i.e., economic profit motives) conflicts with China's distinct socialism (i.e., social profit motives), so they need to be sensitive to cultural differences when conducting business.

• ***Feasibility studies*** focus on the costs and benefits of launching new initiatives and determining whether demand, financial resources, appropriate locations, trained staff, and so on are sufficient to justify proceeding. Small business advisory groups often provide information for entrepreneurs on how to conduct research to determine whether their business plans are feasible. Berrett, Burton, and Slack (1993) have shown that the failure rate for new small businesses, including those related to sport, is over 50%. Research can help an entrepreneur decide whether to start the business in the first place, and data collected and compared over time can assist in planning and decision making as the business unfolds. Accurate estimates of costs and how they might change over time are crucial. Organizers of major sporting events who need government approval and sponsor support also conduct feasibility studies. Showing that facilities are sufficient, that accommodations and restaurants are available to serve tourists, and that a viable financial plan is in place are examples of the research needed to convince stakeholders that the investments will generate the types of spin-offs desired.

• ***Economic impact studies*** are commonly used by organizers of sport events, as you learned in chapters 12 and 19. For example, Bernthal and Regan (2004) conducted a study to estimate the economic impact of multiple events at a NASCAR-affiliated track on the economy of a rural region in the United States. Their results revealed that only 7% of attendees at a weekend race were regional fans, with nonregional fans making up 93% of attendees. Racing fans spent money in a variety of ways including tickets to the event, fuel, track concessions, overnight lodging, shopping, and restaurants. The estimated economic impact was over $30 million USD in addition to the creation of 908 jobs, but it was not clear whether the job opportunities were sustained after the event ended or whether any negative impacts were associated with the hosting of the event.

• ***Evaluation research comprises*** many different types, but all of them address the fundamental question, How are we doing? The research required to answer this question might include an assessment of how well existing policies, programs, and strategies are working or whether improvements are required to increase customer satisfaction levels. Needs assessments, program evaluations, and employee performance appraisals are all examples of applied evaluation research (Chelladurai, 2006). In a program evaluation study, Ashton-Shaeffer, Gibson, Autry, and Hanson (2001) evaluated men and women with physical disabilities who participated in a sport camp for adults with recent spinal cord injuries or lower-limb amputations. The adults were asked questions about their backgrounds and previous experiences in sport, their motivations for attending the camp, their experiences at camp, and their ideas for future camps. The analysis of the data revealed that camp participants faced difficulties in their everyday interactions with able-bodied people, which had resulted in their exclusion from sport in the past. The camp served as an important way of confronting the stereotypes that the adults with disabilities had faced, and it provided them with a sense of empowerment. As one camper in the study said, "I feel like [the camp] opened up a lot of doors to me that had closed when I got hurt" (Ashton-Shaeffer et al., 2001, p. 110).

Quantitative and Qualitative Data

One way to determine whether a study used a systematic approach is to examine the information source to ascertain whether the researchers collected empirical data. We usually associate data with numbers or statistics, but sport managers rely on many different types of data. Data in the form of numbers are known as **quantitative data**, whereas data in the form of words, pictures, or actions are known as **qualitative data**. The choice of data depends on the research question, and sometimes both types of data are required to address the research questions. When investigators collect both quantitative data and qualitative data in the same study, they are using a **mixed methods approach** (Creswell, 2003). For example, a program evaluation might entail tracking the number of new and repeat participants as well as conducting interviews with

Learning Activity

Break into groups of three or four students and create a list of the types of applied research that progressive sport organizations might use to improve their decision making. Consider a wide range of sport organizations, including those in the commercial sector (e.g., professional sport, retail sport companies), the public sector (e.g., schools, sport governing bodies), and the nonprofit sector (e.g., youth groups, advocacy organizations, charities). Compare and contrast your list with the lists that other groups in the class created. Did the types of research vary by sector? In your discussions, be sure to identify how sport organizations can benefit from each type of research listed.

them to determine whether any changes to the program are desired. Common methods of collecting quantitative and qualitative data will be discussed later in this chapter.

quantitative data—Data in the form of numbers.

qualitative data—Data in the form of words, pictures, or actions.

mixed methods approach—Both quantitative and qualitative data are collected to address the purpose of the study.

Research Design

Creswell (2003) defines a **research design** as a strategy or plan of action that links the research questions to the choice of research methods and the desired outcomes of the research. Common research designs in sport management research include experiments, surveys, ethnographies, case studies, and action research. Factors such as the purpose of the research, the research questions, the training and expertise of the researcher, available resources, and how the research will be used determine the choice of research design.

research design—A strategy or plan of action that links the research questions to the choice of research methods and the desired outcomes.

Like exercise scientists, some sport management researchers use **experimental designs** to test the effect of a treatment condition or an intervention on an outcome. By exposing groups to different treatments or interventions, the researcher can examine whether the treatment or intervention is causing a change in an outcome of interest (Creswell, 2003). For example, Chalip, Green, and Hill (2003) used an experimental design to examine the effects of event advertising and event telecasts on viewer images in a sport tourism destination that was hosting a major sport event. They were interested in three outcomes: (1) the participants' images of the destination based on safety, novelty, climate, and a number of other factors; (2) the participants' intentions to visit the destination; and (3) the relevance of televised communications to the viewer. Participants in the study were placed in different groups, and each group was given an intervention that included a six-minute video, with different content for each group. The researchers then asked the participants to fill out a questionnaire about their impressions of the outcomes. The researchers found that the types of media had different effects on impressions and individual's intentions to visit the host destination, and they proposed a number of recommendations for sport managers to consider based on the results.

experimental design—Study participants are exposed to different treatments or interventions to examine changes in outcomes of interest.

Because experimental designs cannot answer all questions of interest, sport management researchers also use other research designs, such as surveys, case studies, ethnographies, and action research. A **survey design** provides a quantitative or numeric description of trends or attitudes of a population of interest (Creswell, 2003). Researchers must carefully consider the questions that they will ask, the strategies that they will use to ensure that as many people as possible in their sample complete and return questionnaires, and the statistics that they will use to analyze the results. For example, Kent and Chelladurai (2001) used a survey design to study the leadership and organizational commitment of athletics directors and their subordinates in intercollegiate athletics. They found that transformational leadership was positively related to organizational commitment, an important finding because committed workers are thought to contribute more to the productivity of organizations than less committed workers do. Armstrong (2002) also used a survey design to understand Blacks' consumption of sport events of historically black colleges and universities (HBCUs). She designed survey questions on psychosocial sport involvement, ethnic identification, frequency of HBCU sport attendance, and frequency of engaging in non-HBCU sport consumption. Her questionnaire was completed by 278 Black spectators at an HBCU sporting event. Armstrong found that ethnic identification and psychosocial involvement with HBCU sports significantly influenced HBCU sport attendance, and she discussed the implications of these findings for sport managers.

As more people gain access to computers, researchers are using online surveys more frequently than mail or telephone surveys. At the 2005 conference of the North American Society for Sport Management, Hoeber, Riemer, Dorsch, and Hoeber discussed the advantages of using a Web-based survey design that tracked the opinions of athletes and their parents over time. This research design was time efficient and convenient both for those who filled out the survey and for the researchers, who could analyze the results efficiently because the questions were programmed so that the data could be automatically coded for statistical analysis.

> **survey design**—Provides a quantitative or numeric description of trends and attitudes of a population of interest.

Research questions are sometimes best answered by going out into the field and studying how sport is managed in a natural setting. **Ethnography** is one such type of field research. The goal is often to understand the context or conditions that shape people's perspectives of their experiences as sport organizers, volunteers, consumers, or sponsors. Theberge's (2000) book chronicles her two-year ethnographic study on the organizational tensions behind the emergence of women's ice hockey in Canada. She observed hockey practices, locker rooms, and games. She also interviewed players and coaches of an elite women's hockey team over time and compared and contrasted the norms governing the women's game with the men's game.

> **ethnography**—Involves research of the perceptions, actions, and experiences of people in a natural setting over time.

Case studies are another popular research design in which the researcher explores a program, event, process, or organization in depth over time using a variety of data collection methods (Stake, 2005). Desbordes (2001) conducted a case study on organizational innovation based on the design and development of downhill skis by the Salomon manufacturing company. He analyzed 10 annual reports from the firm and various media articles about the ski industry. He interviewed various managers including the company director, the quality manager, the marketing director, and the director of a new factory where the skis were produced. Desbordes concluded that continual increases in the research and development budget, multibranding, and a worldwide communication policy contributed to the success of the firm. In another case study, Wilson and White (2002) examined a grassroots movement to revive a defunct professional football team franchise in Canada. They conducted interviews with key members of the revival movement and did a content analysis of media coverage of the group and the football team. The analysis provided interesting insights into the power dynamics between big business, local government, the media, and a group of fans when professional sport teams are being disbanded or relocated.

> **case studies**—The researcher explores a program, event, process, or an organization in depth over time using a variety of data collection methods.

Although sport management has less commonly used **action research**, interest in this research design is growing because it is a way of bringing study participants, practitioners, and researchers together to tackle problems of mutual concern (Frisby, Reid, Millar, & Hoeber, 2005; Greenwood & Levin, 1998). The overall goal of action research is to produce knowledge about how everyday experiences of people can be improved to promote social change and social justice (Reason & Bradbury, 2001). For example, we know that those living below the poverty line are much less likely to participate in sport because of the high costs of programs, apparel, and equipment. By collaborating with those living in poverty on all phases of the research process, community sport managers can identify barriers to participation and develop action strategies for overcoming them (Frisby, Crawford, & Dorer, 1997).

> **action research**—A collaborative approach to research about the everyday experiences of people that is designed to promote social change and social justice.

Learning Activity

Conduct an online literature search of abstracts of recent publications in the leading sport management and management journals to uncover one additional example of each of the following research designs: experimental research, surveys, ethnographies, case studies, and action research. When you find an example of interest, read the full article and write a brief report comparing and contrasting the research questions, research methods, and overall outcomes of each study.

Validity and Reliability

Before determining whether to collect quantitative data, qualitative data, or both, researchers must determine how they are going to measure the various managerial concepts under investigation. Because many concepts are abstract (we cannot

In 2004, Australia announced a program to enhance community and national identity in Oceania by transcending ethnic, religious, language, and other barriers through sport. This effort raises many questions about the effectiveness of sport as a tool for social transformation. Action research conducted among the people targeted by the program, such as these sports-minded nuns in remote western Guadalcanal, would provide valuable data that could help answer these questions.

touch them or observe them directly), coming up with perfect measures or indicators is rarely possible. For example, managerial concepts such as organizational effectiveness and customer satisfaction are abstract and multifaceted and therefore difficult to define and measure. One way to measure abstract concepts is to create appropriate survey questions or other data collection techniques. Note, however, that our measures are rarely perfect indicators of the abstract concept under investigation.

To determine how well our quantitative and qualitative data collection techniques measure abstract concepts of interest, **validity** and **reliability** are important considerations. Validity assesses how well our measures capture the meaning of abstract concepts, and reliability refers to the consistency or dependability of our measures (Neuman, 2003). A sport manager can have more faith in research if the measures used capture the meaning of the abstract managerial concept and hold up over time and across different groups.

validity—The degree to which measures capture the meaning of abstract concepts.

reliability—The consistency or dependability of measures of abstract concepts.

To illustrate, a manager of a fitness facility can assume that low prices, cleanliness, and qualified instructors contribute to customer satisfaction. If customers confirm that only these three factors contribute to their satisfaction, then the measures devised by the manager would have high validity because they fully capture the meaning of the concept. But if customers reveal that other factors such as variety in program offerings and having the latest weight-training equipment also contribute to their satisfaction, then the survey or interview questions should incorporate those additional measures.

Using this same example, the fitness facility manager should also consider whether the measures of customer satisfaction are reliable by testing whether they are consistent over time and across different groups when all other conditions remain constant. If customers were asked to fill out a customer satisfaction survey twice and the results of the two surveys were similar, then the measures are assumed to be dependable over time.

Although quantitative and qualitative researchers often use different terminology and techniques to assess validity and reliability, both groups are interested in producing results that are credible, dependable, and believable (Marshall & Rossman, 1999). Some of the strategies that they use to achieve these goals are carefully defining abstract concepts, examining results over time and across subgroups, and using multiple sources of data.

Besides understanding key concepts, sport managers must also understand what a systematic approach to research entails. The next section offers further information on the various components of the research process.

THE RESEARCH PROCESS

A number of steps should be followed when conducting research. As researchers make decisions at each step, they must usually make adjustments in the other steps. Therefore, we cannot view the research process in a linear fashion because the steps are highly interconnected. As illustrated in figure 20.1, considering each step helps clarify the purpose of the study as well as the other steps that make up the process. An example of each step is provided in "Scenario: An Example to Illustrate the Research Process" on page 457.

Clarifying the Purpose of the Study

Writing a clear purpose statement that is not too broad or vague is the first step of the research process. Sport managers often have specific topics or issues in mind, but they must focus the purpose of the study so that they can make decisions about the other steps in the research process. If the purpose of the study is vague or too broad, researchers will have considerable difficulty determining what research methods are most appropriate. Talking with other members of the organization to clarify the intent of the study, identifying specific information gaps, and determining how the information will be used will help clarify the purpose.

Usually, a study has an overall purpose followed by specific **research questions** to be addressed or **hypotheses** to be tested. Formulating research questions helps guide the process. Questions can arise from a number of sources including theories, observations, experiences, or simple curiosity (Palys, 1997). Note that not all questions are researchable. For example, asking whether affirmative action hiring policies are fair is a philosophical question rather than an empirical question. We can turn this question into a researchable one by asking, Do current male and female athletics administrators support affirmative action hiring policies? The next step for researchers who are operating from a theory and want to measure relationships between variables would be to write a hypothesis. For example, feminist theory might suggest the hypothesis that female athletics administrators would be more likely than male athletics administrators to support affirmative action hiring policies because research has shown females remain underrepresented in

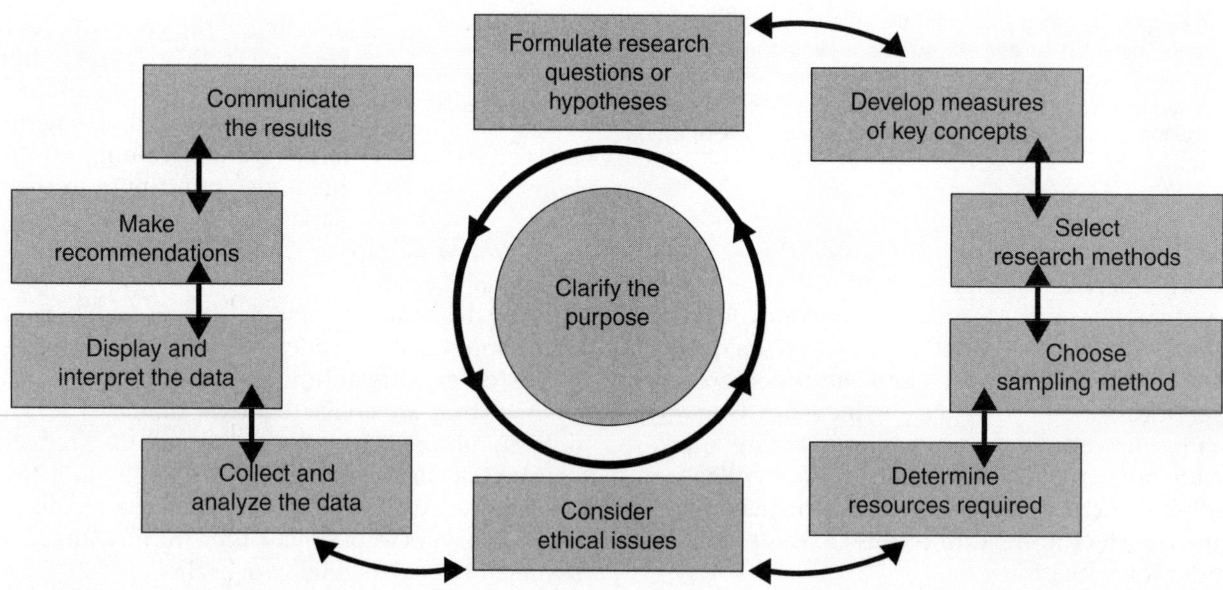

Figure 20.1 The research process.

most senior sport management positions. Note that an unsupported hypothesis can be as informative as a supported hypothesis because the unsupported premise can suggest new theories for future study. That is, if the previously stated hypothesis was not supported and males were found to be more supportive of affirmative action policies than females were, then alternative explanations for this finding would generate additional research ideas. Not all research studies include hypotheses, but their absence is not necessarily a weakness in the study design. The aim of some research is to understand phenomena from the points of view of the people involved rather than predict behavior based on theories. Measuring variables is not the goal of all research. A researcher might want to investigate sport administrators' experiences with affirmative action policies over their careers, so she or he may ask a number of related research questions to guide the study without stating hypotheses.

research questions—Specific questions that researchers ask to address the purpose of the study and guide other decisions to be made about the research process.

hypothesis—A statement about the expected relationships between two or more variables.

Developing Measures of Key Concepts

All key concepts contained in the purpose, research questions, and hypotheses must be clearly defined. Up-to-date management textbooks, journal articles, or research reports can provide definitions. After clearly defining key concepts, researchers can rely on existing research instruments (e.g., survey scales or interview guides) or develop their own questions to measure the concepts.

Selecting Research Methods

Having determined and clearly defined the purpose, research questions, or hypotheses of the study, researchers must then decide what research methods to use. As discussed in more detail later, questionnaires, secondary data analyses, document analyses, interviews, focus groups, and observations are some commonly used research methods in the sport management field.

Choosing a Sampling Method

Sampling is a strategy that researchers use when including all members of the study population is impossible or impractical. For example, to predict voting patterns in a national political election, pollsters would be unable to poll all citizens because the time and cost of doing so would be prohibitive. By careful sampling, researchers can often predict with a high degree of accuracy what the outcome of the vote would be if it were held at a particular time. But because predicting results for a population with 100% accuracy is impossible when sampling, researchers must report the degree of accuracy and margins of error that can be expected.

Researchers approach sampling differently, depending on whether they are collecting quantitative or qualitative data. When the aim is to collect quantitative data, the overall goal of sampling is usually to generalize the findings from a smaller sample to a larger population. In this instance, **probability sampling** methods are employed. Randomness, the key principle underlying probability sampling methods, ensures that each person in the study population has an equal chance of being selected. For example, the manager of a ski resort might be interested in polling snowboarders to determine what new jumps to add to the ski hill. He or she could then put all the names on the membership list in a hat and draw them at random before soliciting opinions. Using this method, each snowboarder who is a current member (i.e., the population) has an equal chance of being selected as part of the sample to participate in the study.

Researchers who collect qualitative data are more interested in obtaining in-depth understanding of topics or issues and are usually not interested in generalizing their findings from a sample to a population. Therefore, they usually use **nonprobability sampling** techniques to study people, events, or situations. The goal is to select study participants who represent the study population, even though it might not be possible to select them randomly. Using the previous example, if membership lists were not available, the ski resort manager could approach snowboarders on the hill on a particular day and ask them to name other snowboarders who frequently use the hill. Then, he or she could ask that second set of snowboarders the same question. This type of nonprobability sampling, known as snowball sampling, is an appropriate choice if the researcher is interested in learning about the social networks of people or organizations. A weakness of this approach is that the views of those selected might not adequately represent the views of the larger study population.

probability sampling—A way of randomly selecting study participants from a larger population; frequently used in quantitative research when the goal is to generalize from a sample to a population.

nonprobability sampling—A way of nonrandomly selecting study participants from a larger population; frequently used in qualitative research when the goal is to understand participants' experiences or perspectives rather than to generalize from a sample to a population.

Determining the Resources Required

Undertaking research requires time, expertise, finances, equipment, and supplies. After calculating the resources required, researchers may have to adjust the purpose, sampling technique, or other dimensions of the study. For example, it might be necessary to select a smaller sample when conducting survey research if, after developing the budget, the mailing costs are found to be prohibitive. Researchers must estimate the resources required before starting a research project to ensure that it can be properly carried out.

Considering Ethical Issues

Researchers must carefully consider several ethical issues. Sport management faculty and students are required to obtain ethical approval from their colleges or universities before conducting research to ensure that they do not violate the rights of study participants. Although sport managers normally do not require this type of formal approval, taking ethics into account will ensure a professional approach to research and help maintain good public relations.

Before deciding whether to participate, study participants have the right to know what the purpose of the study is, who is sponsoring the research, and how the research will be used. Participation in research should be voluntary, and study participants should have the right to decide whether to allow their names or their organizations to be identified in the research. Because sport management research focuses on the practices and policies of sport organizations, investigators should anticipate the possible repercussions of the research. For example, it would be unethical for a sport management researcher to ask employees about problems in their organization and then let their bosses know "who said what." This example shows that research may not benefit everyone, because the employees could face negative consequences, or even be fired, for speaking honestly with a researcher about problems in their organization.

Collecting and Analyzing Quantitative Data

Questionnaires, secondary data analyses, and content analyses are common techniques used in the sport management field to collect quantitative data.

Questionnaires

Questionnaires can be mailed, posted on the Internet, conducted over the telephone or through e-mail, or used when intercepting people at different types of sporting events. Researchers use questionnaires when they are interested in hearing from a sample of people about a particular topic. Those who agree to participate are asked a series of questions, and their responses are usually recorded in a numerical format. For example, in a questionnaire designed to gauge purchasing patterns, researchers might intercept spectators and ask them whether they bought merchandise available at a sporting event. If a respondent says yes, the response could be assigned a value of 1, and if the respondent says no, the response could be given a value of 2. The researcher can then enter the values reported from all respondents into a spreadsheet to determine the percentage of spectators who bought merchandise at the event.

Other common ways of converting responses on questionnaires into quantitative data include asking people to rank-order their preferences or choose a response on a five-point scale that best represents their opinion. Open-ended questions can be used on questionnaires, but responses are often difficult to code numerically. When researchers want to ask a number of open-ended questions, interviews or focus groups are a more appropriate choice of methodology (Neuman, 2003). Depending on the type of numerical data collected, researchers can compute a number of statistics on spreadsheets or with computer software programs to reveal patterns in the data that they can then display in tables, graphs, or charts.

Secondary Data Analysis

Obtaining statistics that were collected previously for another reason, perhaps by a government agency or a research firm, and reanalyzing them to address a research question of interest is called secondary data analysis. To illustrate, entrepreneurs interested in starting new sport-related

Learning Activity

As a class project, construct a one-page questionnaire designed to capture the career aspirations of sport management students. Develop five or six questions that measure different aspects of career aspirations, an abstract concept. Ensure that responses provided for each question can be assigned a numerical value. Have each student fill out the survey. Enter the responses into a computer spreadsheet. Calculate the percentage of students who responded to the different values for each question and compare the findings. Discuss and record possible explanations for the similarities and differences observed.

businesses commonly examine demographic data available through government sources on populations living in a specific geographic area as a way of determining whether demand for their business will be sufficient. Secondary data analysis refers to the fact that the researcher used data previously collected for another purpose, whereas primary data analysis means that the researcher collected the data firsthand.

Content Analysis

Another common way of collecting numerical data is by conducting a content analysis. This method involves examining the content of written materials (e.g., budget statements or newspaper articles) and recording certain information or features about them. For example, a newly hired sport manager who is preparing for an upcoming budget meeting might want to conduct a content analysis of previous financial statements to determine what the major expenditures and revenues have been in the past. Table 20.1 summarizes some of the major advantages and disadvantages of the common methods used to collect quantitative data.

Collecting and Analyzing Qualitative Data

Interviews, focus groups, observations, and content analyses are common techniques for collecting qualitative data to shed light on the meanings that people associate with various sport-related activities. Usually the goal of collecting qualitative data is to obtain a better understanding of people's experiences or how they are thinking or feeling about an issue or situation. For example, a professor can review a sport management student's resume and academic transcripts (i.e., perform a content analysis) to locate a suitable field placement for that student, but an interview with the student will reveal more in-depth information about his or her career goals and interests. Qualitative data are often displayed as direct word-for-word quotations made by respondents, and those quotations can also be used as testimonials to promote key attributes or benefits of products, services, or programs. The professor who is coordinating field placements could conduct follow-up interviews with students upon completion of their placements to determine whether the program was successful. With the students' permission, the professor could use their direct comments in promotional material to advertise the benefits of the program to future applicants (e.g., "This internship was a terrific

Table 20.1

Common Methods of Collecting Quantitative Data

Method	Main advantage	Main disadvantage
Mailed surveys	Can be used on larger samples	Low response rate
Internet or e-mail surveys	Quick response is possible	Only those with computers can participate
Telephone surveys	Immediate response	Respondents might feel their privacy is invaded
Intercept surveys	Immediate response	Ensuring sample is representative
Secondary data analysis	Avoid costs of primary research	Not all data required might be available
Content analysis	Budgets, marketing material, planning documents, and media broadcasts are usually available	Not all data required might be available in these documents

learning experience that helped me clarify my career goals"). Qualitative data can also be displayed in the form of photographs or video clips. Computer software programs are available to help manage and analyze large qualitative data sets.

Interviews

Face-to-face or telephone interviews are commonly used in sport management research because they often have a higher response rate than mail-in surveys do. Researchers are able to clarify confusion resulting from the questions asked, and interviews usually produce more in-depth responses (Palys, 1997). Although making direct contact with people through interviews humanizes the research process, the amount of time required to conduct one-on-one interviews is a major disadvantage of this data collection method. Careful consideration must be given to the interview questions asked, and it is advisable to seek permission from respondents to tape-record interviews so that an accurate recording of responses can be obtained. Using a mixed methods approach, researchers can combine interviews with questionnaires to obtain information about how to word questionnaires properly. Researchers can also conduct interviews after administering questionnaires to uncover possible explanations for the results.

Focus Groups

Focus groups are another method used to solicit qualitative data. A major advantage of this technique is that researchers can speak with 6 to 8 people at the same time (Cassell & Symon, 2004). Focus groups are often used in marketing research when researchers want to test new products or promotional strategies on a specific target group, but they can be used in a variety of contexts. As with interviews, researchers must take care when developing questions. Tape-recording sessions will help ensure accurate recording of the data. Researchers must be trained to manage group dynamics when conducting focus groups. For example, to obtain a full range of views on the topic, the researcher must not allow some participants to dominate the discussion while others remain quiet.

Observations

Although researchers can often quantify observations of different types of behavior or sport settings, they can also record them qualitatively in written field notes. To illustrate, the problem of parental violence at children's sporting events has been receiving considerable media attention. If you were the manager of a sport program or facility and had received a growing number of complaints about parental behavior, you could conduct an observational study to determine whether the complaints were justified. You might decide to attend games randomly and develop an observation checklist to record the numbers and types of inappropriate parental behavior. You could also write your thoughts about what is causing or escalating the problem and make notes about possible strategies for reducing it. By developing a systematic way of collecting data, you would likely arrive at a better solution than you would have otherwise. Conducting interviews and focus groups with parents, players, coaches, and referees and finding out how other sport managers have attempted to handle this problem would produce additional valuable information.

Learning Activity

After developing the questionnaire to examine the career aspirations of sport management students in the previous learning activity, work with your classmates to develop five or six interview questions that would reveal additional information on this topic. Working in pairs, conduct interviews with your classmates and use tape recorders to record the responses. Avoid questions with yes or no answers, and use follow-up questions to probe for in-depth responses. Transcribe the taped responses into a word processing file and compare the responses. How did the interview data augment the survey data collected previously? Compare the advantages and disadvantages of using questionnaires and interviews to examine student career aspirations.

Content Analysis

A content analysis of documents, media broadcasts, and other types of communications can be used to collect both quantitative and qualitative data in a mixed methods approach. To illustrate, a sport management student might be interested in determining whether female and male athletes receive equal television coverage and treatment during the Olympic Games. A content analysis that would generate quantitative data related to this question would entail recording on-air coverage over a designated period and totaling the time devoted to the coverage of each gender. In terms of qualitative data, an analysis of the content of the comments made by Olympic sportscasters could determine whether common stereotypes about male and female athletic performances are still being perpetuated. An emphasis on the physical appearance rather than the athletic accomplishments of female athletes in comparison to male athletes would indicate differential treatment by the media based on the gender of the athlete.

SCENARIO: An Example to Illustrate the Research Process

Laurence Chalip, a professor from the University of Texas at Austin, and Anna Leyns, a marketing executive for PRISM, a sport marketing firm in the United Kingdom, published an article titled "Local Business Leveraging of a Sport Event: Managing an Event for Economic Benefit" in the *Journal of Sport Management* in 2002. The article contained information on four qualitative studies that they conducted to examine the tactics used by local businesses to leverage visitor spending during a major sporting event. The researchers argued that although a growing body of literature touts the economic benefits of hosting sport events, there is little evidence about whether local business managers know how to leverage sales during an event.

- ***Purpose of the study***. The purpose of the study was to determine whether small local businesses on the Gold Coast of Australia attempted to leverage sales when the city hosted the Honda Indy car race. A clear and specific focus is apparent in the purpose statement because leveraging tactics were specified as the abstract managerial concept under investigation, small local businesses in one geographic area were sampled, and a specific sporting event served as the case study.
- ***Measures of key concepts***. The researchers defined leveraging tactics as "the means by which local businesses cultivate spending by event visitors, particularly impulse spending" (Chalip, 2001). Leveraging tactics were measured by asking managers of small local businesses whether their businesses attempted to capitalize on the Indy. If managers identified leveraging tactics, the researchers asked whether those tactics had been effective. If they had not used leveraging tactics, the researchers asked why they had not implemented promotional activities during the Indy.
- ***Research methods***. Given the purpose of the study, interviewing managers of small local businesses was an appropriate choice of methodology. The interviews allowed the researchers to obtain an in-depth understanding of managers' reasons for choosing whether to leverage the event and provided insights into their business practices.
- ***Sampling method***. Because the goal of this study was to understand managerial practices of a select group rather than to generalize the findings to a larger population, the researchers used a nonprobability sampling technique known as quota sampling. Quota sampling helped to ensure that the sample represented the diverse characteristics of local businesses on the Gold Coast. In this case, the researchers wanted to ensure representation from different types of small businesses based on their proximity to the event site. As a result, 22 managers were interviewed, including 8 restaurant managers, 7 retail store managers, and 7 hoteliers. For each industry, the researchers chose businesses located inside the event venue, adjacent to the event venue, and 1 to 3 kilometers (.6 to 1.8 miles) away from the event venue.
- ***Resources required***. The budget required to conduct the study was minimal because the researchers, who had considerable research experience and expertise, conducted the interviews and inputted and analyzed the data themselves. The equipment and supplies required included tape recorders, audiotapes, and a computer. The researchers did invest considerable time traveling to the businesses for the interviews, conducting the 22 interviews, transcribing them, participating in a task force, and writing the journal article.
- ***Ethical issues***. Anonymity was an ethical issue that the researchers had to consider because most managers do not want details about their business operations made public. Obtaining financial statements before and after the event would have allowed the researchers to determine whether sales increased during the event, but understandably, the managers were reluctant to release that information. The researchers assured the managers that the reporting of the results would not divulge their names, the names of their businesses, or business financial information.
- ***Collecting and analyzing the data***. The researchers contacted the managers in person by visiting the businesses to arrange interview times. Interviews were tape-recorded and transcribed word for word into a word processing file. The researchers used Strauss's (1987) open coding technique to generate themes (e.g., efforts to promote businesses during the Indy) and subthemes (e.g., creating displays that captured the atmosphere of the Indy) identified in the interview data.
- ***Displaying and interpreting the data***. Because they collected qualitative data, the researchers displayed the results in the form of direct quotations. For example, the following response was typical of the rationale used by managers for not using leveraging

(continued)

SCENARIO: *(continued)*

tactics during the event: "It sells itself, basically. We get a lot of repeat business. That's about how it works" (p. 139). The researchers found that only 8 of the 22 businesses employed tactics to leverage the Indy. The investigators provided a number of possible explanations for this finding. Businesses close to the event believed that promotions were unnecessary because they assumed that sales would automatically increase during the event, whereas businesses located away from the event believed that they were too far away to be attractive to Indy visitors.

- ***Making recommendations.*** Chalip and Leyns (2002) used an innovative approach to provide managers with recommendations about how to encourage visitor spending at future events. They formed a task force of nine experts (representing tourism, event management, marketing, hotel management, and small business) to consider the challenges of and prospects for leveraging the Indy. One of the task force's recommendations was that neighborhood businesses should band together to implement a coordinated strategy rather than initiate independent efforts.
- ***Communicating the results***. Chalip and Leyns (2002) shared their findings with a larger Gold Coast Visioning Project that involved a partnership with the city and local businesses to reposition the Gold Coast within the tourism industry. In addition, because leveraging tactics are of interest to sport management researchers, educators, and students, the researchers communicated their findings in the *Journal of Sport Management*.

Table 20.2 summarizes some of the main advantages and disadvantages of the methods that sport management researchers commonly use to collect qualitative data.

Displaying and Interpreting the Data

As mentioned previously, quantitative data are usually displayed in graphs, tables, and charts, while qualitative data are usually displayed as direct quotations, photos, or other types of visuals. When interpreting the data, researchers should provide alternative explanations for the results. When alternative explanations contradict one another, further research will be required to determine which competing explanation has more merit.

- ***Making recommendations***. When making practical recommendations, researchers must be sure that the results support their suggestions. Sport managers should be suspicious of recommendations that do not deal directly with the purpose of the study or that generalize the findings improperly. For example, the researchers in "Scenario: An Example to Illustrate the Research Process" took care not to generalize their findings beyond the 22 businesses examined because they used a nonprobability sampling technique. The recommendations they made pertained directly to the businesses studied and provided managers with important information about how to improve their marketing practices.
- ***Communicating the results***. The final step in the research process is determining the best way to communicate the results. A variety of formats can be used such as final reports, journal articles, and oral presentations. Researchers should tailor their communication strategies to the intended audience. For example, sport managers might be more interested in the findings and recommendations,

Table 20.2

Common Methods of Collecting Qualitative Data

Method	Main advantage	Main disadvantage
Interviews	In-depth responses are possible	Time intensive
Focus groups	Less time intensive than interviews	Managing group dynamics
Observations	Can confirm or refute other types of data	Actions are often open to multiple interpretations
Content analysis	Data can be collected without talking to people directly	Data obtained are often open to multiple interpretations

Learning Activity

Locate a recent issue of a sport management journal and determine how many articles contained quantitative data, qualitative data, or a mixed methods approach using both types of data. Choose one article and determine whether questionnaires, secondary data analysis, content analysis, interviews, focus groups, observations, or other techniques were used to collect the data.

whereas academics might be more interested in hearing about the research methods employed.

JUDGING THE QUALITY OF RESEARCH

Sport managers who lack adequate training face considerable challenges when interpreting research. Because of the information explosion that has accompanied the emergence of a knowledge-based economy, sport managers are being bombarded with research from a variety of sources including the media, the Internet, trade journals, academic journals, consulting and governmental reports, workshops and conference presentations, as well as research done for their own organizations. Because research varies considerably in quality, sport mangers must be able to make accurate evaluations of the research methods used and the data analysis techniques employed to judge whether the conclusions drawn and the recommendations made are reliable and credible.

- ***Considering the source***. The source of the research is one element to consider. One might assume that findings reported in an academic journal would be of high quality, but that may not be so. Although most academic journals use a rigorous review process to ensure the high quality of published material, the research design may be problematic. Many people are suspicious of research reported over the Internet, with good reason. Although some Web sites contain research information that has been carefully monitored or reviewed, many do not. Readers often have difficulty determining whether information on the Internet is credible because the source may not report adequate details regarding the research design or the qualifications of the researcher.
- ***Questions to ask to judge research quality***. Many questions must be asked when judging the quality of research, including the following:

1. Are the purpose, research questions, or hypotheses of the research clearly stated?
2. Is a strong rationale for conducting the study provided?
3. Who conducted the research, and what are their credentials?
4. Who sponsored the research, and how will they benefit from it?
5. What is the source of the research, and is a rigorous review process in place for ensuring quality?
6. Are the key concepts or variables under investigation clearly defined?
7. If applicable, was relevant literature or background information drawn upon?
8. Did the researcher consider ethical issues when conducting the research?
9. Were the methods used to collect the data appropriate?
10. What sampling techniques were used, and were they appropriate?
11. Are the measures or indicators of key concepts valid and reliable?
12. How were the data recorded and analyzed?
13. What are the limitations of the study design?
14. Were explanations for the findings provided, and are they justified?
15. Are conclusions and recommendations provided, and are they supported by the findings?

THE FUTURE OF SPORT MANAGEMENT RESEARCH

The amount of research conducted in sport management will increase to meet the needs of decision makers and build the body of knowledge in the field. As Amis and Silk (2005) pointed out in a special issue of the *Journal of Sport Management* on innovative approaches to the study of sport management, we will continue to see new theoretical and methodological approaches to round out how we think about, practice, and teach sport management. Amis and Silk argue that, similar to those who contribute to the business literature (Hinings & Greenwood, 2002), sport management researchers have been preoccupied with research on the effectiveness of organizations and have not paid enough attention to who benefits from these types of studies. Do managers benefit the most by finding more efficient ways of operating? Do researchers benefit the most by publishing their work or being paid for consulting on projects? What about employees, volunteers, athletes, nonparticipants, and citizens at large? Do they also benefit from the research questions being posed? Sport management students, managers, and researchers should continue to grapple with questions like these.

A related issue is that sport management researchers do not effectively communicate much of their research to managers. In part, this problem occurs because researchers associated with academic institutions must publish in academic journals rather than in other sources. In part, some sport managers lack the skills or interest to seek out and interpret sport management research. As noted in chapter 19, grappling with the gap between research and practice is another issue that will be at the forefront in the future.

Advances in technology will continue to have an effect on how research is done. Although computers and other forms of communication will make research more convenient for both the researcher and the study participants, ethical issues remain important. For example, a significant portion of the world's population does not have access to computers for financial and other reasons, and serious questions remain about how they can contribute in meaningful ways to the knowledge production process.

Given the importance of research as outlined in this chapter, research should eventually be included as a content area in National Association for Sport and Physical Education–North American Society for Sport Management curriculum guidelines for undergraduate sport management degree programs. Sport management students should certainly take courses in research methods to prepare themselves for a future based in the knowledge economy.

SUMMARY

Sport management research is available from a variety of sources, and managers are increasingly relying on it to make informed decisions. To assess what types of sport management research are reliable and credible, sport managers need a sound foundation in research. Understanding key concepts such as science and pseudoscience, basic and applied research, qualitative and quantitative data, research design, reliability and validity, and the research process can help sport managers judge the quality of research so that they can make sound decisions.

Engaging in the research process can be stimulating and rewarding. Clarifying the purpose of the study and developing research questions or hypotheses are important first steps. Developing measures that adequately represent the abstract concepts of interest; selecting the research methods and sample; ensuring that research is conducted in an ethical way; and collecting, analyzing, and interpreting the results are other interrelated steps in the research process. The researcher who effectively communicates results and makes well-founded recommendations can help sport managers improve their practices and might advance the body of knowledge in the sport management field.

Besides incorporating research into their course work, sport management students can attend conferences, join associations that promote sport management research, such as the North American Society for Sport Management, and refer to publications within the sport management and business fields.

Review Questions

1. Discuss five key ways that pseudoscience differs from science and then explain why a scientific approach can provide sport managers with more trustworthy information upon which to base decisions.
2. Differentiate between basic and applied research and provide an example of each.
3. Differentiate between quantitative and qualitative data and describe one common data collection technique for each. In your answer, provide one main advantage and one main disadvantage of each data collection technique discussed.
4. What is a research design and what are the key features of the most common research designs used in sport management research?
5. After the purpose of a study has been determined, what are the other nine steps in the research process? Choose one of these steps and discuss how the purpose of the study might be refined after considering this step.
6. Why is it important to consider ethical issues when conducting sport management research?
7. What questions should be asked to judge the quality of sport management research?
8. Do you agree that the need for expertise in sport management research will continue to grow in the future? Justify your argument.

References

Chapter 1—Managing Sport in the 21st Century

Acosta, R.V., & Carpenter, L.J. (2006). *Women in intercollegiate sport—A longitudinal, national study: Twenty nine year update 1977-2006.* Retrieved June, 6, 2006, from http://www.aahperd.org/nagws/pdf_files/longitudinal29.pdf.

Ammon, R., Jr. (2000). The globalization of sport: Preparing sport managers for the 21st century. *International Journal of Sport Management, 1*, 151-153.

Bennett, G., Henson, R.K., & Zhang, J. (2003). Generation Y's perceptions of the action sports industry segment. *Journal of Sport Management, 17*, 95-115.

Board of Certification for the Athletic Trainer (2004). *Education and training.* Retrieved January 28, 2006, from www.bocatc.org/athtrainer/PREP.

Broughton, D., Lee, J., & Nethery, R. (1999, December 20-26). The answer: $213 billion. *Street & Smith's SportsBusiness Journal*, pp. 23, 26.

Chernushenko, D. (with van der Kamp, A., & Stubbs, D.) (2001). *Sustainable sport management*, United Nations Environment Programme. Ottawa, Ontario: Green & Gold.

Clay, B. (1995, February). 8 great careers in the sports industry. *Black Enterprise, 25*(7), 158-160, 162, 164, 166.

Coakley, J.J. (2004). *Sport in society: Issues and controversies* (8th ed.). Boston: McGraw-Hill.

Comfort, G. (2005a). *Directory of graduate programs in sport management.* Morgantown, WV: Fitness Information Technology.

Comfort, G. (2005b). *Directory of undergraduate programs in sport management.* Morgantown, WV: Fitness Information Technology.

Comte, E., & Stogel, C. (1990, January 1). Sports: A $63.1 billion industry. *The Sporting News*, pp. 60-61.

Council of Europe. (2001). *The European Sports Charter (Revised).* Retrieved January 28, 2006, from www.sportdevelopment.org.uk/html/eucharter.html

Cuneen, J., & Schneider, R. (Eds.). (2001a). Sport in the third millennium [Special issue]. *Journal of Sport Management, 15*(4).

Cuneen, J., & Schneider, R. (2001b). Sport in the third millennium: A retrospective and perspective on 1990s and 2000-era sport. *Journal of Sport Management, 15*, 267-274.

Cuneen, J., & Sidwell, M.J. (1998, Winter). Evaluating and selecting sport management undergraduate programs. *The Journal of College Admission*, 6-13.

Cuskelly, G., & Auld, C.J. (1991). Perceived importance of selected job responsibilities of sport and recreation managers: An Australian perspective. *Journal of Sport Management, 5*, 34-46.

Danylchuk, K.E., & Boucher, R. (2003). The future of sport management as an academic discipline. *International Journal of Sport Management, 4*, 281-300.

DeSensi, J.T. (1994). Multiculturalism as an issue in sport management. *Journal of Sport Management, 8*, 63-74.

Ford, G.R. (1979). *A time to heal: The autobiography of Gerald R. Ford.* New York: Harper & Row.

Frank, R. (1984). Olympic myths and realities. *Arete: The Journal of Sport Literature, 1*(2), 155-161.

Gunston, R. (2005, January-February). Play ball! How sports will change in the 21st century. *The Futurist, 39*, 31-36.

Horch, H., & Schütte, N. (2003). Competencies of sport managers in German sport clubs and sport federations. *Managing Leisure, 8*, 70-84.

Josephson Institute of Ethics. (2002). *Making ethical decisions.* Retrieved January 28, 2006, from www.josephsoninstitute.org/MED/MED-intro+toc.htm.

Kidwell, R.E. (2004). "Small" lies, big trouble: The unfortunate consequences of résumé padding, from Janet Cooke to George O'Leary. *Journal of Business Ethics, 51*, 175-184.

Krumrie, M. (2006). *Sports management.* Retrieved February 3, 2006, from http://management.monster.com/articles/sports_management.

Laczniak, G.R. (1985). Frameworks for analyzing marketing ethics. In G.R. Laczniak and P.E. Murphy (Eds.), *Marketing ethics: Guidelines for managers* (pp. 9-26). Lexington, MA: Heath. (Reprinted from *Journal of Macromarketing*, Spring 1983, pp. 7-18.)

Lambrecht, K.W. (1991). A study of curricular preparation needs for sport club managers. *Journal of Sport Management, 5*, 47-57.

Lapchick, R. (2004-2006). *Institute reports and studies.* Retrieved January 27, 2006, from Central Florida University, Institute for Diversity and Ethics in Sport Web site:www.bus.ucf.edu/sport/cgi-bin/site/sitew.cgi?page=/ides/index.htx.

Lawler, E.E., III, & Ledford, G.E., Jr. (1997). New approaches to organizing: Competencies, capabilities and the decline of the bureaucratic model. In C.L. Cooper & S.E. Jackson (Eds.), *Creating tomorrow's organization: A handbook for future research in organizational behavior* (pp. 231-249). New York: Wiley.

Li, M., Hofacre, S., & Mahony, D. (2001). *Economics of sport.* Morgantown, WV: Fitness Information Technology.

Li, M., Kanters, M., & Ammon, R., Jr. (2002). The status of the internationalization of the sport management curriculum in the United States. *International Journal of Sport Management, 3*, 282-289.

Madella, A. (2003). Methods for analysing sports employment in Europe. *Managing Leisure, 8*, 56-69.

Mahony, D.F., & Howard, D.R. (2001). Sport business in the next decade: A general overview of expected trends. *Journal of Sport Management, 15*, 275-296.

Malloy, D.C., & Zakus, D.H. (1995). Ethical decision making in sport administration: A theoretical inquiry into substance and form. *Journal of Sport Management, 9*, 36-58.

Mason, J.G., Higgins, C.R., & Wilkinson, O.J. (1981). Sports administration education 15 years later. *Athletic Purchasing and Facilities, 5*(1), 44-45.

Masteralexis, L.P., & McDonald, M.A. (1997). Enhancing sport management education with international dimensions including language and cultural learning. *Journal of Sport Management, 11*, 97-110.

Mawson, L.M. (2002). The extreme sport challenge for sport managers. *International Journal of Sport Management, 3*, 249-261.

McGee, J.V., & Prusak, L. (1993). *Managing information strategically.* New York: Wiley.

Meek, A. (1997). An estimate of the size and supported economic activity of the sports industry in the United States. *Sport Marketing Quarterly, 6*(4), 15-21.

Moss, C.L., & Parks, J.B. (1991). Athletic training in an undergraduate sport management curriculum. *Athletic Training, 26*, 178, 180-183.

Mullin, B.J. (1980). Sport management: The nature and utility of the concept. *Arena Review, 4*(3), 1-11.

North American Society for Sport Management (1992). *The Code of Ethics. NASSM Constitution.* Retrieved January 28, 2006, from www.nassm.com/index.html.

Parks, J.B., Chopra, P.S., Quain, R.J., and Alguindigue, I.E.. (1988). "ExSport: I: An expert system for sport management career counseling." *Journal of Research on Computing in Education, 21,* 196-209.

Parks, J.B., & Olafson, G.A. (1987). Sport management and a new journal. *Journal of Sport Management, 1*, 1-3.

Parks, J.B., & Parra, L.F. (1994). Job satisfaction of sport management alumnae/i. *Journal of Sport Management, 8*, 49-56.

Parks, J.B., & Roberton, M.A. (2000). Development and validation of an instrument to measure attitudes toward sexist/nonsexist language. *Sex Roles: A Journal of Research, 42*, 415-438.

Parks, J.B., & Roberton, M.A. (2002). The gender gap in student attitudes toward sexist/nonsexist language: Implications for sport management education. *Journal of Sport Management, 16*, 190-208.

Parks, J.B., Russell, R.L., Wood, P.H., Roberton, M.A., & Shewokis, P.A. (1995). The paradox of the contented working woman in intercollegiate athletics administration. *Research Quarterly for Exercise and Sport, 66*, 73-79.

Pitts, B.G., Fielding, L.W., & Miller, L.K. (1994). Industry segmentation theory and the sport industry: Developing a sport industry segmentation model. *Sport Marketing Quarterly, 3*(1), 15-24.

Pitts, B.G., & Stotlar, D.K. (2002). *Fundamentals of sport marketing* (2nd ed.). Morgantown, WV: Fitness Information Technology.

Quain, R.J., & Parks, J.B. (1986). Sport management survey: Employment perspectives. *Journal of Physical Education, Recreation and Dance, 57*(4), 18-21.

Robinson, M.J., Hums, M.A., Crow, R.B., & Phillips, D.R. (2001). *Profiles of sport industry professionals: The people who make the games happen.* Gaithersburg, MD: Aspen.

Robinson, M.J., Peterson, M., Tedrick, T., & Carpenter, J.R. (2003). Job satisfaction of NCAA Division III Athletic Directors: Impact of job design and time on task. *International Sports Journal, 7*(2), 46-57.

Rosner, D. (1989, January 2). The world plays catch-up. *Sports inc,* pp. 6-13.

Schoenfeld, B. (1999, November 8-14). Diversity in sports isn't happening. *Street & Smith's SportsBusiness Journal*, pp. 3, 24-25.

Smucker, M., & Kent, A. (2004). Satisfaction and referent comparisons in the sport industry. *International Journal of Sport Management, 5*, 262-290.

Sports market place directory (2005). Millerton, NY: Grey House Publishing.

Toepfer, K. (2003, December). *Sport and sustainable development.* Paper presented at the 5th World Conference on Sport and Environment, Turin, Italy. Retrieved January 28, 2006, from www.unep.org/Documents.Multilingual/Default.asp?DocumentID=364&ArticleID=4316&l=en.

United Nations (2000-2005). *Resolution 59/10 adopted by the General Assembly.* Retrieved January 27, 2006, from www.un.org/sport2005/resources/resolution.

VanderZwaag, H.J. (1998). *Policy development in sport management* (2nd ed.). Westport, CT: Praeger.

Westerbeek, H., & Smith, A. (2003). *Sport business in the global marketplace.* New York: Palgrave Macmillan.

What will happen to sports in the '90s. (1989, January 2). *Sports inc.*

Chapter 2—Developing a Professional Perspective

Baldrige, L. (1985). *Letitia Baldrige's complete guide to executive manners*. New York: Rawson Associates.

Baldrige, L. (1993). *Letitia Baldrige's new complete guide to executive manners*. New York: Simon & Schuster.

Career Dimensions, Inc. (2004). *FOCUS*. Retrieved February 14, 2006, from www.focuscareer.com/index.cfm.

Carney, C.G., & Wells, C.F. (1995). *Discover the career within you* (4th ed.). Pacific Grove, CA: Thomson Brooks/Cole.

Casella, D.A., & Brougham, C.E. (1995). Work works: Student jobs open front doors to careers. *Journal of Career Planning & Employment, 55*(4), 24-27, 54-55.

Chelladurai, P. (2005). *Managing organizations for sport and physical activity: A systems perspective* (2nd ed.). Scottsdale, AZ: Holcomb Hathaway.

Cuneen, J., & Sidwell, M.J. (1994). *Sport management field experiences*. Morgantown, WV: Fitness Information Technology.

Curtis & Associates, Inc. (1999). *Work culture*. Kearney, NE: Author.

DiMarco, C. (1997). *Career transitions: A journey of survival & growth*. Upper Saddle River, NJ: Prentice Hall.

Dixon, M.A., Cunningham, G.B., Sagas, M., Turner, B.A., & Kent, A. (2005). Challenge is key: An investigation of affective organizational commitment in undergraduate interns. *Journal of Education for Business, 80*, 172-180.

Fletcher, C.A., Kelley, D.R., & Ridinger, L.L. (2005). *Utilizing electronic portfolios in sport management*. Paper presented at the annual conference of the North American Society for Sport Management, Regina, Saskatchewan, Canada.

Gordon, D. (2002). Tracking internship outcomes through comparative quantitative assessment. *Journal of Career Planning and Employment, 62*(2), 28-32.

Herr, E.L., Cramer, S.H., & Niles, S.G. (2004). *Career guidance and counseling through the lifespan: Systematic approaches* (6th ed.). Boston: Pearson/Allyn & Bacon.

Hoff, K.S. (2000). The web of personal career reality. *Proceedings of the Academy of Human Resource Development*, Research Triangle, North Carolina.

Institute of Sport Management. (2005). *Code of ethics & professional conduct*. Retrieved February 5, 2006, from www.ismhome.com/visitor/v_ethics.htm.

Kadlecek, J., and Thoma, J.E. (1999, June). *Sport management student portfolios: What practitioners want included*. Paper presented at the annual conference of the North American Society for Sport Management, Vancouver, British Columbia, Canada.

Lilienthal, S. (2004, June). *Professional etiquette of sport management students: Investigating employer perceptions*. Paper presented at the annual conference of the North American Society for Sport Management, Atlanta, GA.

Mitchell, M. (with Corr, J.) (1998). *The first five minutes: How to make a great first impression in any business situation*. New York: Wiley.

Moore, M.E., & Parkhouse, B.L. (1996, May). *An examination of diversity in sport management professional preparation programs for women, minorities, and individuals with disabilities*. Paper presented at the conference of the North American Society for Sport Management, Fredericton, New Brunswick, Canada.

Nardo, J. (1999). Helping new grads become successful new hires. *Journal of Career Planning and Employment, 59*(3), 45-56.

NASPE. (2006). *Sport Management Program Review Council approved programs*. Retrieved February 6, 2006, from www.aahperd.org/naspe/pdf_files/approvedPrograms06.pdf.

NASPE–NASSM (2000). *Sport management program standards and review protocol*. Retrieved February 5, 2006, from www.aahperd.org/naspe/template.cfm?template=ns_smps.html.

National Association of Colleges and Employers. (2005). *Job outlook 2005*. Retrieved June 10, 2006, from www.naceweb.org/products/jo2005report.htm.

National Commission for Cooperative Education. (2005). *Benefits of cooperative education*. Retrieved February 7, 2006, from www.co-op.edu/aboutcoop.htm.

Parkhouse, B.L. (1987). Sport management curricula. Current status and design implications for future development. *Journal of Sport Management, 1*, 93-115.

Parks, J.B., & Bartley, M.E. (1996). Sport management scholarship: A professoriate in transition? *Journal of Sport Management, 10*, 119-130.

Parks, J.B. (executive producer), Harper, M.C. (writer), & Lopez, P.G. (director). (1994). *One person's struggle with gender-biased language: Part 1* [Videotape]. (Available from WBGU-TV, Bowling Green State University, Bowling Green, OH 43403.)

Parks, J.B., & Sun, J. (2001). *ExSport II: An artificial intelligence sport management career guidance system*. Retrieved February 7, 2006, from http://personal.bgsu.edu/~jparks/ExSport.

Patterson, V., & Allen, C. (1996). Occupational outlook overview: Where will the jobs be in 2005? *Journal of Career Planning and Employment, 56*(3), 32-35, 61-64.

Raths, L.E., Harmin, M., & Simon, S. (1978). *Values and teaching: Working with values in the classroom* (2nd ed.). Columbus, OH: Merrill.

Reardon, R., Lenz, J., & Folsom, B. (1998). Employer ratings of student participation in non-classroom activities: Findings from a campus survey. *Journal of Career Planning and Employment, 58*(3), 36-39.

Sports internship book 2005. (2004). Winston-Salem, NC: Career Education Institutes.

Sukiennik, D., Bendat, W., and Raufman, L. (1995). *The career fitness program: Exercising your options* (4th ed.). Scottsdale, AZ: Gorsuch Scarisbrick.

Sutton, W.A. (1989). The role of internships in sport management curricula: A model for development. *Journal of Physical Education, Recreation and Dance, 60*(7), 20-24.

Williams, J. (2003). Sport management internship administration: Challenges and chances for collaboration. *NACE Journal, 63*(2), 28-32.

Chapter 3—Thinking Critically About Sport Management

Boucher, R.L. (1998). Toward achieving a focal point for sport management: A binocular perspective. *Journal of Sport Management, 12*, 76-85.

Browne, M.N., & Keeley, S.M. (2007). *Asking the right questions: A guide to critical thinking* (8th ed.). Upper Saddle River, NJ: Prentice Hall.

Coakley, J.J. (2004). *Sports in society. Issues and controversies* (8th ed.). Boston: McGraw Hill.

Edwards, A. (1999). Reflective practice in sport management. *Sport Management Review, 2*, 67-81.

Eitzen, D.S. (Ed.) (2005). *Sport in contemporary society: An anthology* (7th ed.). Boulder, CO: Paradigm.

Ennis, R.H. (1995). *Critical thinking.* Upper Saddle River, NJ: Prentice Hall.

Ennis, R.H. (2000). *Super-streamlined conception of critical thinking.* Retrieved January 23, 2002, from www.criticalthinking.net/SSConcCTApr3.html.

Facione, P.A., Facione, N.C., Sanchez, C. (1995). The disposition toward critical thinking. *The Journal of General Education, 44*(1), 1-25.

Frisby, W. (2005). The good, the bad, and the ugly: Critical sport management research. *Journal of Sport Management, 19*, 1-12.

Harris, J. (1993). Using kinesiology: A comparison of applied veins in the subdisciplines. *Quest, 45*, 389-412.

Lapchick, R. (2004-2006). *Institute reports and studies.* Retrieved May 28, 2006, from Central Florida University, Institute for Diversity and Ethics in Sport Website: www.bus.ucf.edu/sport/public/downloads/2004_Racial_Gender_Report_Card_College.pdf.

National Center for Health Statistics. (2004, October 6). *Obesity still a major problem, new data show. Prevalence of overweight among children and adolescents: United States, 1999-2002* [News release]. Retrieved July 15, 2005, from www.cdc.gov/nchs/pressroom/04facts/obesity.htm.

Putnam, D. (1999). *Controversies of the sports world.* Westport, CT: Greenwood Press.

Women's Sports Foundation. (2001-2005). *Coaching—Do female athletes prefer male coaches? The Foundation position.* Retrieved May 28, 2006, from www.womenssportsfoundation.org/cgi-bin/iowa/issues/coach/article.html?record=3.

Chapter 4—Intercollegiate Athletics

Abney, R., & Richey, D.L. (1991). Barriers encountered by Black women in sport. *Journal of Physical Education, Recreation and Dance, 62*(6), 19-21.

Abney, R., & Richey, D.L. (1992). Opportunities for minorities. *Journal of Physical Education, Recreation and Dance, 63*(3), 56-59.

Acosta, V., & Carpenter, L. (2006). *Women in intercollegiate sport—A longitudinal, national study: Twenty nine year update 1977-2006.* Retrieved June 13, 2006, from http://webpages.charter.net/womeninsport.

AEMA. (2005). *Certification.* Retrieved May 26, 2006, from www.aema1.com/cert.html.

Ammon, R., Southall, R.M., & Blair, D.A. (2004). *Sport facility management: Organizing events and managing risks.* Morgantown, WV: Fitness Information Technology.

Armstrong, K.L. (2001). Black consumers' spending and historically black college sport events: The marketing implications. *Sport Marketing Quarterly, 10*(2), 102-111.

Armstrong, K.L. (2002). An examination of the social psychology of blacks' consumption of sport. *Journal of Sport Management, 16*, 267-288.

Bamberger, M. (2003, December). The good times roll: At the Bayou Classic in New Orleans, Grambling State and Southern throw a football party that puts Mardi Gras to shame. *Sports Illustrated, 99*(22), 36-38.

Becker, D. (1992, January 14). Sweet's job surpasses her dreams. *USA Today*, p. 1C.

Berg, R. (1990). The roads less traveled. *Athletic Business, 14*(11), 44-47.

Brooks, D.D., & Althouse, R.C. (1993). Racial imbalance in coaching and managerial positions. In D.D. Brooks & R.C. Althouse (Eds.), *Racism in college athletics: The African-American athlete's experience* (pp. 101-142). Morgantown, WV: Fitness Information Technology.

Burwell, B. (1993, November 26). Bayou Classic gives tradition a new beat. *USA Today*, p. 5C.

Byers, W. (with Charles Hammer). (1995). *Unsportsmanlike conduct: Exploiting college athletes.* Ann Arbor: University of Michigan Press.

Christian, H. (2000). *Leadership styles and characteristics of athletic directors.* Unpublished doctoral dissertation, University of Alabama. Dissertation Abstracts Online. Retrieved November 20, 2002, from www.lib.umi.com/dissertations/results?set_num=1.

CIAA. (2005). The Central Intercollegiate Athletic Association website. Retrieved May 29, 2006, from www.theciaa.com/landing/index.html.

Claussen, C.L., & Lehr, C. (2002). Decision making authority of Senior Woman Administrators. *International Journal of Sport Management, 3*, 215-228.

Copeland, B.W., & Kirsch, S. (1995). Perceived occupational stress among Division I, II, and III athletic directors. *Journal of Sport Management 9*, 70-77.

Crowley, J. (2006). *In the arena: The NCAA's first century.* Indianapolis: The NCAA.

Cuneen, J. (1992). Graduate-level professional preparation for athletic directors. *Journal of Sport Management, 6*, 15-26.

Curtis, M. (2000). *A model of donor behavior: A comparison between female and male donors to men's and women's athletics support organizations at Division I NCAA-affiliated institutions within the Big Ten.* Unpublished dissertation, University of Iowa.

Farmer, S. (2001, January 18). Union may put label on colleges: labor: United Steel Workers get behind effort by former UCLA linebacker to get better treatment for athletes. *Los Angeles Times*, p. 1D.

Fitzgerald, M.P., Sagaria, M.A.D., & Nelson, B. (1994). Career patterns of athletic directors: Challenging the conventional wisdom. *Journal of Sport Management, 8*, 14-26.

Fulks, D. (2005, February). *2002-2004 revenues and expenses of Division I and II intercollegiate athletics programs report.* Indianapolis, IN: NCAA.

Geisler, P.R. (2003, April-June). Multiculturalism and athletic training education: Implications for educational and professional progress. *Journal of Athletic Training, 38*(2), 141-154.

Hardin, R., & McClung, S. (2002). Collegiate sports information: A profile for the profession. *Public Relations Quarterly, 47*(2), 35-40.

Hiestand, M. (2005, February 24). New spinoff ESPNU to get tardy start but has ambitious game plan. *USA Today*, p. 2C.

Howard, D.R., & Crompton, J.L. (2004). *Financing sport* (2nd ed.). Morgantown, WV: Fitness Information Technology.

Huggins, S. (1996). Broad range of talents required for today's athletics directors. *NCAA News, 33*(39), 1, 13.

Hughes, A. (2005, March). The 50 most powerful African-Americans in sports. *Black Enterprise, 35*(8), 88-91.

Irwin, D. (2001). Sport licensing. In B.L. Parkhouse (Ed.), *The management of sport* (3rd ed.) (pp. 353-364). New York: McGraw-Hill.

Irwin, R., Sutton, W., & McCarthy, L. (2002). *Sport promotion and sales management.* Champaign, IL: Human Kinetics.

Jackson, E.N., Lyons, R., & Gooden, S.C. (2001). The marketing of black-college sports. *Sport Marketing Quarterly, 10*, 138-146.

Johnson, R.S. (1999, December 20). How one college program runs the business: Inside Longhorn, Inc. *Fortune, 140*(12), 160-164, 168, 170, 172, 174.

Karlin, L. (1997). *The guide to careers in sports* (2nd ed.). New York: E.M. Guild.

Kinder, T.M. (1993). *Organizational management administration for athletic programs* (3rd ed.). Dubuque, IA: Eddie Bowers.

Knight Foundation Commission on Intercollegiate Athletics. (1991). *Keeping faith with the student athlete: A new model for intercollegiate athletics.* Charlotte, NC: Author.

Knight Foundation Commission on Intercollegiate Athletics. (2001). *A call to action: Reconnecting college sports and higher education.* Retrieved November 25, 2002, from www.ncaa.org/databases/Knight_commission/2001_report/2001_knight_report.html.

Lagesse, D. (2002, March 18). Troubleshooting: Schools are hiring compliance officers to police athletic departments. *US News & World Report, 132*(8), 61.

Lords, E. (2000, April 7). Professors' group seeks to reform college sports. *The Chronicle of Higher Education, 46*(31), A58.

Lucas, J.A., & Smith, R.A. (1978). *Saga of American sport.* Philadelphia: Lea & Febiger.

Maisel, I. (2005, April 25). No detail too small in Syracuse makeover. *ESPN the Magazine.* Retrieved August 9, 2006, from http://proxy.espn.go.com/ncf/columns/story?columnist=maisel_ivan&id+2041480.

Marrs, J.M. (1998). *The phantoms of the arena: A history of collegiate athletic publicity, 1911-1961.* Unpublished doctoral dissertation, University of Washington.

Momentum Media (June/July 1999). *AEMA marks a quarter century.* Retrieved August 10, 2006 from www.momentummedia.com/articles/am/am1104/bbaema25.htm.

Morrison, L.L. (1993). The AIAW: Governance by women for women. In G. Cohen (Ed.), *Women in sport: Issues and controversies* (pp. 59-78). Newbury Park: Sage.

NAIA. (2005a). National Association of Intercollegiate Athletics website. Retrieved May 29, 2006, from http://naia.cstv.com.

NAIA. (2005b). The NAIA Champions of Character Program. Retrieved May 29, 2006, from http://naia.cstv.com/champions-character.

National Association of Academic Advisors for Athletics. (2006). *N4A history.* Retrieved May 29, 2006, from www.nfoura.org/about/about_history.php.

NATA. (2006). What is an athletic trainer? Retrieved August 10, 2006, from http://www.nata.org/about_AT/whatisat.htm.

NCAA. (2005a). Overview. Retrieved August 10, 2006 from http://www2.ncaa.org/portal/about_ncaa/overview.

NCAA. (2005b). Membership. Retrieved August 10, 2006, from http://www2.ncaa.org/portal/about_ncaa/membership.

NCAA. (2005c). 2005 National College Football Attendance Report. Retrieved May 29, 2006, from www.ncaa.org/stats/football/attendance/2005/2005_football_attendance.pdf.

NCAA. (2005d). 2005 NCAA Membership Report. Retrieved May 26, 2006, from www.ncaa.org/library/membership/membership_report/2005/2005_membership_report.pdf.

NCAA. (2006, May 8). *NCAA News Online* retrieved May 29, 2006, from www.ncaa.org/wps/portal/newsdetail?WCM_GLOBAL_CONTEXT=/wps/wcm/connect/NCAA/NCAA+News/NCAA+News+Online/Association-wide/

Association+SWA+announces+staff+departure+-+5-8-06+NCCA=News&TITLE=Assocation+SWA+announces+staff+departure+-+5-8-06+NCAA+News.

NCAA Member Services Staff. (2004a, August). *Division I manual.* Indianapolis, IN: NCAA.

NCAA Member Services Staff. (2004b, August). *Division II manual.* Indianapolis, IN: NCAA.

NCAA Member Services Staff. (2004c, August). *Division III manual.* Indianapolis, IN: NCAA.

NCCAA. (2005). National Christian Collegiate Athletic Association website. Retrieved May 29, 2006, from www.thenccaa.org/

Nichols, W., Moynahan, P., Hall, A., & Taylor, J. (2001). *Media relations in sport.* Morgantown, WV: Fitness Information Technology.

NJCAA. (2006). National Junior College Athletic Association website. Retrieved May 29, 2006, from www.njcaa.org/history.cfm.

Olson, J. (1997). *Facility and equipment management for sport directors.* Champaign, IL: Human Kinetics.

Oriard, M. (2001). *King football: Sport and spectacle in the golden age of radio and newsreels, movies, and magazines, the weekly and daily press.* Chapel Hill: University of North Carolina Press.

Parks, J.B., Russell, R.L., & Wood, P.H. (1993). Marital and other primary dyadic relationships of intercollegiate athletics administrators. *Journal of Sport Management, 7,* 151-158.

Parks, J.B., Russell, R.L., Wood, P.H., Roberton, M.A., & Shewokis, P. (1995). The paradox of the contented working woman in athletics administration. *Research Quarterly for Exercise and Sport, 66,* 73-79.

Pitts, B.G., & Stotlar, D.K. (2002). *Fundamentals of sport marketing* (2nd ed.). Morgantown, WV: Fitness Information Technology.

Posnanski, J. (2001, August 26). Hawking the Heisman: Hey kid, want college football's top prize? Your school had better make one heck of a sales pitch and hope it pays off. *The Kansas City Star,* p. L9.

Q & A: Knight Commission's Hearn touts academic reform. (2005, May 19). *USA Today,* n.p. Retrieved May 30, 2006, from www/usatoday.com/sports/college/other/2005-05-19-hearn_xhtm.

Quarterman, J. (1992). Characteristics of athletic directors of historically Black colleges and universities. *Journal of Sport Management, 6,* 52-63.

Quarterman, J. (1994). Managerial role profiles of intercollegiate athletic conference commissioners. *Journal of Sport Management, 8,* 129-139.

Reese, J. (2003). Ticket operations. In U. McMahon-Beattie and I. Yeoman (Eds.), *Sport and leisure: A service operations approach* (pp. 167-179). London: Continuum.

Robinson, M.J., Peterson, M., Tedrick, T., & Carpenter, J.R. (2003). Job satisfaction of NCAA Division III athletic directors: Impact of job design and time on task. *International Sports Journal, 7*(2), 46-57.

Robinson, M.J., Tedrick, T., & Carpenter, J.R. (2001). Job satisfaction of NCAA Division III athletic directors: A descriptive analysis and examination of gender differences. *International Sports Journal, 5*(1), 25-32.

Ryska, T.A. (2002). Leadership styles and occupational stress among college athletic directors: The moderating effect of program goals. *Journal of Psychology 136,* 195-213.

Sack, A.L., & Staurowsky, E.J. (1998). *College athletes for hire: The evolution & legacy of the NCAA amateur myth.* Westport, CT: Praeger Press.

Sanders, C.T. (2004). *The administrative reporting structure of athletics directors in NCAA Division I, II, and III intercollegiate athletics.* Unpublished dissertation. Bozeman: Montana State University.

Schneider, R.C., & Stier, W.F. (2005, Winter). Necessary education for the success of athletics directors: NCAA presidents' perceptions. *The Sport Journal, 8*(1), n.p. Retrieved May 30, 2006, from www.the sportjournal.org/2005Journal/Vol8No1/robert_schneider.asp.

Shulman, J.L., & Bowen, W.G. (2001). *The game of life: College sports and educational values.* Princeton, NJ: Princeton University Press.

Solomon, J. (2001). *An insider's guide to managing sporting events.* Champaign, IL: Human Kinetics.

Sperber, M. (2000). *Beer and circus: How big-time college sport is crippling undergraduate education.* New York: Henry Holt.

Staurowsky, E.J. (1996). Women and athletic funding raising: Exploring the relationship between gender and giving. *Journal of Sport Management, 10,* 401-416.

Stoldt, G.C., Miller, L.K., & Comfort, P.G. (2001). Through the eyes of athletics directors: Perceptions of sports information directors, and other public relations issues. *Sport Marketing Quarterly, 10*(2), 164-172.

Suggs, W. (2005, April 8). Faces in a mostly white, male crowd. *The Chronicle of Higher Education, 51*(31), 31a.

Tiell, B. (n.d.) *The senior woman administrator.* Unpublished paper retrieved May 30, 2006, from http://bruno.tiffin.edu/btiell/WLS/SWA%20Research/SWA%20Overview.htm.

Tiell, B. (2004, May 18). *Career paths, roles, and tasks of senior woman administrators in intercollegiate athletics.* Retrieved May 30, 2006, from www1.ncaa.org/membership/governance/division_II/SWA_presentation.pdf.

Tillman, K.G., Voltmer, E.F., Esslinger, A.A., & McCue, B.F. (1996). *The administration of physical education, sport, and leisure programs* (Rev. ed.). Boston: Allyn and Bacon.

US Department of Education (2002). *Equity in Athletic Disclosure Act.* Retrieved August 10, 2006, from www.ed.gov/finaid/prof/resources/athletics/eada.html.

US Department of Education. (2005). Institution Data, *Revenues and Expenses: The University of Texas at Austin.*Retrieved August 10, 2006, from http://ope.ed.gov/athletics/InstDetail.asp?CRITERIA=3.

Whisenant, W.A., & Pedersen, P.M. (2004, January). The influence of managerial activities on the success of intercollegiate athletic directors. *American Business Review, 22*(1), 21-26.

Wieberg, S. (1991, January 7). Naming of female president sends message. *USA Today*, p. 2C.

Williams, C. D. (1983, May 4). Eastern college sports merge governing bodies. *TheHarvard Crimson*. Retrieved May 30, 2006, from www.thecrimson.com.

Yow, D.A., Migliore, R.H., Bowden, W.W., Stevens, R.E., & Loudon, D.L. (2000). *Strategic planning for collegiate athletics*. Binghamton, NY: Haworth Press.

Chapter 5—Professional Sport

A history of past women's professional basketball leagues. (1996). *ABL Courtside, 1*, 33.

Adams, R. (2005, March 28). Is MLB extending its reach or overreaching? *Street & Smith's SportsBusiness Journal*, p. 21.

Attendance: 2004 attendance. (2005). Retrieved June 28, 2005, from http://sports.espn.go.com/nfl/attendance.

Bernstein, A. (2002a, January 28). Increases in NBA's new TV deal tied to new net. *Street & Smith's SportsBusiness Journal*, p. 1.

Bernstein, A. (2002b, November 25). DirecTV paying licensing fee for NBA TV, less upfront for League Pass. *Street & Smith's SportsBusiness Journal*, p. 4.

Bernstein, A. (2005, April 25). NFL restores NBC's clout. *Street & Smith's SportsBusiness Journal*, p. 1.

Brockinton, L. (2000, December 25). TV ratings take a slide, many hit all-time lows. *Street & Smith's SportsBusiness Journal*, p. 23.

Brockinton, L. (2001, May 28). NBC/TNT adds 6 big Winston Cup race sponsors to NASCAR advertising roster. *Street & Smith's SportsBusiness Journal*, p. 4.

Browne, L. (1992). *Girls of summer*. Toronto: Harper Collins.

Callahan, K. (2005). *WNBA attendance*. Retrieved June 28, 2005, from http://womensbasketballonline.com/wnba/attendance.html.

Cassady, H. (2003, May 26). After tumultuous offseason, WNBA cleans up with P&G. *Brandweek*, p. 16.

Federal Base Ball Club of Baltimore, Inc. v. National League of Professional Base Ball Clubs, 259 U.S. 200 (1922).

Fraser et al. v. Major League Soccer, 97 F. Supp. 2d 130 (2000).

Freedman, W. (1987). *Professional sports and antitrust*. New York: Quorum Books.

Gorman, J., & Calhoun, K. (1994). *The name of the game: The business of sports*. New York: Wiley.

Greenberg, M.J. (1993). *Sports law practice*. Charlottesville, VA: Michie.

Guterson, D. (1994, September). *Moneyball: On the relentless promotion of pro sports*. Harper's Magazine, p. 38.

Harris, D. (1986). *The league: The rise and decline of the NFL*. New York: Bantam Books, pp. 13-14.

Horovitz, B. (1996, October 18). A basketball league of their own: Women athletes leap through hoops to live their dreams. *USA Today*, p. 1B.

How we see it: MLB up at the plate: Many hits, a few misses. (2005, April 4). *Street & Smith's SportsBusiness Journal*, p. 22.

King, B. (2005, March 7). The 24/7 fan. *Street & Smith's SportsBusiness Journal*, p. 23.

Leagues & teams. (2005). Negro Leagues Baseball Museum Web site. Retrieved July 7, 2005, from www.nlbm.com/s/team.htm.

Lee, J. (2004, March 8). LPGA Tour firms up its global grip. *Street & Smith's SportsBusiness Journal*, p. 1.

Lefton, T. (2005, June 20). Pizza Hut's naming deal rare for fast food. *Street & Smith's SportsBusiness Journal*, p. 5.

Liberman, N. (2005, June 6). Going for the green: An aggressive approach is needed to sell the LPGA to the corporate world. What will it take for the next commissioner to pull it off? *Street & Smith's SportsBusiness Journal*, p. 1.

Lombardo, J. (2002, July 29). NBA will try to make switch to cable TV add up. *Street & Smith's SportsBusiness Journal*, p. 19.

Mandalay Sports Entertainment Information. (2005). Retrieved July 7, 2005, from www.daytondragons.com/mandalay.html.

Media tracker: MLB ticket sales (regular-season totals). (2004, October 11). *Street & Smith's SportsBusiness Journal*, p. 32.

Minor league arena naming rights deals. (2001, August 13). *Street & Smith's SportsBusiness Journal*, pp. 16-17.

Minor league arena naming rights deals. (2003, November 3). *Street & Smith's SportsBusiness Journal*, p. 38.

Mullen, L. (2005, May 30). NFLPA looks at cutting agent fees. *Street & Smith's SportsBusiness Journal*, p. 4.

Mullin, B.J., Hardy, S., & Sutton, W.A. (2000). *Sport marketing*. (2nd ed.). Champaign, IL: Human Kinetics.

Muret, D. (2004, May 17). Lender lands in pricey neighborhood. *Street & Smith's SportsBusiness Journal*, p. 33.

Muret, D. (2005, March 14). Boston naming rights deal raises bar for cash going to arena. *Street & Smith's SportsBusiness Journal*, p. 14.

Naming rights deals at big-league facilities. (2001, August 13). *Street & Smith's SportsBusiness Journal*, pp. 18-19.

National Hockey League: Official guide and record book, 1995-96. (1996). New York: Author.

NBA attendance: 2004-05 attendance. (2005). Retrieved June 28, 2005, from http://sports.espn.go.com/nba/attendance.

Negro League baseball: Timeline of events in professional Black baseball. (2005). Retrieved July 7, 2005, from www.negroleaguebaseball.com/timeline.html.

On the racks. (2000, September 4). *Street & Smith's SportsBusiness Journal*, p. 32.

Rader, B.G. (1983). *American sports: From the age of folk games to the age of televised sports.* Englewood Cliffs, NJ: Prentice Hall.

Rank by capacity. (2005). Retrieved June 28, 2005, from www.infoplease.com/ipsa/A0105606.html.

Roberts, R. (1995, Spring). The salary cap in professional sports. *The Sports Lawyer*, p. 1.

Roberts, R., & Olson, J. (1995). *Winning is the only thing: Sports in America since 1945.* Baltimore: Johns Hopkins University Press.

Rofe, J. (2000a, December 25). Baseball's rich getting richer as economic ills go untreated. *Street & Smith's SportsBusiness Journal*, p. 23.

Rofe, J. (2000b, April 3). What new sponsorship can we sell? *Street & Smith's SportsBusiness Journal*, p. 24.

Salary growth since 1993 in the big four team sports. (2000, January 31). *Street & Smith's SportsBusiness Journal*, p. 29.

Sosnowski, T. (2005, February 1). NFL powerhouse: The NFL is undisputed king of sports licensing. *Playthings*, p. 22.

Staudohar, P.D. (1989). *The sports industry and collective bargaining.* Cornell, NY: ILR Press.

Staudohar, P.D., & Mangan, J.A. (1991). *The business of professional sports.* Urbana: University of Illinois Press.

Tannenbaum, M.B. (1994). An overview of the relationship between major and minor league baseball. *The Sports Lawyer, 11*, 1, 7-11.

TMR's Fan Cost Index: National Basketball Association: 2004-2005. (2005). Retrieved July 7, 2005, from www.teammarketing.com/fci.cfm?page=fci_nba_04-05.cfm.

TMR's Fan Cost Index: National Football League: 2004. (2005). Retrieved July 7, 2005, from www.teammarketing.com/fci.cfm?page=fci_nfl_04.cfm.

Turnstile tracker. (2004, November 1). *Street & Smith's SportsBusiness Journal*, p. 32.

Warfield, S. (2005, March 21). Selling soccer: Adidas has invested heavily in MLS. Kevin Ross will make sure it is money well spent. *Street & Smith's SportsBusiness Journal*, p. 32.

White, G.E. (1996). *Creating the national pastime: Baseball transforms itself.* Princeton, NJ: Princeton University Press.

Zimbalist, A. (1992). *Baseball and billions.* New York: Basic Books.

Zimbalist, A. (2004, April 5). Break up the Yanks? We owe them thanks. *Street & Smith's SportsBusiness Journal*, p. 23.

Zimbalist, A. (2005, February 14). NFL, Kraft make the Super Bowl math add up. *Street & Smith's SportsBusiness Journal*, p. 29.

Chapter 6—Sport Management and Marketing Agencies

Bernstein, A. (2005). ESPN, Big East end long disagreement over change in rights fees. *Street & Smith's SportsBusiness Journal*, p. 13.

Bernstein, A. (2000, May 29-June 4). And the winner is . . . the top sports marketing agencies. *Street & Smith's SportsBusiness Journal*, pp. 27, 37.

Bevilaqua International Inc. (1994). Corporate brochure and sales materials. Atlanta, GA: Author.

Conklin, M. (1994, January 25). Blackhawks' Chelios in spotlight as new ad rep for company. *The Chicago Tribune* (North Sports Final Edition), p. 7.

Conrad, E. (1995, January 10). NFL experience: Super Bowl-related bazaar will be running right next to JRS. *The Sun Sentinel* (Fort Lauderdale, FL), p. 10.

Cortez, J.P. (1992, June 1). Julius keeps the score for sports promotions: Leading marketers rely on consultancy's numbers. *Advertising Age, 63*(22), 10.

Crespo, M. (1995, February 14). You get more eyeballs: Satellite television sports. *Financial World, 164*(4), 94-98.

Damage control: Who was best? (2005, June 20). *Street & Smith's SportsBusiness Journal*, p. 1, 14-17.

International Management Group. (2000). *Corporate Report.* Cleveland, OH: Author.

International Management Group. (2001). *Corporate Report.* Cleveland, OH: Author.

International Management Group. (2005). Retrieved, July 8, 2005, from www.imgworld.com.

Lefton, T. (2003, September 8). Client-centric culture breeds growth at a rapid velocity. *Street & Smith's SportsBusiness Journal*, p. 1.

Lipsey, R.A. (Ed.). (2004). *Sports market place.* Princeton, NJ: Sportsguide.

Menninger, B. (2000, May 29-June 4). Hidden hosts of big events. *Street & Smith's SportsBusiness Journal*, pp. 32-33.

Mullen, L. (2005a, January 31). McNabb marketing agent targets corporate gigs. *Street & Smith's SportsBusiness Journal*, p. 18.

Mullen, L. (2005b, February 28). Octagon closes deal, acquired TMS sports. *Street & Smith's SportsBusiness Journal*, p. 4.

Mullen, L. (2005c, April 4). SFX sports, looking to grow golf and tennis, pursues events. *Street & Smith's SportsBusiness Journal*, p. 14.

Mullen, L. (2005d, October 24). Owner taking Kain's spot at IMG. *Street & Smith's SportsBusiness Journal*, p. 25.

A new era in the NFL: Expansion '95. (1995). *Sport Magazine, 86*(9), 61.

Parascenzo, M. (1993, May 3). Prime time. *Business Week*, pp. 100-103.

Schreiber, A.L. (1994). *Lifestyle & event marketing.* New York: McGraw-Hill.

Schwartz, D. (2000, May 29-June 4). Super concierge to the Olympics, SportsMark claims its niche. *Street & Smith's SportsBusiness Journal*, p. 33.

Sports sponsorship up 11% in '03 according to IEG estimates. (2004, January 8). *Sports Business Daily.*

Chapter 7—Sport Tourism

ABC. (2002, February 10). *ABC evening news*. Report on Nagano, Japan.

Aburdene, P., & Naisbitt, J. (1992). *Megatrends for women*. New York: Villard Books.

Adair, D. (2004). Where the games never cease: The Olympic Museum in Lausanne, Switzerland. In B. Ritchie & D. Adair (Eds.), *Sport tourism: Interrelationships, impacts and issues* (pp. 46-76). Clevedon, UK: Channel View.

Alachua County (2002). *Where nature meets culture*. Retrieved February 20, 2002, from www.visitgainesville.net.

Alm, R. (2001, October 5). Area tourism industry hopes for a big score from Texas-OU game. *The Dallas Morning News*, p. D1.

ANZALS (2001, July 2). Opening session speaker, John Longley. Fremantle, Australia.

Bale, J. (1988). *Sports geography*. London: E and FN Spon.

Blair, S., & Brodney, S. (1999). Effects of physical inactivity and obesity on morbidity and mortality: Current evidence and research issues. *Medicine and Science in Sports and Exercise*, *31*(11), supplement 1:S646-S662.

Bourdeau, P., Corneloup, J., & Mao, P. (2004). Adventure sports and tourism in the French mountains: Dynamics of change and challenges for sustainable development. In B. Ritchie & D. Adair (Eds.), *Sport tourism: Interrelationships, impacts and issues* (pp. 101-116). Clevedon, UK: Channel View.

Buckley, R., Pickering, C., & Warnken, J. (2000). Environmental management for alpine tourism and resorts in Australia. In P. Godde, M. Price, & F. Zimmermann (Eds.), *Tourism and development in mountain regions* (pp. 27-45). Wallingford, UK: CAB International.

Burgan, B., & Mules, T. (1992). Economic impact of sporting events. *Annals of Tourism Research*, *19*, 700-710.

Chalip, L. (2001, February). *Leveraging the Sydney Olympics to optimize tourism benefits*. Paper presented at the International Conference on the Economic Impact of Sports, Athens, Greece.

Chalip, L., & Green, B.C. (2001, June). Leveraging large sports events for tourism: Lessons learned from the Sydney Olympics. *Supplemental Proceedings of the Travel and Tourism Research Association 32nd Annual Conference*, Fort Myers, FL.

Chalip, L., & Leyns, A. (2002). Local business leveraging of a sport event: Managing sport for economic benefit. *Journal of Sport Management*, *16*, 132-158.

Chernushenko, D. (1996). Sports tourism goes sustainable: The Lillehammer experience. *Visions in Leisure and Business*, *15*, 65-73.

Coakley, J. (2004). *Sport in society: Issues & controversies* (8th ed.). New York: McGraw-Hill.

Coccossis, H. (2004, November). *A new look at a friendly destination: Greece*. Paper presented at the First International Meetings Industry Conference, Athens Greece.

Cohen, E. (1974). Who is a tourist? A conceptual clarification. *Sociological Review*, *22*, 527-555.

Cohen, S. (1998, November). Transatlantic allies. *Continental Inflight Magazine*, 30-33.

Crompton, J. (1979). An assessment of the image of Mexico as a vacation destination and the influence of geographical location upon that image. *Journal of Travel Research*, *17*(4), 18-23.

Crompton, J. (1995). Economic impact analysis of sports facilities and events: Eleven sources of misapplication. *Journal of Sport Management*, *9*, 14-35.

Dann, G. (1994). Tourism: The nostalgia industry of the future. In W. Theobold (Ed.), *Global tourism: The next decade* (pp. 56-67). Oxford: Butterworth-Heinemenn.

Davis, F. (1979). *Yearning for yesterday: A sociology of nostalgia*. New York: Free Press.

De Knop, P. (1987). Some thoughts on the influence of sport tourism. In *Proceedings of the International Seminar and Workshop on Outdoor Education, Recreation and Sport Tourism*, pp. 38-45. Netanya, Israel: Wingate Institute for Physical Education and Sport.

Dogan, H. (1989). Forms of adjustment: Socio-cultural impacts of tourism. *Annals of Tourism Research*, *16*, 216-236.

Dovey, K. (1989). Old scabs/new scars: The hallmark event and the everyday environment. In G. Syme, B. Shaw, D. Fenton, & W. Mueller (Eds.), *The planning and evaluation of hallmark events* (pp. 73-80). Aldershot, UK: Avebury.

Doyle, T. (2004). *Areas report notes slope trends*. Retrieved June 23, 2005, from www.nssra.com.

Ebisch, R. (2005, July). Cool mountains: You want peak experiences? We'll give you peak experiences! *Sky Delta Airlines Inflight Magazine*, pp. 42-51.

Elliott-Spivak, S. (1998). Health spa development in the U.S.: A burgeoning component of sport tourism. *Journal of Vacation Marketing*, *4*, 65-77.

Fairley, S., (2003). In search of relived social experience: Group-based nostalgia sport tourism. *Journal of Sport Management*, *17*, 284-304 (Special issue: sport tourism).

Fakeye, P., & Crompton, J. (1991). Image differences between prospective, first-time, and repeat visitors to the Lower Rio Grande Valley. *Journal of Travel Research*, *30*(2), 10-16.

Fisher, J. (2001). *The Gator Shop: In-person interview*. Unpublished student paper, University of Florida, Gainesville.

Foley, M., & Reid, G. (1998). Activities, holidays and activity holidays in Scotland. In N. Ravenscroft, D. Phillips, & M. Bennett (Eds.), *Tourism and visitor attractions: Leisure, culture and commerce* (vol. 61, pp. 61-73). Eastbourne, UK: LSA.

Fowler, P. (1992). *The past in contemporary society: Then and now*. London: Routledge.

Frommer, A. (2001, September 2). On a budget: Yellowstone's hot deals. *Los Angeles Times*, part L, p. 2.

Gammon, S. (2002). Fantasy, nostalgia and the pursuit of what never was—but what should have been. In S. Gammon & J. Kurtzman (Eds.), *Sport tourism: Principles and practice* (pp. 61-71). LSA Publication #76. Eastbourne, UK.

Gammon, S., & Robinson, T. (1997). Sport and tourism: A conceptual framework. *Journal of Sports Tourism*, *4*(3), 8-24.

Garnham, B. (1996). Ranfurly Shield Rugby: An investigation into the impacts of a sporting event on a provincial city, the case of New Plymouth, Taranaki, New Zealand. *Festival Management and Event Tourism*, *4*, 145-149.

Gee, C., Makens, J., & Choy, D. (1989). *The travel industry* (2nd ed.). New York: Van Nostrand.

Getz, D. (1997). Trends and issues in sport event tourism. *Tourism Recreation Research*, *22*, 61-74.

Gibson, H. (1998a). Sport tourism: A critical analysis of research. *Sport Management Review*, *1*, 45-76.

Gibson, H. (1998b). Active sport tourism: Who participates? *Leisure Studies*, *17*, 155-170.

Gibson, H., Ashton-Shaeffer, C., Green, J., & Kensinger, K. (2002, October). *"It wouldn't be long before I'd be friends with an undertaker": What it means to be a senior athlete*. Presented at the Leisure Research Symposium held in conjunction with the National Park and Recreation Association Congress, Tampa, FL.

Gibson, H., Willming, C., & Holdnak, A. (2002) "We're Gators . . . not just a Gator fan:" Serious leisure, social identity, and University of Florida football. *Journal of Leisure Research*, *14*, 397-425.

Gibson, H., Willming, C., & Holdnak, A. (2003). Small-scale event sport tourism: College sport as a tourist attraction. *Tourism Management*, *24*, 181-190.

Goeldner, C., & Ritchie, J.R. Brent. (2003). *Tourism: Practices, principles, philosophies*. New York: Wiley.

Grohmann, K. (2004, July 30). *Athens Games green record is miserable—Greenpeace*. Retrieved July 11, 2005, from www.planetark.com.

Hall, C. (1992). Adventure, sport and health tourism. In B. Weiler & C.M. Hall (Eds.), *Special interest tourism* (pp. 141-158). London: Bellhaven Press.

Hall, C., & Hodges, J. (1996). The party's great, but what about the hangover? The housing and social impacts of mega-events with special reference to the 2000 Sydney Olympics. *Festival Management and Event Tourism*, *4*, 13-20.

Hanis, A. (2000, May 3). Take your home team on a baseball road trip. *Chicago Sun-Times*, p. 60.

Higham, J. (1999). Commentary—sport as an avenue of tourism development: An analysis of the positive and negative impacts of sport tourism. *Current Issues in Tourism*, *2*(1), 82-90.

Hinch, T., & Higham, J. (2001). Sport tourism: A framework for research. *International Journal of Tourism Research*, *3*, 45-58.

Hudson, S. (1996). The greening of ski resorts: A necessity for sustainable tourism or a marketing opportunity for skiing communities? *Journal of Vacation Marketing*, *2*(2), 176-185.

Hudson, S. (2004). Winter sport tourism In North America. In B. Ritchie & D. Adair (Eds.). *Sport tourism: Interrelationships, impacts and issues* (pp. 77-100). Clevedon, UK: Channel View.

Irwin, R., & Sandler, M. (1998). An analysis of travel behavior and event-induced expenditures among American collegiate championship patron groups. *Journal of Vacation Marketing*, *4*, 78-90.

International Union of Official Travel Organizations. (1963). *The United Nations' conference on international travel and tourism*. Geneva, Switzerland: International Union of Official Travel Organizations.

Jago, L., & Shaw, R. (1998). Special events: A conceptual and definitional framework. *Festival Management and Event Journal, 5,* 21-32.

Janofsky, M. (2000, December 3). Environmental groups' ratings rile ski industry. *New York Times*, p. 30.

Kelly, J. (1999). Leisure behaviors and styles: Social, economic, and cultural factors. In E. Jackson & T. Burton (Eds.), *Leisure studies: Prospects for the twenty-first century* (pp. 135-150). State College, PA: Venture.

Kelly, J., & Freysinger, V. (2000). *21st century leisure*. Boston: Allyn & Bacon.

Kim, N., & Chalip, L. (2004). Why travel to the FIFA World Cup? Effects of motives, background, interest, and constraints. *Tourism Management*, *25*, 695-707.

Ladd, S. (1995, July 7). Pinehurst: One man's vision. *Greensboro News and Record*, Weekend, pp. 8-10.

Leiper, N. (1990). Tourist attraction systems. *Annals of Tourism Research*, *17*, 367-384.

Lewis, G., & Redmond, G. (1974). *Sporting heritage: A guide to halls of fame, special collections, and museums in the US and Canada*. New York: Barnes.

Loy, J. (1968). The nature of sport: A definitional effort. *Quest*, *10*, 1-15.

Martin, K. (1995, December 13). The fit and adventuresome can now vacation by skate. *Hartford Courant*, Travel Section, p. 3.

McFee, G. (1990). The Olympic Games as tourist event: An American in Athens, 1896. *Proceedings of the Leisure Studies Association Second International Conference, Leisure, Labour, and Lifestyles: International Comparisons* (pp. 146-157), Conference Papers No. 43. Eastbourne, UK: LSA.

Mintel. (2000, December). *Special interest holidays. Leisure intelligence*. London: Mintel International Group.

Mintel. (2004). *Snow sport holidays*. Retrieved July 9, 2005, from www.mintel.com.

Morse, S., & Lanier, P. (1992). Golf resorts—Driving into the '90s. *The Cornell Hotel and Restaurant Administration Quarterly, 33*, 44-48.

Mules, T., & Dwyer, L. (2005). Public sector support for sport tourism events: The role of cost-benefit analysis. *Sport in Society, 8*, 338-355 (Special issue: Sport tourism: Concepts and theories).

National Golf Foundation (2005). *Frequently asked questions*. Retrieved June 23, 2005, from www.ngf.org.

National Sporting Goods Association (2004). *Sport participation patterns 2004*. Retrieved June 23, 2005, from www.nsga.org.

NBC. (2000, September 9). Today show interview with John Coates, president of the Australian Olympic Committee.

Nogawa, H., Yamguchi, Y., & Hagi, Y. (1996). An empirical research study on Japanese sport tourism in Sport-for-All Events: Case studies of a single-night event and a multiple-night event. *Journal of Travel Research, 35*, 46-54.

North Carolina Travel and Tourism Division (1995). *North Carolina travel guide*. Raleigh, NC: Author.

North Central Florida Almanac (2005, April 17). *The Gainesville Sun*.

Olds, K. (1998). Urban mega-events, evictions and housing rights: The Canadian case. *Current Issues in Tourism, 1*(1), 2-46.

Palmer, C. (2004). More than just a game: The Consequences of golf tourism. In B. Ritchie & D. Adair (Eds.), *Sport tourism: Interrelationships, impacts and issues* (pp. 117-134). Clevedon, UK: Channel View.

Pitts, B.G. (1999). Sports tourism and niche markets: Identification and analysis of the growing lesbian and gay sports tourism industry. *Journal of Vacation Marketing, 5*(1), 31-50.

Pleumarom, A. (1992). Course and effect: Golf tourism in Thailand. *The Ecologist, 22*, 104-110.

Poon, A., & Adams, E. (2000). *How the British will travel 2005*. Bielefeld, Germany: Tourism Intelligence International.

Priestley, G. (1995). Sports tourism: The case of golf. In G. J. Ashworth & A.G.J. Dietvorst (Eds.), *Tourism and spatial transformations: Implications for policy and planning* (pp. 205-223).Wallingford, UK: CAB International.

Reality check: The post-Olympic glow fades amid a new budget squabble. (2004, September 30). *The Economist*. Retrieved July 11, 2005, from www.economist.com.

Redmond, G. (1973). A plethora of shrines: Sport in the museum and hall of fame. *Quest, 19*, 41-48.

Redmond, G. (1991). Changing styles of sports tourism: Industry/consumer interactions in Canada, the USA, and Europe. In M.T. Sinclair & M.J. Stabler (Eds.), *The tourism industry: An international analysis* (pp. 107-120). Wallingford, UK: CAB International.

Ritchie, J.R. Brent. (1984). Assessing the impact of hallmark events: Conceptual and research issues. *Journal of Travel Research, 23*, 2-11.

Ritchie, J.R. Brent. (1999). Lessons learned, lessons learning: Insights from the Calgary and Salt Lake Olympic Winter Games. *Visions in Leisure and Business, 18*, 4-13.

Ritchie, J.R. Brent, & Aitken, C. (1984). Assessing the impacts of the 1988 Olympic Winter Games: The research program and initial results. *Journal of Travel Research, 23*, 17-25.

Ritchie, J.R. Brent, & Lyons, M. (1990). OLYMPUS VI—A post event assessment of resident reaction to the XV Olympic Winter Games. *Journal of Travel Research, 29*, 14-23.

Ritchie, J.R. Brent, & Smith, B. (1991). The impact of a mega-event on host region awareness: A longitudinal study. *Journal of Travel Research, 30*, 3-10.

Roche, M. (1994). Mega-events and urban policy. *Annals of Tourism Research, 21*, 1-19.

Rowan, D., & Sandberg, D. (1990, January). The cosmopolitan future of America's ski resorts. *Ski Area Management, 29*, 76-77.

Schor, J. (1991). *The overworked American: The unexpected decline of leisure*. New York: Basic Books.

Smith, V. (1989). *Hosts and guests: The anthropology of tourism* (2nd ed). Philadelphia: University of Pennsylvania Press.

Snyder, E. (1991). Sociology of nostalgia: Sport halls of fame and museums in America. *Sociology of Sport Journal, 8*, 228-238.

Soutar, G., & McLeod, P. (1993). Residents' perceptions on impact of the America's Cup. *Annals of Tourism Research, 20*, 571-582.

Sparvero, E., Trendavilova, S., & Chalip, L. (2005, June). *An alternative approach to environmental dispute resolution in sport contexts*. Poster presented at the North American Society for Sport Management conference, Regina, Saskatchewan, Canada.

Spencer, R. (2006, January 5). Olympic clean-up hides Beijing's sightseeing gems. *The Daily Telegraph*, p. 20.

Sportbusiness.com (2004, August 18). *Sports tourism is a multi-billion dollar business*. Retrieved July 9, 2005, from www.reports.mintel.com.

Standeven, J. (1998). Sport tourism: Joint marketing—A starting point for beneficial synergies. *Journal of Vacation Marketing, 4*, 39-51.

Standeven, J., & De Knop, P. (1999). *Sport tourism*. Champaign, IL: Human Kinetics.

Stevens, T., & Wootton, G. (1997). Sports stadia and arena: Realising their full potential. *Tourism Recreation Research, 22*(2), 49-56.

Tabata, R. (1992). Scuba diving holidays. In B. Weiler & C. Hall (Eds.), *Special interest tourism* (pp. 171-184). London, UK: Belhaven Press.

Toohey, K., Taylor, T., & Lee, C. (2003). The FIFA World Cup 2002: The effects of terrorism on sport tourists. *Journal of Sport Tourism, 8*, 167-185.

Travel Industry Association of America (1999). *Profiles of travelers who attend sports events*. Washington, DC: Author.

Travel Industry Association of America. (2000). *Tourism works for America*. Washington, DC: Author.

Travel Industry Association of America (2005). *Economic impact of travel and tourism*. Retrieved June 22, 2005, from www.tia.org.

Tourism Industry Association of Canada and Canadian Sport Tourism Alliance. (2004). *2010 Olympics—A call to action for the Canadian tourism industry*. Retrieved June 22, 2005, from www.canadiansporttourism.com.

Travelwirenews.com (2005, July 7). *Olympic wins worth 2 billion pounds to British tourism*. Retrieved July 7, 2005, from www.travelwirenews.com.

Urry, J. (1990). *The tourist gaze*. London: Sage.

US Department of Health and Human Services (1996). *Physical activity and health: A report of the Surgeon General*. Atlanta, GA: Author.

US Travel Data Center (1989). *Discover America 2000: The implications of America's changing demographics and attitudes on the US travel industry*. Washington, DC: Author.

Waters, R. (1989). *Travel industry world yearbook: The big picture—1988-1989* (Vol. 33). New York: Child & Waters.

Watson, G.L., & Kopachevsky, J. (1994). Interpretations of tourism as commodity. In Y. Apostolopoulos, S. Leivadi, & A. Yiannakis (Eds.), *Sociology of tourism* (pp. 281-300). London: Routledge.

Whitson, D., & Macintosh, D. (1993). Becoming a world-class city: Hallmark events and sport franchises in the growth strategies of western Canadian cities. *Sociology of Sport Journal, 10*, 221-240.

Wilson, A. (2004). *The relationship between consumer role socialization and nostalgia sport tourism: A symbolic interactionist perspective*. Unpublished master's thesis, University of Florida, Gainesville.

Wilson, J. (1999). "Remember when . . ." A consideration of the concept of nostalgia. *ETC: A Review of General Semantics, 56*, 296-304.

Wood, S. (2001, November 4). Fort Worth, Texas, area aims for smaller sporting events after losing the Olympics. *Fort Worth Star-Telegram*.

World Cup soccer games finally come to America. (1993, May 17). *Business America*, pp. 2-6.

World Tourism Organization (1994). *Recommendations on tourism statistics*. Madrid, Spain: Author.

World Tourism Organization (2004). *Tourism market trends*. Retrieved June 22, 2005, from www.world-tourism.org

Yiannakis, A., & Gibson, H. (1992). Roles tourists play. *Annals of Tourism Research, 19*, 287-303.

Zachary, J. (1997, March). *Assembling the most attractive sport tourism packages*. Panel session at Teaming for Success: A Forum on Sport Tourism, Arlington, Virginia.

Chapter 8—A North American Perspective on International Sport

A-B paces ad spending, Olympic sponsors climb list. (2005, March 21-27). *Street & Smith's SportsBusiness Journal*, p. 9.

Abelson, J. (2006, February 1). Fireman era ends. *Boston Globe*, p. E2.

Allen, K. (2006, February 20). Minnesota-Duluth women boost Sweden's chance for gold. USA Today, p. 5D.

Andrews, D.L. (Ed.). (2004). *Manchester United*. London: Routledge.

Ashton, C. (2001, November). China comes out to play. *SportBusiness International*, 28-31.

Bale, J., & Maguire, J. (Eds.). (1994). *The global sports arena: Athletic talent migration in an interdependent world*. London: Routledge.

Barnet, R.J., & Cavanagh, J. (1994). *Global dreams: Imperial corporations and the new world order*. New York: Simon & Schuster.

Beckham, D., & Watt, T. (2004). *Beckham both feet on the ground: An autobiography*. New York: Perennial Currents.

Bernstein, A., Shari, M., & Malkin, E. (2000, November 6). A world of sweatshops. *Business Week*, pp. 84-85.

Bosman, J. (2003, June 24). The NBA goes global: Rosters filling up with international talent. *Orlando Sentinel*. Retrieved March 25, 2006, from www.globalpolicy.org/globalis/cultural/2003/0701nba.htm.

Brake, T., Walker, D.M., & Walker, T. (1995). Doing business internationally: The guide to cross-cultural success. Burr Ridge, IL: Irwin.

Burton, R. (2000, Oct. 9-15). Olympic sponsors missing out on special opportunity. *Street & Smith's SportsBusiness Journal*, pp. 40-41.

Chu, Chin-Ning (1991). *The Asian mind game: Unlocking the hidden agenda of the Asian business culture: A westerner's survival manual*. New York: Rawson Associates.

Cronin, S. (2001, July). China's stadia revolution. *SportBusiness International, 6*(Suppl. 59), 9-11.

DePauw, K., & Gavron, S. (2005). *Disability sport* (2nd ed.). Champaign, IL: Human Kinetics.

Echikson, W., Webb, A., & Fonte, D. (2001, July 9). Guess who wants Beijing to get the games. *Business Week*, p. 48.

Elashmawi, F. & Harris, P.R. (1998). *Multicultural management 2000: Essential cultural insights for global business success*. Houston, TX: Gulf Publishing.

Embassy of the People's Republic of China in the United States of America. (2005, February 8). *Lang Ping named head coach of US women's national volleyball team*. Retrieved April 4, 2006, from www.china-embassy.org/eng/gyzg/t183069.htm.

Engardio, P., & Belton, C. (2000, November 6). Global capitalism: Can it be made to work better? *Business Week*, pp. 72-75.

Fay, T.G. (1989). Beyond the medals and fanfare: Nordic skisport—health and excitement for all. *Palaestra, 6*, 37-45.

Fay, T.G. (2001). Strategic approaches to vertical integration & equity for athletes with disabilities: An examination of a critical change factors model. In G. Doll-Tepper, M. Kroner, & W. Sonnenschein (Eds.), *New horizons in sport for athletes with a disability: Proceedings of the International VISTA '99 Conference, Cologne, Germany*. Aachen, Germany: Meyer & Meyer Sport.

Fay, T.G, Hums, M.A., & Wolff, E.A. (2000a, June). *Inclusion of sport for athletes with disabilities into non-disabled sport organizations*. Paper presented at the annual meeting of the North American Society for Sport Management, Colorado Springs, CO.

Fay, T.G., Hums, M.A. & Wolff, E.A. (2000b, September). *Critical change factors model: Understanding the integration process of sport organizations for athletes with disabilities into national governing bodies and the United States Olympic Committee*. Paper presented at the International Congress on Sport Science, Sports Medicine, and Physical Education, Brisbane, Australia.

Fay, T., Legg, D., & Wolff, E.A. (2005, June). *Inclusion of Paralympic events within the Olympic Games*. Paper presented at the annual meeting of the North American Society for Sport Management, Regina, Saskatchewan, Canada.

Foer, F. (2004). *How soccer explains the world: An unlikely theory of globalization*. New York: Harper Perennial.

The great world atlas (3rd ed.). (2004). New York: Dorling Kindersley.

Grevemberg, D., Hums, M.A., & Wolff, E.A. (2001, June). *Integration of Paralympic sport into international sport federations: Comparative international models*. Paper presented at the annual meeting of the North American Society for Sport Management, Virginia Beach, VA.

Grundy, P. & Shackelford, S. (2005). *Shattering the glass: The remarkable history of women's basketball*. New York: New Press.

Guttman, A. (1994). *The Olympics: A history of the modern games*. Chicago: University of Illinois Press.

Hums, M.A., & MacLean, J.C. (2004). *Governance and policy in sport organizations*. Scottsdale, AZ: Holcomb Hathaway.

Jennings, A. (1996). *The new lords of the rings*. London: Pocket Books.

Jennings, A. (2001). *The great Olympic swindle: When the world wanted its Games back*. New York: Simon & Schuster.

Jones, D. (1996, June 6). Critics tie sweatshop sneakers to "Air" Jordan. *USA Today*, p. 1B.

Joukowsky, A.A.W., & Rothstein, L. (2002). *Raising the bar: New horizons in disability sport*. Umbrage Editions Books.

Kaplan, D. (2001, October 8-14). Medal-hungry China loosens grip on athletes. *Street & Smith's SportsBusiness Journal*, pp. 1, 39.

Kaplan, D. (2005, May 30-June 5). Media's Man U questions left unanswered by the Glazers. *Street & Smith's SportsBusiness Journal*, p. 6.

Katz, D. (1994). *Just do it: The Nike spirit in the corporate world*. Holbrook, MA: Adams Media Corporation.

Kaufmann, M. (2001, October 1-7). League tries to tap into Olympic spirit. *Street & Smith's SportsBusiness Journal*, p. 29.

Khermouch, G., Holmes, S., & Ihlwan, M. (2001, August 6). The best global brands. *Business Week*, pp. 50-57.

King, B. (2005a, January 31-February 6). Gambling, steroids rank high on sports lobby's list of issues. *Street & Smith's SportsBusiness Journal*, pp. 1, 10-11.

King, B. (2005b, April 25-May 1). What's up with women's sports? *Street & Smith's SportsBusiness Journal*, pp. 18-23.

Larmer, B. (2003, September 8). The next Yao Ming? *Time, 162*, 66-68.

Larmer, B. (2005). Operation Yao Ming: *The Chinese sports empire, American big business, and the making of an NBA superstar*. New York: Gotham Books.

Lefton, T. (2005, May 30-June 5). The Meal Deal: How Mc Donald's has used sports to package the perfect pitch during most of its 50-year history. *Street & Smith's SportsBusiness Journal*, pp. 15-23.

Lombardo, J. (2004, October 25-31). Global trade: NBA imports talent and exports the game. *Street & Smith's SportsBusiness Journal*, pp. 22-29.

Longman, J. (2000). *Girls of summer: The U.S. women's soccer team and how they changed the world*. New York: Harper Collins.

Maguire, J. (1999). *Global sport: Identities, societies, civilizations*. Cambridge, UK: Polity Press.

Maguire, J., & Nakayama, M. (2005). *Japan, sport & society: Tradition and change in a globalizing world*. London: Routledge.

Maich, S. (2005, July 1). Big-league awakening: Canada is fielding top talent. *Maclean's, 118*, 82-84.

McCloskey, J., & Bailes, J.E. (2005). *When winning costs too much*. Lanham, MD: Taylor Trade Publishing.

Moore, K. (1996, August 5). Munich's message. *Sports Illustrated, 85*, 30-31.

Morrison, T., Conaway, W., & Douress, J.J. (2001). *Doing business around the world*. Paramus, NJ: Prentice Hall.

Mullen, L. (2006a, January 30-February 5). Forstmann turns page at IMG: Pyne in, Johnson out as McCormack's Generals fade away. *Street & Smith's SportsBusiness Journal*, pp. 1, 34.

Mullen, L. (2006b, February 20-26). Agents can leave IMG, take clients. *Street & Smith's SportsBusiness Journal*, pp. 1, 31.

Muret, D. (2005, April 25-May 1). AEG to start building arena inside London's unloved dome. *Street & Smith's SportsBusiness Journal*, p. 14.

Orkin, L. (2004, August 18). Kenteris, Thanou suspended. *USA Today*. Retrieved April 1, 2006, from www.usatoday.com/sports/olympics/athens/track/2004-08-13-greek-sprinters_x.htm.

Payne, M. (2005). *Olympic turnaround.* Westport, CT: Praeger.

Pedulla, T. (2005, June 29). International picks prove there is a world of talent. *USA Today,* Retrieved June 22, 2006, from www.usatoday.com/sports/basketball/draft/2005-06-29-international-picks_x.htm.

Pike, L.L., & Fay, T.G. (1994). Cross-cultural studies: Implications on professional preparation and management training in global sport. In R. Wilcox (Ed.), *Sport in the global village* (pp. 53-72). Morgantown, WV: Fitness Information Technology.

Pitts, B.G., & Stotlar, D.K. (2002). *Fundamentals of sport marketing* (2nd ed.). Morgantown, WV: Fitness Information Technology.

Pound, R.W. (1994). *Five rings over Korea: The secret negotiations behind the 1988 Olympic Games in Seoul.* New York: Little, Brown and Co.

Pound, R.W. (2004). *Inside the Olympics.* Montreal: Wiley & Sons.

Power, S., & Allison, G.T. (Eds.). (2000). *Realizing human rights: Moving from inspiration to impact.* New York: St. Martin's Press.

Powers, J. (1993, February 21). New world borders. *Boston Globe Magazine,* 8-9.

Price, S.L. (2005, May 23). The sprinter. *Sports Illustrated, 102,* 52-61.

Reeve, S. (2000). *One day in September.* New York: Arcade Publishing.

Roberts, R. (2001a, July 30). For China's economic reformers, the 2008 Olympics are gold. *Business Week,* p. 49.

Roberts, K. (2001b, October). Crisis, what crisis? *SportBusiness International,* 36-39.

Roberts, K. (2001c, November). Olympian ambitions? *SportBusiness International,* 35-37.

Roberts, K. (2004a, March). The shape of things to come. *SportBusiness International,* pp. 32 -33.

Roberts, K. (2004b, February). Olympic security will come at a price. *SportBusiness International,* 53.

Robson, D. (2001). Just do...something. *Business Week,* pp. 70-71.

Rubinfeld, A., & Hemingway, C. (2005). *Built for growth: Expanding your business around the corner or across the globe.* Upper Saddle River, NJ: Wharton School Publishing.

Schenkler, M. (2000). *Politics and the Olympic dream.* Retrieved March 25, 2006, from www.queenspress.com/archives/nfp/2000/issue20/nfp.htm.

Schoenfeld, B. (2005, April 25-May 1). Forstmann's IMG: What's next. *Street & Smith's SportsBusiness Journal,* pp. 1, 8-9.

Simson, V., & Jennings, A. (1992). *Dishonored games: Corruption, money, & greed at the Olympics.* New York: SPI Books.

Smith, A., & Westerbeek, H. (2004). *The sport business future.* London: Palgrave Macmillan.

Smith, G. (1992, June 15). A few pieces of silver. *Sports Illustrated, 76,* 64-75.

The sport and environment commission. (2006). Retrieved April 2, 2006, from www.olympic.org/uk/organisation/commissions/environment/index_uk.asp.

Symonds, W.C. (2001, July 9). Guess who wants Beijing to get the Games: Straight talk from a sponsor. *Business Week,* p. 48.

Szymanski, S., & Zimbalist, A. (2005). *National pastime: How Americans play baseball and the rest of the world plays soccer.* Washington, DC: Brookings Institution Press.

Terroux, G., & Brodeur, D. (1972). *Face-off of the century: Canada–USSR.* Montreal: Collier-Macmillan.

Thoma, J.E., & Chalip, L. (1996). *Sport governance in the global community.* Morgantown, WV: Fitness Information Technology.

Ueberroth, P. (1985). *Made in America.* New York: William Morrow.

Ungerleider, S. (2001). *Faust's gold: Inside the East German doping machine.* New York: St. Martin's Press.

United States Olympic Committee. (2005). *2001 fact book.* Colorado Springs, CO: Author.

Wallechinsky, D. (2004). *The complete book of the summer Olympics.* Toronto: Sport Media Publications.

Warfield, S. (2005, March 21-27). Selling soccer. *Street & Smith's SportsBusiness Journal,* pp. 33-34.

Weiler, P.C., & Roberts, G.R. (2004). *Sports and the law: Text, cases, problems* (3rd ed.). St. Paul, MN: West.

Weir, T. (2006, February 18). Cheek's charity for a cause. *USA Today,* p. 1D.

Westerbeek, H., Smith, A., Turner, P., Emery, P., Green, C., & van Leeuwen, L. (2005). *Managing sport facilities and major events.* Melbourne: Allen & Unwin.

Westerbeek, H., & Smith, A. (2003). *Sport business in the global marketplace.* London: Palgrave/Macmillan.

Wharton, D. (2002). *Eye on the storm.* Associated Press Sports Editors. Retrieved April 1, 2006, from http://apse.dallasnews.com/contest/2002/writing/over250/over250.enterprise.second1a.html.

Who's wearing the trousers? (2001, September 8). *The Economist,* 360, 26-28.

Wilson, J. (1994). *Playing by the rules: Sport, society, and the state.* Detroit, MI: Wayne State University Press.

Wise, M. (2005, May 29). Ginobili heads list of Argentina's big shots. *Boston Globe,* p. C7.

Woodward, S., & Muret, D. (2005, April 25-May 1). Changing with the times: Sport facilities overseas shift more emphasis to the spectator experience. *Street & Smith's SportsBusiness Journal,* pp. 17-22.

Yao, M. (with Bucher, R.). (2004). *Yao: A life in two worlds.* New York: Miramax.

Chapter 9—Sport Marketing

Associated Press (2006, February 2). NCAA not backing down on Indian mascots: Despite resistance, restriction on use meant to protect values, Brand says. retrieved on February 21, 2006 from http://msnbc.msn.com/id/11151463.

Armstrong, K.L. (1998). Ten strategies to employ when marketing sport to Black consumers. *Sport Marketing Quarterly, 7*(3), 11-18.

Armstrong, K.L. (2001). Creating multicultural sport spectating experiences: Marketing the sociology of sport consumption. *International Journal of Sport Management, 2*, 183-204.

Armstrong, K.L. (2002). An examination of the social psychology of Blacks' consumption of sport. *Journal of Sport Management, 16*, 267-288.

Barbano, S. (1998, February/March). Women's sports market perspective: Women as spectators of men's sports. *Women's Sport Market Report, 3*(1), 1, 8.

Berfield, S., Brady, D., & Lowry, T. (2003, October 27). The CEO of Hip-Hop. [Electronic version] *Business Week*. Retrieved July 12, 2005, from www.keepmedia.com.

Bernstein, A. (1999). Study: Hispanic tastes are varied, strong. *Street & Smith's SportsBusiness Journal, 2*, 7.

Brooks, C.M. (1994). *Sports marketing: Competitive business strategies for sports*. Englewood Cliffs, NJ: Prentice Hall.

Broughton, D., Lee, J., & Nethery, R. (1999, December 20). The answer: $213 billion. *Street & Smith's SportsBusiness Journal, 2*, 23, 26.

Covey, S.R. (1989). *The seven habits of highly effective people*. New York: Simon and Schuster.

DeSensi, J.T. (1994). Multiculturalism as an issue in sport management. *Journal of Sport Management, 8*, 63-74.

Dyson, M.E. (1996). *Race rules: Navigating the color line*. Reading, MA: Addison-Wesley.

Francese, P. (1990). How to manage consumer information. In D. Crispell (Ed.), *The insider's guide to demographic know-how* (pp. 9-14). Ithaca, NY: American Demographics Press.

Fullerton, R.A. (1988). How modern is modern marketing? Marketing's evolution and the myth of the production era. *Journal of Marketing, 52(1),* 108-125.

Gardyn, Rebecca, "Putting the 'World' in the World Series," American Demographics (April, 2000).

Gray, D.P. (1996). Sport marketing: A strategic approach. In B.L. Parkhouse (Ed.), *The management of sport: Its foundation and application* (pp. 249-289). St. Louis, MO: Mosby.

Grunig, J.E., & White, R. (1992). Communication, public relations and effective organizations. In J.E. Grunig (Ed.), *Excellence in public relations and communications management*. Hillsdale, NJ: Erlbaum.

Hall, M. (2002, August 19-25). Taking the sport out of sports. *Street & Smith's SportsBusiness Journal* (p. 23).

Hardy, S. (1990). Adopted by all the leading clubs: Sporting goods and the shaping of leisure, 1800-1900. In R. Butsch (Ed.), *For Fun and Profit: The transformation of leisure into consumption* (pp. 71-101). Philadelphia: Temple University Press.

Hofacre, S., & Burman, T.K. (1992). Demographic changes in the U.S. into the twenty-first century: Their impact on sport marketing. *Sport Marketing Quarterly, 1*(1), 31-36.

Laczniak, G., Burton, R., & Murphy, P. (1999). Sport marketing ethics in today's marketplace. *Sport Marketing Quarterly, 8*(4), 43-53.

Lopiano, D. (2000). *Marketing trends in women's sports and fitness*. Women's Sports Foundation. www.lifetimetv.com/search/frameset/shtm

McCarthy, L.M., & Stillman, W.P. (1998). Marketing sport to Hispanic consumers. *Sport Marketing Quarterly, 7*(4), 19-24.

McCarville, R.E., & Copeland, R.P. (1994). Understanding sport sponsorship through exchange theory. *Journal of Sport Management, 8*, 102-114.

McLeod, K. (1999). Authenticity within hip-hop and other cultures threatened with assimilation. *Journal of Communications, 49*(4), 134-150.

Midol, N. (1998). Rap and dialectical relations. Culture, subculture, power, and counter-powered. In R. Genevieve (Ed.), *Sport and postmodern times* (pp. 333-343). Albany, NY: State University of New York Press.

Mullin, B.J., Hardy, S., & Sutton, W.A. (2000). *Sport marketing*. (2nd ed.). Champaign, IL: Human Kinetics.

Murphy, E. (2004, July 2-4). NASCAR takes a female turn. *USA Today*, pp. 1A-2A.

Pitts, B.G., Fielding, L.W., & Miller, L.K. (1994). Industry segmentation theory and the sport industry: Developing a sport industry segmentation model. *Sport Marketing Quarterly, 3*(1), 15-24.

Pitts, B.G., & Stotlar, D.K. (2002). *Fundamentals of sport marketing* (2nd ed.). Morgantown, WV: Fitness Information Technology.

Pons, F., Larouche, M., Nyeck, S., & Perreault, S. (2001). Role of sport events as ethnocultural emblems: Impact of acculturation and ethnic identity on consumers' orientations toward sporting events. *Sport Marketing Quarterly, 10*(4), 231-240.

Rowe, A.J., Mason, R.O., & Dickel, K.E. (1986). *Strategic management: A methodological approach*. New York: Addison-Wesley.

Shank, M.D. (2005). *Sports marketing: A strategic perspective* (3rd ed.). Upper Saddle River, NJ: Pearson Education.

Sutton, W.A., & Wattlington, R. (1994). Communicating with women in the 1990s: The role of sport marketing. *Sport Marketing Quarterly, 3*(2), 9-14.

Turco, D.M. (1996). The X Factor: Marketing sports to Generation X. *Sport Marketing Quarterly, 5*(1), 21-24.

Chapter 10—Sport Consumer Behavior

Accenture. (n.d.). *Print advertising.* Retrieved January 20, 2006, from www.accenture.com.sa/Global/About_Accenture/Company_Overview/Advertising/PrintAdvertising.htm.

Baldinger, A.L., & Rubinson, J. (1996). Brand loyalty: The link between attitude and behavior. *Journal of Advertising Research, 36*(6), 22-34.

Brustad, R.J. (1996). Parental and peer influence on children's psychological development through sport. In F.L. Smoll & R.E. Smith (Eds.), *Children and youth in sport: A biopsychosocial perspective* (pp. 112-124). Madison, WI: Brown & Benchmark.

Burnett, J., Menon, A., & Smart, D.T. (1993). Sports marketing: A new ball game with new rules. *Journal of Advertising Research, 33*(5), 21-33.

Cialdini, R.B., Borden, R.J., Thorne, A., Walker, M.R., Freeman, S., & Sloan, L.R. (1976). Basking in reflected glory: Three (football) field studies. *Journal of Personality and Social Psychology, 34*, 366-375.

de Mooij, M.K. (2004). *Consumer behavior and culture: Consequences for global marketing and advertising.* Thousand Oaks, CA: Sage.

Detroit Super Bowl XL Host Committee (n.d.). Retrieved January 20, 2006, from www.sbxl.org/events.

FFToolbox.com LLC. (2006). *How to play fantasy football.* Retrieved June 13, 2006, from www.fftoolbox.com/how_to_play.cfm.

F1 Marketing Group, Inc. (2005). *Home page.* Retrieved June 13, 2006, from www.speedgear.com.

Formula 1. (n.d.). *Home page.* Retrieved June 13, 2006, from www.formula1.com.

Formulapod.com. (n.d.). *Home page.* Retrieved June 13, 2006, from www.formulapod.com.

Grand Prix Supporters Association. (n.d.). *Home page.* Retrieved June 13, 2006, from www.fosagold.org.

Green, B.C. (1996). A social learning approach to youth sport motivation: Initial scale development and validation (Doctoral dissertation, University of Maryland, 1996). *Dissertation Abstracts International, 60.*

Horn, T.S., & Weiss, M.R. (1991). A developmental analysis of children's self-ability judgements in the physical domain. *Pediatric Exercise Science, 3*, 310-326.

Jenkins, C. (2000, March 13). Caught in gambling's web: Colleges fear students easy targets for Internet sports betting sites. *USA Today*, p. 1C.

Kardes, F.R. (2002). *Consumer behavior and managerial decision making* (2nd ed.). Upper Saddle River, NJ: Prentice Hall.

Kerstetter, D.L., & Kovich, G.M. (1997). An involvement profile of Division I women's basketball spectators. *Journal of Sport Management, 11*, 234-249.

Major League Soccer. (2005). *MLS announces team award winners.* Retrieved January 20, 2006, from www.mlsnet.com/MLS/news/mls_events_news.jsp?ymd=20051109&content_id=47822&vkey=mlscuppr2005&fext=.jsp.

Mara, J. (2000). The halo effect. *Brandweek, 41*(20), 86-88.

McDonald, M.G. (2000). The marketing of the Women's National Basketball Association and the making of postfeminism. *International Review for the Sociology of Sport, 35*, 35-47.

Milne, G.R., Sutton, W.A., & McDonald, M.A. (1996). Niche analysis: A strategic measurement tool for managers. *Sport Marketing Quarterly, 5*(3), 17-22.

OuterQuest. (n.d.). Home page. Retrieved August 12, 2005, from www.outerquest.com.

Park, C.W., & Mittal, B. (1985). A theory of involvement in consumer behavior: Problems and issues. *Research in Consumer Behavior, 1*, 201-231.

Racing-Live S.A. (n.d.). *Home page.* Retrieved June 13, 2006, from http://f1racing-live.com/f1.

Raudsepp, L., & Viira, R. (2000). Sociocultural correlates of physical activity in adolescents. *Pediatric Exercise Science, 12*, 51-60.

Roberts, G.C. (Ed.). (1992). *Motivation in sport and exercise.* Champaign, IL: Human Kinetics.

Rogers, M.H. (2000, August). Playing with family values: The attractions of minor league baseball. *Stadia, 4*, 34-38.

Shamir, B. (1992). Some correlates of leisure identity salience: Three exploratory studies. *Journal of Leisure Research, 24*, 301-323.

Sirgy, M.J. (1986). *Self-congruity: Toward a theory of personality and cybernetics.* New York: Praeger.

Snyder, C.R., Lassegard, M., & Ford, C.E. (1986). Distancing after group success and failure: Basking in reflected glory and cutting off reflected failure. *Journal of Personality and Social Psychology, 51*, 382-388.

Soccer Industry Council of America (2005). *National soccer participation survey.* North Palm Beach, FL: Author.

Solomon, M.R. (2002). *Consumer behavior: Buying, having, and being* (5th ed.). Upper Saddle River, NJ: Prentice Hall.

Sportvac Plus Inc. (2006). Home page. Retrieved June 13, 2006, from http://formulatours.com.

Stone, G. (1981). Sport as a community representation. In G.R.F. Lüschen & G.H. Sage (Eds.), *Handbook of social science of sport* (pp. 214-245). Champaign, IL: Stipes.

Sutton, W.A., McDonald, M.A., Milne, G.R., & Cimperman, J. (1997). Creating and fostering fan identification in professional sports. *Sport Marketing Quarterly, 6*, 15-22.

Turner, V. (1986). *The anthropology of performance.* New York: PAJ.

Wann, D.L., Melnick, M.J., Russell, G.W., & Pease, D.G. (2001). *Sport fans: The psychology and social impact of spectators.* New York: Routledge.

Whiting, R. (1989). *You gotta have wa.* New York: Vintage.

Chapter 11—Public Relations in the Sport Industry

Arrington, D. (2005, June 23). Sponsors race to hitch ride to NASCAR's run to riches. *The Sacramento Bee*. Sacramento, CA: Author. Retrieved July 7, 2005, from www.sacbee.com/content/sports/motor/v-print/story/13112493p-13956956c.html.

Associated Press (2003, August 14). Source: Sunoco is NASCAR's new fuel. *Sporting News*. New York: Sporting News. Retrieved July 7, 2005, from www.sportingnews.com/nascar/articles/20030814/487927.html.

Battenfield, F. (2005, June). *Using an ethnography of communication to investigate a paradigmatic change in the communications culture in a Division I-A sports information office*. Paper presented at the meeting of the North American Society for Sport Management, Regina, Saskatchewan, Canada.

BBC. (2002, May 27). Newspapers top reading survey. London: Author. Retrieved June 12, 2006 from http://news.bbc.co.uk/2/hi/uk_news/2009746.stm.

Betts, J.R. (1953). The technological revolution and the rise of sport, 1850-1900. The *Mississippi Valley Historical Review*, *40*(2), 231-256.

Broadcasting and cable yearbook. (2001). New Providence, NJ: Bowker.

Canadian Newspaper Association. (2006). *Newspaper readership remains stable in 2004*. Toronto, Ontario, Canada: Author. Retrieved January 31, 2006, from www.cna-acj.ca/client/can/can.nsf/web/FactsReadership.

Central Intelligence Agency. (2006a, January 10). *Field listing—television broadcast stations*. Washington, DC: Author. Retrieved February 1, 2006, from www.cia.gov/cia/publications/factbook/fields.2015.html.

Central Intelligence Agency. (2006b, January 10). *Field listing—radio broadcast stations*. Washington, DC: Author. Retrieved February 1, 2006, from www.cia.gov/cia/publications/factbook/fields.2013.html.

Communications today. (2001, December 20). *World Wide Web turns 10*. Retrieved February 1, 2006, from www.telecomweb.com/cgi/pub/tnd/ct/2001/ct12200111.html.

Cutlip, S.M., Center, A.H. & Broom, G.M. (2000). *Effective public relations* (8th ed.). Englewood Cliffs, NJ: Prentice Hall.

Dallas Stars. (2000). *Community report*. Arlington, TX: Author.

Deeter, W.R. (1993). Great communicators: The growing importance of corporate communications. In B.J. Morgan (Ed.), *Public relations career directory* (5th ed.) (pp. 53-58). Detroit, MI: Gale Research.

Eastman Kodak Company. (2004, June 22). *Kodak's NASCAR sponsorship spotlights women's health*. Rochester, NY: Author. Retrieved July 7, 2005, from www.kodak.com/US/en/corp/pressReleases/pr20040622-01.shtml.

GlaxoSmithKline. (2005, June 26). *GSK Healthcare races towards NASCAR sponsor history again*. Pittsburgh, PA: Author. Retrieved July 7, 2005, from www.gsk.com/ControllerServlet?appId=4&pageId=402&newsid=596.

Gregory, H. (2005). *Public speaking for college and career* (7th ed.). New York: McGraw-Hill.

Grunig, J.E., & Hunt, T. (1984). *Managing public relations*. New York: Holt, Rinehart and Winston.

Helitzer, M. (2000). *The dream job: $port$ publicity, promotion and marketing* (3rd ed.). Athens, OH: University Sports Press.

Holtz, S. (1999). *Public relations on the net*. New York: American Management Association.

Hopwood, M.K. (2004, September 22-25). Public relations practice in English county cricket: A case study of Durham County Cricket Club and Yorkshire County Cricket Club. *Proceedings of the 12th EASM European Sport Management Congress*. Ghent, Flanders, Belgium: Publicatiefonds voor Lichamelijke Opvoeding vzw. (Hopwood's proceedings, pp. 188-190).

Isidore, C. (2005, April 22). *NFL's rights might*. Atlanta, GA: Cable News Network. Retrieved February 1, 2006, from http://money.cnn.com/2005/04/22/commentary/column_sportsbiz/sportsbiz/index.htm.

Jackowski, M. (2000, October 2-8). Repair, rebuild relationships with your community. *Street & Smith's SportsBusiness Journal*, pp. 40-41.

James Madison University. (2004, July 29). *New research center's first subject: NASCAR sponsorship*. Harrisonburg, VA: Author. Retrieved January 25, 2006, from www.jmu.edu/jumweb/general/news/general4092.shthml.

Leonard, W.M., II. (1998). *A sociological perspective of sport* (5th ed.). Needham Heights, MA: Allyn and Bacon.

Lesly, P. (1998). The nature and role of public relations. In P. Lesly (Ed.), *Lesly's handbook of public relations and communications* (5th ed.) (pp. 3-18). Lincolnwood, IL: NTC Contemporary.

Liberman, N. (2001, June 25-July 1). Once-hot Web hits a cool spell. *Street & Smith's SportsBusiness Journal*, p. 44.

Matuszewski, E. (2000). Tangled Web. *College Sports Information Directors of America Digest*, *50*(2), 7.

McLuhan, M. (1966). *Understanding media: The extensions of man*. New York: McGraw-Hill.

Modestino, L. (2005). *TV times for 6/17-19/05*. MotorSportsNews.net. Covington, KY: Author. Retrieved July 7, 2005, from http://motorsportsnews.net/lm20050615.html.

The money in racing. (2003, September 8). *ThatsRacin.com*. San Jose, CA: Author. Retrieved July 8, 2005 from www.thatsracin.com/mld/thatsracin/sports/special_packages/money/6708615.htm.

Mullin, B.J., Hardy, S., & Sutton, W.A. (2000). *Sport marketing* (2nd ed.). Champaign, IL: Human Kinetics.

National Telecommunications and Information Administration (2004). *A nation online: Entering the broadband age*. Washington, DC: US Department of Commerce. Retrieved March 9, 2005, from www.ntia.doc.gov/reports/anol/NationOnlineBroadband04.htm.

New Balance. (2001). *Community involvement: Giving guidelines*. Boston: Author. Retrieved February 12, 2002, from www.newbalance.com/aboutus/cmnty/guidelines.html.

Newspaper Association of America. (2004a). *U.S. daily and Sunday newspaper readership audience*. Vienna, VA: Author. Retrieved March 9, 2005, from www.naa.org/info/facts04/readership-audience.html.

Newspaper Association of America. (2004b). *U.S. daily newspaper pages or sections usually read*. Vienna, VA: Author. Retrieved March 9, 2005, from www.naa.org/info/facts04/readership-sections.html.

Nichols, W., Moynahan, P., Hall, A., & Taylor, J. (2002). *Media relations in sport*. Morgantown, WV: Fitness Information Technology.

Peak, B. (1998). Community relations. In P. Lesly (Ed.), *Lesly's handbook of public relations and communications* (5th ed.) (pp. 113-136). Lincolnwood, IL: NTC Contemporary.

Schoenfeld, B. (1999, September 27-October 3). Vikings take issue with journalism's new speed. *Street & Smith's SportsBusiness Journal*, p. 21.

Schoenfeld, B. (2000, November 20-26). Snyder, Skins take charity to a new level. *Street & Smith's SportsBusiness Journal*, p. 24.

Schramm, W. (1954). How communication works. In W. Schramm (Ed.), *The process and effects of mass communication* (pp. 3-26). Urbana: University of Illinois Press.

Severin, W.J., & Tankard, J.W., Jr. (1997). *Communication theories: Origins, methods and uses in the mass media* (4th ed.). White Plains, NY: Longman.

Smith, R.D. (2002). *Strategic planning for public relations*. Mahwah, NJ: Lawrence Erlbaum Associates.

SportsBusiness Journal/ESPN Sports poll. (2001, June 11-17). *Street & Smith's SportsBusiness Journal*, p.13.

Stoldt, G.C. (2000). Current and ideal organizational roles of NCAA Division I-A sports information professionals. *The Cyber-Journal of Sport Marketing, 4*(1). Retrieved May 24, 2000, from www.cjsm.com/vol4.stoldt41.htm.

Stoldt, G.C, Dittmore, S.W., & Branvold, S.E. (2006). *Sport public relations: Managing organizational communication*. Champaign, IL: Human Kinetics.

Street & Smith's Sports Group (2005). *Street & Smith's Sports Group upcoming conferences*. Retrieved July 7, 2005, from www.sportsbusinessjournal.com/index.cfm?fuseaction=page.feature&featureId=1485.

US Census Bureau. (2004). Statistical abstract of the United States: 2004-2005 (124th ed.). Washington, D.C.: Author.

Verve Sponsorship Group. (2005). *Mission*. Atlanta, GA: Author. Retrieved July 7, 2005 from www.vervesg.com.

World Almanac. (2002). *Internet basics*. Mahweh, NJ: Primedia Reference. Retrieved January 17, 2002, from OCLC FirstSearch database at http://newfirstsearch.oclc.org.

Chapter 12—Finance, Economics, and Budgeting in the Sport Industry

2001 MLB profits and losses. (2001). Retrieved May 31, 2005, from http://espn.go.com/mlb/s/2001/1205/1290765.html.

2005 salaries. (2005). Retrieved May 15, 2005, from http://cbs.sportsline.com/mlb/salaries/avgsalaries.

About YES Network. (2005). Retrieved May 31, 2005, from www.yesnetwork.com/network/aboutyes.asp.

Ballparks.com. (2005). *PETCO Park*. Retrieved May 1, 2005, from www.ballparks.com/baseball/index.

Bernstein, A. (2004, February 23-29). Daly: Shutdown blots red ink. *Street & Smith's SportsBusiness Journal*, p. 43.

Bernstein, A. (2005, August 22). "NHL rights put OLN in big leagues." *Street & Smith's SportsBusiness Journal,* 1.

Broughton, D., Lee, J., & Nethery, R. (1999, December 20-26). The answer: $213 billion. *Street & Smith's SportsBusiness Journal*, pp. 23, 26.

By the numbers: The authoritative annual research guide and fact book (2004). *Street & Smith's SportsBusiness Journal 6(36)*.

CBS gets tourney for 11 more years. (1999). Retrieved June 6, 2005, from http://espn.com/ncb/news/1999/1118/178535.html.

East Tennessee State preps for finale. (2003, August 23). Retrieved May 1, 2005, from www.sportingnews.com//cfootball/articles/20030823/489123.html.

Fulks, D.L. (2005). *Revenues and expenses of Divisions I and II intercollegiate athletic programs report*. Retrieved August 20, 2006, http://www2.ncaa.org/portal/media_and_events/ncaa_publications/research/index.html#revenues.

Hiestand, M. (1999, November 19). CBS locks in college hoops for $545M. *USA Today*, p. C1.

Howard, D.R., & Crompton, J.L. (1995). *Financing sport*. Morgantown, WV: Fitness Information Technology.

Howard, D.R., & Crompton, J.L. (2004). *Financing sport* (2nd ed.). Morgantown, WV: Fitness Information Technology.

IEG. (2002). 2003 spending to rise as sponsors ask for, receive more for their money. *Sponsorship Report, 21*(24), 1, 4-5.

Kaplan, D. (2000, December 18-24). Pats' tab for stadium is highest ever. *Street & Smith's SportsBusiness Journal*, pp. 1, 48.

Keat, P.G., & Young, P.K. (2000). *Managerial economics: Economic tools for today's decision makers* (3rd ed.). Upper Saddle River, NJ: Prentice Hall.

Keat, P.G., & Young, P.K. (2003). *Managerial economics: Economic tools for today's decision makers* (4th ed.). Upper Saddle River, NJ: Prentice Hall.

Keating, G. (2004, November 8). *NFL extends CBS, Fox broadcast rights for $8bln*. Retrieved December 22,

2004, from http://abcnews.go.com/Entertainment/wireStory?id=237270.

Kress, A., & Sunnucks, M. (2003, December 12). Valley could reap $150 million from bowl game. *The Business Journal Phoenix.* Retrieved May 30, 2006, from www.bizjournals.com/phoenix/stories/2003/12/15/story6.html.

Lee, J. (2001, September 10-16). Football fuels the gravy train at the top. *Street & Smith's SportsBusiness Journal*, pp. 21, 23, 28.

Mahony, D.F., & Howard, D.R. (2001). Sport business in the next decade: A general overview of expected trends. *Journal of Sport Management*, 15, 275-296.

Meek, A. (1997). An estimate of the size and supported economic activity of the sports industry in the United States. *Sport Marketing Quarterly*, *6*, 15-21.

MLB News. (2005). Retrieved June 22, 2005, from http://roadsidephotos.com/baseball/97-2news.htm.

Mock, E.J., Schultz, R.E., Shultz, R.G., & Shuckett, D.H. (1968). *Basic financial management: Text, problems, and cases*. Scranton, PA: International Text.

NCAA. (2001). *2001 NCAA annual report*. Retrieved May 31, 2005, from www.ncaa.org NFL on television. (2006). *Wikipedia*. Retrieved January 23, 2006, from http://en.wikipedia.org/wiki/NFL_on_television.

NFL on television. (2006). Wikipedia. Retrieved January 23, 2006, from http://en.wikipedia.org/wiki/NFL_on_television.

Ozanian, M.K. (2005a). *The business of football*. Retrieved June 6, 2005, from www.forbes.com/sport/2004/09/01/04nfland.html.

Ozanian, M.K. (2005b). *The business of baseball*. Retrieved June 6, 2005, from www.forbes.com/business/2005/04/06/05mlbland.html.

Porter, P. (2001). Super Bowl impact figures a super stretch. *Street & Smith's SportsBusiness Journal*, p. 31.

Rishe, P. (2001). *Economic impact report: 2001 NCAA Division I Women's Basketball Final Four*. Retrieved April 15, 2005, from www.sportsimpacts.com.

Rovell, D. (2003, May 21). Sources: Lebron, Nike agree to seven year deal. *USA Today*. Retrieved January 23, 2006, from http://espn.go.com/nba/news/2003/0521/1557489.html.

Stadiums and arenas under construction. (2002, March 4-10). *Street & Smith's SportsBusiness Journal*, pp. 24-25.

Taylor, J.B. (2001). *Economics*. Boston: Houghton Mifflin.

Turco, D.M., & Kelsey, C.W. (1992). *Conducting economic impact studies of recreational and parks special events*. Arlington, VA: National Recreation & Park Association.

US Bureau of Economic Analysis. (2005). *Real gross domestic product, chained dollars*. Retrieved May 20, 2005, from www.bea.gov/bea/dn/nipaweb/TableView.asp#Mid.

US Census Bureau. (2005). *Statistical abstract of the United States: 2004-2005*.

Zimbalist, A. (1999). *Unpaid professionals: Commercialism and conflict in big-time college sports*. Princeton, NJ: Princeton University Press.

Zimmerman, D. (1997). Subsidizing stadiums: Who benefits, who pays? In R.G. Noll & A. Zimbalist (Eds.), *Sports, jobs and taxes*. Washington, DC: Brookings Institution Press.

Chapter 13—Sport Facility and Event Management

Abernethy, B. (2004, November) Worst-case scenarios. *Stadia*. Retrieved November 27, 2004, from www.stadia.tv/archive/user/news_article.tpl?id=20041124173315.

Ammon, R., Jr., & Fried, G. (1998). Assessing stadium crowd management practices and liability issues. *Journal of Convention & Exhibition Management*, *1*(2-3), 119-150.

Ammon, R., Jr., Southall, R., & Blair, D. (2004). *Sport facility management: Organizing events and mitigating risks*. Morgantown, WV: Fitness Information Technology.

Ammon, R., Jr., & Unruh, N. (2003). Crowd management. In D.J. Cotton & J.T. Wolohan (Eds.), *Law for recreation and sport managers* (3rd ed., pp. 352-362). Dubuque, IA: Kendall/Hunt.

Amsterdam ArenA hosts mock terrorist attack. (2005, April). *Stadia*. Retrieved April 11, 2005, from www.stadia.tv/archive/user/news_article.tpl?id=20050408112335.

Aramark hit with another $75M charge in drunk-driving case. (2005, January 20). *Sports Business Daily*. Retrieved January 21, 2005, from http://sportsbuisnessdaily.com/index.cfm?fuseaction+sbd.main&storyID=SBD2005012013.

Baugus, R.V. (2002, January/February). Roskilde organizers learn from 2000 tragedy. *Facility Manager*, *18*(1), 24, 26.

Cameron, S. (2001, December 17-23). Tales from Europe: Scottish dilemma, naked truth, and indoor windsurfing. *Street & Smith's SportsBusiness Journal*, p. 19.

Court overturns $105 million ruling against beer vendor. (2006, August 3). Retrieved August 7, 2006 from http://sports.espn.go.com/espn/print?id=2538373&type+story.

David, A. (2006). *Olympics security costs at $107 million so far*. Retrieved February 5, 2006, from http://sports.yahoo.com/olympics/torino2006/news?slug=ap-turin-security&prov=ap&type=lgns.

Deckard, L. (2004, April). Bedeviling the competition. *VenuesToday*, *3*(4), 13-14.

Deckard, L. (2005a, January 19). Keynoter stresses customer service to ticketing professionals. *VenuesToday*, *4*(3), 2-3.

Deckard, L. (2005b, June 8). Promoting good sportsmanship is an operational issue at most colleges. *VenuesToday*, *4*(19), 6-7.

Deckard, L. (2005c, June 15). USC Trojans ban beer sales in stadium. *VenuesToday, 4*(19), 14-15.

Deckard, L. (2005d, June 23). SMG adds Idaho Center to its stable. *VenuesToday, 4*(20), 4-5.

Farmer, P., Mulrooney, A., & Ammon, Jr., R. (1996). *Sport facility planning and management.* Morgantown, WV: Fitness Information Technology.

Hiestand, M., & Woods, S. (2001, December 19). Fan conduct rises on NFL agenda: Some see violence at recent games as precursor to soccer-style hooliganism. *USA Today*, p. 3A.

Kurokawa, K. (2001, November). Opening eyes. *Stadia*, 26-30.

Launch of online security initiative for international stadia. (2005, January). *Stadia*. Retrieved January 10, 2005, from www.stadia.tv/archive/user/news_article.tpl?id=20050110162214.

Nagy, T.M. (2001). *Customer service in professional sport.* Unpublished master's project, Bowling Green State University, Bowling Green, OH.

On this day. (n.d.). *1989: Crushed to death.* Retrieved June 14, 2006, from http://news.bbc.co.uk/onthisday/hi/witness/april/15/newsid_2913000/2913355.stm.

Sherborne, P. (2005, January 19). Turner Field will get some new toys, including record-setting video. *VenuesToday, 4*(3), 6-7.

Simonich, M., & Srikameswaran, A. (2005, May 8). A peaceful panic at PNC Park. *Pittsburgh Post-Gazette*, pp. A1, A6.

Staff. (2005, November). *Stadia*'s sampling of major news stories. *Stadia*, 4-5.

Steadman, G., Neirotti, L.D., & Goldblatt, J.J. (2001). *The ultimate guide to sports marketing.* New York: McGraw-Hill.

Steinbach, P. (2004, August). Special operations. *Athletic Business, 28*(8), 24-28.

Supovitz, F. (2005). *The sports event management and marketing playbook.* Hoboken, NJ: Wiley.

This year in *SportsBusiness*: Stories of the year. (December 26, 2005-January 1, 2006). *Street & Smith's SportsBusiness Journal*, pp. 12-29.

Warshaw, A. (2004, March). Making a stand. *Stadia*, 12-14.

Yanchulis, D. (2005, December/January). Improving accessibility and compliance under the ADA and ABA. *Facility Manager, 20*(6), 16, 63.

Chapter 14—Managing Sport Organizations

Agudo, Y. (2004). Factores gerenciales que han influido en el rendimiento deportivo de los atletas venezolanos en los juegos olímpicos 1984 al 2004. Unpublished master's thesis. Universidad Pedagógica Experimental Libertador, Caracas, Venezuela.

Armstrong, K.L. (2002). An examination of the social psychology of Blacks' consumption of sport. *Journal of Sport Management, 16*, 267-288.

Armstrong, K.L., & Stratta, T.M.P. (2004). Market analyses of race and sport consumption. *Sport Marketing Quarterly, 13*, 7-16.

Bello, P. (1977). *Prospectiva del deporte en Venezuela.* Venezuela: Universidad de Carabobo. Valencia, Colorado.

Caza, A. (2000). Context receptivity: Innovation in an amateur sport organization. *Journal of Sport Management, 14*, 227-242.

Chalip, L. (1995). Policy analysis in sport management. *Journal of Sport Management, 9*, 1-13.

Chelladurai, P. (2005). *Managing organizations for sport and physical activity* (2nd ed.). Scottsdale, AZ: Holcomb Hathaway.

Colyer, S. (2000). Organizational culture in selected western Australian sport organizations. *Journal of Sport Management, 14*, 321-341.

Crompton, J.L. (1997). Partnering with business: What's in it for them? *Journal of Park and Recreation Administration, 15*(4), 38-60.

Crompton, J.L. (1998a). Programs that work. Force underlying the emergence of privatization in parks and recreation. *Journal of Park and Recreation Administration, 16*(2), 88-101.

Crompton, J.L. (1998b). Partnering: The complementary assets of businesses and park and recreation agencies. *Journal of Park and Recreation Administration, 16*(4), 73-94.

Cousens, L., Babiak, K.M., & Slack, T. (2001). Adopting a relationship marketing paradigm: The case of the National Basketball Association. *International Journal of Sports Marketing and Sponsorship, 2*, 331-355.

Cunningham, G.B. (2002). Examining the relationship among Miles and Snow's strategic types and measures of organizational effectiveness in NCAA Division I athletic departments. *International Review for the Sociology of Sport, 37*(2), 159-175.

Cunningham, G.B., & Fink, J.S. (2006). Diversity issues in sport and leisure: Introduction to a special issue. *Journal of Sport Management, 20*, tdb.

Cunningham, G.B., & Sagas, M. (2004). Racial differences in occupational turnover intent among NCAA Division I-A assistant football coaches. *Sociology of Sport Journal, 21*, 84-92.

Daft, R.L. (1998). *Organization theory and design* (6th ed.). Cincinnati, OH: Thomson South-Western.

Daft, R.L. (2007). *Organization theory and design* (9th ed.). Mason, OH: Thomson South-Western.

Dass, P., & Parker, B. (1999). Strategies for managing human resource diversity: From resistance to learning. *The Academy of Management Executive, 13*(2), 68-80.

Frisby, W., Thibault, L., & Kikulis, L.M. (2004). The organizational dynamics of under-managed partnerships in leisure service departments. *Leisure Studies, 23*, 109-126.

Jones, G.R. (2004). *Organizational theory, design, and change. Text and cases.* Upper Saddle River, NJ: Pearson Prentice Hall.

Jones, G.R., George, J.M., Hill, C.W.L., & Langton, N. (2002). *Contemporary management* (1st Canadian ed.). Toronto: McGraw-Hill Ryerson.

Kikulis, L.M., Slack, T., & Hinings, C.R. (1992). Institutionally specific design archetypes: A framework for understanding change in national sport organizations. *International Review for the Sociology of Sport, 27*, 343-370.

Kikulis, L.M., Slack, T., & Hinings, C.R. (1995). Sector specific patterns of organizational design change. *Journal of Management Studies, 32*, 67-100.

Legg, D. (2003). Organizational strategy in amateur sport organization: A case study. *International Journal of Sport Management, 4*, 205-223.

Machado, R. (1990). *Gerencia Deportiva*. Caracas, Venezuela: Editorial Miranda.

Matton, J.N., & Hernandez, C.M. (2004). A new study identifies the "makes and breaks" of diversity initiatives. *Journal of Organizational Excellence, 23*, 47-58.

Milton-Smith, J. (2002). Ethics, the Olympics and the search for global values. *Journal of Business Ethics, 35*, 131-142.

Mintzberg, H. (1979). *The structuring of organizations*. Englewood Cliffs, NJ: Prentice Hall.

Mintzberg, H. (1994). *The rise and fall of strategic planning*. New York: The Free Press.

Mintzberg, H. & Quinn, J.B. (1991). *The strategy process. Concepts, contexts, cases* (2nd ed.). Englewood Cliffs, NJ: Prentice Hall.

Olberding, D.J. (2003). Examining strategy content in U.S. Olympic sport organizations. *International Journal of Sport Management, 4*, 6-24.

Papadimitriou, D. (2001). An exploratory examination of the prime beneficiary approach of organisational effectiveness: The case of elite athletes of Olympic and non-Olympic sports. *European Journal of Sport Management, 8*, 63-82.

Pettigrew, A.M. (1987). Context and action in the transformation of the firm. *Journal of Management Studies, 24*, 649-670.

Pettigrew, A.M. (1990). Longitudinal field research on change: Theory and practice. *Organization Science, 1*, 267-292.

Pettigrew, A.M., Ferlie, E., & McKee, L. (1992). *Shaping strategic change. Making change in large organizations. The case of the National Health Service*. London: Sage.

Putler, D., & Wolfe, R. (1999). Perceptions of intercollegiate athletic programs: Priorities and tradeoffs. *Sociology of Sport Journal, 16*, 301-325.

Quinn, R.E., & Spreitzer, G.M. (1991). The psychometrics of the competing values culture instrument and an analysis of the impact of organizational culture on quality of life. *Research in Organizational Change and Development, 5*, 115-142.

Sack, A.L., & Nadim, A. (2002). Strategic choices in a turbulent environment: A case study of Starter Corporation. *Journal of Sport Management, 16*, 36-53.

Schein, E.H. (1985). *Organizational culture and leadership*. San Francisco: Jossey-Bass.

Scott, D.K. (1997). Managing organizational culture in intercollegiate athletic organizations. *Quest, 49*, 403-415.

Slack, T., & Parent, M.M. (2006). *Understanding sport organizations. The application of organization theory* (2nd ed.). Champaign, IL: Human Kinetics.

Theodoraki, E.I. (2001). A conceptual framework for the study of structural configurations of Organising Committees for the Olympic Games (OCOGs). *European Journal for Sport Management, 8*, 106-124.

Theodoraki, E.I., & Henry, I.P. (1994). Organisational structures and contexts in British national governing bodies of sport. *International Review for the Sociology of Sport, 29*, 243-268.

Thibault, L., & Babiak, K. (2005). Organizational changes in Canada's sport system: Toward an athlete-centred approach. *European Sport Management Quarterly, 5*, 105-132.

Thibault, L., Frisby, W., & Kikulis, L.M. (1999). Interorganisational linkages in the delivery of local leisure services in Canada: Responding to economic, political, and social pressures. *Managing Leisure: An International Journal, 4*, 125-141.

Thibault, L., Kikulis, L.M., & Frisby, W. (2004). Partnerships between local government sport and leisure departments and the commercial sector: Changes, complexities, and consequences. In T. Slack (Ed.), *The commercialization of sport* (pp. 119-140). Essex, UK: Frank Cass.

Thibault, L., Slack, T., & Hinings, C.R. (1993). A framework for the analysis of strategy in nonprofit sport organizations. *Journal of Sport Management, 7*, 25-43.

Thibault, L., Slack, T., & Hinings, C.R. (1994). Strategic planning for nonprofit sport organizations: The empirical verification of a framework and location of strategic types. *Journal of Sport Management, 8*, 218-233.

Trail, G., & Chelladurai, P. (2000). Perceptions of goals and processes of intercollegiate athletics: A case study. *Journal of Sport Management, 14*, 154-178.

Wolfe, R., Hoeber, L., & Babiak, K. (2002). Perceptions of the effectiveness of sport organisations: The case of intercollegiate athletics. *European Sport Management Quarterly, 2*, 135-156.

Wolfe, R., & Putler, D. (2002). How tight are the ties that bind stakeholder groups? *Organization Science, 13*, 64-80.

Zeigler, E.F. (1987). Sport management: Past, present, future. *Journal of Sport Management, 1*, 4-24.

Chapter 15—Managerial and Leadership in Sport Organizations

Avolio, B.J., Waldman, D.A., & Yammarino, F.J. (1991). Leading in the 1990's: The Four I's of transformational leadership. *Journal of European Industrial Training, 15*, 9-16.

Ayman, R., Chemers, M.M., & Fielder, F. (1995). The contingency model of leadership effectiveness: Its levels of analysis. *The Leadership Quarterly, 6*, 147-167.

Bass, B.M. (1985). *Leadership and performance beyond expectations.* New York: Free Press.

Bass, B.M. (1991, August). Is there universality in the full range of model leadership? Paper presented at the annual meeting of the Academy of Management, Miami, FL.

Bass, B.M., & Avolio, B.J. (1994). *Improving organizational effectiveness through transformational leadership.* Thousand Oaks, CA: Sage.

Bass, B.M., & Stogdill, R.M. (1990). *Bass & Stogdill's handbook of leadership: Theory, research, and managerial applications* (3rd ed.). New York: Free Press.

Bennett, G., & Hardin, B. (2002). Management behaviors of an elite intercollegiate baseball coach. *International Journal of Sport Management, 3*, 199-214.

Bennis, W., & Nanus, B. (1985). *Leaders: The strategies for taking charge.* New York: Harper & Row.

Blake, R.R., & McCanse, A.A. (1991). *Leadership dilemmas: Grid solutions.* Houston, TX: Gulf.

Blake, R.R., & Mouton, J.S. (1985). *The managerial grid III: A key to leadership excellence* (3rd ed.). Houston, TX: Gulf.

Bourner, F., & Weese, W.J. (1995). Executive leadership and organizational effectiveness in the Canadian Hockey League. *European Journal for Sport Management, 2*(1), 88-100.

Branch, D. (1990). Athletic director leader behavior as a predictor of intercollegiate athletic organizational effectiveness. *Journal of Sport Management, 4*, 161-173.

Broughton, D., Lee, J., & Nethery, R. (1999, December 20-26). The answer: $213 billion. *Street & Smith's SportsBusiness Journal*, pp. 23, 26.

Burns, J.M. (1978). *Leadership.* New York: Harper & Row.

Danylchuk, K.E., & Chelladurai, P. (1999). The nature of managerial work in Canadian intercollegiate athletics. *Journal of Sport Management, 13*, 148-166.

Doherty, A.J. (1997). The effect of leader characteristics on the perceived transformational/transactional leadership and impact of interuniversity athletic administrators. *Journal of Sport Management, 11*, 275-285.

Doherty, A.J., & Danylchuk, K.E. (1996). Transformational and transactional leadership in interuniversity athletics management. *Journal of Sport Management, 10*, 292-309.

Evans, M.G. (1970). The effects of supervisory behavior on the path-goal relationship. *Organizational Behavior and Human Performance, 5*, 277-298.

Fiedler, F.E. (1967). *A theory of leadership effectiveness.* New York: McGraw-Hill.

Glueck, W.F. (1980). *Management* (2nd ed.). Hinsdale, IL: Dryden Press.

Gulick, L., & Urwick, L. (1937). *Papers on the science of administration.* New York: Institute of Public Administration.

Hersey, P., & Blanchard, P. (1969). The life cycle theory of leadership. *Training and Development Journal, 23*(5), 26-34.

Hersey, P., Blanchard, K.H., & Johnson, D.E. (2001). *Management of organizational behavior: Leading human resources* (8th ed.). Upper Saddle River, NJ: Prentice Hall.

Herzberg, R. (1966). *Work and the nature of man.* Cleveland, OH: World.

House, R.J. (1971). A path goal theory of leader effectiveness. *Administrative Science Quarterly, 16*, 321-338.

House, R.J., & Mitchell, T.R. (1974). Path-goal theory of leadership. *Journal of Contemporary Business, 3*, 81-97.

House, R.J., & Mitchell, T.R. (1997). Path-goal theory of leadership. In R.P. Vecchio (Ed.), *Leadership: Understanding the dynamics of power and influence in organizations* (pp. 259-273). Notre Dame, IN: University of Notre Dame Press.

Katz, R.L. (1974). Skills of an effective administrator. *Harvard Business Review, 52*(5), 90-102.

Katz, D., & Kahn, R. (1978). *The social psychology of organizations* (2nd ed.). New York: Wiley.

Kent, A., & Chelladurai, P. (2001). Perceived transformational leadership, organizational commitment, and citizenship behavior: A case study in intercollegiate athletics. *Journal of Sport Management, 15*, 135-159.

Kent, A., & Weese, W.J. (2000). Do effective organizations have better executive leaders and/or organizational cultures? A study of selected sport organizations in Canada. *European Journal for Sport Management, 7*(2), 4-21.

Kerr, S., Hill, K.D., & Broedling, L. (1986). The first line supervisor: Phasing out or here to stay? *Academy of Management Review, 11*, 103-117.

Kirkpatrick, S.A., & Locke, E.A. (1991). Leadership: Do traits matter? *Academy of Management Executive, 5*(2), 48-60.

Koontz, H., O'Donnell, C., & Weihrich, H. (1984). *Management* (8th ed.). New York: McGraw-Hill.

Kotter, J.P. (1990). What leaders really do. *Harvard Business Review, 68*(3), 103-111.

Kumagai, B.T., & Kleiner, B.H. (1995). Managing the transition to supervision. *Work Study, 44*(1), 8-10.

Labich, K. (1988). The seven keys to business leadership. *Fortune, 118*(9), 58-62, 64, 66.

Likert, R. (1961). *New patterns of management.* New York: McGraw-Hill.

London, C., & Boucher, R. (2000). Leadership and organizational effectiveness in Canadian university athletics. *International Journal of Sport Management, 1*, 70-87.

Maslow, A.H. (1954). *Motivation and personality.* New York: Harper.

Mayo, E. (1933). *The human problems of an industrial civilization.* New York: MacMillan.

McCrae, R.R., & Costa, P.T. (2003). *Personality in adulthood: A five-factor theory perspective* (2nd ed.). New York: Guilford Press.

McGregor, D. (1960). *The human side of enterprise.* New York: McGraw Hill.

Mintzberg, H. (1973). *The nature of managerial work.* New York: Harper & Row.

Mintzberg, H. (1990). The manager's job: Folklore and fact. *Harvard Business Review, 68*(2), 163-176. (Reprinted from *Harvard Business Review, 53*(1), pp. 49-61, 1975).

Northouse, P.G. (2004). *Leadership theory and practice.* Thousand Oaks, CA: Sage.

Pavett, C.M., & Lau, A.W. (1983). Managerial work: The influence of hierarchical level and functional speciality. *Academy of Management Journal, 26*, 170-177.

Petit, T.A. (1975). *Fundamentals of management coordination: Supervisors, middle managers, and executives.* New York: Wiley.

Pruijn, G.H.J., & Boucher, R.L. (1995). The relationship of transactional and transformational leadership to the organizational effectiveness of Dutch National Sport Organizations. *European Journal for Sport Management, 2*(1), 72-87.

Quarterman, J. (1994). Managerial role profiles of intercollegiate athletic conference commissioners. *Journal of Sport Management, 8*, 129-139.

Quarterman, J. (1998). An assessment of the perception of management and leadership skills by intercollegiate athletics conference commissioners. *Journal of Sport Management, 12*, 146-164.

Quarterman, J., Allen, L., & Becker, A. (2005). Managerial roles of intercollegiate athletics directors of the NAIA: The Mintzberg model. *International Journal of Sport Management, 6*, 165-182.

Slack, T., & Parent, M.M. (2006). *Understanding sport organizations: The application of organization theory.* Champaign, IL: Human Kinetics.

Snyder, C.J. (1990). The effects of leader behavior and organizational climate on intercollegiate coaches' job satisfaction. *Journal of Sport Management, 4*, 59-70.

Soucie, D. (1994). Effective managerial leadership in sport organizations. *Journal of Sport Management, 8*, 1-13.

Stogdill, R.M. (1974), *Handbook of leadership: A survey of theory and research.* New York: Free Press.

Straw, B.M. (1986). Organizational psychology and the pursuit of the happy/productive worker. *California Management Review, 2,* 40-53.

Taylor, F.W. (1911). *The principles of scientific management.* New York: Harper.

Wallace, M., & Weese, W.J. (1995). Leadership, organizational culture, and job satisfaction in Canadian YMCA organizations. *Journal of Sport Management, 9*, 182-193.

Weese, W.J. (1995). Leadership and organizational culture: An investigation of Big Ten and Mid-American Conference campus recreation administrations. *Journal of Sport Management, 9*, 119-134.

Weese, W.J. (1996). Do leadership and organizational culture really matter? *Journal of Sport Management, 10*, 197-206.

Weisman, L. (1993, November 29). Tagliabue likes to see big picture. *USA Today*, pp. 1C-2C.

Wofford, J.C. (1982). *Organizational behavior: Foundations for organizational effectiveness.* Boston: Kent Publishing Company.

Yukl, G. (1989). Managerial leadership: A review of theory and research. *Journal of Management, 15*, 251-289.

Chapter 16—Legal Considerations in Sport Management

Alford, D. (2000, August 7). Pregame prayer barred. *Christianity Today, 44*(9), 19-20.

Americans with Disabilities Act of 1990, 42 USCA § 12101 et seq. (West, 1993).

Batista, P. (2002). Balancing the First Amendment's Establishment and Free Exercise Clauses: A rebuttal to Alexander & Alexander. *Journal of Legal Aspects of Sport, 12*(2), 87-116.)

Black, M.A. (1990). *Black's law dictionary* (6th ed). St. Paul, MN: West.

The closet atheist. (n.d.). Retrieved September 18, 2005, from www.geocities.com/closetatheist/stats.htm.

MacLeod, L. (2000, September). School prayer and religious liberty: A Constitutional perspective. *CWA Library.* Retrieved September 18, 2005, from www.cwfa.org/articledisplay.asp?id=1266&department=CWA&categoryid=freedom.

Mauro, T. (2000). *Supreme Court bans student-led prayer at football games.* Retrieved September 18, 2005, from www.freedomforum.org/templates/document.asp?documentID=12727.

Moorman, A., & Eickhoff-Shemeck, J.M. (2005). The legal aspects: Is obesity a disability under the Americans with Disabilities Act? *ACSM's Health & Fitness Journal, 9*(1), 1-3.

Myers, D.G. (2000). On assessing prayer, faith, and health [Electronic version]. *Reformed Review, 53*(2), 119-126.

Pederson v. Louisiana State University, 213 F.3d 858 (5th Cir. 2000).

Public schools and religion. (2000, January 15-22). *America, 182*(2), 3.

Restatement (Second) of Torts (1963).

Rosenbloom v. Metromedia, 403 U.S. 29 (1971).

Santa Fe Independent School District v. Doe, 530 U.S. 290 (2000).

Shapo, H.S., Walter, M.R., & Fajans, E. (1999). *Writing and analysis in the law* (4th ed.). New York: Foundation Press.

Sport Agent Responsibility and Trust Act, 15 U.S. { 7801 et seq. 2005.

Ted Stevens Olympic and Amateur Sports Act, 36 USC § 220501 et seq. (2005).

Teply, L.L. (1999). *Legal research and citation*. St. Paul, MN: West Group.

Title IX of the Education Amendments of 1972, 20 USC § 1681-1688 (1990).

Thompson, D.P., & Edmonson, S.L. (2002). Policy alternatives for student pre-activity and graduation messages in light of *Santa Fe ISD v. Doe*. *West's Education Law Reporter, 163*, 541-550.

US Constitution, 1st Amendment.

US Constitution, 14th Amendment.

van der Smissen, B. (2004). Legal liability and risk management for public and private entities (2nd ed.). Cincinnati, OH: Anderson.

Walsh, M. (2001, January 17). Public sees role for religion in schools. *Education Week, 20*(18), 13-17.

Wilde, T.J. (2001). State action. In D.J. Cotton, J.T. Wolohan, & T.J. Wilde (Eds.), *Law for recreation and sport managers* (pp. 415-426). Dubuque, IA: Kendall Hunt.

Chapter 17—Ethical Considerations

Agarwal, J., & Malloy, D.C. (2000). The role of existentialism in ethical business decision-making. *Business Ethics: A European Review, 9*, 143-154.

Bellah, R. Madesen, R., Sullivan, W., Swidler, A., & Tipton, S. (1985). *Habits of the heart: Individualism and commitment in American life.* Berkely: University of California Press.

Bellah, R. Madesen, R., Sullivan, W., Swidler, A., & Tipton, S. (1991). *The good society.* New York: Knopf.

Browne, M.N., & Keeley, S. (2007). *Asking the right questions: A guide to critical thinking* (6th ed.). Upper Saddle River, NJ: Prentice Hall.

DeSensi, J.T., & Rosenberg, D. (2003). *Ethics and morality in sport management* (2nd ed.). Morgantown, WV: Fitness Information Technology.

Frankena, W. (1973). *Ethics* (2nd ed.). Englewood Cliffs, NJ: Prentice Hall.

Heidegger, M. (1962). *Being and time* (J. Macquarrie and E. Robinson, Trans.). New York: Harper & Row.

Heidegger, M. (1966). *Discourse on thinking.* New York: Harper & Row.

Hodgkinson, C. (1983). *The philosophy of leadership.* Oxford: Basil Blackwell.

Hodgkinson, C. (1996). *Administrative philosophy: Values and motivations in administrative life.* Oxford: Pergamon.

Kierkegaard, S. (1975). The first existentialist. In W. Kaufmann (Ed.), *Existentialism from Dostoevsky to Sartre* (pp. 83-121). New York: Times Mirror.

Kohlberg, L. (1984). *The psychology of moral development.* New York: Harper & Row.

Korsmeyer, C. (2002). Seeing, believing, touching, truth. In W. Irwin (Ed.) *The Matrix and Philosophy* (pp. 41-52). Chicago: Open Court.

Kretchmar, R.S. (2005). *Practical philosophy of sport and physical activity* (2nd ed.). Champaign, IL: Human Kinetics.

Lumpkin, A., Stoll, S.K., & Beller, J.M. (2003). *Sport ethics: Applications for fair play* (3rd ed.). New York: McGraw-Hill.

MacIntyre, A. (1984). *After virtue* (2nd ed.). Notre Dame, IN: University of Notre Dame Press.

Malloy, D.C. (2003). Understanding the nature of ethics, values, and purposes of business, health care, and law: Implications and applications for community sport. In *The sport we want: Essays on current issues in community sport in Canada* (pp. 59-79). Ottawa, Ontario, Canada: Canadian Centre for Ethics in Sport.

Malloy, D.C., Ross, S., & Zakus, D.H. (2003). *Sport ethics: Concepts & cases in sport and recreation* (2nd ed.). Toronto, Ontario, Canada: Thompson Educational.

Morgan, W.J., Meier, K.V., & Schneider, A.J. (Eds.). (2001). *Ethics in sport.* Champaign, IL: Human Kinetics.

Morris, W. (1885). *Useful work versus useless toil.* Retrieved October 4, 2005, from www.anglocatholicsocialism.org/work.html.

Nietzsche, F. (1886a/1992). Beyond good and evil: Prelude to a philosophy of the future. In *Basic writings of Nietzsche* (W. Kaufmann, Trans.) (pp. 179-436). New York: The Modern Library.

Nietzsche, F. (1886b/1992). On the geneology of morals. In *Basic writings of Nietzsche* (W. Kaufmann, Trans.) (pp. 437-600). New York: The Modern Library.

Rinehart, J.W. (1987). *The tyranny of work: Alienation and the labour process.* Toronto, Ontario, Canada: Harcourt Brace Jovanovich.

Rokeach, M. (1973). *The nature of human values.* New York: The Free Press.

Sartre, J. (1957). *Existentialism and human emotions.* New York: The Wisdom Library.

Sartre, J. (1966). *Being and nothingness.* New York: Washington Square Press.

Sartre, J. (1975). Existentialism and humanism. In W. Kaufman (Ed.). *Existentialism From Dostoevsky to Sartre* (pp. 345-369). New York: Times Mirror.

Singer, P. (1995). *How are we to live? Ethics in an age of self-interest.* Amherst, NY: Prometheus Books.

Tetsushi, F. (1988). Watsuji Tetsuro, the man and his work (G. Bownas, Trans.). In W. Tetsuro, *Climate and culture* (p. 228). New York: Greenwood Press.

Zeigler, E.F. (2002). *Who knows what's right anymore? A guide to personal decision-making.* Victoria, British Columbia, Canada: Trafford.

Chapter 18—Sociological Aspects of Sport

ABC News Internet Ventures. (2006). *Basketbrawl anniversary highlights changes.* Retrieved November 19, 2005, from www.abcnews.go.com/GMA/print?id=1328687.

Acosta, R.V., & Carpenter, L.J. (1988). *Perceived causes of the declining representation of women leaders in intercollegiate sports: 1988 update*. Unpublished manuscript, Brooklyn College, Brooklyn, NY.

Acosta, R.V., & Carpenter, L.J. (2006). *Women in intercollegiate sport: A longitudinal, national study, 29 year update, 1977-2006*. Retrieved February 11, 2006, from http://webpages.charter.net/womeninsport.

Andersen, M.B. (2001). When to refer athletes for counseling or psychotherapy. In J.M. Williams (Ed.), *Applied sport psychology: Personal growth to peak performance* (4th ed.) (pp. 401-415). Mountain View, CA: Mayfield.

Anderson, E. (2005). *In the game: Gay athletes and the cult of masculinity*. Albany: State University of New York Press.

Anderson, K. (2001, May-June). Starving to win. *Sports Illustrated for Women*, pp. 88-95.

Ashe, A. (1977, February 6). Send your children to the libraries. *New York Times*, p. 2S.

Beck, E. (2002, February 26). *Report: 2002 NCAA National Convention*. Retrieved July 13, 2005, from www.smia-online.org.

Benedict, J. (2004). *Out of bounds: Inside the NBA's culture of rape, violence, and crime*. New York: HarperCollins.

Bernstein, A. (2005a, April 25-May 1). NFL restores NBC's clout. *Street & Smith's SportsBusiness Journal*, pp. 32-33.

Bernstein, A. (2005b, January 31-February 6). Word on the street: "Jimmy's hanging tough." *Street & Smith's SportsBusiness Journal*, pp. 26-28.

Brennan, C. (2005, March 24). *Survey says: E-mails no way to judge Title IX*. Retrieved June 15, 2005, from www.usatoday.com/sports/columnist/brennan/2005-03-24-brannan-title-IX_x.htm.

Bryant, J., Zillmann, D., & Raney, A.A. (1998). Violence and the enjoyment of media sports. In L.A. Wenner (Ed.), *MediaSport* (pp. 252-265). London: Routledge.

Buffington, D. (2005). Contesting race on Sundays: Making meaning out of the rise in the number of Black quarterbacks. *Sociology of Sport Journal, 22*, 19-37.

Burstyn, V. (1999). *The rites of men: Manhood, politics and the culture of sport*. Toronto, Ontario, Canada: University of Toronto Press.

Buysse, J.M., & Embser-Herbert, M.S. (2004). Constructions of gender in sport: An analysis of intercollegiate media guide cover photographs. *Gender and Society, 18*(1), 66-81.

Buzinski, J. (2004, January 27). *Florida settles with lesbian athlete*. Retrieved July 13, 2005, from www.outsports.com/campus/20040227zimbardisettlement.htm.

Campbell, R. (2004). *2001-02 national women's college basketball attendance*. Retrieved August 16, 2004, from www.ncaa.org/stats/w_basketball/attendance/2001-02/#top.

Carpenter, L.J., & Acosta, R.V. (2005). *Title IX*. Champaign, IL: Human Kinetics.

Christopherson, N., Janning, M., & McConnell, E.D. (2002). Two kicks forward, one kick back: A content analysis of media discourses on the 1999 women's world cup soccer championship. *Sociology of Sport Journal, 19*, 170-188.

Coakley, J.J. (1993). Social dimensions of intensive training and participation in youth sports. In B.R. Cahill & A.J. Pearl (Eds.), *Intensive participation in children's sport* (pp. 77-94). Champaign, IL: Human Kinetics.

Coakley, J.J. (2001). *Sport in society: Issues and controversies* (7th ed.). Boston: WCB McGraw-Hill.

Coakley, J.J. (Ed.) (2004). *Sport in society: Issues and controversies* (8th ed.). New York: McGraw-Hill Higher Education.

Curry, T.J. 1998. Beyond the locker room: Campus bars and college athletes. *Sociology of Sport Journal, 15*, 205-215.

Davis, L. (1997). *The swimsuit issue and sport: Hegemonic masculinity in* Sports Illustrated. Albany: State University of New York Press.

de Jong, A. (2005, April 13). *Fighting an image: Female athletes must face lesbian stereotypes in so-called masculine sports*. Retrieved July 13, 2005, from www.dailybruin.ucla.edu/news/articles.asp?ID=32759.

Donlan, F. (2005, March 16). *Style-challenged Sox get "Queer Eye" fashion help*. Retrieved July 21, 2005, from www.usatoday.com/sports/baseball/al/redsox/2005-03-15-queer-eye_x.htm.

Duncan, M.C., & Messner, M.A. (2005). *Gender in televised sports: News and highlights shows, 1989-2004*. Retrieved July 20, 2005, from www.aafla.org/9arr/ResearchReports/tv2004.pdf.

Duncan, M.C., Messner, M.A., & Cookey, C. (2000). *Gender in televised sports: 1989, 1993 and 1999*. Retrieved August 15, 2004, from www.aafla.org/9arr/ ResearchReports/tv2000.pdf.

Eastman, S.T., & Billings, A.C. (2000). Sportscasting and sports reporting: The power of gender bias. *Journal of Sport & Social Issues, 24*, 192-213.

Eitzen, D.S. (1999). *Fair and foul: Beyond the myths and paradoxes of sport*. Lanham, MD: Rowman & Littlefield.

Eitzen, D.S., & Sage, G.H. (2003). *Sociology of North American sport* (7th ed.). New York: McGraw-Hill Higher Education.

ESPN.com Page 2. (2001, June 3). *Outside the lines: The gay dilemma*. Retrieved November 14, 2001, from http://sports.espn.go.com/page2/tvlistings/show62transcript.html.

Everhart, C.B., & Chelladurai, P. (1998). Gender differences in preferences for coaching as an occupation: The role of self-efficacy, valence, and perceived barriers. *Research Quarterly for Exercise and Sport, 69*, 188-200.

Fink, J.S., & Kensicki, L.J. (2002). An imperceptible difference: Visual and textual constructions of femininity in *Sports Illustrated* and *Sports Illustrated for Women*. *Mass Communication & Society, 5*, 317-339.

Flagrant fouls. (2004, November 22). *USA Today*, p. 14a.

Galst, L. (1998, October 26). The sports closet. *Ms.*, *9*(2), 74-78.

Gettings, J. (2002). *Olympics: Civil disobedience*. Retrieved February 4, 2002, from www.infoplease.com/spot/mm-mexicocity.html.

Greenberg, W. (2005, January 10). *Female coaches in short supply, despite Title IX gains: Ursinius symposium to address shortage*. Retrieved July 11, 2005, from www.collegenews.org/x4047.xml.

Greendorfer, S. (2001). Gender role stereotypes and early childhood socialization. In G.L. Cohen (Ed.), *Women in sport: Issues and controversies* (2nd ed.) (pp. 3-23). Reston, VA: National Association for Girls and Women in Sport.

Griffin, P. (1992). Changing the game: Homophobia, sexism and lesbians in sport. *Quest*, *44*, 251-265.

Griffin, P. (1998). *Strong women, deep closets*. Champaign, IL: Human Kinetics.

Griffin, P. (2001). Homophobia in women's sports: The fear that divides us. In G.L. Cohen (Ed.), *Women in sport: Issues and controversies* (2nd ed.) (pp. 279-290). Reston, VA: National Association for Girls and Women in Sport.

Hasbrook, C.A., Hart, B.A., Mathes, S.A., & True, S. (1990). Sex bias and the validity of believed differences between male and female interscholastic athletic coaches. *Research Quarterly for Exercise and Sport*, *63*, 259-267.

Hughson, J. (2001). 'The Wogs are at it again': The media reportage of Australian soccer 'riots.' *Football Studies*, *4*(1), 40-55.

Iannotta, J., & Kane, M.J. (2002). Sexual stories as resistance narratives in women's sports: Reconceptualizing identity performance. *Sociology of Sport Journal*, *19*, 347-369.

Jones, R. (2004, March 21). *Backtalk: First, a word about me and my sponsor*. Retrieved July 21, 2005, from http://query.nytimes.com/search/restricted/article?res=F10E14F93A550C728EDDAA0894DC404482.

Kane, M.J. (2001). Leadership, sport, and gender. In S.J.M. Freeman, S.C. Bourque, & C.M. Shelton (Eds.), *Women on power: Leadership redefined* (pp. 114-146). Boston: Northeastern University Press.

Kane, M.J., & Buysse, J.A. (2005). Intercollegiate media guides as contested terrain: A longitudinal analysis. *Sociology of Sport Journal*, *22*, 214-238.

Kane, M.J., & Disch, L J. (1993). Sexual violence and the reproduction of male power in the locker room: The "Lisa Olson incident." *Sociology of Sport Journal*, *10*, 331-352.

Kane, M.J., & Lenskyj, H.J. (1998). Media treatment of female athletes: Issues of gender and sexualities. In L. Wenner (Ed.), *MediaSport: Cultural sensibilities and sport in the media age* (pp. 186-201). London: Routledge.

Kramer, S.D. (2005, May 2-8). Making choices: Ad buyers direct their dollars to the right mix of broadcast and cable programming. *Street & Smith's SportsBusiness Journal*, pp. 17-20.

Krane, V. (2001). We can be athletic and feminine, but do we want to? Challenging hegemonic femininity in women's sport. *Quest*, *53*, 115-133.

Krane, V., & Barber, H. (2005). Identity tensions in lesbian intercollegiate coaches. *Research Quarterly for Exercise and Sport*, *76*(1), 67-81.

Lapchick, R. (2005a). *The 2004 racial and gender report card: A comprehensive analysis of the hiring practices of the National Basketball Association, National Football League, Major League Baseball, Major League Soccer, Women's National Basketball Association, and College Sport*. Retrieved June 17, 2006, from Central Florida University, Institute for Diversity and Ethics in Sport Website: www.bus.ucf.efu/sport/cgibin/site/sitew.cgi?page=/ides/index.htx.

Lapchick, R. (2005b). *The 2004 racial and gender report card: College sports*. Retrieved June 17, 2006, from Central Florida University, Institute for Diversity and Ethics in Sport Website: www.bus.ucf.edu/sport/cgi-bin/site/sitew.cgi?page=/ides/index.htx.

Lapchick, R., (with Stacy Martin). (2006a). *The 2005 racial & gender report card: Major League Baseball*. Retrieved June 17, 2006, from Central Florida University, Institute for Diversity and Ethics in Sport Website: www.bus.ucf.edu/sport/cgi-bin/site/sitew.cgi?page=/ides/index.htx.

Lapchick, R., (with Stacy Martin). (2006b). *The 2005-06 season racial & gender report card: National Basketball Association*. Retrieved June 17, 2006, from Central Florida University, Institute for Diversity and Ethics in Sport Website: http://www.bus.ucf.edu/sport/cgi-bin/site/sitew.cgi?page=/ides/index.htx.

Lumpkin, A., & Williams, L.D. (1991). *An analysis of sports illustrated feature articles, 1954-1987*. *Sociology of Sport Journal*, *8*, 16-32.

Lynch, R. (1991). Disorder on the sidelines of Australian sport. *Sporting Traditions*, *8*(1), 50-75.

Messner, M.A., & Stevens, M.A. (2002). Scoring without consent: Confronting male athletes' violence against women. In M. Gatz, M.A. Messner, & S.J. Ball-Rokeach (Eds.), *Paradoxes of youth and sport* (pp. 225-240). Albany: State University of New York Press.

Messner, M.A., Dunbar, M., & Hunt, D. (2000). The televised sports manhood formula. *Journal of Sport & Social Issues*, *24*(4), 380-394.

Metheny, E. (1965). *Connotations of movement in sport and dance*. Dubuque, IA: Brown.

Murphy, S. (2005). *The dark side of youth sports*. Retrieved July 11, 2005, from www.momsteam.com/alpha/features/cheersandtears/dark_side2.shtml.

National Association of Anorexia Nervosa and Associated Disorders (NAANAD). (2005). *Facts about eating disorders*. Retrieved July 11, 2005, from www.anad.org/site/anadweb/content.php?type=1&id=6982.

National Federation of State High School Athletic Associations (2005). *2004-05 NFHS high school athletics participation survey*. Retrieved February 20, 2006, from www.nfhs.org/scriptcontent/VA_Custom/SurveyResources/2004-05_Participation_Summary.pdf.

Poynting, S. (2005). Bulldog whistling: Criminalization of young Lebanese-Australian Rugby League fans. *Internet Journal of Criminology*. Retrieved June 19, 2006, from www.internetjournalofcriminology.com/Poynting%20-%20Bulldogwhistling.pdf.

Pronger, B. (1999). Outta my endzone: Sport and the territorial anus. *Journal of Sport & Social Issues, 23*(4), 373-389.

Ray, B. (1996, January 26). Unforgiven: Passage of time can't hide NU's problems. *Daily Nebraskan Online*. Retrieved July 17, 2002, from www.unl.edu/DailyNeb.arch/zzzzz/1-96/1-26-96/opinion/ray.html.

Ryan, J. (2000). *Little girls in pretty boxes: The making and breaking of elite gymnasts and figure skaters*. New York: Warner Books.

Sabo, D., & Grant, C.H.B. (June 2005). *Limitations of the Department of Education's online survey method for measuring athletic interest and ability on U.S.A. campuses*. Retrieved January 30, 2006, from www.dyc.edu/crpash/limits_of_online_survey.pdf.

Samuels, C.A. (2005). *Title IX guidance "problematic," critics say*. [Electronic version]. Retrieved June 15, 2005, from www.edweek.org/ew/articles/2005/03/30/29titleix.h24.html.

Sands, R.R. (Ed.). (1999). *Anthropology, sport, and culture*. Westport, CT: Bergin & Garvey.

Schmid, P. (2003, October 15). *Women to discuss homophobia in women's sports tonight*. Retrieved July 13, 2005, from www.nclrights.org/projects/sp-startribune101503.htm.

Shaw, S., & Hoeber, L. (2003). "A strong man is direct and a direct woman is a bitch": Gendered discourses and their influence on employment roles in sport organizations. *Journal of Sport Management, 17*(4), 347-375.

Snyder, E. (1990). Sociology of sport. In J.B. Parks & R.K. Zanger (Eds.), *Sport and fitness management* (pp. 213-222). Champaign, IL: Human Kinetics.

Sporting Goods Manufacturers Association (SGMA). (2001, May 1). *New survey: 54% of US youngsters play organized sports*. Retrieved December 20, 2001, from www.sgma.com/press/2001/press988721108-30622.html.

Stangl, J.M., & Kane, M.J. (1991). Structural variables that offer explanatory power for the underrepresentation of women coaches since Title IX: The case of homologous reproduction. *Sociology of Sport Journal, 8*, 47-60.

Suggs, W. (2005). *A place on the team: The triumph and tragedy of Title IX*. Princeton, NJ: Princeton University Press.

Theberge, N. (2000). *Higher goals: Women's ice hockey and the politics of gender*. Albany: State University of New York Press.

Tuaolo, E., & Cyphers, L. (2002, October 30). *Free and clear*. Retrieved July 13, 2005, from http://espn.go.com/magazine/vol5no23tuaolo.html.

Turner, B.A., & Chelladurai, P. (2005). Organizational and occupational commitment, intention to leave, and perceived performance of intercollegiate coaches. *Journal of Sport Management, 19*(2), 193-211.

Vamplew, W. (1994) Violence in Australian soccer: The ethnic contribution. *Australian Society for Sports History: Studies in Sports History, 7*, 1-15.

Wellman, S., & Blinde, E.M. (1997). Homophobia in women's intercollegiate basketball: Views of women coaches regarding coaching careers and recruitment of athletes. *Women in Sport and Physical Activity Journal, 6*, 63-82.

Williams, J.M. (Ed.). (2001). *Applied sport psychology: Personal growth to peak performance* (4th ed.). Mountain View, CA: Mayfield.

Women in Higher Education. (2004, August 16). *NCAA to run women coaches academy*. Retrieved July 11, 2005, from www.findarticles.com/p/articles/mi_m0KSO/is_9_13/ai_n6332305/print.

Women's Sports Foundation. (2005). *Her life depends on it: Sport, physical activity and the health and well-being of American girls*. Retrieved July 20, 2005, from www.womenssportsfoundation.org/binary-data/WSF_ARTICLE/pdf_file/990.pdf.

Woodward, J.R. (2004). Professional football scouts: An investigation of racial stacking. *Sociology of Sport Journal, 21*, 356-375.

WUSA Players' Association. (2004). *About WUSA*. Retrieved August 15, 2004, from http://wusa.com/about.

Chapter 19—Questions, Answers, and Sport Management Research

Alexander, D.L., & Kern, W. (2005). Drive for show and putt for dough? An analysis of the earnings of PGA Tour golfers. *Journal of Sports Economics, 6*, 46-60.

Argyris, C., & Schon, D. (1991). Participatory action research and action science compared: A commentary. In W.F. Write (Ed.), *Participatory action research*. Newbury Park, CA: Sage.

Armstrong, K.L., & Peretto Stratta, T.M. (2004). Market analyses of race and sport consumption. *Sport Marketing Quarterly, 13*, 7-16.

Baca, L.R. (2004). Native images in schools and the racially hostile environment. *Journal of Sport & Social Issues, 28*, 71-78.

Barros, C.P. (2003). Incentive regulation and efficiency in sport organizational training activities. *Sport Management Review, 6*, 33-52.

Barton, J. (2000, September). Courses & travel: Great destinations. *Golf Digest*. Retrieved June 17, 2005, from www.golfdigest.com/courses/travel/index.ssf?/courses/great_de_36dq0ibc.html.

Berri, D.J., Schmidt, M.B., & Brook, S.L. (2004). Stars at the gate: The impact of star power on NBA gate revenues. *Journal of Sports Economics, 5*, 33-50.

Bodley, H. (2005, April 7). Annual salary survey: MLB teams armed and ready. *USA Today*. Retrieved June 17, 2005, from www.usatoday.com/sports/baseball/salaries/2005-04-06-pitching-increase_x.htm.

Chang, K., & Chelladurai, P. (2003). Comparison of part-time workers and full-time workers: Commitment and citizenship behaviors in Korean sport organizations. *Journal of Sport Management, 17*, 394-417.

Chelladurai, P. (2006). *Human resource management in sport and recreation* (2nd ed.). Champaign, IL: Human Kinetics.

Cohen, W., Cook, G.G., Daniel, M., Friedman, D., Gest, T., Goode, E.E., et al. (1993, October 25). Beyond 1993: From dream swapping to virtual shopping, the way it will be in 2053. *U S News & World Report, 115*, 70-80.

Costa, G., Tsitskari, E., Tzetzis, G., & Goudas, M. (2004). The factors for evaluating service quality in athletic camps: A case study. *European Sport Management Quarterly, 4*, 22-35.

Council of American Survey Research Organizations. (2002). *Taking responsibility for the future*. Retrieved September 6, 2002, from www.casro.org.

Crompton, J.L. (1995). Economic impact analysis of sports facilities and events: Eleven sources of misapplication. *Journal of Sport Management, 9*, 14-35.

Dew Action Sports Tour (2006, April 11). *About the Dew Action Sports Tour general information: Overview*. Retrieved August 16, 2006, from www.dewactionsports-tour.com/modules.php?name=content&pa=showpage&pid=49.

Dewhirst, T., & Sparks, R. (2003). Intertextuality, tobacco sponsorship of sports, and adolescent male smoking culture: A selective review of tobacco industry documents. *Journal of Sport & Social Issues, 27*, 372-398.

Eitzen, D.S. (1999). *Fair and foul: Beyond the myths and paradoxes of sport*. New York: Rowman & Littlefield.

Evans, D.M., & Smith, A.C.T. (2004). The Internet and competitive advantage: A study of Australia's four premier professional sporting leagues. *Sport Management Review, 7*, 27-56.

Extejt, M.M. (2004). Philanthropy and professional sports teams. *International Journal of Sport Management, 5*, 215-228.

Farrey, T. (2003, February 10). Is sports gambling with its integrity? *ESPN.com*. Retrieved June 21, 2005, from http://espn.go.com/nba/s/2003/0209/1506501.html.

Fink, J.S., Cunningham, G.B., & Kensicki, L J. (2004). Using athletes as endorsers to sell women's sport: Attractiveness vs. expertise. *Journal of Sport Management, 18*, 350-368.

Fort, R. (2004, December 20). How you see it: Dueling answers? No, different questions. *Street & Smith's SportsBusinesss Journal*, p. 26.

Frank, R. (1984). Olympic myths and realities. *Arete: The Journal of Sport Literature, 1*, 155-161.

Getz, D. (1997). *Event management & event tourism*. Elmsford, NY: Cognizant Communication Corporation.

Gibbins, R. (1986). Volunteers and volunteerism in Calgary: A methodological overview. *Volunteers and volunteerism in Calgary series, No. 1*. Calgary, Alberta, Canada: University of Calgary, Research Unit for Public Policy Studies.

Gladden, J.M., Mahoney, D.F. & Apostolopoulou, A. (2005). Toward a better understanding of college athletic donors: What are the primary motives? *Sport Marketing Quarterly, 14*, 18-30.

Haan, P., & Shank, M. (2004). Consumers' perceptions of NFL stadium naming rights. *International Journal of Sports Marketing & Sponsorship*, 5, 269-281.

Harris, J. (2005). The image problem in women's football. *Journal of Sport & Social Issues, 29*, 184-197.

Hopwood, M.K. (2005). Applying the public relations function to the business of sport. *International Journal of Sports Marketing & Sponsorship, 6*, 174-188.

Howard, D.R., & Crompton, J.L. (2004). *Financing sport* (2nd ed.). Morgantown, WV: Fitness Information Technology.

Howell, A. (1986). Why do volunteers burn out and drop out? *Volunteers and volunteerism in Calgary series, No. 8*. Research Unit for Public Policy Studies. Calgary, Alberta, Canada: University of Calgary, Research Unit for Public Policy Studies.

Hoye, R., & Cuskelly, G. (2003). Board-executive relationships within voluntary sport organizations. *Sport Management Review, 6*, 53-74.

Huff, D. (1982). *How to lie with statistics*. New York: Norton.

Huff, D. (1993). *How to lie with statistics*. New York: Norton.

Joyce Julius & Associates, Inc. (2005, April 18). *Nike reaps $10 million of TV exposure during Tiger's triumphant final round at the Masters*. Retrieved June 1, 2005, from www.joycejulius.com/PressReleases/pr_April_18_2005.htm.

Kerlinger, F.N., & Lee, H.B. (2000). *Foundations of behavioral research* (4th. ed.). Orlando, FL: Harcourt.

Késenne, S. (2003). The salary cap proposal of the G-14 in European football. *European Sport Management Quarterly, 3*, 120-128.

Kindt, J., & Asmar, T. (2002). College and amateur sports gambling: Gambling away our youth? *Villanova Sports & Entertainment Law Forum, 8*, 221-252.

King, B. (2004, September 13). Will rise of DVRs change sports TV? *Street & Smith's SportsBusiness Journal*, p. 1.

Klein, M.W. (2004). Work and play: International evidence of gender equality in employment and sports. *Journal of Sports Economics, 5*, 227-242.

Lapchick, R.E. (2005, September 26). *The 2004 racial and gender report card*. Retrieved January 19, 2006, from www.bus.ucf.edu/sport/public/downloads/2004_Racial_Gender_Report_Card.pdf.

Lefton, T. (2005a, January 31). Super chance for a blockbuster: Studios use the big game to generate box office buzz. *Street & Smith's SportsBusiness Journal*, p. 20.

Lefton, T. (2005b, May 23). Retired players still scoring in the latest sports QScores. *Street & Smith's SportsBusiness Journal*, p. 12.

Levin, A.M., Beasley, F., & Gamble, T. (2004). Brand loyalty of NASCAR fans towards sponsors: The impact of fan identification. *International Journal of Sports Marketing & Sponsorship, 6*, 11-21.

Lewin, K. (1946). Action research and minority problems. *Journal of Social Issues, 2*, 34-36.

Liberman, N. (2005, May 9). Putting the pieces together: How the Dew Action Sports Tour went from idea to reality. *Street & Smith's SportsBusiness Journal*, p. 19.

MacLean, J. (2001). *Performance appraisal for sport and recreation managers*. Champaign, IL: Human Kinetics.

Madden, J.F. (2004). Differences in the success of NFL coaches by race, 1990-2002: Evidence of last hire, first fire. *Journal of Sports Economics, 5*, 6-19.

Mahony, D.F., Hums, M.A., & Riemer, H.A. (2005). Bases for determining need: Perspectives of intercollegiate athletic directors and athletic board chairs. *Journal of Sport Management, 19*, 170-193.

Market update: Golf course supply per capita. (2005, May 5). *Golf Course News Magazine*. Retrieved June 17, 2005, from www.golfcoursenews.com/articles/article.asp?Id=419&SubCatID=42&CatID=7.

McKelvey, S.M. (2004). The growth in marketing alliances between U.S. professional sport and legalised gambling entities: Are we putting sport consumers at risk? *Sport Management Review, 7*, 193-210.

Miller, S. (2003a, June 16). Major investment in research part of playing the demographics game. *Street & Smith's SportsBusiness Journal*, p. 23.

Miller, S. (2003b, August 11). Research budgets increase as leagues seek growth. *Street & Smith's SportsBusiness Journal*, p. 17.

Mongrain, A. (2004, January 29). *The ads of Super Bowl XXXVIII: Scarborough looks at the ad categories and the consumers who watch the game*. Retrieved June 6, 2005, from www.scarborough.com/press_releases/Superbowl%20FINAL%201.29.04.pdf.

Muret, D. (2004, November 1). Would stadium pay off for city? Dueling studies reach different conclusions on proposed Cowboys stadium. *Street & Smith's SportsBusiness Journal*, p. 4.

National Golf Foundation (2004). Rounds played. In World Golf Foundation (2004, June 8). *Golf 20/20 industry report for 2003*. Retrieved June 2, 2005, from www.golf2020.com/Reports/2004_frip.pdf.

Nielsen Media Research (2005). *About Nielson Media Research*. Retrieved June 11, 2005, from www.nielsenmedia.com/about_us.html.

Parks, J.B. (1992). Scholarship: The other "bottom line" in sport management. *Journal of Sport Management, 6*(3), 220-229.

Peetz, T.B., Parks, J.B., & Spencer, N.E. (2004). Sport heroes as sport product endorsers: The role of gender in the transfer of meaning process for selected undergraduate students. *Sport Marketing Quarterly, 13*(3), 141-150.

Pitts, B.G., & Slattery, J. (2004). An examination of the effects of time on sponsorship awareness levels. *Sport Marketing Quarterly, 13*(1), 43-54.

Poole, M. (2004, February 16). Sports sponsorship will be the key to connecting with the TiVo generation. *Street & Smith's SportsBusiness Journal*, p. 11.

Popcorn, F. (1992). *The Popcorn report: Faith Popcorn on the future of your company, your world, your life*. New York: Harperbusiness.

Popcorn, F., & Marigold, L. (1998). *Clicking: 17 trends that drive your business—and your life*. New York: Harperbusiness.

Porter, L.W., & McKibbon, L.E. (1988). *Management education and development: Drift or thrust into the 21st century?* New York: McGraw-Hill.

Puckett, A. (2004, October 25). Have a ball: Debates challenge playoffs for viewers. *Street & Smith's SportsBusiness Journal*, p. 12.

Quarterman, J., Allen, L., & Becker, A. (2005). Managerial roles of intercollegiate athletic directors of the NAIA: The Mintzberg model. *International Journal of Sport Management, 6*(2), 165-182.

Quick, S.P., Taylor, T., & Gargalianos, D. (2005). The paradox of politics and sport: Exploring international relations in the context of Olympic sports. *International Journal of Sport Management, 6*(1), 1-14.

Quinn, K.G., Bursik, P.B., Borick, C.P., & Raethz, L. (2003). Do new digs mean more wins? The relationship between a new venue and a professional sports team's competitive success. *Journal of Sports Economics, 4*, 167-182.

Rascher, D., & Rascher, H. (2004). NBA expansion and relocation: A viability study of various cities. *Journal of Sport Management, 18*, 274-296.

Rines, S. (2004). Has adverse publicity affected Beckham's sponsorship potential? *International Journal of Sports Marketing & Sponsorship, 6*, 22-30.

Rishe, P., & Mondello, M. (2004). Ticket price determination in professional sports: An empirical analysis of the NBA, NFL, NHL, and Major League Baseball. *Sport Marketing Quarterly, 13*, 104-112.

Sanderson, A.R., & Siegfried, J.J. (2003). Thinking about competitive balance. *Journal of Sports Economics, 4*, 255-279.

Scarborough Research (2005). *Suite of services: Scarborough Sports Marketing*. Retrieved June 6, 2005, from www.scarborough.com/sports.htm.

Schiesel, S. (2005, June 21). They got (video) game; N.B.A. finals can wait. *New York Times* (Late ed.). Retrieved June 21, 2005, from www.nytimes.com/2005/06/21/arts/television/21vide.html?th&emc=th.

Singleton, R.A., & Straits, B.C. (1999). *Approaches to social research*. New York: Oxford University Press.

Smart, D., & Wolfe, R.L. (2003). The contribution of leadership and human resources to organizational success: An empirical assessment of performance in Major League Baseball. *European Sport Management Quarterly*, *3*, 168-188.

Smith, A.C.T., & Shilbury, D. (2004). Mapping cultural dimensions in Australian sporting organizations. *Sport Management Review*, *7*, 133-165.

Smith, D.R. (2003). The home advantage revisited: Winning and crowd support in an era of national publics. *Journal of Sport & Social Issues*, *27*, 346-371.

SGMA International (2002). *State of the industry report* (2002 ed.). Washington, DC: Author.

SGMA International (2005a). *Sports licensing white paper* (2005 ed.). Washington, DC: Author.

SGMA International (2005b). *Sports participation topline report* (2005 ed.). Washington, DC: Author.

Sutton, W.A., & Watlington, R. (1994). Communicating with women in the 1990s: The role of sport marketing. *Sport Marketing Quarterly*, *3*, 9-14.

Taylor Nelson Sofres (2005a). *TNS corporate fact sheet*. Retrieved June 9, 2005, from www.tns-global.com/corporate/Rooms/DisplayPages/LayoutInitial?Container=com.webridge.entity.Entity[OID[85DAAD60A2B65E4BA3826F9ED9B30436]].

Taylor Nelson Sofres (2005b). *TNS sport clients*. Retrieved June 9, 2005, from www.tns-global.com/corporate/Rooms/DisplayPages/LayoutInitial?Container=com.webridge.entity.Entity[OID[43DEAE59189A9C40B5AF546D5DAA85D1]].

Team Marketing Report (2005). *Fan cost index*. Retrieved June 1, 2005, from www.teammarketing.com/fci.cfm.

Tedrick, T. (1990). How to have the help you need. *Parks and Recreation*, *25*, 64.

Thomas, J.R., Nelson, J.K., & Silverman, S.J. (2005). *Research methods in physical activity* (5th ed.). Champaign, IL: Human Kinetics.

Thompson Tregear. (2006). *About us*. Retrieved January 19, 2006, from www.thompsontregear.com.au/about%20us.htm.

Tinning, R. (1992). Action research as epistemology and practice: Towards transformative educational practice in physical education. In A.C. Sparke (Ed.), *Research in physical education and sport: Exploring alternative visions*. London: Falmer Press.

TNS Intersearch (2004). *2003 ESPN Sports Poll*. White Plains, NY: Author.

Toohey, K., Taylor, T., & Lee, C.K. (2003). The FIFA World Cup 2002: The effects of terrorism on sports tourists. *Journal of Sport Tourism*, *8*, 167-185.

Totty, M. (2005, April 25). Better training through gaming. *Wall Street Journal* (Eastern ed.), p. R6.

Ulseth, A. (2004). Social integration in modern sport: Commercial fitness centres and voluntary sports clubs. *European Sport Management Quarterly*, *4*, 95-115.

Verducci, T. (2000, May 1). Expo 2000. *Sports Illustrated*, *92*, 38-45.

Vizcaino, S.A., Mason, D.S., & McDaniel, S.R. (2005). Online auctions of sports trading cards: How do auction attributes and seller reputations affect final bid prices? *International Journal of Sport Management*, *6*, 99-121.

Wilkinson, D.G. (1988). *The event management and marketing institute*. Willowdale, Ontario, Canada: The Event Management and Marketing Institute.

Chapter 20—Understanding Sport Management Research

Amis, J. (2003). “Good things come to those who wait”: The strategic management of image and reputation at Guinness. *European Sport Management Quarterly*, *3*, 189-214.

Amis, J. & Silk, M. (2005). Rupture: Promoting critical and innovative approaches to the study of sport management. *Journal of Sport Management*, *19*, 355-366.

Armstrong, K. L. (2002). An examination of the social psychology of Blacks’ consumption of sport. *Journal of Sport Management*, *16*, 267-288.

Ashton-Schaeffer, C., Gibson, H.J., Autry, C.E., and Hanson, C.S. (2001). Meaning of sport to adults with physical disabilities: A disability sport camp experience. *Sociology of Sport Journal*, *18*, 95-114.

Bernthal, M.J., & Regan, T.H. (2004). The economic impact of a NASCAR racetrack on a rural community and region. *Sport Marketing Quarterly*, *13*, 26-34.

Berrett, T., Burton, T.L. & Slack, T. (1993). Quality products, quality service: Factors leading to entrepreneurial success in the sport and leisure industry. *Leisure Studies*, 12, 93-106.

Cassell, C. & Symon, G. (2004). *Essential guide to qualitative methods*. London: Sage.

Chalip, L. (2001). Sport and tourism: Capitalizing on the linkage. In D. Kluka & G. Schilling (Eds.), *The business of sport* (pp. 78-89). Oxford, UK: Meyer & Meyer.

Chalip, L., & Leyns, A. (2002). Local business leveraging of a sport event: Managing an event for economic benefit. *Journal of Sport Management*, *16*, 132-158.

Chalip, L. Green, B.C., & Hill, B. (2003). Effects of sport event media on destination image and intention to visit. *Journal of Sport Management*, *17*, 214-234.

Chelladurai, P. (2006). *Human resource management in sport and recreation*. Champaign, IL: Human Kinetics.

Creswell, J.W. (2003). *Research design: Qualitative, quantitative, and mixed methods approaches*. Thousand Oaks, CA: Sage.

Desbordes, M. (2001). Innovation management in the sports industry: Lessons from the Salomon case. *European Sport Management Quarterly, 1*, 124-149.

Frisby, W., Crawford, S., & Dorer, T. (1997). Reflections on participatory action research: The case of low-income women accessing local physical activity services. *Journal of Sport Management, 11*, 8-28.

Frisby, W. (2005). The good, the bad, and the ugly: Critical sport management research. *Journal of Sport Management 19*, 1-12.

Frisby, W., Reid, C., Millar, S., & Hoeber, L. (2005). Putting 'participatory' into participatory forms of action research. *Journal of Sport Management.* 19, 367-386.

Geng, L., Burton, R., & Blakemore, C. (2002) Sport sponsorship in China: Transition and evolution. *Sport Marketing Quarterly, 11,* 20-32.

Gerrard, B. (2003). What does the resource-based view "bring to the table" in sport management research? *European Sport Management Quarterly, 3,* 139-144.

Greenwood, D.J., & Levin, M. (1998). *Introduction to action research: Social research for social change.* Thousand Oaks, CA: Sage.

Hinnings, C.R., & Greenwood, R. (2002). Disconnects and consequences in organization theory? *Administrative Science Quarterly*, 47, 411-421.

Hoeber, O., Riemer, H., Dorsch, K. & Hoeber, L. (2005). The application of web-based survey research methods to longitudinal designs. A paper presented at the North American Society for Sport Management Conference, Regina, Saskatchewan, Canada.

Hums, M.A., & Chelladurai, P. (1994a). Distributive justice in intercollegiate athletics: Development of an instrument. *Journal of Sport Management, 8,* 190-189.

Hums, M.A., & Chelladurai, P. (1994b). Distributive justice in intercollegiate athletics: The views of NCAA coaches and administroators. *Journal of Sport Management, 8,* 200-217.

Kent, A., & Chelladurai, P. (2001). Perceived transformational leadership, organizational commitment, and citizenship behavior: A case study in intercollegiate athletics. *Journal of Sport Management, 15,* 135-159.

Mahony, D.F., & Pastore, D. (1998). Distributive justice: An examination of participation opportunities, revenues, and expenses at NCAA institutions - 1973-1993. *Journal of Sport and Social Issues, 22,* 127-148.

Mahony, D.F., Hums, M.A., & Riemer, H.A. (2002). Distributive justice in intercollegiate atheltics: Perceptions of athletic directors and athletic board chairs. *Journal of Sport Management, 16,* 331-356.

Marshall, C., & Rossman, G.B. (1999). *Designing qualitative research.* (3rd ed.). Thousand Oaks, CA: Sage.

Mauws, M.K., Mason, D.S. & Foster, W.M. (2003). Thinking strategically about professional sports. *European Sport Management Quarterly, 3*, 145-164.

Neuman, W.L. (2003). *Social research methods: Qualitative and quantitative approaches.* Boston: Allyn and Bacon.

Palys, T. (1997). *Research decisions: Quantitative and qualitative perspectives* (2nd ed.). Toronto: Harcourt Brace Canada.

Reason, P., & Bradbury, H. (2001). *Handbook of action research.* Thousand Oaks, CA: Sage.

Shaw, S., & Amis, J. (2001). Image and investment: Sponsorship and women's sport. *Journal of Sport Management, 15,* 219-246.

Shaw, S., & Slack, T. (2002). "It's been like that for donkey's years': The construction of gender relations and the cultures of sport organizations. *Culture, Sport, Society, 5*, 86-106.

Shaw, S., & Hoeber, L. (2003). 'A strong man is direct and a direct woman is a bitch': Analysing discourses of masculinity and femininity and their impact on employment roles in sport organizations. *Journal of Sport Management, 17*, 347-376.

Shaw, S., & Penney, D. (2003). Gender equity policies in National Governing Bodies: An oxymoron or a vehicle for change? *European Sport Management Quarterly, 3,* 78-102.

Slack, T., and Parent, M. (2006). *Understanding sport organizations: The application of organization theory.* Champaign, IL: Human Kinetics.

Smart, D.L., & Wolfe, R.A. (2003). The contribution of leadership and human resources to organizational success: An empirical assessment of performance in Major League Baseball. *European Sport Management Quarterly, 3,* 165-188.

Stake, R.E. (2005). Qualitative case studies. In N.K. Denzin and Y.S. Lincoln (Eds.) *Qualitative research.* Thousand Oaks, CA: Sage.

Strauss, A.L. (1987). *Qualitative analysis for social scientists.* New York: Cambridge University Press.

Theberge, N. (2000). *Higher goals: Women's ice hockey and the politics of gender.* New York: State University of New York Press.

Thibault, L., Frisby, W., and Kikulis, L. (1999) Interorganizational linkages in the delivery of local leisure services in Canada: Responding to economic, political and social pressures, *Managing Leisure*, 4, 125-141.

Wilson, B., & White, P. (2002). Revive the Pride: Social process, political economy, and fan-based grassroots movement. *Sociology of Sport Journal, 19,* 119-148.

Index

Page numbers followed by an *f* or a *t* indicate a figure or table, respectively.

About the Editors

Janet B. Parks, DA, is a distinguished teaching professor emerita, former graduate studies coordinator, and former sport management division chair at Bowling Green State University in Ohio. She was a founding member of the North American Society for Sport Management (NASSM), which has honored her with the Earle F. Zeigler Award for Professional Achievement (1992) and the NASSM Distinguished Service Award (2001). She is a NASSM research fellow; a fellow in the Research Consortium of the American Alliance for Health, Physical Education, Recreation and Dance; and the recipient of the Outstanding Achievement Award from the Sport Management Council (SMC) of the National Association for Sport and Physical Education (NASPE). In 1994-95 and 2002-03 she was an honorary fellow in the Women's Studies Research Center at the University of Wisconsin at Madison.

Dr. Parks is a founding coeditor of the *Journal of Sport Management* and has served on NASPE's Task Force on Sport Management Curriculum Accreditation (1986-93) and Sport Management Program Review Council (1993-94). More recently, she was an SMC/NASPE representative on the Task Force on Sport Management Curriculum Standards (2005-2006).

During her 39 years at Bowling Green, Dr. Parks taught physical education and sport management and coached tennis and golf. Her research interests include sport management career development, sexist language, and gender issues in sport. Her published works include textbooks, book chapters, journal articles, a computer program, and research reports. She serves as a reviewer for several scholarly journals.

Dr. Parks received an undergraduate degree from the University of Chattanooga, a masters from Illinois State University, and completed postdoctoral study at the University of Wisconsin at Madison. She makes her home in Bowling Green, Ohio, where she enjoys working on research that advances the sport management body of knowledge and projects that preserve the history of women in sport. Dr. Park's photo appears courtesy of Craig J. Bell, BGSU.

Jerome Quarterman, PhD, is associate professor of sport management studies at Florida State University in Tallahassee. Before working at Florida State, he was a full-time faculty member at Bowling Green State University in Ohio. In 28 years of teaching, 16 have involved teaching students in sport management courses in undergraduate and graduate courses at both the master's and doctoral levels. He teaches students in a variety of courses, including Organizational Theory in Organizations of the Sport Industry, Intercollegiate Athletics Administration, Research Methods, Ethics in Organizations of the Sport Industry, Organizational Behavior in Organizations of the Sport Industry, Managing Human Resources in Organizations of the Sport Industry, and Managing Diversity in Organizations of the Sport Industry. He has also served as department chair at Southern, Alabama State, Kentucky State, and Hampton universities. His research has appeared in the *International Journal of Sport Management, Sport Marketing Quarterly, Journal of Sport Management,* and *Journal of Teaching Physical Education.* He is also a member of the editorial board for the *International Journal of Sport Management, Athletic Academic Journal, The SMART ON-LINE Journal,* and the *ICHPERSD Journal of Research.* Dr. Quarterman holds a doctoral degree from The Ohio State University, a master's degree from Kent State University, and a bachelor's degree from Savannah State University. He is an active researcher in organizational behavior, organizational theory, and research methods as applied to sport management studies. Dr. Quarterman is the proud parent of Terrance and Michele. His photo appears courtesy of Jerome Quarterman.

Lucie Thibault, PhD, is associate professor and chair at Brock University in Ontario, Canada. Before working at Brock University, Dr. Thibault taught at the University of British Columbia for eight years and the University of Ottawa for five years. She is editor of the *Journal of Sport Management* and was named a North American Society for Sport Management research fellow in 2001. She teaches in the areas of sport policy, globalization of sport, and organizational theory as it applies to sport organizations. Her research interests lie in the formation, management, and evaluation of cross-sectoral partnerships in sport organizations. She also investigates the role of the Canadian government in sport excellence and sport participation and government involvement in developing sport policy. Her research has appeared in the *Journal of Sport Management*, the *International Review for the Sociology of Sport, Journal of Sport and Social Issues, Human Relations, Leisure Studies, European Sport Management Quarterly,* and *International Journal for Sport Management and Marketing.* Dr. Thibault completed her master of arts and doctoral degrees at the University of Alberta. Her bachelor's degree was completed at the Université d'Ottawa. Dr. Thibault's photo appears courtesy of Suzanne Gabriel, Brock University.

About the Contributors

Robertha Abney, PhD, is the associate athletic director, senior woman administrator, and an associate professor at Slippery Rock University. She has distinguished herself as an authority in minorities in leadership roles in sport. She currently serves on the National Collegiate Athletic Association (NCAA) Division II Management Council and Committee on Infractions. She served on the NCAA Division II Nominating Committee from 1997 to 2001 and was president of the National Association for Girls and Women in Sport (NAGWS). Dr. Abney was selected to represent the International Council for Health, Physical Education, Recreation, Dance, and Sport in Beijing, China. She continues to give presentations and publish. Dr. Abney's photo appears courtesy of Images Unlimited Inc.

Omari Donovan Aldridge, a British Columbia native, earned the baccalaureate degree in sports management from Bowling Green State University in 2006. His achievements as an athlete on the men's soccer team have included the Regional All-American Honors from the National Soccer Coaches Association of America, selection to the 2005 All-MAC team, and the Gary V. Palmisano Memorial Award as the most valuable player on the Bowling Green State University soccer team. Mr. Aldridge not only led the university's soccer team in goals in 2006, but he also broke into the Single-Season Goal Top Ten scoring list with his 11th goal of the season. As a student, Mr. Aldridge recommended that *Contemporary Sport Management* have a broader international perspective. His current goals include playing professional soccer in Europe or becoming a sports agent. Mr. Aldrige's photo appears courtesy of Bowling Green State University.

Robin Ammon, Jr. is a full professor and the chair of the department of sport management at Slippery Rock University. He graduated with an EdD in sport administration from the University of Northern Colorado. His areas of research include legal liabilities in sport, risk management in sport and athletics, and management and marketing components for special events. At Slippery Rock University, he teaches undergraduate and graduate courses in risk management, sport law, event and facility management, and senior seminar. Dr. Ammon has written more than a dozen articles in refereed journals, nine chapters in sport management books, and two textbooks. He has presented more than 50 times at local, regional, national, and international conferences on a variety of topics including facility legal, security, and crowd management issues. Dr. Ammon has served as an expert witness in a variety of court cases regarding several of these issues. Dr. Ammon was the 17th president of the North American Society for Sport Management (NASSM) and is currently NASSM's business office manager. Dr. Ammon's photo appears courtesy of Robin Ammon, Jr.

Ketra L. Armstrong, PhD, is an associate professor and the director of the graduate program in sport management at California State University at Long Beach. She is also the president of the National Association for Girls and Women in Sport. Before her arrival at California State University at Long Beach, Dr. Armstrong taught sport marketing courses at Ohio State University. Her research specialization is sport marketing and sport consumer behavior, and her research has been featured in numerous journals: *Journal of Sport Management, Sport Management Review, International Journal of Sport Management, Sport Marketing Quarterly, Journal of Sport Behavior, Journal of Sport and Social Issues, Women in Sport and Physical Activity Journal, Journal of Black Psychology, Quest, Academic Athletic Journal, The Black Coaches Association Journal, The Physical Educator*, and *Future Focus*. Dr. Armstrong coauthored a manuscript that received the Outstanding Research Award by the Sport Marketing Association. She has conducted research for *Essence* magazine on Black women's fitness, and she received the Young Professional Award from the American Association of Active Lifestyle and Fitness.

In addition to Dr. Armstrong's scholarly pursuits, she has amassed a wealth of practical experience in the sport industry. She is a former Division I basketball player, Division I collegiate women's basketball coach, and collegiate athletic administrator. Over the years, she has performed integral roles in the research, management, marketing, and media relations for numerous community, national, and international sport events. Dr. Armstrong is also a freelance sport broadcaster and a former board member of the National Women's Hall of Fame. Her photo appears courtesy of Ketra Armstrong.

F. Wayne Blann, EdD, earned his doctorate from Boston University and is professor and coordinator of the undergraduate sport management degree program at Ithaca College. In 1986, he developed the sport marketing course in the sport management curriculum at Ithaca College, and he continues to teach this course. He also teaches sport marketing in the Ithaca College sport management graduate program. Dr. Blann pioneered research on American collegiate and professional athletes' and coaches' career transitions. He has served as consultant to the NBA, the NFL, the NHL Players' Association, and Major League Baseball Players' Association. Since 1996, the Professional Athletes Career Transition Program (PACTP) developed by Dr. Blann has served as the model for athlete career education programs. He has given several presentations at national and international conferences and has published articles in sport management, applied sport psychology, sport sociology, and applied research in coaching and athletics journals and newsletters. Dr. Blann's photo appears courtesy of Melanie Blann.

Robert Boucher, PhD, professor and dean of faculty at human kinetics at the University of Windsor, Ontario, has extensive experience as a leader in the academic and applied areas of sport management. He cofounded and has served as president of the North American Society for Sport Management (NASSM) and the Canadian Intramural Recreation Association (CIRA). He was the head of the department of athletics and recreational services at the University of Windsor from 1987 to 1996. He served as the chef de mission for the 1997 World University Games in Sicily, Italy, and as the assistant chef for the 1995 World University Games in Fukoka, Japan. He also served as the chair of the organizing committee of the Pan Am Junior Athletic Championships, which were held in Windsor in 2005. Dr. Boucher has published an edited book with Dr. W. James Weese and has written articles that appear in a variety of academic and professional journals. Dr. Boucher received the Dr. Earle F. Zeigler Lecture Award for contributions to sport management by NASSM in 1996 and the Distinguished Service Award in 2002. Dr. Boucher's photo appears courtesy of the University of Windsor.

Carla A. Costa, PhD, is an assistant professor in the department of kinesiology and health education at the University of Texas at Austin. She has completed a funded research project on the participation of youth in sport, and she is experienced in the area of event and destination leveraging. As the coauthor of *Adventure Sport Tourism in Rural Revitalization,* she explores several assumptions that are commonly present in the use of sport as a tool for community revitalization in rural areas. She is active in organizations including the North American Society for Sport Management (NASSM) and the European Association for Sport Management. Dr. Costa's photo appears courtesy of Magdalena Zavala.

Corinne M. Daprano, PhD, is an assistant professor in sport management at the University of Dayton. She has more than 15 years of experience working in the sport and recreation industry. Her extensive study includes topics such as human resource management in sport and recreation organizations, organizational change associated with the changes in the sport and recreation industry, and the study of service learning in higher education and its relation to sport management programs. She has coauthored a book on the topic of service learning, and she has authored a case study on collaboration in sport research. Dr. Daprano participates in the North American Society of Sport Management (NASSM) and the Academy of Management (AOM). Dr. Daprano's photo appears courtesy of Larry Burgess, University of Dayton.

Timothy D. DeSchriver, PhD, is an assistant professor of sport management in the department of health, nutrition, and exercise sciences at the University of Delaware. He earned his doctor of education degree in physical education with an emphasis in sport administration from the University of Northern Colorado. He has worked as a field economist for the U.S. Department of Labor, served as interim associate athletic director at the University of Northern Colorado, and spent four years as an assistant professor at Western Carolina University. He currently teaches classes on sport finance and sport economics at both the undergraduate and graduate levels. Dr. DeSchriver's research interests are sport consumer demand, pro sport ownership incentives, and sport facility financing. He has published articles in the *Journal of Sport Management, Eastern Economic Journal, Sport Marketing Quarterly, International Sports Journal,* and *Street & Smith's SportsBusiness Journal.* He has been involved in research projects for the NCAA, the Major Indoor Soccer League, and the National Steeplechase Association. He was also coauthor of the textbook *Sport Finance*. Dr. DeSchriver is a member of the North American Society for Sport Management (NASSM) and the Sport Marketing Association (SMA). He has made numerous presentations at the North American Society for Sport Management annual conferences as well as at international conferences. Prior to his position at the University of Delaware, Dr. DeSchriver was an assistant professor at the University of Massachusetts at Amherst. Dr. DeSchriver's photo appears courtesy of the University of Massachusettes.

Joy T. DeSensi, EdD, is professor and head of the department of exercise, sport, and leisure studies at the University of Tennessee. She earned her doctoral degree from the University of North Carolina at Greensboro. Her research interests include ethics in sport management; women in sport; and gender, race, and ethnicity in sport. She is coauthor of *Ethics and Morality in Sport Management* and has authored numerous book chapters and articles. She has served on the editorial review boards of scholarly journals, was the editor of the *Journal of Sport Management,* and is the current editor of *Quest*. Dr. DeSensi is a founding member of the North American Society of Sport Management (NASSM). She has served as the president of the Southern Academy of Women in Physical Activity, Sport, and Health; the International Association for the Philosophy of Sport; and the National Association for Kinesiology and Physical Education in Higher Education. She received an award for the Most Outstanding Book in Sport Management from the European Association for Sport Management for her work on *Ethics in Sport Management*. Her other professional achievements include Distinguished Alumna awards from the University of Memphis and the University of North Carolina at Greensboro; NAGWS Pathfinder and Presidential Awards; and Teaching, Research, and Service Awards from the University of Tennessee. Dr. DeSensi's photo appears courtesy of the University of Tennessee.

Stephen W. Dittmore is an assistant professor in the department of sport studies at East Stroudsburg University of Pennsylvania. He will graduate in May 2007 with a PhD from the University of Louisville. He has 10 years of practitioner experience in various sport public relations roles, and coauthored Sport Public Relations: Managing Organizational Communication. His experience includes crisis communications and community, government, and media relations in sport. He served as a director of the Salt Lake Organizing Committee for the 2002 Olympic Winter Grams, and he belongs to the North American Society of Sport Management (NASSM). He has been awarded the Order of Excellence from the Salt Lake Organizing Committee for the 2002 Olympic Winter Games and the Practitioner of the Year Award in 2002 from Wichita State University Sport Administration. His photo appears courtesy of Steve Dittmore.

Jess C. Dixon, MHK, is an assistant professor of sport management in the department of kinesiology at the University of Windsor. He is nearing the completion of his doctor of philosophy degree in sport management from the University of Massachusetts at Amherst. Over the past several years, he has coordinated and instructed courses in sport management at the University of Windsor, the University of Massachusetts, and Brock University. His primary research and scholarly interests are in the areas of strategic management, business policy, and human resource management. He has experience working within the golf and retail sport goods industries, as well as with a boutique sport agency. He belongs to the North American Society for Sport Management (NASSM) and the Sport Marketing Association (SMA), and has made several research presentations at their respective annual conferences. His photo appears courtesy of Jess Dixon.

Ted G. Fay, PhD, is an associate professor and international coordinator for the sport management program at SUNY Cortland (NY). He served as program head from 1999 to 2005 and was responsible for developing the undergraduate major in sport management and a corresponding graduate program including a special focus on international study. He earned his doctoral degree from the University of Massachusetts at Amherst. He serves as a senior research fellow and strategic consultant at the Center of the Study of Sport in Society at Northeastern University where he is cofounder of the Disability in Sport Initiative. His research and scholarly interests include international sport management and international sport policy; the Olympic and Paralympic movements; and comparative strategic management and policy studies examining social justice issues in management with respect to diversity issues as related to race, gender, disability, social class, sexual orientation, sectarianism, classism, and ageism. Dr. Fay has worked in a variety of coaching, marketing, and administrative positions with a number of national sport governing bodies in the United States including having served for eight years as national team hockey head coach and program director for the US Disabled Ski Team from 1983 to 1991. He remains actively involved as a researcher, technical classifier, and sport official with the International Paralympic Committee including eight Winter Paralympic Games. He served as the executive director of the IIHF 1996 World Junior Ice Hockey Championship held in the United States and as a cross country ski coach as a member of the 1988 US Winter Olympic Team in Calgary, Alberta. Dr. Fay also created the Sport Media & Technology Learning Center (SMTLC) at SUNY Cortland through the support of a $6.2 million (USD) corporate gift from Pinnacle Systems Team Sports (now XOS Technologies) in 2002 and further supported by a $500,000 (USD) gift from Dartfish USA in 2005. He was primarily responsible for negotiating the move of the US Women's National Team Handball Team's residency program from the Lake Placid Olympic Training Center to SUNY Cortland in 2005. Dr. Fay's photo appears courtesy of Eric Poggenpohl Photography.

Carol A. Fletcher, PhD, assistant professor of sport management at St. John's University, has an extensive background in curriculum development, athletic administration, intercollegiate athletics, and event and facility management. Dr. Fletcher initiated the sport management curriculum in the school of business at Teikyo Post University and instructed the first sport management course. She also established a revenue-generating swimming instruction program at Teikyo Post University and reorganized the St. John's University sport management curriculum. She participates in the North American Society for Sport Management (NASSM) and the National Association for Sport and Physical Education. Her photo appears courtesy of Carol Fletcher.

Wendy Frisby, PhD, is associate professor and chair in the department of women's studies at the University of British Columbia, where she teaches the third-year research methods course. Dr. Frisby has also helped to develop a fourth-year practicum course that includes a research component. She earned her doctoral degree in kinesiology (sociology of sport) from the University of Waterloo, Canada. Dr. Frisby was the editor of the *Journal of Sport Management* from 2000 to 2003 and currently serves on the editorial boards of *Journal of Sport Management, European Sport Management Quarterly,* and *Leisure/Loisir.* She is a research fellow in the North American Society for Sport Management (NASSM) and a member of the International Institute for the Study of Sport Management and the Canadian Association for Leisure Studies. She has published more than 30 articles in refereed journals and conference proceedings and has written several book chapters and government reports. Dr. Frisby participated in a collaborative research effort with several public sector partners and women living below the poverty line. The study identified community organizing practices that include women living in poverty in local physical activity and recreation programs as a health promotion strategy. She received the Earle F. Zeigler Lecture Award in 2004. Dr. Frisby's photo appears courtesy of John MacLeod, University of British Columbia.

Heather Gibson, PhD, is an assistant professor in the department of tourism, recreation, and sport management at the University of Florida at Gainesville. She has an international reputation as a scholar in sport tourism and has presented keynote addresses at international conferences in Finland and the United Kingdom. Her educational background encompasses both sport and tourism studies. She earned her doctoral degree in sport, leisure, and exercise science from the University of Connecticut. She has published both conceptual and empirical work on sport tourism and is the author of one of the most widely cited articles in sport tourism, "Sport Tourism: A Critical Analysis of Research," which was published in *Sport Management Review* in 1998. Dr. Gibson, together with Laurence Chalip of the University of Texas, has been instrumental in bringing sport tourism to the attention of sport management professionals in the North American Society for Sport Management (NASSM). She is a member of the National Recreation and Park Association, World Leisure, and the Leisure Studies Association. Dr. Gibson's photo appears courtesy of Donna Walker.

James M. Gladden, PhD, is an associate professor and graduate program director of sport management at the University of Massachusetts. Dr. Gladden has more than 15 years of sport marketing research and consulting experience and is an expert in brand management as applied to sport. He has published articles in academic journals and in sport industry publications. He coauthored the article "Managing North American Major Professional Sport Teams in the New Millennium: Building, Sharing, and Maintaining Equity," which was published in the *Journal of Sport Management* in 2001. The article emphasizes the importance of generating assets through strategic alliances and the importance of focusing on and serving consumer needs. Dr. Gladden has also provided brand management consulting to several organizations, including the National Basketball Association and the Ladies Professional Golf Association. He was the project director for DelWilber+Associates from 1991 to 1994. He earned his doctoral degree from the University of Massachusetts at Amherst and is a member in both the North American Society for Sport Management (NASSM) and the Sport Marketing Association. Dr. Gladden's photo appears courtesy of Tom Kendall, kendallphoto.com.

B. Christine Green, PhD, is an active researcher studying consumer behavior of sport event volunteers, active sport participants, and fans in a variety of sport settings. An assistant professor in the department of kinesiology and the director of the sport development lab at the University of Texas at Austin, Dr. Green earned her doctoral degree in sport management from the University of Maryland. She has published more than 25 articles that span a variety of contexts, including sport participants, fans, event volunteers, and sport tourists. Her article in *Sport Management Review* in 2001 focuses on using key consumer behavior constructs to better market and promote sport events. She designed and implemented the volunteer management system for the British Olympic Association's pre-Games training camp and participated in the strategic planning efforts to redesign the Australian university sport system. Dr. Green was the head of the research team that studies the motivation and commitment of the 2000 Sydney Olympic volunteers. She supervised student-run marketing projects that significantly increased student attendance at women's basketball games. She is a member of the American Marketing Association and the Sport Marketing Association, and she is a research fellow in the North American Society of Sport Management. She has been honored with the Academic Innovation Award from the RGK Center for Philanthropy and Community Service and is a fellow in the Judy Spencer Tate Fellowship for Excellence. Dr. Green's photo appears courtesy of Magdalena Zavala.

Kathryn S. Hoff, PhD, is an associate professor of human resource development in the college of technology at Bowling Green State University, where she earned her PhD in higher education administration and MEd in human resource development. She spent more than 20 years as a human resource development practitioner responsible for internship and cooperative education programs, college relations and recruiting, career development and management of employees, organizational change management, and training and development. Dr. Hoff currently serves as the managing director for the Academy of Human Resource Development (AHRD), an international association of scholars and practitioners whose mission is leading human resource development through research. She is a contributor and reviewer for the AHRD's journals. Dr. Hoff's photo appears courtesy of Bowling Green State University.

Mary Jo Kane, PhD, is full professor and director of the school of kinesiology at the University of Minnesota; she also serves as director of the Tucker Center for Research on Girls & Women in Sport. In 1996, Dr. Kane was awarded the first distinguished professorship related to women in sport and physical activity, the Dorothy McNeill and Elbridge Ashcraft Tucker chair for women in exercise science and sport. Professor Kane was elected by her peers as a fellow in the American Academy of Kinesiology and Physical Education, the highest honor in her field. She is an internationally recognized scholar on sport and gender. She is particularly interested in the media's treatment of female athletes. Professor Kane authored a groundbreaking publication in 1995 which argued that sport should be seen as a continuum, devoid of the popular gender binary. This publication helped to fundamentally alter traditional notions of male superiority in sport as a biological given. Professor Kane received the Scholar of the Year Award from the Women's Sport Foundation in 2004. She is a member of the North American Society for the Sociology of Sport (NASSS) and the National Association for Girls and Women in Sport (NAGWS), and has served on the editorial review boards of the *Journal of Sport Management, Sociology of Sport Journal*, and the *Journal of Sport & Social Issues*. Dr. Kane's photo appears courtesy of the University of Minnesota.

Stuart M. Keeley, PhD, is professor emeritus at Bowling Green State University. He was designated Distinguished Teaching Professor of Psychology by the Bowling Green State University Board of Trustees in 1999, primarily on the basis of his commitment to the teaching of critical thinking to undergraduates both in a stand-alone course and as a component of all the courses he teaches. Dr. Keeley is coauthor of the textbook *Asking the Right Questions: A Guide to Critical Thinking,* which is now in its eighth edition. He is also the author of *Asking the Right Questions in Abnormal Psychology.* He has presented numerous workshops on various topics related to critical thinking at the International Conference on Critical Thinking and Educational Reform; his workshops emphasized tips for teaching critical thinking and designing assignments for critical thinking courses. His photo appears courtesy of Stuart Keeley.

JoAnn Kroll is the director of career services at Bowling Green State University. Her department is responsible for career planning, student employment, cooperative education and internships, job placement, and alumni career management services for a student population of 18,000. She earned her MEd in higher education administration from Kent State University. The National Association of Colleges and Employers has twice honored her department with its prestigious Award of Excellence for Educational Programming. She served as a consultant in Russia, helping to establish the first career services center and a national network of career services professionals. She has written several book chapters and is a frequent speaker at professional conferences. She has written and produced a job search manual for college students for over 20 years and is an ongoing contributing author for the leading graduate textbook in college student personnel, the *Student Affairs Practice in Higher Education.* She is a member of the National Association of Colleges and Employers and the American Association for Employment in Education. Her achievements include receiving the 2001 Gerald L. Saddlemire Mentor Award from the Ohio College Personnel Association, the 2003 University Community Fellowship Award from the Division of Higher Education and Student Affairs, and the 2004 Michael R. Ferrari Award from the Bowling Green State University Administrative Staff Council. Her photo appears courtesy of Bowling Green State University.

Ming Li, EdD, is the director of the school of recreation and sport sciences at Ohio University and a professor in sports administration. He received his bachelor's degree in education from Guangzhou Institute of Physical Culture, his master's degree in education from Hangzhou University, and his doctor of education degree in sport administration from the University of Kansas. Li has memberships on the editorial boards of several professional journals, including *Journal of Sport Management, International Journal of Sport Management,* and *Sport Marketing Quarterly.* He was recently appointed as assistant editor for the *ICHPERSD Journal.* He has published more than 25 articles in refereed journals, two books *(Economics of Sport* and *Badminton Everyone),* and four book chapters. He has made numerous refereed presentations at state, national, and international conferences. Li is an honorary guest professor of the Guangzhou Institute of Physical Education in Guangzhou, China. He was an Olympic envoy for the Atlanta Committee for the 1996 Olympic Games and is a member of the North American Society for Sport Management (NASSM) and the National Association for Sport and Physical Education. He was the recipient of the Young Scholar Award in 1997 and the Taylor Dodson Award in 1999. Dr. Li's photo appears courtesy of the Ohio University.

Daniel F. Mahony, PhD, is a professor of sport administration and the assistant university provost for institutional effectiveness at the University of Louisville. Dr. Mahony has a B.S. in accounting from Virginia Tech, an M.S. in sport management from West Virginia University, and PhD in sport management from Ohio State University. He has worked for the accounting first of Peat Marwick Main & Co., the North Hunterdon High School athletic department, the West Virginia University athletic department, and the University of Cinncinati athletic department. Dr. Mahony has taught classes in a variety of areas, including sport finance and athletics in higher education. Dr. Mahony is an active researcher in the areas of sport consumer behavior and intercollegiate athletics and has published over 40 articles in various journals including *Journal of Sport Management, Sport Management Review, Sport Marketing Quarterly, International Sports Journal, International Journal of Sport Marketing and Sponsorship, International Journal of Sport Management, Professional Ethics, European Journal of Sport Management, Journal of Academic Ethics, Journal of Contemporary Athletics,* and *Journal of Sport and Social Issues.* He was also coauthor for Economics of Sport. Dr. Mahony's photo appears courtesy of the University of Louisville.

David Cruise Malloy, PhD, is a full professor in the faculty of kinesiology and health studies and the associate dean in the faculty of graduate studies and research. His research focuses on applied ethics and philosophy in administrative contexts in health, nonprofit organizations, and sport. Specifically his interests include ethical decision making, codes of ethics, and ethical climate and culture. He has published numerous refereed articles and is the coauthor of two texts dealing with applied ethics: *Biomedical Ethics for Health Care Professionals* and *Sport Ethics* (Thompson Educational Publisher). Dr. Malloy's current research is funded by both the Social Sciences and Humanities Research Council of Canada (SSHRCC) and the Canadian Institutes of Health Research (CIHR). Dr. Malloy's photo appears courtesy of Don Hall, University of Regina.

Mark A. McDonald, PhD, is an associate professor of sport management at the University of Massachusetts at Amherst, where he received a PhD in 1996. Dr. McDonald has published in the *Journal of Sport Management, Sport Marketing Quarterly, International Journal of Sports Marketing and Sponsorship,* and *Journal of Sport and Social Issues.* He served as coeditor for the special *Sport Marketing Quarterly* issue on relationship marketing in sport and is on the editorial boards for the *European Sport Management Quarterly* and *Sport Marketing Quarterly.* He has given more than 35 presentations in the United States and abroad, and his research interests include sport sponsorship, relationship marketing, and leadership in sport organizations. He has published 20 refereed journal articles and has coauthored two books, *Cases in Sport Marketing* and *Sport Marketing: Managing the Exchange Process.* Dr. McDonald is a North American Society for Sport Management (NASSM) research fellow. Dr. McDonald's photo appears courtesy of Janis Ori.

Lori K. Miller, EdD, is the associate dean of the college of education and a professor in sport administration at Wichita State University. She has published more than 40 works on legal issues, including "The Non-Lawyer Educator Teaching Legal Issues in Higher Education: Legally and Educationally Defensible?" in the *Journal of Legal Aspects of Sport* in 2002 and "Online Sports Gambling: Regulation or Prohibition?" in *Journal of Legal Aspects of Sport* in 2001. She has made numerous presentations on sport and legal issues at international, national, and local conferences. Dr. Miller is a member of the Society for the Study of Legal Issues, which awarded her the 2000 Leadership Award. She also belongs to the North American Society for Sport Management, which recognized her as a research fellow in 2001. She has been honored with the Sport Management Outstanding Achievement Award in 2005; the Sport, Recreation, and Law Association Honor Award in 2004; and as Teacher of the Year in 1996 by the University of Louisiana school of education. Dr. Miller's photo appears courtesy of Dr. Alan Aagaard.

Anita M. Moorman, JD, is an associate professor in Sport Administration at the University of Louisville where she teaches sport law and legal aspects of sport. She joined the faculty at the University of Louisville in 1996. Professor Moorman has a law degree from Southern Methodist University and prior to her academic pursuits, she practiced law in Oklahoma City, Oklahoma in the areas of commercial and corporate litigation for ten years. Professor Moorman also holds an M.S. in sport management from the University of Oklahoma, and a B.S. in political science from Oklahoma State University.

Professor Moorman is the editor of a feature column in the Sport Marketing Quarterly entitled "Sport Marketing and the Law" and is co-author of the text, *Sport Law: A Managerial Approach*. Professor Moorman's research interests include commercial law issues in the sport industry; and legal and ethical issues related to sport marketing practices, brand protection, and intellectual property issues in sport. She has published more than twenty articles in academic journals, including the *Sport Management Review, Sport Marketing Quarterly, Journal of Legal Aspects of Sport, JOPERD, Leisure Science, International Sport Journal, Journal of Sport and Social Issues; Journal of the Academy of Marketing Science; and ACSM's Health and Fitness Journal*; and has given more than forty presentations at national and international conferences. Her photo appears courtesy of Anita Moorman.

Catherine Pratt, PhD, directs marketing, event planning, and media counseling for Communications Ink. She began covering sports as an undergraduate at Bowling Green State University. Her extensive marketing and public relations experience includes working for Carl Byoir and Associates in New York City, where she provided media training for Olympic and professional athletes and produced radio documentaries, TV news clips, and corporate video for clients such as RCA, Hallmark, Post Cereals, Johnson Wax, Borg-Warner, and Honeywell. She hosted and coproduced a weekly sports television show while serving on the journalism faculty at BGSU and completing her doctoral degree in mass communications. Dr. Pratt's photo appears courtesy of James R. Gordon.

David L. Snyder, JD, PhD, is a tenured associate professor of sport management at the State University of New York (SUNY) College at Cortland, where he also serves as interim chair of the sport management department. He is also a part-time associate professor in the sport management program at Tompkins Cortland Community College. Professor Snyder received his JD from the University of Tennessee and has been licensed to practice law in New York since 1986. Before accepting his current position at SUNY Cortland, he served as president of an international sport marketing company headquartered in Tokyo, Japan. He is currently pursuing his doctoral degree in sport management at the Deutsche Sporthochsule Köln in Germany. His doctoral research focuses on the relationship between Japanese sociocultural values and the business of professional baseball in Japan. He is a member of the Sports Lawyers Association (SLA); the American Alliance for Health, Physical Education, Recreation and Dance (AAHPERD); the Sport Marketing Association (SMA); and National Association for Sport and Physical Education (NASPE). He is an executive member of the International Academy of Sports Law Practitioners & Executives (ASPE). Professor Snyder serves on the Asian Baseball and Business of Baseball Research Committees of the Society for American Baseball Research (SABR). He is a program reviewer for the Sport Management Program Review Council (SMPRC) and serves as a member of the editorial board for the *International Journal of Sports Marketing and Sponsorship*. He received the 2005 Excellence in Teaching Award in Sport Management at SUNY Cortland. His photo appears courtesy of SUNY.

Ellen J. Staurowsky, EdD, is professor and graduate chair of the department of sport management and media at Ithaca College. She received her doctoral degree in sport management and psychosocial aspects of sport from Temple University. On 75 occasions, Dr. Staurowsky has presented to learned societies, professional associations, and conferences on gender equity and Title IX, pay equity and equal employment opportunity, the exploitation of athletes, the faculty roles in reforming college sport, representation of women in sport media, and the misappropriation of American Indian imagery in sport. She has published numerous articles in scholarly and professional journals. In 1998, she coauthored the book *College Athletes for Hire: The Evolution and Legacy of the NCAA Amateur Myth.* Dr. Staurowsky is a member of the editorial board for the *Journal of Sport Management, Women in Sport and Physical Activity Journal,* and *Athletic Management.* She is past president of the North American Society for the Sociology of Sport. She is a founding member of the Drake Group, a group of faculty around the country interested in college sport reform. She is the former college field hockey and lacrosse coach at Oberlin College and was the director of athletics at Daniel Webster College and William Smith College for 9 years. She is currently president elect of the AAHPERD Research Consortium. Dr. Staurowsky's photo appears courtesy of Ithaca College.

G. Clayton (Clay) Stoldt, PhD, is an associate professor and serves as coordinator of the graduate sport administration program at Wichita State University. He teaches classes in sport public relations and sport marketing. Stoldt is the co-author of Sport Public Relations: Managing Organizational Communication and his research activities have focused on sport public relations issues such as crisis communications, the roles of sport public relations professionals and the application of advanced public relations practices in the field. As graduate coordinator, he administers a program that includes more than 80 graduate students. Stoldt received his Doctor of Education from the University of Oklahoma in 1998. His master's degree was in sport management and his bachelor's in journalism/mass communication.

Prior to coming to Wichita State, Stoldt worked in the athletic department at Oklahoma City University where he served as sports information director, radio play-by-play broadcaster, and development officer. He also served as an adjunct instructor at both Oklahoma City and the University of Oklahoma, teaching courses in sport management and mass communication. During his tenure as sports information director, Stoldt earned several national awards for sports information publications. Stoldt's background also includes experience as a radio sportscaster and sales executive. His photo appears courtesy of Ryan Stoldt.

David K. Stotlar, EdD, is a professor of sport management in the areas of sport marketing and sport law at the University of Northern Colorado. He has had more than 50 articles published in professional journals and has written several book chapters in sport marketing, fitness risk management, and sport law. He is the author of several textbooks, including *Developing Successful Sport Sponsorship Plans,* which was published in 2001. He has made numerous presentations at international and national professional conferences and has conducted international seminars in sport management and marketing for various sport councils, federations, and institutes. Dr. Stotlar served as the media subcenter supervisor for the Soldier's Hollow venue at the 2002 Winter Olympic Games in Salt Lake City. He received the Dr. Earle F. Zeigler Award from the North American Society for Sport Management in 1999 and was named an NASSM research fellow in 2001. Dr. Stotlar's photo appears courtesy of Sylvia Stotlar.

William A. Sutton is professor and associate director of the Devos sports business management program at the University of Central Florida. Prior to this position, he served as vice president of team marketing services for the National Basketball Association (NBA) and held an appointment as professor in the sport studies department at the University of Massachusetts at Amherst. He is principal of Bill Sutton & Associates and has worked for such clients as the NBA, NFL, NHS, Major League Baseball Properties, LPGA, NCAA, Hoop-It-Up, IBM, Mazda, and Sprint. A former president of the North American Society for Sport Management (NASSM), Dr. Sutton has also served as coeditor of *Sport Marketing Quarterly* and serves on the editorial board of the *International Journal of Sports Marketing and Sponsorships.* Dr. Sutton is widely published in sport marketing and has made more than 100 national and international presentations. He is coauthor of the texts *Sport Marketing,* published in 2000, and *Sport Promotions and Sales Management,* published in 2002. He is a regular contributor to *Sport Business Journal* and *Gigant del Basket,* an Italian basketball production. Dr. Sutton's photo appears courtesy of University of Central Florida.